HISTORY OF THE NORWEGIAN PEOPLE

THE MACMILLAN COMPANY
NEW YORK · BOSTON · CHICAGO · DALLAS
ATLANTA · SAN FRANCISCO

MACMILLAN & CO., LIMITED
LONDON · BOMBAY · CALCUTTA
MELBOURNE

THE MACMILLAN CO. OF CANADA, LTD.
TORONTO

HISTORY

OF THE

NORWEGIAN PEOPLE

BY

KNUT GJERSET, Ph.D., Litt.D.

(HEIDELBERG)

PROFESSOR OF HISTORY IN LUTHER COLLEGE
DECORAH, IOWA

TWO VOLUMES IN ONE

WITH MAPS AND ILLUSTRATIONS

New York

THE MACMILLAN COMPANY

1932

PRINTED IN THE UNITED STATES OF AMERICA

Set up and electrotyped. Published August, 1915.
Two volumes in one, September, 1927. Reprinted
April, 1932.

Norwood Press
J. S. Cushing Co. — Berwick & Smith Co.
Norwood, Mass., U.S.A.

PREFACE

THE growing interest in Norwegian language, literature, and culture in this country has created a special need for a history of the Norwegian people in the English language devoting sufficient attention to the more important phases of the people's life to show the development of their institutions and culture, their life at home, and their activity and influence abroad. It has been my aim in this work to meet this demand by having constantly in mind what questions an intelligent reader might be expected to ask, and by trying, as far as possible, to answer them. In the Middle Ages the Scandinavian peoples were potent factors in developing navigation, commerce, municipal life and government, literature and culture in northern Europe. But nothing has been taken for granted, nor has any theory been advanced beyond what is clearly established by the investigations of the best scholars. The way to the original sources has, therefore, always been pointed out, and these have been used in a conservative spirit. The views of the leading scholars have been followed, and sometimes preference has been purposely given to the more conservative views on points where there is or might be a difference of opinion. On the whole I have deemed it advisable to adhere to Snorre Sturlason's healthful principle: "It seems better to us that something should be added later than that anything should have to be stricken out."

The period of the union with Denmark has been treated with some fullness of detail. The preservation of the people's personal freedom amidst general national decay, the germs of a new development distinctly traceable in social life has been especially dwelt upon, not only because these features are characteristic of the life of the Norwegian people in that period, but because they constitute the basis of their political and social development in modern times.

Regarding Norway's long struggle for complete independence after 1814 an attempt has been made to state facts fearlessly and impartially, without any spirit of antagonism against the noble and heroic Swedish people, who are and will be Norway's truest friends.

In proper names the original spelling has been preserved, except in a few cases where a distinct English form has been developed; as, *Copenhagen, Gottenborg, Charles John.* The attempt to give Norwegian names an English form, or to translate appellatives, destroys their euphony and character as names, and leads to many difficulties. An aid to the pronunciation of Norwegian names will be found under a separate heading.

KNUT GJERSET.

LUTHER COLLEGE, DECORAH, IOWA,
August 1, 1914.

CONTENTS

LIST OF PLATES

LIST OF MAPS

LIST OF ILLUSTRATIONS IN THE TEXT

xiii

AID TO CORRECT PRONUNCIATION OF NORWEGIAN PROPER NAMES

A, a pronounced *ah*, like English *ä* in *arm*.

E, e pronounced *ay*,[1] like English *ā* in *day*.

I, i pronounced *ee*, like English *ē* in *eve*.

O, o pronounced *oo*, like English *ō* in *only*.

U, u pronounced *ou*, like English *ou* in *you*.

$Æ$, $œ$ is an open sound like English *ă* in *at*, but usually lengthened.

$\emptyset$, ϕ like German *ö* in *söhne*, or English *ē* in *fern*.

AA, aa pronounced *awe*, like English *aw* in *awful*; *Aasen* pronounced *Aw'sen*.

Y, y is a vowel like English *ў* in *ўt'rium*: example, *Ўgg'dräsil*, *Ўng'vär*.

The consonants have their simple Latin sound, except *j*, which has the sound of English *y* in *year*: example, *Jœmtland* pronounced *Yämt'länd*. Final *e* is always sounded and forms a distinct unaccented syllable: examples, *Lerche* pronounced *Lĕrch'ë*, *Gĭm'lë*.

The digraph *ie* is pronounced like English *ie* in *field*: example, *Friele* pronounced *Free'lë*. The *ei* is pronounced like English *i* in *ice*; example, *Einar* pronounced *Ī'när*. The *au* is pronounced like English *ou* in *out*: example, *Aud* pronounced *Oud*.

Skj is pronounced like *sh*: example, *Jernskjegge* pronounced *Yern'sheggë*.

Kj is pronounced like *ch*: example, *Kjartan* pronounced *Chär'tän*.

---

[1] Pronounced without the vanishing sound.

HISTORY OF THE NORWEGIAN PEOPLE

VOLUME I

HISTORY OF THE NORWEGIAN PEOPLE

1. THE COUNTRY AND ITS RESOURCES

THE kingdom of Norway forms a part of the Scandinavian peninsula, embracing its mountainous western slope.[1] It consists of a rock-bound coast region 1700 miles in length when measured along the outer belt of rocks. In the southern part it is about 260 miles wide, in the northern about sixty miles, though the extreme northern province, Finmarken, is considerably wider. Measured in a straight line, the distance north and south from Vardø to Lindesnes is 1100 miles, so that if the country were swung around, its northern extremity would reach the Pyrenees. Norway is a little larger than the United Kingdom of Great Britain and Ireland, its total area being 124,495 sq. m., or about the same as that of our New England States together with New York and New Jersey. The country consists of a mountain plateau broken by two larger depressions: one in the southeastern part; another, and smaller one, around the Trondhjemsfjord. These two tracts—Østlandet and Trøndelagen—consisting of undulating mountain slopes, contain extensive and valuable forests of coniferous trees, and are especially well adapted to farming and cattle raising. The southern coast region — Vestlandet — as well as the northern part — Nordland and Finmarken — is inter-

---

[1] *Norway, Official Publication for the Paris Exhibition*, Christiania, 1900. Paul B. Du Chaillu, *The Land of the Midnight Sun*. Joh. Dyring, *Kongeriget Norge, dets Geografi, Samfundsindretninger og Næringsveie*, 1894. Jens Kraft, *Historisk-topografisk Haandbog over Kongeriget Norge*. Professor Dr. Sophus Ruge, *Norwegen*. Yngvar Nielsen, *Reise-haandbog over Norge*. *Norges officielle Statistik, utgit av det Statistiske Centralbyraa*, Christiania. Einer Haffner, *Bogen om Norge*. Amund Helland, *Norges Land og Folk topografisk-statistisk beskrevet*. M. Braun Tvethe, *Norges Statistik*, 1848. A. Schweigaard, *Norges Statistik*, Christiania, 1840.

sected by narrow fjords extending far into the country. These deep cuts in the rocky plateau continue inland as narrow, fertile valleys, abounding in streams and waterfalls, and are often of incomparable beauty and grandeur. Fringing these valleys are large mountain-tracts unfit for agriculture, bearing timber, grass, and wild berries. These tracts are valuable as pasture and timberlands, while an abundance of wild game lends them a special charm as excellent hunting grounds. The high inland plateau is uninhabitable, being for the most part covered by glaciers and perpetual snow. This is the undisputed domain of birds and wild deer, which exist here in such numbers as to render even these large areas of frozen desolation of considerable importance to domestic economy.

Norway lies north of the 58th parallel; its southern extremity, Lindesnes, being at 57° 59′ N. L., while in the north it reaches a latitude of 71° 11′. If the country were applied to the North American continent in the same latitude, its southern part would be found to lie in the region of central Labrador, while its northern extremity would reach the magnetic pole. Considering its high latitude, the climatic conditions of the country are unique. The Gulf Stream, passing up through the Atlantic to the west of the Scandinavian peninsula, so affects conditions in this respect, that nowhere else in the world is the average temperature so high in the same latitude. The climate varies a great deal with the elevation above the sea, as well as with the latitude, but south of the arctic circle the average temperature is about the same as in our northern tier of states, being cooler in summer, and warmer in winter, than in our states; resembling more closely the climate of the state of Washington and British Columbia. Thunderstorms are rare, even in the southern part. The coast is often swept by strong winds or severe storms, especially in winter, but in the inland districts the air is almost always calm, owing to the uniform temperature. The winter is long and dark; in the northern part of the country an almost unbroken night. A deep covering of snow then spreads over mountains and woodlands, affording unequaled opportunity for sleighing and skiing, which form the most characteristic features of winter life in Norway.

The summer, with its almost continuous daylight, is very beautiful. From the last days of May till the end of July the sun never sets on northern Norway, and even in Christiania day fades so gently into night that they can scarcely be told apart. The summer landscape of fjords and wooded mountain sides, dark headlands and green islands, which break the evening sunlight into various hues and tints, has the ethereal mystic beauty peculiar to high latitudes.

Fishing, farming, and cattle raising were the chief occupations from early times, and they still continue to be the people's principal means of subsistence, though many new pursuits, such as lumbering, commerce, and manufacturing, have become of great importance in later years. According to the sagas, splendidly painted ships with many-colored sails carried fish from Norway to England over 1000 years ago, and fish still continues to be one of the chief articles of export. Especially important are the herring and cod fisheries, though mackerel, halibut, salmon, seatrout, sardines, and lobster are also caught in large quantities. The most noted fishing grounds are the Lofoten Islands, where thirty-six fishing stations are located. In the early months of winter about 40,000 fishermen gather here to take part in the cod fisheries. The average value of the yearly catch of herring, cod, and other varieties of fish, when ready for the market, is estimated at $12,000,000. Agriculture is one of the leading pursuits in Norway, and is carried on in all parts, except in the extreme northern region north of the 70th parallel, where no grain can be raised. Scarcely 3 per cent of the total area of the country is under cultivation, and of this area the greater portion is meadow; only $\frac{7}{10}$ per cent of the total area being devoted to the cultivation of grain. But although the acreage is small, a remarkably large number of people devote themselves to farming. According to the census of 1900, 993,000 persons, or 44.7 per cent of the population, were connected directly or indirectly with this occupation. The average yearly value of agricultural products in the period from 1895 till 1900 was $17,496,000.

Of the cereals wheat, barley, oats, and rye are raised. Wheat and barley were cultivated on the Scandinavian peninsula as early as in the Younger Stone Age, prior to 1500 B.C. Oats was introduced in the Bronze Age (1500–500 B.C.), and rye in the Iron Age (after 500 B.C.). Oats is the chief grain in most districts, being cultivated more extensively than any other cereal; the average annual yield is

9,500,000 bushels. Barley, which ripens as far north as 70° N. L., yields annually about four million bushels. The wheat-growing area is small, being restricted chiefly to the southern district. The yield is about 255,000 bushels annually. Rye is the chief food grain in Norway, and ripens up to 69° or 70° N. L. But it is not raised extensively, as spring rye gives a small yield, and the winter rye is not reliable. The annual yield is about 900,000 bushels. A considerable area is devoted to the raising of pease and potatoes. The pease crop is 220,000 bushels; the potato crop about 23,000,000 bushels annually.

Fruit raising is carried on in many parts of Norway, but not on a very extensive scale. Apples, pears, and cherries are raised, and berries, such as currants, gooseberries, and raspberries, are grown in great abundance. Of wild varieties the blueberry, cloudberry, and whortleberry are found in inexhaustible quantities in the mountain districts. The home market is often glutted with these delicacies at certain seasons of the year, and the export of berries is a growing source of income.

The raising of cattle and other domestic animals is of even greater importance than agriculture, because this branch of husbandry can be carried on with success in places where grain cannot be cultivated. During the last few years the income from this source has been about $40,500,000 a year, or more than the income from fishing and agriculture combined. In connection with cattle raising, dairying has, especially of late years, become of great importance, and may almost be said to be a new branch of husbandry. It has been greatly stimulated through the organization of coöperative dairies with scientific methods of butter making, and by the building of cheese factories and milk-condensing stations. In the period from 1885 till 1900 the number of dairies increased from 249 to 650.

In olden times wild game was so plentiful in the mountain regions of Norway that hunting was an occupation of considerable importance. The Anglo-Norman historian Ordericus Vitalis,[1] who visited Norway in the first part of the twelfth century, writes: " Rural home-

---

[1] Ordericus Vitalis, *Historia Ecclesiastica*, edited by A. le Prevost, *Société de l'Histoire de France*, vol. V., Paris, 1838–1855.

A large part of this work, dealing with the history of the Anglo-Saxons and the Normans, is translated into Danish by P. Kierkegaard, Copenhagen, 1889.

PLATE 1

A MODERN NORWEGIAN FARM, SEIERSTAD, TOTEN.

LUMBERING IN EASTERN NORWAY.

steads are found in large numbers around the lakes of the interior. The people have plenty of fish, fowl, and meat of wild animals. They keep strictly the Commandments and strict laws of the Christian faith, and punish severely any violation of these. From all quarters their ships bring treasures into the country." Hunting has lost its former significance, being now carried on mainly as a sport, but wild game is still very plentiful in all parts of the country, and a considerable income is derived from this source in many districts. The red deer, the elk, and the reindeer still inhabit the mountains and forests in large numbers. The total of 2033 head killed in 1897 may be regarded as a fair yearly average. Still greater are the number and varieties of birds and small game. The grouse is, no doubt, the most important wild game in the country. So plentiful is it that about two million birds are shot or snared every year. The coast of Norway is yearly visited by hosts of wild geese, swans, eider ducks, and other aquatic fowl, and great quantities of eggs and down are gathered.[1]

Commerce reached a high development in Norway in very early times. Through the Viking expeditions new trade routes were developed, and the Norsemen soon became clever merchants, as well as able seamen, and bold warriors. In "The King's Mirror" ("Kongespeilet," "Speculum Regale"), written in Norway about 1250, a father gives advice to his son, who wishes to become a merchant. "Both knowledge and experience is necessary," says the father, "as a merchant must travel in distant lands and among strange peoples. He should be courteous, pleasing in manners, generous, a good judge of goods, and honest and upright in all his dealings. He should avoid gambling and bad company, and whatever might create the impression that he is a mere barterer and an uncultured person. He should set a good table, dress well, and seek the company of the best people wherever he comes." "Study carefully all laws," says the father; "but if you want to be a merchant, there is no law which you should study more carefully than the *Bjarkeyjarréttr*,[2] or laws of trade."

[1] J. N. Gregersen, *Jagt i Norge*, Christiania, 1898. *Norges Fuglevildt, og Jagten paa samme*, Copenhagen, 1881. J. B. Barth, *Erfaringer fra Jagten paa det mindre Vildt i Norge*, 2d edition, Christiania, 1891.

[2] In the trade centers and chief market places there grew up in very early times rules and regulations governing business intercourse. These rules were known by the common name of *Bjarkeyjarréttr*, a word found in Old

"Though I have been more a king's man than a merchant," he says, "yet I find no fault because you choose this occupation, for it is now chosen by many of our best men."[1] Norway's shipping and commerce are, however, at present of far greater economic importance than at any earlier period. In 1913 her merchant marine consisted of 2133 steamships, 1040 sailing vessels, and 205 motor boats, representing altogether a capacity of 2,586,030 tons.[2] Only Great Britain, Germany, and the United States have a larger merchant marine than Norway. The greater number of this large fleet of vessels are engaged in the carrying trade in different parts of the globe. The earned profits of this trade for the year 1900 were $38,853,000.

The forests of Norway are very extensive, covering about 24 per cent of the entire area of the country. About three-fourths of this area is covered with coniferous, and one-fourth with deciduous trees. The value of the annual export of timber and other forest products is estimated at about $15,740,000.

Mining has not hitherto been engaged in on any extensive scale. The most important mines are the Kongsberg silver mines, which have been worked since 1624, the Røros copper mines, operated since 1646, and the Sulitjelma copper mines, which were opened in 1887. Iron ores occur in large quantities in many places, and the mining of this metal is rapidly increasing.

Manufacturing is of comparatively recent development in Norway. In olden times manufactured articles were either imported, or they were supplied through private industry carried on in the homes by members of the family or by skilled laborers. A high degree of skill

Swedish and Old Danish, as well as in Old Norse. The word seems to be derived from Bjarkø or Birka, in Mälaren, Sweden, presumably the oldest important commercial center in the North. The rules of trade here in vogue came into use also in other trading centers and market places, and when these, in course of time, developed into towns and cities, the *Bjarkeyjarréttr* became a code of municipal laws, distinct from the other laws of the country. Alexander Bugge, *Studier over de norske Byers Selvstyre og Handel før Hanseaterne*, Christiania, 1899. The *Bjarkeyjarréttr* or *Bjarkø-Ret* is found in *Norges gamle Love*, published by R. Keyser and P. A. Munch, Christiania, vol. I., part III.

[1] *Kongespeilet*, the *King's Mirror*, Christiania, 1848.

[2] B. E. Bendixen, *Et Omrids of Norges Handelshistorie*, p. 58. *Decorah-Posten*, Decorah, Iowa, July 17, 1914.

and artistic taste had been developed in many handicrafts long before the times of recorded history. Weaving of homespun cloth, both of wool and linen, was common, and the farmers made their own tools and implements. It was the pride of the women then, as it is still in Norway, to embroider with taste, and there were artisans skilled in blacksmithing, wood carving, and in the making of ornaments of precious metals. Ship-building and the making of weapons were national arts which were held in high esteem, and were carried on with surprising skill in design and workmanship. With the development of towns and cities in the eleventh and twelfth centuries, and through the influx of skilled foreign artisans in the thirteenth, fourteenth, and fifteenth, a system of crafts and guilds originated which gained full control of the different lines of manufacture. This system of corporations produced a new industrial growth. Each guild had a monopoly on its specialty, to which the members were limited by strict laws, and which they did much to develop. The old native artisans, not able to compete with these new organizations, lost their importance, and also much of their former skill; but to some degree they have survived all industrial changes, so that even at the present time workers in wood, silver, and brass can be found here and there in the rural districts, whose art seems to have been inherited through successive generations from those early times.

The development of manufactures is limited chiefly to the nineteenth century, the growth having been especially rapid during the last sixty years. In 1850 only 12,700 persons were employed in the factories of Norway; in 1900 the number had risen to 70,000. With the cheap and almost unlimited waterpower available, and with a rich supply of minerals and other raw materials, manufacturing seems destined to become the great future occupation of the Norwegian people. But hitherto, during all the centuries of the past, the location, as well as the general character of the country, has been favorable to the development of the seafaring life along the extensive coasts, and the husbandry in the inland districts which have given Norwegian national life its distinctive features, both economically and socially.

2. SCANDINAVIA IN PREHISTORIC TIMES

How long Scandinavia has been inhabited cannot be determined. When history, about 800 A.D., first lifts the veil of darkness which envelops the remote past, we find a people far advanced in civilization, possessing a high social organization, art, laws, and even some degree of luxury and refinement. No detailed account can be given of the people's life and development prior to this period, but archæology has been able, through numerous finds of relics of antiquity, to establish some important data regarding prehistoric conditions which make it possible to trace in large outlines the greater phases of progress and the mode of life.[1] Iron has been in use in Scandinavia since about 500 B.C., and the period from 500 B.C. to 1050 A.D. is called by archæologists the *Iron Age*. Other metals were in use earlier. Articles of gold, copper, and bronze were brought to Scandinavia from southern Europe as early as 2000 B.C.

About 1500 B.C. bronze seems to have come into general use in the making of weapons and edged tools. The period from 2000 B.C. to 500 B.C., when iron makes its appearance, is, therefore, known as the *Bronze Age*. Prior to this era weapons and implements were made of stone, wood, bone, and horn, and this earliest period is called the *Stone Age*. In this period two different epochs are noticeable; the *Older Stone Age*, and the *Younger Stone Age*. In the Older Stone Age people seem to have lived almost exclusively by hunting and fishing. Their clothes were made of skin; their tools

---

[1] *Annaler for nordisk Oldkyndighed*, Copenhagen. J. J. A. Worsaae, *Nordens Forhistorie*, Copenhagen, 1881. Oscar Montelius, *Om Livet i Sverige under Hednatiden*, Stockholm, 1905. Reinert Svendsen, *Fortidsmindesmerker i Ringsaker paa Hedemarken*, Christiania, 1902. *Skrifter udgivet af Videnskabs-Selskabet i Christiania*, II historiske klasse, 1910; *Den antike Stenalder i Norge*, A. W. Brøgger. Paul Du Chaillu, *The Viking Age*, Scribner's, New York, 1889. Gabriel Gustafson, *Norges Oldtid*, Christiania, 1906. Sophus Müller, *Vor Oldtid*, Copenhagen, 1897. Alexander Bugge, *Norges Historie*, vol. I, 1. Sophus Müller, *De forhistoriske Tider i Europa, Verdenskulturen*, edited by Aage Friis, vol. II., p. 1 ff. Sven Nilsson, *Skandinaviska Nordens Ur-invånare*, 1838–1843. Sven Nilsson, *Udkast til Jagtens og Fiskeriets ældste Historie i Skandinavien*. J. J. A. Worsaae, *Danmarks Oldtid*, 1843. Ingvald Undset, *Jernalderens Begyndelse i Nord-Europa*, Christiania, 1881.

FIG. 1. — Flint ax from Skåne.　　FIG. 2. — Flint ax from Skåne.　　FIG. 3. — Flint ax from Bohuslen.

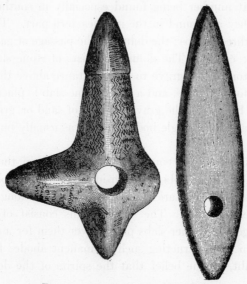

FIG. 4. — Stone axes from Bohuslen.

and weapons of horn and bone. They had only one domestic animal, the dog, probably a domesticated jackal.

No graves have been found from this period. The most important remains are the great shell-heaps (avfaldsdynger, kjøkkenmøddinger). These heaps consist of mussel and oyster shells, and of bones of fish, birds, and animals, such as the bear, urox, wild boar, deer, wolf, fox, etc.; embedded in which are found arrowheads, spear points, and other stone weapons and implements, together with fragments of earthenware, and articles made of bone and horn.

The Younger Stone Age gives evidence that great progress had been made in many ways. Stone weapons and tools were made, as a rule, of flint, which was the best-known material for edged tools. They are nicely polished and graceful in form, bearing evidence of the taste and skill of the makers. Agriculture may be said to have begun, since both wheat and barley are known to have been cultivated. Nearly all the domestic animals were introduced, which can be seen from bones found in the graves from this period. The importation of flint from Denmark to the Scandinavian peninsula, of which there is evidence, seems to show that navigation, too, was in the process of development. Of special importance to the study of the Younger Stone Age are the many graves preserved from this epoch, a great number being found especially in southern Sweden. In Norway they are found in the southeastern part. They may be divided into three groups: the dolmens, the passage or gallery graves, and the stone coffins. The dolmen consists of stone slabs reaching from the bottom of the grave to some distance above the ground, so placed as to form a circle, and a great stone slab is placed on top as a roof. The bottom of the grave is made of sand or gravel. These graves are made for a single body, which was usually buried in a sitting posture.

The gallery graves are constructed very much in the same way, but they are burial chambers of considerable size, supplied with an entrance passage. They are sometimes twenty feet long, twelve feet wide, and six feet high. The stone coffins consist of stone slabs placed on edge, with other slabs placed over them for a cover.

The custom of constructing such permanent abodes for the dead rests, no doubt, on the belief that the spirits of the departed con-

FIG. 5. — Stone ax from
Bohuslen.

FIG. 6. — Stone ax
from Skåne.

FIG. 7. — Flint saw from Bohuslen.

FIG. 8. — Grindstone from Skåne.

tinued to exist after death, much in the same way as in this present life. The grave was to be a suitable habitation, supplied with such

FIG. 9. — Dolmen in Bohuslen.

necessaries as they might need. Clothes, weapons, ornaments, even food and drink were placed in the grave with the dead body, and

FIG. 10. — Passage grave in Vestergötland.

offerings, probably connected with the worship of the spirit of ancestors so common among early peoples, were, no doubt, performed on the flat stone forming the roof of the grave.

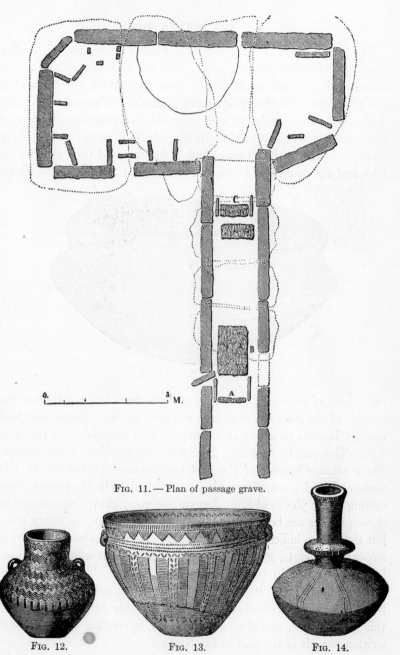

FIG. 11. — Plan of passage grave.

FIG. 12.   FIG. 13.   FIG. 14.

Vessels found in an old burial chamber in Denmark.

3. THE BRONZE AGE

The introduction of bronze, and the livelier intercourse with other countries, of which this is a proof, gave rise to a new culture in the Scandinavian North much higher than that which the Stone Age had produced. Weapons, ornaments, vessels, and utensils were now made with a taste in design and ornamentation sometimes worthy of the skilled artisans of Rome itself. Most of these articles were made at home, but the bronze had to be imported from the British Isles and the countries of central and southern Europe. This shows

FIG. 15. — Bronze bowl.

that ships of considerable size must have been built, and that the peoples of the North were able to navigate the sea, though they had not yet learned to use sails, which were first introduced in the Iron Age. This can be seen also from the rock tracings of this period. These strange records of the past are pictures chiseled on the flat surface of rocks, sometimes, also, on stone slabs in the graves, illustrating many phases of life. Among the many things represented in these pictures are boats, carrying sometimes as many as thirty men, but there is no indication of mast or sail. Horses can be seen drawing two-wheeled carts, spans of oxen hitched to four-wheeled wagons, farmers engaged in ploughing, warriors on horseback, etc. The full meaning of this system of picture writing has not been deciphered, but the pictures themselves throw considerable light on the life of this early period, and they are especially interesting as the earliest written records of the past in the North.

PLATE II

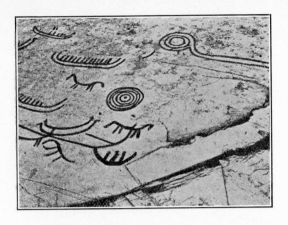

ROCK TRACING IN BOHUSLEN.

Besides bronze, ornaments of gold and many other articles were imported. Many of these articles of foreign make show that the Scandinavian countries already at this time must have been in communication with southern Europe. The earliest routes of intercourse seem to have followed the large rivers of southern Russia from the Black Sea into Poland, and thence along the Vistula to the shores of the Baltic Sea.

The mode of burial was also changed. During the first centuries of this era the bodies of the dead, together with weapons and ornaments, were placed in coffins made of hollowed oak logs which were deposited in mounds. To this mode of burial we owe the fortunate circumstance that garments have been found in so remarkable a state of preservation that not only the material, but also the style, can be determined. The garments found are made of woolen cloth; in one instance of linen. The women wore cap, waist, and skirt, very much of the same style as they still wear them in our time. The men's dress, besides cap and footwear, consisted chiefly of a cloak-shaped garment fastened about the waist with a belt. No trousers were yet worn.

FIG. 17. — Bronze spear point.

FIG. 16. — Bronze ax.

It became customary quite early in the Bronze Age to burn the bodies of the dead, a custom which also marks a great change in the ideas regarding the life hereafter. It is believed that the body was burned in order that the soul might the more quickly be liberated from the fetters of the natural world, and begin

FIG. 18. — Ornamental bronze disk.

FIG. 21. — Rock tracing in Bohuslen.

FIG. 19. — Bronze buckle.

FIG. 20. — Rock tracing in Bohuslen.

its own separate existence; but the graves still contained weapons, ornaments, and other articles needed by the departed, which shows that, though the body was burned, the spirit was thought to continue its existence after death. Women were buried with the same elaborate care as the men, which indicates that already in this early

FIG. 22. — Oak coffin from the Bronze Age, found at Treenhøi in Denmark.

period they were held in high esteem in Scandinavia, and that their position in society was one of dignity and honor.

4. THE IRON AGE

About the beginning of the fifth century B.C. iron replaced bronze as the most important metal. Throughout the Bronze Age the peoples of the North had been in communication with the countries of southern Europe, and through this intercourse they became acquainted with iron, as they had learned to know bronze in the same way at a still earlier period. The Iron Age may be divided into several quite distinct periods. During the *pre-Roman period*, embracing the earlier centuries of the era from about 500 B.C. to the birth of Christ, the influence of the Celtic peoples of Gaul and the Alpine region is especially noticeable, but this influence ceased when the Romans, by extending their sway over Gaul and Britain, came into direct contact with the Germanic world. From that time to the fall of the Roman Empire the superior Latin civilization exerted a preponderating influence on the development and culture in the North. This period has, therefore, been called the *Roman Iron Age*.[1] The

[1] It should be observed that the time limits fixed for these various ages are admitted by archæologists themselves to be purely tentative. No ulti-

culture which developed under the influence of Roman civilization unfolded itself of a sudden with a certain gaudy splendor produced by the influx of Roman customs and ideas. Richly ornamented

swords, coats of ring mail, metal helmets, spurs, elegantly mounted bridles, and rich trappings for war horses give evidence of the splendor of war accouterments which now came into use. Silver, lead, zinc, and glass were introduced, and money of Roman coinage makes its appearance.[1] A variety of articles for domestic use, such as elegantly designed vases and drinking-horns of glass, metal mirrors, bronze statuettes, strainers,

FIG. 23.— Ornamented drinking-horn.

silver goblets, bronze vases, razors, shears, tweezers, and costly ornaments of gold and silver, furnish an even stronger proof of the luxury which had been developed in the North long before the Viking Age.

mate criterion exists according to which these dates can be determined, and it is natural that there should be considerable divergence of opinion among the authorities. Montelius estimates:

Older Stone Age, prior to 5000 B.C.
Younger Stone Age, 5000–2000 B.C.
Bronze Age, 2000–500 B.C.
Older Iron Age, 500 B.C.–800 A.D.
Younger Iron Age, 800 A.D.–1050 A.D.

Sophus Müller estimates:

Older Stone Age, prior to 3000 B.C.–2500 B.C.
Bronze Age, prior to 1000 B.C.–after 500 B.C.
Older Iron Age, ca. 400 B.C.–800 A.D.
—*Vor Oldtid*, Copenhagen, 1897.

[1] About 6000 Roman coins from this period have been found on the islands in the Baltic, and in Denmark, Sweden, and Norway. The most noteworthy finds are the following: In 1842, 600 Roman silver coins from the first and second centuries A.D. were found at Kanes, in the island of Gothland. In 1871 a similar find of 550 Roman denarii was made at Hagestadborg, in southern Sweden. At Bagsværd, near Copenhagen, forty-five Roman

FIG. 25. — Ring mail.

FIG. 26. — Shield boss.

FIG. 24. — Bronze statuette.

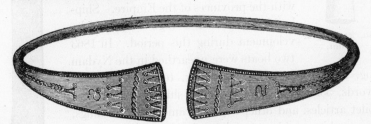

FIG. 27. — Gold ring.

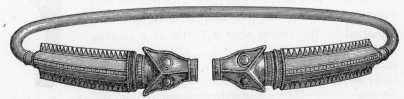

FIG. 28. — Gold ring.

The mode of burial remained much the same as it was in the later Bronze Age. The bodies of the dead, together with weapons and ornaments, were usually burned on a funeral pyre, and the ashes and other remains were deposited in bowl-shaped graves, over which sometimes a mound was thrown up, on which a rune-stone was placed, bearing the name of the dead. The swords and other articles found in these graves have been damaged by fire; often they have been purposely bent and twisted, so as to be rendered useless. Sometimes the body was not burned, but was buried with weapons and ornaments in grave-chambers made of stone slabs.

Fig. 29.—Spear point.

The contact of the North with the Roman world, though not a direct one, exerted a great influence. Trade was greatly stimulated; possibly also ship-building and navigation. The great number of Roman coins and other articles of Roman make brought to Scandinavia by traders show that a lively intercourse must have been maintained with the provinces of the Empire. Ship-building reached a high stage of development during this period. In 1863 two boats were unearthed in the Nydam bog, near Sundeved in Schleswig, together with 106 swords, 552 spear points, seventy shield bosses, coins, toilet articles, and other objects; among other things, also, a shirt, or blouse, and a pair of trousers made of woolen cloth were found, which show that trousers were worn at this time. The collection seems to have been deposited by the victors after a battle as a sacrifice

coins from the period 69–218 A.D. were found in 1850, and the same year thirty-six Roman gold coins were found in the island of Bornholm. *Antiquarisk Tidsskrift udgivet av det Kongelige nordiske Oldskriftselskab*, Copenhagen, vol. for 1849–1851. Oscar Montelius, *Livet i Norden under Hednatiden.*

Fig. 30.—Iron sword.

FIG. 31. — Part of a sword found in Upland, Sweden.

FIG. 32. — Boat found near Sundeved in Denmark.

to the gods, and is thought to date from about 400 A.D. One of the boats is of oak, the other of pine. The oak boat is about eighty feet long, and eleven feet wide at the middle. It is made for fourteen pairs of oars, and is riveted together with iron rivets. It has no mast. The prow and stern are both sharp and of equal height, so that it is difficult to tell which is the rear, and which is the front end of the vessel. It is of the same shape as the ships of the Suiones (Swedes) described by Tacitus. "The states of the Suiones (Swedes), situated in the ocean itself, are strong in fleets as well as in men and arms. Their ships differ from ours in this respect; that both ends present a front always ready for landing. They do not equip their ships with sails, nor do they join the oars in due order to the sides. The oarage is loose, as on certain river boats, and can be changed from one side to the other as circumstances demand." [1]

The most striking evidence of the development of culture during this period is the introduction of the runic alphabet and the art of writing. The older runic alphabet consists of twenty-four characters, divided into three equal groups, as follows:

f ut h a r c gw : h n i j e p – R s : t b e m l ng o d

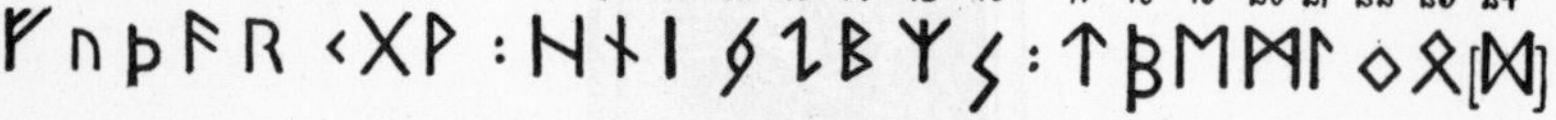

FIG. 33. — Early runic alphabet.

The first six characters form the word *futharc*, which is often used instead of the word *alphabet* to designate the system of runic letters. The resemblance between the runes and the letters of the Latin alphabet is, in several cases, quite apparent, and the Danish scholar L. F. A. Wimmer advanced the theory, which was for some time everywhere accepted, that the runes have been derived from the Latin alphabet, and that they first came into use in southern Germany. The change in the form of the Latin letters was occasioned by the fact that the runes were carved on wood, or cut in stone or metal, which made the use of the angle and straight line much more convenient than the curve or circle. Later the Norwegian scholar Sophus Bugge advanced the opinion that they originated among the Goths, in the region

[1] Tacitus, *Germania*, ch. 44.

north of the Black Sea,[1] an idea which gained further support through the investigations of the Swedish archæologist Bernhard Salin. He showed that the runes must have been brought to the North along the old routes of intercourse between the Black Sea and the Baltic, known to have existed even in the Bronze Age, as they first made their appearance in those regions. Professor von Friesén, of Upsala University, has since shown that the runes have been derived from a system of Greek letters, the so-called cursive or running hand, which was much used in everyday life in the eastern part of the Empire. Of the twenty-four runes in the older runic alphabet, fifteen are surely derived from this Greek alphabet, and five more are, presumably, traceable to the same source. Only four are derived from the Latin alphabet, with which the Goths may have become acquainted in the Latin colony of Dacia, north of the Danube.[2]

Runic inscriptions have been found wherever Germanic peoples have dwelt, but they are especially numerous in the Scandinavian countries, and in Great Britain. The runic inscriptions on stone are by far the most important, and these are found principally in the Scandinavian countries. One hundred inscriptions in the older runic alphabet, from 300 to 700 A.D., are found in Denmark, Norway, and Sweden, some of which are of great length. The language is everywhere the same, showing that, as yet, no difference in speech existed in the three countries. Besides Wulfilas Bible translation, and a few loan-words in the Finnish and Lappish languages, these earliest runic inscriptions are the oldest remains in the Germanic tongue that have been preserved to us.

As a result of the closer contact of the Empire with the Germanic peoples of the North, the Romans became better acquainted with this part of the world hitherto so unknown. The enterprising Greek explorer Pytheas from Massilia, in southern Gaul, made voyages to Britain and northern Europe about 330 B.C. On one of these expeditions he also visited Thule and the Amber Coast. His own accounts

---

[1] L. F. A. Wimmer, *Runeskriftens Oprindelse og Udvikling i Norden*, Copenhagen. Sophus Bugge, *Norges Indskrifter med de ældre Runer*, Christiania. G. Stephenson, *The Old Northern Runic Monuments of Scandinavia and England*, London, 1866–1884.

[2] Otto v. Friesén, *Om Runskriftens Härkomst; Sprokvetenskapliga Sällskapets Förhandlingar*, 1904–1906.

of these voyages have been lost, but brief notices are given by the Greek geographer Strabo in his "Geographica,"[1] and by Plinius the Elder in his "Historia Naturalis."[2] According to Pytheas, Thule was situated six days' sailing from Britain, and one day's sailing from the frozen, or half-frozen, ocean called *mare cronium*. He regards Thule as the most northern country, and relates that summer is a continuous day, and winter a continuous night, there for six months. "The people live on hirse and garden vegetables, as well as on wild fruit and roots. Those who have grain and honey make also a drink from these. When they have cut the grain, they bring it into large houses and thrash it there, because they have no bright sunshine, and thrashing-floors in the open would be useless because of excessive rains." Strabo, lib. IV., ch. V. That Thule is identical with Norway can scarcely be doubted, but the description given of the people may apply to Britain and the North in general.

This was about the only knowledge which the world possessed of Scandinavia prior to the Christian era. In the year 40, or 44, A.D., Pomponius Mela, a Roman geographer, wrote a book, "De Chorographia," describing the countries of the then known world, in which he also mentions Scandinavia. This is the first time the name is employed by Roman writers.

"In that bay which we have called Codanus, Scandinavia is prominent. It is still occupied by the Teutons, and surpasses the other islands in fertility and size." — "Chorographia," III., 54.

Plinius the Elder (23–79 A.D.) also uses the name in his "Historia Naturalis." He had served as cavalry officer in the German campaigns, and had visited the shores of the North Sea. He manifests a real interest in Scandinavia, which he believes to be an island, or a group of islands, in the northern sea. "There the Mount Særvo, itself of great height, and not lower than the Riphæic[3] Mountains,

---

[1] Strabo, *Geographica*, lib. I., ch. IV.; lib. III., ch. V.; lib. IV., ch. V. W. Bessell, *Ueber Pytheas von Massilien*, Göttingen, 1858. D. Gustav Moritz Redslob, *Thule, die phönicischen Handelswege nach dem Norden, die Reise des Pytheas von Massilien*, Leipzig, 1855. Strabo did not receive his information directly from Pytheas' own works, but from the writings of Eratosthenes, Polybios, and Hipparchos.   [2] *Historia Naturalis*, II., 75, IV., 16.

[3] The Riphæic or Rhipæic Mountains were fabulous mountains supposed to represent the northern boundary of the then known world. To the north

forms a bay with the promontory of the Cimbri. This bay, which is called Codanus, is full of islands, the most noted of which is *Scatinavia*, of unknown size." — Lib. IV., 96.

"There are those who tell of other islands, Scandia, Dumnam, Bergi, Berice, or Nerigon,[1] the largest of all, whence one sails to Tyle. One day's sailing from Tyle lies the frozen ocean called Cronium by some." — Lib. IV., 104. The name *Scandia* is still preserved in Skåne, southern Sweden.

Tacitus, in his "Germania," written 98 A.D., distinguishes between the Suiones (Swedes) and their neighbors, the Sitones.

"Beyond the Suiones lies another ocean, sluggish, and almost without motion, which is thought to terminate and encompass the sphere of the earth, since the light of the setting sun continues so bright till it rises, that it makes the stars dim." — "Germania," 44, 45.

In the second century A.D. Claudius Ptolemy of Alexandria mentions Scandia and Thule.

"North of the Orcades lies Thule, of which the western part is in the latitude 63°, o., longitude 29°." — "Geographia," lib. II., ch. III.

"East of the Cimbrian peninsula (the Danish peninsula) there are four islands called Scandiæ; three indeed are small; the middle one is in the latitude 58°, longitude 41° 30'. The one which is largest and farthest to the east, near the mouth of the river Vistula, is properly called Scandia. Its western part is inhabited by the Chaideinoi, the eastern part by the Phanonai and the Phiraisoi, the southern part is occupied by the Gautai and the Dauchiones, and the middle part by the Lenonoi." — "Geographia," lib. II., ch. XII.

These peoples are unknown, except the Gautai, or Götar, here mentioned for the first time as the inhabitants of Scandinavia, and the

of these, the ancients thought, lay the frozen ocean, and the icy regions towards the borders of the earth. According to later ideas, the Hyperboreans dwelt north of these mountains. The sky was clear, and the climate ideal there, as the region lay north of the north wind, which was supposed to come from the Rhipæic Mountains. The Hyperboreans were thought to live in groves, in a state of perfect innocence and uninterrupted happiness.

[1] The form *Nerigon*, found in one manuscript, might be the same as Norway. But the name *Noregr* or *Norvegr* (= the northern way) seems not to have been in use till about 800 A.D.

Chaideinoi or Heiner, the inhabitants of Hedemarken, in eastern Norway.

Denmark and southern Sweden had up to this time been the most densely populated portions of the North, but throughout the Iron Age the population was growing rapidly, and the remoter parts of Norway and Sweden were cleared and settled. Norway, which had hitherto had the smallest population, made gains during this period which placed her on a more equal footing with the other two northern countries.[1]

5. THE MIGRATIONS

From 400 A.D. Rome was fighting her last desperate battles with the conquering hosts of Germanic warriors, and, like a bleeding gladiator, was fast tottering to her fall. The legions were withdrawn from Gaul and Britain for the defense of the Italian peninsula, but this served only to give the untiring victors new vantage ground. The weakened defenses of the frontiers were forced, Gaul and Spain were overrun, Rome was sacked, the Empire was crumbling to pieces before the onset of this new race, destined to wrest the scepter of empire from the withering hands of Rome that they might teach the world new lessons. The peoples of Germany were no longer unskilled barbarians, unacquainted with culture. Since the days of the Emperor Augustus

[1] Amund Helland has given estimates of the population of Norway in the different periods of prehistoric times based on the number and distribution of archæological finds, and on calculations made by the historians P. A. Munch and Ernst Sars from the size and number of ships in the Norwegian navy in the Younger Iron Age. His investigations give the following general results:

At the end of the Stone Age, 1200 B.C. (Sophus Müller)	2,500
In the middle of the Bronze Age, 800 B.C.	4,700
At the beginning of the Iron Age, 400 B.C.	9,000
At the time of the birth of Christ	17,400
200 A.D.	24,200
400 A.D.	80,000
800 A.D. (the beginning of the Younger Iron Age)	146,000
925 A.D. (the middle of the Younger Iron Age)	212,000
1050 A.D. (at the end of the Younger Iron Age)	242,000

This seems to be a very small population, but it must be remembered that all countries in northern Europe had a very small population at that time, measured by modern standards. Amund Helland, *Oldfundene og Norges Folkemængde i forhistoriske Tider*, Christiania, 1908.

they had followed the Roman eagles as soldiers of the legions, from the prætorian guard in Rome to the remotest provinces of the Empire. They now possessed great skill in the art of war; they had great leaders, excellent arms, and an efficient military organization, as they had attained to a high degree of general culture, gained through long periods of development, and, finally, through direct contact with the Roman world. This accounts for their victory over Rome in this most notable contest for world power. That the warriors from Scandinavia also took part in the expeditions against the Roman Empire can be seen from the great treasures of gold brought to the North during this period. At Tureholm, near Trosa, in Sweden, were found, in 1774, articles of gold weighing all together 25 pounds; the actual metal value of which at the present time would be $7214. So many similar treasures have been found, that it is regarded as certain that they are the spoils of warlike expeditions against Rome, or part of the tribute paid the Germanic peoples by the emperors of the East Roman Empire during the fifth century. The first Germanic peoples who crossed the borders of the Roman Empire were the Cimbri and the Teutones. They came from the peninsula of Jutland, and appeared in the Roman province of Noricum in 113 B.C. Their combined fighting force is said to have numbered 300,000 men, and they repeatedly defeated the Roman armies sent against them. The terror in Rome was so great that the expression *terror cimbricus* became proverbial. In 104 B.C. Gaius Marius, the hero of the war against Jugurtha, was made consul and general. He took the field with a large and well-disciplined army. In 102 he met the Teutones in southern Gaul, and destroyed them in the battle of Aquæ Sextiæ. The next year he annihilated the Cimbri, who had penetrated into the Po valley in upper Italy. The size of the fighting forces of these great migrating hosts indicates that other tribes must have joined them on their southward march.[1]

The Herules, a people who played a conspicuous part in the

---

[1] Ptolemy knows the Cimbri, who, according to him, inhabited the northern part of Jutland (*Cimbri Chersonesus*). Their name is thought to be preserved still in Himmerland, a region south of the Limfjord. Near them dwelt the Charudes, whose name is still preserved in *Hardesyssel*. *Geographia*, lib. II., ch. XI., tabula IV. See also Alexander Bugge, *Vikingerne*, Christiania, 1904.

migrations, came from southern Scandinavia. Jordanes [1] says that they were driven from their homes by the Danes, and Procopius [2] states that when their king died they sent to their own royal race in Thule for a leader. Very early in the period they migrated southward into the region north of the Danube, where they founded a kingdom. A part of their force joined the army of Odovacer, and aided him in destroying the West Roman Empire. According to Procopius, their kingdom was destroyed by the Longobards, with whom they were waging war; some of them sought refuge in the East Roman Empire, and some returned to Scandinavia, taking up their abode near the Gautar, where they seem to have had their original home.[3]

The Gautar [4] and the Swedes (Swear, Sviones) are the first peoples in the Scandinavian North which passed out of mere tribal organization, and founded kingdoms of some strength and importance. The Gautar inhabited Götaland, a region around the great lakes Venern and Vettern in Sweden. The Swedes founded the kingdom of Svitiod, which embraced the tribes and territories farther north,

[1] An historian of the sixth century, of Gothic descent, known from his work, *De Origine Actibusque Getarum*. Jordanes had read Flavius Cassiodorus' history of the Goths, which is now lost. In his work he supplements what information he had thus gathered with what he himself knew, or believed to be true, about the Goths and their neighbors. The work contains many interesting things, but it is not reliable.

[2] Procopius, a Greek historian of the sixth century A.D., much more reliable than Jordanes, wrote *Historiae* (*History of his own Time*), in eight books.

Jordanes tries to show that the Goths originally came from Scandinavia. "Therefore, from this island of Scandza, as if from a workshop of peoples, or as if from the womb of nations, the Goths, led by their king Berig, are known at one time to have gone forth " (ch. IV.). He evidently considered the Goths to be identical with the Gautar, the inhabitants of Götaland, in southern Sweden, but this is, no doubt, erroneous. The Goths seem to have called themselves *gutans*. Tacitus writes *gothones*, Plinius *guthones*, Ptolemy *gotones*. *Gutans* corresponds to the Old English *gotan*, Old Norse *gotar*, Old High German *gozzen*, still preserved in *Gossensass* (= Gotensitz), name of a village in Tyrol. The inhabitants of Götaland in Sweden are called in Old Norse *gautar*, a form which in Gothic would be *gautôs*. Ptolemy writes *gautai*.

[3] Alexander Bugge thinks that the Herules were not a single people, but that the name is used as a common designation for all the Scandinavian peoples who took part in the migrations into southern Europe.

[4] The Gautai (Gautar) are mentioned by Ptolemy. Procopius says that they are the most numerous of the thirteen tribes inhabiting Thule.

around Lake Mälaren. They gradually enlarged their dominions until all Sweden was united under the rule of their kings. The Swedes were closely related to the Goths, among whom kingship had reached a much higher development than in western Germany, where the kings were still mere tribal chieftains and leaders of the armed host. Among the Goths the king was the ruler of his people — a national sovereign, who traced his lineage to the gods themselves. This institution of national kingship also obtained among the Swedes, and it is probable that they had adopted it from their Gothic kinsmen. The royal seat and center of the kingdom was Upsala, the oldest and most famous sanctuary in Sweden. The king served also as priest in the great temple there, and this union of the priestly with the royal office must have tended to strengthen greatly the power and influence of the kings of Upsala. They were of the Scilfing family,[1] a royal race which had ruled in Svitiod long before historic times, and were supposed to be the descendants of the god Frey, who, according to tradition, had built the temple at Upsala.[2]

The Angles, Saxons, and Jutes, who effected the conquest of England, came from the Cimbric peninsula. The Saxons were a German tribe dwelling north of the Elbe, in what is now Holstein. Ptolemy says that they lived "on the neck of the Cimbric Chersonesus."[3] From the third century they are frequently mentioned by Roman historians as marauders in the North Sea.

North of the Saxons, in what is now Schleswig, dwelt the Angles. Their name is still preserved in *Angeln*, a district in southern Schleswig. They are mentioned by Ptolemy, and Tacitus speaks of them in connection with several other tribes, as worshipers of the goddess Nerthus.[4] King Alfred says that northwest of the Saxons lies the land called Angle (Angeln), and Sillende (Seeland), and a part of the Danes.[5] Bede, in his account of the conquest, says: "From the Angles, that is, from the region which is now called 'Angulus,' and which is said to have remained from that day till now depopulated, lying between the boundaries of the Jutes and the Saxons, came the East Angles, the Mid Angles, the Mercians, and all the race of North-

---

[1] Sometimes also called Ynglings.
[2] Snorre Sturlason, *Kongesagaer* (*Heimskringla*).
[3] *Geographia*, lib. II., ch. XI.   [4] *Germania*, ch. 40.   [5] Alfred's *Orosius*.

umbrians who dwell north of the river Humber."[1] They seem to have inhabited the greater part of Schleswig, possibly also some of the Danish islands. They must have migrated to Britain during the conquest, since Bede states that their country was depopulated from that day.

The Jutes are a more obscure people. They have given their name to Jutland, the northern part of the Cimbric peninsula, where they are thought to have dwelt as early as 100 A.D., though they are not mentioned by Ptolemy. They are believed to be the Eudoses mentioned by Tacitus. To them belonged Hengist and Horsa, the chiefs of the Anglo-Saxon host which invaded Britain. The Angles and Saxons were related Low-German tribes, but the Jutes seem to have been of Danish origin.

The Danes inhabited southern Sweden and the Danish isles. The first account of them is given by Jordanes, who says that they came from Scandinavia, and that they drove away the Herules. Procopius states that a part of the Herules returning northward to their old homes came to the ocean; no doubt, the Baltic Sea. From there they wandered through the Danish territories, whence they returned to Thule. From about 500, the Danes entered upon a period of remarkable development and greatness. Their kings, the Skjoldungs (Scyldings), dwelt at Leire in Seeland, where they built the royal hall *Heorot*, celebrated in the Old English poem "Beówulf." In 515 their king Hygelâc (Hugleik) made an expedition against the Hetware near the mouth of the Rhine, where he fell in battle. He is, no doubt, the *Chochilaicus* mentioned by Gregory of Tours and the "Gesta Regum Francorum," who, on an invasion of the lower Rhineland, lost his life in a battle against the Frankish prince Theodebert in 515.[2] In 565 the Danes made another similar expedition westward. They fought many hard battles, especially with the Heathobeards dwelling south of the Baltic Sea. These landed on Seeland at one time, and advanced almost to Heorot, but they were defeated by King Hrôthgâr (Roar) and his nephew Hrôthulf (Rolf Krake). Rolf Krake became

---

[1] Bede, *Historia Ecclesiastica*, I., 16.

[2] In *Beówulf* he is called the king of the Geátas, or Gautar, who dwelt in Götaland in Sweden. See Hermann Paul's *Grundriss der germanischen Philologie*, 2d ed., vol. III., p. 817.

the ideal king and semi-mythical hero of tradition, who is said to have been slain in his royal hall, together with his twelve champions, in a treacherous night attack.[1] The Danes were at this time the most renowned people in the North, though the Swedes rivaled them in warlike achievements, as well as in wealth and power. The Swedish kings [2] waged war with the Danes, and made expeditions into Esthonia, and other regions east of the Baltic. Their royal family was the oldest in the North, and their kingdom, Svitiod, had risen into prominence before that of the Danes. No such united national kingdom had yet been founded in Norway as in Sweden and Denmark, but kings ruled here also, and the tribes had formed larger unions in different parts. Jordanes speaks of the Norwegian king Rodulf, who, fleeing from his own country, went to Theoderic the Great in Italy and became his man. Rodulf seems to have ruled over a confederation of tribes in southern Norway.

The Old English poem "Wídsíth," and more especially "Beówulf," preserves many traces of historic events, and of social life in Denmark and southern Scandinavia in the sixth century. The detailed descriptions of arms and customs given in "Beówulf," no doubt, reflect quite accurately many features of the life of the chieftains and their followers during the sixth and seventh centuries. Heorogâr, Hrôthgâr, and Hâlga are the sons of Healfdene, of the dynasty of the Scyldings (Skjoldungs).

Hrôthulf, son of Hâlga, is the Rolf Krake so famous in Danish tradition. Hrôthgâr builds the hall Heorot at Leire in Seeland, a feature of the tradition which preserves the memory of the power of the Danish kings at that time. Beówulf, a nephew of King Hygelâc, comes with a band of followers to help Hrôthgâr against the monster

---

[1] See *Hrólfssaga* and Saxo Grammaticus.

[2] A number of remarkable graves have been found at Vendel, a little to the north of Upsala, which are believed to be the graves of ancient Swedish kings. The mode of burial shows that the persons interred here must have been princes of wealth and power. This can be seen, also, from the richly ornamented helmets which have been found in three of the graves. At this time (about 600 A.D.) such helmets were worn only by persons of royal blood. From 1881 till 1893 fourteen of the graves were examined. In all cases the body of the dead person was buried in a boat, together with his helmet, shield, sword, war horse with saddle, dogs and hawks for the chase, food and drink, and all necessary utensils.

Grendel. After the military guards of the coast have permitted him to land, he proceeds to Heorot with his companions. They have shields, helmets, and brynies of ring-mail, and are in every way well armed and trained warriors. They are courteously received, and are entertained in the most hospitable manner.

"Then Wealhtheów, the queen, entered, the lady mindful of good manners. Adorned with golden ornaments she came to greet the guests. She first gave the drinking cup to the king of the Danes, and asked him to partake of their banquet. He gladly took the cup, and accepted the entertainment. She went all about, this highminded lady from the country of the Helmings, and gave gifts to young and old, till the opportunity came when the ring-adorned queen handed the meadcup to the prince of the Geátas, and she thanked God that her wish had been fulfilled, that at last she could expect from an earl help out of their difficulties." — "Beówulf," 608-629.

When Beówulf had succeeded in killing Grendel, there was great joy at Heorot, and many came from far and near to see what had happened. When the festivities at the hall were at their height, a *scop*, or *scald*, arose. Every one became silent, and listened to what he might have to say. He sang of Beówulf's journey, and

"Every old song which he had heard of Sigemund, and of many an unknown heroic deed; about Wølsung's combats and distant journeys, about battles and malice, of which none of the children of men yet knew, save he and Fitela alone." — "Beówulf," 872-880.

Sigemund the Wølsung is the father of Siegfried, or Sigurd, the slayer of Fafnir, so well known from the "Elder Edda," the "Vølsungasaga," and the "Nibelungenlied," and Fitela is Sinfjotle, Sigurd's half-brother.

"Then the king himself, the giver of rings, stepped from his queen's apartment, rich in glory, with an excellent band of followers, and the queen walked with him into the festive hall with her train of maids." — "Beówulf," 920-925.

The cultural life of this period must not be judged by twentieth century standards, still there was among these early ancestors of ours, not only a very considerable civilization in the externals of life, but intellectual culture and a spirit of refinement were not wanting. They appreciated art and fine manners. They had lofty sentiments and noble virtues, less polished, but, probably, no less vigorous and constant than those which have graced society in later ages.

The Migrations checked the peaceful intercourse which the Germanic peoples had hitherto maintained with the Roman Empire, and the necessity of supplying their wants through their own skill and industry, created by this change, made itself more strongly felt. The ideas and cultural elements which had been borrowed from the Romans could now be better assimilated, and the native mind began

FIG. 34. — Gold bracteate found in Bohuslen.

to put its own impress even on articles of luxury, which were now, to a great extent, produced at home. The gold bracteates of this period bear evidence of this transition from Roman to native industry and art. These are ornaments and amulets of gold made in imitation of Roman coins. Besides the original image of the Roman Emperor they are often ornamented with runes, and sometimes with quite original designs representing Thor driving his goats, or Odin with his horse and ravens. The beautifully decorated helmets, swords, shields, buckles, necklaces, and other articles made by native metal workers show these to have been veritable masters in their art. These articles are made with artistic skill and taste. Some are of pure gold, others of gold-plated bronze, or silver, with ornaments of filigree and inlaid jewels. Pictures on helmets show the style of dress worn both by men and women in this period. The men wore a coat reaching to the knees, and fastened about the waist with a belt. It was edged

VOL. I — D

with fur, it had sleeves, and was ornamented in various ways. Trousers were also worn. The lady wore a dress, sometimes ornamented in front with embroidered bands. She wore shawl and necklace, while her hair seems to have hung loose over the shoulders.

Different modes of burial prevailed during this period. The bodies of the dead were sometimes burned, and a mound was, as a rule, thrown up over the charred remains, and a rune-stone was erected on the mound. Sometimes the body, together with weapons and ornaments, was buried in a carefully constructed grave. Over the grave a mound might be constructed, or stones might be set up around it. The dead, both men and women, were often buried in boats. In 1880 a ship was found in a burial mound at Gokstad, near Sandefjord, in Norway, the blue clay of the mound having preserved it from decay. The vessel, which is made of oak planks, is eighty feet long, and sixteen feet wide. It has a mast, and sixteen pairs of oars. Around the ship was hung a row of shields colored black and yellow alternately. A chieftain, no doubt the owner of the vessel, had been buried in it. A burial chamber is constructed in the stern, where the body was placed on a bed furnished with a feather mattress. The grave had been robbed of all ornaments of precious metals, but a complete supply of articles belonging to the outfit of a ship at that time was found. Among these articles were: several bedsteads, a sleigh, a bronze kettle, and many kitchen utensils; also the bones of twelve horses, six dogs, and some birds, which, evidently, had been sacrificed at the burial. The ship is supposed to date from about 900.[1]

Fig. 35. — Rune-stone from Tune, Norway.

In 1904 another ship was unearthed in a large mound at Oseberg, near Tunsberg, in southern Norway. Two women were buried in it; one of high birth — possibly a queen — the other evidently a maid servant. The ship was packed with goods, both fore and aft. Sev-

[1] N. Nicolaysen, *Langskibet fra Gokstad ved Sandefjord*, Christiania, 1882.

PLATE III

The Oseberg Ship, and Wagon found in It.

eral bedsteads, a sleigh, a four-wheeled wagon, the queen's shoes, and her trunk containing toilet articles were among the objects found. Most of the articles, as, for example, the sleigh and the wagon, are decorated with wood carvings so exquisitely done that they are real treasures of beauty. The ship, which is now fully restored, is sixty-eight feet long, and had been beautifully ornamented. It is more tastefully made than the Gokstad ship, and it is regarded as certain that it is the queen's own pleasure yacht. The find dates from about 800 A.D. Together, the articles present a picture of civilization most interesting and impressive.[1] It is quite evident that the districts around the Baltic Sea, and, more particularly, the Scandinavian countries, possessed a culture superior in many ways to that of any other region of the Continent north of the Alps. The population seems to have been denser here than elsewhere. Nowhere else are the graves from early periods so numerous as in this region, and nowhere are the relics of stone, bronze, and other metal work so tastefully designed, or so skillfully made. When Tacitus says of the Esthonians that they raise more grain than is otherwise customary among the Germans, it is only another bit of evidence of the superior culture then existing on the shores of the Baltic Sea.

6. THE PEOPLE

In 1677–1698 the Swedish scholar Olof Rudbeck published a large work, "Atlantica s. Manheim vera Japheti Sedes et Patria," in which he sought to prove that the Atlantis described by Plato was Sweden, the original home of the descendants of Japhet, i.e. the Europeans. The work was held in high esteem until more scientific methods were introduced in archæological research. Since then it has been regarded merely as a literary curiosity. The theory that Scandinavia was the original home of the Indo-European race was again revived by K. Penka, who treated the question in a scientific way in his work "Die Herkunft der Arier," 1886. The theory that the Indo-Europeans migrated from India into Europe has of late years been discarded by many scholars, who hold that the original home of this family of peoples must be sought in northern Europe. Of recent years some

[1] *Saga-Book of the Viking Club*, London, 1908.

scholars have come to regard the region of the Baltic Sea as the original home of this race. Noteworthy is the theory advanced by Matthæus Much that Europe is the original home of the Indo-Europeans, since, in Denmark and the region of the western Baltic, relics have been found showing every stage of development from the earliest to the latest Stone Age, without break or interruption.[1] This continuous development is not found in southern Europe, or in western Asia. The Indo-Europeans raised cattle, and tilled the soil in their original home, says Much, and the domestic animals which have been thought to come from Asia are, no doubt, native to Europe.

The attempted solutions of this difficult problem will, probably, never be much more than more or less plausible conjectures.[2] A similar difficulty confronts us when we ask how long the Scandinavians have lived in the countries which they now inhabit. Archæology shows a gradual and unbroken development from the Stone Age to later eras, with no interruption to indicate any invasion or sudden immigration of any new people. This would tend to prove that the Scandinavians have dwelt in their present home since the Younger Stone Age.[3] Philology holds, on the other hand, that the

[1] "Fragt man sich nun, wo sich uns innerhalb des Steinalters die ältesten, die schönsten und am meisten entwickelten, endlich die zahlreichsten Belege für die Thätigkeit und Befähigung in der Herstellung von Werkzeugen bieten, so besteht kein Zweifel, dass dies die Küsten sind, welche Festland und Insel des westlichen Ostseebeckens umsäumen. Hier treten uns die ältesten und einfachsten Zeugnisse entgegen, welche wir nach Abschluss des paläolithischen Steinalters kennen." *Die Heimat der Indogermanen*, p. 18 f. J. Schmidt, *Urheimat der Indogermanen und das europäische Zahlsystem*, Berlin, 1890. Hermann Paul, *Grundriss der germanischen Philologie*. 2d ed., vol. III., p. 756.

[2] See Eduard Meyer, *Geschichte des Alterthums*, 1909. Vilhelm Thomsen thinks that the original home of the Indo-Europeans was somewhere in the great belt between the Hindu-Kush Mountains and the Indus, to the southeast, and the Baltic Sea, including southern Scandinavia, to the northwest; probably in the region of the lower Danube rather than close to the Baltic. India, as well as the south-European peninsulas, Greece, Italy, and Spain, are excluded, as the immigration of the Indo-Europeans to these regions is clearly traceable. Vilhelm Thomsen, *Oldarisk Kultur*, *Verdenskulturen*, edited by Aage Friis, vol. I., p. 178 ff.

[3] Oscar Montelius says : "As shown by finds of later periods, no new people has immigrated into our country after the close of the Younger Stone Age. This proves that the ancestors of the people now living in Sweden dwelt in this country already at that time." *Om Livet i Sverige i Hednatiden*.

peoples now living in the Scandinavian North have migrated into these regions at a much later period.[1] The Norwegians are not a wholly unmixed people, any more than are other European nations of to-day. A considerable foreign element has immigrated into Norway from various countries, at different periods in historic times, and far back of all history there may have been migrations and a consequent mixing of races about which we know little or nothing. The theory that there have been in Scandinavia since prehistoric times two ethnically distinct elements is as old as the "Rígsþula" of the "Elder Edda," which tells of the *thrall*, with his yellow skin and black hair, of the fair-faced and light-haired *karl*, or freeman, and of the *jarl*, with light hair, bright cheeks, and eyes like a serpent. This idea of two distinct racial elements in the Norwegian people has been advanced by many leading scholars and anthropologists, notably by O. Rygh, Montelius, Wibling, A. M. Hansen, and O. Almgren.

The theory of a migration from the east into Scandinavia was held even earlier by Schøning,[2] Keyser,[3] and P. A. Munch.[4] A. W. Brøgger remarks that the older and more commonly accepted form of this theory is not verified by his investigations.[5] What can be shown from

[1] But A. W. Brøgger says: "Neither in Norway nor in Sweden can philology show any immigration of foreign elements in early periods. We only know from the runic inscriptions that a Germanic people lived in Scandinavia in the Older Iron Age. Neither does there exist any probability that any proof of any considerable immigration after the Older Stone Age can be adduced from the archæological material. The conclusion seems, therefore, justified, that an Indo-Germanic people lived in southern Scandinavia also in the Stone Age. But some scholars are still inclined to hold the opinion that an immigration has taken place in the Younger Stone Age." *Skrifter utgivet af Videnskabs-Selskabet i Christiania*, 1909.

[2] Gerhard Schøning, *Norges Riges Historie; Afhandling om de Norskes og nordiske Folks Oprindelse.*

[3] Rudolf Keyser, *Om Nordmœndenes Herkomst og Folkeslegtskab, Samlinger til det norske Folks Sprog og Historie*, vol. VI., p. 258 ff.

[4] P. A. Munch, *Samlede Afhandlinger*, vol. I., p. 173 ff., and *Om den saakaldte nyere historiske Skole i Norge.*

[5] Dr. A. M. Hansen advances the hypothesis that in the Older Stone Age a pre-Aryan people lived in Scandinavia, ethnically different from the Indo-Europeans who came later. About 4000 years ago our Aryan forefathers came to Scandinavia. In the period 1000–500 B.C. they settled in Norway. The pre-Aryan inhabitants were not destroyed, but were reduced to subjection and slavery, hence they continued to form a part of the Norwegian people. This pre-Aryan race is the same, he thinks, as the Jenisei-Ostiakian people

archæological finds, thinks Brøgger, is that away back in the Stone Age there were two groups in Scandinavia, ethnically somewhat different. The south Scandinavian group, who at one time must have come from the south, had fixed homes, and were engaged in agriculture. The northern or arctic group inhabited the northern part of the peninsula, and must have come from the east, or northeast. They lived by hunting and fishing. From Sweden they penetrated farther to Trøndelagen, and spread along the coast of Norway from Jæderen to Finmarken. The south Scandinavian group advanced northward, and the northern group were either absorbed or driven out, and ceased to exist as a distinct element. How great the difference was between the two groups, and how far down in time distinct traces of the northern group existed, we do not know. Scientific research has not yet been able to throw full light on these problems, but in so far as it is possible to determine distinct racial traits in modern nations, we are justified in saying that the Scandinavians belong to the Germanic branch of the Indo-European race. Anthropological investigation shows that they have preserved more fully the characteristic Germanic traits than have any other people. Skeletons found in the graves from early periods show them to have been at all times a tall race, and all early accounts describe them as blue-eyed, with light hair and fair complexion. The song "Rígsþula," of the "Elder Edda," says of the lady whom the god Heimdall visits:

> Her eyebrows were light,
> her bosom lighter,
> her neck whiter
> than the white snow.

Of her son it says:

> Light was his hair,
> bright were his cheeks,
> and sharp his eyes
> like the serpent's.

still to be found in Siberia. The language of this people is, he thinks, essentially that of the pre-Aryan inhabitants of Norway, and he claims to have discovered a marked resemblance between this language and the Norwegian. See *Aftenposten*, May 22 and 23, 1908. A. M. Hansen, *Oldtidens Nordmænd, Ophav og Bosætning*, Christiania, 1907. Professor A. Thorp shows in

These characteristics have been well preserved to the present time. The first extensive anthropological investigation of the Norwegians was made during the American Civil War. They were then found to be the tallest of all Europeans, the Americans and Indians alone surpassing them in height. In chest measurement they were surpassed by none.[1] For the last thirty-five years the Norwegian recruiting statistics give complete data. A great improvement in the physical condition of the recruits is noticeable during this period. The increase in height has been so marked that the Norwegians are now the tallest of all peoples, surpassing even the Americans in this respect. Military statistics show that the emigration of the last thirty or forty years, which has been thought to be so detrimental to

articles in *Aftenposten*, May 27 and June 3, 1908, that Hansen's linguistic theory remains unproven. His theory, in general, has not been accepted by archæologists.

[1] The following figures show the result of these investigations in the Union armies:

	NUMBERS	HEIGHT	CHEST MEASUREMENT
Americans	365,670	171.9 cm.	84.9 cm.
Norwegians	2,290	171.4 cm.	87.2 cm.
Swedes	1,190	169.9 cm.	87.2 cm.
Scotch	3,476	170.3 cm.	85.9 cm.
Irish	50,537	169.5 cm.	85.8 cm.
English	16,186	169.1 cm.	84.8 cm.
German	34,996	169.0 cm.	86.1 cm.
French	3,243	168.3 cm.	85.9 cm.

	COMPLEXION	
	NUMBERS	DARK-LIGHT RATIO
Scandinavians	6,782	2 : 10
Germans	89,021	4 : 10
Scotch	7,313	4 : 10
English	30,037	4 : 10
Irish	83,128	5 : 10
Americans	544,000	5 : 10
French	6,809	10 : 10
South Europeans	897	27 : 10

the physical efficiency of the nation, has had the opposite effect. In districts where emigration has been especially heavy, the number of narrow-chested and weak-bodied persons has rapidly decreased, and fewer are now unfit for military service than formerly.[1]

The extreme northern part of Norway is inhabited to a large extent by two peoples of Mongolian race, the Finns[2] and the Kvæns. The Finns are small, the men averaging about five feet in height. Their face is broad, with prominent cheek bones. Their complexion is dark, their hair generally chestnut brown, the growth of beard scant. In the inland districts they live as nomads on their flocks of reindeer, with which they move about from the mountains to the seacoast and back again, as the seasons require. The greater number, however, live in permanent homes near the coast, where they are engaged in fishing. In 1891 the Finnish population in Norway numbered 20,780. Of these 2912 spoke the Norwegian language, the rest still use their own Finnish tongue. The Bible has been translated into their language, and the government has, especially of late years, done much to Christianize and educate them.

The theory that the Finns once occupied the whole of Scandinavia, and that they were gradually forced northward when the Scandinavians entered the peninsula, can no longer be maintained.[3] They seem to have immigrated from Asia at a time when the Scandinavians already dwelt in the peninsula, and they have never occupied a territory much larger than at the present time.[4]

[1] See the Norwegian government's official publication, *Norway*, published for the Paris exposition, 1900.

[2] They are also called Lapps.

[3] Sven Nilsson and P. A. Munch held this view.

[4] See W. A. Brøgger's article in *Skrifter udgivet av Videnskabs-Selskabet i Christiania*, 1909. Also, *Lappernes Fremrykning mod syd i Throndhjems Stift og Hedemarkens Amt*, Yngvar Nielsen, *Det norske geografiske Selskabs Aarbog*, 1889–1890. When the Finns first entered Scandinavia is a question which is still unsettled. The Danish philologist V. L. P. Thomsen thinks that they are the *Scridefinni* described by Procopius and Jordanes. An account of these Scridefinni is also given by Paulus Warnefridus, a Lombard historian, 750–800. See also A. M. Hansen, *Oldtidens Nordmænd*, Christiania, 1907.

The first reliable account of the northern part of Scandinavia and of its non-Aryan inhabitants is given by the Norwegian explorer Ôhthêre (Ottar) to King Alfred the Great of England, of his expedition around the North

The Kvæns are a large and well-built people. Like the Finns, they are found mostly in the two northern provinces, Tromsø and Finmarken. Norway has at different times received immigrants from this Finno-Ugrian race. In the thirteenth century some Permians came from northern Russia into the Tromsø province, but no trace of them can be found at the present time. More important was the emigration from Finland about 1600 to the forest regions along the eastern borders of Norway. Most of the immigrants settled in Sweden, but some located on the Norwegian side of the border, and the tract has since been known as the Finn-forest. They have now been so far assimilated that only a few individuals speak the Finnish language.

The most important emigration from Finland to the northern provinces of Norway took place in the eighteenth century. It began during the great Northern War, 1700–1720, when the Finns who lived in what was then Swedish territory were so sorely harassed by the Russian soldiery that many fled from their homes. The movement increased about the middle of the nineteenth century, but of late years it has ceased.

7. THE DAWN OF HISTORIC NORWAY

Many invaluable finds of relics of antiquity have helped to throw light on the life and customs of the Scandinavian peoples in prehistoric ages, but, valuable as this evidence is, it is circumstantial and indirect. No account was left by the people themselves of their life and institutions, or of the vicissitudes and struggles through which they passed. But about 800 A.D. the silence of the past is broken by the *scalds*, who in their songs celebrate the exploits and great qualities of chieftains and rulers, and recount many important historic events. As an historical source the scaldic songs are of the highest value. The scalds were, as a rule, members of the king's *hird*, or court, and followed him on his military expeditions. They were not only contemporary with the events which they describe, but were often eyewitnesses of, or even partakers in them.

Cape, and his exploration of these northern regions. King Alfred included the report in his translation of *Orosius*. Other valuable early accounts are given by Adam von Bremen, and by the *Egilssaga*.

Another important and, generally, quite reliable source for the early history of Scandinavia are the accounts given of the Norsemen by early writers in other European countries. In many lands old chroniclers have recorded, often with glowing colors, but usually with solemn brevity, the unwelcome visits of the bold warriors of the North. Fragmentary and often one-sided as such accounts necessarily are, they furnish many valuable data regarding the life and doings of the Vikings in foreign lands.

It was left, however, for the saga writers to give comprehensive and detailed accounts of the persons and events during the Viking Age. The *sagas* are narratives written in excellent prose style, and in many instances they are based on the songs of the scalds as a source. Though very similar in form and style, they differ widely in contents and character. Some resemble more closely the historical novel, others are still more imaginative productions, dealing with mythological and heroic elements, while some are history in a strict sense, where the author pursues his narrative with critical method, and with strict regard for truth and accuracy. With consummate skill the writer pictures the character and psychological traits of the persons in the narrative. Life and customs, thoughts, sentiments, social and political institutions, are described with never erring insight, and with nicely measured regard for detail and coloring. The events are narrated with simple straightforwardness, but the circumstances and motives giving rise to them, and the long train of results following them, often lend the story dramatic features cast in a calm and somber epic mold. The sagas which deal with fabulous, or mythological, heroes and traditions are held by many to be a later growth in saga literature. Such are: the "Vølsungasaga," the "Hrólfssaga," the "Ragnar Lodbrokssaga," the "Friðþjófssaga," and others. The earlier sagas were written about distinguished men and their families, for the purpose of recounting their great achievements, and especially for the sake of perpetuating the knowledge of the family relationship so important in all early Germanic society. Many of these sagas furnish important historical material. Among these may be mentioned the "Egilssaga," the "Laxdølasaga," the "Njálssaga," and the "Gunlaugssaga." Sagas were also written about the Norwegian kings, and about discoveries, and colonies founded in the western islands. "Olafssaga Tryggvasonar," "Olafssaga ins Helga," "Sverrissaga"; "Orkneyingasaga," narrating the history of the Orkney Islands; "Landnámabók," dealing with the colonization of Iceland; "Sigmund Brestissonssaga," containing the early history of the Faroe Islands; and the "Saga of Eirik the Red," or "Thorfinn Karlsevnessaga" (found in the "Hauksbók"), which tells about the discovery of America by the Norsemen, are among these.

Some authors undertook more ambitious works, and wrote in connected narrative the whole history of Norway from about 850 to their own time. Of such works may be mentioned: "Historia de Antiquitate Regum Norwagiensium," written in Latin by the monk Thjodrek (Theodricus Monachus), and "Historia Norwegiae," also in Latin, by an unknown author; "Ágrip af Noregs Konungasøgum," "Morkinskinna," "Fagrskinna," and, above all, Snorre Sturlason's masterly work, "Heimskringla." Snorre was an historian of high rank. He is a writer of rare ability, and a scholar with historical and critical method. Most of the sagas were written in Iceland during the twelfth and thirteenth centuries. Some were written in Norway, partly by Icelanders, and partly, also, by native sagamen. As the sagas do not always describe contemporary events, but often deal with periods long past, it need cause no wonder that in these narratives the real historic occurrences are often hidden by a growth of fiction which only the most careful critical analysis can pare away. Where the saga writers describe the institutions, life, and customs of their own time, they generally give a most vivid and realistic picture, but in the finer details of historic events it is often difficult to separate fact from fiction, a weakness common to all early historians.

The new period of development which began in the eighth century is heralded by many important changes which show that cultural life in the North had begun a new and more independent growth. The language, which hitherto had been but slightly differentiated from the Germanic tongue, now became a distinct Scandinavian dialect. The runic alphabet of twenty-four characters, common to all Germanic peoples, was replaced in the North by the younger runic alphabet of sixteen characters about 850.

f u th o r k h a i n s t,d p,b m l r(y)

Fig. 36. — Later runic alphabet.

This system is developed from the older runic alphabet, and has been used exclusively in the Scandinavian countries.

At this time, also, began the Viking expeditions, which became of such far-reaching importance to the development of the North. The word *viking* means warrior, not, as hitherto generally held, a dweller by a *vik*, or bay.[1] The word was applied earlier, also, to other Germanic peoples. It is found in the Old English poem "Widsíth," [2] and in South Germany it occurs as a man's given name. From now on it was used to designate the bold Scandinavian sea rovers. Their journeys across the sea into foreign lands, which hitherto had occurred rather sporadically, now took more definite shape. The Scandinavian peoples began a great forward movement eastward, southward, and westward, which can only be regarded as a continuation of the great Migrations. Just when the movement started cannot be definitely stated, neither is it possible to determine with accuracy when it terminated, but it is certain that it began prior to 800, and that about 1050 it had spent its force. This period, called by archæologists the *Younger Iron Age*, is known in history as the *Viking Age*.

Ship-building had reached a high stage of development in the North even prior to this era. The Norsemen had well-constructed seagoing vessels, fitted out with mast and sail. Their home environment pointed to the sea as the surest and quickest road to wealth and conquest. Hitherto it had been regarded as a barrier behind which the peoples could dwell secure, and hamlets and monasteries nestled in profound quiet along the unprotected shores. The Norsemen made it a highway from island to island, and from coast to coast. When their well-equipped fleets, tired of coasting along their own shores, turned their sharp prows westward in search of conquest and adventure, it marked, not only the beginning of the Viking Age, but the dawn of ocean navigation, and the development of naval warfare, which was gradually to produce the formidable navies and the interoceanic commerce of modern times.

[1] Alexander Bugge, *Norges Historie*, vol. I., 2d part, p. 71.
[2] About 800. "Mid Wenlum ic wæs and mid Wærnum and mid Wícingum."

8. THE EARLY VIKING EXPEDITIONS

The Viking expeditions began about 790. The "Anglo-Saxon Chronicle" mentions the Vikings even earlier. For the year 787 it records the following:

"In this year King Breohtric married King Offa's daughter Eadburge. And in his days came the first three ships of the Northmen from 'Hereðalande.'[1] . . . These were the first Danish ships which visited the land of the Anglian people." King Breohtric ruled from 787 till 800. The chronicle does not say that the ships came in 787, but in his day.

In 793 the Vikings plundered the monastery of Lindisfarne. They came from the North, that is, from Norway, or the islands north of Scotland. The next year they appeared in Northumbria, where they attacked the monastery of Jarrow, near the mouth of the Tyne, but this time they were driven away. We are also told that in 795 a fleet numbering more than a hundred ships came to South Wales, but they were driven off by King Maredudd. The spirited resistance which they met with may have been the reason why no further attempts were made against England for many years. Instead, they turned their attention to Ireland, and to the islands along the coast, which proved to be an easier prey. In 795 the Norwegian Vikings appeared on the coast of Leinster, where they seized the island of Rachru, which they called Lambay, a name which it still bears. Two years later they took the island Inis-Padraig, which they gave the Norwegian name Holm-Patrick. The home of these Vikings is called "Hirotha" by the Irish annalists, which is, no doubt, a corrupted form of Hereðaland (Hordaland), on the southwest

---

[1] Hereðaland = Hordaland, on the west coast of Norway. Steenstrup has conjectured that Hereðaland is an orthographical mistake for oferherian þæt land, but Sophus Bugge has shown that this has nothing to support it. Dr. Todd, in the introduction to the Irish saga Cogadh Gœdhel re Gallaibh (The War of the Gædhill with the Gaill), points out that the name Hirotha or Irruth is used in the Irish writings, and he identifies it with Hereðaland. Dr. Zimmer has further shown in " Keltische Beiträge," Zeitschrift für deutsches Alterthum, XXXII., 196–334, that the expression King Lugir of Hirotha or Hereðaland is found in the Legend of St. Patrick from 807, as well as in the Irish sagas from 800. See Taranger, Den angelsaksiske Kirkes Indflydelse paa den norske, p. 17 ff.

coast of Norway. From year to year the ravages were renewed. The shrine of St. Columba in the island of Iona was plundered in 802, and again in 806. The treasures were carried away, and many of the monks were slain. The survivors fled to Ireland, bringing with them the bones of the saint. Lindisfarne and Iona were still regarded as the greatest sanctuaries in the western Christian Church, and the wanton destruction of these holy places filled the minds of the Christian nations of western Europe with an almost superstitious fear of this hitherto unknown enemy.[1]

These early expeditions to the British Isles, which, evidently, came from the west coast of Norway, were undertaken for the sole purpose of plunder. The Shetland and Orkney Islands served as vantage points from which the marauders would sweep down on the unprotected coasts, plunder some town or monastery, and depart with their booty as suddenly as they came. Seldom did the terror-stricken inhabitants offer any effective resistance.

9. The Vikings in Ireland and in the Islands

The success which the Vikings met with encouraged them to renewed attempts. Year by year their fleets grew larger, and their attacks soon changed from mere piratic forays to well-organized expeditions aiming at conquest and colonization. The year after the

[1] Of especial importance to the student of the Viking period is Johannes Steenstrup's *Normannerne*, Copenhagen, 1876. This is a very scholarly work, the result of a careful examination of all the sources dealing with the expeditions, culture, and institutions of the Vikings, though it cannot be said to be wholly free from a tendency to credit the Danes with achievements which later investigations have shown may with more justice be claimed for the Norwegians.

Of equally high excellence are Professor Alexander Bugge's works: *Vikingerne*, Christiania, 1904; and *Vesterlandenes Indflydelse paa Nordboernes, særlig Nordmændenes ydre Levesæt og Samfundsforholde i Vikingetiden*, Christiania, 1905. These works deal especially with the cultural side of Viking life and history. Among other scholarly works of the highest value must also be mentioned: Gustav Storm's *Kritiske Bidrag til Vikingetidens Historie*, Christiania, 1878. J. J. A. Worsaae, *Minder om de Danske og Nordmændene i England, Skotland og Irland*, London, 1852; *Den danske Erobring af England og Normandiet*, 1863. A. Fabricius, *Danske Minder i Normandiet*, Copenhagen, 1897. Konrad Maurer, *Die Bekehrung des norwegischen Stammes zum Christenthume*, München, 1855. Charles Oman,

sack of Iona they landed on the west coast of Ireland, and destroyed the monastery of Innishmurray. From 812 till 814 they appeared far inland in Munster, Ulster, and Connaught, defeating the bands of the Irish kings, and plundering churches and monasteries. Their fleets soon swarmed around all the coasts of Ireland. In 826 they made the first permanent settlement in the county of Meath, and during the next decade they extended their marauding expeditions almost to the heart of the country. In 836 two fleets, numbering in all about sixty ships, sailed up the rivers Liffy and Boyne. Torgils or Turgeis, the great sea-king, was the leader. He became king of all the Norsemen in Ireland, and began a systematic conquest of the country. He built fortified strongholds, both inland and along the coasts, and founded the city of Dublin,[1] which soon became the center and seat of government of the Norwegian colonies in the island. Limerick, a second Norwegian city, was founded on the Shannon River, in the north of Ireland, where Viking colonies were springing up.

Turgeis evidently aimed at destroying Christianity in Ireland; monasteries were destroyed, and churches were plundered and turned into heathen temples. For a while it looked as if the Asa faith would triumph over the Cross, but in 845 the Viking king fell by chance into the hands of Maelsechlainn, high-king of Erin, who put him to death. He was long remembered as the founder of the Viking dominion in Ireland. On these westward expeditions the Vikings had discovered the Faroe Islands, the Orkneys, and the Shetland Islands prior to the year 800.[2] These barren and inhospitable island

History of England, vol. I., *England before the Norman Conquest*, 1910. Hermann Paul, *Grundriss der germanischen Philologie*, 2d edition, vol. III., section XII. Valtýr Guðmundsson and Kristian Kålund, *Skandinavische Verhältnisse*.

[1] *On the Fomorians and the Norsemen by Duald MacFirbis*, the original Irish text edited with translation and notes by Alexander Bugge. The obscure village of Ath Cliath had existed there before, but Dublin first came into prominence as a Norwegian city. L. J. Vogt, *Dublin som norsk By*, Christiania, 1896.

[2] Jakob Jakobsen, who has made a special study of the nomenclature, and of other remnants of Norse language on the Shetland Islands, claims that the Norsemen must have come to the islands as early as 700. Many place names show word formations which were out of use at the time Iceland was colonized. *Shetlandøernes Stedsnavne, Aarbøger for nordisk Oldkyndighed*, 1901. See also Alexander Bugge, *Vesterlandenes Indflydelse*, 307 ff.

groups had at the time a few Celtic inhabitants, but the Norsemen took full possession of them, and planted settlements there, and the population soon became wholly Norwegian. The Hebrides, too, were settled. From 820 to 830 the Vikings came in such numbers that the islands were called by Irish annalists "Innse Gall" (*i.e.* the islands of the strangers). The new settlers accepted the Christian faith and culture of the native Celtic population in the Hebrides, but Norwegian customs and mode of life prevailed. The original inhabitants gradually adopted the ways of the conquerors, and Norwegian social organization became general throughout the islands.

10. The Vikings in France and Spain

In 810–820 the Vikings began to visit the island of Noirmoutier, near the mouth of the Loire, on the west coast of France. That they came from Ireland, where the Norwegian Vikings were gathering in great numbers, seems the more certain, because the northern coasts of France were not disturbed at this time. In 843 a fleet of sixty-seven ships came to the Loire directly from Norway, and a permanent colony was established on Noirmoutier.[1] They called themselves Westfoldingi, *i.e.* men from Vestfold, in southern Norway. From this base of operations they ascended the Loire, and captured and sacked the city of Nantes. Returning to Noirmoutier with their booty, they made another expedition up the Garonne River in 844, under their leader Asgeir, attacking the cities of Toulouse (844), Bordeaux (848), Nantes and Tours (853). They also ascended the Adour, in Gascogne, as far as to Tarbes, but lost many men in battles with the mountaineers. Leaving southern France for a time, they made an attack on the coast of Spain. After an unsuccessful siege of Lisbon, they followed the coast to Cadiz,

---

[1] Professor Alexander Bugge has brought quite conclusive proofs that these Vikings on the Loire were Norwegians, and not Danes. See *Morgenbladet*, April 4, 1911. Many of the chieftains of the Loire Vikings are known to have been in Dublin, at that time a Norwegian settlement, such as Baard, who plundered Orleans in 865, Baard and Eirik, who sacked Tours in 903, and Ragnvald, 923–925. Baard Jarl is spoken of as the leader of the Norwegians in their fights with the Danes in northern Ireland in 878. Keary, *The Vikings in Western Christendom*, London, 1891. Du Chaillu, *The Viking Age*, New York, 1890.

plundered the city, and ascended the Guadalquivir to Sevilla, in Andalusia. They besieged the city, and captured the suburbs, but they were unable to take the city itself. In Spain they fought many battles with the Saracens, whose prowess they soon learned to respect. From their settlements on the Loire the Norsemen made repeated expeditions into southern France. In 877 they took permanent possession of a region along the coast, and founded a colony which long maintained its independent existence. The colonies on the Loire acknowledged the supremacy of the Norwegian kings of Dublin, who were regarded as overlords of all the Norwegian colonies in the West.

In 859 a new Viking expedition was fitted out in western France for a voyage to Spain and the Mediterranean Sea, possibly, also, for the purpose of attacking Rome itself. The wealth and glory of the Eternal City must have presented special attractions to these bands of professional warriors, who sought in hazardous adventure both honor and pastime. Danish Vikings seem to have joined with the Norwegians from the Loire colonies in the enterprise, as the renowned Hasting, or Haastein, the son of Atle Jarl in Fjalafylke (Søndfjord), in western Norway, and Ivar Boneless, son of the famous Danish chieftain Ragnar Lodbrok, were the leaders of the expedition. Hasting is well known in the annals of western Europe, which describe him as the incarnation of all that was fierce and terrible in Viking character.[1] Ivar, who later became the leader of the great Viking army which invaded England in 866, was one of the most renowned of Ragnar Lodbrok's sons.

The fleet sailed around Spain to the mouth of the Rhone River, in southern France, where they seized and fortified the island of

[1] The French writer Dudo mentions only Hasting as the leader of the expedition, but Irish annals make it clear that the Danes also took part under the leadership of Ivar, the son of Ragnar Lodbrok.

Ragnar Lodbrok seems to have lived in the early part of the ninth century. He figures as a semi-mythical hero in numerous exploits described in *Ragnar Lodbrokssaga*. Most of these seem to be historical, but many of them have, no doubt, been performed by his sons. According to the saga he was shipwrecked on an expedition to England, and was captured by the usurper Ælla, of Northumbria, who threw him into a pit full of serpents, where he perished. This seems to be an ingenious invention by the saga writer to explain later historic events in England.

Camargue. From here they made an attack on the coast of Italy, where they captured the city of Luna, mistaking it for Rome.

Through these expeditions the Norsemen came into contact with the Saracens in Spain, and communications were established between Dublin and southern Europe. In 844 the Norwegian king in Dublin sent an embassy to Emir Abderrhaman II. of Spain, who, in return, sent the poet Alghazâl as special envoy to the "King of the Pagans" in Ireland. Alghazâl has left an account of his mission, in which he speaks of the many conversations he had with the queen, whom he praises highly for her beauty and courtly manners. When he expressed anxiety lest their conversations should arouse the king's jealousy, the queen replied : "It is not customary with us to be jealous. Our women stay with their husbands only as long as they please, and leave them whenever they choose." "The Vikings brought a large number of Moors as prisoners to Erin," says the chronicle; "these are the blue men in Erin . . . long indeed did these blue men remain in Erin." Commercial relations were also established between Spain and the Norwegian colonies in Ireland, and merchants sailed from Dublin to Spain to buy silk, leather, and costly cloth from the Arabs.

The geographical location of the Scandinavian countries determined, very largely, the routes taken by the Viking bands from each, as well as the localities to which their operations were chiefly confined. Those coming from Norway followed, as a rule, a northerly route, leading to Ireland, Scotland, and the islands in the northern ocean. From Ireland this route led farther to the west coast of France, to Spain, and the coasts of the Mediterranean Sea, and there can be little doubt that the hosts who directed their warlike activities to these regions were, in the main, Norwegians, led by Norwegian chieftains.

The Danish Vikings usually followed a more southerly route, leading to Friesland, Flanders, England, and the north coast of France. That Danish Vikings in early centuries took part in the great Migrations is possible. The expedition of Chochilaicus (Hygelâc) into the Rhine country in 515 has already been mentioned, but their powerful kinsmen, the Saxons, dwelling to the south of them, seem to have been an effective barrier against extensive operations in that direction, and no general movement is noticed before the beginning of the Viking Age. During the reign of Charlemagne, Viking fleets were seen to hover around the northern shores of the Empire, but the energetic Emperor, who discerned the danger, established military posts to guard the coasts. He even ordered fleets to be built, but the order was not carried out. His aggressive policy on the southern borders of Denmark aroused, however, the hostility of the Danes, and King Sigfred gave aid and shelter to those who had rebelled against Charles. In 810 a Danish fleet of 200 ships ravaged Friesland. Later the powerful King Godfred began war against the Emperor, but he was killed by one of his own men in the midst of the campaign (811).[1] While Charles lived, no other general advance against the Empire was attempted, but when he died, the opportunity came. The strength of the Empire was soon lost through weak rulers and internal dissensions; maladministration and disorder prevailed, and the Vikings were quick to seize the opportunity. The attack began in 834, when a Danish fleet sailed to the Rhine, and ascended the river to the rich city of Dorstadt, which was seized and plundered. In rapid succession new attacks were made during the years following. In 837 the Vikings also captured the island of Walcheren. These events led the emperors Lewis the Pious and Lothair to grant Dorstadt, Walcheren, and neighboring districts to a Danish prince, Harald Klak, with the understanding that he should defend the coast of Friesland against the Vikings, but this only served to give them a new foothold. The Danes were soon masters of Friesland, whence they could fit out new expeditions into the wrecked Empire. The Frankish kings, who were unable to meet them on the field of battle, were forced to buy peace by paying a yearly tribute, which was often made oppressively high by the victorious Viking chieftains. In 845 an expedition led by Ragnar Lodbrok captured Rouen, advanced up the Seine, and fortified themselves on some islands in the river. King Charles the Bald hastened to Paris to defend the city, but he failed to bring with him a sufficient military force, and was obliged to seek refuge in the fortified monastery of St. Denis. Most of the inhabitants fled from the city, and the Vikings plundered the suburbs

---

[1] Jacobus Langebek, *Scriptores Rerum Danicarum*, II., p. 25 ff.

and penetrated far into the neighboring districts, practically unmolested. Again the old method of buying peace had to be resorted to. King Charles agreed to pay Ragnar 7000 pounds of silver on condition that he should leave France, and that he should not again attack the country. Ragnar returned to Denmark, it seems, but new hosts soon appeared under new leaders. Following the large rivers, they penetrated far inland, and plundered large districts. Paris was again attacked in 857, and once more heavy taxes had to be levied to buy off the enemy. The leader of the Viking host now operating on the Seine was Bjørn Ironside, a son of Ragnar Lodbrok, whom King Charles the Bald sought in vain to drive from his fortified camp on the island of Oissel, above Rouen. Piratic expeditions were constantly undertaken into the neighboring country, and in 861 Paris was again sacked. King Charles now offered the Norsemen on the Somme River 3000 pounds of silver to attack the Viking camp on Oissel, and the attack was also made, but the two Viking hosts soon came to an understanding, we are told, and left France in the spring of 862. The Viking inroads in France continued. In 885 a large army assembled on the Seine and laid siege to Paris, but they were, finally, persuaded to withdraw upon receiving a tribute of 700 pounds of silver. They were, however, allowed to advance, and plunder the rich districts of Burgundy. The great Viking army met with no real check till it was finally defeated by the German Emperor, Arnulf, near Louvain, in 891.

11. THE VIKINGS IN ENGLAND

After their first visits to the coasts of England an interval of some forty years passed, during which the Vikings made no further attempt to gain a foothold there. They pressed with vigor their conquests in Ireland and France, and England was given a respite, during which ample preparation might have been made to meet the coming storm. But internal strife between petty kingdoms, and ceaseless feuds among princes and other men of quality gradually wore down the strength of the Anglo-Saxons, and left them weak and disorganized. One thing had been achieved, however, in these forty years, which became of far-reaching importance in the coming struggle. King Ecgbert of Wessex succeeded in uniting all the Anglo-Saxon kingdoms in 827, and could now rule as "King of the English." But of more immediate importance than this weak union, and Ecgbert's precarious supremacy, was the fact that the kingdom of Wessex now became the center of English national life and development, and that a dynasty of kings of superior ability ascended the throne, and made this small kingdom a tower of strength which ultimately broke the force of the coming invasion.

In 834 [1] the Vikings began their attack on England in earnest by ravaging the island of Sheppey,[2] at the mouth of the Thames. In 836 they returned to the coast of Wessex with thirty-five ships, and near Charmouth, in Dorsetshire, where King Ecgbert resided, a bloody battle was fought in which the Vikings were victorious. It is noteworthy that this attack occurred almost simultaneously with the plundering of Dorstadt, and the expeditions against the Frankish kingdom. It can scarcely be doubted that it was the same armed host which operated on both sides of the English Channel, and that the Vikings who now appeared in England were Danes.

In 838 a great fleet came to the land of the West Welsh, made an alliance with them, and attacked Wessex. King Ecgbert marched against the allies, and defeated them with great slaughter at Hengestesdune, near Plymouth, but this was his last exploit. He died the following year, and was succeeded by his son Æthelwulf, a pious and conscientious, but weak man, who was unable to cope successfully with the invaders. After Ecgbert's death the Vikings began more extensive operations in England. In 840 they made two successful raids on the coast of Wessex, and in the year following they entered the Wash, defeated and slew the ealdorman of Lindesey and plundered his land. They then turned south to ravage the coasts of East Anglia and Kent. London and Rochester were attacked in 842 by a large fleet, and the following summer King Æthelwulf was defeated in the second battle of Charmouth, in Wessex. Northumbria, too, was attacked in 844, and King Redwulf was slain by the invaders.

---

[1] "Wrongly called 832 by the Anglo-Saxon Chronicle," says Charles Oman, *A History of England*, 1910, vol. I., p. 399.

[2] Sheppey, *Sceapige* (sheep island).

Norwegian Vikings, too, seem to have taken part in these raids on the English coasts; but, as a rule, no distinction between Norwegians and Danes is made in the early English annals, and it is left for us to draw what conclusions we may from the general direction of the attacks. In 846 a Viking band attempted to land on the coast of Somersetshire, but they were defeated by Bishop Ealhstan and two ealdormen at the mouth of the Parret. The locality of the fight makes it probable that this band, at least, were Norsemen from the coast of Ireland. The "Three Fragments of Irish Annals" states that in the year 851 the Norsemen attacked Devonshire, while the Danes harried Kent and Surrey. This agrees in the main with the "Anglo-Saxon Chronicle," which records for the same year the fact that the ealdorman Ceorl fought with heathen men in Devonshire, near Wicgeanbeorge, killed many of them, and gained the victory. These raids on the coast seem to have been mere skirmishes preliminary to the more general advance which began in 851, when a fleet of 350 ships entered the Thames River.[1] A force was landed, which captured Canterbury, while the fleet proceeded to London, which was stormed and plundered. The invading host began to spread over the inland districts, but King Æthelwulf and his son Æthelbald arrived with the whole military force of Wessex, and defeated the Vikings in the bloody battle of Aclea. This produced a brief lull in the invasion, but a new host appeared in 854, and, taking up quarters on Sheppey Island, in the Thames, they were now able for the first time to spend the winter in England. Every summer the attacks were renewed, until, in 866, the great Viking army led by Ivar Boneless and Ubbe or Hubba, the sons of Ragnar Lodbrok, arrived and began a conquest which placed the greater part of England under Viking dominion before another decade had passed. This time the attack was directed against Northumbria, which was more torn by internal troubles than any other part of England. Wars between rival candidates for the throne had been waged there constantly for many years, and were still in progress when the Vikings arrived. They mixed merrily in the fight, and made themselves masters of the important city of York, a calamity so great that it even brought the two fighting rivals, Osbeorht and Ælla, to their

---

[1] *Two of the Saxon Chronicles*, edited by Charles Plummer, p. 64.

senses. They patched up their differences, united their forces, and made an assault upon York in an attempt to recapture the city. But they were both killed, their army was cut to pieces, and Northumbria submitted to the conquerors, 867. In 868 the Viking chieftains advanced with their army to Nottingham, and wintered in Mercia. In 870 they entered East Anglia. King Edmund met them in the battle of Hoxne, but lost both his army and his life. The story is told that he was captured, and, being unwilling to pay tribute, and to submit to Ivar Boneless, he was tied to a tree and shot to death with arrows. This may be true, since he was worshiped as a saint not long after his death. The Danes at York invited the Norwegian kings Ivar and Olav of Dublin to join in the conquest of England. They accepted the invitation, harried northern England, and captured Dumbarton on the Clyde; but they soon had to return to Dublin to defend their own dominions against the Irish. In 870 a large army came from Denmark to join in the conquest. It was led by Halvdan (Halfdene), Hubba (Ubbe), Guthrum (Guttorm or Gorm), and many other kings and jarls. The next year they advanced through Mercia to attack Wessex, and pitched their camp at Reading, which they took care to fortify. A fierce campaign was now fought. The men of Wessex, led by King Æthelred and his younger brother, Alfred,[1] advanced to attack them, and a series of sharp engagements were fought which forced the Danes to retire to their fortified camp at Reading. An attempt to take the camp by assault proved unsuccessful, and the English were driven back with great slaughter. The Danes now emerged from their camp, but were again met by Æthelred and Alfred on the hills of Æscesdun (Ashdown), where they were defeated, after a desperate battle in which the young Alfred especially distinguished himself. The Danes lost one of their kings, Bægsceg, five jarls, and many thousand men. The remaining king, Halvdan, shut himself up in the camp at Reading with the remnant of his army to await reën-

[1] Æthelwulf died in 858, and was succeeded by his four sons:

Æthelbald, 860;
Æthelbert, 866;
Æthelred, 871;
Alfred the Great, 871–900.

forcements. In two weeks he was again able to take the field, fighting a successful engagement at Basing, and the battle of Bedwyn soon followed, in which the Danes were again victorious. King Æthelred died shortly after from wounds received in the battle, as it seems, and Alfred the Great succeeded to the throne of Wessex. As he had but a small army, and no navy, he was forced to buy peace from the victorious Vikings. They received a tribute, and withdrew from Wessex, and the kingdom was left unmolested for about four years. During this time Alfred began to organize a navy, which in future contests was to develop strength and efficiency in the hard school of sharp naval warfare with the powerful Viking admirals, who regarded the sea as their own undisputed domain.

The Viking army, after leaving London and subjugating Mercia, was divided into two parts, one under King Halvdan, and the other under Guthrum, Aasketil, and Aamund. Halvdan raided Bernicia, Strathclyde, and parts of Scotland, and settled permanently at York, in 875. The other part of the army camped in Mercia. All England was now in the hands of the invaders, save the kingdom of Wessex, south of the Thames.

During the eighty or ninety years which had passed since the first Viking bands visited the shores of England, great changes had taken place both in the extent and character of their operations in foreign countries. The early piratic attacks changed in time into well-planned expeditions undertaken by large fleets and armies bent on permanent conquest. Wars were waged which were often attended by wanton destruction of life and property, but the Vikings now fought for the purpose of gaining full dominion over territory in which they wished to live and rule. They were no longer a mere destructive force. The conquest once accomplished, they settled down to till the soil, to build cities, and to develop the country. In the various pursuits of peace they often showed an energy, a practical insight, and a talent for organization not exhibited by the native inhabitants. In many fields they exerted a stimulating influence which made future progress possible. During the winter which King Halvdan spent in London after retiring from Wessex, he minted coins bearing sometimes his own name, sometimes that of the city. The designs were later used on English coins struck by Alfred the

Great, and by Ceolwulf, king of Mercia. In 875 Halvdan took up his permanent abode in York. The "Anglo-Saxon Chronicle" states that he portioned out the lands of Northumbria, and that his followers henceforth continued to plow and to till them. Every Dane received his allotment of land, while the original inhabitants continued to exist as a dependent class. According to Viking custom York was strongly fortified, and became again the great city which it had been in the days of Roman dominion in Britain. This custom of walling in the cities, and of building fortified strongholds, which was so important, both in warfare and for the development of cities, was first introduced into England by the Vikings. The coining of money was also carried on here, and the crude copper coins heretofore used were soon replaced by coins of silver. Deira, the southern part of Northumbria, was organized into the Danish kingdom of York, while Bernicia, the northern part, was tributary to the kings of York, but formed no integral part of their kingdom.

12. ALFRED THE GREAT AND THE VIKINGS

After Alfred had entered into an agreement with the Vikings, Wessex enjoyed peace for some years, but in 875 the Viking host was again collected for a new attack on the kingdom. The invaders marched across Wessex to Wareham, on the south coast, where they constructed a fortified camp. Alfred met them here with a large force, and the two armies lay watching each other for some time. The Danes finally agreed to depart if they received a tribute, and a treaty was concluded, but a part of their force escaped from Wareham and marched to Exeter, which they seized and fortified. Alfred followed close on their heels, and besieged the town. The remainder of the force at Wareham soon evacuated their camp and put to sea to join their besieged companions, but their fleet was destroyed in a storm, and the detachment at Exeter, being hard pressed by Alfred, promised to leave Wessex. Alfred allowed them to depart, and they advanced into Mercia, where they forced King Ceolwulf to give them a large part of his kingdom. This land was divided among many jarls; the five most important divisions being: Stamford, Lincoln, Derby, Nottingham, and Leicester, which were later known as the "Five Boroughs." All the divisions formed together a loose confederacy embracing the eastern half of Mercia.

The great Viking army was still kept united under the command of King Guthrum (Guttorm). Aided by other forces operating in the Irish Sea, they again advanced to attack Wessex. An auxiliary squadron was led by Hubba (Ubbe), a brother of Halvdan and Ivar Boneless, and Guthrum began his campaign in the middle of January, 878. The unexpected attack at this season of the year caused the greatest panic. Many fled the country without thinking of resistance, and King Alfred with his military household was forced to take refuge on the island of Athelney,[1] in the Parret River in Somerset. During the remaining months of the winter of 878 the Vikings were masters of all Wessex, but when spring came, the tide began to turn. Hubba fell in Devonshire in an attack on the English stronghold Cynuit, and his force was cut to pieces. Shortly after Easter, Alfred left Athelney, gathered all forces possible, and attacked the Danish army at Ethandun, gaining a complete victory. Guthrum submitted, and received baptism with twenty-nine other leaders. The treaty concluded received its name from the royal manor of Wedmore, where the baptismal feast was celebrated. According to its stipulations, a region including Northumbria, East Anglia, and all central England east of a line stretching from the mouth of the Thames River along the River Lea to Bedford, along the Ouse to Watling Street, and along Watling Street to Chester, was ceded to the Vikings. This region was henceforth known as the "Danelag" (Danelaw). Guthrum seems to have carried out quite faithfully the agreement entered into. He left Wessex, and took possession of East Anglia and Essex, where he founded a kingdom similar to that established in York by King Halvdan. He took part in Viking expeditions to France, and even aided Danish Vikings operating on the coast of England, but he never again attacked Wessex. He died in 890. After the treaty of Wedmore, in 878, Alfred's kingdom enjoyed comparative peace until 892, when the "Great Army" undertook a

---

[1] The well-known story that Alfred, in the darkest hour of his misfortunes, was alone; that he found shelter in a cowherd's hut, where the episode with the burned cakes occurred, is found in late chroniclers. It is surely nothing but fiction, like many similar stories often invented to adorn the lives of great men.

new invasion of England. This permanently organized host of Danish Vikings had been operating in Brabant and Flanders, where it had been defeated by Emperor Arnulf, in 891. The names of the leaders of the "Great Army" are not mentioned, but it was joined by a smaller detachment of eighty ships, evidently coming from the Norwegian colonies on the west coast of France led by the famous Viking chieftain Hasting. The war lasted for three years, but the Vikings could gain no permanent advantage over Alfred's well-organized armies. Alfred captured their fleet, and besieged them closely in their camps. Finally, worn out by fruitless fighting, the "Great Army" broke up, and joined their countrymen in East Anglia and Northumbria, but a detachment sailed across the sea to the Seine. These must have been the Norsemen under Hasting, with whom Alfred seems to have concluded a treaty of peace. Alfred had broken up the great organized host of invasion, and had created an efficient fleet which was able to cope successfully with Viking detachments along the coast. Hasting left England in 897, and the peace was not again disturbed during the remaining four years of Alfred's reign.

King Halvdan of York had ruled his kingdom only one year (876–877), when he was expelled by his own people. His successor, Gudrød, died in 894, and Knut, who was then placed on the throne, had to share his authority with the Norwegian jarl, Sigurd, who had gained great power in northern Scotland. This shows that there were Norsemen, as well as Danes, in the Viking kingdom at York, an assumption which is borne out by the many names of Norwegian origin found in Northumbria.[1] Snorre Sturlason says in the "Heims-kringla" that Northumbria was mostly settled by Norsemen after the sons of Lodbrok had conquered the land. Norwegians and Danes must often have fought side by side, and, the conquest once completed, a period of immigration followed in which men and women from both countries flocked across the sea to settle in the new and invit-ing land which they had won. During the first stages of the struggle the invading armies were almost exclusively Danish, but the Nor-

---

[1] Of Norwegian origin are names ending in -fell (fjeld = mountain), -haugh (haug = hill), -tarn (= lake), -force (foss = waterfall), -nes (= pen-insula), etc.

wegian element must have grown rapidly in importance, especially in the North, and their leaders soon gained the ascendancy in Northumbria.

13. NAMES APPLIED TO THE VIKINGS

Long before the beginning of the Viking Age the Gautar (Götar), Swedes, and Danes seem to have been quite well known as distinct peoples, occupying clearly defined regions of the Scandinavian North. The names are used frequently both by early Old English authors and by Latin writers of the early centuries of the Christian era.[1] But *Norway*, as a term applied to the western half of the Scandinavian peninsula, and *Norsemen*, or *Norwegians*, as a name used to designate all the inhabitants of this region, are terms which do not occur till in the Viking period. The notice in the "Anglo-Saxon Chronicle" for the year 787, already mentioned elsewhere, uses the name *Norð-manna:* "On his dagum comon III scipu Norðmanna of Hereðalande." King Alfred uses the name *Norðmenn* in his writings (880–900), and Ôhthêre (Ottar), the Norwegian explorer, who stayed at his court, uses the names *Norðmannaland* and *Norðweg* for the whole of Norway.[2] The Irish monk Decuil, who wrote in 825, states that the Irish monks on the Faroe Islands had to flee because of the *Latronum Normannorum*. It seems, then, that these names must have been quite commonly used about 800. Norway (Noregr, Norvegr, Norge) means the northern way, and Norsemen, men from the North. These names seem first to have been applied to the Norwegians and their country by their neighbors in southern

---

[1] The author of *Beówulf* must have been singularly well informed regarding the early history of Denmark and southern Scandinavia. He gives a detailed account of the royal houses, of family relationship, and of political and military affairs, such as we can only find in the sagas several centuries later. The author of the poem *Widsith* shows a similar knowledge of the peoples and countries of the North:

"Ic wæs mid Húnum and mid Hréðgotum,
mid Sweóm and mid Geátum and mid Suðdenum.
Mid Wenlum ic wæs and mid Wærnum and mid Wícingum."

[2] Hé sæde ðæt Norðmanna land wære swýðe lang and swýðe smæl. . . Þonne is þis land oð hé cymð tó Scirincgesheále, and ealneweg on þæt bæcbord Norðweg." Alfred, *Orosius*. See also Gustav Storm, *Kritiske Bidrag til Vikingetidens Historie*, Christiania, 1878.

Sweden and Denmark. On the Continent the Vikings, both Danes and Norwegians, were, as a rule, called Northmen, or Norsemen, while in England and Scotland they were called Danes.[1]

In Ireland they were called Gall (strangers) or Normanni (Norsemen). Later, when the Danes also began to harry the country, the Irish called the Norsemen Finn-Gall (fair strangers), and the Danes Dubh-Gall (dark strangers). The country whence the Norsemen came is called Lochlann (the land of the fjords) by the Irish annalists already in the ninth century. From this word a new name was in time formed for the Norwegian Vikings, namely Lochlannac or the people from Lochlann.[2]

14. NORSEMEN AND DANES IN IRELAND

The Norwegian Vikings overran Ireland with astonishing rapidity. Shortly after the close of the eighth century they were found in nearly every part of the island. Dr. Zimmer says:[3] "If we read the annals of the period 795–950, we are compelled to ask if there were a cloister, a lake, a mountain, a valley, a brook on the island where the Vikings had not been, or where they had not dwelt in great numbers for a longer or shorter period." Year by year colonists arrived with their families from Norway to take possession of districts where the army of conquest had gained more or less firm control. The Irish

---

[1] The reason why the Vikings were called Northmen in France, and Danes in England, seems to have been the fact that the first Viking hosts which invaded western France were Norwegians, while the first invasion of England was made by the Danes. The names have then come into use as a general designation for all strangers of the same type. In a similar way the name of the Alemanni, a tribe in southern Germany, has become in French *Allemands* (Germans), *Franks* has become French, and *Angles*, English. This is the view of the Norwegian historian Gustav Storm. The Danish historian Steenstrup holds that the people on the Continent called them Northmen because they came from the North. He also cites parallels: The Norwegians were called Eastmen (*Austmenn*) by the Icelanders, and the Norwegians called the Irish Westmen (*Vestmenn*), and the Germans Southmen (*Suðrmenn*).

Concerning the names applied to the Vikings, see also *Afhandlinger om hvilke Benævnelser Landet, Folket og dets Sprog findes tillagte, Samlinger til det norske Folks Sprog og Historie*, vol. II, p. 379 ff.

[2] See L. J. Vogt, *Dublin som norsk By*, Christiania, 1896.

[3] *Zeitschrift für deutsches Alterthum und Literatur*, vol. 35.

were warlike, and could often meet the invaders in overwhelming numbers, but they were unable to carry on a successful campaign of defense for want of systematic organization. It would have required the united strength of the whole country to withstand so formidable an invasion, but the obsolete Irish clan system stood in the way of centralization of power, and of effective coöperation in the common cause. The high-king (Ard Righ) was indeed regarded as over-king of all Erin, but his exalted station was at the time an empty title which carried with it no real authority. Civil strife between hostile clans and petty princes was the normal condition throughout all Ireland. Many of the natives even abandoned Christianity, and joined the Vikings, aiding them in the attacks upon their own country. They were called "Gall-Gædhel" or "Irish strangers." The Irish people often fought with reckless bravery, and gained many a victory over the enemy, but their planless efforts could not stay the progress of the invaders. Not till complete subjugation or ultimate extermination stared them in the face did they think of seeking refuge where alone it can be found under such circumstances, in unselfish and systematic coöperation; and even then the lesson was but indifferently learned.

The Norsemen operated, on the whole, with skill and caution, employing tactics which we have observed in Viking expeditions elsewhere. With their fleets they entered the fjords and estuaries, where they constructed fortified camps, or founded cities, and built strong castles, as at Dublin. Sometimes they would establish their camps and naval stations on islands near the coast, where they could not be attacked by the Irish, who possessed no war vessels of any kind. From such a fortified base of operations they would ascend the rivers to the lakes of the interior, where they would build other strongholds at well-selected strategic points, from which they were able to control the neighboring districts with a comparatively small force. Turgeis sent a part of his fleet up the Bann River into Loch Neagh, in the northeastern part of Ireland, and with another part he ascended the Shannon River to Loch Ree, in the very heart of the island, where, according to the annals, he built a number of strongholds. Their firmest hold was on the coast region, where colonists and reënforcements could be received at any time. In the shelter of their camps at Strangford, Carlingford, Dublin, Wicklow, Limerick, and other places, permanent Norwegian colonies sprang up which, in course of time, extended themselves along the coast from the Boyne River to Cork, while more isolated areas were settled at Dundalk and Limerick. The numerous Norwegian names of islands, bays, headlands, cities, and localities along the Irish coast, which in anglicized form have been preserved to the present time, attest to the thorough and permanent occupation of these parts by the Norsemen.[1]

15. THE VIKING EXPEDITIONS EASTWARD. FOUNDING OF THE RUSSIAN KINGDOM. THE VARANGIANS IN CONSTANTINOPLE

When the Scandinavians entered into communication with the peoples dwelling east of the Baltic Sea cannot be determined, but it is quite certain that such an intercourse existed from very early times, since even the oldest historic traditions mention expeditions made by Swedish kings to the countries across the Baltic. The first account of the old Yngling dynasty is given by the Norwegian scald Thjodolv af Hvin[2] in his song "Ynglingatal."[3] Among the old kings of Svitiod here mentioned is Vanlande, a great warrior who visited many foreign lands, and at one time spent the winter in Finland.

[1]
Present Form :	Dublin	Norse Form :	Dyflinn
Present Form :	Dalkey	Norse Form :	Dalkey
Present Form :	Glandore	Norse Form :	Grandeyrr
Present Form :	Waterford	Norse Form :	Veðrafjǫrðr
Present Form :	Ireland	Norse Form :	Iraland
Present Form :	Limerick	Norse Form :	Hlymrek
Present Form :	Howth	Norse Form :	Hǫfuð
Present Form :	Carlingford	Norse Form :	Kerlingarfjǫrðr
Present Form :	Strangford	Norse Form :	Strangifjǫrðr
Present Form :	Smerwick	Norse Form :	Smjǫrvik
Present Form :	Wexford	Norse Form :	Veisufjǫrðr
etc.		etc.	

[2] Thjodolv af Hvin was born in southern Norway about the middle of the ninth century, and lived at the court of the Norwegian king Harald Haarfagre.

[3] The elaborate account of the Yngling dynasty given by Snorre Sturlason in his *Heimskringla* is based on Thjodolv's poem, which, however, is quite brief. Where Snorre got the more detailed information is not known. The old Swedish dynasty is usually called Scilfings.

Agne, another king of the same dynasty, subjugated Finland, and brought with him home the daughter of the Finnish prince. Ingvar and his son Anund, two other kings of the Yngling family, made expeditions to Esthonia, and brought great booty home. These traditions point to a connection between Scandinavia and the regions east of the Baltic in very early ages. This is further verified through the more reliable evidence of archæological finds, which prove that the Scandinavians must have paid frequent visits to the eastern shores of the Baltic, that their civilization was transplanted to those regions, and that they must have founded settlements there in many places. These finds are especially numerous in Tavastland and Satakunda, in southern Finland, but they have also been made in many other places.

Of special interest is the account given by the Russian chronicler Nestor of the founding of the kingdom of Russia by the Swedes. Nestor was a monk in Kief in the latter part of the eleventh century. He tells the story as follows: "In the year 6367 after the creation of the world (859 A.D.),[1] the Varangians [2] came across the sea and exacted tribute from the Tchouds and the Slavs, from the Merians, Vesses, and Krivitches. In the year 6370 (862 A.D.) they (i.e. the Slavs) drove away the Varangians across the sea, paid them no tribute, and began to rule themselves; but disorder prevailed. One tribe rose against the other, there was enmity between them, and they began to wage war on each other. Then they said to each other: 'Let us get a prince who can rule over us, and who can judge rightly.' And they went across the sea to the Varangians, to the Russians, for so the Varangians are called, while some are called Swedes, others Norsemen, others Angles, and Goths. And the Tchouds, the Slavs, the Krivitches, and the Vesses said to the Russians: 'Our land is

---

[1] The Byzantine and Russian annalists used the Constantinopolitan era, counted from the creation of the world. The year began Sept. 1st. The birth of Christ was supposed to have occurred in the year 5509 of that era. This number subtracted from the given number of years gives the year of the Christian era.

[2] Russian Varjag, Byzantine Varangoi, Arabic Varank, Scandinavian Væring, O. N. plu. Væringjar, O. N. vár = a pledge or oath, A. S. wær. Varangians or Værings signify those who have pledged themselves, evidently to a chief or leader.

large and fertile, but there is no order there; come, therefore, and rule over us.' Three brothers were chosen, and they took with them all the Rus, and they came. And the oldest, Rurik, settled in Novgorod, and the second, Sineus, at Biéloe-Ozéro, and the third at Izborsk; his name was Trouvor. From these Varangians the Russian kingdom received its name; that is the Novgorodians; these are the Novgorodian peoples of Varangian descent; before the Novgorodians were Slavs. After two years had passed, Sineus died, and also his brother Trouvor. Rurik then became ruler in their stead, and gave cities to his men; to one he gave Polotsk, to another Rostof, to a third Biéloe-Ozéro. Into these places the Varangians had immigrated; the former inhabitants in Novgorod being Slavs, in Polotsk Krivitches, in Rostof Merians, in Biéloe-Ozéro Vesses."

The Frankish annals tell of an embassy sent by the Byzantine Emperor, Theophilos, to the Frankish Emperor, Louis the Pious. Along with this embassy came some men who said that they were from a people by the name of Ros,[1] that they had been sent as messengers by their king to the Emperor at Byzantium, and wished now, with Louis' aid, to return to their own country, because the route which they had followed to Constantinople led through the lands of strange and barbarous peoples, where it was very dangerous to travel. Upon closer investigation Louis found that they were Swedes.[2]

That Rurik and his followers, the Varangians, or Russians, came from Scandinavia is seen also from the great number of names of unmistakable Scandinavian origin in early Russian history. The names of Rurik's successors, Oleg and Igor, are but slightly altered forms of the Scandinavian names Helge and Ivar, or Ingvar. The representatives sent by these rulers to conclude peace with the Byzan-

---

[1] The Varangians or Ros (Russians) probably came from Roslagen in Sweden. *Ros* or *Rus* is thought to mean rowers. The seacoast districts of Uppland and Östergötland in Sweden were in olden times called *Roþer* (*Roþin*), and had to furnish rowers for the *leding*, or military expeditions at sea. From these words the form *Rus* (Russian) seems to have been evolved. Alexander Bugge, *Vesterlandenes Indflydelse*, p. 132. V. L. P. Thomsen, *The Relations between Ancient Russia and Scandinavia, and the Origin of the Russian State.* P. A. Munch, *Samlede Afhandlinger*, vol. II., p. 184 ff.

[2] *Annales Bertiniani.* See R. Keyser, *Om Nordmœndenes Herkomst og Folkeslœgtskab, Samlinger til det norske Folks Sprog og Historie*, VI., 259 ff. Also P. A. Munch, *Samlede Afhandlinger*, II., 184 ff.

tine Emperor in 912 and 945 had Scandinavian names. As examples may be mentioned: Karl, Inegeld, Ivar, Vuefast, Uleb, Bern, Schigbern, Turbern, Grim, Kol, Sven, Gunnar, etc.[1] As late as in the eleventh century the name Oleg was still used in the Russian dynasty.

In the beginning Novgorod or Holmgard was the chief city in the new Russian kingdom, but soon Kief grew into great importance, and became the real capital.

Great trade routes were opened along the Volga to Astrakhan, and along the Dnieper to the shores of the Black Sea. Here the Varangians met the Arab tradesmen, and a lively commercial intercourse sprang up, through which a great number of coins and other articles of value were brought to Scandinavia.[2] Kief, which was situated on this main trade route, reached its highest splendor in the time of King Jaroslaf. He wished his capital to rival Constantinople, and Kief became famous as the "city of four hundred churches."

The Varangian prince Ivar of Novgorod concluded a treaty of commerce with the Emperor of the Byzantine Empire, and traders and slave dealers carried on a steadily growing traffic along the Volga and the Dnieper to Novgorod and the shores of the Baltic Sea.[3] Many names of towns and waterfalls along these routes still preserve the memory of the Scandinavian traders and travelers who sojourned in those regions in ages past.[4] As an illustration may be mentioned

---

[1] The Scandinavian forms are: *Karl, Inggjald, Ivar, Vigfast, Ulf, Bjørn, Sigbjørn, Torbjørn, Grim, Kol, Sveinn,* and *Gunnar.*

[2] Especially interesting are the Kufic coins, brought to the North in great numbers. These are generally counterfeit coins minted in Central Asia in the tenth century. They are made of copper, and are coated with silver.

A grave opened at Tchernigof contained the remains and weapons of an unknown prince of the tenth century. He was, no doubt, a Varangian. His helmet and coat of mail resemble quite exactly the armor of the Vikings.

[3] An interesting illustration of the slave trade of this period is the pathetic story in the *Laxdǿlasaga* of Melkorka, an Irish princess sold as a slave to Hoskuld Dalakollsson of Iceland.

[4] One of the most interesting early accounts of the Russians is given by Emperor Constantine Porphyrogenitus in his work *De Administrando Imperio,* written in the middle of the tenth century. He tells how they descended the river Dnieper in boats, and that they carried their boats past the waterfalls. The names of these waterfalls are given both in Slavic and Russian, with Greek translation, and the Russian forms are clearly of Scandinavian origin. The names of the second and third, for example, are written $O\dot{v}\lambda\beta o\rho\sigma\iota$ and $\Gamma\epsilon\lambda\alpha\nu\delta\rho\iota$ = O. N. *Ulforsi* and *Gjallandi* (the noisy waterfall).

Bjarkowitz, a Russian form of the Scandinavian Bjarkø, an island near the coast of Ingermanland, where a trading station was located. The kings of Sweden and Norway were related to the Russian princes through marriage, and often sent them troops when needed, or they sought refuge with them in times of trouble at home. A lively intercourse between Scandinavia and Russia, or Gardarike, as it was usually called in the North, continued till the death of Jaroslaf in 1045. The Slavs then gained the ascendancy, and Scandinavian influence in Russia came to an end. Through the Varangians these dark and far-off regions were brought into the daylight of history; colonies were founded, cities were built, commerce and government were established, and this hitherto unknown domain was opened to the forces of civilization and progress. Russia became under Varangian rule a European kingdom, aspiring to rival in culture the nations most advanced in those times, something that cannot be said of Russia through many centuries after the Scandinavians had ceased to rule.

After having penetrated the wilds of Russia, and established permanent communication with the Black Sea, it was comparatively easy for the enterprising Vikings to push across that sea to Constantinople, or Myklegard (the great city), as they called it. Nestor says that a number of Varangians in the service of Vladimir the Great of Russia became dissatisfied and went to Constantinople. This is said to have happened about 980, but these were not the first Varangians in the Byzantine Empire. The Emperor had already at that time an army of Scandinavian warriors who served, not only as his bodyguard, but were also used in active warfare in different parts of the Empire. Most famous of all the Scandinavians in Constantinople was Harald Sigurdsson, son of the Norwegian king, Sigurd Syr, and a half-brother of King Olav Haraldsson (St. Olav). He became chief of the Varangians in Constantinople, and took part in many campaigns in Syria, Armenia, Palestine, Sicily, and Africa. He captured many fortified cities, and gathered immense treasures. Snorre says that there was a law, that when the Greek Emperor died, the Varangians should have *polata-svaro*.[1] They were then allowed to go through all the royal palaces where the treasures were

---

[1] *polata = palatium. polata-svaro* = robbery of the palace.

stored, and take what they could seize with their hands. Harald Sigurdsson had three times taken part in such a *polata-svaro* in Constantinople. He returned to Novgorod with great treasures, married King Jaroslaf's daughter, and became later king of Norway. As such he is known as Harald Haardraade.

FIG. 37. — The marble lion of Piræus with runic inscription.

An object which preserves in an interesting way the memory of the Vikings in the Byzantine Empire is the great marble lion from Piræus, now standing at the entrance to the arsenal in Venice, where it was brought by the Venetians in 1687, after they had captured Athens. On this monument is found a delicately carved runic inscription in the snake-loop design so familiar from Scandinavian rune-stones. The characters are so nearly effaced that the inscription cannot be read, but it silently points to the days when Harald Sigurdsson and the Varangians served the Byzantine Emperor in Constantinople and Jerusalem, and measured swords with the Saracens in Asia and Africa.[1]

[1] See *Harald Haardraade og Væringerne i de græske Keiseres Tjeneste,* Gustav Storm, *Norsk Historisk Tidsskrift,* anden række, 4, 1884. *Nordboernes Forbindelse med Østen i det niende og nærmest følgende Aarhundreder.* Carl C. Rafn, *Antiquarisk Tidsskrift,* 1852–1854, Copenhagen. P. A, Munch, *Samlede Afhandlinger,* vol. I., p. 505 ff.

16. Life and Culture of the Viking Age

Intellectual culture is a complex and delicate fabric into which the fibers of experience and the finer filaments of secret and mysterious influence are deftly woven. Social environment and native talent fashion the texture, but the threads have been brought from many climes, and every age has been laid under tribute. Wherever higher culture has been produced, a process of absorption of new elements, an accumulation of new experience, a borrowing and importation, have freely taken place. The stimulus produced by the new, with the attendant reaction of the native mind upon it, primarily determines all new cultural growth. The Greeks borrowed from the Orient, the Romans from the Greeks; from both came culture and Christianity to the rest of Europe. Even the far North had felt the thrill of this influence long before the Viking Age began, but the process of absorption of new elements had been slow, and the development uneventful. No sudden changes are noticeable till the Migrations sweep over Europe, and roll high the billows of general tumult and upheaval. The quickening effect of this great movement tore the peoples of the North from their ancient moorings, and as Vikings they burst forth, adding new terror to this dark and bloody period. In this first outburst of pent-up energy and unrestrained passions we see the worst instincts of a primitive race let loose in savage warfare which often throws the deepest shadow on the pages of Viking history. But justice even here constrains us to admit that it is but a shade deeper than a similar shadow which falls over the history of all human warfare. To consider minutely all the acts of vandalism and cruelty perpetrated by the Vikings would not even give us the satisfaction of having shown that their system of plunder and bloodshed differed essentially from that of the Roman generals, of the pious crusaders, the defenders of the faith, and most Christian princes of later, and more enlightened, ages. It must also be borne in mind that on these expeditions we meet the Vikings as warriors, and that the outrages often committed can furnish no adequate criterion for judging their life and culture in general.

The nature of the Viking campaigns furnishes an easy explanation of the panic which seems to have seized the inhabitants of the countries exposed to their attacks. A cruel fate usually befell the towns and cities they seized. Not only did they kill and plunder, and carry women off into slavery, but they spared no sanctuary, and nothing holy could stay their rapacious and destructive hands. When the battle was over, and the victory won, they would celebrate the event in drunken carousals in which the skulls of their fallen enemies often served as wine bowls, and other acts equally gruesome were committed, which might well strike Christian hearts with horror. Even human beings are known to have been sacrificed to the gods, and when a city was taken, children would be transfixed with spears, and "given to Odin" amid wild outbursts of triumphant rejoicing. If we add that by means of their fleets they could depart at will, only to reappear at the most unexpected moments, that the inhabitants often felt powerless over against this dreaded enemy, we can understand the people's superstitious fear, the sad laments and exaggerated stories of the old writers, and the prayers offered up in the Christian churches: "From the fury of the Northmen, Lord God, deliver us!" Intellectually and culturally the whole period was one of general contraction and retrogression, in which ancient arts and civilization were forgotten, and ignorance and rude manners prevailed. Viewing the period thus, we may justly term it the Dark Ages. A tone of retrospection and sadness was prevalent among those who possessed learning and culture. They looked backward to the days of Greece and Rome as to a golden age that would never return. The sun had set, they thought; the world would never again become what it had been in ancient times; their only consolation was that after death there awaited the Christian a blissful life in heaven. But these dark centuries represent not only the downfall of the old, but also the birth of the new. Viewed from this side, we find the period to be an era of expansion and development in which old barriers were broken, and new opportunities were given to the peoples which had hitherto been regarded as dwelling outside the pale of civilization.

On their expeditions the Vikings had come into direct communication with nearly every part of the then known world. Their sphere of activity was thus immensely widened, and their ideas of the world were altered correspondingly. New ideas from the Christian faith, from Græco-Roman civilization, and from Irish poesy and learning poured into the North, and became the leaven which brought the half-slumbering energies of the Scandinavian peoples into full activity. A new culture was produced which soon placed the peoples of the North in the front rank of enlightened and progressive nations. Norway and her colony Iceland became the center of literary activity in northern Europe during the Middle Ages, and Norse mythology was elaborated into a system which, though inferior to that of Greece in beauty, surpasses it in depth and grandeur. The Scandinavians became leaders in navigation, commerce, and discovery, and developed a system of laws and government which has left deep and lasting traces wherever permanent Viking settlements were founded.

The maritime enterprise and naval warfare attending the Viking expeditions gave a great stimulus to ship-building and navigation in the North. We have seen that even before this period the Scandinavians possessed great skill in ship-building, and could construct vessels of considerable size. In the Viking Age a great demand made itself felt for vessels suited for long voyages, and able to carry as large a number of warriors as possible. In the Mediterranean Sea they became acquainted with Greek and Roman ships, and every effort was now made to construct ships of large size, and of improved type.

The larger sea-going ships were of two kinds: merchant ships and war vessels. An early type of merchant ship was the *kjóll* (A. S. *ceól*), but during the greater part of the Viking Age the *knarre* (*O. N. knǫrr*) and the *byrding* were common types. Later a larger-sized vessel, the *busse*[1] (O. N. *búza*), came into use, and still later the *kogge* (O. N. *kuggr*), which soon developed into a war vessel. The merchant ships were quite broad and high in proportion to their length, with half-decks in the prow and stern. The goods were placed in the undecked middle part of the vessel. The ship had one mast and a four-cornered sail. The mast could be folded down, and would then rest on supports high enough so that a person could conveniently pass under it.[2] The oar-shaped rudder was fixed

---

[1] Cf. medieval Latin *bussa*.

[2] Valtýr Guðmundsson, *Nordboernes Skibe i Viking- og Sagatiden*, Copenhagen, 1900. Hermann Paul, *Grundriss der germanischen Philologie*, 2d edition,

to the right side of the vessel, near the stern. This side was, therefore, called the *steerboard* (O. N. *stjórnbordi*), while the left side, which was at the back of the helmsman, was called the *backboard* (O. N. *bakbordi*). Oars were used only in the front and rear ends of the vessel.

Of the warships the *askr* [1] and the *elliði* were older types, which seem to have differed little from the ordinary merchant vessel. A later type was the *long ship*,[2] so called, because it was long and narrow, with high prow and stern. This type seems to have come into use in the tenth century. These ships were beautifully painted in various colors, and were ornamented with wood carvings. Oars were used along the whole ship, and on both sides hung a row of shields painted black and yellow alternately. The prow was gilt and shaped like the head of a bird or animal; usually like that of a dragon. The sails were usually striped, red, blue, and green, and were often made of costly material. The warships were divided into various classes according to their shape and size, and the service for which they were intended. The *skeið* [3] was a narrow, swift sailing vessel. The *snekkja* was supplied with a sort of snout. The *drage* (O. N. *dreki*) [4] or dragon ship was larger than ordinary, with a prow like a dragon's head, and a stern often shaped like a dragon's tail. The *barði* was also a large ship, built for the special purpose of ramming and sinking the ships of the enemy. It had iron rams, both on prow and stern. The warships had a full deck, and second half decks in bow and stern. The forward half deck was called the *forstavnsdæk*, and the rear half-deck *løftingen*. Another classification was made according to size by counting the number of row-benches on one side of the ship. In this classification the ships were known as thirteen-bench, fifteen-bench, twenty-bench, thirty-bench; etc., with twenty-six, thirty, forty, and sixty oars. The most common size was the twenty-bench, with forty oars, and a crew of

---

Skandinavische Verhältnisse, von Valtýr Guðmundsson und Kristian Kålund (§§ 49–60 Schiffe, von V. G.)   N. E. Tuxen, *De nordiske Langskibe, Aarbøger for nordisk Oldkyndighed og Historie*, 1886.   Alexander Bugge, *Vesterlandenes Indflydelse paa Nordboerne i Vikingetiden*, p. 199 ff.

[1] Cf. Latin *askus*. *Askmenn* (sailors) was a term often applied to the Vikings in foreign lands.

[2] Cf. Latin *navis longa*.   [3] Cf. Greek σχεδια.   [4] Latin *draco*.

PLATE IV

VIKING WARSHIP.

THE GOKSTAD SHIP RESTORED.

ninety men. On the thirty-bench there were two men to each oar, or 120 rowers, the crew consisting all together of about 260 men. King Olav Tryggvason's famous ship, the *Long Serpent*, is said to have had a crew of 300 men.

The scattered Viking bands, which operated in a more desultory way at the beginning of the period, were gradually united under able leaders into fleets and armies of great size. "The Anglo-Saxon Chronicle" shows how the Viking fleets in England were growing:

Year 787. In his (King Breohtric's) days came three ships of Northmen from Hereðaland.

Year 833. In this year King Ecgbyrht fought with the crews of thirty-five ships at Carrum.

Year 840. In this year King Æthelwulf fought at Carrum against the men of thirty-five ships.

Year 851. In this year 350 ships came to the mouth of the Thames, and the men landed and took Canterbury and London by storm.

Year 877. 120 ships were wrecked at Swanawic.

Year 893. In this year the great army . . . returned, . . . and came to land at Limenemouth with 250 ships.

At this time the ships must have been of the older and smaller types; but if we assume that each ship had a crew of only 40 men, 350 vessels would bring an army of 14,000 warriors. Similar numbers of ships are mentioned by many other sources. The chroniclers describe in glowing colors the vast numbers of the invaders. They are compared to swarms of grasshoppers that cover the earth. The Viking ships, says an Arabian writer, fill the ocean like a flock of red birds. An Irish annalist says that the ocean rolls billows of strangers over all Erin. Fleet upon fleet is spewed out by the sea, so that there is not a spot in the island where their ships are not found.[1]

Excepting the ships of the Saracens in Spain, and the small beginning made by King Alfred in England, the peoples of western Europe had as yet no fleets. These great naval armaments, therefore, gave

[1] See Steenstrup, *Normannerne*, vol. I., p. 209 ff.

the Vikings an advantage which largely explains the success which they achieved in their campaigns.

The size of the army was no less imposing than that of the fleet. At the siege of Paris in 885 the Vikings had 40,000 men, of which 30,000 probably constituted the actual fighting force, if we may believe the old sources. In the battle of Saucourt 9000 Vikings are said to have fallen. But the success of the Vikings was due to their superior training and equipment rather than to the size of their

FIG. 38. — A Viking warrior.

armies, which in many cases seems to be exaggerated. Professor Oman says: "But no less important than the command of the sea was the superiority of the individual Viking in battle to the average member of the host that came out against him. The war bands of the invaders were the pick of the North, all volunteers, all trained warriors. In a Frankish or an English host the only troops that could safely be opposed to them, man to man, were the personal following of the kings and ealdormen of England — or the dukes and counts of the Continent. And these were but a small fraction of the hasty levy that assembled, when news came that the Danes were ashore at Bremen or Boulogne, at Sandwich or Weymouth. The majority of the *hereban* of a Frankish county, or the *fyrd* of an English shire, was composed of farmers fresh from the plow, not of trained fighting men. Enormous superiority of numbers could alone compensate for the differences in military efficiency. If that superiority existed, the raider quietly retired to his ships, or to his fortified island base. If it did not, he fell upon the landsfolk and made a dreadful slaughter of them. How could it be expected that the ceorl, who came out to war with spear and target alone, should contend on equal terms with the Northmen equipped with steel cap and mail shirt, and well trained to form the shield wall for defense and the war wedge for attack? Working against the hastily arrayed masses of the landsfolk, the Viking host was like a good military machine beating upon an ill-compacted earthwork." [1]

The Viking army was a strong and permanent organization, with able commanders and officers. It had infantry and cavalry, spies, sappers, and a well-organized commissariat. It had catapults and battering rams, and other machinery for the carrying on of sieges. Military tactics were well developed; there was strict discipline, and perfect obedience to authority.

17. CAUSES OF THE VIKING EXPEDITIONS

The Viking expeditions may have been due to a number of causes. In the Scandinavian countries, with their limited area of tillable soil, and their extensive seacoast, a seafaring life was necessitated from the start, which produced a hardy and energetic race, and fostered the spirit of daring and adventure which expresses itself in the whole movement. The size of the Viking armies indicates clearly that the population in the North was increasing at a very rapid rate during this period, owing, no doubt, to polygamy, which, in one form or another, was extensively practiced. The number of those who found it necessary to follow war as a permanent occupation was growing. According to the old laws ("Frostathingslov" and "Gulathingslov") all sons shared equally in the inheritance, but as both political power and social standing depended on wealth, and especially on the ownership of land, the aristocracy would not sell their estates, nor would they destroy them by dividing them into small parcels. The young men were partly encouraged, partly driven by necessity to seek their fortune on expeditions to foreign countries. Led by love of adventure, and encouraged by the prospects of wealth and fame, they flocked to the standards of the Viking chieftains in such numbers that the movement soon became a migration, and extensive campaigns were waged for conquest and colonization. The women and children usually accompanied the men, and were left in fortified camps while the army advanced to the attack.[2]

[1] Oman, *England before the Norman Conquest*, p. 415.

[2] The "Great Army," led by Hasting, was ravaging King Alfred's kingdom in England in 893. While Hasting and the army were absent, the

It often happened that the women dressed in warriors' garb, and joined their husbands and brothers in the battle.[1] As they were forced to share the perils and hardships with the men, they became inured to danger, and showed an alertness and bravery equal to that of the best warriors.[2] Sometimes women would even become leaders of armies, like the "red maiden," a Norwegian amazon who led an army in Ireland in the tenth century.

It is an error often repeated that the Vikings came to foreign lands as bands of adventurers, married the women there, and soon forgot their own customs and language. As a rule they brought their families with them, and settlers, both men and women, came to the new colony as soon as it was safely established. The social organization of the home country was reproduced in the colonies, and there is ample evidence to show that the Vikings clung to their own customs and national identity with a tenacity not unworthy of so proud a race.

18. TOWNS AND COMMERCE

The military operations of the Vikings constitute, in many ways, the great features of the period. This fact, together with the fallacious idea that they were only buccaneers and adventurers, has often diverted the attention from their peaceful pursuits and extensive friendly intercourse with other nations, so important to the development of Europe. We have seen that in very early times they had maintained extensive trade relations with peoples dwelling

English fell upon his camp and captured it, taking a great amount of booty, besides the wives and children, both of Hasting's own force and of the men of the "Great Army." Among the prisoners were Hasting's own wife and his two young sons. The prisoners were later returned to Hasting by Alfred. See Oman, *England before the Norman Conquest.* The Irish annals state that "the foreigners were gathered from all the western part of Europe, envoys having been sent into Norway, the Orkneys, and the Baltic Islands, so that a great number of Vikings came from all Scandinavia with their families for the purpose of making a permanent settlement."

[1] This custom may have led the early Greek and Latin writers to describe the Scandinavian North as the land of the Amazons.

[2] Kedren, a Greek writer of the eleventh century, in describing a battle between Svjatoslav's Varangians and the Greeks, says that when the Greeks plundered the bodies of the barbarians, they found among the dead many women in the garb of warriors, who had helped the men in the fight.

east and south of the Baltic Sea, that they had visited the British
Isles, and, no doubt, also the coasts of Friesland and northern France
as merchants long before they were heard of as Vikings. Towns and
trading places, such as Upsala, Sigtuna, and Birka, on Mälaren in
Sweden, Wisby in Gothland, Skiringssal in Norway, Schleswig or
Hedeby in Jutland, and Dorstadt in Friesland, are known to have
existed at the beginning of the Viking period. Through the Viking
expeditions these early trade relations were so stimulated and developed as to become a systematized commerce, the first of the kind
in northern Europe. With their fleets of merchant ships the Vikings
opened new routes of trade. They brought the products of Russia
to the West, those of southern Europe, Spain, and France to the
North, and found new markets for their own articles of export.
Many of their expeditions were undertaken for the sake of trade,
rather than for war. When they came to a foreign land, they often
entered into an agreement with the inhabitants that for a certain
number of days or weeks perfect peace should be maintained, and
as long as this lasted, a lively trade was carried on. Only after the
period of peace was at an end, did they consider it legitimate to plunder.[1] During this period Norway had more products for export
than most other countries, the more important being dried codfish,
herring, furs, walrus skin, from which rope was made, falcons, used
extensively in hunting at that time, and walrus teeth, which were
considered very valuable. To the colonies and home markets the
Vikings brought the much-prized products of southern Europe,
such as fine cloth, leather, wines, saddles, etc., and these new wares
produced a hitherto unknown demand for articles of luxury. "In
968 the Irish plundered Limerick," says the chronicler, "and carried

[1] "The plan adopted by them on this occasion was to equip three captains, sprung from the noblest blood of Norway, and to send them with a
fleet to Ireland, for the object of obtaining some station for the purpose of
trade. And with them they accordingly embarked many tempting wares,
and many valuable jewels, — with the design of presenting them to the men
of Ireland, in the hope of thus securing their friendship." From Keating,
by Aug. J. Thebaud, *Ireland, Past and Present.*

Brynjolv Herse would not give his son a warship, "but a merchant ship
and goods will I give you," he says — "Go with that south to Dublin, for this
traffic is now most spoken of." *Egilssaga*, ch. 22. Aage Friis, *Verdenskulturen*, vol. IV., Alexander Bugge's article *Vikingetidens Handel*, p. 113.

away the treasures and most valuable possessions of the Vikings; their fine foreign saddles, their gold and silver, their beautifully woven cloth of all kinds and colors, their silk and satin, both scarlet and green, and all kinds of cloth in the same way." [1] These were all articles which the Norsemen had imported. The foreign saddles and the fine Cordovan leather (leather from Cordova), which was in great demand, show that they carried on trade with Spain, where they would get from the Arabs the products of the Orient.

Before the arrival of the Norsemen, the Irish had no ships, only boats made of skin, frail craft in which, however, they had been able to reach the distant islands. They had no cities or commerce, and they coined no money. To facilitate trade, the Norsemen introduced in Ireland a system of weights and measures, and here, as in Britain, they began to coin money. The words *mark* (O. N. *mǫrk*) and *penning* (O. N. *peningr*) have been incorporated into the Irish language as *marc* and *pingind*.[2] The growth of towns as centers of trade followed as a direct result of Viking settlement and the development of commerce. Waterford, Cork, Limerick, and other cities founded by the Vikings became important trading places, while Dublin developed into one of the leading emporiums of commerce in northern Europe. Silks, and costly cloth of all kinds, leather, wines, and other products from the South were imported to Dublin, whence they were again brought by merchants to Norway, Denmark, Sweden, and Iceland. How rich and flourishing the Viking cities in Ireland were can be seen also from accounts of contemporary writers. In 941-942 King Muirchertach made a journey through all Ireland; he also visited Dublin, and nowhere did he receive such presents as there. In a song written by a contemporary poet his reception is described as follows: [3]

"A supply of his full store was given
to Muirchertach, son of Niall,

---

[1] *War of the Gœdhel*, p. 78. See also Alexander Bugge, *Vikingerne*, I.

[2] It is noteworthy that silver was the metal most used in the Viking period, while earlier, gold was the chief precious metal. The silver was usually weighed and used in bulk. Gold was used for ornaments, especially for spiral arm rings. The kings, who often made presents of these to show their munificence, were called by the scalds "dispensers of rings."

[3] Alexander Bugge, *Vesterlandenes Indflydelse*, p. 184.

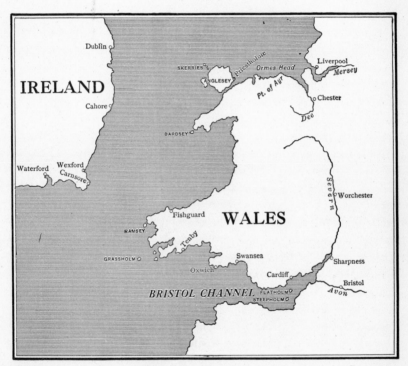

NORSE SETTLEMENTS AND TOWNS IN WALES AND ON THE BRISTOL CHANNEL.

of bacon, of good and perfect wheat;
also was got a blood-debt of red gold.

Joints (of meat), and fine cheese (were given)
by the very good and very pure queen,
and then was given, (a thing) to hear,
a colored mantle for each chieftain."

After the battle of Glenmama, in the year 1000, King Brian captured Dublin. "In this one place," says the old writer, "there were found the greatest treasures of gold, silver, and findrun (a sort of white bronze), of precious stones, carbuncles, drinking horns, and beautiful goblets." [1]

"The Norsemen brought with them to Ireland the ideas of cities, commerce, and municipal life hitherto unknown," says Aug. J. Thebaud.[2] "The introduction of these supposed a total change necessary in the customs of the natives, and stringent regulations to which the people could not but be radically opposed. . . . No more stringent rules could be devised, whether for municipal, rural or social regulations; and, as the Northmen are known to have been of a systematic mind, no stronger proof of this fact could be given."

Also in the Scandinavian countries at home, and elsewhere along all the routes of trade, cities sprang into existence under the stimulating influence of Viking commerce. Rouen, in Normandy, became the most important trading center in France, and merchant vessels from Norway and Iceland anchored in the Seine. In Norway the new commercial town of Tunsberg, on the Christianiafjord, soon outdistanced the older Skiringssal; and Konghelle, a new trading town, was founded in the southeastern part. Haløre, probably located on the coast of Skåne, in Sweden, and Brännøerne, near the mouth of the Göta River, became important commercial centers.

A lively intercourse was also maintained between Ireland and the English seacoast towns across the Irish Sea, which had either been founded or developed by the Vikings. Several of these towns grew into prominence, such as Swansea,[3] Tenby, Chester, and especially Bristol, which had become a great trading center, and in course of

---

[1] *Cogadh Gœdhel*, p. 114 ff. [2] *Ireland, Past and Present*, p. 122.
[3] Swansea = Sweins-ea (*i.e.* Swein's river).

time superseded Dublin and Waterford as the greatest commercial city on the shores of the Irish Sea.[1] In the Midlands the towns of the "Five Boroughs," Lincoln, Leicester, Nottingham, Stamford, and Derby (O. N. Dýrabýr) became cities of importance, and on the east coast of England, Grimsby and York grew into prominence. At the time of the "Domesday Book," York was, next to London and Winchester, the largest city in England.

In speaking of the influence of the Vikings on the development of English commerce, Mr. W. Cunningham says: "The English were satisfied with rural life; they were little attracted by the towns which the Romans had built, and they did not devote themselves to commercial pursuits or to manufacturing articles for sale. The Danes,[2] though so closely allied in race, appear to have been men of a different type. They were great as traders and also as seamen. We may learn how great their prowess was from the records of their voyages to Iceland, Greenland, and America, from accounts of their expeditions to the White Sea and the Baltic, and from their commerce with such distant places as the Crimea and Arabia. Their settlements in this country were among the earliest of the English towns to exhibit signs of activity. Not only were the Danes traders; they were also skilled in metal work and other industrial pursuits. England has attained a character for her shipping and has won the supremacy of the world in manufacturing; it almost seems as if she were indebted, on those sides of life on which she is most successful, to the fresh energy and enterprise ingrafted by Danish settlers and conquerors. By the efforts of Roman missionaries she had been brought into contact with the remains of Roman civilization, but by the infusion of the Danish element she was drawn into close connection with the most energetic of the Northern races."[3] Aug. J. Thebaud says: "Endowed with all the characteristics of the Scandinavian race, deeply infused with the blood of the Danes and the

---

[1] Alexander Bugge, *Contributions to the History of the Norsemen in Ireland*, III., *Skrifter udgivet af Videnskabs-Selskabet i Christiania*, 1900.

[2] *Danes* is used by many English writers as a common designation for all Vikings, Danes and Norwegians.

[3] W. Cunningham, D.D., Fellow and Lecturer of Trinity College, Cambridge, and Tooke Professor of Economic Science in King's College, London, *Outlines of English Industrial History*, 1905.

Northmen, she (England) has all the indomitable energy, all the systematic grasp of mind and sternness of purpose joined to the wise spirit of compromise and conservatism of the men of the far North. She, of all nations, has inherited their great power of expansion at sea, possessing all the roving propensities of the old Vikings, and the spirit of trade, enterprise, and colonization of those old Phœnicians of the arctic circle." [1]

A similar influence was exerted by the Norsemen on the naval development of France. "It is the great achievement of the Normans," says Depping, "that they gave France a navy. There was no longer any navy in France, and she had ceased to be numbered among maritime nations. The Normans reëstablished the marine, and William the Conqueror succeeded in forming a fleet, the like of which France had not seen. The conquests made by the Normans in Sicily were due in part to their superiority in navigation." [2] It may be due to the same influence that Normandy furnishes more sailors and pilots than any other part of France, and that many of the leading French admirals have been Normans.

We have seen that the Vikings had early learned to build fortifications and stone towers of great strength, that, besides the fortified camps, and strongholds built for military purposes, they also surrounded their towns and cities, especially in the colonies, with walls and moats which virtually made them fortresses of great military importance. The building of castles was first developed in Normandy, and the *donjon* or square tower, so typical in medieval castles, is thought to be of Viking origin. In Ireland the Norsemen began to build fortified strongholds as early as 840. Cork was fortified in 866, and in a saga of the eleventh century Limerick is called "the city with riveted stones." [3] Dublin, where stood the royal

---

[1] *Ireland Past and Present*, p. 54.

[2] George Bernhard Depping, *Histoire des Expeditions Maritime des Normands, et leur Établissement en France au X Siècle*, liv. IV., ch. III.

[3] *Caithreim Cellachain Caisil*. The original Irish text edited with translation and notes by Alexander Bugge, Christiania, 1905.

> "Come to Limerick of the ships,
> O Clan Eogan of the noble deeds!
> Around the gentle Cellachan,
> To Limerick of the riveted stones."

hall or castle, with its massive stone tower, was surrounded by walls and moats, and was called "the strong fortress." Waterford, too, had walls and moats, and a royal castle where the king used to dwell. An old stone tower is still found there called Reginald's Tower (Ragnvalds taarn) supposed to be the *donjon* of the old royal castle. It is known to have stood there in 1170, when the English captured Waterford.[1] York and the cities of the "Five Boroughs" in England were also well fortified.

The Roman towns in early Britain were destroyed by the Anglo-Saxons when they conquered the country. "Of the fifty-six cities of Roman Britain," says W. Cunningham,[2] "there is not one in regard to which it is perfectly clear that it held its ground as an organized center of social life through the period of English conquest and English settlement." Many of these old ruined cities were rebuilt by the Vikings, and many new ones were founded. These Viking cities were the first to show the signs of municipal and urban life, both in Great Britain and Ireland. They became centers, not only of trade, but also of industry, as the Danes and Norsemen also devoted themselves to industrial pursuits, and produced wares of their own make for the general market. The Vikings had a keen sense for legal justice, and maintained strict order in their towns. They developed a system of city laws of which traces are still found in English city government.[3]

---

[1] See Alexander Bugge, *Vesterlandenes Indflydelse*, and L. J. Vogt, *Dublin som norsk By*, Christiania, 1896, p. 193.

[2] *Outlines of the English Industrial History*, p. 47.

[3] The legal term *by-law* (a law governing local and private affairs) is the same as the Danish *by-lov* = city law. The *husting* (O. N. *húsþing*) also reveals its Scandinavian origin. Originally it was a council held by a king or earl, and attended by his immediate followers. Later the *husting* was a council held at the Guild-hall in London of the Lord Mayor, Recorder, and sheriffs; long the supreme court of the city. It was also a court of common pleas. It is now convoked only for the purpose of considering and registering gifts to the city. A court of local jurisdiction in Virginia, U. S. A., was also called the Court of Hustings. *The Oxford Dictionary.*

In the cities of the "Five Boroughs"; in Cambridge, Chester, and other towns, there were twelve sworn lawmen (O. N. *lǫgmenn*), who, acting as judges, conducted all trials at the *thing* or court, and prepared all decisions. "Many scholars have of recent years come to regard this institution of twelve sworn men who conducted the legal proceedings in the general assembly of the

PLATE **V**

REGINALD'S TOWER (RAGNVALDS TAARN)
WATERFORD.

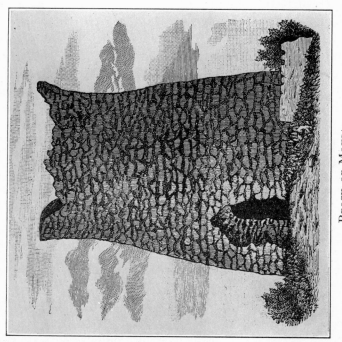

BROCH OF MOUSA.

19. Dress, Houses, Food and Drink

The many new wares brought to the North by enterprising Viking merchants increased the comforts of daily life, and created among the higher classes a taste for fine clothes, ornaments, and luxury in various forms which exerted a marked influence on cultural life in this period.[1] From early ages the Norsemen had woven their own woolen cloth, but it was a coarse and common fabric which they had not learned to dye in striking or delicate colors; linen (lérept) was also in common use. The new commerce brought rich supplies of costly fabrics from abroad: silk, satin, and fustian, a cotton cloth; scarlet (Lat. scarlatum), pell, and purple were brought from Spain, France, Flanders, and England. Men of higher rank took great pride in wearing scarlet mantles embroidered with gold, and trimmed with costly furs. The scald Gunlaug Ormstunge, received such a mantle from King Sigtrygg, in Dublin,[2] and Egil Skallagrimsson received "a costly mantle" from King Æthelstan for composing a song in his honor.[3] When Kjartan Olavsson from Iceland came to King Olav Tryggvason in Norway, he wore a scarlet mantle, and, when he left, the king gave him a complete dress of scarlet cloth.[4] From Arinbjørn Herse,[5] Egil Skallagrimsson received a silk cloak ornamented with gold buttons. The women exhibited the traditional feminine predilection for ornaments and fine dresses.

people as very strong evidence that the jury originated in England, and has not been introduced by the Normans. If this view is correct . . . it is of Scandinavian, not of Anglo-Saxon origin." Alexander Bugge, Vikingerne, II., p. 331.

[1] Paul, Grundriss der germanischen Philologie, vol. II., p. 235 ff., 2d ed., vol. III., p. 407 ff., Skandinavische Verhältnisse, Guðmundsson and Kålund. Alexander Bugge, Vesterlandenes Indflydelse, p. 142 ff. Alexander Bugge, Vikingerne, II., 156 ff. R. Keyser, Nordmœndenes private Liv i Oldtiden. Valtýr Guðmundsson, Privatboligen paa Island i Sagatiden, samt delvis i det øvrige Norden, Copenhagen. N. Nicolaysen, Noget om Skaalebygningen, Norsk Historisk Tidsskrift, vol. I., 1871. P. A. Munch, Det norske Folks Historie, vol. I. M. Mallet, Northern Antiquities, ch. X. R. Keyser, Nordmœndenes Boliger og daglige Sysler i œldre Tid, Lange's Norsk Tidsskrift, vol. I.

[2] Gunlaugssaga, ch. 7.   [3] Egilssaga, ch. 55.
[4] Laxdølasaga, ch. 40.   [5] Herse, pronounced hâr'sa.

The song "Rígsþula," in the "Elder Edda," describes the lady visited by Rig [1] (the god Heimdall) as follows:

> The wife sat
> mindful of her arms,
> smoothed the veil,
> stretched straight the sleeves,
> made stiff the mantle.
> A brooch was on her bosom;
> long was the train
> on her silk-blue dress.
>
> The wife bore a son,
> and swaddled him in silk,
> sprinkled him with water, [2]
> and called him jarl.

When the Irish sacked Limerick in 868, they carried away the "beautiful Viking women dressed in silk."

The saga writers often dwell with pride on the elegant attire of the persons prominent in their narrative. "Gunnar of Lidarende rode to the *thing* with all his men. When they came there, they were so well attired that there was nobody there so well dressed, and the people came out of the booths to look at them. . . . One day when Gunnar came from the *thing*, he saw a well-dressed woman approaching. When they met, she greeted Gunnar. He returned her greeting, and asked what her name was. She said that her name was Hallgerd, and that she was the daughter of Hoskuld Dalakollsson. She was rather forward in her speech, and asked him to tell her about his travels. This request he did not refuse, and they sat down and talked together. She was dressed in the following manner: She had a red skirt well ornamented, and over it she wore a scarlet cloak embroidered with gold. Her hair hung over her bosom, and it was both long and beautiful. Gunnar wore the scarlet clothes which King Harald Gormsson had given him, and on his arm he had the

---

[1] *Rig* is an Irish word meaning king. In the introduction to the poem he is said to be identical with Heimdall. E. Mogk thinks that Rig is Odin himself.

[2] A heathen ceremony probably introduced in imitation of Christian baptism. The jarls were of noble birth. The word is here used as an eponym.

gold ring which he had received from Haakon Jarl."[1] The Norsemen were quick at imitation, and soon learned to dye their own homemade cloth in various colors. New fashions, too, were introduced from abroad, which becomes apparent from many foreign names of articles of dress which came into use at this time; such as, *sokkr* (A. S. *socc*), *kyrtill* (A. S. *cyrtill*) = coat, *kápa* (Med. Lat. *capa*), cloak, *mǫttul* (Med. Lat. *mantellum*), mantle, etc. The tailor makes the gentleman, says the proverb, and true as this seems to be, the Norsemen had fully learned to appreciate this side of culture. Neither did they forget to lay stress on fine manners and courtly bearing. Tall, blond, stately, and self-conscious, they were manly and striking figures, and when in foreign lands they stepped before the kings and rulers in their finest attire, with gilt helmets and richly ornamented swords, they were not easily mistaken for barbarians. In "Ravnsmaal," a song by King Harald Haarfagre's hirdscald, Thorbjørn Hornklove, composed after the battle in Hafrsfjord (872), a raven and a valkyrie describe in a dialogue King Harald and his men. Says the valkyrie:

> About the scalds I wish to ask,
> those who follow King Harald,
> since you seem to know
> so much about brave men.

The raven:

> From their dress you may know,
> and from their rings of gold,
> that they are the king's friends;
> red mantles they wear,
> they have fine striped shields,
> silver-decorated swords,
> brynies of ring mail,
> gold embroidered shoulder-straps,[2]
> and ornamented helmets
> which Harald selected for them.

---

[1] *Njálssaga*, ch. 33. See also the *Saga of Olav the Saint* in the *Heimskringla*, the description of Olav's visit to his stepfather King Sigurd Syr. This description, however, pictures the customs of the saga writer's time, rather than of King Olav's own days.

[2] Two leather straps worn over the shoulders, and crossed in the front and in the back. In one was carried the sword, in the other the shield.

The description of the famous Norman warrior Robert Guiscard, given by Anna Comnena, the gifted daughter of Emperor Alexius, would fit just as well his Viking ancestors of a couple of generations earlier. She finds fault with his fierceness and his greed, but his manly qualities won her highest admiration, though he was her father's enemy:

"The Robert here mentioned was a Norman of quite humble extraction. He coveted power; in character he was cunning, in action quick and energetic. He eagerly desired to get possession of the wealth of the rich, and he carried out his wishes with irresistible energy, for in the pursuit of his aims he was resolute and inflexible. He was so tall that he carried his head above the largest men. He had ruddy cheeks, blond hair, broad shoulders and clear blue eyes, which seemed to flash fire. He was slender where he should be slender, and broad where he should be broad — in short, he was from top to toe as if molded and turned, a perfectly beautiful man, as I have heard many declare. Homer says of Achilles that when he spoke it was as if a multitude of people were making noise, but they say that Robert could shout so fearfully that he could drive away thousands. It is natural that a man with such physical and intellectual qualities would not bend under the yoke, nor submit to any one." [1]

The higher classes in Norway did not live in castles like the feudal aristocracy in France or Germany, but dwelt on their country estates, where they engaged in farming and cattle raising when they were not absent on Viking expeditions, or occupied in commercial pursuits. The farm labor was done by slaves, but even men of high station would put shield and sword aside and join in the work. We read in the sagas that Gunnar fra Lidarende was in the field sowing grain; that Thorbjørn Øxnarmegin was in the meadow making hay, and that King Sigurd Syr was superintending the harvest when his stepson, King Olav Haraldsson, visited him. The life in the home was still one of patriarchal simplicity. The wife managed the household, looked after the work, and waited on her guests at the table. As a token of her dignity as head of the household she carried in her belt a bunch of keys. In the "Rígsþula" she is called the *hangin-*

---

[1] Anna Comnena, *Alexiadis libri XIX*, translated into Danish by O. A. Hovgård, Copenhagen, 1879–1882, p. 59.

lukla, or "the lady with the dangling keys." Besides the regular household duties, the women, even of the highest standing, spent much time in weaving fine linen, and in embroidering tapestries of beautiful design. The men spent much of their spare time at metal work, wood carving, and the making of weapons, in which arts they possessed great skill. The houses were simple but well built log

FIG. 39. — Loom from the Faroe Islands.

structures. The principal house was the *skaale* (O. N. *skáli*), a long rectangular hall, often of great size. The gable over the main entrance was ornamented with carved dragonheads or deer horns. In the front end, in or near which the main entrance was located, were two smaller rooms, the *forstua* and the *kleve*, over which there was a loft. In the gables there were usually windows made of a thin membrane, as glass was not yet used for that purpose.[1] On

¹ The O. N. word *vindauga* (window) has been incorporated in the Irish language as *fuindeog,* which proves that also with regard to the construction of dwelling houses the Irish learned much from the Norsemen.

the side walls of the hall there were no doors or windows. If the hall was large, the roof rested on two rows of pillars. Along the middle of the hall was a fireplace, *arinn*, and above it in the roof was an opening, the *ljori*, through which the smoke escaped. Benches were placed along the side walls, and at the middle of one of these walls was placed the high-seat for the head of the family (*háscæti, ǫndvegi*), with high carved pillars on each side, the *ǫndvegissúlur*. Across from this seat, by the opposite wall, was a second and simpler high-seat for distinguished guests. Across the rear of the hall was

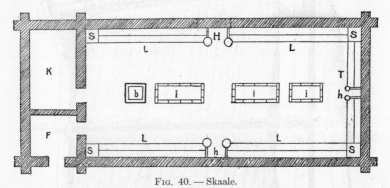

Fig. 40. — Skaale.

F, forstua; *K*, kleve; *H*, principal high-seat; *h*, second high-seat; *i, i, i*, fireplace; *T*, tverpall; *L, L, L, L*, benches; *S, S, S, S*, beds built in the wall; *b*, table to place food on.

placed a bench for the women, the *tverpall*, behind which were inclosed sleeping chambers. The benches along the walls were also used as beds at night by the men. At mealtime tables were placed in front of the benches on both sides along the hall, and when the meal was over, they were removed.

The walls were hung with shields, weapons, and woven tapestries. Sometimes they were ornamented with elaborate woodcarvings, like Olav Paa's hall at Hjarðarholt in Iceland, described in the "Laxdølasaga." Of other houses the most important were the *dyngja*, or *skemma*, where the women spent most of their time, and where they did their weaving and needlework, and the *svefnbúr*, where the lord of the household slept with his family. Usually there was also a *búr, jungfrúbúr*, where the young women stayed. The slaves had their own houses.

Great delight was taken in feasting and social entertainments, and the most generous hospitality was shown every wayfarer. It was regarded, not only as a sacred duty, but as a pleasure and a privilege to entertain strangers. Instances are mentioned in the "Landnámabók" where the *skaale* was built across the road, so that no stranger could pass without entering the house. The husband and wife would then stand ready to invite the travelers, and to offer them food and drink. Says the "Hávamál," in the "Elder Edda":

> "Fire needs he
> who enters the house
> and is cold about the knees;
> food and clothes
> the man is in need of
> who has journeyed over the mountains."

Festivals were held in connection with religious exercises, weddings, funerals, and other home events, and also in the winter, especially at Christmas time. The "Saga of Olav the Saint," in the "Heimskringla," relates how Asbjørn Selsbane continued the old practice of his father of having three festivals every winter. To such festivals a number of guests were invited. Before they assembled, the tables were set up in the hall, and covered with beautifully embroidered linen tablecloths. Thin wafer-like bread served as plates. Ordinarily the men and women took their meals apart, but at festivals the women sat with the men at the table, occupying the inner end of the hall, to the left of the main high seat, while the men were seated at the outer end, toward

FIG. 41. — Drinking-horn.

the main entrance. Bowls of water and towels were passed around, so that the guests could wash their hands both before and after the meal. Wine and ale were served with the food, which was both abundant and well prepared. Again we must quote the "Rígsþula," which describes how Rig (Heimdall) was entertained at the home of a man of higher social standing:

> Then took Móðir [1]
> an embroidered tablecloth
> of white linen,
> and covered the table;

[1] The lady of the house.

took she then
thin leaves
of white wheat-bread
and put on it.

And she set
filled dishes
and silver-plated vessels
on the table,
and fine ham
and roasted fowls;
wine was in the can,
they drank and talked
till the day ended.

The women took pride in filling their chests with fine table linen, sheets, bed curtains, and fine clothes, but they also devoted themselves to more intellectual pursuits. As the designs with which they adorned linen and tapestry generally represented events from history or tradition, they had to become acquainted with mythology and the lives and deeds of the heroes and great men of their people. The practice of medicine and surgery was left to them; they bandaged the wounded, and healed and nursed the sick. At times the woman would also be priestess, superintending the sacrifices and religious ceremonies, and, especially in early times, she might be *vǫlva* or *seiðkona*, a woman who was believed to possess the power of witchcraft and prophecy, and a knowledge of the supernatural.[1] Woman's position in society was, on the whole, one of great freedom and independence. Among the higher classes, at least, she was looked upon as man's equal. She might be his companion in battle and in the banquet hall; when she married, she received a dowry from her father, and a nuptial gift (*mundr*) from her bridegroom, which remained her own property throughout her married life. In the management of the household she had full authority. So great an influence did women exercise on the ebullient passions of the Norsemen that they appear as the easily discerned cause of bloody domestic feuds and dramatic historic events, like the fates themselves, breed-

---

[1] See the *Vǫluspá* in the *Elder Edda* (*Vǫluspá* = the vølva's prophecy).

ing discord and bloodshed, or fostering peace and blessing by petty intrigues, by a nod or a smile. The sagas have pictured most vividly a gallery of interesting women; some beautiful, jealous, plotting, and revengeful, causing endless feuds, like Hallgerd, Gudrun Usvivsdotter, Freydis, and Queen Gunhild; some proud and ambitious, like Bergthora, Queen Aasta, and Sigrid Storraade; some affectionate, mild, and devoted, like Helga the Fair and Thorgerd Egilsdotter. We hear of domineering wives and hen-pecked husbands, like Aake and Grima, but also of women truly great, like Aud the Deepminded (Unnr), a lady of rare talents, who, as widow, became the acknowledged head of the family, and managed both her own affairs and those of her daughters and relatives so well under all difficulties that no one did anything of importance without seeking her advice and assistance.[1] These heroic and self-assertive women of the Viking Age have a certain romantic charm, still woman had not yet been accorded her proper privilege in society or in the home. The most sacred relations were yet marred by harsh and corrupt primitive customs. Marriage was not based on mutual love and affection, but on wealth and social standing. It was a business affair, a contract concluded between the bridegroom and the bride's father and relatives. The bride's consent was necessary, it is true, but it was often a matter of form, rather than the result of natural inclination. Many a touching love affair is recorded in the sagas and elsewhere in Old Norse literature, but they usually represent the revolt of the human heart against harsh and selfish social laws.[2] Love was re-

[1] Hallgerd . . . . . *Njálssaga*	Thorgerd . . . . . *Egilssaga*
Bergthora . . . . . . *Njálssaga*	Aasta . . . . . *Heimskringla*
Gudrun . . . . . . *Laxdølasaga*	Gunhild . . . . . *Heimskringla*
Aud . . . . *Laxdølasaga*	Sigrid . . . . . *Heimskringla*
Freydis . . . *Saga of Eirik the Red*	Aake and Grima . . *Vølsungasaga*
Helga . . . . . . *Gunlaugssaga*	

[2] The *Gunlaugssaga* is a typical love romance. So is, also, the *Friðþjófssaga*, and the story of Kjartan Olavsson and Gudrun Usvivsdotter in the *Laxdølasaga*. Other instances are numerous. The scald Kormak, famous for his love lyrics, could not forget his beautiful Steingerd even after she had become the wife of another. Harald Haarfagre's hirdscald, Ølve Hnuva, ceased to be a Viking and turned poet, because he had been thwarted in a love affair. The scald Thormod wrote a song to the lady of his heart, Thorbjørg Kolbrúna, and as a result he was nicknamed Kolbrúnarskald.

garded as a weakness, and a young woman was considered as being disgraced if a young man mentioned her name in a love song. The husband often had concubines besides his legally wedded wife. It also happened that men traded wives, or that a man gave his wife away to a friend if he did not like her. Divorce was common and easily obtained. There was nothing sacred in this most intimate and important relation into which human beings can enter. In Viking culture we find the shadows and blemishes characteristic of pagan civilization at all times. The Norseman had a keen and well developed mind, but his heart was as hard as the steel of his sword. He loved the battle and the stormy sea; he admired the strong, the brave, the cunning, the intellectual; for the old and feeble he had no interest, for the suffering no sympathy; the weak he despised. He sang of valor and of heroic deeds; not of love and beauty. The sagas of the rich and powerful have been written, the poor and unfortunate classes are passed over in silence. But in the Viking Age the lifegiving spirit of Christianity was breathed gently also upon the pagan North. Unconsciously at first the hard heartstrings were loosened, and the soul was stirred by a new life. Notes of love and sadness steal into their songs, words of affection and sorrow are chiseled on their tombstones, woman gradually rises to new dignity, and the rights of the heart gain recognition. Even religious life is deeply affected by this gentle influence. The Light of the World had cast its first faint glimmer upon the intellectual and moral life of the North, — the Viking expeditions had begun to bear their greatest fruit.

20. RELIGION AND LITERATURE

Wherever the Vikings settled they established a well-developed social organization, infused new vigor into the peoples with whom they came in contact, and imparted to them ideas which germinated into new cultural growth. Along practical lines they were often much farther advanced than the nations which were subjected to their attacks. This was especially manifest in Ireland, where the people at the time of the Viking inroads yet lived under a tribal organization, amid most primitive economic and social conditions.

Not only did they lack a well-organized army, ships, commerce, cities, roads, and bridges, but they paid little attention to agriculture, living for the most part on their herds and flocks, with which they moved from place to place. They were, as a rule, cruel and sensual; their warfare was savage, the position of woman was low and degrading, their houses were usually miserable huts. Yet this people possessed a remarkable intellectual culture, and became in this field the teachers and benefactors of their enemies, the Norsemen.

FIG. 42. — Irish monastery on the west coast of Ireland.

They had been Christians for many centuries before the Vikings began their conquests. Their missionaries were laboring, not only in Scotland and England, but had penetrated to the remote forest regions of Germany and France, to Switzerland and northern Italy.[1] Even in the solitudes of the Faroe Islands and Iceland pious Irish monks had erected their hermitages. They had great scholars who diligently studied Greek and Latin authors, and profound philosophers like John Scotus Erigena. During the seventh, eighth, and

[1] Alexander Bugge, *Kelternes Kulturbetydning, Verdenskulturen*, edited by Aage Friis, vol. III., p. 211 ff.

St. Columba, the apostle of the Scotch, died in 597 as head of the Caledonian church. He was born in Ireland in 521.

St. Columbanus, born in Ireland in 545, was the first Christian missionary among the Germans. He founded the monastery of Bobbio in Lombardy, where he died in 615.

St. Gallus of Hibernia, a disciple of Columbanus, labored as missionary in Switzerland. He is thought to have founded the monastery of St. Gallen on the Bodensee.

ninth centuries the Irish schools became celebrated all over Europe. Not only Greek and Latin, but philosophy, astronomy, mathematics, and geography were studied. The Irish cloister schools became the refuge of those who loved intellectual culture in the Dark Ages, and scholars from many countries flocked to them. Alcuin, the great scholar at the court of Charles the Great, corresponded with one of the professors of the Irish school at Clonmacnois, whom he calls his dear master and teacher. Also in their own native tongue they produced a rich literature, both in prose and poetry. Heroic tradition flourished, sagas were written to commemorate the deeds of great chieftains, or to preserve the knowledge of the clan and of family relationship, and songs were composed by scalds in honor of their kings. They sang, too, of love and of the beauty of nature with a sweet tenderness strange in those days when such poetry was almost unknown. But both their poetry and their prose suffered from an overflow of fancy and feeling, uncontrolled by artistic taste. The wildest exaggerations abound, the characters are grotesque, superhuman, and indistinctly drawn. There is an obscurity and lack of form which stand in the sharpest contrast to the brief, lucid style, and psychological character painting in the Norse sagas.

That the religious and literary life so highly developed among the Irish, their love of nature, their lyric sentimentality, and sympathetic and emotional character made a deep impression on the stern Norsemen is certain. They, who came to conquer, were in turn conquered by this new and gentle influence. Long before they were converted to Christianity, their lives and views were deeply affected by ideas acquired in the Christian countries which they visited, and especially through their sojourn in Ireland.[1] It was largely due to this new stimulus that Norse scaldic poetry and the saga literature began to flourish in the Viking period, and that Norse mythology assumes at this time a distinctly new form in which we find embedded in the strata of pagan thought many unmistakable fragments of Christian ideas; as, the conceptions of creation, of righteousness, of good

---

[1] King Harald Haarfagre would bring no offering to any god save the one who had created the sun and fashioned the heavens. *Fagrskinna*, 17. When Ingmund the Old was mortally wounded by Rolleiv, he advised him to flee lest his sons should do him harm. *Vatsdølasaga*, 23.

and evil, as well as views of the life hereafter, which can have their origin only in the realm of Christian faith and morality.

The scaldic poetry falls into two general groups: the scaldic songs, so called because they are written by scalds whose names and careers are known, and a body of old songs by unknown authors, called the "Elder Edda" or "Norrœn Fornkvæði." The scalds were usually connected with a king's *hird* or court, and produced songs to extol the person and achievements of their patrons, on whose munificence they lived.

These songs, which contain much valuable information regarding persons and events of early Norwegian history, are usually composed in a most intricate verse form, the *drottkvætt*, which abounds in word transpositions, allusions, and metaphoric expressions (*kenningar*), which offer many difficulties to the modern reader. This verse seems to have been invented by Brage Boddason (Brage the Old), who lived in the first part of the ninth century and is the first Norwegian scald of whom we have any record. There were also scalds who did not stay at the courts, and who composed songs on more varied subjects. Egil Skallagrimsson, one of the great masters in scaldic song, and Ulv Uggason, the author of the "Húsdrápa," may be mentioned. Egil is well known from his songs "Hǫfuðlausn" and "Arinbjørnsdrápa," but especially for his great poem "Sonatorrek," in which he laments the loss of his sons. Noteworthy are also Kormak's "Mansǫngsvisur," love songs to the beautiful Steingerd. Many of the saga writers were also scalds, notably Snorre Sturlason and Sturla Thordsson. Snorre, the author of the "Heimskringla," has also written the "Younger Edda," [1] a most important work intended as a book of instruction for young scalds. The work has preserved the names of a great number of scalds, together with fragments of their songs, and furnishes a key to the many difficulties

---

[1] *The Prose or Younger Edda*, translated by G. W. Dassent, Stockholm, 1842. Rasmus Flo, *Gamle Skaldar og Kvad*, 1902. *Corpus Poeticum Boreale*, edited by G. Vigfússon and Y. Powell, Oxford, 1883. *Carmina Norrœna*, edited by Th. Wisén, Lund, 1886. Finnur Jónsson, *Den oldnorske og oldislandske Litteraturs Historie*, Copenhagen, 1894–1902. Eugen Mogk, *Geschichte der norwegisch-isländischen Literatur*, Strassburg, 1904. Hermann Paul, *Grundriss der germanischen Philologie*. Sophus Bugge, *Norrœn Fornkvæði eller Sæmundar Edda*. Sophus Bugge, *Helgedigtene i den ældre Edda*, Copenhagen, 1896.

in scaldic poesy. It gives a review of mythology (Gylfaginning) which a scald must necessarily know, it explains the poetical and metaphorical expressions (*heiti, kenningar*) used in scaldic poetry, and a poem written to King Haakon Haakonsson and Skule Jarl illustrates all the verse forms used by the scalds.

The "Elder Edda" consists of two series of songs, the mythological and the heroic, written by scalds whose names are not known. Besides the poems about Helge Hundingsbane and Helge Hiǫrvarðsson, the heroic songs deal with the great Nibelungen tradition, and constitute the first literary embodiment known of this great Germanic epic. The Eddic poems have preserved a much older form of this tradition than that found in the "Nibelungenlied." [1] In the mythological poems we find clearly set forth in verse of classic simplicity and beauty the Norsemen's ideas of creation, the lives and character of their gods, the destruction of the world, and of man's destiny after death. In the "Hávamál" we find outlined also their moral conceptions, and their view of life in general. The grandest of all these old songs is the "Vǫluspá" (the prophecy of the vǫlva). [2]

This vǫlva can be none other than Urd (O. N. Urðr), one of the three *norns*, or goddesses of fate (Urðr, Verðandi, and Skuld). The gods are assembled in council at the Well of Urd. Odin calls the vǫlva from the grave, and the great sibyl comes forth to reveal to the god of wisdom what even he does not know — the mysteries of

---

[1] The Ms. Codex Regius, which contains the Eddic poems, is no longer complete, some songs dealing with the Nibelungen tradition having been lost. The *Vǫlsungasaga*, whose author has known the Codex Regius in complete form, gives in prose the contents of all the songs in the *Elder Edda*, dealing with the Nibelungen tradition. The title *Edda* is a misnomer. Edda means poetics, or the art and doctrine of poetry. The word is properly used as the title of Snorre's book, the *Younger Edda*, but it is in no way applicable to these old songs. It has also been called *Sœmundar Edda*, owing to an old erroneous belief that Sæmund Froði was the author.

[2] Vǫlva (plu. *vǫlur*) = a sorceress.

Julius Hoffory says: "The Vǫluspá is not only, as Müllenhoff said, the greatest poem in the North to the present time; it is a work which has never been equaled, not to say surpassed, by any production of its kind. The world has not yet seen another poem like it."

Of the many works dealing with Norse mythology may especially be mentioned: Jac. Grimm, *Deutsche Mythologie*, 4te Ausg., 1878. N. M. Petersen, *Nordisk Mythologi*, Copenhagen, 1842. R. Keyser, *Normændenes Religionsforfatnina i Hedendommen*. Christiania, 1847. P. A. Munch,

creation, the destruction of the gods, the end of the world, and the happy existence in the life to come. She commands silent attention, and tells the assembled gods that in the beginning there was neither sand, nor sea, nor cool billows; the earth did not exist, nor the heavens above; there was a yawning abyss,[1] but nowhere grass, before the sons of Bur [2] lifted up the dry land, they who created the beautiful earth. The sun shone from the south on the stones of the hall,[3] and the earth was covered with green herbs. The sun, the moon, and the stars did not know their proper courses, but the mighty gods held council, and gave them their right orbits, dividing time into night, morning, midday, and evening. The "Gylfaginning" presents a more complete account of creation, giving in fuller detail a myth which is outlined also in the "Vafþrúdnismál." Here we learn that in the beginning there were two regions, one of fire and heat, called "Muspelheim," ruled over by Surt, who watches the borders of his realm with a glowing sword. When the end of the world comes, he will conquer the gods, and destroy the earth with fire. The other was a cold region, "Niflheim" (O. N. Niflheimr), from which twelve rivers issue, called "Élivágar." Between these two regions is the great abyss "Ginnungagap." The masses of ice which had accumulated on the northern side of this abyss finally caught the spark of life from the heat issuing from Muspelheim, and a great man-shaped being, Yme (O. N. Ymir), was produced,

---

Nordmændenes Gudelære i Hedenold, 1847. Henry Petersen, *Om Nordboernes Gudsdyrkelse og Gudetro i Hedenold*, Copenhagen, 1876.

These are all works of high excellence, but the views of these earlier scholars must be regarded as antiquated since Sophus Bugge published his epoch-making work: *Studier over de nordiske Gude- og Heltesagns Oprindelse*, Christiania, 1881–1889. Translated to German by O. Brenner.

Hermann Paul, *Grundriss der germanischen Philologie*, vol. III., 2d ed., section XI., Eugen Mogk, *Mythologie*. Konrad Maurer, *Bekehrung des norwegischen Stammes zum Christenthume*, vol. II., München, 1855–1856. N. F. S. Grundtvig's *Nordens Mythologi*, 1808, is an interesting and inspiring work, written with patriotic enthusiasm, but it has no scientific value. R. B. Anderson's *Norse Mythology*, Chicago, 1876, is a very useful book. Ivar Mortenson, *Edda-Kvæde paa Nynorsk*. M. Mallet, *Northern Antiquities*, translated by Bishop Percy, London, 1909. Axel Olrik, *De nordiske Folk i Vikingetid og tidlig Middelalder*, *Verdenskulturen*, edited by Aage Friis, vol. III., p. 253 ff.   [1] Ginnungagap.

[2] Odin, Hœnir, and Lodur; or Odin, Vili, and Vé.   [3] The mountains.

from whom the Jøtuns descended. The gods killed Yme, and from his body they created the earth, from his blood the ocean, from his bones the mountains, and from his skull the heavens. From sparks from Muspelheim they made the sun, moon, and the stars, and placed them on the heavens. Again the gods assembled in council, says the vǫlva, and created the dwarfs in the earth. From two trees, ash and elm, they created man and woman. Odin gave them the spirit, Hønir gave them reason, and Lodur color and warmth of life. The gods were amusing themselves at the gaming tables, and there was no lack of gold until the three powerful maidens came from Jøtunheim.[1] These maidens are the three *norns* or goddesses of fate, already mentioned. Strife had not yet begun; the gods were happy in this golden age, which lasted until the fates appeared to determine the destiny of gods and men. But the elements of discord had entered the world: gold, woman, and witchcraft. The goddess Gullveig, who seems to be a personification of all three, was killed in Odin's hall, and this caused the first war, that between Æsir and Vanir, the two tribes of gods, who now contended for supremacy. "Odin threw his spear into the throng, this was the first combat in the world." A peace was finally concluded, according to which the two tribes were united on equal terms. The personification of evil itself is Loke and his children with the giantess Angerboda (O. N. Angrboða), the three monsters Hel, goddess of the underworld, the wolf Fenre (O. N. Fenrir), who at the end of the world will kill Odin, and the Miðgarðsormr, or Jørmungand, the world serpent, a personification of the ocean encircling the earth. The world, in which there is now continual strife, is represented under the symbol of a giant ash tree, the Yggdrasil, whose top reaches into the heavens, whose branches fill the world, and whose three roots extend into the three important spheres of existence outside the world of man. One root is where the Æsir dwell. Under this root is the Well of Urd, where the gods assemble in council. Another root

---

[1] Jøtunheim (O. N. Jǫtunheimr), the home of the Jøtuns or giants. Midgaard (O. N. Miðgarðr), the dwelling place of man, was thought to be surrounded by high mountains, beyond which was Jøtunheim. In the heavens is Aasgaard (O. N. Ásgarðr), the home of the Æsir (*Æsir*, plu. of *ás* = god). In the lower world is Niflheim (O. N. Niflheimr), the home of the dead, ruled over by the goddess Hel.

reaches to the home of the Jøtuns, or Rimthuser (O. N. Hrímþursar), under which is the Well of Mimer, the fountain of wisdom. The third root is in Niflheim, and under it is the terrible well Hvergelme, by which is found the snake Niðhǫggr, which, together with many others, continually gnaws at the roots of the world tree, and seeks to destroy it. Niðhǫggr is the symbol of the destructive forces operating in the world.

> An ash tree I know,
> Yggdrasil [1] called,
> a tall tree
> sprinkled with water;
> from it comes the dew
> that falls in the valleys,
> ever green it stands
> by the fountain of Urd.

> Much do they know
> the three maidens
> who come from the hall
> which stands by the tree;
> one is Urd,
> the other Verdande,
> Skuld is the third;
> laws they make,
> they determine life
> and the fate of men.

The *norns* are not only in the world, but they are the real rulers of it; even the gods must submit to their decrees. They rule over life and death, and man's destiny; no one can escape the calamities which they have preordained. But they have not the absolute power attributed to the fates in Greek and Roman mythology. They are also subject to an ultimate fate. They disappear at Ragnarok (O. N. Ragnarøkkr) together with this present world.

Again the gods assembled, says the vǫlva, to consider how evil had come into the world. Odin, who is interrogating her, tries to

---

[1] Regarding the name *Yggdrasil* see *The Origin and Meaning of the Name Yggdrasil*, by S. N. Hagen, *Modern Philology*, vol. I., 1903.

conceal his identity, but she recognizes him, and tells him the great secrets of his life. In Norse mythology Odin is the chief divinity and the father of many of the other gods, but it is evident that in earlier periods other gods have held the highest position. Ty[1] (O. N. Týr), the god of war (A. S. Tius, O. H. G. Ziu), seems to be the same divinity as the Greek Zeus, and has, no doubt, at one time been the principal god. Thor,[2] the god of thunder and lightning, must also have ranked higher than Odin, but in Norse mythology he has become Odin's son. He is constantly fighting the wicked Jøtuns, at whom he hurls his hammer Mjølner (the thunderbolt). He is the farmer's special protector and benefactor. He shields them against the hostile forces of nature, and furthers husbandry and all peaceful pursuits. In Norway he was worshiped more extensively than any other god. Odin (A. S. Wôdan, O. H. G. Wuotan, Germ. wüthen) seems originally to have been a storm god, but in later periods he becomes so prominent that he pushes the older divinities from their throne. Odin is an embodiment of the spirit of the Viking Age. Even in appearance he is a chieftain; tall, one-eyed, graybearded, attired in a blue mantle, carrying a shield and the spear Gungne (O. N. Gungnir), which never misses its mark. His life is rich in all sorts of adventures. He loves war, and is generally found in the midst of the battle. He is also the god of wisdom, and his desire for knowledge is almost a passion. His two ravens, Hugin and Munin, bring him daily notice of everything that happens in the world. No sacrifice is too great if thereby he can gain more knowledge. How did he lose his eye? It is a great secret, but the vǫlva reveals it. He drank once from the Well of Mimir, the fountain of wisdom, and had to give one of his eyes as a forfeit. Odin is the personification of the heavens; his one eye is the sun, the other, which Mimir took, is the sun's reflection in the water. He also discovered the runes, but only by making

---

[1] Sk. Dyâus, Gk. Zeus, Lat. Ju-piter, O. E. Tius, O. N. Týr.

[2] "Now we will speak about the superstition of the Swedes. This people has a very famous temple called Ubsala, not very far from the city of Sictona, in which they worship the images of three gods. Thor, who is the greatest of these, has his throne in the middle of the hall, and on his right and left sit Wodan and Fricco." Adam v. Bremen, *Gesta Hammaburgensis Ecclesiae Pontificum*, IV., 26, 27.

another great sacrifice. The "Hávamál" gives the following account of it:

"I know that I hung on the windy tree nine nights together, wounded by a spear, sacrificed to Odin, myself to myself, on the tree which no one knows from what roots it springs. Neither with food nor with drink was I refreshed. I looked carefully down and raised up the runes; crying I raised them up, and fell then down."

Even this great pain Odin is willing to undergo to discover the runes, for through them he gains occult knowledge, and becomes the god of sorcery, the wisest and most powerful of all the gods. From his throne Lidskjalv (O. N. Hliðskjálf) he overlooks the whole world. He is always thoughtful, and meditates on great problems. Evil and good are equally interesting to him, for both reveal some secret of life. He contemplates the mystery of existence and the approaching end of things; he is never glad, because he knows too much.

In Aasgaard (O. N. Ásgarðr) the gods built a beautiful hall, Gladsheim, for the gods, and another, Vingolv (O. N. Vingólf), for the goddesses, but greater than any of these was Odin's own hall, Valhal (O. N. Valhǫll). To this hall the valkyries [1] bring the dead warriors who fall on the field of battle, and they are feasted and entertained by Odin himself. All who die a natural death are excluded. The heroes find their pastime in fighting, and many fall every day, but they rise again unharmed, and return to feast in Valhal as the best of friends.

Another divinity who in the Viking period must have undergone a great change, and who seems to reflect the new spirit of that age, is Balder. The opinions of scholars with regard to the Balder myth are hopelessly at variance. A. Olrik thinks that Balder is an old sungod, that his death signifies the victory of darkness over light, while H. Schück thinks that he was not a real god till shortly before the advent of Christianity. According to Saxo Grammaticus, he was a young and impetuous warrior who waged many combats with

---

[1] Valkyries < val = dead bodies on the field of battle, and kyria < kjósa = to choose, i.e. "the choosers of the dead." They are virgin goddesses on horseback, armed with helmets, shields, and spears. They are sent by Odin, and ride through the air to be present in the battle, where they choose those who are to fall, and bring them to Odin in Valhal. The fallen heroes are to help Odin in his last great battle at Ragnarok.

his rival Hother, by whom he is finally slain. He is a son of Odin, but lives on the earth. Sophus Bugge considers this to be the older form of the myth. In the "Vǫluspá" and the "Gylfaginning" he is pictured as the gentle god of innocence and righteousness, so bright that a light of glory surrounds him. He dwells in the hall Breidablik (the far shining hall), where nothing impure is found. He is wise, kind, and eloquent, and so just that his decrees cannot be altered. His wife is Odin's granddaughter, the faithful Nanna; his son is Forsete, the god of justice and reconciliation. While Balder lives, evil can gain no real control in the world, but bad dreams begin to trouble him, and as this portends some great misfortune to the Æsir, Odin saddles his eight-legged horse, Sleipne (O. N. Sleipnir), and rides to Niflheim to learn what evil is thus foreboded. He calls the vǫlva from her grave, and asks her for whose reception they are making preparations in Hel's kingdom, and she answers that it is for Balder, who will soon die. This news causes great consternation among the Æsir, and they assemble in council to discuss the matter. Frigg, Balder's mother, requires everything in the world to take an oath not to harm her son. The gods now feel secure, and in their joy that the danger is averted, they amuse themselves by throwing all sorts of things at Balder to show that nothing will hurt him. But Loke comes disguised to the assembly, and learns from Frigg that there is a tiny plant, the *mistilteinn*, which she has not required to take the oath, because it seemed too small. He pulls up the plant, brings it to the assembly, and asks the blind god Hød (Hǫðr) to throw it at Balder. Hød does so; the plant pierces him through, and he falls dead. The greatest misfortune has happened; Nanna's heart breaks of sorrow, and she is buried together with her husband, who is received by Hel in her kingdom. But there is a hope even in this great calamity. While Balder lies on the bier, Odin whispers something in his ear. This episode is mentioned in the "Vafþrúdnismál," [1] where Odin asks the wise Vafþrudne:

> What did Odin
> whisper in his son's ear
> before he was laid on the funeral pyre?

[1] In this song, which is thought to be one of the oldest in the *Elder Edda*, Odin examines Vafthrudne to test his knowledge in mythology. The song,

This is a riddle which even Vafþrudne cannot solve. He answers:

> No one knows
> What, in the beginning of time,
> thou didst whisper
> in thy son's ear.

No one knows; but it was, no doubt, a promise that he should not remain forever in Hel's realm, but that he should return when the world of strife had passed away, and the new life of peace and righteousness had begun.[1]

In Norse mythology, as elsewhere in old religious systems, the ideas of the life hereafter are often vague, even contradictory. Mythology is a growth, a product of long periods of a people's intellectual development, in which old ideas have constantly been mixed with new conceptions. It represents a march of the human mind forward to new light, rather than a once for all perfected system. The Hel myth is an illustration. Hel, the name both of the goddess and of the realm over which she rules, is sometimes thought of as the home of all the departed, where even Balder goes after death. Hence the Norwegian expression *at slaa ihjel, i.e.* to kill, to deprive one of life so that he goes to Hel. But Hel is also thought of as the place for the wicked.[2] Hel, the goddess, is white on one side and black on the other, and her hall is described as a frightful place. We have seen that from the earliest times the Norsemen believed in a life after death, which is shown by many burial customs. In course of time they began to construct large burial chambers where all the members of the family could be interred together. Professor H. Schück thinks that these graves first engendered the idea of the lower world. He says: "A primitive people does not think of

which consists of questions and answers, resembles a catechism, and must have been written for the purpose of instructing people in the essentials of mythology.

In the *Hervararsaga*, Odin, who is disguised as the blind Gest, asks King Heidrek the same question.

[1] The Balder myth is found especially in the song *Baldrsdraumar* in the *Elder Edda*.

[2] "The wicked go to Hel, and thence to Niflhel, which is below, in the ninth world." *Gylfaginning.* Niflhel, or Niflheim, in Hel's kingdom, the underworld.

death as annihilation, but rather as an entrance into new life. Only by premising such a belief can a number of antique burial customs be explained. . . . At first the dead person lived this new life in the grave itself, and these large family graves gave origin to the idea of the realm of the dead." According to the oldest belief, then, all the dead came to this realm where Hel ruled.[1] But it was a shadowy, joyless existence, and the feeling that heroes and good people deserved something better gave rise to new creations; to Valhal, Odin's hall; Folkvang and Sessrymne (Sessrymnir), where Freyja entertains one half of all the fallen heroes; Vingolv (Vingólf), where all heroes are entertained by the goddesses, and to the idea that all women who die unmarried go to the goddess Gefjon. Hel and her kingdom fell into disfavor, and were painted in ever darker colors.

Loke did not escape punishment. He was tied by the Æsir in a rocky cavern where poisonous adders drop venom into his face, and there he will have to lie till Ragnarok, or the end of the world. But his faithful wife, Sigyn, stands always by him, and gathers the dripping venom in a cup. Only when she empties the cup does it drop into Loke's face, and then he writhes in pain so that the earth quakes. Høi, the slayer of Balder, is also punished. With the goddess Rind, Odin has the son Vaale, who kills Høi. But revenge cannot remedy the mischief done. Balder the Good has perished, and evil triumphs. In her hall Fensale Frigg weeps for her son; the end is approaching, Ragnarok,[2] when gods and men must perish, and the present world will be destroyed.

Another divinity which, especially in Sweden, was worshiped more extensively than Odin himself, was Frey, the son of Njørd the god of the sea. He was the god of weather and of harvests, and was regarded as the giver of riches. He became so enamoured with the beautiful Jøtun maiden Gerd that he could neither eat nor sleep. One day he sat on Lidskjalv in Aasgaard and saw her far to the north, and so beautiful was she that she made sky and ocean resplendent with light. He sent his servant, Skirne (Skírnir), to woo her, but

---

[1] The word helvede, O. N. helviti < hel and viti (punishment), has been brought to the North by German missionaries, says Alexander Bugge.

[2] Ragnarökkr, the darkness of the gods. Ragna, gen. plu. of regin (gods), rökkr (darkness). Cf. Goth. riquis.

in order to win her he had to surrender his greatest treasure, his sword, and when Ragnarok comes, he will be slain by Surt, because he has no weapon with which to defend himself.

Heimdall, one of the oldest deifications of the heavens, is the sentinel of the gods, and lives at Bifrøst,[1] the celestial bridge over which gods and men ride to Valhal. Vidar, the silent one, is, next to Thor, the strongest of the gods. Æge (Ægir) is the ocean god, and Brage the god of poesy and eloquence.

In Norse mythology there are twelve or thirteen principal gods, and an equal number of goddesses (ásynjur). Frigg is Odin's wife and the queen of heaven, and dwells in Fensale, far to the west where the sun sets in the sea. Freyja, the beautiful goddess of love, lives in Folkvang, where the great hall Sessrymne is found. To her belongs one half of the warriors who fall on the battlefield, and she is accorded the right of first choice. Idun, Brage's wife, called the good goddess, keeps the apples from which the gods eat to preserve their youth. Thor's wife is the beautiful Siv (Sif), with hair of gold. Skade, Njørd's wife, was, like Gerd, of Jøtun race, and Snotra was the goddess of good sense and womanly graces.

Before Ragnarok evil passes all bounds. For three years there is perpetual strife. Brothers fight and kill each other, the ties of blood relationship are broken, morals are corrupted, and one person has no compassion for the other. Then follow three years of constant winter, the Fimbulwinter (the great winter). Finally Yggdrasil trembles, Fenre breaks his fetters, and the Midgardsorm comes out of the ocean. Surt, the fire demon, comes; Loke is free again and leads the sons of Muspell [2] and other forces of destruction to the final battle with the gods on the plain Vigrid. Fenre kills Odin, but is in turn slain by the powerful Vidar. Thor and the Midgardsorm kill each other; Frey is slain by Surt; Ty fights against Hel's hound Garm, and both fall. Surt finally hurls fire over the earth;

---

[1] *Bifrøst*, the rainbow.

[2] Sophus Bugge thinks that *Muspell* is the fire region from which Surt also comes. The word is used in the *Heliand*, and also in the O. H. G. fragment *Muspilli* from about 900. The word as here used means the destruction of the world. See W. Braune's *Althochdeutsches Lesebuch*. The word probably means the great world-destroying fire, but its origin is by no means clearly understood.

the sun grows dark, the earth sinks into the ocean, fire consumes all — the world of strife and bloodshed has disappeared.

Out of the ocean, says the vǫlva, rises a new green earth, where grain fields grow without being sown, and where no evil exists. Here, on the Fields of Ida, the gods who have survived Ragnarok reassemble. Balder, who has returned from Hel, is there; also Vidar, Høð, Hønir, and Thor's sons, Mode and Magne. A new race of men are also born.

Pursuing her story, the vǫlva says:

> A hall I see
> on the heights of Gimle,[1]
> brighter than the sun,
> and covered with gold;
> righteous men
> shall dwell there
> in endless happiness.

This hall is a perfect contrast to Valhal, where the heroes even after death amuse themselves by fighting and slaying each other; in Gimle the righteous live in peace and happiness. Gimle is the safe and secure home ornamented with precious stones. Sophus Bugge thinks that the Fields of Ida are in reality the Christian Garden of Eden, and that Gimle is the heavenly Jerusalem described in Revelation, xxi., 10–21.

"10. And he carried me away in the spirit to a great and high mountain, and shewed me that great city, the holy Jerusalem, descending out of heaven from God,

"11. Having the glory of God: and her light was like unto a stone most precious, even like a jasper stone, clear as crystal.

"21. And the twelve gates were twelve pearls; every several gate was of one pearl: and the street of the city was pure gold, as it were transparent glass."

And, says the vǫlva, bringing her narrative to a closing climax:

> From above comes
> to the great judgment
> the powerful one,
> the ruler of all.

---

[1] *Gimle* is the name of the hall and of the mountain on which it stands.

This is the ruler of the new world whose name not even the vǫlva knows. In Norse mythology the world is pictured as a scene of perpetual struggle between good and evil, a never-ending combat between the powers of life and the forces of destruction, and it is especially noteworthy that this struggle is a great tragedy in which the gods suffer complete overthrow. Balder was killed, Loke and Fenre broke their fetters; the struggle against evil has been unsuccessful on every point. Most of the leading gods themselves are destroyed by the forces of evil in the great final battle at Ragnarok. But evil, too, passes away with the world of strife in which it has existed. This thought of the overthrow and destruction of the greatest gods seems to be a new feature which could not very well have been developed until the faith in the old divinities was beginning to waver, and people began to feel that there was a heaven higher than Valhal and Vingolv, that true happiness was not to be found in strife, but in peace and righteousness, and that there was a god whom they did not yet know, who was more powerful than the Æsir, and who, in the new world, would establish a reign of justice, peace, and happiness.

The "Hyndluljóð" says:

> Then comes another god
> still mightier,
> but his name
> I dare not mention;
> few can now
> see farther
> than to Odin's
> meeting with the wolf.[1]

The worship might be carried on privately in the home, where the head of the family would sacrifice to the gods, and bring offerings to their images, but it was usually conducted in temples, *hov* (O. N. hof), or in simpler sanctuaries, *horg* (O. N. hǫrgr), of which no description is given in the old writings.[2] They seem to have

---

[1] Odin's meeting with the wolf is Ragnarok. Few can see farther than to the end of the present world. The new ideas about a world of peace and righteousness they had not yet become acquainted with.

[2] R. Keyser, *Samlede Afhandlinger*, p. 324. R. Keyser, *Nordmændenes Religionsforfatning i Hedendommen*, p. 89. Reinert Svendsen, *Fortidsmindesmerker I Ringsaker*, Christiania, 1902.

been simple structures, stone altars, or the like, erected in the open, and dedicated especially to the worship of goddesses. In the "Hyndluljóð" Freyja says:

> Horg he built me,
> made of stone,
> now the stones have turned to glass;
> with fresh blood
> of oxen he sprinkled them.
> Ottar always believed in goddesses.

R. Keyser and P. A. Munch are of the opinion that many of the stone circles found in Norway are remnants of this kind of sanctuaries.[1] These circles, which are formed by placing great stones in an upright position, are often very large, and may have had an altar in the center.

The temple consisted of two parts; the large assembly hall, or nave, and the shrine, a smaller room in the rear end of the building, corresponding to the choir of the Christian churches. The images of the gods were placed in a half-circle in the shrine. At the center stood the altar (stallr), upon which lay a large gold ring (baugr), upon which all solemn oaths were sworn. The bowl containing the blood of the sacrificed animals (hlautbolli) was placed on the altar by the priest (goði), who, with a stick (hlautteinn), sprinkled it on the images of the gods, and on the persons present. The meat of the animals was boiled, and served to the assembled people in the large hall of the temple, where toasts were drunk to the gods for victory and good harvests. The sanctuary and the grounds belonging to it was called vé, a holy or sacred place, and any one who violated its sanctity was called varg i véum (wolf in the sanctuary), and was outlawed. Three religious festivals were held each year: one at the beginning of winter (October 14), the vinternatsblót, or haustblót, to bid winter welcome; another at midwinter (January 14), midvintersblót,[2] for peace and good harvest; and a third, som-

---

[1] P. A. Munch, Det norske Folks Historie, vol. I. Munch calls attention to the fact that in Vestergötland in Sweden such a stone circle is still called Hargene (i.e. the horgs). Harry Fett, Norges Kirker i Middelalderen, Christiania, 1909.

[2] The sacrifice was called blót = Goth. blôtan, A. S. blôtan, to worship It is not related to the word blood.

merblót, held on the first day of summer (April 14), for victory on military expeditions.

The temples seem to have been quite numerous, but especially well known were the ones at Sigtuna and Upsala in Sweden, at Leire (Hleidra) in Denmark, and at Skiringssal in Norway. There was in the North no distinct class of priests.[1] The priestly functions were exercised by the *herser* and the *jarls,* and even by the king himself. Women, too, might serve as priestesses (*gyðja*). In Iceland the *gode* (O. N. *goði*) held about the same position as the *herse* in Norway. He was a chieftain, and the temple in which he served as priest was built on his estates.

21. EARLY SOCIAL CONDITIONS IN NORWAY

The first account of early Norwegian society is given by the "Rígsþula," which describes the various social classes, and pictures conditions which resemble those of early Germanic society elsewhere. Rig (the god Heimdall) comes to a hut where he finds Aae and Edda,[2] an old couple, gray-haired from work and hardship, sitting by the fire. Edda, who wore an old headgear, set before the visitor coarse bread and other simple food. Their son Thrall was stoop-shouldered and coarse-featured, with dark complexion and wrinkled skin. They evidently belonged to some foreign race, brought to Norway either as prisoners of war, or as slaves bought in the numerous slave markets. Thrall married without much ceremony the flat-nosed and sunburnt Thir.[3] Their children were called Fiosnir (stable boy), Drumbr (the clumsy one), Ambátt (slave), Tǫtrughypja (the ragged one), etc. When they grow up, they do all sorts of menial labor; they manure the fields, build fences, and herd goats and swine. This is the slave class, which must have been quite numerous.

[1] German antiquarians have shown that neither among the Germans was there a distinct priesthood in early pagan times. Müllenhoff, *Deutsche Alterthumskunde,* IV., p. 230 f., 237 ff.

[2] The *Rígsþula* is thought to have been written in the period 890–920. It describes social conditions in Norway at that time, giving most valuable information with regard to this side of national life. Aae and Edda = great-grandfather and great-grandmother. [3] Thir = servant girl, slave.

Rig proceeded on his way, and came to the home of Ave and Amma.[1] The man was busy making parts for a wooden loom; he wore a tight-fitting shirt, his beard was in order, his locks hung over his forehead. The wife sat spinning, and was well dressed. Their son was called Karl.[2] He was married to Snor[3] with due ceremony, according to custom. He tamed oxen, made wagons, built houses and barns, and drove the plow. Their children were Hal,[4] Bonde, Hauld, Tegn, Bodde, etc. This is the farmer class, those who own land, and devote themselves to agriculture. The *karls* were the lowest class of landowning freemen, peasants. Below them were the freedmen and renters. The *haulds* (*stórbóndi*) were an aristocratic class of landowners, a gentry who held their land by inherited right and title, *odel*, and were said to be odel born.[5] At the head of the *haulds* stood in each *herred*, or district, an hereditary chieftain, the *herse*, who was their leader in war, and commanded the local subdivision of the army. He exercised also priestly functions, and presided at the *thing* (O. N. *þing*), or the assembly of the people.

Rig then came to a hall where Faðir and Moðir lived. The man was engaged in making bows and arrows. He belonged to the aristocracy. The wife decked the table with a fine linen tablecloth, placed silver vessels on it, and served wine, wheat bread, ham, and roasted fowl. She was blonde, and was elegantly dressed.

> Her brows were light,
> her bosom lighter,
> her neck whiter
> than the white snow.

Their son was the golden-haired Jarl, who married the blonde and beautiful Erna, daughter of Herse. From them the king descends.[6]

[1] Ave and Amma = grandfather and grandmother.

[2] Freeman who owns land.   [3] Snor = the son's wife.

[4] Hal = man.   Bonde = farmer.   Hauld = landed proprietor.   Tegn = one who follows a chieftain.   Bodde, same as Bonde.

[5] The *Hyndluljóð* classifies the *haulds* with the *hersir* and kings as the choicest men on the earth.   P. A. Munch, *Det norske Folks Historie*, vol. I. J. E. Sars, *Udsigt over den norske Historie*, vol. I., 144 ff.   Alexander Bugge, *Vikingerne*, vol. II., 316.   Ebbe Hertzberg, *En Fremstilling af det norske Aristokratis Historie indtil Kong Sverres Tid*.

[6] Finnur Jónsson thinks that the *Rigspula* is written to glorify the institution of national kingship as the best form of government, and to represent

Over against their neighbors, the Swedes and Danes, the Norsemen felt themselves to be a distinct people from times which far antedate the beginning of authentic history, but they did not at first constitute a united nation. They consisted of a number of independent tribes, occupying quite well-defined districts. The names of many of these tribes are given by Jordanes, and Procopius says that thirteen tribes live in Scandinavia, the Gautar being the most numerous. The names of Egder, Ryger, Horder, Raumer, Heiner, etc., are still preserved in names of provinces and districts in Norway, like Agder, Rogaland, Hordaland, Romerike, and Hedemarken. The tribe consisted of families to whom belonged the greater part of the land, and who, by virtue of wealth, influence, and tradition, possessed all religious and political power. The title to the land was held by the head of the family, but the real ownership was vested in all the members jointly. It was called *odel*, and the principle seems to have prevailed that it could not pass out of the possession of the family. All the sons shared equally in the inheritance, but the old homestead was not divided, but was usually inherited by the oldest son. The younger sons received other portions of the estate, or they sold their interest and sought their fortune elsewhere. The village system did not obtain in Norway, as among the Anglo-Saxons and Germans. Each family dwelt on its own separate estate. In Anglo-Saxon the word *tûn* means town. In Norse it means the place on which the dwelling is located. The people were divided into *fylker* (O. N. fylki < folk = people), and each *fylke* placed in the field an organized military force under its own commander. The *fylker* constituted the larger units of the army. A parallel to this system is found in the Anglo-Saxon tribal organization, and, especially, in the division of the tribes into smaller groups: East Saxons, South Saxons, West Saxons, North-folk, and South-folk. The *fylke* had its own temple, and its own *thing*, or assembly of the people, where suits at law were tried and decided. The *fylke* was divided into *hereder* (O. N. heraδ < her — ráδ, a military command), which corresponds to the *hundreds* among the Anglo-Saxons,

the king as the chief personage in the whole kingdom, holding a position above all social classes. This national king must, he thinks, be Harald Haarfagre, who united all Norway under his rule.

and the *centena* among the Franks. This seems to have been a district large enough to furnish a hundred [1] warriors, which formed the unit of military organization. The *herse* was the hereditary tribal chieftain, while the jarls had about the same powers as petty kings, and ruled over larger districts. Before Harald Haarfagre's time most districts were governed by kings (*fylkeskonger*) who ruled over larger tribes, such as Ryger, Horder, Egder, Raumer, etc., but not till after the union of Norway did the king become distinctly superior to the jarls.

The movement towards a union of independent, but closely related tribes into a *þjóð* (A. S. *þeod*, Goth. *þiuda*), or people, seems to have been well under way, both in Sweden and Denmark, already in the early centuries of the Christian era. Svitiod, the kingdom of the Swedes dwelling around Mälaren, has already been mentioned, also Gautiod, the Gautar or Gøtar, inhabiting the districts farther south, about the great lakes Venern and Vettern. Denmark was united into one kingdom under the Skjoldung dynasty prior to 500 A.D. In Norway, where deep fjords and snow-covered mountains made inland travel in early times difficult, and laid great obstacles in the way of closer intercourse between the different districts, national unity was effected later and with more difficulty. But from very early times the trend of social development towards ultimate union is clearly seen in the growing tendency to merge the isolated tribes into larger confederacies, and to adopt for these a uniform system of laws which were gradually made operative in larger districts.

The oldest confederacy was, probably, that of the Heiner [2] (O. N. Heiðnir) dwelling in Hedemarken by the great lake Mjøsen, in the eastern part of Norway. They are mentioned in the O. E. poem "Widsíth," and the runic inscription on the Rökstone in Östergötland, Sweden, states that, together with Horder and Ryger, they made a warlike expedition to Seeland in Denmark, under a common king. Their confederacy must have existed as early as at the time

---

[1] It should be noticed that hundred in Old Norse means $10 \times 12 = 120$, the so-called large hundred. Alexander Bugge, *Vesterlandenes Indflydelse*, p. 15. P. A. Munch, *Det norske Folks Historie*, vol. I., p. 93 ff.

[2] Ptolemy mentions the Finns in the northern part of Scandinavia, the Gautar, or Götar, in the southern part, and the Chaideinoi, or Heiner, in the western part. See also Alexander Bugge, *Norges Historie*, vol. I. 2, 49 ff.

of the birth of Christ, and seems to have embraced, besides the Heiner, also Raumer,[1] Ringer, and Hader in Romerike, Ringerike, Hadeland, and other districts. Together they constituted the Eidsivalag, *i.e.* the people united under a common law called the "Eidsivathingslov."[2] The place of the common assembly, or *thing* (Eidsivathing) was Eidsvold, at the lower end of Lake Mjøsen. The name of the place of assembly brought about a change of the name "Heiðsævislǫg" to Eidsivalag.

More powerful was the confederacy Trøndelagen, formed by eight *fylker* dwelling in old Þróndheimr, the district around the Trondhjemsfjord. This region, which has been inhabited as long as records can trace the existence of Norsemen, is one of the best agricultural districts in Norway. The large areas of fertile soil, which form an undulating plain around this great fjord, explain sufficiently the fact that in very early times Trøndelagen was one of the wealthiest and most densely populated districts, and was regarded as the heart and center of the country. Snorre calls it the "center of the country's strength." The Trønders took little active part in the Viking expeditions. They regarded their own districts as the most desirable place to live in, and were too strongly attached to their own homes to be fond of adventure or emigration.[3] Trøndelagen consisted of two parts: Indtrøndelagen, or the four inner *fylker*: Sparbuen, Værdalen, Eynafylke, and Skogn; and Uttrøndelagen, the four *fylker* situated towards the mouth of the fjord, Stjørdalen, Strinden, Guldalen, and Orkedalen. Trøndelagen had two *things*: Ørething, on Bratøren, in the present city of Trondhjem, and Frostathing, on the peninsula Frosta, in Indtrøndelagen. Every farmer who had a manservant had to attend the Ørething, which assembled once a year. At the Frostathing 400 representatives met from the eight *fylker*, forty from each *fylke* in Indtrøndelagen, and sixty from each *fylke* in Uttrøndelagen.[4] The Frostathing grew in impor-

---

[1] Jordanes mentions them as *Raumaricii.*

[2] The older form is *Heiðsævislǫg* < *Heiðsær*, the sea of the Heiner.

[3] Henr. Mathiesen, *Det gamle Trondhjem. Festskrift udgivet i Anledning af Trondhjems 900 Aars Jubilæum*, 1897. H. G. Heggtveit, *Trondhjem i Fortid og Nutid*, 1897. A. Helland, *S. Trondhjems Amt, Norges Land og Folk.*

[4] *Frostathingslov, 1, 2, Norges gamle Love*, edited by R. Keyser and P. A. Munch. J. E. Sars, *Udsigt over den norske Historie*, I., p. 224. P. A.

tance, and gave its name to the body of laws called "Frostathingslov," which was adopted by the whole northern part of Norway. Each *fylke* had its own temple and *fylkesthing*, and governed itself in all local matters. The *thing* (O. N. þing) was the assembly of the people in which the freemen met to decide matters of common interest. It was also a court of law. The *lagthings* or larger assemblies, like Ørething and Frostathing, tried all cases of greater importance; they were also appellate courts to which cases were brought from the lower courts. The president of the *lagthing* appointed a body of judges, the *lagrette*,[1] usually thirty-six in number, chosen for one session, who served under oath, and had to interpret and apply the law in the cases that came up for trial. The decision prepared by the *lagrette* was submitted to the whole assembly for approval. The institution of *lagmand* (plu. *lagmænd*) was also found in Norway, though it was not so important as it became later in Iceland. At first the laws were not written, and the *lagmand* was one learned in the law, who could recite it to the assembly. It seems that in Norway several *lagmænd* acted together in declaring the law. The place of assembly was one of peace and sanctity. "Every man must go fasting into court, and no drink shall be brought to the *thing*, either for sale or otherwise," says the "Frostathingslov." [2] The place where the *lagrette* sat was regarded as a sanctuary, and was surrounded by ropes, *vebønd*, the sacred cords.

Munch, *Det norske Folks Historie*, part I., vol. II., p. 147. Johan Fritzner, *Ordbog over det gamle norske Sprog.* William Forsyth, *History of Trial by Jury.*

   [1] *Lagrette*, O. N. lǫgrétta < rétta lǫg, to properly interpret and apply the law in given cases, and to propose changes in the law. *Glossar til Norges gamle Love*, vol. V. See Falk and Torp, *Etymologisk Ordbog, lov.*

   "The men who are chosen for the *lagrette* shall judge according to law in the cases brought before this tribunal, according to what the lawbook says. In all matters which the lawbook does not decide, that is to be followed in each case which all the *lagrette* men agree on." *Frostathingslov*, I., 2.

   The *lagrette* resembled the jury in that it was a popularly constituted tribunal of 3×12 men selected for one session only. But as the *lagrette* men interpreted and applied the law, they were judges, and not jurors. They also had legislative functions, in that they could amend the laws when it was found necessary.

   Ebbe Hertzberg, *Glossar til Norges gamle Love*, vol. V., dómr and tólf.

   [2] *Frostathingslov*, I., 3.

Dueling with swords was not infrequently resorted to in settling disputes. It was called *holmgang*, because the duels were generally fought on a holm, or small island. When blood was drawn, the affair was regarded as settled, and the losing party had to pay a sum previously stipulated. A duel between the scald Gunlaug and his rival Ravn led to its abolition in Iceland by the *Althing*, in 1006.[1] In Norway it was abolished about 1012. After Christianity was introduced, the ordeal became a mode of trial occasionally resorted to. Its best known form in Norway was the *jernbyrd*, which consisted in carrying a redhot iron, or in walking barefooted over hot plowshares. This mode of trial was abolished in 1247. In Trøndelagen, with its two *lagthings*, and dual arrangement in general, there were, besides the *fylkes-hov*, two great sanctuaries; one at Mæren in Sparbuen, one of the most renowned heathen temples in Norway, and one at Lade in Uttrøndelagen, near the present city of Trondhjem. Before King Harald Haarfagre's time there were no kings in Trøndelagen. At the head of each *fylke* stood a chieftain, who was also priest and leader of the people at the *thing*. His office was hereditary, but whether he bore the title of *herse*, which was customary in Norway, or was called *gode*, like the chieftains in Iceland, is not known. The two *fylker* Nordmør and Romsdal, petty kingdoms from very ancient times, also belonged in a general way to the Frostathingslag. The people of Romsdal had their temple on the little island of Véey (the island of the sanctuary) in the Romsdalsfjord.

South of Romsdal lies Søndmør, a *fylke* which had its own king, and was the home of some of the most powerful families in the early history of Norway. Especially noteworthy is the great Arnmødling family, the descendants of King Arnvid who fell in the battle of Solskjel fighting against Harald Haarfagre. They resided on the island of Giske, near the present city of Aalesund, where a number of interesting archæological finds have been made. The Søndmørings were great seamen, and took active part in the Viking expeditions.

North of Trøndelagen a large seacoast region fringed with thousands of islands stretches for many hundred miles towards the borders of Finmarken. This is Nordland, or, as it was called in earlier times,

[1] *Gunlaugssaga*, ch. 11.

Haalogaland. The great cod and herring fisheries for which this region is still noted, made it in early days one of the most populous districts in Norway. Whale and walrus were caught here in large numbers, and the district was for centuries the center of the rich fur trade of the North, until it was finally surpassed by Novgorod, in Russia, in the eleventh century. The powerful chieftains in Haalogaland carried on a lucrative fur trade with the Finns in Finmarken, on whom they also levied a tribute which brought them a large income. Ôhthêre [1] says that the most precious thing for the chieftains in Haalogaland is the tribute paid them by the Finns. This consists of furs, feathers, whalebone, robes, and ship ropes made from walrus hide. The people of Haalogaland were enterprising merchants and sailors. They went on trading expeditions to southern Norway, Denmark, and the British Isles, and followed routes across the mountains to the Gulf of Bothnia. Many trading centers sprang up, like Vágar (Kabelvaag), and Tjotta, noted later as the seat of the great chieftain Haarek af Tjotta, still one of the largest country seats in northern Norway; also Sandness, and Bjarkey, later the home of the powerful Tore Hund. Wealth was accumulated, and literature and culture flourished. Three of the Edda songs, "Vølundarkviða," "Hýmiskviða," and "Grímnismál," are known to have been written in Haalogaland, and here lived also the great scald Eyvind Skaldaspiller. The jarls of this district were among the most powerful chieftains in Norway at that time; they had large fleets, and ruled over the whole region from Finmarken to the Trondhjemsfjord, including, also, the district at the mouth of the fjord.

In the southwestern part of Norway the three *fylker*, Firðafylke (Nordfjord and Søndfjord), Sygnafylke, or Sogn, and Hordaland (including Nordhordland, Søndhordland, Hardanger, and Voss) were united in the Gulathingslag, a much looser confederacy than the Trøndelag. Firðafylke and Sogn are named after the fjords, while Hordaland bears the name of the Horder, one of the oldest known peoples in Norway. They are mentioned by Cæsar,[2] in the

---

[1] Alfred's *Orosius*.

[2] *Gallic War*, I., 31. Ptolemy mentions them as Charudes, *Geographia*, lib. II., 50.

year 58 B.C., when, according to his account, 24,000 Harudes arrived, and joined Ariovistus. Hordaland was a very mountainous region, with numerous fjords, and but a small area of tillable soil, and the Horder became great seamen and Vikings from very early times. It has already been noted that the "Anglo-Saxon Chronicle" mentions them as the first Vikings in England, and from that time on, this region remained the center of Viking activity in Norway.[1] They extended their power over neighboring tribes and districts, and Firðafylke and Sogn seem to have been new settlements founded by them. The Gulathing was held every spring. Twelve men were chosen from each of the three *fylker* as a *lagrette* by the chieftains who presided over the *thing*. In the mountain valleys farther inland the old organization, with petty kings and full tribal autonomy, still existed unmodified by any tendency towards union.

In southern Norway the Christianiafjord, known in earlier times as the Foldenfjord, extends for a distance of about sixty miles into a fertile and beautiful region called Viken. This district, which lies in close proximity to Sweden and Denmark, and faces the Skagerak and the Baltic Sea, was most favorably located for intercourse with other states. Rich soil, a fine climate, fisheries, and trade made it an attractive and populous region. In early ages it became a harbor for foreign influence and new ideas, a center of progress and development, in which was found all that was highest of art and culture in the North at that time. To the west of the fjord lay two *fylker*, Grenland (the land of the Grannii) and Vestfold; to the east Vingulmark, and southward from Svinesund to the Göta River stretched Ranrike, the land of the Ragnaricii,[2] also called Alfheimr in the sagas, which in later times became a Swedish province. In the southern part of Vestfold, near the coast, lay the famous sanctuary Skiringssal,[3] around which a town had grown up. Ôhthêre says in his report to King Alfred the Great that he lived in Haalogaland,

---

[1] The Horder were found both in Norway and in Denmark. Their original home seems to have been on the Cimbric peninsula, where their name is still preserved in *Hardesyssel*, south of Limfjord. Their name was also given to King Knut the Great's son Hardeknut. See Alexander Bugge, *Norges Historie*, I., 238 ff.   [2] Jordanes, III., p. 19.

[3] *Historisk Tidsskrift udgivet af den norske historiske Forening*, Christiania. Gustav Storm, *Skiringssal og Sandefjord*, fjerde række, vol. I., p. 214.

and that there is in southern Norway a town called Skiringssal
(Sciringes heál), to which one can sail in a month by resting in the
night, if the wind is favorable. As a commercial town it was soon
outstripped by Tunsberg, not far away, on the west side of the Christianiafjord. In the neighborhood of Tunsberg lay a number of
sanctuaries, dedicated to various divinities, whose names are still
traceable in Basberg (Baldersberg), Hassum (Haðsheimr), Horgen,
and Oseberg (the land of the Æsir), where the Oseberg ship was
found. The art and wealth exhibited in the grave chamber of the
queen, or princess, buried in this ship furnish singular evidence of
the culture and power of the princes of Vestfold in early ages. The
kings of Denmark had won supremacy over this province. When
this happened is not known, but in 813 the ruling native princes
acknowledged the Danish king's overlordship, and Vestfold became
a Danish province. But the powerful King Godfred of Denmark,
who ventured to begin war even against Charlemagne, was killed
by one of his own men in 810, and a period of confusion and strife
between rival claimants to the throne was the result. During this
period the Ynglings came into power in Vestfold, a family which was
destined in time to rule over all Norway, and to unite it into one
kingdom. They quickly seized the opportunity, and made Vestfold
independent, but the Danish kings continued to claim it, even as
late as in the reign of Valdemar the Victorious.

22. The Origin of the Yngling Dynasty

According to Thjodolv af Hvin's "Ynglingatal," and the "Yng-
lingasaga" in Snorre's "Heimskringla," the Yngling family were
descendants of the Swedish kings at Upsala. But the Swedish dynasty were, usually, called Scilfings, and the Norwegian kings of
the Yngling family may not, therefore, be descended from them.
In the "Hyndluljóð" in the "Elder Edda" the Scilfings and Ynglings are mentioned as different families.[1] Ynglings means de-

[1] Þadan eru Skiolldungar
Þadan eru Skilfingar
Þadan Audlingar
Þadan Ynglingar.
See *Norræn Fornkvæði*, by Sophus Bugge.

scendants of the god Yngve, who was worshiped in Jutland and northern Germany. He was later considered identical with the god Frey, from whom the Scilfings were supposed to descend, a circumstance which probably gave rise to the idea that the Scilfings and the Ynglings were the same family. Alexander Bugge thinks that the Ynglings originally came from Vestergötland. They came to Norway through marriage, and Vestfold became their real home. Gudrød Veidekonge was the first ruler of Vestfold who called himself king, a title which he assumed after he had succeeded in freeing himself from Danish overlordship. His son Olav Geirstad-Alv, who succeeded him as king of Vestfold and Grenland, became the father of the great sea-king Ragnvald Heidumhære, in honor of whom Thjodolv wrote his "Ynglingatal," and from whom the Norwegian kings of Dublin descended. But better known than Olav Geirstad-Alv is his younger brother Halvdan Svarte, the father of King Harald Haarfagre, who seems to have been a gifted and energetic man with some of the lofty ambition and talent for organization which distinguished his great son. Halvdan was only one year old at his father's death, but when he became of age he forced his brother to share the kingdom with him. Through successful wars he made himself master of one district after another, until he ruled over nearly the whole of Østlandet (southeastern Norway). Tradition says that King Halvdan organized the Eidsivathingslag, but this is much older, though Halvdan, no doubt, increased its significance by adding to it the districts of his kingdom in order to strengthen its organization. Through the marriage of a daughter of King Harald Guldskjeg of Sogn, he was also able to add that district to his kingdom, and at the time of his death in 860 his kingdom was the largest and best organized in all Norway. He had introduced a system of general taxation which the people considered very oppressive, because they were not used to paying taxes, but he seems, nevertheless, to have been held in high esteem. According to the sagas he was drowned while crossing the Randsfjord on the ice in the winter of 860.

23. Harald Haarfagre. — Unification of Norway

When Halvdan Svarte died, his ten-year-old son, Harald Haarfagre, ascended the throne of the kingdom which he had founded. Harald's reign marks the beginning of a new epoch in the history of Norway, in which the union of the whole country under the rule of the Yngling dynasty was effected. The petty kingdoms, jarldoms, and aristocratic confederacies were welded by Harald into a national monarchy with a system of government and administration which placed great power in the hands of the ruling sovereign. What Charlemagne had done on the Continent, and Ecgbert and Alfred in England, King Harald Haarfagre did for Norway. It can scarcely be doubted that the example of these great rulers, as well as that of the neighboring states of Sweden and Denmark, which for long periods had been united and strong kingdoms, fired Harald's ambition, and that many important features in his system of government were due to foreign influence.

About Harald's early life comparatively little is known, but all sources agree that at the death of his father he was ten years of age. The "Fagrskinna"[1] says that at that time he was young in years, but fully developed in the manly bearing which befits a king. He had a luxuriant growth of light hair which looked like silk. He was tall, strong, and beautiful; wise, prudent, and energetic. Old men admired him, and young and vigorous men sought him because of his renown and generosity, and the splendor of his court. According to the sagas, his mother's brother Guttorm was his adviser and the leader of the army, and Ragnvald Mørejarl must also have been his counselor and assistant. When Halvdan Svarte died, the kings and other petty princes in eastern Norway, who had been forced to acknowledge his overlordship, rose in rebellion against his youthful successor. King Gandalv of Ranrike made an expedition against Harald, but he was defeated and slain, and his kingdom was seized. Somewhat later the Swedish king occupied the territory between

---

[1] *Fagrskinna*, or *Noregskonungatal*, narrates the history of the kings of Norway from Halvdan Svarte until 1177. It was written in Norway in the period 1220–1230. It is older than the *Heimskringla*, but the author, though he is a careful and reliable writer, lacks Snorre's ability as historian.

the Glommen and the Göta River, but Harald made a successful campaign against him, and recovered the territory, over which he now placed Guttorm as a sort of *markgraf* to protect the borders. The kings of Ringerike and Hedemarken, aided by Toten and Hadeland, also rebelled. It is said that they made an agreement with Gudbrand, the *herse* of Gudbrandsdal, that they should combine to resist Harald. They assembled to form an alliance against him, but Guttorm fell upon them and destroyed them by setting fire to the house in which they were assembled, and Harald also added Gudbrandsdal to his kingdom.[1] By such vigorous measures he soon overcame all opposition, and not only preserved intact his father's kingdom, but even enlarged its borders. Snorre, in the "Heimskringla," tells how through a fortuitous circumstance he hit upon the idea of making himself king of all Norway. He sent messengers to woo a young maiden by the name of Gyda, the daughter of King Eirik of Hordaland. But she answered proudly that she would not marry a king who ruled over only a few *fylker*. She was surprised, she said, that no king was found who wished to rule over Norway, as King Gorm did over Denmark, and King Eirik in Upsala. She told the messengers that she would marry Harald when he had made himself the ruler of all Norway. This message they brought back to Harald, who thought that she had spoken wisely. "She has reminded me of those things," he said, "which I am surprised have not occurred to me before," and he made a vow that he would not cut or comb his hair before he had conquered the whole country. When this was accomplished, he again sent messengers to Gyda, who now gave her consent, and the two were married. This little romance is ingenious invention, like so many other poetic stories connected with the name of the great king. In the "Fagrskinna" a similar story is told about Ragna, the daughter of Adils the Rich. The ultimate union of Norway was already clearly foreshadowed by the trend of political development which formed a part of a general European movement toward a form of monarchy in which the king possessed as near as

---

[1] Harald's hirdscald, Thorbjørn Hornklove, describes these early campaigns in his poem *Glymdrápa*, of which, however, only a fragment has been preserved. Five of the seven or eight existing stanzas are found in Snorre's *Heimskringla*.

possible the totality of governmental powers. Halvdan Svarte had manifested a similar ambition, and might have come much closer to its realization but for his untimely death. Harald's kingdom was the largest in Norway; he was young and ambitious; he was surrounded by energetic men and wise counselors. Nothing could seem more natural to him under the circumstances, than to continue the work which his father Halvdan had begun.

Harald permitted the districts in Oplandene [1] to retain their own local kings, who now, in a sense, became his vassals. The *herse* of Gudbrandsdal was also allowed to retain his old dignity upon paying taxes, and acknowledging the king's overlordship. Harald now crossed the Dovre Mountains to Trøndelagen, which submitted to him without difficulty, as did also Haalogaland and Namdalen, where the powerful jarl Haakon Grjotgardsson ruled. Jarl Haakon was the king's friend, and aided him in establishing his authority over this part of Norway. Harald spent the winter in Trøndelagen, which he now considered as his real home.[2] He built a residence at Lade, near the present city of Trondhjem, which later became the seat of the powerful Ladejarls, and spent his time in building a fleet, and in systematizing the administration. In the spring he set sail with his fleet for Nordmør and Romsdal. One decisive battle was fought at Solskjel, where King Hundtjov of Nordmør fell; his son, Solve Klove, saved himself by flight, and the two provinces submitted to Harald. Out of these districts he created a jarldom, to which he added a little later also the district of Søndmør, and placed his friend Ragnvald Mørejarl in charge of the administration. From him descended the Orkney jarls, and the dukes of Normandy.

In Vestlandet, where by this time the Viking activity held full sway, the love of local autonomy and of unrestricted personal independence was most intense. The aristocracy feared nothing so much as a possible restriction of their old rights, and the overlordship of a national king. As Harald's success greatly alarmed them, they united their entire strength, and sought assistance even in

[1] Oplandene (the Uplands) is a name applied to the districts Hadeland, Land, Gudbrandsdal, Valders, Hedemarken, Østerdalen, Toten, Vinger, Odalen, and Solør, constituting at present the two *amts* Kristian and Hedemarken.   [2] *Heimskringla, Harald Haarfagre's Saga*, ch. 9.

the Viking colonies in the West for a decisive combat with the ambitious king. No single district could assemble a larger fleet, nor raise a stronger force of well-trained warriors with able leaders than Vestlandet, and when the hostile forces finally met in Hafrsfjord, on the coast of Rogaland, in southwestern Norway, in 872, King Harald well knew that he faced the most critical struggle of his life. The battle is described in a poem by the scald Thorbjørn Hornklove, who tells how King Luva fought against Kjøtve (the stout one) and Haklang (the one with the long chin), whose men were armed with white shields,[1] Gaelic swords, and spears made in the West. Luva (O. N. *lúfa* = thick hair) was a nickname applied to Harald Haarfagre in his younger days, because of his heavy growth of hair. Kjøtve seems to be a nickname by which the scald designates King Gudrød of Agder, while Haklang, from whom he received aid, seems to have been his son Olav the White of Dublin. King Olav, who had driven out the Danes, and had reëstablished the power of the Norsemen, ruled in Dublin for many years, together with Ivar, probably Ivar Boneless, the son of Ragnar Lodbrok, with whom he seems to have formed an alliance. In 871 he left Ireland and never returned, which indicates that he must have died on his expedition. The "Three Fragments of Irish Annals," found in 1860, states that in 871 King Amlaib (Olav) went from Erin to Lochlann (Norway) to wage war with the Lochlannaig (Norsemen), and help his father, Gotfried, because the Lochlannaig had begun war against him, and he had come to ask his son for aid. Haklang (Olav) fell in the battle, says Hornklove. This explains why Olav never returned to Ireland. It is clear that the kings of Vestlandet, with their combined forces under the leadership of Gudrød, and assisted by a Viking army from Ireland under King Olav, met Harald in the Hafrsfjord, but they were defeated after a fierce battle in which King Olav fell. The overthrow of the opposition was complete, and Harald was acknowledged king of united Norway.[2]

[1] When Irish annalists call the Norsemen *Finn-Galls* or white strangers, to distinguish them from the Danes, who are called *Dubh-Galls* or dark strangers, it is probably due to their custom of carrying white shields.

[2] Gustav Storm, *Slaget i Hafrsfjord. Historisk Tidsskrift* anden række, vol. II., 313.

Many kings and chieftains mentioned by Snorre as partakers in the battle

During these wars Harald had created both an army and a navy, and it became necessary to maintain these military organizations to protect the kingdom from foreign and domestic enemies. Piratic expeditions within the borders of Norway were now forbidden, and all inhabitants had to swear fealty to the king or leave the country. Many of the chieftains in the districts which had offered the stoutest resistance chose to emigrate rather than submit to Harald. Their estates were confiscated, and became royal demesne lands, the property of the king. Of these estates he retained a number, which he placed in charge of royal overseers, *aarmænd*, and these lands became one of his chief sources of income. The greater part of the confiscated lands he gave to his followers as a payment for services rendered or to be rendered. They received the lands, not in full ownership, but in *veitsle*, which means that they were entitled to the income from them, in return for which they should collect taxes, furnish fully equipped men for the army, and be of aid and service to the king. King Harald derived income also from various other sources. The trade with the Finns, and the tribute paid by them, was made a royal monopoly. All derelict property belonged to the king. He also levied a personal tax on his subjects; probably, also, a tax on certain special privileges and incomes. The *aarmænd* were the local collectors of these taxes. This royal office, or *syssel*, together with that of overseer, was later given to officers called *sysselmænd*.[1]

Snorre says that Harald placed a jarl in each *fylke*, who should maintain law and order and collect taxes, of which he should retain one-third for his expenses and for the maintenance of his household. Under each jarl there should be four *herser*, who should have an income of twenty marks a year. Each jarl should furnish sixty men for the king's army, and each *herse* should furnish twenty.[2] This arrangement seems to have been made, however, only in the districts which had offered the most determined resistance, in consequence of which the old institution of fylkes-king was abolished, and

are unhistoric characters; like Roald Rygg, Hadd den Haarde, King Sulke, and his brother Sote Jarl.

[1] R. Keyser, *Efterladte Skrifter*, vol. II., *Norges Stats- og Retsforfatning i Middelalderen.* T. E. Aschehoug, *Statsforfatningen i Norge og Danmark indtil 1814*, p. 12 f.

[2] Snorre, *Heimskringla, Harald Haarfagre's Saga*, ch. 6.

royal officers were placed in charge of the local administration. We have seen that in Oplandene and in Gudbrandsdal the old system was retained, and the same was, no doubt, the case in Trøndelagen, and, in fact, in all districts which had submitted voluntarily to the king. The name and office of *herse* was retained, but later the *herser* became *lendermænd* (O. N. *lendr maðr*), an office which corresponded in general to their old dignity. But while the *herse* was an hereditary chieftain and a leader of the people, the *lendermand* was a royal official who held his position by appointment, and, as a rule, this new dignity never became fully hereditary.[1] The jarls were no longer independent rulers, as of old, but became the highest officials under the king. They were the leaders of the army in war, conducted the deliberations at the *thing*, collected the taxes, and had charge of the local administration in larger districts. Especially powerful were the king's old friends and assistants; Guttorm, Haakon Grjotgardsson, and Ragnvald Mørejarl, who ruled over many *fylker*.

The sagas, especially the "Egilssaga," which is very hostile to Harald, pictures his government as a usurpation of power, a veritable tyranny. Snorre says that wherever Harald acquired any territory, he took the *odel* away from the people, and forced them to pay a land tax.[2] The *odel* was a right to full ownership of land, vested permanently in the family, the members of which had a right to redeem the property, if it should be sold to any one outside of the family.

[1] *Heimskringla, Harald Haarfagre's Saga*, ch. 6. J. E. Sars, *Udsigt over den norske Historie*, I., 161. R. Keyser, *Norges Retsforfatning*, p. 112–113. P. A. Munch, *Samlede Afhandlinger*, vol. I., p. 77 ff.

[2] Older scholars have accepted, in the main, the statement of the sagas that King Harald deprived the people of their right of *odel*. "Harald appropriated to himself as king the right of *odel*, *i.e.* the supreme right of ownership of all the land, with a corresponding right to levy taxes." R. Keyser, *Efterladte Skrifter*, vol. II. *Norges Stats- og Retsforfatning i Middelalderen*, p. 30.

"With the right of the conqueror Harald took with armed hand all the lands in the districts which he seized. He did not drive away the former owners, but he deprived them of their *odel*, and made them pay a land tax." T. H. Aschehoug, *Statsforfatningen i Norge og Danmark indtil* 1814, p. 12. Later investigations have led to the conclusion that Harald did not deprive the people of their right of *odel*.

"The freeholders (*bønder*) thought that if they should pay taxes they were no longer free odelsbønder, but the king's tenants. This is the real meaning

This was a very important right, which secured the power and independence of the large class of freeholders. To judge from the statement in the "Egilssaga" that in every *fylke* Harald took all the *odel*, and all land, inhabited and uninhabited, even the sea and the waters, and that all freeholders (*bønder*) should henceforth be his tenants, one might be led to think that the king was the owner of all the land, and had introduced the feudal system in Norway. But this is a manifest exaggeration. The feudal system was not at that time developed anywhere in Europe, and it was never introduced in Norway. With the exception of the confiscations already mentioned, the people, no doubt, retained their *odel* now as heretofore, and there is no evidence that they even had to pay a land tax, such as the sagas complain of. Harald left undisturbed the *things* and the old legal system, and the "Egilssaga" states that shortly after the king's death Egil Skallagrimsson brought a suit on behalf of his wife against Bergamund at the Gulathing, maintaining that she was entitled to inherit one-half of the estate left by her father, Bjørn Herse, both of real and personal property. This shows that the right of *odel* existed at that time. What Harald did was to levy a personal tax on the freeholders, possibly, also, a tax on certain incomes. This had been done before by his father Halvdan, but it was otherwise an innovation. As people had never been accustomed to paying taxes, they regarded this as a sign of dependence, and as so great an encroachment on their liberty that it was tantamount to depriving them of their *odel* and their rights as freemen, and of reducing them to tenants under the king.

From very early times the kings and chieftains had a band of personal followers called *drott*, or *verðung*, corresponding to the *comitatus* of the early German chieftains.[1] In Harald's time the name "hird"[2] came into use, and many foreign manners and cus-

of the complaint that Harald took the *odel* away from them. That King Harald levied a tax which the *bønder* could call a land tax, there is nothing to show." Alexander Bugge, *Norges Historie*, vol. I., second part, p. 125. Yngvar Nielsen, *Historisk Tidsskrift*, fjerde række, vol. IV., p. 1 ff. Absalon Taranger, *Historisk Tidsskrift*, fjerde række, vol. IV., p. 98 ff.

[1] "It was their honor and power always to be surrounded by a large body of select young men, their pride in peace, and their protection in war." Tacitus, *Germania*, 13.

[2] *Hird*, O. N. *hirð* < A. S. *híred*, or *hírd*, = family.

toms were introduced. Ambitious young men flocked to Harald, and the *hird*, which originally had been a very simple institution, became a real court, famous for its splendor and fine manners. "King Harald Haarfagre was the strictest of all kings with regard to conduct and courtly etiquette," says the saga.[1] Liberal gifts, some high office or other good fortune, awaited those who gained the king's favor. The "Egilssaga" tells that King Harald sent word to Kveldulv fra Fjordene that he wished that one of his sons might become a *hirdmand*. Kveldulv, who had been an opponent of the king, told his son Thoralv that he thought they would reap nothing but misfortune from it. But Thoralv answered: "Things must then take another turn than I expect. I think that the king will give me great advancement, and I have determined to go to him and become his man. I have heard that his *hird* consists of the very best men, and it seems to me a great advantage to be among them, if they will receive me. They are also better provided for than any other men in the land. The king is said to be very generous, and always willing to promote those who deserve it. But I have heard that those who resist him, and do not seek his friendship, accomplish nothing. Some leave the country, and some become tenants."[2]

Like Charlemagne and Alfred the Great, King Harald was also a patron of literature. Many scalds came to his court, and the *hird* became the center of intellectual life and literary activity. We hear of scalds before this time, but the *hirdscald* poetry, which consisted mainly of laudatory songs composed to commemorate great events and the lives and deeds of kings and princes, seems to have been developed at Harald's court, where new themes and opportunities were offered the poets. The union of Norway, and Harald's great achievements created a new national pride, which is freely voiced in the songs of the *hirdscalds*. Hitherto the poets had sung about mythology and heroic traditions; their songs were composed in

---

[1] *Nornagestssaga*, ch. 9. Alexander Bugge, *Vikingerne*, II., 208 ff. *Kongespeilet* (the *King's Mirror*), Christiania, 1848, 59–60. R. Keyser, *Norges Stats- og Retsforfatning*, Christiania, 1867, 77 ff. T. H. Aschehoug, *Statsforfatningen i Norge og Danmark indtil* 1814, Christiania, 1866.

[2] See Thorbjørn Hornklove's song about Harald, also called the *Ravnsmaal*, *Fagrskinna*, 5.

the clear and classic alliterative verse; their names they gave to oblivion with a certain proud disdain which does not covet honor, as did the authors of the songs of the "Elder Edda." The *hirdscalds* sang of the great events of the day, and praised the achievements, and extolled the renown of the kings and princes who were their patrons, and who rewarded them liberally for their songs. They sought honor as well as reward, and their names have been handed down to posterity. They composed their songs in a new and intricate verse form, the *drottkvætt*, abounding in word transpositions and metaphoric expressions (*kenningar*), in which Irish influence can be recognized, Ireland being the only country where a like verse form and a similar poetic literature was found. The most noted scalds at Harald's court were: Thjodolv af Hvin and Thorbjørn Hornklove, who have already been mentioned. Less known are Ølve Hnuva, Ulv Sebbason, Guttorm Sindre, and Audun Illskelda, the oldest of them all, who had been scald at the court of Harald's father, Halvdan Svarte. Court jesters were introduced to create diversion and entertainment for the *hird*, and games, resembling dice and chess (*terning* and *brætspil*), were much indulged in. Music, especially the playing of the trumpet and the harp, declamation of poems by the scalds, rich ornaments, fine clothes, and courtly manners added charm to this circle of gifted and prominent men who constituted the *hird* of King Harald Haarfagre.

Many features of Harald's great work are, as already indicated, clearly traceable to the influence of Charlemagne and Alfred the Great, from whose constructive statesmanship he gathered both inspiration and ideas. His plan of making Norway a united kingdom, and of dividing the country into jarldoms, or larger administrative districts, are ascribable, in the main, to this influence. The revival of learning produced by Charlemagne after the darkness and confusion of the Migrations must have inspired him, also, with the noble ambition to become a patron of literature, and a teacher of good manners, to make his court an intellectual center, and to foster in his people a true appreciation of the ennobling influence of higher culture. The stirring events at home, together with the stimulus given by the Viking expeditions, and the influence of the art and culture of the nations with whom the Norsemen now came into more immediate contact, produced in Norway a great intellectual awakening, the fruit of which was the scaldic poetry, the Eddas, the sagas, valuable historical works, and collections of old laws. In the field of literature, as in the domain of seamanship and maritime enterprise, the Norsemen manifested the most original and versatile genius of the age. King Harald learned, indeed, from others, but he was not a mere imitator. All accounts of him, whether friendly or hostile, agree in describing him as a gifted and truly great man. He was tall and strong, and a rich growth of flaxen hair crowned his majestic brow. He was a kingly and imposing figure, who inspired confidence and respect. In peace, as in war, he exhibited the same talent for organization which made him able to shape a well-ordered system in every field to which he devoted his attention. He pursued his aim with great energy and perseverance, and his hand fell heavy on those who resisted. In many cases he might have been arbitrary, even cruel and despotic, but he possessed, on the whole, a mixture of sternness and moderation which made it possible for him, not only to accomplish his first great aim, but to overcome all opposition, and to rule in peace during a long reign.

24. Events outside of Norway. The Norse Colonial Empire. The Orkney and Shetland Islands

Many men of influence and power left Norway after the battle of Hafrsfjord in 872. They emigrated to the Faroe Islands, the Orkney [1] and Shetland (Hjaltland) groups, the Hebrides (Sudreyjar), to Iceland, and to the Viking colonies in the West. Olav the White's son, Eystein, and Ivar Boneless ruled in Dublin, and possessed large districts in Scotland, while Ketil Flatnev, father of Aud the Deep-minded, the wife of Olav the White, had established a sort of independent sovereignty in the Hebrides.[2] These opponents of Harald harbored and aided the fugitives, who used their new homes as a base of operations from which they would send out piratic expeditions to harry the coasts of Norway. Irritated by these constant

---

[1] The Orkneys (O. N. *Orkneyjar*) were called by the Romans *Orcades*. The Norsemen retained the first part of the name *Orc*, or *Ork*, and added *eyjar* (*i.e.* islands).   [2] The *Laxdølasaga*.

VOL. I — K

ravages, Harald at length fitted out a large fleet, and sailed westward to punish the Vikings. He attacked the Norse settlements in Scotland, chased away the Viking bands from Shetland, the Orkneys, and the Hebrides, and seems to have visited even the Isle of Man. Shetland and the Orkneys were annexed to Norway, and Ragnvald Mørejarl's brother Sigurd was made ruler of the new provinces. This expedition against the Vikings made Harald a friend of the English king, Æthelstan, with whom he concluded a treaty. The two kings sent each other valuable presents, and each sought to rival the other. Harald also sent his son Haakon to England to be reared at the court of King Æthelstan, not, as the sagas would explain it, in order to insult the king, but because he wished the boy to become acquainted with English manners and culture. Jarl Sigurd and Thorstein the Red, a son of Olav the White of Dublin, soon gained possession of Caithness (Katanes), Sutherland (Suðrland), and other districts of northern Scotland, as far as to the river Oikel, says the "Orkneyingasaga." [1] Sigurd died in Scotland, and was succeeded by his son Guttorm, but he lived only a year, and Torv-Einar, a son of Ragnvald Mørejarl, became jarl of the Orkneys.[2] From him descended the powerful Orkney jarls, prominent both in Scotch and Norwegian history.[3] He was a half-brother of Gange-Rolv, who founded the Norse dukedom of Normandy.

[1] Alexander Bugge shows that there is a manifest error in the saga, as the son of Olav the White of Dublin was called Eystein, and not Thorstein.

[2] He was nicknamed Torv-Einar (Peat-Einar), because he taught the people to use peat for fuel. He was a practical man and a powerful warrior. He soon drove out the Viking freebooters, and established peace and order in the islands. *Orkneyingasaga*, translated by Jon A. Hjaltalin and Gilbert Goudie, edited with notes and introduction by Joseph Anderson, Edinburgh, 1873.

[3] L. Dietrichson, *Monumenta Orcadica, the Norsemen in the Orkneys and the Monuments They Have Left*, Christiania, 1906. J. Wallace, *Description of the Isles of the Orkneys*, 1673, new edition, London, 1884. Fea, *Present State of the Orkney-Islands*, London, 1885. J. J. A. Worsaae, *Minder om de Danske og Nordmændene i England, Skotland og Irland*, p. 177 ff., Copenhagen, 1851. Torfæus, *Orcades*, 1700. Peder Claussøn Friis, *Norriges og omliggende Øers sandfærdige Beskrivelse*, 1632. Joseph Anderson, *Scotland in Early Christian Times*, vol. I. *Islandske Annaler*, edited by Gustav Storm. P. A. Munch, *Erindringer fra Orknøerne. Samlede Afhandlinger*, III., 52–59. P. A. Munch, *Geografiske Oplysninger om de i Sagaerne forekommende skotske og irske Stedsnavne*, III., 79–181.

PLATE VI

RUINS OF THE BISHOP'S PALACE AT KIRKWALL.

THE ST. MAGNUS CATHE-
DRAL AT KIRKWALL.

NOTLAND CASTLE IN WESTRAY.

Harald Haarfagre's son Halvdan Hálegg, who had killed Ragnvald Mørejarl in Norway, came to the Orkneys to drive away Torv-Einar. Einar fled to Caithness, but returned to the islands with a large force, and defeated and killed Halvdan. As a punishment King Harald demanded of the people of the Orkneys a tax of sixty marks of gold. This tax Einar undertook to pay on condition that the people should surrender to him their right of *odel, i.e.* the right of private owner- ship of the land which they tilled. When Torv-Einar died, about 910, his three sons, Arnkell, Erlend, and Thorfinn Hausakljuv, suc- ceeded him. During their time King Eirik Blood-Ax, son of Harald Haarfagre and his queen Ragnhild, sought refuge in the Orkneys, having been banished from Norway. Arnkell and Erlend helped King Eirik in his battles in England, and fell there, but Thorfinn Hausakljuv remained jarl of the Orkneys till 963. He married Gre- laug, daughter of the Scotch maormor Dungad, or Duncan, and received with her Caithness, which from now on was united with the Orkneys. He was mound-buried on the northwest coast of South Ronaldsay, at Hoxa. Thorfinn's five sons succeeded one an- other as jarls of the Orkneys. King Eirik Blood-Ax's daughter Ragnhild married in course of time three of the brothers, but caused the death of all her husbands. Her evil influence brought about a period of feuds and bloodshed in which many of the leading men of the islands met their death. At length Lodve, the fifth and only remaining son of Thorfinn Hausakljuv, became jarl. He died about 980, and was succeeded by his son Sigurd Lodvesson, the famous Orkney jarl who fell in the battle of Clontarf. King Olav Trygg- vason forced Sigurd to acknowledge his overlordship, and to accept Christianity, 995. The island jarldom had been a Norse dependency since Harald Haarfagre's time, but the suzerainty of the Norwegian kings was not always firmly maintained till in the reign of Olav Haraldsson (1015–1030). Jarl Sigurd ruled, not only over the Ork- neys and Caithness, but also over Sutherland, Ross, Moray, and Argyle in Scotland, as well as over the Hebrides and Man. He was often hard pressed in his wars with the Scotch earls or maormors, and in order to get more active support from his people, he gave them back their right of *odel* which Torv-Einar had taken from them. He defeated Findlay, the father of Macbeth, at Skida Myre, and in the battle of Duncansby Head he defeated the two Scotch maormors Hunde and Maelsnechtan, but being unable to defend his Scotch possessions, he made peace with Scotland, and married the daughter of King Malcolm II. She was his second wife, and bore him the son Thorfinn. When Sigurd fell at Clontarf, in 1014, three sons of a former marriage, Sumarlide, Bruse, and Einar Vrangmund, divided the Orkneys among themselves, but none of them lived long, and Thorfinn soon became the ruler of his father's possessions. But he soon had to surrender two-thirds of the Orkneys to Ragnvald, the son of Bruse, who returned to the island in 1035. For some time Thorfinn and Ragnvald were friends, and made Viking expeditions together, but when Thorfinn suddenly demanded that Ragnvald should give up one-third of his possessions to Kalv Arnesson of Norway, hostilities began in which Ragnvald was defeated and slain.

After Thorfinn's death about 1064, his two sons, Paul and Erlend, ruled jointly till 1098, a period during which the islands enjoyed peace and prosperity. They were succeeded by their sons, Haakon Paulsson and Magnus Erlendsson, or St. Magnus, but in 1115 the selfish and violent Haakon slew Magnus, who was afterward venerated as a saint. The direct line of Norse jarls in the Orkneys became extinct in 1231 upon the death of John Jarl, but the islands remained a Norwegian dependency till 1471.[1] In 1468 the Orkney Islands were mortgaged by Christian I., king of Denmark and Norway, to King James III. of Scotland as security for 50,000 Rhenish gulden; this sum being part of the dowry of 60,000 Rhenish gulden which his daughter Margaret was to receive upon her marriage to King James. In 1471 the last Orkney jarl, William Sinclair, ceded the islands to the Scotch king, and received in return extensive possessions on the mainland of Scotland.

Numerous remains from the Norse period are still found in the islands. Burial mounds, ship burials, stone monuments, and ruins of churches and other old buildings attract the attention of scientists and travelers. The town of Kirkwall (Kirkjuvágr) was

---

[1] *The Orkneyingasaga*, which is the chief source for the early history of the Orkneys, was written not before 1250. The *Islandske Annaler* contain some notices of events in the Orkneys after the period dealt with in the *Orkneyingasaga*. See also *Njálssaga*, and *Olav Tryggvasonssaga* in the *Flateyjarbók*.

founded by Jarl Ragnvald, the son of Bruse. It is built on the same plan as the early Norwegian cities of Tunsberg, Nidaros, Oslo, Bjørgvin, and Stavanger. The St. Olaf cathedral in Kirkwall was erected by Jarl Ragnvald, who was a friend of St. Olav Haraldsson, king of Norway.

In 1050 Jarl Thorfinn went on a pilgrimage to Rome, where he received Pope Leo IX.'s permission to establish a separate bishopric for the Orkneys. The Christ church at Byrgisaa, the first bishop's church in the islands, is thought to have been erected by Thorfinn. The bishop's residence was later removed to Kirkwall. The church at Orfjara was built by Jarl Haakon Paulsson, 1118–1122, in expiation of the murder of St. Magnus. Among other conspicuous ruins are those of the Magnus church on Egilsey, the bishop's palace in Kirkwall, and Notland castle on Westray. The grandest building in the Orkneys is the Magnus cathedral in Kirkwall, a truly magnificent structure erected by Ragnvald Jarl, the second Orkney jarl of that name, 1137–1156. "It is the mightiest monument left by the Norsemen in the West, indeed, next to Trondhjem cathedral, the oldest monument of the whole ancient Norway." "Here, too," says L. Dietrichson, "is a confirmation of what may generally be said of the Viking expeditions; namely, that although in themselves wild and barbaric, they always contained the germ of a new, rich cultural development, that stirred as soon as the warlike spirit sank to rest, and left room for the play of the intellectual strength and civilizing power that also dwelt in the Vikings. St. Magnus' cathedral is the living expression of this thought." [1]

The people of the Orkneys have retained to the present time their Norse character. They are proud of their Norse descent, and refuse to be called Scotch. They live on their country homesteads, as of old, and the freeholders are still called "udallers" (i.e. odelsmænd). They are great sailors and fishermen, and show a preference for a seafaring life. In the course of the eighteenth century the Norse language disappeared, and English is now spoken exclusively, but many Norse words and idioms have been preserved. The Orkney peasants still say, "luk the grind!" for "shut the gate," and their accent strongly resembles that of the western districts of Norway.

[1] Dietrichson, *Monumenta Orcadica.*

Professor P. A. Munch, who traveled in the Orkneys in 1849, writes : [1] "The Norse era, isolated by a new linguistic period, stands surrounded by a mystic glory in the memory of the people of the Orkneys. They exalt it to the skies at the expense of the English-Scotch period. Everything belonging to that time, and, in general, everything which is called "Norn" (from Norrøn, or Norse) they regard as better and nobler than the English or Scotch. I experienced many very touching examples of the devotion with which the people still cling to Norway and to the memories of this their motherland."

When the Orkneys came under Scotland, a number of Scotchmen came over to the islands, and through the aid and connivance of the rulers they secured large estates, and became in time a landed aristocracy. The original Norse settlers became more and more dependent on the great landowners, and were oppressed by heavy taxes. This engendered a spirit of ill feeling between the Scotch and the Norse elements, which increased when the Scotch law was substituted for the old Norse law of St. Olav. Tenaciously the people clung to their old rights. Even in 1903 an Orkney farmer so stoutly defended his rights according to St. Olav's Norse law in regard to some fisheries in dispute, that the English authorities made inquiries of a Norwegian professor of jurisprudence at the University of Christiania to secure information regarding this old law.[2] The Orkney group consists of about eighty islands, all of which have Norse names, with the exception of two or three. The islands have a population of about 30,000. The two cities are Kirkwall with 4000 inhabitants, and Stromness with 2000. The Orkneys are divided into eighteen parishes, and together with the Shetland Islands they have one representative in the English Parliament.

The Shetland archipelago (O. N. Hjaltland) was settled by the Norsemen on their early expeditions to the British Isles. The islands were inhabited at that time by the Picts (called Petar by the Norsemen), who had been converted to Christianity by Irish monks prior to the arrival of the Vikings. Many ruins and stone

---

[1] *Samlede Afhandlinger*, III., p. 52 ff.   Jakob Jakobsen, *Nordiske Minder paa Orknøerne*, in *Maal og Minne, Festskrift til H. Feilberg*, 1911, p. 318.

[2] A. Taranger, *Aftenposten*, September 13, 1903, quoted by L. Dietrichson, *Monumenta Orcadica*, p. 13.

PLATE VII

INTERIOR OF ST. MAGNUS CATHEDRAL AT KIRKWALL.

monuments still preserve the remembrance of these early inhabitants.[1] Cairns (burial mounds of stone) and stone circles from this period are found both in the Shetland Islands and the Orkneys, but the most noteworthy Pictish monuments in the Shetland Islands are the round stone towers, "Pictish towers," built of undressed stone, without the use of mortar. Several ruins of such towers are still found, and one, the Broch of Mousa, is still preserved entire. In the "Egilssaga" it is called "Moseyjarborg." The old tower has derived its name from the Isle of Mousa (O. N. Mosey), on which it is situated. The story is told that while Harald Haarfagre ruled in Norway, a prominent Viking merchant, Bjørn Brynjulvsson, eloped with the beautiful Thora Roaldsdatter fra Fjordene. The two fled to Shetland to escape the wrath of the angry parents. The wedding was celebrated in the Broch of Mousa, and the young couple spent the winter there. In the spring Bjørn learned that he had been outlawed by the king, and that the jarls in the Orkneys and the Hebrides had received orders to seize him. He accordingly continued his flight to Iceland, where he arrived safely with his bride. A couple of centuries later the chieftain Erlend Ungi fled from the Orkneys with Margaret, the mother of Jarl Harald Madadsson, famous alike for her beauty and her frivolity. They were pursued by the angry jarl, and sought refuge in the Broch of Mousa. Jarl Harald was unable to take the tower by force, and an agreement was made, according to which Erlend was allowed to marry Margaret on condition that he should swear fealty to Harald.

In course of time the original Celtic inhabitants disappeared. The Norsemen gradually took full possession of the islands, and gave them the Norse names which they still bear. Most of the names of mountains, islands, rocks, and skerries in the Shetland archipelago are Norse, which is seen from the usual Norse terminations *firth* (fjord), *wick* (vik), *ness* (nes), *daill* (dalr), *voc* (vágr), etc., found in

---

[1] J. J. A. Worsaae, *Minder om de Danske og Nordmændene i England, Skotland og Irland*, p. 277, § 5, and p. 286, § 6. Cowie, *Shetland*, Edinburgh, 1880. J. Jakobsen, *Det norrøne Sprog paa Shetland*, Copenhagen, 1897, Salmonsen's *Konversations-Leksikon*, "Shetland." Arthur Laurenson, *Om Sproget paa Shetlandsøerne, Annaler for nordisk Oldkyndighed*, 1860. K. J. Lungby, *Om Sproget paa Hjaltlandsøerne, Annaler for nordisk Oldkyndighed*, 1860.

names like Hillswick (Hildisvik), Thorness (Þorsnes), Lax-Voc (Laxa-vágr), Hamna-Voc (Hafna-vágr). In the southern part of the island of Mainland lies the estate Howff (O. N. Hof). The name indicates that a heathen temple was once located there. In the reign of King Olav Tryggvason the Shetland Islands were united with the kingdom of Norway; Christianity was introduced, and the Norse system of law and government was established here as elsewhere in the Norse colonies. The *Althing* of the islands was held in the present parish of Thingvall (Þingvǫllr), where the place of meeting is still seen on a little island in a lake near the church. The island is connected with the mainland by a row of stones called the "stepping stones." The island of Mainland was divided into seven judicial districts, or *things*. The names of five of these have been preserved, namely Sandsthing (Sandsþing), Aithsthing (Eiðsþing), Delthing (Dalaþing), Lunzeisthing (Lundeiðisþing), and Nesthing (Nesþing). The two others, Rauðarþing and Þvei-taþing, are known only from the sagas.

The Norse language died out in the islands in the eighteenth century, but the English, which is now spoken, is still mixed with many Norse words and idioms. According to Jakob Jakobsen about 10,000 Norse words are still used in the Shetland Islands. In the Orkneys not quite as many. Words like *quern* (N. kvern), a hand-mill; *haaf-fishing* (N. hav-fiske), ocean fishing; *tows* (N. toug), rope; *hogan* (N. hagi), a pasture; *hoy-sæde* (N. høisæte), high-seat, the seat of the lady of the house; *bysmer* (N. bismer), a steelyard, are interesting examples. In dress and mode of life many Norse customs still prevail.

The Shetland Islands continued to be a Norse colony till 1468, when they were mortgaged to Scotland by King Christian I. by the same documents in which he also included the Orkneys. Here, as in the Orkneys, a feudal system was introduced whereby English and Scotch lords took possession of the soil. The independent free-holding Norse farmer class disappeared, and the Norse population became tenants under the great landlords.

Of the 117 islands which form the Shetland archipelago only twenty-nine are inhabited. The large island of Mainland embraces the greater portion of the inhabitable area. In 1890 the Shetland

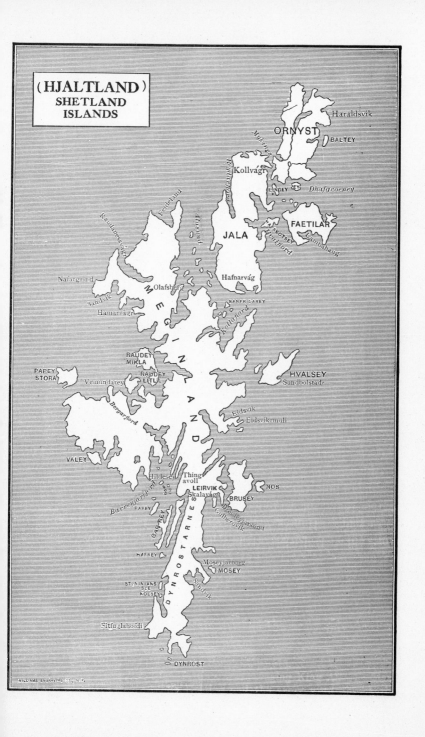

(HJALTLAND) SHETLAND ISLANDS

Haraldsvik
ORNYST
BALTEY
Kollvagr
EY
ENGEY
Dhafgroeney
JALA
FAETILAR
Hafnarvág
Nafargrind
Olafsberg
SANFRIDAREY
Sandvik
Hamarvágr
MEGINLAND
RAUDEY MIKLA
PAPEY STORA
RAUDEY LITLA
HVALSEY
Sundbolstadr
Vemundarey
Borgarfiord
Eidsvik
Eidsvikrmuli
VALEY
Thing avoll
Hildesey
NOS
LEIRVIK
Skalavága
BRUSEY
Barreyiarfiord
PAPEY
BARREY
DYNROSTARNES
HAFREY
Moseyjarborg
MOSEY
ST NINIANS SLE
KOLSEY
Sitfuglahofdi
DYNROST

Islands had a population of 28,711. The cities are Lerwick and Scalloway, with 4000 and 600 inhabitants respectively.

25. ICELAND AND THE FAROE ISLANDS

Decuil, an Irish monk living in France, wrote in 825 a work on geography, "Liber de Mensura Orbis Terræ," in which he describes the islands in the northern ocean which, he says, he has not found mentioned by any other writer. After having described what appears to be Iceland and the Shetland Islands, he says: "There are also some other small islands, almost all divided from each other by narrow sounds, inhabited for about a century by hermits proceeding from our Scotia (Ireland); but as they had been deserted since the beginning of the world, so are they now abandoned by these anchorites on account of the northern robbers, but they are full of countless sheep, and swarm with seafowl of various kinds." The sheep must have been left there by the Irish hermits, and the Norsemen, appropriately enough, called the islands "Fær-eyjar" (Sheep-isles), the Faroe Islands. The Irish monks seem to have come to the islands about 700, and about a century later they had to leave because of the Vikings.[1] The "Færeyingasaga" tells us that Grim Kamban was the first Norseman to settle in the islands. This was, probably, in the early part of the ninth century. When Aud, the widow of Olav the White, went to Iceland, she stopped on the Faroe Islands to celebrate the wedding of her son's daughter Aalov. From her descended the Gateskjegger, the greatest chieftains in the islands. After the battle of Hafrsfjord many emigrants from Norway settled in the Faroe Islands. It is not stated that Harald, on his expedition against the Vikings, annexed the islands to Norway, but a little later they are spoken of as a Norwegian dependency.

According to Decuil, Iceland was also discovered by Irish monks prior to 795. Are Frode, the earliest Icelandic historian, who has written a very reliable work on the early history of Iceland, the "Íslendingabók," says that at the time when the Norsemen first began to visit the island "they found Christian men there whom

[1] C. Rafn, *Færeyingasaga*, contains all the accounts of the Faroe Islands found in the Icelandic sagas. Fridtjof Nansen, *Nord i Taakeheimen* (*In Northern Mists*), p. 124 ff.

they called *papa*, but they soon left because they did not wish to dwell among the heathens. They left Irish books, bells, and crosiers, from which one must judge that they were Irish."[1] The "Landnámabók" also mentions these Irish monks, and the name of the island of Papey, off the east coast, still brings to memory their stay in Iceland.[2]

Iceland was discovered by the Norsemen in the period 860–870. Are Frode says that Iceland was first settled in the days of Harald Haarfagre, 870 years after the birth of Christ, by people from Norway.[3] According to Sturla's "Landnámabók," the Norseman Naddod first reached the island, having lost his way while on a voyage from Norway to the Faroe Islands. According to the "Historia Norwegiae" and Hauk's "Landnámabók" the Swede Gárdar first discovered Iceland. But neither the story of Naddod, nor that of Gardar, can be regarded as anything but tradition. A little later than Naddod's and Gardar's reputed voyages a Norseman, Floke Vilgerdsson, sailed to Iceland from the Hebrides where Norse colonies already existed. He spent two winters in the island, and gave it the name of Iceland.[4]

---

[1] *Íslendingabók*, ch. 1.   Jacobus Langebek, *Scriptores Rerum Danicarum*, II., p. 31 f.   [2] *Landnámabók*, p. 2.

[3] *Íslendingabók*, ch. I.

The *Landnámabók* exists in two slightly different versions, one by Sturla Thordsson, from about 1250, and another by Hauk Erlendsson, from about 1400. An older edition by Styrmer Frode is lost, as is, also, the original version. It is a unique work of great importance, containing a detailed account of the early Norse settlements in Iceland, as well as the names of the settlers.

Of special interest and importance is Fridtjof Nansen's new work, *Nord i Taakeheimen*, or *In Northern Mists*. An interesting account of Iceland and the Faroe Islands is also found in Daniel Bruun's work, *Det høie Nord*, Copenhagen, 1902. Among other helpful works may be mentioned: N. Winther, *Færøernes Oldtidshistorie*, Copenhagen, 1875. J. R. Rønne, *Færøerne*, Copenhagen, 1900. Salmonsen's *Konversations-Leksikon*, articles on Iceland, and the Faroe Islands. Hans Reynolds, *Hos gammelt norsk Folk*, *Reiseskildringer fra Færøerne*, Christiania, 1905.

[4] Besides the *Íslendingabók* and the *Landnámabók*, which relate the early history of Iceland, valuable contributions to the history and geography of the island are found in Th. Thoroddsen's *Oversigt over de geografiske Kundskaber om Island før Reformationen*, *Geografisk Tidsskrift*, 10. aarg., 1888–1889. Th. Thoroddsen, *Islands Beskrivelse*, Christiania, 1883. *Lýsing*

The first permanent settlement was made by Ingolv Arnarsson and his friend Leiv Hrodmarsson, who came to Iceland in 874. The "Landnámabók" says that Ingolv brought with him the pillars of the high seat (ǫndvegissúlur), and when he came near the coast he threw them into the sea, and resolved to build his home where they should drift ashore, as he regarded this as a divine omen. He settled temporarily on the south coast, but the next year the pillars were found in Fakse Bay, on the west coast. Here he built a permanent home, calling the place Reykjavik (Smoky Bay), from some hot springs in the neighborhood. This became the site of the present city of Reykjavik, the capital of Iceland. The period of colonization, which began in 874, is considered to have lasted till 930, when about 20,000 people were dwelling in Iceland. The emigration from some districts in western Norway was so great that King Harald feared that the country would be depopulated, and collected a tax of five øre [1] from every one who sailed for Iceland, in order to check the movement. The loss to the country must be measured not only by the number, but also by the quality of the emigrants. They were generally the best families, both intellectually and economically the leaders in their communities. Vestlandet, which hitherto had been a center of strength, was so weakened that it never again recovered its former importance.

When Harald made his expedition against the Vikings in the western islands, a great number of those who had sought refuge there had to flee. They went to Iceland, and with them came a number of Irish and Scotch emigrants. Aud, the widow of Olav

Islands, Ágrip, efter Th. Thoroddsen, Copenhagen, 1900. C. Rosenberg, Træk af Livet paa Island i Fristadstiden. N. M. Petersen, Fortællinger om Islændernes Færd hjemme og ude. Fr. Winkel-Horn, Billeder af Livet paa Island. Valtýr Guðmundsson, Islands Kultur ved Aarhundredskiftet, Copenhagen, 1902. Jón Thorlaksson, Om Digtningen paa Island i det 15de og 16de Aarhundrede, Copenhagen, 1888. G. Storm, En Sommerreise paa Island, Christiania, 1883. P. E. Kristian Kålund, Bidrag til en historisk-topografisk Beskrivelse af Island, Copenhagen, 1877. Konrad Maurer, Island von seiner ersten Entdeckung bis zum Untergang des Freistaats, München, 1874. Konrad Maurer, Zur politischen Geschichte Islands, Leipzig, 1880.

[1] Øre (O. N. eyrir, plu. aurar) = $\frac{1}{8}$ mark = 3 ørtugar.
The mark was about $8.65, but money at that time had a much greater purchasing power than in our time. Gold was from sixteen to twenty-two times as valuable as at present.

the White, and her son Olav Feilan came from Scotland with a large company of Norse, Irish, and Scotch emigrants.[1] These *landnámsmænd*, or first settlers, who, as a rule, were men of wealth and power, came to Iceland with one or more ships, bringing with them their families, relatives, servants, slaves, cattle, household goods, and supplies of various sorts. After having selected a place of settlement, they took formal possession of a large tract of land extending from the mountains to the shore, passing fire around it to show that they had established ownership of it. Inside of this tract each freeman in the company received his allotment. The system of *odel* was not introduced in Iceland. The first settlers took such large tracts that those who came later complained that they had taken too much. King Harald Haarfagre was made arbitrator, and he decided that no one should take more land than he and his ship's crew could carry fire around in one day. The chieftains, who claimed large tracts of land by right of settlement and occupation, were an aristocracy who took possession of the soil, while the freemen, who, with their consent, settled in their *landnám* (the territory which they had taken), held only a secondary title. The chieftains generally built a temple (*hov*) near their home, and the people in the surrounding district became in religious matters a sort of congregation, with the *hov* as a center. The chieftain was priest, and managed, also, the administration of laws and public affairs. He was called *gode* (*goði*), and his office (*godord*) was hereditary. It corresponded to that of *herse* in Norway, and it is probable that the title of *gode* had also been used there. There were thirty-nine *godord*, or chieftains with rank of *gode*, in Iceland, and as no general government yet existed, the country was a collection of independent settlements. Each locality had its own laws, borrowed, no doubt, from the settlers' home district in Norway. But the necessity soon made itself felt of having a *thing*, or general government, where disputes might be settled. Thorstein Ingolvsson established the *thing* at Kjalarnes, which became a general court for many districts, but it was of little avail, as there existed no uniform system of laws. In 927 a man by the name of Ulvljot was sent to Norway to study the Norwegian laws. Aided by his uncle Thorleiv Spake, he pre-

---

[1] *Landnámabók*, part V., ch. 1.

pared a code based on the "Gulathingslov," and returned to Iceland in 930. A general *thing* for all Iceland, the *Althing* (O. N. Allsherjarþing), was now established, and Ulvljot's laws were adopted. This *thing* should meet every year at midsummer at Þingvellir, near the mouth of the river Øxará, in southern Iceland, for a period of two weeks. The *thing* consisted, in the beginning, of the *goder*, each of whom was accompanied by two men, making in all 108 members. The *Althing* was the highest court of justice, and it dealt also with the more important questions touching lawmaking and general administration. The power was placed in the hands of the *lagrette*, which was chosen by the *goder*. They also elected a *lovsigemand* (O. N. *lǫgsǫgumaðr*), who was the head of the *lagrette*, and whose duty it was to recite the laws to the assembled *thing*. This was of great importance at a time when the laws were not yet written, or read by the people in general.[1] The *lovsigemand* was elected for a term of three years, and his office was the highest in the country. He presided over the *thing*, but had no administrative functions. The country was divided into four districts, or quarters, each with its own *thing, fjórðungsþing*, and twelve minor *thing* districts were established, each having three *goder*. The northern district, or *fjórðung*, had four *thing* districts, making in all thirty-nine *godord*. The island had now become an organized state — a sort of federal republic with a central government created through election, but exercising very limited power, the greatest possible autonomy being retained by the local communities.

The fact that the early settlers in Iceland made King Harald Haarfagre the arbitrator in so important a question as the proper distribution of land shows that, although they had left Norway because of his tyranny, they still had confidence in his good judgment and sense of justice. They soon felt their dependence on the mother country, and sought to maintain close relations with it. They seem to have come to a friendly understanding with Harald, who was, evidently, planning to extend his authority over Iceland. It appears

---

[1] Konrad Maurer, *Island von seiner ersten Entdeckung bis zum Untergang des Freistaats.*

The old Icelandic laws have been preserved in a codex called *Grágás*, published by the Nordiske Literatur-Samfund in the series *Nordiske Oldskrifter*, Copenhagen, 1855

that they agreed to pay him the five øre tax (landøre) once for all for the privilege of coming and going between Iceland and Norway, and they probably acknowledged him as their overlord. In return for this, Harald granted them the right of self-government, and, also, the right of citizenship in Norway. When they came back to the mother country, they had the haulds-right (the right of a storbonde, or landed proprietor). They could join the king's hird; they could own and inherit property in Norway, and could bring suits in the Norwegian courts. Norway had become not only a united kingdom, but, in fact, an empire with extensive colonial possessions, including, besides the island groups mentioned, also Finmarken and Iceland; and later the Hebrides, Greenland, and Jæmtland were also added. The people in the colonies felt themselves united with the mother country, not only by the strong ties of kinship, language, laws, and customs, but also through commercial and economic interests, and by the privileges which were still theirs in the old home. They were still citizens of Norway, and took pride in recognizing the king and his court as the center of national life. The king came to be regarded by the colonists as the preserver of the strength and continuity of the whole Norwegian people. They felt how closely their life and history were bound up with that of the mother country, and the most complete history of the kings of Norway has been written by the Icelanders. The thriving colonies in Ireland, Scotland, and France must also be regarded as belonging to this "Greater Norway." The story of the Norwegian colonial empire forms, indeed, an instructive as well as an interesting chapter in colonial history.

26. FINMARKEN

The Norsemen had, from early times, occasionally visited Finmarken to trade with the Finns, and to fish and hunt along the coast, but little was known about the region till Ôhthêre explored it in King Harald Haarfagre's time. In 880 Ôhthêre went to England, where he joined King Alfred's court. He gave the English king, who was much interested in history and geography, an account of his voyage around the North Cape, and his exploration of Finland and Bjarmeland (the land of the Permians). When Alfred translated Orosius' history of the world,[1] he added a fuller description of the countries of northern Europe to this old author's scant and vague notices, and included also Ôhthêre's account of his explorations in the far North, as well as the account given by the Danish or English seafarer Wulfstan (Ulvsten) of his voyages in the Baltic Sea. The countries around the Baltic were quite well known already at that time, but Ôhthêre's voyage is of extraordinary interest and importance, being the first voyage of exploration into the arctic regions. King Alfred says in part:

"Ôhthêre said to his lord King Alfred that he dwelt farthest north of all Norsemen. He said that he dwelt on the northward side of the land by the western ocean. He said that the land stretched thence far to the northward, but it was all desolate, except in a few places where the Finns dwell in scattered groups, hunting in the summer and fishing in the winter in the ocean. He said that at one time he wished to find out how far the land extended northward, or if any people dwelt north of this desolate region. He sailed then northward along the land, so that he had the waste on the starboard, and the open sea on the larboard for three days. He was then as far north as the whalers ever go. He continued on his northward course as far as he could sail in three more days. There the land turned to the east,[2] or a bay projected into the land, he did not know which, but he knew that he there awaited wind from the west, or a little to the north, and he followed the land eastward as far as he could sail in four days. There he had to await winds from the north, because the shore turned southward, or a bay projected into the

---

[1] Paulus Orosius, a Christian presbyter, born in Spain in 390, wrote a work *Historiarum Adversus Paganos, Libri VII.*, in which he narrates the history of mankind from the creation of the world till 417 A.D., giving what brief notices he can of the countries which the Romans knew. He shows little knowledge, and emphasizes strongly the misery of the world in pagan times.

[2] P. A. Munch has discussed Finmarken's political and commercial relations with Norway from the earliest times in *Annaler for nordisk Oldkyndighed og Historie*, 1860, p. 336. Ôhthêre's account is found in Jacobus Langebek's *Scriptores Rerum Danicarum*, vol. II., p. 106 ff. A. Halvorsen, *Billeder av Livet i Finmarken i Fortid og Nutid*, 1911. Axel Magnus, *Samlinger til Finmarkens Historie*, 1889. Knud Leem, *Beskrivelse over Finmarkens Lapper.*

land, he did not know which.[1] He then sailed straight southward as far as he could sail for five days, and came to a big river;[2] and they sailed up the river, because they did not dare to sail past the river along the coast for fear of enemies, because the land was all inhabited on the other side of the river. He had not before found inhabited country since he left his own land. But all the time he had had on the starboard a waste, except some fishermen, fowlers, and hunters, and these were all Finns. The Permians (N. Bjarmer) had built their land well, but thither they did not dare to go. But the land of the Terfinns was a waste, except where hunters, fishermen, and fowlers were staying. The Permians told him much, both about their own and neighboring lands, but he did not know what was true, for he had not himself seen these lands. His chief object in making the voyage, besides exploring the country, was to find walrus, because these animals have very precious teeth (of which he brought the king a few), and their skin is very good for ship ropes. This whale is much smaller than other whales, for it is not above seven ells [3] long. But in his own country is the best whale fishery; there are whales which are forty-eight ells, and the largest are fifty ells. Of these he said he could kill sixty in two days with a crew of five men.

" He was very rich in the kind of property which constitutes their wealth, that is, in reindeer. When he came to the king, he owned six hundred tame animals; six of these were decoy animals. These are very dear among the Finns, for with them they catch the wild reindeer. He was among the foremost men in his country, still he had no more than twenty cows, twenty sheep, and twenty swine, and what little he plowed he plowed with horses. But their most precious possession was the tax paid them by the Finns. This tribute consisted of robes, feathers, whalebone, and ship ropes made of walrus hide or of sealskin. Each pays according to his rank. The person of the highest rank must pay fifteen marten skins, five reindeer robes, one bear skin, and ten ambra of feathers, and a mantle of bear skin or of otter skin, and two ship ropes, each sixty ells long, either of walrus hide or of sealskin."

---

[1] He had now rounded the North Cape and had reached the White Sea.
[2] The Dvina. The people dwelling on the other side of the river were the Permians (Bjarmer).   [3] O. N. *ǫln*, plu. *alnir*.

This account shows that the Norsemen carried on a lucrative trade in these northern regions, and that Finland had in part become a Norwegian dependency, since the Finns had to pay a yearly tribute. From Harald Haarfagre's time this trade became a royal monopoly which the king granted to his *sysselmænd* in Haalogaland. Ôhthêre's voyage opened a new trade route to the land of the Permians (called Bjarmeland by the Norsemen), which was one of the centers of the fur trade of the North. About 965, King Harald Graafeld made an expedition to the land of the Permians, and fought a battle with them on the banks of the Dvina, and from that time the whole of Finland and the Kola peninsula were under Norwegian rule. The fur trade with Finland and the Permians continued till in the thirteenth century.

27. NORMANDY AND THE NORMANS

The great Viking army, consisting chiefly of Danes, which had harried the Netherlands and the region about the Seine in northern France, suffered a great defeat in 891, and left France for England. In 896 it was again defeated by Alfred the Great, and a large part of the army disbanded and settled in East Anglia and Northumbria. A small band returned to the mouth of the Seine; this was constantly joined by other Viking forces, and a new army of invasion was soon formed, of which the Viking chieftain Rollo, or Rolv (Gange-Rolv), became the leader some time before 911. He was defeated in a campaign against Chartres, but the army was held ready for a new attack at any favorable moment. The king of France, Charles III., also called Charles the Simple, was too sorely troubled by rebellious nobles to bring an efficient force into the field against the Vikings. He probably pursued the best plan possible under the circumstances when he offered Rolv a large tract in northern France, and the hand of his daughter Gisela in marriage, on condition that he should swear fealty to the king of France and embrace Christianity. Rolv accepted the offer, and in 911 a treaty was concluded at Claire-sur-Epte by which he received the territory between the river Epte and the sea, a grant which the Norsemen interpreted to mean the lands between the Somme and the borders of Brittany. In the following year Rolv was baptized. The tract embraced in this new duchy of Normandy had been devastated by repeated Viking incursions, and many districts were almost depopulated, but Rolv, with the energy and talent for organization characteristic of the Vikings, soon established peace and order in his dominions. The land was parceled out among his followers, serfdom disappeared here a couple of centuries earlier than in the rest of France, agriculture began to flourish, and the population increased rapidly.[1] The cities were rebuilt, and trade and commerce developed as never before, so that Rouen, the capital of the province, soon became one of the great commercial centers of northern Europe. Rolv established the laws used in the Viking settlements elsewhere, and these were felt to be so wise and equitable that he was called the great lawgiver. He was harsh, but just, and his reign was long remembered as a period of prosperity and peace. He seems to have possessed the resolute will, the energy, and talent for government which characterized his descendants, the illustrious race of Norman dukes, kings, and crusaders. The story is told that the bishop requested Rolv to kiss the king's foot in token of his gratitude for having received so great a gift. But he answered: "Never will I bend the knee before the knees of any, and I will kiss the foot of none." He ordered one of his followers to kiss the king's foot, but the man did it so awkwardly that the king fell backward, and great merriment resulted.

The question as to Rolv's (O. N. Hrólfr), or Rollo's identity, whether he was a Dane or a Norseman, has been much discussed by historians and scholars in the North, ever since the sixteenth century. The earliest account of Rolv and the dukes of Normandy is a work written by Dudo of St. Quintin,[2] completed about 1015. Dudo says that Rollo's father was a great chieftain in Dacia who had

[1] See Leopold Delisle, *Étude sur la Condition de la Classe Agricole et l'État de l'Agriculture en Normandie.*

[2] Dudonis S. Quintini Decani, *De Moribus et Actes Normannorum*, found in Duchesnius' *Historiae Normannorum Scriptores Antiqui.* Wace's rhymed chronicle, *Le Roman de Rou*, and Benoit de Sainte More's *La Chronique des Ducs de Normandie*, follow Dudo's account.

In the sagas, the Norman dukes are called Rudejarls (from Ruda = Rouen). *Chronicon de Gestis Normannorum in Francia*, Jacobus Langebek, *Scriptores Rerum Danicarum*, tom. II.

never bent his knee before a king, therefore, the king hated him, and at his death attacked his dominions and his two sons Rollo and Gorm. Rollo had to flee, and went first to the island of Scandza (Scandinavia). Later he came to England and Friesland, and, finally, to France. Later Danish historians, as Worsaae,[1] Fabricius,[2] and, especially, Steenstrup,[3] have sought to prove that Dacia is the same as Denmark, that Rollo was a Dane, and that he is not the same person as Rolv, or Gange-Rolv.[4] The Norse sagas have preserved another tradition, according to which Rolv, or Rollo, was a Norwegian, the son of Ragnvald Mørejarl, the friend of King Harald Haarfagre. The "Fagrskinna"[5] says: "Gange-Rolv Jarl was the son of Ragnvald Mørejarl, and a brother of Jarl Thore Tegjande, and of Torv-Einar in the Orkneys." "Harald Haarfagre's Saga" in the "Heimskringla"[6] says that Ragnvald Mørejarl had the sons Rolv and Thore with his wife Hild. But he had also some bastard sons, among them Torv-Einar. Rolv was a great Viking, and was so big that no horse could carry him, and he was, therefore, called Gange-Rolv (Rolv the Walker). One summer, coming from a Viking expedition in the East, he ravaged a district in Viken (the district around the Christianiafjord). This aroused King Harald's wrath, and he banished him. Rolv then went to the Hebrides (Sudreyjar), and thence to northern France (Valland), where he won for himself a great jarldom, since called Normandy. From him descended the dukes of Normandy.

The Norwegian historians P. A. Munch, E. Sars, and, especially, G. Storm and Alexander Bugge, uphold the account of Rolv given in the sagas, and maintain that it must be accepted as true in its main features.[7] They have shown that Dudo is very unreliable, that he considers Dacia to be the Dacia of the ancients, and that he uses Daci as a name to designate both Danes and Norsemen. It is

---

[1] *Den danske Erobring af England og Normandi.*
[2] *Danske Minder i Normandiet.*   [3] *Normannerne.*
[4] This view has also been taken by Walter Vogel in his work *Die Normannen und das fränkische Reich*, 1906.   [5] *Fagrskinna*, 142–143.
[6] *Heimskringla, Harald Haarfagre's Saga*, ch. 24. Also *Laxdølasaga*, ch. 32.
[7] The same view is held by Sophus Bugge, Konrad Maurer, and Finnur Jónsson.

also noteworthy that Rolv, or Rollo, is not mentioned by Saxo Grammaticus, or any other old Danish writer. Alexander Bugge, who has lately published the results of his thorough researches touching this question, makes the significant remark that the trouble has been that in the discussion of the question the two accounts have been placed over against each other, and the question has been, "which one is true?" whereas the effort must be made to explain both in the light of Viking history. This he has done with a lucidity and thoroughness which leaves little doubt that Rolv and Rollo are the same person, and that the first duke of Normandy was the Rolv, or Gange-Rolv, the son of Ragnvald Mørejarl, spoken of in the sagas. That Rolv and Rollo are the same name cannot be doubted, says Bugge. William the Conqueror's standard-bearer in the battle of Hastings was called Turstinus (Torstein), son of Rollo, and he is also called Turstinus, son of Rolv (filius Rolv). Rollo is also called Rolus. Bugge shows that the Norsemen founded colonies in the island of Noirmoutier, and in the region by the mouth of the Loire in western France. This is also admitted by Steenstrup.[1] Hasting, son of Atle Jarl of Fjalafylke, in southern Norway, has already been mentioned as the great chief of the Loire Vikings and the leader of the expedition against Rome. Dudo devotes the first book of his chronicle to Hasting, and describes him as the one who began the conquest of Normandy. The chronicler

[1] Alexander Bugge, *Gange-Rolv og Erobringen av Normandie*, *Historisk Tidsskrift*, femte række, vol. I., p. 160 ff.

Morgenbladet, March 25, 1911, *Gange-Rolv og Erobringen av Normandie*, Alexander Bugge; also *Morgenbladet*, April 4, 1911, Bugge. Lecture by Professor Ebbe Hertzberg of the Library of Public Documents, before the Historical Society, Christiania, March 30, 1911.

Bugge cites an interview in *Berlingske Tidende*, in which Steenstrup says: "We Danes also know that when Normandy fell under Danish rule it was because the Norsemen had attacked the Frankish kingdom, especially from the Loire region, so that finally the Frankish king was compelled to cede the Seine province to the Danes 'as a protection for the kingdom,' as it was termed."

That the Vikings on Noirmoutier and the Loire were Norsemen is seen also from a Viking grave recently found on the island of Groix, near the south coast of Brittany. Among other relics found were the remains of a boat in which the person had been buried. The archæologist G. Gustafson has shown that this mode of burial was practised by the Norsemen, but that it was unknown in Denmark.

Adamar of Chabannais (988–1030) also makes it appear that the conquest of Normandy was begun by the Loire Vikings, first under Baard, and later under Hasting. William of Malmesbury,[1] who wrote about 1120, mentions Hasting, and after him Rollo, as the leaders of the Vikings who conquered Normandy. He says that the leaders of the Normans were "first Hasting, and, soon after, Rollo, who descended from a noble family among the Norsemen; but its name had in course of time been forgotten; he was outlawed at the king's command, and left his native country with many who were outlawed and in debt, and who had joined him in the hope of better times. This account, written before Snorre's "Heimskringla," or the "Fagrskinna," agrees with the saga narrative. After the defeat in 891, the "Great Army" left France for England, as has already been stated. That Hasting and the Norse Vikings also joined it on this expedition seems certain, for shortly afterwards Hasting is found fighting in England against Alfred the Great, who finally defeated the whole Viking army in 896. The greater part of the army then disbanded, but a part returned to France. This part consisted of the Norsemen under Hasting. The Old English St. Neots' chronicle, written in the twelfth century, but based on still older Frankish annals which have been lost, states that Hasting sailed across the sea "without gain and without honor," and, after having lost many of his followers, he reached the mouth of the Seine. After Hasting one by the name of Hundeus, or Huncdeus, became leader of these Vikings at the mouth of the Seine. Sophus Bugge has shown that Hundeus is the very rare name Huntjov (O. N. Hunþjófr), found in Norway, but not in Denmark. He seems to have been a relative of the King Huntjov of Nordmør, who fought the battle of Solskjel against King Harald Haarfagre. The Frankish king, Charles the Simple, negotiated with Hundeus and his Vikings, and in 897 an armistice was concluded, and the Vikings went into winter quarters at the mouth of the Loire. This shows that they came from the Loire colonies, and that they were Norsemen. In 910 Rollo appeared as the leader of the Vikings at the mouth of the Seine, and the following year King Charles the Simple ceded to him the district which

---

[1] An early English historian. His principal work is *De Gestis Regum Anglorum*, a history of the kings of England from the Saxon invasion till 1127.

was later called Normandy.[1] Professor Bugge shows that it is a Norman as well as a Norse tradition that Rollo was a Norseman. The Old English laws, known as the laws of Edward the Confessor, state that "King William the Conqueror said that the ancestors of nearly all the Norman barons came from Norway." These laws were written in 1130, and the words quoted show that the Norman kings regarded themselves as descendants of the Norsemen. All scholars agree that the Danes settled in Normandy in great numbers, but they seem to have arrived after the conquest was completed.[2] Gustav Storm has shown that the old Danish writers have not preserved a single tradition about the colonization of Normandy by the Danes, but that the Roskilde Chronicle states that *Nordmanni* plundered Gaul, and that for fear of them King Charles of Francia granted them lands to inhabit which they still possess. And Ebbe Hertzberg states that if the colonists in Normandy had been Danes, they would not have called themselves Normans, or Northmen, but Danes.[3]

When Rolv died in 931, he was succeeded by his son William Longsword, who had been reared in the Christian faith by his French mother. Paganism was disappearing in Normandy, though many of the settlers still clung to the faith and customs of their ancestors. The Bayeux district, which had been settled almost exclusively by the followers of Rolv, and by later emigrants from Scandinavia, was, especially, a Norse center. The people of this district retained their Norse speech and culture for many generations. They used old pagan devices on their shields, and in going into battle they would raise the old warcry, "Thor aide!" William Longsword's son and successor was Richard the Fearless, whose daughter Emma married King Knut the Great of Denmark and England in 1017. His son,

[1] The name *Normandy* came into use about the year 1000. It is found in an old document from 1025.

[2] Professor Fridtjof Nansen has shown quite conclusively in a spirited discussion with Professor Steenstrup that whale fishery was carried on by the Normans on the coasts of Normandy in the same manner as along the coast of Norway, and that the methods and technical expressions used by the Normans were distinctly Norwegian. See *Nationaltidende,* April 24 and 29, 1911. *Tidens Tegn,* April 29, 1911.

[3] Ebbe Hertzberg, *Traditionen om Gange-Rolf, Historisk Tidsskrift,* femte række, vol. I., p. 197 ff.

Duke Richard III., also called Richard the Good, was William the Conqueror's grandfather. Sometime before the conquest of Normandy the Vikings had settled in the Channel Islands; Jersey, Guernsey, Chansey, and Alderney, the only islands on the French coast which still have the Norse termination *ey* (island). Jules Lair [1] has shown that Rolv received from the king of France the whole of present Normandy, and that Brittany became a dependency under the overlordship of the Norman dukes. Before many generations had passed, the Viking settlers accepted Christianity, and with it the French language and Christian culture; but their names, both personal and geographical, still showed their Northern origin, and many of these are still in use. [2] Their laws and social institutions were long preserved. They introduced into Normandy their own system of private ownership of land, and feudalism was not established there till in the eleventh century. Here, as in the North, the laws were unwritten. Decisions were made according to common practice, which was proclaimed at the *thing* by a *crieur* (*lovsigemand*). These old laws were collected in *le Vieux* or *le Grand Coutumier*, in 1270–1280. They were in use till in the sixteenth century, when they were, in great part, replaced by the Roman law. Both in spirit and in appearance the Normans retained their Northern traits, which even at the present time characterize the people of Normandy. [3] They were tall and well built, with blonde hair and blue eyes. Frequently over-jealous of their own personal independence and honor, they were often quarrelsome, revengeful, and hard to govern; but they were honest and hospitable, loved adventure, and excelled in

[1] Lair, *Étude sur Dudon*, p. 58.

[2] As examples may be mentioned the names of the cities: *Quetteville, Teurteville, Toqueville, Tourgeville, Toutainville, Tremauville, Trouville,* and *Turqueville.* According to old documents the older forms were: *Ketilsvilla, Torquetelvilla, Tokevilla, Turgisvilla, Turstenivilla, Tormotvilla, Turulfivilla,* and *Torclevilla,* from the personal names Ketil, Torketil, Toke, Torgils, Torstein, Tormod, Torolf, and Torkil. Worsaae, *Den danske Erobring af England og Normandiet,* p. 179.

[3] "If one, on leaving Paris, suddenly finds himself, after a few hours' ride on the train, in the middle of Normandy, he will be surprised to see the remarkable change in the racial type, and to see the Northern traits so prominent in these strong, well-built, blonde, and blue-eyed people." Fabricius, *Danske Minder i Normandiet,* p. 156. See also Amélie Bosquet, *Normandie illustrée,* and Worsaae, *Den danske Erobring af England og Normandiet.*

ship-building.[1] Neither Christianity nor their own homes in pleasant and fertile Normandy could eradicate their bent for war and travel. Trading expeditions and pilgrimages to the Holy Land offered opportunities for some diversion of this kind, till the crusades, knight-errantry, and a new series of conquests made the old spirit blaze forth in new martial achievements. In 1016 forty tall and handsome Norman pilgrims returning from Palestine landed in southern Italy, where the Greeks and Lombards were fighting, and where the Arabs, who had conquered Sicily, were plundering. The Viking pilgrims helped Gaimar of Salerno to drive the Arabs away from his dominions. When he learned that these brave men were from Normandy, he sent messengers to induce more Norman warriors to come to Italy. Soon well-equipped fleets were headed for southern Italy, where new fields were found for warlike enterprise. The Normans gained permanent foothold by taking a castle in the swamps of Campania, and, also, the castle Aversa la Normanna. Soon the whole of Apulia and Calabria was in their hands, and Sicily was also taken. They also extended their conquests to the shores across the Adriatic. In 1082 Robert Guiscard took a large part of Albania, and his son, Bohemund, continued the conquest.[2] Many of the chieftains fighting in southern Italy had Norse names; as, Asmund Drengot, Anqvetil, Rolf, Thorstein, and Stig. William Iron Arm, one of Tancred of Hauteville's twelve sons, became Count of Venossa and Apulia, in 1042, and Roger, another son, became ruler of Sicily. William's successors were his three brothers: Drogo (1046), Humphrey (1051), and Robert Guiscard (1057). These warrior knights, and others of their kind, like William the Conqueror, and the great crusaders, Robert of Normandy, Bohemund of Tarent, and his nephew Tancred, were types of Norman knights of the eleventh century. Also in Norman literature the old Viking spirit continued

---

[1] Many Norse loan-words in French naval terminology bear witness to the influence exerted by the Norsemen on the naval development of France: *bateau* (bátr), *esturman* (stýrimaðr), *esneque* (snekkja), *matelot* (mǫtunautr = a comrade), etc.

[2] Colonel H. Angell writes in *Aftenposten* of Nov. 26, 1912, in a correspondence from Albania: "In the public library at Podgoritza I found in an Italian book much about the history of the city under the Normans. The city, like the whole Albanian coast, was at one time in their hands."

to live and express itself, especially in the historic, epic romances of the *trouvers*, the somber and ponderous *chansons de gestes*, in which, as in the sagas and the scaldic songs, great events and heroic deeds form the great theme.

28. THE NORSE COLONIES IN GREAT BRITAIN AND IRELAND

The defeat and death of Olav the White, and the unification of Norway after the battle in the Hafrsfjord in 872, weakened the Viking power in the West. If recruited only in the colonies, their armies could not long maintain their old efficiency. Hitherto they had depended on the mother country for the supply of new forces, but these could not easily be obtained after the whole country was once united under King Harald's rule. The peoples in whose countries the Norsemen were such unwelcome visitors had also learned many valuable lessons in ship-building and military tactics during a hundred years of almost incessant warfare. They were now able to put well-equipped and organized armies in the field against the Vikings, who were the more vulnerable because they had occupied large districts where they now dwelt in permanently established homes. Henceforth their campaigns would require defensive, as well as offensive, tactics.

Olav the White, son of the king of Vestfold in Norway, came to Ireland in 853, where he became king of the Vikings. The struggle between the Norsemen and the Danes in the colonies, which had begun in 848, was still going on, but when Ivar Boneless, the son of the Danish Viking chieftain Ragnar Lodbrok, soon after arrived in Ireland, he and Olav became friends and allies, and peace was made between the Danes and the Norsemen in 856. The two kings coöperated both in Ireland and in Scotland, and we are told that in 870–871 they returned together from a campaign in England, Scotland, and Wales with a fleet of 200 vessels, and with many prisoners of war. When Olav died on his expedition to Norway in 872, Ivar continued to rule as king of Ireland, together with Olav's son Eystein.[1] Ivar died in 873, and Eystein, who was yet young, became

---

[1] It has been held that Ivar was a brother of Olav, but Alexander Bugge holds that he was Ivar Boneless, the son of Ragnar Lodbrok. Alexander Bugge, *Norges Historie*, vol. I., 2, p. 292.

king under the guardianship of the Norse Viking chieftain Baard Jarl. Dublin was now attacked by Halvdan, another son of Ragnar Lodbrok, who has already been mentioned as the founder of the kingdom of York, in 876. After having ruled in York about a year, he was expelled by his own subjects, and he sought to mend his fortunes by gaining possession of his brother's throne at Dublin. The young King Eystein was treacherously murdered, and the fight between Norsemen and Danes was renewed, in which also Halvdan lost his life in 877. Ten years later the sons of Ivar Boneless had gained control of Dublin, but ceaseless strife had so far weakened both factions that in 902 King Cerbalh of Leinster attacked and captured the city. The Viking power in Ireland was for a time overthrown, and many Norsemen emigrated to Cumberland and Northumbria.

In 914 the Vikings began a new conquest of Ireland; both Norsemen and Danes now united under new leaders, Ragnvald and Sigtrygg, of the family of Ivar Boneless, and the Norse jarls Baard and Ottar. A great fleet under Ragnvald and Ottar came to Waterford (O. N. Veðrafjǫrdr), and, in the battle of Cennfuait, which took place soon after, the united forces of the kings of Munster and Leinster, and King Niall, high-king of Ireland, were completely defeated; even the archbishop of Armagh was among the slain. Another army was led by King Sigtrygg against Dublin. In 919 a decisive battle was fought at Cilmashogue. The Irish army was defeated, the high-king, Niall, fell, and the Vikings again seized Dublin, and reëstablished their control over the districts which they had before held. In Limerick another Viking kingdom arose, with Baard Jarl and his sons as rulers.

The Dublin dynasty became rulers also over the kingdom of York. While Sigtrygg became king of Dublin, Ragnvald succeeded to the Yorkish throne. In 912 he conquered Bernecia and the northern part of Northumbria. In 920 Sigtrygg left Dublin on a Viking expedition to southern England. On the death of Ragnvald, which probably occurred in 921, he was made king of York. Sigtrygg's two sons were Gudrød[1] and Olav Kvaaran (the sandal). Gudrød ruled as king of Dublin till 934, and was succeeded, first by his son Olav Gudrødsson, and later by a second son, Blakar. But more

[1] This name is written also Godred, Godfred, Gothfraid.

famous than all of them was Olav Kvaaran, one of the most conspicuous and romantic figures in Viking history.

29. The Fall of the Kingdom of York

The last four years of King Alfred the Great's reign (887–900) seem to have been peaceful. The "Great Army" had disbanded, Hasting had retired into France, and the Vikings showed no disposition to renew their attacks on Wessex. When King Alfred died, his son Edward was chosen king by the Witan, but Æthelwald, a son of Alfred's elder brother Æthelred, attempted to make good his claim to the throne. He was unable to cope with Edward, but fled to York, where he was hailed as king. This meant a renewal of war between the Danelag and the king of Wessex. King Æthelwald came southward to Essex with a large Northumbrian fleet, and was joined by the Danes of East Anglia under their king, Eirik. Mercia was ravaged, and the combined forces crossed the Thames into Wiltshire, in Wessex. In the meantime Edward had marched northward, and attacked the Danish settlements. This compelled Æthelwald to return to defend his own dominions. A battle was soon fought, in which Æthelwald and Eirik both fell, and a treaty of peace terminated the war in 903. In 910 hostilities were renewed, and Edward and his sister Æthelflæd undertook to conquer the whole Danelag. The building of fortified strongholds, or burghs, which had been introduced by the Vikings, became a great feature in this war. Æthelflæd built a number of burghs along the borders, and the conquest was pushed steadily forward. By 919, the chronicle tells us, King Edward was acknowledged as overlord by King Ragnvald of York, by Donald, king of the Welsh in Strathchlyde, by Ealdred of Bamborough, and even by Constantine, king of the Scots. Whether these kings really submitted to Edward may well be doubted, but Mercia was joined permanently to Edward's possessions. Edward died in 924, and was succeeded by his son Æthelstan, then over thirty years of age. King Sigtrygg of York acknowledged himself the vassal of the new king, and received his sister in marriage, but he died the following year, and Æthelstan formally annexed Northumbria. The kings of Strathchlyde and Scotland

and many princes of Wales submitted to Æthelstan, who now called himself *Rex totius Britanniae.* Olav Kvaaran, the son of King Sigtrygg, who had been living in Scotland, planned to recapture his father's kingdom. He gathered a large armament from all parts of the Viking dominions for an attack on Northumbria. His father-in-law, King Constantine III. of Scotland, joined him, Olav Gudrødsson of Dublin came with a large fleet; from the Orkneys, the Hebrides, and even from Brittany forces were gathered. In 937 he sailed up the Humber with a large fleet, and captured York. But King Æthelstan and his half-brother Edmund also gathered their forces, and many Norse Vikings joined the standards of the English king; among others, the great scald Egil Skallagrimsson from Iceland, and his brother Thoralv.[1] The latter fell in the great combat which Egil has described in his songs. The armies met at Brunanburh, or Vinheid, as Egil calls it, and here was fought one of the most renowned battles in Viking times. From morning till evening the bloody struggle lasted. Five kings and seven Viking jarls are said to have fallen. King Æthelstan was finally victorious. Olav Gudrødsson of Dublin fled back to Ireland with the remnant of his army, and King Constantine returned to Scotland. An old English poet has described the battle in a well-known old song.

30. "THE BATTLE OF BRUNANBURH"

"Here King Æthelstan, lord of earls,
warriors' ring-giver, and also his brother,
Edward the ætheling, life-long glory
gained in battle with the edge of the sword
by Brunanburh. They split the shield wall,
they hewed the war shields with hammered swords,
the sons of Edward; such was their noble nature
from their ancestors, that they in battle oft
'gainst every foe the land defended,
hoards and homes. The foe they crushed,

---

[1] The *Egilssaga*, ch. 40–45 and 54–56, tells how Egil and Thoralv, with 300 men, joined King Æthelstan, and rendered him important service in the battle. Æthelstan, who was a friend of King Harald Haarfagre, seems to have maintained cordial relations with the Norsemen, probably for the purpose of obtaining their aid in these wars.

the Scots fell and the army of seamen,
marked for death. The field grew slippery
with warriors' blood, from the time that the sun rose
at morning tide, that the glorious star
glided over the world, God's bright candle,
the eternal Lord's, and until the noble luminary
sank to its setting. There lay many a man
hurt with the sword, Northern warriors,
shot over the shields, and also Scotchmen,
weary of warfare. The West-Saxons
throughout the day, in chosen bands,
pursued eagerly the hated enemy,
hewed from behind the fugitives from battle,
with sharpened swords. The Mercians refused not
the hard hand play with any hero
who with Anlafe (Olav) over the billowy ocean,
on the ships' bosom sought this land,
to meet their death. Five kings
lay dead upon the battlefield,
put to sleep with swords, and, also, seven
of Anlafe's earls, and countless numbers
of Scotch and seamen.[1] Put to flight
was the chief of the Northmen, forced by necessity
to seek the ship's prow with a small band.
The ship drove afloat: the king departed,
on the dark sea he saved his life.

*　　　*　　　*　　　*　　　*　　　*

The Northmen departed on their nailed barks,
bloody leavings of the spears, Dublin to seek,
and afterward Ireland, much ashamed."

In the battle of Brunanburh the power of the kingdom of York was broken. Æthelstan died in 940, and was succeeded by his half-brother Edmund, who had taken a prominent part in the great battle. The Vikings rose again in rebellion, and chose Olav Gud-rødsson of Dublin king of York. Edmund consented to recognize him as king, but he had to receive baptism, and do homage to Edmund. His reign was short, as he attacked Bernicia, where he met his death

[1] Seamen, or sailors, means Norsemen.

in 942. The same year Edmund subdued the "Five Boroughs," and annexed them to the English kingdom. During the period 890–920 the Norse Vikings had settled Cumberland, which appears to have been a sort of vassal state under the kings of Dublin and York. It seems that Edmund attacked Cumberland in 944, drove away Olav Kvaaran, who ruled there, and turned this state over to King Malcolm III. of Scotland. The growing weakness of the Viking colonies, which led to the fall of the kingdom of York, manifested itself also in Ireland. King Blakar had succeeded his brother Olav Gudrødsson on the throne, but he was driven from Dublin by the Irish king Congelach. The houses of the Norsemen were plundered, their property destroyed, and many women and children were carried into slavery. When Blakar attempted to recapture the city, he fell, together with a number of his men.

After his defeat at Brunanburh Olav Kvaaran led a roving life, spending some time in Scotland and Cumberland, but he seems to have returned to Northumbria, and to have ruled there as king of York from 949 till 952. This can be seen from a number of coins bearing the inscription, *Anlaf Cununc M.*, ✠ *Anlaf Cununc*, ✠ *Onlaf Rex, etc.* His successor as king of Northumbria was Eirik, no doubt Eirik Blood-Ax, son of King Harald Haarfagre.[1] Olav Kvaaran must have been driven away again from Northumbria. In 952 he seized Dublin, where he married an Irish princess, and joined the Irish Church. He extended his sway over a great part of Ireland, and ruled till 980, when he was defeated in the battle of Tara by King Maelsechnaill of Tara, in Meath. Old and gray-haired, he departed from Ireland on a pilgrimage to Iona, where he died as monk in 981.

Olav Kvaaran is, in many ways, a typical representative of the Viking character of that period. These Viking kings did not persecute the Christians, but sought to gain the influence and good will of the church. In religious matters they were generally indifferent, as they had long since ceased to believe in the old gods, without having acquired the Christian faith and spirit. Christianity had, however, exercised a great influence upon them. It had softened their hearts and tempered their fierce spirit. The preparation for

[1] Alexander Bugge, *Vesterlandenes Indflydelse*, p. 283 ff.

their final conversion to the Christian faith had been made, and during the last half of the tenth century most of the colonists seem to have joined the Christian Church.

31. THE LAST YEARS OF KING HARALD HAARFAGRE'S REIGN

Polygamy, which was quite common among the Vikings, was practiced, also, by King Harald. During his long life he was married many times, and, especially in his younger years, he had a number of wives, and raised a large family of sons and daughters. The sagas say that he had twenty sons; the "Historia Norwegiae" says sixteen. When he became king of all Norway, he wooed Ragnhild, daughter of King Eirik of Denmark, but she would not marry him unless he put away his other wives. This he consented to do, and she became his queen. She bore him the son Eirik, later known as Eirik Blood-Ax, but died within three years after her marriage. The story is told that in his old age Harald fell in love with a Finnish maiden, Snefrid, whom he married. He loved her to such a degree that he neglected his kingdom, and when she died, he sat by her bier day and night for three years, because her face retained its natural color and beauty. This story undoubtedly came to Norway from the British Isles, but Harald must have had a queen by that name, since Snefrid's sons are historic persons.[1]

In 912 Harald assembled a *thing* at Eidsvold, where he gave his sons the royal title, and divided the whole realm among them. A couple of years before his death he made his son Eirik Blood-Ax over-king, not because he was the oldest, but because he was of royal blood also on the mother's side. By introducing such a system of an over-king and several subordinate kings, an arrangement hitherto wholly unknown in Norway, and clearly an imitation of Charlemagne's and Louis the Pious' plan of succession, King Harald destroyed his own great work. The unity of the kingdom of Norway was sacrificed, and the new principle of equal inheritance produced here, as in the Frankish empire, endless bloodshed and confusion.

[1] Halvdan Koht, *Harald Haarfagre's Sønner, Historisk Tidsskrift*, fjerde række, vol. II., part 2, p. 242. Sophus Bugge, *Mythiske Sagn om Halvdan Svarte og Harald Haarfagre, Arkiv for nordisk Filologi*, 1900, p. 1 ff.

At the time of his death, the great king was over eighty years old. Are Frode, in the "Íslendingabók," says that he died in 933, but the year cannot be fixed with certainty. He was buried at Haugar, near the present city of Haugesund, in southwestern Norway, and a great mound was raised over his grave. On this mound a stately monument was erected in 1872.

32. EIRIK BLOOD-AX

To rule successfully as over-king over a number of jealous and ambitious kings of inferior rank, who had an equally good claim to the throne, would, probably, have been beyond the power of the wisest and most moderate of sovereigns; for Eirik Blood-Ax even a less difficult task might have been impossible. The "Fagrskinna" describes him as follows: "King Eirik was tall and well-built, courageous and good looking. He was surly and taciturn, covetous and reckless, but a great and very successful warrior." These are traits which would be more commendable in a Viking chieftain than in a king of Norway. He married Gunhild, daughter of King Gorm of Denmark. The sagas say that she was beautiful and dignified, though not very tall; she was cunning, talkative, and evil-minded.[1] Tradition has made her a veritable Lady Macbeth in Norwegian history; a crafty and ambitious woman, a daughter of Assur Tote of Haalogaland, reared among the Finns, who were masters of witchcraft.[2] History places her in a different light. She appears as the faithful wife and good mother, a gifted and heroic woman, who clung to her husband in evil days, as in good. She governed her sons; she was their constant adviser, and kept them united under all difficulties. So great an influence did she exercise over them that they were always known as the sons of Gunhild. But it is more than likely that a woman so gifted and energetic, a princess of an old royal family, might be haughty and overbearing as queen of Norway, and that, when trouble came, she would fight for her throne, her husband, and her sons with all the intrigues and secret weapons which she, as woman, could command. Eirik tried to continue the system of government established by Harald, but his brothers re-

---

[1] *Fagrskinna*, p. 14.   [2] *Heimskringla, Harald Haarfagre's Saga*, ch. 33.

fused to submit to him. Halvdan, king in Trøndelagen, severed all connections with him, and Olav became independent king in Viken. Halvdan died soon, and people claimed that Queen Gunhild had hired a sorceress to poison him. He was succeeded by Sigfrød, another son of Harald, who formed an alliance with King Olav against Eirik, but they were defeated and slain. Sigurd, the son of Jarl Haakon Grjotgardsson, was now jarl in Trøndelagen, residing at Lade. He did not wish to submit to King Eirik, but sent for Haakon, a younger son of Harald, to come to Norway. Haakon, who was reared at the court of King Æthelstan of England, is known as Haakon Adelstensfostre, and, also, as Haakon the Good. He promised to restore to the people their right of *odel*, *i.e.* to do away with that feature of Harald's system of government which was regarded as especially oppressive. This aroused the greatest enthusiasm, and he was hailed as king at the Ørething in Trøndelagen. Oplandene and Viken joined him, and the following spring he advanced southward with a large fleet. Few remained faithful to the unpopular Eirik, and he left Norway without even attempting to resist his successful rival. Haakon was made king over all Norway, and became the real successor of King Harald.

After Eirik left Norway, he spent several years on Viking expeditions. The scald Guttorm Sindre says that he was a great sea-king, who won gold with the sword in Scotland and elsewhere. In 948 he came to Northumbria,[1] where he was made king, but the people, who feared the wrath of King Eadred, the successor of Edmund, forced him to leave, and chose Olav Kvaaran king. He ruled till 952, when he was driven away, and Eirik again became king of York. Coins have been found bearing on the front side the inscription Ericus Rex, and on the back side the name of the city of York. These had, evidently, been coined by Eirik while he was king of York. He extended his sway over a great part of Northumbria, and it appears that he was baptized, and that he acknowledged King Eadred as his overlord.

An incident occurred while Eirik ruled at York which gives some

---

[1] The sagas state that he left Norway in 935, two years after King Harald's death, but this reckoning must be erroneous. See *Caithreim Cellachain Caisil*, edited with translation and notes by Alexander Bugge, p. 148.

ground for the opinion that he was, probably, better than his reputation. The "Egilssaga" tells us that the great scald Egil Skallagrimsson and King Eirik were bitter enemies. Once when Egil came sailing from Iceland, he was shipwrecked on the coast of Northumbria, and was taken prisoner by King Eirik, who, according to custom, would have had him executed. But during the night, Egil composed a song in praise of the king. The next morning Egil was allowed to recite his song before Eirik, who was so moved that he granted the scald his life, and permitted him to depart unharmed. The poem is called "Hǫfuðlausn" (the ransom of the head).

In 954 King Eirik was driven from Northumbria. He again turned Viking, gathered an army in Ireland, in the Orkneys, and the Hebrides, and attempted to regain his throne. But in Westmoreland he met an army under Oswulf of Bamborough and Maccus Olavsson. A fierce battle was fought, in which Eirik fell, and York ceased to be a distinct Viking kingdom.[1] Jarls continued, however, to rule in York and Northumbria, and they often owed but slight submission to the kings of England.

In the tenth century a stream of Norse emigrants from Ireland and the Hebrides poured into England. These new settlers were especially numerous in Cumberland, Westmoreland, and Northumbria. Anglesey, on the coast of Wales, was settled by Norsemen, and bears still its Norse name. Chester, which had long been in ruins, was seized and rebuilt, and became an important commercial town. The Danes and Norsemen, at first two distinct peoples, rapidly merged on English soil into one foreign element. In the twelfth century they still spoke their own Northern tongue, the Norse laws were still in use in the districts where they had settled, and the people maintained a democratic government. All freeborn men able to bear arms met at the *thing*, where they elected the king or ruler, and adopted the laws which were proposed. The *alls herjar mót*, or meeting of the armed host, was the general *thing*, but there were also local *things* in each shire, triding, wapentake, and

---

[1] The ever faithful Gunhild caused a scald to compose a song in memory of her husband. It is called the *Eiriksmál*, and describes the preparations made in Valhal for the reception of the great warrior. It is one of the finest songs in scaldic poetry, but only a fragment of it has been preserved. See *Fagrskinna*.

hundred. In the division of the country into smaller administrative districts, northern England still shows traces of Viking influence. Yorkshire and York are still divided into ridings, a later corruption of the Old Danish, or Old Norse, *thrithing* or *triding*, as each *thinglag* in Iceland, and elsewhere in the North, was divided into three *tridings* or districts, each with its own *gode*.

Personal liberty was highly prized by the Vikings, and, although they kept slaves, and were great slave traders in early days, slavery died out earlier in the Danelag than elsewhere in England. In the "Domesday Book" only 2524 slaves are recorded for the Danelag, while southern England had 25,156 male and 467 female slaves, or ten times as many. In Lincolnshire and Yorkshire there was not a single slave at the time of the Domesday survey. A. Bugge says : "As soon as the Vikings settled in England they began to give their freed slaves land to till. In the treaty of peace between Guttorm and King Alfred, the Viking freedmen (*leisinger*) were considered equal to the Anglo-Saxon ceorls, or peasants, who were renters. That the two classes, the freedmen and the ceorls, were considered equal, shows the contrast between Viking and Anglo-Saxon society. The freedman had been a slave, but he rose to personal freedom and a better social condition. The ceorl was a freeborn man whose ancestors had wielded the sword in the conquest of Britain. But gradually his condition grew worse; he had ceased to own lands, and he was about to lose his personal freedom. Then came the Viking period, and arrested the development of large estates, and planted in the conquered districts a large class of freemen. What difference is there not in the 'Domesday Book' between Cornwall with its 1160 slaves, its more or less dependent 2355 *bordari*, and its 1730 *villani*, who, in the records, are placed even below the slaves ; or Devonshire, where there were 4847 *bordari*, 3294 slaves (*servi*), and 8070 *villani*, named after the slaves, and no freemen, save the citizens of the towns, the vassals, and the subvassals; and Lincolnshire with 11,503 freeborn *sochemanni* (freeholders), as against 4024 *bordarii* and 7723 *villani;* or Norfolk with its 4277 freemen (*libri homines*), and 4571 *sochemanni*, as against 9537 *bordarii*, 4656 *villani*, and not more than 995 slaves; and Suffolk, where one-half of the rural population were freeholders.

" When the condition of the rural population in England, even in the darkest days of the Middle Ages, was better than in France and Germany, it was due to the Danes and Norsemen, who brought with them to England their love of personal rights and liberty, and to their kinsmen, the Christian and French-speaking Normans." [1]

33. HAAKON THE GOOD

By raising Haakon to the throne, and by hailing him as successor of King Harald, the people of Norway had expressed in a formal way their approval of the work done by Harald Haarfagre. In their consciousness Norway was now a united country, but the system of succession adopted could not safeguard the future stability of the kingdom. It had already led to fratricidal strife, and gave promise of weakness and disintegration. The first revolution had been accomplished without violence and bloodshed; the people gave their united support to the popular Haakon, and the struggle was over, but at any future moment, similar revolutions might occur for no weightier reason than personal rivalry among the claimants to the throne.

King Haakon was a man of many excellent qualities. The sagas describe him as tall, strong, and flaxen-haired. He was of a milder temper than his father, but resembled him strikingly in physical appearance. He was well skilled in the use of arms, but the people knew him as gentle, wise, and peace loving. At the court of King Æthelstan he had been reared in the Christian faith, and had acquired a culture which, no doubt, tended to soften the martial Viking spirit, and to incline his heart and mind to the pursuits of peace. His promise to the people to restore to them their right of *odel*, in other words, to redress their grievances, and grant what they considered to be their just demands, was an acknowledgment on his part that henceforth the king was not to rule as a conqueror, but according to the will of the people and the laws of the land   It appears that the king was no longer to tax the people arbitrarily, according to his own pleasure, but that taxation should be regulated by the *things*. He exercised his kingly power with great moderation.

¹ Alexander Bugge, *Vikingerne*, II., 321 ff.

In the beginning of his reign Jarl Sigurd of Lade ruled in Trøndelagen with almost sovereign power, and the fylkes-kings in Oplandene enjoyed a high degree of autonomy. Over the Norwegian dependencies in the West he exercised little control. His personal rule was largely limited to the southwestern districts of Norway — Vestlandet. The most abiding result of his reign was his work as lawgiver, and his effort to organize the military forces of the country into a strong national army. He surrounded himself with a body of advisers, a sort of council of wise men, to which Sigurd Jarl and Thorleiv Spake belonged.[1] Such changes were made in the *lagthings* (Frostathing, Gulathing, and Eidsivathing) that they became, in a measure, representative bodies. Each *fylke* was henceforth to send a certain number of men to the *thing* (*nefndarmenn*), who were to receive a fixed salary.

The danger which always threatened the kingdom from the sons of Eirik Blood-Ax, who had taken refuge with their grandfather, King Gorm, in Denmark, and who now watched for an opportunity to attack Norway to regain their father's throne, made it necessary for Haakon to pay special attention to the development of both army and navy. He divided the *fylker* along the coast into *skibreder*, or naval districts, and made regulations in regard to the size and number of the warships to be built and equipped by each district. The *nefgildi*, a personal tax levied by Harald Haarfagre, was made a shipmoney tax by Haakon for this purpose. The whole armament, consisting of ships, warriors, weapons, and provisions, was called *leding* (O. N. *leiðangr*). The full number of ships and warriors in each district was called *almenning*. In time of war it was the duty of the people in these districts to meet in full *almenning*, while for military service in time of peace they were required to furnish half *almenning*, together with the necessary equipment and provisions. Every freeman capable of doing military service should own shield, spear, and battle-ax. The military burdens of the coast districts took the place of the *nefgildi*, or shipmoney tax, in this part of the country, but in the inland districts, where there was less military service, this tax was maintained. It is quite evident that the *leding*

---

[1] Whether Torleiv Spake can be regarded as an historical character has been doubted by some, but he seems to have been a *herse* in Hordaland.

system had existed before King Haakon's time, but he gave it a better organization, and extended it to all districts along the coast. He also organized a system of war signals. Fires, called *varder*, should be lighted on the mountain tops when an enemy was approaching the coast. In seven days the warning could, in this way, be given to all parts of the country, and the *almenning* could be held ready everywhere.

The people of Jæmtland had also heard of King Haakon's benign rule. This large district, lying on the border between Norway and Sweden, had first been settled by people from Trøndelagen. In Harald Haarfagre's time many had sought refuge there, and the population was rapidly increasing. King Haakon sought to gain the good will of the leading men in Jæmtland. "They came to visit him," says Snorre,[1] "promised him obedience, brought him presents, and became his men. They had heard good reports about him, and would rather be subject to him than to the king of Sweden, because they were Norsemen. But he established law and justice among them." The foundation was thus laid for the final absorption of the district, but it did not become an integral part of the kingdom of Norway till the time of Eystein Magnusson and Sigurd the Crusader.

King Haakon made an unsuccessful attempt to introduce Christianity in Norway. Centuries of intercourse with the Christian nations in Great Britain and elsewhere had wrought a change in the religious views of many people, even at home. Many had ceased to worship the old gods, and had substituted a sort of new faith in a higher god, the *Alfader*, or creator of all things. Some were indifferent, and believed in nothing but their own strength and prowess, while the majority, especially of the common people, still clung to the old worship. But the old religion was not only a matter of faith. It was closely bound up with the political and social life. The *herser*, or local chieftains, were priests in the *fylkes-hov*, and much of their influence and power depended on their priestly office. A change of religion would bring with it far-reaching alterations in the whole social structure, and it is not surprising that a suggestion of this kind should meet with the most determined resistance. It is said that Haakon brought priests from England, and built churches

[1] *Heimskringla, Haakon den godes Saga*, ch. 12.

in Romsdal and Nordmør, but when he finally proposed at the Frostathing that the people should accept Christianity, it caused a storm of indignation. Sigurd Jarl gave him no support, and Asbjørn of Medalhus, who made himself the spokesman of the people, threatened that they would all rise against him, if he urged the point. He had to join in the sacrifice to the gods, and felt compelled to give up the plan. To carry it through by force was impossible, for he soon needed the support of his people to repel the attacks of the sons of Eirik Blood-Ax. In 955 the brothers Gamle, Harald, Ragnfrød, Gudrød, and Sigurd Sleva led an expedition against Norway, but Haakon defeated them in a battle near the island of Frei, in Nordmør. Gamle fell, and the other brothers returned to Denmark, but they continued to harry the southern coasts. In 961 they renewed the attack. With a large fleet they landed at Fitje, on the island of Stord, where King Haakon was staying. A bloody battle was fought, in which the sons of Eirik were again defeated, but King Haakon, who fought valiantly in the midst of the fray, was wounded in the arm by an arrow, and died shortly after the battle. He had no sons to whom he could leave the throne, and the story is told that, when he felt death approaching, he sent messengers to his fleeing nephews, and invited them to return and take the kingdom. He regretted much, says the saga,[1] that he had been compelled to depart from the Christian faith. His men offered to bring his body to England, and give it Christian burial, but he answered: "I am not worthy of it. As a heathen I have lived, and as a heathen you must bury me." The wounded king was brought to his birthplace, Haakonshelle, where he died at the age of forty-six, after a reign of twenty-six years. His friend and comrade in arms, the great scald Eyvind Skaldaspiller, composed a great song to his memory, the "Haakonarmaal," in which he says:

> Freed from his fetters,
> against the world
> the wolf Fenrir shall come,[2]
> before such another king
> shall follow in his footsteps.

[1] *Fagrskinna*, p. 26. *Heimskringla, Haakon den godes Saga*, ch. 32.
[2] This will happen at Ragnarok, or the end of the world. Then Fenrir will break loose from the fetters with which the gods have bound him.

> Friends die,
> cattle perish,
> desolated is the land;
> since Haakon went
> to heathen gods
> people live in serfdom and bondage.

34. THE SONS OF EIRIK BLOOD-AX. HAAKON JARL THE LEADER OF THE ARISTOCRACY. LOSS OF NATIONAL UNITY AND INDEPENDENCE

After Haakon's death the sons of Eirik Blood-Ax became kings of Norway. They all bore the royal title, and each maintained his own *hird*, but Harald Graafeld, the oldest living brother, was regarded as over-king. After their father was driven from the throne, they had been in foreign lands, and they were known in Norway mainly as Viking chieftains and as enemies of the country. This, together with the general odium in which Eirik and Gunhild were held, made them very unpopular, and they showed no ability to win the people's good will by their own conduct as kings. They were disposed to be rash and violent; they showed little wisdom, or self-control, and would resort to mean plots and bloody assaults, in true Viking fashion. The best one was Harald Graafeld, who seems to have been generous, good-natured, and well-intentioned. The aristocracy, who still held firmly to their own inherited rights and privileges, who were opposed to a strong central government exercised by a national king, and watched with more jealousy their own interests than the welfare of the nation, tolerated the new kings, and, probably, found their unpopularity convenient. As Harald Graafeld and his brothers could find little popular support, their kingship could be little more than an empty title. The aristocracy, who had been compelled to bow under the mailed fist of Harald Haarfagre, but who had driven Eirik from the throne, and had elected Haakon the Good, could now find new opportunity to fully regain their old prestige and power. Even in Haakon's time, Sigurd Jarl had exercised almost sovereign power in Trøndelagen. Now he did not even swear allegiance to the new kings, but ruled his large domain as an independent sovereign. Tryggve Olavsson, a grandson of Harald Haarfagre, ruled as independent king in Romerike, and in the districts east of the Foldenfjord (Christianiafjord). The districts west of the fjord were ruled by Gudrød Bjørnsson, another grandson of Harald, and in Oplandene the fylkes-kings exercised their old unrestricted authority. The sons of Eirik were, in fact, kings only in the districts of southwestern Norway. But they aspired to maintain the unity of the kingdom, and to rule, as King Harald had ruled, over all Norway. First of all they would curb the pride and arrogance of the powerful Jarl Sigurd. They enticed to their side his younger brother, Grjotgard, and with his aid King Harald Graafeld suddenly fell upon the unsuspecting Sigurd, and burned him and his men in the house where they were assembled for a feast. Sigurd's son, Haakon Jarl, gathered a large following, and after a struggle lasting for three years he made himself master of Trøndelagen. But he was unable to successfully continue the conflict, and fled to Denmark. The kings had also defeated and slain the kings Tryggve and Gudrød in southern Norway, and together with their mother Gunhild, they now established their residence in Viken.

In 964 King Harald Graafeld made an expedition to the Permians (Bjarmeland), and defeated them on the banks of the Dvina, thus pushing the boundaries of Norway to the White Sea (Gandvik). The expedition was much talked of, and was mentioned with praise in the songs of the scalds.[1] Harald seems to have made an earnest effort to rule well, but the popular ill-will was, nevertheless, growing. The brothers had been baptized in England, but they were unable to introduce Christianity in Norway, and undertook, instead, to destroy the heathen temples, and to heap other indignities upon the old religion. This, together with many acts of violence, committed especially by the younger brothers, tended to further alienate the people, who complained that the kings did not respect the laws of King Haakon the Good. King Sigurd Sleva was killed by his irate subjects in southwestern Norway. There were crop failures and hard times, and the people blamed the kings, who were thought to have aroused the anger of the gods by their wickedness and misrule. Haakon watched closely the developments in Norway. This

---

[1] The Trollbotn, in popular belief the abode of the trolls, where no sun shines, was henceforth thought to be located in these far-off northern regions.

able but crafty and unscrupulous jarl was a more formidable opponent than the kings imagined. He was, in all respects, a representative of the old order of things, a strict adherent of the Asa-faith, and a champion of the rights of the aristocracy. He despised, no doubt, the new religious tendencies, as thoroughly as he hated the idea of submission to a national king.

Harald Blaatand (Bluetooth) had succeeded his father Gorm on the Danish throne. Gorm had ruled both long and well, and at the end of his reign Denmark was the most populous and powerful of the Northern kingdoms, a circumstance which, probably, gave rise to the not uncommon misconception that he had brought about the union of the Danish kingdom. His queen was the able and popular Thyra Danebod, who rebuilt Danevirke, a castellated wall, stretching across the narrowest part of the peninsula, from the city of Schleswig to the mouth of the River Eider; forming the old boundary between Denmark and Germany. Harald Blaatand seems to have emulated his great contemporary Otto the Great of Germany. He was dreaming of empire, and sought to enlarge his possessions, especially in northern Germany, which at this time was inhabited by the Wends, a Slavonic people. In 960 he made an expedition to the mouth of the Oder, where he is said to have won a great jarldom. On the island of Wollin, over against the river mouth, lay the important commercial town Julin. Close to this town Harald built a strong castle called "Jómsborg," which later became famous [1] as the seat of a remarkable body of Viking warriors, the Jómsvikings. Jómsborg was, doubtless, built to protect Julin and the neighboring districts

[1] An account of Jómsborg and the Jómsvikings is found in the *Jómsvikingasaga*, which is, however, a romance rather than a history, and is, consequently, of little value as an historical source. The laws and social organization of the Jómsvikings here described must, however, be true. Similar laws were used by other Viking organizations, and in the Viking army similar rules were also followed. Bravery, not rank or birth, was the qualification required for membership. No one would be accepted who was under eighteen or over fifty years of age. No woman was allowed to enter the castle and no warrior could be absent more than three days at a time. Friendship and good understanding should prevail among the warriors, and no one should offend the other. They should all avenge the death of their comrades, and no one was allowed to speak a word of fear. All news should first be brought to the chieftain, and all booty should be divided among th warriors. *Jómsvikingasaga*, sec. IV., ch. III.

against the Wends. It had a fine harbor, where 300 Viking vessels could ride at anchor, and was surrounded by great walls.[1]

Harald Blaatand, who had received baptism, labored earnestly, and with great success, to introduce Christianity in Denmark. During his reign the greater part of the people seem to have accepted the Christian faith. It was natural that in his efforts to enlarge his kingdom he should also think of Norway as a legitimate field for conquest. The district of Vestfold had been a Danish province since very early times, and circumstances in Norway seemed to offer an opportunity to regain at least this province. A son of his elder brother returned to Denmark from his many Viking expeditions, and claimed a share in the kingdom. He was known as Gold Harald, because of his wealth. Haakon Jarl saw his opportunity. He persuaded King Harald to rid himself of this inconvenient rival by seizing Norway, which he then might make a tributary kingdom under the rule of his nephew. The plan was accepted, and Harald Graafeld was enticed to Denmark, where he was killed by Gold Harald. Now the plotting Haakon Jarl came forward with his real plan. He showed the king that his ambitious nephew would, as king of Norway, be a dangerous rival rather than a faithful vassal; why not make Haakon Jarl ruler of Norway? He could not aspire to kingship in either country, and all danger of a rival would be averted. After he had come to some sort of understanding with the king, Haakon attacked Gold Harald, who was defeated and slain. The king now set sail for Norway with a fleet of 700 ships. The two remaining sons of Eirik Blood-Ax could offer no resistance, but fled to the Orkneys with their mother Gunhild, and Harald Gormsson Blaatand was hailed as over-king of Norway. Haakon Jarl was to rule a large part of the country as King Harald's vassal. According to agreement he should pay the king a tax amounting to half of the income from the lands which he received, but Haakon reduced it to the nominal sum of twenty falcons a year. King Harald himself ruled Viken through his own jarls, and Oplandene maintained their own autonomy. Trøndelagen and Haalogaland were Haakon's own patrimony, where he exercised full authority.

[1] Many coins and other articles of interest have been unearthed on the site of the old castle, and remnants of the old walls have also been laid bare.

From the king he received seven *fylker*: Rygafylke, Hordafylke, Sogn, Firdafylke, Søndmør, Romsdal, and Nordmør. Norway had ceased to be a united kingdom even under Danish overlordship. Harald Haarfagre's great work was destroyed.

The new rule was welcomed by the aristocracy, who had now regained their former power. Haakon Jarl was one of their own number, and the Danish king's overlordship was a mere name, as he was too far away to exercise any control. Haakon was now very popular. He rebuilt the temples which the sons of Eirik Blood-Ax had destroyed, and tried, as far as possible, to establish the old conditions. But nothing is more difficult than the attempt to arrest a development caused by the forces of life and growth. Haakon might rebuild the temples, but he could not revive the old faith. It was dying; in many people's minds it was already dead; the outer forms alone remained. The aristocracy might feel elated over their success, but new thoughts of a national kingdom were germinating and striking roots. Such ideas are in league with destiny. Haakon tried to buttress the old social structure, only to be finally buried under its ruins.

For a time he was loyal to his overlord, the king of Denmark. When the German emperor, Otto the Great, died, war broke out between his successor, Otto II., and King Harald Gormsson.[1] As a vassal Haakon was called to Denmark, where he fought valiantly in defense of Danevirke. After the campaign was over, King Harald demanded of Haakon that he should be baptized, and exacted from him a promise that he would introduce Christianity in Norway. Haakon seems to have consented with all desirable alacrity, and, on his return, priests went along to do missionary work in Norway. But, as soon as he touched the home shore, Haakon drove away the priests, and declared himself and Norway independent of Denmark. King Harald made efforts to reconquer the country, and to introduce Christianity in Viken; the work of the missionaries which he sent to this district bore some fruit, but he failed in the attempt to regain the lost territory. Harald Blaatand died about 986 from a wound received while he was fighting against his rebellious son, Svein Tjugeskjeg (Forkbeard). As soon as Svein became king, he

[1] *Danmarks Riges Historie*, vol. I., p. 339 ff.

renewed the attempt to subdue Norway. The Jómsvikings, who seem to have promised to aid him in this undertaking, moved swiftly to the attack with a fleet of sixty ships and an army of professional warriors led by their chief, Sigvalde Jarl.[1] They found Haakon in Hjørungavaag, near the present city of Aalesund, where he had collected 180 ships. But this armament had been gathered in a hurry, and most of the vessels were merchant ships. Haakon was assisted by his sons, Eirik, Svein, and Arnljot. A fierce battle ensued, in which Eirik Jarl especially distinguished himself both by bravery and generalship. The outcome of the battle was long doubtful. Tradition says that Haakon Jarl even sacrificed his son to the gods to gain victory, but this is, no doubt, an invention. The Jómsvikings finally suffered a crushing defeat. Twenty-five of their ships were taken, and Sigvalde Jarl made good his escape with the remaining thirty-five. This battle became very famous. Eyvind Skaldaspiller composed the song "Háleygjatal" about Haakon Jarl and his victory, after the pattern of the "Ynglingatal," [2] to show that Haakon's family, the Háleygings, also descended from the gods. Through this memorable victory Norway had successfully maintained her independence.

After the battle of Hjørungavaag, Haakon Jarl exercised full sovereign power, but he did not assume the title of king. As he was now relieved of the pressure of foreign enemies, he paid little heed to the aristocracy, and attempted to rule with all the authority of Harald Haarfagre himself. This kind of rule, which the aristocracy had regarded as tyranny when exercised by a national king,

[1] According to tradition the Jómsviking chieftain, while at a feast, where he had been drinking too much to carefully weigh his words, had promised to attack Haakon, and drive him from Norway. *Heimskringla, Olav Tryggvasonssaga,* ch. 35.

[2] Haakon Jarl was fond of scaldic poetry, and, like Harald Haarfagre, he kept a number of scalds at his court. Of these, Einar Skaalaglam was the most noted. He was with Haakon at Hjørungavaag, and has described the battle in a long poem, the *Vellekla,* twenty stanzas of which are found in the *Heimskringla.* Tin Halkelsson, Thorleiv Raudfeldarsson, and Vigfus Vigaglumsson also wrote songs about the fight with the Jómsvikings, but only fragments of these songs have been preserved. Bishop Bjarne in the Orkneys was a great scald. He has written *Jómsvikingadrápa,* and it is thought that he is also the author of the *Jómsvikingasaga.* The description of the battle of Hjørungavaag in the saga seems to be reliable.

they considered as unbearable arrogance in a mere jarl, who was of no higher lineage than many others of their number. Haakon Jarl's popularity soon waned, and his greed, cruelty, and licentiousness further aggravated the growing discontent. The hearts of the people again turned to the Ynglings, who, since King Harald's time, had stood as the representatives of a national kingdom and other progressive ideas.

35. OLAV TRYGGVASON. THE INTRODUCTION OF CHRISTIANITY IN NORWAY

Tryggve Olavsson, a grandson of Harald Haarfagre, who ruled over the districts east of the Christianiafjord, was slain by the sons of Eirik Blood-Ax, as already stated. His wife Astrid fled, says the saga,[1] and sought refuge on a lonely island where her son Olav Tryggvason was born.[2] His birth occurred, probably, in 963 or 964. With her child she came to her father, Eirik Bjodaskalle at Oprudstader, in the district of Jæderen, in southwestern Norway, but as the wicked Queen Gunhild sent spies to learn her whereabouts, she continued her flight to her father's friend, Haakon Gamle, in Sweden. But even here she felt unsafe, because of Gunhild's machinations, and she determined to seek refuge at the court of Grand Duke Vlademir of Gardarike (Russia), where her brother Sigurd was staying. On the voyage across the Baltic Sea they were attacked by Vikings, and Queen Astrid and her boy Olav were taken prisoners. Mother and child were separated, and both were sold as slaves in Esthonia. Not very long afterward, a merchant by the name of Loden, a wealthy man of good family from the district of Viken, found Astrid at a slave market in Esthonia, and brought her back to Norway, where they were married. Olav remained in slavery about six years, until his uncle Sigurd finally found him and brought him to Holmgard (Novgorod), where he was reared at the court of Grand Duke Vlademir. That Olav was reared at the court of the grand duke seems to be true. It is mentioned also by Hallfrød Vandrædaskald in his "Olavsdraapa," which deals with Olav's life prior to his arrival in Norway. But the numerous legendary tales which cluster about

---

[1] Heimskringla, Olav Tryggvasonssaga.   Odd Munk, Olav Tryggvasonssaga, p. 22.

[2] Agrip states that Olav was three years old when his father died.

the magic figure of Olav Tryggvason throw about his early youth a deep twilight of romance, which renders obscure even what little is known about this period of his career.[1] From this obscure background he enters the historical arena as a young man, "tall, beautiful, strong, and athletic beyond all Norsemen ever mentioned," says Snorre.[2] At the age of twelve he began his career as Viking chieftain in the Baltic Sea. The saga states that sometime afterward he came to Vendland to King Burislav, and married his daughter Geira.[3] He aided his father-in-law in his wars, but Geira died, and he left Vendland to seek new fields for enterprise in the British Isles. He must have gained great renown as a warrior during these years, for we find him now at the head of a great armament, the nucleus of another "Great Army," which was to begin a new conquest of England.

The vicious and incompetent Æthelred the Unready was now king of England. He made no attempt to maintain the efficiency either of army or of navy, though he had been warned of impending danger by repeated Viking attacks which began anew in 978. Iona was sacked, a bloody battle was fought off the Isle of Man in 986, and in 989 a Viking fleet ascended the Severn, and the king was forced to pay tribute to the intruders. These Viking squadrons operating in British waters were led by Jostein, a brother of Olav's mother Astrid, and Gudmund, a Danish chieftain. When Olav arrived, they were united into a great fleet under his command. In 991 they came to Staines on the Thames, with ninety-three ships, and plundered Kent and Suffolk. Following the coast the fleet again came to anchor at the mouth of the Blackwater, where Ealdorman Brihtnoth met them with the levies of Essex. A bloody battle was fought at Maldon, in which Brihtnoth lost his life, and his forces suffered a disastrous defeat. The details of the battle are vividly described in the Old English poem "The Battle of Maldon."[4] The

[1] Alexander Bugge observes that the adventurous flight of Astrid, and Gunhild's relentless pursuit, remind us strongly of the fairy-tale about the wicked step-mother. *Norges Historie*, vol. II., p. 239.

[2] *Heimskringla, Olav Tryggvasonssaga*, 8.

[3] Burislav, no doubt King Boleslav of Poland, 992–1025, has been substituted for Miesko, 964–992, through a mistake by the saga writer.

[4] *Two of the Saxon Chronicles*, ed. Plummer, Oxford, 1892, p. 126.

poet tells how Brihtnoth with his hirdmen came riding at the head of his host. Near the Blackwater he dismounted, and addressed words of encouragement and advice to his warriors. The Vikings, who were stationed on the opposite side of the river, sent a herald who addressed Brihtnoth and his army as follows:

> "The bold seamen send me to you
> and bid me say that you must at once
> send rings in return for peace; better it is for you
> to buy off this combat with tribute
> than that we fight so hard a battle."

> Brihtnoth raised his shield and answered:
> "Hearest thou, seafarer, what this people say?
> Spears will we give you for tribute,
> poisonous arrows and tried swords.
> Tell thy people the unwelcome news,
> that here stands the earl and his brave army,
> who will defend this land.
> Rather shall sword and spear unite us
> in grim war-play than we will pay tribute."

The Vikings waited for low tide and crossed the river.

> Then was the time come when doomed men should fall.
> A cry went up which brought thither the ravens
> and the eagles hungry for carrion; great was the alarm.
> The hard spears were hurled, the sharp arrows flew,
> the bows were busy, the shields received the spear points,
> bitter was the battle tumult, heroes fell,
> on every hand lay fallen warriors.

Brihtnoth fell, but the young Ælfwine rallied the hirdmen, who rushed to the attack to avenge their fallen lord, till all of them were cut down. Old Brihtnoth's heroic fight stands in sharp contrast to Æthelred's weakness and planless inactivity. After the battle of Maldon he bought peace from the invaders by paying them 10,000 pounds of silver,[1] an enormous sum at that time, when the taxes of

---

[1] The text of the treaty has been preserved. The heading reads as follows "This is the peace which King Æthelred and his whole Witan made with the army which Olav, Jostein, and Gudmund, Stegita's son, led." Lieber

the whole kingdom were only half that amount. The following year "the king and the Witan decreed that all ships which were worth anything should be gathered together at London, in order that they might try if they could anywhere entrap the Army from without," says the "Anglo-Saxon Chronicle." But the attempt failed. About this time Olav Tryggvason must have accepted the Christian faith. It is said that on a little island he met a hermit who foretold him his career, and that he and his men were baptized.[1]

At this time King Svein Tjugeskjeg of Denmark also came to England. Olav and Svein united their forces, but Olav still remained the real leader. In 993 Bamborough was taken by storm, and Lindsey was harried. The following year a large Viking army was organized, and Friesland and the northern coasts of Germany were harried. Who the leaders of this host were is not stated, but scaldic verses point to Olav Tryggvason and Svein Tjugeskjeg. In the fall of 994 Olav and Svein again appeared in the Thames with a fleet of ninety-four ships, and tried to take London. In this attempt they failed, but they harried the neighboring districts, and Æthelred bought peace by granting them Southampton for winter quarters, and by paying them 16,000 pounds of silver. The king now sought to win Olav Tryggvason, and sent a bishop to negotiate with him. Olav visited the king at Andover, where he was confirmed by Bishop Ælfeah of Winchester,[2] and a treaty of peace was made, in which he solemnly promised never again to wage war on England, a pledge which he loyally kept. A great ambition now fired his zeal for worthier undertakings. He would no longer be a Viking chieftain, but a crusader. To regain the throne of his fathers, and to convert his people to Christianity became his great aim. He separated from Svein Tjugeskjeg, and took no further part in the conquest of England.

Olav Tryggvason was the most chivalric and heroic of all the early

mann, *Gesetze der Anglo-sachsen*, I., 220–223. *Diplomatarium Norwegicum, Oldbreve*, edited by Alexander Bugge, Christiania, 1910, nittende samling, part first, p. 1.

[1] *Historia de Antiquitate Regum Norwagiensium*, by Theodricus Monachus, says that Olav was baptized in the Scilly Islands. See *Monumenta Historica Norwegiae*, published by Gustav Storm, Christiania, 1880.

[2] *Two of the Saxon Chronicles*, Plummer, Oxford, 1892, p. 126.

kings of Norway. Saga and tradition extol him as a leader of men, a beau ideal of a hero. The "Olav Tryggvason's Saga" says: "King Olav was in all respects the most capable man in Norway of whom there is any record; he was stronger and more dexterous than any other person, and many stories are told about him; one being that he scaled the Smalsarhorn [1] and fastened his shield near the top of the mountain; another, that he helped one of his *hirdmænd*, who had climbed up the mountain so far that he could neither ascend nor descend. The king climbed up, and carried him down under his arm. The king could walk on the oars on the outside of his ship, the 'Long Serpent,' while his men were rowing; he could play with three swords at a time in such a way that one would always be in the air. He could wield the sword equally well with both hands, and could throw two spears at the same time. He was the most cheerful and jovial of men, kind and condescending, impetuous in everything, generous and distinguished among his men. He was the bravest of all in battle, but very cruel when he became angry." [2] Both at home and in the British Isles he became a hero in tale and tradition. In England his name was changed to Havelock. It has been thought that Havelock was Olav Kvaaran,[3] but Alexander Bugge holds that the life of Kvaaran could furnish no basis for the Havelock poem, but that the incidents narrated in the poem correspond point for point with the stories told of Olav Tryggvason's early life.[4]

Early in the summer of 995 Olav Tryggvason set sail for Norway with a small fleet.[5] The "Heimskringla" tells us that Haakon Jarl sent his agents to lure him to Norway, where he had laid plans to kill him; but as Olav, the scion of the royal house of the Ynglings, probably would be the last person whom Haakon would wish to see in Norway at that juncture, the story must be an invention of the enemies of Haakon, who wished to paint him as black as possible. It was, no doubt, the people of Trøndelagen who sent agents to Olav

[1] A mountain peak on the coast of Nordfjord, in Norway.

[2] *Heimskringla*, *Olav Tryggvasonssaga*, 85.

[3] Gustav Storm, *Havelock the Dane, and the Norse King Olav Kvaaran.*

[4] See Odd Snorreson Munk, *Saga Olafskonungs Tryggvasonar*, published by P. A. Munch, Christiania, 1853.

[5] *Heimskringla* says five ships; Odd Munk says nine ships.

to invite him to come to Norway and rid them of the hated jarl. Olav took several missionaries along: Bishop Sigurd, Teodbrand (Thangbrand), and Thormod,[1] who were to aid him in Christianizing Norway. He went by way of the Orkneys, where he forced the powerful Jarl Sigurd Lodvesson to acknowledge his overlordship, and to accept Christianity. When he finally landed in Trøndelagen, the people hailed him with enthusiasm. Haakon Jarl was soon deserted, and fled, accompanied by his slave, Kark. The "Heimskringla" tells how Haakon and Kark hid in an underground pigsty on the estate Rimol, where Kark assassinated the sleeping Haakon to get the prize which Olav had placed on the jarl's head. The story is too dramatic to be taken literally, but all sources, including the songs of contemporary scalds, agree that Haakon Jarl was ignominiously done to death by treacherous hands. Olav was now proclaimed king of Norway at the *Ørething*, in Trøndelagen. No one could be better qualified to become the representative of the new progressive ideas than he. He had spent all his life in foreign lands, and was not bound up in the old traditions of his fatherland, nor was he, like Haakon the Good, indebted to a party for his position as king. He was a convert to Christianity, and was well acquainted with the Christian culture of the British Isles. Famous for his great achievements as a military leader he came like a man of destiny at a moment when the people hailed him as a deliverer, and rejoiced that a prince of the royal race of the Ynglings had come to rule over them. To the popular mind he was the hero especially protected by fortune. "Olav had favorable wind wherever he sailed," says his old biographer.[2] He possessed the indomitable energy of a crusading warrior, he was the brilliant man of action, who dazzled his followers with ever new exploits. His charming and inspiring personality won the hearts and fascinated the minds of his countrymen, and he became popular as no other king of Norway. "He was one of those fortunate individuals," says E. Sars, "before whom destiny places great problems, and who possesses the ability to solve them."

There was no one in Norway at this moment who could openly resist so able and popular a king. Haakon Jarl's sons, Eirik and

[1] Theodricus Monachus, *Historia de Antiquitate*, 15. *Ágrip*, 36.
[2] Odd Munk, *Olav Tryggvasonssaga*.

Svein, had left the country, the Danish officials in the southern districts were driven away, and the whole kingdom of Norway was once more united, under Olav Tryggvason's rule.

King Olav entered upon his great task of Christianizing Norway with true crusading zeal. To what extent political motives strengthened his resolve to bring about this great change it is impossible to say, though statesmanlike foresight must have made it clear to him that the new national kingdom could find but little support in the old system of worship and social ideas, while the Christian Church, if once established, would give the king new dignity, and increase the stability of the kingdom. Christianity was no longer wholly unknown to the Norwegian people at this time. We have seen how communication with the Christian countries during the Viking period had produced an ever increasing influx of new ideas, which had already effected great changes both in the social and religious life of the people. Belief in the old gods was waning, and rationalism and religious indifference were rapidly spreading among the higher classes; the myths themselves were in a stage of transformation and decay. Christian captives of war had told the story of Christ and the saints to many an interested listener; missionaries had preached the Christian faith in the days of Haakon the Good, and King Harald Blaatand's efforts to introduce Christianity in Viken had borne fruit. Still the common people, who, perhaps, never had grasped the intricate and lofty myths of the Asa-faith, whose religious life consisted, chiefly, of fetish worship and of various forms of sorcery practiced by means of incantations, amulets, and the like, were probably wholly untouched by these new ideas.[1] Among the upper classes

---

[1] The sun, fire, running water, cattle, and even strong men were worshiped. A dish of butter was placed on the roof of the house to make the sun shine warmer; salt, flour, milk, or beer was thrown into the fire to prevent conflagrations, and articles of value were brought as offerings to springs and brooks. See Bishop A. Chr. Bang, *Udsigt over den norske Kirkes Historie under Katholicismen*, p. 26, Kristiania, 1890. Runic characters were used as amulets. They were carved on swords and spear points to make the weapons more effective, on rings and drinking goblets as a charm against evil influences of all kinds. *Galdr*, or magic songs, were used as a wonder-working remedy in the art of healing, and *seid*, or sorcery, was supposed to loosen all the diabolic powers of the spirit world. Many features of this side of pagan religious belief have perpetuated themselves in folklore and popular super-

the old worship still retained its political importance as a state institution closely bound up with the old social order. The time had, indeed, come when the new religion would be received by many without resistance, but the conversion of the whole people could not be accomplished rapidly without the use of coercion and force. It seems that King Olav never thought that it could be brought about by teaching and persuasion alone. The true inwardness of the Christian faith and spirit was still foreign to him; he was yet to such an extent a Viking that he had no hesitation in bringing his subjects to the baptismal font by bribes or by force, where gentler means had failed, and baptism and conversion he regarded as identical. His missionaries labored zealously, but the people often cared little for their preaching, and understood it still less. The king is the central figure, always busy directing the work of conversion, intimidating some, gaining the friendship and good will of others, coming to the rescue with his influence and power, and often dealing hard blows when preaching and persuasion proved unavailing.[1] Sigurd, or John, as he was called in Latin, held the rank of bishop, and was the leader of the missionaries. He was a gentle and Christian-spirited man, who represented the best features of the Anglian Church. It appears that he was of Norse descent. He probably came from the Viking settlements of Northumbria, and he could, no doubt, address the people in their own vernacular, which was an advantage, though the language at this time offered no great difficulty. "There was one language in England and Norway until William the Bastard

stitions to the present time. See Dr. A. Chr. Bang, *Norske Hexeformularer og magiske Opskrifter.*

[1] In judging the harsh measures often employed by Olav Tryggvason, and also by his great successor, Olav the Saint, it is necessary to bear in mind that the medieval Christian spirit was of the militant and martial kind, foreign to the modern world. Charlemagne's conversion of the Saxons, and the crusades of the Teutonic Knights and the Knights of the Sword in Livonia, Curland, and Prussia bear the same general character as Olav Tryggvason's missionary work. Chr. Bruun has shown that the theory that the heathens should be compelled to accept the Christian faith was a well established tenet of the church in the Middle Ages, based on the passage in Holy Scripture (Luke xiv., 23), "Go out into the highways and hedges and compel them to come in, that my house may be filled." This view of missionary work was established by the great church father Augustine. Chr. Bruun, *Olav den hellige, For Kirke og Kultur*, vol. IV., p. 321 ff.

conquered England," says the saga.[1] This must not be taken too literally, but the Norse and Anglo-Saxon tongues were yet so nearly alike that the two peoples seem to have been able to converse freely together. The priest Thangbrand, supposed to have been the renegade son of a Saxon count, was a harsh and violent man, to whom the true Christian spirit seems to have been wholly unknown.

It is deserving of special mention that the first missionaries to Norway came from England, where the gospel was preached, not in the Latin church language commonly used at that time, but in the people's own tongue, and where the church still retained its popular and apostolic character to a degree unknown on the continent. Bishop A. Chr. Bang says:[2] "Of all the nations which in the first half of the Middle Ages accepted the Christian faith, probably no other people developed so genuine, warm, and deep a Christianity as the Anglo-Saxons. Christian life flourished among them, the word of God was translated into their own tongue, and they had many gifted poets who sang their praise to the Lord in their own vernacular. What especially gave Anglo-Saxon Christianity its distinguishing features was the delightful blending of Christian with popular elements, which we still admire. We need not study long their religious literature to be deeply touched by observing how the Northern heroic spirit had become transfigured by the holy Christian spirit. The daughter church of Norway could, therefore, receive a valuable inheritance from the mother church of England. I need not mention the practical features of church organization which were transplanted from English to Norwegian soil. It was more important that the Old Norse church language found in Anglo-Saxon a natural starting point, and a closely related pattern. And still more significant, perhaps, was the circumstance that later Norwegian ecclesiastics learned from their Anglo-Saxon predecessors to honor and esteem their mother tongue, and to be as eager as they were able to preach to the people in their own language. That the kings themselves introduced Christianity was of no small importance to the future development. Most significant in this connection was the fact

---

[1] *Gunlaugssaga Ormstungu*, ch. 6.
[2] *Udsigt over den norske Kirkes Historie under Katholicismen*, p. 37 ff.

that Christianity thereby from the beginning was closely linked to the state as a popular church, a state church." [1]

In the early Anglo-Saxon Church the Christian doctrines are often found expressed in a heroic strain which echoes the dying martial notes of primitive Germanic poetry. Christ is often represented as a young hero who vanquishes evil, and conquers his enemies, rather than as the suffering Savior atoning for the sins of mankind. The runic inscription on the old Ruthwell cross represents the cross as saying: "Stripped himself, God Almighty, when he wanted to mount the cross, courageously in the sight of all men. (I) bent," etc.

A very similar inscription is found in the old poem "Dream of the Rood," by some attributed to Cynewulf:

> Stripped himself then the young hero,
> that was God Almighty,
> strong and brave:
> he mounted the high cross
> courageously in the sight of many,
> when he wanted to set mankind free.
> I trembled when the hero embraced me.
> I dared not bend to the earth.

Such a view of Christ would, naturally, appeal to the warlike Norsemen. This was a Christianity which they could understand. Their quick imagination seized upon these popular features by means of which they could span the gulf between the old and new spheres of thought. Christ, the heroic new god of the Christians, more powerful than Thor, superior in every way to the old divinities, would ultimately gain the victory, they thought. The "Njálssaga" [2] tells how, in Iceland, a woman by the name of Steinvor disputed with the missionary Thangbrand, saying: "Have you not heard

---

[1] P. A. Munch, *Det norske Folks Historie*, vol. II. Absalon Taranger, *Den angelsaksiske Kirkes Indflydelse paa den norske*, Kristiania, 1890. A. D. Jørgensen, *Den nordiske Kirkes Grundlæggelse og første Udvikling*, Copenhagen, 1874–1887. Dr. Konrad Maurer, *Die Bekehrung des norwegischen Stammes zum Christenthume*, München, 1855. R. Keyser, *Den norske Kirkes Historie under Katholicismen*, Christiania, 1856. Henry Goddard Leach, *The Relations of the Norwegian with the English Church, 1066–1399, and their Importance to Comparative Literature, in Proceedings of the American Academy of Arts and Sciences*, vol. XLIV., May, 1909. [2] *Njálssaga*, ch. 100.

that Christ was challenged to a duel by Thor, and that he dared not fight with him?" "I have heard," said Thangbrand, "that Thor would be but dust and ashes unless God would let him live." A man by the name of Finn, who had heard of the power of Christ, disputed with the bishop, but, as he was convinced by his arguments, he exclaimed: "This is something different from what I have heard before, that no god was equal in power to Thor and Odin. Now I understand from what you say of Christ, about whom you preach, that while he was in this world any one could treat him almost as he pleased, but after death he became so powerful that he raided hell, and bound Thor, the chieftain of the gods, and since that time nothing can resist him." [1] Christ can bind Thor. He is that powerful god foreshadowed even in the Edda songs as the one "coming from above to rule over all." "Christianity," says Keyser, "no longer appeared at this time in its original purity. A covering of human inventions, superstitions, and errors had been wrapped about its divine kernel. But the covering was brilliant, inviting to the senses, impressive to the feelings. This form of Christianity was, probably, better suited to appeal to a people in the stage of intellectual development of the old Norsemen than if it had been preached in a purer form." [2]

King Olav began his missionary work in Viken, where his father Tryggve had been king, and where Christianity, because of early missionary efforts, was best known. Here he could count on greater good-will and more general support than elsewhere.[3] After winning his own relatives for the new faith, he secured the coöperation of the powerful chieftains, the brothers Hyrning and Thorgeir, by giving them his half-sisters Ingerid and Ingegerd in marriage, and by bestowing on them great honors and rich estates. When the leaders

[1] See R. Keyser, *Den norske Kirkes Historie under Katholicismen*, vol. I. B. Kahle, *Das Christenthum in der altnorwegischen Dichtung*, *Arkiv for nordisk Filologi*, 1890.

[2] *Den norske Kirkes Historie under Katholicismen*, vol. I., p. 47.

[3] The statement made by Odd Munk in *Olav Tryggvasonssaga*, ch. 17, that Olav landed at Moster, and began missionary work there, must be erroneous, and is probably due to a misunderstanding arising from the fact that Olav built the first Christian church there. Compare A. Chr. Bang, *Udsigt over den norske Kirkes Historie under Katholicismen*, p. 46, and Alexander Bugge, *Norges Historie*, vol. I., 2, p. 257 ff.

had been won by the granting of such favors, the people could more easily be persuaded to follow their example, and receive baptism. The church service was made as showy as possible. The rich vestments worn by the priests, the burning incense, the impressive ceremonies, appealed strongly to the listeners.[1] The hell torments were pictured in vivid colors, and the missionaries showed how God and the saints were aiding King Olav. The people were rapidly won for the Christian faith, but not a few resisted obstinately. Odd Munk tells how Olav dealt hard blows to those who offered resistance. "Those who opposed Christianity," says Snorre,[2] "he punished severely; some he killed, some he caused to be maimed, and some he drove out of the country." The people were summoned to the *thing*, where the king bade them receive the Christian faith, and after they were baptized, he destroyed the temples, and everything that reminded them of the old worship. Before long the whole district of Viken was Christianized. The "Heimskringla" states that he also visited the district of Ringerike, where King Sigurd Syr reigned, and King Sigurd was baptized, together with his wife, Aasta, and her little boy of a former marriage, Olav Haraldsson, who later became King Olav the Saint.

From Viken King Olav proceeded to the districts of Gulathingslag, on the southwest coast. Here, as in Viken, he seems to have won the chieftains through private negotiations. The powerful Erling Skjalgsson of Sole married the king's half-sister Astrid, became the king's ardent supporter, and received great preferments and honors. In the little island of Moster, on the coast of Hordaland, where a

[1] Odd Munk, *Olav Tryggvasonssaga*, ch. 11. The younger *Olav Tryggvasonssaga* relates that when the priest Thangbrand preached in Iceland, Sidu-Hall, the man at whose house he was staying, arose one morning with all his people, and stood before the tent where the priests were saying mass. When they heard the chiming bells and the sweet voices of the singers, the like of which they had never heard before, they were much impressed. Still greater was their wonder when the mass began, and they saw the priests in beautiful garments, with burning candles, and perceived the sweet scent of the burning incense. When they returned, Hall asked his people how they liked the customs of the Christians, and they all said that everything that they had seen and heard seemed to them pure and beautiful.

[2] Snorre, *Heimskringla, Olav Tryggvasonssaga*, ch. 53. *Historia Norwegiæ*, ed. G. Storm, p. 116.

famous heathen temple was found, the king assembled a great *thing*, probably in 996, to confer with the people regarding Christianity. The saga [1] tells that three men were chosen to speak in opposition to the proposal made by the king that they should accept the Christian faith. But when the first one tried to speak, he was seized with a violent cough, the second speaker began to stammer, and the third became so hoarse that he could say nothing. This caused great merriment, and the people agreed to accept the king's proposal. King Olav built a church at Moster, the first Christian church building in this part of Norway.[2] A

little later the king summoned another *thing* at Dragseid, near Stadt, on the west coast, where the people from Sogn, Firdafylke, Søndmør, and Romsdal met. The king had a strong military force, and gave them the choice between receiving baptism, and fighting with him. When they saw that they could not resist him, they submitted and were baptized. After these meet-

FIG. 43. — Old church at Moster thought to have been erected by Olav Tryggvason.

ings in Moster and Dragseid, Olav summoned the Gulathing, where Christianity was declared to be the lawful religion of the whole Gulathingslag.

The legend of St. Sunniva originated in Olav Tryggvason's time, and seems to have been first officially published at the *thing* at Dragseid. In the rocky caverns on the Norwegian coast in these parts, human bones and skeletons have been found, often in a good state of preservation. They may be the remains of persons who have sought refuge in these places, or of people who in prehistoric times have used these caverns as dwellings. Such a find was made in a cavern in the island of Selja, and the rumor spread that the bones were the remains of St. Sunniva, a pious Irish princess, who fled to

[1] *Heimskringla, Olav Tryggvasonssaga*, ch. 55.
[2] It has been thought that the old stone church still standing in the island is the one erected by King Olav, but it is not certain. The church built by Olav may have been a wooden structure.

escape a vicious suitor, and of the holy persons who accompanied her across the sea. Miracles were said to happen in this place. King Olav and Bishop Sigurd visited the cavern while the *thing* was in session at Dragseid, and found there the bones referred to. A church was erected there, and July 8th, supposed to be the saintly princess' death day, was consecrated as the St. Sunnivamas in 996. Norway had thus received her first national saint. A monastery was also founded there, the ruins of which are still to be seen in the island.[1]

King Olav had now introduced Christianity in southern and southwestern Norway. The way had here been paved for the new faith, and the resistance offered to it had been weak and half-hearted. But Trøndelagen, with its famous old temples at Lade and Mæren, still remained the great bulwark of the Asa-faith. Here lived many of the great leaders of the old aristocracy, and the ideas of local autonomy were kept alive. If these populous and well-organized districts, which were properly regarded as the center of military and economic strength in the country at that time, should present a united front against the missionary efforts of the king, the opposition would be formidable enough to endanger the whole movement. Olav was, no doubt, aware of this, and when he entered Trøndelagen, his tactics quickly assumed a military character, as if he well knew what would happen. Odd Munk [2] tells that at Christmas time he prepared a feast at Lade, where he was now staying, and invited all the chieftains of Trøndelagen. When they were seated at the table, the king arose and spoke to them about the religious situation. He said that if he should return to the old faith, he would revive the very ancient custom of human sacrifice, but he would not sacrifice slaves, but the chieftains themselves. He told them that an armed force had surrounded the house, and stood ready to do his bidding.

---

[1] The name Sunniva is English, and the legend is the same as that of Ursula and the 11,000 maidens. *Historiske Afhandlinger tilegnet Professor Dr. J. E. Sars.* Yngvar Nielsen, *De gamle Helligdomme paa Selja.* See A. Taranger, *Den engelske Kirkes Indflydelse paa den norske*, 155. Gustav Storm, *Monumenta, Acta Sanctorum in Selio.* Ludvig Daae, *Norges Helgener*, 137 ff. Konrad Maurer, *Die Bekehrung des norwegischen Stammes*, I, 287 ff. Odd Munk, *Olav Tryggvasonssaga.* Sunniva is not mentioned in *Heimskringla, Fagrskinna*, or the larger *Olav Tryggvasonssaga.*

[2] Odd Munk, *Olav Tryggvasonssaga*, ch. 23.

The chieftains understood the situation, and submitted to the king. Olav destroyed the temple at Lade, and carried away its treasures, but the people gathered an army, and he proceeded to the district of Haalogaland till the storm blew over. In this far northern province the old pagan religion still flourished in all its original vigor. The chieftains, Haarek of Tjotta, Eyvind Kinnriva, and Thore Hjort, met the king with an armed force, and he returned to Trøndelagen. The situation looked threatening. The people kept a large force in the field, and the king lived as if in a military camp, always surrounded by his army. He tried to win the leaders in various ways, but with little success. In 998 he summoned the Frostathing, where all the chieftains in Trøndelagen met, but when he asked them to accept the Christian faith, their leader, Jernskjegge, answered that if the king did not desist from his attempt to introduce Christianity, they would do with him as they had done with Haakon Jarl. Olav spoke words of conciliation and promised to meet them again at the *thing* in Mæren. The *thing* assembled in 999, and Olav came with a force of 300 men. All the chieftains who were most determined in their resistance to Christianity had also met with an armed force. When the *thing* was called to order, says the "Heimskringla," the king spoke, and asked the people to accept the Christian religion. Jernskjegge again answered him in behalf of the people, and said that they were of the same opinion now as before, that the king should not break the law. "We demand," he said, "that you take part in the sacrifice as other kings before you have done," and the people shouted their assent.[1] This scene reminds us of the one enacted on a similar occasion between Asbjørn of Medalhus and Haakon the Good. But Olav was not Haakon. He did not answer Jernskjegge, but said that he would go into the temple and look at the sacrifices. As soon as Olav disappeared in the temple, one of his men cut Jernskjegge down at the entrance, and Olav came out and offered the people the choice of receiving baptism or of fighting with him. Discouraged by the loss of their leader, they submitted and were baptized.

Olav did not wish to stay at Lade, where he was constantly reminded of the old pagan worship. Across the river Nid he founded,

---

[1] *Heimskringla, Olav Tryggvasonssaga*, 68.

in 997, the city of Nidaros, later called Trondhjem. Here he built a royal hall, and erected a church dedicated to St. Clemens, the patron saint of commerce. The city became in time a great center of commercial activity and religious life in Norway.[1]

Haalogaland was also Christianized. The king won the greedy Haarek of Tjotta for the Christian faith by granting him large possessions. The stories told in the sagas that Olav caused Eyvind Kinnriva and Raud den Ramme to be tortured to death, because they refused to be baptized, are fiction — literary ornaments of the kind often used by the saga writers.[2]

Norway was now, in a way, Christianized. The heathen temples were destroyed, sacrifices and the practice of sorcery were forbidden by law; churches were built, and Moster, Selja, and Nidaros became centers of Christian life and missionary activity. But the church was still but an infant. No church organization existed, few were the missionaries who were to instruct the people in the Christian faith, and the old paganism had not been very deeply shaken by King Olav Tryggvason's crusade. And yet, the people had seen, though faintly, the new light, which was now no longer a dream, but an experience. Christianity, this strange force, had entered into the people's life and development as a new and recognized factor, under the seal and sanction of the law.

36. INTRODUCTION OF CHRISTIANITY ON THE FAROE ISLANDS AND ICELAND

The "Fagrskinna" says that Olav Tryggvason Christianized Norway, and, also, several other lands: the Orkneys, the Faroe Islands, the Shetland Islands (Hjaltland), Iceland, and Greenland.[3] Whether he Christianized the Shetland Islands is doubtful, and missionary work seems to have been done in the Orkneys before his reign; but it is quite certain that through his efforts Christianity was introduced in the Faroe Islands, and in Iceland, and, probably, also in Green-

---

[1] Henrik Mathiesen, *Det gamle Trondhjem.* H. G. Heggtveit, *Trondhjem i Fortid og Nutid*, Horten, 1897. *Festskrift udgivet i anledning av Trondhjems 900 aars Jubilæum*, 1897, Trondhjem.

[2] *Heimskringla, Olav Tryggvasonssaga*, chs. 76 and 80.

[3] *Fagrskinna*, p. 57.

land. The Faroe Islands had in course of time become a Norwegian dependency, but in Haakon Jarl's days the powerful and cunning chieftain Trond i Gata had gained complete control of the islands. He was the head of the Gateskjegger, the most powerful family in the islands, who traced their descent from King Olav the White of Dublin, and his queen, Aud the Deepminded. The chivalrous Sigmund Brestesson, the national hero of the islands, whose father had been slain by Trond, and who had subsequently spent a long time in exile in Norway, received aid from Haakon Jarl, and returned to the Faroe Islands, where he defeated Trond. He received the islands as a fief from Haakon, and became his *lendermand*. Sigmund was now the most powerful and popular chieftain in the islands. He resembled Olav Tryggvason in prowess and accomplishments, and was highly admired by his people. Even at this time he seems to have been among those who had practically repudiated the pagan faith. When Haakon Jarl asked him concerning his religious views, he answered that he believed in his own strength and power.[1] Olav invited Sigmund to come to Norway. Here he was baptized, and at the request of the king, he undertook to introduce Christianity in the Faroe Islands. But the task was made difficult by his old rival and enemy Trond i Gata, who stirred up the people against him, and troubled and embarrassed him in every way. Finally, on a dark and stormy night, Sigmund with thirty followers proceeded to the rocky island of Austrey, where Trond was dwelling, took him prisoner, and forced him to receive baptism. The work of Christianizing the islands was now quickly accomplished, but this form of conversion brought with it no great change of heart. Though the outer forms of Christianity had been accepted, life long continued to be heathen in spirit in these islands.

The time had been when the Christian faith was not wholly unknown in Iceland. Many of the early settlers came from the colonies in the British Isles, where they had spent a great part of their life in more or less close contact with the native Christian population, and not a few had been so far influenced by the new faith and culture that they were regarded as Christians, at least by their own

[1] *Færeyingasaga*, ch. 23. Konrad Maurer, *Bekehrung des norwegischen Stammes*, I., 339–346.

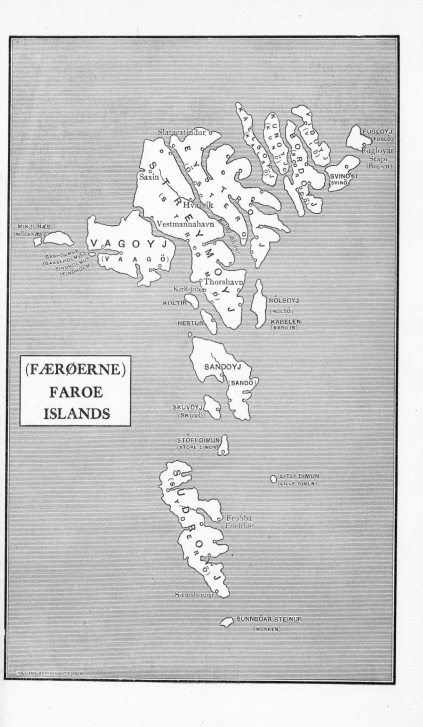

(FÆRØERNE)
FAROE
ISLANDS

countrymen, while some, no doubt, were baptized. The "Land-námabók" says:[1] "It is said by men who are well informed that many of the *landnaamsmœnd* who had migrated to Iceland were baptized, especially of those who came from the West across the sea; among these are mentioned: Helge Magre, Orleyg Gamle, Helge Bjolla, Jørund Kristne (the Christian), Aud the Deepminded, and Ketill Fiflske, and many others who came from the West across the sea; and some of these remained Christians till their death day; but their descendants did not long continue in the faith, for even the sons of some erected temples, and sacrificed to the gods. The land was entirely heathen for well-nigh a hundred years."[2] Those who at this time were regarded as Christians must, however, have been comparatively few in number, and, as they lived scattered among a heathen people, they could not have exercised any marked influence on the life of their fellow countrymen.

A German bishop, Friedrich, and his friend, the Icelander Thorvald Vidførle, who had traveled far and wide, were the first missionaries to Iceland. They arrived there in 981, and succeeded in baptizing a few persons, but when Thorvald ventured to preach at the Althing, he was so twitted and ridiculed that he slew two of his antagonists, and both he and the bishop were outlawed, and had to leave the island.[3]

Many Icelanders came to Norway every year. They were generally influential men at home, and King Olav Tryggvason used every opportunity to win them for the Christian faith. The sagas mention many leading Icelanders who in this way became Christians. The most notable instances of this kind were, probably, the conversions of the poet Hallfrød Vandrædaskald, and of Kjartan Olavsson, a hero famous in saga literature, and one of the leading men in Iceland.[4]

In 996 King Olav sent Stevne Thorgilsson as missionary to Ice-

[1] *Landnámabók*, V., ch. 15.
[2] A great hundred, or $10 \times 12 = 120$. A similar account is found in the younger *Olav Tryggvasonssaga*, ch. 119.
[3] See *Kristnisaga*, the younger *Olav Tryggvasonssaga*, ch. 165. Konrad Maurer, *Bekehrung des norwegischen Stammes*, I., 201 ff.
[4] See *Laxdølasaga*, ch. 40. *Heimskringla*, *Olav Tryggvasonssaga*, ch. 82 and 83. Odd Munk, ch. 30.

land. He marched about the country with an armed force, destroying the temples, pulling down the altars, and raiding the country in true Viking fashion. This was Stevne's idea of missionary work. The Althing passed a law that any one who spoke disrespectfully of the gods, or harmed their images, should be outlawed. In accordance with this measure Stevne was outlawed, and had to leave Iceland. But Olav did not abandon the idea of Christianizing Iceland. The priest Thangbrand, who had come with Olav to Norway, had aroused the king's displeasure by his violent and unchristian conduct, and as a punishment he was ordered to go to Iceland as a missionary. Thangbrand spent the first winter with the thoughtful and influential Sidu-Hall at Þottaa, in eastern Iceland, and Hall was baptized, together with his family. The next spring, 998, Thangbrand began the missionary work in earnest. He was a strong and courageous man, always ready for a fight whenever he encountered opposition. The sagas say that he carried a crucifix before his shield, a wise thing to do, no doubt, or he might have been mistaken for a real Viking.[1] More than once it came to blows, and Thangbrand killed many persons, but the people were impressed by his rough and ready way of dealing with his opponents, and many of the leading men accepted the Christian faith. Dissatisfaction with his methods was, nevertheless, growing, and he was finally outlawed, and had to return to Norway. King Olav was very angry when he learned that Thangbrand's mission also had proved a failure, but two leading Icelanders, Gissur Hvite and Hjalte Skjeggesson, who were then staying in Norway, promised the king to return home, and renew the attempt. In the year 1000 they set sail for Iceland, accompanied by the priest Thormod. The Christians had already become so numerous that they met at the Althing as a strong and well-organized party. But the hostility between the adherents of the two religions was so intense that when Gissur and Hjalte spoke in favor of Christianity, civil war was with difficulty averted. The wise and moderate Sidu-Hall, and the still heathen *lovsigemand*, Thorgeir Ljosvetningagode, succeeded in bringing about a compromise between the contending factions. Thorgeir spoke of the evils which would attend a civil war. Perhaps he pointed out to them, also, what effect it might

---

[1] For an account of Thangbrand see *Njálssaga*, ch. 100 ff.

have on their future autonomy if they continued to resist King Olav in this matter. He suggested a way of settling the difficult question, to which both factions finally agreed. All the people of the island should accept Christianity and be baptized, the heathen temples should be destroyed, and any one who sacrificed publicly to the gods should be outlawed for three years. But any one might sacrifice to the gods privately, eat horse meat, and expose infants as heretofore. Christianity was now the officially acknowledged religion of Iceland, but in thought and spirit the greater part of the people were yet heathen. Generations were still to pass before the precepts of Christian teaching gained full and general recognition.

That no greater change was effected in the people's life and ideas by the first preaching of Christianity was of importance to the development of the saga literature. Had the change been deep and sudden, this literature could never have been produced. The period 930–1030 is known as the great Saga Age. In this period lived the greater number of the renowned persons and families about whom the sagas have been written; such as, Egil Skallagrimsson, Olav Paa, Kjartan Olavsson, Njál paa Bergthórshvál, Gunnar paa Lidarende, Sidu-Hall, Snorre Gode; Bergthora, Hallgerd, Gudrun Usvivsdotter, Aud the Deepminded, and Helga the Fair. Commerce was maintained, not only with Norway and Denmark, but also with Ireland, England, and Normandy. It was a time of enterprise and great achievements, and wealth and luxury could be found among the better families in Iceland in those days. The "Laxdølasaga" tells us that the sons of Hjalte of Hjaltadal entertained twelve hundred (= 1440) guests at their father's funeral. When Hoskuld Dalakollsson died, his son, Olav Paa, invited all the leading men in that part of Iceland to the funeral. Nine hundred guests came (= 1080), and the festival lasted for two weeks. Olav built himself a famous residence, Hjardarholt, the walls of which were decorated with wood carvings representing myths of the Asa-religion. The pictures were later described in the poem "Húsdrápa." The proud memories of this great age were preserved by oral tradition for a couple of centuries; the greater number of the best sagas were not written till in the period 1200–1300, which is regarded as the classic period of Old Norse prose literature. When pagan life is still so perfectly reflected in the sagas, and the Old Norse literary style is found in its classic purity, unmarred by Latin influence, it is due to the fact that paganism survived in Iceland for centuries after Christianity had been officially recognized as the state religion.

King Olav had reunited and Christianized Norway, and all colonial possessions had pledged their submission and loyalty to the mother country. As king he was strong and popular, but the integrity and independence of the kingdom were threatened by powerful enemies. The Danish king was still looking for an opportunity to recover Viken, and the kings of Sweden had reluctantly surrendered their claims to the border province of Ranrike, or Bohuslen, between Svinesund and the Göta River. Eirik and Svein, the sons of Haakon Jarl, had sought refuge in Sweden and Denmark after leaving Norway, and were trying to form a powerful alliance against King Olav. Svein was engaged to Holmfrid, the daughter of the Swedish king, Eirik Seiersæl, and Eirik married Gyda, the daughter of King Svein Tjugeskjeg of Denmark. Olav seems to have been aware of the impending danger. He formed an alliance with Jarl Ragnvald Ulvsson of Vestergötland, and gave him his sister Ingebjørg in marriage, a step which he would scarcely have taken without some political motive. The same is probably true of his courtship of Queen Sigrid Storraade, widow of the Swedish king, Eirik Seiersæl. Both affairs reveal a desire to strengthen the friendly relations with the neighbor state. Sigrid is described as a rich and powerful queen, very proud and haughty. The marriage had been arranged, says the saga,[1] and she came to meet King Olav in Konghelle, in southeastern Norway, but when he asked her to accept the Christian faith, she refused, whereupon he struck her in the face with his glove, and called her a heathen. This ungallant act aroused the temper of the proud queen, and she retorted angrily that it might cost him his life. She returned home, and soon afterward married King Svein Tjugeskjeg of Denmark, while Olav married Thyre, Svein's sister, as it appears, without her brother's consent. From this time on Sigrid continually plotted against King Olav, from motives of revenge. Through her efforts an alliance was formed against him by the kings of Denmark and Sweden, and the jarls Eirik and Svein. It is true that Sigrid

[1] *Heimskringla, Olav Tryggvasonssaga*, ch. 61.

married King Svein of Denmark, and that Olav married Thyre, but the story that Olav struck Sigrid in the face with his glove, because she refused to accept Christianity, is a bit of conventional fiction used in various forms also about other persons both in Norse and Irish sagas. Neither does it seem to be true that the alliance against King Olav was the work of the revengeful Sigrid. The warlike and ambitious Svein Tjugeskjeg was, no doubt, the prime mover in the affair. Already as prince he returned to paganism, and rebelled against his father. He hated King Olav, and felt especially offended because he had married Thyre without obtaining his consent; but the chief motive was his desire to reconquer Viken, and, possibly, all Norway. The time for forming an alliance was especially opportune. His queen, Sigrid, was the mother of the young king of Sweden, Olav Skotkonung, and the jarls Eirik and Svein were ready to join in an undertaking which gave them hope of regaining their power and possessions in Norway. Sigvalde Jarl of Jómsborg, who had suffered defeat in Hjørungavaag, also became a secret partner to the compact. In the harbor of Nidaros Olav Tryggvason had for several years been busy building a new fleet of ships of a size and elegance in equipment hitherto never seen in the North. Especially conspicuous were the ships "Tranen" (the "Crane"), "Ormen Korte" (the "Short Serpent"), and "Ormen Lange" (the "Long Serpent"). In the year 1000 he sailed with a fleet of seventy-one ships southward to Vendland for the purpose, as the sagas have it, of collecting an inheritance belonging to his queen, Thyre, who had formerly been married to Duke Miesco of Poland. The larger ships, especially, were manned by the most select warriors in Norway at that time. Olav's brother-in-law, Erling Skjalgsson of Sole, commanded a squadron of the fleet. His other brothers-in-law, Thorgeir and Hyrning, and his half-brother, Thorkel Nevja, were with Olav on the "Long Serpent." Here were, also, a band of distinguished chieftains, such as Ulv Røde, Kolbein Stallare, Thorgrim Thjodolvsson of Hvin, and Einar Tambarskjælver, a giant in strength, and the best archer in Norway, though only eighteen years of age. Queen Thyre also accompanied Olav on the expedition. What the real purpose of the expedition may have been is not apparent, though it seems reasonable to suppose that it was something more weighty than the collection of the queen's inheritance. The "Historia Norwegiae"[1] states that Olav had forty missionaries with him on the "Long Serpent." This gives it, to some degree, the appearance of a crusade undertaken, possibly, for the purpose of Christianizing the Wends. Certain it is that Olav formed an alliance with Boleslav, king of Poland, doubtless against King Svein of Denmark. He also negotiated with Sigvalde Jarl of Jómsborg, who treacherously promised to aid him, being at the time a secret ally of the Danish king. Unconscious of danger, Olav set sail for the homeward voyage. He allowed a great part of his fleet, consisting of the lighter and swifter vessels commanded by Erling Skjalgsson of Sole, to proceed at full speed, and thus to separate from the squadron of heavier vessels under his own command. Sigvalde Jarl, who was playing the rôle of a friend and ally, followed the king's squadron with a number of ships, and succeeded in decoying him into the estuary of Svolder, where the kings of Sweden and Denmark, and the jarls Eirik and Svein with a great fleet lay ready to attack him. Too late King Olav discovered the plans of his enemies, but he scorned to seek safety in flight. He quickly placed his ships in order of battle, and on the 9th of September, in the year 1000, was fought the memorable battle of Svolder, still famous in the songs and annals of the North. Though overwhelmed by numbers, King Olav and his men fought with prodigious valor until his enemies finally boarded the king's ship, the "Long Serpent," and Olav leaped overboard with his few remaining followers. Queen Thyre is said to have died of grief a short time afterward.[2] Thus ended Olav Tryggvason's short but brilliant career, and the unity and independence of the kingdom of Norway perished with him. "He came from the unknown, and disappeared in the dark," says Alexander Bugge, "but his reign was of epoch-making importance. It represents the transition from the Viking Age to the Middle Ages."

After the battle of Svolder Norway was divided among the victors. King Svein of Denmark got Viken, excepting the province of Ranrike, which was incorporated in the kingdom of Sweden. The Swedish king also received the four *fylker* in Indtrøndelagen, together with Nordmør, Romsdal, and Søndmør. These possessions he gave as a

[1] *Historia Norwegiae*, p. 118.
[2] *Heimskringla, Olav Tryggvasonssaga*, ch. 102 ff.

fief to Svein Jarl, who had married his sister Holmfrid. Eirik Jarl became independent sovereign over the whole coast region, from Finmarken to Lindesnes. Raumarike and Vingulmark, and two districts in Viken, he received as a fief from his father-in-law, King Svein Tjugeskjeg. In Oplandene the kings regained their old autonomy, and the island possessions, too, drifted away from the mother country in the period of disintegration and weakness which was now inaugurated. Jarl Sigurd Lodvesson ruled the Orkney and Shetland Islands as an independent prince, and in the Faroe Islands the old pagan party, led by Trond i Gata, rose against Sigmund Brestesson, who was finally slain. Trond gained full control in the islands, and paid no heed to Norway, which was now divided among foreign princes and self-seeking jarls — a dismembered kingdom with an empty throne.

37. The Discovery and Colonization of Greenland

About the year 900 a man by the name of Gunbjørn, while on a voyage to Iceland, was driven out of his course far to the westward, where he claimed that he discovered a new land.[1] In Iceland stories were told of his adventure, and the land which he claimed to have seen was called Gunbjørn's Skjær (skerry, rock). In 982 Eirik the Red, a settler near the mouth of the Breidafjord in northwestern Iceland, was outlawed for killing a man in a brawl. He left Iceland with a few followers, and undertook to find the land which Gunbjørn had seen. He reached the ice-bound east coast of Greenland, and, finding it uninhabitable, he continued the voyage southward along the coast, rounded the southern extremity of the island, and came finally to a fjord on the west coast, which he called Eiriksfjord (Tunugdliarfik). During the following three years he explored the west coast of Greenland, and sought out the places where colonies might be established. He then returned to Iceland to induce people to migrate to the new land. He called it Greenland, because he thought that it would be easier to persuade people to go there, if the land had a fine name.[2]

[1] The O. N. documents dealing with the colonization of Greenland and the discovery of America are found in the *Antiquitates Americanae*, Copenhagen, 1837, edited by Carl Christian Rafn.

[2] Are Frode, *Íslendingabók*, ch. 6. *Eyrbyggjasaga*, ch. 25.

In 986 [1] twenty-five ships sailed for Greenland, but only fourteen reached their destination. The rest were lost, or had to return. It is possible that the fleet was caught in the great earthquake which is known to have occurred at that time. The "Flateyjarbók" mentions a Christian colonist from the Hebrides who accompanied Herjulv, one of the early settlers, on his voyage to Greenland. He wrote a poem, the "Hafgerðingadrápa," about the great breakers in the ocean, from which he prays God to protect him. Only a single stanza of the poem has been preserved.[2]

The colonists found no native inhabitants where they settled, but numerous traces of human beings convinced them that Greenland was inhabited. The reliable old writer Are Frode [3] says: "They found remnants of human dwelling places both eastward and westward in the land, stone weapons and fragments of boats, from which it was evident that the same people who inhabit Vinland, and whom the people of Greenland call Skrælings,[4] had also sojourned here." Two settlements were founded on the west coast. The Eastern Settlement, in 60°–61° N. L., corresponding to the present Julianehaab district; and the Western Settlement farther up the coast, in 64°–65° N. L., located in the present district of Godthaab.[5]

The Eastern Settlement numbered at one time 190 dwellings, twelve churches, a cloister, and a monastery; the Western Settlement had ninety dwellings and four churches. The number of inhabitants in the two settlements probably never exceeded 2000.

In Greenland the winters are long and cold, and the sea is covered with huge icebergs till quite late in the spring. But in the summer months a green belt of vegetation stretches along the western coast,

---

[1] *Islandske Annaler*, edited by Gustav Storm, p. 104 and 464.

[2] See *Landnámabók*, V, ch. 14; also, *Voyages of the Norsemen*, edited by Professor Julius E. Olson in *Original Narratives of Early American History*, p. 47.

[3] *Kongespeilet*, ch. 16, gives a more detailed account of this phenomenon. Are Torgilsson Frode, born in Iceland 1067, wrote the *Íslendingabók*, probably in the period 1120–1130. It is a work of fundamental importance in Old Norse history writing. The work has been preserved in a somewhat abridged form of a later date.

[4] Skræling, from O. N. *skral*, puny, thin, small.

[5] Daniel Bruun, *Det høie Nord, Færøernes, Islands og Grønlands Udforskning*, Copenhagen, 1902.

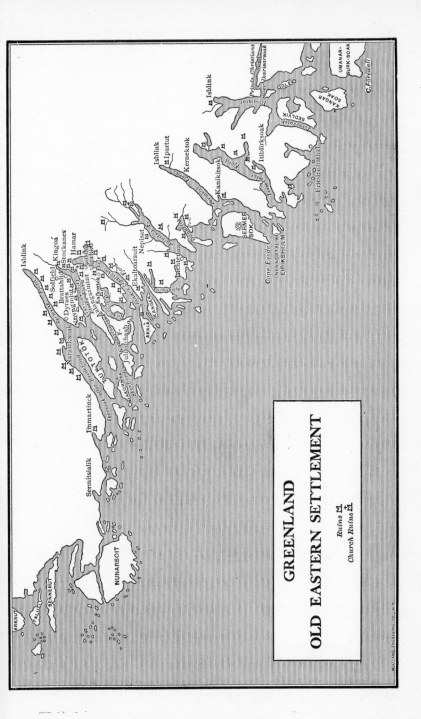

GREENLAND
OLD EASTERN SETTLEMENT

Ruins ⌂
Church Ruins ⛪

behind which tower the immense glaciers, and huge, snow-covered mountains.[1] The weather during this season of the year is agreeable, and the scenery beautiful. Explorers claim that those who have stayed long enough to become acquainted with conditions, always like to return to Greenland. The vegetation in the summer is quite varied. There are no forests, but birch trees reach a diameter of six inches, and a height of twenty feet, and they are numerous enough to form considerable groves. There is an abundance of grass, flowers, berries, and brush. The blue fjords and green valleys, the calm, clear air, the sun shining on glaciers and snow-covered mountains, give the region in the summertime a serene and tranquil beauty. Fish are found in abundance in the streams, as well as in the sea, and seals, walrus, polar bears, and furbearing animals are plentiful. Cattle, sheep, goats, and horses thrived well, and were kept in goodly numbers by the settlers. "The King's Mirror" says: "It is said that in Greenland there is good pasturage. The people have many sheep and cattle, and make cheese and butter in large quantities." But no grain could be raised, and we are told that many of the people living there, especially those of the poorer class, had never tasted bread.

By the Eiriksfjord lay Brattahlid, the home of Eirik the Red, the first chieftain's residence erected in Greenland. By the Einarsfjord (Igaliko) lay Gardar, where the Althing met every summer. The Icelandic laws and system of government were introduced. The settlements were divided into districts, or *sysler*, and all important matters were brought before the Althing, where the *lovsigemand* presided.

The settlers continued to explore the west coast of Greenland. In the summer they sailed northward to a place called Norðrsetur, in the region about Disco Bay, to hunt seal, and to gather driftwood. How far north they penetrated is not known, but in 1824 a rune-stone was found in the island of Kingigtorsuak, 72° 55′ 20″ N. L., which shows that they reached this latitude. Professor Magnus Olsen thinks that the stone dates from about 1300.[2]

[1] Finnur Jónsson og Helga Pettursson, *Um Grønland að Fornu og Nyju*, Copenhagen, 1899.

Kongespeilet gives a lengthy description of the climate of Greenland, which is equally correct at the present time.

[2] The stone has the following inscription: "Erling Sighvatsson, Bjarne Thordarsson and Endride Oddsson Saturday before gagndag (April 25)

The colonists built their houses and churches of stone, and many ruins of these early buildings are still found. Their dwelling houses were of good size, and separate stables were built for horses, cattle, and sheep. Intellectual life flourished, and literature was produced also in Greenland. The "Atlamál" of the "Elder Edda" was, no doubt, composed there in the second half of the eleventh century. Kostbera's dream of the polar bear coming into the house and devouring the people shows that the poem was written in Greenland. It may, indeed, happen that polar bears reach the coast of Iceland on cakes of ice, but such instances are rare, and it could not have occurred to an Icelandic poet to describe such a bear as coming into the houses and devouring people. A few lines of a "Norðrsetudrápa" written in Greenland have also been preserved. Stories and sagas were told at the Althing in Greenland as well as in Norway and Iceland.

Navigation between Greenland and Iceland was often difficult and dangerous, and was at times entirely interrupted by ice. In 999 Leiv Eiriksson, the son of Eirik the Red, struck boldly across the Atlantic, and sailed from Greenland to Norway by way of the Hebrides. This was the first voyage made directly across the Atlantic Ocean, and marks the beginning of ocean navigation. When we consider that the voyage was made in open boats, and without compass, we can understand the daring of these northern sailors. It is an achievement which ranks with the greatest in the history of navigation. A new route of commerce and travel was thus opened between Norway and Greenland, and a lucrative trade soon sprang up between the two countries. "The King's Mirror" ("Kongespeilet") says that "some go to Greenland because of the renown which they gain by exposing themselves to great dangers; others go to satisfy their curiosity, but some for the sake of profit. The Greenlanders have to import nearly all things needed in the colonization of the country: iron, building material, and other necessaries; but they sell hides, seal skins, walrus teeth, and ropes of walrus hide."[1] Grain was also a leading article of import.

While Leiv Eiriksson was in Norway, he visited King Olav Tryggva-

---

built these varder (cairns) and cleared . . ." Then follow a few runes which have been erroneously interpreted to mean 1135. Professor L. Fr. Löffler interprets them to mean ice.   [1] *Kongespeilet*, ch. 17.

son, who persuaded him to receive the Christian faith. He undertook to introduce Christianity in Greenland on his return, and the king sent a missionary along to aid him in the work. The people received the new faith without much difficulty, but their moral and spiritual life was at first but slightly influenced by the change, and heathen customs continued to prevail. Leiv's father, Eirik the Red, refused to be baptized, and continued to worship an old polar bear staying in the neighborhood of Brattahlid. Greenland became a bishopric, probably about 1110, though Arnaldr, who was ordained bishop in Lund, in Skåne, 1124, is the first bishop of Greenland known to have been ordained. A cathedral was erected at Gardar, where the bishop resided, but the foundations alone remain of the once proud structure. Its massive walls of red sandstone have been used as a quarry where the inhabitants in modern times found convenient

FIG. 44. — Ruins of the church at Kakortok, Greenland.

building material. The foundations and ruins of five churches from this period have been found, among others a well preserved ruin at Kakortok of a church, which, probably, was never completed. Excavations have been made in these ruins, and a number of relics have been brought to light.[1] In the Eastern Settlement the ruins of about 100 dwellings have been found.

In perusing the later history of the colonies it grows constantly darker, until, at length, the light completely fails. When modern intercourse again brings this remote region to view, it presents to the inquisitive eye of the traveler, not flourishing settlements, but a graveyard where all traces of the colonists are lost. What, we ask, became of the now extinct colonies? In 1261, in the reign of King Haakon Haakonsson, Greenland became a Norwegian dependency, or crown colony. Till the beginning of the fourteenth century con-

[1] Daniel Bruun, *Udgravninger paa Grønland. Grønlands historiske Mindesmerker.*

siderable traffic was maintained between Greenland, Iceland, and Norway, but the Black Death, which reached Norway in 1349, gave this traffic a severe blow. Great harm had already been done by making colonial trade a royal monopoly, so that no trading vessels could go to the colonies, except a few which were in the king's service. This monopoly stopped all enterprise, and virtually put an end to commercial intercourse with Greenland. When the Hanseatic merchants finally gained control of Bergen, the most important commercial city in Norway at that time, and swept Norwegian commerce from the sea, the colonies in Greenland were completely cut off from all communication with the mother country, on which they depended for so many of the necessaries of life. Nothing more was heard about them, and they were soon entirely forgotten. The last mention of the colonies is found in a papal letter issued by Pope Alexander VI., in the first year of his pontificate (1492–1493), dealing with the appointment of a new bishop for Greenland. "For eighty years, or thereabouts," says the Pope, "absolutely no bishop or priest governed that church (of Greenland) in personal residence," and he complains that Christianity has almost died out there.[1] Being left without aid by the mother country, the settlers were in sore straits, and were, probably, forced little by little to adopt the mode of life of the Eskimos. The Western Settlement seems to have been abandoned prior to 1340. A priest, Ivar Baardsson, from Norway, came to Greenland in 1341, and was sent to the Western Settlement with a small force to aid the settlers, but he did not find a person there. The colony was entirely destroyed, says the account, only a few almost wild sheep and cattle were found and brought to the Eastern Settlement. For the year 1379 the "Icelandic Annals" contain the following notice: "The Skrælings attacked the Greenlanders, killed eighteen of them, and carried away two boys, whom they made slaves."[2] Where this fight took place, or what was the cause of it, is not known. In 1418 the Skrælings again attacked the settlers, killed many people, and burned

[1] The letter is printed in the *Flatey-book and Recently Discovered Vatican Manuscripts Concerning America as Early as the Tenth Century*, published by the Norrœna Society, New York, London; etc., 1908. Also in *Original Narratives of Early American History*, New York, 1906.

[2] *Islandske Annaler*, edited by Gustav Storm, Christiania, 1888, p. 364. *Grønlands historiske Mindesmerker*, III., p. 258.

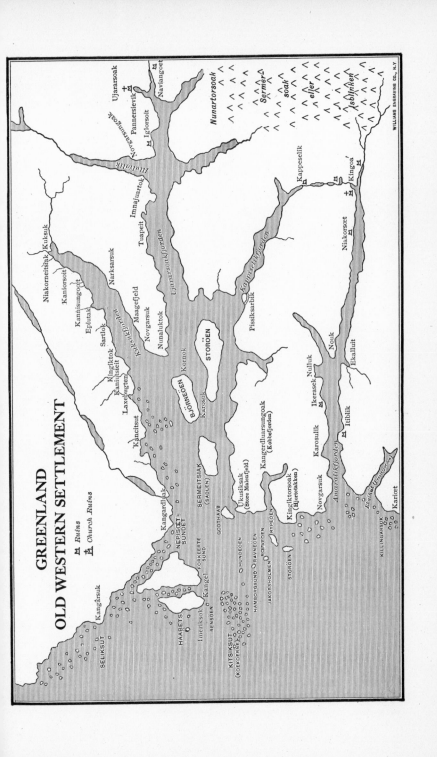

GREENLAND
OLD WESTERN SETTLEMENT

⌂ Ruins ⌂ Church Ruins

WILLIAMS ENGRAVING CO., N.Y

houses and churches. References to these events are found in a letter by Pope Nicolaus V., dated Sept. 20, 1448,[1] in which he speaks of the calamities which befell the church and people of Greenland thirty years earlier. What, finally, became of the settlers is left to conjecture. Did they all perish ? or did they finally join the Eskimos after all hope of aid from the mother country had to be abandoned? The Danish explorer, Normann Hansen, in a lecture on his investigations of the ruins of the Old Norse colonies in Greenland recently delivered at Copenhagen, states that at the head of one of the fjords he and his companions made their way up a fork-shaped river, and found, in a place difficult of approach, a ruin which, from its situation, seems to have been the last place of refuge of the Norse colonists. The buildings in this remarkable retreat were constructed in a more substantial way than elsewhere. On the top of a high mountain, Igdlerfigsalik, two stone circles are found which seem to be the remains of stone huts erected there by the Norse colonists. Mr. Daniel Bruun thinks that these huts have been used by watchmen who year after year maintained the fruitless outlook for aid from the mother country, which never came till the last colonist had perished. Professor Nansen maintains that the views hitherto generally held, that the colonists were exterminated by the Eskimos, are untenable for many reasons. The attacks on the colonists which the Eskimos are reported to have made must have been provoked by the settlers themselves, as the Eskimos are a very peaceful people, and these conflicts could scarcely have been so serious as to lead to the destruction of the colonies. The report that Ivar Baardsson in 1341 found the Western Settlement destroyed rests on a misconception, according to Nansen. The report says that he found no people, but only some sheep and cattle. This does not prove that the people

---

[1] The letter is printed and translated in *Original Narratives of Early American History*, Scribner's Sons, New York, 1906. Also in *Flatey-book and Recently Discovered Vatican Manuscripts Concerning America as Early as in the Tenth Century*, Norrœna Society, New York, 1908. Nansen shows that the Pope has not been well informed about conditions in Greenland, and that many statements in the letter are erroneous. The events as here described can scarcely be regarded as historical, though there may have been conflicts between the Skrælings and the settlers. See *Nord i Taakeheimen*, p. 373. (English title, *In Northern Mists*.)

had been killed. But the report itself seems to be erroneous. The sheep and cattle could have existed in Greenland uncared-for but a short time during the summer months. If the settlement had been destroyed, this must have happened, then, shortly before Baardsson's arrival, in which case traces of the final conflict would still have been visible. Norse loan-words and traditions still found among the Eskimos indicate that the Norse settlers finally joined them. During long periods the colonists had no priests to maintain the Christian religion among them, and they gradually returned to paganism. This can be seen, both from Pope Alexander VI.'s letter, and from an entry in "Gisle Oddsson's Annals," written in Iceland in 1637: "The people of Greenland fell away from the true faith and the Christian religion, and after having lost all good customs and true virtues they returned to the American people." [1] This can only mean that they turned to the ways of the native inhabitants. Professor Nansen shows that the Eskimos' mode of life was the only one possible for the colonists in Greenland after the connections with the mother country had been severed.

In 1406 a ship sailing from Norway to Iceland strayed from its course, and finally landed in Greenland, where it remained till 1410, when it returned to Norway. This is the last definite mention of a voyage from Norway to Greenland. But the letter of Pope Alexander VI., 1492, indicates that news had been brought from Greenland regarding conditions there shortly before the letter was written. There are also other indications that a voyage was made to Greenland in the latter part of the fifteenth century.[2] Some sources even state that the expedition took place in 1476. After this time no mention is made of voyages to Greenland. When John Davis, in 1585, reached the coast of Greenland, the "Land of Desolation," six hundred years after Eirik the Red had first discovered it, he found Eskimos there, but the white settlers had disappeared, and Davis thought he was the real discoverer of the country.

---

[1] *Grønlands historiske Mindesmerker*, III., p. 459.
[2] Daniel Bruun, *Det høie Nord*, p. 176. Fridtjof Nansen, *Nord i Taakeheimen*, p. 376 f.

38. The Discovery of the Mainland of North America

After the Norsemen had succeeded in establishing colonies in Greenland; after ocean voyages were successfully made across the North Atlantic to Norway, and their exploring expeditions found the way northward through Davis Strait into the polar regions, it is by no means surprising that they should also have found the neighboring coast of the mainland of North America. Though no relic has been found which can be offered as a proof that the Norsemen ever visited these shores, the fact that they discovered America about the year 1000 is so well established as to leave no room for doubt or controversy. Professor Fridtjof Nansen, who in his work "In Northern Mists" (1911) has subjected all accounts of the Vinland voyages and the discovery of America by the Norsemen to a most searching criticism, says: "Icelandic literature contains many remarkable statements about countries to the southwest or south of the Greenland settlements. They are called 'Helluland' (*i.e.* slate or stone-land), 'Markland' (*i.e.* wood-land), 'Furðustrandir' (*i.e.* the marvel-strands), and 'Vínland' (also written 'Vindland,' or 'Vinland'). Yet another, which lay to the west of Ireland, was called 'Hvítra-manna-land' (*i.e.* the white men's land). Even if certain of these countries are legendary, as will presently be shown, it must be regarded as a fact that the Greenlanders and Icelanders reached some of them, which lay on the northeastern coast of America; and they thus discovered the continent of North America besides Greenland, about five hundred years before Cabot (and Columbus)." [1]

Vinland is first mentioned by Adam v. Bremen about 1070. In the fourth chapter of his church history of the archbishopric of Hamburg, "Gesta Hammaburgensis," is found a description of the lands and islands in the far North, "Discriptio Insularum Aquilonis." Adam's geographical knowledge is derived from various sources: from old classic authors, from Bede, Paulus Warnefridus, and other old writers, and partly from information gathered at the court of the Danish king, Svein Estridsson, where he was staying at the time. He says about Vinland:

[1] Nansen, *In Northern Mists*, vol. I., p. 312.

"He (the king of Denmark) mentioned also another island which has been discovered by many in this ocean, which is called Winland, because grapevines grow wild there, and yield the best wine. That self-sown grain is found there in abundance, we have learned, not through fabulous conjecture, but through reliable accounts given by the Danes. Beyond this island there is no habitable land in that ocean, but all which lies beyond is full of unbearable ice and boundless gloom. Of this circumstance we are reminded by Marcian: 'Three days' sailing beyond Thule the ocean is congealed.' Harald, the king of the Norsemen, a prince very desirous of knowledge, experienced this when he explored the whole width of the northern ocean with his ships, and as the disappearing edge of the earth grew dark before his eyes, he scarcely escaped in safety the great abyss by returning." [1]

The next mention of Vinland is found in Are Frode's "Íslendingabók" (1120–1130):

"The land which is called Greenland was discovered and colonized from Iceland. Eirik the Red, a man from Breidafjord, went thither, and took land in a place since called Eiriksfjord. He gave the land name, and called it Greenland, saying that it would entice people to go there, if the country had a fine name. They found human dwelling places both east and west in the land, remnants of boats, and stone implements, from which they could judge that the same people had wandered about here, which inhabit Vinland and which the Greenlanders call Skrælings. But he began to colonize the country fourteen or fifteen winters before Christianity was introduced in Iceland,[2] according to what was told Thorkel Gellisson in Greenland by one who had accompanied Eirik the Red thither." [3]

Hvítramannaland and Vinland are mentioned in the "Landnámabók" about 1250.

"Hvítramannaland, which some call Ireland the Great, lies in the western ocean near Vinland the Good. It is considered to be six days' sailing west of Ireland." [4]

The Hauk version of the "Landnámabók" also states that Karlsevne found Vinland the Good.[5]

---

[1] Adam v. Bremen, *Gesta Hammaburgensis*, IV., 38.

[2] According to Are, Christianity was introduced there in the year 1000.

[3] *Íslendingabók*, ch. 6.

[4] *Landnámabók*, part II., ch. XXII.   [5] Part III., ch. X.

A most interesting allusion to Helluland, Markland, and Vinland is found in an old Icelandic geography, thought to have been written, in part at least, by Abbot Nikulás Bergsson of Thverá, who died in 1159. "South of Greenland," he says, "lies Helluland, then comes Markland, and not very far from there lies Vinland the Good, which some believe to be connected with Africa; but if this is the case, then the great ocean must come between Markland and Vinland. It is said that Thorfinn Karlsevne chopped a tree for a *husa-snotra* (an ornament on a building), and that he afterwards set out to find Vinland the Good, and came to the place where this land was supposed to lie, but he was not able to explore it, and did not establish himself there. Leiv the Lucky first discovered Vinland, and he rescued some merchants whom he found in the sea in great danger. He also introduced Christianity in Greenland, which so prospered that a bishopric was established at Gardar."

We find, then, in the oldest existing form of the tradition the following quite distinct features: South of Greenland three lands had been discovered; Helluland, Markland, and Vinland. The discovery is attributed to Leiv Eiriksson, called Leiv the Lucky, who also introduced Christianity in Greenland. Thorfinn Karlsevne led an expedition to Vinland, but no permanent colony was established there.

Vinland is mentioned also in several sagas from the classic period of saga literature. In the "Eyrbyggjasaga," of about 1250, the following statement is found: "Snorre went to Vinland the Good with Karlsevne. They fought there with the Skrælings, and Thorbrand Snorresson, the bravest of men, was killed."

The same saga tells also of a merchant by the name of Gudleiv, who sailed from Norway to Dublin. From there he was going to Iceland, but was driven by strong winds far westward into the ocean, where he finally came to an unknown land. The warlike natives met them in large numbers, but the chieftain, who proved to be an Icelander, soon addressed them in their own language, and made inquiries about his relatives in Iceland. After a long conversation he advised them to leave the country, and sent with them presents to his friends at home.[1]

---

[1] *Eyrbyggjasaga*, chs. 48, 64.

Vinland is mentioned in the "Heimskringla," written about 1230, in the "Kristnisaga," prior to 1245, and in the "Grettissaga," from 1290. The only lengthy description existing of the discovery of America, and the subsequent voyages to Vinland, are found in the "Saga of Eirik the Red," [1] written in the thirteenth century, and in the "Grønlendingaþáttr" in the "Flateyjarbók," dating from about 1387, but the narratives in these two sources differ in many respects. According to the "Grønlendingaþáttr," it was Bjarne Herjolvsson who first discovered Vinland. On a voyage from Norway to Greenland he was driven out of his course towards the American coast. He finally reached Greenland, but he said nothing about his discovery till several years afterward, when he was staying in Trondhjem, in Norway, at the court of Eirik Jarl. He was criticized by many because he had not spoken about it, and Leiv Eiriksson bought a ship, and set out to discover the land which Bjarne had seen. The "Saga of Eirik the Red" says that Leiv Eiriksson discovered America. The "Flateyjarbók" describes five different voyages to Vinland. The "Saga of Eirik the Red" mentions only two; the discovery by Leiv Eiriksson, and Karlsevne's attempt to colonize the new land. Professor Gustav Storm has subjected all the sources dealing with this question to a critical examination in his excellent work "Studier over Vinlandsreiserne" (1887), in which he shows that the "Saga of Eirik the Red," written in the classic period of Icelandic literature, has preserved the tradition regarding the discovery of America in its most reliable form. He points out that this saga bears all the marks of general truthfulness, that it agrees in the main with independent older sources, and that, therefore, the account given must be accepted as reliable in its main features. The "Flateyjarbók" is a later production, written at a time when the saga literature was fast degenerating, and the tradition had been partly forgotten. He shows that where it differs from the "Saga of Eirik the Red" it stands unsupported by other evidence, that it often relates things in themselves quite incredible, and that it must be discarded as a reliable historical source.

By following the more reliable "Saga of Eirik the Red" the account

[1] Finnur Jónsson is of the opinion that this saga was written about 1200, while Gustav Storm regards the period 1270–1300 as a more likely date.

of the events connected with the discovery of the mainland of North America, and of the attempts to found a colony somewhere on the coast will be as follows: [1]

Leiv Eiriksson, the son of Eirik the Red, sailed from Greenland to Norway in 999. He came to the court of King Olav Tryggvason, and was well received. The king persuaded him to accept the Christian faith, and Leiv undertook to proclaim Christianity in Greenland on his return. In the spring of 1000 Leiv started on the homeward voyage.

"Leiv put to sea when his ship was ready for the voyage. For a long time he drifted about in the sea, and he came upon lands of which he previously had no knowledge. There were self-sown wheat fields, and vines grew there. There were also the trees which are called *masur* (*mǫsurr*), and of all these they had some specimens. Some trees were so large that they were laid in houses" (*i.e.* used as housebeams).

"On his homeward voyage Leiv found some men on a wreck, and took them home with him and gave them all shelter for the winter. He showed much nobility and goodness, he introduced Christianity into the country, and rescued the men; he was called Leiv hinn heppni (the Lucky)."

After Leiv's return home "there was much talk that they ought to seek the land which Leiv had found. The leader was Thorstein Eiriksson,[2] a good man, and wise, and friendly."

Eirik the Red was also asked to join in this undertaking.

"Eirik was asked, and they trusted in his good fortune and foresight being greatest. He was against it, but did not say no, as his friends exhorted him to do it. . . . They drifted about the sea for a long time and did not arrive where they had desired. They came in sight of Iceland, and they had also birds from Ireland; their ship was carried eastward over the ocean. They came back in the autumn, and were then weary and worn."

Thorstein Eiriksson now married Gudrid, a young woman who shortly before had come over from Iceland. They settled in Lysefjord,

---

[1] *The Saga of Eirik the Red*, also called the *Saga of Thorfinn Karlsevne*, is translated in *Original Narratives of Early American History*.

[2] A brother of Leiv Eiriksson.

in the Western Settlement, but Thorstein died that same winter, and Gudrid returned to Eirik the Red, in Brattahlid in 1001.

The following summer two ships came from Iceland. One was owned by Thorfinn Karlsevne. Along with him came Snorre Thorbrandsson. The other ship belonged to Bjarne Grimolvsson and Thorhall Gamlason. They came to Brattahlid to Eirik the Red, and remained there that winter. After Christmas Karlsevne married Gudrid, Thorstein Eiriksson's widow. In the spring he prepared an expedition for the purpose of establishing a colony in Vinland.

In 1003, three ships were fitted out; one by Karlsevne and Snorre Thorbrandsson, another by Bjarne Grimolvsson and Thorhall Gamlason, and a third by Thorvald, a son of Eirik the Red, and Thorhall Veidemand (the Hunter). Karlsevne's wife, Gudrid, accompanied him, and Freydis, a daughter of Eirik the Red, also joined the expedition.

"They had in all 160 men when they sailed to the Western Settlement and thence to Bjarneyjar (Bear Islands). From there they sailed away with a north wind. They were on the sea two *dægr*.[1] Then they found land, and rowed along it in boats, and examined the country, and found there on the shore many flat stones so large that two men might easily lie stretched upon them sole to sole. There were many white foxes there. They gave the land a name and called it 'Helluland' (*i.e.* Land of Flat Stones)."

This land is thought to have been Labrador.

Then they sailed for two *dægr* towards the southeast and south, and then a land lay before them, and upon it were great forests and many beasts.

An island lay to the southeast off the land, and there they found a polar bear, and they called the island "Bjarney"; but the country they called "Markland" (*i.e.* Woodland) on account of the forests.

This is thought to have been Newfoundland, where extensive forests are found, and where red deer still exist in large numbers. Polar bears occasionally reach the coast of Newfoundland on large cakes of ice, but have not been found farther south.

"After they had sailed again for two *dægr*, they sighted land and sailed under the land. There was a promontory where they first

---

[1] *dægr* = 12 hours.

came. They cruised along the shore, which they kept to starboard (*i.e.* to the west). It was without harbors, and there were long strands and stretches of sand. They went ashore in boats, and found there on the promontory a ship's keel, and called it 'Kjalarnes' (*i.e.* Keelness). They also gave the strands a name and called them 'Furðustrandir' (*i.e.* Marvel Strands, or the wonderful, strange strands), because it took a long time to sail by them."

Gustav Storm held that Kjalarnes was located somewhere on the coast of Cape Breton Island, and that the ship's keel must have been carried thither by the ocean currents. Fridtjof Nansen thinks that the name has, probably, been suggested by the shape of the cape, which may have resembled a keel. This was the more common way in which such names originated.[1]

South of the Furðustrandir " the land was indented by bays (vágskorit) and they steered the ships into a bay." Karlsevne put on shore the Gaelic runners (the man Haki and the woman Hekja) whom Leiv and Eirik had given him. They were to run southward, and examine the condition of the country, and return before three days were past. Karlsevne cast anchor and waited during their absence; "and when three days were past, they came running down from the land, and one of them had grapes in his hand, the other self-sown wheat. Karlsevne said that they seemed to have found a fertile country. They sailed along the coast and came to anchor in a fjord."

"There was an island outside, and round the island strong currents. They called it 'Straumsey.' There were so many birds there that one could hardly put one's foot between the eggs. They held up the fjord, and called it 'Straumsfjord,' and unloaded the ships, and established themselves there. They had with them all kinds of cattle, and sought to make use of the land. There were mountains there, and fair was the prospect. They did nothing else but search out the land. There was much grass. They stayed there the winter, and it was very long; but they had not taken thought for anything, and were short of food, and their catch decreased. Then they went out to the island expecting that there they might find some fishing, or something might drift up (*i.e.* a whale be driven ashore?). There was, however, little to be caught for food, but their cattle thrived

---

[1] Nansen, *In Northern Mists*, vol. I., p. 324.

there. Then they prayed to God that he might send them something to eat; but no answer came so quickly as they had hoped." The heathen Thorhall the Hunter then disappeared for three *dœgr*, and doubtless held secret conjurations with the red-bearded one (*i.e.* Thor). A little later a whale was driven ashore, and they ate of it, but were all sick. When they found out how things were with Thorhall and Thor, "they cast it over the cliff, and prayed God for mercy. They then made a catch of fish, and there was no lack of food. In the spring (1004) they entered Straumsfjord, and had catches from both lands (*i.e.* from both sides of the fjord), hunting on the mainland, eggs on the island, and fish in the sea."

Thorhall the Hunter seems to have been much disappointed. He quarreled with Karlsevne, and wished to go northward in search of Vinland, while Karlsevne decided to go southward. With nine others, who probably wished to return home, he left the expedition. While he was preparing his ship for the voyage, he sang the following lay:

> "Let us go homeward,
>   where we shall find fellow countrymen;
>   let us with our ship seek
>   the broad ways of the sea,
>   while the hopeful
>   warriors (those who praise
>   the land) on Furðustrandir
>   stay and boil whales' flesh."

"Then they parted (from Karlsevne, who had accompanied them out) and sailed north of Furðustrandir and Kjalarnes, and then tried to beat westward. Then the westerly storm caught them, and they drifted to Ireland, where they were made slaves and ill-treated. There Thorhall lost his life, as merchants have reported.

"Karlsevne, with Snorre, Bjarne, and the rest, continued southward along the coast.

"They sailed a long time, until they came to a river, which flowed down from the interior into a lake, and thence into the sea. There were great sandbars before the mouth of the river, so that it could only be entered at high water. Karlsevne and his people sailed to the mouth of the river and called the country 'Hóp' (*i.e.* a small land-locked bay).

There they found self-sown wheat fields, where the land was low, but vines wherever they saw heights. As every brook was full of fish, they dug trenches on the shore below high-water mark, and when the tide went out, there were halibuts in the trenches. In the forests there was a great quantity of beasts of all kinds. They were there half a month amusing themselves, and suspecting nothing. They had their cattle with them. But early one morning, when they looked about them, they saw nine hide-boats [1] (hudkeipa), and wooden poles were being waved on the boats, making a noise like threshing-flails, and they were moved with the sun. Karlsevne's men took this to be a token of peace, and bore a white shield towards them. Then the strangers rowed towards them, and wondered, and came ashore. They were small (or black) men,[2] and ugly, and they had ugly hair; their eyes were big, and they were broad across the cheeks. They stayed there awhile, and wondered, then rowed away and went south of the headland."

Professor Nansen says of this first meeting of white men with the North American Indians: "This, then, would be the description of the first meeting in history between Europeans and the natives of America. With all its brevity it gives an excellent picture; but whether we can accept it is doubtful. As we shall see later, the Norsemen probably did meet with Indians; but the description of the latter's appearance must necessarily have been colored more and more by greater familiarity with the Skrælings of Greenland when the sagas were put into writing. The big eyes [3] will not suit either of them, and are rather to be regarded as an attribute of trolls and underground beings; gnomes and old fairy men have big, watery eyes. The ugly hair is also an attribute of the underground beings." [4]

[1] Storm thinks that the saga writer has failed to distinguish between bark canoes and skin canoes. So, also, John Fiske, *Discovery of America*, I., 191. Professor Yngvar Nielsen has advanced the theory that the natives which the Norsemen met in America were Eskimos, a theory which has not been accepted. See *Historisk Tidsskrift*, fjerde række, vol. III., p. 277 ff.

[2] The Vellum A.M. 557 says "smair menn" (small men). The *Hauksbók* says "svartir men," meaning, probably, black-haired and dark-eyed.

[3] Storm suggests that the expression "eygðir váru þeir mjǫk" (they had large eyes) may refer to the size of the eye sockets. *Studier over Vinlandsreiserne, Vinlands Geografi og Ethnografi*, p. 54 ff.

[4] Nansen, *In Northern Mists*, vol. I., p. 327.

"Karlsevne had built their houses above the lake, some nearer, some farther off. Now they stayed there that winter (1004–1005). No snow fell at all, and their cattle were out at pasture."

Regarding the probable location of Vinland there has been much difference of opinion. In the "Flateyjarbók" the statement is made that day and night are of more equal length there than in Greenland or Iceland. "The sun had there $eyktarstaðr$ and $dagmálastaðr$ on the shortest day of the year"; $i.e.$ the sun was up at $eyktar$ time and $dagmála$ time in the darkest season of the year. According to the interpretation of the passage by the scholars the shortest winter day would be of such a length that Vinland would have to be located in latitude $41°\ 24'\ 10''$, or on the coast of Rhode Island. This was the interpretation given by Torfæus in his "Vinlandia," 1705, and later writers followed it, until it was regarded as quite firmly established that Vinland was located on the coast of Rhode Island or Massachusetts.[1] In conformity with this view it was also thought that the inscription on the Dighton Rock, on the Taunton River, was a runic inscription made by the Norsemen, and that the old stone tower at Newport, R. I., was the remains of a building erected by them.[2] Gustav Storm has shown that this passage in the "Flateyjarbók" has been misinterpreted, and that no theory as to the location of Vinland can be adduced from it. He shows that

[1] Professor Eben Norton Horsford in his work, $Discovery\ of\ America\ by\ the$ $Northmen$, 1888, tries to show that many place names along the coast of Massachusetts are of Norse origin. See also $The\ Defenses\ of\ Norumbega$, 1891, and $The\ Problem\ of\ the\ Northmen$, 1890, by the same author.

To this effort Justin Windsor remarks: "We can see in Horsford's Dis-$covery\ of\ America\ by\ the\ Northmen$ to what fanciful extent a confident enthusiasm can carry it." $Narrative\ and\ Critical\ History\ of\ America$. Rev. B. F. De Costa, $The\ Northmen\ in\ Maine\ and\ a\ Chapter\ on\ the\ Discovery\ of$ $Massachusetts\ Bay$, Albany, 1870.

[2] Carl Christian Rafn, $Antiquitates\ Americanae\ sive\ Scriptores\ septentrio$-$nales\ rerum\ ante$-$Columbianarum\ in\ America$, Copenhagen, 1837. Carl Christian Rafn, $Abstracts\ of\ the\ Historical\ Evidence\ for\ the\ Discovery\ of\ America\ by$ $the\ Scandinavians\ in\ the\ Tenth\ Century$, London, 1838. Rev. Abner Morse, A.M., $Further\ Traces\ of\ the\ Ancient\ Northmen\ in\ America,\ with\ Geological$ $Evidences\ of\ the\ Location\ of\ their\ Vineland;$ read before the New England Historico-Genealogical Society, and published at their request, Boston, 1861. North Ludlow Beamish, $The\ Discovery\ of\ America\ by\ the\ Northmen\ in$ $the\ Tenth\ Century$, London, 1841. T. H. Webb, $Descriptio\ vetusti\ Monumenti$ $in\ Regione\ Massachusetts\ reperti$, $Antiquitates\ Americanae$, p. 355 ff. B. F. De

Helluland, in all probability, was Labrador, that Markland must have been Newfoundland, and that Vinland, which according to the saga narrative was located as far north as wild grapes were growing, in all likelihood was the coast of Nova Scotia. The Newport stone tower has been shown to have been an old stone mill, and the Dighton Rock inscription has been found to be Indian picture writing.

"When spring came, they saw early one morning a number of hide-boats rowing from the south past the headland, so many that it seemed as if the sea had been sown with coal in front of the bay, and they waved wooden poles on every boat. Then they set up shields and held a market, and the people wanted most to buy red cloth; they also wanted to buy swords and spears, but this was forbidden by Karlsevne and Snorre." The Skrælings gave them untanned skins in exchange for the cloth, and trade was proceeding briskly when "an ox, which Karlsevne had, ran out of the woods and began to bellow. The Skrælings were scared, and ran to their boats and rowed south along the shore. After that they did not see them for three weeks. But when that time was past, they saw a great multitude of Skræling boats coming from the south, as though driven on by a stream. Then all the wooden poles were waved against the sun, and all the Skrælings howled loudly. Then Karlsevne and his men took red shields and bore towards them. The Skrælings leaped from their boats, and then they made towards each other and fought; there was a hot exchange of missiles. The Skrælings also had catapults (valsløngur). Karlsevne and his men saw that the Skrælings hoisted upon a pole a great ball about as large as a sheep's paunch, blue in color, and slung it from the pole upon the land over Karlsevne's people, and it made a great noise when it came down.[1] At this, great terror

Costa, *The Pre-Columbian Discovery of America by the Northmen*, Albany, 1868. The views of Horsford, De Costa, Morse, T. H. Webb, Beamish, and others of their school regarding Vinland must now be regarded as wholly abandoned.

[1] Speaking of this remarkable style of fighting, John Fiske says: "According to Mr. Schoolcraft, this was a mode of fighting common among the Algonquins in New England and elsewhere. This big ball was what Mr. Schoolcraft calls the 'balista,' or what the Indians themselves call the 'demon's head.' It was a large round bowlder, sewed up in a new skin and attached to a pole. As the skin dried, it enwrapped the stone tightly; and then it was daubed with grotesque devices in various colors.

"'It was borne by several warriors who acted as balisteers. Plunged upon

smote Karlsevne and his people, so that they had no thought but of getting away and up the river, for it seemed to them that the Skrælings were assailing them on all sides; and they did not halt until they had reached certain crags. Then they made a stout resistance. Freydis came out and saw that they were giving way. She cried out: 'Wherefore do ye run away from such wretches, ye gallant men? I thought it likely that ye could slaughter them like cattle, and had I but arms, I believe I should fight better than any of you.' None heeded what she said. Freydis tried to go with them, but she fell behind, for she was with child. She nevertheless followed them into the woods, but the Skrælings came after her. She found before her a dead man, Thorbrand Snorreson, and a flat stone was fixed in his head. His sword lay unsheathed by him, and she took it up and defended herself with it. Then the Skrælings came at her. She then took her breasts out of her sark and whetted the sword on them. At that the Skrælings became afraid, and ran away back to their boats, and went away. Karlsevne and his men met her and praised her happy device. Two out of Karlsevne's men fell, and four of the Skrælings; but nevertheless, Karlsevne had suffered defeat. They then went to their houses to bind up their wounds, and to consider what swarm of people it was that came against them from the land. It seemed to them now that there could have been no more than those who came from the boats, and that the other people must have been glamour."

It was probably a well planned Indian ambush, a mode of warfare with which the Norsemen were not acquainted.

"The Skrælings also found a dead man, and an ax lay beside him; one of them took the ax and struck at a tree, and so one after another, and it seemed to delight them that it bit so well. Then one took and smote a stone with it; but when the ax broke, he thought it was of no use, if it did not stand against stone, and he cast it from him.

"Karlsevne and his men now thought they could see that although

a boat or canoe, it was capable of sinking it. Brought down upon a group of men on a sudden, it produced consternation and death.' This is a most remarkable feature of the narrative, for it shows us the Icelandic writer (here manifestly controlled by some authoritative source of information) describing a very strange mode of fighting, which we know to have been characteristic of the Algonquins." *The Discovery of America*, I., p. 192.

the land was fertile, they would always have troubles and disquiet with the people who dwelt there before. Then they prepared to set out, and intended to go to their own country. They sailed northward and found five Skrælings sleeping in fur-jerkins, and they had with them kegs with deer's marrow mixed with blood. They thought that they could understand that these were outlaws and they killed them. Then they found a headland and a multitude of deer, and the headland looked like a crust of dried dung, from the deer lying there at night. Now they came back to Straumsfjord, and there was abundance of everything. It is reported by some that Bjarne and Gudrid remained behind there, and a hundred men with them, and did not go farther; but they say that Karlsevne and Snorre went southward with forty men and were no longer at Hóp than barely two months, returning the same summer.

"Karlsevne then set out with one ship in search of Thorhall the Hunter, but the greater part of the company remained behind. They sailed to the northward around Kjalarnes, and then bore to the westward, having land to the larboard. The country there was a wooded wilderness as far as they could see."

On this voyage Thorvald Eiriksson was killed by an arrow shot from the shore — by a uniped,[1] says the saga. They returned to Straumsfjord, and remained there that winter. The next summer (1006) they sailed for Markland, and thence to Greenland. The winter (1006–1007) they spent at the home of Eirik the Red, at Brattahlid.

Professor Fridtjof Nansen holds that the "Saga of Eirik the Red," though it contains features which show that the Norsemen must have visited the American continent, and that they met with North American Indians, is, nevertheless, a piece of fiction;[2] that the description

[1] A fabulous being with only one leg.

[2] Nansen's views have hitherto met with strong opposition from many leading scholars in Norway and Denmark; especially from Finnur Jónsson, *Erik den rødes Saga og Vinland, Historisk Tidsskrift,* femte række, vol. I., p. 116 ff., and Alexander Bugge, *Spørgsmaalet om Vinland,* in *Maal og Minne, Festskrift til H. F. Feilberg,* 1911, p. 226 ff.

Professor Bugge holds that Nansen, assisted by Professor Moltke Moe, has treated the question from a standpoint of literature rather than from that of history. Many features of the "Saga of Eirik the Red" may have been borrowed from legendary tales, but this cannot be the origin of the story of

of Vinland is patched together from traditions about the Insulae Fortunatae, found in many old Latin writers. "To sum up, it appears to me clear that the saga's description of Wineland must in its essential features be derived from the myth of the Insulae Fortunatae." [1] The description of the grapes and the self-sown wheat said to have been found in Vinland he regards as features borrowed from these old traditions.[2] The name Vinland has its origin, he thinks, in the Irish legend of St. Brandan, or it is, possibly, simply a translation of the name Insulae Fortunatae, while the description of the Skrælings shows them to have been imaginary beings with the characteristics usually ascribed to such beings in popular superstition. About Leiv Eiriksson he says:

"In the year 999, according to the saga, Leiv, the son of Eirik the Red, sailed from Greenland to Norway. This is the first time we hear of so long a sea voyage being attempted, and it shows in any case that this long passage was not unknown to the Icelanders and Nor-

---

Vinland. The name Vinland is older than the story *Navigatio S. Brandani*, and Bugge thinks that it is the actual name of the country discovered by Leiv Eiriksson. He also points to the fact that Nansen himself holds that the Norsemen discovered America. The main features of the saga, that the Norsemen found the continent of North America, that they met the Indians, and that they reached a point so far south that they found wild grapes (probably south of Nova Scotia), he says, seem wholly trustworthy.

See also Juul Dieserud, *Vinlands Beliggenhed nok engang*, Symra, 1909, p. 35 ff. Julius E. Olson, *Nansens Angreb paa Vinlands-sagaerne*, Symra, vol. VII., p. 129 ff. Henrik Nissen, *Vinlands-taagen*, Symra, vol. VIII., p. 193 ff. P. P. Iverslie, *Gustav Storms Studier over Vinlandsreiserne*. P. P. Iverslie, *Kvartalskrift udgivet av det norske Selskab i Amerika*, VI., p. 6 ff. William H. Babcock, *Early Norse Visits to North America*, Washington, 1913.

[1] Fridtjof Nansen, *In Northern Mists*, vol. I., p. 352. Professor Carl Marstrander supports Nansen's views in an article in *Aftenposten*, Feb. 6, 1913. He holds that the name "Vinland" is derived from old Irish *Find*, the land of the blessed (*i.e. Insulae Fortunatae*).

[2] Nansen thinks that M. L. Fernald's theory, that what the sagas call grapes was really whortleberries, and the self-sown wheat was wild rye (*Elymus arenarius*), must be rejected for many evident reasons. See *Rhodora, Journal of the New England Botanical Club*, vol. 12, 1912, February number, *Notes on the Plants of Wineland the Good*, by M. L. Fernald.

Schübeler, *Om den "Hvede" som Nordmændene i aaret 1000 fandt vildtvoxende i Vinland*; Forhandlinger i Videnskabs-Selskabet i Christiania, 1858, p. 21 ff. Schübeler believes that this grain which is called wheat was *Zizania aquatica* or wild rice.

wegians. Formerly the passage to Greenland had been by way of Iceland, thence to the east coast of Greenland, southward along the coast, and round Hwarf. But capable seamen like the intrepid Leiv thought they could avoid so many changes of course and arrive in Norway by sailing due east from the southern point of Greenland. Thereby Leiv Eiriksson becomes the personification of the first ocean voyager in history who deliberately and with settled plan steered straight across the open Atlantic, without seeking to avail himself of harbors on the way. It also appears clearly enough from the sailing directions for navigation of northern waters which have come down to us, that voyages were made across the ocean direct from Norway to Greenland. It must be remembered that the compass was unknown, and that all the ships at that time were without fixed decks. This was an exploit equal to the greatest in history; it is the beginning of ocean navigation." [1]

The claim, however, that Leiv Eiriksson first discovered the North American mainland rests, according to Nansen, on weak and unreliable evidence. He says about the "Saga of Eirik the Red": "It will therefore be seen that the whole narrative about Wineland voyages is a mosaic of one feature after another gathered from east and west. . . . It looks as though the tale of Leiv had been inserted without proper connection. In the 'Grønlendingaþáttr,' too, this discovery is attributed to another man, Bjarne Herjolvsson, which shows that the tradition about Leiv had not been firmly rooted." [2]

The question then arises: Is there anything in the saga narrative which must be regarded as reliable? Nansen answers that although the saga in its main features must be regarded as invention, the chief personages in the narrative may be historical. The description of the barren and stony Helluland (Labrador), of the forest covered Markland (Newfoundland), and of Kjalarnes seems to rest on local topographical knowledge. The oldest and most original features of the saga are the verses found in it, which give a different, and as it appears, a more realistic picture of the newly discovered land, where the explorers drank water, and ate the flesh of whales which had drifted ashore. He points out that the trading with the natives described in the saga, and the subsequent war with them, must rest on

[1] *In Northern Mists*, vol. I., p. 315.   [2] *Ibid.*, vol. I., p. 315; vol. II., p. 21.

actual experience. These features cannot be explained by the traditions about the Insulae Fortunatae, nor can the ideas of bloody battles with the natives in which the Norsemen were defeated have originated in Greenland. It must represent an actual encounter with the Indians. It is impossible that the Greenlanders or Icelanders should have described a battle with the unwarlike Eskimos of Greenland in this way. There can be no doubt that the Norsemen had reached America, and had met the North American Indians. This is further substantiated by the description of so remarkable a weapon as the "balista," known to have been used by the Algonquin Indians. The references to the discovery of America found in the "Landnámabók" and in the "Íslendingabók" by the reliable old writer, Are Frode, show that the tradition was old and firmly established before the "Saga of Eirik the Red" was written.[1]

The most reliable evidence that these discoveries were actually made is found, according to Nansen, not in the sagas, but in an entry in the "Islandske Annaler" (Skálholt-Annals) for the year 1347: "There came also a ship from Greenland smaller in size than the small vessels that trade to Iceland (*i.e.* ships plying between Norway and Iceland). It came to the outer Straumfjord (on the south side of Snefellsnes in Iceland); it was without an anchor. There were seventeen men on board, and they had sailed to Markland, but afterwards (*i.e.* on the homeward voyage to Greenland) they were driven hither (*i.e.* to Iceland)." Nansen thinks that, as the "Skálholt-Annals" were written not very long after the event here mentioned (probably about 1363), it must be regarded as certain that this ship had been

---

[1] Nansen thinks that the game of ball, "Lacrosse," found among many Indian tribes, was introduced in America by the Norsemen, as Ebbe Hertzberg has before maintained. (*Historiske Skrifter tilegnede Professor Ludvig Daae*, p. 186.) This theory finds additional support in the fact that a very similar game, which they seem to have learned from the Norsemen, was played by the Eskimos in Greenland. Dr. W. J. Hoffmann has described the game as it is found among the various Indian tribes. See *Fourteenth Annual Report of Ethnology*, 1892–1893, Washington, 1896, vol. I., p. 127 ff. Also *American Anthropologist*, vol. III., p. 134 f. Hoffmann thinks that the game originally came from the Algonquins in the St. Lawrence Valley, and from there to the Hurons, the Iroquois, the Cherokees, etc. This is the way it must have spread, if it were introduced by the Norsemen. See Nansen, *In Northern Mists*, vol. II., p. 38 ff.

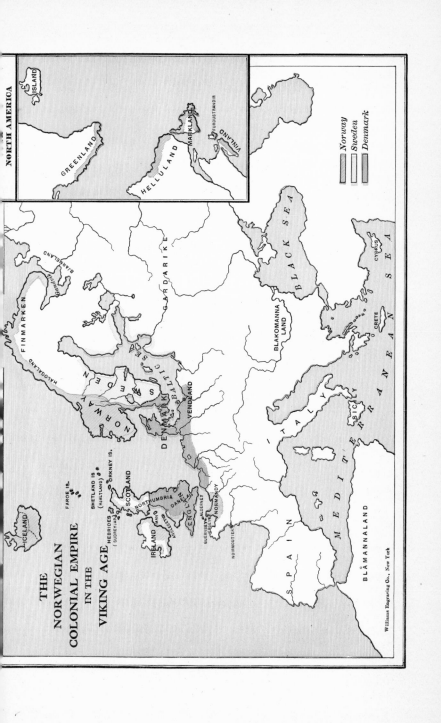

THE
NORWEGIAN
COLONIAL EMPIRE
IN THE
VIKING AGE

Norway
Sweden
Denmark

William Engraving Co., New York

in Markland, probably for the purpose of bringing home wood and timber. The driftwood which could be found did not supply the demand, and for bows and the like it was useless. He says: "But if this voyage took place in 1347, and we only hear of it through the accident of the vessel getting out of her course, and being driven to Iceland, we may be sure that there were many more like it; only that these were not the expeditions of men of rank, which attracted attention, but everyday voyages for the support of life, like the sealing expeditions to Norðrsetur, and when nothing particular happened to these vessels, such as being driven to Iceland, we hear nothing about them. We must therefore suppose that, even if they had given up the idea of forming settlements in the West, the Greenlanders occasionally visited Markland (Newfoundland or the southernmost part of Labrador), perhaps chiefly to obtain wood of different kinds.

"In the so-called 'Greenland Annals,' put together from old sources by Bjørn Jónsson of Skardsá (beginning of the seventeenth century), it is said of the districts on the west coast of Greenland, to the north of the Western Settlement, that they 'take up trees and all the drift that comes from the bays of Markland.' This shows that it was customary to regard Markland as the region from which wood was to be obtained. The name itself (= woodland) may have contributed to this view. But the fact that it survived long after all mention of Wineland had ceased, may probably be due to communication with the country having been kept up in later times, and to this name being the really historical one on the coast of America." [1]

On the farm Hønen, in the district of Ringerike, in southern Norway, a rune-stone was still to be seen in 1823. The stone is now lost, but the inscription has been copied and preserved. It reads as follows, according to Sophus Bugge:

"They came out (into the ocean) and over wide expanses (vítt) and needing cloth to dry themselves on, and food, away toward Wineland, up into the ice in the uninhabited country. Evil can take away luck, so that one dies early."

Bugge thinks that the inscription dates from the period 1000–1050, but it is difficult to decipher it, and the interpretation will always remain doubtful. The inscription seems to have been chiseled on the

[1] *In Northern Mists*, vol. II., p. 37.

stone in commemoration of some man of note who had lost his life on a voyage to the Far West. On this voyage they were driven far into the ocean in the direction of Vinland. After having suffered shipwreck they had left their ships, and had probably tried to save themselves on the drifting ice off the coasts of Greenland. Some perished, but some one must have survived to tell the story. If the interpretation of the inscription is correct, this is the first known mention of Vinland.

The last mention of a voyage to Vinland is an entry in the Icelandic annals for the year 1121, stating that in that year Bishop Eirik (Eirik Gnupsson) went to search for Vinland.[1] This Eirik may have been the first bishop in Greenland. He must have lost his life on the expedition, as nothing more was heard of him, and in 1122 or 1123 the Greenlanders were making efforts to get another bishop.

That the Norsemen failed to establish colonies in America is in nowise remarkable. There was at this time no general emigration from Norway to the colonies, and the new and poorly equipped settlements in Greenland had neither the means nor the population to successfully carry out such an undertaking. They had few ships, and lacked the materials for building new ones. Arms, implements, and supplies were scarce, and were difficult to procure. Their scant resources had to be employed in procuring the necessaries of life on those bleak and inhospitable shores where they maintained a precarious existence for well-nigh five hundred years.

However the sagas may be interpreted in detail, all scholars agree that the mainland of North America was discovered by the Norsemen about the year 1000. But this discovery led to no abiding results.[2]

---

[1] See *Islandske Annaler*, edited by Gustav Storm, p. 19, 59, 112, 252, 326, 473.

[2] The theory that Columbus, in undertaking his great voyage of exploration, profited by his knowledge of the discovery of the New World by the Norsemen was first advanced by Finn Magnusen in an article *Om de engelske Handel paa Island*, in *Nordisk Tidsskrift for Oldkyndighed*, II., 1833. The same has been maintained also by Axel Emanuel Holmberg in his work *Nordbon under Hednatiden* (1852–1854); by R. B. Anderson in his work *America not Discovered by Columbus*; and by Marie A. Brown, *The Icelandic Discoverers, or Honor to Whom Honor is Due*, Boston, 1888. It has been shown however, that this theory rests wholly upon conjecture. See Gustav Storm *Christopher Columbus og Amerikas Opdagelse; Christopher Columbus pac*

It is one of the closing episodes of the Viking Age, not the beginning of a new era. The world was not yet ready to profit by so auspicious an event. The Viking colonial empire had reached its final limits, both in extent and power, and the nations of Europe had to slumber and gather strength for another five hundred years before empire building in the New World could be begun.

39. THE DOWNFALL OF VIKING DOMINION IN IRELAND. THE BATTLE OF CLONTARF

The final overthrow of the Vikings in Ireland is connected chiefly with the name of Brian Borumha, the greatest of Irish kings. Muirchertach had fought with great success against the strangers, but he fell in 944 in a battle with the Vikings of Dublin. Brian's older brother, Mathgamhain, king of Munster, carried on an unsuccessful struggle against the Vikings of southwestern Ireland, and was compelled to make peace, but Brian refused to yield. He withdrew with his followers into the forests, and from his retreats he carried on a successful guerrilla warfare against the enemy. The struggle waxed more serious, and King Ivar of Limerick finally took the field with all available forces, but was defeated by Mathgamhain in 968; Limerick was taken and sacked by the Irish king, who captured great quantities of gold, silver, fine cloth, and other valuable wares which the Norsemen had brought home to their city through commerce with many lands. After some time the Vikings again succeeded in regaining possession of the town, but the redoubtable Brian, who, upon the death of his brother Mathgamhain had become king of Munster, defeated and slew King Ivar and his sons, and Limerick became a dependency of Munster, under Brian's overlordship. Maelsechnaill, king of Tara, also styled Ard-Righ, or high-king of Erin, inspired by Brian's success, attacked King Olav Kvaaran in 980, defeated him in the battle of Tara, in Meath, and even seized the city of Dublin. Brian and Maelsechnaill had hitherto been rivals, but in 998 they came to a friendly understanding. Brian became king of southern Ireland, and, in return, acknowledged Maelsechnaill ruler of the

Island og vore Forfædres Opdagelser i det nordvestlige Atlanterhav, Det norske geografiske Selskabs Aarbog, IV., p. 67 ff. H. Weitemeyer, Columbus, Copenhagen, 1892.

northern half. The hitherto independent Leinster now joined the
Norsemen of Dublin, but their united forces were defeated by the
two kings in the bloody battle of Glenmama, where 1200 Norsemen
are said to have fallen. Olav Kvaaran's son and successor, Sigtryg
Silkbeard, had to flee, but on submitting to Brian he received again
the throne of Dublin as a vassal king. Maelsechnaill was deposed a
Ard-Righ, and Brian became high-king of all Ireland.

The life of the Norsemen had undergone a great change during
their long stay in Ireland. They were no longer mere invaders, dwell
ing in military camps. The occupations of trade and traffic had
especially absorbed their attention, and they had settled down to
peaceful and well regulated urban life in the cities which they had
built or developed. Dublin, Waterford, Wexford, Cork, and Limerick
had become important centers of trade, and the Norsemen, who wer
ever fond of seafaring, now spread their sails chiefly as enterprisin
merchants who sought the markets of Chester, Bristol, France, and
Spain, of the countries around the Baltic Sea, and even of distant
Novgorod, whence they brought home to Ireland such valuable good
as wheat flour, costly embroidered mantles, swords, furs, and wine
A part of the tribute which they had to pay the victorious Brian Bo
rumha, according to a contemporary Irish poet, Mac Liag, was 15
butts of wine from the Norsemen of Dublin, and a tun of wine fo
every day in the year from the Norsemen of Limerick. "This tribute
of wine," says Alexander Bugge, "presupposes a considerable trad
with southwestern France, as the place where any one from Irelan
might most easily obtain his wine." In the glossary of Cormac, from
about 900, mention is made of a vessel for measuring wine, spoke
of in the "sea laws." This can only refer to Norse sea laws, as neithe
the Franks nor the Irish were seafaring nations, and it seems to ind
cate that already at this time the Norsemen had a maritime code
The many terms of weight and measure and money, such as *pundar*
bismari, mǫrk, pennigr; and naval terms, as *knǫrr, karfi, leiðang
lypting, stýrimaðr, þilja,* and *þopta,* which have been incorporated i
the Irish language, show that the development of trade and commerc
in Ireland was due to the Norsemen.

¹ Alexander Bugge, *Contributions to the History of the Norsemen in Irelan*
III., p. 4., Christiania, 1900.

The Viking cities in Ireland were surrounded by stone walls. In Dublin the royal castle, with its formidable stone tower, was conspicuous in the center of the city. Another prominent building was the temple, erected for the worship of the gods of the Asa-faith. But at this time paganism was fast disappearing; the Norsemen were being converted to Christianity, and the temples were replaced by Christian churches. It has already been noted elsewhere that King Olav Kvaaran of Dublin became a Christian in his old age, and died as a monk on the island of Iona. His son and successor, Sigtrygg Silkbeard, was married to Brian Borumha's daughter, and his court resembled in every way that of Knut the Great in England. In his *hird* were found both Icelandic scalds and Irish bards, who vied with each other in the art of song, and great splendor was maintained in dress and accouterments of war. The king's *hirdmænd*, equipped with helmets and shirts of mail, fought on horseback like William the Conqueror's mounted knights, but King Sigtrygg himself lacked the warlike spirit to such a degree that he did not even take part in the great battle of Clontarf, fought beneath the very walls of Dublin, but stood with his queen on the battlements of the city, and watched the great combat as an idle spectator.

The Norse system of laws and government was introduced also in the Norse colonies in Ireland. In Dublin the *thing* was regularly assembled at a place known throughout the Middle Ages by the name of "Thengmota" (the meeting place of the *thing*). A *lagrette*, consisting of thirty-six members, of whom twelve seem to have acted at a time, was chosen to act as a tribunal in deciding cases brought before the *thing*. This institution so impressed the Irish that they called the Norsemen the "Twelve Judges Tribe." [1]

But the Irish were also benefited in no small degree. Ireland had hitherto never experienced such a period of progress in commerce

---

[1] "Soon his twelve judges tribe before
my valiant troop shall flee;
and their proud king shall fall, no more
his isles of boars to see."

From the Irish ballad "Laoidh Maghnuis moir, righ Lochlainn," *i.e.* "Lay of Magnus the Great, King of Lochlainn" (King Magnus Barefoot), translated by Miss Brooke in her *Reliques of Irish Poetry*, Dublin, 1739. See Alexander Bugge, *Contributions to the History of the Norsemen in Ireland*, II.

and navigation, in the building of cities, and the development of urban life, wholly due to the enterprise and activity of the practical Norsemen, who possessed less lovable, but more distinctly masculine qualities. The old writer Geraldus Cambrensis says that the Norsemen were allowed to build cities in Ireland on condition that they should bring to Ireland from other lands the merchandise which the Irish wanted.[1] Norse influence had left deep traces, also, in Irish literature and intellectual life. Professor Alexander Bugge says that "many of the Irish mythical conceptions have been formed under the influence of the Norsemen."[2] In speaking of Irish literature he says: "Professor Zimmer,[3] by his admirable investigations, has thrown fresh light upon the ancient Irish sagas, and has shown in how many ways they are interwoven with Norse elements and reminiscences from the Viking Age. But we see that the Norse influence on Gaelic tradition and story-telling is not confined to the Viking Age. A recollection of the Norsemen has been retained for centuries and down to the present time Lochlann (Norway) still plays a very conspicuous part in Irish and Gaelic ballads and fairy-tales."

Though a spirit of hostility naturally prevailed between the Irish and the Norsemen, a quiet amalgamation was, nevertheless, going on which would ultimately have led to the complete absorption of the Norse element. Not infrequently the two peoples would meet as good friends and neighbors in convivial gatherings, and many Norse loan-words in the Irish language relating to social life show that in daily intercourse they were coming into closer touch.[4] The Norsemen would often select Irish foster-fathers and foster-mothers to rear their children; but still more important was the growing frequency of intermarriage.[5] Had the process of amalgamation, with the attendant blending of the traits characteristic of both peoples, been allowed to proceed uninterrupted, it might have produced a national character of the right temper to carry Ireland successfully through

---

[1] *Topographia Hibernica*, dict. III., ch. XLIII.

[2] *Contributions to the History of the Norsemen in Ireland*, II., *Norse Elements in Gaelic Traditions of Modern Times*, Christiania, 1900.

[3] Zimmer, *Keltische Beiträge*.

[4] Zimmer, *Keltische Beiträge*. See also W. A. Craigie, *Oldnordiske Ord de gœliske Sprog*, *Arkiv for nordisk Filologi*, 1894, p. 1 ff.

[5] L. J. Vogt, *Dublin som norsk By*.

all future struggles. But the possibility of such a solution of the difficult situation was, to a great extent, removed by the battle of Clontarf.

The Norsemen, who, after the defeat at Glenmama, were sinking into a state of dependency, could not, as in earlier days, lean on the mother country for support. But there were numerous Viking settlements around the Irish Sea, and the powerful Jarl Sigurd Lodvesson in the Orkneys, and the people elsewhere in the colonies felt the necessity of coöperation at so critical a juncture, since the overthrow of Norse dominion in Ireland would weaken the Viking power everywhere in the West. When King Sigtrygg Silkbeard came to the Orkneys to solicit aid, Jarl Sigurd promised to bring an army to Ireland. The Viking chieftain Broder also promised to support him. About the middle of March a great Viking armament began to gather before Dublin. Ships and warriors came from the Orkneys, the Shetland Islands, Caithness, and the Hebrides, and from the Norse settlements on the coast of Scotland, Cumberland, and Wales. They were joined by the men of Leinster, and by the Norse forces raised in Ireland, except those of Limerick, who were now King Brian's subjects, and joined his standards. Brian had collected a large army, and Maelsechnaill also came to his aid with a considerable force. On Good Friday, April 23, 1014, the two armies met at Clontarf, a little village lying a short distance north of Dublin, and here was fought the last great battle of the Viking Age, generally known as the battle of Clontarf, but in the Norse songs and traditions it is usually called the Brian battle. The right wing of the Viking army was led by Broder; in the center stood Sigurd Lodvesson and Maelmorda, the king of Leinster, with their forces; the left wing was formed by the men of Dublin. Brian's son, Murchad, led the Irish left wing against Broder, and his grandson, Tordelbach (the Kertjalfad of the sagas), commanded the center. On the right wing stood the Viking chieftain Uspak and the men of Connaught. Brian, who was now a very old man, was present on the field of battle, but did not lead the army in person. From morning till evening the combat raged with unabated fury, and the men fell on both sides like a field of grain that is being harvested. But towards evening the Viking right wing gave way, and Broder fled with his men into the forest of Thor, in the neighbor-

hood of Dublin. On their retreat they accidentally found King
Brian, who was too feeble to participate in the battle, and had been
left there almost unguarded. He was pointed out to Broder, who
slew him with his battle-ax; but Broder was soon after killed by his
pursuers. Soon Sigurd Lodvesson also fell in a fierce dash against
Magduna, where Brian was staying. He was met by Murchad's
forces, and in the mêlée Murchad was also mortally wounded. The
Norsemen were now thrown into complete rout. Their retreat was
cut off except toward the sea, and great numbers were slain in the
headlong flight which ensued. According to the "Ulster Annals,"
Brian's army lost 4000 men and the Norsemen 7000. Nearly all
the prominent leaders of both armies lay dead upon the field. Besides
Broder and Sigurd Lodvesson, the Norsemen had also lost Dugald
Olavsson, who led the men of Dublin, and Maelmorda, king of Leinster, a brother of King Sigtrygg Silkbeard's Irish mother, Gormflaith,
(the Kormlød of the sagas). The Irish had lost Brian, Murchad,
and Turlogh, Brian's grandson.

Many omens are said to have preceded the battle of Clontarf.
The most noteworthy is the frightful vision described in the "Darrad-
song" in the "Njálssaga," in which Darrad, at Caithness in Scotland,
on the day of the battle saw twelve valkyries weave the web of the
bloody conflict at Clontarf with human entrails on a loom of swords
and spears. The song contains this remarkable prophecy, which,
for Ireland, has become but too true:

"Those will now soon rule the land,
    who formerly had the naked head-lands for a home.

Such sorrow shall come to the Irish people,
    as men never shall forget."

The battle of Clontarf had no very noteworthy immediate results.
Maelsechnaill succeeded Brian as high-king of Ireland, but Dublin
was not captured, and the Norsemen continued to occupy the same
cities and territories as heretofore. They devoted themselves very
extensively to commerce, and retained their laws and national customs. When the English began their conquest of Ireland in 1170
Norse commerce still flourished there. At the capture of Waterford

a Norse ship was taken in port, laden with wheat and wine.[1] As late as 1292 we still hear of the wine trade of the Norsemen at Waterford.[2] The English expelled the original inhabitants from the cities which they captured, and assigned them quarters outside the old towns. This is the origin of the Ostmantown (Oxmantown) of Dublin and Waterford. The Norsemen chafed under such oppression, and when King Haakon Haakonsson of Norway came to Ireland with a fleet, in 1263, they sent messengers to him asking him to deliver them from the English yoke. This is the last mention of any attempt on their part to maintain relations with the mother country. Their saga in Ireland was ended.

But although the Norsemen continued to live and thrive in Ireland so long after their defeat at Clontarf, their power was, nevertheless, destroyed in this great battle, and in others immediately preceding it. Their leaders were gone, and their fighting force was annihilated. Henceforth they existed as isolated settlements, unable to unite in a common effort, or to exercise any influence on the trend of events in Ireland. The Irish had won a notable victory, and had regained full control of affairs in their own country, but this display of strength was due to a single great leader — Brian Borumha. No one was able to continue his work; the customary feuds between the native princes were renewed, and Ireland quickly lapsed into the old confusion. Clontarf was a brilliant feat of Irish arms, but in the light of subsequent history it must be regarded as a calamity, rather than as a national victory. This overwhelming defeat of the Norsemen weakened Ireland's sinews of strength, and, when the English conquest began, the Irish showed no greater ability to repel foreign invasion than they had done several centuries earlier when the Vikings bore down upon the island.

40. THE NORSEMEN IN THE HEBRIDES, AND IN THE ISLE OF MAN

During the great invasion of the British Isles in the early part of the Viking Age, the Norsemen took possession also of the Isle of Man, and of the Hebrides, which they called Sudreyjar (Southern

[1] Vogt, *Dublin som norsk By*, p. 386.
[2] Alexander Bugge, *Contribution to the History of the Norsemen in Ireland*, III., p. 4. *Njálssaga*, ch. 155 f.

Islands), because they lay south of the Orkneys and the Shetland Islands. The story of the Norse settlements in these islands is imperfectly told in the sagas, and but little is known of their history.[1] The "Landnámabók" states that King Harald Haarfagre sent Ketil Flatnev to the Sudreyjar to win the islands from some Vikings who had established themselves there. Ketil subdued the Vikings, but made himself ruler of the islands, and paid the king no taxes. According to the "Laxdølasaga," Ketil Flatnev, *herse* in Romsdal in western Norway, had to leave the country because he would not submit to King Harald. He became a man of great power and influence in the island colonies, and his daughter Aud married King Olav the White of Dublin.[2] On his expedition against the Vikings, King Harald Haarfagre also subjugated the Hebrides and the Isle of Man, and many of the leading men of these islands fled to Iceland. Among those who emigrated to Iceland at this time was, also, Ketil Flatnev's daughter Aud, widow of King Olav the White.

It appears that King Harald's successors did not maintain the suzerainty over the distant possessions of Man and the Hebrides. Professor P. A. Munch thinks it likely that the islands for a time were a part of the dominions of the Norse kings of Dublin. But from the middle of the tenth century we meet with independent "kings of Man and the Isles." Among the names of these are Ragnvald, Harald, Gudrød, Olav, and Maccus. After Olav Kvaaran was driven away from Northumbria in 952, he seems to have remained for some time in the Isle of Man or in the Hebrides, before he gained the throne of Dublin. About 970 Maccus, son of Harald, became king of Man and the Isles. He is mentioned in 973 as one of the eight kings who at Chester did homage to Eadgar, king of England, and rowed him in his barge to and from church on the river Dee. He took possession of the island of Inniscathaig at the mouth of the Shannon, and delivered from captivity King Ivar of Limerick, but he was defeated

---

[1] The chief sources of information are the *Chronica Regum Manniae et Insularum* (The Chronicle of Man and the Sudreys) contained in a manuscript codex in the British Museum, edited with historical notes by Professor P. A. Munch, Christiania, 1860; and the *Orkneyingasaga;* but neither of them is very reliable in details. See also Alexander Bugge, *Vikingerne*, I.

[2] It appears from other sources that Ketil Flatnev was a son of Bjørn Buna, of Sogn.

and slain by Brian Borumha in 976. He was succeeded by Gudrød, who seems to have been his brother. Gudrød captured Anglesea on the Welsh coast, which now received its Norse name.[1]

In 980 Sigurd Lodvesson, great-grandson of Torv-Einar, became jarl of the Orkneys. He was ambitious to enlarge his dominions, and succeeded in capturing Caithness, Ross, Moray, and Argyll in Scotland. He also extended his sway over the Hebrides, which hitherto had paid taxes to the king of Norway.[2] These islands were now ruled by a tributary jarl, Gilli, who had married Sigurd's sister. Sigurd Lodvesson acknowledged himself the vassal of Haakon Jarl in Norway, and, later, of King Olav Tryggvason, but when Olav, in the year 1000, fell in the battle of Svolder, he seems to have remained wholly independent till his death in the battle of Clontarf, in 1014. His four sons now divided his possessions, but no mention is made of the Hebrides. Thorfinn Jarl, the youngest son, became even more powerful than his father. He lived longer than the other brothers, and finally united the Orkneys, the Shetland Islands, the Hebrides, and large parts of Scotland under his rule. He died in 1064.

Gudrød Crowan, son of Harald Svarte of Islay and the Hebrides, was the founder of a dynasty which ruled Man, and sometimes, also, the Hebrides for about two hundred years. He took part in the battle of Stamford Bridge, and after the defeat he fled to the Isle of Man. After several unsuccessful efforts he finally conquered the island in 1079, and made himself king.

On his expeditions to the British Isles, 1093–1103, King Magnus Barefoot of Norway again established Norse suzerainty over these island possessions, but the ties between them and the mother country were henceforth gradually weakened, and in 1266 King Magnus Lagabøter ceded the Hebrides to Scotland for a money consideration by the treaty of Perth, but their ruler, who bore the title "Lord of the Isles," was still almost independent. Man passed in course of time under English control. In 1405 King Henry IV. of England granted the island as a fief to Sir John Stanley. In 1825 it came under direct control of the English crown. The Hebrides and the Isle of Man constituted together the bishopric of Sodor[3] and Man, which

---

[1] It was formerly called *Mon. Angles -ea* from O. N. *Qnglus -ey.* O. N. *Qngull* = fishhook, *ey* = island. [2] See *Floamannasaga.* [3] Sodor from *Sudreyjar.*

was joined to the archbishopric of Nidaros, in Norway, when this was created in 1152.

The Norsemen found in Man and the Hebrides a dense native population, which never entirely disappeared during the many centuries of foreign occupation. The remarkable mixture of Norse and Gaelic names on these islands attests to the gradual amalgamation of the two peoples.[1] Many of the islands of the Hebrides group have Norse names, easily enough recognized still through the endings -ay, or -a (= Norwegian øy or ø, O. N. ey = island). Wiay is derived from Norse Vé-ey (holy island), Vist from Vist (dwelling), Gighay from Guðey (island of the gods), Lewis from Ljóðhus, Eriksay from Eiriks-ey, Grimisay from Grims-ey, Trodday from Tronds-ey, Ulva from Ulvs-ey, Sanda from Sand-ey, Fladda from Flat-ey, Heist from Hestr (i.e. the horse), etc. In Lewis four-fifths of all place-names are Norse. In the southern islands the proportion is smaller. The blond type prevalent in many districts, the temperament of the people, and many customs and traditions still existing among them, clearly bespeak their Norse origin. After the Hebrides were ceded to Scotland, the Gaelic population again increased in the islands, and the Norse language has long since disappeared, but a vague tradition still exists among the people that their ancestors came from Lochlann (Norway).

In the Isle of Man the Norse influence is still more clearly seen in the names, speech, and character of the people. In stories and fairy-tales the Manx have preserved a multitude of interesting reminiscences of their Norse ancestry. A number of place-names in Man have the Norse termination -by (= O. N.býr, bœr = dwelling place), as Kirby from Kirkeby, Dalby, Jurby from Ivarby, Sulby, etc. The suffix -garth (= O. N. garðr = dwelling place) is found in Fishgarth. In the names of fjords, mountains, promontories, bays, valleys, etc., the Norse forms are strongly represented, which is shown by endings like -wick (O. N. vík = bay), -fell (O. N. fell, fjall =

[1] Skene states that there was frequent intermarriage between the two races who occupied the islands, "and this would not only lead to the introduction of personal names of Norwegian form into families of pure Gaelic descent in the male line, but must, to a great extent, have altered the physical type of the Gaelic race in the islands." Skene, Celtic Scotland, I., 39.

mountain), and -way (O. N. vágr, = fjord or bay), thus Ronaldsway from Rognvaldsvágr, Fleshwick, Garwick, and Snæfell.[1]

Of special interest are the various rune-stones and stone crosses of Norse workmanship found in the Hebrides and the Isle of Man. Prior to the arrival of the Norsemen a number of stone crosses had been made by Celtic monks in various parts of the British Isles. These crosses are carefully chiseled, and are decorated with pictures representing persons and scenes from the Bible. The Norse settlers began to imitate them, and a number of ornamented crosses of Norse origin are found, especially in the Isle of Man. They are less carefully made than the Celtic crosses, but there is a variety of new ideas in the designing of ornaments, and the pictures generally portray scenes from Norse mythology and tradition. Gaut Bjørnson is mentioned as the first representative of this art in Man. The inscriptions, which are always in the Norse language, are usually short, and present a strange mixture of Christian and pagan ideas.[2] Alexander Bugge says that these runic monuments show more clearly than anything else that the Norsemen and Celts in the Isle of Man dwelt peaceably side by side, that they intermarried, and that they mutually influenced one another. "We can observe, not only that men of Norse descent had Celtic wives, but that men with Celtic names erected crosses with pictures representing the gods of the Asa-faith and heroes of Norse tradition." [3]

The government of the Isle of Man is still, in its essential features, a continuation of the Norse institutions established by the Viking colonists. The governor is the representative of the crown, and the chief executive. The law-making assembly, called the Court of Tynwald (Tynwald < O. N. Þingvǫllr), consists of two chambers; an upper house, the Council, consisting of the governor, the bishop, and six other leading officials; and a lower house, the House of Keys, consisting of twenty-four members chosen by popular vote. Until

[1] A. W. Moore, Manx Names, 2d ed., London, 1903. Alexander Bugge, Vikingerne, I., p. 172 ff. P. A. Munch, The Chronicle of Man and the Sudreys, p. xx., and historical notes.

[2] P. A. Munch, Runeindskrifter fra Øen Man og Suderøerne, Samlede Afhandlinger, III., 181–199.

[3] Alexander Bugge, Vikingerne, I., p. 196. George Henderson, Norse Influence on Celtic Scotland, p. 40 ff.

1866 this house was self-elective. When a member died, a new member was chosen by the house. The members are called "Keys," because, at the time when the laws were yet unwritten, they should keep the words of the law in their bosoms, and maintain law and justice. The Court of Tynwald meets at Douglas, the capital city, but all new laws must be proclaimed on Tynwald Hill (Þingvǫllr), near Peel, the old capital. This hill was constructed by the early Norse settlers for this purpose. Around it lies a level plain where the people could assemble. The governor and the law-making assembly meet here every year, and after religious service has been held, they are escorted by soldiers to the top of the hill. The governor is seated on a chair with a drawn sword before him, and the court is formally opened. The House of Keys is clearly a continuation of the *lagrette* of the old Norse *thing*. The *lagrette*, which prepared all decisions and other measures to be voted on by the assembly, sat in a circle hedged in by ropes, the *vébǫnd*, or sacred cords, inside of which no strife or disturbance was tolerated. When the Court of Tynwald has assembled on Tynwald Hill, the coroner still proclaims the peace by declaring loudly: "I fence the court." The two deemsters (thought by some to be O. N. *dómstjori*), or judges, are members of the Council. Till in the eleventh century they judged according to unwritten laws, called the "breast laws," of which they were the depositaries.[1]

We observe again how the Norsemen, whenever they founded colonies, whether in Man, in France, or in distant Greenland, established a system of laws and government of a high type, and maintained order and justice, and an efficient administration of all public affairs. Their government, though not truly representative in form, approached so near to it in spirit that we feel the popular will and sense of justice expressed in their laws, and in the legal decisions rendered by the *thing*. It was their talent for organization, and their sense of legal justice and good government, as much as their enterprise in navigation and commerce, which enabled them to establish the Norse colonial empire at this early period.

[1] J. J. A. Worsaae, *Minder om de Danske og Nordmændene.* Alexander Bugge, *Vikingerne*, I.; *Norges Historie*, I.

41. THE NORSEMEN IN SCOTLAND

The earliest predatory attack by Viking bands in Scotland of which we possess definite information, was the ravaging of Icolmkill, or Iona, in 794. Four years later we hear of an attack on Ireland and Alban (Scotland), and Iona was repeatedly ravaged during the early decades of the next century. Galloway was laid waste in 823 by Norse Vikings, who were also instrumental in placing Kenneth McAlpin on the Pictish throne. According to the "Ulster Annals," Olav and Ivar, two Norse kings, attacked Dumbarton Rock in 870, and took it after a four months' siege. We have already seen how a general emigration from Norway was set on foot during the reign of Harald Haarfagre, when many left the country because they would not submit to the powerful king. According to the "Laxdølasaga," Ketil Flatnev, who finally established himself as independent ruler in the Hebrides, came first to Scotland about 890, and was well received there. He was accompanied by his daughter, Aud the Deepminded, who later married King Olav the White of Dublin. According to the "Orkneyingasaga" Thorstein the Red, a son of Aud and Olav, invaded the northern mainland of Scotland.[1] "He ravaged the country far and wide, and was always victorious," says the saga. "Later he made an agreement with the king of the Scots by which he received half of Scotland, over which he became king." [2] Thorstein seems to have been the first to establish Norse influence on the mainland of Scotland, and his power probably extended over Caithness, Sutherland, and Ross. The "Heimskringla" states that Thorstein the Red, and Sigurd, a son of Ragnvald Mørejarl, took possession of Caithness and Sutherland as far as Eikkjalsbakke, i.e. the region about the Oikel River. When Sigurd died, "his son Guthorm ruled the lands one winter, and died childless. Afterwards the Vikings established themselves in these lands, Danes and Norsemen." [3]

[1] Who Thorstein the Red was is not clear. Olav the White's son was called Eystein, not Thorstein.

[2] *Laxdølasaga*, ch. 4. *Orkneyingasaga*, edited by Joseph Anderson. *Landnámabók*, part 1, ch. XI.

[3] *Harald Haarfagre's Saga* in *Heimskringla*, ch. 22.

When Sigurd Lodvesson became jarl of the Orkneys, he took possession of the Scotch districts of Caithness, Moray, Ross, and Argyll. He married a daughter of King Malcolm II. of Scotland, who became the mother of Thorfinn Jarl. At this time the district of Galloway, in southwestern Scotland, was also extensively colonized by Norse settlers who came over from the neighboring Isle of Man. The Norse influence in this district is apparent, especially in many personal names of Norse origin, such as M'Ketterick, M'Kittrick, from Norse Sigtrygg, Sitric; M'Eur, M'Cure, from Norse Ivar, or Ingvar; M'Burney from Bjørn; etc.[1] When Sigurd's fall at Clontarf, 1014, was rumored in Scotland, King Malcolm II. gave the earldom of Caithness to Thorfinn, his daughter's son by Sigurd, then twelve years of age, while Sigurd's three other sons by a former marriage, Sumarlide, Bruse, and Einar, divided the Orkneys among themselves. Sumarlide died soon, and the unpopular Einar was slain. Thorfinn acquired the possessions of both, and when Bruse died, he became jarl of all the Orkneys. Upon the death of King Malcolm II., his maternal grandfather, he also seized Sutherland, Ross, and Galloway. The saga states that he also took possession of the Sudreys (Hebrides), and that he sent his friend and relative Kalv Arnesson to maintain his authority there. Thorfinn had married Ingebjørg, daughter of Finn Arnesson, Kalv's brother. "Jarl Thorfinn retained all his dominions till his dying day," says the saga, "and it is truly said that he was the most powerful of all the jarls of the Orkneys."[2]

"He was a man of large stature, uncomely, sharp-featured, darkhaired, and sallow and swarthy in his complexion. Yet he was a most martial-looking man, and of great energy; greedy of wealth and of renown; bold and successful in war, and a great strategist."

Thorfinn's cousin,[3] Duncan, the son of another daughter of Malcolm II., succeeded his grandfather, but Macbeth, well known from Shakespeare's drama of the same name, who was also Duncan's cousin, had, probably, an equally valid claim to the throne. He

---

[1] George Henderson, *Norse Influence on Celtic Scotland*, 1910, p. 18.

[2] *Orkneyingasaga*, ch. 22.

[3] In the sagas he is called Karl Hundason, "a name which is clearly a translation," says George Henderson.

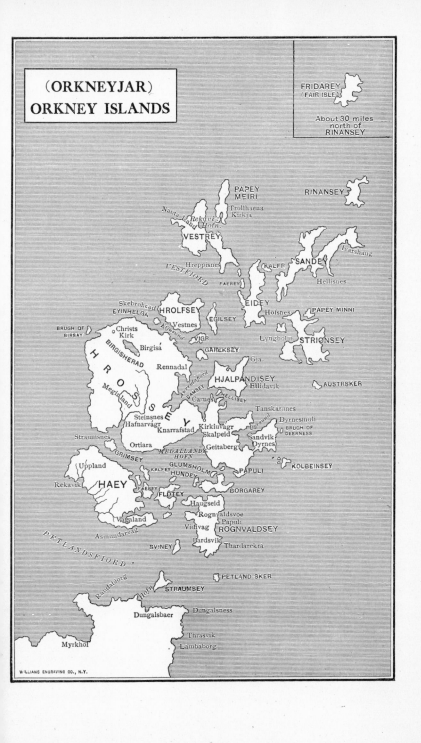

(ORKNEYJAR)
ORKNEY ISLANDS

FRIDAREY
(FAIR ISLE)

About 30 miles
north of
RINANSEY

was maormor [1] of Moray and Thorfinn's firm friend and ally. When Duncan became king, he claimed suzerainty over Caithness and Sutherland, but Thorfinn refused to acknowledge his overlordship, because Malcolm II. had granted him this earldom in full possession. Macbeth, who, no doubt, also coveted the throne, supported Thorfinn, also because he feared that Duncan would do as Malcolm II. had done, who increased his power at the expense of the maormors. Duncan attacked Thorfinn, but was entirely discomfited in the sharp naval engagement at Dyrness, in the Orkneys. Earl Moddan, who led Duncan's land forces into Caithness, was slain by Thorkel Fostri, at Thurso. Duncan fled, but he soon gathered a large army and renewed the attack. He met Thorfinn at Torfness, in northern Scotland, but suffered a crushing defeat. According to Scotch sources Duncan was slain in 1040, near Elgin. George Henderson says: "The probability is that he was attacked and slain by Macbeth in the confusion and discord following upon the defeat at Torfness, which has been identified with Burghead." [2]

Upon the death of Duncan, in 1040, Macbeth became king of Scotland, and ruled for many years. He was a just and equitable prince, with none of those dark traits of character portrayed by the great dramatist. In 1050 King Macbeth made a pilgrimage to Rome to obtain absolution from his sins, and as Thorfinn also went to Rome for the same purpose, it is likely that the two friends made the journey together.[3] Skene shows that, although Macbeth occupied the throne, his sway in Scotland rested on the power and influence of Earl Thorfinn and the Norsemen of the Orkneys.[4] Malcolm Canmore, the son of Duncan, finally took the field against Macbeth, who was defeated in the battle of Dunsinane in 1054. In 1057 he was slain in the battle of Lumphanan. Malcolm had married Ingebjørg, the daughter of Thorfinn and his wife, who was a daughter of Finn Arnesson of Norway, and when Malcolm ascended the throne, the Norwegian girl became queen of Scotland. Thorfinn,

[1] Mormaer or maormor = earl.

[2] *Norse Influence on Celtic Scotland*, p. 31.

[3] George Henderson, *Norse Influence on Celtic Scotland*, p. 29. *Orkneyingasaga*, edited by Joseph Anderson, Introduction, p. xxxii, p. 43 n. P. A. Munch, *The Chronicle of Man and the Sudreys*, p. 47.

[4] Skene, *The Highlanders in Scotland*, I., p. 113 ff.

who, undoubtedly, had aided Macbeth, also met with reverses, and
probably had to give up his possessions in southern Scotland. The
strife between Malcolm and Thorfinn continued until the latter's
death in 1064. The colonies in Caithness and Sutherland continued
to exist as distinct Norse settlements ruled by Norse jarls, but after
Thorfinn's death they passed permanently under the overlordship
of the king of Scotland. Thorfinn's sons, Paul and Erlend, succeeded
to the government of the Orkneys. As vassals of the king of Norway
they were called upon to aid King Harald Sigurdsson (Haardraade)
when he invaded England in 1066. They were both present at
the battle of Stamford Bridge, where King Harald fell. In 1098
Magnus Barefoot, king of Norway, came to the British Isles with
a large fleet. He subdued the Sudreys (Hebrides), and seized
Løgman, the son of Gudrød, king of the Isles. The king of Scotland sent messengers to him to offer peace. "They said that the
king of the Scots was willing to give him all the islands lying west
of Scotland, between which and the mainland he could pass in a
vessel with the rudder shipped. Thereupon King Magnus landed
in Satiri (Cantire), and had a boat drawn across the isthmus, he
himself holding the helm, and thus he gained possession of the whole
of Satiri, which is better than the best island of the Sudreys, Man
excepted." [1] Magnus seized, also, jarls Paul and Erlend, and sent
them to Norway, where they died. Their sons Haakon and Magnus
then became rulers of the Orkneys for some time, but trouble arose
between them, and Haakon captured Magnus and had him executed.
When Haakon died, his sons succeeded him. One of them, Harald,
"held Caithness from the king of the Scots, and he resided frequently
there, but sometimes, also, in Scotland (Sutherland?), for he had
many friends and kinsmen there." In the reign of William the Lion,
who was crowned king of Scotland in 1166, Harald Ungi came to
Scotland with his followers. "Jarl Harald requested King William
to grant him half of Caithness, which Jarl Røgnvald had held. The
king granted him this, and Jarl Harald went, then, down to Caithness to gather troops." ("Orkneyingasaga," ch. cxiii.) When
Harald Ungi died, Harald Madadsson took forcible possession of
Caithness without asking the king's leave. He was also ruler of

[1] *Orkneyingasaga*, ch. xxx.

the Orkneys and the Shetland Islands. But King Sverre of Norway seized the Shetland Islands, and King William the Lion forced Harald to hold Caithness on the same terms as his predecessor, Harald Ungi. The "Orkneyingasaga" relates, also, how the Norse people in Caithness killed Bishop Adam, because he increased their taxes. This event, which happened in 1222, is recorded in the "Islandske Annaler," [1] and, also, in a letter from Pope Honorius, dated February 13, 1223. The Norse settlers gradually ceased to stand apart as a distinct foreign element. They lost their national identity, and mingled with the native population, but only after influencing the language, culture, and character of the people of Scotland so deeply and permanently that the Scotch were henceforth a mixed people, showing clearly the characteristic traits of both races. In speaking of the Norse influence in Scotland Dr. George Henderson says: "The influence was so mighty that had the Gaelic language not been one of the most vigorous forms of speech, it must have died out; but the Gaelic people at the time were martial and powerful to an extent that afterwards made the perfervid genius of the Scots proverbial in Europe. But the result of this racial fusion is that Celtic Scotland of to-day holds a mediating position in point of race, and is much better equipped than it otherwise could have been for adapting itself to the requirements of the world. Carlyle once called the Highlanders a Norse breed, and he was in a rough way nearer the truth than many imagine." [2]

The Norse influence in various fields of Scotch culture is so extensive that only a few prominent features can be mentioned here by way of illustration. A more detailed and complete discussion of this subject will be found in Dr. George Henderson's excellent work, "Norse Influence on Celtic Scotland," which has already been quoted.

In Scotland, as well as in Man and the Hebrides, remnants have been found of decorated Viking stone crosses with runic inscriptions. "Most interesting of all is a stone with Scandinavian art-work, found by Mr. Collingwood in the chapel of St. Oran, and now deposited in the cathedral of Iona, an isle which is the burial-place of eight

---

[1] *Islandske Annaler*, edited by Gustav Storm; 1222, I. III. IV. V. VII. VIII. IX. (1220 X). [2] *Norse Influence on Celtic Scotland*, p. 2.

Norse kings. This Iona cross-shaft of the Viking Age has the usual Scandinavian dragon, with irregular interlacing, as also a galley with its crew, a smith with his hammer, anvil, and pincers — and so greatly resembles the Manx crosses that it may have been the tombstone of one of the Norse kings of Man," says Dr. Henderson. Sword-hilts and rare brooches and other ornaments of Norse origin have been unearthed in many Viking burial-places. These articles are so exquisitely designed, and wrought with such consummate skill that they prove the makers to have been adepts in the goldsmith's and jeweler's art. A sword-hilt of the Viking time found in Eigg is especially fine. Dr. J. Anderson says of it: "I know no finer or more elaborate piece of art workmanship of the kind either in this country or in Norway." [1]

The number of personal and place names of Norse origin in Scotland is so large that the few which can be cited as illustration cannot well convey any idea of the extent of Norse influence on this point. Huisdean, from the older form *Huisduin*, Anglicized Hugh, is from the Norse *Eystein;* M'Iver from *Ivar*, or *Ingvar;* MacAndy from Norse *Andi*, a form found in *Andabú* and *Andestad;* MacSwan from *Sveinn;* M'Siridh from Norse *Sigridr;* MacUsbaig from *Uspakr;* M'Asgill, or MacAskill from *Asketill;* Lamont from *Lagman;* Mac-Aulay from *Anlaf, Olave;* MacLeod, or M'Cloyd, from the older form *Macljotr* from Norse *Ljotr;* MacCrimmon from Norse *Rumun;* MacCodrum from *Guttormr*. In speaking of Norse place-names in Scotland, Dr. Henderson says: [2] "Many of the chief features in the Scottish mainland, from Eskadale, Norse *Eskidalr*, 'Ash-dale,' by the Beauly River, of old Uisge Farrar, and northwards round the coasts of Ross and Sutherland and Caithness, and along the western border, southward to Galloway and Liddesdale, the *Hlið-dalr* of the Viking settlers, are Norse. As soon as we cross from the Beauly valley into Urray we have Tarradale, from Norse *Tarfr-dalr*, 'bull-dale'; Alcaig in Urquhart from N. *Alka-vîk*, 'auks-bay'; Culbo in Resolis from N. *Kúla*, a ball or knob, and *ból*, 'a farm-stead'; Udale in Cromarty, N. *Y-dalr*, 'yew-dale.' Scatwell in Contin is from N. *scat-vǫllr*, 'the scat-field' or land which yielded tax, *i.e.*

---

[1] *Scotland in Pagan Times, The Iron Age*, p. 48–49. Quoted by Dr. Henderson.   [2] *Norse Influence on Celtic Scotland*, p. 152.

scat to the Northern earls whose seat of justice is commemorated prominently in Dingwall, N. *þing-vǫllr*, the field of the *þing* or Norse court of justice. N. *vǫllr* meets us in Brae-langwell, N. *lang-vǫllr*, 'longfield,' in Resolis, repeated again in Lang-well, Caithness. Cadboll, Catboll (1561), is from N. *kattar-ból*, 'cat-stead.' When we cross to Sutherland, Norse names abound with the Norse terminations in *-dale*, *-boll* ('homestead'), *-gil*, *-vǫllr*, *-bakki* ('bank'), *-ery* (-ary, 'shieling'), *á* ('river'). A few prominent names may suffice for illustration, such as Swordale = *Sward-dale*; Helmsdale = *Hjalmund's dale*; Strath Halladale = *helga-dalr*, 'holy-dale'; Torrisdale = *þorir's-dale*; Ceoldale = cold-dale, or 'keel'-dale."

Norse influence on the Scotch language has been both extensive and lasting. A large Norse vocabulary has been incorporated in the original Gaelic tongue once spoken in Scotland, so that the Highland Scotch speech is no less a composite language than the people themselves are a mixed race. The words referring to dress and armor, pasture, agriculture, peat, trees, carpentry, fish and fishing, birds and animals, time, measure, house, household, family life and government, sea and ships, are Norse to a very large extent. The more rapid discarding of inflectional endings in northern Scotland is also due to Norse influence. But "above all," says Henderson, "it is the difference in intonation, in modulation in the use of the voice between speakers from Central Lochaber, say, where there are no Norse place-names, and between Sutherland or Lewis speakers, where Norse influence is strong, that makes one instinctively feel the presence of the foreigner. . . . One thing is certain : there are great similarities between Norse accentuation and that of the Highland area. This has been noted by Dr. Waltman, of Lund, in a contribution to the Swedish "Nordiska Studier" entitled "Nordiska aksentformer i Gäliska." [1] "Not only Ireland, Bretland, or Wales came to know the Vikings," says the same author; "they had made a great part of Scotland their own." He quotes the following words from Dasent, in the introduction to the "Njálssaga." "To this day the name of almost every island on the west coast of Scotland is either pure Norse, or Norse distorted so as to make it possible for Celtic lips to utter it. The groups of Orkney and Shetland are

[1] *Norse Influence on Celtic Scotland*, p. 109 f.

notoriously Norse, but Lewis and the Uists, and Skye and Mull are no less Norse; and not only the names of the islands themselves, but those of reefs and rocks and lakes and headlands bear witness to the same relation, and show that, while the original inhabitants were not expelled, but held in bondage as thralls, the Norsemen must have dwelt, and dwelt thickly, too, as conquerors and lords."

Norse influence may also be traced in charms, fairy-tales, and popular beliefs, and in many quaint customs still to be found in Scotland. Noteworthy is the idea of hell as a cold place, which is repeatedly met with in Highland poetry. Dr. Henderson calls attention to Mackenzie's "Beauties of Gaelic Poetry," from which he cites, among other illustrations, a stanza from an old Caledonian poem which in translation reads as follows:

"Woe to the one who chooses cold Hell, for it is a cavern with sharp thorns: I abhor Hell, with its cold and wet, a place of bitterness everlasting, where bitter is the drink for aye." [1]

Incantations were used in Scotland to charm away sickness and evil from the cattle as late as 1767, a heathen practice which has been in vogue among the peasantry of Norway till in very recent years. In the Hebrides the old custom, well known from Iceland, of carrying fire around the possessions belonging to each family has been in use within the memory of people still living. The numerous traces of Norse influence in the culture and temperament of the people of Scotland show the permanent importance of the Norse element to their whole development as a nation. Dr. Henderson says: "The Scottish love of freedom, in short, has been intensified by the advent of the Norseman, who within his lights was law-abiding at home if cruel as Viking abroad." "Perhaps to him," says Dr. Magnus Maclean, "we owe our continuance as a race to this day. He has carried with him over the wave the breath of freedom and strenuous endeavor, and fused them into the life of this great nation, helping Britain to build up and maintain a world-wide empire and the supremacy upon the seas." [2] The benefit which the Vikings themselves derived from their prolonged efforts to conquer and colonize new territory may seem relatively small. Their voyages brought them to countries where permanent colonization was impossible, and it is an apparently tragic feature of Viking history that their marvelous expenditure of energy during several centuries brought them no other permanent possessions than the barren islands in the North Atlantic. But if the permanent territorial acquisitions were limited, the Norsemen were richly compensated in other ways. They stimulated the slumbering nations to new activity, engendered a spirit of liberty and enterprise, and furnished ideas which became important factors in the development of western Europe. "They carried strength to others," as the poet expresses it. This was, indeed, no misfortune, but a victory more lasting and glorious than the mere conquest of territory. The Norsemen had become a nation great in fame and power, in culture, and in conscious self-reliance. The Viking expeditions had given them the opportunity to develop in a broad way their latent powers, and to mold on a wide theater of action the national character which has been the vital force in all subsequent Norwegian history.

42. Conditions in Norway during the Reign of the Jarls Eirik and Svein

The creation of the united kingdom of Norway by Harald Haarfagre and the introduction of Christianity by Olav Tryggvason were the two epoch-making events in the national development of the Norwegian people prior to the year 1000. But the new ideas of a united and Christian Norway represented by these two great kings had as yet failed to gain the active support and conscious loyalty of the whole people. There had always been much secret opposition and silent ill-will on the part of the aristocracy, and the common people, who were yet strangers to the idea of national patriotism, allied themselves with their own local chieftains. The battle of Svolder was a result of existing conditions. The opportunity came, and the new national kingship received a crushing blow. The aristocracy regained its power; Norway was divided between the kings of Sweden and Denmark, and the jarls Eirik and Svein, who ruled the country as their vassals. Independence was lost as well as national unity, but no word of protest or complaint was heard. The people seemed to be well satisfied with the new arrangement. One great element necessary to national growth was still wanting — patriotism, which makes a people a nation, conscious of its own distinct life and destiny. The entrance of this new force into the history of the Norwegian people is associated with the name of King Olav Haraldsson, commonly known as Saint Olav.

The rule of the jarls was, in general, a return to the old ways. Nominally they were Christians, but they showed no interest for the new faith, and did nothing to promote or to maintain it. "Eirik Jarl and Svein Jarl were both baptized, and received the true faith," says the saga, "but so long as they ruled Norway, they let each man do as he pleased with regard to Christianity." [1] As a result of this indifference Christianity was soon forgotten, and the people returned to their pagan worship.

Eirik Jarl resided at Lade, and Svein Jarl dwelt at Stenkjær, at the head of the Trondhjemsfjord. The commercial town Nidaros (Trondhjem), which Olav Tryggvason had founded, was allowed to decay. In Oplandene (southeastern Norway) the *herser* and petty kings regained their old independence, and in Vestlandet (southwestern Norway) Erling Skjalgsson of Sole, the brother-in-law of Olav Tryggvason, ruled with unrestricted authority without submitting to the jarls. The king of Sweden collected taxes in Trøndelagen, but King Knut the Great of Denmark, the son of Svein Tjugeskjeg, who was now engaged in the conquest of England, paid little attention to his Norwegian possessions. Eirik and Svein were unable to exercise any great authority. They were satisfied with enjoying the privileges and emoluments of their high office, due them according to ancient custom. The people seem to have been well pleased with their mild rule and the gradual return to the old order of things. "They maintained well the old laws and all customs," says the saga, "and they were popular men and good rulers." [2]

An important change was, nevertheless, taking place at this time. The aristocracy had learned the necessity of united action, if they wished to maintain their old privileges against a national king, who

[1] *Heimskringla. Olav Tryggvasonssaga*, ch. 113.   [2] *Ibid.*

might at any time appear upon the scene. In France and the British Isles they had also become acquainted with a social system in which the aristocracy owned nearly all the land, and exercised a far greater authority over the common classes than did the Norwegian chieftains, who had hitherto stood in a more or less patriarchal relation to the people. These lessons were not forgotten. The more powerful families, of which there were many in Norway at this time, now made an effort to become more firmly united through intermarriage, and the great chieftains began to enlarge their estates to a hitherto unknown extent. One of the most powerful chieftains was Thore Hund of Bjarkey in northern Haalogaland (Nordland). He had a monopoly on the trade with the Finns, and became very wealthy through the export of furs to England. His brother was the powerful Sigurd of Trondanes, who was married to a sister of Erling Skjalgsson. His sister was married to Ølve of Egge, the greatest chieftain in Indtrøndelagen. Haarek of Tjotta was another man of great note in Haalogaland. Many free-holders lived in the island of Tjotta, but he gradually bought them out, until he finally owned the whole island. He made much money by trade, and became very rich. Few men in Norway at this time wielded greater influence than Einar Tambarskjælver in Uttrøndelagen, who had been with Olav Tryggvason at Svolder. He was married to a daughter of Haakon Jarl, and lived at Gimsar in Guldalen. In Søndmør dwelt the great Arnmødling family. The brothers Thorberg, Kalv, Finn, Arne, and Arnbjørn Arnesson played an important part in public affairs in the reign of Olav Haraldsson. Their sister Ragnhild was married to Haarek of Tjotta, and Thorberg, the lord of Giske, was married to the daughter of Erling Skjalgsson, who was the greatest of all the chieftains. The saga says that Erling always had a force of men with him, resembling a king's *hird*. He was tall, strong, and beautiful; and in all manly sports he resembled Olav Tryggvason. On his estate he had thirty slaves and a number of serfs. He gave the slaves a piece of land to till. This piece they worked during spare hours, and they were allowed to sell the grain which they raised. They could purchase their freedom for a fixed price, and when they had become free, Erling either retained them in his service, or gave them land which they might clear and cultivate. When Erling traveled by sea, he always had a fully equipped war ship, and when Eirik Jarl or Svein was near, he had with him two hundred men (240) or more. "It is the common opinion," says the saga, "that Erling Skjalgsson was the greatest of all *lendermænd* in Norway." In Gudbrandsdal the great *herse* Dale-Gudbrand ruled as an independent prince. Of the many petty kings which ruled in southeastern Norway may be mentioned King Sigurd Syr of Ringerike, Saint Olav's stepfather; and King Rørek in Hedemarken.

The aristocracy, which controlled the greater part of the wealth and resources of the country, could now present a united front against a king who should presume to encroach on their established rights. Eirik and Svein were of their number, and ruled in the interest of their class; the two brothers seem to have been worthy representatives of that old class of chieftains. Eirik Jarl had especially distinguished himself as a warrior. He had borne the brunt of the battle against the Jómsvikings at Hjørungavaag, and had taken Olav Tryggvason's famous ship, the "Long Serpent," at Svolder. He was a man of great prowess and ability. The more it is to be regretted that he had drawn his sword against his king and his country for motives of sordid gain and self-aggrandizement.

> "Then faded away his old renown,
> Till in foreign lands a grave he found.
> The death-knell sounds in the breast of the man
> Who draws his sword 'gainst his native land." [1]

43. OLAV HARALDSSON OR OLAV THE SAINT

Olav Haraldsson, son of King Harald Grenske and Aasta, descended from Harald Haarfagre.[2] His father died before he was born, and Aasta was married a second time to King Sigurd Syr of Ringerike, where Olav was raised. The people of this fertile inland district had taken little part in the Viking expeditions, but they dwelt near the centers of trade in southern Norway, and the new

---

[1] From the poem "Eirik Jarl" by Peer Sivle.

[2] Harald Haarfagre > Bjørn Farmand > Gudrød Bjørnsson > Harald Grenske > Olav Haraldsson.

ideas and elements of culture which trade and commerce brought from foreign lands were easily accessible. Ringerike and the neighboring districts, like Hadeland and Toten, became at this time a center of culture, which is still evidenced by the many decorated rune-stones which were erected here during this period. Two of the finest specimens are the Dyna stone from Hadeland, and the stone at Alstad in Toten.[1] These districts were also making great progress economically. King Sigurd Syr, who seems to have been a peaceful man of no great ability, was more devoted to farming than to military exploits; but Aasta was a high-minded and ambitious woman, who wished her sons to gain power and renown. Her words to her son Olav are characteristic: "If I had the choice I would rather that you become over-king of Norway, though you should live no longer in the kingdom than did Olav Tryggvason, than that you should become no greater king than Sigurd Syr, and die of old age."[2] The sagas state that when Olav was three years old, Olav Tryggvason visited Ringerike, and Sigurd Syr, Aasta, and Olav were baptized; but according to the Norman chronicles and the Catholic legends he was baptized much later at Rouen. Alexander Bugge thinks that the saga statement may be true, since

FIG. 45. — The Dyna rune-stone at Hadeland, Norway.

[1] On the estate Alstad lived, about the year 1000, a lady of high birth by the name of Jørund. In memory of her husband she erected a stone monument decorated with pictures of a falcon-chase, which had been his favorite sport. The monument bears the following runic inscription: "Jørund erected this stone in memory of —— [the name is nearly effaced] who had her for a wife; and brought the stone from Ringerike, from Hole; and she caused it to be ornamented with pictures."

The stone from Dyna was erected by another lady of noble birth, Gunvor Trireksdatter, in memory of her daughter Astrid. It is richly ornamented with pictures and bears the following runic inscription: "Gunvor Trireksdatter made a bridge in memory of her daughter Astrid. She was the most dexterous in using the hand of all maidens in Hadeland."

[2] *Heimskringla, Saga of Olav the Saint*, ch. 35.

the boy was called Olav, a name not before found in the family.[1] Olav was still very young when he went on Viking expeditions together with his foster-father Rane Vidførle. They went first to Denmark, where they joined some Viking bands in a descent on the shores of Sweden and Finland. On their return they visited Jómsborg, where Thorkel the Tall, a brother of Sigvalde Jarl, was preparing an expedition to England. Olav joined Thorkel's forces, and they sailed southward along the coast of Jutland. After a battle at Søndervik, they proceeded to the coast of Friesland and Holland.[2] Tiel, an important commercial town, was sacked and burned, and the suburbs of Utrecht were plundered, 1008 or 1009. From Holland Thorkel sailed for England, and arrived there in August, 1009.[3]

After Olav Tryggvason had concluded peace with King Æthelred, and had returned to Norway in 995, Svein Tjugeskjeg of Denmark continued military operations against England. In 997 and the following years the southern districts were continually ravaged by Viking bands. A number of Danes and Norsemen had settled in England, and Æthelred feared that they might make common cause with the invaders. His fear and cowardice led him to secretly arrange a general massacre of the Danes, which was carried out on St. Brice's Day (Nov. 12), 1002. How far the slaughter extended, is not known, but it must have been confined to southern England, where the Danish settlers were few. This event again brought King Svein to England with a large fleet in 1003. A war began which ended in the final conquest of England. King Æthelred fled to Normandy, and Svein was hailed as king of England in 1013. During these ten years the war had been continuous, but in 1009, when the fleet of Thorkel the Tall arrived, Svein was not in England, and it is possible that the fleet had been sent with his aid and approval. At Southwark they made a fortified camp, but failed in an attempt to take London. The next year they ravaged the country exten-

---

[1] Norges Historie, I. 2, p. 325.   [2] Bloch, Geschichte der Niederlande.

[3] In Senja, in northern Norway, a number of old articles of silver were found some years ago. Among these was a collar of silver with the following runic inscription: "We went to visit the men of Friesland, and to divide the war-clothes with them." The inscription, which dates from about the year 1000, must have been made by one of Olav's followers on the expedition to Friesland. See A. Bugge, Norges Historie, I., p. 327.

sively and defeated Ulvkel Jarl and the East Anglians at Ringmere, and King Æthelred was forced to promise them a tribute of 48,000 pounds of silver. In 1011 the Vikings besieged Canterbury. Through treachery they gained entrance to the city and they carried away, among numerous other captives, Archbishop Ælfeah, who had confirmed King Olav Tryggvason. They held him for a ransom, but as neither this, nor the Danegeld granted by Æthelred, was paid, they stoned the unfortunate archbishop to death. He was buried in St. Paul's church at London, and became one of the most venerated of English saints. The Danegeld was finally paid, and the Viking army gradually disbanded. Thorkel the Tall and Olav Haraldsson entered the service of King Æthelred with forty-five ships. They defended London against King Svein in 1013, and made such brave resistance that he failed to take the city. But after Æthelred had fled, and all England had been subjugated, London also submitted to King Svein.

In this way Olav Haraldsson had been schooled in the art of war, and had lived through a period of youthful storm and stress. He had seen the wildest kind of Viking warfare in company with the professional buccaneers of the Jómsborg, but he had also come into direct touch with European life and ideas in Friesland, Holland, Normandy, and England. What impression this had made on him we do not know. He was still a Viking, but nobler thoughts and higher ideals soon made him turn away from the adventurous path of rude Viking warfare. The spirit of Christianity, and the charms of a new and better culture inspired him with the ambition to devote his life to the attainment of higher aims. The lost cause of Christianity and national unity in Norway was still waiting for a leader strong enough to break the evil spell which had fallen upon it. To wrest the leadership in national affairs from the unwilling hands of a strong and reactionary aristocracy, and to launch the nation upon a period of national development in compact with new ideas was the great end to which destiny seems to have consecrated the life, the heroic courage, and singular devotion of this remarkable prince.

King Svein died suddenly in 1014, and his oldest son Harald succeeded him as king of Denmark. But the Anglo-Saxons recalled King Æthelred and his son Edmund Ironside, and Svein's son Knut, later called Knut the Great, who was in East Anglia, was forced to leave the country. In 1015 he returned with a large fleet. Thorkel the Tall had now joined him, and he had also called to his assistance Eirik Jarl of Norway. Some hard campaigns were fought with the English forces led by Edmund Ironside, but King Æthelred and Edmund both died in 1016. Knut became king of England, and married Emma of Normandy, King Æthelred's widow.

Olav Haraldsson left England in 1013 in company with King Æthelred, and went to Normandy to aid Duke Richard II. in a war against Count Odo of Chartres. He accompanied Æthelred back to England, but left again shortly after on an expedition to France and Spain. He sailed southward along the coast of France, fought a battle with William V. of Aquitaine, and then proceeded to the northern coast of Spain, where he captured Gunvaldsborg, and took Jarl Geirfinn prisoner and forced him to pay a ransom. He seems also to have visited Portugal and southern Spain. The saga tells us that Olav sailed into the Guadalquivir (Karlsaaerne). "But while he was lying there waiting for favorable wind to sail into the Strait of Gibraltar (Norvasund), and thence to the Holy Land, he dreamed that a strange and powerful, but also fearful man appeared and bade him give up the plan of going into foreign lands: "Go back," he said, "to your *odel*, for you shall become king of Norway forever." [1] This is, of course, a legend. But Olav returned to Normandy, where he was well received. He spent the winter in Rouen, where he is said to have been baptized; but it is probable that he was confirmed here by Archbishop Robert, a brother of Duke Richard.

In the spring of 1015 Olav sailed from Normandy to England, and thence to Norway, where he would take up the struggle to reëstablish Christianity and to regain the throne of his ancestors. He had only two merchant vessels, about 140 men, and a few missionaries. The moment was opportune. Eirik Jarl had gone to England to aid King Knut, and had left his son Haakon in charge of his possessions at home. The two merchant vessels which arrived from England created no suspicion. Haakon was at this time in Vestlandet with only one war vessel, and Olav entrapped him and took him prisoner. He was liberated on the condition that he should

[1] *Heimskringla, Saga of Olav the Saint*, ch. 18.

leave the country and never again bear arms against Olav. Haakon went to England, where his uncle King Knut made him jarl of Worcestershire. Eirik Jarl was made ruler of Northumbria, where he died in 1023. Olav sailed southward along the coast of Norway, entered the Foldenfjord (Christianiafjord), and came to his step-father, King Sigurd Syr, in the autumn. He was now about twenty-two years of age. He was of middle size, but strong and well-built, with auburn hair, red beard, and ruddy cheeks. He had large bright eyes and a majestic look. The saga says that he was well skilled in all manly sports, but it does not state that he surpassed others in this respect. In speech he was wise and eloquent. He lacked, however, the charm of personality and the chivalric qualities which had made Olav Tryggvason so popular. He was less cheerful, less willing to compromise; at times he was irritable and unnecessarily obstinate; but he possessed the resolute will and singleness of purpose which accomplishes great things. He had a strength of character and an ability to sacrifice all for a lofty aim, which makes him a great and tragic figure in history. Olav acquainted King Sigurd with his plans, and received his promise of support. By rich presents and persuasion he gained many friends and adherents in Oplandene, and Sigurd Syr gave him all possible aid. The saga says that Sigurd held a meeting with the other kings of Oplandene in Hadeland, where Olav was present. He urged upon them the necessity of throwing off the foreign yoke which the Swedes and Danes had laid upon them. They could now get a man who could take the lead in this affair, and he told them of Olav Haraldsson's many exploits. King Rørek of Hedemarken expressed his regret that Harald Haarfagre's kingdom had fallen to decay, but they were well satisfied, he said, with the present arrangement. The over-kings were now so far away that they did not oppress them. It was doubtful if their condition would be better if a native prince became over-king of Norway. They yielded, however, to persuasion, and Olav was proclaimed king of Norway at a general *thing* assembled in Oplandene. The powerful Dale-Gudbrand, *herse* in Gudbrandsdal, also pledged him his allegiance. In the winter before Christmas, Olav crossed the Dovre Mountains, and surprised Svein Jarl, who dwelt at Stenkjær in Trøndelagen. Svein had to flee, and Olav seized the food which he had prepared for the Christmas feast. He also advanced to Nidaros, and began to restore the buildings of the deserted town. Here he met the scald Sighvat Thordsson, who had just arrived from Iceland. Sighvat became Olav's hirdscald and his lifelong friend and companion. But Svein Jarl and Einar Tambarskjælver soon appeared on the scene with a large force, and Olav had to return to Oplandene. He now went to Viken, where he drove away the Danish officials. It appears that these districts submitted without offering any resistance; but a decisive combat would yet have to be fought with the powerful Svein Jarl, and both prepared for the inevitable struggle. In the spring of 1016 Olav sailed through the Foldenfjord (Christianiafjord) to meet Svein, who was approaching with a large fleet, and on Palm Sunday they met at Nesjar, near Tunsberg, where Svein was defeated after a sanguinary battle. He fled to Sweden, and died on an expedition to Russia the following year. The battle of Nesjar marks the final overthrow of the rule of jarls in Norway. Olav, who was now master of the whole realm, went to Trøndelagen, where he was proclaimed king of Norway at the Ørething, according to old custom.

44. FOREIGN RELATIONS

Olav had ascended the throne of his ancestors, and Norway was again a united kingdom; but the kings of Sweden and Denmark, who, since the fall of Olav Tryggvason, had exercised sovereign authority in the country, had not recognized its integrity, or independence. The situation was extremely difficult. The powerful nobles at home might seize the first opportunity to join King Olav's enemies, as Eirik Jarl and Svein had done in the days of Olav Tryggvason; and such an opportunity was sure to come, since Olav would have to defend his kingdom against his powerful neighbors, who now claimed it with some show of right. The king of Sweden sent tax collectors into Trøndelagen, as before, and held Jæmtland and Ranrike, which he had seized. King Olav refused to pay him taxes, and prepared for war. At the Sarp Falls of the Glommen River, in southeastern Norway, he erected a walled fortress, called "Borg" (later Sarpsborg), inside of which he founded a city, and built a church to St. Mary. The ruins of the fortifications are still visible. Olav gathered stores at Borg, or Sarpsborg, and remained there during the winter of 1017–1018. He carried on secret negotiations with the people in Ranrike, and as the chieftains gave him their support, the province soon renewed its old allegiance to Norway. Olav advanced with an army, drove out the Swedish officials, and war began along the border. Ragnvald Ulvsson, jarl of Vestergöt-land, who was married to Olav Tryggvason's sister Ingebjørg, felt himself bound to King Olav through this bond of relationship, and became his faithful friend. Olav and Ragnvald agreed that peace should be maintained between them, and, as the war was unpopular on both sides of the border, Olav sent an embassy to the Swedish king to negotiate peace. In the spring of 1018 a *thing* was held at Upsala where Ragnvald Jarl was present, and urged the king to conclude peace with King Olav. The powerful Torgny Lagmand also arose and spoke in favor of peace with such authority that the king yielded. The agreement was made that the king of Sweden should give Olav his daughter Ingegerd in marriage, and that the wedding should be celebrated at Konghelle in the fall; but Olav Skotkonung did not keep his word. He married his daughter to Grand Duke Jaroslaf of Gardarike (Russia), and when King Olav came to Konghelle to celebrate his nuptials, the bride did not arrive. Olav was very angry and wished to renew the war, but he was, finally, persuaded to send another embassy to Sweden. Sighvat Scald was intrusted with the mission. He came to Ragnvald Jarl, where he saw the beautiful Astrid, another daughter of the Swedish king, and Ragnvald undertook to arrange a match between her and King Olav. He took the princess to Sarpsborg, where she was married to Olav without her father's consent. Olav Skotkonung of Sweden would, probably, have continued the war, but circum-stances forced him to make peace with Olav Haraldsson King Knut, who ruled all England, had also been chosen king of Denmark on the death of his brother Harald; and he might seize Norway and, possibly, also Sweden unless some balance of power was maintained. The Swedish king, therefore, met Olav at Konghelle, where peace was concluded, 1019. The independence of Norway was recognized, and the borders were fixed between the two kingdoms.

45. KING OLAV ESTABLISHES CHRISTIANITY IN NORWAY. HIS LAWS AND ADMINISTRATION

After the peace of Konghelle King Olav ruled for many years without being molested by foreign enemies. It was his ambition to make Norway a strong Christian monarchy like other Christian states of Europe, and he labored assiduously to carry through a great program of organization and reform by which the foundations were laid for the future national development of Norway. The problems confronting him were many and difficult. Norway would have to regain its integrity and independence, Christianity had to be reëstablished, the laws were in need of revision, and the aristocracy had to be reduced to submission and to full obedience to the laws.[1] In the years prior to 1019, while he was yet engaged in the struggle with the king of Sweden, he introduced Christianity in Oplandene. He visited every district and petty kingdom, placed missionaries there to instruct the people, and punished severely all those who refused to accept the Christian faith. The kings of these districts were much displeased, and assembled to form an alliance against him; but a friend informed him of their plot. He surprised them and took them prisoners while they were still deliberating upon the uprising, and punished them severely. Some he banished, others he maimed or blinded, says the saga; the rule of petty kings in Norway was ended. Oplandene, which hitherto had been nearly independent, was now placed immediately under the crown. After the treaty of peace with Sweden in 1019, Olav could devote himself to the missionary work with greater energy, and he was ably assisted by the bishops which he had brought from England and Normandy. Of those mentioned, — Rudolf, Bernhard, Grimkel,[2] and Sigurd, — Grimkel was the most important. He was a man of learning, tact, and ability. The name indicates that he was of Norse descent, but

[1] Konrad Maurer, *Die Bekehrung des norwegischen Stammes zum Christenthume*, vol. I., 39. A. D. Jørgensen, *Den norske Kirkes Grundlæggelse og første Udvikling*, p. 476 ff. P. A. Munch, *Det norske Folks Historie*, part I., vol. II., 589 ff. R. Keyser, *Den norske Kirkes Historie under Katholicismen*.

[2] Adam v. Bremen mentions Sigurd, book II. c. 55, together with Grimkel, Rudolf, and Bernhard; but it is not certain that Sigurd came to Norway with King Olav.

he must have been born in England. He was King Olav's chief adviser and assistant both in the missionary work and in lawgiving. Among the king's most powerful and devoted friends were also: Bjørn Stallare (*comes stabuli*), Sighvat Thordsson the great scald, Thord Foleson, Aslak Fitjaskalle, Thormod Kolbrunarskald, and Hjalte Skjeggesson.

In 1019 Olav went to Nidaros, where he remained that winter. The following summer he introduced Christianity in Haalogaland, the most northern district of Norway, and Haarek of Tjotta and Thore Hund of Bjarkey, the most powerful chieftains in those parts, pledged their submission to the king. In Uttrøndelagen Christianity had been maintained since the days of Olav Tryggvason, but in Indtrøndelagen the people had returned to paganism, and the powerful Ølve of Egge continued to officiate as priest in the heathen temple in spite of King Olav's warning. Olav, therefore, marched against the Indtrønders while they were assembled for the spring sacrifices, captured Ølve, and caused him to be executed. He gave his widow and his estates to Kalv Arnesson, whom he made a *lendermand*. The people of Gudbrandsdal were converted to Christianity in 1021, after some resistance. When the army which they sent against the king was defeated at Breidevangen, south of Sell, a *thing* was assembled at Hundtorp, where the *herse* Dale-Gudbrand was baptized, and the people accepted Christianity. Dale-Gudbrand built a church at Hundtorp, and Olav left missionaries to instruct the people. The story told in the sagas that the people carried out an idol representing the god Thor, thinking that it would frighten King Olav, and that Kolbein the Strong, one of Olav's men, demolished it with a club, is a piece of fiction introduced by Snorre for dramatic effect. It symbolizes the combat of Christianity against heathenism, and King Olav's war against the idols. It marks the beginning of a whole literature of folk-tales connected with the name of Saint Olav.[1] In 1023 Olav also introduced Christianity in the Gula-

---

[1] The story is found in the *Saga of Olav the Saint* in the *Heimskringla*, and also in the *Olavssaga ins helga*. This saga is also written by Snorre, and differs little from the *Saga of Olav the Saint* in the *Heimskringla*. It is but a new revised edition of it. See Gustav Storm, *Snorre Sturlasons Historieskrivning*.

thingslag and in Valdres. In many places, as in Viken, in Uttrøndelagen, and in localities on the west coast where churches had been
built by Olav Tryggvason, Christianity had not altogether disappeared, but it had been obscured and corrupted through heathen
ideas and customs, It, therefore, became King Olav's second great
task to give the Church of Norway a permanent organization, and
to establish for it a code of church laws according to which it might
be governed. With the assistance of Bishop Grimkel and other ecclesiastics, he produced such a code of laws written in the Norwegian
language. The "Heimskringla" says: "The church laws he made
according to the advice of Bishop Grimkel and other teachers, and
devoted all his energy to eradicate heathenism and old customs which
he considered contrary to the Christian spirit."[1] He called a general
thing in the island of Moster, where people from Viken, Gulathingslag, and Frostathingslag were present. Here King Olav and Bishop
Grimkel explained the new laws to the people, and they were finally
adopted. For the Eidsivathingslag Olav made a new code in which
the church laws were incorporated. The districts of Viken were
also organized into a *thinglag*, called "Borgarthingslag," because
the *thing* met at Borg, or Sarpsborg. It received a code of laws to
which the church laws were also added.[2] It is not certain, however,
that the Borgarthingslag was originally organized by King Olav.
In the Gulathingslag and Frostathingslag there was one principal
church in each *fylke;*[3] in the Borgarthingslag two, and in the Eidsivathingslag three. The principal churches had resident priests
who received the income from church lands set aside for their maintenance. The final step taken by King Olav in the organization of the
Church of Norway was to place it under the higher ecclesiastical

[1] These church laws are found in the *Gulathingslov*, the *Frostathingslov*,
and as supplements to the *Eidsivathingslov*, and the *Borgarthingslov*. See
Norges gamle Love, vol. I.

[2] The Eidsivathing's code and the Borgarthing's code have been lost,
but the church laws of both codes have been preserved. See *Norges gamle
Love*, vol. I.

[3] "The next is that we should maintain all the churches and the Christianity which Saint Olav and Bishop Grimkel established on the Moster-
thing, and all since built. But there is one church in each fylke which we
call the main church which all men in the fylke must maintain." Gulathingslov, ch. 10.

authority of an archbishop. This might have led to a closer affiliation with the Church of England, since Christianity had been brought to Norway from that country, but the political situation proved unfavorable. Knut the Great, who was now king of England, had not relinquished his claim on Norway, and any closer relations between the two countries, even in religious matters, might have contributed to strengthen his hold. King Olav, therefore, sent Bishop Grimkel to negotiate with Archbishop Unvan of Bremen, with the result that the Church of Norway was placed under the supervision of the Archbishop of Bremen.

Christianity began henceforth to gain general favor. The old pagan conceptions were not eradicated, however, through the hasty conversion. They gradually assumed Christian forms and continued to live in the religious life as well as in the songs and stories of the people. Christ was substituted for Odin as the divine ruler. The poet Eiliv Gudrunsson sang about Christ the mighty king of Rome, who sits in the South at the Well of Urd, and rules over the lands of the mountain kings. King Olav takes the place of Thor as the red-bearded champion of light, who is ever victorious in his war against trolls and evil spirits. Freyja reappears as the Virgin Mary, who rules over the animals of the forest. She is also the midwife, and assists at the birth of children.[1] This naïve but poetic blending of Christian forms and pagan ideas marks the advent of the intellectual life of the Christian Middle Ages, from which the folk-songs and fairy-tales have sprung.

It became necessary for Olav also to revise the civil laws, to bring them into closer conformity with Christian principles. The "Heimskringla" states that "he made the laws according to the counsel of the wisest men; he took away, or added, as he considered it just." We have already seen that he gave the Eidsivathingslag a new code, and it is probable, though not certain, that he established the Borgarthingslag. The laws of the Gulathingslag and of the Frostathingslag were so thoroughly revised that these old codes were henceforth known as the "Laws of Saint Olav." The revision of the laws by the king and his learned assistants, who were familiar,

[1] Dr. A. Chr. Bang, *Udsigt over den norske Kirkes Historie under Katholicismen*, p. 77 f.

not only with Christian principles, but also with the laws of the Christian kingdoms of western Europe, was a legal work of the greatest importance. The "Laws of St. Olav" were destined to become the foundation of future Norwegian jurisprudence. King Olav's lawgiving represents in itself a centralization of power, and a growth of royal authority which carries with it the greatest change in the political institutions of Norway. King Haakon the Good had, indeed, been a lawgiver, but not to the extent which this function was now exercised by King Olav. The old laws were regarded as having been given by the gods themselves; they were inherited, time-honored custom, the expression of the sense of legal justice of the whole people, who originally had exercised the power of lawmaking. But after the union of Norway, and the introduction of Christianity, when the laws had to be revised and brought into harmony with the new conditions, the king gradually assumed this power; and after Olav Haraldsson's time the people had little direct influence on legislation. The old *lagthings*, which had been well suited to the old tribal organization, were conspicuously defective as lawmaking assemblies for the united kingdom of Norway. They were four in number, not a single assembly for the whole country, and they were provincial, not national in character.[1] They had no power of taxation, and the laws were introduced by the king, or in his name. The powers of administration, taxation, and legislation were, therefore, quite naturally united in the hands of the sovereign. The king, not the *lagthings*, became the exponent of the national will. But he was not an absolute monarch; the people still exercised indirectly no small influence on legislation. If they desired a new law, or the revision of an old one, they negotiated privately with the king, and when an understanding was reached, the measure was proposed at the *lagthing* in the king's name. If he wished to propose a new law, he negotiated with men of influence to gain the necessary support. In these preliminary negotiations the people could exercise considerable influence through their spokesmen. To become a law, the new measure had to be proposed at the *lagthing* and accepted by the people. In matters of taxation the king was also dependent on the will of the people. If new taxes had to be

[1] T. H. Aschehoug, *Statsforfatningen i Norge og Danmark indtil 1814.*

levied, even for special emergencies, a proposal was brought before the various local or *fylkesthings*, where the assent of the people had to be secured.

The establishment of the kingdom of Norway based on the theory of a strong national monarchy with centralized legislative and administrative powers necessitated many important changes in the whole system of government. Many new departures of far-reaching importance had been made, especially by Harald Haarfagre, and Olav Haraldsson continued his great predecessor's work of reorganization. The *herser*, or tribal chieftains, who had ruled over larger local districts, were now replaced by *lendermænd* (= men holding lands from the king), or officials appointed by the king. The *herser* had been the leaders of the people — an old aristocracy; the *lendermænd* became the representatives and adherents of the king. The *aarmænd*, who in Harald Haarfagre's time were men of humble station, appointed as overseers of the royal estates, were now replaced by *sysselmænd*, or royal officials. They collected the taxes in their districts, and arrested and punished criminals in the name of the king.

The *hird* was also reorganized. Three classes are mentioned: *hirðmænd*, *gestir*, and *huskarlar*. The *hirðmænd*, usually sons of *lendermænd* and other leading men in the country, constituted the king's court. The *gestir* were sent on difficult and dangerous missions, and executed the police duties exercised by the king throughout the kingdom. The *huskarlar* had charge of the work about the royal residence, and furnished the necessaries for the king's household. This class does not seem to have belonged to the *hird* proper. The "King's Mirror" says: "All men who serve the king are called 'huskarlar,' but honor and power are divided among them according to their ability to serve him, and according as he wishes to grant preferments to each. There are some *huskarlar* in the king's *hird* who receive no salary, neither are they permitted to eat or drink with the rest of the *hird*. They must do all things about the royal residence which the overseer demands."[1] They seem to have been

---

[1] See the description of the *hird* in *The King's Mirror*, XXV. ff. R. Keyser, *Norges Stats og Retsforfatning i Middelalderen*, p. 77 ff. T. H. Aschehoug, *Statsforfatningen i Norge og Danmark indtil 1814*, p. 33. Ebbe Hertz-

young men of good family, who sought this kind of service as a possible road to promotion and royal favor. At the head of the *hird* stood the great officials of the king's court, who acted in the capacity of ministers of state. They were called *hirðstjórar* (leaders of the *hird*). The chief officials were: the *stallari*, who had charge of the royal equipages, and acted as the king's representative at the *thing*; the *merkismaðr*, or royal standard-bearer, the *féhirðir*, or treasurer, and the hirdbishop, who was the king's adviser in ecclesiastical affairs. All public offices, from the lowest to the highest, had thus been organized into an articulate system of national administration.

During the reign of Eirik Jarl and Svein, the powerful chieftains in the colonies had cast off all allegiance to Norway, and ruled as independent princes. The task of reuniting these island possessions with the kingdom required, therefore, the most vigilant attention. Through energetic and tactful measures King Olav soon succeeded in bringing the Orkney and Shetland Islands back to their old allegiance. The Faroe Islands accepted the king's code of church laws, but so long as the crafty Trond i Gata lived, no taxes were paid to the king of Norway. King Olav investigated diligently how Christianity was maintained in Iceland. He persuaded the Icelanders to abolish many heathen customs which were still practiced, but his church laws do not seem to have been established there. He sought to gain the friendship of the Icelandic chieftains, and many of them visited him in Norway. He negotiated with them in regard to the relation between Norway and Iceland, and an agreement was made about 1022, called "The Institutions and Laws Which King Olav Gave the Icelanders." According to this agreement the Icelanders should virtually enjoy the rights and privileges of citizens of Norway. They had the same right of *odel* as other freeholders, and could inherit property in Norway on the same terms as native citizens. They paid no taxes except the *landøre*, which was paid for the privilege of trade and intercourse with Norway. In return, the king's men should have the same rights in Iceland as native citizens, and the suits at law should be brought directly to the highest court. In

berg, *En Fremstilling af det norske Aristokratis Historie*, p. 58 ff. *Hirðskrá*, 43–45, *Norges gamle Love*, vol. II., and Glossary, vol. V. P. A. Munch, *Det norske Folks Historie*, part I., vol. II., p. 639 f.

time of war the Icelanders who happened to be in Norway owed the king military service, and could not leave the country. Two out of every three would then have to join the royal standards. This arrangement lasted till 1262, when Iceland was finally united with Norway. King Olav rebuilt the city of Nidaros, which Olav Tryggvason had founded, and restored the royal hall and the St. Clemens church, which had been erected in Olav Tryggvason's time.

More difficult than any other task in King Olav's great work of reorganization was that of reducing the recalcitrant aristocracy to proper submission. Many of the great chieftains who reluctantly had pledged the king a nominal allegiance, soon manifested a hostile opposition to his plans, but King Olav, none the less, proceeded with characteristic energy to restrict their power to what he considered reasonable limits. The powerful Haarek of Tjotta had to divide his *syssel* with King Olav's friend Osmund Grankelsson, and Aslak Fitjaskalle was made *sysselmand* in Hordaland, in southwestern Norway, where Erling Skjalgsson of Sole ruled with almost royal power. The king enforced the laws with strict impartiality, and punished with uncompromising severity even the most powerful offenders. The "Heimskringla" says: "He meted out the same punishment to the powerful and to the small, but the great men of the country regarded this as arrogance, and they were greatly offended when they lost their kinsmen through the king's just decision, even if the case was true. This was the cause of the uprising of the great men against King Olav, that they could not tolerate his justice. But he would rather surrender his kingdom than his uprightness." [1] Erling Skjalgsson and others sent their sons to King Knut the Great in England, who received them well, gave them rich presents, and did what he could to encourage the defection of the Norwegian chieftains. King Knut was a powerful monarch who ruled over England, Scotland, Wales, and Denmark. He, also, called himself king of Norway, and claimed even the throne of Sweden. He was tall and stately, with light hair and bright eyes, generous and sociable, a king whom the young nobles loved to serve. So long as Knut was fully occupied with affairs in England, the aristocracy did not venture to rebel openly against King Olav, but the growing power

[1] *Heimskringla, Saga of Olav the Saint,* ch. 181.

and influence of King Knut was a steadily growing menace to Norwegian independence. The new king of Sweden, Anund Jacob, was a brother of Olav's queen, Astrid. The two kings made a joint attack on Denmark in an endeavor to seize the country, but King Knut met them with a large fleet, and an undecisive battle was fought by Helgeå, near Skåne, after which all thought of conquering Denmark had to be abandoned. Erling Skjalgsson and Haarek of Tjotta had thrown off all allegiance to King Olav, so that he could find no support in northern and western Norway. King Knut, who had made active preparations to invade the country, left England with a fleet of fifty ships, in 1028, and a Danish fleet lay ready to join him. When this news reached Norway, the chieftains of Trøndelagen assembled the Ørething and proclaimed Knut king, and Erling Skjalgsson hastened to his assistance at the earliest opportunity. But Olav would still strike a blow for his throne and his country. He left Viken with thirteen ships, and met Erling Skjalgsson's squadron near Utstein in southwestern Norway. A battle was fought which resulted in the defeat and death of Erling. It was now late in the fall, and a great fleet was advancing against him from Trøndelagen. All further resistance was useless. He steered his ships into a fjord in Søndmør, took leave of his friends, and through the winter's snow he made his way across the mountains to Sweden. He spent some time in the island of Gothland, where he introduced Christianity. From there he proceeded to Novgorod, and finally to Kief, where he found refuge at the court of his brother-in-law, Duke Jaroslaf of Gardarike.

46. Norway under Danish Overlordship. The Battle of Stiklestad. King Olav the Saint

King Knut the Great, who was now over-king of Norway, placed Haakon, the son of Eirik Jarl, in charge of the kingdom as his deputy or vassal. Haakon went to England, where he married Gunhild, a daughter of King Knut's sister, but on his return voyage he was drowned in the Pentlandsfjord, and the great Ladejarl family became extinct in the male line. Both Kalv Arnesson and Einar Tambarskjælver aspired to become his successor, but Knut let them understand that he intended to make his own son king of Norway. This was a great disappointment to the ambitious nobles. It became apparent that the benefit which they were to derive from their rebellion against King Olav would be considerably smaller than they had been led to anticipate. Einar Tambarskjælver became quite disgusted, and remained absent from Norway till after the battle of Stiklestad.

Olav Haraldsson languished in exile at Grand Duke Jaroslaf's court. He was moody and unhappy, and could never wholly relinquish the idea of rescuing Norway from foreign rule. The "Heimskringla" states that Olav Tryggvason appeared before him in his dreams, and told him to return to Norway and claim the kingdom which God had given him. "It makes a king renowned to gain victory over his enemies, but it is a glorious death to fall on the battlefield with one's men." Many of Olav's men had joined him in Gardarike, and they encouraged him to attempt to wrest Norway from the foreign conquerors. When the news spread that Haakon was dead, he determined to return to Norway. He left his son Magnus at the court of Jaroslaf, and proceeded to Sweden, where King Anund Jacob gave him great aid, though he did not dare to form an alliance with him against King Knut. He gave him a number of soldiers, and allowed him to recruit many more.[1] His adherents in the eastern districts of Norway also aided him. His halfbrother Harald Sigurdsson, son of King Sigurd Syr and Aasta, the later chieftain of the Varangians in Myklegard (Constantinople), joined him with a force of 720 men. People of all sorts drifted to his standards, and he was able to enter Norway with a considerable army. He had some good troops, but the greater portion of these hasty levies were of inferior quality.[2] In Trøndelagen the chieftains, on hearing of King Olav's return, had gathered a large army of the

[1] Queen Astrid remained in Sweden at the court of her brother, King Anund, and did not return to Norway till in the reign of Magnus the Good. She was accompanied by their only daughter, Ulvhild, who later married Ordulf, son of the Duke of Saxony, of the House of the Welfs.

[2] Alexander Bugge, *Norges Historie*, vol. I, 2, p. 404. Olav, who had made Christianity his special cause, possessed the ardor and vehemence of a crusader, but the *Heimskringla* is evidently in error when it states that before the battle of Stiklestad he sent away 600 men who would not accept

best forces in the country under such able generals as Kalv Arnesson, Tore Hund, and Haarek of Tjotta. Kalv Arnesson had the chief command. The "Heimskringla" states that their army numbered 12,000 men, while Olav had only 3600 men; but these figures are, no doubt, too large. Henrik Mathiesen [1] estimates the forces of the chieftains to have numbered about 5000 men. Sighvat Scald says that they gained the victory because they had twice as many men as King Olav, who, accordingly, must have had a force of about 2500 men. Olav marched across the mountains to Værdalen in Trøndelagen, and selected a very advantageous position at Stiklestad. According to the "Olavssaga ins helga " he remained here a few days before the arrival of the chieftains and their forces, waiting for Dag Ringsson, who was bringing reënforcements; but Dag reached Stikle-stad too late to be of any assistance. On the morning before the battle, legend tells, while the army was still resting, King Olav fell asleep, leaning his head upon the knee of Finn Arnesson, Kalv Arnesson's brother, who had remained faithful to him. He dreamed that a ladder reached from the earth to heaven, and that he had reached the highest round. Here Christ stood and beckoned to him, and promised him reward for his faithful work. At noon, on July 29, 1030, the two armies faced each other on the field of Stikle-stad in full battle array. King Olav stood in the midst of his army in brynie and gilt helmet. He carried the sword "Hneiter" and a white shield on which a golden cross was painted. His white stand-ard with a dragon in the center was carried by his standard-bearer, Thord Foleson. About one o'clock, the war trumpets sounded the signal for advance. The serried columns of warriors rushed down the sloping ground to the combat; the most notable battle in Nor-wegian history had begun. Olav's plan was to throw his opponents into disorder by a vigorous assault, and in this he was partly success-ful. The lines in his front yielded before the furious onset, and great confusion resulted. But the experienced generals and well dis-ciplined forces of the enemy soon regained their foothold. Olav's

the Christian faith. The scald Sighvat, who was with him in the battle, says: "Not all the warriors believed in God; the army was divided into two parts; the famous king asked the Christians to stand on his right hand."

[1] *Det gamle Trondhjem*, p. 104 ff.

small army was outflanked and surrounded, attacked in front and rear, and overwhelmed by superior numbers. The king was soon wounded in the mêlée. He had dropped his sword and stood leaning against a stone when Kalv Arnesson and Tore Hund, who pressed forward toward the royal standard, found him and cut him down. Thord Foleson the standard-bearer, Bjørn Stallare, and many other leading men of the royal army were now dead, and many were wounded. Among the latter were Thormod Kolbrunarskald, who on the morning of the battle had awakened King Olav's army with a song. He withdrew from the conflict with an arrow in his bosom and died before evening.[1] Dag Ringsson now arrived and made a spirited attack, but he could not prevent the complete rout of the royal forces. Those who could sought safety in flight; among others Harald Sigurdsson, who was severely wounded. After his recovery, Harald went to Russia to Grand Duke Jaroslaf, and later he proceeded to Constantinople, where he became captain of the Varangians in the service of the Greek Emperor.

Christianity was no longer the issue in the battle of Stiklestad. The Christian faith had been so firmly established that the chieftains did not attempt, and, probably, did not even desire, to subvert it. The memorable battle was a struggle between the old system of aristocratic rule, and the new royalty leagued with the ideas of national union, independence, and progress toward higher cultural ideals. For this cause King Olav had labored, and in devotion to it he gave his life. But the aristocracy had triumphed. The king lay dead on the field of battle, and the national cause seemed hopelessly lost when the rumor got abroad that Olav was a saint. The glory of his martyrdom emanating from the battlefield of Stiklestad kindled the first sparks of patriotism, and gave the lost national cause a new and sacred consecration. Those who had opposed Olav the king now willingly bent the knee before Olav the saint. His name became the rallying cry of patriots; his great work and still greater sacrifice for his high ideals had united all hearts; his defeat at Stiklestad had turned into a national victory.

An English lady Ælfgifu (N. Alfiva) bore King Knut a son, Svein,

[1] The story of Thormod's death is told in the *Heimskringla, Saga of Olav the Saint*, ch. 234.

who was now about fourteen years of age. Svein was made viceroy of Norway, and his mother accompanied him, acting as his adviser, though it is generally acknowledged that she was the real ruler during Svein's short reign. The old form of aristocratic government was not reëstablished as might have been expected. King Knut was not satisfied with maintaining merely a nominal overlordship, as Harald Gormson had done in earlier days, but demanded for his son powers and privileges far exceeding those which King Olav had claimed. Svein and Alfiva established Danish laws, and began to rule as if they were exercising unlimited dominion over a conquered people, though it was the Norwegian nobles, and not the Danes, who had defeated King Olav. No one was permitted to leave the country without permission from the king. The property of persons convicted of murder was confiscated by the king, and the inheritance of persons outlawed for crime was swept into the royal coffers. The fishermen had to give a part of their catch to the king; a tax called "Christmas gifts" was levied; all ships leaving Norwegian harbors had to pay a tax called "landøre," and the people had to erect all buildings needed on the royal estates. Each seventh man had to do military service, and the testimony of a Dane (a member of the king's *hird*) was to be worth that of ten Norsemen. King Knut's failure to keep his promise to the Norwegian nobles had caused great disappointment, but the government which he established added insult to injury, and awakened the bitterest resentment even among the chieftains who had given him the kingdom. King Olav, who had fought so bravely for national independence, was contrasted with the foreign oppressors. His justice and heroism were extolled, and the deep mutterings of popular discontent soon grew into angry avowals that disloyalty to him was treason, and that slavery under foreign rulers had been substituted for national independence. The rumor that King Olav was a saint added new strength to the growing storm of discontent. The eclipse which occurred on August 31st, a month after the battle of Stiklestad, was thought to be in some way connected with King Olav's defeat and death, and the association of ideas soon established the conviction that the eclipse took place at the time of the battle. Miracles were said to have happened while the king's body was lying on the battlefield. Thorgils Halmason and his son Grim, who were living near Stiklestad, saw on the night after the battle a light issue from the place where the king's body was lying. They carried the corpse away, and hid it carefully from his enemies, but the same light was seen every night. King Olav's cheeks did not fade, but retained their ruddy color. His hair, beard, and fingernails continued to grow, and sick persons who prayed to the dead king were healed. King Svein and his mother made every effort to hush down and explain away these stories about Olav, but this only nursed the wrath of the people against the enemies of their patriotic and sainted king. The disappointed nobles supported the growing opposition to the Danes. "It was Einar Tambarskjælver's boast that he had not taken part in the uprising against King Olav. He remembered that King Knut had promised him a jarldom in Norway, and that he had not kept his word. Einar was the first of the chieftains to maintain that King Olav was a saint." [1] Olav's body was brought to Nidaros and interred in the St. Clemens church, which he had built. Bishop Grimkel proclaimed him a saint, and the 29th of July, the day of his death, was dedicated as a church holiday, the Olavmas, in his honor.[2] A pretender by the name of Tryggve now appeared, who claimed to be a son of Olav Tryggvason. He came to Norway with a small force, but was defeated and slain by Svein. But the powerful *lendermænd* gave the king no support. They summoned a *thing*

---

[1] *Heimskringla, Saga of Olav the Saint,* ch. 241.

[2] In early Christian times the congregation had the right to declare a person a saint, but canonization by an act of the Pope originated as early as 975, and in the twelfth century, in the pontificate of Alexander III., the Holy See claimed the sole power of canonization. In later times, the local saints, who had not received papal sanction, were called "beati," while those who were canonized by the Pope were called "sancti," or saints of the highest order. Bishop Grimkel's declaration was still at this time the only official act necessary to make King Olav a saint of the first rank, and his saintship was later recognized in papal letters by Alexander VI., 1255, and by Clemens IV, 1266. The sagas tell us that King Olav had been buried a year and five days before he was finally interred in the St. Clemens church. Before the interment Bishop Grimkel opened the coffin, and showed the king to the assembled people. His cheeks had not faded, but he looked as if he slept, and a pleasant odor arose from the body. It seems certain that the priests had embalmed the body before it was buried, as it is known to have existed 500 years later. Ludvig Daae, *Norges Helgener,* p. 5.

at Nidaros, where the people presented their complaints, but Svein and his mother were unable to give any answer. Einar Tambarskjælver arose and said, "Go home, ye people! A bad errand you have now, as you have had before when you appealed to Alfiva and King Svein. You might as well await injustice at home as to seek it all at once in this one place. Now you listen to the words of a woman, but you refused to listen to King Olav, who was in truth a saint. A vile treason was committed against him, and our punishment has been severe, while such great humiliation has fallen on our people since this rule was established over them. God grant that it may not last long! It has already lasted too long." [1]

King Svein and his mother tried in vain to assemble a new *thing*. No one came in answer to their summons. They began to fear a general uprising, and in the winter (1033–1034) they left Nidaros, and Danish dominion in Norway was ended. The people of Trøndelagen determined to place St. Olav's son, Magnus, on the throne. Einar Tambarskjælver and Kalv Arnesson were sent to Gardarike as special envoys to offer him the crown. He accompanied them to Norway, and was proclaimed king in 1034, or 1035.

Olav's canonization was an event of the greatest importance, not only because of the immediate results which it produced, but also through the influence which St. Olav was destined to exercise on the religious and national development in the future. The hero-king and great lawgiver had become the patron saint and supreme representative of the nation, the *perpetuus rex Norwegiae* under whose egis both royalty and hierarchy could henceforth exercise permanent and unquestioned authority. The old church still standing at Stiklestad was built, it is thought, on the very spot where King Olav fell, and the rock near which he suffered death is said to have been inclosed in the altar of the church. But Nidaros, where the king was buried, became the chief St. Olav sanctuary in Norway, and pilgrims from many lands visited the saint's grave every year. They came from Sweden, Denmark, and Russia; from the Baltic Sea countries, and from the British Isles.[2] In course of time their

---

[1] *Olavssaga ins helga*, ch. 102. *Fagrskinna*, ch. 119.

[2] "The capital of the Norsemen is Trondensis, which is beautified by many churches, and which is visited by a great number of people. There

rich offerings to the Saint enabled the archbishop of Norway to erect a cathedral in Trondhjem, the most magnificent in the Scandinavian North. Crosses and chapels were erected in various places made sacred by Olav; but the commemoration of the saint spread also to other countries, and many churches were dedicated to him in foreign lands. In the island of Gothland; in Ångermanland, Helsingland, Upsala, and other districts in Sweden he was especially honored. There were St. Olav churches in Norrköping and Lödöse, and the monasteries in Åbo, Strengnes, Skara and Enköping were dedicated to him. In Denmark the commemoration of St. Olav was very widespread, which can be seen from the number of churches dedicated to him in all parts of the Danish kingdom. In England a number of churches were named in his honor. In London alone there were four St. Olav churches: one in Southwark, one in Silver street, and two in the eastern part of the city. There was also a Tooley (= St. Olav) street, and Exeter had a St. Olav church. Chester has still an Olaf's church and an Olaf street. York has an Olaf's church, and Norfolk a St. Olave's bridge. Churches were also dedicated to St. Olav in Reval in Esthonia, in Novgorod and Constantinople, and there is evidence that he was commemorated also in Ireland, Scotland, and Normandy.[1]

47. MAGNUS THE GOOD. THE UNION OF NORWAY AND DENMARK

Magnus Olavsson met with no resistance on his arrival in Norway. King Knut the Great died in England in 1035, and Svein and Alfiva (Ælfgifu) fled to Denmark, where Svein died the year following. What plans King Knut had with regard to the succession is not

rests the body of Olav, the blessed king and saint, at whose grave God till this day performs great wonders of healing, so that many people journey thither from distant lands, hoping to receive help through the merit of the holy martyr." Adam v. Bremen, *Gesta Hammaburgensis*, IV., ch. 39.

"His day of commemoration, which is the 29th of July, is held sacred by all the people dwelling about the northern ocean: Norsemen, Swedes, Götar, Danes, Sembs and Slavs, by perpetual celebration." Adam v. Bremen, *Gesta Hammaburgensis*, II., ch. 59. Kristian Bing, *Norsk Tradition om Middelalderens Olafsfest, Bergens historiske Forenings Skrift*, no. 8.

[1] P. Nordmann, *St. Olavs Dyrkan i Finland*. Jacobus Langebek, *Scriptores Regum Danicarum, Legendae aliquot de Sancto Olavo Rege Norwegiae*.

known, but it is probable that he desired his realm to remain united under his one legitimate son Hardeknut, son of Emma, who had already been crowned king of Denmark.[1] But Harald Harefoot, the son of Knut and his English mistress Alfiva, the mother of Svein, was staying in England, and when Knut died he became an active candidate for the throne. Hardeknut was, therefore, compelled to come to an understanding with King Magnus. In order to terminate the hostilities between Norway and Denmark, which had already been in progress for some time, the two kings met at Brennøerne, near the mouth of the Göta River, in 1038, and concluded a treaty of peace. Hardeknut recognized the independence of Norway, and a compact was entered into by the kings that if one of them died without an heir, the other should inherit his kingdom, and twelve leading men of each country took an oath to maintain the compact. The treaty of Brennøerne is a counterpart of the treaty of Konghelle concluded with Sweden in 1019. The integrity and independence of Norway had now been duly recognized, and the kings of the Yngling dynasty were regarded as possessing the same full legitimacy as the royal families of Denmark and Sweden. King Olav's great fame both as king and saint had made a deep impression on the whole Scandinavian North, and contributed greatly to win for Norway an unqualified recognition as a sovereign and independent state. When Magnus returned to Trondhjem, says the saga, he placed King Olav's body in a beautiful casket ornamented with gold, silver, and precious stones. He also began the erection of a St. Olav's church, in which the remains of the saint were to be deposited; but this structure was not completed till in the next reign.

Before Magnus became king, he had to promise full amnesty to those who had taken part in the armed opposition to his father. It seems that he also agreed to abrogate the noxious laws introduced by King Svein, and to reëstablish the laws of King Olav. But youthful impetuosity soon led him to deal harshly with his father's old enemies. When Haarek of Tjotta was killed by a personal

[1] Laurence M. Larson, *The Efforts of the Danish Kings to Recover the English Crown after the Death of Harthacnut. Annual Report of the American Historical Association*, 1910.

enemy, the offender was not punished. Tore Hund died on a pilgrimage to the Holy Land, and Kalv Arnesson had to flee to the Orkneys to Thorfinn Jarl, who was married to Ingebjørg, the daughter of his brother Finn Arnesson. There had been much secret rivalry between Kalv and Einar Tambarskjælver, both of whom had aspired to become jarl. Einar, who had taken no part in the uprising against King Olav, gained the friendship of Magnus, but the young king was unable to forgive Kalv, who had been the leader of the opposition to his father. Einar was styled the king's fosterfather, or chief councilor, and exercised great influence. Many who had taken part in the battle of Stiklestad against Olav were made to feel the king's wrath, and the laws of Svein were not repealed as quickly as had been expected. The people grew dissatisfied and chose as their spokesman the scald Sighvat Thordsson, who had been King Olav's closest friend, and who now occupied a similar position of honor and confidence at the court of King Magnus. In a song called "Bersøglisvísur" [1] the scald reminded the young king of his promises to the people, showed him how ill it befits a king to break his word, and pointed to the growing dissatisfaction and the danger of such a situation. So deeply was Magnus impressed with the song that he immediately changed his ways. He became so just and kind that the people henceforth called him Magnus the Good. He granted amnesty to all, and promised to improve the laws by gradually revoking the more oppressive measures of King Svein's reign.

The ties which united the island colonies with the mother country were weakened by the repeated overthrow of the government, as

---

[1] Sighvat was one of the foremost scalds, and the "Bersøglisvísur" is one of the finest specimens of scaldic poesy. Others excelled him in imagination and brilliant word-painting, but Sighvat thinks deep and fine thoughts, and we see behind his lines a wise and high-minded man. He sings less about war and battles than do other scalds, but more about lofty aims, and the ends to be attained by man's efforts. The greater part of the song has been preserved. Nine stanzas are found in the *Heimskringla*.

Accounts of the events of this period are found in the *Ágrip*, in Theodricus Monachus' *Historia de Antiquitate Regum Norwagiensium*, *Morkinskinna*, *Flateyjarbók*, *Fagrskinna*, and in *Heimskringla*. The relation of these sources has been discussed by Professor Gustav Storm in his work *Snorre Sturlasons Historieskrivning*.

well as by the establishing of foreign dominion in Norway. As the Danish kings paid little attention to the Norwegian colonies, the jarls and chieftains who ruled over the island groups found opportunity to make themselves independent. In the Orkneys Thorfinn Jarl had regained his old independence after the fall of St. Olav, and the crafty and powerful Trond i Gata had ruled the Faroe Islands according to his own pleasure since the death of Sigmund Brestesson. But when Trond died in 1035, Leiv Assursson, another Faroe chieftain, went to Norway and tendered his submission to King Magnus, who placed him in charge of the colony. Thereby Norwegian sovereignty was again established in the Faroe Islands.[1] The king's measures with regard to the Orkneys proved less successful. It has been noted elsewhere that, on the death of Sigurd Lodvesson, the Orkneys were divided among his sons Sumarlide, Bruse, and Einar; but none of them lived long, and their half-brother, Thorfinn Sigurdsson, became jarl, and seized all their possessions. Bruse's son, Ragnvald, who was staying at the court of the Grand Duke Jaroslaf, in Gardarike, had accompanied Magnus to Norway. Magnus gave him the title of jarl, and granted him his father's possessions in these islands. Ragnvald was well received by Thorfinn, who at this time was engaged in wars in Scotland. He granted him two-thirds of the islands, and they became friends and allies. But while Kalv Arnesson, the uncle of Thorfinn's wife Ingebjørg, was staying in the Orkneys, Thorfinn and Ragnvald became enemies, and hostilities resulted in which Ragnvald lost his life. The colony did not return to its allegiance to Norway till in 1066, in the reign of Harald Haardraade.

King Knut the Great is thought to have been about forty years old at the time of his death. He came to England as a conqueror, but proved to be one of the ablest and wisest of English kings. During the last five years of his reign he ruled over a great empire including England and Scotland, Denmark, Norway, the Orkney Islands, and the Viking colonies in the Hebrides and the Isle of Man. The

---

[1] The memory of the three great chieftains, Brester, Sigmund Brestesson, and Leiv Assursson has been preserved in a runic inscription on a rune-stone found in the Faroe Islands. N. Winter, *Færøernes Oldtidshistorie*, p. 154 ff. P. A. Munch, *Det norske Folks Historie*, part I., vol. II., p. 859.

extensive possessions under his own immediate rule he governed with a wisdom and moderation which entitles him to be numbered with the greatest monarchs.[1] He did not confiscate the people's lands for the benefit of his own followers, or in other ways treat England as a conquered country. His soldiers received a money payment, and the people were allowed to keep their lands. He established the old English laws, known as the "Laws of Edward the Confessor," and ruled as a native English sovereign. He was one of the wisest and most prolific of early English lawgivers; he became an earnest Christian, and remained throughout his reign deeply attached to the intellectual life and higher culture of western Europe. But Knut's worthless sons did not walk in their father's footsteps. In 1036 Harald Harefoot (son of Ælfgifu or Alfiva) succeeded him on the throne of England, but his reign was short and inglorious. He was ambitious and violent, and seemed more devoted to hunting than to the affairs of the state, wherefore the people, fitly enough, nicknamed him Harefoot. He died at Oxford in 1040 at the moment when his half-brother Hardeknut (son of Emma) finally arrived in England. Hardeknut was, if possible, even less qualified to occupy a throne than his worthless brother. He promised amnesty to all who had hitherto sided with Harald Harefoot, but as soon as he was crowned king he began to levy heavy taxes to pay his large army. He was harsh and narrow-minded, and lacked every kingly quality. When this unworthy son of the great King Knut suddenly died in his twenty-fifth year, in the second year of his reign, the people felt it as a riddance. He was succeeded by his half-brother, Edward the Confessor, the last surviving son of King Æthelred and Emma.

According to the treaty of Brennøerne, King Magnus of Norway succeeded Hardeknut as king of Denmark. King Knut's family was now extinct in the male line, and Svein Ulvsson, or Svein Estridsson, a son of Ulv Jarl and Knut's sister Estrid, who was the nearest heir to the throne, was unable to rally the people to his support. King Magnus Olavsson was now eighteen years old, a well-built young man with light auburn hair and noble features. He was brave, well skilled in the use of arms, and had already gained a reputation for justice. The Danes welcomed him with unfeigned enthusi-

[1] Laurence Marcellus Larson, *Canute the Great.*

asm, mixed with a veneration accorded him as the son of the greatest saint in the North. With characteristic generosity King Magnus made Svein Estridsson a jarl, with the understanding that he should defend the borders of Jutland against the Wends. He married his sister Ulvhild to Ordulf, son of the Duke of Saxony, and secured thereby the friendship and support of that powerful family. Magnus, who enjoyed great power and renown, claimed also the throne of England as the heir of King Hardeknut according to the treaty of Brennøerne. The "Saga of Magnus the Good"[1] states that he sent the following message to King Edward the Confessor: "You may have heard of the agreement which was made between King Hardeknut and myself, that the one who lived longest should inherit the lands and subjects of the other, if he died without a male heir. Now it has come to pass, as I know you have learned, that I have fallen heir to all the Danish possessions of King Hardeknut. But at the time of his death he held England no less than Denmark, and I, therefore, claim England according to the agreement made. I desire that you give up the kingdom to me, otherwise I will attack it with an army both from Denmark and Norway, and he will then govern it who wins the victory." The "Anglo-Saxon Chronicle" shows that in 1046 an invasion from Norway was expected, and that the English fleet was stationed at Sandwich ready to defend the coast. But "Svein's fight with him (*i.e.* with Magnus) hindered him from coming hither," says the chronicle. Subsequent events in Denmark prove the correctness of these statements. Einar Tambarskjælver is said to have shaken his head when he heard that Magnus had made Svein Estridsson a jarl. "Too powerful a jarl," was his comment. Svein was soon tempted to begin an uprising against King Magnus. He made an alliance with the Wends, against whom he was to protect the borders, and Magnus had to call out half the military forces of Norway to put down the rebellion. Svein was compelled to flee, but at any favorable moment he might renew the attack, and with so dangerous an enemy at his back Magnus did

---

[1] *Heimskringla, Saga of Magnus the Good*, ch. 36. *Diplomatarium Norwegicum, Oldbreve*, edited by Alexander Bugge, Christiania, 1910, nittende samling, part I., p. 25. Letter of King Magnus to King Edward, p. 26, King Edward's answer.

not venture to undertake an invasion of England. The fortified city of Jómsborg was also an inconvenient neighbor. So long as this independent Viking stronghold did not submit to King Magnus it was a constant source of danger to his kingdom, and he resolutely marched against it and captured it after a spirited resistance. In the meanwhile the Wends,[1] who had not been held in check by Svein Estridsson, poured over the borders, and committed fearful depredations in southern Jutland. Magnus gathered a large army at Hedeby, and his brother-in-law, Ordulf of Saxony, came to his assistance with a considerable force. On Michaelmas, Sept. 29, 1043, he faced the Wendish host on Lyrskog Heath, and defeated them in a most sanguinary battle. Under these circumstances the intended invasion of England had to be abandoned, but Magnus had won great renown through his many victories. He had overcome all opposition, and the peace and security of the Danish kingdom was safely established. Everything now augured well for a prosperous and peaceful reign, but Magnus was still to learn that "uneasy lies the head that wears a crown." A most formidable rival suddenly appeared to place new difficulties in his path. This was Harald Sigurdsson,[2] a half-brother of St. Olav, son of Aasta and King Sigurd Syr. During the fifteen years which had passed since the battle of Stiklestad, he had gained great renown as chief of the Varangians in the service of the Greek Emperor at Byzantium. He had married Elizabeth (Ellisiv), daughter of Grand Duke Jaroslaf of Gardarike, and brought great treasures with him to Norway. Elizabeth seems to have died soon after their marriage, as Harald married Thora of the Arnmødling family shortly after his arrival in Norway. Harald was a talented leader of the old martial type, who never hesitated to make the sword the arbiter of every controversy. The sagas describe him as

[1] In the early centuries of the Christian era the Germanic peoples on the south shores of the Baltic Sea began a general migration towards the borders of the Roman Empire. The Slavs pushed westward and occupied the vacated territory as far as the mouth of the Elbe. They were generally known as the Wends. They were still heathens, and were often very troublesome neighbors.

[2] Peter Friedrich Suhm, *Forsøg til Forbedringer i den gamle danske og norske Historie, Harald Haardraade. Heimskringla, Harald Haardraade's Saga.* Theodricus Monachus, *De Antiquitate Regum Norwagiensium*, ch. XXV. *Fagrskinna*, p. 106 ff. *Morkinskinna*, p. I. ff. *Ágrip.*

very tall and strong, resolute and energetic. He possessed in an eminent degree the spirit of enterprise and reckless daring which characterized the great Viking chieftains, and his military achievements in the Levant were soon extolled in a whole literature of fictitious tales, in which he is represented as the central figure in every historic event with which he was in any way connected. The saga narratives, based partly on these tales, and partly on scaldic songs which were often misunderstood, because they told of unknown and distant lands, are wholly unreliable in details. Only the more general features which are corroborated by other sources can be accepted as history. P. A. Munch has shown that the scaldic songs agree in all main features with the Byzantine writers, and that a reliable account of Harald's early career can be extracted from these sources.[1] The correctness of Munch's position was later proven

[1] In his *Samlede Afhandlinger*, vol. I., p. 505 ff., and in *Det norske Folks Historie*, part II., Professor P. A. Munch has examined critically all the sources dealing with Harald Sigurdsson's sojourn in the far East. He finds that the most elaborate account is found in the *Flateyjarbók*, which is a comparatively late production from about 1380. But the account is, evidently, borrowed from the *Morkinskinna*, which, with the exception of the fragment *Ágrip*, is the oldest existing connected history of the Norwegian kings written in the Norse language, dating from about 1220. The chapters in the *Morkinskinna* treating of King Magnus the Good and Harald Sigurdsson have been lost, but the corresponding chapters in *Flateyjarbók*, III., 251–441, have preserved the Morkinskinna version, which is the oldest existing form of the narrative. The *Fagrskinna*, which is somewhat younger, and which is written with more critical ability, has eliminated many of the more legendary features; and Snorre in his *Heimskringla*, from about 1230, has discarded many more of the untrustworthy features. He says that he has left much unwritten about Harald's great deeds. "This is due partly to our lack of knowledge, and partly because we do not want to record in books stories which rest on no sure testimony. Even though we may have heard things told, or spoken of, it seems better that something should be added later, than that anything should have to be stricken out." *Heimskringla, Harald Haardraade's Saga*, ch. 36.

The account of Harald's exploits in the Orient is also found in the two fragments of history of the Norwegian kings *Hrykkjarstykki* and *Hrokkinskinna*, on which the text of the *Fornmanna Søgur*, vol. VI., has been based. The Byzantine sources are the *Chronicle of Kedren* (George Kedrenos), and the *Annals of Zonaras*, who lived in the middle of the twelfth century. His contemporary, Glykas, follows Kedren. The most reliable Norse sources are the songs of the scalds. Many stories about Harald's exploits are found in Saxo Grammaticus and William of Malmesbury.

through the discovery of a document which threw new light on the subject. In 1881 Professor Wassilievsky of Moscow published a treatise on a newly discovered Greek manuscript from the eleventh century, written by a contemporary of Harald Sigurdsson.[1] The author tells us that Araltes (Harald) was a son of the king of Varangia, and that his brother Julavos (Olav) had made him next to himself in rank. But Araltes, who was young and had learned to admire the power of the Romans, wished to do homage to Emperor Michael Paflagōn (also called Michael Katalaktus), and came to Constantinople with 500 brave warriors. This agrees with the "Heimskringla," which states that Harald had many men. The author further states that the Emperor sent him to Sicily, where the Roman army was carrying on war. He must have served under the imperial general Georgios Maniakes, whom he aided in the conquest of Sicily, 1038-1040. He performed great feats of arms, says the author, and on his return the Emperor gave him the title of "manglabites." Then it happened that Delianos in Bulgaria rose in rebellion. Harald accompanied the Emperor into that province, and performed such deeds as befitted his rank and valor. On his return to Constantinople the Emperor conferred on him the title of "spatharo-kandidatos." [2] Harald's campaign in Bulgaria is not mentioned in the sagas, but it is referred to in a song by the scald Thjodolv Arnorsson. Harald was staying in Constantinople when the Emperor died in December, 1041, and also during the short reign of Michael Kalifates, who was dethroned April 21, 1042. He did military service for a while also under the next Emperor, Konstantin Monomachos, but he sought permission to leave, "because he wished to return to his own country." This request was refused, but Harald made good his escape, 1043 or 1044. The author is also able to state that Harald became king in his own country after his brother Olav, and that as king he maintained his old friendship with the Romans. From the scaldic songs, which corroborate the statements of the author, and on many points supplement the account, we learn that Harald also took part in

---

[1] Gustav Storm, *Harald Haardraade og Væringerne i de græske Keiseres Tjeneste, Historisk Tidsskrift udgivet af den norske historiske Forening,* Christiania, vol. IV., p. 354 ff.

[2] *Spatharo-kandidatos* = officer of the swordsmen, or officer of the Emperor's bodyguard.

campaigns in Syria and Mesopotamia, and that he went to Jerusalem with a body of Varangians, probably to guard the architects and laborers sent by the Emperor to erect a new church in that city.

After Harald left Constantinople, he went to Grand Duke Jaroslaf in Gardarike. He married Ellisiv, the grand duke's daughter, as already stated, and after having spent some time at his court, he crossed the Baltic with a single ship, and came to Sigtuna in Sweden. Here he met Svein Estridsson, who sought to persuade him to join in an attack on King Magnus; but Harald decided to try negotiations. He proceeded to Denmark, and found Magnus stationed with his fleet in Øresund (the Sound), on the coast of Skåne. Harald had a stately vessel, beautifully painted, with gilt dragon head and dragon's tail, and with a sail of costly material. The sudden appearance of such a ship caused no small surprise on the royal fleet, and King Magnus sent a vessel forward to hail the stranger. In answer to the inquiry of the king's messengers a tall and stately man came forward and told them that he was sent by Harald Sigurdsson, King Magnus' uncle, to learn how he would receive him. The tall stranger was Harald Sigurdsson himself. When this news was brought the king, he immediately sent word that he would receive his uncle with open arms. Harald then landed and was received by King Magnus and all his leading men. In a few days negotiations were begun. Harald asked if Magnus would recognize his right of succession to the throne, and grant him one-half of his kingdom; to which Magnus replied that in such matters he would follow the advice of his chief counselors. Einar Tambarskjælver then arose and said that if Harald received half the kingdom, it was but fair that he should divide his treasures with King Magnus; but this Harald refused to do. Einar, who was ruffled by the refusal of so generous an offer, said to him: "Far away you were, Harald, while we won the kingdom back from the Knytlings (King Knut and his sons), and we have no desire to be divided between chieftains. Hitherto we have served only one at a time, and so it shall be as long as King Magnus lives. I will do all in my power to prevent you from getting any part of the kingdom." Harald now returned to Sweden, where he formed an alliance with Svein Estridsson. Denmark was attacked, and Harald harried the Danish islands in true Viking fashion, as it appears, against the will of Svein, who could only gain the people's ill-will through such depredations. When Magnus came with a fleet, Harald made his way to Norway, where he hoped to be proclaimed king in Magnus' absence. He first tried to win his own home districts in Oplandene, but the people remained indifferent. In Gudbrandsdal he was more successful. His powerful relative, the youthful Thore of Steig, aided him. Harald called a *thing*, where Thore gave him the royal title, which, together with the band of followers which he had gathered, gave him new prestige. When Magnus learned of Harald's whereabouts, he quickly returned to Norway, but a clash of arms was averted by the chieftains, who did not want to see two near relatives wage war against each other. A meeting was arranged, and negotiations were renewed. It seems that the chieftains were determined not to divide the kingdom, and not to tolerate two kings except as joint sovereigns. An agreement was finally reached on the basis of Einar Tambarskjælver's earlier proposition. Harald should share the throne of Norway with Magnus, and in return he should divide his treasures with him. The joint sovereignty appears to have been limited to Norway, which was now for the first time to be ruled by two kings exercising equal authority. The kings had each their own *hird*, but rivalry and jealousy between their followers and adherents soon bred serious trouble. Harald, who was harsh and uncompromising, was nicknamed Haardraade (Hard-ruler), and was often contrasted in a disparaging way with the kind and generous Magnus the Good. The people, especially the chieftains, sided with Magnus, and Harald grew very embittered against Einar Tambarskjælver, who became the leader of an opposition to the new king, whom he regarded as an usurper. In 1047 Magnus and Harald made an expedition to Denmark, and drove out Svein Estridsson, but Magnus died suddenly in Seeland. According to Saxo Grammaticus, Svein Aagesson, and Adam v. Bremen, he was thrown from his horse while pursuing Svein, and received so severe an injury that he died shortly after on board his ship, 1047. Before he died he willed the kingdom of Denmark to Svein Estridsson, whom he had learned to respect as a courageous and able prince. Magnus was highly beloved by the Norwegian people, and his death caused general mourning. He left no son to succeed him

on the throne; a fortunate circumstance, perhaps, as civil strife
between rival candidates was thereby averted. Harald immediately assembled all the warriors of the fleet, and announced to them
that he did not want to abide by the decision of King Magnus, as
he regarded Denmark as well as Norway his rightful inheritance.
But the warriors refused to follow him on a campaign in Denmark
until he had properly buried King Magnus. Einar Tambarskjælver
told him that he would rather follow Magnus dead than any other
king living. With a large part of the fleet he left King Harald, and
set sail for Trondhjem, where Magnus was interred in the St.
Clemens church by the side of his father, St. Olav. Harald could
do nothing against Denmark for the present. He went to Viken in
southern Norway, and assembled the Borgarthing, where he was
proclaimed king of all Norway. He was also proclaimed King Magnus' successor at the Ørething, in Trøndelagen, according to old
custom, and the following year he married Thora, the daughter of
Thorberg Arnesson of Giske, as already mentioned.[1]

48. The Reign of Harald Haardraade

Olav Tryggvason and Olav Haraldsson had to win the throne as
a prize in armed conflict with the aristocracy, but Harald Sigurdsson
Haardraade became king of Norway without opposition, though he
was very unpopular. Since St. Olav's time a complete change had
taken place in the people's attitude towards the centralized power of
monarchical government. Kingship was now looked upon as a fully
legitimated national institution, and Harald succeeded to the throne

---

[1] The *Heimskringla* is authority for the story that King Harald had two
wives at the same time. In 1045 he married Ellisiv (Elizabeth), daughter
of Grand Duke Jaroslaf, and three years later he married Thora, daughter
of Thorberg Arnesson of Giske. Snorre says that when Harald departed
on his expedition to England, he left Queen Thora in Norway, but Queen
Ellisiv and her daughters, Maria and Ingegerd, accompanied him. *Heimskringla, Harald Haardraade's Saga*, ch. 82. That Harald, who was a Christian king, could live in open bigamy without protest from the Pope or the
clergy is quite incredible, and as it is nowhere stated that Ellisiv followed
Harald to Norway, it is safe to assume that she was dead when Harald married Thora. The statement in the *Heimskringla* is due to some strange
error in the tradition. See Gustav Storm, *Harald Haardraades paastaaede
Dobbeltgifte, Historisk Tidsskrift*, tredie række, vol. III., p. 424 ff.

by right of inheritance, or *odel*, which no one ventured to challenge. There was no longer any organized opposition to the king. The aristocracy had accepted the new form of government, and submitted loyally to the king's authority when it was exercised with proper moderation. They had given King Magnus their undivided support in all his undertakings, and he was very popular and highly beloved by all. But his rule had been benign, and the nobles had exercised a great influence in public affairs. During his minority Kalv Arnesson had acted as regent, and later Einar Tambarskjælver became his chief counselor. Magnus was not a tool in the hands of the nobles, but he listened to their advice, and showed them no unnecessary effrontery. King Harald Haardraade was of a different type. He was harsh and greedy, not always conscientious as to the means which he employed, disposed to be arbitrary and to have slight regard for others. His character was of the kind that breeds discord, and quarrels with recalcitrant nobles were numerous in his reign. But he was able and ambitious, and came to the throne with the fixed purpose of making the royal power supreme in church and state, and of extending full authority over all the lands which belonged or which had belonged to the Norwegian crown. He was a most able and energetic ruler, who brooked no interference from nobles at home or from powers abroad. He loved independence as passionately as he coveted renown, and wielded the sword of state with a grim recklessness, like a soldier's broadsword, to gain for himself and his kingdom the greatest possible prestige and power. From the outset he met with considerable opposition and ill-will, caused by his own greed and harshness. He was greatly chagrined by what he considered the arrogant behavior of some of the chieftains. One of the principal offenders was Einar Tambarskjælver in Trøndelagen, who acted as the spokesman of the people, and on more than one occasion forced the king to recede from his harsh, and sometimes unjust, demands. King Harald had a suspicion that many of the chieftains were carrying on secret negotiations with King Svein of Denmark. In order to test their loyalty he engaged spies who claimed to be secret agents sent by King Svein to offer the Norwegian nobles riches and great honors if they would aid him against King Harald. When these spies came to Einar Tambarskjælver, he told them that although he was not Harald's friend, he would do everything in his power to aid him in defending the kingdom against King Svein. The king praised Einar for his loyalty, and invited him to a festive gathering in Nidaros. It now looked as if old differences would be forgotten, that peace and friendship would, finally, be established between them. But King Harald gave the great noble new offense, as if from pure love of mischief. The old enmity was still further aggravated, and Einar and his son Eindride were treacherously murdered at the instigation of the king. This wanton deed caused the greatest resentment in Trøndelagen, and the people threatened to rise in open rebellion. Einar's widow, Bergliot, sent word to her powerful relative, Haakon Ivarsson in Oplandene, and asked him to avenge Einar's death. Harald sent Finn Arnesson to Haakon, who promised to remain loyal if the king would give him Ragnhild, the daughter of Magnus, in marriage, together with a dowry suitable to her rank. This was promised him, and the threatened uprising was averted. Finn Arnesson, who had been St. Olav's special friend, and who had adhered no less faithfully to his successor, was not much better rewarded than Einar Tambarskjælver. His brother Kalv, who at Finn's request had been permitted to return from his exile, accompanied Harald on an expedition against Denmark, but the king sent him against the enemy with a handful of men, and he was overpowered and slain. Finn felt so aggrieved that he abandoned both his king and his country, and went to King Svein in Denmark, who made him jarl over the Danish province of Halland, on the southwest coast of Sweden. After some time Haakon Ivarsson asked King Harald to fulfill his promise of giving him Ragnhild, King Magnus' daughter, in marriage. Harald said that he had no objection, but Haakon would have to obtain the maiden's own consent. Haakon agreed to do this, but he was unsuccessful in his courtship. Ragnhild told him that although he was a handsome and noble-looking man, she, being a princess, could not marry him so long as he was only a *lendermand*. He then asked Harald to give him the rank of jarl, so that he could marry Ragnhild, but this he would not do. It had been a rule, he said, ever since the time of St. Olav, not to have more than one jarl in the kingdom at one time. Orm Eilivsson was now jarl, and he could not deprive him of his title and dignity. This strange answer convinced Haakon that Harald did not intend to keep his promise, and he went to King Svein in Denmark, where he was well received. He was later reconciled to King Harald, and married Ragnhild, who had learned to love him, and now accepted him without interposing any conditions. Harald promised to raise him to the rank of jarl on the death of Orm Eilivsson, but when Orm died, he again failed to keep his promise, and Haakon and Ragnhild returned to Denmark to King Svein, who invited them to stay at his court, and welcomed St. Olav's granddaughter with special fondness. Haakon was made jarl of Halland to succeed Finn Arnesson, who had died.

It is quite clear from these and other similar episodes that Harald Haardraade was bent on destroying the power of the aristocracy, and he could ill conceal his feeling of satisfaction when the powerful nobles one after another disappeared. He is even said to have stated in scaldic verse that he had caused the death of thirteen men, but who they were is not mentioned. It cannot be doubted that by pursuing such a policy of removing the old chieftains who possessed sufficient prestige to be able to offer resistance, the king gradually strengthened his own power. He possibly even gave the throne increased stability, but this practice weakened Harald in his foreign wars. It deprived him of the aid of many of the ablest men. Some left the country to use their influence in stirring up opposition to him both at home and abroad, and many who remained at home gave him but a half-hearted support.

The enmity between Harald and King Svein developed into a feature of European politics, and shaped Harald's attitude in the administration of church affairs. In order to strengthen his position, Svein allied himself more closely with Archbishop Adalbert of Bremen, and with the German Emperor, while Harald continued in the old friendship with the Saxon dukes. He severed all connections with Archbishop Adalbert, received bishops from the Greek Church, and maintained friendly relations with Byzantium. The Norwegian bishops were no longer consecrated by the Archbishop of Bremen,[1] but in Rome, England, France, or in the Orient.

[1] Hamburg became an archbishopric in 834, and St. Ansgar, the misionary who had introduced Christianity in Denmark and Sweden, became

Archbishop Adalbert protested to Pope Alexander II. against Harald's flagrant disregard of the authority of the archbishop over the Church of Norway, and the Pope wrote a letter reprimanding the king. Adalbert also sent messengers to Harald to protest against his course of action, and threatened him with ban and other punishments, but Harald replied: "I know of no archbishop in Norway except myself, King Harald." He maintained the independence of the Church of Norway throughout his whole reign with such unbending pertinacity that he was accused of all sorts of vile practices by his angry opponents. Adam v. Bremen, who stayed at the court of Archbishop Adalbert, indulges in the bitterest invectives against Harald, whom he pictures as the most cruel and unprincipled tyrant.[1] This is not history, but the expression of acrimonious partisan spirit. Konrad Maurer[2] quotes the following from Kemble[3]: "Every wise and powerful government has treated with deserved disregard the complaint that the 'Spouse of Christ' was in bondage. Boniface, himself an Englishman, papal beyond all his contemporaries, laments that no church is in greater bondage than the English,— a noble testimony to the nationality of the institution, the common sense of the people, and the vigor of the state!"

The hostility existing between Harald Haardraade and King Svein seems to have led Harald to establish the city of Oslo (now incorporated in the city of Christiania) on the Foldenfjord in Viken. Here he would be within more easy reach of Denmark, and in better position to defend the country than if stationed in the far-away Nidaros. A new national sanctuary was established in the city to give it greater prestige, as Harald seems to have entertained the hope that Oslo might become to southern Norway what Nidaros and the shrine of St. Olav was to Trøndelagen. The saint interred in the new city was Halvard, a native of the district, and a cousin of the

the first Archbishop of Hamburg. The city was sacked by the Norsemen in 845, and in 848 the archbishop's see was moved to Bremen. In 864 Pope Nicolas I. united Bremen and Hamburg into an archbishopric usually called Bremen.

[1] *Gesta Hammaburgensis*, III., ch. 16.

[2] Konrad Maurer, *Die Bekehrung des norwegischen Stammes*, II., p. 65; P. A. Munch, *Det norske Folks Historie*, vol. II., p. 208 ff.

[3] Kemble, *The Saxons in England*, II., p. 373.

king.[1] He is said to have been the son of a landed proprietor, Vebjørn, and his wife Torny, a sister of Aasta, the mother of St. Olav and King Harald Haardraade. Already in his youth he was noted for great piety and purity of life. His father was a merchant, and Halvard assisted him in his work, but he was so conscientious that he made two weights, a lighter one for weighing the part which he himself was to receive, and a heavier for weighing his brother's part. One day, as he left home to go across the Drammensfjord, a woman came running to him, beseeching him to rescue her. She was pursued by three men who claimed that she had committed theft in their brother's house. She protested her innocence, and Halvard took her into his boat and started across the lake, but the pursuers soon caught up with them. In vain he pleaded for the woman. When he refused to give her up, they killed both him and her, fastened two millstones to his body and lowered it into the lake. Some time afterward, his body, with the millstones still fastened to it, was found floating on the lake, and twigs, which had been used in searching for the corpse, budded several times in succession. The Icelandic annals state that St. Halvard was slain in 1043, and Adam v. Bremen says that many miraculous cures occurred at his grave. He must, therefore, have been generally regarded as a saint at the time when Adam v. Bremen wrote (about 1070), but when and in what way he was proclaimed a saint is not known. His body was probably interred in the St. Mary's church erected by King Harald. In the twelfth century a new cathedral church, dedicated to St. Halvard, was erected at Oslo. King Harald also built a St. Mary's church in Nidaros, in which the shrine of St. Olav was deposited. As the city had grown, and private houses were erected around the St. Clemens church and the royal hall, the king selected for the new church a location farther from the center of the city. Here he also erected a new royal residence. He completed the St. Olav's church which King Magnus had begun, and the unfinished royal hall from King Magnus' time was remodeled into a church dedicated to St. Gregorius.

King Harald maintained the supremacy over the colonies with

[1] Ludvig Daae, *Norges Helgener*, II., p. 163, *Den hellige Halvard. Acta Sanctorum*, tom. III. *Heilagramannasøgur*, I., p. 396 ff.

energy and firmness. Thorfinn, the powerful jarl of the Orkney and Shetland Islands, who had remained independent since the death of St. Olav, hastened to Norway as soon as he heard of the death of Magnus the Good, and was well received at the court. It must be inferred that he submitted to Harald, and that these island colonies returned to their old allegiance as dependencies under the king's overlordship. Thorfinn seems to have been the more willing to offer his submission, because King Macbeth of Scotland, with whom he was closely associated, was threatened by Malcolm Canmore the son of Thorfinn's cousin King Duncan. Thorfinn was sure to be involved in the struggle in Scotland, and he would not risk the possibility of coming into collision with King Harald. Hostilities between Macbeth and Malcolm began in 1054. Aided by his foster father, the powerful Earl Siward of Northumbria, Malcolm defeated Macbeth at Dunsinane the same year, and in 1057 Macbeth was slain in the battle of Lumphanan. What part Thorfinn played in the struggle cannot be stated, but it is quite certain that he aided his old friend Macbeth. Thorfinn had also added the Hebrides (Sudreys) to his dominions, and when he submitted to the king, they became a Norwegian dependency. Kalv Arnesson acted as governor in the islands till his return to Norway in Harald Haardraade's reign.[1] The Faroe Islands remained in firm allegiance to Norway. Since Leiv Assursson was made governor by King Magnus after the death of Trond i Gata, no attempt was again made by the colony to assert its independence. Harald also made earnest efforts to attach Iceland more closely to the crown. He sought by rich gifts to gain the good-will of the leading men, and when a famine occurred in Iceland, he sent several shiploads of provisions. Many Icelandic scalds became his *hirdmœnd* and were shown great honors. As a result of these favors the Icelanders held Harald in high esteem, but they did not formally acknowledge themselves subject to the king of Norway. The intercourse with the colonies in Greenland was

---

[1] "Jarl Thorfinn subdued all the islands, and made all the inhabitants his subjects, even those who had sworn allegiance to Jarl Ragnvald. Thor finn then fixed his residence in the Orkneys, keeping a great number of men about him; he imported provisions from Caithness, and sent Kalv Arnesson to the Sudreys and ordered him to remain and maintain his authority there." *Orkneyingasaga*, ch. 16.

vell maintained, and voyages were made every year across the Atlantic directly from Norway to Greenland.

Harald refused to abide by the arrangement made by King Magnus that Svein Estridsson should receive the kingdom of Denmark, and continued to claim the Danish throne. He repeatedly harried the coasts of Denmark, but as these attacks, which seem to have been mere raids, proved unavailing, Harald finally challenged Svein to a pitched battle. The challenge was accepted, and a naval engagement was fought off Nisaa near the mouth of the Göta River on the 9th of August, 1062. Throughout the whole bright summer night the combat raged. Harald gained the victory, but he returned to Norway immediately afterwards, and this battle was as barren of results as former expeditions.

King Anund Jacob of Sweden had died, and his successor, Stenkil Ragnvaldsson, had granted Vermland to Haakon Ivarsson, who had been made jarl of Halland by King Svein. At the head of an army Haakon entered Ringerike in southeastern Norway, and collected taxes as if he were a jarl. Haakon was popular in these districts, while Harald was disliked, because he levied excessive taxes and deprived the people of many old rights and privileges. A serious uprising seemed imminent, and Harald finally decided to make peace with Denmark, 1064. King Svein was henceforth left in undisturbed possession of the Danish throne. Harald attacked and defeated Jarl Haakon, and the uprising in Oplandene was speedily put down.

49. THE SECOND CONQUEST OF ENGLAND

The weak King Edward the Confessor, who succeeded Hardeknut on the throne of England, was better fitted to be a monk than a king, and throughout his reign he was a tool in the hands of the powerful earls, Godwin of Wessex, Leofric of Mercia, and Siward of Northumbria. Godwin, who was his father-in-law and the most powerful man in England, exercised for a long time almost regal powers, and his sons Sweyn, Harold, and Tostig were granted large possessions. Harold was a man of eminent ability, and his generosity and uprightness of character made him very popular. When his father died 1051, he was about thirty-one years of age, and during the declin-

ing years of Edward the Confessor he administrated the affairs of
the realm with great wisdom and ability. His brothers Sweyn and
Tostig were men of a different type — greedy and lawless ruffians,
who were a constant source of strife and mischief. Sweyn abducted
the beautiful abbess Eadgifu from a nunnery, and committed other
vile deeds, for which he was finally banished. Tostig, who was
King Edward's favorite, was made Earl of Northumbria on the death
of Earl Siward, but he seldom visited his possessions except to extort
unjust taxes. The long-suffering people finally rebelled and drove
him away, and Morkere, a grandson of Leofric, was chosen to succeed him. King Edward died on the 5th of January, 1066. As he
left no son, the kingdom of England became a prize to be contended
for by a number of rival candidates, all men of fame and ability, whose
claims to the throne were equally clouded and uncertain. The four
candidates who claimed to be the lawful heirs of the deceased king
were: Duke William of Normandy, Earl Harold, son of Godwin
King Svein Estridsson of Denmark, and King Harald Haardraade
of Norway. Earl Harold claimed that King Edward had bequeathed
him the kingdom. This would give him no valid title to the throne
since the king could not elect his successor. But Harold was the
only native English candidate who could be considered at this critical
moment, and he was chosen king by the Witenagemot, which alone
possessed the right of choice. This made Harold rightful king of
England, but it did not extinguish the title which the other candi
dates claimed to have. Duke William urged that King Edward
the Confessor had promised him the throne of England. He also
maintained that Harold had sworn fealty to him, and had solemnly
promised to support his claim. Harold had been shipwrecked on
the coast of Ponthieu in France some years before. The count of
that district took him prisoner, and turned him over to Duke Wil
liam of Normandy, and he was forced to give William the stated
pledges to obtain his liberty. Neither of these reasons gave Duke
William any right to the throne of England, as neither King Edward
nor Earl Harold could give away the kingdom, but what he needed
was a fair pretext; for the rest he trusted to his valiant sword
Svein Estridsson of Denmark claimed the English throne as the
heir of his cousin King Hardeknut, and of his uncle King Knut the

Great. Harald Haardraade of Norway based his claim on the treaty of Brennøerne by which Hardeknut made Magnus the Good his heir. This was, in a way, the same claim which Magnus himself had urged against Edward the Confessor, but it had been reduced to an empty pretense, since Magnus on his death-bed had surrendered Denmark to Svein Estridsson. The plotting Earl Tostig had negotiated with all the three foreign pretenders, and stood ready to sell his support to the highest bidder.

As soon as rumor got abroad that Harold had been crowned at London, January 6, 1066, Duke William of Normandy sent messengers to remind him of his promise, and began active preparations for an invasion of England. He mustered all his barons, and induced a great number of knights from Anjou, Brittany, Poitou, Flanders, and other places to join in the enterprise by offering them lands and treasures. He had prevailed on Pope Alexander II. to issue a bull approving of the expedition, and ships were built to carry the army across the English Channel. According to William of Aquitaine,[1] he also sent an embassy to Svein Estridsson to solicit his aid. This must have been Tostig, who, according to the sagas, went to King Svein as soon as his brother Harold was crowned king, to induce him to invade England. Svein did not venture upon such an undertaking, and Tostig then turned to King Harald Haardraade of Norway without any authority from Duke William. Harald is said to have promised to send an expedition to England in the summer, and Tostig promised to aid him with all the forces which he could gather. When the conquest was completed, he was to be made jarl over one-half of England as King Harald Haardraade's vassal.[2] But Tostig, who was as impatient as he was unreliable, hastened to Flanders, and before either Duke William or King Harald were ready to set sail, he gathered a fleet of sixty vessels, manned partly by his own adherents, partly by adventurers and freebooters of all sorts, and made an attack on the southern coast of England. King Harald came against him with a large fleet and army, and he

---

[1] P. A. Munch, *Det norske Folks Historie*, vol. II., p. 314.

[2] Accounts of these negotiations are found in the *Morkinskinna*, 18 *a* and *b*, in *Fagrskinna*, ch. 119; in Theodricus Monachus, *Historia de Antiquitate Regum Norwagiensium*, ch. 28; and in Ordericus Vitalis, *Historia Ecclesiastica*.

fled northward, and entered the Humber, where his fleet was destroyed by Earl Edwin of Mercia. With twelve ships he reached Scotland, where he was harbored by King Malcolm III.

In the summer of 1066 Harald Haardraade was busy making preparations for his expedition to England. He had chosen the Solund Islands, on the coast of Sogn, in southwestern Norway, as the rendezvous for his fleet, and by the beginning of September he had gathered a large armament of 250 war vessels and about 20,000 men. Before his departure he made his eldest son, Magnus, regent, and caused him to be crowned king. His younger son, Olav, accompanied him on the expedition. He sailed first to the Shetland Islands, and thence to the Orkneys. The Orkney jarls, Paul and Erlend, had to join the expedition with a large number of ships and troops. When he reached the Tyne in Scotland, about the 10th of September, he was also joined by Tostig, who acknowledged him as his lord. They landed at various places along the coast, captured Scarborough after some resistance, and took possession of the coast districts as far as the Humber. The fleet ascended the Humber and the Ouse, but came to anchor at Riccal, eight miles south of York. Here Harald landed his army, and marched along the river towards the city. The earls Morkere of Northumbria and Edwin of Mercia, who had gathered a large army in York, came out to meet Harald at Fulford, about two miles from the city. A bloody battle was fought in which the earls suffered a crushing defeat. The remnants of their army fled back to York, while Harald took possession of the neighboring district, and intrenched himself at Stamford Bridge on the Derwent River. The city of York offered to capitulate, and on September 24 Harald advanced with his army to meet the citizens outside the city, where the terms of peace were arranged. They acknowledged him their lord, promised to supply him with provisions and agreed to give 500 hostages. In the evening Harald returned to his fleet, but planned to advance on the following morning to Stamford Bridge, where the hostages were to be delivered.

In the meantime Harold Godwinson had arrived at York with his army, and had been watching Harald's movements. In the

¹ According to various sources, Harald had now no less than 300 war vessels and 30,000 men.

night he was secretly admitted into the city. The next morning Harald advanced with a part of his army; the other part was left in charge of his son Olav and the Orkney jarls Paul and Erlend to guard the fleet. The day was warm, and, as no hostilities were anticipated, the men marched without their brynies. When they arrived at Stamford Bridge, Harold suddenly fell upon them with his whole force. The saga says that Harald did not follow Tostig's advice to retreat to the ships, but sent messengers to bring the rest of the army to his support. This was a fatal mistake. Before help arrived, Harald's forces were overwhelmed and defeated, and he was mortally wounded in the fight. The "Heimskringla" gives a vivid description of the battle of Stamford Bridge. It tells how Harald, when he found himself face to face with the whole English army, planted his banner, formed a shield-ring, and made ready for the combat. But before the battle began, a horseman rode up, spoke to Earl Tostig, and offered him the earldom of Northumbria if he would join the English. Tostig asked how much he would give Harald Sigurdsson, the Norwegian king. The horseman said that he would gladly give him six feet of ground, and as much more as he was taller than other men; [1] but Tostig rejected the offer, says the saga. When the horseman rode away, they discovered that it was King Harold Godwinson himself. The fight commenced, and the Norsemen in their shield-ring resisted stoutly the attack of the English cavalry. But when they thought that the attack had failed, and that the English began to retreat, they rushed eagerly forward in pursuit. The shield-ring was broken, and they were attacked from all sides. A fearful carnage resulted. King Harald rushed into the midst of the fray, but an arrow pierced his throat, and he fell mortally wounded. Tostig now assumed command. Supported by the reënforcements which arrived from the fleet, he rallied the broken columns to renewed efforts, but the men had become exhausted on the forced march from the fleet. Towards evening the Norse army broke and fled in wild disorder, and darkness alone saved the broken remnants from destruction.

This dramatic description of the battle is manifestly erroneous.

[1] Harald Sigurdsson Haardraade is said to have been almost seven feet tall.

The English are represented as fighting on horseback, though we know that their army was very deficient in cavalry. The English were foot-soldiers, as we see from the battle of Hastings, which occurred less than three weeks later. The saga writer seems to have confused the battle of Stamford Bridge with that of Hastings, where the Norman mounted knights made repeated attacks on the English foot-soldiers, who stood firm behind their shield-wall, until by a feint they were led to pursue the enemy, and suffered a crushing defeat. The cavalry fight in the battle of Stamford Bridge is not mentioned in the older Norse sources,[1] nor in the "Anglo-Saxon Chronicle." We are left completely in the dark, therefore, as to the details of the battle. We only know that at Stamford Bridge King Harald Haardraade suffered an overwhelming defeat. "There King Harald of Norway and Earl Tostig were slain," says the "Anglo-Saxon Chronicle,"[2] "and a great number of men with them, both Norsemen and English." The chronicle states that Harold Godwinson suffered Harald's son Olav and the Orkney jarls to depart with twenty-four ships and the remnant of the army. We may well doubt the accuracy of the statement that only twenty-four ships left. Olav and the jarls, who were in charge of the fleet, had both time and opportunity to hold the ships in readiness, as they knew that a battle was in progress. That the whole large army of 30,000 men should be so utterly destroyed that only twenty-four ships could be manned seems quite incredible. The statement in the "Heimskringla" that Harold let Olav depart with the fleet and the remnant of the army seems more worthy of belief. Harold had no time to waste. On Sept. 28th, three days after the battle of Stamford Bridge, Duke William landed at Pevensey, in southern England, with 60,000 men, and on the 6th or 7th of October Harold was again in London making preparations for the still greater battle fought at Hastings.

---

[1] Ágrip, Theodricus Monachus, Historia de Antiquitate Regum Norwagiensium.

[2] Plummer, Two of the Saxon Chronicles, p. 199. Harald Haardraade is called Harald Haarfagre in the Chronicle. This may be an error, but it is possible that the epithet "Haarfagre" was applied to Harald Sigurdsson by his contemporaries, because of his long flaxen hair. This seems the more likely as he is called "Haarfagre" also by Ordericus Vitalis, book III., p. 116 P. Kierkegaard's translation.

October 14, 1066. In this hard-fought battle Harold Godwinson fell, and William the Conqueror became king of England.

The defeat and death of the warlike Harald Haardraade changed the political situation in the North. Svein Estridsson of Denmark felt that all danger of an attack from Norway was now removed, and as he considered his claim to the throne of England as valid as ever, he resolved to invade England and expel King William. Many Danes who had been banished from England, or had suffered other wrongs, were also urging him to assert his claim. But the preparations proceeded very slowly, and three years passed before the expedition was finally ready to start. In the month of August, 1069, 240 ships set sail for England, led by Svein's brother Asbjørn, his sons Harald and Knut, and Jarl Thorkil. After attacking Dover, Sandwich, and Norwich without success, the fleet entered the Humber, and advanced toward York. Northern England, where the Viking element still was strong, had not submitted to King William. The boy Eadgar the Ætheling, grandson of Edmund Ironside, was chosen king when Harold fell at Hastings, but he had fled to Scotland after the battle. He was now in Northumbria, where the earls Morkere and Edwin were aiding him in organizing a great revolt against William. The arrival of the Danish fleet in the Humber became the signal for a general uprising. York was taken by the combined forces of Danes and Northumbrians, but the Norman garrison burned the city before surrendering, and the victors leveled the fortifications with the ground. When King William arrived, the Danes retreated to their ships, and the Northumbrians returned to their homes, but as soon as he departed the attack was renewed. William was unable to assail the Danish fleet for want of ships, but he succeeded in bribing the Danish commander, Asbjørn, to remain inactive, and finally to depart from England. On northern England he wreaked a fearful vengeance, wasting it with fire and sword. No such devastation had ever passed over an English community as that wrought by William the Conqueror in Northumbria. The prosperity of this flourishing district was wiped out, and its spirit and power of resistance was broken. Asbjørn returned to Denmark with his ships laden with booty, but the enterprise had failed, and his own conduct had been reprehensible. In 1075 another Danish fleet of 200 vessels, led by Svein's son Knut, and Jarl Hagen, again visited England, and entered the Humber, but not a hand was raised to aid or welcome them, and they returned home after collecting some booty in the neighborhood of York. This was the last Viking expedition to England.

50. Olav Kyrre. A Period of Peace

Olav, Harald's son, spent the winter 1066-1067 in the Orkneys, and returned to Norway in the spring. His brother Magnus had been crowned king before the expedition left for England, but Olav was also made king on his return. The "Heimskringla" says that they were made joint kings, but Magnus was to rule the northern and Olav the southern half of the country.[1] The loss of the great army sent to England was a severe blow; nothing less than a national calamity. The country's resources were badly drained, and the available stores and military forces were gone. Under these circumstances King Svein of Denmark found the time opportune to put forward a claim to overlordship over Norway. Magnus and Olav refused to listen to these demands, and he gathered a fleet and prepared to invade the country. This he could now do without violating any agreement, since the treaty of peace concluded between him and King Harald in 1064 should remain in force only so long as the kings lived. Hostilities commenced, but the peace-loving Olav began negotiations with King Svein, which resulted in a new treaty of peace between Norway and Denmark in 1068. This treaty should be binding for all times, and neither kingdom should claim supremacy over the other. King Magnus, who had been sickly for some time, died in 1069, and Olav became king of all Norway. The "Heimskringla" describes him as follows: "Olav was a large man, and well built. It is a common opinion that no one has seen a man better looking, or of nobler appearance. His yellow, silky hair fell in rich locks; he had fair skin, beautiful eyes, and well proportioned limbs. He was, generally, reticent, and spoke little

---

[1] The kingdom was still looked upon as the *odel*, or property of the king, which could be divided among his heirs, like another private estate. This division is the beginning of a long series of partitions of the kingdom between the sons and heirs of the ruling king.

at the *thing*, but he was glad and talkative at the drinking-feast. He drank much, and was cheerful and peace-loving to the end of his days." [1] Because of his quiet disposition and peaceful reign he was called Olav Kyrre (the quiet). His efforts to maintain peace at home and abroad had a most beneficent effect at this time, not only because the kingdom needed to recover from the heavy losses incurred in the fruitless military exploits of his martial father, but also because the people's mind needed to be turned away from the strut and vainglory which usually attends war and adventure, to seek employment and honor in peaceful pursuits. Conditions in the neighboring kingdoms were also favorable to the maintenance of peace, as both Denmark and Sweden were so occupied with internal strife or foreign conquests that they could not pursue any aggressive policy in their relations with Norway. Christianity had not been firmly established in Sweden, and many people were displeased because of King Stenkil's efforts to promote the missionary work. The violent reaction against the church which occurred when he died in 1067, was caused, perhaps, in part by the overzealous Bishop Egino of Skåne, who had threatened to destroy the great heathen temple at Upsala. Many people returned to their old faith, and sacrificed to the heathen gods. Several rival candidates were also contending for the throne, and the country was torn by civil strife for many years, until Inge Stenkilsson finally overpowered his rivals, and succeeded his father on the throne. In Denmark King Svein was engaged in preparing his great expeditions to England, which brought him only loss and disappointment. When he died in 1076, his son Harald became his successor, but he soon died, and a younger brother, Knut, became king of Denmark. He was an ambitious and warlike young man, who could not forget that his ancestors had occupied the throne of England. Not discouraged by his father's fruitless attempts at conquest, he determined to send a new expedition to England. He was a great friend of Olav Kyrre, and solicited his aid for the undertaking. Olav refused to join the expedition, but as a good friend he placed sixty warships fully manned at his disposal. In 1084 Knut began to collect a large fleet, but time passed, and when the preparations finally were near

[1] *Heimskringla, Olav Kyrre's Saga*, ch. I.

completion, most of the Danish chieftains grew impatient and returned to their homes. Norway was thereby saved from renewed hostilities with England. King Knut, who thus suddenly found himself deserted, was very wroth. He began to rule harshly, and collected unjust and excessive taxes. This produced a general rebellion, and he was killed by an angry mob in St. Alban's church in Odense where he had sought refuge. In the reign of his successor, Olav Hunger, he was declared holy, and he soon became the national saint of Denmark, though his only merit seems to have been that he was slain in a church.[1]

Olav Kyrre, who was pious as well as peaceful, was deeply interested in the labors of the clergy, and worked zealously throughout his long reign to give the Church of Norway a more stable and efficient organization. The defiant attitude which his father Harald Haardraade had assumed over against the Archbishop of Bremen he seems to have regarded as improper, if not unfortunate. His own disposition, as well as his friendly relations with Denmark, which was a part of the archdiocese of Bremen, inclined him to favor the archbishop, and to uphold his authority over the Norwegian clergy. He was also encouraged in his loyalty to the Roman See and its representative the archbishop by the Pope himself, who in his letters to the king expressed deep solicitude for the church in the North. The powerful Gregory VII., who occupied the papal throne at this time (1073–1085), was the real founder of the papal power, and the organizer of the Roman hierarchy. The constant strife between ruling princes, the violence and turmoil everywhere rampant convinced him that the church alone possessed the wisdom and authority to maintain peace, and to act as arbiter in every controversy. He wished to reform the world by organizing a universal religious monarchy with the Pope as supreme ruler. "Human pride," he wrote, "has created the power of kings. God's mercy has created the power of bishops. The Pope is the master of the

---

[1] Olav, who had been imprisoned by his brother, King Knut, was made king of Denmark. In his reign a drought produced a great famine, which the people regarded as a chastisement sent upon them by the angry God because Knut had been slain in the St. Alban's church. They began to venerate the dead king as a saint, and Olav was called King Olav Hunger because of the famine.

emperors. He is rendered holy by the merits of his predecessor, St. Peter. The Roman Church has never erred, and Holy Scripture proves that it can never err. To resist it is to resist God." [1] The growing power of the hierarchy, and the increased devotion to the Roman Church, which was the result of Pope Gregory's activity, was fast ripening into the great religious movement which culminated in the crusades, the impulse of which was felt in every land in western Europe. Cathedrals were built, and crusading missionary work was carried on with zeal, while all nations were drawn closer to Rome, which was the center of religious and intellectual life.

That Olav Kyrre was imbued with the spirit of the age is rendered evident by his labors to organize the Church of Norway according to the general plan of the Catholic Church in other countries, as well as by his efforts to introduce in Norway the culture and refinement of the aristocratic circles in England and continental Europe. His reign marks a final victory of medieval ideas, which found their best expression in crusades and knight-errantry, but the Roman incubus, which was so potent in controlling the governments, and in shaping the intellectual life of the age, was far less marked in Norway than elsewhere in Europe. Celibacy of priests, which the Pope now enforced as a part of the Roman church discipline, was not introduced in Norway. The clergy remained subject to the king, who exercised firm control in ecclesiastical affairs. The scaldic poetry flourished, the national saga literature and history writing were yet to blossom forth, and there were but scant traces of a religious literature fostered under the influence of the church. The separation of the North from the archdiocese of Bremen gave the Norwegian people a new opportunity to preserve their independence in church affairs, and to develop a strong national spirit. The attempt of Pope Gregory VII. to assert his supremacy over the German Emperor precipitated the famous struggle between the Pope and Emperor Henry IV., which divided the whole Empire into the warring factions of Welfs and Ghibellines, friends of the Pope and supporters of the Emperor. Archbishop Adalbert of Bremen was one of the Emperor's stanchest supporters. His successor, Liemar, also adhered to the Ghibelline party, even after the Emperor had been excommunicated,

[1] T. F. Tout, *The Empire and the Papacy*, p. 126.

and Pope Gregory VII. punished the disobedient prelate by depriving him of his office. King Svein Estridsson of Denmark and his successors were adherents of the Pope, and this finally led to the separation of the Scandinavian countries from the Bremen archdiocese, and the creation of a new archbishopric in the Danish city of Lund, in Skåne, in 1104. During this period of strife, which paralyzed the power of the Archbishop of Bremen, the highest ecclesiastical authority in Norway was exercised by the king. The state-church principle, which had been practiced by St. Olav, and which had been so imperiously maintained by Harald Haardraade, was now further strengthened by circumstances which made the king the natural leader of the Church of Norway. King Olav Kyrre divided Norway into three bishoprics: Nidaros, Selja, and Oslo, each with its diocesan bishop, who received the rank of jarl. New incumbents were chosen by the chapters of the diocese, but they had to present themselves before the king, who in reality selected the candidates. Each diocese had its own saint: Nidaros, St. Olav; Oslo, St. Halvard; and Selja, St. Sunniva. In Trondhjem Olav erected a cathedral church on the spot where St. Olav was thought to have been buried the first time. It was dedicated to the Trinity, but was generally called the Christ church. The altar was placed on the spot where St. Olav's body was supposed to have rested, and the shrine of the saint was moved to the new church. On the foundations of this church the Trondhjem cathedral was later erected. King Harald Haardraade's body, which had been brought back to Norway, was interred in the St. Mary's church, which he had built. On the west coast of Norway, Olav Kyrre founded the city of Bergen (O. N. Bjørgvin),[1] which, because of its favorable location, soon became one of the chief commercial towns in the North. The bishop of the diocese was to reside here, and the king began the erection of a

[1] The exact time is not given, but the city is thought to have been founded somewhere between 1070 and 1075. See Yngvar Nielsen, *Bergen fra de ældste Tider indtil Nutiden*, Christiania, 1877. P. A. Munch, *Det norske Folks Historie*, II., 433 ff. Alexander Bugge, *Studier over de norske Byers Selvstyre før Hanseaternes Tid*, Christiania, 1899. *Fagrskinna*, p. 149. *Heimskringla, Olav Kyrre's Saga*, ch. I.; *Morkin kinna*, p. 125. *Historisk Tidsskrift*, tredie række, vol. V., p. 433, Gustav Storm, *De kongelige Byanlæg i Norge i Middelalderen*.

large cathedral of stone, the Christ church. This was finished in 1170, and the St. Sunniva relics were then transferred from Selja to Bergen. In the Orkneys Jarl Thorfinn founded a bishopric and built a cathedral church at Birgsaa 1050–1064.[1] In Iceland Gissur Isleivsson, who became bishop in 1081, erected a cathedral on his estate Skálholt, which he donated to the church as a permanent bishop's residence.

The long period of peace during the reign of Olav Kyrre produced a marked improvement in economic conditions. The cities grew, and commerce increased; no extra taxes were imposed for military purposes, and good harvests seem to have added to the general prosperity. It is evident from the saga accounts that this reign was long remembered as a sort of golden age of peace and plenty. "In the reign of Olav Kyrre there were good harvests and such abundant good fortune that Norway had never been more prosperous under any king since the days of Harald Haarfagre," says the saga.[2] Under these circumstances a taste for luxury and comfort was naturally developed, and the king labored earnestly to bring the civilization and culture of his people into full harmony with the Christian spirit, and to introduce in Norway the elegance and courtly manners which were being developed everywhere in Europe during this age of chivalry. The *hird* was doubled in number, so that it consisted of 120 *hirdmænd*, sixty *gestir*, and sixty *huskarlar*. The *hirdmænd* were divided into groups, at the head of which stood *skutilsveinar*,[3] or officers of the king's guard. After the creation of this new office the *lendermænd* do not seem to have sought the king's *hird* as before, but they held now the highest rank in the country, as King Olav did not appoint any jarls after the death of Haakon Ivarsson. The *kertisveinar*,[4] corresponding to the French pages, waited at the king's

[1] See L. Dietrichson, *Monumenta Orcadica*, p. 19; *Orkneyingasaga*, ch. xxi.

[2] *Morkinskinna*, *Olav Kyrre's Saga*, 20 b.

[3] *Skutilsveinn*, from *skutill* (Lat. *scutula*, a dish), a plate, or small table placed before a guest. The title does not properly indicate the duties of the office. The *skutilsveinar* were officers of the guards, not waiters at the table, though they may have waited on the guests at the table on special occasions. About their duties see *Hirðskrá*, *Norges gamle Love*, vol. II.

[4] *Kertisveinn* from *kerti* = candle. Their duties are mentioned in the *Hirðskrá* (the laws of the court), ch. 25, *Norges gamle Love*, vol. II.

table. Behind each guest at the table stood a *kertisveinn*, with a burning candle.

The people of the higher classes began to wear costumes of foreign pattern borrowed especially from England and Normandy. "The people began to dress with great splendor according to foreign fashions," says the saga. "They wore fine hose ruffled about the knee. Some put gold rings about the legs; many wore long mantles with slit sides tied with ribbons, and with sleeves five ells long, and so narrow that they had to be pulled on with a cord, and arranged in folds up to the shoulders. They wore high shoes, embroidered with silk and even ornamented with gold." [1] From the upper classes, who were in sympathy with the spirit and higher culture of the age, the new tastes and ideas were soon communicated to the common people, who through a natural instinct for imitation gradually adopted as much of the new customs as environment and circumstances would permit. King Olav also introduced many improvements in the construction of dwelling-houses. Hitherto the fireplace, *arinn*, was placed in the center of the house, and the smoke escaped through an opening in the roof, the *ljóri*. Olav built houses with stone floors and introduced the oven, which was erected in a corner of the room with a flue for carrying away the smoke. The *ljóri* disappeared, and the houses received a loft, the beginning of a second story. Windows became more common, though glass windows seem yet to have been limited to the king's own dwellings.

From the earliest times the Norsemen took great delight in social and religious festivities; their great hospitality and the liberal entertainment of friends and travelers have already been mentioned as a conspicuous national trait. The period of prosperity and peace in the time of Olav Kyrre gave new stimulus to the development of social life. Permanent clubs or guilds (N. *gilde*, O. N. *gildi*), organized under the protection of the church, were instituted by King Olav to afford better opportunity for social intercourse.[2] These guilds

---

[1] *Heimskringla, Olav Kyrre's Saga*, ch. 2.

[2] Professor Alexander Bugge says: "It is, in fact, nowhere in the sagas mentioned that Olav Kyrre introduced the first guilds into Norway, but only that he instituted guilds in the Norwegian towns. On the contrary, the sagas seem to presuppose that guilds existed at a still earlier date, *i.e.* in the younger saga of St. Olav where Ølver á Eggju answers King Olav :

had their own guild halls, women were also members, the rules were strict, and much attention was paid to fine manners and good conversation. Christian spirit was also fostered in the guilds, as they were placed under the supervision of the church. The members were mutually pledged to assist one another in times of need, a very fortunate arrangement at a time when municipal government was yet in its infancy. Thereby the guilds became the forerunners of political clubs, insurance companies, pension funds, and like organizations which have sprung from the feeling of social interdependence. The members were jointly responsible for each other's houses and stables. If a member suffered loss of house or stable by fire, the guild would rebuild it. If a man's granary burned, he received a certain amount of grain; if he lost three head of cattle or more, each member should give him a measure of grain; if the member

'sagði at bǿndr hefði engar veizlur haft þat haust, nema gildi sin ok hvirfings drykkjur' (Fornmannasǿgur, IV., ch. 102), or where the holy bishop Martin in a dream says to Olav Tryggvason: 'þat hefir verit háttr manna her i landi sem vida annarstoðar, þar sem heidit folk er, at Þór ok Oðni er ǫl gefit, þar sem samdrykkjur eðr gildi ero haldin.' I believe like Hegel (Städte und Gilden, I., p. 412), and Munch (Det norske Folks Historie, II., p. 442 f.), that Olav Kyrre in imitation of western European fashion, erected guild halls in Norwegian towns. But I also believe that the guilds themselves existed at a still earlier time and that they were connected with the heathen sacrificial banquets (blotveizlur)." The Earliest Guilds of Northmen in England, Norway, and Denmark, in Sproglige og historiske Afhandlinger viede Sophus Bugges Minde, Christiania, 1908.

The origin of the guilds is very obscure. They are known to have existed in the Empire of Charlemagne in the ninth century, and probably even earlier. A. Bugge says: "I regard the Empire of the Franks as the birthplace of the guilds, the country from which this most typical institution of the Middle Ages has spread to all parts of western and northern Europe." The Earliest Guilds of the Northmen in England, Norway, and Denmark, in Afhandlinger viede Sophus Bugges Minde, p. 197 ff. See also Alexander Bugge, Studier over de norske Byers Selvstyre og Handel fǿr Hanseaterne. W. A. Wilda, Das Gildenwesen im Mittelalter, Halle, 1831. O. P. K. Hartvig, Untersuchungen über die ersten Anfänge des Gildenwesens, Göttingen, 1860.

Various influences contributed to their later development. Alexander Bugge has shown that the guilds of England have been strongly influenced by the Danes and Norsemen. "First of all," he says, "the word 'guild' itself is probably a Scandinavian word (= O. N. gildi). The Thanes' Guild of Cambridge from the first half of the eleventh century bears especially the impression of being influenced by Scandinavian institutions." See also Falk og Torp, Etymologisk Ordbog, "gilde."

was a merchant, and lost his goods by shipwreck, he also received a compensation. If a member was imprisoned in a foreign land, he was ransomed by the guild; if he was slain by one who did not belong to the guild, the other members would assist in prosecuting the slayer; but if a member committed murder, he was expelled from the guild, and was not again allowed to appear in the guild hall. When a member died, all the other members were present at the funeral. The guilds were generally named after patron saints, under whose special protection they were supposed to stand. In Bergen they were especially numerous, and the names of many are still familiar in that city. The most important was the St. Jatmund's (St. Edmund's) Guild, to which, according to an old writer, even "kings, dukes, counts, barons, knights, and other noblemen belonged." In Trondhjem the oldest was the Mykle Guild (the Great Guild), organized by Olav Kyrre, and dedicated to St. Olav. Tunsberg had the St. Olav's Guild and the St. Anna's Guild; Oslo, the Guild of the Holy Body, St. Anna's Guild, and the Shoemakers' Guild. The country districts, too, had their guilds. They are mentioned as having existed in Salten, Aalen, Opdal, Medalen, in Herø in Søndmør, and in many other places. That many guilds existed of which no records have been preserved can be seen from place-names like Gildeskaale, Gildehus, Gildevang, Gildevold, Gildesaker, etc. In course of time when the cities became industrial centers, the guilds very naturally developed into craft-guilds, in which men of the same profession or handicraft were associated together.[1] But in Norway the guilds were controlled by the king and the church, and at no time did they become independent political organizations hostile to the ruler, something which happened not infrequently in some countries of Europe.

---

[1] Of the statutes (skrá) of the guilds only two have been preserved: the skrá of the Olav's Guild in Gulathingslag, and the skrá of the St. Olav's Guild in Onarheim, Søndhordland. *Norges gamle Love*, vol. V., p. 7–13. These statutes are the chief source of our knowledge of the guilds and their work. Accounts of the guilds are found in Christian C. A. Lange, *De norske Klostres Historie i Middelalderen*, and P. A. Munch, *Det norske Folks Historie*, vol. II. Alexander Bugge, *Studier over de norske Byers Selvstyre og Handel før Hanseaterne*. Alexander Bugge, *The Earliest Guilds of the Northmen in England, Norway, and Denmark*, published in *Afhandlinger viede Sophus Bugges Minde*, Christiania, 1908.

Among the more prominent men in Norway in Olav Kyrre's time may be mentioned especially Skule Kongsfostre, the king's chief adviser, a man of high rank, who had followed him from England. He seems to have been the king's foster-father, not the son of Earl Tostig, as some sources have it. Skule was placed at the head of the *hird*, and he was also sent to England to bring back the body of King Harald Haardraade. The king gave him the old royal hall in Oslo, when a new royal dwelling was erected, and he granted him also a number of estates at Oslo, Konghelle, and Trondhjem; and also Rein in Nordmør, from which his descendants derived their name. From Skule Kongsfostre descended Duke Skule (Skule Jarl), famous in the reign of King Haakon Haakonsson. Dag Eilivsson, the father of Gregorius Dagssøn, in Viken, Sigurd Ulstreng in Trøndelagen, the son of Rut af Viggen who fell at Stiklestad, Thore af Steig, in Oplandene, who was the king's secret opponent, and Sveinke Steinarsson, who ruled the border districts on the Göta River, were among the most powerful men in the kingdom at this time. King Olav Kyrre died in 1093, in the twenty-seventh year of his reign.

51. A REVIVAL OF THE VIKING SPIRIT. MAGNUS BAREFOOT

When Olav Kyrre died, his son Magnus was proclaimed king in Viken, while the people of Oplandene were led, as it appears, by Thore of Steig, to choose his nephew Haakon. The arrangement of joint kingship, first introduced in the time of Magnus the Good and Harald Haardraade, was now repeated. The kingdom does not seem to have been divided, though some sources seem to indicate it. According to the "Morkinskinna," [1] the two kings ruled together for two years, but the older sources, Theodricus Monachus and "Ágrip," state that the joint kingship lasted only one winter. Haakon was then killed by a fall from his horse. Thore of Steig, the old opponent of Olav Kyrre, did not even now acknowledge King Magnus, though, after the death of Haakon, the young king was the only legitimate heir to the throne. Thore formed an opposition party in support of the pretender Svein, and started a revolt; but this was easily

---

[1] *Morkinskinna, Magnus Barefoot's Saga.* Theodricus Monachus, ch. xxx. *Ágrip*, 72–73.

put down, and the two leaders, Thore of Steig and Egil Askelsson, were captured and executed.

The king found another opponent in Sveinke Steinarsson, who was a *lendermand*, a sort of *markgraf* in the border districts on the Göta River. In these far-off districts his will was law, and he protected the people against the robbers and outlaws who infested the region along the border. He had not taken part in the revolt, but he did not submit to the king, and managed all affairs according to his own mind. He was summoned to the Borgarthing, where the *stallare*, Sigurd Ulstreng, represented the king. After the *thing* was assembled, they saw a body of warriors approaching, dressed in steel so bright that they looked like a moving block of ice.[1] This was Sveinke, who came to the *thing* with 500 armed followers. He ridiculed the *stallare*, and after some altercations, Sigurd had to flee. The king marched against the arrogant *lendermand*, but hostilities were averted through the intercession of friends. Sveinke was banished for a short period, but he was soon recalled, and became one of the king's best friends.

Magnus Barefoot was a warrior like his grandfather Harald Haardraade. In his reign the air was again filled with the sounds of war trumpets and the din of arms. The Viking spirit flared up anew from the smoldering embers, fanned into life by the martial spirit of the young king, who is reported to have said that a king ought to court honor rather than a long life. King Magnus was brave to foolhardiness, and energetic to rashness, a sort of demigod, who was loved by his followers even for his faults. But it would be manifestly unjust to regard him as a mere Viking chieftain, or as a romantic dreamer, who spent the ten years of his reign in the pursuit of the phantom of military glory. It is evident that he followed a clearly conceived plan, and that he was never led by vain ambition to waste his means in rash and impossible adventures. He did not aspire to the throne of England, like his grandfather had done, nor did he attempt to conquer Ireland, as some old writers would have us believe. The chief, if not the only, purpose of his expedition to the British Isles seems to have been to reduce the Norse island possessions to full submission to the home government. But the

[1] *Morkinskinna*, p. 137.

ever recurring war expeditions increased the burdens of taxation, removed great numbers of the ablest men from productive employments, and retarded the peaceful development inaugurated by Olav Kyrre. The history of Magnus Barefoot's reign is a record of his military campaigns; of the internal affairs of the country in his time little is known; of real progress history has nothing to record.

As soon as Magnus was securely seated on the throne, he provoked a war with Sweden by claiming the Swedish province of Dal, or Dalsland, lying between Ranrike and Lake Venern. He crossed the Göta River with an army, and harried the districts until they had to offer their submission. On Kåland Island, in Lake Venern, he built a fort, and left a garrison of 360 men, but when he returned home for the winter, the Swedish king, Inge Stenkilsson, captured the fort and drove away the garrison. The following spring Magnus renewed his campaign, and a battle was fought at Fuxerna, on the Göta River. According to "Ágrip," Magnus was victorious, but according to Theodricus Monachus he lost the battle. The last version is probably correct, since a peace conference was called at Konghelle in 1101, where the three kings, Magnus Barefoot of Norway, Inge Stenkilsson of Sweden, and Eirik Eiegod of Denmark were all present. According to the terms of the treaty here concluded, the kings should retain the territories which their predecessors had held, but Magnus should receive the hand of Margaret, King Inge's daughter, in marriage, and her dowry should be the districts in dispute.[1] She was nicknamed Fredkulla (the peace maiden). Snorre gives the following description of the three kings as they appeared together at Konghelle: "Inge was the largest and strongest, and looked most dignified, Magnus seemed the most valiant and energetic, but Eirik was the handsomest."

The most noteworthy features of King Magnus' reign were his expeditions to the British Isles. Two earlier expeditions, which Magnus was thought to have made in 1092 and 1093–1094, have been described by the old scholar Torfæus. Buchanan, a Scotch

---

[1] Theodricus Monachus, *De Antiquitate*, ch. xxxi. *Ágrip*, 79, found in Gustav Storm's *Monumenta Historica Norwegiae*. The terms of the treaty are stated both by Theodricus and by the *Ágrip*, and seem to be correct, though the dowry is not mentioned by Snorre, who simply states that Magnus married Margaret, the daughter of the Swedish king.

historian of the sixteenth century, who bases his account on Fordun's "Scotichronicon," also tells how King Magnus in 1094 aided Prince Donaldbane to gain the throne of Scotland. The account of the last-named expedition has been considered to be historic also by the great Norwegian historian P. A. Munch, but Gustav Storm has shown that Magnus made neither of these expeditions. The passage in the "Scotichronicon" is shown to be an interpolation by a late writer, and the foundation for the statement referring to Magnus' operations in Scotland in 1094 disappears wholly when it is made clear that at this time he was still in Norway, busily engaged in securing his succession to the throne.[1] Norse sagas mention only the two expeditions in 1098–1099 and 1102–1103, about which Welsh chronicles, Irish annals, and verses of contemporary scalds give the most reliable information.

After the peace at Konghelle, Magnus sailed to the British Isles with a fleet of 150 ships. He landed in the Orkneys, where he deposed the jarls Paul and Erlend, and sent them to Norway, possibly, because they had been neglectful of their duties as vassals. Soon afterward he took King Gudrød Crowan of the Hebrides prisoner, and forced him to submit. He then proceeded to the Isle of Man, which was regarded by the Norsemen as belonging to the Hebrides group (Sudreyjar). Civil strife between rival chieftains had here been in progress, and he found on the battlefield of Sandvad the corpses still lying unburied, says the chronicle.[2] He took possession of the island and erected a number of houses and castles. According to Ordericus Vitalis,[3] he brought over a large number of colonists from Norway, because the inhabitants had been greatly reduced in numbers by the incessant feuds. The real reason for the new colonization may have been that he could put little trust in the loyalty of the Manx, who were partly of Gaelic descent, and who had lived isolated in their island homes too long to feel any attachment for Norway.

During the reign of William Rufus (1087–1100) the Normans in

[1] Gustav Storm, *Magnus Barfods Vesterhavstog, Historisk Tidsskrift*, anden række, vol. III. Ordericus Vitalis, *Historia Ecclesiastica. Orkneyingasaga*, ch. xxviii ff.

[2] *Chronica Regum Manniæ et Insularum*, p. 6.

[3] Ordericus Vitalis, *Historia Ecclesiastica*, p. 767.

England were engaged in subduing Wales.[1] The king was unsuccessful in his campaigns against the Welsh mountaineers, but Norman barons and adventurers had gradually pushed their way into the country, where they seized one district after the other, and erected castles. When the king of South Wales fell in the battle of Brecknock, in 1093, three Norman lordships came into being in South Wales. In Northern Wales the Normans had been less successful, but the conquest was pressed with energy. The Earl of Chester had pushed across the Menai Strait to Anglesea, where he built a castle at Aberlleiniog. But the Welsh rallied in 1095–1096, and destroyed all the Norman castles on Welsh soil except that of Pembroke. King William marched against them, and vowed that he would exterminate the entire male population, but he had to return home without having won a single victory. The Norman earls were more successful. In 1098 the earls of Shrewsbury and Chester marched through northern Wales, crossed over to Anglesea, and rebuilt the castle of Aberlleiniog. The Welsh turned to Magnus Barefoot for aid. He accepted the invitation, and quickly crossed over from the Isle of Man with his fleet. In attempting to prevent the Norsemen from landing, the Earl of Shrewsbury was mortally wounded, and the Normans, who had become thoroughly alarmed, evacuated Anglesea. Magnus returned to the Orkneys for the winter. King Lagman of Man, whom he had taken captive, was made vassal king of Man and the Hebrides, and he seems to have ruled till 1101.

When the king and his men returned to Norway, they wore Scotch national costumes. As these had never before been seen in Norway, they attracted much attention, and the people, who were ever fond of descriptive nicknames, called the king Magnus Barefoot.

King Lagman of Man and the Hebrides disappears in 1101. Whether he died in that year, or departed on a pilgrimage to the Holy Land as stated in the "Chronica Regum Manniæ" cannot be definitely determined. The chronicle also states that Magnus sent another king, Ingemund, to Man; but he was slain, and Magnus went to the Islands to restore order and submission. This gives

[1] H. C. W. Davis, *England under the Normans and Angevins*, p. iii ff., London, 1909.

a credible explanation of Magnus' second expedition, which he seems to have undertaken for the purpose of organizing the western possessions for his son Sigurd, who was made "king of the Islands" in 1102. His plan seems to have been to make Sigurd ruler of this new island kingdom, while his older son Eystein was to inherit the throne of Norway. The Welsh chronicle states that Magnus visited Anglesea, cut a great deal of timber, and brought it to Man, where he built three castles, which he garrisoned with his own men. From Man he sailed to Dublin in 1102. The "Heimskringla" states that he captured Dublin and Dublinshire, and spent the winter with King Myriartak (Muirchertach) in Kunnakter (possibly Connaught), but this is wholly erroneous. The "Ulster Annals" have the following entry for the year 1102: "In this year King Magnus came to Man, and he made peace with the Irish for one year." The Four Masters give a more detailed account: "An Irish army was assembled at Dublin to resist Magnus and the Norsemen, who came to ravage the country, but they made peace for one year, and Muirchertach gave King Magnus' son Sigurd his daughter in marriage, and many costly presents with her." [1] This shows that Magnus' second expedition could not have been undertaken with a view to conquer Ireland, but that it has been his aim to attach the island possessions more closely to the Norwegian crown. In these efforts he had been very successful. He reëstablished order in the islands, built and garrisoned forts for the maintenance of peace, brought in new colonists to settle and develop the districts which had been laid waste during the period of anarchy and misrule, and united the islands under a king, who was to govern them, subject to the authority of the king of Norway. These wisely conceived and ably directed efforts to establish an efficient government in these distant islands which had hitherto been the spoils of reckless adventurers, and the haunts of freebooters, might have had abiding results; a new era of peace and development might have dawned for them, had not death suddenly cut short King Magnus' career. It appears that in the summer of 1103 he left the Isle of Man, bound on a homeward voyage. He landed on the northeast coast of Ireland, where he made

[1] Sigurd's marriage must have been arranged with a view to strengthen his power and prestige as king.

a raid into the country with but a small force. After he had penetrated quite a distance inland he was suddenly attacked by an Irish army. Trusting in his bravery he refused to retreat, but his men were overpowered by superior numbers in the marshes where the battle was fought, and Magnus himself fell. He was at this time thirty years of age. The accounts of this raid into Ireland as given by the different sources are much at variance. The sagas describe it as a foraging expedition, and state that Magnus was waiting for cattle to be brought him "ofan af Kunnöktum," [1] when the Irish suddenly fell upon him. Ordericus Vitalis relates that Magnus landed on the coast of Ireland. The Irish were much afraid, and did not dare to meet him in battle, but, speaking fair words, they prevailed on him to debark, and when he had marched two miles into the country he was ambushed and slain.[2] The "Chronica Regum Manniæ" states that Magnus hastened ahead of his fleet with sixteen ships; that he imprudently landed in Ireland, where he was surrounded by the Irish, who slew the king and nearly all his men. He was buried at the St. Patrick's church at Down (Downpatrick), the chronicle adds. The essence of the whole matter seems to be contained in the statement of the "Ulster Annals" that Magnus was attacked and killed by the Ulstonians on a plundering expedition.

When Sigurd heard of his father's death, he became disheartened and returned to Norway. King Muirchertach had formed an alliance with King Henry I. of England, as both seem to have regarded Magnus as a dangerous neighbor, and Olav Bitling, a son of the former King Gudrød Crowan, was placed on the throne of Man.

Though Magnus' plans thus suddenly came to naught, his work had, none the less, produced permanent results. The jarls of the Orkneys and the kings of Man and the Hebrides became more closely attached to Norway than hitherto, and the system and organization introduced by King Magnus continued to exist in the Islands for well-nigh 150 years.

The closer relations established with the lands in the West gave a great stimulus, also, to commercial intercourse between Norway and the British Isles, and new costumes and articles of luxury were introduced from Scotland and England. Magnus himself had formed a

---

[1] *Morkinskinna*, 24 *a*. *Fagrskinna*, 240.
[2] Ordericus Vitalis, *Historia Ecclesiastica*, XI. 8. *Orkneyingasaga*, xxxii.

sort of partnership with an English merchant in Lincoln, who kept his treasury, and supplied him with arms, ornaments, and other necessary articles. After King Magnus' death, Henry I. of England forced the merchant to turn over to him 20,000 pounds of silver.

52. The Norwegian Coat of Arms

The Norwegian coat of arms, which consists of a golden lion with crown and battle-ax in a red shield, was thought to have originated on Magnus Barefoot's expeditions to the British Isles. Snorre says that when Magnus fought and fell in Ireland, "he wore a helmet, and carried a red shield on which appeared a lion wrought in gold. He was girded with the sword 'Leggbit,' the best of weapons. Its hilt was of walrus teeth, decorated with gold. He carried a spear, and over his shirt of mail he wore a cloak of red silk on which a lion was embroidered both on the front and in the back." [1] Professor Gustav Storm observes [2] that the oldest account of Magnus' last battle in Ireland, found in the "Ágrip af Norregs Konungasøgum," not in the "Heimskringla," mentions neither the red cloak nor the lions, but states that he had helmet, sword, and spear, and that he wore kilt (silkihjup) and stockings (stighosor) — the Scotch dress in which he was usually attired. The later saga writers are evidently guilty of the anachronism of describing Magnus as wearing the royal attire, adorned with the coat of arms used in Snorre's own time by King Haakon Haakonsson and Skule Jarl, a very common failing of the saga writers. The question then confronts us: When and how did the Norwegian coat of arms originate? We have seen that the Norsemen usually decorated their ships and weapons with figures representing beasts and birds of prey, like the dragon heads on their warships, and the raven (Odin's bird) on their sails and banners. These figures were symbols of bravery, and were employed to strike terror into the hearts of the enemy, but they had no heraldic character. In the twelfth century the knight errants began to decorate their shields and banners with heraldic figures and devices, and in

---

[1] *Heimskringla, Magnus Barfotssaga*, ch. 24.

[2] Gustav Storm, *Norges gamle Vaaben, Farver og Flag*, Christiania, 1894. Dr. G. L. Baden, *Undersøgelse om Ælden af Flags Brug i vort Norden, Samlinger til det norske Folks Sprog og Historie*, vol. IV., p. 514 ff.

the course of the thirteenth century these devices became family coats of arms.[1] Professor Storm shows that the golden lion on a red shield as a royal coat of arms is traceable to the time of Haakon Haakonsson and Skule Jarl (*i.e.* not earlier than 1217). Both King Haakon's and Skule Jarl's seals, though damaged, have been preserved. Their device is a golden lion, without crown or battle-ax, on a red three-cornered shield. King Haakon's son, Crown Prince Haakon Haakonsson the younger, chose the eagle as his coat of arms, but his younger brother, Magnus, who on Haakon's death became heir apparent to the throne, had selected the lion, which thereby became the coat of arms of the royal family. Magnus' son and successor, Eirik Magnusson (Priesthater), retained this device, but the lion appears in his seal with the crown and the battle-ax of St. Olav.

53. NORWAY PARTICIPATES IN THE CRUSADES. EYSTEIN MAGNUSSON AND SIGURD THE CRUSADER

King Magnus Barefoot had many sons, but none of them was born in lawful wedlock. Eystein, the oldest, who was fourteen years of age, Sigurd, the next oldest, and Olav succeeded their father as joint kings. The *hird* and *lendermænd* were divided among the kings, perhaps also the royal estates. But Olav was a mere child under the guardianship of his brothers, and as he died before he became of age, he may be left out of account. Harald Gille, who was still a child staying with his Irish mother in Ireland, is also generally acknowledged to have been a son of King Magnus, though his own assertion is about the only evidence of his royal descent. His mother called him Gillchrist, *i.e.* the servant of Christ. A later pretender, Sigurd Slembediakn, also claimed to be a son of Magnus, but he was generally regarded as an impostor, and was finally captured and put to death. The principle prevailed that all the king's sons, illegitimate as well as legitimate, had an equal right to the throne. Kingship was regarded as an inherited right; the kingdom was looked upon as an inheritance which could be held in joint ownership, or divided

---

[1] The *Thidrikssaga*, ch. 172–185, describes the coats of arms of King Thidrik and all the heroes in his hall. King Thidrik has a red shield decorated with a golden lion. Hildebrand has a red shield on which is painted a white castle with golden towers, etc.

among the heirs.[1] The practice of joint kingship, established in the time of Magnus the Good and Harald Haardraade, was adhered to. The kings kept their own *hird*, and shared equally in the royal revenues, but the kingdom was not divided. The reign of the joint kings was regarded as lasting while any of them remained on the throne.

With the death of Magnus Barefoot, and the accession of his young sons, a period of peace was again inaugurated, which lasted till the outbreak of the civil wars in 1130. During this period the archbishopric of Lund in Skåne was established, as already stated. Norway and Sweden, as well as Denmark, were included in this new church province, and the Scandinavian North was thereby separated from Germany with regard to ecclesiastical affairs.[2] The intense religious enthusiasm which had been awakened through the efforts of the Pope, and especially by the crusaders, and the zeal of the monastic orders had also reached the North, and the two kings, who were deeply influenced by the general spirit of the age, gave their most zealous efforts to the causes and ideals which had been created by the new awakening. The more warlike Sigurd became a crusader, while the peace-loving Eystein, who ruled the kingdom during his brother's absence, revived the policy of his grandfather Olav Kyrre. He built churches and monasteries, improved the laws, maintained peace and order in the kingdom, and devoted special attention to useful internal improvements.

In 1095 Pope Urban II. preached at Clermont in France the first holy war against the infidels. The religious fervor was soon fanned into white heat by zealots like Peter the Hermit and Walter the Penniless, and large numbers of pilgrims gathered on the Rhine and in northern France to march against the Turks. The sovereigns of western Europe took no part in the first crusade. Two of them,

---

[1] T. H. Aschehoug, *Statsforfatningen i Norge og Danmark indtil 1814*, p. 14 ff. R. Keyser, *Norges Stats- og Retsforfatning i Middelalderen*, p. 41 ff.

[2] In theory the Archbishop of Bremen was still the head of the church in the North. His supremacy was confirmed by Pope Calixtus II. in 1123, and when a dispute arose on this point between the archbishops of Lund and Bremen, Pope Innocent II. sent a cardinal to investigate the matter, whereupon he confirmed the supremacy of the Archbishop of Bremen through a letter of May, 1133. But this supremacy was merely nominal, and was soon transferred to the Archbishop of Lund.

the Emperor Henry IV. and King Philip I. of France, were under the ban of the church, the king of Spain was fighting against the Saracens at home, and the vicious William Rufus of England was hostile. The crusading hosts were, therefore, led by the great feudal magnates of Lotharingia, Burgundy, Normandy, Flanders, and the Norman colonies in southern Italy; men like Raymond of Toulouse, Hugh of Vermandois, a brother of King Philip I. of France, Robert, Duke of Normandy, his cousin Robert II. of Flanders, Stephen of Blois, the son-in-law of William the Conqueror, Godfrey of Bouillon, and the Italian Norman, Bohemund of Tarent, a son of Robert Guiscard. The armies marched overland to Constantinople, where Emperor Alexius Comnenus had them transported across the Bosphorus into Asia Minor, after the leaders had taken an oath of fealty to him. Nicæa was captured in 1097, Antioch fell into their hands in 1098, and on June 15, 1099, Jerusalem was stormed by the sick and starving crusaders. Jerusalem was organized into a kingdom, and Godfrey of Bouillon became ruler, with the title of "Baron and Advocate of the Holy Sepulchre." Bohemund the Norman became Prince of Antioch, and Baldwin, brother of Godfrey, became Count of Edessa. Warriors from the Scandinavian kingdoms also participated in the first crusade, but as they joined the main army in smaller bands, little is known of their fate or achievements. In 1097 a Danish noble, Svein by name, a member of the royal family, led a band of crusaders to Palestine. They took part in the capture of Edessa, and marched to join in the siege of Antioch, but on the way they were betrayed into the power of the Mohammedans, who cut them down to the last man.

In 1102 the Norwegian *lendermand*, Skofte Agmundsson, who had quarreled with King Magnus Barefoot, organized a crusading expedition to the Holy Land. Accompanied by his sons Finn, Agmund, and Thor, he sailed southward with five ships to Flanders, where he wintered. The next summer (1103) they sailed for Italy, but Skofte died in Rome. His sons also found their graves on Italian soil. "Thor died in Sicily," [1] says the saga, but whether this happened before they reached Palestine, or on the homeward journey, is not stated, though the saga narrative seems to show that the expedition

---

[1] *Heimskringla, Magnus Barefoot's Saga*, ch. 20.

reached the Holy Land. "When the sons of Magnus became kings, some men who had followed Skofte Agmundsson came from Jorsala-land (Jerusalem), and others from Myklegard (Constantinople). They were very renowned, and brought many new tidings, and these accounts made many desirous of going thither." [1] The news of the crusades, which by this time had reached Norway through many channels, reawakened the old spirit of martial adventure among the Norsemen at home no less than among their kinsmen in Normandy and southern Italy. The transition from Viking expeditions to crusades, already noticeable in Olav Tryggvason's career as crusading Christian king, was neither great nor sudden, and it was now finally accomplished through the general change of conditions as well as through the growth of Christian spirit. We cannot doubt that many were eagerly awaiting an opportunity to go to Palestine to fight against the Mohammedans, but we hear nothing of any great religious enthusiasm, and it appears that most of them were actuated less by Christian zeal than by love of war and adventure, and the prospects of gain and renown. "They asked of the kings that one of them should be the leader of those who wished to join in this enterprise," says the saga. "The kings agreed to this, and both of them together fitted out an expedition in which many leading men took part, both *lendermænd* and *storbønder*. When everything was ready, it was decided that Sigurd should lead the expedition, but Eystein should rule the kingdom in the name of both." [2] This undertaking was a regularly planned and prepared crusade against the Turks in Palestine. The preparations lasted four years. A fleet of sixty ships was fully equipped and manned with 10,000 volunteer warriors from all parts of Norway. King Sigurd set sail from Horda-land, possibly from Bergen, in the fall of 1107, and went to England, where he was well received by King Henry I., who offered him his

[1] *Heimskringla, The Saga of the Sons of Magnus*, ch. I.

[2] *Morkinskinna*, 25. King Eirik Eiegod of Denmark, and his queen Bodil, made a pilgrimage to the Holy Land in 1103. Eirik did not reach his destination. He died of fever in the island of Cyprus. Queen Bodil died on the Mount of Olives, at Jerusalem, and was buried in the valley of Josaphat. The fame of these royal pilgrims may have done much to stimulate the kings of Norway to undertake a crusade. See *Danmarks Riges Historie*, vol. I., p. 505 ff. Peter Friedrich Suhm, *Forsøg til Forbedringer i den gamle danske og norske Historie*, p. 159 ff.

friendship and assistance, since he was engaged in so praiseworthy an undertaking.[1] Sigurd spent the winter at the gay English court, and gave many rich presents to various English churches. In the spring (1108) he continued his voyage, but he was much retarded by stormy weather, and did not reach Spain till late in the summer. He therefore decided to spend the winter there, and the governor of Galicia not only gave him permission to establish his winter quarters in that province, but promised, also, on certain conditions, to supply him with the necessary provisions throughout the winter. But the governor took this promise rather lightly, and by Christmas time King Sigurd and his men were in want. With sword in hand they decided to pay the governor a visit in his own castle, but he very discreetly abandoned it in haste, and they provisioned the fleet with the abundant stores which they found.

Early in the spring (1109), as they sailed southward along the west coast of Spain (now Portugal), they met a fleet of Moorish freebooters. The two fleets joined in battle, and after a hard fight, in which a great number of Moors fell, King Sigurd captured eight galleys, while the rest succeeded in making their escape.[2] He thereupon landed at Cintra in Portugal, which had been taken by the Moors, and aided Count Henry in capturing the city. He offered the Moorish garrison their lives if they would accept the Christian faith, but when they refused, he had them all put to death in the true fashion of crusaders. From Cintra he marched to Lisbon, which was also in the hands of the Moors. The sagas state that he battered down the walls and took the city, but this seems to be erroneous, since the place is known to have remained in the possession of the Moors after King Sigurd left.[3] The contemporary scald Haldor Skvaldre, who seems to have accompanied Sigurd, simply states that King Sigurd won his third victory by the *borg* which is called Lisbon.[4] It seems likely that he won a victory over the Moors

---

[1] *Morkinskinna*, 25. [2] *Fagrskinna*, ch. 243.

[3] *Morkinskinna*, 25 b. *Fagrskinna*, ch. 243.

[4] In the South a third victory,
able descendants of kings;
you won when you landed;
Lisbon the burh is called.
— *Heimskringla, Saga of the Sons of Magnus*, ch. 5.

outside of the city, but he did not capture the city itself. The sagas state, quite correctly, that Lisbon was the boundary between heathen and Christian Spain. The Moors had seized that part of Portugal which lies south of the River Tejo, while the rest was still in the hands of the Christians. In the so-called heathen Spain Sigurd captured a castle which is called "Alkasa" in the sagas, but as this name is only a corruption of *alcazar*, a Spanish loan-word from Arabic, meaning castle, as shown by Professor P. A. Munch, it is impossible to determine where this fortress was situated.

After leaving Spain he fought another successful engagement with the Moorish freebooters, who at this time controlled the Mediterranean Sea. He then continued his voyage eastward till he reached the Island of Formentera, in the Balearic Isles. Here the freebooters had established a stronghold in a cave in the side of a mountain. The steep ascent leading to the entrance of the cave was protected by a breastwork of stone, and the cave itself was divided into two parts, or chambers, of which the innermost seems to have served as a storehouse for the booty which they gathered from all the Mediterranean coasts. Sigurd tried to capture the cave, but his men were unable to ascend the steep incline against the showers of stones and missiles hurled upon them by the freebooters, who felt so secure in their inaccessible retreat that they jeered and ridiculed the Norsemen, and showed them costly articles to betoken their contempt. King Sigurd then took two boats, filled them with warriors, and lowered them by ropes from the top of the mountain before the entrance to the cave. The men in the boats shot with arrows, and compelled the Moors to abandon the breastwork and retreat into the cave. The assailants were now able to break through the stone wall in front of the entrance, and gain accession to the cave. The Moors fled to their inner chamber, but the Norsemen kindled a fire, and smoked them out. They were all killed, and all their booty fell into the hands of the Norsemen.[1] After visiting the islands of Iviza, Minorca, and, possibly, also Majorca,[2] where they also fought with the Moors,

---

[1] *Heimskringla*, *Saga of the Sons of Magnus*, ch. 6.

[2] "Sigurd, the king of the Norsemen, who in his earlier days deserved to be numbered among the bravest, tarried on his voyage to Jerusalem a whole winter in England after he had asked for the king's peace. He gave much

PLATE VIII

NORWEGIAN WOVEN TAPESTRY REPRESENTING THE ENTRANCE OF KING SIGURD THE CRUSADER INTO CONSTANTINOPLE.

they sailed to Sicily and Apulia, where they met their kinsmen the Normans, who had gained control of those parts of southern Italy. The Normans in Italy still felt themselves akin to the Norsemen, and Duke Roger of Sicily was married to Edla, the widow of King Knut the Saint of Denmark. King Sigurd and his army of crusaders were, therefore, received with the greatest joy and hospitality. "There was a splendid reception, and every day Duke Roger himself waited on King Sigurd at the table," says the saga. "But on the seventh day of the feast, after the men had taken a bath, King Sigurd took the duke by the hand and led him to the high-seat and gave him the title of 'King of Sicily.'"

Sigurd spent the winter in Sicily and arrived at Ascalon in Palestine in August, 1110.[1] Fulker of Chartres gives the following account of his achievements in Palestine:[2]

"In the meantime there had landed at Joppa (Jaffa) a people called the Norsemen, whom God had stirred up to journey from the western ocean to Jerusalem. Their fleet consisted of sixty ships. Their leader was a young man of exceedingly fine appearance, a

gold to the churches, and after the west wind had opened the gates of spring and quieted the ocean, he again went on board and set sail. He terrified with his sword the Balearic Isles, called Maiorica and Minorca, and left them an easy prey for William of Montpellier. From there he went to Jerusalem, which he reached successfully with all his ships except one." William of Malmesbury, *De Gestis Regum Anglorum*, V.

[1] The *Heimskringla* and other sagas state that Sigurd landed at Akersborg (*i.e.* Acre), but many contemporary ecclesiastics in other countries have written about the crusades, and as they seem to have had better knowledge of the geography of Palestine, their statements on such points must be regarded as reliable. These sources are found in *Samlinger til det norske Folks Sprog og Historie*, vol. I. The *Historia Hierosolymitanae Expeditionis*, by Albert Canonicus of Aachen, says: "In the meantime Magnus, a brother of the Norwegian king (Magnus is a mistake for Sigurd Magnusson), arrived in the harbor of Ascalon with a well equipped and strong army with forty warships and 10,000 warriors, after having spent two years on the voyage over the great ocean from his kingdom. He anchored for a day near the city to see if any one would come against him, either by sea or land, with whom he might come into a fight either purposely or inadvertently, but as the people of Ascalon remained quiet and did not dare to come out, he landed the following day at Joppa (Jaffa), as he was desirous of worshiping in Jerusalem," ch. 26.

[2] *Gesta Peregrinatium Francorum cum armis Hierusalem Pergentium*, ch. 36.

brother of the king of that country. As the king (Baldwin) had
returned to Jerusalem, he rejoiced exceedingly over their arrival,
spoke kindly to them, admonished them, and asked them out of
love of God to stay a while in the land to which they had come,
and help him to spread Christianity; they could then, after having
served the cause of Christ in some way, give thanks to God when
they returned to their own country. They assented gladly, and
answered that they had come to the Holy Land with no other intention; they promised to follow him with their fleet wherever he would
go with his army, if he would provide them with the necessary provisions. This was agreed to and fulfilled. They first decided to
go to Ascalon, but later they laid the better plan of attacking and
besieging the city of Sidon. The king led his army from Ptolemaida,
which is now generally called Achon, while the Norsemen, well armed,
sailed from the harbor of Jaffa. The fleet of the emir of Babylonia
lay at that time hidden in the harbor of Tyre. The Saracens annoyed the Christians, our pilgrims, on their buccaneering expeditions, and they provisioned by various routes the sea coast towns
which were still in the hands of the king of Babylonia, but when
they heard about the Norsemen, they did not venture to leave the
harbor of Tyre, for they did not dare to fight with them. When the
king came to Sidon, he laid siege to the city, while the Norsemen
attacked it from the sea. With war machines they so terrified the
inhabitants that the garrison asked the king to be permitted to depart
unharmed, he could then, if he wished, keep the people of the city,
and use them for tilling the soil. This was asked and granted. The
garrison retired, but the landsfolk remained in peace according to
the agreement. The sun had visited the archer (the constellation)
nineteen times when the Sidonians in the month of December (19th
of December, 1110) surrendered their city." This account, which
is in full accord with the sagas, is substantiated also by a number of
other sources.[1] Sigurd claimed no reward for aiding in the capture

---

[1] *Heimskringla, Saga of the Sons of Magnus*, ch. II. *Fagrskinna*, 245.
Albert of Aachen, *Historia Hierosolymitanae Expeditionis*, lib. xi., ch.
31–34. Archbishop William of Tyre, *Historia Rerum in Partibus Trans-
marinis Gestarum a Tempore Successorum Mahumeth usque ad Annum Domini
mclxxxiv.*, lib. xi., ch. 14. *Secunda Pars Historiae Hierosolimitanae*, A.D. 1110.

of Sidon, but Baldwin distributed rich presents among his men, and gave him a chip of the Holy Cross, which Sigurd promised under oath to preserve at the shrine of St. Olav. He also made a vow to introduce the system of tithes in Norway, and to do everything in his power to secure the establishment of an archbishopric in Nidaros. King Sigurd left Palestine shortly after the capture of Sidon, and went to Constantinople, where he was magnificently entertained by Emperor Alexios Comnenos (called Kirialax in the sagas). Sigurd and his men were escorted through the golden portal, *porta aurea*, through which the Emperors alone entered the city when they returned in triumph from successful military campaigns. They were quartered in the Blachernæ palace, and were entertained with games in the hippodrome at the Emperor's expense. When Sigurd left, he gave Alexios all his ships, and many of his men remained in Constantinople, and entered the service of the Emperor. Sigurd and his crusaders returned through Bulgaria, Hungary, Austria, and Germany. About midsummer they arrived in Schleswig, where the Danish jarl Eiliv entertained them. King Nicolas (Nils) of Denmark, who was married to Sigurd's stepmother, Margareta Fredkulla, received him with the greatest hospitality, accompanied him through Jutland, and gave him a fully equipped ship on which he returned to Norway in July, 1111. He was received with great rejoicing, and his brother Eystein, who had ruled the kingdom during his three and a half years' absence, cheerfully surrendered to him the share of the kingship which he had held in trust. "It was a common opinion," says the saga, "that no one had made a more memorable expedition from Norway." He was called Sigurd Jorsalafarer (Jorsal = Jerusalem), a name by which he is generally known in history.[1]

54. King Eystein Magnusson's Reign. The Acquisition of Jæmtland

During Sigurd's absence Eystein ruled the kingdom with great ability. He showed rare talent for administration, and furthered a

[1] Paul Riant, *Skandinavernes Korstog og Andagtsreiser til Palestina*, Copenhagen, 1868.

peaceful development with such devoted interest that his reign is remembered as one of the most benign and prosperous in the history of
the country. He is described as a man of medium size with blue
eyes and light curly hair. He had acquired extensive legal knowledge, and he distinguished himself through equanimity and great
wisdom in council. The people loved him highly for his friendly
and cheerful disposition and his love of peace and justice.

His brother Sigurd Jorsalafarer (Crusader) was not like him
He had auburn hair, and was tall and well-built, but not good looking. He was a great athlete and a very ambitious prince, but usually
gloomy and reticent. At times he showed a violent temper, and he
often punished offenders severely; but he was generous to a fault,
frank, brave, and upright. The more untoward traits of his character can only be explained as an inception of insanity, which in his
later years enveloped him in mental darkness.

With the instinct of a statesman King Eystein soon took steps
to join the province of Jæmtland to the Norwegian kingdom. This
independent border district had been settled in early days by colonists from Trøndelagen, and when Harald Haarfagre had won all
Norway, many people who were dissatisfied with the new order
of things emigrated into Jæmtland and the neighboring districts,
Helsingland and Herjedalen. We have seen that in the time of
Haakon the Good the people of Jæmtland voluntarily placed themselves under the authority of the king of Norway, as they preferred
his overlordship to that of the Swedish king. This step proves
that they considered themselves as Norsemen. The province belonged to Norway till in the time of King Olav the Saint, when it
was seized by the king of Sweden, and it remained a Swedish dependency until it was reunited with Norway in Eystein's reign.[1]

In ecclesiastical affairs, however, it always formed a part of the
diocese of Upsala. Herjedalen, which is often mentioned together
with Jæmtland, belonged to the diocese of Trondhjem, and seems
always to have been a Norwegian province. "King Eystein sent
messengers to Jæmtland to the wisest and most powerful men,"

---

[1] P. A. Munch, *Det norske Folks Historie*, vol. II., p. 596 ff. *Samlinger
til det norske Folks Sprog og Historie*, vol. I., p. 34 ff., *Nye Bidrag til den
gamle norske Provins Jæmtlands Historie.*

says the saga, "and invited them to visit him. He received with great cordiality those who came, and gave them valuable gifts. He also sent presents to some who did not come, and in this way he gained the friendship of all those who ruled that country. He spoke to them and showed them that the people of Jæmtland had acted unwisely in withdrawing their allegiance and their taxes from the kings of Norway. He mentioned that the people of that province had given their allegiance to Haakon Adalsteinsfostre (Haakon the Good), and had long remained subject to the Norwegian kings. He pointed out how many necessary articles they could get from Norway, and how much trouble it would cause them to get what they needed from the king of Sweden. He succeeded so well with his arguments that the people of their own accord made an offer, and asked that they might be allowed to pledge their allegiance to King Eystein, which they termed their need and necessity. The union was brought about in the following manner: The leading men asked the people to take an oath of fealty, and afterwards they went to King Eystein and gave him the country." [1]

How the province of Jæmtland could be enticed away from Sweden and joined to Norway without causing an open rupture between the two countries it is not easy to explain, even if according to Eystein's view of the matter Norway still had a valid claim to this border district which Sweden had unrightfully seized. The inactivity of the Swedish king must have been due to circumstances which made it impossible for him to pay attention to this distant province, but what these circumstances were is left to conjecture. If King Inge Stenkilsson was still alive, which is not known, he was now an aged man, possibly too weak to take a very active part in the affairs of state. If he was dead, it is not improbable that jealousy between rival candidates for the throne had temporarily crippled the government, and that King Eystein used such a moment of weakness for his shrewd and well-planned move.

Monasticism made its appearance in Norway at this time, and several monasteries of the Benedictine order were built during the twelfth century. Sigurd Ulstreng founded a monastery of this order, probably in 1104, and King Eystein began the erection of a St. Michael's

---

[1] *Heimskringla, The Saga of the Sons of Magnus*, ch. 15.

church and monastery at Nordness, near Bergen. The buildings were large stone structures, but it is not known whether they were finished in Eystein's time. It has been thought that the St. Albanus monastery at Selja, and the three nunneries, Gimsø at Skien, Nonnesæter in Oslo, and Bakke in Trondhjem, were also founded in Eystein's reign,[1] but this is doubtful. The St. Albanus monastery is not heard of till in King Sverre Sigurdsson's reign, and the nunneries are not mentioned till in the second half of the twelfth century. The rules of the order required the Benedictine monks to divide the time not spent in devotional exercises between physical labor, especially gardening and horticulture, and study, which consisted chiefly in the copying of books and manuscripts. They introduced many new varieties of plants and trees, and the fruit raising which now flourishes in many districts of Norway was developed mainly by their skillful and painstaking efforts. To their literary activity we are indebted especially for some valuable works on the early history of Norway, the most noteworthy of which is the "Historia de Antiquitate Regum Norwagiensium," by Theodricus Monachus.

Owing to the interest of the kings in religious matters, Norway was fast swinging into line with regard to church organization and ecclesiastical affairs generally. The diocese of Bergen was divided, and a new bishopric was established at Stavanger. No city had yet been founded there, but wharves had been built on the fine harbor, which was visited by merchant ships in great numbers. When the bishop's residence was located there, a new development began, and Stavanger is spoken of as a city already in the latter half of the twelfth century. Reinald (Reginald), a Benedictine monk from Winchester, England, was made bishop, and his first thought seems to have been to erect a cathedral church, which of necessity had to adorn every bishop's seat in those times. It was a great undertaking, as the cathedrals were built by the church, not by the state, but the Catholic bishops were men of wealth and power; they had the rank of jarls, and enjoyed a princely income. Large tracts of land had been granted to the diocese, and when King Sigurd the Crusader introduced the system of tithes, the bishops also received one-fourth of

[1] Chr. C. A. Lange, *De norske Klostres Historie i Middelalderen*, p. 17 f.

PLATE IX

THE STAVANGER CATHEDRAL.

INTERIOR OF THE STAVANGER CATHEDRAL.

this new revenue. They had also a considerable income from royal fiefs and from fines paid by those who transgressed against the ordinances of the church. For undertakings of special importance the bishop could also call upon the people for a general contribution. A cathedral was erected, which is still the pride of the beautiful city of Stavanger. It was built in the Romanesque style after the pattern of the Winchester cathedral in England, and seems to have been completed about 1150.[1] It was dedicated to St. Swithun, bishop of Winchester in England (837–862), and a shrine containing some relics of the saint, which had been brought from England for the purpose, was deposited in the church. A new bishopric was also established at Hólar in Iceland in 1106,[2] and a cathedral was erected at Kirkebø in the Faroe Islands, where a diocese was now permanently established. The attempt of Bishop Eirik Gnupsson of Greenland to Christianize the Skrælings in Vinland has already been mentioned elsewhere. He was, evidently, lost on the voyage, as he was never again heard of. King Eystein erected churches in Trondhjem, and at Trondenes in Nordland. In Bergen he built a royal residence, which was said to be the finest wooden structure in Norway. Close to this hall he built the Apostle church, which was used as a royal chapel. Eystein's efforts were wholly directed towards the peaceful upbuilding of the kingdom through internal improvements and the encouragement of commerce. He constructed a new harbor at Agdenes, at the entrance to the Trondhjemsfjord, and improved the harbor of Sundholm Sound near Bergen. On the mountain tops along the coast he caused beacons to be erected for the guidance of mariners. These improvements were of importance to commerce, which was developing rapidly at this time, especially through the increased export of herring and codfish.

The numerous pilgrimages to St. Olav's shrine had increased travel across the Dovre Mountains, but as the journey through the wilds from eastern Norway to Trondhjem was difficult and dangerous,

---

[1] Tveteraas, *Stavanger Domkirke, Stavanger Aftenblad*, April 12, till June 1, 1911. *Stavanger Domkirke, etc., udgivet av Foreningen til norske Fortidsmindesmerkers Bevaring, med Text av N. Nicolaysen*, Christiania, 1896.

[2] A. D. Jørgenson, *Den nordiske Kirkes Grundlæggelse og første Udvikling*, p. 875.

Eystein erected three mountain stations, where travelers could find shelter and refreshments. Though primarily intended for pilgrims, these stations proved to be such an aid to all travelers that the traffic across the mountains was greatly increased.

The relation between the kings, though peaceful, was not cordial, and at times it was marred by more serious clashes provoked by Sigurd's jealous disposition and violent temper. Snorre has pictured an altercation between them in the "Heimskringla," in the happiest vein of his inimitable style. The episode as he describes it must be regarded as drama rather than history, but it gives a most vivid picture of the temper and character of the two kings: "One winter the kings Eystein and Sigurd were entertained in Oplandene, and each had his own residence. But as the estates where they were to dwell were not far apart, their followers agreed that the kings should stay together, and that they should visit one another in turn. At first they were all assembled at the home of King Eystein; but in the evening when the drinking-feast began, the ale was not to their liking, and the men were reticent. Eystein said: 'The men are silent, but it is more in keeping with custom to be merry over the drinking-cup. Let us have some merriment, and there will still be good cheer among the men. It is proper, brother Sigurd, that we should begin some jocular conversation.' But Sigurd replied curtly: 'Be as talkative as you please, but allow me to be quiet.' King Eystein said: 'It has often been customary at the drinking-feast that one compares himself with another, so let it be now.' But Sigurd remained silent. 'I see,' said Eystein, 'that I have to begin this diversion. I will compare myself with you, brother. I must mention that we are equal in honor and possessions, and there is no difference in our descent or education.' King Sigurd answered: 'Do you remember that I could throw you in a wrestling match whenever I pleased, though you are a year older?' Eystein said: 'But I also remember that you did not win in the contests which require agility.' Sigurd said: 'Do you remember that when we were swimming I could duck you under whenever I pleased?' Eystein answered: 'I swam as far as you did, and I could swim equally well under water. I could also skate so well that I know of no one who could compete with me in that sport, but you could not skate better than an ox.' Sigurd said: 'It seems to me that it is a sport better fitted for chieftains to be able to shoot well with bow and arrow, but you cannot use my bow if you draw it with your feet.' Eystein answered: 'I am not so strong with the bow, but there is little difference in our ability to hit the mark. In skiing I am your superior, and that has hitherto been accounted a fine sport.' Sigurd said: 'It seems to me especially befitting a chieftain that he, who is to be the leader of others, should be tall and strong, and better able to wield the weapon than other men, so that he can be easily recognized where many are assembled.' King Eystein said: 'It is no less important that a man is handsome, he is then easily recognized in a multitude; that, too, appears to me to be a quality of a chieftain, for fine clothes suit well a handsome man. I am also better versed in the laws than you are, and when we speak, I am more eloquent.' Sigurd said: 'It may be that you know more tricks in law than I do, for I have had other things to contend with. No one denies that you have a smoother tongue, but many say that you do not always keep your word, but that you take your promises lightly; that you seemingly agree with every one you talk with, and that is no kingly conduct.' King Eystein said: 'When people bring their suits before me, my first thought is to bring the cause of each party to a conclusion that will seem best to him; but then comes also the counterpart, and the quarrel is then often adjusted in a way satisfactory to both. It often happens that I promise to do what people ask of me, for I desire that all should go away well pleased. But I have the choice, also, if I wish, to do like you, and threaten everybody with punishment, and I have heard no one complain that you do not keep your promise.' King Sigurd said: 'It has been generally recognized that the expedition which I made when I left our land was an achievement worthy of a chieftain, but you stayed at home like your father's daughter.' King Eystein answered: 'Now you touched the ulcer. I should not have started this conversation if I could make no reply on this point. It should almost seem as if I sent you from home like my sister when you were equipped for the expedition.' King Sigurd said: 'I suppose you have heard that I fought many battles in Turkey, which you have heard mentioned. I was victorious in all of them, and secured a great deal of valuable booty, such as never has been brought to this land. I was most honored where I met the best men, but I am afraid that you are still the home-bred greenhorn.' King Eystein said: 'I have heard that you fought some battles abroad, but it was of more value to our country that I erected five churches from the very foundations. I also constructed a harbor at Agdenes where there was no harbor before, and where every sailor had to pass in going north or south along the coast. I also built the stone tower in Sundholm Sound, and the royal hall in Bergen, while you sent Saracens to the devil in Turkey, which, I think, was of little benefit to our kingdom.' King Sigurd said: 'On my expedition I went even as far as the river Jordan, and I swam across the river; but on the river bank are some small trees, and among these I tied a knot, and spoke over it, that you, my brother, should untie it, or you should be spoken of accordingly.' King Eystein said: 'I will not untie the knot which you have tied for me, but I might have tied you a knot which you would have been far less able to untie, the time when you sailed with one ship into my fleet on your return.' After this they remained silent, and both were angry." [1]

A more serious collision between the two kings occurred in connection with the suit brought by King Sigurd against his *lendermand* Sigurd Ranesson, whom he accused of defalcation and fraud. Ranesson had been a faithful friend and companion of King Magnus Barefoot, and he was married to Skjaldvaar, King Magnus' sister. He had been appointed royal tax collector in Finmarken,[2] and had a monopoly on the trade with the Finns. King Sigurd accused him of having withheld sixty marks of silver yearly which rightfully

---

[1] *Heimskringla, The Saga of the Sons of Magnus,* ch. 21.

[2] Finmarken, as far as to the White Sea, was at this time a Norwegian dependency, and the Finns had to pay tribute to the kings of Norway. This tribute was farmed out to powerful nobles in Haalogaland in northern Norway. They agreed to pay the king a certain sum every year, and in turn they were granted exclusive right to trade with the Finns, and to collect what tribute they might get from them. This *syssel,* or office of royal tax collector, was regarded as very profitable.

The original sources dealing with this noted case have been collected and edited by Gustav Storm in his work *Sigurd Ranessons Proces,* Christiania, 1877. See also *Samlinger til det norske Folks Sprog og Historie,* vol. I., p. 112 ff.

belonged to the royal treasury, and Ranesson feared that, although he was innocent, the decision might go against him when the suit was brought before the *thing*. He therefore hastened to Viken, placed his case before King Eystein, and asked his assistance. Eystein investigated the matter carefully, and advised Ranesson as to what course to pursue.

In the spring King Eystein went to Trondhjem for the purpose of bringing about a reconciliation between Ranesson and King Sigurd. But Sigurd summoned a *bything* where he accused Ranesson of having collected taxes, and of having seized the trade with the Finns without authority. Eystein pointed out that the case was of such a character that it could not be tried at a *bything*, but would come under the jurisdiction of a regular *thing*, and Sigurd had to postpone the matter. He summoned a *thing* to meet within two weeks, and left the meeting with his men. At the appointed time both kings appeared at the *thing* with a large number of armed followers, and Sigurd reiterated his accusations against Ranesson, who maintained that he was innocent, and that the king had been misinformed. Eystein spoke very eloquently in Ranesson's behalf, and showed that if the case was to be settled according to law and justice, it would have to be brought before the Thrandarnesthing, as the *thing* which King Sigurd had summoned had no jurisdiction over a vassal. After the *lagmænd* (those learned in the law) had carefully weighed the matter, they declared the point raised by King Eystein to be well taken. The *thing* had to be adjourned, and King Sigurd summoned Ranesson to plead his cause at the Thrandarnesthing within a fortnight.

Both kings gathered strong forces and met on the day appointed. "When King Eystein approached the *thing*, he said to Ranesson: 'What offer doest thou intend to make, and how wilt thou defend thyself to-day at the *thing?*' Ranesson answered: 'From you I expect to get counsel and help.' Eystein said: 'Come now hither, if thou wilt follow my advice, and give me thy hand as a token that thou wilt transfer thy cause to me. It is proper that we brothers should look each other in the eye, and see who is best versed in the law.' This was done, and Eystein went to the *thing* with his men." King Sigurd repeated his charges against Ranesson, and Eystein again spoke in his defense, but when Sigurd declared that he was determined to have the case settled according to law, King Eystein said: "I have indeed said, brother, that you should bring this case against Ranesson before the Thrandarnesthing, but since a slight change has now taken place, so that the kings themselves are parties in the case, it cannot be decided at a *fylkesthing*, but must be brought before the *lagthing*. The Frostathing alone has now jurisdiction in this case, and there it must be decided, if it must absolutely be decided according to law. I have taken upon myself this case against Sigurd Ranesson, so that we kings are now parties in it. This you cannot gainsay." King Sigurd declared that he would not yield, and he summoned Eystein to appear before the Frostathing. But this *thing* had already been adjourned, and would not assemble again till the following summer.

When the *lagthing* convened, King Sigurd preferred his charges against Ranesson in the most carefully prepared legal form, and Eystein undertook to conduct the defense. The *lendermand* Jón Mornev, a man very learned in the law, was leader and spokesman for the *lagrette*.[1] It is clear that *lagmænd* were also present at the thing.[2] Ranesson was able to prove that King Magnus Barefoot had granted him the trade with the Finns as a monopoly, and that he had made the provision that this grant should also continue throughout the reign of his sons. It was for the *thing*, then, to decide whether Magnus could make a grant for a period extending beyond his own reign. The *lagmænd* found that the king could make permanent grants, but in order to be valid such grants had to be published at all the *lagthings* (Frostathing, Gulathing, etc.), but Ranesson had no witnesses to prove that he had complied with the law on this point. King Sigurd declared that he would not recognize this to be the law, that a

---

[1] The *lendermænd* were not chosen to the *lagrette* except with the consent of the *haulds* or *bønder*.

[2] The *lagmænd* were a sort of judges who declared and interpreted the law. The decisions to be voted by the *thing* were prepared by the *lagrette*. The office corresponded somewhat to that of *lovsigemand* in Iceland. About the age of the institution of *lagmænd* in Norway there has been considerable discussion, but it is clear that it existed at this time, and even much earlier. See Konrad Maurer, *Das Alter des Gesetz-sprecheramtes in Norwegen;* Ebbe Hertzberg, *Grundtrækkene i den ældste norske Proces;* Gustav Storm, *Sigurd Ranessons Proces.*

king could make a grant for a longer period than his own reign, and maintained that it had now been proven that Ranesson had no right to the trade with the Finns. Eystein maintained that the king had the right to make such grants, but as it seemed impossible to wholly remove all doubt on this point, the chieftains proposed that the kings should cast lots as to whose view should prevail. To this they consented. Sigurd was successful, and he declared his view to be adopted. The point was now raised whether Ranesson had gained possession of the wares which he had collected, without the consent of the owners. The *lendermand* Bergthor Bokk testified against him on this point, and King Sigurd demanded that the defendant should be declared guilty and punished. But Eystein had not yet exhausted all his resources in this legal duel. He said that it seemed to him to be very unjust to find Ranesson guilty when King Magnus had made the grant in behalf of his sons, and it had hitherto not been revoked. He requested the *thing* to pause a few moments before rendering a decision, and this was granted. He then called witnesses to prove that the case had already been dismissed at three previous *things*, and showed that when a case, because of irregular procedure, had been dismissed thrice it could not again be brought before a *thing*. This law point was accepted by the *lagrette* as applying to the case, and no decision could be given by the *thing*. We can scarcely blame King Sigurd for waxing wroth when he again found himself worsted in this way. He left the *thing*, and vowed that since Eystein had blocked justice by shrewd tricks he would now seek it in some other way.

The relations between the brothers were now strained to the breaking point, and civil war seemed imminent. In the evening after the *thing* adjourned Eystein returned to his residence, and talked with his men about the trial just concluded. He asked Ranesson what he thought of the outcome, and Ranesson answered that he was very thankful to the king for what he had done for him. The "Morkinskinna" continues: "Shortly afterwards Sigurd Ranesson found an opportunity to leave the house. It was late in the evening, and when he had assured himself that no one noticed him, he walked hastily away alone. He had no mantle, he wore a scarlet coat and blue trousers buttoned outside the coat and buckled about the waist; in his hand he carried a javelin with a handle so short that his hand touched the iron. He walked down the street, and did not stop until he came to the wharf which touched the stern of King Sigurd's ship. A man sat there keeping guard. Ranesson asked permission to enter the ship, but the guard refused. 'Choose then,' said Ranesson, 'leave the wharf now, or this spear will pierce you.' The guard withdrew, and he entered the ship and walked forward towards the front. There the men were seated by the tables, and no one noticed him until he knelt before the king and said: 'I do not wish, King Sigurd, that you brothers, as it now appears, should begin war against one another for my sake. I will rather give myself and my head into your power. Do with me as you please, for I will rather die than cause hostilities between you and your brother.' Many of the men interceded for him, and begged Sigurd to show him mercy since he had surrendered himself to the king. King Sigurd said: 'You are truly a noble man, Sigurd Ranesson, and you have taken a course which is best for us all. It looked as if a misfortune was about to happen, so great that God alone could know the outcome. I had decided to go up to Julvold in the morning with my men, and fight with King Eystein. I am now willing to bring about a reconciliation if you will leave the matter to my decision.' This Ranesson did. King Sigurd said: 'I will not delay settlement, for this case has been long drawn out. You must pay a fine of fifteen marks, which sum is to be paid in full to-morrow before the services are at an end in the Christ church. My brothers intended to disgrace me, but I will guard their honor as carefully as my own. You must pay five marks to King Eystein and five marks to King Olav,[1] and you must pay them before you pay me. This fine you are to pay in pure gold, for I have been told that you have grown rich in gold from taxes which you have collected. But if you do not pay this money exactly in the manner which I have now stated, the reconciliation between us is at an end.' Sigurd Ranesson answered: 'I thank you, my lord, for your willingness to become reconciled, howsoever it may be with my wealth.' Sigurd Ranesson had no gold,

[1] The boy king was still living. He died in 1115, fifteen years of age. Since Ranesson was fined for fraudulently appropriating to his own use money collected as royal taxes, it was proper to divide the fine equally among the kings, as Sigurd did.

but he succeeded in borrowing five marks from his friends. This sum he first offered King Eystein, but he refused to accept it, and told Ranesson that he would make him a present of it. When he brought the gold to King Olav, he said that he would do as his brother Eystein had done. Finally he offered Sigurd the five marks. The king said that he would give him the gold, if he would be his friend in case hostilities should ever break out between him and Eystein. Ranesson answered: 'I hope that you will never again disagree, for I wish both you and your brothers well; but however much gold will be at stake, yes, even if it should cost me my life, I will esteem no one higher than King Eystein as long as I live.' The king then gave him the gold without condition. Ranesson thanked him, and invited the king to dine with him that same day with as many followers as he wished to bring, and King Sigurd accepted the invitation. After mass he went to Ranesson's house with forty men. When they entered the hall, they found it beautifully decorated with tapestries and weapons; the walls were hung with shields, and everything was so elegantly arranged that the king and his men were quite surprised. The feast was very magnificent and lasted the whole day. Ranesson and his men waited on the guests, carried in beverages and everything which they wanted. When they were gone, so that the king was alone with his followers, he said to them: 'Where have you ever seen a house of a vassal furnished like this? You will not find the like even in the halls of kings. It surpasses anything that is to be seen anywhere.' Bergthor Bokk answered: 'Fine weapons these are, indeed, and everything is beautifully arranged, but it would have been a greater honor for our host if he had owned some of these fine things himself and had not borrowed them all.' King Sigurd became offended and replied: 'We can see how many friends the man has, when we notice that he can get from others everything which he wishes; but thou hast not spoken kindly.' Ranesson now stepped into the hall, and he had heard what had been said. When the bells tolled for the vespers, the king prepared to leave. Ranesson gave him costly presents and invited him to return after the vespers to drink a toast to the memory of Christ.[1] This invita-

---

[1] This was a continuation of an old heathen custom of drinking toasts to the honor of the gods.

tion the king accepted. When King Sigurd and his men returned to the hall, all the shields had been removed except an old shield and a mantle which hung by the table where the drinks were served. 'A sudden change has taken place while we were gone,' said Sigurd. 'It is but to be expected, my lord,' said Ranesson, 'that each one wants his articles returned. I own no shield save this old one which hangs yonder, and whether or not I am to keep that you shall decide. The story of this shield is as follows: We accompanied your father, King Magnus, on his expedition to Ireland, and we landed for the last time on the Irish coast, which we should not have done. An invincible Irish army came against us; a battle began, as you know, and the great misfortune happened that King Magnus your father, Stallare Eyvind Olboge, and many other brave heroes fell. Our army fled, and all hurried to the ships as fast as they could; but I was not among the first to flee. As they hurried to the ships, a deep swamp near the coast retarded their flight. They attempted to jump over it, and some succeeded, but others did not, and many of those who did not get across were stabbed with spears. When we approached the swamp, I saw a man in front of me; he had this shield on his back, and this mantle about him. When he noticed that it was difficult to cross the swamp, he first threw away the shield, then he tore off his mantle He wore a silk cap, and the most honorable thing he did, it seemed to me, was that he did not also throw away the cap. It seemed to me that this man was Bergthor Bokk; but Vidkun Jónsson knows, for he was present when I picked up the shield and the mantle. In the battle I had had no shield. Since then I have kept this shield, and now, my lord, you may decide whether I or Bergthor should own it.' The king answered curtly: 'Keep thou the shield.' The king left, and Bergthor was very angry. Shortly afterward King Olav died, as has already been told; Sigurd and Eystein were both kings, but from this time on they were not real friends, though peace was maintained while they lived."

King Eystein died in 1122, thirty-three years of age, at Hustad in Romsdal, and was interred in the Christ church in Trondhjem. "At no man's bier had there been so many mourners since the death of King Magnus the Good, the son of St. Olav," says the "Heimskringla."

The report of the case against Sigurd Ranesson is one of the most valuable documents in all saga literature dealing with Norse jurisprudence. It brings to view a highly developed legal system adapted to an intricate court procedure by astute lawyers, whose skillful pleadings remind us of the proceedings in modern common-law courts. The laws had not been made by great law-givers, but had been gradually evolved from the sense of justice of the whole people. The *things*, both local and superior, gave the people an opportunity to participate directly in the deliberations on all important public questions. All controversies were adjudicated there, and the decisions rendered expressed the best sentiment and most intelligent will of the community. This system developed in time an intimate knowledge of the law, the love for its details, the pride in its intricacies, but also the profound respect for its authority which was the virtue and strength of the Norse social organization. The thing-system developed in the people an ability for self-government, a sense for legal justice, a regard for the rights of the individual which made arbitrary decisions and tyrannical government impossible. The people in council at the *thing* was the highest tribunal and authority in the land, before which even kings had to plead their cause. During the centuries in which the life and traits of the Norsemen were rapidly fashioned into a permanent national character, these institutions of popular self-government were developing in the Norwegian people the spirit of freedom which expresses itself in an intense love for individual autonomy and national independence in all subsequent Norwegian history.

55. THE REIGN OF KING SIGURD THE CRUSADER

After Eystein's death, Sigurd ruled Norway for seven years, pursuant to the policy of peace and cultural development inaugurated by his brother. He made a crusade against the Swedish province of Småland, and forced the yet heathen inhabitants of this district to accept the Christian faith, but the expedition seems to have been undertaken for the purpose of fulfilling a promise which he had made in Palestine that he would do everything possible to further the cause of Christianity. Sigurd was imbued with a religious zeal of the crusading type characteristic of the age, and he sought earnestly to improve the organization of the church, and to give the clergy more power and greater independence of secular authorities. By these efforts he was clearly assisting the church in its efforts to establish itself as an independent power and supreme authority, though he was, possibly, unable to foresee that this new power, once securely established, would recoil most forcibly against the royal authority which had been instrumental in creating it. The statement of Ordericus Vitalis [1] that Sigurd first built monasteries in Norway and established permanent bishoprics there is, indeed, erroneous, but he established a fourth bishopric at Stavanger, though the year when this happened cannot be determined. He continued the work on the Christ church in Bergen, and completed the St. Halvard's church in Oslo. He had also promised, while in Jerusalem, to make his kingdom an archbishopric, but this promise he could not fulfill, as the Church of Norway was still too little developed to be organized into an independent ecclesiastical province. The most important step taken by Sigurd in church affairs was the introduction of the system of tithes. This was a tithe on incomes, and was to be substituted for the salaries which had hitherto been paid the priests and functionaries of the church. But the salaries were collected as before, and the clergy could now rejoice over a great increase in their income.

King Sigurd established his permanent residence in the trading town of Konghelle, in southeastern Norway, which through his efforts soon ranked with the most important cities in the kingdom. He erected a large castle there, and surrounded it with walls and moats. Inside the walls he built a royal residence, and erected the church of the Holy Cross, to which he gave the chip of the cross of Christ which he had received in Jerusalem. He had promised to deposit it in the Christ church in Trondhjem, but he donated it to this new church, as it seems, for the purpose of giving the growing town of Konghelle increased prestige. On the altar of the church he placed a costly chest which he had received from Prince Eirik Emune of Denmark, and also a *plenarium* [2] written with golden letters, which

---

[1] Ordericus Vitalis, *Historia Ecclesiastica*, X., p. 767.

[2] Plenarium (= complete book), so called because it contained a complete collection of texts for all Sundays in the year.

the patriarch of Jerusalem had given him. In speaking of the Norwegian cities at this time Ordericus Vitalis says: "Along the coast of Norway, by the sea, are found the following five cities: Bergen, Konghelle, Kaupang (Nidaros), Borg (Sarpsborg), and Oslo. There is also a sixth city by the name of Tunsberg, which lies eastward towards the Danes." Stavanger is not mentioned.

King Sigurd had suffered at times from serious mental aberrations which plunged him into the deepest anguish and despondency. As years passed, his mental condition grew worse, until he was seized with violent fits of insanity. On Pentecost Sunday, as he sat in his hall with his queen, Malmfrid, surrounded by many friends and guests, his men noticed to their horror that the king had suddenly become insane. He rolled his eyes wildly and stared around the hall and at his men. He grabbed a costly book written with golden letters, which he had brought from Constantinople, looked at the queen and said: "How much can be changed in a person's lifetime. When I came to this land, I had two things which I considered more precious than all others, this book and my queen. Now it seems to me that one is worse than the other. The queen does not know how horrid she looks. She has a goat-horn in her forehead, and the more lovely she looked then, the more horrid she looks now. This book is worth nothing." With these words he threw the book into the fire, and struck the queen in the face. She wept, but more because of the king's illness than because of his conduct towards her. Before the king stood a young *kertisveinn* (page), Ottar Birting, small in stature, but handsome and dark-haired. He snatched the book from the fire, and said to the king: "It is different now, my lord, from the day when you returned with honor and glory to Norway, and all your friends hastened to meet you, and greeted you with reverence as their king. Now days of sorrow have come. Many of your friends have assembled to celebrate this festival, but they cannot be glad because of your sad condition. Be good, my lord, and take my advice. Console with your kindness the queen, whom you have grievously wronged, and also your chieftains, your *hird*, your friends, and your servants." "What!" shouted the king, "darest thou ugly peasant boy of the humblest descent to give me advice?" He jumped up and raised the sword with both hands over the boy's head. But Birting looked at him calm and fearless, and the king dropped the side of the sword on his shoulder, and sat down without saying a word. Everybody in the hall was silent. The king had now regained his composure and looked around with calmness. "But late one tries his own men, and learns how they really are," he said. "Here my best friends are assembled: *lendermænd, stallarer, skutilsveinar*, and the foremost men in the land, but no one served me as well as this page, whom, I suppose, you consider very inferior to yourselves. This page is Ottar Birting; he has shown me the greatest devotion. Here I, an insane man, was about to destroy my treasure, but he saved it so that it was not damaged. Neither did he fear death, but he spoke to me in such words that I felt honored. He did not mention anything that could arouse my anger, although he had good reason to do so. He spoke so well that no one present could have spoken better. I jumped up in a rage and was going to strike him with the sword, but he was so brave that he showed no fear, therefore I did him no harm, for he ought not to die because of his virtue. But now, my friends, I will let you know how I intend to reward him. Hitherto he has been my *kertisveinn;* now he shall be my *lendermand*, and, more than that, he shall from this moment be the foremost among the *lendermænd*. Take, therefore, Ottar, thy seat among the *lendermænd*. Thou shalt serve no longer." Ottar became afterwards a prominent and highly honored man.[1]

It may have been largely due to his diseased state of mind that Sigurd finally put away Queen Malmfrid, and married a young lady, Cecelia, with whom he had fallen in love. Bishop Magne of Bergen refused to allow this marriage to be performed, but Sigurd finally induced Bishop Reinald of Stavanger to grant permission, by offering to contribute liberally to the Stavanger cathedral which the bishop was building.[2] King Sigurd died in Oslo in the spring of the year 1130, and was interred in the church of St. Halvard.

56. THE PERIOD OF CIVIL WARS. MAGNUS THE BLIND, HARALD GILLE, AND SIGURD SLEMBEDIAKN

King Sigurd the Crusader had his faults, but he was an able ruler, and was loved and respected by his subjects. His expeditions abroad had won him honor and distinction; at home he continued with ability and upright purpose the policy of peaceful development inaugurated by Eystein, which made the reign of the sons of Magnus Barefoot one of the most benign and prosperous in the early centuries of Norwegian history. The darkness of the long period of civil strife, bloodshed, and confusion which followed upon the death of Sigurd becomes still deeper when we view it against the background of the prosperous and peaceful era which preceded it. Instead of great national kings, the period of civil wars ushers past with kaleido-scopic rapidity arrogant and incompetent heirs to the throne, con-temptible pretenders, daring fortune-seekers, and worthless puppet kings who hold the throne for a day, to be swept from the political chessboard by plots and assassinations. Progress is retarded, and the energies of the nation wasted by the endless strife between rival candidates for the throne. The old writers look upon the period as if the wrath of heaven had suddenly fallen upon the country. Saxo Grammaticus compares the coming of Harald Gille to Norway with a destructive thunderstorm which suddenly swept over the country; [1] and the "Morkinskinna" lets King Sigurd prophesy that evil days would come after his death: "Unfortunate are you, Norsemen, that you have an insane king to rule over you, but the time will come when you would give red gold to have me for a king rather than Harald Gille or Magnus, the one cruel, the other foolish." [2]

But we need not explain the evils of this period either as the wrath of an offended deity, or as the result of the wickedness or in-competence of a single man. The civil wars were only a revival of old evils in an aggravated form, and they were due, in the main, to the same causes which had produced civil wars in earlier days. The circumstance that there was no regulated succession to the throne, but that all the sons of the king or kings had an equal claim to the kingship whether they were born in lawful wedlock or not was in

---

[1] Saxo Grammaticus, part III., book XIII. [2] *Morkinskinna*, p. 196.

itself sufficient cause for civil strife, as it became possible for any bold adventurer to put forward a claim to the throne, based on the assertion that he was of royal blood. During this period the various aspirants to the throne were weak and worthless men, children, or ill-starred adventurers. In such hands royal power could become nothing but a name and a shadow. The aristocracy gained control, and willingly aided the worthless kings in weakening and destroying one another. The chieftains fought, indeed, under various standards with seeming zeal for the claims and rights of the candidates whose cause they espoused, but in reality they sought their own advantage, and strengthened their own influence at the expense of the crown, which gradually lost its luster. The clergy, too, were eagerly reaching out for more prestige and power, and would gladly despoil the king of the authority and supervision which he had hitherto exercised in the church. This tendency became especially marked after the creation of the Norwegian archbishopric of Nidaros in 1152. In their efforts to despoil royalty of its power, we soon find the clergy firmly leagued with the aristocracy, and in time these two allied forces ruthlessly swept away the last vestige of real significance of the crown.

With a young woman of good family, Borghild of Dal, King Sigurd had the illegitimate son Magnus, whom he caused to be proclaimed successor to the throne. King Eystein had only one child, a daughter, Maria, and as Magnus was Sigurd's only son, it was expected that he would become sole king without opposition. But two years before the death of Sigurd a young man of Irish birth, Harald Gille, or Gilchrist, came to Norway, and claimed to be an illegitimate son of King Magnus Barefoot. Harald was tall and slender, with dark hair, and looked in all respects like an Irishman; he spoke the Norwegian language imperfectly, and never learned to speak it well; his whole career showed him to be a man of weak character and small ability. He asked King Sigurd to grant him permission to prove his royal extraction by ordeal, and after some deliberation Sigurd, strangely enough, granted this request, as he seems to have felt convinced that Harald was really his half-brother. Harald passed successfully through the ordeal of walking over red-hot plowshares, and Sigurd made him a member of his *hird* and became quite attached to him, though he made him swear a solemn oath that he would never attempt to become king of Norway as long as Magnus lived. Magnus seems to have regarded Harald Gille as a rival, and felt intense hatred for him from the start. This was in itself natural enough, but Magnus' own vicious character aggravated the situation, and foreboded serious trouble. Though yet very young he was avaricious, proud, quarrelsome, violent, and intemperate. This must have made it easy for the profligate but cheerful Harald Gille to secure a large number of friends and followers. When Sigurd died, Magnus succeeded to the throne, but Harald, who was in Tunsberg at the time, assembled a *thing* there, and when it became apparent that he had as many adherents as Magnus, he was also proclaimed king in spite of the oath he had taken. Magnus was forced to give his consent, and the two became joint kings, each with his own *hird*. The first few years passed quietly, but it was evident from the start that peace could not long be maintained. In 1134 hostilities commenced. Magnus collected a large army, and Harald Gille crossed the Dovre Mountains into Viken and Bohuslen, where he hoped to get support from his friend King Eirik Emune of Denmark. But he was completely defeated by Magnus, and fled to Denmark, where he received the province of Halland as a fief from the Danish king. The shortsighted and arrogant Magnus would listen to no advice, and he took no precaution to guard his kingdom against attack. Harald Gille gathered a new army and received substantial aid from King Eirik Emune. He came to Norway the same year, and quickly gained control of the southeastern districts, where he had many friends. When he reached Bergen, Magnus was still busy trying to gather an army, but he had no force to put in the field against his rival. Harald took him prisoner, caused him to be maimed and blinded, and imprisoned him in a monastery at Nidarholm, near Trondhjem. He was afterwards known as Magnus the Blind. The vicious Harald Gille pursued with innate cruelty the adherents of Magnus; killed, maimed, and blinded many of them to get possession of the royal treasures. He seized Bishop Reinald of Stavanger, and hanged him, because he could not pay the sum of twelve marks of gold which Harald Gille demanded when the bishop could not reveal the place where King Magnus had hidden his treasures. To hang a bishop like a common thief was regarded as the vilest of crimes, but we hear of no bull of excommunication issued against Harald, though a provincial church council was assembled shortly afterwards. Harald Gille had, indeed, become king, but during his short reign he was a tool in the hands of his followers. He spent his treasures with lavish hands, and let his men do as they pleased. This gave him a certain popularity among the leaders, who felt that he was weak and pliant enough to leave them in actual control. During his inglorious reign the foundation was gradually laid for a rule of the aristocracy through their most powerful representatives, the *lendermænd*.[1]

Very little is known of Harald Gille's reign. In 1135 the Wends appeared on the coast of Norway with a large fleet. They attacked the city of Konghelle, but it is nowhere recorded that King Harald made an attempt to aid the city. The castle was besieged and taken, the church and king's residence were burned, the city was pillaged, and a large number of the inhabitants were carried into captivity. The prosperity of the town was destroyed, and it never regained its prestige. It became henceforth an ordinary trading place, as it probably had been before the days of Sigurd the Crusader. An event of some importance was the successful attempt of Kale Kolsson, or Ragnvald Jarl, to get possession of the Orkneys. King Sigurd

---

[1] The office of *lendermand* was not hereditary. The king might make any one a *lendermand*, as we see in the case of Ottar Birting; but this was an exception. The son was generally appointed to succeed his father, and the *lendermænd* as a class belonged to the old aristocracy. They received the total income from large estates, and in return for these grants they had to entertain the king and his court when he traveled through the country, and in time of war they had to serve him with a certain number of armed men. In war the *lendermænd* commanded the military levies of their districts. According to the *Hirðskrá*, they were allowed to keep forty armed men, *huskarlar*, even in time of peace, as they had to exercise police authority and maintain peace and order in their districts. They were of higher rank than the *hirdmænd*, and when at court, they were *hirðstjórar*, or the chief officials of the *hird*. Together with the jarl, *stallare*, and *merkismaðr* they constituted the king's chief council. The rank of the *lendermænd* resembled that of the lords and barons in England, while the position of the *hirdmænd* resembled that of the knights. P. A. Munch, *Samlede Afhandlinger*, vol. I., p. 77 ff.; vol. III., p. 444 ff. See *Hirðskrá*, 19. *Norges gamle Love*, vol. II., p. 407. Gustav Storm, *Om ¦Lendermandsklassens Talrighed i tolvte og trettende Aarhundrede, Historisk Tidsskrift*, anden række, vol. IV., p. 129 ff. Ebbe Hertzberg, *En Fremstilling av det norske Aristokratis Historie*.

had granted Kale one-half of the Orkneys, and he gave him the name and title of Ragnvald Jarl, after Ragnvald Bruseson, one of the most renowned of the Orkney jarls. The grant seems to have been made for the purpose of uniting the islands more closely with Norway, since Jarl Paul, who ruled them at this time, sought to gain the friendship of the king of England, for the purpose, no doubt, of becoming able to throw off all allegiance to King Sigurd. When Magnus became king, he deprived Ragnvald both of his title and his possessions, but Harald Gille renewed the grant, and Ragnvald captured Jarl Paul, and made himself ruler over both the Shetland and Orkney groups. As he owed full allegiance to the king of Norway, the danger of a separation of these colonies from the mother country was averted.

Harald Gille had not been king very long when a new pretender appeared and claimed the right to share the throne with him. This was Sigurd Slembediakn, who also claimed to be a son of Magnus Barefoot. His mother, Thora, daughter of Saxe of Vik, was married to the priest Adalbrecht, and it does not appear with what show of right he called himself the son of King Magnus. He had been considered the son of Adalbrecht, and had been brought up for the church, but he began a life of adventure, visited the Holy Land, and engaged in trading expeditions to Ireland, Scotland, and the Orkneys. In Denmark he proved his paternity by ordeal, as Harald Gille himself had done in Norway, but when he presented himself before the king in Bergen, and asked him to recognize him as his brother, Harald refused. The leading men also refused to believe the story, though they were, probably, not troubled so much by the doubt of his veracity as by the fear that this gifted and resolute man might be able to exercise authority over them, if he were allowed to ascend the throne. Sigurd was imprisoned and placed on trial for killing Thorkel Fostre, the son of Sumarlide, in the Orkneys, and it seems that Harald sought to rid himself of the inconvenient rival by having him secretly carried away at night and drowned. But Sigurd, who suspected the design, pushed two of the guards into the sea, jumped from the boat and escaped to the mountains. For some time nothing was heard of him, but on the night of the 13th of December, 1136, he gained access with a few followers to the house where Harald Gille was sleeping after a drinking-feast, and killed him in his bed.

From the deck of a vessel in the harbor Sigurd addressed the people of Bergen, as soon as day dawned, and asked them to accept him as their king, but they refused. They gathered in large numbers on the shore and proclaimed him an outlaw. Sigurd then left Bergen and went to Hordaland, in southwestern Norway, where he was well received by the people. But Harald Gille's queen, Ingerid, hastened to Viken and assembled the Borgarthing, where her one-year-old son, Inge, was proclaimed king. In Trøndelagen the Ørething assembled as soon as the people heard of Harald Gille's death, and his illegitimate son Sigurd, three years of age, was placed on the throne. He was later known as Sigurd Mund.

When Sigurd Slembediakn saw that he had no chance to gain the throne for himself, he resolved to take Magnus the Blind from the monastery, and present him as a candidate. On a dark night, shortly after Christmas, in 1137, he landed at Nidarholm, took Magnus from the monastery, and sailed southward along the coast to the mouth of the Romsdalsfjord, where they parted. Magnus proceeded up the Romsdal valley into Oplandene, where he spent the winter, and Sigurd set sail westward across the sea, hoping that he would be able to rally a strong party around the blind king. In this expectation he was not disappointed. The return of Magnus awakened once more the loyalty to the son of Sigurd the Crusader, and many of the chieftains joined him. But in Viken Thjostolv Aalesson and other leaders, who were guarding King Inge, gathered an army, marched against King Magnus, and defeated him in a battle at Minne. Thjostolv Aalesson carried the child-king, Inge, with him in the battle, and he was hurt so that he grew up to be a lame and crippled hunchback. In history he is usually called Inge Krokryg (Hunchback). Magnus fled to Jarl Karl Sunnesson in Vestergötland, and persuaded him to espouse his cause. The jarl invaded Norway, but Thjostolv Aalesson and Aamunde Gyrdsson met him at Krokaskog and defeated him. Magnus now fled to Eirik Emune of Denmark, and employed all his power of persuasion to stir this tyrannical and ambitious king to lead his forces against the Norwegian chieftains. He told him that the country was now ruled by children, and that if he came with his whole army, no one would venture to raise a sword against him. King Eirik found the moment favorable and the outlook tempting. He gathered a large fleet of 250 ships, and sailed for Oslo, where Thjostolv Aalesson was stationed with a small garrison. Aalesson retreated, bringing with him the shrine of St. Halvard. The St. Halvard church was destroyed by fire and the city was sacked and burned, but the *lendermænd* soon met King Eirik with large forces, and he was unable to make further progress. All his attempts were unsuccessful, and he lost a number of men. Finally he returned to Denmark, deeply chagrined at his failure. The people's ill-will against him had increased, and he was assassinated at the Urnehovedthing, in Schleswig, shortly after his return. Eirik Haakonsson, generally known as Eirik Lam, was chosen his successor.

Sigurd Slembediakn, who had been in the Orkneys, returned too late to aid Magnus in his campaigns. When he reached Norway, and heard of Magnus' defeat, he turned southward to Denmark, where King Eirik Lam allowed him to gather ships and warriors. His operations henceforth can scarcely be characterized as anything but piratic expeditions, carried on with great cleverness and daring, but leading to no definite results. He attempted to get a footing at Konghelle, but was driven away by Thjostolv Aalesson. In another attempt at Portør, in Viken, he was equally unsuccessful. With seven ships he then made a descent on Lister in southern Norway, and killed the *lendermand* Bentein Kolbeinsson, but the people soon drove him away, and he sailed northward to Bjarkey, in Haalogaland, where he was well received by Vidkun Jónsson, Magnus the Blind's fosterfather. In the spring of 1139 he again joined Magnus in Denmark, and the two gathered what forces they could find for a new attack on Norway. They had in all thirty ships, of which twelve were Norwegian, while eighteen were auxiliary Danish forces. The kings Inge and Sigurd sent twenty ships against them, and at Holmengraa, near Bohuslen, the battle was fought on November 12, 1139. The Danes sailed away before the battle began, and Sigurd and Magnus were soon overpowered. Magnus fell, and Sigurd Slembediakn was captured and put to death in a most cruel manner. This terminated the first period of the civil wars, and the country enjoyed peace for a few years. The aristocracy, now secure in their power, had nothing to fear so long as the kings were young, but when they grew to manhood they might become more difficult to manage. Inge Krokryg proved to be weak and tractable, but Sigurd Mund was a dissolute and violent youth. His first act when he became of age was to cause the assassination of Ottar Birting, the leading man in Trøndelagen. In order to further weaken the power and influence of the crown, the *lendermænd* sought to create as many kings as possible. Six years after Sigurd and Inge had been placed on the throne, Eystein, an older son of Harald Gille, came from Scotland with his mother, Beathach. Harald had told his men of this son, and no other evidence of his royal descent was demanded. He was speedily proclaimed king at the Ørething in Trøndelagen. Harald Gille had a fourth son, Magnus, who was reared by the old chieftain Krypinga-Orm of Stødle, and he was also proclaimed king, though he was a sickly cripple, and did not live long. Norway had now four kings at the same time, and if this system of succession was to be followed, the kingdom might be blessed with four times four kings before another generation had passed. When we observe such a canker of weakness and decay eating at the very vitals of the state, we can understand the feelings of the old historian, Theodricus Monachus, when he cuts short his "Historia de Antiquitate Regum Norwagiensium" at the close of the reign of Sigurd the Crusader, and says that he will not record for posterity all the dastardly and lawless acts committed in the period which followed that reign.

These struggles between rival candidates for the throne do not seem, however, to have disturbed the peace and contentment of the rank and file of the people. The armed conflicts were carried on by the kings, the pretenders, the greater chieftains, and their personal followers. That there was no general war can be seen from the small number of ships and men engaged even in the more serious encounters, as in the battle of Holmengraa, where Sigurd and Magnus had only twelve small vessels, and the united forces of King Inge Krokryg and Sigurd Mund numbered only twenty ships. There is evidence that general prosperity and contentment prevailed, and that commerce was rapidly developing. The commercial towns of Véey in Romsdal, Skien (Skidan), in southern Norway, and Kaupang in Sogn sprang into existence, and the cities of Stavanger and Hamar also began their first real growth at this time.

The Cistercian monastic order was introduced in Norway during this period, not from France, but from England. Two monasteries of this order were founded: the Lyse monastery at Bergen, and the Hovedø monastery at Oslo (Christiania); also a cloister for nuns of the same order, the Nonneseter cloister in Bergen.[1] Lyse monastery, which was founded by Bishop Sigurd of Bergen, July 10, 1146, was the first monastery of this order in Norway. The Hovedø monastery was founded May 18, 1147. The Nonneseter cloister seems also to have been founded by Bishop Sigurd about the same time as the Lyse monastery.

57. THE INNER ORGANIZATION AND GROWTH OF THE CHURCH OF NORWAY

Among pagan nations, religion has always been regarded as an affair properly belonging within the domain of state administration. In pagan Norway, public worship was a state affair to such an extent that there was not even a distinct priesthood. The kings and chieftains performed the priestly functions in the temples, and as they were the leaders of the people in war and at the *thing*, they were also the custodians of the sanctuaries, and the wardens of the old faith. The feeling that the king was the highest authority in religious matters as well as in affairs of government grew out of the oldest traditions of the nation, and it was only intensified through the introduction of Christianity. The new faith was established by the kings themselves, who exercised full authority in all matters pertaining to the church, and made laws governing its organization and future work. Christianity had become their special cause, in the opinion both of friends and opponents a part of the new system which they sought to establish. When the aristocracy suffered defeat, and the old political and religious opposition disappeared, the king became the head of the church as well as of the state, not only because of the power which he exercised, and the organization which he had created, but also because the tradition and sentiment of the nation freely

[1] Christian C. A. Lange, *De norske Klostres Historie i Middelalderen.* N. Nicolaysen, *Om Lysekloster og dets Ruiner*, udgivet av *Foreningen til norske Fortidsmindesmærkers Bevaring.* N. Nicolaysen, *Hovedø Kloster og dets Ruiner.* B. E. Bendixen, *Nonneseter Klosterruiner.*

accorded him that position.[1] Even after the Church of Norway was placed under the supervision of the Archbishop of Bremen, and later under the archbishopric of Lund in Skåne, which was created in 1104, the king continued to be its real head. King Harald Haardraade's answer to Archbishop Adalbert of Bremen: "I know of no archbishop in Norway except myself, King Harald,"[2] is characteristic, and illustrates well the situation. The archbishop, who was far away and wholly unknown to the people, could exercise but a nominal authority; all real power was in the hands of the king. This gave the Church of Norway a somewhat unique position. The character of its organization was determined by the laws issued by the king, and its complete dependence on royal authority stood in sharp contrast to the supremacy of the Roman Catholic Church in other countries of Europe.

The bishops were at first missionaries without fixed dioceses. They were chosen by the king, and were called hird-bishops, as they were regarded as belonging to the king's *hird*. They were his advisers in ecclesiastical affairs, but owed him the same obedience as other *hirdmœnd*. The "Heimskringla" says of St. Olav:[3] "The church laws he made according to the advice of Bishop Grimkel and other teachers, and he devoted all his energy to the eradication of paganism and old customs, which he considered contrary to the Christian spirit." The necessity of obtaining the consent of the people to the laws thus made constituted, however, an effective check on the royal authority.[4] Even after permanent dioceses had

---

[1] Konrad Maurer, *Die Bekehrung des norwegischen Stammes*, II. A. D. Jørgensen, *Den norske Kirkes Grundlæggelse*. P. A. Munch, *Det norske Folks Historie*. J. E. Sars, *Udsigt over den norske Historie*, part II. R. Keyser, *Norges Stats- og Retsforfatning i Middelalderen*, p. 183 ff. R. Keyser, *Den norske Kirkes Historie under Katholicismen*.

[2] Adam v. Bremen, Book III., 16.   [3] *Saga of Olav the Saint*, ch. 58.

[4] "In each of the three (Scandinavian) countries, separate, though not very complete codes of church laws were enacted, which should take the place of the canonical code. The oldest of these laws were enacted, at least in Norway and Denmark, by coöperation of the king, the bishops, and the people. They gave the church no right to inflict civil punishments, neither did they exempt the clergy from trial by the regular courts of justice." T. H. Aschehoug, *Statsforfatningen i Norge og Danmark indtil 1814*. These old Norwegian church laws are found in *Norges gamle Love*, published by R. Keyser and P. A. Munch.

been established the choice of bishops was still controlled by the king. They were still dependent on him for their maintenance as well as for their office, and when they traveled through the country superintending the church work, they came as the king's representatives.

The churches erected during the early Christian period were of three kinds. Each *fylke* had one or more principal churches, *fylke's* churches. These received grants of land from the king, and the people were also required to contribute to their support. In course of time churches were also built in the *herreds*, or local districts, and many of the leading men erected chapels, *høgende's* churches, on their own estates. The priests of the *fylke's* churches were chosen by the king, and received an income, partly from the church lands, and partly in form of contributions and fees from their parishioners. The *herred* priests were chosen by the people, and were wholly dependent on the parishioners for their salary. The priests in the *høgende's* churches were appointed and paid by the owner of the church, or by the *fylke's* or *herred's* priests whom they served as assistants. This very democratic church organization differed widely in character from the hierarchic system of the Church of Rome. The bishops exercised authority, each in his own diocese, but they were not leagued together in any higher unity. They were dependent on the king, as the priests were dependent on their parishioners, both for their office and their subsistence. The clergy were amenable to the state laws, like other citizens, as the church laws were only a part of the civil code. The church had no laws of its own, and exercised no separate jurisdiction. In social life the priests and bishops were still bound closely to the rest of the people through intermarriage, as celibacy was not enforced in Norway till in the latter part of the thirteenth century. But in time the influence of the Roman hierarchy, which dominated all intellectual and spiritual life of the age, made itself more strongly felt also in Norway. The religious enthusiasm aroused by the crusaders inspired kings like Olav Kyrre and Sigurd the Crusader with ardent devotion to the cause of the church, and they were easily persuaded to enlarge its privileges even at the expense of their own power. The spirit of the times, the zeal and ability of the popes, together with the conditions at home gave the Church of Norway a hierarchic character, and made it an organization independent of the state, able to exert a controlling influence over state affairs. The religious fervor of the kings originated this new development. The introduction of the system of tithes in the reign of Sigurd the Crusader made the clergy independent economically, and the period of the civil wars hastened the growth of the power and independence of the church. The weak and worthless kings who occupied the throne in that period were as unfit as they were unable to exercise supreme control over religious affairs. In struggles with their rivals they willingly bartered away powers and principles for temporary advantages; the royal power was weakened, and the government demoralized. In such a period of anarchy and commotion the church would, naturally, assume control of its own affairs, not only because of the opportunity, but as a matter of necessity.

The chief step towards a hierarchic organization of the Church of Norway was the establishing of the archdiocese of Nidaros in 1152, and the new regulations then made for the Norwegian Church.[1] Cardinal Nicolaus Brakespeare of England[2] was sent by Pope Eugenius III. as papal legate with instructions to establish archbishoprics in Norway and Sweden, and he also brought with him the pall for the new archbishops. The archdiocese of Nidaros should include the five bishoprics of Norway,[3] and also the six bishoprics in the Norwegian colonies: Skálholt and Hólar in Iceland, Kirkwall (O. N. Kirkjuvágr) in the Orkneys,[4] Gardar in Greenland, Kirkebø

[1] We hear of Reidar who was appointed Archbishop of Norway in 1150, but he died in southern Europe and never reached his archdiocese. According to the "Icelandic Annals" he died in 1151. He is not mentioned in the sagas, but he seems to have been appointed by the Pope before the archbishopric of Nidaros was formally established. All sources agree that Jón Birgersson, Bishop of Stavanger, became the first archbishop. Chr. Lange, *Norsk Tidsskrift*, vol. V., p. 41. P. A. Munch, *Samlede Afhandlinger*, II., 555. *Festskrift udgivet i Anledning af Trondhjems 900 Aars Jubilæum 1897.* Ludvig Daae, *En Krønike om Erkebiskopperne i Nidaros. Diplomatarium Norwegicum*, III., no. 2, 3.

[2] In 1154 Cardinal Nicolaus was elected Pope, and assumed the name of Adrian IV.

[3] The diocese of Oslo was divided, and a new bishopric was established at Hamar. The five bishoprics were: Trondhjem (Nidaros), Bergen, Oslo, Stavanger, and Hamar.

[4] The Orkneys were originally a part of the archbishopric of York. Thorfinn Jarl, while on a pilgrimage to Rome about 1050, succeeded in having

(O. N. Kirkjubœr) in the Faroe Islands,[1] and the bishopric of the Hebrides (Sudreyjar) and Man (Sodor and Man). New regulations were also made for the election of bishops in the five bishoprics of Norway proper. A chapter, or college of priests, was organized in each diocese. The members of this chapter (*canonici*) should constitute the bishop's council; they were also to perform the duties of his office in case of vacancy, and should elect his successor without interference from secular authorities. The archbishop was chosen by the chapter of the diocese of Nidaros, but he was consecrated by the Pope, and received the pall from him. The colonial dioceses had no chapters, and their bishops were chosen by the chapter of the diocese of Nidaros. The tax called "Peter's Pence" was introduced, and each grown person should pay a penning to the church. Regulations were also made for disposing of property by testament, which had not hitherto been customary, and it must be inferred that the church hoped to profit by this arrangement. A person should have the right to give away by testament one-tenth of his inherited property and up to one-fourth of property which he himself had acquired. A woman might grant by will one-tenth of her dowry, and up to one-fourth of her one-third share of the property which she held in joint ownership with her husband. Celibacy of the clergy was also established, but it was not yet enforced. The priests were to be appointed by the bishops, but it is not clear to what extent the bishops exercised this right.

The Roman Church asserted everywhere its spiritual supremacy over the state, and claimed certain privileges and powers as its own indisputable right. The chief of these were: The right of the church to legislate in all ecclesiastical matters. The church law consisting of the canonical code, supplemented by the decrees which the Pope and the church councils might issue from time to time, should be independent of the civil law, and should govern all affairs pertaining to the church and the clergy. Separate ecclesiastical courts were to be established, and the church should exercise full jurisdiction in

a bishop appointed for the islands. The bishop's seat was at first at Birgsaa, but it was transferred to Kirkwall, where the Magnus cathedral was built. The Orkneys became a part of the archbishopric of Nidaros in 1152.

[1] The bishopric of the Faroe Islands seems to have been established in 1103. Gudmund was the first bishop, and served from 1103 till 1139.

all cases involving religion, the church, and the clergy. The church
was to enjoy freedom from any but voluntary contributions to the
state.

By the new regulations of 1152 these "rights" were established in
theory, at least, and the bishops henceforth claimed them in the
name of the church. But neither the kings nor the people were at
first willing to grant the clergy such privileges. The claims remained for a while only the abstract principles of the spiritual supremacy of the church, and its independence of all secular authority.
But the time came when the church arrayed itself against the state
in an effort to enforce its claims, and we find the bishops themselves
fanning the flames of civil strife. This new power, which had been
nursed under the king's special care, allied itself, after 1152, with the
reactionary aristocracy in opposition to the crown. The energies of
the clergy were largely devoted to the perfecting of its outward
organization, and to the incessant combats waged for new privileges
and increased influence. The priests were often poorly qualified for
their calling, worldliness grew, and more emphasis was laid on the
outer form than on the inner spirit of Christian life and faith. As
Christianity had been introduced by royal decree, as the knowledge
even of the fundamentals of the Christian faith was more than imperfect, and the bishops and priests were often more intensely interested in politics and other temporal affairs than in the religious
instruction of the people, Christianity was generally regarded as a
new law which the king had proclaimed. The new faith became a
sort of witch's chaldron in which remnants of paganism, superstitions, and fragments of Christian belief were hopelessly mixed. In
too many cases it could scarcely be called Christianity. The hierarchic organization of the church probably increased at first its
efficiency as a moral agent. It could now act with great authority
and could display a power and splendor which made a strong impression on the popular mind. But its missionary spirit gradually gave
way to love of wealth and power, and the attention was gradually
directed to the outward forms of the church service which could
work no regeneration of spirit. The work of conversion was begun
but the Roman hierarchy showed itself unable to lead the people
forward to full spiritual daylight.

The religious and moral growth, so slow in Norway, was, if possible, even more behindhand in the colonies. Christianity was accepted as the state religion in Iceland in the year 1000, but the legislative act of the Althing which abolished the old worship produced no perceptible change in the moral life or the religious views of the people. The Christian church in Iceland was too poorly organized to become even a fair substitute for the old temples which were torn down. The churches were all built by influential chieftains, who often took holy orders and served as priests in their own churches, when no priests could be had. In this way they could combine the priestly functions with their political and social leadership, as in pagan times. If they found this arrangement inconvenient, they took boys into their homes, and instructed them sufficiently so that they could read the church service, and made them priests in their churches. These boys had no social standing, but were classed with the servants of the household. It is quite evident that under such circumstances Christianity could be but a thin varnish over a completely pagan life. The loss of the old faith and the lack of instruction in the new produced, not immediately, but in due course of time a religious indifference and general moral laxity which comes so prominently into the foreground in the bloody Sturlung period 1160–1262, a complete counterpart to the period of civil wars in Norway. In speaking of this period Professor J. E. Sars says : " In the so-called Sturlung period the country was more and more torn by the wildest party strife, the final result of which was that the Icelandic people — exhausted, torn, and despairing — gave up their independence and threw themselves into the arms of the kingdom of Norway. The accounts of these feuds reveal a bloodthirstiness, hardheartedness, and violent desire for wealth and power which is not surpassed in pagan times, and furthermore a faithlessness and treachery, a lack of respect for law and justice, a licentiousness, and a dissolution of domestic life, to which the saga period prior to 1030 furnishes no parallel." [1]

Konrad Maurer says of the Sturlung period : "The fearful disorders are ascribable in part to the political situation, but in part, and perhaps for the greater part, they are due to another circum-

[1] J. E. Sars, *Udsigt over den norske Historie*, part II., p. 57.

stance, namely the change to the new faith, as paradoxical as this may sound. The more completely paganism as a thoroughly national religion had grown together with the whole life of the Norsemen, the more definitely and comprehensively it had embraced and shaped the people's moral and legal conceptions, the more grievous was the loss caused by abandoning it. On the other hand, the more outward the motives had been which had led the masses of the people to change their faith, the less the new faith, we must admit, was able to compensate for the loss. During the first decades after the introduction of Christianity this misfortune would be less keenly felt, since, on the one hand, paganism still continued for a time to dominate the minds of the people, while, on the other hand, the glowing fervor and truly Christian conduct of the few who from a deep inner conviction professed the new faith won for Christianity, as far as their influence went, a powerful influence also over external life. But after the generation which had been brought up under paganism had passed away, and also their nearest descendants, who through lack of priests had been reared to a large extent in the pagan spirit; after Christianity, on the other hand, had become a custom, represented, not by zealous neophytes, but by priests who were poorly trained, and who generally were so occupied with the outward forms of the new religion that they could pay but little attention to its inner contents, while their great political importance, and their unfortunate social position turned their thoughts from their religious calling, the gap produced in the people's minds by the change of faith, outwardly accomplished, but inwardly far from completed, showed itself in all its fearful significance. It is easily understood that the unrest caused by this sudden rupture of all existing conditions brought to the surface the worst elements of the people and the most objectionable traits of their national character." [1]

It would be erroneous, however, to think that the blight thrown upon Christianity by these conditions was altogether general. Long before the introduction of the Christian faith, many of the most earnest and intelligent had ceased to believe in the old gods, and were searching for new light. To many of them Christianity must have

[1] Konrad Maurer, *Island von seiner ersten Entdeckung bis zum Untergang des Freistaates*, p. 278–280. The passage is quoted by Sars.

come as glad tidings, and though their Christian knowledge was very imperfect, it must have chastened their spirit, and inspired them with new love for the goodness which is heaven born. The new moral standards established by the Christian teaching could not long remain a secret to those who had dreamed of virtues which paganism did not know, and the force of their example, and their words of admonition and counsel would not be lost on those who suffered from all the evils of a dark and lawless age. Through the tumult of the civil wars we hear nothing of these, but we are, nevertheless, sure that they were found, yes, that they were numerous, and that they were gradually bringing about a great change in the social, religious, and moral life of the nation. The effect of this new spiritual and moral leaven is shown among other things by the disappearance of slavery. It happened even in pagan times that a man would grant a slave his liberty on certain conditions, especially if the slave had done him some great service; or the slave might buy his freedom. But new ones were constantly bought in the numerous slave markets. But with the advent of Christianity the slave markets were gradually closed. In the old laws, usually called the "Laws of St. Olav," it was enacted that at the meeting of every *lagthing* a slave should be given his freedom, "to the honor of God," and the remuneration given the owner should be paid by the whole *lagdømme*. In Olav Kyrre's time this law was so amended that each *fylkesthing* should liberate a slave every year.[1] This had a great influence on public opinion, and in the twelfth century, before the civil wars were ended, slavery had ceased to exist in Norway. Although religious life made slow progress during the period of storm and stress caused to some degree by the change of faith, a new cultural life, born in part of the new spirit, was growing, budding, and giving promise of the great intellectual awakening, the luxuriant unfolding of literature, art, and national greatness in the period that followed; an age of almost unparalleled productivity which in a hundred years gave Norway and Iceland the great Old Norse literature, which saw great cathedrals erected, science and learning cultivated, and Norway, politically strong and economically prosperous, highly honored among the

---

[1] *Gulathingslov*, p. 5 f., *Norges gamle Love*, I. *Frostathingslov*, III., 19 *Norges gamle Love*, I.

states of Europe. Such conditions could not be produced suddenly, as if by accident, but followed as a result of a development which, though obscured and retarded, was not interrupted by the tumultuous feuds of the civil wars, and which gives even that period a tinge of hopefulness and a touch of wayward charm.

The period which was marred by so much domestic turmoil showed marked signs of an awakening of literary activity. The books were usually written in Latin, which was the literary language elsewhere in Europe. The mass, which was the most important part of the church service, was also conducted in that language, but the custom of preaching to the people in their own tongue had been introduced from England by the first missionaries in the time of Olav Tryggvason and Olav the Saint, and homilies were written in Old Norse to be read in the churches. The legends about the Norwegian saints were also embodied in writing. The oldest St. Olav legend [1] was written in Latin about 1140. It seems to have been composed by a priest in Trondhjem to be read to pilgrims and visitors on St. Olav's day, and it was soon followed by a whole literature of similar character. Einar Skúlason's poem "Geisli," a drápa written about St. Olav, which the poet recited in the Christ church in Trondhjem in 1153, was also based on this legend.

The most important literary work of the period was the embodiment in writing of the old laws of Norway in the great codes: the "Frostathingslov," "Gulathingslov," "Eidsivathingslov," and "Borgarthingslov." [2] These codes, together with the "Bjarkeyjarréttr," or municipal laws, the "Hirðskrá," and other old laws were all written in the Old Norse language. The time when they were written can be determined only approximately from internal evidence from the codes themselves, as the sources contain no direct statement with regard to it. The old writers regarded it as certain that the old laws were first written by St. Olav himself. Theodricus Monachus says of Olav: "Leges patria lingua conscribi fecit," and the "Legenda de Sto. Olavo" says: "Leges divines et humanas scripsit et promul-

---

[1] Edited by Metcalf. Jacobus Langebek, Scriptores Regum Danicarum, vol. II., Legendae de Sancto Olavo.

[2] These codes have been published by R. Keyser, P. A. Munch, Gustav Storm, and Ebbe Hertzberg in five stately volumes with glossary.

gavit." Saxo Grammaticus holds the same opinion.[1] But Konrad Maurer has shown that this opinion has nothing to support it except St. Olav's great reputation as lawgiver, while the wording of the codes themselves proves that they could not have been written by him or under his direction.[2] Ebbe Hertzberg finds that the church laws (Kristenret), which form a supplement to all these codes, were written before the system of tithes was introduced by Sigurd the Crusader (1111–1120), and as the other laws must have been written as soon as possible after the task was once begun, the whole work was probably finished in Olav Kyrre's reign, prior to 1111.[3]

58. RAGNVALD JARL'S CRUSADE

In 1150 the young *lendermand* Eindride Unge returned from Constantinople, where he had served in the Varangian guard of the Emperor, and he could tell much about the exploits of the Varangians, and also about the second crusade, led by King Louis VII. of France, and Emperor Conrad III. of Germany, 1147–1148. Eindride met Ragnvald Jarl of the Orkneys, who was then in Norway, and encouraged him to lead a crusade to the Holy Land. Erling Ormsson Skakke and others also spoke in favor of the undertaking, and agreed to join in it. Ragnvald agreed to go, and when it became known that he and Erling were organizing a crusade, many prominent men joined them. Ragnvald should be the leader, and Eindride Unge, who had already been in the Orient, should act as guide for the expedition.[4] Two years were to be devoted to preparations, and Ragnvald returned to the Orkneys in the fall. In 1152 he came again to Norway, and the ships were made ready for the voyage. They set sail from Bergen, but when they reached the Orkneys, they decided to remain there that winter, as it was already late in the

---

[1] Saxo Grammaticus, book X.
See Ebbe Hertzberg, *Vore ældste Lovtexters oprindelige Nedskrivelsestid, Historiske Afhandlinger tilegnede Professor dr. J. E. Sars*, Christiania, 1905.

[2] Konrad Maurer, *Gulathingsløg, Ersch and Gruber's Encyclopedia*.

[3] Ebbe Hertzberg, *Vore ældste Lovtexters oprindelige Nedskrivelsestid, Historiske Afhandlinger tilegnet Professor dr. J. E. Sars*. Of the *Eidsivathingslov* and the *Borgarthingslov* the church laws alone remain.

[4] *Orkneyingasaga*, translated by John A. Hjaltalin and Gilbert Goudie, edited with notes and introduction by Joseph Anderson, ch. lxxx, ff.

season. The arrogant Eindride Unge, who, contrary to agreement, had fitted out more splendid ships than the others, was shipwrecked on the coast of Shetland, and had to get a new ship from Norway. In the summer of 1153 all preparations were completed, and Ragnvald and his followers set sail from the Orkneys with fifteen large ships. As each ship must have had a crew of 120 men or more, they were in all probably about 2000 men.

"They then sailed till they were south of England, and thence to Valland (west coast of France). There is no account of their voyage until they came to a seaport called Verbon.[1] There they learned that the earl who had governed the city, and whose name was Geir-björn, had lately died; but he had a young and beautiful daughter, by name of Ermingerd, and she had charge of her patrimony under the guardianship of her noblest kinsmen. They advised the queen (i.e. the earl's daughter) to invite Jarl Ragnvald to a splendid ban-quet, saying that her fame would spread far if she gave a fitting recep-tion to noblemen arrived from such distance. The queen left it to them; and when this had been resolved upon, men were sent to the jarl to tell him that the queen invited him to a banquet, with as many men as he himself wished to accompany him. The jarl received her invitation gratefully, and selected the best of his men to go with him. And when they came to the banquet there was good cheer, and nothing was spared by which the jarl might consider himself specially honored. One day, while the jarl sat at the feast, the queen entered the hall, attended by many ladies. She had in her hand a golden cup, and was arrayed in the finest robes. She wore her hair loose, according to the custom of maidens, and she had a golden diadem round her forehead. She poured out for the jarl, and the maidens played for them. The jarl took her hand along with the cup and placed her beside him, and they conversed during the day. The jarl sang:

> Lady fair! thy form surpasses
> All the loveliness of maidens,
> Though arrayed in costly garments,
> And adorned with costly jewels:

---

[1] Where this seaport was located is not known.

> Silken curls in radiant splendor
> Fall upon the beauteous shoulders
> Of the goddess of the gold-rings.
> The greedy eagle's claws I redden'd.

The jarl stayed there a long time and was well entertained. The inhabitants of the city solicited him to take up his residence there, saying that they were in favor of giving him the queen in marriage. The jarl said that he wished to complete his intended journey, but that he would come there on his return, and then they might do what they thought fit. Then the jarl left with his retinue, and sailed round Thrasness. They had a fair wind, and sat and drank and made themselves merry. The jarl sang this song:

> Long in the prince's memory
> Ermingerd's soft words shall linger;
> It is her desire that we shall
> Ride the waters out to Jordan;
> But the riders of the sea-horses,
> From the southern climes returning,
> Soon shall plow their way to Verbon
> O'er the whale-pond in the autumn.

"They went on till they came west to Galicialand, five nights before Jule-tide, and they intended to spend Christmas there. They asked the inhabitants whether they were willing to sell them provisions; but food was scarce in that country, and they thought it a great hardship to have to feed such a numerous host. It so happened that the country was under the rule of a foreigner, who resided in the castle, and oppressed the inhabitants greatly. He made war on them if they did not do everything he wished, and menaced them with violence and oppression. When the jarl asked the inhabitants to sell him victuals, they consented to do so until Lent, but made certain proposals on their part — to wit, that Jarl Ragnvald should attack their enemies, and should have all the money which he might obtain from them. The jarl communicated this to his men, and asked them what they would be inclined to do. Most of them were willing to attack the castle, thinking that it was a very likely place to obtain booty. Therefore Jarl Ragnvald and his men agreed to the terms of the inhabitants."[1]

The castle was taken, but the chief (Gudifrey, or Godfred) escaped.

"They plundered far and wide in heathen Spainland," that is in the part of Spain occupied by the Saracens, and they sailed then through the Strait of Gibraltar into the Mediterranean Sea. Here the wrongheaded Eindride Unge left the expedition with six ships, and went to Marseilles in France. With the remaining nine ships Ragnvald continued the voyage. "Over against Sardinia they met two very large Saracen ships of the type called dromones." One of these ships escaped, but the other one was attacked by the Norsemen and captured after a hard fight. After this battle Ragnvald landed on the coast of Africa, where he concluded a seven-day peace with the inhabitants, and sold the booty which he had gathered. He then sailed to Crete, where he was detained for some time by bad weather. As soon as they got favorable wind they continued their voyage to Palestine, and landed at Acre in 1154; but soon after their arrival they were smitten with a contagious fever, and many died. They were now so far reduced in numbers that they do not even seem to have attempted military operations. After visiting the holy places they left Palestine for Constantinople, where they were well received by Emperor Manuel I. On their homeward journey they visited Apulia and Rome, whence they returned by the customary overland route through Germany and Denmark. The visit to Verbon and the fair Ermingerd seems to have been abandoned.

59. THE SECOND STAGE OF CIVIL WARS. THE RULE OF ERLING SKAKKE AND MAGNUS ERLINGSSON

The difference in character between the kings Inge Krokryg, Sigurd Mund, and Eystein became very marked when they grew to manhood. Sigurd was tall and well built. He was of a jovial disposition and carried himself well among his men; but he was of a violent temper, perverse, capricious, imprudent, and hard to please. Eystein was also a well-built and athletic young man, but he was of an imperious disposition, had a violent temper, and was very covetous.

[1] *Orkneyingasaga*, ch. lxxx.

The crippled Inge, on the other hand, was very meek and mild-tempered.[1] He had also the advantage of being born in lawful wedlock. His very weakness and his gentle disposition attached to him a great number of powerful nobles who virtually ruled in his name. The most influential of his adherents was the powerful Gregorius Dagssøn, who reminds us of Erling Skjalgsson and Einar Tambarskjælver in earlier days. But while Erling and Einar had been the leaders of the old aristocracy in opposition to the king, Gregorius was the leader of a faction, and acted as the king's representative. Inge's weakness proved to be his strength, and he became the most powerful and influential of the three kings. Sigurd and Eystein formed a secret alliance against him, and agreed to dethrone him, because he was a cripple.[2] But the alert Gregorius Dagssøn frustrated their plans. With King Inge he hastened to Bergen, and shortly after King Sigurd also arrived. A *thing* was assembled, and Gregorius appeared in gilt helmet with a great number of armed men. Inge told the people of the plot, and asked their help, which was cheerfully promised. Sigurd also addressed the *thing*, and said that the report of the plot was wholly unfounded, that it had been circulated by Gregorius Dagssøn to hurt him and Eystein, but he hoped that he would soon meet Gregorius in such a way that his gilt helmet should roll in the dust. No hostilities seem, however, to have been seriously contemplated, but bloody encounters which took place ᴌ few days afterwards between the followers of the two kings precipitated a general fight, in which King Sigurd was killed. Some days later King Eystein arrived in Bergen with thirty ships, but no further hostilities occurred at this time. Inge went to Trondhjem, and Eystein sailed southward to Viken. Shortly after this meeting in Bergen Eystein made an unsuccessful attempt to surprise and capture Gregorius Dagssøn, and, as a result, the relations between the two kings grew constantly more strained. Inge succeeded in winning over many of Eystein's most influential adherents, and Eystein, who was less popular, revenged himself by committing many dastardly acts. Finally, in 1156, open hostilities commenced, and both kings gathered forces for a decisive struggle. Inge collected eighty ships, while Eystein had only forty-five, and when the two

---

[1] *Heimskringla, Ingessaga.*   [2] *Fagrskinna,* ch. 260.   *Morkinskinna,* p. 223.

fleets met, most of Eystein's ships deserted, and he was compelled to flee without fighting a battle. The following year he was captured and put to death.

No reasonable objection could now be made to Inge Krokryg as sole king of Norway. According to the rule of succession the reign of the joint kings should be a single reign, which should continue so long as any one of them lived. The sons of the deceased kings could, therefore, not rightfully succeed to the throne as long as King Inge lived. He had, moreover, been very popular, and had won the support of the greater part of the people and the aristocracy because of his mild rule and gentle disposition. But some of the followers of King Eystein refused to submit to him, and chose Haakon Herdebreid, the illegitimate ten-year-old son of Sigurd Mund, as their candidate for the throne.[1] The struggle was no longer waged for any principle. It was not even a contest between rival candidates for the throne, but a feud between hostile and rival factions of the aristocracy. The leaders of King Inge's party were Gregorius Dagssøn and Erling Skakke. Among the leaders of the comparatively small faction which still remained in opposition were Sigurd of Reyr, a personal enemy of Gregorius Dagssøn, and Eindride Unge, who had partaken in Ragnvald Jarl's crusade together with Erling Skakke, but the two had parted as bitter enemies. The struggle was kept up by such rivalries and animosities between ambitious nobles, and new pretenders were put forward in the interest of the contending factions. Professor Sars says: "In earlier days the kings had created the parties, at least in an external way, but now the king was created by the party.[2] The king had ceased to be anything but a name. The aristocracy had gained full control, and the only issue was which faction should wield the greater power."

King Inge Krokryg sought to strengthen his position as far as possible. He stationed Gregorius Dagssøn in Viken to defend the southern districts against Haakon Herdebreid and his party. He carried on negotiations with the king of Denmark, and succeeded in

---

[1] *Orkneyingasaga*, ch. lxxxiii.

[2] J. E. Sars, *Udsigt over den norske Historie*, part II., p. 88. P. A. Munch, *Det norske Folks Historie*, II., p. 860. *Heimskringla, Haakon Herdebreidssaga. Fagrskinna*, p. 175.

having his chaplain, Eystein Erlendsson, elected Archbishop of Trondhjem. The new archbishop was a man of extraordinary ability, and could wield great influence in his behalf in that part of the kingdom. Haakon Herdebreid's party, which, to begin with, was quite small, had sought refuge across the Swedish border, and when they made an attempt to capture Konghelle, they were defeated by Gregorius Dagssøn. But they soon advanced into Trøndelagen, where they received reënforcements, and Haakon Herdebreid was proclaimed king over one-third of Norway, to which he was regarded as being entitled as the heir of his father, King Sigurd Mund. His chance of success now rapidly improved. In 1161 Gregorius Dagssøn fell in a skirmish against Haakon's followers at Bevja (Bevera), in Bohuslen, — a severe blow to Inge's party. The saga states that when Inge heard of Gregorious' death he shed tears and said: "The man has fallen who has been my best friend, and who has done the most to preserve my kingdom for me. But I have always thought that we should not long be parted." [1] This foreboding proved prophetic. In February of the same year, while Inge was in Oslo celebrating the marriage of his brother, Orm Kongsbroder, to Ragna Nikolasdotter, the widow of King Eystein, Haakon suddenly marched against the city. A battle was fought on the ice of the fjord, near Oslo, in which King Inge fell, at the age of twenty-six.

The able and ambitious Erling Skakke now became leader of Inge's party. He belonged to one of the most powerful families, and was married to Christina, the daughter of Sigurd the Crusader and his queen Malmfrid. He had won renown as a crusader, and was at this moment the most sagacious and powerful noble in the kingdom. When he had heard of King Inge's death, he called a meeting of the party leaders in Bergen to lay plans for the future. They were not willing to submit to Haakon Herdebreid, who counted among his followers many of their bitterest enemies. They agreed, therefore, to keep the party together, and promised under oath faithfully to support each other. The most difficult task was to find a suitable candidate for the throne around whom the party could rally. In casting about among several not very available candidates, they finally selected the five-year-old Magnus Erlingsson,

[1] *Heimskringla, Haakon Herdebreidssaga*, 15.

the son of Erling Skakke and his wife Christina, daughter of Sigurd
the Crusader.   But by this choice they set aside all rules of succession.
Magnus, the son of Erling Skakke, was not a king's son, and had no
right whatever to the throne.   This choice, in flagrant violation of
the law, was dictated by Erling's own ambition, and by party interests.
In order to gain additional support Erling hastened to Denmark to
negotiate with King Valdemar, who promised to aid him on condition that the province of Viken should be ceded to Denmark, and
Erling, in his eager desire for power, committed the treasonable act
of subscribing to this condition.[1]

While Erling was absent, Haakon Herdebreid was proclaimed
king of Norway at the Ørething in Trøndelagen, and Sigurd of
Reyr, one of his chief supporters, was made jarl.   Haakon stationed
himself at Tunsberg, and sent Jarl Sigurd to Konghelle to guard the
southern districts of Norway against Erling, but on his return from
Denmark Erling seized Tunsberg without difficulty.   Haakon retreated in haste to Trøndelagen, and Jarl Sigurd joined him there
soon afterward.   In the spring of 1162 Haakon equipped both fleet
and army, and prepared to meet Erling Skakke.   He advanced
southward along the coast, gathering men and ships in the adjoining
districts, but at Véey, in Romsdal, he quite unexpectedly encountered
Erling's whole fleet.   A battle was fought near the island of Sekken
in the Romsdalsfjord, where Haakon fell, and his forces suffered a
complete defeat.   Haakon was only fifteen years of age, and the saga
describes him as playful and boyish; tall, broad-shouldered, and
good looking.   After the battle Erling Skakke sailed to Nidaros
and summoned the Ørething, where his son Magnus was proclaimed
king of Norway.

Haakon's party was defeated, but it was not crushed, and as the
old royal line was not extinct, they were able to find a new candidate
for the throne who had some legitimate claim to it.   This was
Sigurd Sigurdsson, another illegitimate son of Sigurd Mund, who
seems to have been a mere child.   He was staying in Oplandene
with his foster-father, Markus of Skog, and is generally known as
Sigurd Markusfostre.   But now as before they were unable to cope
with the redoubtable Erling Skakke.   In 1163 he defeated and slew

[1] *Heimskringla, Magnus Erlingssonssaga*, ch. 2.

Sigurd Jarl in a battle at Ree, northwest of Tunsberg, and shortly after he captured Markus of Skog and the young King Sigurd, and caused them both to be executed. But Erling saw that his son Magnus would find it difficult to maintain himself on the throne as a mere usurper. It was necessary to create the impression that he was a lawful king, and he hoped to secure for him an appearance of legitimacy by having him anointed and crowned. This would give him the support of the church, which would thereby officially approve his elevation to the throne. For this purpose he entered into negotiations with Archbishop Eystein Erlendsson, but the sagacious and powerful prelate drove a hard bargain, and granted his request only after Erling had subscribed to conditions which destroyed both the power and the dignity of the crown. In the summer of 1164 a council of magnates was assembled at Bergen consisting of the archbishop, the bishops, and a certain number of representative and influential men from each lagdømme.[1] The newly elected bishop, Brand Sæmundsson of Hólar, and the great chieftain Jón Loftesson of Odda, in Iceland, were also present. Before this assembly the seven-year-old Magnus Erlingsson was crowned king of Norway, and all questions regarding the succession to the throne were now discussed and settled. King Magnus had to subscribe to the following conditions: He surrendered himself and his kingdom for all times to St. Olav (i.e. to the church), and promised to rule as his vicar and vassal.[2] As a sign of submission, his crown, and those of his successors, should be placed as an offering on the altar of the cathedral in Nidaros, at their death.[3] By this agreement the king virtually became a feudal tenant under the church. But his influence and independence would be still further limited by enforcing

---

[1] Heimskringla, Magnus Erlingssonssaga, ch. 21. Fagrskinna, ch. 268.

[2] " Deo namque in hac die gloriose resurreccionis me cum regno in perpetuum et glorioso martyri regi Olao. cui integraliter speciali deuocione secundo post dominum. regnum assigno Norwegie. et huic regno. quantum deo placuerit. velut eiusdem gloriosi martyris possessioni hereditarie. sub eius dominio. tamquam suus vicarius et ab eo tenens presidebo."

[3] " In perpetue quoque subieccionis testimonium. hoc pro me et pro omnibus meis catholicis successoribus priuilegium huic metropolitane ecclesie concedo et literis meis sigillatis confirmo. ut post voccacionem meam regale diadema et meum. quod hodierna die sacro altari in confirmacionem offero. et omnium mihi succedencium. presenti delegetur ecclesie."

the new rules of succession which were now adopted. These almost shattered the old principles of an hereditary monarchy, since the king in many instances was to be elected, and the church was given full control of the election. When the king died, a council of magnates should be summoned to meet in Trondhjem to determine whether the heir to the throne possessed the required qualifications. This assembly should consist of the archbishop, his suffragan bishops, the abbots, the *hirðstjórar* and the *hird*, and twelve men from each bishopric, to be appointed by the bishops. The king's eldest legitimate son should succeed to the throne, as sole king, but if the assembly found him to be unworthy, or otherwise disqualified, that legitimate son which the assembly considered best qualified should become king. If the king had no legitimate son, they might choose the nearest heir, or any one else whom they considered well qualified. The choice should be decided by a majority vote, provided the archbishop and the bishops consented.[1] The arrangement that the king's oldest legitimate son should inherit the throne was a good feature, as it did away with the most flagrant fault of the old system, that any illegitimate son, or any bold adventurer, might aspire to the crown. But this single good feature was vitiated by giving the assembly, or in fact the clergy, the power of deciding who was worthy or qualified to become king. This enabled them to exclude at will any legitimate heir to the throne, while the election of a new candidate was delegated to them. The king of Norway, the successor of Harald Haarfagre and St. Olav, could scarcely be reduced to a more impotent shadow. The aristocracy and the clergy, who had now joined hands in their effort to divest the crown of all real power, could rejoice in a complete triumph.

Archbishop Eystein Erlendsson sprang from a noble family in Trøndelagen. He was related to the powerful Arnunge family, and

---

The document is found in *Norges gamle Love*, I, 442. Ebbe Hertzberg, *Den første norske Kongekroning, Historisk Tidsskrift*, fjerde række, vol. III, p. 29. Gustav Storm, *Om Magnus Erlingssøns Privilegium til Nidaros Kirke 1164, Videnskabs-Selskabets Skrifter*, Christiania, 1895.

[1] *Gulaþingsbók 2., Norges gamle Love*, vol. I. R. Keyser, *Norges Stats- og Retsforfatning i Middelalderen*, p. 45 ff. T. H. Aschehoug, *Statsforfatning i Norge og Danmark indtil 1814*, p. 19. Ebbe Hertzberg, *En Fremstilling af det norske Aristokratis Historie*, p. 126 ff.

through them also with the royal family itself. According to the standards of those times he was well educated, and there can be no doubt that he had studied in foreign lands for many years, though no record is found of it. He was in every way a chieftain, a gifted and ambitious man, who set his mind on the accomplishing of great things. When he was chosen archbishop in 1157, he went to Italy, as it seems, to get the pall from the Pope, but he must have encountered some difficulty, as he was not consecrated till in 1161. The delay may have been caused by the struggle between Alexander III. and Victor IV., who were rival candidates for the papal throne. Pope Adrian IV. died in 1159, and Alexander III. was elected by a majority of the cardinals; but Emperor Frederick Barbarossa would not sanction his election, and caused Victor IV. to be chosen. A bitter fight was waged by the two popes, but Alexander III. was quite generally regarded as the true Pope. Even the new antipopes chosen after the death of Victor IV. were finally forced to withdraw. In Italy and elsewhere in southern Europe, Eystein had seen the Roman Church in all its outward splendor, and he returned to Norway with a firm resolve that the cathedral church of his own archdiocese of Nidaros should betoken by its outward appearance the dignity and power of the Church of Norway. The Christ church which Olav Kyrre had built was too plain and small, and he immediately commenced to reconstruct it. He began the work by rebuilding the transepts in the Anglo-Norman style in vogue at the time. A great architectural work was thus begun, which led to the erection of the magnificent Trondhjem cathedral, the grandest structure ever built in the Scandinavian North.[1] In order to get the necessary means for so ambitious an undertaking he increased in many unusual ways the revenues of his diocese. His income grew with the building, and the taxes were constantly increased. He made the regulation that the taxes paid to the church should henceforth be paid in pure silver, not in coin, which had been debased. This nearly doubled his income. He shipped grain to Iceland without paying export duty, and infringed in other ways on the royal preroga-

[1] P. A. Munch and H. E. Schirmer, *Trondhjems Domkirke*, Christiania, 1859. A. Freiherrn von Minutoli, *Der Dom zu Drontheim*, Berlin, 1853. Hermann Schirmer, *Kristkirken i Nidaros*, Christiania, 1885.

tive. Erling Skakke was much displeased, but he had to acquiesce in these arbitrary innovations. This was, no doubt, one of the conditions on which the archbishop finally agreed to crown Magnus Erlingsson at the assembly of magnates in Bergen in 1164. Erling, who controlled the crown lands and the royal estates, found a compensation by driving his opponents into exile and confiscating their estates.[1]

When Magnus Erlingsson was crowned, King Valdemar of Denmark sent messengers to Norway to demand the district of Viken, which Erling Skakke had promised in return for the aid which he had given him. But Erling gave an evasive answer. The people of the district would have to speak for themselves, he said. When the Borgarthing was assembled, the people declared loudly that they would never consent to being transferred to Denmark. Valdemar was very wroth when he discovered Erling Skakke's deceitfulness, and as Erling's personal enemies encouraged Valdemar to attack him, he sent spies to Norway to learn what the popular sentiment was. They came as pilgrims to Nidaros, and many of Erling's opponents promised to aid Valdemar. When Erling found this out, he seized those who had implicated themselves, and punished them most severely. Valdemar made an expedition to Norway in 1165, and visited Sarpsborg and Tunsberg, but when he found that the people were almost unanimously opposed to Danish overlordship, he returned home without attempting to forcibly occupy the district.

Haakon Herdebreid's party in the southern districts put a new pretender in the field against Erling and his son Magnus. This was

---

[1] The great minster in Bergen, the Christ church, which was begun in the time of Olav Kyrre, was completed in 1170, and St. Sunniva's shrine was brought from Selja and placed on the altar of the church. It remained there till 1531, when the church was destroyed. The Maria church in Bergen, which is still standing, and which is now the oldest building in the city, must also have been erected in Archbishop Eystein's time, as it is mentioned in 1183. *Kunst og Haandverk fra Norges Fortid, udgivet af Foreningen for norske Mindesmerkers Bevaring,* IV., Kirker, pl. XIV–XXI. The Elgeseter monastery near Trondhjem, and the Castle monastery at Konghelle, both of the order of St. Augustine, were also founded by Eystein. He was a special friend and admirer of Thomas à Becket, the fearless and headstrong Archbishop of Canterbury, whom he sought to emulate. When Becket was killed, he was regarded as a martyr also in Norway, and his biography, the *Thomassaga,* became very popular reading.

Olav Ugæva, the son of King Eystein's daughter Maria. He gathered formidable bands of followers called "Hettusveinar," who avoided pitched battles, but levied tribute on the people for their maintenance, and exercised great power in the southeastern districts and in Viken. At one time Erling himself barely escaped falling into their hands. These bands were the forerunners of the Birkebeiner (Birchlegs), who were to play such an important part in future events.

Olav Ugæva and his followers sought support in Denmark, and Erling, who feared the powerful King Valdemar, was evidently alarmed, and eagerly grasped what seemed to him an opportunity to avert the danger. While Valdemar was absent on an expedition against the Wends, Buris, one of his vassals, a descendant of King Svein Estridsson, formed a treasonable plot to overthrow him. He negotiated with Erling, who promised to attack Denmark with the Norwegian fleet. The plot was revealed in time, and Valdemar called Buris before him and accused him of treason. Buris denied the charge, but the king kept him in custody until the Norwegian fleet arrived on the coast of Denmark. This proved his guilt, and he was imprisoned as a traitor. Erling captured some Danish ships at Dyrsaa, in Jutland, plundered Grindhøg (Grenaa), and arrived before Copenhagen. But the vigilant Bishop Absalon met him with a strong force, and Erling did not attack the town. A peace was concluded between him and the bishop, and after an unsuccessful attack on Holland Erling returned home.

King Valdemar decided to punish the Norsemen for this attack on his kingdom. The following spring he sailed with a large fleet to Viken, where, according to Saxo Grammaticus, he was well received by the people; no doubt, by the adherents of Olav Ugæva. At Tunsberg the townsmen even marched in procession to meet him. But Erling arrived with a fleet, and Valdemar was forced to take to sea. His men became mutinous and wished to return home, but the voyage was continued along the coast "until they came so far north that at the summer solstice the nights are as light as the day, and one can read at midnight the finest writing without difficulty," sagely remarks the learned Saxo. It may be supposed that they were somewhere on the southwestern coast of Norway. As he was short of provisions, and as the resistance and ill-will on the part of his men continued to trouble him, he sailed back to Denmark; but for the future he laid an embargo on all trade between Denmark and Norway.

Although hostilities had ceased, a state of war still existed between the two countries. But worse than the war was the interruption of the trade with Denmark, on which the southern districts of Norway were especially dependent. The people in Viken demanded that peace should be concluded with King Valdemar, and Erling sent his wife Christina, a cousin of Valdemar, to Denmark, ostensibly on a visit, but really for the purpose of quietly gaining information as to the prevailing sentiment. She was well received by the king, and Erling sent Bishop Helge of Oslo to negotiate peace. Bishop Stephanus of Upsala also became his representative. Erling was summoned to Denmark, and the peace was concluded at Ringsted in 1170. According to the "Heimskringla" the district of Viken was given to Valdemar, who in return made Erling a jarl, and gave him the district as a fief under the Danish crown. Through his selfish and unpatriotic policy Erling Skakke had alienated a part of the kingdom of Norway, something which had not happened since the days of his prototypes, Haakon Jarl and his sons.[1] The authority exercised over the district by King Valdemar was purely nominal, it is true, but Erling's system of statesmanship was of the most pernicious sort, and might have led to very serious consequences if he and his party had remained in power.

After he had made peace with Denmark he guarded eagerly against all pretenders, and with the eye and spirit of a tyrant he sought to exterminate the family of Harald Gille. This aroused the hostility of the Swedish jarl Birger Brosa, who was married to Harald Gille's daughter Bergitta, and henceforth his opponents found en-

---

[1] Saxo Grammaticus says that Erling became King Valdemar's vassal, and promised to furnish him sixty ships in time of war. He promised also to rear his young son, Valdemar (Valdemar the Victorious), to give him the title of duke, and to have him elected king of Norway, if Magnus died without legitimate heirs. He does not mention Viken, but it is evident that it was only as jarl of Viken that he was Valdemar's vassal, as this conforms to the original agreement between him and King Valdemar. *Historia Danica*, part III., book XV. *Fagrskinna*, ch. 273–274.

couragement and support in Sweden. No one wielded a mightier sword than Erling Skakke. He combined craft and resourcefulness with great energy and courage; but he had the tyrant's fear, and as his heart grew harder and his methods bloodier, his real power decreased, and an opponent mightier than he arose to overthrow him.

60. THE ENGLISH CONQUEST OF IRELAND. EVENTS IN THE COLONIES

After the battle of Clontarf the Norsemen ceased to rule in Ireland. Their military power was broken, and they submitted to the Irish kings. They continued, however, to hold their fortified cities, and as the Irish, because of incessant feuds, were able to exercise but a nominal overlordship, they continued their commerce, governed themselves according to their own laws, and remained a distinct nationality as before. By old Irish and English writers they are generally called Ostmen (*i.e.* men from the East), a name still preserved in Oxmantown (= Ostmantown) in Dublin. Giraldus Cambrensis speaks of them as a distinct people given to seafaring and commerce ("gens igitur haec, quae nunc Ostmannica gens vocatur").[1] About the middle of the twelfth century the Irish feuds raged with their accustomed fury, and led finally to the conquest of Ireland by the Anglo-Normans in 1169–1171. The principal resistance to the invaders was offered by the fortified Norse towns, but as there was no national government and no general leadership, each town fell in turn, and the conquest was easily accomplished.

In 1166 Ruaidhri O'Connor became high-king of Ireland. He went to Dublin, where he was also hailed as king by the Ostmen; but this was scarcely more than a ceremony, since the men of Dublin were still ruled by their own king, Askell (Hasculf) Ragnvaldsson. With O'Connor's aid Diarmait MacMurchadha, king of Leinster, a very restless and troublesome chief, was driven away from Ireland. He hastened to King Henry II. of England for aid, found him in Aquitaine, and promised to do homage to him for his kingdom, if he would help him to regain it. This gave Henry a welcome opportunity

---

[1] Giraldus Cambrensis, *Topographia Hiberniae*. J. J. Worsaae, *Minder on de Danske og Nordmændene i England, Skotland og Irland*, p. 432.

to undertake the conquest of Ireland, which he seems to have planned for some time. He had already obtained a bull from Pope Adrian IV. (the former Cardinal Nicolaus Brakespear), in which the Pope permitted him to take possession of the country, and blessed the undertaking as one prompted by "ardor of faith and love of religion." King Henry promised the Pope to "subject the people to laws, to extirpate vicious customs, to respect the rights of the native churches, and to enforce the payment of Peter's Pence." He could not leave for Ireland at once, but he gave Diarmait a letter granting his vassals permission to aid him. With this letter Diarmait returned to England, and Richard Clare, Earl of Pembroke, also called Strongbow, and many other Anglo-Norman barons promised to assist him. Strongbow bargained for the hand of Diarmait's daughter, and was to become heir to the throne of Leinster.

In 1169 the half-brothers Robert Fitz-Stephens and Maurice Fitz-Gerald went to Ireland with a small force and captured Wexford. Strongbow followed the next year with 1000 men and 200 mounted knights. Waterford was stormed, and a large number of the inhabitants were put to death. After celebrating his wedding with Diarmait's daughter, Aife, Strongbow made haste to attack Dublin. The city was taken by a stroke of perfidy executed during an armistice arranged for the purpose of negotiating about the terms for capitulation. Askell (Hasculf) and some of the Ostmen who succeeded in escaping to the ships sought refuge in the Orkneys and the Hebrides, but the city was sacked, and a great number of people were slain. The victors made Dublin their headquarters, and it was clearly their plan to subdue the whole country; but King Henry's jealousy of Strongbow's success, and the resolute resistance offered by both Norsemen and Irish, threw new obstacles in their path. Henry ordered the barons to return to England, and when Diarmait died, the people of Leinster chose his nephew as their king, and turned their backs on Strongbow, who was, thereby, placed in a most difficult situation, as he could get no further reënforcements.

In the meantime Askell, who had gone to the Orkneys, had gathered a fleet of sixty ships and a large number of warriors, who, according to Giraldus Cambrensis, wore shirts of mail, and carried round, red shields.[1] The leaders of this army were Askell Ragnvaldsson and Jón Ode, a chieftain from the Orkneys. They made a vigorous assault on Dublin, but were finally defeated. Jón Ode fell, and Askell, the last Norse king of Dublin, was captured and put to death.

Archbishop Laurentius, who still hoped to rid Ireland of the enemy, sent messengers to King Gudrød of Man, and to the chieftains of the Hebrides, and asked for help. King Gudrød came with a fleet of thirty ships, and invested Dublin from the seaside, while the high-king besieged it with an army of 30,000 men. Strongbow, who was in command of the garrison, was brought to desperate straits, and he even began negotiations for surrender; but the siege was not pushed with vigor, and by a sudden sally from the city he defeated and drove away the Irish army, and returned with rich booty. The high-king had to yield, and Strongbow took possession of Leinster as Diarmait's heir. But the garrison at Wexford had been overwhelmed, and Strongbow, who saw that he could not succeed without reënforcements, hastened to England to offer his submission to King Henry II. While he was away, the Irish made another unsuccessful attempt to capture Dublin. We hear also about this time of the last Viking expedition led by the last Viking, Svein Asleivsson of the Orkneys, who undertook to capture Dublin. It is possible that the expedition was undertaken to avenge the death of Askell Ragnvaldsson, and that it was made while Strongbow was in England. The "Orkneyingasaga" gives the following account of it: "They went all the way south to Dyflin (Dublin), and took the inhabitants by surprise, so that they did not know till they were in town. They took a great deal of plunder, and took captive the rulers of the city, and their negotiations ended in the surrender of the city to Svein, and they promised to pay as much money as he might levy on them. He was to quarter his men in the town, and have the command of it, and the Dyflin men confirmed this arrangement with oaths. Svein and his men went down to their ships in the evening, but in the morning they were to come into the town and receive hostages from the inhabitants.

[1] Giraldus Cambrensis (Gerald de Barri) was a priest, who accompanied the Anglo-Norman barons to Ireland, and wrote a chronicle of the expedition and a description of the country, *Topographia Hiberniae.*

"Now it is to be told what was going on in the town during the night. The rulers of the town had a meeting, and considered the difficulties in which they were placed. They thought it a grievous hardship that they should have to surrender their town to the Orkneymen, especially to him whom they knew to be the most exacting man in the whole West; and they came to the determination to play him false if they could. They resolved to dig a large pit inside of the city gates, and in many other places between the houses, where it was intended that Svein's men should come in, and armed men were hidden in the houses close by. They placed such coverings over the pits as were sure to fall in when the weight of the men came upon them. Then they covered all over with straw, so that the pits could not be seen, and waited till morning.

"Next morning Svein and his men arose and armed themselves, and went to the town; and when they came near the gates, the Dyflin men ranged themselves on both sides from the gates along by the pits. Svein and his men, not being on their guard, fell into them. Some of the townsmen ran immediately to the gates, and others to the pits, and attacked Svein's men with weapons. It was difficult for them to defend themselves, and Svein perished there in the pit, with all those who had entered the town." [1]

When Strongbow arrived in England, King Henry was already preparing an expedition to Ireland. The earl obtained the king's pardon by surrendering to him the Irish seaports; he did homage to him for Leinster, and accompanied him to Ireland. Henry placed English garrisons in Dublin, Wexford, and Waterford, received the homage of the Irish chieftains, and returned home.

But although the Norsemen were conquered, they were not driven from Ireland.[2] They are mentioned in the "Annals of the Four

[1] *Orkneyingasaga*, translated by Jon A. Hjaltalin and Gilbert Goudie, edited by Joseph Anderson, ch. cxi–cxii. Svein Asleivsson is also mentioned in the *Annals of the Kingdom of Ireland by the Four Masters* about 1174.

[2] The Norsemen were forced to withdraw from the cities, and they built new towns outside the city walls as at Dublin. The Ostmantown (Oxmantown), which thus originated, merged in course of time with the original city. See Alexander Bugge, *Contributions to the History of Ireland*, no. 6., p. 4. J. J. Worsaae, *Minder om de Danske og Nordmœndene i England, Skotland og Irland*, p. 435 ff.

Masters," 1174, and also by Giraldus Cambrensis, who states that the same year the English asked the Ostmen for help against the Irish, and in a battle near the city 400 Ostmen from Dublin fell. J. J. A. Worsaae says: "Over a century later many Ostmen were yet found in the larger towns of Ireland, where they, as it appears, still preserved their Norse characteristics which distinguished them from the Irish and the English. In the year 1201 a decision was rendered at Limerick by twelve Irishmen, twelve Englishmen, and twelve Ostmen regarding Limerick church lands, churches, and other belongings, which show that the Ostmen were still so numerous that they were accounted equal to the Irish and English.[1] Even from the year 1283 there is found preserved in the Tower of London a document issued by King Edward I., ordaining that the Ostmen of Waterford, in conformity with the regulations made by King Henry II., should be amenable to the same laws as the English who were living in Ireland." [2] This shows that the Ostmen were still a distinct people.[3] In 1292 the wine trade of the Ostmen is still spoken of in old documents, which shows that this once flourishing commerce was not yet dead, though over a hundred years had passed since the Norse towns in Ireland had fallen into the hands of the English.

After the Norsemen lost their independence, they gradually mixed with the Irish and English inhabitants. "The Irish annals," says Worsaae, "mention several clans which were of Norse descent, or strongly mixed with Norse blood. In the annals and genealogical tables from the Middle Ages we find many, both among the clergy and outside, with Norse names. In the fourteenth and fifteenth centuries we find among the canons and monks of the Christ church in Dublin, which was erected by the Norsemen, such names as Harold, Olaf, Siwird (Sivard), Regenald (Ragnvald), Iwyr, etc." The old

---

[1] "As late as 1251 Magnus Mac Olav Duff proposed to raise a force in Ireland to invade the territory of the king of Norway in the Isle of Man," says Alexander Bugge. *Contributions to the History of Norsemen in Ireland*, no. 5, p. 24; *Calendars of Documents relating to Ireland*, I., no. 3206.

[2] This document, from *Patent Roll II.*, Edward I., no. 9, is printed as an appendix to Worsaae's book.

[3] Worsaae, *Minder om de Danske og Nordmœndene*, p. 432 f. Alexander Bugge, *Contributions to the History of the Norsemen in Ireland*, III., p. 10 f. *Historical and Municipal Documents of Ireland.*

chronicler Duald MacFirbis, who wrote in the middle of the seventeenth century, says: "And as for the greater part of the merchants in the city of Ath Cliath up to the present day they are of the family of Amhlaibh Cuaran (Olav Kvaaran), and of the family of Sadhbh, daughter of Brian Borumha, who was his wife when the battle of Clontarf was fought." And he adds: "Thus the race of this Amhlaibh Cuaran in the town of Ath Cliath (Dublin) is opposing the Gaedhels (Irish) of Erin." [1] Mr. Worsaae points out that traces of the Norsemen are still found in Ireland, especially in personal names of Norse origin still in use, as MacHitteric or Shiteric (son of Sigtrygg), O'Bruadair (son of Broder), McRagnall (son of Ragnvald), Roailb (Rolv), Auleev (Olav), Manus (Magnus), Harrold (Harald), Iver (Ivar), Cotter or McOtter (Ottar), and others.

The civil wars had a tendency to weaken the ties which still bound the colonies to the mother country. The Orkney jarls continued to do homage to the kings of Norway for their possessions, but during such a period of weakness and confusion they could exercise sovereign authority without much interference or restraint. King Gudrød of Man and the Hebrides had long been waging war with his rival Sumarlide. In 1154, or 1155, he made an expedition to Ireland, where he defeated King Muirchertach's brother, and was hailed as king of Dublin. He returned to Man, but became so tyrannical that many people in the Sudreys turned away from him, and chose Sumarlide's son, Dugald, as king. This brought about a permanent partition of the kingdom of Man and the Hebrides, 1158. Gudrød was finally defeated by Sumarlide, and went to King Inge

---

[1] *On the Fomorians and Norsemen by Duald MacFirbis*, the original Irish text edited with translation and notes by Alexander Bugge, p. 11.

Lindssay's *The Coinage of Ireland*, Cork, 1839, enumerates the following Norse kings of Dublin: Anlaf (Olav) 853, Ifar (Ivar) 870, Ostinus (Eystein) 872, Godfred (Gudrød) 875, Sihtric (Sigtrygg) 893, Sihtric 896, Regnald (Ragnvald) 919, Godfred 920, Anlaf 934, Blacar 941, Godfred 948, Anlaf 954, Godfred 960, Anlaf 962, Regnald, Gluniaran 981, Sihtric 989, Ifar 993, Sihtric 994, Anlaf 1029, Sihtric 1034, Anlaf 1041, Ifar 1050, Eachmargach 1054, Mælnambo 1064, Godred Crovan 1066 (?), Godfred Merenach 1076, Gilalve 1094, Thorfinn 1109, Regnald 1125, Godfred 1147, Oicterus (Ottar) 1147, Broder 1149, Askel 1159, Roderick 1171–1200. Of the kings of Waterford and Limerick only a few are mentioned. See Worsaae, *Minder om de Danske og Nordmændene*, p. 395.

Krokryg in Norway, who confirmed his title to his kingdom. But Gudrød deserted his suzerain in the battle of Oslo, and joined his opponent Haakon Herdebreid. He remained in Norway till Sumarlide fell in 1164, when he returned with a large military force, and seized Man and a part of the Hebrides, which possessions he ruled till 1187, while the other part of the island kingdom was ruled by Sumarlide's son Dugald.[1]

61. SVERRE SIGURDSSON AND THE BIRKEBEINER

Erling Skakke's harsh régime, and his attempt to exterminate all descendants of Harald Gille created a most determined opposition to his rule, and brought new forces into the field against him. Many had no choice but to resort to armed resistance in their own self-defense, for although they were convicted for no wrongdoing, they knew that Erling was plotting their destruction, and with their band of followers they sought refuge in mountains and forests, where they led a life almost like brigands in constant want and danger. They were called "Birkebeiner" (Birchlegs), because they were sometimes forced to wrap their feet in birch bark for want of shoes. In their fight against the tyrannical Erling and the puppet king, Magnus, the Birkebeiner stood forth as persecuted patriots, who under the guidance of an extraordinary leader brought about a revolution, and revived the lost ideal of a united and independent Norway.

The Birkebeiner first rallied around Eystein, a grandson of Harald Gille. He was small and fair-faced, and was nicknamed Meyla (i.e. maiden). Jarl Birger Brosa, who was married to Brigida, a sister of Eystein's father, promised to aid him, and furnished him with both men and money. Eystein and his men spent two years in Viken and neighboring districts, and in 1176 he sailed to Nidaros, captured the city, and was proclaimed king.

He had assembled an army of 2400 men, and with this force he crossed the mountains into southern Norway, but in January, 1177, King Magnus Erlingsson met him at Ree, where Eystein was defeated

---

[1] *Orkneyingasaga*, ed. by Anderson, p. 181 and note. *Chronica Regum Manniæ*, ed. by Munch, p. 12, note p. 81. *Heimskringla, Haakon Herdebreid's Saga*, ch. 17. P. A. Munch, *Det norske Folks Historie*, vol. II., 940.

and slain. His followers were scattered, and many of them sought refuge across the Swedish border.

A more formidable leader now appeared on the scene to champion the lost cause of the Birkebeiner. This was Sverre Sigurdsson, who claimed to be an illegitimate son of King Sigurd Mund. The "Sverressaga,"[1] which gives a full, though not impartial, account of King Sverre's life and deeds,[2] states that Unas Kambari, a brother of Bishop Hroi (Roe) in the Faroe Islands, married a Norse wife named Gunhild, in the reign of the sons of Harald Gille. She bore a son, who was called Sverre, and he was thought to be the son of Unas. When he was five years old, he was sent to the Faroe Islands, where he was reared by Bishop Hroi, who educated him for the priesthood, and ordained him as priest. Sverre did not know who was his real father until he was twenty-four years of age. At that time his mother Gunhild went to Rome, where she made the confession that Sverre was not the son of Unas, but of King Sigurd Mund. This confession was laid before the Pope, and she was commanded to inform her son of his real parentage. She returned to Norway, and sailed thence to the Faroe Islands, where she told Sverre that he was King Sigurd's son.[3] The next year he went to

---

[1] The Saga of King Sverri of Norway, translated by J. Sephton, M.A., London, 1899.

[2] The Sverressaga was written by Abbot Karl Jónsson of Thingeyre in Iceland, who was staying at the court of King Sverre, and began the work in 1185. The prologue states that it was written "according to the book which Abbot Karl Jónsson wrote when King Sverre sat over him and settled what he should write." This seems to make clear also the question of the authorship, but the prologue in the "Flateyjarbók" says that "Priest Styrmi the historian followed that book (Abbot Karl's) when he wrote." Professor P. A. Munch held that Karl Jónsson did not write the whole saga, but that Styrmi wrote the last part. Det norske Folks Historie, part III., p. 395. Dr. Vigfusson has made it quite clear, however, that Abbot Karl has written the whole work. See J. Sephton's translation of the Sverressaga, Introduction, p. XVII.

As the Heimskringla, Fagrskinna, Morkinskinna, and other collections of sagas of the Norse kings stop with the year 1177, the Sverressaga is the most important source for the reign of King Sverre.

[3] Whether King Sverre was of royal blood was a much debated question in his own day, and there is no more unanimity of opinion on this point among modern scholars. R. Keyser says: "Whether Sverre really was a son of King Sigurd Mund, as he claimed to be, could scarcely be determined with

Norway to see what he could do. He mingled with the people, visited Erling Skakke, spoke with the king's bodyguard, and learned to know the general sentiment, but he did not disclose his plans or his identity. At last he made his way through Gautland to Jarl Birger Brosa, where he arrived three days before Christmas, weary and exhausted. The jarl's wife, Brigida, was a sister of Sigurd Mund, and he confided his troubles to her and Jarl Brosa, but they

certainty in his own day, and it is still more difficult to do so now." (*Norges Historie*, II., p. 166.) Professor P. A. Munch is inclined to regard Sverre's assertion regarding his descent as true, though he points to the lack of positive evidence, and says that it is a question which cannot be definitely settled. (*Det norske Folks Historie*, part III., p. 50 ff.)

Dr. G. Vigfusson (*Corpus Poeticum Borcale*, II., p. 255 f.) held that the story of Sverre's royal descent was pure invention. J. E. Sars finds Sverre's assertions untrustworthy, but he considers it probable that he was a son of King Sigurd Mund, or at least that he thought he was. (*Udsigt over den norske Historie*, II., p. 122 ff.) In 1901 Professor Gustav Storm wrote a treatise on this subject: *Kong Sverres fœdrene Herkomst* (*Historisk Tidsskrift*, fjerde række, vol. II., p. 163 ff.), in which he takes the position that Sverre was really what he claimed to be, a son of Sigurd Mund. He finds the best evidence of this in the *Gesta Henrici Secundi*, written by a contemporary of King Sverre, the English abbot Benedict of Peterborough, 1169–1181. Benedict gives an account of the political events in Norway which is quite accurate, and shows that the author was well informed. He says that Sigurd Mund had three illegitimate sons : Haakon, Sigurd, and Sverre, and they had different mothers. Another contemporary English writer, Robert de Hoveden, who wrote a history of England up till 1201, and partly used Benedict as a source, gives a similar account of Sverre's descent. Storm holds that these English historians were impartial, while other old writers, like William Parvus of Newburgh, who wrote his *Historia Rerum Anglicarum*, 1196–1198, and likewise Saxo Grammaticus, have received their information from Sverre's enemies, the adherents of Magnus Erlingsson and the Norwegian hierarchy. In *Historisk Tidsskrift*, fjerde række, vol. III., 1905, Professor Ludvig Daae has written a reply to Gustav Storm's treatise under the title: *Var Sverre Kongesøn?* in which he states that he has not been convinced by Storm's arguments. Among those who hold an opposite view of Sverre's descent he mentions Vigfusson, Dahlmann (*Geschichte von Dänemark*, Hamburg, 1840–1843), and Werlauff (*Anecdoton, Historiam Sverreri, Regis Norwegiae Illustrans*, Copenhagen, 1815). In the story which sets forth how Sverre discovered that he was a son of Sigurd Mund, Daae finds so many features which he considers wholly incredible that he regards the whole as a fabrication, and holds that the probability of Sverre's royal descent is very slight. It is probably correct when Vigfusson sees in Sverre's great talents a proof that he was "no chip of the Gilchrist block," and with Dahlmann we can most properly regard him as "the son of his own deeds.",

would not help him, because they had promised to support Eystein
Meyla (his cousin), and because they had heard that Erling Skakke
had sent this young man to them in mockery. But Sverre stayed
with them during Christmas, and spoke to them constantly about
his plans. After Christmas he went to Vermland to visit Sigurd
Mund's daughter Cecilia, the wife of Folkvid Lagmand, and she
received him with great joy. Rumors had already reached him of
Eystein Meyla's defeat and death, and the Birkebeiner, who had
learned that Sverre, a son of Sigurd Mund, was staying in Vermland, sent messengers to him and asked him to be their leader. At
first he refused, because the Birkebeiner were small disorganized
bands in want of everything, but when they threatened to kill him
to gain King Magnus' good-will if he did not join them, he consented.
With a band of seventy men he started for Viken in southern Norway, and the number increased on the march till he had 420 men.
A *thing* was called, and the Birkebeiner hailed Sverre as king, though
he was opposed to assuming the royal title under so unfavorable
circumstances. He soon resumed his march, following the Swedish
side of the border to Trøndelagen. He kept strict discipline, and
forbade his men to plunder. On these weary marches he was deserted
by all but his most resolute followers, so that his little force again
dwindled to seventy men. With this small band he suddenly appeared before Trondhjem; but the city was well garrisoned, and the
commanders marched against him with a force of 1450 men. Sverre
retreated, but bewildered them with circuitous marches until he had
secured some reënforcements. He then attacked them in a position
well suited to his tactics, and won a decisive victory. He seized the
ships in the harbor, and defeated several small squadrons which were
coming to join the fleet in defending Trondhjem. King Magnus'
lendermænd fled, the city surrendered, and Sverre was received by
the people in festive procession to the chiming of bells. He assembled
the Ørething (twelve representatives from each of the eight *fylker*),
and was proclaimed king of Norway according to St. Olav's law; that
is, according to the old law of succession which did not exclude a
king's illegitimate son from the throne. The law of 1164 was not
recognized, and King Magnus would be treated as an usurper.
Archbishop Eystein Erlendsson, who is not mentioned in connection

with these events, must have been absent from Norway at this time, a circumstance which, probably, enabled Sverre to seize Trondhjem.

The rumors of the events in Trøndelagen had reached Magnus and Erling, who hastened with their fleet northward along the coast. Sverre did not await their arrival, but marched across the mountains into Gudbrandsdal, and advanced to Lake Mjøsen, where he found Magnus' *lendermænd* stationed with 1400 men and eighteen ships. He did not venture to attack them, but sent a detachment to the Randsfjord; the vessels on that lake were seized, and the local forces defeated. But Orm Kongsbroder, Magnus' chief lieutenant in southern Norway, was advancing from Viken with a strong force. With great difficulty Sverre succeeded in transporting some of the small vessels overland from Randsfjord to Mjøsen. With these he attacked the *lendermænd*, surprised and defeated them, and captured all the vessels on the lake. All the districts of Oplandene now submitted to him, but as his force was so small that he could leave no garrisons, he was unable to hold permanently any of the territory which he had won. For some time this indecisive guerrilla warfare continued with forced marches and daring exploits in which Sverre proved himself a peerless leader, but his forces were too small to risk a decisive engagement, and his daring ventures represented no substantial progress. King Magnus and Orm Kongsbroder, who had united their armies in Viken, soon compelled Sverre to withdraw from Oplandene. In the winter of 1177 he crossed the mountains in an effort to capture Bergen, but the city had been warned; a fleet was patrolling the coast, and at Voss an army confronted him which he could not hope to cope with. He had no choice but to retrace his steps across the snow-covered mountains. For weeks they struggled through the pathless wilds, without fire or shelter. Horses and military stores were lost, and many of his men perished from cold or exhaustion before they finally reached the settlements in Valdres. Even here he did not dare to tarry, as all avenues of escape might be cut off. He continued his retreat to Østerdalen, where he camped during Christmas; but when he learned that Erling Skakke was approaching, he withdrew across the Swedish border.

Sverre began the campaign of 1178 in Jæmtland, where he forced the Jamts to swear allegiance to him. It seems to have been his plan to secure a base of operations from which he might attack Trondhjem, which again had fallen into the hands of King Magnus and Archbishop Eystein, but he entertained no great hope of success. When he reached Namdalen, a district north of Trondhjem, he assembled his men and discussed the situation with them. Three courses, he thought, now remained open: "One to make a voyage north to Haalogaland, obtain friends and ships, and then sail south to Bergen to see if he could win a victory over his foes; the second course, to leave the land, and sail to the Western Isles, where there were good prospects, he considered, of obtaining support; the third course, to go on a plundering expedition to Ireland, or other western lands, for he was of the opinion that the popularity of King Magnus and Erling Jarl would grow less the longer they ruled over the country. 'But at present,' he said, 'their power is great, and to contend with them will be a hard matter.'"[1] The Birkebeiner would not listen to Sverre's advice, but thought that they could capture Trondhjem now as easily as they had done before. But Archbishop Eystein was at home, and urged the Trønders to resist the Birkebeiner to the utmost. "I have been told," he said, "that their numbers are few and their ships small; the men, moreover, are in an exhausted and wretched condition. It befits not yeomen and merchants to give up their clothes or goods to such thieves and evil-doers as Sverre has scraped together." King Sverre risked the attack, but he suffered a crushing defeat, and narrowly escaped losing his life. After this mishap he again sought refuge in the mountains, but marched slowly southward towards Viken. When King Magnus heard of the approach of the Birkebeiner, he hastened to meet them with a strong force. Sverre, who saw that he could gain no further support until he gained a victory over his opponents, told his men that he would rather die now in an honorable battle with King Magnus than to be constantly driven from pillar to post. At Hirta Bridge he resolutely attacked King Magnus' forces. Both the king and Orm Kongsbroder were wounded, many of their men fell, and they retreated from the field. Shortly afterwards he also succeeded in destroying a

[1] *Sverressaga*, ch. 22.

part of King Magnus' fleet at Konghelle. These successes inspired his men with new confidence, and he stationed himself in Viken, where he could obtain both provisions and reënforcements. From this time on his fortunes began to mend. In the fall of 1179 he returned to Trondhjem, where he defeated the forces of King Magnus, captured the city, and took ten ships; but this victory was in no way decisive. The great leaders—King Magnus, Erling Skakke, Orm Kongsbroder, and Archbishop Eystein—were staying in Bergen, and when they heard of Sverre's success they collected a large fleet with which they intended to attack him as soon as the new campaign should open in the spring. When winter was past, Sverre sailed southward with the fleet which he had collected, but off Stadt he met Magnus, Erling, Orm, and Eystein with so overwhelming a force that the only question became how to avoid falling into their hands with the whole fleet. To save himself Sverre steered for the open sea. In a fog his pursuers lost sight of him, and as they were unable to determine what course he had taken, Orm Kongsbroder and Eystein were sent with a part of the fleet to protect Bergen, while King Magnus and Erling proceeded to Trondhjem. Sverre was already in the city when they arrived, but they landed without opposition, and took up a position on the Kalveskind, a peninsula formed by the river Nid and the sea, while Sverre held the opposite bank of the river. After some fruitless parleying Sverre marched away, and the rumor spread that he had retreated into the mountains. So confident was Erling Skakke that he would not return that he allowed his men to feast and drink in the town, and did not heed the warning of his lieutenants that he should keep good watch. Sverre, who well knew the significance of the combat now imminent, had hastened into Guldal to collect reënforcements. On the night of the 18th of June he returned to Trondhjem. He reached the city at daybreak, halted a few moments and addressed his men, telling them how much depended on the battle which was to be fought, and what they might gain if they were victorious. "I will now make known to you what is to be gained," he said: "whoever slays a *lendermand*, and can bring forward evidence of his deed, shall himself be a *lendermand*; and whatever title a man shall cause to be vacant, that title shall be his; he shall be king's man who slays a king's man, and he shall receive good honor beside." [1] King Magnus' sentinels had noticed the approaching Birkebeiner, and the war trumpets called the men to the standards. The first onset was so fierce that Erling's men were forced backward, his standard was cut down, and he received a halberd thrust in the abdomen, and fell mortally wounded. King Magnus' forces broke into disorderly flight. In rushing past, Magnus noticed his father; he bent down and kissed him and said: "We shall meet again on the day of joy, my father." Erling's lips moved, but he could not speak. Magnus had to flee for his life, and Erling soon breathed his last among his enemies. Magnus boarded a ship and sailed away from Trondhjem. His defeat was overwhelming. Ten *lendermænd* had fallen, and half of his *hird*. The decisive battle between the two parties had been fought. Erling Skakke was buried near the south wall of the Christ church, but his burial place now lies inside the much larger Trondhjem cathedral which was erected later.[2]

After the battle of Nidaros Magnus fled to Bergen, which was held by Archbishop Eystein and Orm Kongsbroder. Sverre fortified Trondhjem with palisades, and took special care to strengthen his fleet, knowing that this branch of the military service would be of the greatest importance in the future. Magnus and Eystein spent the winter in Viken, and the following spring they assembled again a large fleet and sailed to Trondhjem to try conclusions with the victorious Sverre. He proposed that they should make peace; that he and Magnus should rule as joint kings, but the offer was rejected. On the 27th of May, 1180, another battle was fought at Ilevoldene in Trondhjem, in which Magnus was again defeated. His army was torn up, six *lendermænd* fell,[3] and Magnus retreated to Bergen with the remnants of his forces. But his victorious pursuers followed close on his heels, and as he was unable to offer any effectual resistance, he abandoned the struggle and fled to Denmark. Archbishop Eystein also left Norway, and sought refuge in England. King Henry II. was no special friend of prelates, but he, nevertheless,

---

[1] *Sverressaga*, ch. 35.

[2] King Sverre's speech at the grave of Erling Skakke is a fine specimen of eloquence, spiced with playful wit and biting sarcasm. See *Sverressaga*, translated by J. Sephton, ch. 38.

[3] Gustav Storm, *Historisk Tidsskrift*, anden række, vol. IV., p. 156.

treated the archbishop with due respect, and assigned him the monastery of Edmundsbury for a residence; but he granted him but a small allowance, probably because he did not want to make it appear that he was supporting King Sverre's enemies.

The great defeats had weakened the aristocracy, but had not destroyed their power of resistance. Not only could the chieftains still raise forces in nearly every district in the kingdom, but they did not hesitate to seek the support of the king of Denmark, who was willing enough to aid them as long as they were opposing the representative of a strong national government and an independent Norway. Sverre had indeed gained control of the whole kingdom, but his task was only rendered more difficult, as he had to defend it against the combined attacks of domestic and foreign enemies. In the spring of 1181, while sailing from Bergen to Viken, he suddenly encountered King Magnus and Orm Kongsbroder, who came from Denmark, with a fleet of thirty-two large ships.[1] His own fleet was much smaller, and he fell back to Bergen, where a bloody naval engagement was fought. By superior generalship he won the victory, but the battle was not decisive, as both sides suffered heavy losses. To know where the next attack would be made was impossible. Sverre hastened to Trondhjem, garrisoned the city and marched overland to Oslo for the purpose of defending Viken; but Magnus attacked Trondhjem, overwhelmed the garrison, and captured Sverre's whole fleet of thirty-five ships. When Sverre returned to aid the city, Magnus sailed away to Bergen, and Sverre could not pursue him for want of ships. The situation had once more become critical, as everything which Sverre had gained in many hard-fought campaigns was lost by one fell swoop. But he wasted no time in mourning his losses; with characteristic energy he set about repairing them as far as possible. The necessity of strengthening the defenses of the city so that it could be held by a garrison of reasonable size had become apparent. He greatly strengthened the fortifications, and erected a castle which he called "Zion," generally known as the "Sverreborg," where he stationed a part of the garrison.

[1] The followers of Magnus were called "Heklunger," from *hekla*, a chasuble.

"In the spring he caused palisades to be set up, so that a complete line stretched (from the castle) along the sea-coast, then inland along the guild-halls, and over the Eyra (Øren) across to the river, and along the river to the quays. A catapult was fixed on Bratøren by the sea, and a blockhouse was erected close to the sea." [1]

In the meantime Sverre had collected twenty small vessels, and with a strong north wind he set sail for Bergen. Magnus' ships were riding at anchor in the harbor. He entered quite unexpectedly, cut the anchor ropes, and towed the fleet out into the fjord, while a vigorous assault was made on the city. King Magnus fled after a short resistance, and again sought refuge in Denmark. Archbishop Eystein, who had returned to Norway after a three years' exile, was in Bergen at this time. He tendered his submission, and was allowed to return to his archdiocese in Trondhjem. The terms imposed by Sverre are not known, but it is quite certain that the constitution of 1164 was annulled, and that Eystein acknowledged him to be the rightful king of Norway.

Archbishop Eystein's political career was now ended. For eighteen years he had helped to keep Magnus Erlingsson on the throne. He had suffered defeat, he had languished in exile, and the great work which he had dreamed of accomplishing in his new archdiocese had been interrupted. He longed to return to his beloved Nidaros, and the last few years of his life were devoted to the erection of the great Trondhjem cathedral. Before his exile he had rebuilt and greatly increased in height the transepts of the Christ church which Olav Kyrre had erected; but during his sojourn in England and Normandy he was greatly impressed by the beauty of the Gothic architecture of the magnificent cathedrals which were built during this period.[2] When he returned to Trondhjem, he razed the choir of the Christ church, and built a new magnificent choir in the Gothic

---

[1] *Sverressaga*, ch. 71.

[2] In the neighborhood of Edmundsbury, where Eystein was staying, the Norwich cathedral was being repaired, and the Peterborough cathedral, which was begun in 1117, was nearing its completion in 1177–1180. The cathedral of Canterbury had been damaged by fire in 1174, and the work of restoration was begun in the following year. In Normandy the choir of the St. Etienne cathedral, in Caen, was erected 1180, and the Notre Dame in Seéz had been completed in 1126. See M. Schirmer, *Kristkirken i Nidaros*.

PLATE X

RUINS OF THE TRONDHJEM CATHEDRAL.

THE TRONDHJEM CATHEDRAL AS IT LOOKS AT PRESENT.

style. To this was joined the octagonal Lady's chapel, a minor choir (retrochorus). The main altar was placed in the choir proper over the grave of St. Olav. The Lady's chapel contained a minor altar for the Virgin Mary and her image, richly ornamented with precious stones. Underneath the walls of the Lady's chapel is the holy St. Olav's well, which, according to the legend, "welled up" on the spot where St. Olav's body was buried. It is forty-four feet deep, and walled with stone from the bottom. The reconstructed transepts, the new choir, and the Lady's chapel were probably finished when Eystein died in January, 1188.[1] The work of erecting a new nave in harmony with the other new parts of the cathedral was not begun till 1248.

After receiving aid from King Knut Valdemarsson of Denmark, Magnus returned to Norway in the spring of 1184 with twenty-four ships and a force which must have numbered about 3000 men. At Fimreite in Norefjord (a narrow arm of the Sognefjord) he met King Sverre, who at that moment had only fourteen ships and a force not exceeding 2000 men. The fierce battle which began in the afternoon of the 15th of June lasted till midnight. Twenty-one hundred and sixty men are said to have fallen, but Sverre was finally victorious. King Magnus perished together with the flower of the aristocracy, and Bergen and the districts of southwestern Norway which had given him the most loyal support hastened to tender their submission to King Sverre. After the battle Magnus' body was brought to Bergen, and buried in the Christ church. "Fair speeches were made over the grave. Nicolas Sultan spoke, a brother of King Sverre's mother, and one of the most eloquent of men. The king himself made a long speech in which he said: 'We stand here now at the grave of one who was kind and loving to his friends and kinsmen; though he and I, kinsmen, had not the good fortune to

---

[1] In 1229 Eystein was proclaimed a saint by a church council held in Trondhjem. His body was placed in a shrine, and deposited in the Trondhjem cathedral, where it remained till the time of the Reformation. His silver coffin was then brought to Copenhagen and given to the royal treasury. On an old oak confessional in the north transept of the cathedral is still found painted in gold the three saints: *St. Olaus, St. Halvardus, and St. Augustinus* (*i.e.* Eystein). See Peter Friedrich Suhm and Gerhard Schøning, *Forsøg til Forbedringer i den gamle danske og norske Historie,* p. 449 ff.

agree. He was hard to me and my men; may God forgive him now all his transgressions. Yet he was an honorable chief in many respects, and adorned by kingly descent.' The king spoke with many fine words, for he did not lack them on whatever course he was bent. The burial of King Magnus was put in careful order by King Sverre, coverlets were spread over the tombstone, and a railing was set up around it."[1]

62. KING SVERRE'S REIGN

While the struggle between Sverre and Magnus had the appearance of a personal contest for the possession of the throne, even a casual observer would soon discern that a revolution had been set on foot in which the Birkebeiner, or common people, under the leadership of Sverre had undertaken to wrest the power from the aristocracy and the clergy. Sverre could assert his right to the throne only according to the old rule of succession as the illegitimate son of Sigurd Mund, while Magnus Erlingsson wore the crown by the special arrangement of 1164, which virtually transferred the sovereign power to the church and the nobility. With Sverre on the throne the era of puppet kings and the rule of the nobility would be at an end; the constitution of 1164 would be overthrown, and a régime would be inaugurated to which Sverre himself gave the keynote in his speech at the funeral of Erling Skakke: "Times are greatly changed, as you may see, and have taken a marvelous turn, when one man stands in the place of three — of king, of jarl, of archbishop — and I am that one." Sverre would rule in the spirit of Harald Haarfagre and St. Olav, as the sovereign of a national and independent kingdom exercising the highest authority in ecclesiastical and state affairs within the realm. But although he had gained the power, and was fully resolved to use it, he did not exercise it in a harsh or arbitrary way. With the instinct of a true statesman, he took care to gradually lessen the influence of the nobility, to put more power into the hands of the common people, and to organize the administration and the judicial procedure in such a way as to lodge the power more firmly with the central government, and leave less to the whim of the individual or the caprice of fortune.

[1] *The Saga of King Sverri*, J. Sephton, ch. 97.

We have seen that the local administration was originally controlled by the *herser,* or hereditary chieftains. The *lendermœnd,* who succeeded them, were appointed by the king, but exercised to a large extent the same power. They controlled the local military organization, and exercised extensive police power; they attended the *thing* in the capacity of police officers to maintain peace and order, and they were still regarded by the people as their chieftains. They usually belonged to the old aristocracy, and although they exercised their power in the name of the king, they were quite independent of royal authority because of their rank and influence. The *aarmœnd* were the king's real representatives in local administration. They were overseers of the royal estates, collectors of taxes, and procured the necessaries for the entertainment of the king and his *hird* when he stayed in their district. They had to meet at the *thing* to maintain the king's cause; they should see to it that the *thing* was assembled at the right time, and should arrange for the election of *nefndarmenn,* or members of the *lagthing;* it was their duty, also, to keep in custody persons under arrest, and to inflict on them the punishments imposed by the *thing.* But they were of low birth — often they were freed slaves — and they were neither loved nor respected by the people. When determined resistance was offered, they were often unable to execute efficiently the duties of their office. In such a case the *lendermand* might from sheer kind-heartedness condescend to aid them; but as the *aarmœnd* stood under the supervision of the king, not of the *lendermœnd,* we may be sure that such assistance was both rarely and grudgingly given. In cases of special lack of efficiency in the local administration, or for special purposes, the king would appoint one of his trusted men as his *sysselmand,* or personal representative, clothed with an authority superior even to that of the *lendermœnd.* But such appointment was not permanent except in far-away districts like Haalogaland and Jæmtland. The *sysselmœnd* were royal officials, men of standing and ability. They had all the duties and powers of the *aarmœnd,* except that of acting as overseers over the royal estates, which was considered menial service. They also performed many of the duties of the *lendermand.* They had police power, collected fines and taxes, and assembled the *thing,* where they proclaimed new laws in the king's name. They acted as prosecutors, and defended the people in their rights over against the clergy; as royal deputies they had numerous duties, and possessed great power.[1] The appointment of *sysselmand* grew more common in the twelfth century, but during the period of the civil wars, while the king exercised only a nominal authority, this institution could not be of very great importance. Not till in King Sverre's time can it be said to have developed into a general and permanent system of local administration. After the battle of Nidaros he appointed *sysselmænd* in the whole of Trøndelagen. The office does not seem to have been established everywhere in the kingdom in his reign, but it was rapidly extended under his successors. The *aarmænd* continued for a time to act as subordinate officials under the *sysselmand*, but as the more important functions of their office were delegated to him, they became superfluous and gradually disappeared. The *lendermand* institution was left intact. Sverre pursued a conciliatory policy, and left the *lendermænd* in undisturbed possession of their lands and powers. He even appointed many of them as his *sysselmænd*. But in the civil wars their ranks had been greatly thinned, and Sverre rewarded many of his own men by elevating them to this high rank even if they were men of humble birth. Many of his followers he married to the widows and daughters of those who had fallen in the wars. He thereby attached the *lendermand* class more closely to himself, and by appointing them *sysselmænd*, they became royal officials dependent on the king, while the office of *lendermand*, stripped of its old significance, gradually became an empty title.

Of no less significance was the change made by King Sverre in the hitherto obscure office of *lagmand* (O. N. *lǫgmaðr*). Much difference of opinion has prevailed regarding the origin of this institution in Norway. R. Keyser, P. A. Munch, and Fr. Brandt held that the office of *lagmand* was created by Sverre, that before

---

[1] In regard to the various duties of *aarmænd*, *lendermænd*, and *sysselmænd* see *Norges gamle Love*, vol. V. Glossary under *ármaðr*, *lendrmaðr*, and *sýslumaðr*. See also T. H. Aschehoug, *Statsforfatningen i Norge og Danmark indtil 1814*, p. 49 ff. R. Keyser, *Norges Stats- og Retsforfatning i Middelalderen*, p. 209 ff. T. H. Aschehoug, *De norske Communers Retsforfatning før 1837*, p. 8 ff. E. Hertzberg, *Len og Veitzla i Norges Sagatid, Festskrift for Konrad Maurer, Germanistische Studien*, p. 283–331.

his time the word "lagmand" signified a man well versed in the law, who exercised no prescribed function in the judicial system.[1] Konrad Maurer held that the *lagmænd* were a separate class, distinct from the *lendermænd* and the people. He points to the very closely related institution of *lovsigemand* (*lǫgsǫgumaðr*), the leader of the *thing* in Iceland; and the *lagmand* in Greenland, the Faroe Islands, and Jæmtland, and finds that the existence of this institution in the Norwegian colonies can only be explained by supposing that it also existed in the mother country. Ebbe Hertzberg does not fully agree with either view, but holds that the office of *lagmand* dates from an earlier period than Sverre's reign,[2] which is shown especially by Sigurd Ranesson's noted case, where the *lagmænd* are mentioned several times. "Then King Eystein asked the *lagmænd* if it was law in Norway that *bønder* should judge kings. The *lagmænd* answered that suits between kings would have to be tried at the Ørething." When the laws in course of time became more numerous and complicated, few knew them well, and those who were to render decisions at the *thing* would, naturally, ask the opinion of those who were well versed in the law. "In course of time," says Hertzberg, "the word 'lagmand' came to designate one who was well versed in the law, who at the *thing* was requested to give his opinion as to the law, and thus for the occasion acted as *lagmand*." This view must be regarded as the one which is best supported by the evidence of the old writers. Several such *lagmænd* were present both at the *fylkesthing* and the *lagthing*, but they were not officially appointed. Archbishop Eystein attempted also to give the clergy control over the courts of law by making a regulation that at the *thing* the lawbook should be read by a priest, who would thereby get the office of principal *lagmand*. King Sverre's attention had, probably, been directed to this important office by Eystein's attempt. He reduced the number of *lagmænd*, and made them royal officials appointed by

[1] Keyser, *Norges Stats- og Retsforfatning*, p. 247. Munch, *Det norske Folks Historie*, II., p. 106. Brandt, *Langes Tidsskrift*, vol. V., p. 106.

[2] Maurer, *Kritische Vierteljahrsschrift für Gesetzgebung und Rechtswissenschaft*, München, 1868, p. 374. Ebbe Hertzberg, *Grundtrækkene i den ældste norske Proces*, edited by Dr. Fr. Brandt, Christiania, 1874, p. 156 ff. Maurer, *Die Entstehungszeit der älteren Gulathingslǫg*, München, 1872. *Egilssaga*, ch. 57.

the king. The duty of the *lagmand* should be to give his *orskurd*, *i.e.* to state the law according to which the *lagrette* should decide the case. It became customary, also, to bring cases before the *lagmand* outside of the *thing*, and to settle them according to his *orskurd*, or legal opinion. This relieved people of the burden of expensive litigation at the *thing*. At first the contending parties would not necessarily have to abide by the *orskurd* of the *lagmand*, but by a law of 1244 a fine of three marks was imposed on any one who disregarded the *orskurd*.[1] The *lagmand* had become a high judicial functionary appointed by the king. He exercised great influence over the judiciary, and tended to strengthen greatly the monarchic principles.

Over against the hierarchy King Sverre asserted the principle of the sovereign power of the king in all affairs within the realm with more uncompromising vigor. He not only annulled the agreement of 1164, but also all the laws inspired by Archbishop Eystein, by which this prelate had sought to enhance the privileges of the clergy at the expense of royal power. The struggle with the church soon waxed very bitter, since Eystein's successor, Archbishop Eirik, who had been elected in spite of Sverre's protest, was an avowed opponent of the king, and a most determined advocate of church supremacy. The archbishop based his claim on the new code of church laws called "Gullfjǫðr," a revision of the older laws, completed under the supervision of Archbishop Eystein, in which many privileges were granted the church. Sverre refused to acknowledge these laws, and appealed to the laws of St. Olav as they were found in the old code "Grágás" from the time of Magnus the Good. He declared "that Erling Skakke ought not to have broken the laws of Olav the Saint to have his son appointed king. For Magnus was not rightly chosen, inasmuch as never before since Norway became Christian had one been king who was not a king's son, nor yet in heathen times."[2] King Sverre regarded as unlawful usurpation every innovation introduced by Erling Skakke and King Magnus, and would

---

[1] *Frostathingslov*, 16, *Norges gamle Love*, vol. I. Konrad Maurer, *Die Entstehungszeit der Frostathingslǫg*. Ebbe Hertzberg, *Grundtrækkene i den ældste norske Proces*. See under *lǫgmaðr* and *órskurðr*, *Norges gamle Love*, Glossary; and Johan Fritzner, *Ordbog over det gamle norske Sprog*.

[2] *Sverressaga*, ch. 112.

force the church to surrender its illegally obtained privileges. "One subject of dispute between them was the old law and practice by which the king and the yeomen should build churches, if they wished, on their own homesteads and at their own cost, and should themselves have control of the churches and appoint priests thereto. But the archbishop claimed rule and authority in each church as soon as it was consecrated, and over all those whom he permitted to officiate in them. The king requested that the law should hold, but the archbishop refused." [1] Sverre also demanded that the taxes which the archbishop levied in his diocese should be reduced to what they had been before the time of Magnus, and that he should not keep more than thirty armed followers, the number prescribed by law. "The archbishop," he said, "has no need of a bodyguard, or of warriors, or of a ship all bedecked with shields; and he so far exceeds what the law says, that he sails in a smack having twenty benches manned by ninety men, or more, and bedecked with shields from stem to stern. We Birkebeiner will call to mind the ship sent by the archbishop to attack us under the Hattarhamar, and that we thought the same too hardily manned by his huscarls. So, too, in Bergen, when we attacked the fleet, the archbishop's ship and his company were much readier with their weapons to fight against us than were the king's company. I should think it more righteous before God if the archbishop had no guardsmen beyond what is lawful, for no one will plunder him or the church property, and if he used the cost to set men to the quarries to transport stone, to do mason's work, so as to advance the building of the minster for which preparations have already been made." The archbishop made an arrogant reply, and Sverre declared that within five days he would outlaw the men which he might have in excess of the prescribed number. The archbishop thereupon fled to Denmark.

Another controversy arose over the election of bishops. Sverre claimed the right to control their election, and maintained that in early Christian times the bishops were chosen by the king. This practice had been adhered to in the time of St. Olav, and even in the days of Eystein, Sigurd, and Inge, the sons of Harald Gille.[2] The

---

[1] *Sverressaga*, ch. 117.

[2] See Sverre's *En Tale mod Biskopperne*, edited by Gustav Storm, p. 22.

concessions made by King Magnus he wholly disregarded, and the right of the clergy to elect the bishops, which had been conceded in principle even in the reign of the sons of Harald Gille, he interpreted to mean that in case two or more kings ruled jointly, and could not agree on a candidate, the clergy might elect. He says about the right of election in his speech against the clergy: "We have heard these people (the clergy) state that the king has surrendered this right, and has given it to them. But any one will perceive, whom God has given understanding in the bosom, that even if the king would relinquish this power he could not do so, inasmuch as he must account for it to God himself. For God will call the king to account for everything which he has given the kingdom, and, in like manner, he will hold the bishop responsible for everything which he has given the bishopric. One cannot alter it for the other by giving or receiving, as this is contrary to God's own disposition and command." [1]

When a new bishop was to be elected for the diocese of Stavanger, the choice fell on Nicolas Arnesson, a half-brother of King Inge and Orm Kongsbroder. Nicolas was a staunch adherent of King Magnus, and had fought against Sverre in the battle of Ilevoldene. The king, who feared that he would use his influence to support the archbishop and to strengthen the hierarchic party, refused to sanction the election. But the cunning Nicolas wrote a letter to the queen, and she interceded for him. Sverre yielded to her pleadings, and sanctioned the choice. The bishop elect was transferred to the diocese of Oslo, and in later events he comes into the foreground as the most sinister figure in Norwegian history. His misfortune has been that little is known about him save what is told in the "Sverressaga," which was written by his enemies, and all posterity has learned to regard him as the treacherous arch-conspirator, the very incarnation of evil. This view is, no doubt, both erroneous and unjust, but it finds its explanation in the fact that he became the real organizer and leader of the hierarchic-aristocratic opposition party known as the "Bagler," and fanned into flame the passions of party spirit and civil strife. Nicolas exhibited talent mixed with cunning and selfishness. He must have been educated, but he had, probably, no specific religious training. His martial spirit indi-

[1] *En Tale mod Biskopperne*, p. 21.

cates that he lacked true religious feeling, and he seems to have been partisan and narrow. His career shows him to have been a chieftain of the old type rather than a bishop. The "Sverressaga" relates that it happened one day while Sverre lay in the Seimsfjord that his men rowed him in a cutter close under the land. Bishop Nicolas exclaimed to him: "Why don't you come on land, Sverre? Are you not willing to fight now, you renegade? You think no life equal to that of robbing and harrying. Now I will wait for you here. Behold my sleeve" (and with that he held up his shield); "the miter and staff which by the Pope's command I bear against you are this helmet and sword; I will carry these weapons until you are slain or driven from your realm."[1] However we may regard the words quoted by the saga writer, they probably give a correct picture of the warlike prelate in martial array, hostile and bitter in his opposition to King Sverre.

That the position taken by Sverre would produce a renewed conflict with both the hierarchy and the aristocracy might be expected. Archbishop Eirik was well received in Denmark by the powerful Archbishop Absalon, who gave him all possible aid. He instructed Abbot William of Ebelholt to write a letter to the Pope in Eirik's behalf, and describe the king's action against the archbishop and the church.[2] The letter emphasized especially that Sverre had requested the archbishop to crown him, but he had refused to do so except with the consent of the Pope. This had made Sverre and his whole army angry, as he claimed that in such an affair he was not dependent on the favor of the Pope, since kings might let themselves be anointed wherever and by whomsoever they pleased. The letter received no immediate answer. Pope Clement III. died in April, 1191, and the new Pope, Celestine III., was too much occupied with affairs in Germany and Italy to devote much attention to the far-away province of Norway. In 1193 the two archbishops sent men to Rome with a new letter, and now the Pope issued a bull in which he placed Archbishop Eirik and his successors under his apostolic protection, confirmed all rights and privileges of the Norwegian clergy, and made new regulations.[3] The bull concludes with the threat that

---

[1] Sverressaga, ch. 131.   [2] Diplomatarium Norwegicum, vol. VI., no. 3.
[3] The document is found in the Diplomatarium Norwegicum, vol. II., no. 3.

whoever resists it shall lose his authority, his title of honor, and shall be excommunicated.

Sverre did not long enjoy peace even after the overthrow of the Heklungs, and the death of Magnus Erlingsson. New armed hosts were constantly placed in the field against him by the nobles. These strong bands, which were usually recruited from the most lawless elements, did much harm, and Sverre's ability as a general was often taxed to the utmost to defend the various sections of the kingdom against them. But their operations were planless raids, which the saga gives undue prominence, and pictures with unnecessary minuteness of detail. After the battle of Fimreite the followers of Magnus took from the Hovedø monastery at Oslo a monk known as Jón Kuvlung [1] whom they hailed as king, claiming that he was a son of Inge Krokryg. The clergy and aristocracy supported him, and as all adventurers and lawless elements joined his standards, Sverre found it difficult enough to cope with the "Kuvlungs," as these bands of rebels were called. They captured Bergen and took the Sverreborg, which the king had built in the city. Another time they seized Trondhjem and destroyed the Sverreborg of that city. But they were finally taken unawares by Sverre in Bergen; Jón Kuvlung fell, and he was proven to be a simple impostor, the son of a man by the name of Peter and his wife Astrid.

Even before the Kuvlungs had been scattered, a new band of rebels and marauders, the "Varbelgs," made their appearance in Marker, a border district of southeastern Norway. Their leader, Sigurd, an Icelander of low birth, claimed to be a son of King Inge Krokryg. He was defeated and slain by the angry farmers; but after the fall of the Kuvlungs the chieftains put forward another pretender, Vikar, a mere child, who had been brought from Denmark, and was said to be a son of Magnus Erlingsson. The Varbelgs were finally defeated at Bristein by the men from Tunsberg, and Vikar was slain.

During the next two years (1190–1192) no band of rebels disturbed the kingdom, and a joint crusade to the Holy Land was organized in Denmark and Norway. After Jerusalem had been

[1] Kuvlung, from kuvl (= cowl), a name given him in derision by the Birkebeiner.

captured by the Turks in 1187, Pope Gregory VIII. preached a new crusade against the infidels, and the three most powerful sovereigns in Europe at that time: Frederick Barbarossa of Germany, Philip Augustus II. of France, and Richard Cœur de Lion of England became the leaders of the third crusade. The papal legates also came to Denmark with letters from the Pope, and met King Knut Valdemarsson at a diet assembled in Odense. The great noble Esbern Snare arose and urged the Danes to forget their domestic quarrels, and to use their strength and resources to rescue the Holy Sepulcher. Many Danish nobles took the cross, and sailed to Konghelle in Norway, where Ulv af Lauvnes, one of King Sverre's ablest Birkebein chieftains, lay ready to join them. Warriors from all the three Scandinavian countries joined in this crusade; Bernardus Thesaurarius says: "Norsemen, Götar, and the other inhabitants of the islands which lie between the North and the West, tall and warlike people, despising death, came armed with battle-axes, and sailing on round ships called snekkjar."[1] Ulv af Lauvnes became the leader, as he was the most experienced seaman. They first sailed to Bergen, where the Danish chieftains visited King Sverre and asked his forgiveness for having aided the rebel bands which had risen against him. Sverre readily granted them his pardon, embraced them as his friends, and wished them a safe journey. On their voyage across the North Sea they suffered much from stormy weather, and when they reached Friesland, they decided to leave their damaged ships, and journey overland. They marched along the Rhine, and finally reached Venice, where they chartered a ship to transport them to the Holy Land. They reached Palestine in September, 1192, just as Richard Cœur de Lion had made a truce with Saladin, and was about to depart for home. They could, therefore, take no part in military operations, and after visiting the Holy City and the river Jordan, some returned to Constantinople, where they were well received by the Greek Emperor, Isaac Angelus, and his Varangian guards, while others returned by way of Rome. Ulv af Lauvnes is not mentioned in later events in Norway, and it is possible that he lost his life on the expedition.

The brief period of peace which followed the overthrow of the

[1] Quoted by P. A. Munch, *Det norske Folks Historie*, vol. IV., p. 224

Kuvlungs and Varbelgs was but a lull before the storm. In the spring of 1193 a new band of rebels had been organized. They were called "Eyskjegger," because they had assembled in the Orkney Islands. Hallkel Jónsson, who was married to Ragnhild, a sister of Magnus Erlingsson, Sigurd Erlingsson, a son of Erling Skakke, Olav Jarlsmaag, a brother-in-law of Jarl Harald Madadsson of the Orkneys, and Bishop Nicolas Arnesson were the leaders of this new uprising, and the boy Sigurd, a son of Magnus Erlingsson, was their candidate for the throne. After successful operations in Viken they sailed to Bergen, and tried to capture the city, but they were unable to take the Sverreborg, and on Palm Sunday the following spring King Sverre defeated them in the battle of Florevaag, west of Bergen. Hallkel Jónsson, Sigurd Erlingsson, Olav Jarlsmaag, and the pretender Sigurd Magnusson lost their lives. King Sverre went to Viken, and summoned before him Bishop Nicolas, who had to admit that he was implicated in the rebellion. To appease the irate king he agreed to crown him. Sverre summoned the bishops of Hamar and Stavanger to meet in Bergen, where he was crowned by Bishop Nicolas, June 29, 1194. He also caused an English clerk, Martin, to be chosen Bishop of Bergen to succeed Bishop Paul, who died before the battle of Florevaag. In the summer of the same year the Pope excommunicated Sverre, and on the 18th of November he also published a bull of excommunication against the Norwegian bishops, which should take effect if they continued to show obedience to the king. Sverre summoned the bishops to meet at a council of magnates assembled in Bergen to confer with him about the situation. They all promised to remain faithful to him, and it was decided to send messengers to the Pope to place the situation in Norway in its right light. Bishop Nicolas Arnesson seems to have protested his faithfulness to the king, like the other bishops, but as soon as he had returned to Oslo, he went to Denmark, joined Sverre's enemies, and received absolution from Archbishop Eirik for having crowned him. Jarl Harald Madadsson of the Orkneys was also present in Bergen to obtain King Sverre's pardon for having tolerated the Eyskjegger in his dominions. The king granted him pardon, but did not let him escape unpunished. He confiscated the estates of those who had taken part in the uprising, and separated the Shetland Islands permanently from the jarldom of the Orkneys, and joined them to the kingdom of Norway. These islands were henceforth governed by a royal *sysselmand*.

63. BIRKEBEINER AND BAGLER. KING SVERRE AND POPE INNOCENT III.

Sverre had shown that he could cope successfully with rebellious bands of the kind which had hitherto opposed him. His enemies saw that no hope could be pinned on future efforts of that sort, and Archbishop Eirik and Bishop Nicolas Arnesson, who were in Denmark at this time, undertook in 1196 to unite the supporters of the aristocratic-hierarchic principle into a strong party called the "Bagler" (from begall, baculus = crozier) in a final effort to overthrow the king. Archbishop Eirik had become blind, and Bishop Nicolas became the soul and real leader of the new party. No bloodier civil war had ever been fought in Norway than the struggle which now began between the Bagler and the king's party, the Birkebeiner. King Sverre was placed in a most trying position. He had gained the throne by the aid of the common people, the Birkebeiner, but he now found himself opposed by the most opulent and powerful aristocracy as well as by the Pope and the clergy. The people were, moreover, divided geographically. The Bagler gained the support of the southern and western districts, while the Birkebeiner controlled only Trøndelagen and the northern districts. The struggle between the Birkebeiner and Bagler is a parallel to the contest between Welfs and Ghibellines in Germany, the only difference being that Sverre was opposed by nearly the whole nobility.

The Bagler appeared in Norway in 1196, and reënforcements were ready to join them. They took Viken and assembled the Borgarthing, where the pretender Inge Magnusson, whom they claimed to be a son of Magnus Erlingsson, was proclaimed king. The *lendermand* Halvard of Saastad, in Oplandene, joined them, and when Bishop Thore of Hamar died in February, 1197, they chose Ivar Skjaalge, one of their own party, to succeed him. By his remarkable skill as a strategist Sverre was able to defeat the Bagler at Oslo, but the victory was of no avail, for they soon captured Trondhjem,

destroyed the Sverreborg, and seized his fleet. Bergen was burned,
and one district after another fell into their hands until they controlled
the whole coast. Only the *fylker* of Trøndelagen proper still remained in Sverre's possession. He seemed to be hopelessly defeated,
and Bishop Nicolas could say with a boast: "Priest Sverre now
holds no more of Norway than a single ness; it would be a very fit
lot for him to govern the part of Eyra outside the palisades, and be
hanged there on the gallows. We Bagler care very little, I should
suppose, where he goes with his sea rams that he has got together
in the town. Before the Trønders receive any good from them, I
expect all their buildings will be charcoal. We will roam over the
fjord as we please, in spite of them, quite free from fear, for they
have no force to bring against us." [1]

To make a desperate situation seem still more hopeless, Sverre
was at this time attacked also by the powerful Pope Innocent III.
This great pontiff, who succeeded Celestine III. on January 8, 1198,
made all the monarchs of Europe tremble, and in course of time the
kings of Aragon, Portugal, Poland, and England had to bow in submission, and acknowledge themselves his vassals. In the quarrel
between Philip of Swabia and Otto IV. in Germany he claimed the
right to "examine, approve, anoint, consecrate, and crown the Emperor elect, if he be worthy; to reject him, if unworthy." Nothing
could escape his attentive eagle eye, and he was determined to humble the refractory King Sverre, as he did humble every prince who
resisted him. In the fall of 1198 the storm broke loose in earnest.
Innocent placed Norway under interdict, declared Sverre to be excommunicated and deposed, and hurled the most violent anathemas
against him.[2] He also sent letters to the kings of Denmark and
Sweden, and to Jarl Birger Brosa, in which he recounted Sverre's
"crimes," and asked them to arm themselves in defense of the
churches and the clergy, and to overthrow this monster, and thereby
earn God's reward and the gratitude of the Pope. None of the bishops dared any longer remain loyal, and an opportunity was given,

---

[1] *Sverressaga*, ch. 155.

[2] *Diplomatarium Norwegicum*, VI., p. 7–14, XVII., no. 1233. The bull
of excommunication is found translated in P. A. Munch's *Det norske Folks
Historie*, vol. III., p. 331.

not only those who were at heart disloyal, but all the indifferent and faint-hearted to sever their allegiance. But Sverre could yet count on his war-scarred Birkebeiner. They had placed him on the throne, and had followed him in all his campaigns. They feared no one, not even the Pope in distant Romaborg, and their religion was not of a kind to make them over-scrupulous in doctrinal matters. They trusted in their swords, and clung to their leader with a faithfulness which had been their forefathers' prime virtue of old.

King Sverre's courage rose with the danger, and his clear intellect sought out the loftiest and most effective means to neutralize the effect of the Pope's attack. He would fight the hierarchy with their own weapons. In answer to the Pope's anathema he published his "Speech against the Bishops," a remarkable document, written in the Norse language, in which he appeals with great eloquence and consummate skill of argument to the Norwegian people, places before them the principles involved in the controversy, shows them the fallacies of the clergy and the arrogance of their claims, and asks them to judge. He compares the church to the human body whose members have their special functions. "Christ himself is the head, the church is the trunk of this body. The eyes should be our bishops, who should point us to the right way and the safe road, free from all erring paths, and should moreover have a careful oversight of all the members. The nostrils should be the archdeacons, who should perceive the scent of all the perfume of righteousness and sacred truth. The ears should be the deans and provosts, who should hear and decide causes and difficult suits in holy Christianity. The tongue and lips should be our priests, who should preach to us sound doctrine, and themselves afford good example by their conduct. The heart and breast should be the kings, whose duty lies in solicitude, in deliberating and in acting, in emboldening and defending all other members.

"But," he continues, "now exists the evil, that all the members suffer change in their nature, and each forsakes the office and service which it should perform. The eyes look sideways, and see dimly. The same scales have fallen upon the eyes of our bishops that fell on the eyes of the apostles the night when God was taken. The same drowsiness and heaviness is come upon them, and they see all things as in a dream, where they distinguish neither clear light nor true appearance. The nostrils perceive only a stench, and not a perfume or sweet smell. The ears are now dull of hearing, and can hear neither truth nor good sense. Indeed, truth is neither heard nor seen. Our bishops and other rulers, who should watch over Christianity, are blinded by covetousness, excess, ambition, arrogance, and injustice. There have now arisen bishops such as those whom God himself slew aforetime, Hophni and Phineas, sons of Eli, high-priest in Shiloh, who did violence to the holy sacrifices which the people would offer to God, and seized with wrong and robbery all His offerings and holy sacrifices from God's holy people. And it has now come to pass that in the same manner our tithes and charitable offerings are demanded with threats and ban and excommunication. We are urged to build churches, and when they are built, we are driven from them like heathens. We are urged to undertake the cost, but are given no rule over them. Sins and offenses into which men fall are used as rent-producing farms; sinners are not chastised with right punishments, as every one is at liberty to compound for his sins if he wishes, for silence is at once kept when money is offered. We are deprived of some of our property with the sanction of the law; but where the law fails to apply, it is taken unjustly and by laying charge against us; and the wealth that is obtained and amassed is removed out of the country on an evil errand, for it is transmitted to Rome to purchase excommunication and anathemas, which are sent to our land as recompense for our Christianity and the consecration of churches. These are the gifts and presents brought to us in return for our tithes and other property. We are given gall to drink instead of wine, and poison instead of God's blood."

After having indicted the hierarchy in this strain he says that he does not blame the Pope, who knows no more about what happens in Norway than in other distant lands, but he blames the bishops and the clergy, who have misrepresented things to him. He quotes from the Decretals of the Popes to prove that an unjust decree issued by the church cannot hurt the innocent person against whom it is directed, but recoils on those who issued it. "To the same effect Pope Gelasius bears witness in the same cause when he speaks: 'An innocent man subjected to ban and anathemas shall pay the less heed to it, because a misplaced ban injures no one before God and holy church, nor weighs upon him. He shall not seek absolution to be released from the ban, for he knows himself guiltless and not subject to it, inasmuch as it was unjustly pronounced.'

"These examples, and many others, bear witness that wrong judgments cannot injure us, though the deceitful wickedness of our clergy has had the power to put us to shame, for they flee from us and from this land as if we were heathens. Either the wise rulers of the holy church and Christendom have pronounced no excommunication though they have been urged, or else excommunication has been pronounced, and it has certainly fallen upon those who by injustice and wickedness requested it, and has not fallen upon us, who certainly deem ourselves innocent, and certainly believe ourselves free from all excommunication."

He urges those who are not guilty of treason or of spreading false reports to remain loyal, and asks those who may be implicated in wrong-doing against the king and the nation to depart from those evil ways.

"All should know, clerical and lay, that the clerical leaders are not set over God's people to tread scornfully upon their necks, to cast shame in their teeth, to regard them as good to be pillaged and wrongfully plundered of their goods. Still less are they set over God's people to turn them away from God to hell, as into the mouth of the ravenous wolf, either by wrongful ban and anathema or by false persuasion."

In discussing the power of the king he shows by quotations from Holy Scriptures and the Decretals that royal power is divinely instituted, and that he exercises the highest authority in church and state by God's appointment.

"So great a mass of examples show clearly that the salvation of man's soul is at stake when he does not observe complete loyalty, kingly worship, and a right obedience; for kingly rule is created by God's command, and not after man's ordinance, and no man obtains kingly rule except by divine dispensation. A king would not be more powerful or mightier than others if God had not set him higher than others in his service; for in his kingly rule he serves God, and not himself. Now, inasmuch as duty binds him to answer to God himself, and to render an account of his protection and care of holy church, according to the cause just quoted; and as duty binds a minister of holy church to be obedient to the king, to afford him hearty worship and a guileless loyalty; therefore we cannot understand with what reason our clergy wish to remove the king from the oversight which he should have in holy church, and for which God requires him to answer, when we certainly know that men of inferior rank to the king have to exercise power in holy church. For knights and guardsmen, and even yeomen, have oversight in holy church if they are patrons of churches. There are three cases in which a man comes to have such oversight in holy church — the first, if he inherits an estate after his father, or mother, or other kinsmen, and the upholding of the church goes with the inheritance; the second is when a man buys an estate, and the upholding of the church goes with the lands which he buys; the third is when a man builds a church at his own pains and cost and endows it with lands for its future upholding. It must now be made clear so that all may fully understand, what oversight it is which those whom we have just mentioned lawfully exercise in holy church, according as it is said in *xvi. causa et ultima questione ejusdem cause*, and found in other places in the writings of the apostles (popes) themselves; 'This oversight in holy church has to be exercised by the sons, grandsons, and other fit heirs of the man who built the church or has been its upholder. Those who are rightful heirs shall have a care that no one through deceit or transference remove anything which the upholder of the church gave to it at the outset. That which was set apart for the maintenance of the priest at the beginning shall so remain; and that which was set apart at the beginning for tar, for lights, and for vestments in the church shall so remain. And if the priest makes any change in what was thus set apart at the beginning, so that the church is injured thereby, then shall the patrons whom I have just named make the matters known to the bishop, and ask him to devise a remedy, if they themselves are unable to devise one; and if the bishop will not devise a remedy, or if he himself does such things as those I have mentioned, then shall the patrons of the church make the matter known to the archbishop, and ask him to devise a remedy. If the archbishop will not devise a remedy, or if he himself does such things, then shall the patrons lay the matter before the king, and cause him to rectify it by the authority which God has placed in his hands.' Now, this bears witness that the king is set above all other dignitaries; for the king has here to direct the bishop or archbishop to do justice, if they themselves will pay no heed to it. This, be it said, relates to direction and guardianship of holy church, and not to those other violations of law which might occur in secular matters. How great is the king's power in secular matters may thus be seen, since he sits even in the highest seat of judgment in matters relating to holy church, which would have been thought, if men had not heard this quotation, to lie under the direction of the bishop." He shows that it is usually the bishops, and not the kings, who lead the people into errors in religious matters.

"It may now be seen whether the king is to blame, and claims their rights to rob them of their dignity, or they quarrel with the king's honor, and wish to deprive him of it and render him honorless. And if this unrest turns into heresy, as seems too likely, heresy and the profanation of Christianity will be seen to proceed from a source whence they have aforetime proceeded. We know few instances where kings have originated heresies, but we know many where kings have overthrown them when bishops have originated them. You may now hear the names of those who in various ways have been heretics."

Then follows an exposition of the fallacies of many ecclesiastics who have been regarded as heretics; among others, Arius, Bishop of Alexandria, Macarius, Bishop of Antioch, Donatus, Bishop of Numidia, Tertullian and Pelagius. But "the very worst, the cause of most harm, was called Nicolas Advena, a disciple of the Lord himself. He was afterwards bishop in Serkland (Saracenland), and is now known as Mahomet." Professor P. A. Munch thinks that Sverre especially emphasizes the name of this reputed founder of Mohammedanism, because he bears the same name as Bishop Nicolas Arnesson.

"Not many kings will be found who have originated heresy, for kings ever talk of their realm, of their kingly rule, and the defense of their lands. Bishops are appointed to proclaim truth and Christianity, and whether they preach in church, or at the assemblies (*things*), they declare before the people that all they preach must be followed; to fail in carrying out all they command is wrong, they say, and opposed to Christianity.

"Let these encroachments now cease which for a time have found place among men, and be just to one another. When both parties observe what stands in the holy writings, there is freedom for both; but when they wish to transgress what is written, they practice unrighteousness, and will be rejected by God, by good men, and by equity." [1]

The document sets forth clearly the doctrine of the divine right of kings in opposition to the claim of Pope Innocent III. that the rule of the whole world had been given to the Pope, and that "no king could reign rightly unless he devoutly served Christ's vicar."

It was clearly the intention that this document should be read in the churches and at the *things* wherever this could be done, as many copies of it are known to have been distributed. In this speech King Sverre not only exhorts his people to remain loyal, but he instructs them as to the legitimate power and the proper sphere of activity of king and clergy. His logic seems to have disconcerted his opponents, and the people listened as to a man inspired. Many of the Birkebeiner who had left the king returned to their old allegiance; Bishop Nicolas was henceforth called "the heretic," and his party "the excommunicated Bagler." The king had been able to awaken the people's patriotism, and to turn public sentiment against his opponents — a more signal victory than could be gained by arms.

Sverre succeeded in maintaining friendly relations with the neighboring kingdoms in spite of the letters sent by the Pope. King Knut Valdemarsson of Denmark did not attempt to attack Norway, though he had lost his supremacy over Viken, and King Sverker of Sweden remained friendly. His son Karl married Sverre's daughter Ingebjørg, and Sverre himself was married to the Swedish princess Margaret, daughter of King Eirik the Saint. Jarl Birger Brosa

---

[1] *En Tale mod Biskopperne*, edited by Gustav Storm, Christiania, 1885. *Anecdoton Sverreri*, translated by J. Sephton, *The Saga of King Sverri of Norway*, Appendix II. P. A. Munch, *Det norske Folks Historie*, vol. III., p. 335–348.

remained friendly, and Sverre made his son Philip jarl of Oplandene and Viken, and kept him at his court. Even with regard to the relation of the neighboring powers to the kingdom of Norway the mandate of the Pope had produced no startling effect.

In the winter of 1199 Sverre stayed in Trondhjem, where he was busily engaged in building a new fleet. Each of the eight *fylker* of Trøndelagen had promised to build one large war vessel, and he remodeled many merchant vessels into warships. In the spring he left Trondhjem with the new fleet, and met the Bagler in the Strindenfjord near Frosta. A fierce battle was fought, in which pardon was neither asked nor granted. The Bagler were defeated, all their larger ships were taken, and many of their chieftains fell; but Bishop Nicolas escaped to Denmark, and did not return to Norway while Sverre lived. Some of the Birkebeiner pursued the fleeing Bagler northward, and recovered Haalogaland, while the king himself with the main fleet proceeded southward to Viken, where he spent the summer. He had now regained control of the whole kingdom, but the Bagler were not yet annihilated. In the winter of 1200, while Sverre was staying in Oslo, great forces from Oplandene, Viken, Telemarken, and Tunsberg joined in an attack on the city. The campaign was well planned, and the enemy was approaching the town from different sides when Sverre became aware of the movement. Now, as many a time before, he went in disguise to the enemy's lines to learn their plans, and he set his men to cut a passage through the ice-bound harbor, so that the fleet might be extricated in case of defeat. He found that three armies were converging on the city, each one larger than his own. One had already gained the mountain heights east of the town, another was marching up the fjord on the ice, and a third was approaching from the west. Sverre's strategic skill, and the superior discipline of his veterans enabled him to keep the armies apart, and to defeat each in turn, but the struggle was long and desperate, and the victory could not have been decisive, as Sverre left Oslo and sailed to Bergen. The Bagler also attacked Bergen and Trondhjem, but they met with small success. Before the winter was over, the king began a new campaign against them in Ranrike and the southeastern districts of Norway. He forced them to retreat, and placed strong garrisons in Viken.

They made their last stand in Tunsberg, where one of their ablest leaders, Reidar Sendemand, intrenched himself in the citadel of the town, which was erected on a steep mountain height. Sverre could not take this strong citadel by storm, and in September, 1201 he laid siege to the place with 1000 men. After five months Reidar had to surrender, and Sverre, who was always ready to show clemency to his defeated enemies, pardoned the whole garrison, and cared well for the half-starved men. Reidar was ill for a long time, and Sverre kept him at his court, and gave him the best care and medical attendance. "Thus," says Munch, "this prince, who was excommunicated and decried by a political party among the clergy as an infidel, showed a conciliatory Christian spirit, and a humaneness which his opponents would scarcely have shown under like circumstances, and which in that age was extremely rare. But he showed that herein as in so many other respects he was far in advance of his times."

With the surrender of Reidar Sendemand at Tunsberg the war with the Bagler may be said to have ended, and Sverre returned victorious to Bergen. He had freed all parts of the kingdom from foreign overlordship; he had successfully resisted the encroachments of the hierarchy, and the attacks of the Pope; he had wrested the power from the aristocracy, and had reëstablished the sovereignty of the crown in harmony with the monarchic principles of Harald Haarfagre, Olav Tryggvason, and Olav the Saint; but he was not to enjoy the fruits of his victory. He fell sick at the siege of Tunsberg, and returned to Bergen only to die. There is a tone of sadness in the words which he spoke on his death-bed: "The kingdom has brought me labor and unrest and trouble, rather than peace and a quiet life. But so it is, that many have envied me my rank, and have let their envy grow to full enmity. May God forgive them all; and let my Lord now judge between me and them, and decide all my cause." He passed away on the 9th of March, 1202, and was laid to rest with elaborate ceremonies in the cathedral at Bergen. King Sverre was one of Norway's greatest sons. His character was of the highest type, combining courage with prudence and perseverance. He was witty and eloquent, wise, just and humane; great as statesman and general, noble and amiable as a man. His saga, which was written by a contemporary, characterizes him as follows: "King Sverre was most polished in manner. He was low of stature, stout and strong, broad of face and well featured. His beard was usually trimmed, and his eyes were hazel in color, set deeply and handsomely. He was calm and thoughtful. He was most eloquent in speech, and when he spoke, the ring of his voice was so clear that though he did not appear to speak loud, all understood him, though they were far off. He was a seemly chief as he sat in his high-seat grandly dressed; for though his legs were short he sat high in the seat. He never drank strong drink to excess, and always ate but one meal a day. He was valiant and bold, very capable of enduring fatigue and loss of sleep." In comparing him with his supposed father, King Sigurd Mund, the saga writer further says of him: "Sverre was steadfast and calm, careful in the choice of his friends, staunch and even-tempered. He was true to his word, reserved, sagacious, and conscientious."

64. King Sverre's Immediate Successors

When Sverre died, his only living son, Haakon Sverresson, ascended the throne. Sigurd, Haakon's older brother, who died some time previous, left a young son, Guttorm, but no attempt was made to secure for him any share in the kingdom. The principle that the realm should be ruled by a single king was thus tacitly accepted by all. On his death-bed Sverre had written a letter to his son, in which he advised him to bring about a reconciliation with the church, and Haakon invited the bishops, who were still staying in Denmark, to meet him for the purpose of arranging a satisfactory settlement. The bishops gladly accepted the offer, as they were tired of living in exile, and the archbishop even revoked the interdict without awaiting the permission of the Pope. An agreement was reached, the terms of which were embodied in a proclamation issued by the king, but this document was couched in a language so vague that it is impossible to determine definitely what concessions were made by either side. It is quite clear, however, that the king did not recede from the position taken by Sverre, except on minor points, while the bishops were required to swear allegiance to him as their lawful sovereign. The clergy seem to have been anxious to bring about a reconciliation on almost any terms. The Bagler party had been so weakened by defeats that they could have little hope of success if the struggle were renewed, and they learned to their sorrow that the dreaded weapons of the Pope — excommunication and interdict — had been of little real aid. The clergy ceased to oppose the king, and kept aloof from future struggles for the throne. The Bagler, who were still led by the doughty Bishop Nicolas, became a political faction, and their conflict with the Birkebeiner lost all real significance. While Haakon Sverresson lived, the Bagler did not attempt any new uprising, as his right to the throne could not be questioned; but his peaceful reign was cut short by his sudden death on New Year's day, 1204.

Haakon Sverresson was thought to have died childless, and his brother Sigurd's four-year-old son, Guttorm, was chosen king. Haakon Galin, son of King Sverre's sister Cecilia, a brave warrior and dashing noble, was made regent during his minority. The Bagler party now thought that the opportunity had come for them to regain their lost power. Bishop Nicolas sought to persuade them to place his nephew, Philip Simonsson, on the throne, but he was merely a noble, and they chose instead the pretender Erling Steinvæg, who claimed to be an illegitimate son of Magnus Erlingsson, and Philip Simonsson was elevated to the rank of jarl. Thereby the Bagler also repudiated the constitution of 1164, which excluded illegitimate sons from the throne. King Valdemar the Victorious of Denmark promised to aid Erling on condition that he should acknowledge him his suzerain. He came to Tunsberg with a fleet of 360 ships in 1204, and Erling Steinvæg, Philip Simonsson, and the rest of the Bagler chieftains, true to their unpatriotic policy of former years, did homage to him as their overlord. Valdemar gave them thirty-five war vessels and returned to Denmark. This might have seriously endangered Norwegian independence, but Valdemar's wars with the Wends, and his campaigns in northern Germany, so completely absorbed his attention that he took no steps to maintain his supremacy over any part of Norway. Guttorm Sigurdsson died in August, and, as the Birkebeiner would not recognize Erling Steinvæg, a new king had to be chosen. A posthumous son, Haakon, had in the meantime been born to Haakon Sverresson by Inga of Varteig, probably in the month of June, but this was not yet known, and the choice fell on Inge Baardsson, a son of King Sverre's sister Cecilia. His half-brother, Haakon Galin, was made jarl and commander of the army, and one-half of the royal income should fall to him.[1]

The struggle between the Birkebeiner and the Bagler was renewed. The Birkebeiner, who had Sverre's fleet, were the stronger party, but they nevertheless suffered heavy losses. In 1206 the Bagler surprised and took Trondhjem, and captured their whole fleet. Many of the leading Birkebeiner fell, and King Inge Baardsson barely escaped being taken prisoner. When Erling Steinvæg died at Christmas time, 1206–1207, Philip Simonsson was proclaimed king by the Bagler. They captured Bergen twice and destroyed the Sverreborg; but their campaigns were mere raids, undertaken at favorable moments, when the Birkebeiner were stationed in other parts of the country. After years of bloodshed and destruction of property neither side had any signal advantage to its credit. Both parties finally tired of this bloody feud, in which both were losers, and a peace was concluded in the summer of 1208 at Hvittingsey. Philip received Viken as a fief, for which he did homage to Inge Baardsson as his overlord, and Ranrike was placed directly under King Inge. Thereby the independence and integrity of Norway was assured. Nothing seems to have been said about what title Philip was to bear, but he retained his royal seal, and continued to call himself King Philippus. He received Sverre's daughter Christina in marriage, and their wedding was celebrated in Oslo in 1209.

When the civil wars had been terminated by the peace of 1208, friendly relations were established with Denmark, and both parties

---

[1] The chief sources for this period are the *Saga of the Three Kings*, or the *Bǫglungasǫgur*, and the *Haakon Haakonssonssaga*, written by Sturla Thordsson. The *Saga of the Three Kings* (Haakon Sverresson, Guttorm Sigurdsson, and Inge Baardsson) is found in two editions: a longer version, found only in translation by Peter Claussøn Friis, from 1633, and a briefer version dealing with the period 1202–1210. The short version is only an epitome of the more complete version, which has been written by a well-informed Icelander belonging to the Bagler party. These sagas are found in translation by P. A. Munch, *Norges Kongesagaer fra de ældste Tider, etc.*, edited and continued by O. Rygh, vol. II., Christiania, 1871.

united in an expedition to the Orkneys, where Jarl Harald Madadsson had made himself independent, and had reëstablished his authority over the Shetland Islands. His sons David and Jón, who were now jarls, submitted without resistance, and they were allowed to retain the Orkneys on the condition that a great part of their income was granted the king of Norway. King Ragnvald Gudrødsson of Man and the Hebrides, who had thrown off all allegiance, was also forced to submit. He went to Norway, swore fealty to King Inge, and promised to pay tribute.

Such military expeditions furnished a welcome employment for the hosts of idle warriors who would have been a source of disturbance and danger in a period of peace. After the expedition returned from the Orkneys, many went on a crusade to Palestine under the leadership of the Bagler chieftain Reidar Sendemand, and Peter Steyper, a nephew of King Sverre. Steyper died on the way, but Reidar reached the Holy Land. Later he entered the service of the Emperor at Constantinople, where he died in 1214. During the last years of his pontificate Pope Innocent III. preached another general crusade in all the countries of western Europe. Many leading men in Norway took the cross, and King Inge, who was too ill to leave home, promised to send ships and warriors to aid the crusaders, but he died in Trondhjem, April 23, 1217, before the fifth crusade had commenced.

65. King Haakon Haakonsson and Skule Jarl

King Haakon Haakonsson came from the unknown like his great predecessors Olav Tryggvason, Olav the Saint, and Sverre Sigurdsson. He was an illegitimate child, born in obscurity by Inga of Varteig after King Haakon Sverresson's death. Had he fallen into the hands of King Sverre's old enemies, his history would, probably, have been short, but the faithful Birkebeiner guarded the child against the plotting Bagler chieftains. The "Haakon Haakonsson's Saga" gives the following account of Haakon's early years: "Thrond Priest knew that Haakon Sverresson was the child's father. He baptized it and kept this so secret that he did not dare to let any one bring it to the baptism, save his two sons and his wife.

He reared the child in secrecy. There was a man called Erlend of Husabø, a relative of King Sverre, of Guttorm Graabarde's family. Thrond Priest sought Erlend, and spoke to him about the child, and they agreed that it had to be kept hidden as well as possible. The first year the child stayed with Thrond Priest; but the next winter before Christmas Thrond and Erlend made ready to go northward from Borgarsyssel, and they took the prince and his mother with them. They went with the greatest possible secrecy to Oplandene. On Christmas eve they came to the city of Hamar, in Hedemarken, where there were two Birkebein *sysselmænd*, Fredrik Slaffe and Gjavald Gaute. They had a large number of men, and were much afraid because the Bagler were round about in Oplandene. Bishop Ivar was in Hamar at the time, and he was then as always a bitter enemy of Sverre's family and of all the Birkebeiner. However secretly they went with the child, the bishop soon learned that a king's son had come to the city. The bishop then invited the prince and his mother to stay with him during Christmas, saying, as in sooth was the case, that the prince was his relative. But the Birkebeiner did not trust him, and answered, saying that the king's son should come to him after Christmas, that both he and his mother were now too tired from the journey to stay where so many people were assembled. But as soon as Christmas day was over, the *sysselmænd* took three horses, and brought the prince and his mother away from the city. They did not stop until they came to Lillehammer, where they remained on a little farm in the greatest secrecy till after Christmas. During Christmas the Birkebeiner sent word to Toten and all neighboring districts, and summoned all the Birkebeiner to meet them. After Christmas they left Hamar and came to Lillehammer, and took the prince and his mother with them, and went to Østerdalen, whence they would go to Trondhjem. On this journey they suffered much from cold, snow, and bad weather; at times they had to spend the night in forests and in uninhabited wilds. One evening the weather became so bad that they did not know where they were. They then sent Thorstein Skevla and Skervald Skrukka, two of the best ski-runners, in advance with the prince; they got two men who were well acquainted with the locality to act as guides. They traveled as fast as they could, but

did not find the way to the settlements; they came then to some
out-farm sheds, made fire, and prepared a bed there for the child
Later the guides returned to find the others, and they came back
to the sheds about midnight. It was uncomfortable to stay there
for it was dripping everywhere when the snow was melted by the
fire, and most of them thought they might as well stay outside as
inside. They had no other food for the child than snow, which they
melted and poured into its mouth. The place where they stayed
was called Navardal. Afterwards walking became so difficult that
they could not break a path through the snow otherwise than by
pounding it down with their spear-handles. In Østerdal the people
helped them in every way; wherever they came they lent them
horses, and guided them on the road.

"Thoughtful men have said that the troubles and difficulties which
the Birkebeiner encountered on this journey, and the fear they
also had for their enemies until they came to Trondhjem with the
prince, could best be compared with the dangers to which Olav
Tryggvason and his mother Astrid were exposed when they fled
from Norway to Svitiod from Gunhild and her sons."[1] The Birkebeiner brought Haakon to Trondhjem to King Inge Baardsson, who
reared him, and acknowledged him to be the son of Haakon Sverresson, and rightful heir to the throne. Among Sverre's old veterans
the boy was a great favorite. "He was very lively, though small
and young in years; he was very mature in his speech, so that the
jarl and all who knew him had great fun over his comical sayings.
Often two of the Birkebeiner took him, one by the head and the
other by the feet, and stretched him in fun, saying that this would
make him grow; for it seemed to them that he was growing too
slowly."

When King Inge died, the ambitious Skule Baardsson, his brother,
openly aspired to the throne, although he supported for a time King
Inge's eleven-year-old son Guttorm. But the Birkebeiner, led by
Vegard af Veradal, a prominent man within the *hird*, rallied around
Sverre's young grandson Haakon Haakonsson, who proved to be a
more popular candidate. Skule pretended to doubt Haakon's
royal descent. He sought the support of the clergy, reaffirmed

[1] *Haakon Haakonssonssaga*, ch. 3.

the constitution of 1164, which excluded illegitimate sons from the throne, and sought to prevent the choice of a king as long as possible. Haakon's supporters grew impatient. The *hird* assembled under Vegard's leadership, and demanded that Haakon should be proclaimed king without further delay. A letter was also brought from the Gulathingslag by the Birkebein chieftain, Dagfinn Bonde, stating that if the Trønders hesitated to proclaim Haakon king, who was the rightful heir to the throne, they would immediately hail him as king at the Gulathing. The Ørething was then assembled, and Haakon was proclaimed king of Norway, 1217, at the age of thirteen. Accompanied by Skule Jarl, Haakon then went to Bergen, where he was also hailed as king. It was decided that Skule should receive one third of all the royal revenues, but he was jealous and dissatisfied. He plotted with the Bagler, persuaded King Philippus in Viken to demand one-half of the revenues of the kingdom, and without Haakon's knowledge and consent he used the royal seal, which was still in his possession. Archbishop Guttorm and the bishops would not acknowledge Haakon before he had given better proof of his royal birth, and the matter was referred to a council of magnates which was assembled at Bergen in 1218, where the archbishop, bishops, and *lendermænd* were present. Inga of Varteig had to submit to trial by ordeal to prove that Haakon was the son of Haakon Sverresson. She passed the ordeal successfully, and Haakon's elevation to the throne was sanctioned by the council; the archbishop and the clergy acknowledged him the lawful king of Norway, and Skule Jarl could no longer resist with any show of right. The king granted favors without partiality to the leaders of all groups, and the Bagler now disappeared as a distinct party. In 1218 a new rebel band, the Slitungs, had assembled in the border district of Marker, and had chosen as their leader a pretender by the name of Bene, or Benedict. They caused great disturbance in many districts, but were finally dispersed by the united forces of the Bagler and Birkebeiner. The Ribbungs, who appeared later, were more powerful, and their leader, Sigurd Ribbung, who claimed to be a grandson of Magnus Erlingsson, carried on a guerrilla warfare in the southeastern districts for many years. They did not disappear until 1227, after Sigurd Ribbung's death. In order to

establish a more permanent friendship between the king and Skule
Jarl, Haakon was betrothed to Skule's daughter Margaret in 1219,
but she was at that time only nine or ten years of age, and their
marriage was not solemnized till 1225. The new distinction of
being the king's father-in-law flattered the ambitious jarl, and for
a time he seems to have been well disposed towards King Haakon.
It must have been evident even to Skule Jarl that it would be impossible at that moment to organize a successful revolt against the popular grandson of King Sverre. The whole nation was weary of the
endless feuds between rival pretenders, and longed to bind up their
many wounds. With intuitive foresight, born of secret but earnest
longing, they were soon able to prognosticate that Haakon Haakonsson would inaugurate a new era of peace, towards which many looked
as to a promised land after many generations of bloody civil strife.
The martial notes died away in song and saga, and the writers tell
us with rejoicing how Haakon's peaceful and benign reign made
the land blossom, and nature grow suddenly fruitful as if awakened
by a new impulse. "When Haakon was made king it was such a
good year in the land that it was general that fruit-trees blossomed
two times, and that the birds laid eggs twice," says the saga.[1] The
scald Sturla Thordsson says in a song about King Haakon: "It is
certain that twice blossomed the fruit-trees in one summer, and that
from the beginning of the year wild birds laid eggs twice without
suffering from cold, when the ruler, desirous of glory, had taken the
name of king, and his good fortune, destined to reach the highest
fame, began to grow.

"Saw, then, all that the elements on the wide ocean-encircled earth
would welcome the noble king."

All might now have been well, but ambition gave Skule Jarl no
rest. It stole the contentment from his heart, and filled his mind
with treasonable thoughts. In 1223 he went to Denmark to visit
King Valdemar the Victorious, who was at that time the most powerful monarch in the North. It seems to have been his plan to make
himself king of southern Norway by Valdemar's aid, and to acknowledge him as his overlord. But Valdemar had been taken prisoner

[1] *Haakon Haakonssonssaga*, ch. 28 (25). *Det norske Oldskriftselskab
Samlinger*, xv., *Konungasøgur*, edited by C. R. Unger.

by one of his own vassals, Henry of Schwerin, and Skule had to resort to his old method of intriguing against Haakon. In 1223 the king would be of age (eighteen years old); Skule could no longer act as his guardian, and the last remnant of royal power would slip from his hands. He had not abandoned his claim to the throne, and his attitude grew more hostile as the time approached when Haakon would hold the reins of power, but even under these circumstances Haakon showed the wise moderation which distinguished him throughout his whole reign. No one could justly question his title to the throne, but he, nevertheless, summoned a council to meet at Bergen on Olavmas, July 29, 1223, where all pretenders should meet and have their claims carefully examined. A greater meeting of notables had never assembled in Norway. Beside the king sat the *lendermænd, sysselmænd,* and *lagmænd* from the whole kingdom; the archbishop, the bishops, and many other ecclesiastics. The Orkneys were represented by Jarl Jón and Bishop Bjarne, the Faroe Islands by Bishop Sørkve, and the Shetland Islands by Archdeacon Nicolas, and the royal *sysselmand* Gregorius Kik, who was married to King Sverre's daughter Cecilia. The pretenders present were: Skule Jarl, Guttorm, son of Inge Baardsson, Sigurd Ribbung, and Junker Knut, son of Haakon Galin, and a nephew of King Sverre. After all claims had been carefully examined, the *lagmænd* declared that Haakon Haakonsson was the rightful heir to the throne, and the archbishop solemnly proclaimed him the lawful king of Norway. Skule was to rule over one-third of the kingdom, but had to swear fealty to the king. He received Trøndelagen, Haalogaland, Nordmør, Romsdal, and Søndmør. In these northern districts where the people were very loyal to King Sverre's family, he would find small opportunity to secure aid from Denmark if he should venture to attempt an uprising against the king.

In the opinion of posterity as well as in the eyes of his own times Haakon Haakonsson was a truly great king, who ruled with wisdom and carried himself with dignity. In his day Norway reached the zenith of her power. The great activity in literature and architecture, the splendor of his court, and the high honor which he enjoyed among the crowned heads of Europe made his reign the Augustan Age in Norwegian history. King Haakon was rather short of stature, says the saga, but he was well-built and broad-shouldered. In appearance he resembled King Sverre. He had a broad face and fair complexion, fine hair and large, beautiful eyes. He was cheerful, quick, and lively; always kind to those who were poor and in distress. "Wise men who were sent to him from other rulers said that they had seen no prince who seemed to be more truly both companion, king, and lord." We notice in King Haakon a quiet dignity and calm judgment coupled with magnanimity and rare mental equipoise. He adhered firmly to the policy inaugurated by Sverre, but his statesmanship was broad-minded and clear-sighted. Though firm in principles, he was generous and conciliatory in minor matters. He reconciled and united all factions, built, legislated, and improved; and rounded into completion the work of his great predecessors Harald Haarfagre, Olav Tryggvason, St. Olav, and King Sverre. Even his family life was an ideal one. In 1225 he married Skule Jarl's daughter, Margaret, who was then about seventeen. She was a most affectionate wife, and clung to her husband with the greatest tenderness even when her father turned traitor and became Haakon's implacable enemy. The feeling that he held the throne by unclouded title, and ruled a prosperous and united people by their full consent and undivided support, gave Haakon a confidence, and threw about his life and reign a halo of harmony and dignified repose to which Skule's ill-starred career, torn by unsatiated ambition and treasonable plots, forms a most tragic contrast. Unable to remain satisfied within his proper sphere, though the magnanimous king granted him the greatest honors, knowing that he could not openly gain the throne to which he had no title, Skule's heart was torn by doubt; he hatched plots, used underhand means, tried finally open revolt, and paid for it all by yielding his life to his pursuers in a last obscure retreat.

In the fight between the Ghibellines and the Welfs, the kings of Denmark supported the latter, as they feared the German Emperor, who attempted to make their kingdom a vassal state under the imperial crown. But the Danes in turn sought to establish an overlordship over Norway, or its southern provinces, and, as Skule Jarl solicited King Valdemar's aid in his ill concealed efforts to obtain the crown, King Haakon endeavored to counteract this move by entering into closer relations with the Ghibelline Emperor Frederick II. of Germany, the most powerful monarch in Europe at that time. Frederick sent ambassadors to Norway; Haakon called the Emperor his friend, and it is quite apparent that he counted on his support if Valdemar and Skule Jarl should venture to attack him. He also entered into friendly relations with Henry III. of England, and an agreement was made by which restrictions on trade between the two kingdoms were removed.[1]

After Haakon had taken the reins of government into his own hands, he had to devote much time and energy for several years to put down the Ribbung uprising. When Sigurd Ribbung died in 1226, Junker Knut became the leader of these rebels. They had always received aid from the border provinces in Sweden, and Knut's mother, Christina, who was married to *lagmand* Eskil, in Vestergötland, aided her son liberally; but Haakon pushed the campaigns against him with such vigor that Knut submitted, and disbanded the Ribbungs in 1227. Haakon now returned from Oslo to Bergen. Near Lindesness he met Skule Jarl, who was on his way to Denmark with many large ships to aid Valdemar the Victorious. The Danish king had regained his liberty, and was endeavoring to punish his rebellious vassals, and regain the territory which he had lost. Haakon did not upbraid Skule, though he met him on so suspicious an errand, but he could inform him that Valdemar had just suffered a crushing defeat at Bornhøved. Skule, who understood that he could accomplish nothing in Denmark under these circumstances, returned with Haakon to Bergen.

For some time the relations between the two were, seemingly, friendly, but Skule built a fleet of his own, and conducted himself in a way which awakened grave suspicion as to his loyalty. In 1233 he was summoned before a council at Bergen to answer to charges preferred against him, but he boldly denied every accusation, and no further action was taken in the matter.

[1] In a letter to the bailiffs of Lynn, dated Aug. 31, 1225, Henry III. instructs them to receive the Norwegian merchants in a friendly way, as he has granted the Norwegians permission to bring their wares to Lynn without hindrance for a period of three years. *Diplomatarium Norwegicum*, vol. 19, 1, p. 128.

King Haakon still treated Skule with considerate regard, but the
jarl's conduct became more and more openly disloyal, especially after
an illegitimate son, Peter, was born to him. In 1235 he took a step
which might have plunged the country into civil war. For a second
time he was summoned before a council of magnates at Bergen to
explain his conduct. He left Trondhjem with twenty warships, but
spent the whole summer in Steinavaag, in Søndmør, and did not go
to Bergen, though repeatedly requested to appear. The king finally
sailed northward with a fleet of forty ships to meet him. Skule
hesitated for a while. Some advised him to come to an understanding
with the king, others appealed to his pride and whetted his jealousy.
He followed the advice to which his nature inclined him, left his
ships on Haakon's approach, and crossed the mountains into Oplandene and the southern provinces. In order to avoid an open
conflict the king made him the offer that he could collect the royal
revenues of the southern one-third of the kingdom if he would not
begin hostilities until a peaceful settlement could be negotiated.
This offer was accepted by Skule, who used the respite thus granted
to organize a new band of rebels called "Varbelgs." After repeated
efforts a reconciliation was again brought about between Haakon and
Skule Jarl. A new division of territory was made by which Skule
should have one-third of all the *sysler*, or administrative districts, in the
kingdom, and at the Ørething in 1237 he was given the title of duke
(hertug = dux). He received no additional power, but the new
title must have been granted him as the greatest honor which could
be bestowed upon a subject, as it had never before been used in Norway. But even this new honor could not long satisfy the ambitious
jarl. The following year he took the decisive step. After collecting
a large military force in Trøndelagen, and levying heavy taxes for
its support, he assembled the Ørething, where he was proclaimed
king of Norway. He took the oath on the shrine of St. Olav, which
his son Peter and a few others had forcibly removed from the Christ
church. In the opinion of many this desecration of the sanctuary
was a rather inauspicious omen for the rebellion thus set on foot.
Skule sought to prevent word from being sent to the king of the
step which he had taken, but the news was brought King Haakon
in Bergen on the night of the 15th of November by Grim Keikan

one of his *hirdmænd*, who had succeeded in eluding the Varbelgs. The saga says: "There were not many with the king when he received this news. He sat a while silent and then said: 'God be praised that I now know the situation from this day on, for that which has now come to light has long been planned.' He went to the queen's lodging and asked to be admitted. Light was burning in her apartments, and some of her servants and maids were sleeping there. The king approached her bed where she was standing in a silk sleeping-gown. She threw a red cloak about her and greeted the king, and he returned her greeting cordially. She took a silk pillow and bade him be seated, but he declined. The queen then asked him if he had received any news. 'Nothing very important,' he said, 'but now there are two kings in Norway.' She said: 'Only one can be the rightful king, and that is you. God and St. Olav grant that it may always be thus!' The king then told her that her father had been proclaimed king at the Ørething. 'Things must still be better than that,' she said; 'believe it not, for God's sake, until you have received full assurance.' Then she burst into tears, and she could say no more. The king bade her be of good cheer, and said that she should not suffer for her father's conduct. Shortly afterwards he left; and as soon as day came, he caused mass to be said, and then summoned his counselors. Grim was present, and told them the news which he brought. It was then decided to send war-bulletins both north and south from Bergen, and call thither half the *almenning*." [1]

Skule Jarl sent his Varbelgs into many districts to burn and pillage. He left Trondhjem, and went to the southern provinces, where he gained some advantages over the king's *sysselmænd*, but Haakon soon arrived and defeated him in the battle of Oslo. With a few followers Skule fled northward to Trondhjem, but the city was soon taken by the royal forces, and his son Peter was killed. For some days Skule roamed about in the forests, not knowing what course to pursue. He finally sought refuge in the monastery of Elgesæter, but the angry Birkebeiner set fire to it, forced him to come out, and slew him, May 24, 1240. This was the closing episode of the civil wars. Skule had attempted rebellion in an age which would not

[1] *Haakon Haakonssonssaga*, ch. 207.

be disturbed. The uprising did not prove dangerous, and Haakon treated with the greatest leniency all those who had taken part in the revolt.

66. King Haakon's Coronation. Colonial Affairs

King Haakon had long desired to be crowned, but because of his illegitimate birth, he had to obtain the Pope's dispensation, and so long as Skule Jarl lived, his efforts in this direction were frustrated. After Skule's death he renewed the negotiations regarding the coronation, and Pope Innocent IV., who ascended the throne of the popes in 1243, encouraged him by a most friendly attitude. Innocent had maintained with more than usual vigor the supremacy of the Pope, and as a result he soon quarrelled with Emperor Frederick II. In his struggle with this powerful monarch he felt the necessity of keeping on friendly terms with other princes. To gain Haakon's good-will he sent Cardinal William of Sabina as a legate to Norway to crown him. He also wrote a letter by which he removed all blemish with regard to King Haakon's birth, so that it should neither mar his royal dignity nor the right of his legitimate sons to inherit the crown.[1] When the cardinal arrived in Norway, he tried to persuade Haakon to acknowledge the overlordship of the Pope, but when the king refused, he did not urge the point. The coronation took place in Bergen with great ceremony July 29, 1247.[2] The ceremonies in connection with the coronation are vividly described by the author of the "Haakon Haakonssonssaga": "The Olavmas-eve was a Sunday. On the Olavsday mass was sung in the whole city whereupon the people were summoned to the Christ church by the blowing of trumpets. Eighty *hirdmænd* in military attire cleared the way to the church. The royal procession was arranged thus First came the *hirdmænd* who were to clear the way, two abreast then the standard-bearers with standards, the *skutilsveinar* and the

---

[1] *Diplomatarium Norwegicum*, I., 29.

[2] According to the *Haakon Haakonssonssaga*, ch. 247, the bishops of Norway tried to force King Haakon Haakonsson to take the same oath which Magnus Erlingsson had taken when he was crowned in Bergen in 1164 This would have made Haakon, like Magnus Erlingsson, a helpless tool in the hands of the church. The statement is manifestly erroneous.

sysselmænd in fine attire, and the *lendermænd* with beautiful swords; thereupon came four *lendermænd* carrying aloft a table on which were placed the coronation robes and all the royal insignia; after them came Sigurd, the king's son, and Munaan Bishopsson carrying two silver scepters, one ornamented with a golden cross, and the other with a snake of gold; then came the younger King Haakon [1] with the crown, and Jarl Knut carrying the coronation sword. Archbishop Sigurd and two bishops escorted King Haakon. At the entrance to the royal residence the priests in procession met the king, and chanted the responsory: *Ecce mitto angelum meum;* after which they proceeded to the church. The cardinal with his clerks and two bishops stood by the church door, where they sang a song, whereupon they followed the king to the altar. Mass was then sung, and the coronation was carried out in the usual manner. After the mass the archbishop and the bishops followed the king to his residence in the same order as before, singing hymns in praise of God. The king took off the coronation robes, and put on the royal robes and insignia. The crown he wore the whole day. He then proceeded to the hall, where the royal banquet was prepared, together with all those who were to take part in it. The walls of the hall were hung with colored cloth, and cushions were placed there covered with pell and gold-inwoven silk. The seats were so arranged that the king sat by the north wall between the inner pillars. At his right sat the cardinal, the archbishop, the bishop of Bergen, and other bishops. On the right side, toward the sea, sat the abbots, the priors, the provosts, and other learned men. In the middle of the hall, over against the high-seat, was a second high-seat, where the younger King Haakon sat, together with Jarl Knut and Sigurd, the king's son; and many *lendermænd* sat on either side of them. On the king's left sat the queen, and next to her sat her mother, Ragnhild, then Christina and Cecilia, the king's daughters, Abbess Rangrid, the abbesses, and other ladies. Along the southern wall sat the king's *hird.* Two rows of tables extended along the middle of the hall from one end to the other. Outside of these sat the guests, also by two rows of tables. In all there were thirteen rows of tables

---

[1] King Haakon's son, Haakon, had received the title of king in 1240.

along the hall. The multitude, who did not find room inside, stayed in tents around the hall." [1]

Cardinal William of Sabina spoke at the royal banquet of the impressions which he had received on his visit to Norway. He said: "God be praised that I have now fulfilled the errand which was given in my charge by my lord the Pope. Your king is now crowned, and honored more highly than any king in Norway before. God be praised, also, that I did not turn back on the way, as I was urged to do. I was told that I would find few people here, and if I found any, they would resemble animals in their conduct more than human beings. Now I see here a great assembly of the people of this country, and it appears to me that they show good manners. I see here so many men from foreign lands and such a multitude of ships that I have never seen a greater number in any harbor; and I believe that most of these ships have been laden with good things for this country. They scared me by saying that I would get little bread or other food, and what I would get would be of poor quality; but it seems to me that there is such an abundance of good things that both houses and ships are full. I was told that I would get nothing to drink here but water and diluted milk, but I see an abundance of all good things. God keep our king, the queen, the bishops, the learned men, and the whole people. He grant that my errand to this land may so terminate that it may be an honor to you, and a joy for us all both in this life and in the life to come."

The council of magnates which had gathered in Bergen for the coronation found opportunity, also, to discuss many features of state and church polity, and by the aid of the cardinal many important reforms were carried through. The laws regarding the strict observance of Sunday and church holidays were modified. The cardinal found that the weather and the general environment had to be taken into due consideration, and that the people ought to be allowed to fish and to harvest their grain when there was an oppor-

---

[1] The *Haakon Haakonssonssaga* was written in the reign of King Haakon's son Magnus Lagabøter, at his request, and under the supervision of the king and the leading men of his court. Haakon's letters and the documents of the archives were placed at the disposal of the historian. The saga is based on reports given by the king himself and his contemporaries.

tunity, except on the principal holidays.[1] Trial by ordeal (*jernbyrd*) was abolished, "as the cardinal said that it was not proper for Christians to summon God as witness in human affairs." It is very probable that this reform was initiated by the king, who must have been as anxious as the cardinal to see this mode of trial abolished. His own mother, Inga of Varteig, had been forced to submit to ordeal to prove his royal descent, and many bold pretenders had, by means of it, made good their claim to the throne. Those who rebelled against the king should be punished by excommunication. The queen was granted the right of advowson over three royal chapels which the king had built, and also over missionary churches built on the border of the kingdom for the conversion of the heathens.[2] This was an important concession, since the priests of these churches would stand under direct supervision of the king. The cardinal also adjusted many minor complaints of the people and the lower clergy against the bishops, and he finally issued a proclamation regarding the relation of church and state in Norway, or what he considered to be their relation. He said that he found the church in full and peaceful possession of separate jurisdiction in all ecclesiastical affairs, whosoever were the parties in the case, and over the clergy in all cases whatsoever. He also found that the church had full right of advowson, except in case of the royal chapels above mentioned; and, finally, that the election of bishops and prelates was made by the clergy according to the right granted them by the canon law, without interference of secular authority.[3] These rights were universally claimed by the Catholic Church at that time, but it is by no means clear that the church of Norway possessed them in

[1] In regard to herring fishery on Sunday a concession was granted in 1184 by Pope Alexander III. It is found in the *Frostathingslov*, ch. 26. "This is the relief and grace which Pope Alexander granted and confirmed about herring fishery in Norway; that herring may be caught at any time when it approaches the shores, except on the principal holidays." These days are then enumerated. [2] *Diplomatarium Norwegicum*, I., no. 37.

[3] See Keyser, *Den norske Kirkes Historie under Katholicismen*, p. 382. P. A. Munch, *Det norske Folks Historie*, vol. IV., p. 36 ff.

The cardinal's document, both in the original Latin text and in Norse translation, is found in *Norges gamle Love*, vol. I., p. 450. The translator has greatly modified the expressions of the original, probably because he found that they exceeded the truth.

the degree here stated by the cardinal. King Sverre, and likewise his successors, maintained the right of the king to sanction the choice of bishops. The bishop-elect had to be presented to the king, who in this way exercised great influence on the election. As to the right of advowson there was much dispute, and the old Norse church laws recognized no ecclesiastical courts. Keyser thinks that the proclamation was a secret document placed by the cardinal in the hands of the bishops, to be used at some future moment. After a generation or two it could be appealed to as an authority. To further please King Haakon the cardinal sent a letter to Iceland, requesting the Icelanders to acknowledge the overlordship of the king of Norway. He did this, also, because the Roman church did not recognize a republic as a legitimate government. Haakon immediately sent a governor, or *sysselmand*, to Iceland to assert the king's authority over the island.

The Norse colonial empire, which had been founded in the Viking Age, was still intact. The colonies in Ireland and Normandy, as well as the settlements along the coast of Scotland, Wales, and northern England, were no longer Norse communities; but Man and the Hebrides, the Orkneys, the Faroe Islands, and the Shetland Islands were still Norse colonies; and Greenland and Iceland, though politically independent, were tied to the mother country as closely as ever before. Norway's commerce and her power at sea depended in a large measure on her colonial possessions, through which she still maintained an open highway of trade and communication with the countries of the West. The revenues directly obtained were often in arrears when measured with the cost of fitting out military expeditions to keep the chieftains in these island possessions in due submission, but the kings of Norway guarded the colonies, not only because they were felt to be in a sense a part of Norway, but because they never lost sight of their real importance.[1] The protracted civil

---

[1] P. A. Munch says: "It is a significant circumstance that from the moment when Norway lost the Sudreys (Hebrides), 1266, we note the beginning of the Hanseatic influence, the decay of national commerce, and the entering of Norway into the continental political system." *Det norsk Folks Historie*, vol. II., p. 529.

See also Alexander Bugge, *Handelen mellem England og Norge indti Begyndelsen af det 15de Aarhundrede*, *Historisk Tidsskrift*, tredie række vol. IV.

wars had diverted the attention from affairs in the colonies, and tended to weaken the ties which bound them to the kingdom, but though their allegiance was severed at times, it was reëstablished quickly and without difficulty. A greater danger to Norse overlordship was the close proximity of many of these island groups to England and Scotland. That future development would lead to an absorption of these islands by the kingdoms to which they geographically belonged could not fail to be apprehended by foresighted statesmen.

In 1158 the kingdom of Man and the Hebrides was divided between King Gudrød and Sumarlide's son, Dugald. Ragnvald (Reginald) Gudrødsson, who succeeded his father in 1187, threw off all allegiance to Norway, but the expedition to the Orkneys and Hebrides in 1209–1210 forced Ragnvald and his son Gudrød to repair to Norway and offer their submission to King Inge Baardsson. Ragnvald took his oath of allegiance lightly. In 1219 he swore fealty to King Henry III. of England, and in obedience to a request made by the papal legate, Pandulf, he issued a document, dated September 1, 1219, by which he transferred the kingdom of Man to the church of Rome, and received it back as a fief from the Pope, promising to pay a yearly tribute of twelve marks Sterling.[1] The Pope formally accepted the gift May 23, 1223, and placed Ragnvald and his kingdom under the protection of St. Peter.

A war now broke out between Ragnvald and his brother Olav Svarte, whom he had imprisoned and ill-treated. Olav, who had regained his liberty, attacked Ragnvald with a fleet of thirty-two ships, and forced him to divide his kingdom with him. Ragnvald sought aid in Scotland, and Earl Alan of Galloway, the most powerful of the Scotch magnates, acting, as it appears, under the instructions of the energetic King Alexander II., came to his support. In the bloody conflict which ensued, Ragnvald lost his life, and Gudrød, who had been maimed and blinded by Olav, fled to Norway. But Alan made great preparations to attack Olav, and even threatened to attack Norway, saying, that it was no more difficult to go from Scotland to Norway than from Norway to Scotland, there being no less facility of finding ports or shelter for a fleet there than in

_____
[1] *Diplomatarium Norwegicum*, XIX., no. 123.

the firths of Scotland. It was clearly the plan of King Alexander II. to seize the islands, and Olav, who was unable to cope with so powerful an enemy, hastened to Norway to seek aid. When news was brought by fugitives of the situation in Man and the Hebrides, King Haakon took the matter in hand. Olav's most trusted lieutenant, Paul Baalkesson, had sought the support of Skule Jarl, and the king could not trust one party much more than the other. He therefore divided Ragnvald's possessions between Olav and Gudrød. Over the portion which had belonged to Sumarlide's son Dugald, he placed Uspak, Sumarlide's grandson, who was a veteran Birkebein chieftain in the king's service. He bestowed on him the title of king and gave him his own name, Haakon. When Olav arrived in Norway, a fleet of thirteen ships commanded by Uspak-Haakon was ready to sail to the colonies. Both Olav and Gudrød returned with the fleet, which in the Orkneys received reënforcements till it finally numbered eighty ships. They sailed past Cantire to Bute, where the Scots had strongly garrisoned Rothesay castle. The castle was taken, but the Norsemen lost 360 men. Uspak-Haakon was wounded, and died shortly afterwards. Olav, who succeeded him as commander of the fleet, sailed to Man and took possession of that island. The division of the islands between Olav and Gudrød was now consummated, and after Torquil Mac Dermot had been expelled from the island of Lewis (Ljodhus), the fleet returned to the Orkneys. Hostilities immediately broke out between the two kings in Man and the Hebrides. Gudrød was slain, and Olav seized the whole kingdom; but when the fleet returned to Norway, 1231, King Haakon thanked his men for what they had achieved. Norse sovereignty over these colonies had been maintained, and Alan of Galloway did not again attack Man or the Hebrides.

In the Orkneys there were also feuds between rival chieftains and hostile factions. Jón Jarl was killed, and his successor Magnus held Caithness as a fief from the king of Scotland. The Orkney jarls became more and more closely connected with Scotland and Scotch interests, and Caithness became the most important part of their possessions. The inhabitants, both in this province and in the Orkneys, were beginning to lose their Norse nationality. The number of Scotch settlers increased, and Scotch language and customs were gaining ground; an indication that Norse influence in these colonies was waning.

67. CRUSADES AND CRUSADERS

In the summer of 1217 the fifth crusade began, and many chieftains from Norway took the cross and went to Palestine. Sigurd Kongsfrænde, a nephew of King Sverre, seems to have been the first to depart. He journeyed through Denmark to Germany, and joined the army of crusaders which assembled at Spalato under the leadership of King Andrew of Hungary. The army reached the Holy Land, but accomplished nothing of importance, and King Andrew led his forces back to Europe.

Erlend Thorbergsson and Roar Kongsfrænde, another nephew of King Sverre, sailed with two ships for Palestine. The saga says:[1] "The same summer that the king and the jarl were in Viken, Roar Kongsfrænde went to Jerusalem. He had a large and beautiful ship. With him went a man by name of Erlend Thorbergsson, who had another ship, which the townsmen had built at their own expense.[2] Roar's ship came to Acre, but the townsmen's ship reached even Darmat (Damietta in Egypt), and both were successful on this expedition."

Roar and Erlend joined the large fleet collected in Germany, Holland, Denmark, Scandinavia, and England, which sailed from the Netherlands in the spring of 1217. On the way they stopped in Portugal, where they captured the strong castle Alcazar from the Moors. The siege lasted until October, and they spent the winter in Lisbon. The next spring they sailed for the Levant, and joined the crusaders who were operating against Egypt. Damietta was taken in November, 1219, after a long siege in which the capture of the chain-tower was the most notable event. It is quite certain that the Norsemen played a prominent part in the capture of this stronghold, as they possessed great skill in that kind of warfare. Wilkens says that in order to capture this citadel a remarkable tower was constructed on two ships.[3] This corresponded to the *húnkastali*

[1] *Haakon Haakonssonssaga*, ch. 30.
[2] Probably the people of Trondhjem.
[3] *Geschichte der Kreuzzüge*, vol. VI., p. 126, 127, 163–179. P. A. Munch, *Det norske Folks Historie*, vol. III., p. 593 ff.

(*i.e. turris ambulatoria*) which the Norsemen were accustomed to construct when they attacked fortified cities. "The King's Mirror" gives an elaborate account of the weapons and tactics employed in sieges. The father says to his son :

"When one is to attack a castle with the weapons which have been mentioned, then he needs also to have catapults (*valslǫngur*) along, both stronger and weaker; the stronger to throw big stones against the walls, that they, perchance, may be made to fall by the great impact; the weaker to throw stones over the walls to destroy the houses within the castle. But if the stone-walls can not be broken down or rent asunder by the catapults, one must try to use a machine called *veðr* (*i.e.* a battering-ram), covered in the end with iron; few stone-walls can stand against it. But if the stone-wall should not be shaken apart or fall, then one can use, if he wishes, the *grafsvín*.[1] A tower built on wheels (*i.e. turris ambulatoria*) is also good to capture a castle with, if it is higher than the one which is to be taken, even if it is only seven ells, but it is better to take the castle with the higher it is. Ladders on wheels, which can be pulled back and forth, well covered with boards below, and with railings on both sides, are also good for this use. In short, all weapons are good in the taking of a castle, but one who wishes to take part must know just when to use each weapon.

"But those who defend a castle may use most of the weapons here mentioned and many others; both big and small catapults (*valslǫngur*), hand-slings, and stave-slings. Crossbows (*lásbogi*) are also good weapons for them, and likewise all other bows, and other weapons to shoot with, lances and palstaves, both light and heavy. Against catapults and *grafsvín*, and against that which is called *veðr* (battering-ram) it is well to strengthen the walls inside with oak timbers, but if there is enough earth or clay, that is the best. Those who defend a castle make also great hurdles (*flaki*)[2] of big oak branches and cover the walls with three to five layers of them, but these hurdles should be well filled with sticky clay. Against the impact of the battering-ram they fill big sacks with hay and chaff, and lower them

---

[1] A musculus constructed of boards and hides to protect the men while they undermined the walls.

[2] Crates made of boards and branches, and filled with clay.

in light iron chains in front of the ram where it would strike the wall. There may be so much shooting that the men cannot stand in the embrasures (*vígskarð*), then it is well to make hanging embrasures of light hurdles; they should be two ells higher than the real embrasures of the castles, and three ells deeper, and they must hang so far from the wall that the men can use all kinds of weapons between the real embrasures of the castle and the hanging ones. They must also hang on light beams which they can pull back and shove out again whenever they wish. An *igulkǫttr* [1] is also a good weapon for those who are to defend a castle; it must be made of big and heavy trees with oak spines along the back, like a brush; it is fastened outside the walls by the embrasures, and it is dropped on those who approach the castle. *Slagbrandar*, made of long, heavy trees, with sharp teeth of hard oak, are raised on end near the embrasures so that they may be dropped down on the men who approach the castle. A *brynklungr* (spider) is also a good weapon; it is made of good iron with bent teeth of steel, and on each tooth there is a barb. It must be so made that the ropes which are nearest to it, and higher than a man can reach, should be barbed iron chains so that they can neither cut them nor hold them fast. Above this point one may use any kind of rope, if it is strong enough. Such a contrivance is good to throw down among the men to try to grab some and pull them up." [2]

The author mentions several other kinds of weapons together with hot water, and molten glass and lead, which may be thrown upon the besiegers; also a war-machine called *skjoldjǫtun*, which spews out fire and flames. How this was constructed is not known, but it must have been a machine by which fire and hot objects were hurled at the enemy.

Even in earlier centuries the Vikings showed great engineering skill both in constructing and capturing fortified strongholds; and the high military science familiar to the author of "The King's Mirror," who wrote his work in Haakon Haakonsson's reign, probably in 1250–1260, justifies the assumption that the Norse crusaders played an important part in the capture of the fortresses at Damietta and other places. When the Norsemen returned from the crusade is

---

[1] *Igulkǫttr* = porcupine, so called because of its resemblance to this animal.
[2] *The King's Mirror*, XXXIX.

not known, but the saga says that they came home in safety. The *lendermand* Gaut Jónsson returned from a crusade in 1218, and Agmund of Spaanheim, who made an expedition to the land of the Permians (O. N. Bjarmeland) and journeyed through Russia by way of Novgorod and the Black Sea, to Constantinople and Palestine, must also have taken part in the fifth crusade.

Haakon was a statesman of high rank. He showed, indeed, less originality than his grandfather, King Sverre, but he acted with greater moderation, and managed foreign as well as domestic affairs with such wisdom and firmness that he won for his kingdom high honor and great influence among the powers of Europe. He continued to strengthen his fleet, until Norway ranked all nations as a naval power; a circumstance which, together with the king's great reputation as a statesman and ruler, gave his kingdom an influence which can best be seen in the efforts of the crowned heads to gain his friendship. He took no part in the struggle between the Welfs and the Hohenstaufers (Guelfs and Ghibellines) in Germany, but remained a friend both of the Pope and the Emperor.

The throne of Germany was considered vacant by the church, since the Pope had declared Emperor Frederick to be deposed, and the cardinal was empowered by the Pope to offer King Haakon the imperial crown, an honor which Haakon had wisdom enough to decline. He seems also to have been interested in the crusading movement which was now drawing to a close. At this time the sixth crusade to the Holy Land was being prepared by St. Louis, king of France, as the quarrel between the Pope and the Emperor prevented the organization of a general crusade. Matthew Paris says that St. Louis invited Haakon to accompany him on the crusade, and offered him as "the powerful and experienced on the sea " the command of the whole French fleet.[1] Louis IX. sent Matthew Paris to Norway with a letter to the king,[2] but Haakon declined the honor. It seems that, although Haakon had pledged himself, probably in good faith, to embark on a crusade to the Holy Land, the

---

[1] *Chronica Majora* (London, 1877), IV., p. 651.
[2] The letter of Louis IX. to King Haakon, in which he invites him to take part in the crusade, and offers him the command of his whole fleet, is found in *Diplomatarium Norwegicum*, 19, 1, p. 160.

Pope took no umbrage at his refusal to accompany King Louis; and it is not strange that the king hesitated to leave his kingdom, and to spend his resources in distant lands at a moment when northern Europe was threatened by a grave danger. At the beginning of the thirteenth century the great Tartar conqueror Genghiz-Khan united the tribes of central Asia into a great empire. He subjugated China, Turkestan, India, and Persia; and after his death his son Oktai continued the work of conquest and devastation. He sent his nephew Batu-Khan to subdue the countries of the West. In 1240 Kief was sacked, and Russia, Poland, and Hungary were soon overrun by their hordes; but at Liegnitz in Silesia their further progress was checked by the Germans under Henry the Pious. Batu-Khan returned to Asia, but Europe was in great alarm. Many fugitives from Russia, especially Permians from the White Sea region, flocked into the districts on the Baltic Sea, and also into Finmarken, where King Haakon permitted them to settle.

The relations with the neighboring kingdoms, Sweden and Denmark, had not been good. Since the time of the Ribbung revolt the king of Sweden had maintained a hostile attitude, but Haakon finally succeeded in effecting a reconciliation. A treaty was concluded between the two kingdoms, and the bond of friendship was further strengthened by the marriage of Crown Prince Haakon to Rikitza, the daughter of Birger Jarl of Sweden.

Denmark had also been unfriendly since the time of Valdemar the Victorious, and sharp commercial competition aggravated the situation. For some time Haakon tried in vain to arrange a peaceful settlement; the growing enmity culminated in open hostilities, and Haakon sailed with a strong fleet to Copenhagen. A more serious clash was averted, however, by timely concessions made by the Danish king, and a treaty of peace was signed in 1257. During these troubles the crown prince, Haakon the Younger,[1] died, and his brother Magnus succeeded him as heir apparent to the throne. In 1261 his marriage to Ingebjørg, the daughter of the king of Denmark, was celebrated at Bergen. After the wedding festivities King Haakon caused Magnus to be proclaimed king, and the young

[1] In the sagas King Haakon is generally called Haakon the Old, to distinguish him from his son, Haakon the Younger.

royal pair were crowned with elaborate ceremonies. With England Haakon maintained very friendly relations, and King Alfonso X., the Wise, of Castile sought to gain his friendship and support. He sent an embassy to Norway to bring about the marriage of Haakon's daughter Christina to his son Don Philip. Christina was escorted to Spain, and the wedding was celebrated at Valadolid. An alliance was formed between the two kings, in which it was stipulated, however, that Haakon should not be asked to aid Castile against England, Sweden, or Denmark; nor should Alfonso X. be requested to help Haakon against Aragon or France.

King Haakon's life and reign reflect the high ideals, the Christian character, and true religious sentiment which gave his public acts, and all his measures of social and legal reform a mark of moderation and good-will. He held firmly to the principle that the king was the highest authority in church as well as in state, and placed himself squarely against every attempt to place new restrictions on the royal authority. But he had a high regard for the church. He adopted the measures which it advocated, when he found them to be just and beneficial; he dealt conscientiously with all ecclesiastical matters, and it was said to his praise that no king since St. Olav had done so much to further Christianity in Norway. He accepted in part the plan so long advocated by the clergy regarding the succession. He adhered firmly to the principle that Norway should be an hereditary kingdom, but he recognized the expedience and wisdom of excluding illegitimate sons from the throne, so far as this could be done without endangering the hereditary principle. The new law of succession given at the Frostathing in 1260 makes the provision that "the one shall be king of Norway who is the king's oldest legitimate son, odel-born to realm and thanes; but if there is no legitimate son, then the king's son shall be king even if he is not legitimate, and if there is no son, then the one shall be king who is odel-born, nearest in inheritance, and of the royal family."[1] It was established, then, by this law that Norway in the future should be an undivided kingdom with a single king. In the succession preference was given to the king's oldest legitimate son, but in order to preserve the strict principle of an hereditary monarchy, illegitimate

[1] *Hákonarbók, Norges gamle Love*, vol. I., p. 263.

sons, or other members of the royal family, might succeed to the throne.

The king retained the old right of legislating for the church, and the code of church laws in the "Frostathingslov" was prepared under his supervision.[1] This code was more in harmony with the canon law than the older church laws, and Haakon enforced it throughout the whole kingdom. The relation between the king and the church was thereby made clear. Since the king could make and amend the laws of the church, and since no ecclesiastical courts existed, but all cases had to be tried in the secular courts, where the king's *lagmand* declared and interpreted the laws, the Church of Norway was a state church, subject to the authority of the king and the laws of the realm.

King Haakon's legal reforms and his revision of the old codes of law was a work of the greatest importance. The change which had taken place in social conditions and in the moral and religious spirit of the nation made many of the old laws seem antiquated and even adverse in spirit to the prevailing public sentiment. It seems to have been Haakon's aim to revise the old laws both in church and state so as to bring them into harmony with the more enlightened conception of justice. In 1244 he published an amended edition of the "Frostathingslov" together with a code of church laws (*kristenret*) which seems to have been written by Archbishop Sigurd Eindridesson of Trondhjem with the advice and sanction of the king.[2] In 1260, a new revision of the "Frostathingslov" appeared together with many new laws placing restrictions on feuds and the execution of personal vengeance. Hitherto the friends and relatives of a person killed

[1] An old law from the reign of King Magnus Eiriksson, of September 14, 1327, mentions this code "which the worthy Lord Haakon the Old and Archbishop Sigurd of Nidaros established with the advice and consent of the worthiest men." *Norges gamle Love*, vol. III., p. 153.

[2] Konrad Maurer says that the publication of these church laws must be placed in the year 1244 for weighty reasons, "and as no other date of publication can be assigned for the other parts of the code, it must be assumed that Haakon in this year revised the whole law (Frostathingslov) and divided it into sixteen books, and that with the advice of Archbishop Sigurd he has caused the church laws to be revised." *Udsigt over de nordgermanske Retskilders Historie*, p. 28. See also P. A. Munch, *Det norske Folks Historie*, vol. IV., p. 110 ff.

might proceed, not only against the slayer himself, but against his whole family, and instead of having recourse to legal justice, they often sought satisfaction for the injury by killing a near relative of the slayer. This often led to protracted and bloody feuds, which brought sorrow and suffering in their trail. This evil custom could not be abolished at once, but Haakon established the principle that the wrongdoer alone could be punished for his crime, a fundamental element of legal justice, which, when once recognized, would form a new foundation for criminal jurisprudence.

68. THE ANNEXATION OF ICELAND AND GREENLAND

After the completion of the colonization of Iceland, after a system of laws and government had been established, and Christianity had been acknowledged to be the state religion, the throes of organization were over, and the people enjoyed a period of peaceful development, which may be said to have lasted from about 1000 till 1150. By the adoption of the laws of Ulvljot in 930 the new state received its constitution. The Althing and the *fjórðungsthings* were organized, and the local *thing* districts were limited to twelve; each with three *goder*, except in the northern district, or *fjórðung*, where there were four *thing* districts, making in all thirty-nine *godord* in Iceland. In 1004 a supreme court of appeal, the *fimtardómr*, was created in connection with the Althing to decide cases which could not be settled at the *fjórðungsthings*, and twelve new *goder* were created to sit in this tribunal. The *fimtardómr* should consist of nine *goder* from each of the four districts (*fjórðungar*) and the twelve new *goder*, in all forty-eight; but as the prosecution could discard six and the defense six, only thirty-six rendered the decision. This new tribunal proved to be very beneficial. The resorting to duels (*holmgang*) in settling disputes had become very common, but after the creation of the *fimtardómr* duels were abolished in Iceland, 1006. In 1022 the relations between Iceland and the mother country were definitely established by the agreement known as the "Institutions and Laws which St. Olav gave the Icelanders." We have already seen that by this agreement a quasi Norwegian citizenship, which, indeed, they had enjoyed since Harald Haarfagre's reign, was granted the Icelanders; *i.e.* the right of *odel*, the right to join the king's *hird*, to bring suits before the *thing*, to cut wood and timber, to inherit property, and to trade and traffic in Norway. In return for these privileges they had to pay a small tax, *landøre*, and of those who happened to stay in Norway in time of war, two of every three had to do military service. The intellectual, no less than the economic and commercial relations, tended to strengthen the bonds between the colony and the mother country. Every year ships from Iceland entered the harbors of Norway to carry back the wares needed at home, but still stronger were the ties knit by common religious and literary interests, a common language, and intimate intercourse in the fields of intellectual activity, which nursed strong the feeling that the people of the two countries were one nation. Christianity had been introduced in Iceland by Norwegian missionaries, sent by the Norwegian kings, and the two bishoprics in the island were joined to the archdiocese of Nidaros. In Iceland saga literature and scaldic poetry flourished as nowhere else in the North, but most of the Icelandic scalds and sagamen stayed in Norway, where they found welcome, honor, and reward at the king's court. The Icelanders felt as keenly as did any Norseman at home that the king of Norway and his court were the center of Norse intellectual and national life, and the embodiment of the strength and unity of the Norse nation. Of this they have given ample proof in their songs and sagas about the kings of Norway. But the old love of freedom and local autonomy was also kept alive in the aristocratic republic of Iceland, and their political independence was lost only after internecine strife had paralyzed law and government, and created unbearable conditions which made a strong central government a paramount necessity. Two principal defects in the political institutions of Iceland, the alienability of the *godord*, and the absence of a central government, led gradually to the disappearance of popular government and the destruction of law and order. The thirty-nine *goder* of the minor *thing* districts were, besides the *lovsigemand*, the only officials in the Icelandic state.[1] Their office (*godord*) was hereditary; they were the wealthiest and most influential and powerful men in their com-

---

[1] The twelve new *goder* created for the *fimtardómr* had no duties or powers except in connection with this tribunal.

munity, and usually kept a band of forty to sixty armed followers. They had charge of the local administration, and were to maintain law and order in their communities; they sat in the *lagrette*, where they exercised all legislative power, and they also appointed the judges, who performed the judicial functions at the various *things*. The *lagmand* and the *goder* had to attend the Althing, and the *bønder* (farmers) who had a small amount of property were also required to attend. It is clear that the *goder*, who had well-nigh all the powers of government, were the pillars of the state. The more pernicious was the right which they possessed of alienating their office and of placing it in the hands of grasping and ambitious chieftains. Rival families gathered into their possession one *godord* after another, until a few powerful chieftains had usurped all political power, and ruled with sovereign power, each in his own district.[1] As no central government existed, their private feuds developed into a permanent state of civil war. They brought armies in the field, and fought pitched battles; houses were burned and property destroyed; the laws were a dead letter, since they could not be enforced. In 1217 a powerful family, the Oddaverjer, in southern Iceland, felt themselves offended by the Norwegian merchants, and attacked and plundered some Norwegian merchant vessels. The Sturlungs sided with the merchants, and killed many of the Oddaverjer. The news of these disturbances was brought to Norway by the great saga writer Snorre Sturlason, who had to promise King Haakon to use his influence to bring Iceland under Norwegian overlordship. He was made *lendermand*, and returned to Iceland, but he did not seem very eager to fulfill his promise, and as his countrymen resisted all attempts of that kind, nothing was accomplished. The struggle between the Icelandic chieftains continued. Snorre Sturlason's brother, Sighvat Sturlason, and his son Sturla Sighvatsson became very prominent in the century 1160–1262, which is also called the Sturlung period. Sturla forced Snorre and his son Urøkja to leave Iceland, but his arrogance so angered the other chieftains that they combined against

[1] Konrad Maurer, *Island von seiner ersten Entdeckung bis zum Untergang des Freistaates*. P. A. Munch, *Det norske Folks Historie*. R. Keyser, *Norges Historie*, vol. II. Salmonsen, *Konversations-Leksikon;* "Island," "Althing," "Gode."

the Sturlungs, and defeated and killed both Sturla and his father in the battle of Ørlygsstad, in 1238.[1]

Snorre and his son had repaired to Norway to the court of Skule Jarl, and when they heard that Sturla was dead, they made ready to return to Iceland. King Haakon had sent Snorre a message requesting him not to leave before he could make some arrangements with him regarding Iceland, but Snorre paid no heed, and departed without seeing the king. After Skule Jarl's death Haakon instructed the Icelandic chieftain Gissur Thorvaldsson to send Snorre to Norway, or else to kill him. Gissur had been married to Snorre's daughter, but had parted from her, and he and his father-in-law were bitter enemies. He marched with an armed band to Snorre's home, Reykholt, in Borgarfjord, and killed the great saga writer, who was then sixty-three years old (1241). Snorre was a great historian, but his contemporaries describe him as self-seeking and treacherous.

When King Haakon found that he could accomplish nothing in Iceland by the aid of the chieftains, he decided to strengthen his influence in the island by the assistance of the clergy. The bishops of Iceland had hitherto been chosen by the clergy and the people, but as this was contrary to the canon law, Haakon got the right of election transferred to the Archbishop of Nidaros and the cathedral chapter. By 1238 Norwegian ecclesiastics had been made bishops in Iceland, and they naturally sought to strengthen the hold of Norway in the island. While the bloody feuds continued unabated, Haakon summoned two of the leading chieftains, Thord Kakale and Gissur Thorvaldsson, to Norway and retained them there for some time. In 1255 he sent one of his own men, Ivar Englesson, to Iceland, who, by the aid of Bishop Henrik of Hólar, succeeded in getting the people of the northern districts to submit to the king. In 1258 Haakon made Gissur Thorvaldsson jarl, and permitted him to return to Iceland after he had solemnly promised to bring the whole island into submission. Gissur did not act with much energy in the matter, and in 1261 the king sent Halvard Guldsko to Iceland. Through his

---

[1] The principal source for the history of Iceland during the Sturlung period is the *Sturlungasaga*, written in Iceland about 1300. This is not a family saga, but an historical work dealing with the affairs of Iceland during this period. See also *Haakon Haakonssonssaga*.

efforts all the people of Iceland, save the eastern districts, were persuaded to take the oath of allegiance, and to acknowledge themselves subjects of the king of Norway. A compact was made between the king and the people of Iceland stipulating what rights and privileges they were to enjoy. According to this compact they were to pay taxes to the king. They should keep their own laws, and they could not be summoned before a court outside of their own country. Six ships should sail from Norway to Iceland every year; the *landøre* tax should be abolished, the *lovsigemand* and the *sysselmænd* should be Icelanders, and the island should be governed by a jarl appointed by the king.[1] In 1264 the people of the eastern districts also tendered their submission to King Haakon. In 1261 Greenland had formally placed itself under the king of Norway. The "Haakon Haakonssons-saga" says: "That fall Odd of Sjalte, Paul Magnusson, and Knarrar-Leiv came from Greenland. They had been gone four winters. They said that the Greenlanders had resolved to pay the king taxes as well as fines for manslaughter, whether the person killed was a Norseman or a Greenlander, and whether the murder happened in the settlements or in Norðrsetur, so that the king now received wergeld as far north as under the polar-star."

69. HAAKON HAAKONSSON'S EXPEDITION TO THE HEBRIDES. THE CLOSE OF HIS REIGN

King Alexander II. of Scotland had manifested great desire to gain possession of the Hebrides. He was even on the point of beginning a war for this purpose, when he suddenly died in 1249. His son, Alexander III., was then a mere child, and a regency was appointed to rule during his minority. The kings of Man and the Hebrides were loyal to King Haakon, and for a time no danger seemed to threaten the colonial possessions; but when Alexander III. became old enough to control the affairs of government, he revived his father's plan of joining the Hebrides to the Scotch kingdom. In 1261 he sent two envoys to Norway, as it appears, for the purpose of persuading King Haakon to cede the islands, but the attempt was unsuccessful. In the summer of the following year news was

---

[1] *Norges gamle Love*, vol. I., p. 460.

brought to Norway that William Earl of Ross, together with many other Scotch chieftains, had attacked the island of Skye, and harried it most cruelly, the report adding that it was King Alexander's intention to conquer all the isles. The attack was evidently made by his orders, since hostages were carried to Scotland, where they were kept in custody at the Iverness castle at the expense of the government.[1] This made Haakon very angry, and by the advice of his council he decided to declare war. In the spring of 1263 he began to make preparations for an expedition to Scotland. He committed the government at home to his son Magnus, and collected a large fleet at Bergen. An advance squadron of eight vessels was dispatched to aid King Magnus Olavsson of Man, but because of stormy weather it did not reach its destination before the main fleet arrived on the coast of Scotland. On the 5th of July the king sailed from Bergen, accompanied by Magnus Jarl of the Orkneys, who had been called to Norway, as it seems, for the purpose of assisting in the undertaking. How large the fleet was is not definitely stated in the saga, which says that "Haakon had over 120 ships" when the whole fleet was assembled in the Hebrides. The old Scotch historian Fordun states that he had 160 ships and 20,000 men,[2] which agrees quite well with the saga. This was probably the largest army ever sent from Norway to the British Isles, and great alarm spread through the coast districts of Scotland, where the attack might be expected at any time. Haakon sailed by way of the Shetland Islands to the Orkneys, where he stopped for a few days to work out a more detailed plan of campaign. He would divide his fleet into two squadrons, one of which should go to Moray Firth and attack the eastern districts of Scotland, while the king himself would proceed to the Hebrides with the other. But his captains refused to go anywhere except under the king's direct command, and the plan had to be abandoned. While waiting for the forces from the Orkneys to complete their preparations, he went to Caithness,

[1] *The Chronicle of Man and the Sudreys*, ed. Munch, p. 27; and notes, p. 110. P. A. Munch, *Det norske Folks Historie*, part IV., vol. I., p. 387. *Haakon Haakonssonssaga*, ch. 314. Skene, *The Highlanders in Scotland*, vol. II., p. 225.

[2] Fordun X., 15 (vol. II., p. 97); see P. A. Munch, *Det norske Folks Historie*, vol. IV., p. 396. *Haakon Haakonssonssaga*, ch. 319.

and compelled the people to pay tribute, because they had accepted the overlordship of the king of Scotland. He offered them peace if they would pay a certain amount, probably of stores and provisions, and they promptly accepted the terms. King Alexander III. strengthened the garrisons and defenses of the castles in all the districts where an attack might be expected. At Iverness, on Moray Firth, at Ayr and Wigtoun, in the southern part, and even at Stirling the garrisons were strengthened, and energetic measures were taken to collect ships, and to build new ones.

On the 10th of August Haakon left the Orkneys. The forces of these islands had not yet completed their armament, but they were ordered to follow as soon as they could. He sailed by the way of Lewis into the Sound of Skye and came to anchor at the little island of Cailleachstone (N. Kerlingarstein), where he was joined by the king of Man, and the forces which had been dispatched to that island. When he entered the Sound of Mull, King Dugald of the Hebrides met him in a light craft, and piloted the fleet to Kerrera, where the forces from the islands had assembled to join the main fleet. Both King Magnus Olavsson of Man and King Dugald Mac Rory (Ruaidhri) of the Hebrides were loyal to King Haakon, but Eogan of Argyll,[1] whom he had given the title of king, and invested with the island of Mull, had joined Alexander III. Eogan held large fiefs on the mainland of Scotland, and as he found it impossible to serve two masters, he dropped his royal title, and with it his allegiance to King Haakon. From Kerrera Haakon sent fifty ships in command of King Dugald, King Magnus, and some Norwegian captains to Cantire, and fifteen ships to the castle of Rothesay, in the island of Bute; with the rest of the fleet he advanced to the island of Gigha. The lords Murchaed and Angus of Cantire came to Haakon to offer their submission, and took an oath of allegiance to him, but they had to pay a tribute of 1200 head of cattle. The castle of Rothesay also capitulated without much resistance. Envoys now also came from Ireland to King Haakon, and offered the submission of the people of Ireland, if he would deliver them from

---

[1] In *Haakon Haakonssonssaga* he is called Jón, by Matthew Paris, Oneus or Genus, in the *Chronicle of Man and the Sudreys*, Johannes. See this Chronicle, notes, p. 112 ff.

the oppressive English rule. It is not stated who these envoys were, but it is quite clear that they came from the Norse colonies, who felt sorely oppressed under English rule. It has already been stated elsewhere that the English had taken their cities, and had forced the Norsemen to withdraw and found new settlements outside the city limits. Haakon sent Sigurd from the Hebrides to Ireland with some light vessels to investigate the conditions, while he moved his fleet around Cantire to the island of Aran. Haakon's large fleet, as well as the victories which he had already won, so alarmed King Alexander III. that he sent messengers to sue for peace, and Haakon welcomed this opportunity to terminate the hostilities. The summer was nearly spent, and he foresaw the danger of exposing his fleet to the severe autumn storms in these dangerous waters. An armistice was arranged, but King Alexander would not accept the terms offered, and much time was wasted in fruitless negotiations. Finally Haakon grew impatient, and gave notice that he would renew the campaign. He had advanced up the Firth of Clyde, whence he sent sixty ships into Loch Long, while the main force was to land at Largs to fight the Scotch army stationed there. The forces sent into Loch Long brought boats to Loch Lomond, and ravaged the country as far as Stirling; but on the 1st and 2d of October a hurricane swept over western Scotland, and put a sudden end to further operations. Ten ships of the squadron in Loch Long foundered, and of the main fleet at Largs many ships were damaged or driven ashore. The king sought refuge in the island of Cumræ (Kumrey), but many ships drifted to the mainland, where they were attacked by the Scots. When the storm abated somewhat, the king again went on board the ships, and sent aid to the men on shore. The Scots were driven off, and the Norse detachments spent the night on land. In the morning, October 2, the Scotch main army came up. About 1000 Norsemen were now on shore, of whom 240 were stationed on a hillock. They were attacked by overwhelming numbers. Many fell, and the rest fled to the shore, where they made a spirited resistance. At last two captains succeeded in landing fresh troops, and the Scots were driven back upon the hill, and finally put to flight. The battle was over, and the Norsemen returned to their ships. The next morning they landed again, removed the dead from the battlefield, and buried them near a church, probably in the island of Bute. The squadron from Loch Long again joined the fleet, and Haakon destroyed his stranded ships, and moved his fleet to Lambash harbor. Sigurd of the Hebrides, who had been sent to Ireland, now returned with a message from the Irish people to the king that they would keep his army the whole winter if he would come and deliver them from the English. He called a *thing* to consider this proposal, but his men were opposed to it, as it was late in the season, and they were short of provisions. He decided, therefore, to go into winter quarters in the Orkneys, and many of his men were permitted to return to Norway. After a very stormy voyage, he reached these islands during the last days of October.

King Haakon, who was now fifty-nine years old, seems to have overexerted himself in this strenuous naval campaign. Not long after his arrival in the Orkneys, sickness confined him to his bed. "During his illness," says the saga, "he had the Bible and Latin books read to him; but it soon seemed to fatigue him to catch the meaning of the words. He then let Norwegian books be read, day and night, first the sagas of the saints, and when there were no more of them, the sagas of the kings of Norway from Halvdan Svarte, one after the other."[1] He died, deeply mourned by the whole nation, December 15, 1263, and was succeeded by his son Magnus Lagabøter. His body was brought to Bergen, and interred in the Christ church by the side of his father and grandfather.

The celebrated battle of Largs was in reality only a skirmish, in which the Norwegians were victorious; but this great expedition, and the disaster which overtook it, seems to have brought the leading men to ponder the situation more carefully. They began to see how difficult it was to defend the Hebrides, lying snug to the shores of Scotland, when even vassals like Eogan of Argyll sided with the king of Scotland. Could Norway afford to keep a dependency like the Hebrides, when her whole naval force would have to be kept in constant service to defend it? King Magnus Lagabøter and his advisers were wise enough to see that such a cause would not only be futile, but ruinous, and steps were soon taken to conclude peace with Scotland. After negotiations had been carried on for some

---

[1] *Haakon Haakonssonssaga*, ch. 329.

time, King Alexander agreed to buy the Hebrides and Man. By the treaty of Perth, signed July 2, 1266, Magnus transferred these islands to Scotland for the sum of 4000 marks sterling, payable in four annual installments. Scotland also agreed to pay every year perpetually 100 marks to the crown of Norway. A fine of 10,000 marks sterling was to be paid by the party who violated, or did not fulfill, the treaty.[1] At the time when the treaty was concluded, King Magnus Olavsson of Man was already dead. This island was never formally united with Scotland, but was held by the kings of Scotland as a personal possession until it was finally transferred to the crown of England.

70. LITERATURE AND CULTURE IN THE AGE OF HAAKON HAAKONSSON

The old Norse poetic literature (*i.e.* the "Elder Edda" and the songs of the scalds) flourished principally in the period from Harald Haarfagre until the middle of the eleventh century. After Harald Haardraade's time the scaldic poesy began to decay. Many familiar names are, indeed, met with later, but they indicate no revival of the old art of poetry. The three great scalds of Haakon Haakonsson's own time, the historian Snorre Sturlason and his two nephews, Sturla Thordsson and Olav Hvitaskald, possessed great ability as poets, but the vigor and spontaneity had gone out of their verse, and Snorre and Sturla are famous principally as historians and prose writers. Snorre wrote his "Younger Edda" as a textbook for scalds with the intention, as it seems, of creating new interest in the noble old art. It is one of the most valuable works in Old Norse literature, but it failed to produce the result intended; the age of Norse poetry and song was fast drawing to a close. The chief interest now centered upon history and romance, and in the course of the thirteenth century the Old Norse prose literature reached its fullest development. It embraces works on the most varied subjects — history, biography,

---

[1] The text of the treaty is found in *Diplomatarium Norwegicum*, 8, 1; *Acts of Parliaments of Scotland*, vol. I., p. 78, 101. Torfæus, *Orcades*, p. 198. Torfæus, *Historia Norwegiae*, IV., p. 343. Peterkin, *Rentals of Orkney*, Johnstone's *Antiq. Celto-Normannicae*, p. 52. See P. A. Munch, *The Chronicle of Man and the Sudreys*, p. 132. *Islandske Annaler*, ed. Gustav Storm, p. 258.

geography, legend, and romance — all known by the common name of "saga" (*i.e.* narrative); to which must also be added treatises on grammar, mythology, and poetry, codes of laws, and other miscellaneous works. The sagas are written in a style of noble simplicity and classic beauty. Rich in contents, fascinating in form and diction, they rank with the Eddic songs among the greatest achievements in the domain of literature. "Few persons in our day adequately realize the extent of the early Icelandic literature or its richness," says Professor John Fiske. "The poems, legends, and histories earlier than the date when Dante walked and mused in the streets of Florence survive for us now in some hundreds of works, for the most part of rare and absorbing interest. The 'Heimskringla,' or chronicle of Snorre Sturlason, written about 1215 [should be about 1230], is one of the greatest history books in the world." [1]

The historical sagas may be divided into three great groups: the Icelandic family sagas, dealing with the history and biography of the great families in Iceland; the sagas about the kings of Norway; the sagas about the Norwegian colonies. This literature began to flourish both in Norway and Iceland towards the middle of the twelfth century, and reached its zenith in Haakon Haakonsson's reign. The old Icelandic writer, Are Frode (1148), has been called the father of Old Norse history writing. He wrote the "Íslendinga-bók" about 1134, and some scholars have held that he also began the "Landnámabók," which was finished by later writers.[2] About 1150 Eirik Oddsson wrote the "Hrykkjarstykki," a history of Harald Gille and his successors, which has been lost. In the latter part of the same century Odd Snorrason wrote the elder "Olavssaga Tryggvasonar," Gunlaug Leivsson wrote another saga by the same name, Karl Jónsson wrote the "Sverrissaga," and some unknown Icelander wrote the "Bǫglungasǫgur," or "Saga of the Three Kings" (Haakon Sverresson, Guttorm Sigurdsson, and Inge Baardsson). In Norway the monk Thjodrek (Theodricus Monachus) wrote a history of the

---

[1] *The Discovery of America*, vol. I., p. 154.

[2] G. Vigfusson and Bjørn Olsen regarded Are as the author of the *Landnámabók*, but Konrad Maurer, Eugen Mogk, and others find this view untenable. Mogk thinks that it was written in the period 1200–1225, and that Sturla Thordsson is the author. See *Geschichte der norwegisch-islandischen Literatur*, p. 788.

kings of Norway, " De Antiquitate Regum Norwagiensium," in the
latter part of the twelfth or the beginning of the thirteenth century,
and about the same time an unknown Norwegian ecclesiastic, probably
in the Orkneys, wrote the " Historia Norwegiae." The "Ágrip af
Noregs Konungasøgum," the first attempt at a connected account
of the kings of Norway in the Norse language, was also written about
this time, but only a fragment of this work has been preserved.[1]

From the close of the twelfth century the Latin language, which
hitherto had been used occasionally, ceased to be employed in saga
literature; the Old Norse classic prose had been developed, and the
taste for history writing had been fully awakened. The "Morkinskinna," a compilation of sagas about the Norwegian kings, was
written by some unknown Icelandic author about 1220. A more
critical work is the "Fagrskinna," also by an unknown Icelandic
author, from the period 1220–1230. It gives the connected history
of the kings of Norway from Halvdan Svarte till 1177. On these
earlier works Snorre Sturlason based his " Heimskringla," the greatest
work of the Icelandic historiographers, written about 1230. Snorre's
history is supplemented by the works of his nephew Sturla Thordsson,
the last original Icelandic historian. He wrote the " Íslendingasaga,"
which constitutes the nucleus of the great "Sturlungasaga," or the
history of Iceland during the Sturlung period (1160–1262); also the
"Landnámabók," one of the most important sources of our knowledge
of Germanic life, religion, and jurisprudence.[2] King Magnus Haakonsson became acquainted with Sturla Thordsson, and urged him,
while on a visit in Norway, to write the history of his father's reign,
the "Haakon Haakonssonssaga" ("Hákonarsaga Hákonarsonar").
This saga, which is based on letters and documents of the royal
archives, "is the most important source of the history of the Scandinavian North in the thirteenth century, and gives a vivid picture
of Haakon Haakonsson's reign. Because of King Haakon's friendship with Emperor Frederick II., and his relations to the Lübeckers
and others, it is also of importance to the history of Germany." [3]

[1] Gustav Storm thinks that the author of the Ágrip was a Norwegian,
Konrad Maurer and Eugen Mogk have held that he was an Icelander, but
that he, perhaps, was staying in Norway when he wrote his work.

[2] E. Mogk, Geschichte der norwegisch-islandischen Literatur, p. 788.

[3] Eugen Mogk, Geschichte der norwegisch-islandischen Literatur, p. 814 f.

This saga seems to have been written shortly after 1263. On a second visit to Norway Sturla was persuaded to write the history of Magnus Haakonsson's reign, the "Magnussaga Hákonarsonar," but only a fragment of this saga remains. To the historical works written about the kings of Norway belongs also the historical "Ólavssaga ins helga" from about 1250, while the legendary "Olavssaga" must be classified with the legendary and religious literature. Several later works like the "Hulda," the "Hrokkinskinna," the "Gollinskinna," and the "Eirspennill" bear no longer the marks of critical and original scholarship.

The sagas which deal exclusively with the Norwegian colonies are: the "Færeyingasaga," found in the sagas of Olav Tryggvason and Olav the Saint in the "Flateyjarbók." The original, which no longer exists, may have been written in Iceland about 1200 or a little later. The "Orkneyingasaga," also found in the "Flateyjarbók," is thought to have been written before 1250. The "Saga of Eirik the Red," which deals with the history of the Norse colonies in Greenland, and the discovery of the mainland of North America, is found in two manuscripts; the older from the thirteenth century, in the "Hauksbók," the later dates from the fifteenth century. The "Flateyjarbók" is a great collection of sagas and short stories (þættir) written in 1387–1395 by two Icelandic priests, Jón Thordsson and Magnus Thorhallsson. The compilers show little originality or critical ability, still the "Flateyjarbók" remains one of the most fruitful sources of our knowledge of Norwegian history and culture.[1]

Of special importance for the history of Iceland are the sagas dealing with the church history of the island; the "Kristnisaga," which treats of the introduction of Christianity and the early history of the church in Iceland; the "Biskupasøgur" and "Hungrvaka," which give the history of the bishops of Iceland.

The Icelandic saga writers have also devoted some attention to the history of Denmark. The "Jómsvíkingasaga" narrates the history

---

[1] Hermann Paul, *Grundriss der germanischen Philologie*, vol. II., p. 130. Eugen Mogk, *Geschichte der norwegisch-islandischen Literatur*. Finnur Jónsson, *Den oldnorske og oldislandske Literaturs Historie*. R. Keyser, *Nordmændenes Videnskabelighed og Literatur i Middelalderen, Efterladte Skrifter*, I. A. Gjessing, *Undersøgelse af Kongesagaens Fremvæxt*.

of the Jómsvikings and the Jómsborg, and the "Knýtlingasaga" contains the history of the Danish kingdom from 950 till 1202.

Most of the Icelandic family sagas were written in the period 1200–1300. The more important are: "Egilssaga," "Laxdølasaga," "Gunlaugssaga," "Eyrbyggjasaga," "Fóstbrøðrasaga," "Ljósvetningasaga," "Reykdølasaga," "Vápnfirðingasaga," "Harðarsaga," "Víga Glúmssaga," "Hønsaþórissaga," "Gíslasaga Súrssonar," "Njálssaga," "Vatsdølasaga," "Kormakssaga," "Grettissaga," "Gullþórissaga," "Svarfdølasaga," "Bjarnarsaga Hítdølakappa," and "Floamannasaga."

A second main division of the Icelandic saga literature is formed by the large number of mythological sagas dealing with the heroic traditions of the Scandinavian North, the "Fornaldarsøgur Norðrlanda." Among the best known of these are: "Vølsungasaga," "Friðþjófssaga," "Ørvar Oddssaga," "Hervararsaga," "Ragnarssaga Loðbrókar," and "Hrólfssaga."

Another important part of the Icelandic prose literature are the numerous works of a religious character, such as collections of homilies, and sagas or stories about the apostles and saints. In this extensive literature we find the sagas, or stories, of Virgin Mary, John the Baptist, the "Heilagramannasøgur" (sagas of the saints), "Postulasøgur," or lives of the apostles, besides a long list of sagas about persons prominent in the New Testament, such as Peter and Paul, John and James, Simon and Jude, Martha and Mary Magdalene, Stephen, Pilate, and others. To this literature belongs, also, the "Stjórn," a large work consisting of translations of the historical books and other portions of the Old Testament, together with commentaries. The greater portion of this Bible translation dates from about 1250.[1]

---

[1] Professor Gustav Storm analyses the contents of the *Stjórn* as follows:

1. A Norwegian translation of the historical books of the Old Testament from about 1250 or earlier.

2. An Icelandic translation of the books of the Maccabees, written in Norway 1262–1263 by Brandr Jónsson.

3. A Norwegian commentary together with a translation of the Genesis and half of the Exodus, written at the court of the king of Norway about 1310.

4. An Icelandic edition of the history of Joshua and of the history of the Hasmoneans (Maccabees) and the Idumæans (Edomites) according to

Aside from the Latin historical works already mentioned, the Norwegian sagamen devoted themselves almost exclusively to the writing of fiction, consisting largely of translations or elaborations into prose narratives of chivalric metrical romances introduced from England and the Continent, especially from France. These have been called "Fornsøgur Suðrlanda." E. Sars says : "The Norwegian court seems to have given the first impulse to the activity which in the course of the thirteenth century transplanted many French chivalric romances and other foreign literary productions into the Norwegian tongue. About 'Tristan and Isoldes Saga,' one of the earliest chivalric romances in the Norse language, it is specifically stated in one of the manuscripts that it was written at the request of Haakon Haakonsson. The same seems to be true of the 'Elissaga,' 'Íventssaga,' and many other works translated from the French. King Haakon's relatives and successors, who, like himself, had been well educated, also seem to have been interested in this kind of literary activity, and to have acted as its patrons and promoters. According to an old source the 'Barlaamssaga ok Josaphats,' is supposed to have been written by King Haakon Sverresson, who seems, however, to have been confounded with Haakon the Younger, King Haakon Haakonsson's eldest son." From Norway this literary activity of recasting foreign stories into narratives in the Norse tongue was also introduced into Iceland, but these stories did not become popular there, as the style was best suited to the tastes of knights and courtiers. The Icelanders usually based their narratives on Norwegian translations, not on the original text, and many of these sagas, such as the "Þiðrekssaga," the "Karlamagnússaga," and others are, therefore, found in widely different Norwegian and Icelandic versions.

One of the most important and interesting works in Old Norse literature is "The King's Mirror" (O. N. Konungs-Skuggsjá, Lat.

the *Historia Scholastica*, written in the middle of the fourteenth century as a supplement to no. 2 and 3.

5. A short résumé of the later books of Moses by an Icelandic author from the latter part of the fourteenth century, written as a supplement to no. 3. *Arkiv for Nordis Filologi*, 1886, p. 244 ff. See also Eugen Mogk, *Geschichte der norwegisch-islandischen Literatur*. Finnur Jónsson, *Den oldnorske og oldislandske Literaturs Historie*.

Speculum Regale), written in the reign of Haakon Haakonsson, about 1250–1260, by an anonymous Norwegian author, who must have lived in Namdalen, near Trøndelagen. This work occupies a unique position in Old Norse literature. It is a didactic-philosophic treatise in the form of a dialogue between a father and his son, in which the author planned to describe the education, culture, and manners of the four classes of Norwegian society — merchants, courtiers, farmers (*bønder*), and clergy. The father gives this description so that the son may choose his calling with insight, and that he may know what he must learn in order to become successful and honored in his profession. Only two parts have been written, but even in its fragmentary form it gives the most vivid picture of medieval Norwegian society, especially of the upper classes, of any work in existence. It is worthy of note that the agricultural class (*bønder*) is treated, not only as an independent and highly respected class, but as a separate estate, equal in rank to the courtiers and the clergy. This was something quite unusual at this time, when the agricultural classes elsewhere in Europe had sunk into abject serfdom. It is equally worthy of attention that the merchants, also, formed a distinct class, no less highly regarded than the others. The father says to his son: "Though I have been more a king's man (*i.e.* a courtier) than a merchant, still I would find no fault if you would choose this profession, for it is now often chosen by the best men." That the agricultural and merchant classes should stand so high is quite remarkable, when we consider that even the third estate (the citizen of the larger cities) had gained but scant recognition elsewhere in Europe. The father goes on to outline to his son what he must study if he wishes to become a real merchant. He points out the necessity of avoiding drinking and gambling, of being upright, Christian-minded, well-dressed, polite, and cultured, as this constitutes the general basis for a successful career. He must also study the laws, especially the "Bjarkeyjarréttr," or Norwegian municipal laws. He must know the manners and customs of every country where he travels, and, if he wishes to be especially well qualified, he "should study all languages, especially Latin and French, for they reach farthest, but neither must thou neglect thine own language."

VOL. I — 2 G

He advises his son, also, to get a thorough knowledge of the courses of the heavenly bodies, of the tides, and other natural phenomena of importance to navigation. He must become especially well versed, also, in arithmetic, which is indispensable to merchants. He instructs him how to equip his ships for the voyage, in what seasons of the year he should sail, and what rules he is to observe in doing business. He gives the young man very detailed and elaborate instruction in political and physical geography, in which branches he shows deep interest and remarkable knowledge. He discusses the ocean currents, the prevailing winds, the aurora borealis, the volcanoes, geysers, warm springs, and earthquakes in Iceland, and the glaciers and icebergs in Greenland. He gives a description of Ireland and Iceland, and discusses the climate and the conditions in Greenland with great minuteness and with considerable accuracy. He says to his son: "But since thou doest ask if the sun shines in Greenland, or whether it happens that there is fine weather as in other countries, then thou must know, forsooth, that there is fine sunshine, and that the climate there in the summer time may be called good. But there is great difference in the seasons, for the winter is almost a perpetual night, and summer almost a continuous day. But when the sun is highest, it is strong enough to give light, but it gives but little heat; still it is so strong that where the ground is free from ice, it is warmed so much that it produces good and fragrant grass, therefore people can easily inhabit the land where it is thawed up, but that is indeed only a small area." [1] He describes the fishes and animals in the ocean near Iceland and Greenland, and discusses in detail the fauna of Greenland, the domestic animals of this country, its products, exports and imports, and the mode of life of the people. In the second part, in which he discusses the courtier class, he speaks of the manners and customs of the court, of the power of the king, of the nature and value of the government, and instructs his son in military science and the use of arms.

If we compare this system of education with the established curriculum of the schools in other countries of Europe at that time, we are struck by its superiority over all school plans then existing. The schoolmen were yet confining instruction to their *trivium* and

[1] *The King's Mirror*, ch. xix.

quadrivium, which embraced little more than Latin and scholastic dialectics. Of geography there was none, excepting what might be incidentally mentioned as explanatory notes to Latin texts. The mother tongue was banished from the schools, as were all modern languages; natural science was not taught. "Natural science was very much neglected in the Middle Ages. With extraordinary credulity the people regarded the most incredible as true, and, being prepossessed by a belief in invented phantasms and wonders, they did not see God's true wonders in creation," says Karl von Raumer.[1]

The author of "The King's Mirror" finds it necessary for the young man — the prospective merchant — who wishes to be well educated, to study, not only Latin, but French, and especially his own mother tongue, yes all languages, which simply means as many languages as possible. He has to learn the laws of trade and commerce; he must study the courses of the heavenly bodies, and the changing seasons, *i.e.* astronomy. He must learn practical navigation, and he must devote especial attention to the study of nature: climate, ocean currents, glaciers, icebergs, volcanoes, earthquakes, and animal life on sea and land. He must also study political geography, the customs and manners of all nations which he comes in contact with; their products, their imports and exports. Besides acquiring such training, both practical and theoretical, he should also be a Christian and cultured gentleman. This system of education is so modern in spirit and general purpose that with but few modifications we might well accept it to-day without much hesitation. A little reflection and comparison make us feel the truth of the great scholar Sophus Bugge's statement that "The King's Mirror" "was five centuries ahead of its time." Strong evidence, indeed, that no people in Europe were better educated than the Norwegians.

The remarkable growth of Norse prose literature in the thirteenth century represents the culmination of a long literary development, and cannot be directly attributed to the influence of the reign of Haakon Haakonsson. Still the court of the king of Norway was in this period, as heretofore, the center of the intellectual life of the Norwegian people. It was the place where men of learning and ability met, where the impulses from abroad were most directly felt,

---

[1] *Geschichte der Pädagogik*, erster teil, p. 7.

and where many of the leading works were written. Karl Jónsson wrote the "Sverressaga" at King Sverre's court, and by his aid. Sturla Thordsson was persuaded by King Magnus Haakonsson (Lagabøter) to write the "Haakon Haakonssonssaga" at King Magnus' court, and by his assistance. The "Vølsungasaga" is thought to have been written at the court of Haakon Haakonsson for the entertainment of the king, and a part of the "Stjórn" was written at the request of King Haakon Magnusson († 1319). It is certain, also, that Snorre Sturlason was encouraged, especially by Skule Jarl, to write the "Younger Edda" and the "Heimskringla." King Haakon's peaceful and glorious reign and his lofty example proved a powerful stimulus. He was well educated, and could read Latin as well as Norse. He was intensely interested in literature and art; anxious to further the intellectual development of his people, as he was careful to preserve the power and honor of his kingdom, and the prosperity of the nation. The king of Norway was to the Norwegian people what King Arthur was to the Knights of the Round Table — the source of national unity and strength, by whose influence and power they felt themselves united into one nation. The king was the bond of union between the colonies and the mother country, and the source of national tradition and honor. This would alone explain the great influence which the king and his court exerted on the development of literature and culture and the growth of a national spirit.

King Haakon took great interest, also, in commerce and the development of cities. On the coast of Bohuslen he founded the city of Marstrand, probably because of the great herring fisheries along this coast.[1] He improved the harbor of Agdenes at the entrance to the Trondhjemsfjord, and constructed wharfs there. He also sought to protect Norwegian commerce by treaties with England and Lübeck. King Valdemar the Victorious and his successors had not been friendly to Norway, and when war broke out between Denmark and the German city of Lübeck, Norwegian shipping was injured by both parties. Haakon, therefore, seized the ships both of the Danes

---

[1] Alexander Bugge, *Studier over de norske Byers Selvstyre og Handel før Hanseaternes Tid*, Christiania, 1899. Gustav Storm, *De kongelige Byanlæg i Norge i Middelalderen*, *Historisk Tidsskrift*, tredie række, vol. V., p. 433.

PLATE XI

RUINS OF THE HOVEDØ MONASTERY.

KING HAAKON HAAKONSSON'S GUILD-HALL IN BERGEN, AND THE VALKENDORF TOWER.

and the Lübeckers in Norwegian harbors, a measure which proved so effective that the merchants of Lübeck sent John de Bardevik as ambassador to Bergen to apologize to King Haakon. The result was a commercial treaty between Norway and Lübeck, concluded October 6, 1250.[1] Treaties of commerce were also signed with the king of England.[2]

Haakon devoted much attention to the improvement of the coast defenses. It seems to have been his plan to construct a system of fortresses which would safeguard all important harbors, and protect the whole coast. He rebuilt the Sverreborg at Bergen, reconstructed the Sverreborg at Trondhjem, erected a fortress at Ragnhildarholm, near Konghelle, and fortified Oslo and Tunsberg. The many churches, monasteries, hospitals, and other public buildings erected during this reign testify to Haakon's great interest in cities and city culture. At Bergen he erected the Haakon's hall, a large, two-story royal hall of stone, built in Early English style. It stood completed in 1261 when the wedding of his son Magnus was celebrated there. In later centuries this fine piece of early Norwegian architecture suffered much through neglect, but it has been restored, and it remains one of the proudest old structures which adorns the city. The "Haakon Haakonssonssaga" gives the following account of his activity as a builder:

"He built a church in Tromsø, and Christianized the whole parish belonging to it. Many Permians came to him, who had fled from the East because of the inroads of the Tartars. These he Christianized, and he permitted them to settle on the Melangerfjord. He built a church at Ofoten, a redoubt and piers for wharfs at Agdenes. In Nidaros he built a hall in connection with the royal residence, as well as a chapel over against the royal hostelries. In Bergen he built the Apostle church of stone near the royal residence. He also built a St. Olav's church and a monastery at his own expense. He improved the royal residence at Bergen by erecting two stone halls, and by surrounding it with a stone wall with castles above the portals.

[1] The text of the treaty is found in *Diplomatarium Norwegicum*, vol. V., no. 4.

[2] That very friendly relations existed between Norway and England at this time can be seen from Haakon's correspondence with Henry III. *Diplomatarium Norwegicum*, vol. XIX., no. 153 ff.

He built the St. Catherine church at Sandbru, together with a hospital, and gave to it property yielding an income of 200 mán-aðrmatr.[1] In the castle at Bergen he rebuilt all the houses which had been destroyed by fire. He erected two-thirds of the surrounding stone wall with embrasures, and built the outer castle. The All Saints' church at the upper end of the Vaag (*i.e.* the fjord) was also built according to the king's advice, and he gave to it 100 mánaðrmatr during his illness. At Agvaldsnes he built a stone church, the fourth in size of all the parish churches in Norway. At Tunsberg he constructed a castellated stone wall around the mountain, and built the Gaute castle across the Daneklev. He built, also, the necessary houses on the mountain, erected a royal residence near the St. Lawrence church, and built a hospital near the St. Olav's church, to which he gave property yielding an income of 300 marks. He caused the channel at Skeljastein to be deepened, so that *kuggr* (*i.e.* merchant ships) now could sail where ferry boats could scarcely float before. He built the Barefoot-brothers' church at Tunsberg, but moved it later to Dragsmark, where he erected a St. Mary's cloister and a stone church, to which he gave property yielding an income of fifty marks. In Oslo he built a castle on the Vaalkaberg, and moved the St. Nicolas church thither; he also built the royal residence in the islands. On the Valdisholm he also built houses. At Konghelle he erected a castle on the Ragnhildsholm; he built a royal dwelling in the city, and houses on Gulløen. He cleared the Eker Islands, and built houses and a wooden church there. He likewise founded Marstrand, and erected buildings in many islands in Viken. He erected a stone castle at Ringsaker on Lake Mjøsen, and built houses there. He built, also, a hall at Steig, and repaired the church, which was nearly in ruins. He also built a hall at Hov, in Breiden, and donated property to it, and at Tofte he built a hall and a chapel. He bought Lo, in Opdal, and built dwelling houses, hall, and chapel there. In Hedemarken he erected halls, at Husabø, in Skaun, and at Ringsaker, and he caused dwelling houses to be built at Vidheim, in Øyer. He also constructed a stone wall around

---

[1] *Mánaðrmatr* literally means provisions for a month, but the word denotes a certain measure, especially of flour and butter, or in a more general sense, the value of a given amount of these articles.

the Sverreborg, at Stenbergene, and built houses there, since the Bagler had destroyed the castle." [1]

This catalogue of the great king's many achievements furnishes all necessary evidence of his remarkable energy, and proves how great was his solicitude for the intellectual development as well as for the social and economic welfare of the nation. The greatest architectural work of King Haakon's reign was the building of the nave of the Trondhjem cathedral. After the death of Archbishop Eystein, in 1188, the work on the cathedral seems to have been discontinued. His successor, Archbishop Eirik Ivarsson, engaged in a bitter controversy with King Sverre, and was forced to leave the country in 1190. Sverre charged him with keeping a large force of armed followers, as if he feared an attack upon himself or his church; that he thus spent the money which he should have used to keep workmen in the quarries carrying and cutting stone for the construction of the cathedral according to the original plan. Whether Eirik's successors, Thore Gudmundsson (1206–1214) and Guttorm (1215–1224) continued the work is not known, but it was not resumed with vigor till in the time of Archbishop Sigurd Eindridesson (1231–1252). He began the erection of the nave, which seems to have been nearly completed in the time of Archbishop Jón (1268–1282).[2] The nave, which, like the chancel, was built in the Gothic style, was the most ornate and imposing part of the great cathedral. According to the old writer Absalon Pederssøn Beyer (1530–1574), the west front had "a large gilt circular window cut in stone." Peder Claussøn Friis (1545–1614), a priest in southern Norway, says of it: "But about that same cathedral, how it is built, or how large it is, I can write nothing save what I have heard of others; namely, that it is built in the form of a cross, of cut stones which are chiseled into all sorts of figures round about the whole church, both inside and outside, so that it is astonishing, and in the west front, which is gilt, large images of the twelve apostles are cut in stone and gilt, and there are numerous pillars of polished

---

[1] *Haakon Haakonssonssaga*, p. 451 ff.

[2] Hermann M. Schirmer, *Kristkirken i Nidaros. The Cathedral of Trondhjem*, published by order of the Norwegian government, text by Professor P. A. Munch, drawings by Architect H. E. Schirmer, Christiania, 1859. *Teknisk Ugeblad*, Arkitektafdeling, Dec. 4, 1908. Freiherrn *v.* Minutoli, *Der Dom zu Drontheim*, Berlin, 1853.

marble, both inside and outside in the church, both white and black, and of different color, so smooth that one might think that they had been cast. In the southern portal there are about sixty pillars ingeniously wrought, so that one cannot well estimate what this single door has cost, not to mention the whole church." [1] How the nave looked when completed, it is difficult to determine, for it was scarcely finished when a series of accidents gradually reduced the proud edifice to a melancholy ruin.[2] But the Norwegian people, who have always cherished piously the memories of their past history, have long since made its restoration a national cause. Since 1869 the work of rebuilding the great cathedral has been in progress under the leadership of the best architects and sculptors in the country. Large sums are contributed yearly to the cause by individuals and private organizations as well as by the state, and before many years have rolled by, the old church will again lift its proud towers over the city of Trondhjem.

71. MAGNUS HAAKONSSON LAGABØTER. A NEW SYSTEM OF JURISPRUDENCE

Magnus Haakonsson, generally called Magnus Lagabøter (the Lawmender), was twenty-five years of age when his father, King Haakon, died in 1263. He had acted as regent during his father's absence, and as he had been crowned king in 1261 at the time of his wedding, he ascended the throne without proclamation or ceremony. He continued Haakon's peaceful policy, not only because wise statesmanship dictated such a course, but also because of his own inclination, since his interest was chiefly centered on lawmaking and

[1] Peder Claussøn Friis, *Samlede Skrifter*, edited by Gustav Storm, Christiania, 1881, p. 348.

[2] The cathedral was damaged by fire, April 31, 1328. It suffered still more in the next fire caused by lightning in 1432. After these accidents it was repaired to some extent, but in 1531 it was again set on fire by lightning, and great damage was done. The steeple, which was still standing, was wrecked by lightning in 1687. Two years later it fell and demolished the chapter house, near the church. The hasty repairs which had been attempted from time to time were of little avail. Two more fires, 1708 and 1719, left the church a ruin, and it was abandoned to its fate till in 1869, when the work of restoration was begun.

PLATE XII

The Trondhjem Cathedral as it will appear When Restored.

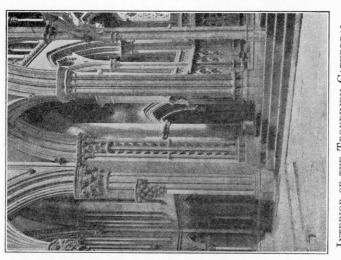

Interior of the Trondhjem Cathedral.

judicial reforms. He labored earnestly to promote the welfare of his people, and devoted special attention to the reorganization of the judicial system which constitutes the chief feature of his reign; but he lacked his father's robust energy and self-confident grasp of international affairs. He found his kingdom a field sufficiently large for his ambition, and the maintenance of peace seems to have been his chief concern in his whole foreign policy. The peace with Scotland, resulting in the cession of the Hebrides by the treaty of Perth in 1266, has already been mentioned. As soon as the war with Scotland was terminated, King Magnus began his legal reforms by publishing a revision of the "Gulathingslov," which, according to the "Islandske Annaler," was accepted by the Gulathing in 1267. The following year the revision of the laws of the Eidsivathingslag and the Borgarthingslag was also completed. According to Konrad Maurer, the two codes of church laws, the "Younger Gulathings Kristenret" and the "Younger Borgarthings Kristenret," are also to be ascribed to King Magnus' lawmaking activity during these early years of his reign.[1] In the Frostathingslag the king was permitted to revise the secular laws, but the church laws were left untouched because of the determined resistance of the arrogant prelate Jón Raude, Archbishop of Trondhjem, who maintained that no secular authority had the right to legislate for the church. The papacy, which had finally vanquished the Hohenstaufen emperors, stood at this time at the very zenith of its power. Archbishop Jón had witnessed the conclusion of this struggle while on a journey to Rome to receive the archbishop's pall, and he returned deeply impressed with the glory of the Roman Church and the power of the Holy Father, eagerly bent on asserting the hierarchic principles in his archdiocese with the utmost vigor. In Norway the state-church principle had been maintained since the introduction of Christianity, with but a short interruption in the time of Magnus Erlingsson. The king, as the head of the church, had also legislated for it, with the advice and assistance of the bishops. In conformity with the principles everywhere urged by the Roman hierarchy at that time. Archbishop Jón denied the king's right to legislate for the church,

[1] Konrad Maurer, *Udsigt over de nordgermanske Retskilders Historie*, p. 34 f.

and King Magnus, with characteristic weakness, yielded to the resolute prelate. In the negotiations between the two regarding the new lawmaking it may have been the archbishop who first suggested that uniform codes of laws for the whole kingdom, both civil and ecclesiastical, ought to be prepared, and it is possible that a compromise was reached, whereby the archbishop was suffered to prepare the code of church laws, though he received no formal authority to do so.[1]

The first fruit of this new system of legislating for the whole kingdom was a code of laws for Iceland, the "Jarnsíða," which was sent to Iceland, and accepted by the Althing in 1271.[2]

On March 29, 1272, Pope Gregory IX. issued a circular letter in which he summoned a church council to meet May 1, 1274, and he also requested all the bishops to report to this council all irregularities within their dioceses. Archbishop Jón believed that many abuses existed in his archdiocese, and he undertook to remedy them in the code of church laws which he was preparing. By his advice Bishop Arne of Skálholt wrote a similar code for Iceland, which was accepted at the Althing in 1275. Jón negotiated with King Magnus with regard to some points concerning which controversy was sure to arise. As a worthy successor of archbishops Eystein and Eirik he sought to make the church independent of the state, but Magnus, nevertheless, was quite manageable and conciliatory. At a council assembled in Bergen, 1273, a concordat was arranged in which the king yielded to the archbishop on nearly every point, modifying slightly only his most unreasonable demands. But because of these

---

[1] Konrad Maurer thinks that a code of church laws generally attributed to King Sverre dates from a later period, that it is an attempt of King Magnus and Archbishop Jón to agree upon a uniform code of church laws for the kingdom. The incomplete sketch has no heading or conclusion, and was never adopted as law. *Udsigt over de nordgermanske Retskilders Historie,* p. 37.

[2] *Biskop Arnessaga. Islandske Annaler,* ed. Storm, p. 49.

Because of the erroneous belief that this code was prepared by King Haakon Haakonsson, it has also been called the *Hákonarbók.* The *Jarnsíða,* with a Latin translation by Th. Sveinbjørnsson, was published at Copenhagen in 1847 under the title *Hin forna Lǫgbók Íslendinga sem nefnis Jarnsíða eðr Hákonarbók.* See also, *Norges gamle Love,* vol. II., p. 339, *Erkebiskop Jóns Kristenret.*

modifications the Pope would give only a conditional sanction. This action of the Pope ruffled even the pliant and peace-loving Magnus, and he interpreted it to mean that he had refused to sanction the agreement. Another council was called at Tunsberg in 1277,[1] where the concordat was subscribed to by both the king and the archbishop without going to the trouble of asking for the Pope's sanction. The archbishop's code of church laws may also have been accepted, though this is doubtful, but in his joy over the settlement of the difficulty Magnus showered additional favors on the church.

At the council of Bergen, 1273, King Magnus published a new law regulating the succession to the throne. According to this law, which was later incorporated in the general code, the throne might pass to twelve different heirs in due order of succession. The first five were the following:

1st. The king's oldest legitimate son.[1]
2d. The king's oldest legitimate grandson.
3d. The king's oldest legitimate brother.
4th. The king's oldest legitimate uncle (father's brother).
5th. The king's oldest legitimate nephew (son of the king's brother).

If none of these twelve heirs was found, then the one which was the nearest heir according to the general law of inheritance was to succeed, but always a man, not a woman.[2]

[1] The agreement entered into at Tunsberg, 1277, as well as that of Bergen, 1273, is found in *Norges gamle Love*, vol. II., p. 455 ff.

[2] Councils, like the one at Bergen in 1273, and at Tunsberg, 1277, had been assembled at various times to settle important questions of general interest. The scope of their power was not defined, nor is it known who were regarded as constituent members. They seem to have been assembled by the king as an advisory body. The advice given was of the greatest weight, and the king would not venture to oppose the council, which acted on behalf of the whole people. Its consent was necessary in order to alter the written laws of the kingdom, as in this case when the king proposed a change in the law of succession, and it was regarded as settled that the king could promulgate no measure which the council refused to sanction. The ordinary administrative work was done by the king, who would ask advice of his *hirðstjórar* (leaders of the *hird*), prelates, and other leading men of his immediate surroundings. His chief adviser and assistant was his chancelor, or the keeper of the great seal (*sigillum*) which was affixed to all royal documents and communications. Those whom the king thus consulted acted

Magnus Lagabøter's code of laws for the kingdom of Norway was based on the older codes, especially those of the Gulathingslag and the Frostathingslag, but it is not as well written as the old laws. It was accepted as the laws of the kingdom in 1274, in the eleventh year of King Magnus' reign. This code marks a new epoch in the development of Norwegian jurisprudence. Although many of the laws are borrowed almost verbatim from the old codes, new principles of judicial procedure were introduced which were wholly unknown to earlier lawmakers. These new features represent a change in the views regarding the punishment of crime, brought about by the rapid social development after the close of the civil wars. The heathen conceptions had given place to Christian ideas; the old warlike aristocracy was disappearing, and in its place the yeoman class was increasing in numbers and social importance. This class was less able to maintain their rights by force. They trusted in the security which the laws could give, and welcomed every change in the codes which would render justice more easily accessible to the common man. It was, no doubt, the purpose of King Magnus to adjust the legal system of the kingdom to the changed social conditions, and the people seem to have been conscious from the start of the need and importance of his legal reforms. This is revealed also in the prologue to the new code where the king says: "You know how the most discreet men of the Gulathingslag have said to us repeatedly that they have heard that we are engaged in revising the lawbooks of the land with the advice of the best men, and they have asked us that their lawbook may be revised in the same way." [1]

In the old jurisprudence crime was not regarded as a wrong against the state, but as an injury to the individual and the family to which he belonged.[2] The peace was regarded as broken between the

as a royal council (concilium generale), which could be assembled only on special occasions. T. H. Aschehoug, Statsforfatningen i Norge og Danmark indtil 1814, p. 140 ff.

[1] Norges gamle Love, vol. II., Nyere Landslov, prologus.

[2] Fr. Brandt, Nordmændenes gamle Strafferet, Historisk Tidsskrift, første række, vol. IV., p. 327 ff.; anden række, vol. IV., p. 20 ff. J. E. Sars, Udsigt over den norske Historie, vol. II., p. 217 ff. Konrad Maurer, Udsigt over de norske Retskilders Historie. P. A. Munch, Det norske Folks Historie, vol. IV., p. 488 ff. R. Keyser, Norges Stats-og Retsforfatning i Middelalderen, p. 237, 359. E. Hertzberg, Grundtrækkene i den ældste norske Proces.

family of the offender and the family of the party injured, and a state of feud, or private war, existed until a settlement was agreed upon. But it was a private affair which concerned only the families and parties involved. The injury done could be compensated for by a fine, which was agreed upon, either by the parties themselves, or by men selected by them for the purpose of giving an estimate. Only when the crime was of a more serious character, so that the offender would be outlawed, or sentenced to pay fine to the king, did the case have to be brought before the *thing*. Here both parties had to produce their own witnesses. The *thing* secured the observance of the necessary legal formalities, and rendered the decision, but there was no prosecuting authority, and whether the injured party sought redress through vengeance, which was considered lawful, or through private settlement, or at the *thing*, it had to be done through his own initiative, and at his own expense, which made justice costly and difficult to obtain.

The "Code of Magnus Lagabøter" introduced great changes in the principles of Norwegian jurisprudence by altering fundamentally the conception of crime, as well as the method of punishing the criminal. It greatly reduced the opportunity of the aggrieved party to seek redress through personal vengeance. In case of murder the criminal should be turned over to royal officials, who would cause him to be tried and sentenced by the *thing*. If guilty he was declared an outlaw, and any one might kill him; but the relatives of the person slain could not harm the slayer before he was tried and sentenced. The king had the power to pardon the offender, and the plaintiffs in the case would then have to be satisfied with a money payment. In case of other personal injuries personal revenge was also forbidden. The injured party should complain to the royal officials, whose duty it should be to appoint judges to decide the case, and fix a date for the payment of the fine. If the fine was not paid, the plaintiffs might resort to revenge, but the punishment inflicted should be in proportion to the injury. Crime was no longer regarded as a private affair, but as a violation of the laws, and an offense against the state, which should be punished by a fine paid to the king in addition to the fine paid to the party injured. These fines should be assessed by persons chosen by the royal officials, and not by the parties in the case. The public officers were given greatly increased powers of apprehending, detaining, and punishing criminals. The code also created a system of public prosecution, according to which the *things* might take the initiative in bringing the criminal to trial. It established the following principle: "Every freeborn man who is of age shall bring his own suit, but if he lacks the necessary knowledge or ability, the royal officials shall bring the suit in his behalf." [1] The judges were not only to hear the witnesses and pronounce the decision, as heretofore, but they were instructed to examine carefully the motives of the person accused, and the circumstances in the case; whether the crime was committed without provocation, whether it was done in self-defense, or whether other extenuating circumstances existed. The code says: "For this purpose courts of law are instituted that there the wrong and misdeeds are to be measured, and the decision should be rendered according to the circumstances of the case, as the *thingmænd* and the leader of the court find the truth to be before God and according to their own conscience, and not as many a fool has hitherto answered, that they judged only according to the law."

This new system of jurisprudence, which placed the administration of justice almost exclusively in the hands of the state, increased greatly also the power and dignity of the king. J. E. Sars says: "In the provincial laws (*i.e.* the Gulathingslov, the Frostathingslov, etc.) he was still regarded as a semi-private person. His authority had the character of certain well-defined rights which once for all had been given to the royal family, a sort of private domain whose well-defined borders he could not overstep without coming into collision with the rest of society. The 'Code of Magnus Lagabøter,' on the other hand, placed him as an exalted majesty above the people. It says that he has his authority from God, and from this theory it deduces a duty of obedience to him to which no fixed limits can be given." [2] The code expresses this principle as follows: "The king has received from God authority in secular matters, but the bishop has received spiritual authority in spiritual matters. . . .

---

[1] *Norges gamle Love*, vol. II., *Nyere Landslov*, 8. (*i.e. Code of Magnus Lagabøter*). *Norges gamle Love*, vol. II., *Nyere Landslov*, 17.
[2] J. E. Sars, *Udsigt over den norske Historie*, vol. II., p. 227.

Because they are God's officials; secondly, because all recognize that they can in no way dispense with them; thirdly, that God himself deigns to call himself by their name, he is, indeed, in great danger before God, who does not with perfect love and reverence uphold them in the authority to which God has appointed them." [1] Together with the conception that the king was divinely appointed followed also, as a natural corollary, the idea that he was the fountain of justice. The *lagmænd*, who were royal appointees, presided over the *lagthings*. Civil cases could either be brought before the *herredsthing* (local *thing*), or it could be submitted to the *lagmand*. From his decision an appeal could be taken to the *lagthing*, which could only lay the matter before the king. The *herredsthings* were assembled and presided over by the *sysselmænd*, who appointed the judges and executed the decrees of the court. In criminal cases in which the extreme penalty was inflicted, an appeal could be made to the king, who possessed the power of pardon.

The change which was thus quietly brought about in the character both of government and jurisprudence was probably greater than the people themselves realized. In pagan times the laws were regarded as springing from the gods themselves, hence they were considered as being permanent, almost unchangeable. In reality the old laws were the embodiment of old customs and usages expressing the nation's sense of legal justice at an earlier stage of development. These customs had, indeed, been modified by early lawgivers, but their fundamental common law character still remained. The new code, though sanctioned and adopted by the people, regarded laws and justice as emanating from the king, whom the people owed loyalty and obedience, not only because he was the head of the state and occupied the throne by inherited right and with the people's sanction and consent, but because he was God's anointed, and ruled by divine right. This view is most clearly expressed in the "King's Mirror," written, as already stated, about 1250. The father says to his son: "Now the king, as thou saidst, ought to be wise, well informed, and also upright, so that he fully understands that he is only God's servant, though, he is so highly honored, and elevated to such great dignity in God's service that all bow before him as before

[1] *Norges gamle Love*, vol. II., p. 23.

God himself; because all serve God and the holy name which he (the king) bears, but not his own person. It is therefore the very essence of royalty that all have great fear and awe before the king, so that no one is irreverent when they hear him mentioned." [1] "The king is appointed to watch over this holy house (*i.e.* the courts of law), and he is placed in the holy seat to guard God's holy decrees. He shall so judge between men in matters pertaining to the body that he may receive eternal salvation, and likewise all others who watch over the decrees which are justly rendered. In his hands God has placed the sword of punishment, with which he is to strike when it is necessary, as we said that King Solomon did when he subjected Joab to the punishing sword, and many others, with just punishment." [2]

This development of kingship was not due to a sudden innovation by Magnus Lagabøter. The idea was latent in the nationalism introduced into Norwegian political life by Harald Haarfagre and his successors, Olav Tryggvason and Olav the Saint. Harald Haard-raade and Olav Kyrre had nursed it; but King Sverre's triumph over clergy and aristocracy, and his position as head of both church and state brought it to full unfolding. In Haakon Haakonsson's reign it was so fully established that he could proclaim it officially in his code without a word of protest being uttered.

After publishing the general code, King Magnus also undertook to revise the "Bjarkeyjarréttr," or city laws, a work which was no less urgently demanded. In earlier days the towns and trading places, yet in their infancy, did not constitute independent communities, but belonged to the districts in which they were situated. Nidaros stood under the jurisdiction of the Frostathing, Bergen under the Gulathing, Oslo and Tunsberg under the Borgarthing. The growth of commerce, and the development of town life necessitated special legislation for the regulation of the growing urban communities. The "Bjarkeyjarréttr" gave them a character distinct from the rural districts to which they originally belonged, and may be re-garded as their first distinct organization as cities. They received their own *mót*, corresponding to the *thing* of the rural districts, where matters pertaining to trade and to the public peace and order were decided. The *mót* consisted of all permanent residents, *húsfastir*

_____
[1] *The King's Mirror*, p. 105.   [2] *Ibid.*, p. 171.

menn, all of whom enjoyed equal political rights. The cities also had their own courts of law; the *xii. manna dómr,* a tribunal of arbitration for settling legal disputes; and courts for trial of civil suits; but in matters of more general character they were still subject to the *lagthings,* the city courts being legal tribunals of secondary rank. The chief executive officer was the *gjaldkeri,* who acted as major and chief of police.[1] This first development of city government took place, as it seems, in the eleventh century during the period of commercial progress in the peaceful reign of Olav Kyrre.

The new code of municipal laws, which was published in 1277, was based on the old laws of Bergen, and seems to have been intended primarily for that city. Bergen was at that time the largest city in Norway, and one of the most important commercial centers on the shores of the North Sea. Its municipal government was highly developed, and might well serve as a model for the municipal laws for all the cities of the kingdom. One of the chief features introduced by the new code was the creation of a *byraad,* or city council of twelve members, which together with the *lagmand* and *gjaldkeri* had charge of the administrative affairs, and acted as judges at the townmót. The cities received also their own *lagthing* and *lagmænd, i.e.* their own superior courts of law, corresponding to the general *lagthings,* which hitherto had exercised jurisdiction also over the cities. The *lagthing* should consist of twelve members from each quarter or precinct, appointed by the *gjaldkeri,* and the *sysselmand,* a new city official who shared with the *gjaldkeri* the highest administrative authority. The power of the *sysselmand* was gradually increased until he became chairman of the council, and the most important official in the city.[2] The liberties granted the cities by the " Code of Magnus

[1] Alexander Bugge, *Studier over de norske Byers Selvstyre og Handel før Hanseaternes Tid.* Ebbe Hertzberg, *Glossarium, Norges gamle Love,* vol. V. T. H. Aschehoug, *De norske Communers Retsforfatning før 1837.* P. A. Munch, *Det norske Folks Historie,* vol. IV., p. 569 ff. R. Keyser, *Norges Historie,* vol. II., p. 271 ff. T. H. Aschehoug, *Statsforfatningen i Norge og Danmark indtil 1814,* p. 125 ff.

[2] "The *sysselmand* is mentioned in Magnus Lagabøter's municipal code in many instances together with the *gjaldkeri,* but he was, evidently, the latter's superior. He was himself appointed by the king, and according to the provisions of 1346 he took part in the appointment of the *gjaldkeri.*" T. H. Aschehoug, *De norske Communers Retsforfatning før 1837,* p. 106.

Lagabøter" made them wholly independent of the rural districts, and facilitated the development of city life and government. Even before this time the merchant class, or citizens of the larger towns, had been regarded as a separate fourth estate, distinct from the nobility, the yeomanry (bønder), and the clergy.[1] The new municipal code of laws for the *hird* was also revised by King Magnus. Laws defining the rights and duties of *hirdmænd* had existed from very early times. Occasionally revisions had been undertaken to bring them into harmony with more advanced culture and increased refinement of courtly etiquette. Such revisions had been made especially by Olav the Saint and Olav Kyrre, and the old laws were finally collected in a single code, the "Hirðskrá," which was again altered and enlarged by Magnus Lagabøter. In this revised edition we find first the law governing the succession to the throne as it had been changed and adopted in the reign of King Magnus. Then follow the laws dealing with the organization of the *hird*, and the duties and privileges of the various classes of *hirdmænd*. Next to the duke, or jarl, in dignity were the *lendermænd*, who were the king's advisers, and could keep forty armed followers, or *húskarlar*. Equal in rank with the *lendermænd* was the king's chancellor, who was keeper of the great seal, and prepared all royal letters and documents. He was usually an ecclesiastic. Next to the chancellor in dignity was the *stallare*, who represented the king at the *thing*, and acted as the leader of the *hird*. With these is classed also the *merkismaðr*, or royal standard-bearer, and the *skutilsveinar*, or officers of the *hird*, who on special occasions waited at the king's table. To the *skutilsveinar* belonged also the *dróttseti* and *skenkjari*, who had charge of the king's household. The different classes of the *hird: hirdmænd, gestir, húskarlar*, and *kertisveinar*, have already been spoken of. In 1277 King Magnus gave his *lendermænd* the foreign title of "barons"; the *skutilsveinar* were called "knights"; and both classes were styled "lords." This was not only a change of name, but marks the beginning of a new nobility, which appears later besides the king as the real rulers of the kingdom. Professor Aschehoug shows that the new nobility developed from the *hird*, which afforded the chieftain class the opportunity to win honor and promotion in the personal

---

[1] *The King's Mirror*, Introduction.

service of the king; but the real foundation for their power was their ownership of land.[1] The system of *leding* (O. N. *leiðangr*) was also changed. The people of the sea-coast districts had hitherto been required to supply the navy with arms and provisions, while in time of war they had to furnish armed men, and to render military service in proportion to the value of their land. But as the navy was now but seldom called into active service, the *leding* was changed into a general yearly tax of the same name, which corresponded to the *visøre* tax for the inland districts. An attempt was also made to strengthen the military forces of the kingdom. The *sysselmænd* were instructed to keep a certain number of armed men in each *skibrede*, or naval military district, and those who held benefices under the crown were required to furnish one warrior for every three marks income. But the standing army thus created was not very large.[2]

Many features of Magnus Lagabøter's reign are imperfectly known, owing to the loss of one of the chief sources for this reign, namely the "Magnus Haakonssonssaga," of which only a fragment now remains.[3] King Magnus' oldest son, Olav, died in 1267. His remaining sons were: Eirik, born in 1268, and Haakon, born in 1270. At a *thing* assembled at Bergen in 1273 the five-year-old Eirik received the title of king, as heir apparent to the throne, while Haakon was given the rank of duke. This was, evidently, done to secure an undisturbed succession in conformity with the provisions of the law.

72. THE GROWTH OF TRADE AND THE ORIGIN OF A DISTINCT COMMERCIAL POLICY

In Magnus Lagabøter's reign Norwegian commerce reached the greatest volume and the highest development to which it ever attained before its revival in modern times. A definite public policy with

---

[1] T. H. Aschehoug, *Statsforfatningen i Norge og Danmark indtil 1814*, p. 95 ff.

[2] P. A. Munch, *Det norske Folks Historie*, IV., 535, 549, says 3284 men. T. H. Aschehoug says that this is a misprint for 2284, *Statsforfatningen i Norge og Danmark*, p. 123.

[3] The other sources of this reign are: The *Bishop Arnessaga*, the *Islandske Annaler*, the public documents, royal letters, and the old laws. Accounts of the closing episodes of the war with Scotland must be gathered chiefly from Scotch chronicles and public documents.

regard to the regulation and promotion of commerce was now developed for the first time. Each city received a fixed territory within which it had a trade monopoly, as trading in the rural districts was gradually restricted, and trafficking with other cities was prohibited. With this centralization of trade in the cities followed also a regulation that only persons possessing a fixed amount of wealth could become merchants. This hastened the development of a well-organized and opulent merchant class. Commerce was carried on, not only with the Norwegian colonies, especially Iceland and Greenland, but also with England and Flanders, and other countries around the North Sea, as well as with Wisby in Gothland, and other commercial towns on the Baltic coast. The English Custom Rolls show that the merchants of Tunsberg, Oslo, Bergen, and Nidaros carried on a lucrative trade with England, and many families, especially in Bergen, seem to have subsisted exclusively on the traffic with the British Isles. "About the year 1300 Lynn was one of the most important commercial towns in England," says Alexander Bugge. "The oldest Custom Roll for this town covers a period from Feb. 5, 1303, till May 19, 1304. In this period there arrived in Lynn and neighboring smaller towns 235 foreign ships." [1] These ships brought goods to the value of £2036. 4s. 9d. The Norwegian ships alone brought goods to the amount of £1067. 386s. 12d., or over one half of the total amount. In the year 1304–1305, according to the same source, goods were imported to the same towns to the value £3688. 12s. 10d. Of this amount the wares brought by Norwegian ships represented the sum of £834. 27s. For the year following, 1305–1306, the figures are: Goods imported, £2798. 14s. 2d.; Norwegian goods, £913. 508s. Other English documents show that the Norwegians carried on a lively trade with London, Boston, Yarmouth, Newcastle, and other towns on the east coast of England. The chief articles of export from Norway to England were timber, herring, dried codfish, furs, falcons, etc.[2] The trade between Norway and

---

[1] *Studier over de norske Byers Selvstyre og Handel*, p. 134 ff.

[2] Alexander Bugge, *Handelen mellem England og Norge indtil Begyndelsen af det 15de Aarhundrede, Historisk Tidsskrift*, tredie række, vol. IV. In regard to Norway's export of timber see *Patent Rolls*, 31, Edward I., number 45. *Pl. of Patent Rolls*, Edward III., 1334–1338, p. 350. Vogt, *Historisk Tidsskrift*, anden række, vol. V.

England developed in the latter part of the eleventh century after
Olav Kyrre had founded the city of Bergen, and this commerce,
which was of great importance to both countries, continued to increase until it was destroyed by the Hanseatic League in the fourteenth century. The earliest English commercial treaties were
concluded with Norway, and embassies were frequently sent to England by the kings of Norway to bring greetings and presents to the
English king. An alliance was formed between King John of England and King Sverre, which seems to have been more than a mere
treaty of commerce, since John sent a hundred English engineers to
aid Sverre in the siege of Tunsberg in 1201. In the early years of
Haakon Haakonsson's reign this treaty was renewed, and King
Haakon and Skule Jarl sent many presents and friendly messages to
the English king. In a letter to King Haakon, Henry III. says:
"We rejoice greatly, and will continue to rejoice, because our realms
are so united that merchants from your kingdom may unhindered
come to us, and ours likewise to your realm." [1] The treaty seems
to have been ratified in 1222. A very lively commerce was also
carried on with Flanders and neighboring provinces, at this time the
most densely populated districts in northern Europe. Ypres and
Gent were famous for their manufacture of fine cloth, and Bruges
was one of the chief commercial cities of Europe, where merchants
from all countries met. The traders from France, England, Spain,
Italy, Lübeck, Hamburg, Norway, etc., did business here in separate
streets which were wholly controlled by them. A report of the im-

[1] Alexander Bugge, *Handelen mellem England og Norge, Historisk Tidsskrift*, tredie række, vol. IV.

King Haakon sent Archdeacon Anders of Bergen, and two other men,
Asgaut and Asgeir (Osgoð and Askerus), to England to negotiate with
King Henry III. Haakon sent with them a number of falcons as a present
to King Henry, and he also wrote him a very friendly letter. The messengers remained in England till 1225, when they returned home, bringing rich
presents of grain and malt which Henry III. sent King Haakon. King
Henry also wrote to the royal officials of Lynn that he had granted permission to the subjects of his dear friend the king of Norway, notwithstanding
the embargo, to export from England 1000 quarteria of grain. He also
wrote to the bailiffs of Lynn instructing them to receive the Norwegian merchants in a friendly way, as he had granted them permission to bring their
wares to Lynn for a term of three years, beginning with the next Michaelmas.
Diplomatarium Norwegicum, vol. XIX., no. 172, 173, 174.

portation to Bruges for the year 1304 enumerates also the articles brought from Norway: "From Norway come falcons, barrel staves (merrins), butter, tallow, codliver oil, or whale fat (oint?), tanned hides (cuir bouli?) and goat-skins, of which cordovan leather is made."[1] Timber was also exported in ever larger quantities, especially to Friesland and Holland. From about 1300 it became one of the leading articles in the export trade of Norway. Norway's commercial relations with Gothland and the regions around the Baltic Sea date from very early times, when the trade in this quarter was carried on almost exclusively by the townsmen of Skiringssal and Tunsberg.[2] At the close of the eleventh century Bergen became the chief seat of the trade with Gothland, and soon grew to rival Wisby, the only great commercial city in the Baltic. It was especially the dried codfish which brought merchants from all lands to Bergen, and the Gothlanders, who had built up a great commerce, were among the first to profit by the trade with Norway. Danish crusaders who visited Norway in 1191 say about Bergen: "Because of its wealth and power it is the most important city in the land. It has a great number of inhabitants, and many monasteries and cloisters. There is such an abundance of dried codfish that it surpasses measure and number. There one can see a multitude of people who come from all quarters; Irish, Greenlanders, English, Germans, Danes, Swedes, and Gothlanders, and yet many more which it would be too difficult to enumerate."[3] Matthew Paris states that there were 200 ships at one time in the Bergen harbor.[4] It is evident that the trade with Gothland continued to flourish in the thirteenth and also in the fourteenth century, but no account of it has been preserved.

In few countries did commerce ever play so important a part in the economic welfare of the people as in Norway, where even many of the necessaries of life had to be imported. Alexander Bugge says:

[1] Alexander Bugge, Studier over de norske Byers Selvstyre og Handel, p. 155.
[2] Alexander Bugge, Gotlændingernes Handel paa England og Norge omkring 1300, Historisk Tidsskrift, tredie række, vol. V.
[3] De Profectione Danorum in Terram Sanctam, found in Langebek's Scriptores Rerum Danicarum, V. P. A. Munch, Det norske Folks Historie, vol. III., p. 225 ff. Monumenta Historica Norwegiae, ed. by G. Storm, p. 155.
[4] Matthæus Parisiensis, vol. V., p. 36 (Rerum Brittannicarum medii Aeve Scriptores), The Haakon Haakonssonssaga, translated by O. Rygh, ch. 258.

"Norway imported especially grain. As our country has never been able to produce this necessary article in sufficient quantity, it has had to import it from abroad. This circumstance, together with the fact that Norway possessed a rich supply of raw materials, led the Norsemen to develop navigation and commerce in very early times. Grain was usually carried unground; flour is not often mentioned in the Custom Rolls. Malt was also an important article of importation. Nearly all ships which sailed from England to Norway carried grain and malt. Of other imported articles may be mentioned especially: cloth, more seldom costly fabrics, lead, spices, fancy articles, ale, beans, and honey." [1] The chief articles of export were herring, codfish, timber and lumber, hides and furs, tallow, codliver oil, etc.

Commerce has not only been necessary for the prosperity of the Norwegian people, but it has always been a fair index to the health and vigor of their national life. When commerce flourished, it imparted new stimulus, and roused the latent energies to the accomplishment of great things; its decline was an indication of national weakness and decay. At this time the Norwegian fleets of merchant ships spread their sails on all the seas, and crowded every important harbor in northern Europe. Prosperity had increased rapidly, and the great achievements in literature, art, and culture had not failed to create a reserved but self-conscious national pride. But a dangerous rival was already looming broadly into sight to the southward. This was a growing union of German merchants, which later developed into the Hanseatic League, a powerful organization with which the Norwegian merchant marine waged a long but losing contest. King Sverre seems to have hated the German merchants who visited Bergen in his day, probably as much through a general instinct as because they imported wine which increased drunkenness and corrupted public morals. The "Sverressaga" relates that the German merchants brought large quantities of wine to Bergen, that many people drank to excess, and that in a brawl many were killed or wounded. King Sverre then assembled a *thing*, and addressed the townsfolk as follows: "We desire to thank the Englishmen, who have brought hither linen or flax, wax or caldrons. We

[1] Alexander Bugge, *Studier over de norske Byers Selvstyre og Handel*, p. 166.

desire next to make mention of those who have come from the Orkneys, Shetland, the Faroe Islands or Iceland; all those who have brought here such things as make this land the richer, and we cannot do without. But there are Germans who have come here in great numbers, with large ships, intending to carry away butter and dried fish, of which the exportation much impoverishes the land; and they bring wine instead, which the people strive to purchase, both my men, townsmen, and merchants. From that purchase much evil and no good has arisen, for many have lost life through it, and some their limbs; some carry marks of disfigurement to the end of their days; others suffer disgrace, being wounded or beaten. Overdrinking is the cause. To those Southmen I feel much ill-will for their voyage here; and if they would preserve their lives or property, let them depart hence; their business has become harmful to us and to our realm." The king concludes his speech with a very eloquent plea for temperance. His animosity against the German merchants seems, however, to have had a deeper cause than the not very serious disturbance here mentioned. The keen-eyed king has probably discerned in the thrifty, able, and arrogant German merchants a dangerous rival to Norwegian commerce, "whose business had become harmful" to Norwegian commercial interests. We have seen that his grandson Haakon Haakonsson came into armed conflict with them, but that they sent an ambassador to Norway to make peace with the king, and a commercial treaty was concluded between Norway and Lübeck. From a letter written by King Haakon during the negotiations with Lübeck it appears that the trade with the German cities had already become of great importance to Norway, and that the king was anxious to reëstablish peace and friendly relations with them. He says: "You may be assured that we in our kingdom will not injure your citizens in their lawful rights, but that we will readily show you all proper favors, if you will keep the friendship with us inviolable. Send, therefore, in the summer, as usual, your ships to us with the goods which are necessary for our kingdom, namely grain and malt, and permit also our merchants to buy these articles as long as scarcity lasts in our realm." Owing to the growing importance of the German trade King Magnus Lagabøter granted the merchants of Lübeck their

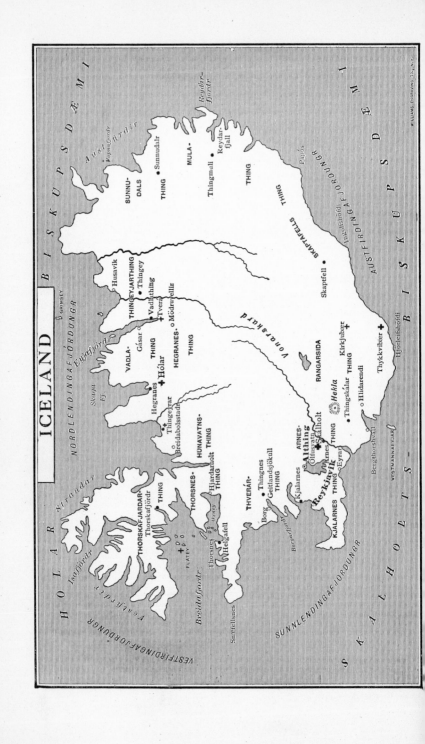

first charter in Norway, July 18, 1278, in which he calls them his special friends.[1] In August the following year he granted the merchants of Bremen a similar charter. The privileges which they received were not very important, "Magnus was a wise and careful man," says Alexander Bugge. "He saw how dangerous it would be to grant the Germans too great liberties; therefore the privileges which Lübeck and Bremen received were quite insignificant, barely enough to avoid making them his enemies." The initial step was, however, taken in granting special rights to these foreign merchants, who used every future opportunity to tighten their hold on Norwegian trade.

Magnus Lagabøter considered Bergen his capital, and spent most of his time there. He maintained a luxurious court, and as he gave liberal donations to the church and to various religious institutions, because of his great piety, he was often in great financial difficulties, and had to resort to the mischievous practice of debasing the coin to replenish his depleted treasury. But his love of peace, his kind and generous disposition made him very popular, and there was general mourning when he died on the 9th of May, 1280.

73. THE REIGN OF EIRIK MAGNUSSON

King Magnus Lagabøter's son Eirik succeeded to the throne at the age of eleven. As he was still too young to rule, a regency was formed consisting of his mother, Queen Ingebjørg, an able and talented lady, and a circle of influential nobles, who acted as her assistants.[2] The most powerful of these were Bjarne Erlingsson, Gaute of Tolga, Bjarne Lodinsson, Hallkel Øgmundsson, Jón Brynjolfsson, Andres Plytt, and the selfish and greedy Audun Hugleiksson Hestakorn, a sinister character, ambitious and unsympathetic, who, like an un-

---

[1] P. A. Munch, *Det norske Folks Historie*, IV., p. 72 f. The letter is found in *Urkundenbuch der Stadt Lübeck*, vol. I., p. 142. P. A. Munch, *Det norske Folks Historie*, vol. IV., p. 667 ff.

[2] According to the old custom followed in Norway, the king was of age when he became twelve years old. This age limit was extended to eighteen years in the beginning of the thirteenth century, but Eirik was declared to have reached his majority when he became fourteen years old. T. H. Aschehoug, *Statsforfatningen i Norge og Danmark indtil 1814*, p. 31. P. A. Munch, *Det norske Folks Historie*, III., p. 637.

lucky constellation, trails a deep shadow across the life and reign of the gentle King Eirik Magnusson. The queen and her assistants formed from the start a distinct party. They were the representatives of the aristocracy, they were bitterly opposed to the growing power of the clergy, and exercised great influence over the young king, who was docile almost to weakness. Eirik's younger and more gifted brother, Haakon, had been made duke before King Magnus died, and when the two brothers became old enough to rule, they seem to have exercised the royal power jointly, though Haakon acted alone in all affairs pertaining exclusively to his dukedom. King Eirik was to be crowned in the summer of 1280,[1] but trouble at once arose between the clergy and the nobility as to the nature of the coronation oath which the king should be requested to take. The haughty and inflexible Archbishop Jón demanded that the liberties of the church should be duly acknowledged; especially the concessions which had been obtained during the reign of Magnus Lagabøter. The queen and the nobles were opposed to this, but they finally yielded, and the coronation took place at Bergen on the 2d of July. Archbishop Jón had hoped to secure a permanent ratification of the privileges claimed by the church, the chief of which were exemption from taxation, and freedom from the authority of the secular courts; but he soon learned to his sorrow that the nobles were not disposed to be bound by their promises on this point. Instead of yielding to the archbishop, who would abate nothing of his high claims, the queen and her advisers requested him to submit to them a copy of the resolutions, or statutes, which had been recently adopted at a provincial church council, under the directions of the archbishop and the bishops.[2]

In this document the principles of the canon law regarding the independence of the church and the power of the clergy were set forth in the most uncompromising spirit, and as this had been adopted without consulting the king or his advisers, it gave great offense. A law was promulgated in the king's name for the purpose, as it

[1] In a letter of May 14, 1280, written in the king's name to Edward I. of England, Eirik Magnusson notifies the king of England of his father's death, and of his approaching coronation. *Diplomatarium Norwegicum*, vol. XIX., no. 303.

[2] The document is found in *Norges gamle Love*, vol. III., p. 227–241.

was claimed, of amending the "Code of Magnus Lagabøter" on certain points where it was not sufficiently explicit. But the new law made many important provisions, especially with regard to the *leding* tax involving the taxation of church property, by which the concordat, entered into by King Magnus and Archbishop Jón, was broken. No one could doubt that the aristocracy intended this as an open defiance to the archbishop's hierarchic policy.

During the summer of 1281 preparations were made for the king's marriage to Margaret, daughter of Alexander III. of Scotland. The "Chronicon de Lanercost" [1] states that she was so beautiful that King Eirik could not rest before he had sent envoys to Scotland to ask for her hand in marriage; but as he was only in his thirteenth year, and never had seen the princess, he could scarcely be so deeply interested. It was, no doubt, a political marriage, arranged by the nobles, who could, perhaps, figure out that some advantage might be gained through this marriage, as Margaret, in case her only brother should die before her, would fall heir to the throne of Scotland. The wedding was celebrated in the summer of 1281, and Margaret, who was about twenty years old, soon became very popular. She devoted herself to the care of her youthful husband, on whom she exercised a most beneficial influence. But, unfortunately for him, she died in 1283 before he reached the age of mature manhood.

After the royal wedding the struggle between the barons and the clergy was renewed with increased bitterness. The archbishop seems to have demanded that the provisions in the new law which he deemed prejudicial to the interests of the church should be repealed. This request was promptly refused. The king's party refused, also, to accept the code of church laws which the archbishop had prepared, and repealed the privileges granted by Magnus Lagabøter in a letter of September 13, 1277. The cunning Audun Hugleiksson Hestakorn seems to have been the soul in this aggressive anti-church policy. He was related to the royal family, and the king called him his dear relative (*carus consanguineus*). While yet young he came to court, where he rose rapidly through royal favor. Because of his ability and great legal learning he became

---

[1] *Norges gamle Love*, vol. III., p. 3–12. See P. A. Munch, *Det norske Folks Historie*, vol. IV., 2, p. 19 ff.

the king's *stallare*. He seems to have planned the whole campaign against Archbishop Jón, but he left its execution to others, and when the vengeance of the church fell upon those who were considered its special enemies, Audun Hugleiksson passed unscathed. The archbishop appealed to Pope Martinus IV., but the king's party also sent envoys to plead with the Pope. The Pontiff had heard of Norway as a great naval power, and as he was much taken up with European politics at the time, he gave the archbishop no support. This only added fuel to the fire. When Bishop Arne of Stavanger refused to pay the *leding* tax he was promptly outlawed. Archbishop Jón now resorted to the extreme measure of excommunicating the king, his mother (Queen Ingebjørg), and many of the leading members of the regency, but they answered by driving the archbishop and two of his stanchest supporters, Bishop Anders of Oslo and Bishop Thorfinn of Hamar, into exile. Their possessions were confiscated, and Jón Brynjulfsson was placed in charge of the archbishop's residence and the prebends of the cathedral of Trondhjem. The archbishop fled to Sweden, where he died in December, 1282. His body was not brought back to Trondhjem for interment until the year following, when the excitement caused by the controversy had subsided. Bishops Anders and Thorfinn, who had repaired to Rome to prevail on Pope Martinus IV. to intervene, received but slight satisfaction. After they had waited two years, the Pope finally wrote a letter to King Eirik, admonishing him in a friendly and fatherly tone to have due regard for the rights and liberties of the holy church; but no bull of excommunication was issued. Thorfinn left Rome before the Pontiff had affixed his seal to this letter, and he died shortly afterwards in the monastery of Doest, in Flanders. Bishop Anders returned to Norway, sought reconciliation with the king, and was again installed in his diocese. In 1287 Bishop Jørund of Hamar was finally chosen to succeed Jón as Archbishop of Trondhjem. It is quite evident that King Eirik, who was a mere boy, took no part in this controversy. If he could have ruled, he would, undoubtedly, have continued his father's conciliatory policy. The epithet "Priest-hater" which has been attached to his name is, therefore, wholly undeserved. The clergy was unable to offer further resistance, and the storm of controversy quickly subsided, as matters of graver importance began to attract general attention. Ever since Queen Ingebjørg had left Denmark in so unceremonious a way to marry Magnus Haakonsson of Norway, strained relations had existed between the two kingdoms. Ingebjørg had received no income from the large estates which were her rightful patrimony, and when she became regent for her son, King Eirik, she took steps to recover her possessions, which the king of Denmark would not surrender. It soon became evident that war could not long be averted, and the Danish king sought to gain the support of the merchants of Lübeck and Hamburg by granting them privileges in the province of Skåne. In Norway the German merchants were growing more unpopular. The queen and her assistants endeavored to enforce the laws against them to the letter, and sought instead to strengthen the friendship with England and Scotland. The marriage of King Eirik to Margaret of Scotland was probably due to this policy, as new ties of friendship between the two kingdoms were thereby created. Before her death Queen Margaret had given birth to a daughter, who was also christened Margaret, and when the only son of Alexander III. died in 1284, this little princess became the nearest heir to the throne of Scotland. The Scotch magnates pledged themselves to acknowledge her as heir to Scotland, Man, and the Hebrides, and to defend her right to the crown.[1] In the summer of 1284 the regency sent an embassy to King Edward I. of England to renew the treaty which had long existed between Norway and England. They were very cordially received, and Edward hoped to bring about a marriage between his son and the Norwegian princess.

The king of Denmark, Eirik Glipping, was opposed by a number of dissatisfied nobles at home, but he showed no disposition to grant the demands of Queen Ingebjørg. With her connivance, but unauthorized by the government, Alv Erlingsson of Thornberg,[2] one of the most powerful of the Norwegian barons, began a series of bold raids on the coast of Denmark. From his castle, Isegram, at the mouth of the Glommen River, he sallied forth into Cattegat and

[1] *Diplomatarium Norwegicum*, vol. XIX., no. 309. *Acts of Scotland*, I., p. 82. *Rymeri fœdera*, I., p. 638. See P. A. Munch, *Det norske Folks Historie*, vol. IV., 2, p. 96.

[2] Alv Erlingsson is the hero of numerous folk-songs, in which he is known as Mindre-Alv.

the Belts, where he took special pleasure in capturing or destroying German merchantmen. Great damage was done by the bold corsair, who is said even to have entered the enemies' ships in disguise, and to have bargained for the prize set on his own head. A number of leading German cities united, and sent a large fleet towards the coast of Norway to stop all Norwegian commerce. In a fight with the Germans Alv at one time captured nine ships, if we may trust the old folk-song, but he was unable to cope with such large forces. The blockade almost isolated Norway commercially, and the government was forced to sue for peace. In the treaty concluded at Kalmar in 1285 Norway agreed to pay an indemnity of 6000 marks of silver, and the merchants of the German cities in question should have the right to buy unhindered whatever they pleased, and export it from Norway. The Norwegian merchants should enjoy the same right in the German cities. Norway was yet able to compete with the Germans, but these foreign merchants had gained a stronger foothold, and their presence soon proved injurious to Norwegian trade.

Even after peace had been concluded with the Germans, the hostility with Denmark continued, and extensive preparations were made to renew the war with that kingdom. Queen Ingebjørg's favorite, Alv Erlingsson of Thornberg (Mindre-Alv, a corruption of Milde Hr. Alv), who had plunged the country into war without authority, was not called to account for his strange conduct, but was instead created jarl, and went to England as special envoy to King Edward I. to secure his help in the war. Alexander III. of Scotland died March 19, 1286, and Princess Margaret of Norway was to succeed to the throne, in conformity with the agreement of 1284. Edward I., who was anxious to bring about a marriage between Margaret and his son Edward, received Alv Jarl very cordially, furnished him a war loan of 2000 marks sterling, and granted permission to knights and others who were willing, to go to Norway to help King Eirik in the war with Denmark. Alv also tried, though without success, to raise military forces in Iceland. Soon after Alv Jarl's return to Norway the Danish king, Eirik Glipping, was assassinated by his rebellious nobles, and the war was thereby averted for a time. Queen Ingebjørg did not live to carry out her plans. She died in March, 1287. The impetuous Alv of Thornberg, who may have been her secret lover, and who owed his power and influence to her favor, immediately started a revolt in his customary desperate style. He burned a part of the city of Oslo; but King Eirik, aided by his brother Duke Haakon, quickly quelled the uprising, and banished the violent jarl.

Hitherto Queen Ingebjørg and her favorites had shaped, to a large extent, the policy of the government, especially as to its relations with foreign powers, though the king had been of age for some time. But the influence by which he had been dominated ceased at the queen's death, and he could now take the reins into his own hands. The hostile attitude towards Denmark was, nevertheless, continued also by King Eirik, and war broke out in 1289; but the only result of two successive campaigns was a further increase of the growing financial embarrassment of the government. In the second campaign, 1290, the banished Alv Erlingsson of Thornberg again found opportunity to renew his piratic raids, but he was captured by the Danes, and put to death.[1]

King Eirik's attention was more and more absorbed by the question of his daughter Margaret's succession to the throne of Scotland, and the operations against Denmark were for a time discontinued. Edward I. of England was making strenuous efforts to bring about a marriage between his son Edward and Margaret, as he hoped thereby to unite the crowns of Scotland and England. This may have been the reason why the Scotch magnates were no longer willing to abide by their former agreement to defend Margaret's title. Eirik sent an embassy to Edward I. to solicit his aid in securing her recognition, and the king showed his good-will by summoning a council at Salisbury, where the three Norwegian envoys met four Scotch and four English representatives to consider the matter. The Scotch representatives, the bishops of St. Andrews and Glasgow, Sir Robert Bruce the Elder, and Sir John Comyn, agreed to acknowledge Margaret as queen of Scotland, if she came to their country without having contracted any obligation as to marriage, a condition to which the Norwegian envoys agreed. In September or October, 1290, the little six-year-old princess, also called the Maid of Norway, was sent to Scotland, but she fell sick on the stormy voyage across the sea, and died shortly after reaching the Orkneys.[1]

[1] Among the common people a tradition prevailed that the Maid of Norway was not dead, but that she had been sold for a large sum of gold by those

Edward I. now began to act the part of overlord of Scotland. He persuaded the Scotch pretenders, Robert Bruce the Elder, John Balliol, John Comyn, and others, to acknowledge him as the paramount lord of the kingdom, and to submit their claims to his decision. King Eirik also sent ambassadors to urge his claim to the vacant throne as Margaret's heir, but it soon became clear that the only candidates who would be seriously considered were Robert Bruce and John Balliol. Edward I. decided in favor of the latter, who received the crown of Scotland as his vassal. The cordial relations between Norway and England ceased from that moment, and Eirik pursued a policy which brought him into ever closer relations with King Edward's enemies. In 1293 he married Isabella Bruce, granddaughter of Robert Bruce the Elder, and sister of the later King Robert Bruce of Scotland. She bore him a daughter, Ingebjørg, but no son. It seems to have been Eirik's intention to strengthen again the bonds between Norway and Scotland by this marriage, but all closer relations between the two kingdoms now rapidly ceased. Among the common people of Scotland the tradition, nevertheless, continued to live that since the time of the Maid of Norway, the Norwegians claimed Scotland, and would some day return with an armed force, and endeavor to take possession of the country. The Scotch poet, Thomas of Erceldoune (Thomas Rymer), wrote a popular ditty about the black fleet of Norway which would enter the Firth of Forth. Not till it had left again could they build castles which would last.

> It will be seen upon a day
> Between the Bass and Bay
> Craigin and Fidderay —
> The black fleet of Norroway;
> Quhen the black fleet is come and gane
> Then may they bigg thair burgh of lime and stane,
> Quhilk they biggit of straw and hay,
> That will stand till doomesday. [1]

who had her in charge. Ten years later a woman came from Germany to Norway, and claimed to be Princess Margaret. She was tried as an impostor and executed, but she was later regarded as a saint by the common people.

[1] P. A. Munch, *Det norske Folks Historie*, vol. IV., 2, p. 204. Bass, or Bass Rock, Craig, and Fidderay, or Fiddra, are isles at the entrance to the Firth

The war with Denmark was renewed in 1293, and after some indecisive campaigns during the following two years a truce was arranged
at Hegnesgavel, according to which King Eirik and his brother Duke
Haakon should have free use of the Danish estates belonging to their
mother, Queen Ingebjørg, and merchants should be allowed to carry
on trade unmolested between the two kingdoms. The truce expired
in 1298, but it was renewed, and Eirik did not continue his attacks
on Denmark.

It is impossible to discover any statesmanlike policy in this protracted quarrel with Denmark, as the advantages which could have
been gained even under the most favorable circumstances would
scarcely have compensated for the heavy war expenses and the losses
incurred by the interruption of commerce. The indemnity to be
paid the German merchants for the damages done by Alv Erlingsson
of Thornberg, and the outlay incident to the war brought King
Eirik into most serious financial difficulties. He was unable to
pay the indemnity when it fell due, and the Germans used the opportunity to obtain new privileges in Norway.[1] These were secured
to them by a charter of 1294. In 1295, while Edward I. of England
was at war with France, King Eirik sent Audun Hugleiksson Hestakorn as plenipotentiary to France for the purpose, as it seems, of
obtaining a loan. Audun had risen to great power after Queen Ingebjørg's death. He was the king's favorite, as Alv of Thornberg had
been the queen's. He had received the title of jarl, and held the
important office of féhirðir, or royal treasurer. There can be no doubt
that this powerful and unscrupulous baron exercised great influence
over the manageable King Eirik, who had learned only too well to
submit to those who possessed a will stronger than his own. Audun
concluded with France a most remarkable treaty. In consideration
of a yearly subsidy of £30,000 he engaged for the kingdom of Norway to furnish for the war with England 200 galleys and 100 large

of Forth. When the black fleet of Norroway is come and gone, they can
build their castles of lime and stone, which they before built of straw and hay.

[1] Alexander Bugge, *Studier over de norske Byers Handel og Selvstyre før
Hanseaterne*, p. 183 ff. P. A. Munch, *Det norske Folks Historie*, vol. IV.,
p. 234 ff. Alexander Bugge, *Handelen mellem England og Norge indtil Begyndelsen av det 15de Aarhundrede, Historisk Tidsskrift*, tredie række, vol. IV.,
p. I ff.

ships with arms and provisions for four months of the year, together
with 50,000 warriors. He well knew that this was far in excess of
Norway's entire military force at this time, and that he contracted
for his country obligations which it could not fulfill; but he accomplished his purpose of obtaining money, as the sum of 6000 marks
sterling was paid to him immediately. The second part of his mission was to obtain for Duke Haakon the hand of Countess Isabella
of Joigny. This request was also granted, but the marriage was
never solemnized. Audun returned to Norway about Christmas
time, and the king ratified the treaty in March, 1296. If he knew
the character of the document when he signed it, and if he acted of
his own free will, which is very doubtful, it shows what kind of influence Audun exercised over him. In 1297–1298 Eirik was able to
pay the indemnity due the German cities, and it must be inferred
that he used the money obtained from France to liquidate this debt.
Fortunately the war between France and England stopped, and Norway was never called upon to meet the obligations created by Audun's
perfidious bargain. Audun's later career is wrapped in mystery.[1]
In 1299 he was imprisoned. Three years later, in the reign of Haakon
Magnusson, he was condemned to death and executed, and all his
possessions were confiscated. This extreme penalty could be inflicted
only for the greatest crime, and although nothing is known as to
the nature of his offense, it has been thought that he was convicted
of high treason.

About 1287 Duke Haakon built the castle of Akershus, at Oslo.
The exact time of its erection cannot be determined, but it is known
to have existed in 1300. The building of this castle seems to have
been a part of a general plan to enlarge and beautify the city of
Oslo. The strategic importance of this town had been repeatedly
demonstrated; its beautiful location, its fine harbor, and its proximity to Denmark, Sweden, and the Baltic Sea would also insure its
growth as a commercial center. It shows considerable foresight on
the part of the young duke when he selected this town for his future
capital.

[1] P. A. Munch, *Det norske Folks Historie*, vol. IV., 344 ff. Gustav Storm
Audun Hestakorn og St. Margrete paa Nordnæs, Historisk Tidsskrift, anden
række, vol. IV., p. 209 ff.

PLATE XIII

AKERSHUS.

King Eirik Magnusson died in Bergen on the 13th of June, 1299, thirty-one years of age. He had always been sickly, and through a fall from his horse he received in his boyhood severe injuries which further impaired his delicate system. Both physically and intellectually he seems to have been quite insignificant, and though he bore the title of king during the long period of twenty-six years, the helm of state had been controlled by other hands throughout the greater part of his reign. His queen, Isabella Bruce, who at the time of his death was a young woman of twenty, spent her long widowhood quietly at Bergen, where she died about sixty years later.

74. HAAKON MAGNUSSON THE ELDER. THE CHANGE OF NORWAY'S FOREIGN POLICY

King Eirik Magnusson had no sons, and his brother, Duke Haakon, succeeded him on the throne. Haakon was not in Bergen when the king died, as his marriage to Euphemia, daughter of Gunther of Arnstein, Count of Rupin, had just been celebrated at Oslo, but when he received the news, he hastened to Bergen, where he was proclaimed king, August 10, 1299. Later in the fall he and his queen were both crowned in his residence city of Oslo.[1] Haakon

[1] Hitherto the coronation had always taken place at Bergen, where the following kings had been crowned:

Magnus Erlingsson	1164
Sverre	1194
Haakon Haakonsson	1247
Magnus Lagabøter	1261
Eirik Magnusson	1280

This custom was broken when Haakon Magnusson was crowned at Oslo, 1299. R. Keyser, P. A. Munch, and later historians have accepted the account of the *Laurentiussaga* that Haakon was crowned in Trondhjem. The saga says: "Then King Eirik Magnusson died on the 10th of July (should have been the 13th, 1299), and his brother Haakon received the title of king, and he was crowned in Trondhjem with royal consecration. Thither came the most prominent men from Norway and from many other countries. There could be seen the greatest concourse of people in the North." Professor Gustav Storm has shown that the account of the saga is erroneous, that a more trustworthy account is given by another, hitherto unnoticed source found in *Biskop Jens Nilssøns Visitatsbøger og Reiseoptegnelser*, edited by Y. Nielsen, which states that Haakon was crowned in Oslo, 1299. Gustav Storm, *De ældre norske Kongers Kroningsstad, Historisk Tidsskrift,*

Magnusson the Elder, or Haakon V., was twenty-nine years of age when he became king. He had been well educated according to the standards of the times; he could speak and write both Latin and French, and both in appearance and ability he formed a contrast to his weak and sickly brother. The Icelanders called him "Hálegg" (Longlegs), which indicates that he was tall and well-built. His determination to rule according to his own ideas, to make the king's power absolute, and to weaken the power and influence of the aristocracy proves that he was a man of great energy and will-power. But he was rather harsh and autocratic — something of a pedant, and he seems to have lacked the intuitive foresight of a great statesman. "His reign," says Alexander Bugge, "is a turning-point in the history of Norway. With him the older period closes, and a new period begins, not only in the external history, but also in the development of spiritual and material life in Norway." Haakon was the last male member of the royal family, as all side-lines had become extinct. During his brother's reign he had seen the barons exercise an influence in the government which he viewed with deep regret, and in the neighboring kingdoms, Denmark and Sweden, the nobles had formed a strong oligarchy. He feared nothing so much as the recurrence of the conditions which had obtained in the time of Eirik. The establishing of a regency, or the election of a king, if the royal family became extinct, might endanger the stability of the throne. It became his great care, therefore, to secure the succession to the royal family; but this problem became very difficult, as the only child born to him in wedlock was a daughter, Ingebjørg. But neither Ingebjørg, nor his illegitimate daughter Agnes, who was a few years older, could inherit the throne. If Ingebjørg had a legitimate son he would stand in order of succession, but Ingebjørg herself was excluded, as well as Agnes and her children. Haakon succeeded, finally, in bringing about a change in the law of succession by which Ingebjørg

tredie række, vol. IV., p. 397 ff. As coronation was not prescribed by law, it was optional with the king whether he would be crowned or not. Storm gives the following table of the coronations of early Norwegian kings:

Bergen	1164	1194	1247	1261	1280
Oslo	1299	1337	1360?	1442	1514
Nidaros	1449	1450	1483		

See also *Islandske Annaler*, edited by Gustav Storm.

herself and her children, and, also, the legitimate sons of Agnes could succeed to the throne. In case a regency had to be created, it should consist of twelve members, whose duties and powers were strictly determined, and the king should not be of age until he was twenty years old. But although the question of succession had been settled, the possibility of a regency had not been eliminated. He feared the *lendermænd*, whose rank and titles had now become almost heredi- tary. In case of a regency they might again gain the ascendency, he thought. In order to prevent this he determined to abolish the titles of "jarl" and "lendermand," and to retain only that of "knight." Thereby the old hereditary aristocracy would be destroyed, and the knights, who received their titles from the king, would become personally attached to him. This plan was carried out by a royal decree issued in 1308; but the provision was made that the *lender- mænd* then living should retain their title and dignity during their lifetime. He also organized the priests of the royal chapels into a distinct clergy, which should stand under the direct supervision of the king. P. A. Munch observes that Haakon Magnusson was manifestly emulating King Philip the Fair of France, who, at this time, was engaged in humbling the clergy and the aristocracy, and in making the royal power supreme.[1]

Haakon waged no great wars, but the hostile entanglements with Denmark were continued, and to these were also added serious trou- bles with Sweden, growing out of the closer relations established with that kingdom through the marriage of King Haakon's daughters to Swedish dukes. Aside from the humdrum of these petty wars, carried on at intervals with the neighboring states, in which no clearly defined policy of statesmanship is visible, Haakon's reign was un- eventful enough. But in his time, as well as in the days of his brother Eirik, Norway's whole foreign policy underwent a complete change, which was fraught with the gravest consequences to the country's future history. Norway had hitherto maintained the closest rela- tions with the British Isles. New intellectual impulses had been carried over the waves from the West ever since the Viking expedi- tions began. Great trade centers, like Dublin and Bristol, had been developed by the Norsemen, and the British Isles had formed

[1] P. A. Munch, *Det norske Folks Historie*, IV., 2, p. 474 ff.

the pivot of their commercial activity. When England developed her own commerce, her merchants established a lucrative trade with Norway, and the friendly relations always maintained between the two countries prove the importance of this traffic to both peoples. The Norwegians had hitherto been a seafaring and commercial nation. Norway had maintained an insular policy, and had taken no direct part in continental affairs. But Eirik Magnusson and Haakon V. severed the bonds which for centuries had existed between Norway and England, and plunged their country into continental wars and political intrigues. Henceforth the Norwegians ceased to be a maritime nation, and Norway became politically a part of the continent. Personally the kings, no doubt, had the best intentions, and were guided by the most upright motives, but they ruled in a critical period, and had to deal with problems which would have put more sagacious statesmen to a severe test.

We have seen that when Eirik's daughter, the Maid of Norway, died, Edward I. established his overlordship over Scotland. But Eirik, who had hitherto been his friend, married Isabella Bruce, and allied himself thereby with the Scotch. Through the treaty negotiated by Audun Hugleiksson he had also entered into alliance with France. This agreement with France proved to be void of significance, but Eirik had identified himself with Edward's enemies at a moment when England was about to begin her long wars with France and Scotland, and when she was strong enough to wage a successful combat with both of them combined.

The English pursued their trade with Norway very energetically, but they had found dangerous rivals in the German merchants, who had already received important charters and privileges in Norway. The English merchants, conscious of their strength, demanded similar rights, but King Haakon would grant no such concessions. They regarded this attitude of the king as evidence of partiality and ill-will, and began to act with great arrogance. Many outrages were committed which aroused the bitterest resentment among the Norwegians, who made not a few reprisals on English shipping. As long as Edward I. lived, no serious clashes occurred, but when the incompetent Edward II. ascended the throne, the situation grew serious. In 1312 English fishermen on the coast of Bohuslen killed the royal *sysselmand* and ten others. In Bergen it seems that the *sysselmand*, Bottolf, arrested some English merchants and confiscated their goods, but they resisted to the utmost, and some of the king's men were killed. Exaggerated reports of these disturbances reached England. In a letter to King Haakon Edward II. complains that 400 Englishmen had been imprisoned, and that goods worth £6000 had been confiscated. Haakon answered that he had not imprisoned King Edward's subjects, but that he had permitted them to stay with their friends, and that he had now allowed all, with the exception of six, to return to England.[1]

While the estrangement between Norway and England was growing, Haakon was strengthening the ties of friendship with Scotland. He was still at war with Denmark, at times also with Sweden, and prudence would naturally lead him to welcome every opportunity to establish amicable relations with other powers. Robert Bruce of Scotland, who was waging his heroic fight against England, studied carefully the political situation, and made advances to win Haakon to his side. It is possible that he was aided in this attempt by his sister Isabella, the widow of King Eirik, who was still living quietly at Bergen. The yearly sum which, by the treaty of Perth, Scotland had engaged to pay Norway in return for the cession of the Hebrides had not been paid since Edward I. established his overlordship over Scotland. This also added to Haakon's displeasure with England, and we may suppose that Bruce offered to carry out the provisions of the treaty, if Haakon would recognize him as king of Scotland. Haakon finally decided to act. In 1312 he accepted Bruce's invitation to send envoys to Scotland, and on the 29th of October the treaty of Perth was renewed at Iverness, and most cordial relations were established between the two kingdoms. This did not mend the already strained relations with England, but Edward II. was a weak king, and the important trade relations existing between the two countries contributed to the maintaining of peace.

Over against the German merchants Haakon acted with more energy than his weak predecessor. In 1315 he enforced the already existing rule that only those who imported malt, flour, and grain to

---

[1] Alexander Bugge, *Handelen mellem England og Norge, Historisk Tidsskrift*, tredie række, vol. IV., p. 1 ff.

Norway should be allowed to export from the kingdom fish and butter. The year following he imposed a high export duty on articles bought and shipped from the country. If any one failed to pay the duty, his ship and goods should be seized. No foreign merchants were allowed to remain in Bergen, Oslo, or Tunsberg longer than the term fixed by law.[1] But the king's quarrel with England proved advantageous to the Germans. With the falling off of English trade their traffic became of ever greater importance to Norway. In the early part of his reign Haakon had been forced by circumstances to treat them with great leniency, and he soon found it necessary to modify the measures by which he had hoped to keep their traffic under control.[2] But to the English merchants he would make no concessions. Haakon had chosen between the German merchants and the English people. Time proved that he had chosen most unwisely. He had estranged the nation with which Norway had hitherto maintained the closest and most profitable relations; he had granted favors and concessions to the country's most dangerous enemy, which before the middle of the century destroyed Norway's commerce and power at sea; and his affiliation with Scotland proved as valueless as that with France.

The war with Denmark, which had lasted about twenty years, was still continued. Haakon was supported by the exiled slayers of King Eirik Glipping and their adherents in Denmark. The exiles held the castles Hunehals and Varberg on the coast of Halland, and the stronghold of Hjelm, built by their leader Mark Stig Anderssøn in the island of Hjelm, near the coast of Jutland. Haakon made repeated expeditions to Denmark, but no important battles were fought. The Danish king, Eirik Menved, could not resist the Norwegian fleet, and Haakon seems to have made these hostile visits mainly for the purpose of enforcing his claims.

In his anxiety to preserve the royal family from extinction, one of Haakon's great cares was to find suitable husbands for his daughters.

---

[1] O. A. Øverland, *Norges Historie*, vol. IV., p. 344 ff. J. E. Sars, *Hanseaternes Handelsherredømme, Udsigt over den norske Historie*, III., p. 1 ff. P. A. Munch, *Det norske Folks Historie*, part four, vol. II., p. 578 ff.

[2] Alexander Bugge, *Handelen mellem England og Norge, Historisk Tidsskrift*, tredie række, vol. IV. O. A. Øverland, *Norges Historie*, vol. IV., p. 347 ff.

In 1302 Princess Ingebjørg was betrothed to the dashing knight-errant Duke Eirik, son of King Magnus Ladulaas, and brother of King Birger Magnusson of Sweden, while she was a mere child. Duke Eirik visited Oslo, where he spent Christmas, and Queen Euphemia, who found her chief pastime in reading chivalric romances, became quite infatuated with the brilliant duke, in whom she discovered all the knightly qualities of King Arthur's famous knights of the Round Table. Her fondest wish was to see her daughter finally united in marriage with this personified ideal of her dreams. King Haakon does not seem to have been without some suspicion as to his prospective son-in-law's qualities of character, but in 1304 he granted him the important Konghelle as a fief. Duke Eirik was very ambitious, and he felt in no way restrained by any spirit of loyalty. He planned to make himself ruler of all the Scandinavian kingdoms, and Konghelle would form a convenient center for his operations. By marrying Ingebjørg he would secure the throne of Norway; he would drive his brother King Birger from the throne of Sweden, and later he might conquer Denmark. He won his brother, Duke Valdemar, to his side, and the two soon began to quarrel with King Birger, who was less able, and, also, less popular than his more brilliant brother Eirik. They sought aid in Norway, and described the trouble in such a way to Haakon as to gain, for a time, his sympathy and support. But things soon took a turn which he had not expected. In 1306 the dukes treacherously captured King Birger, threw him into prison, and made themselves masters of the kingdom of Sweden. They formed a secret compact, also, with Duke Kristoffer of Denmark, a brother of King Eirik Menved, who was to rebel against his brother and drive him from his throne, and Duke Eirik promised to give Konghelle to the traitorous duke, although this fief did not belong to him, but to King Haakon. Eirik also sought secretly to create a party in Norway, which would favor him, and he attempted to stir up the Norwegian barons against King Haakon. These events led to a complete rupture between the king and his prospective son-in-law. Haakon demanded that Eirik should return to him the fief of Konghelle, but he refused, and war broke out between Sweden and Norway, 1308. King Haakon laid siege to Konghelle, and constructed over against this stronghold a wooden castle, Bohus, the beginning of the later fortress of Bohus, but after some weeks he marched away without having captured the place. He now concluded peace with Denmark, and entered into alliance with King Eirik Menved. King Birger of Sweden, who had escaped from prison, and had sought refuge in Denmark, was to be restored to his throne, and Princess Ingebjørg was promised in marriage to his son Magnus. Duke Eirik invaded Norway, and captured Oslo, but he could not take the castle of Akershus. He also attacked Jæmtland, and defeated a part of Haakon's fleet at Kalfsund, at the mouth of the Göta River, where it had sought refuge in a storm. But the next year, 1309, the dukes found themselves in a most dangerous situation. King Eirik Menved invaded southern Sweden with a large army, and Haakon captured Konghelle. If the two kings had coöperated properly, the dukes would, no doubt, have been defeated, but Haakon paused, and undertook nothing further. Duke Eirik had a powerful ally in Queen Euphemia, who probably used her influence to save her favorite. The Danes could not take the castle of Nyköping, and when winter approached they withdrew and returned home. Haakon also withdrew from Konghelle, and this stronghold again fell into Duke Eirik's hands. In 1310 the dukes concluded peace with King Haakon, and agreed to cede to him Konghelle, Hunehals, Varberg, and the northern part of Halland. King Haakon again agreed to give his daughter Ingebjørg in marriage to Duke Eirik, and his niece, the daughter of King Eirik Magnusson, to Duke Valdemar. The marriage of the two princesses was celebrated at Oslo, September 29, 1312; but Queen Euphemia did not live to see this happy consummation of her fondly cherished hopes, as she died in the month of May the same year. In 1316 a son was born to each of the dukes, and Haakon V. could rejoice to see the succession secured in his own family, as Ingebjørg's son, Magnus Eiriksson, now became heir apparent to the throne. But before long his joy was again turned to grief. The restored King Birger of Sweden, who had not forgotten the ignominy heaped upon him by his brothers, the dukes Eirik and Valdemar, invited them to a feast of reconciliation at the castle of Nyköping, where he seized them and threw them into a dungeon, where they perished. The manner of their death is unknown, but the rumor spread that they were starved to death, as no marks of violence were seen on their bodies. The shock of this quite unexpected tragedy seems to have shortened King Haakon's life. He died May 8, 1319, forty-nine years of age.

Norway still appeared to be as strong and prosperous as ever heretofore. The hereditary principle, which had been so firmly adhered to, gave the throne great stability and contributed to the centralization of government in the hands of the king, whereby an efficiency in administration and a public order were secured which Denmark and Sweden, torn by internal strife, might well have coveted. The Norwegian fleet was still the strongest in the North, and the colonies were firmly united with the kingdom. But unmistakable signs of decadence, like the creeping shadows of approaching darkness, heralded the passing of Norway's national glory. The growing influence of the Hanseatic merchants, the shrinkage in Norwegian shipping and commerce, and the unhappy change of foreign policy, were not more ominous signs than the decay of the national literature during the first part of the fourteenth century. In King Haakon's reign a considerable literary activity was still maintained. Haakon V., no less than his queen, Euphemia, showed great interest in literature, and stimulated greatly the writing of chivalric romances. "He took great delight in good stories, and caused many romances to be translated from French or Greek to Norwegian." [1] This branch of the Old Norse literature had flourished, especially in Norway, while the historic literature was almost exclusively Icelandic. Through the Viking expeditions, and still more through a lively commercial intercourse, the Norsemen came in direct contact with intellectual life in the British Isles and northern France. In earlier days their scaldic poesy showed marked traces of Irish influence, and we find the same causes still operating later when they produced their great literature of prose romances under the influence of French and English poems of chivalry. When the saga literature produced in Norway is romance, and not history, it only proves what intimate relations the Norsemen maintained with their neighbors across the sea. In many respects the romantic sagas written in Norway bring

[1] E. Sars, *Udsigt over den norske Historie*, II., p. 343. Keyser and Unger, *Strengeleikar*, Introduction, p. XI.

evidence of no less originality and literary talent than the histories written by the Icelanders, for although the themes and plots of these stories are of foreign origin, many of the romantic sagas are admirably written, and show many of the best features of the sagaman's art. King Sverre and his successors were well educated. They were thoroughly in sympathy with the cultural life of western Europe, and found great delight in reading these chivalric and romantic tales, as well as the history of their own country, and the lives of the saints. We have seen how they encouraged the writing of history, which is a sufficient proof that they fully appreciated the value of this branch of the old literature; but they also encouraged the writing of romantic sagas for diversion and entertainment. The writing of romances is, therefore, a part of the original and creative literary activity which produced the great Old Norse literature, and when Haakon V. "took great delight in good stories, and caused many romances to be translated from the French or Greek to Norwegian," he only continued the literary activity of his illustrious ancestors. But a notable change had, nevertheless, come. The saga style had ceased to be a suitable vehicle for the thoughts and sentiments engendered in an age of chivalry. Adapted to this purpose it rapidly degenerated, and the romances were becoming verbose and formless nonsense. Before the middle of the century literary productivity ceased, and as the classic saga literature became foreign to the changed spirit of the age, it was no longer read, and was gradually forgotten. At the same time a new literature was springing up among the common people, fostered by impulses received from Germany and Denmark. This new literature of tales, ballads, and folk-songs — half epic and half lyric — afforded new opportunity for a suitable expression of the thoughts and feelings of the age. Norway's first great literary period was closed. The shrill blasts of the war trumpets died away, and the martial notes of the scaldic poetry changed into cooing love-songs and plaintive ballads. The manly vigor which had raised the Norsemen to power and prominence was ebbing, and growing decay had fallen upon national life like an evil destiny. But the old forms of culture passed, only to germinate after a period of rest into more perfect growth. It is the ebb and flow of human life, both alike necessary to its constant rejuvenation and its permanent progress.

INDEX

493

Bergen, founded, 298; chief commercial center, 470–472; considered capital by Magnus Lagabøter, 473.

Bergthora, 193.

Bernicia, raided by the Vikings, 56.

"Bersøglisvisur," 271.

Bevja, battle of, 361.

Bifrost, the celestial bridge, 105.

Birger Brosa, jarl, 377.

Birger Magnusson, king of Sweden, 489–490.

Birka on Mälaren in Sweden, 6, 77.

Birkebeiner, 375, 378–386, 408–410.

Bjarkey in Nordland, 116.

Bjarkeyjarréttr, or Norwegian laws of trade, 5, 464.

Bjarkowitz (Bjarkø), near the coast of Ingermanland Russia, 67.

Bjarne, Bishop of the Orkneys, 173.

Bjarne Erlingsson, 473.

Bjarne Grimolvsson, 210.

Bjarne Herjolvsson, reputed discoverer of America, 208, 219.

Bjarne Lodinsson, 473.

Bjarneyjar (Bear Islands), 210.

Bjørn Ironside, Viking chieftain, 52.

Bjørn Stallare in the battle of Stiklestad, 265.

Black Death in Norway, 202.

Blakar, 154, 158.

Blót, sacrifice, 108.

"Boglungasogur," "Saga of the three Kings," 409, 444.

Borghild of Dal, mother of King Magnus, 338.

Bordeaux attacked by the Vikings, 48.

Brage, the god, 105.

Brage Boddason (Brage the Old), scald, 95.

Brattahlid, 199.

Breidablik, Balder's hall, 102.

Brennøerne, 79; treaty of, 270.

Breohtric (Beorhtric), 45.

Brian Borumha, Irish king, 223–229.

Brihtnoth, 175–176.

Bristol made a great commercial city by the Vikings, 79.

Broch of Mousa, 135.

Bronze Age, agriculture in, 14–17; estimated duration of, 18.

Brunanburh, battle of, 156–157.

Bruse Sigurdsson, jarl in the Orkneys, 132.

Burgundy, ravaged by the Vikings, 52.

Burial, mode of, 10–12; coffins made of hollowed oak logs, 15; of women, 17; mode of, in Bronze Age, 20; in the migrations, 34.

Bylaw, from Norse by-lov, 82.

Caithness, in Scotland, a Norse settlement, 238.

Camargue, island of, seized by the Vikings, 49–50.

Canterbury, captured by the Vikings, 54.

Castle, monastery at Konghelle, 366.

Cecilia, daughter of Sigurd Mund, 378, 408.

Cecilia, daughter of King Sverre, 415.

Celibacy of the clergy introduced, 349.

Celtic influence in pre-Roman period, 17.

Cennfuait, battle of, 154.

Chaideinoi (Heiner), inhabitants of Scandia, 25.

Charlemagne and the Vikings, 51.

Charles the Bald and the Vikings, 51.

Charmouth, battle of, 53.

Charudes (Horder), neighbors of the Cimbri in Jutland, 26, 116–117.

Chester, in England, grows into prominence in Viking times, 79.

Chochilaicus (Hygelâc), 30, 50.

Christina, daughter of Sigurd the Crusader, married to Erling Skakke, 361–368.

Christina, King Sverre's daughter, 409.

Christianity, character of, in Norway and Iceland, 350–353.

Churches, kinds of, in Norway, 347.

Church of Norway, its relation to the archdiocese of Bremen, 296–298; organization of, 345.

Cilmashogue, battle of, 154.

Cimbri, 25; invades the Roman empire, 27; terror cimbricus.

Cities, great development of, by the Vikings, 78–82; Viking city laws, 82.

HISTORY OF THE NORWEGIAN PEOPLE

VOLUME II

CONTENTS

v

LIST OF PLATES

ix

LIST OF MAPS

xi

LIST OF ILLUSTRATIONS IN THE TEXT

HISTORY OF THE NORWEGIAN PEOPLE

THE MIDDLE PERIOD

1. POLITICAL UNION AN ERA OF TRANSITION

WHEN the royal family of Norway became extinct in the male line upon the death of Haakon V. in 1319, the kingdom still appeared to possess its former strength. Internal disturbances no longer threatened, as the aristocracy had submitted unconditionally to the king, who had firmly established the principles of hereditary kingship and a strongly centralized government. In Sweden and Denmark, where royalty had become elective, rival pretenders, aided by powerful nobles, found opportunity to maintain civil strife in ceaseless struggles for the crown. But Norway enjoyed peace, a fair degree of prosperity existed, and its commerce, though somewhat impaired, was still fairly well maintained. This apparent strength and stability of the kingdom was, nevertheless, a mere illusion. In reality the nation was gradually sinking into a state of lethargy and weakness which soon affected every part of the national organism. The once so remarkable energy of the Norwegian people shriveled as if touched by a withering blight, and without any dramatic struggle they lost their political and economic independence. There can be no doubt that the rise of the Hanseatic merchants, and the change in Norway's foreign policy contributed to this growing national decay, but the main cause is to be sought in the extinction of the old line of kings, who had been leaders of the people, and the center of national life and greatness. In their long struggle with the aristocracy, the kings had been victorious. Not only had they lodged all power in the crown, and created a body of administrative and judicial officers wholly subservient to it, but the aristocracy, weakened

by wars and dispirited by constant defeats, had gradually lost significance as leaders of the people. Haakon V. wiped out the remnant
of the old hereditary aristocracy when he abolished the titles of
jarl and *lendermand,* in 1308, while he retained that of *knight,* as
this new rank depended on appointment and royal favor. Had
the circumstances in Norway been favorable to the growth of chivalry, the disappearance of the old aristocracy might have produced
no serious change; but the new nobility never became numerous
or strong enough to assume leadership in a new national development. While Sweden and Denmark fostered a proud and powerful aristocracy, Norway was urged, also by her natural environment,
along the path towards democratic conditions. In comparing the
growth of the Swedish and Norwegian nobility P. A. Munch says:
"The already mentioned circumstance that war in Sweden was
usually waged on land, while in Norway it was generally waged on
the sea, would, when we consider the customary mode of fighting,
make the separation between the mounted nobles and the common
foot soldiers or peasants more distinct and conspicuous than in Norway. The more highly developed land war in Sweden, as well as
the stronger influence of German knight-errantry, also led to the
erection of numerous royal and private castles, a feature almost
unknown in Norway. For years together private knights and
squires, as well as feudal lords, ensconced behind the walls of these
castles, might successfully defy law and justice, oppress the neighboring districts, and maintain an independent existence. It is also
clear that it was in their power to make their privileges hereditary,
and to transform them into rights which were real as well as personal.
This is best seen in cases where some powerful knight received a
fief and castle as security for a debt, which was often not paid during
his lifetime. These estates with the castle were then, as a matter
of course, inherited by his sons, or heirs. In this way there had
been formed in Sweden at the time when it was united with Norway
under Magnus Eiriksson in 1319 a larger and more compact circle
of noble families than in Norway; in other words, a real hereditary
aristocracy whose members, indeed, did not regard themselves superior to the Norwegian nobles, and hence often intermarried with
them; but against their own countrymen they assumed a more

aristocratic and distant attitude than did the Norwegian nobles against their people. We find in Sweden also family names and family coats of arms used much earlier than in Norway, which shows that an aristocracy of birth with inherited privileges was established there, while in Norway nobility as a mere personal honor still prevailed."[1] Professor T. H. Aschehoug shows that the Norwegian nobility was much weaker than the same class in Sweden and Denmark both in wealth and number. "The great and permanent cause of the inferiority of the Norwegian aristocracy in wealth lay in the different natural conditions of the three countries. The wealth, which should be the mainstay of the noble family, consisted at that time more than ever in land. But whether we consider the area or the productivity of the tillable soil, Norway has, without comparison, a more scant supply of land than the neighboring kingdoms."[2]

The growth of royal power had wrought the unification of the people, and the establishing of a national kingdom. An efficient government had been created which enabled Norway to rise to greatness. But the aristocracy had been crushed, and when the kings disappeared, the orphaned nation no longer had competent leaders to shape its career, or to protect its interests. The country's foreign policy was guided by weak and unskilled hands, if it could be said to be guided at all, while in commerce, and in economic life in general, timidity and torpor replaced the earlier spirit of enterprise. For want of men, strong and self-reliant enough to attempt the solution of new problems and to face altered conditions with resolute hopefulness, the people grew unprogressive, and clung to old forms with a tenacity which made successful competition with spirited rivals impossible. The Norwegians had hitherto accomplished great things, because they had been stimulated to efforts by ambitious leaders, and their energies had been wisely directed by able kings. When this stimulus and direction ceased, the decadence began, not because the people's native ability was lost, but because it became inoperative and latent.

[1] P. A. Munch, *Samlede Afhandlinger*, III., p. 504 ff. Yngvar Nielsen, *Af Norges Historie, VI., Borge og Kirker.*
[2] T. H. Aschehoug, *Statsforfatningen i Norge og Danmark indtil 1814*, p. 118 ff.

2. KING MAGNUS SMEK. THE UNION OF NORWAY AND SWEDEN

On the death of Haakon V., May 1, 1319, his grandson Magnus Eiriksson, heir to the throne of Norway, was yet a child only three years of age. King Birger of Sweden, who had been compelled to flee from his kingdom after the treacherous imprisonment and tragic death of his brothers, the dukes Eirik and Valdemar, was still living in exile in Denmark, while his son Magnus had been imprisoned in Stockholm. So bitter was the feeling against the exiled king that there seemed to be no hope for him to regain the throne either for himself or his son. When Haakon died, Magnus Eiriksson was staying with his mother in Sweden, and the leading Swedish nobles immediately took steps to elect him king of Sweden. The royal Council [1] summoned a general council of magnates, which met at Oslo in the month of June. The Duchess Ingebjørg and seven members of the Swedish royal Council met to negotiate a union between Sweden and Norway, and the election of Magnus Eiriksson to the throne of both realms. An act of union was soon agreed upon, and Magnus was proclaimed king of Norway at the Haugathing, at Tunsberg, and about the same time he was also elected king of Sweden. Thus Norway and Sweden were united for the first time "by an accident which looked like a plan." Nothing but family interests had dictated this course, and the two kingdoms had nothing in common but the king, who, according to the act of union, should spend an equal length of time in each kingdom.[2] During the king's

[1] It had been customary for the king to ask advice of his *lendermænd* and other prominent persons in important state affairs, but in the thirteenth century we find traces of a smaller number of men acting as the king's advisers, though they were not required to meet as a body. When Haakon V. abolished the title of "lendermand," he seems to have chosen a few prominent men to act as a *concilium regis*. In the first half of the fourteenth century this council grew rapidly in power, especially during periods when it also acted as a regency during the minority of the kings. From a *concilium regis*, or royal council, it developed into a *concilium regni*, or council of the kingdom, which shared the power with the king, and he was, henceforth, not expected to act except with the advice of the Council. See T. H. Aschehoug, *Statsforfatningen i Norge og Danmark*, p. 140 ff. Yngvar Nielsen, *Det norske Rigsraad*, Christiania, 1880.

[2] *Samlinger til det norske Folks Sprog og Historie*, vol. V., p. 321 f., *Kong Magnus Eriksøns Valgact.* P. A. Munch, *Det norske Folks Historie, Unionsperioden*, vol. I., p. 7 ff. Yngvar Nielsen, *Det norske Rigsraad*, p. 135 f.

minority, his mother, Duchess Ingebjørg, and the Council, which according to the act of succession should consist of twelve members, was to act as a regency. A similar arrangement was also made in Sweden.[1]

The Council showed great laxity in administering the government of the kingdom. The Duchess Ingebjørg, who was a thoughtless and pleasure-loving young woman, got possession of the royal seal, and she was able to exercise such an influence in public affairs, that she might be called the real regent, although she hastened to establish her residence in Sweden, where she also kept the king, contrary to the act of union. She became enamored of a Danish nobleman, Knut Porse, and spent the money in the treasury in pursuit of pleasure, or in furthering the wild and ambitious schemes of her paramour. Without submitting the matter to the councils of regency, she even promised him the support of the united kingdoms in a war with Denmark, which he was about to undertake for the most selfish reasons. Supplied with a document bearing the seal of the kingdom of Norway, he was even enabled to hire mercenaries in Germany for an attack on the Danish kingdom. The public funds had been squandered, the treasury was empty, the laws were disregarded, and the people were oppressed by unlawful taxes. The seal of the kingdom was misused in foreign affairs, and Knut Porse had begun war with Denmark in the name of the king of Norway and Sweden.[2] Discontent grew loud on every hand. In 1322 a council of magnates, which assembled at Skara in Sweden, deprived the duchess of her political power in that kingdom. The following year a similar assembly in Oslo chose Erling Vidkunsson regent to rule the kingdom of Norway with the advice and assistance of the Council.[3] But a difficult situation confronted the new regency. Through the machinations of Knut Porse and the duchess, Norway had been placed in a hostile attitude to Denmark, the relations with England were strained, the treasury was empty, and war had broken

[1] *Diplomatarium Norwegicum*, VIII., no. 50. Yngvar Nielsen, *Det norske Rigsraad*, p. 135.

[2] C. G. Styffe, *Bidrag till Skandinaviens Historia ur utlandske arkiver*, I., p. 2 ff., 6 f. C. E. F. Reinhardt, *Valdemar Atterdag og hans Kongegjerning*, p. 24.

[3] *Samlinger til det norske Folks Sprog og Historie*, V., p. 534 f.

out with Russia as a result of border disputes in Finmarken. In 1323 the Russians and Karelians invaded and harried Haalogaland, but the regent was unable to act with energy for want of necessary funds. Three years later peace was concluded at Novgorod for a period of ten years.[1] What had happened in the meantime is not known, but the hostilities seem to have practically ceased, since Sweden made a treaty with the Russians, 1323. The boundaries in these remote regions were at that time very vague, and the treaty, which was a mere temporary arrangement, did not bring the question much nearer to a final solution. A truce was also concluded between Norway and Russia at Novgorod in 1326, for the period of ten years, and envoys sent to England had been able to come to a friendly understanding with Edward II. in 1325.

The law made by King Haakon V. that the king should not be of age until he was twenty years old seems to have been set aside, as Magnus Eiriksson seized the reins of government in 1332 at the age of sixteen. His reign began auspiciously by the acquisition of Skåne and Blekinge, which had hitherto been Danish provinces. The worthless King Kristoffer II. of Denmark, who had succeeded Eirik Menved, had granted these provinces temporarily to Count John of Holstein as security for a loan of 34,000 marks of silver. As the people were grievously oppressed by the Holsteiners, they appealed to King Magnus, and asked him to become their ruler. Magnus consented, and they hailed him as their lawful king. Count John could not begin war against the provinces while they were supported by the king of Sweden and Norway, and he gladly accepted the offer to relinquish his title for a sum equal to the amount due him by the king of Denmark. Sweden had at least temporarily secured title to these important districts, though it is doubtful if this can be attributed to the king's own energy and foresight.

In 1335 Magnus married Blanca or Blanche of Namur, who bore him two sons; Eirik, 1339, and Haakon, 1340. Very little is known of King Magnus Eiriksson's character. By some contemporaries he was decried as dissolute and incompetent, but it is now generally admitted that he was earnest and conscientious, that he tried to

<hr/>

[1] P. A. Munch, *Samlede Afhandlinger*, Vol. II., p. 626 ff., *Om Grœndse-Traktaterne mellem Norge, Sverige og Rusland i det 14de Aarhundrede.*

rule well, but that he failed, not for want of good intentions, but because he lacked the ability to guide the two kingdoms through a most difficult period. During the long regency, the Swedish nobles had carried on their private feuds without restraint, and Magnus soon met with determined resistance when he attempted to limit their privileges, and to increase his income by levying new taxes. The large sums paid for the newly acquired provinces, as well as Magnus' poor management, had brought him into serious financial difficulties, but his attempt to seek relief in this way only aggravated the situation. The hostile nobles accused him of vice and extravagance, and in contempt they nicknamed him Magnus Smek, a name by which he is generally known in history.[1] Magnus was born and reared in Sweden, and was in all respects a Swedish king. The acquisition of new territory, together with financial difficulties, involved him so deeply in Swedish politics that he seldom visited Norway, or paid any attention to the affairs of that kingdom. But though he remained a stranger to its real needs, he nevertheless continued to settle Norwegian affairs with a stroke of the pen and the use of the royal seal without even consulting the Norwegian Council of State. This caused great dissatisfaction, not only because of the injury done by this careless and irresponsible management of public affairs, but also because this kind of rule did not conform to the people's ideas of the character and dignity of Norwegian kingship. A strong opposition party was formed[2] under the leadership of Erling Vidkunsson, Ivar Agmundsson, Sigurd Hafthorsson, and other powerful barons. They demanded nothing less than a dissolution of the union, and asked that King Magnus' youngest son, Haakon, should be made king of Norway. The king was forced to yield. By a royal decree issued at Varberg, 1343,[3] it was decided that Haakon should succeed to the throne of Norway as soon as he reached his majority, that the older brother Eirik should be elected to succeed his father as king of Sweden and Skåne, and that the kingdoms should remain separated from the time that Haakon became of age (1355). Until that time Magnus should act as regent

---

[1] Smek, pronounced Smäke, from Swedish *smeka*, to fondle or caress.
[2] Gustav Storm, *Islandske Annaler*, p. 348.
[3] *Diplomatarium Norwegicum*, II., no. 258.

in Norway. The following year Eirik was elected king of Sweden, and Haakon was proclaimed king of Norway. Thereby the royal decree annulling the act of union was ratified by the people of both kingdoms.[1] The royal seal was returned to Norway and given to the new chancellor, Arne Aslaksson. This virtually terminated King Magnus Smek's rule in Norway. Nominally he remained regent, but the affairs of the government were henceforth directed by the chancellor and the Council.

After the peaceful settlement of the troubles with Norway, Magnus devoted himself earnestly to social and legal reforms in Sweden. The last remnants of slavery were removed; he prepared a uniform code of laws for the kingdom, "Medal-Lagen," and also a code of city laws. The work was very praiseworthy, and shows that he meant to rule well; but new troubles were soon created both in Sweden and Norway by the growing power and arrogance of the Hanseatic merchants. The foreign affairs of Norway were still controlled by Magnus, while the domestic affairs of the kingdom were managed by the Council. They tried to enforce the tariff laws and other restrictions which aimed at preventing undue encroachments on Norwegian trade, but the Hanseatic League, which was rapidly developing into a great commercial monopoly, possessed great capital and superior business methods, and they did not hesitate to treat the weak government with contempt. The "Icelandic Annals" mention many bloody encounters between the German merchants and the citizens of Bergen; 1332: "The Germans burned a large part of Bergen;" 1333: "A fight between the priests and the German shoemakers (sutara), and two priests killed." [2] Other lawless acts were committed, so that the city of Lübeck in 1341 finally found it necessary to send envoys to King Magnus to arrange

---

[1] Haakon was not proclaimed king at the Ørething, nor at a thing assembled for the purpose, but representatives from the cities and from the country districts were summoned to Bohus, where they signed a written agreement to accept him as their king when he became of age. A copy of this document is still in existence. See Diplomatarium Norwegicum, I., no. 290. This copy bears the signatures of the representatives of the cities and a part of the country districts. Other copies must have contained the signatures of the other representatives.

[2] Alexander Bugge, Studier over de norske Byers Selvstyre og Handel før Hanseaterne. Gustav Storm, Islandske Annaler, p. 220 and 349.

a settlement.[1] King Magnus describes the conduct of the Hanseatic merchants as follows: "When they come to the harbors of Norway, they ill-treat, wound, and kill people, and depart without a thought of amends for their wrong-doings to God or the king, or even of restitution to those whom they have injured. Where they land, they pull down houses belonging to the king or other people, and use them for fuel without asking permission. They do not permit other goods to be exported from their cities than spoiled ale, poor flour, and adulterated hops, but they import from Sweden, Norway, and Skåne grain and other valuable articles. The Germans look with contempt on the inhabitants of Norway, and in Sweden even on those who have formerly belonged to their own class (*i.e.* those who have married in Sweden, and who have established homes there), so that they never admit them to their feasts, or to other social intercourse." [2]

In 1342 Norway and Sweden became involved in a war with King Valdemar Atterdag, who did not seem willing to abide by his agreement regarding the Danish provinces which had been ceded to King Magnus. The Hanseatic cities aided Valdemar, and the "Icelandic Annals" mention a fight between the German merchants and the citizens of Bergen, in which many merchants were killed.[3] In the peace treaty of 1343, Valdemar ceded to Magnus, Skåne, Halland, Lister, Blekinge, and Hven, for the amount of 49,000 marks. In his dealings with the Hanseatic merchants Magnus was less successful. He was unable to pay the stipulated amount for the acquired provinces, and had to seek the financial aid of the Germans, in return for which he granted to a number of German cities a charter (1343) in which he confirmed all the privileges which had been given them by Eirik Magnusson and others of his predecessors. He abolished the high duties, which had been imposed by Haakon V., and henceforth they were not required to pay higher duties than in the days of Eirik Magnusson.[4] The efforts which had hitherto

[1] P. A. Munch, *Det norske Folks Historie*, vol. V., p. 269.
[2] R. Keyser, *Norges Historie*, vol. II., p. 575.
[3] Gustav Storm, *Islandske Annaler*, p. 222.
[4] The document by which the king grants the German merchants of Bergen these privileges is found in *Diplomatarium Norwegicum*, vol. V., no. 197.

been made to control the traffic of the Hanseatic merchants were thereby adjusted in their favor, and they exercised henceforth almost unrestricted control over the country's trade. The general economic conditions seem, however, to have been quite good. The conspicuous lack of energetic activity had at least the advantage of producing a period of comparative peace, in which the people were able to direct their attention to their own domestic affairs. The distribution of land according to the law of *odel*, and the comparative weakness of the aristocracy insured the people against oppression, and maintained a large class of freeholders (*bønder*), who continued to be the mainstay of the nation, and the custodians of the national traditions and spirit of liberty. Even the renters who owned no land were protected in their rights by the laws, and were not left to the mercy of the larger landowners. Roads and bridges were maintained by the people, subject to the direction and supervision of the authorities of the *fylke*, and the laws were so well enforced that no one was in danger of being robbed or otherwise molested, even in journeying along the lonely mountain paths of remote inland districts. But, aside from this fair degree of prosperity and general social wellbeing, a weakening of the people's energies took place in nearly every phase of national activity. Literary productivity ceased, and no books seem to have been read, save legends and translations of chivalric romances. Through the influence of the king and the court and Norway's intimate relations with Sweden, the Swedish language came to be regarded in higher social circles as more refined than the Norse, in which so many great works had been written, and which had been most highly developed as a literary language. Norse was still exclusively used, but many Swedish words were introduced, especially in the diplomatic language and in public documents. The literary language shows very little change, however, during the whole Old Norse period, which lasted till 1350. It retained throughout great purity of vocabulary and constancy of forms and idioms. The Old Norse language was divided into a few not very sharply differentiated dialects, especially during the latter part of the period. East Norse was spoken in Trøndelagen and Østlandet; West Norse in Vestlandet (Gulathingslag) and North Vestlandet (*i.e.* Romsdal, Søndmør, Søndfjord, Nordfjord, and Ytre

Sogn) as well as in Iceland and the rest of the colonies. About 1300 Østlandet developed its own dialect, distinct from that of Trønde-lagen with which it had hitherto been almost identical. The West Norse had been divided into two dialects, a southern and a northern, at a much earlier date. The southern dialect of the West Norse was identical with that of Iceland until about 1400, and is the one used with but few exceptions in Old Norse literature. But when the unifying influence of literary activity disappeared, the number of dialects rapidly increased, and the greater uniformity of forms and idioms was lost. The language of Norway entered upon a new development, like other languages of Europe at that time, while the more conservative Icelandic became a distinct language.[1]

3. Other Causes Contributing to the Intellectual and National Decadence

It is quite evident that in the growing competition with the new sea-power, the Hanseatic League, the Norwegians soon found them-selves outclassed, both as to their merchant marine and their mili-tary power at sea.[2] Hitherto Norway had been a leading naval power. The fleet had been her main strength in war — as necessary to the maintenance of her political power and independence as her mer-chant marine and commerce were to the nation's economic well-being. Shorn of these locks of strength, the nation inevitably sank into a state of languor and debility. The more surprising it is to notice with what indecision and lack of energy the government waged this decisive contest for naval and commercial supremacy. Norway's navy had become hopelessly antiquated. The old *leding* system, which had proven very advantageous a century or two earlier, still remained unaltered, though wholly impractical under the changed conditions of the fourteenth century. According to this system, the coast provinces were divided into 309 *skibreder* (O. N. *skip reiður*), or naval districts, and each *skibrede* should build and man one ship. In this way the full quota of vessels could be secured, but no progress

---

[1] Marius Hægstad, *Det norske Maalet fyre 1350, Indledning til Gamalnorsk Ordbok*, Christiania, 1909. *Norsk Konversations-Leksikon*, "Norge," vol. V.

[2] J. E. Sars, *Hanseaternes Handelsherredømme, Udsigt over den norske Historie*, vol. III.

was made in the art of ship-building. The *bønder* (freeholders), who furnished the required vessels and equipments as a regular *leding* tax, continued to build ships of the same size and type as had been furnished hundreds of years earlier. In the Hanseatic cities, in Flanders, France, and the Netherlands a new type of vessel, the *kogge* (Old Fr. *coque*, Italian *cocca*), had been introduced.[1] This vessel had one or two stationary masts, and was wholly propelled by sails. It was of the size of a brig or small schooner. Such a vessel could travel faster and maneuver easier than the Norwegian longships, which had only one sail, and had to be partly propelled by oars. The *kogge* was also harder to enter; it was well supplied with war machines of different kinds; and as the men did not have to ply the oars, the fighting force on these new ships was relatively much larger than on the old war vessels. About 1350, gunpowder was also introduced, and the Hanseatic merchants were not slow in making use of it. The art of ship-building and the science of war had changed. In a contest with a fleet of sailing vessels of the new type the Norwegian fleet soon proved comparatively useless. After the inferiority of the older type of ships had been thoroughly demonstrated, the longship was discarded about 1350, and sailing vessels of the new type were built; but the change came too late to save Norway's prestige as a naval power.

In the Norwegian merchant marine similar conditions prevailed. Small ships of the old type were still used, while the Hanseatic merchants were introducing large sailing vessels of improved type. Alexander Bugge says: "The Norwegian ships which came to England during the fourteenth century not only became fewer and fewer, but also smaller and smaller," — a sad evidence of Norway's failing strength.

While the nation was sinking into such a lethargic state, its remaining strength was suddenly broken by the fearful ravages of the Black Death. In 1347 this plague had reached southern France from the Orient, and it quickly spread to Italy and Spain. In 1348 it appeared in England, whence it seems to have been carried

---

[1] Alexander Bugge, *Et lidet Bidrag til Spørgsmaalet om Norges Nedgang i det 14de Aarhundrede*, published in *Historiske Afhandlinger tilegnet Professor J. E. Sars*, Christiania, 1905.

to Scotland, the Orkneys, Hebrides, Shetland, and Faroe Islands, while Iceland and Greenland escaped its ravages. The disease was so malignant that people died after a few days', or even a few hours', illness, and many districts lost the greater part of their population. According to the "Icelandic Annals," the disease was brought to Norway by a merchant vessel which came to Bergen from England. The exact date is not given, but it must have been in the summer of 1349.[1] The people on the ship died before the cargo was unloaded, and the ship sank in the harbor, says the annalist. The plague seems to have spread to all parts of the kingdom. In 1350 it harried Sweden, and the following year Finland and Russia. When it reached the districts around the Black Sea, it finally ceased, after having visited all parts of Europe on its deadly mission. How large a part of the population of Norway died from this scourge it is impossible to determine with any degree of accuracy. Many tales were later told by the people, of whole settlements which became wholly depopulated, of churches which were later discovered in dense forests, which had grown up on formerly cultivated areas, of children who had been left alone in depopulated districts, where they grew up in a wild state.[2] It is not difficult to see that these tales are later creations, based largely on imagination; but the mortality must, nevertheless, have been very large. Even public documents show evidence of this.[3] Of the bishops of Norway only one survived the Black Death, and even in 1371 the Archbishop of Nidaros complained to the Pope that while there used to be about three hundred priests in his diocese, there were, after the great plague, not above forty. The "Icelandic Annals" contain the following statement: "Then the disease spread over all Norway, and caused such mortality that not one-third of the people of the country remained alive."[4] This statement is, however, an exaggeration. Oscar Montelius, who has investigated the decrease of the population in Sweden on the basis of the Peter's Pence paid before and after the Black Death, finds that the plague

---

[1] *Islandske Annaler*, p. 275.

[2] *Scriptorum Rerum Danicarum*, VII., 2. Rasmus Nyerup, *Historisk Skildring af Tilstanden i Danmark og Norge i ældre og nyere Tider*, Copenhagen, 1808, vol. I., p. 228 ff. A. Faye, *Norske Sagn*.

[3] *Diplomatarium Norwegicum*, V., 1, p. 166; XI., 1, p. 40 f.; XII., 1, p. 76.

[4] Gustav Storm, *Islandske Annaler*, p. 275.

carried away from one-third to one-half of the population in that country.[1] Professor J. E. Sars, who has made a similar investigation in Norway, finds that the decrease of the population in that kingdom was considerably less than in Sweden, probably because it was less densely populated; that the loss did not exceed one-third.[2] The calamity was, nevertheless, overwhelming. Commerce was almost at a standstill, the voyages to Greenland almost ceased,[3] many estates lay uncultivated, and a number of leading men in church and state were dead. There is, indeed, evidence that the ordinary affairs of life were carried on in the customary routine way, but a stunning blow had been dealt all optimism and enterprise, and the consequences were the more serious because of the low ebb of national vigor.

After the expiration of the ten years' truce which had been concluded at Novgorod in 1326, hostilities with the Russians had been renewed. In 1348 King Magnus crossed the Baltic Sea with an army, and fought a campaign in Finland, but the Black Death put

[1] Oscar Montelius; *Forsell och Wirsen, Svensk Tidsskrift för Literatur, Politik, och Ekonomi,* 1870, p. 219–20.
In Sweden one penning in Peter's Pence was paid yearly by every household. In the period 1333–1350 the average sum per year was $221\frac{3}{5}$ marks, while in the years 1351–1353 the average sum was $132\frac{1}{3}$ marks. The population would, therefore, stand in the same ratio.

[2] In Norway the Peter's Pence was one penning from every man and woman who owned property to the value of three marks. J. E. Sars, *Til Oplysning om Folkemængdens Bevægelse i Norge fra det 13de til det 17de Aarhundrede, Historisk Tidsskrift,* anden række, vol. III., p. 281 ff. Dr. H. Hildebrand, *Sveriges Medeltid,* vol. I., p. 58 ff. C. G. Styffe, *Skandinavien under Unionstiden,* 2d ed., p. 94. P. A. Munch, *Det norske Folks Historie,* anden hovedafdeling, *Unionsperioden,* første del, p. 888 ff. J. E. Sars, *Nyt Historisk Tidsskrift,* vol. V., p. 243 f. A. L. Faye, *Den sorte Død i det 14de Aarhundrede,* Christiania, 1880. J. E. Sars, *Hanseaternes Handelsherredømme og den store Mandedød, Udsigt over den norske Historie,* vol. III.

[3] After Iceland and Greenland were united with Norway, they became crown colonies, and the king regulated all commerce with these islands. In the charter granted the German merchants in 1294, it was stipulated that they should not sail north of Bergen, except where it was granted as a special favor. Alexander Bugge considers it probable that the crown established a monopoly of the trade with these colonies for the benefit of companies in Bergen and Trondhjem. Only one merchant ship was dispatched to Greenland every year, and if this failed to reach its destination the colony remained wholly isolated from the rest of the world.

a stop to the war. The exhausted and afflicted kingdoms needed peace above all things, but the king immediately undertook a new expedition, which was as unsuccessful as the first. In 1351 the Pope instructed the clergy of Sweden and Norway to preach a crusade against the Russians,[1] and Magnus raised a small army of volunteers with which he again entered Finland; but instead of gaining renown as a defender of the Catholic faith, he only proved his incompetence. The treasury was empty, his debts had increased, and new dissatisfaction had been created, especially among the nobility.

4. THE REIGN OF HAAKON MAGNUSSON THE YOUNGER

Haakon Magnusson ascended the throne of Norway in 1355, having reached the age of fifteen years.[2] The two kingdoms were not completely separated, as might have been expected, as several provinces were still retained by Magnus. Besides Vestfold and Skienssyssel, which he retained in his own name, his queen, Blanche, kept Ranafylke, Borgarsyssel, and Iceland as her Norwegian dowry. This was an important modification of the Act of Varberg of 1343, according to which the two kingdoms should be separated as soon as Haakon became of age, but it seems that the Norwegian magnates made this concession without protest, as Magnus had yielded to their demand that the union should be dissolved. The districts retained by King Magnus and his queen were not severed from Norway, but were to revert to the crown upon the death of the royal pair. But through this parceling out of the provinces and possessions of the kingdom, Norway continued to be affected by the subsequent checkered fortunes of Magnus Smek.

The expeditions to Russia had left Magnus in great financial difficulties. Money could be borrowed only in small quantities for short periods, and these distress loans aggravated rather than relieved the deplorable financial situation. In 1355 he was excommunicated by the Pope for failure to pay his debts, and he had already been obliged to pawn his two crowns to the city of Lübeck

---

[1] *Diplomatarium Norwegicum*, vol. VI., no. 200; vol. VII., no. 245.
[2] *Detmars Chronik herausgegeben von Grautoff*, p. 234. P. F. Suhm, *Historie af Danmark*, XII., p. 228 ff.

for a small loan. The political outlook was not encouraging. King Magnus' brother-in-law, Duke Albrecht of Mecklenburg, had entered into a secret compact with King Valdemar of Denmark to wrest from Magnus the province of Skåne.[1] At home he was opposed by the discontented nobles, who for some time had pursued a well-defined policy of increasing their power and privileges at the king's expense. The violent and often disloyal nobles found a new opportunity to nurse their growing discontent when Magnus bestowed the greatest honors on his favorite, Bengt Algotsson, whom he made Duke of Halland and Finland, and governor of Skåne.[2] His motives for doing this are left wholly to conjecture. Did he attempt to win a competent ally for the struggle with the nobility, the approach of which he must have foreseen? It is not improbable, but this move hastened the crisis. The nobles easily persuaded Prince Eirik that he had been slighted. His younger brother Haakon was already king of Norway;[3] the royal favorite, Bengt Algotsson, had been made duke, while Eirik had neither titles nor possessions. In 1356 he raised the standard of revolt. Aided by the nobles, he surprised and captured Bengt, and forced Magnus to cede the whole of southern Sweden. Albrecht of Mecklenburg, who had encouraged him with a view to his own benefit, secured for himself and his sons southern Halland and a part of Skåne. But not even these liberal concessions satisfied the rebellious Eirik, who now assumed the title of king. He broke without hesitation the agreements which he had made, and seized one district after another of his father's remaining possessions until he ruled all Sweden. But in 1359 both he and his queen suddenly died.[4] Magnus again mounted the throne, and

[1] C. E. F. Reinhardt, *Valdemar Atterdag*, 228 f.

[2] *Scriptores Rerum Danicarum*, VI., p. 530.

[3] St. Birgitta, who voiced the general sentiment of her people, expressed disapproval of the arrangement by which the younger brother Haakon received the hereditary kingdom of Norway, while Eirik had to be satisfied with Sweden, where the kingship was elective. The hereditary kingship was regarded as the more stable and honorable, hence Norway was regarded as the more desirable of the two kingdoms.

[4] The rumor was spread that Eirik and his queen were poisoned. (See *Islandske Annaler*, p. 277.) But the report seems to be only an attempt of the common people to account for their sudden death. They probably died in the small-pox epidemic raging at the time.

the nobles, whom he summoned to a council, agreed that everything should be as before, even as if the uprising started by Eirik had not taken place. This agreement was subscribed to also by King Haakon of Norway. But Magnus was not even now suffered to enjoy the blessings of peace. Not long after he had regained the throne, King Valdemar of Denmark entered Sweden with an army and besieged the castle of Helsingborg.

Albrecht of Mecklenburg, who was playing the double rôle of Magnus' friend and Valdemar's secret ally, seems to have been placed in command of the castle by the unsuspecting Magnus, and as soon as the king withdrew to the northern districts of his realm, Albrecht surrendered Helsingborg to King Valdemar, who also seized Skåne and Blekinge. A Danish chronicle says that, "taking advantage of Magnus' lack of penetration, Valdemar gained possession of Skåne through fraud and deceit."

Magnus' weakness encouraged Valdemar to continue his operations. In the summer of 1361 he captured the island of Öland, and seized Gothland, where he sacked the rich city of Wisby. This bold and unexpected move greatly alarmed the Baltic cities of the Hanseatic League, who feared that a similar fate might befall them. Negotiations were begun with a view to bring about an alliance between the Hanseatic cities and the kingdoms of Norway and Sweden against Valdemar, but the greed and selfishness of the cities frustrated the plan. In the fall of 1361, Haakon, who had always been a loyal son, had a serious quarrel with his father, and even imprisoned him for a time.[1] The "Icelandic Annals" state that "Haakon imprisoned Magnus because he promised to cede a part of his kingdom to Valdemar."[2] However this may be, he seems to have been prompted to the act by the nobles. His resolute action won their

---

[1] Enea Silvio Piccolomini (Aeneas Sylvius), later Pope Pius II., wrote in 1457 that Haakon was a superb man and wonderfully loved by his people; that all his deeds show him to have been a good son, father, man, and king, except that in his youth he suffered himself to be persuaded by the Swedish Council to imprison his father, which deed he recompensed later by filial obedience and support. *Samlinger til det norske Folks Sprog og Historie*, vol. III., p. 613. *Diplomatarium Suecanum*, III., p. 708 ff. A. Huitfeldt, *Danmarks Riges Krønike*, p. 493.

[2] Gustav Storm, *Islandske Annaler*, p. 226.

favor, and he was made king of Sweden a few months later, to rule
that kingdom jointly with his father. In their war with Denmark
the Hanseatic cities were unsuccessful. Valdemar captured the
greater part of their fleet, and after an unsuccessful attempt to take
Helsingborg, their commander, John Wittenborg, was forced to
conclude an armistice and withdraw his forces. On his return to
Lübeck he was condemned to death and executed.

Both Magnus and Haakon had learned to understand the advantage of maintaining cordial relations with Valdemar, for they were
now opposed by the Hanseatic League as well as by the nobles at
home, who sought to destroy their power. In 1363 a friendly agreement was finally concluded between the three kings. Magnus ceded
to Valdemar the provinces which had been seized by the Danes,
and the friendship was further cemented by the marriage of King
Haakon to Valdemar's ten-year-old daughter Margaret.[1] Two
months later the Danish prince, Kristoffer, died, and Margaret
became eligible to the throne of Denmark, a circumstance which
ultimately led to the union of the three Northern kingdoms.

The Swedish nobles were deeply offended, as they regarded the
concessions made to King Valdemar as a treasonable sacrifice of
the interests of their country, and they decided to offer the crown
of Sweden to Albrecht of Mecklenburg. He offered them his next
oldest son, Albrecht, who was chosen king of Sweden in 1364 after
Magnus and Haakon had been formally deposed. They received
no aid in their effort to defend their throne. King Valdemar was
absent on a visit to Pope Urban V. in Avignon, and the Norwegian
nobles would not begin a war to keep them on the throne of Sweden.
They succeeded, nevertheless, in raising a small army, with which
they took the field against King Albrecht; but they were defeated
in the battle of Gata, March 3, 1365. Haakon escaped, severely
wounded, but Magnus was captured and imprisoned in Stockholm
castle, where he was confined till 1371, when he was finally set free
on the payment of a ransom of 12,000 marks of silver.[2] Both he

---

[1] C. E. F. Reinhardt, *Valdemar Atterdag*, p. 324.

[2] A mark of silver was half a pound of pure silver, Cologne weight, or
233.858 grams. It was worth about thirty-seven crowns or ten dollars.
But as the purchasing power of money was over eight times as great at that

and Haakon had to relinquish their claim to the throne, but Magnus received the income from the provinces Vestergötland, Dalsland, and Vermland during his lifetime. After he regained his liberty, he spent his remaining years in Norway, where the people liked his kindness of heart, and called him Magnus the Good. He perished in a shipwreck on the Bømmelfjord, in western Norway, December 1, 1373.[1]

5. THE HANSEATIC LEAGUE GAINS ASCENDENCY IN THE NORTH

When Valdemar Atterdag, in 1360, seized Skåne, and shortly after also Öland and Gothland, Magnus Smek and his son, King Haakon of Norway, formed an alliance with the Hanseatic cities against him. This alliance did not last long, as neither of the kings aided the cities in their war against Valdemar in 1362, but the Hanseatic merchants had been able to obtain a new charter (1361), in which they were granted unrestricted permission to trade in both kingdoms whenever and in whatsoever manner they pleased. They could even remain with their wares as long as they pleased, without being obliged to bear the burdens of ordinary citizens. This charter enabled them to gain final control over all trade in every part of the country. They not only seized all commerce, but they began also to do the retail trade with the people of the country districts, which had hitherto been reserved for the Norwegian merchants. In this way they destroyed all competition by forcing the Norwegian merchants even out of the local trade. It was, indeed, always stated in the charters that the Norwegian merchants should enjoy the same privileges in the German cities as the Hanseatic merchants enjoyed in Norway, but these were only meaningless phrases, as Norwegian commerce was already destroyed. Bergen, the great depot of the trade with the North, became one of the most important cities of the League. The Hanseatic colony in Bergen seems to have been definitely organized about 1350.[2] Its three thou-

time as at present, a mark of silver would have a real value of about $80 in our money. Hence the ransom would amount to about $960,000.

[1] *Islandske Annaler*, p. 363.

[2] Friedrich Bruns, *Die Lübecker Bergenfahrer und ihre Chronistik* (Berlin, 1900), *Die Begrundung der hansisch-lübeckischer Machtstellung in Bergen.* Ludvig Holberg, *Bergens Beskrivelse*, p. 202 ff.

sand merchants, masters, and apprentices, all armed and robust men, were not allowed to marry, or mingle socially in any way with the townspeople. They formed a distinct community — a state within the state — governed wholly by their own laws. If a member of the colony committed any misdeed, he could not be brought to justice by the city authorities, and if the offense was a grave one, he could easily be smuggled out of the city on a German merchant vessel. At times these foreign merchants would carry on a veritable reign of terror in the city, as they well knew that the authorities did not dare to resist. In 1365 they broke into the royal residence, and forced the commander of the city to grant every request; whereupon they dragged one of his servants from a monastery, and beheaded him without a trial. They then forced the bishop to grant them absolution for their deeds, and compelled the city council to decide the case in their favor. In case resistance was offered, they threatened to burn the bishop's residence and the whole city. It is true that this species of tyranny and brigandage affected directly only the city of Bergen, that it was a local evil which did not imperil the peace and liberty of the people in general; but it was, nevertheless, a national humiliation, and furnished positive proof of the nation's failing strength. It was a foretaste of the kind of blessing which Norway was to enjoy under the galling commercial yoke of the Hanseatic League.[1]

---

[1] J. E. Sars, *Hanseaternes Handelsherredømme, Udsigt over den norske Historie*, vol. III. Schäfer, *Die Hansestädte und König Waldemar von Dänemark*. Ludvig Daae, *Det tyske Hanseforbund, Historiske Skildringer*, II. Alexander Bugge, *Handel og Byliv nord for Alperne; Verdenskulturen*, edited by Aage Friis, vol. IV., p. 109 ff. W. Cunningham, *Growth of English Industry and Commerce*. W. Vogel, *Nordische Seefahrten im früheren Mittelalter*. P. A. Munch, *Det norske Folks Historie*, part II., vol. I., 804–805. Alexander Bugge, *Handelen mellem England og Norge indtil Begyndelsen af det 15de Aarhundrede, Historisk Tidsskrift*, tredie række, vol. IV. William Christensen, *Unionskongerne og Hansestæderne*, Copenhagen, 1905. O. A. Øverland, *Norges Historie*, vol. IV., p. 489 ff. Kr. Erslev, *Danmarks Riges Historie, Den senere Middelalder*, p. 345 ff. Wolfgang Menzel, *Germany from the Earliest Period. Islandske Annaler*, edited by Gustav Storm. Yngvar Nielsen, *Bergen fra de ældste tider indtil Nutiden*. Yngvar Nielsen, *Af Norges Historie, Norge og Hansaforbundet*, 95 ff. Sartorius, *Geschichte des hanseatischen Bundes*. Friedrich Bruns, *Die Lübecker Bergenfahrer und ihre Chronistik (Hansische Geschichtsquellen*, Neue Folge, Band II.), Berlin, 1900.

When Haakon Magnusson was deprived of the throne of Sweden, he devoted more special attention to the affairs of his own kingdom of Norway. He had seen the injurious effects produced by the charters and liberties granted the Hanseatic merchants; he was loath to keep the agreements which he had made with them; and looked for an opportunity to shake off their commercial yoke. He made regulations which favored the native merchants, and infringed on the rights of the Germans granted in their charters; and in the hope of resisting them, if they attempted to use force, he made an alliance with King Valdemar of Denmark. The Hanseatic cities saw the danger, and determined to break the opposition of the two Northern sovereigns.[1] Already in 1366 they were uttering loud complaints about encroachments made by the kings of Denmark and Norway on their charters and trade privileges, and made extensive preparations for a decisive war against the two realms. The cities of the Baltic seacoast were the leaders in the undertaking, but they also persuaded the other cities of the League to join. In 1367 a general Hanseatic meeting, the largest of the kind ever held, was assembled at Cologne, and a coalition for war was organized in the name of the whole League. The cities agreed to assist each other faithfully against the kings of Denmark and Norway; no city should carry on negotiations, or conclude peace separately, and the compact should remain in force three years after peace was concluded.[2] The

---

[1] The German merchants feared lest they should be shut out from the lucrative trade with the North on which they depended for many of their staple articles, such as fish, herring, furs, hides, etc.   Dried codfish, one of the chief commercial articles, was exported from Bergen.   The herring fisheries on the coast of Bohuslen were especially important at the time. Fishing boats and fishermen from Germany, the Netherlands, Denmark, and Scandinavia would assemble in large numbers during the fishing season in the two towns Skanør and Falsterbo, where they built storehouses and depots, and where great markets were held.   These two towns, situated less than two miles apart on a jutting peninsula, became one of the leading trading places in the North.   A French nobleman who sailed through the Sound in the fourteenth century on his way to Prussia states that 40,000 boats and 300,000 people took part in the herring fisheries during the months of September and October.   Alexander Bugge, *Handel og Byliv nord for Alperne, Verdenskulturen*, edited by Aage Friis, vol. IV., p. 170.

[2] Jacobus Langebek, *Scriptores Rerum Danicarum*, VI., p. 522.   *Detmars Chronik*, von Grautoff, p. 214.

warships should assemble at Easter, 1368, in the Sound. Duke Albrecht of Mecklenburg and his son, the king of Sweden, the counts of Holstein, and many nobles in Jutland, led by Claus Limbek, were also persuaded to join the coalition. The courage of the allies rose with their numbers. They agreed to partition Denmark so that the king of Sweden should receive Skåne and the island of Gothland; Albrecht of Mecklenburg, Seeland and some of the smaller islands; and the counts of Holstein should receive Jutland, Fyen, Langeland, etc. King Valdemar must have been aware of the grave danger which threatened his kingdom, but there is no indication that he took any decisive steps to safeguard his realm.[1] Valdemar was a sagacious though unscrupulous statesman — a great ruler, but not really a warrior, and when so many, even of his own nobles, joined the coalition against him, he seems to have despaired of success in the war. He turned the government over to the Lord High Constable (*drost*), Henning Podbusk, and left the kingdom.[2] He went to Germany, but what he had in mind is not clear. He may have sought to get aid, or he may have thought that the Council would be able to make peace on better terms if he were not present.

Off the Island of Rügen the League collected in 1368 a fleet of seventeen large war vessels and many smaller ones, carrying 200 horses and 1540 warriors. This force was to operate against Denmark, and the victory was swiftly and cheaply won, as no Danish fleet appeared to offer battle. Copenhagen was captured and sacked, a German garrison was placed in the castle, and the harbor was obstructed by sinking ship-hulls at the entrance. Elsinor (Helsingør), Aalholm, Nyköping, Malmö, Skanör, and Falsterbo were captured. Seeland was harried with fire and sword. The king of Sweden took

---

[1] Tradition says that when he received the Hanseatic cities' declaration of war, he improvised as an answer this Low Dutch stanza:

> Seven unde seventig hensen
> Hefft seven unde seventig gensen;
> Wo mi di gensen nichten biten,
> Nah den hensen frage ick nichten schiten.

This is without doubt only invention, but the impression seems to have prevailed that Valdemar was overconfident and failed to make preparations. C. E. F. Reinhardt, *Valdemar Atterdag og hans Kongegjerning*, Copenhagen, 1880.

[2] Jacobus Langebek, *Scriptores Rerum Danicarum*, vol. VI., p. 631.

Skåne, and the counts of Holstein seized the greater part of Jutland. "The Germans harried Jutland and all the possessions of the Danish king," says the old annalist.[1]

A second fleet of six war vessels and 1100 men was organized in the Netherlands to operate against Norway, and this force met as little resistance as the first. The old *leding* system in Norway had fallen into such complete decay that the country no longer had a fleet worthy of the name. The districts east of Lindesnes were ruthlessly harried, and fifteen parishes are reported to have been laid waste. Marstrand, Konghelle, and Ljodhus were burned, and as King Haakon had no means of resisting the enemy, no alternative but the negotiation of peace remained. On August 10, 1368, an armistice was arranged at Wismar, which should last till Easter the following year. During this interval the hostilities should cease, but the embargo on commerce with Norway was to be maintained, a proviso which would ultimately compel the Norwegians to accept peace on any terms offered. But the stipulations regarding the cessation of hostilities were not kept. The seacoast, as far as Bergen, was harried, houses and forests were burned, and an effort was made to so terrorize the people that they would never again attempt to offer resistance to the Hanseatic merchants.

Before the war broke out, the Hanseatic League ordered all the German merchants in Norway to leave the country.[2] The English merchants seized the opportunity, and tried to reëstablish their trade with Norway, but the Germans returned and drove them away.[3]

A new armistice was concluded in 1369, which should last till 1370,

---

[1] *Islandske Annaler*, edited by Gustav Storm, p. 361 f.

[2] The order recalling the merchants from Bergen was issued at Lübeck, Feb. 2, 1368. *Diplomatarium Norwegicum*, vol. VIII., no. 182. In a letter to the League, of May, 1368, the merchants of Bergen say that they have obeyed the order, but that it has brought them irreparable loss. *Diplomatarium Norwegicum*, vol. VIII., no. 184. P. A. Munch, *Det norske Folks Historie*, part II., vol. I., p. 804 f. *Islandske Annaler*, edited by Storm, p. 279.

[3] The English complained of this in 1375, when an embassy from the Hanseatic League arrived in England, and sought to obtain a renewal of the trade privileges of Edward I.'s time. *Hanserecesse*, 1st series, III., no. 318, § 1. Alexander Bugge, *Handelen mellem England og Norge, Historisk Tidsskrift*, tredie række, IV., p. 85.

when peace negotiations should begin at Bohus castle. These negotiations at first led only to the prolongation of the armistice, and permanent peace was not concluded till 1371. Peace with Denmark was concluded at Stralsund, 1370, the most humiliating which any Northern kingdom had ever been forced to conclude. The victorious Hanseatic merchants secured the renewal of all their trade privileges. They got full control of the important herring fisheries on the coast of Bohuslen, and the towns and castles of Skanör, Falsterbo, Malmöhus, Helsingborg, and Varberg were ceded to them for fifteen years as a war indemnity. Their trade privileges were now so extensive and well protected that all competition could be excluded; their commercial supremacy in the North was absolute and uncontested.[1] The only trade which still remained to the native merchants was the traffic with the colonies and with Nordland (the northern districts of Norway, except Finmarken). From Nordland fish and other products were brought to Bergen, and sold to the German merchants. But even this trade was soon brought under the control of the merchants at Bergen.[2] The "Norderfahrer" (Nordfarere), as the Germans called the native traders and fisher-

---

[1] Friedrich Bruns in his excellent work, *Die Lübecker Bergensfahrer und ihre Chronistik*, gives the statistics of the trade between Bergen and Lübeck. Summed up it shows the following results:

	IMPORTED TO BERGEN	EXPORTED FROM BERGEN
1369–1370	$11,058\frac{1}{2}$ marks value	10,586
1378	6,881 marks value	$18,955\frac{1}{2}$
1379	7,564 marks value	17,629
1381	9,369 marks value	19,072
1383	$5,783\frac{1}{2}$ marks value	7,856
1384	$7,920\frac{1}{2}$ marks value	$20,623\frac{1}{2}$
1385	9,211 marks value	12,269

It will be seen that after the Hanseatic merchants gained control of the trade, they exported from Bergen goods worth about twice the amount of the goods imported. As trade at this time was a mere barter, Norway received only half of what her exported goods were worth, and the German merchants were reaping an immense profit.

[2] *Norske So*, an allegory by an unknown author, describing conditions in Norway; quoted by Rasmus Nyerup in *Historisk-statistisk Skildring af Tilstanden i Danmark og Norge i ældre og nyere tider*, Copenhagen, 1803, vol. I., p. 327–340. Ludvig Holberg, *Bergens Beskrivelse*, p. 265 ff.

PLATE I

KRINGEN.

BOHUS IN THE SEVENTEENTH CENTURY.

men who carried on the traffic with Nordland, were often in need. Their capital was small, and the merchants at Bergen gladly furnished them the needed supplies, after an agreement had been made that the fish brought to Bergen should be sold for a fixed price, which was always very low. In this way the Nordfarere were kept in a sort of commercial serfdom, an evil which lasted long, and which was eradicated with great difficulty.

As to the nature of the influence exerted by the Hanseatic merchants on Norway's commercial development there has been difference of opinion among historians. P. A. Munch and J. E. Sars have held that, as Norway at this time had no distinct merchant class, the Hanseatic merchants filled an empty gap, and stimulated Norwegian trade and commerce to new growth. They had more capital and better business methods than the native traders, and although their control of Norwegian commerce proved ruinous to individual traders of Bergen, Tunsberg, and Oslo, forcing them out of business, it was not injurious to the nation as a whole.

It must be admitted that Norway's decline cannot be ascribed to the operations of the Hanseatic merchants; but it can, nevertheless, not be doubted that a strong foreign commercial supremacy established at a time of transition and national weakness tended to prolong the weakness, and hindered the free unfolding of native enterprise which might have produced a new national development. Alexander Bugge shows that already at the time of Haakon Haakonsson and Magnus Lagabøter a new and quite numerous and enterprising Norwegian merchant class was springing into existence, but its further development was cut short by the Hanseatic commercial and naval ascendency.[1] In speaking of the Norwegian merchants, Bugge says:

"Who, then, were the Norwegians who carried on trade and sent their ships to foreign lands? Here, as in regard to cultural life in general, the reign of Haakon Haakonsson forms a period of transi-

---

[1] "But if you acquire a great deal of goods on your trading expeditions, then divide it into three parts; put one part into a partnership with men who always stay in the cities, and are trustworthy and well versed in trade." — *The King's Mirror*, ch. 4. Alexander Bugge, *Handelen mellem England og Norge, Historisk Tidsskrift*, tredie række, IV.

tion. We learn from 'The King's Mirror' (written by a courtier at the time of Haakon Haakonsson) that it was customary for members of the chieftain class to make trading expeditions to foreign countries. But foreign ideas of knight-errantry and nobility gained a firmer hold, and according to these it was considered inconsistent with the dignity of a nobleman to carry on trade. Ever more seldom did the Norwegian chieftains trade in foreign lands, even though we find such instances even in the century following (the fourteenth). . . . There was, then, a place vacant for a real urban merchant class in Norway. But did no such class exist in the country? The answer will, I think, be both yes and no. . . . There can be no doubt that at the time of Haakon Haakonsson such a class was springing into existence in Norway, or rather, perhaps, in the city of Bergen. Trade was so brisk and extensive, and the concourse of strangers so great, that the townspeople could no longer be made amenable to the same laws with the country people, as hitherto. Under Haakon Haakonsson, and especially under his son, Magnus Lagabøter, the cities (*i.e.* Bergen, Nidaros, Oslo, and Tunsberg) were organized as distinct communities, separate from the country districts; they received their own laws, and even a degree of self-government. And what we learn from unmistakable facts of history points in the same direction — that in the cities, especially in Bergen, there was a class, a very numerous class, whose business it was to carry on trade with foreign countries, or rather with England; a class of men who were not at the same time craftsmen and farmers, but merchants exclusively. The well-informed author of 'The King's Mirror' tells us that there were men who resided permanently in the cities and carried on trade. In the privileges granted the Norsemen in England, and in the treaties concluded between the kings of Norway and England, the merchants (*mercatores*), but not the subjects of the king of Norway, are mentioned. In the time of Magnus Eiriksson there was in Bergen a separate guild of 'Englandsfarere,' traders who were engaged in the regular traffic between England and Norway (no such guild of 'Tysklandsfarere or Hollandsfarere' is mentioned). Not only from Bergen, but also from other Norwegian cities, was trade carried on with foreign countries. In 1225, for example, there came to Lynn a trader from Nidaros who called himself 'Skule Jarl's merchant,' who was permitted to buy 200 *quarteria* of grain in the city. But these sprouts were not allowed to thrive and grow. Had it only been a century earlier! Now it was too late. The strangers had gained too great a power, and had become indispensable to the country."

There is reason to believe that peaceful rivalry would have reawakened the spirit of competition and stirred Norwegian commerce to new activity and growth. This rivalry would have been furnished by the uninterrupted intercourse with England, where native commerce was developing. But the forcibly maintained trade monopoly of the German merchants removed every opportunity, and left Norwegian traders and ship owners helpless in the tightening grip of the Hanseatic League, which was not progressive in spirit, but which maintained its supremacy by coercion and force.

6. OTHER FEATURES OF HAAKON MAGNUSSON'S REIGN

When King Magnus and his queen died, the provinces which they had held in Norway were again placed under the administration of the Norwegian government, and various measures adopted show an earnest desire also to strengthen, as far as possible, the ties between the colonies and the mother country. In Iceland and the Orkneys the people, as well as the *sysselmænd*, were required to take an oath of allegiance to the king, and Henry of St. Claire was made Jarl of the Orkney and Shetland Islands in preference to Alexander de le Ard, who failed to respond to a request to come to Norway, where he would be granted an opportunity to prove his title to the jarldom. St. Claire went to Norway, and did homage to the king, subscribing also to a document which imposed great obligations upon him, and placed strict limitations upon his rights and powers in the colony. But such agreements were more easily made than kept. There is no evidence that St. Claire did not intend to keep his word, but Scotch influence was growing, and as Norway's naval strength was broken, the Norwegian kings found it ever more difficult to exercise any real authority in the colonies. Even commercially the ties were weakening, as fewer ships now sailed between Iceland, Greenland, and Norway than formerly. Of nine ships scheduled for Iceland in 1376, only six reached their destination, the others being driven back by storm. Greenland was visited but once a year by the "Greenland-knarre," and if this failed to cross the stormy North Atlantic, the colony remained isolated from the rest of the world till the following year, or till the ship succeeded in making the voyage. That such periods of isolation grew ever more frequent and protracted was evident, and proves that Norway's hold upon her distant colony was weakening, but it is not strange that commerce with Greenland was maintained with difficulty. The fact that the Norwegians were still able to cross the Atlantic Ocean at more or less regular intervals proves that their old-time skill and daring in navigation was not yet lost.

The union with Sweden and the closer relations with Denmark and Germany, established through the altered foreign policy, brought a change also in the character and title of the higher officials in the kingdom. Norway had few castles, it is true; the chief ones, and in a strict sense the only ones, were: Akershus, Bohus, Bergenhus, and Tunsberghus, but these became of greater importance than formerly. One or more *herreds*, or districts, were placed under the castle, and the income from these was collected by the officer in command, who received the German title of *vogt, foget (foged)*, and the district belonging to the castle was called *fogetie (fogderi)*. Even the *sysselmænd* in districts where there were no castles were often called *foget*, and the *gjaldkeri* in the cities was sometimes called *byfoget*. In Norway this new system was of little real significance, however, when we compare it to that of Denmark or Sweden, where the whole kingdom was parceled out among the numerous castles of the nobles. Over cities and larger districts, and also over the colony of Iceland, the king placed royal governors called *hirðstjórar*, whose duties are but imperfectly known.

It has already been stated that Haakon married Margaret, the daughter of King Valdemar Atterdag, in 1363. She was reared in Norway by a Swedish lady, Märta Ulfsdotter, a daughter of St. Birgitta, and seems to have resided permanently at Akershus castle in Oslo, where her son Olav was born in 1370, when the young queen was in her eighteenth year. After peace had been concluded with the Hanseatic cities and Duke Albrecht of Mecklenburg, in Stralsund, 1370, King Valdemar returned to Denmark and devoted himself to the reorganization of his shattered kingdom.[1] Among the many problems which engaged his attention was also that of the succession. As his only son had died some years previous, Albrecht,[2] the son of his elder daughter Ingebjørg, and Olav, the son of King Haakon and Margaret, were both eligible, but in order to obtain a favorable peace with Mecklenburg, Valdemar had promised to support Albrecht.[3] This seemed to give him the better chance of the two candidates, but when Valdemar died in 1375, Albrecht imprudently assumed the title of " King of Denmark " before he had been elected. He thereby violated the principle of elective kingship, and offended the Danish nobles, while the gifted Queen Margaret, who seems to have been charming to a very unusual degree, and knew how to win their favor, secured the election of her five-year-old son Olav. The young king's parents should act as regents during his minority; but as King Haakon always remained in Norway, the queen herself became the real regent and the guardian of her son.[4] Olav was already crown prince of Norway, and his election to the throne of Denmark would ultimately lead to a union between the two kingdoms similar to that which had before existed between Norway and Sweden.

King Haakon VI. had been forced to cede the throne of Sweden to Albrecht of Mecklenburg, but he refused to acknowledge the German prince as rightful king. When his father, Magnus Smek, died, he seized the provinces which that king had been suffered to retain during his lifetime, and hostilities between Norway and Sweden continued, though no real campaigns were fought till shortly before King Haakon's death in 1380.

---

[1] Albrecht, also called Albrecht the Younger, was a nephew of King Albrecht of Sweden.

[2] C. E. Reinhardt, *Valdemar Atterdag*, p. 471; appendix 12 contains King Valdemar's letter regarding terms of peace with the Hanseatic cities and the succession.

[3] Yngvar Nielsen, *Det norske Rigsraad*, p. 248.

[4] C. Paludan-Müller, *Observationes Criticae*, 198 f. *Diplomatarium Norwegicum*, III., no. 484.

7. The Union of Norway and Denmark. Queen Margaret

The sudden death of Haakon VI. placed his ten-year-old son Olav on the throne. Queen Margaret, who was in Denmark at the time, hastened to Norway to arrange for the succession of her son, and Olav was proclaimed king at the Ørething in Trøndelagen. A formal act of union of the two kingdoms must also have been drawn up, but no such document now exists, nor is it anywhere mentioned. A union was thus brought about between Norway and Denmark which was destined to last for 433 years, but the future consequences of so important a step seem to have caused no great concern. Margaret, who was very ambitious, hoped that the union would be permanent; while the leading men of the two kingdoms seem to have regarded the union as a temporary expedient, as the two realms had nothing in common but the king. During Olav's minority Margaret was to act as regent whenever she was in Norway, but when she was not in the kingdom, the administration was to be directed by Agmund Finnsson as regent, assisted by the chancellor, Henrik Henriksson.[1] This precaution was probably taken to prevent the queen from managing the affairs of Norway while she was staying in Denmark, as the situation in that kingdom was still so difficult that it would absorb the greater part of her attention. Many castles and provinces were still in the hands of the allies, who had fought against Denmark in the Hanseatic war, and Margaret had to employ all her skill to win back what had been lost. A contemporary Lübeck chronicler writes:

"In the year 1386 the queen of Norway gained possession of the kingdom of Denmark as completely as her father Valdemar had held it. This she did with great ability in that she first gained possession of Skåne, and then negotiated with her enemies, the counts of Holstein, concluded a permanent peace, and granted them the duchy of Schleswig as a fief. When this was done, a fear and trembling seized all the nobles of the kingdom, as they saw the wisdom and power of this lady, and with their sons they now offered to serve her. She summoned before her all the *fogeds* of the kingdom, and she

---

[1] P. A. Munch, *Det norske Folks Historie*, part II., vol. II., p. 131.

went from one castle to the other to be hailed as queen. She also transferred *fogeds* from one castle to the other, even as abbots move the monks from monastery to monastery. This happened even within a quarter of a year, before Candlemas, and it is quite astonishing that a woman, who before was so poor that she could give no one a meal except by the aid of her friends, because all her castles were encumbered, more by force than by debts, now, together with her son, became so powerful in a quarter of a year that she lacked nothing in the whole kingdom."

Making due allowance for the metaphoric expressions of the chronicler, it is, nevertheless, clear that Margaret was a worthy successor of her illustrious ancestors. Munch says: "The more closely we examine the political events in the North at this time the more prominently Margaret comes into the foreground as the one who surveys and controls events, and whose superior mind directs the whole."

The relations with Sweden continued to be hostile. In 1385 King Olav became of age, and with the advice of his mother he assumed the title of "King of Denmark and Norway and Heir to the Kingdom of Sweden," an open avowal that he would maintain his father's claim to the Swedish throne. Albrecht's power in Sweden was fast declining. He had attempted to place some restrictions on the growing power of the nobles, and this caused such a resentment that a strong party wished to place Olav on the throne in the same manner in which Albrecht himself was made king in 1364. The repetition of this kind of *coup d'état* was, however, averted for the time being by the sudden death of King Olav at Falsterbo castle, in Skåne, 1387.[1] This was a great calamity for the kingdom of Norway as well

---

[1] The cause of Olav's sudden death is unknown. The belief that he had been killed or imprisoned by his own mother is wholly without foundation. An impostor claiming to be King Olav appeared some years later, but he was tried and executed. See H. C. Behrman, *Beretning om den falske Kong Oluf Hagensøn's Død*, Copenhagen, 1846. Chr. Lange, *Litteraturtidende*, Christiania, 1846, p. 298 ff. A. Fabricius, *Minder fra Nordens Historie*, p. 72, Odense, 1898.

According to the law of succession, the heirs to the throne were divided into twelve classes. Albrecht, the son of Margaret's elder sister, Ingebjørg, had no right to the throne, as neither of his parents belonged to the Nor-as for Queen Margaret personally. As Olav was her only living child, the royal family became so nearly extinct at his death that for the first time in centuries a successor had to be placed on the throne by election.[1] King Albrecht of Sweden, a great-grandson of Magnus Smek, was the only heir to the throne of Norway according to the law of succession, but he was not even considered, owing to his great unpopularity and the enmity which had existed between him and the late kings of Norway, who regarded him as an usurper. Queen Margaret had no direct claim to the throne. She was not a member of the royal family of Norway, and hitherto no woman had ruled the

wegian royal family. Professor Gustav Storm has made the following diagram of the situation:

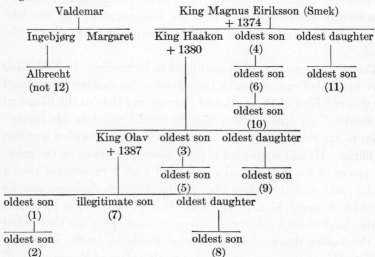

Albrecht, king of Sweden, was number nine in order of succession. Gustav Storm, *Dronning Margretes Valg i Norge, Historisk Tidsskrift,* fjerde række, vol. I.

[1] The election of Queen Margaret was in harmony with the Norwegian law of succession which provided that, when no heir to the throne was found, the one who had the best claim according to the general law of inheritance should be chosen. Since King Albrecht of Sweden was not considered, no heir existed, and Margaret had the best claim as the heir of her son, King Olav. In the Norwegian letter of homage, issued Feb. 2, 1388, it was expressly stated that she was chosen because she was Haakon's queen and the mother of King Olav. Suhm, Nye Samling, III., 387. *Norsk Tidsskrift for Videnskab og Litteratur,* vol. I., p. 230, note 2.

kingdom, but her ability and popularity counted strongly in her favor.[1] Seven days after King Olav's death she was chosen ruling queen of Denmark, and when the Council assembled at Oslo she was also elected regent in Norway, while Eirik of Pomerania, a son of her sister's daughter, was chosen heir to the Norwegian throne.[2] She also assumed the title of "Queen of Sweden," to show that she would continue the policy of her predecessors in her attitude to that kingdom. The Swedish nobles, who had intended to place Olav on the throne, now turned to Queen Margaret. At a meeting at Dalsborg castle, in Dalsland, where she was present, they chose her queen of Sweden, and she promised in return to aid them in driving Albrecht from the kingdom, an agreement which was swiftly carried out. At Aalsed near Falköping, the nobles met King Albrecht's weak forces, defeated him, and carried him and his son, Eirik, as prisoners to Lindholm castle, where they remained incarcerated for six years. King Albrecht's rule had ended, and the queen had won the throne which her son and husband had claimed, though the struggle was still protracted for a time. The novelty of a ruling queen, who had been able to unite all the Northern kingdoms, seems to have impressed the people deeply. A chronicler records with almost superstitious solemnity that "God placed an unexpected victory in the hands of the woman." Queen Margaret had been able to accomplish, both in Denmark and Sweden, what her late predecessors had attempted in vain — a sufficient proof of her ability and diplomatic skill. In 1389 Eirik of Pomerania was formally elected king of Norway at a new meeting of the Council, but Queen Margaret should act as regent until the young king became of age,[3]

---

[1] *Diplomatarium Norwegicum*, III., no. 477. C. Paludan-Müller, *Observationes Criticae*, 106. Yngvar Nielsen, *Det norske Rigsraad*, p. 259. T. H. Aschehoug, *Statsforfatningen i Norge indtil 1814*, p. 153.

[2] *Diplomatarium Norwegicum*, III., no. 484. C. Paludan-Müller, *Observationes Criticae*, 108. Yngvar Nielsen, *Det norske Rigsraad*, p. 261.

[3] J. E. Sars, *Udsigt over den norske Historie*, vol. III., p. 64. Kr. Erslev, *Danmarks Historie under Dronning Margrete og hendes Efterfølgere*, p. 428 f., 504. *Danmarks Riges Historie*, vol. II., p. 358 ff. Christian C. A. Lange, *Norsk Tidsskrift for Videnskab og Litteratur*, vol. I., p. 217 ff. *Bidrag til Norges Historie under Unionen*, af Christian Lange.

Arild Huitfeldt, *Kong Olav, Dronning Margrete og Eirik af Pommern*, p. 135 ff.

and she secured from the nobles concessions which greatly strengthened the royal power both in Sweden and Denmark. In Sweden no more castles should be built, and those that had been erected in Albrecht's time should be razed. More important still was the provision that all crown lands which had been alienated in Denmark in the reign of Valdemar Atterdag, and in Sweden in the reign of Albrecht, should revert to the sovereign, and the income from them should go to the royal treasury. In Denmark a new tax was levied to secure a better coinage, and in Sweden the queen received large personal possessions. It is quite evident that Margaret, the first great ruling queen in European history, possessed skill in administration as well as in diplomacy, but her system of statesmanship was, nevertheless, only a continuation of that of her predecessors, Magnus Smek and Valdemar Atterdag. It was her ambition to rule over a large realm, to gather the threads of administration and political power into her own hands. When the three kingdoms were finally united under her sway, she sought to perpetuate her dominion by strengthening the power and influence of the crown, and by increasing her revenues and private possessions. In these efforts she directed her attention to politics rather than to details of administration, and the local needs of each kingdom continued to be neglected. The efficiency of the local administrative authorities was even purposely weakened, to insure increased influence of the sovereign. Many of the highest offices both in Norway and Sweden were left vacant; the queen was staying in Denmark, and the old administrative system in both kingdoms was falling into decay. In Norway many Danes were appointed to fill the highest positions in the church, until it awakened merited resentment. In Sweden the queen appointed Danish *fogeds*, lawlessness increased, and for want of proper supervision by the royal authorities these foreign administrative officers became ever more arrogant and arbitrary, and wrung from the oppressed people loud and well-founded complaints. A contemporary remarks: "The Germans were expelled (*i.e.* King Albrecht and his Mecklenburgers); the Danes then got the power in the land for many years, and then the Germans were lauded by the people." The Danish *fogeds* were called "tyrants whose cruelty, never to be forgotten, brings them eternal perdition." The three kingdoms were associated on equal terms under the same sovereign, but through Margaret's influence a foreign overlordship was even now being established both in Norway and Sweden, a feature which was to make the political partnership with Denmark so expensive and profitless a business, especially for Norway. Even the defeat and imprisonment of King Albrecht was not to pass without a most unfortunate sequel, which caused much loss and suffering both in the North and elsewhere. The city of Lübeck had sided with Queen Margaret, but the two Hanseatic cities Rostock and Wismar undertook to aid Albrecht. They issued a proclamation that any one who wished to undertake raids into the Northern kingdoms, and would aid in carrying provisions to the city of Stockholm, which was besieged by the queen, would be given protection in their harbors. The invitation proved very tempting to hundreds of lawless adventurers who gathered from all parts of the Baltic seacoast, and a league of professional buccaneers, known as the "Victual Brothers," sprang into existence, which gravely endangered all commerce, not only in the Baltic, but also in the North Sea. The demon of lawlessness once let loose ran its own riotous course. Without discrimination the wild corsairs robbed and plundered remorselessly. They seized Gothland and captured Wisby, which they made their chief stronghold. In 1393 they captured Bergen, sacked and burned the city, and committed the greatest outrages.[1] Malmö and Nyköping were burned, Hanseatic merchant ships were everywhere attacked, and the danger to commerce finally became so great that the fisheries on the coast of Bohuslen and Skåne had to be abandoned for three years. In 1395 Bergen was sacked and burned a second time, "and the robbers," says the chronicler, "gathered great stores, treasures of gold and silver, costly cloth, household goods, and fish, which they brought to Rostock and Wismar, and sold with great profit, as the people of those cities did not care whether the goods were gotten honestly or dishonestly." Because of constant losses and increased hazards

[1] Gustav Storm, *Vitaliebrødrenes Plyndringstog til Bergen i 1393, Historisk Tidsskrift*, tredie række, vol. IV., p. 428 ff. Yngvar Nielsen, *Bergen*, p. 221 ff. Voigt, *Die Vitalienbrüder in Raumers historischem Taschenbuch*, 1841. Gustav Storm, *Islandske Annaler*, p. 422. Helen Zimmern, *The Hansa Towns*, p. 124 ff. P. A. Munch, *Det norske Folks Historie*, part II., vol. II., p. 338 ff. L. Daae. *Historiske Skildringer*, p. 18 ff. *Vitaliebrødrene*.

connected with navigation, prices rose, and many districts suffered for want of supplies, but Queen Margaret was quite helpless against this enemy. The Hanseatic cities made determined efforts to suppress the sea-robbers. Hundreds were captured and executed, but new bands appeared. In 1400 the cities of Hamburg, Bremen, and Lübeck thought that they had succeeded in sweeping the sea clean of pirates, but they soon had to send out a new expedition. In 1402 the notorious pirate chief, Claus Stortebecker, and two of his associates, together with a large number of followers, were captured and put to death. Again the Hamburgers sallied forth and captured Goedeke Michelson, Wichman Wigbold, and eighty pirates, who were all promptly beheaded.

Through such energetic measures the strength of the pirates was finally broken. They sacked Bergen a third time in 1428, and yet a fourth time in 1429, but after that their names disappear from history. The Victual Brothers destroyed the last remaining strength of the native Norwegian merchants, and when the Hanseatic cities revived their trade, they gained exclusive control. This marks the beginning of the period of their greatest prosperity and power in Norway, which lasted for about a hundred years. In 1395 Queen Margaret made peace with the cities of Rostock and Wismar, and Albrecht and his son were liberated. Thereby the war for the possession of Sweden was formally terminated, but the Victual Brothers still continued their ravages, and Stockholm did not open its portals to the queen till in 1398.

8. The Kalmar Union

After Eirik of Pomerania had been raised to the throne also in Denmark and Sweden, Queen Margaret took steps to bring about a formal union of the three kingdoms. In 1397 a meeting of magnates, councilors, and ecclesiastics of the three kingdoms was assembled at Kalmar in Sweden to negotiate about the formation of a union. At this council Eirik of Pomerania was crowned king of all the three kingdoms, and a joint seal was also prepared; but the queen's hope of uniting the three realms in a federal union with an hereditary king was not realized. A rough draft of an act of union, a sort of constitution, was, indeed, drawn up, but it was never completed in the necessary documentary form, or supplied with the required seals. It was expressly stated in the draft that "for the greater assurance that all these points shall forever be loyally kept, the document shall be written on parchment, two copies for each kingdom, and to these shall be affixed the seals of the king, the queen, the councilors of the kingdom, the lords, and the cities." As this was not done, the first draft of the points on which an agreement had been reached could not be legally binding.[1] It is possible that after

[1] *The Proposed Kalmar Act of Union*

This document, which is written on paper, still exists. It contains the following points:

1. The three kingdoms shall henceforth have one king and shall never be parted.

2. After the death of the king a successor shall be elected jointly by the three kingdoms. If the king dies without issue, a successor shall be chosen according to the best judgment and conscience.

3. All the three kingdoms shall continue in love and unanimity, and one shall not withdraw from the others; that which befalls one, as war or attack by foreign enemies, shall be regarded as befalling all three, and each kingdom shall help the other with full faith and energy.

4. Each kingdom retains its own laws, and the king shall rule according to them. He shall not import from one kingdom to the other what has not formerly been law and justice there.

5. One who has been outlawed in one kingdom shall be considered an outlaw in the others.

6. If negotiations are carried on with foreign lords or states, the king has the power to decide the matter with the advice of the Council of the kingdom in which he happens to be, or with a few councilors from each kingdom.

7. All these articles should be kept as prescribed, and they should be so interpreted that they will be to the honor of God and the peace and well-being of the king and the realm. If any one acts contrary thereto, then shall all the three kingdoms aid the king and his officials to remedy the wrong.

8. Queen Margaret shall have and hold with full royal right all that which her father and her son granted her in Denmark, her dowry in Sweden and what the Swedes have given her, together with what her husband and her son have granted her in Norway. At her death the castles shall revert to the crown, but otherwise she may, through her testament, dispose of what she has.

9. These articles shall be embodied in a document written on parchment, two copies for each kingdom, and to these shall be affixed the seals of the king, the queen, the councilors of the kingdom, the lords, and the cities.

This preliminary draft, written on paper, was to be signed by seven Swedes, six Danes, and four Norwegians; but only ten seals appear on the

the queen had failed to carry the chief points of the proposed plan she abandoned the whole of it, and preferred to rule without being bound by a document which gave the union no strength, and the sovereign no increased power; but it is also possible that, since the four Norwegian seals are lacking in the original document, the Norwegian councilors refused to sign, owing to the clause which made the king elective. This would change Norway from an hereditary to an elective kingdom, a serious step to which the Norwegian councilors would not willingly subscribe. A union had, nevertheless, been effected through the election of a joint king for the three kingdoms. This was solemnly ratified at Kalmar by the coronation of Eirik as king of Norway, Sweden, and Denmark, and the new relation of the three realms was also betokened by the use of the common seal. But the principle of elective kingship was retained, and each kingdom kept its full sovereignty and autonomy, its system of laws and administration. With the exception of the king no central government for the united kingdoms existed, and nothing was specified as to any duties which they owed each other as members of the union, except what was found in the unfinished draft of the points on which an agreement had been reached. As to the outward evidences of the compact entered into, the three realms could not have been united by more slender ties. But what Margaret had failed to do directly might in time be done indirectly, since the council had failed to adopt a constitution defining the relation of the kingdoms to each other, or limiting the power of the sovereign. The kingdoms had become associated under the same ruler; the ever present force of circumstances might do everything else that an ambitious and autocratic ruler might wish, since no written constitution existed to remind the people of the limit of his power, or of the extent of their own rights. Even a poor constitution could have been amended, and would have taught the people the art of constitutional government, but the magnates assembled at Kalmar, who

document. Three Danish and all of the Norwegian seals are lacking. Paludan-Müller, *Observationes Criticae de Foedere inter Daniam, Sueciam et Norwegiam Auspiciis Margaretae Reginae Icto.* T. H. Aschehoug, *Statsforfatningen i Norge og Danmark indtil 1814,* p. 174 ff. R. Keyser, *Den norske Kirkes Historie under Katholicismen,* II., 441 ff.

seem to have guarded so jealously against any encroachments on their own liberties, failed with almost childish fatuity to safeguard those liberties for the future.

When King Eirik was eighteen years old, he was declared of age by a council assembled at Vadstena, Sweden, in 1400; but Margaret continued to reign until her death. In 1401 negotiations were begun with the queen and King Henry IV. of England regarding the marriage of King Eirik to Henry's daughter Philippa.[1] As Henry IV. was seated none too securely on the English throne, he sought to strengthen his position through foreign alliances and by the marriage of his children to members of the royal houses. He had watched with much interest the growing power of Queen Margaret, and the consummation of the union of the three Northern kingdoms seems to have made him desirous of gaining the friendship of this new power. After prolonged negotiations Philippa finally came to Denmark in 1406, and the marriage was solemnized at Lund, in Skåne. The young king is described as a man of fine appearance. "He had yellow or golden hair, large eyes, blond complexion, and a broad white neck," writes Enea Silvio Piccolomini, the later Pope Pius II.; and an account to the English Council of the conditions in the North, dated August 8, 1400, evidently written by English envoys, states that "the three kingdoms, which have now been united, enjoy a hitherto unknown peace, whereas before, while they remained separated, they suffered much from war and unbearable evils. The young king is highly loved by his subjects because of his charming and noble personality."[2] The English envoys had evidently not discovered that the gallant young king very early showed signs of that rashness, ill-temper, and lack of good judgment which made his reign so inglorious a failure.

A new era seemed now to have dawned for the Northern peoples, or, rather, a new era might have dawned, if the rulers who were guiding their destinies had possessed the necessary wisdom and

---

[1] L. Daae, *Erik af Pommerns, Danmarks, Sveriges og Norges Konges, Giftermaal med Philippa, Prindsesse af England, Historisk Tidsskrift*, anden række, vol. II., p. 332 ff. A. Fabricius, *Minder fra Nordens Historie, Filippas Giftermaal med Erik af Pommeren.*

[2] *Samlinger til det norske Folks Sprog og Historie*, III., p. 481.

foresight. The union of three peoples, so closely related in language and nationality that no appreciable difference yet existed, augured well for the future. By combining their strength, which had hitherto been wasted in wars and rivalries, the united Scandinavian kingdoms might have risen into new prominence as one of the powers of Europe. Careful amalgamation would soon have obliterated the existing differences, as a friendly feeling already existed between the three peoples. Commercially their interests were identical, and a wisely conceived public policy would have sought means to strengthen the love for the union, and to stimulate the spirit of coöperation against foreign rivals, which would soon have welded the neighbors into one nation. But no such idea seems to have dawned even upon the keen-witted and practical Margaret; her worthless successors were wholly incapable of conceiving it.[1]

After the kingdoms had been united, and cordial relations had been reëstablished with England through the marriage of Eirik and Philippa, the opportunity seemed to have come to revive the naval strength of the Scandinavian realms, to throw off the Hanseatic yoke, and to reëstablish commercial relations with England. But Margaret attempted none of these things. No steps were taken even to strengthen the navy or the coast defenses, though the whole realm lay exposed to the attacks of the Victual Brothers, against whose ravages the queen had been so helpless that she had asked permission of King Richard II. of England to hire three ships at Lynn for the defense of the kingdom. The lack of means could scarcely be urged as a reason for this strange neglect, as the queen constantly increased her revenues, so that in a single year (1411) she could donate 26,000 marks to various religious institutions. Her failure to utilize the new opportunities in the right way was rather due to her system of statesmanship, which was wholly guided by dynastic and personal interests. It was of the general type of the statescraft of the Middle Ages, according to which the sovereign did not regard himself as the servant of the state, but as its owner. The realm was his private property, and it was his main care to secure as much revenue as possible, and to defend his title to the crown.

The thought of developing a united Scandinavian nation was as

[1] A. Fabricius, *Minder fra Nordens Historie*, p. 61 ff.

remote from the mind of Margaret as the idea of nationality was foreign to the whole age. The possibility of amalgamation of the three peoples was precluded from the outset by the queen's effort to make Denmark the principal country in the union, and to reduce Norway and Sweden to the position of provinces. Danish ecclesiastics were appointed to the highest offices in the church in both countries, and swarms of Danish officials were sent, especially to Sweden, while no Norwegians or Swedes were appointed to office in Denmark. We have seen how this policy awakened the bitterest resentment in both countries. The Danes were soon looked upon as oppressors and enemies, and Margaret was unjustly described as cunning and greedy. A Swedish monk calls her the daughter of the "Wolf" (*i.e.* King Valdemar). "Albrecht," he continues, "levied heavy taxes, but Margaret made them still heavier. What he left, she took; the peasant's horse, ox, and cow; in short, all his possessions." Another contemporary annalist states that she was very covetous. "With incredible craft she made herself ruler of all the three kingdoms, which she reduced to almost nothing, and no one could resist her cunning." [1] These outbursts of indignation do not serve to enlighten us as to the real character of the queen, for it is evident that the statements of these annalists are as unjust as they are incorrect. In her dealings with her subjects, she was in no sense the daughter of the "Wolf," as she was not harsh or tyrannical, but cautious and generous. Her varied activity as ruling queen bears the marks of moderation and good-will, and not seldom of true womanly kind-heartedness. But she had created a system of administration, the pernicious character of which she probably never fully knew or understood; and it is with some justice that the queen, who originated the system, should be made directly responsible for its attendant evils, which could neither be controlled nor abated. In Sweden the spirit of rebellion again raised its head. The Norwegians were more tranquil, not because they were better satisfied, but because the weak Norwegian nobility were less able to resist oppression, or to take the reins of government into their own hands.

In Norway the administration had been strongly centralized by the able kings of Harald Haarfagre's line. But the success of such a

---

[1] *Icelandic Annals*, edited by Storm, p. 290.

system depended on the continual presence of the sovereign, and the close supervision by the central government; but as this supervision ceased when the Kalmar union was established, Norway might almost be said to be without a government. During the last fifteen years of her reign, Margaret visited the kingdom only twice, and King Eirik came to Norway only once after he became of age. When the *drotsete*, or regent, Agmund Finnsson, died, no successor was appointed to this most important office for several years, and the

Fig. 1. — Queen Margaret.

chancellor's office was also left vacant for some time after Henrik Henriksson's death. The Council was seldom assembled; the country was ruled from Denmark, and the foreign officials, who were constantly increasing in numbers, could disregard the laws, and practice their extortions with impunity. The queen erred when she established such a system, but it was, perchance, an error of judgment, not one of heart.

Queen Margaret died quite suddenly on board her ship in the neighborhood of Flensborg, October 28, 1412. She was buried at Sorø, but her remains were later transferred to the cathedral of Roskilde, where her beautiful sarcophagus still stands. Nothing is known as to her personal appearance. The marble figure on her

tomb is a decoration, not a portrait; as it seems to have been made
to order by some foreign artist who probably never saw the queen.
But the noble and majestic face makes us feel that thus she must
have looked, this great queen who once ruled the whole Scandinavian
North.

9. KING EIRIK OF POMERANIA

When King Eirik assumed the duties of ruling sovereign, circumstances gave promise of a most successful reign. The newly established union was winning favor in all the three kingdoms, the revenues
were large, and the people were well disposed towards the king, as
they hoped that he would prove to be a wise and kind ruler. But
these fair hopes were soon shattered by the worse than worthless
Eirik. The only question which threatened to produce complications at the beginning of his reign was that of the relation of Schleswig to the crown of Denmark, but this molehill of difficulty grew in
King Eirik's hands into a mountain of trouble. Queen Margaret
had been obliged to cede this province to the counts of Holstein in
1386, but at the time of her death she was on the point of regaining
control of the duchy. An armed conflict had been precipitated;
but the queen had concluded peace, though the question was still
left unsettled. Eirik was opposed to the queen's cautious policy.
He would drive out the Germans, who had migrated in large numbers
into the duchy, and would unite it permanently with the kingdom of
Denmark. He submitted the question to a council (danehof) assembled at Nyborg, 1413, and this assembly decided, that as the counts
had been in arms against their sovereign, they had committed felony,
and had forfeited their fief to the king. Schleswig was thus reunited
with Denmark, but the counts would not abide by the decision of
the council, and a long and expensive war was the result. Hostilities
commenced in 1416. Eirik gained some success, and captured the
city of Schleswig; but he was unable to take the fortified strongholds
of the duchy, and the situation became critical when the Hanseatic
cities, because of the damage done their commerce, cut off all trade
with the North, and threatened to join the Holsteiners in active war
operations against the king. In 1424 the question was finally submitted to the arbitration of the German emperor, Sigismund, who

decided that the duchy of Schleswig belonged to the king. Eirik, who had gone to Hungary to visit the Emperor, was so pleased with what he considered the happy termination of the quarrel, that he journeyed to Jerusalem to offer thanks to God for the victory. But upon his return from Palestine in 1425, he still found Count Henry of Holstein in possession of the duchy of Schleswig, and when he attempted to enforce the decision of the Emperor, the war was renewed. The Hanseatic cities now joined the Holsteiners. Throughout the whole struggle the Victual Brothers had carried on their raids, not only through the connivance, but even upon direct invitation of the Holsteiners, and such damage had been done to commerce that conditions became unbearable. But the united forces of the allies suffered serious defeats. King Eirik gained a notable victory over their fleet in the Sound, 1427. Many of their ships ran aground, many were captured, and the commander, Tidemand Sten, fled with the remainder. The great Hanseatic merchant fleet, which arrived shortly after the battle on its northward voyage, was captured. In an attack on Flensborg Count Henry of Holstein lost his life, and a second Hanseatic fleet failed in its operations against Copenhagen the following year. In two campaigns the allies accomplished nothing. In 1425 King Eirik had seized the opportunity to levy a toll (*Øresundstolden*) on every ship which passed through the Sound, and he might now have concluded peace on very favorable terms, but he stubbornly insisted on enforcing to the letter Emperor Sigismund's decision with regard to Schleswig. His subjects, especially in Norway and Sweden, were tired of this war from which they could derive nothing but harm. Few reënforcements were furnished, and the king was not able to continue the struggle successfully. Flensborg fell into the hands of the allies, and in 1432 he was at length forced to enter into peace negotiations, in which he abandoned his plan of enforcing the Emperor's decision against the counts of Holstein. The peace was concluded at Vordingborg, 1435.

Colonial affairs were not wholly neglected by King Eirik, but the commerce with the Norwegian island possessions was, nevertheless, falling into decay. In 1410 the last ship of which any definite record is preserved came from Greenland to Norway, and no further communications with those distant settlements seem to have been maintained.[1] Holberg says that after Queen Margaret's time the kings were so occupied that they had no time to think about old Greenland.[2] The trade with the colonies continued to be a royal monopoly, and all foreign merchants were forbidden to trade with them, but after Norway's sea-power was broken, and the Hanseatic merchants gained control of the trade, the kings could no longer successfully defend even this last remnant of Norwegian commerce. In 1413 King Eirik protested to King Henry V. of England against the operations of foreign merchants in the Norwegian colonies. In 1431 he again complained to Henry VI., that for twenty years the English had carried on unlawful trade with "Norway's lands and islands" (Iceland, Greenland, the Faroe Islands, Shetland, the Orkneys, Haalogaland, and Finmarken), that they had plundered and burned, that they had carried away many ships with fish and other goods, and that many people had been slain.[3] In Eirik's reign English merchants were beginning to gain control of the trade with Iceland.[4] This trade had always been of some importance, as the Icelanders imported grain and other staple articles, while they exported wool, sheepskins, sulphur, etc. At this time great cod-fisheries, which

[1] The Norwegian nobleman Didrik Pining, who was *hirðstjóri* in Iceland, and commandant of Vardøhus about 1490, was a bold sailor and buccaneer. According to an old Icelandic source, Pining and his companion Pothorst, about whom nothing is known, "carried on trade with Greenland," but this statement seems to be a mere conjecture. Very little is known about Pining's operations in the Arctic waters. The humanist Olaus Magnus says that "Pining and Pothorst were excluded from all intercourse with humanity by the severe decrees of the kings of the North, and they were outlawed because of their violent robberies and many wicked deeds committed against all sailors, which they would seize both far and near." "They then sought refuge in the mountain Hvitserk, which lies between Iceland and Greenland," he continues.

Ludvig Daae, *Didrik Pining, Historisk Tidsskrift*, anden række, vol. III., p. 231 ff. Daae thinks that after peace was concluded between England and Denmark-Norway in 1490 in King Hans' reign, all preying on English commerce by Danish and Norwegian sailors had to stop. But Pining seems to have continued his buccaneering activity; and, as a result, he was outlawed.

[2] Ludvig Holberg, *Danmark's Riges Historie*, II., 531.

[3] *Grønlands historiske Mindesmerker*, III., p. 160 ff.

[4] *The Libell of Englishe Policye*, p. 93 f., a little English work, written in 1436, states that so many English ships had sailed to Iceland that the goods brought back did not pay the expenses.

gave this trade increased importance, were also developed near the coasts of Iceland. The commerce with Iceland was carried on especially by the Norwegian colonists of Bristol, who in earlier times had controlled this trade. They now ventured to disregard the restrictions which the kings had placed on the trade with the Norwegian colonies, hence their trading expeditions often turned into piratical raids; but whether these were extended to Greenland, as indicated in Eirik's complaint, is doubtful. In 1432 King Eirik concluded a treaty with England, in which King Henry VI. agreed to pay the damages which English traders had done in the Norwegian colonies. The people who, during the last twenty years, had been carried away by force, wherever they were found in the kingdom of England, should receive pay for the services they had rendered, and should be allowed to return to their homes. The interdiction of trade in the Norwegian colonies was renewed, but after this prohibition had been repeated by Henry VI. in 1444, and by a treaty between Henry VI. and King Christian I. in 1449, the trade with Iceland was finally made free, on certain conditions, in 1490.[1]

King Eirik continued Margaret's administrative policy. Norway and Sweden were still ruled from Denmark, leading public offices were left vacant, the Council always met in Denmark whenever it was assembled, and as the councilors from the two other kingdoms had to make long and expensive journeys, few attended its meetings, and they could exercise but slight influence, as the Danish members were always in the majority. Norwegian and Swedish affairs were left in the hands of the king and his Danish councilors, who were neither familiar with local circumstances, nor much interested in the affairs which they were called upon to settle. The increased burdens of taxation resulting from the wars, the interruption of commerce,[2]

---

[1] Fridtjof Nansen, *Nord i Taakeheimen (In Northern Mists)*, p. 377 ff. Alexander Bugge, *Nidaros's Handel og Skibsfart i Middelalderen, Festskrift udgivet i Anledning av Trondhjems 9000 Aars Jubilæum 1897.*

[2] During the war the trade with the Hanseatic cities had ceased; but King Eirik had encouraged the English merchants, who sought to revive the trade with Bergen, and also the merchants of the city of Bremen, who had left the Hanseatic League. *Diplomatarium Norwegicum,* vol. V., no. 580. Ludvig Holberg, *Bergens Beskrivelse,* Copenhagen, 1750, p. 126 f. *Norges gamle Love,* anden række, vol. I., p. 91.

and the ravages of the Victual Brothers, from which both Norway and Sweden had suffered much, especially in 1428–1429, soon made Eirik hated in both countries. The great popularity of Queen Philippa had hitherto been a saving feature of his reign. To her the oppressed could turn with their complaints, and her great kindness had won the people's heart. During the king's absence in Palestine she had acted as regent, and she had shown the same energy and high courage which distinguished her brother, King Henry V. of England. But no child was born to the royal pair, and in 1430 the good queen suddenly died at Vadstena in Sweden at the age of thirty-seven. She had been King Eirik's wisest councilor, the only person who could shield him against the growing wrath of his oppressed subjects. Now he stood alone, shortsighted, violent, hated, and always stubborn.

In vain the people now complained of their wrongs. Twice the Swedish nobleman, Engelbrecht Engelbrechtsson, was sent to Denmark by the people of Dalarne to obtain relief from the oppression of the Danish *fogeds;* his pleas fell upon the deaf ears of the shortsighted and obstinate king. Engelbrecht's return from his last unsuccessful mission became the signal for revolt. The peasants assembled at Vesterås, and chose him their leader, and soon all Sweden was in arms to throw off the Danish yoke. On August 16, 1434, the Swedish Council, compelled by Engelbrecht Engelbrechtsson, issued a document in which they renounced their allegiance to the king,[1] but on the 24th of the same month the Norwegian Council gave notice that it found this step to be untimely and ill-advised, and asked the Swedish Council to reconsider its action, as it was contrary to the happy union of the three kingdoms. The king, it continued, had not erred from ill-will, but was ready to right all real wrongs.[2] On the 12th of September the Swedish Council issued a second document, addressed to the Council and people of Norway, in which they stated forcibly and in detail the reasons for renouncing their allegiance to King Eirik, and asked the Norwegians to join them in resisting oppression.[3] No better opportunity could have been offered the Norwegians to sever the unprofitable partnership with Denmark,

---

[1] *Diplomatarium Norwegicum*, vol. V., no. 644.
[2] *Ibid.*
[3] *Ibid.*, no. 647. *Norges gamle Love*, anden række, vol. I., p. 142 f.

but the invitation of the Swedish Council elicited no response. In Norway the hereditary kingship, and the strength and stability of the central government had, in course of time, created a spirit of loyalty to the king, which had ripened into a well-established tradition. The Swedes, who had elected and dethroned their kings in rapid succession, could start a new rebellion without much compunction; to the Norwegians such a course seemed violent and treasonable.

But Engelbrecht Engelbrechtsson continued the war against the Danes with great success. In three months he drove out the Danish *fogeds*, and destroyed a number of their castles. King Eirik finally came to Stockholm with a fleet; but as the city was closely hemmed in by Engelbrechtsson's forces, he found the situation hopeless, and agreed to submit the whole question to the arbitration of a committee of four councilors from each kingdom. On a Rigsdag assembled at Arboga, 1435, Engelbrechtsson was chosen regent until an agreement should be made with the king, and at a council assembled at Stockholm, where also many Norwegian councilors were present, Eirik agreed to the terms submitted. He had to give assurance that he would rule in conformity with the laws, that the castles of the kingdom should be granted only to native lords, and that Sweden should have its own government, at the head of which should stand the *drotsete* and the *marsk*, two new officials. For the former office the Council chose Kristen Nilsson Vasa; for the latter the king appointed Karl Knutsson Bonde. All might now have been well, but King Eirik soon violated the agreement, and war broke out anew. Engelbrechtsson fought a second campaign as successfully as the first, but on April 27, 1436, this great leader was assassinated by a personal enemy, and Karl Knutsson Bonde, a dashing young nobleman, more ambitious than gifted, assumed the management of the uprising.

The Danish misrule, and the failure of the king to listen to the often repeated complaints of the people, finally produced an uprising also in Norway.[1] The successful rebellion in Sweden, and the concessions

---

[1] In a letter of June, 1424, the *bønder* of Skaun complained to King Eirik of the *foged* Herman Molteke, whose oppressions they could no longer endure. They report that they have to leave their homes unless the king sends them

which Eirik had been forced to make at the council of Stockholm, inspired some noblemen of the southeastern districts with the hope that they might be able to compel the king to redress their grievances. The revolt which took place in 1436 was led by Amund Sigurdsson Bolt, from Borgarsyssel, and five other noblemen from neighboring districts.[1] A letter written by Engelbrechtsson, dated March 19, 1436, shows that Amund Sigurdsson and his associates sought an alliance with Engelbrechtsson and the Hanseatic cities against King Eirik, and the uprising seems to have been organized shortly after the Norwegian councilors returned from Stockholm.[2] Amund Sigurdsson marched to Oslo, and seized the fortified bishop's residence, but after an undecisive fight with the garrison of the city, led by Svarte-Jøns, the Danish commander of Akershus castle, the rebels withdrew. King Eirik, who was notified of the uprising, seems to have been alarmed, and full and complete pardon was offered the leaders if they would submit. An armistice was concluded June 23, 1436;[3] and a council was summoned to meet at Tunsberg to negotiate with the leaders of the uprising. Amund Sigurdsson and two other leaders met, together with twenty-six of their followers, and presented to the council the demand that the foreign lords and *fogeds* should be expelled from the country before the 29th of July. This condition was accepted, and peace was formally concluded between Amund

another *foged. Diplomatarium Norwegicum*, vol. II., no. 680. Later they notify the king that they have driven Herman Molteke from their district. *Diplomatarium Norwegicum*, vol. II., no. 681 and no. 683.

[1] Gustav Storm, *Om Amund Sigurdsson Bolt og Urolighederne i det sydlige Norge. Historisk Tidsskrift*, tredie række, vol. II., p. 101 ff., IV., 395 ff. L. Daae, *Nye Studier til Oprørshøvdingen Amund Sigurdssons Historie. Historisk Tidsskrift*, tredie række, vol. I., p. 488 ff.

[2] The letter reads in part: "Likewise the kingdom of Norway has written us and asks to enter into alliance with private Hanseatic cities and with the kingdom of Sweden. We did not know that the kingdom of Norway would join us when our messengers visited the cities; and they (*i.e.* the Norwegians) have now joined us to be allied with Sweden, living or dead. We ask you that you give them your assistance, that they may enter into the same relations with the cities." As the Norwegian Council was still loyal to King Eirik, the term "kingdom of Norway" can only mean Amund Sigurdsson and his party. The letter, which is printed in *Hanserecesse*, part II., vol. I., p. 525, is quoted by L. Daae, *Historisk Tidsskrift*, tredie række, vol. I., p. 490.

[3] *Diplomatarium Norwegicum*, vol. III., p. 525, no. 733.

Sigurdsson and the council.[1] The stipulations of the agreement were carried out to the letter, it seems, as the Danish lords and *fogeds* were expelled from Norway in July, 1436. The uprising had been successful to some degree, but as it gained no general support, it became a local affair of no great national significance. Professor J. E. Sars says of it:

"The Norwegian uprising corresponded in many ways to the Swedish. Like the latter, it was especially directed against foreign lords and *fogeds*, and, like it, it proceeded chiefly from the common people, while the nobles kept aloof, or assumed a hostile attitude, as they regarded the movement with fear and ill-will. . . . But as closely related as the two uprisings — the Norwegian and the Swedish — seem to be in regard to origin and early success, so different were they in regard to historic importance and political consequences. The Swedish developed into a truly national movement, and forms a new epoch in the nation's history; the Norwegian was a mere episode without any permanent or important result. . . . The chief reason why the Norwegian movement died away without results while the Swedish continued to grow, and placed state and nation upon new paths of progress,was that Sweden had an ambitious aristocracy, while the aristocracy in Norway had long been on the decline both politically and otherwise."[2]

In 1436 a council was assembled at Kalmar to bring about a new reconciliation between King Eirik and the Swedes, but the Norwegian councilors were not present, owing, no doubt, to the uprising at home. The Danish councilors supported the Swedes in their demands, and King Eirik had to promise to abide by a new settlement to be made at a meeting in Söderköping, September 29th. At this council the three archbishops of the united kingdoms, and one councilor from each realm drew up a new act of union, the "Draft of 1436," which among other things provided for a government when the king did not reside in the kingdom; but this draft never got beyond the embryo state.

---

[1] *Diplomatarium Norwegicum*, vol. II., no. 727; vol. VI., no. 465. The peace agreement accompanied by a proclamation of the council is dated Feb. 18, 1437.

[2] J. E. Sars, *Udsigt over den norske Historie*, vol. III., p. 128 f.

King Eirik, who had sailed to Gothland, did not return to Söderköping to receive a new oath of allegiance from his subjects. After spending the winter in the island, he went to Prussia to raise a military force for the purpose of compelling the Danes to accept his cousin, Duke Bogislaus of Pomerania, as heir to the throne. In the fall of 1437 he returned to Denmark, but acted more arbitrarily than ever before. In June, 1438, the Swedes assembled a new council at Kalmar, and urged the king to be present, so that a final settlement could be made, but this invitation he disregarded, and sailed again to Gothland, where he now established himself permanently. When it became apparent that he would not return, the council of Kalmar made the agreement that he should still be regarded as king of the three realms, and that perfect friendship should exist between the kingdoms; but the Swedes summoned him to appear at Mora Stenar to declare that he would respect the laws and liberties of the kingdom, or he would be deposed, and in October, 1438, Karl Knutsson Bonde was chosen regent.

Disturbances again broke out both in Norway and Denmark. In Norway the men of Telemarken and Bamble, led by Halvard Graatop, marched against Oslo, but they were defeated and scattered by Svarte-Jøns, the commander of Akershus castle.[1] In Denmark the peasants rose in rebellion against the nobility and clergy. The situation was so alarming that the Council invited King Eirik's nephew, Duke Christopher of Bavaria, and promised him the crowns of the three kingdoms, an assurance which was contrary both to the spirit and the letter of the act of union. In 1439 King Eirik was formally deposed both in Sweden and Denmark; Christopher of Bavaria was hailed as king of Denmark at the Viborgthing in 1440, and the following year he was also elected king of Sweden, and crowned at Stockholm, but only after he had made such concessions to the Swedish nobles that he became the mere shadow of a king. The revolution in Sweden, which had been set on foot by the common people, led by Engelbrecht Engelbrechtsson, had been carried to completion by the aristocracy under the leadership of Karl Knutsson Bonde. The strong royal power established by Queen Margaret had

---

[1] Gustav Storm, *Historisk Tidsskrift*, tredie række, II., p. 119 ff. Ludvig Daae, *Historisk Tidsskrift*, første række, IV., p. 86.

been shattered, and the monarchic union established at Kalmar had been replaced by an aristocratic union. The nobles of Sweden and Denmark had agreed that the two realms should remain united under a shadow king, while the nobility in both kingdoms retained all real power.

In this important revolutionary movement Norway took no part, aside from the two local disturbances mentioned, although King Eirik had virtually ceased to rule the kingdom. "The reins had slipped from his hands here as elsewhere, but there was no one to seize them." Though Sweden and Denmark had deposed King Eirik, and had chosen Christopher of Bavaria as his successor, the Norwegian Council adhered to their old worthless sovereign with a loyalty which would have been pathetic, if it did not furnish evidence of lack of national self-consciousness and clear-sighted political leadership. Time and again the Council sent messages to Eirik in his voluntary retirement, assured him of the loyalty of the Norwegian people, and asked him to help them, but the eccentric old king did not even answer. The only evidence that he still regarded himself as king of Norway was a few appointments which he seems to have made to please the Norwegians. In 1438, before he established himself permanently in Gothland, he appointed two Norwegian nobles, Olav Buk and Olav Nilsson, commandants, respectively, of Akershus castle and Bergen; and in 1439 he finally appointed a new *drotsete*, Sigurd Jonsson, and also a new chancellor, Gunnar Holk.[1] When it finally became evident that Eirik had altogether ceased to rule, the Norwegian Council consented to elect King Christopher. In 1442 the Councils of the three kingdoms assembled at Lödöse, where Christopher was chosen king of Norway, and he was shortly afterwards crowned in Oslo.

In his retreat in Visborg castle in the island of Gothland, King Eirik was now left alone to muse over the strange vicissitudes of human affairs; but his spirit was not of the kind that is chastened by misfortune. He turned pirate and robbed without discrimination Hanseatic merchants and his former subjects. In his castle he defended himself stoutly against attacks, but prudence finally led him to cede Gothland to King Christian I., Christopher's succes-

---

[1] *Samlinger til det norske Folks Sprog og Historie*, vol. IV., p. 545.

sor, and to retire to Pomerania, where he died at the age of seventy-seven.

The internal conditions in Norway during Eirik's reign reveal an increasing decadence, which was further accelerated through the maladministration due to foreign rule. This is, perhaps, most distinctly noticeable in the church, which up to the period of union had retained a distinctly national character. The prelates, as well as the lower clergy, were native-born, and as the king exercised great influence over the election of bishops, the state church principle was

FIG. 2. — Visborg Castle

maintained in practice, however vigorously it might be assailed in theory. Both Sverre and Haakon Haakonsson had successfully defended the principle that the king was the head of the Church of Norway. The bishops, who were elected by the chapters of the dioceses, had to be presented to the king to receive his sanction before they were consecrated by the Pope. It is true that at the council of Tunsberg, 1277, King Magnus Lagabøter renounced the right to influence the election of bishops; but this act was not sanctioned by the Norwegian magnates, and during succeeding reigns the bishops who resisted the king were driven into exile. During the fourteenth century the king does not seem to have interfered with the election of bishops, but he received the right to appoint the priests of the royal chapels. Thereby was created a new class of clergy, the "chapel priests," who were wholly dependent on the king, and, hence, loyally attached to him. From among these priests the king could select his chancellor and other secretaries, and when the Council of the Kingdom came into existence, the leaders of this clergy also received a seat in that body besides the bishops. The Provost of the Apostle church in Bergen was member of the Council as *magister capellarum*, and the office of chancellor should always be held by the Provost of the St. Mary's church in Oslo. In this way the national character of the Church of Norway had been maintained prior to the union. Especially after King Sverre's time the clergy were quite loyal to the sovereign. The sagas of the kings of Norway, and other great works in the national prose literature, were written by them; they were not only the spiritual teachers, but also the spokesmen and leaders of their people.

When the Kalmar union was established, the process of denationalization of the Norwegian Church took its beginning. The union kings maintained with renewed energy the state church principle, and sought to influence the election of bishops, not for the sake of maintaining the national independence of the Norwegian Church, but in order to strengthen their influence in the Council of the Kingdom. Their chief aim was to secure the election of Danish ecclesiastics, who would, naturally, be staunch supporters of the king and his policy. This practice was begun by Queen Margaret, who in 1381 made the Dane, Nicholas Finkenov, Archbishop of Nidaros, although the Norwegian ecclesiastic, Haakon Ivarsson, had been unanimously chosen by the chapter.[1] Nicholas did not attend to the duties of his archdiocese, but returned to Denmark, taking with him the books and treasures of the church. In a similar way, a Danish monk, Benedict, was chosen Bishop of Bergen (1371), and later another Dane, Jacob Knutsson, was chosen bishop of the same diocese (1400), but in 1407 he was transferred to the diocese of Oslo. King Eirik pursued the same policy, and meddled in church affairs in a much more arbitrary way than the more discreet Queen Margaret.

---

[1] Chr. Lange, *Bidrag til Norges Historie under Unionen, Norsk Tidsskrift for Videnskab og Litteratur*, vol. I., p. 217 ff. *Islandske Annaler*, edited by Storm, p. 285.

When Aslak Bolt, the Bishop of Bergen, was chosen archbishop, King Eirik named as his successor the immoral and wholly unworthy Arne Clementsson, whom he later forced upon the Swedes as Archbishop of Upsala. It seems, however, that Arne was never consecrated Bishop of Bergen. In 1422 the king secured the election of another Dane as Bishop of Oslo, and he also made him chancellor, though that office belonged to the Provost of the St. Mary's church. This was a most important office, as the chancellor was the keeper of the seal, which had to be affixed to every royal document to make it valid. The practice thus originated by Margaret and Eirik of Pomerania was continued by their successors, who often used their power very arbitrarily to secure the election of Danes. The clergy became more and more foreign in character, and the church lost its distinct national traits; it grew apart from the people, and ceased to be the nation's intellectual leader.

A similar downward trend is noticeable in all departments of administration. Prior to the union the authority exercised by the king and the Council had articulated well with the local administrative authorities, by whom the behests of the central government could be efficiently carried out. After the union was established, this first principle of good government was destroyed, not only through the negligence and lack of insight of the sovereigns, but even purposely in order to strengthen the royal power. With undisguised efforts the union kings sought to gather all power into their own hands, and to rule by issuing royal decrees to be carried out by *fogeds* whom they themselves had appointed. The old system of local administration was suffered to fall into decay; the principle of government by the people and for the people was disappearing. Henceforth the nation was to be ruled by a wise and divinely inspired *landesvater*, who was rising to the position of a sort of benevolent despot. In Sweden and Denmark this march towards absolutism was arrested by the revolution of 1434–1440; Norway was unable to profit by this opportunity. The weakness of the nobility, which made it possible for the king to exercise full control in Norway, was further augmented by the appointment of foreigners to the highest positions of trust and honor both in church and state. Thereby the leading Norwegians were gradually excluded from public life, and forced into inactivity and obscurity, while the government, which became wholly extraneous to the people, grew paternal and despotic. From the beginning of the union both the sovereign and the Danish Council sought to increase their power and influence in Norway. The offices of the kingdom were treated as a royal possession, and donated at will to Danish nobles and courtiers, while no Norwegians were appointed to office in Denmark. In 1415 the German Hans Kröpelin had been made *foged*, or commandant, of Bohus, and Baltazar van Dem had received Søndhordland as a fief. In 1424 Tideke Rust was commandant of Akershus, and later Svarte-Jøns was appointed to the same position. John Ummereise and Henrik Schacht, though they were foreigners, were made members of the Norwegian Council. From whatever side we view conditions in Norway, it becomes evident that the Danes were gaining the ascendancy. Many Danish nobles and courtiers flocked to Norway, and married Norwegian heiresses.[1] In this way they became the owners of rich estates, and as royal favors were always accorded them whenever an opportunity presented itself, these dashing foreigners with wealth and titles soon elbowed their way to the foremost positions in the land. As illustrations of this kind of fortune seekers may be mentioned Diderich Wistenakker, who received as a fief the whole of Telemarken, and Hartvig Krumedike, who in the reign of Christian I. became the richest man in Norway.

10. An Embryo Democracy

The sources dealing with social conditions in this period are very meager, but an important document has, however, been left us by the Italian sea-captain Pietro Quirini, who wrote an account of the life and customs of the common people of the seacoast districts of northern Norway as he found them in 1432. Quirini was shipwrecked in the North Sea on a voyage to Flanders, and with a few surviving companions he finally reached the islands off the north coast of Norway in a boat. They landed on the uninhabited island of Santi (Sandø), where they suffered much from hunger and cold; but some men who came to the island to look after their sheep found the shipwrecked men, and they were brought to the island of Røst

[1] *Samlinger til det norske Folks Sprog og Historie*, vol. III., p. 608.

where they spent the winter.[1] Quirini says that Røst was only three (Italian) miles in circumference, and had 126 inhabitants, who supported themselves by fishing, as no fruit or grain grew there. They caught a great deal of codfish, which they salted and dried in the sun. This they prepared for the table by pounding it until it became tender, whereupon they mixed it with butter and spices, which made it very palatable. They also had milk and beef, and by mixing meal into the milk they made a dough from which cakes were baked. Usually they drank sour milk, which the strangers did not find to their taste, but they also had beer. Their houses were round, wooden structures with an opening in the roof through which light was admitted, and in winter the opening was covered with a translucent membrane. Their clothes were mostly of coarse London cloth, but not of skin. The author speaks also of the vast number of wild birds, especially wild geese, which were so tame that they would make their nests close to the houses, so that when the people wanted eggs, they lifted the birds off the nests, and took as many as they needed, but otherwise they left the birds undisturbed. Their wealth, he says, consists, not in money, but in fish, two kinds of which were especially important; namely, halibut and codfish. In the month of May when the codfish is dry, they load it on ships, and sail with it to Bergen, which is an important trading center. Thither come ships laden with articles of food and clothing from Germany, England, Scotland, and Prussia, and these goods, such as leather, iron, cloth, and various articles of food, the inhabitants of Røst receive in exchange for their fish. The people, both men and women, he says, are well-built and good-looking, and they live together in the greatest innocence and brotherly love, and usually help one another without any thought of profit. They are good Christians; they

---

[1] Røst is a small island between 67° and 68° N. L. Quirini's account is found in Italian in Ramusio's *Racolte della Navigationi*, tom. II., and in German in J. R. Forster's *Geschichte der Entdeckungen im Norden*, p. 251 ff. Gustav Storm, *Venetianerne paa Røst i 1432*, *Det norske Geografiske Selskabs Aarbog*, VIII., p. 37 ff.

Accounts of their stay in Norway were also written by two of Quirini's companions, Christopher Fioravante and Nicholaus Michele. Schøning, *Det norske Videnskabers-Selskabs Skrifter*, vol. II., p. 95 ff. Rasmus Nyerup, *Historisk-statistisk Skildring af Tilstanden i Danmark og Norge i ældre og nyere Tider*, vol. I., p. 303 ff. *O. A. Øverland Norges Historie*, vol. V., p. 83 ff.

attend church regularly, and keep the fast-days; they never use profanity or mention the name of the devil; they are so honest that they take no care to hide their property behind locks and bars, but leave all doors and drawers unlocked; neither do they fear that their sons and daughters shall transgress against virtue. All of them, young and old, lead such virtuous lives, and live in such perfect obedience to the moral law that they do not know what incontinence is. They marry only to fulfill the commandment of God, and not from carnal appetite, which can get no power over them because of the cold air and the cold country in which they live. When their father, mother, husband, wife, children, or other near relatives die, they go to church and praise God because he suffered the deceased to dwell so long among them; and neither in word nor deed do they betray any sorrow or sadness any more than if the dead were only sleeping. When a woman's husband dies, the widow makes a great feast for all the neighbors on the day of the funeral. They are then attired in their best clothes, and the widow encourages the guests to eat and drink heartily, and to be of good cheer in memory of her husband's departure into eternal rest and peace.

In the month of May the people of Røst began to prepare for their yearly trip to Bergen, whither the strangers were to accompany them. A few days before their departure a noble lady, the wife of the governor of the district, who had heard that some strangers were staying on the island, dispatched her chaplain to Quirini and his companions with a present consisting of sixty dried codfish, three loaves of rye bread, and a cake. She also sent her greetings, saying that as she had learned that the people of Røst had not showed so great a hospitality as they should have done, they should report to her any wrong which they might have suffered, and full restitution would be made them. The inhabitants of Røst were also instructed to show the strangers the greatest courtesy and hospitality, and to bring them along to Bergen. Quirini and his men expressed their heartfelt gratitude to the lady for her kindness. They testified to the people's innocence of any wrongdoing, and praised them most highly for their great hospitality. Quirini sent the lady a paternoster chain of amber as a present, and asked her to pray for their happy return to their own country.

On the 14th of May they set sail for Bergen, and on the way they met Archbishop Aslak Bolt, who was making a tour of inspection in his diocese. When he heard the tale of the strangers, he was filled with compassion and gave them a letter of recommendation to the people of Nidaros (Trondhjem), where they were received with the greatest kindness. On Ascension day they attended mass in the great cathedral, and they were afterwards invited by the *sysselmand* to a banquet, where they were well entertained. After a ten days' visit in the city, they began their journey overland to Stegeborg in Östergötland, Sweden, where an Italian, Giovanni Franco (called in Swedish John Valen), was commandant. Quirini gave the *sysselmand* some small trinkets which he still had in his possession, and the *sysselmand* gave him in return a pair of boots with spurs, a little ax with the picture of St. Olav, a saddle, a hat, four Rhenish gulden, and a sack of provisions. The archbishop had given the people instructions to supply Quirini with a horse, and the *sysselmand* gave him two more. Thus provided, they started on their journey, accompanied by a guide, and they traveled eastward for fifty-three days.

The kingdom was thinly settled, says the author, and they often came to houses where the people lay sleeping, as it was nighttime, though the sun was shining. The guide, who knew the custom of the country, entered without knocking at the door, and they found the table decked, and chairs around it. There were also fur ticks filled with down or feathers to sleep on. Everything was open, so that they could eat what there was, and lie down to sleep; and it often happened that the man of the house came and found them sleeping, and when the guide told them where they were from, and who they were, he became astonished and gave them food without pay, so that the twelve men with three horses did not spend more than the four Rhenish gulden, though they traveled for fifty-three days. On their way they found huge mountains and deep valleys, where they saw great numbers of animals which resembled roebucks, swarms of snow-white birds of the size of heath-cocks, and partridges and pheasants as large as geese. Other birds, as hawks and falcons, were all white, due to the very cold climate of the country. They had also seen in the St. Olai church a white-bear skin about fifteen feet long.

In Stegeborg they were well received by their countryman Giovanni Franco. He sent them to Lödöse, whence they went to England, and they finally returned to Italy in safety.

Captain Quirini's account of the life and customs in these remote seacoast settlements is the more interesting since we still find in the country districts of Norway the same generous hospitality, the mutual helpfulness, the unsuspecting honesty, and with no great modifications, also the customs which he describes. The traits which attracted the captain's attention were not limited to a single locality or period of time, but are general characteristics of the Norwegian people in all ages. These traits bespeak a people leading a healthy rustic life, free from oppression or class struggles; whose simple virtues have been reduced to time-honored customs, the origin of which is hidden in a remote antiquity. Norway's commerce and sea-power had fallen into decay, her national greatness had suffered a total eclipse, and even her political independence was being gradually sacrificed in the interest of an unprofitable union with Denmark; but the social and economic life of the people in its local environment was left almost untouched by these changes, and retained its former health and vigor. The growing weakness and inefficiency of the public régime, to which the rapid deterioration of the military and national power of Norway must be ascribed, reflects in no way any inner social decay.

Nowhere did the people govern themselves in national matters in this period. The central government was either vested in a king and his advisers, as in Norway, or in an aristocracy, as in Sweden and Denmark. If this government was unwarlike and inactive, the state was weak, though the people might be relatively prosperous and well content. If the government was aggressive, and maintained an efficient military organization, the state was strong, as people at that time counted strength. Great wars could be fought, castles and palaces could be built, the nobles could display a dazzling pomp, and the national greatness was commensurate with their number and power; but with the development of this intense military activity followed in the Middle Ages the feudalization of society, by which the people were deprived, not only of their local autonomy, but of their personal freedom. They were gradually reduced to serfdom, and forced to shoulder intolerable burdens, which left them in hopeless poverty and intellectual apathy. In Denmark, where the aristocracy was strong, the nobles owned two-fifths of all the land besides their large family estates. Serfdom and socage were introduced, and the *bønder* were reduced to a most wretched condition.[1] The nobles who devoted themselves to military exploits could place in the field well-drilled armies of mailed horsemen, capable of waging successful campaigns even beyond the borders of the kingdom ; but the burdens fell upon the unfree tillers of the soil, who were wholly at the mercy of their feudal masters. This kind of national greatness, though it produced a rather showy intellectual activity among the upper classes, and a few heroic and interesting personalities, was unquestionably attended with social retrogression and growing internal decay. The people's strength was gradually sapped, society was stratified into hostile classes, and difficult social problems were created which had to be solved before the life of the nation could be lifted to a higher plane. It is quite evident that national strength in the feudal, medieval sense must not be confounded with national progress, and it follows that national weakness, taken in the same sense, need not be associated with economic and social decay. In Norway the aristocracy had been almost destroyed by the king, and when the royal family died out, a vigorous government, which was tantamount to a strong Norway, was impossible. The people seem to have had no regrets. They welcomed cheerfully a Swedish or a Danish king, if he would not violate their laws, or infringe on their local autonomy. They had lost their kings and their nobility, which might have maintained their national greatness, but they had also been relieved of the classes which could oppress them and reduce them to serfdom, and Norway thereby escaped the evils of

---

[1] The old historian Peder Friedrich Suhm says: "The great lords, clergy as well as others, oppressed here as elsewhere the poor, who thereby were brought to despair, so that they frequently revolted. But in Norway this occurred much more seldom than in Denmark, because the lords were not so numerous there, and their estates were smaller, hence they demanded less service." *Samlede Skrifter*, VIII., p. 361.

"Agriculture was declining, and likewise the population. The continual strife between the nobility and the common people was the cause of this." *Samlede Skrifter*, Vol. VIII., p. 359.

the feudal system. The union government, which was exercised at a distance, was paternal and inefficient rather than oppressive, and although greedy *fogeds* might commit individual acts of injustice, they lacked the power, if they did possess the will, to oppress the whole people. Cut off from international conflicts, with the exception of the wars forced upon them through their union with Denmark, the Norwegians were left to themselves to lead an uneventful rustic life among their own fjords and mountains, where they preserved their own laws, local institutions, love of freedom, and robust spirit of independence. With the disappearance of the court and the nobility a leveling of social conditions followed which gradually obliterated the old class distinctions, and consolidated the people into a hardy, plain-spoken yeomanry. In their homes around the fjords and in the mountain valleys, the Norwegians were as much their own lords in the period of union as they had been in the Viking Age; and their irrepressible love of freedom was often whetted into violent resistance to oppression, and jealous hatred and distrust of the new upper class of Danish priests and officials which sprang into existence in the period of union with Denmark. Whatever the Norwegians might have lost through the disappearance of military power and national prestige, the unimpaired manhood and womanhood of the people, than which nothing is better worth preserving, remained to live and grow in a free and healthy domestic environment. It is true that the spirit of the nation no longer found expression in great achievements, but whenever opportunity was offered, it manifested itself in a way which created respect and admiration. We see it in the great naval heroes Kort Adelaer and Peter Tordenskjold, and in the great respect which the Norwegian soldiers always enjoyed in Denmark. The Danish kings in the union period surrounded themselves with a Norwegian bodyguard, and the Danish naval forces were largely recruited in Norway. Molesworth says: "The best seamen of the King of Denmark are the Norwegians."[1] The rather bombastic patriotic songs of a later period praising the bravery, fidelity, and intense love of liberty of the Norwegians need not be

---

[1] Robert Molesworth, *An Account of Denmark as It Was in the Year 1692*, London, 1694, p. 130. Molesworth was an English writer and diplomat. Anathon Aal, *Henrik Ibsen als Dichter und Denker*, Halle, 1906, p. 41 ff.

taken literally, but we would wholly misunderstand them if we failed to recognize that they express in an almost stereotyped and conventional way a well-established general opinion. Anathon Aal says: "The people were always free, the *bønder* (yeomanry) much more so than elsewhere in Europe, but they lacked political leaders who could maintain the national principle." This was a loss, but it was also a gain. When the aristocracy and the national kingship disappeared, the defense of their rights and liberties, and the future destiny of the nation was placed for the first time in the people's own hands. Those who ruled and those who led were gone; the people had to rely upon themselves. However this may be interpreted, it was a social revolution which necessarily marks the beginning of a new era in the people's social and political development. The yeoman class grew strong and numerous. They loved their old freedom, they cherished their rights, they were united by common customs and the equality of economic and social conditions. They lacked the means as well as the ability to seek the glory of military exploits or international politics, but they learned to act together in resisting encroachments, and in managing their own domestic affairs. They were not only freer than the people elsewhere, but they were also more independent economically. We have seen that natural conditions, especially the small and scattered areas of tillable soil, had hindered the growth of a feudal aristocracy in Norway. Few castles were built, and a fairly equitable distribution of land was maintained by the law of *odel*, which safeguarded the *bønder* in the possession of their land. The absence of feudal lords, and the division of the land among the *bønder*, who owned and tilled their own little farms, made the large class of freeholders economically independent, and gave Norwegian society a distinctive democratic character.[1] Because they were left without such an aristocratic upper class, they also developed a love for independent action, and a spirited self-reliance which forms the theme of the patriotic national songs, and which won the admiration of the Danes in the union period. This was not national greatness, but it can safely be called social progress. The only trouble was that this development in Norway came in an age which was not yet able to profit by democratic con-

[1] See Bjørnstjerne Bjørnson's poem, "Norge, Norge."

ditions, and make them a new force in national development. But although centuries were yet to pass before this life, under unfavorable political circumstances, ripened into a new self-conscious nationalism, we find in the Norwegian people after the completion of this great social and political change the future Norwegian democracy in embryo. We see nursed in the quiet the social conditions and the traits of character which so quickly placed Norway in the front rank of political and social democracies when the great awakening finally came.

11. KING CHRISTOPHER

When Christopher of Bavaria finally succeeded King Eirik of Pomerania on the thrones of the Northern kingdoms, the three realms were again united under a common king, but the idea of uniting them into a single Danish kingdom under the personal rule of the king, which had been Queen Margaret's plan, was now abandoned. Separate administration for each kingdom was emphasized, and the only frail strand of the union idea yet remaining was that of a common sovereign, who under the new arrangement had but limited power. In Sweden and Denmark the nobility forced Christopher to subscribe to charters which greatly reduced his power and strengthened the influence of the Council. Sweden secured full autonomy. The kingdom should be left in full enjoyment of its laws, liberties, privileges, and ancient customs; the taxes collected should be used in the kingdom, the king should have only Swedish councilors and courtiers, the castles of the kingdom should be given to Swedes, and upon the king's death they should be turned over to a committee consisting of six of the leading men of the realm. In Norway no specific agreement was signed, but the king never visited the country after his coronation. The administration was left in the hands of the Council, which now acted with greater authority than it had ever done since the union was first established in 1397. Fortunately, King Christopher seems to have coveted peace and comfort rather than power. He is described as short and stout, merry, and good-natured, and he evidently sought to rule in full harmony with the conditions to which he had subscribed. But for all his good intentions, he was not popular in Sweden, where the powerful Karl Knutsson Bonde coveted the throne. It had become a fixed belief among the common people that Karl Knutsson would become king. An old clairvoyant woman had told him so, and a little girl had seen a crown settle on his head while he was sitting in church. The taxes were unjust, it was claimed, and the hard times due to crop failure caused great dissatisfaction. The people said that the grain was fed to the king's horses, while they had to make bread of bark, and they nicknamed him Christopher Barkking. In Norway there was also great unrest, especially in the southeastern districts. The people rose against their *fogeds*, and in Gudbransdal Bengt Harniktsson Gyldenløve, a member of the Council, was slain.

The Hanseatic League still controlled Norwegian commerce, and the Hanseatic factory at Bergen enjoyed at this time its greatest prosperity and power. Its members treated the native population and even the city government with unbearable arrogance, and lawlessness and licentiousness passed all bounds, but the local authorities were unable to enforce the laws. The members of the Hansa had even entered the town hall, sword in hand, and had forcibly ejected the city council.[1] In 1444 the Council of the kingdom met in Bergen to discuss the situation. The opinion prevailed that the German merchants should no longer be tolerated as a state within the state, that their privileges should be reduced to what they had been in the thirteenth and fourteenth centuries.[2] Some of the councilors went to Copenhagen, and placed this proposition before the king, who sanctioned it in a royal rescript of 1444 relative to the trade of foreign merchants in Bergen. Nothing was gained, however. In 1447 the king granted the most unrestricted privileges to the Rostock merchants to trade in the city of Oslo and Tunsberg in southern Norway, while in Bergen the commandant, Olav Nilsson, the leader of the opposition to the Hanseatic merchants, struggled with determination, but under great difficulties, to enforce the new regulations. A most critical situation had been created when King Christopher suddenly died in 1448.[3]

[1] Yngvar Nielsen, *Bergen*, p. 257. *Diplomatarium Norwegicum*, I., no. 801.
[2] *Bergens Fundats*, written about 1580; published by N. Nicolaysen in *Norske Magasin*, I. *Diplomatarium Norwegicum*, vol. VII., no. 417.
[3] The Hanseatic merchants resented the attempt to restrict their privileges. In 1447 they issued a document in which they accused Olav Nilsson of the

In Trondhjem the Hanseatic merchants had gained no foothold, as they were forbidden to trade north of Bergen. Trondhjem had always been the chief center of trade with the Norwegian colonies, especially with Iceland, but this trade declined with the decay of Norwegian commerce and sea-power, and in the later Middle Ages almost nothing is known of the city's commercial activity.[1] The Hanseatic supremacy resulted, very naturally, in a stagnation of the Norwegian cities, as the native merchants were driven out of business, and the population could not grow while the trade was in the hands of unmarried foreigners, who were strictly confined within the precincts of the factory, cut off from all social intercourse with the townspeople. The attempt of Olav Nilsson and the Norwegian Council to assert Norway's sovereign authority over these foreigners was a move in the right direction, but their zeal was greater than their strength, and the effort ended in dismal failure.

12. Christian I. of Denmark and Karl Knutsson of Sweden

As King Christopher left no children, the question arose who should be chosen his successor, if the union were to be maintained. Denmark favored the union because it was considered to be the leading kingdom. In the late reigns the candidates for the throne had been selected by the Danish Council, and the kings, who resided for the most part in Denmark, had sought to give that kingdom great preponderance in the union. This time the Danes selected Christian of Oldenburg, another German, as their candidate, but this created great ill-will among the Swedes, who claimed that the Danes had broken the union agreement by constantly selecting the royal candidates without conferring with the other kingdoms. A small party in Sweden were favorably disposed towards the union, but many Swedish nobles coveted the throne. In Norway some were in favor

most arbitrary and unlawful procedure. The document is published by Professor Yngvar Nielsen in the *Christiania Videnskabs-Selskabs Forhandlinger*, 1877 and 1878. See also Yngvar Nielsen, *Af Norges Historie*, p. 110 ff. *Diplomatarium Norwegicum*, vol. XVI., no. 160.

[1] Alexander Bugge, *Nidaros's Handel og Skibsfart i Middelalderen, Festskrift udgivet i Anledning af Trondhjems 900 Aars Jubilæum, 1897, Trondhjem,* 1897. Alexander Bugge, *Studier over de norske Byers Selvstyre og Handel,* p. 131 ff. *Norges gamle Love,* anden række, vol. I., p. 116 ff.

of placing the native-born Sigurd Jonsson on the throne, but the majority were ready to abide by the choice made by the other kingdoms. In the meanwhile Karl Knutsson had matured his plans. On May 23, 1448, he entered Stockholm with 800 armed men. A mild spring rain was falling, and this was interpreted by the common people as an auspicious omen; the great noble was the man of the hour. On June 20 he was elected king of Sweden, and he was soon after crowned at Upsala. The Danes were quite surprised to learn that the union had been dissolved, but they nevertheless chose their own candidate, Christian of Oldenburg, king of Denmark.

In Norway great indecision prevailed. Sigurd Jonsson, the richest noble in the kingdom, had been chosen regent, but he would not be a candidate for the throne, though he descended from King Haakon V. The Council was divided into a Danish and a Swedish party. Archbishop Aslak Bolt and many of the councilors favored a union with Sweden, but Bishop Jens of Oslo, and the powerful baron Hartvig Krumedike, both of Danish birth, were eager to maintain a union with Denmark. They even went to Denmark as representatives of their party, and acknowledged Christian of Oldenburg king of Norway. But Archbishop Aslak Bolt with the Swedish party met at Bohus in February, 1449, and chose Karl Knutsson of Sweden.[1]

In the meantime Bishop Jens of Oslo and Hartvig Krumedike had returned from Denmark with an armed force, and the Council was summoned to meet at Oslo. None of the Swedish party would meet under these circumstances, except Archbishop Aslak Bolt, who happened to be in the city. At this meeting June 3, 1449, the Danish party chose Christian of Oldenburg king of Norway, and at a second meeting at Marstrand in July King Christian granted the Norwegians a charter with the following main stipulations:

1. The Norwegian people should retain their laws and liberties, and the Church of Norway its rights and privileges.

2. No foreigners should receive fiefs in the kingdom, nor should they be members of the Council, excepting those who already resided in Norway, or those who in the future should acquire the right of citizenship through marriage within the kingdom.

[1] Ludvig Daae, *En Krønike om Erkebiskopperne i Nidaros, Festskrift udgivet i Anledning af Trondhjems 900 Aars Jubilæum, 1897*, p. 158 ff.

3. No important matter touching Norway should be decided except with the advice of the Norwegian Council.

4. Norway should henceforth be a free elective kingdom.

5. The king should visit the kingdom every three years.

6. The trade between Norway and Denmark should be free from duties.

7. Only in cases of emergency could the Norwegian Council be summoned to meet in Denmark, and its stay there should be as short as possible.[1]

The Swedish party would not recede from their position, as they resented the use of force by the leaders of the Danish party. In the fall of 1449 Karl Knutsson came to Hamar, where he was proclaimed king of Norway. On November 20th, he was crowned in Trondhjem by Archbishop Aslak Bolt, after giving a charter in which he granted the prelates and the cathedral many privileges.[2] Fifteen Norwegian nobles were knighted, and the king even sanctioned the Tunsberg concordat of 1277 to please the archbishop. While affairs remained thus unsettled, Aslak Bolt died in 1450, and Olav Throndsson was chosen to succeed him as Archbishop of Nidaros.

After his coronation Karl Knutsson returned to Sweden, but shortly after New Year, 1450, he came to southern Norway with an army, and tried to seize Oslo, which was held by Christian's chief adherent, Hartvig Krumedike.[3] He was unable, however, to take Akershus castle, and an armistice was concluded until a council could be assembled at Halmstad, where all disputes should be settled.[4] When the Swedish and Danish councilors assembled in that city, May 1, 1450, the Swedish councilors sided with the Danes, and a treaty was concluded by which it was agreed that Karl Knutsson should surrender Norway to King Christian of Denmark;[5] that

[1] Diplomatarium Norwegicum, vol. VIII., no. 345. Arild Huitfeldt, Danmarks Riges Krønike, II., p. 845 ff.

[2] Diplomatarium Norwegicum, vol. VI., no. 530; vol. V., no. 762.

[3] Ibid., vol. X., no. 201; vol. IX., no. 308. Eirik Salmundsson, who had been made regent in Norway by King Karl Knutsson, labored hard to overcome the resistance of the Danish party in southern Norway.

[4] Ibid., vol. V., no. 765.

[5] Ibid., vol. III., no. 809; vol. VIII., no. 340. This promise was later ratified by King Karl. See Diplomatarium Norwegicum, vol. III., no. 809, no. 810.

when one of the kings died, the one surviving should be king of both realms, or a regency might be established, and the choice of a king postponed until both the kings were dead, when twelve Swedish and twelve Danish councilors should meet at Halmstad, and choose a king for both realms, who should be either a Dane or a Swede. About Norway it was stated, as a sort of afterthought, that "when it shall please God to unite again the three realms under one king, if it shall please the Norwegian Council and people to remain in the union, they shall enjoy with us, and we with them, all liberty and intercourse as stated." That Norway would remain in the union under all circumstances was, of course, taken for granted by the worthy nobles who directed the political affairs of the kingdoms.

Christian I. was crowned in Denmark October 28, 1449, and on the same day he was married to the eighteen-year-old widow of King Christopher, Dorothea of Brandenburg. The following year he arrived in Norway, and the Hanseatic merchants of Bergen, who received the young king with great pomp, gave him an escort of 300 men and five ships to accompany him to Trondhjem. After the Council had formally declared the election of Karl Knutsson to be null and void,[1] King Christian was crowned in that city with elaborate ceremonies August 2, 1450.

A new act of union drawn up in Bergen, dated August 29, 1450, specified the terms on which the two kingdoms should henceforth remain united. After a rather elaborate introduction the document goes on to say:

"We have now with our gracious lord and high-born prince, the said King Christian's counsel, will, and consent formed a firm, perpetual, and unbreakable union between the said kingdoms of Denmark and Norway, for us and many of our brethren, the Archbishop of Lund, bishops, prelates, knights and squires, the councils and inhabitants of both kingdoms, both those who now live, and those who will be born hereafter, both born and unborn, with such preface and conditions that both kingdoms, Denmark and Norway, shall henceforward remain united in brotherly love and friendship, and one shall not lord it over the other, but each kingdom is to be ruled by native-born magistrates, as shown by the privileges of both kingdoms; in

[1] *Ibid.*, vol. VIII., no. 342.

such wise that each kingdom enjoys, keeps, and uses freely its written laws, freedom and privileges, old and new, which they now have, or hereafter may receive, and that both kingdoms, Denmark and Norway, shall henceforth remain under one king and lord forevermore. And the Council of each kingdom, and its inhabitants, shall aid and assist the Council and inhabitants of the other. And one kingdom and its people shall give the other aid and consolation as the need may be. But neither kingdom shall make war without obtaining the consent of the Council of the other. But the kingdom which asks for assistance shall supply provisions and means of sustenance, and the king shall guarantee against loss. And when it shall please God to let so sad a thing happen that the king dies, then shall the kingdom in which the king dies at once invite the Council of the other kingdom, that the Councils of both may speedily assemble at Halmstad according to the stipulations in the earlier agreement regarding this place. If the king then has one legitimate son or more, then the Councils shall choose the one to be king whom they consider to be the best qualified, and the others shall be properly provided for in both kingdoms. But if such an unfortunate circumstance should occur, which God forbid, that the king has no legitimate son, then shall the Councils of both kingdoms nevertheless meet in said city, and choose the one for king whom, on behalf of both kingdoms, they consider to be best qualified. In these stipulated articles neither kingdom shall suffer any slight or neglect, and especially in the choice of the king the Council of each kingdom shall have full liberty, power, and free will, without let, hindrance, or deceit, and they shall not part until they have agreed upon the choice of a lord and king over both realms, and only one; but in such a way that each kingdom retains its old laws and justice, liberty and privileges."[1]

By this agreement an important change was made in the Norwegian constitution. The old principle of an hereditary monarchy was abandoned, and an elective kingship was substituted. This change had, however, already been made in practice. After the Norwegian royal line became extinct, circumstances had made it necessary to repeatedly place kings on the vacant throne by election. In

---

[1] *Diplomatarium Norwegicum*, vol. VIII., no. 345. *Samlinger til det norske Folks Sprog og Historie*, vol. IV., p. 344 ff.

theory the principle of hereditary kingship had, indeed, been adhered to, but as it could no longer be carried out in practice, it was becoming a mere tradition. It must be observed, however, that this tradition continued to live, and it was even strengthened by the union kings of the House of Oldenburg, who called themselves heirs to the throne of Norway, and spoke of Norway as an hereditary kingdom. If the impression could be created that, in spite of the Bergen agreement, the Oldenburg kings succeeded to the throne of Norway by right of inheritance, it would, naturally, tend to safeguard the union, and to bind Norway more closely to the kingdom of Denmark.[1]

In the articles of union the equality of the two kingdoms was strongly emphasized. One should not lord it over the other, but each should keep its laws, freedom, and privileges. The autonomy and sovereignty of Norway seemed thereby fully safeguarded, so far as this could be done on paper, but circumstances could not fail to operate against the maintenance of such an equality. The king resided in Denmark, where he was constantly surrounded by Danish councilors and officers of state, and in a not distant future he would naturally regard Denmark as the principal kingdom, if he did not already do so. Bygone events had already illustrated this so clearly that no doubt could exist as to the final outcome. The true character of the political situation soon revealed itself. Though King Christian had agreed to come to Norway once every three years, he did not visit the kingdom above four times after his coronation during a long reign of thirty-one years, but the administration of Norwegian affairs he, nevertheless, took into his own hands, and left the Council of the Kingdom almost wholly out of consideration. He even attempted to force upon the people the unscrupulous adventurer Marcellus as Archbishop of Trondhjem, though the chapter had already chosen Olav Throndsson. Only the refusal of the Pope to consecrate that unworthy candidate saved the Church of Norway from this humiliation.[2] His royal edicts were always prefaced with the autocratic phrases: "We, Christian, by the grace of God, King of Denmark-Norway, of the Wends and Goths, Count of Oldenburg

---

[1] T. H. Aschehoug, *Statsforfatningen i Norge og Danmark indtil 1814,* p. 197 f.

[2] R. Keyser, *Den norske Kirkes Historie under Katholicismen,* II., p. 548 ff.

and Delmenhorst," etc. The Council is seldom mentioned in these documents, as if its advice or consent was a matter of slight importance. The seal of the kingdom was kept by the Danish chancellor, while the Norwegian chancellor became a mere judicial officer, and the office of *drotsete*, the highest in the kingdom, was virtually abolished. The Council, too, was allowing the control of public affairs to slip from its weakening grip. This became especially true after a number of immigrated Danes had become members. They had settled permanently in Norway, where they had gained wealth and social standing by marrying Norwegian heiresses, but they were still Danes in sympathy, and as they were not deeply concerned with affairs of local administration, their presence in the Council rapidly destroyed its last vestige of efficiency and usefulness, and it gradually became a mere appendix to the Council of Denmark. The Norwegian clergy was still native-born and national-spirited, but it had been weakened like the aristocracy, and could no longer assert its former independence. Coming events cast their shadows before. Christian, the king by divine right and the grace of God, had given the Norwegian people a first installment of Oldenburg absolutism.

King Christian's policy was wholly dictated by dynastic and Danish interests. In Bergen Olav Nilsson had struggled earnestly, though not with proper moderation, to enforce the laws against the Hanseatic merchants. Sometimes he had even used violent and lawless means to subdue them. While Christopher lived, he supported Nilsson, but Christian changed this method. He needed the support of the Hansa towns in a war with Sweden, and he considered it more important to win their friendship than to compel obedience to the laws of Norway. In 1453 he arrived in Bergen accompanied by his queen, and summoned Nilsson to answer to charges preferred against him by the merchants. Nilsson sought safety in flight, and only after the king had issued a safe-conduct did he return to Bergen to answer the accusations. King Christian confiscated all his fiefs, and appointed a Swede, Magnus Gren, commandant in Bergen. But the doughty baron would not submit. He seized the strong castle of Elfsborg at the mouth of the Göta river, and threatened to hand it over to the Swedes, if the king did not return to him his fiefs, and reinstate him as commandant. The king now found it advisable to yield, and Olav Nilsson returned to Bergen. But while at Elfsborg he had sent out privateers to prey upon Hanseatic merchant ships, and the merchants conspired to kill him. When he appeared at the city *thing*, he was attacked by an armed force, and when he fled to the monastery of Munkeliv, the merchants, to the number of 2000, stormed the monastery, slew Bishop Thorleiv and several priests before the altar of the church, and killed in all sixty men. Nilsson had sought refuge in the tower, but they set fire to the buildings. The monastery was destroyed, and he was seized and put to death.[1] King Christian did nothing to punish the offenders, though they were sentenced to rebuild the monastery at their own expense. "The king did not care much about it, as it pleased him that Olav was killed, because he had opposed the king, and had offended him by seizing Elfsborg castle," says the chronicler.[2] In 1469 he even granted them full pardon upon the request of the cities of Lübeck and Hamburg, and released them, on behalf of the kingdom, from any obligation to pay damages. He had, indeed, earned the praise of the Lübeck chronicler, who calls him "ein gnädich, myldich, sachtmodich vorste." [3]

Other arbitrary and unstatesmanlike acts of the king were equally prejudicial to the interests of the realm. In 1469 his daughter Margaret was married to King James III. of Scotland, but Christian I., who spent money lavishly, and always was in financial difficulties, could not pay the stipulated dowry. In the marriage contract he agreed to annul the annuity payable to the kingdom of Norway in

---

[1] William Christensen, *Unionskongerne og Hansestæderne*. Munkeliv monastery of the Benedictine order was founded about 1110. It suffered much from the ravages of the Victual Brothers, and in 1421–1434 it was changed to a monastery of the order of St. Birgitta with double convent, one for monks, and one for nuns. With the permission of the Pope this was done by King Eirik of Pomerania and his queen, Philippa, who introduced this order in Norway and Denmark. Lange, *De norske Klostres Historie*. Ludvig Daae, *Kong Christiern den førstes norske Historie, 1448–1458*, Christiania, 1879.

[2] *Ditmars Chronik*, edited by Grautoff, II., 180. Quoted by Lange.

[3] J. P. Willebrandt, *Hansische Chronik*, Lübeck, 1748, III., 81. See also *Samlinger til det norske Folks Sprog og Historie*, vol. IV., p. 300. *Lübeckische Chroniken*, edited by Grautoff, II., p. 429. Quoted by J. E. Sars in *Udsigt over den norske Historie*, III., p. 157. Ludvig Daae, *Christiern den førstes norske Historie*, p. 109; *Historiske Skildringer*, p. 33 ff.

consideration of the cession of the Hebrides according to the treaty of Perth, and also the unpaid arrear of this annuity. Of the 60,000 gulden to be paid as dowry only 10,000 should be paid immediately, and as security for the balance he mortgaged the Orkneys to Scotland by a document dated September 8, 1468. When a fleet arrived in Copenhagen to bring the bride home, he was not able to pay more than 2000 gulden, and as security for the remaining 8000 he also included the Shetland Islands in the mortgage, 1469. All this was done without consulting the Norwegian Council, and as these debts were never paid, the mortgaged islands were annexed to Scotland, and Norway was thus made to pay the whole expense of the marriage of the king's daughter.[1]

King Christian I. was a tall and stately man, fond of luxury and display. R. Keyser characterizes him as follows: "He was a shrewd statesman according to the standards of his times, but he lacked sincerity and mental depth. He was active, but cannot be called a good ruler; he was brave without being a great general; he was, finally, such a wretched manager of the finances of his kingdoms that the Swedes very aptly called him 'the bottomless purse.' "[2] In his administrative policy he was guided by family interests and love of power and dominion rather than by true concern for the welfare of his realm and the happiness of his subjects. The year after his coronation as king of Norway, we find him engaged in a war with Sweden, which was begun for the most trivial reasons, the real cause being jealousy and rivalry between the two kings. An armed force from Norway attacked Vermland even before war had been declared, but in 1452 Karl Knutsson formally declared war against Christian I. and marched with an army into Skåne. Trøndelagen was occupied by a Swedish force under Göran Karlsson, and another attack was directed against Bohus in southeastern Norway.[3] An armistice was concluded in 1453, which lasted for two years, but in 1455 the war was renewed.

Karl Knutsson was a weak and unpopular king. He had

[1] Fredrik Scheel, Ørknøerne og Hjaltland i Pantsættelsestiden 1469-1667, Historisk Tidsskrift, femte række, vol. III., p. 381 ff.

[2] R. Keyser, Den norske Kirkes Historie under Katholicismen, II., p. 569 f.

[3] Ludvig Daae, Kong Christiern den førstes norske Historie.

failed to secure the throne of Norway, Gothland had been taken by Christian I., and he had many powerful opponents among the nobles, who reluctantly had placed him on the throne. In 1457 his old enemy, Archbishop Jöns of Upsala, nailed a proclamation on the door of the cathedral, renouncing his allegiance to him. Stockholm was quickly invested, and Karl Knutsson, who found the situation hopeless, fled to Danzig, where he was harbored by King Casimir IV. of Poland. Christian I., who by fair promises had gained strong support among the nobility, was placed on the throne of Sweden. In 1460 he was also elected Duke of Holstein and Count of Schleswig and Stormarn, whereby these provinces were united with the crown of Denmark. No king in the North had ever ruled so large a realm as the one now united under his scepter, but it was loosely knit together and badly governed. The outward greatness represented no corresponding internal strength. J. E. Sars says: "Never has Norway been governed so wretchedly as under the first king of a dynasty which, to such a remarkable degree, should become the object of the Norwegian people's loyalty and devotion. The thirty-one years during which this king ruled belong to the saddest in our history, not only because of the many harmful measures due to his weakness and recklessness, his lack of will and ability to do his duty to Norway, but also of the perfect tranquillity which continued to exist in spite of his maladministration. But that great ill-will had been quietly stored up became manifest when the king died." [1]

In Sweden King Christian's government was no less unpopular than in Norway. His purse was always empty, and as he agreed to pay claims to the heirs of the former princes of Schleswig-Holstein to the amount of 103,000 gulden, he resorted to the levying of heavy taxes and loans, secured by mortgages in castles and crown lands, to increase his revenues. These heavy burdens created the greatest discontent. In 1463, while the king tried to levy an extra tax for an expedition against Russia, a revolt broke out, led by Archbishop Jöns of Upsala, who was an irreconcilable opponent both of Karl Knutsson and the Danes. The uprising was suppressed with great severity, and the archbishop was brought captive to Denmark, but King Christian returned home only to find that new trouble had

[1] J. E. Sars, *Udsigt over den norske Historie*, III., p. 159 ff.

broken out. In the winter of 1464 he led an army into Sweden, but was defeated at Helleskog by the Swedish peasants under Sten Sture. When he also found that Stockholm was closely besieged, he abandoned the campaign and returned home. Karl Knutsson was recalled, but Archbishop Jöns, who had returned from his captivity, stirred up his partisans against him, and when he found the situation as hopeless as before, he formally abdicated, promised never again to aspire to the throne, and retired to his estates in Finland, 1465. The ambitious archbishop was now chosen regent, but he did not long retain the high office, as other nobles also aspired to the honor. The following year Eirik Axelsson Thott succeeded him, and the crafty prelate died soon after on the island of Öland, "poor and in exile; mourned by none, hated by many, and feared by all." [1] Karl Knutsson again became king of Sweden, but Christian I. would not give up the hope of regaining the Swedish throne, an aim which had become more difficult of attaining since the struggle was no longer a mere contest between rival aspirants to the throne, but a patriotic endeavor of the Swedish people to rid themselves of Danish overlordship. On his death-bed Karl Knutsson exhorted the people to fight to the utmost against the Danes, and Sten Sture, who was chosen regent by the Council, rallied the people round his standards to fight for the national cause. King Christian does not seem to have fully grasped the situation. In 1471 he arrived before Kalmar with a fleet of seventy ships, and advanced a little later to Stockholm. He still hoped to accomplish his purpose through negotiations, but if this failed, he trusted in his armed knights. He landed his forces, and took up a strong position at Brunkeberg, but on the 10th of October he was attacked by Sten Sture, and suffered a crushing defeat. Christian himself was brought to his ships severely wounded. The victory was decisive; Sweden had successfully maintained her independence.

In 1474 King Christian made a journey to Rome with a large escort. In Rotenburg in Germany he visited Emperor Frederick III., who received him well, hoping to gain his support against Charles the Bold and the Turks. The Emperor united Holstein and Stormarn into a dukedom, into which he also incorporated Dit-

---

[1] O. A. Øverland, *Norges Historie*, vol. V., p. 161.

marsken, which had hitherto been an independent republic, and this new duchy of Holstein he granted King Christian I. as a fief, evidently for the purpose of gaining his good will. Why Christian undertook this journey is not known, and little good came of it. His expenses were large, and when he came to Italy, he had to borrow money from the Hanseatic merchants, who were willing enough to grant him the necessary loans, knowing that they would be able to obtain charters and trade privileges in return. By a letter of September 6, 1474, the king annulled all restrictions placed on the trade of the Hanseatic merchants in Oslo and Tunsberg, "for the good will and love which the Rostock merchants had shown him," and confirmed all the privileges which had been granted them by his predecessors. In 1469 he had issued a letter which insured them against competition from the Hollanders, by restricting the trade of Holland merchants in Bergen to one or two cargoes a year. King Christian had diligently sought to please the Hanseatic merchants, and to maintain their hated commercial monopoly. In vain the people of Bergen complained of outrages committed by them. The king would not be annoyed. He suffered the laws to sleep and his own pledges to remain a dead letter, but the ill-will created by his wretched rule did not find expression until after his death, which occurred May 22, 1481.

13. THE REIGN OF KING HANS (JOHN)

At the time of King Christian's death his son and successor Hans was twenty-six years old. As early as 1458 the Norwegian Council had made a written promise that he should succeed his father on the throne of Norway. "When it shall please God," says the letter, "to call our gracious lord from this world, then will we in love and obedience accept and receive his eldest son, if God lets him live; but if he dies, then his gracious son who is the next oldest, son after son, to whom we now, one after another with this our open letter and power pay homage and receive as our rightful lord and king of Norway, and we will faithfully serve and obey him."[1] In 1480 this

---

[1] *Diplomatarium Norwegicum*, III., no. 842. Christian I. had four sons: Knut and Olav, who died in childhood, and Hans and Frederick, who survived him.

promise was renewed by the Norwegian Council in Halmstad, where Hans was made coregent with his father.[1] Even in his father's lifetime he had been in Norway, where he had exercised royal administrative authority, and had styled himself "The son of King Christian, elected King of Denmark, and rightful Heir to the throne of Norway," but when Christian died, the Norwegians showed no inclination to accept Hans as their king in spite of these promises. Misgovernment had made them cautious, and they were now fully determined to seek redress for past wrongs before another king was placed on the throne. On February 1, 1482, sixteen members of the Norwegian Council entered into an agreement with deputies from Sweden that the two kingdoms should aid one another in defending their rights and liberties, and that in the election of a king neither should take any step not sanctioned by the Council of the other. The Norwegian councilors at the same time issued a letter in which they recounted the injuries which the kingdom of Norway had suffered in King Christian's reign: the mortgaging of the Orkney and Shetland islands, the outrages committed in Bergen by the Hanseatic merchants in 1455, when no attempt was made by the king to punish the guilty parties, the privileges granted by Christian I. to the German cities, the harmful journeys by which the Council had been compelled to leave the kingdom, the numerous wars which had been forced upon the people without the consent of the Council, that the revenues of the kingdom had been sent out of the country, that Bohus and other fiefs had been granted to foreigners against the advice of the Council, and that these foreigners had received greater powers and privileges in Christian's time than ever at any time before. "When we made complaints against the foreigners, we could receive no justice, but if one of our own citizens broke the laws, he was most severely punished."[2] This indictment of the late king breathes a bitter resentment which could not easily be appeased.

In former elections the Danish Council had at times acted too hastily; this time it proceeded with greater caution. The situation

[1] J. E. Sars, *Udsigt over den norske Historie*, III., p. 160. R. Keyser, *Den norske Kirkes Historie under Katholicismen*, II., p. 570, 580.

[2] Hadorph, *Två gambla Rijmkrönikor, Bihang*, p. 302 ff., quoted by J. E. Sars, *Udsigt over den norske Historie*, III., p. 161.

was difficult. Sweden had already broken away from the union, the duchies of Schleswig-Holstein were but loosely connected with the crown, and in Norway great dissatisfaction prevailed. Under these circumstances Denmark could not proceed to elect a king alone without incurring the risk of destroying the union. In August, 1482, the Danish and Swedish councilors met at Kalmar, where they agreed that peace should exist between the two kingdoms, and that they should be united under the same king, but the Swedes would not elect a king, as the Norwegian councilors were not present. A new meeting was to be assembled at Halmstad, January 13, 1483, as it was hoped that Norway would then be represented. In the meantime the Danes tried to persuade the Norwegian councilors to join them in electing Hans, but this they would not do until they received full assurance of redress of grievances. They were especially aggrieved, because a Danish noble, Jørgen Larensson, had been made commandant of Bohus castle without the consent of the Council. They determined to drive away the hated commandant by force, and the people of the neighboring districts rallied to their support. The Council wrote to their Swedish colleagues complaining of the humiliations and grievances which Norway had suffered. The Danes urged the Norwegians to desist from the siege of Bohus castle, but the councilors replied in a second letter to their Swedish brethren that "it would be a harmful peace if each realm did not maintain its rights at home, or defend its own thanes and territories. According to the terms of the act of union, each kingdom should aid the other herein instead of placing obstacles in its way." [1] The Swedes gave them no support in the attack on Bohus, but invited them to meet with the Swedish and Danish councilors in Halmstad, January 13, 1483, to negotiate regarding the interests and welfare of the three realms.[2] The besiegers were unable to capture the strong castle, and as the Danes removed the commandant, the Council found that under the circumstances they could do no better than to attend the Halmstad conference. Sixteen Danes and nine Norwegians met on

[1] J. E. Sars, *Udsigt over den norske Historie*, III., p. 162. Hadorph, *Två gambla Rijmkrönikor, Bihang*, p. 309 f.

[2] *Diplomatarium Norwegicum*, III., no. 939. Hadorph, *Två gambla Rijmkrönikor, Bihang*, p. 314 f.

the date fixed. Two weeks later four Swedish delegates arrived, but as they had no power to participate in the election of a king, the Danes and Norwegians chose Hans to be king of Denmark and Norway, and issued a charter according to which he should rule both kingdoms. In this document, signed and sworn to by the king, every precaution seems to have been taken to safeguard the privileges of the church, to guarantee the laws, liberties, and full equality of the two kingdoms, and to secure full assurance of redress of grievances. The king promised to maintain the rights and privileges of the church and the clergy as they had been confirmed by the Pope, and to rule each kingdom according to its own laws and charters. No foreigners should be made members of the Council of the Kingdom, nor should castles or fiefs be granted to foreigners, but the kingdom should be ruled by native-born men. No taxes should be levied, no city, castle, lands, or fiefs should be mortgaged or sold, no officials appointed, no one should be made a member of the Council, no privileges should be granted to foreign merchants except by the advice and consent of the Council of the Kingdom. Each kingdom should have its own archives and treasury, and each should mint its own coin, which should be of equal value. The king should spend an equal length of time in each kingdom, and when he was not present in the realm, a commission consisting of four members of the Council should have full authority to maintain law and order. The king also promised to redeem the lands and revenues belonging to the kingdom of Norway, which had been alienated in the reign of his father, King Christian I., and to see that full restitution was made for the outrages committed in Bergen against Olav Nilsson and others. The Norwegian Council, furthermore, was to meet once every two years in Bergen and Oslo alternately, whether the king was present in the kingdom or not, and the king pledged himself to sanction and enforce all its decrees.[1]

King Hans was crowned in Copenhagen, May 18, 1483, and in Trondhjem July 20 of the same year.

[1] C. G. Styffe, *Bidrag til Skandinaviens Historie*, IV., p. lx. Yngvar Nielsen, *Det norske Rigsraad*, p. 341. Arild Huitfeldt, *Kong Hans*, p. 37 ff. King Hans' charter is found in *Samlinger til det norske Folks Sprog og Historie*, vol. IV., p. 347 ff.

In Sweden the able Sten Sture was regent. He did not attempt to seize the crown, as Karl Knutsson had done, but he did not favor the election of Hans, and seems to have opposed a union with Denmark on any conditions. The councilors had, indeed, agreed to a union with Denmark and Norway under a joint king, but in consenting to accept Hans as king of Sweden, they submitted a charter which would place all power in the hands of the nobles, and reduce the king to a mere name. As these terms could not be accepted by the Danish councilors, no choice was made, and the question continued to be agitated. Sten Sture was supported by the common people, but the nobles opposed him, and in order to drive him from power, they organized a strong party of opposition against him, and turned to King Hans for aid. Sture, who still championed Swedish independence, would not yield, and war broke out in 1497. The struggle could not last long, as the forces placed in the field by King Hans and his supporters were too strong to be successfully resisted. Elfsborg was taken, and a large Danish army advanced against Kalmar. Sture hastened to Stockholm to defend the capital, but the Danes seized Brunkeberg, and after defeating a force of Dalkarlean peasants who were marching to his aid, they took Stockholm; Elfsborg fell, and Sture was forced to give up the struggle. On November 25, 1497, Hans was proclaimed king of Sweden, and the union of the three kingdoms was again established, although Sweden, as represented by Sten Sture's party, had entered into the new compact as a most unwilling partner. In order to make the union stable and permanent, the Swedish Council agreed that Prince Christian, the son of King Hans, should succeed his father on the throne, and he was formally hailed as heir to the throne of Sweden at Stockholm in 1499.

The commercial affairs of the North were at this time in a chaotic state. Hostilities had broken out between England and Denmark-Norway, because English merchants continued to trade with Iceland, although the trade with the Norwegian colonies was a crown monopoly. In Norway the ill-will against the Hanseatic merchants had been increased by the outrages in Bergen, and the murder of Olav Nilsson in 1455, to such a degree that in the charter issued by King Hans in 1483 most important trade regulations were made, which, if carried out, would have destroyed the commercial monopoly of the Hanseatic League. Merchants from all countries should be allowed to trade in Norway without hindrance, and the Hollanders, especially, should enjoy the same freedom as of old, but the Hanseatic merchants should not be allowed to carry on trade with Iceland, nor should the king grant any privileges to foreign merchants, except with the advice of the Council.[1] Lübeck and the other Hansa towns understood what the ultimate result would be if this provision was carried into effect, and a struggle began between Denmark-Norway and the Hanseatic cities, which resulted in the discomfiture of the Hanseatic League in the first part of the next century. The contest, which began as diplomatic negotiations, soon turned into a struggle between buccaneers, supported secretly or openly by both sides, and finally it developed into an open war in which large fleets fought great naval battles. During the buccaneering activity in the early part of the conflict, the Baltic and the North Sea were swept by professional corsairs like Pining and Pothorst, and great damage was done to commerce. Loud complaints were made, especially by the Hanseatic merchants of London, of these freebooters, who preyed extensively on English commerce; but peaceful conditions gradually returned only after Denmark and Norway in 1489 modified the charter regarding trade in the interest of the Hanseatic merchants. On January 20, 1490, King Hans and Henry VII. of England concluded a treaty of peace and friendly intercourse between their realms. The trade with Iceland was made free, not only for the English, but also for the Hollanders and the Hanseatic cities.[2]

King Hans had been willing enough to subscribe to charters, but in the keeping of them he emulated his father King Christian I. He had agreed not to grant castles or fiefs to foreigners, but in his reign Danish nobles held Akershus, Bohus, and Bergen; the Dane Anders Muus became Bishop of Oslo,[3] and another, Erick Valkendorf, was

[1] B. E. Bendixen, *Tyske Haandverkere paa norsk Grund i Middelalderen, Skrifter udgivet af Videnskabs-Selskabet i Christiania*, 1911. King Hans' charter, *Samlinger til det norske Folks Sprog og Historie*, IV., p. 347 ff. Arild Huitfeldt, *Kong Hans*, p. 9.

[2] *Diplomatarium Norwegicum*, VI., no. 609.

[3] R. Keyser, *Den norske Kirkes Historie under Katholicismen*, II., p. 594.

made Archbishop of Trondhjem. Now as before the charters remained a dead letter, though the king had pledged himself in the strongest terms to rule according to them. No such overt harm was done the kingdom in Hans' reign as in that of his predecessor, but the disappointment was, nevertheless, great and the dissatisfaction general. Danish *lensmænd* and *fogeds* still remained in charge of the local administration, though the charter stated that the kingdom should be ruled by native-born men, and as these foreign officials used their office to enrich themselves, they often treated the people with intolerable injustice. The *bønder* knew how to resist. When their patience was exhausted, they seized the *fogeds* and put them to death.[1] They lacked neither the will nor the ability to defend their rights, but there were no leaders like Sten Sture in Sweden to organize a general uprising, and give it a national consecration. The leading men of the kingdom were divided into two parties, one favoring Denmark, and the other Sweden, but there was no national Norwegian party to maintain the autonomy of the realm and the chartered rights of the people. The leader of the Danish party at this time was Hartvig Krumedike, commandant of Bohus castle, and a special favorite of the king. The leader of the Swedish party was Knut Alvsson, commandant of Akershus castle, who on the mother's side was of Swedish descent. The fight between the nobles and their adherents has been interpreted by some writers as a national struggle in which Knut Alvsson represented the cause of Norwegian national independence, but this episode can scarcely be regarded as anything but a feud between rival factions without any deeper national significance. Alvsson lacked the qualities of a leader, and the struggle with Krumedike seems to have been inspired by personal enmity rather than by lofty ideas of an independent Norway.[2] The direct

---

[1] O. A. Øverland, *Norges Historie*, V., p. 189 ff.

[2] "There is nothing to indicate that Knut Alvsson was prominent in any respect except through his wealth and family connections. In a contemporary Danish chronicle he is characterized as a simple-minded man, a tool in the hands of Swedish traitors, *i.e.* the anti-union party in Sweden with the regent, Sten Sture, at its head, and there is reason to believe that this characterization agrees with actual conditions." J. E. Sars, *Udsigt over den norske Historie*, III., p. 171. See also R. Keyser, *Den norske Kirkes Historie under Katholicismen*, II., p. 590.

cause of this revolt was a local disturbance in Romerike, where the *foged*, Lasse Skjold, had so exasperated the people by his extortions that they rose against him, and put him to death. The uprising, although not dangerous, assumed such proportions that Knut Alvsson, who was commandant of Akershus, feared that he would be unable to cope with it, and he asked Henry Krumedike of Bohus for aid. Krumedike not only failed to respond, but it seems that he had succeeded in arousing the king's suspicion as to Alvsson's loyalty, and that he had been secretly encouraged by the king to watch his movements. Alvsson lost the king's favor; he was relieved of his command of Akershus, and a Danish noble, Peder Griis, was appointed to succeed him. A bloody feud ensued, and Alvsson turned to Sweden for aid. He raised an armed force in that kingdom, and made a raid into Norway, but he was driven back by the king's adherents. Those who were dissatisfied flocked to his standards, and Erick Gyldenstjerne, the Danish commandant of Elfsborg, joined him; likewise, also, Nils Ravaldsson of Olavsborg in Viken. Akershus, Tunsberg,[1] Marstrand, and Sarpsborg were taken, and Krumedike was striving to hold his own at Bohus. King Hans could not come to Norway, but he sent his son Christian, now twenty-one years old, to take command.[2] The prince showed a most resolute spirit, and soon got the situation under control. Bohus was relieved, and Gyldenstjerne surrendered Elfsborg after a few days' siege, though a Swedish army under Alvsson had arrived in the neighborhood to support him. When he arrived in the Swedish camp, he was killed by the angry soldiers, who looked upon him as a traitor. After an expedition into Vermland, Prince Christian returned to Denmark, leaving Krumedike in command. Tunsberg was soon captured, and Knut Alvsson hastened to the support of Akershus, but as he feared the outcome of an armed conflict, he decided to try negotiations. Provided with a safe-conduct, he boarded Krumedike's ship. But a quarrel between the rivals ensued, and Alvsson was slain, 1502. For this misdeed Krumedike was

---

[1] Ludvig Daae, *Historisk Tidsskrift*, vol. I., p. 500 ff. The castle of Tunsberghus was destroyed in this feud.

[2] Iver Hesselberg, *Christian den anden i Norge, Samlinger til det norske Folks Sprog og Historie*, II., p. 3 ff.

compelled to leave Norway, and the uprising was not put down till 1504.

In 1506 Prince Christian returned to Norway with full royal [1] power.[2] He was a man of great energy and ability, influenced by the new ideas of humanism and the Renaissance. Disposed by nature to brook no restraint, he paid little attention to conventionalities. In Bergen he became enamored with a fair damsel, Dyveke (the little dove), whose mother, Sigbrit Villums, was shopkeeper in the city. She was introduced to the prince at a ball, and being greatly impressed with her rare beauty, "he danced with her," says the old historian, "and this was the cause of his dancing away from these three kingdoms, Denmark, Sweden, and Norway." This is undoubtedly an exaggeration, but Dyveke became his mistress, and the attachment of the prince for the girl and her mother plays an important part in his reign. In public as in private life he was guided by his own impulses, which inclined him to favor the common people. He soon became their favorite, and many a goblet of ale was drunk to the health of the good Prince Christian. He sought to encourage Norwegian trade, and granted the merchants of Amsterdam permission to trade in Bergen and everywhere in Norway.[3] In 1508 he annulled the special privileges of the Rostock merchants in Oslo and Tunsberg, and granted them the same rights as native citizens, when they settled permanently in the city, and bore their share of the public burdens. The following year he placed important restrictions upon the Hanseatic merchants of Bergen and increased the privileges of the native traders. The castle of the city was also rebuilt, so that the commandant ultimately became able to force the Hanseatic factory into submission. The people of the cities might have reason to be satisfied with Prince Christian's efforts to improve conditions, but in the country districts the Danish *fogeds* were still allowed to continue their extortionate practices unmolested. In 1508 a new revolt broke out in southeastern Norway. Under the leadership of one of their own number, Herlog Høfudfat, the *bønder* of Hedemarken rose against the Danish *fogeds*, slew one of them, and

[1] C. F. Allen, *De tre nordiske Rigers Historie*, I., p. 436, 674.
[2] Yngvar Nielsen, *Bergen*, p. 267 ff. Arild Huitfeldt, *Danmarks Historie*.
[3] *Diplomatarium Norwegicum*, VI., no. 647.

drove away another. Christian suppressed the revolt with the cruel severity usually practiced in those days, when the rulers knew better how to punish offenses than to remove their cause. The leaders of the uprising were captured and brought to Akershus, where they were put to the torture and executed as traitors. The heads of the unfortunate offenders were put on stakes, and exhibited to the gaze of the multitude; that of Herlog Høfudfat was placed in the center and crowned in mockery with an iron crown. Even Bishop Karl of Hamar, who on very slight evidence was held to be implicated in the uprising, was thrown into prison, and it is a singular manifestation of the growing weakness of the church that he was suffered to remain incarcerated till his death without being convicted of any wrong-doing, even without being granted a trial.[1] This unnecessary harsh-ness reveals in the prince an innate cruelty, an irresponsible fierce-ness of temper, which proved his undoing after years of struggles had fully awakened the bloodthirstiness of his savage heart. In his administration of state affairs Prince Christian was as despotic as he was hard-hearted in dealing with opponents and offenders. The Council was almost wholly disregarded, and could exercise no influence; Norwegian nobles were deprived of their fiefs, and Danes were appointed in their place in open violation of the charters. The kingdom was not ruled by native-born officials according to the charters, but by the king with the aid of the Danish nobles, while the power of the Council was chiefly limited to judicial matters.[2] But Christian's impulsive nature and democratic manners had gained for him a reputation as the people's friend, and he became a great favorite of the common classes,[3] a distinction of which he was not wholly undeserving; for though a tyrant at heart, he possessed an instinctive appreciation of justice, and as his habits inclined him to favor the common people, he often championed their rights, if for no other reason than out of spite against the nobles, whom he hated. The kingdom of Sweden was tied to King Hans and the union by

---

[1] Ludvig Daae, *Biskop Karl af Hamar, Historisk Tidsskrift*, fjerde række, III., p. 327 ff.

[2] Yngvar Nielsen, *Det norske Rigsraad*, p. 305.

[3] R. Keyser, *Den norske Kirkes Historie under Katholicismen*, II., p. 595 ff. *Danmarks Riges Historie*, III., p. 116 ff. J. E. Sars, *Udsigt over den norske Historie*, III., p. 175. H. Behrmann, *Kong Kristiern den andens Historie*.

very slender threads of loyalty, and these were suddenly rent by the king's unfortunate expedition to Ditmarsken.

It has already been stated elsewhere that Emperor Frederick III. incorporated this province together with Stormarn in the duchy of Holstein, which he granted King Christian I. of Denmark in 1474. Ditmarsken was a marshy district between the rivers Elbe and Eider, protected against inundations by great dikes along the North Sea. The land had to be ditched and drained, but as the Ditmarskers were industrious and intelligent, their land was well tilled, and their country was a republic, where the people governed themselves. To the rapacious nobility and land-hungry kings this morsel was very tempting, but King Christian died before he could take possession of it. King Hans was determined to make good his claim, and the nobles joined his standards in unusually large numbers in anticipation of the rich booty which they were sure to secure. In 1500 Hans marched against Ditmarsken with an army of 15,000 men, consisting of nobles and German mercenaries.[1] The Ditmarskers retreated before this large force, but on the road to Hemmingstedt, their leader, Wolf Isebrand, fortified himself with a force of 500 men, and placed some guns in position. When King Hans arrived on February 17th, rain was falling in torrents, and the Danish army was crowded together on the narrow road, on either side of which were broad ditches filled with water. The Ditmarskers opened fire. The Danes could neither advance nor retreat, and a fearful panic ensued. All order and discipline vanished, and the army was converted into a struggling mass of horses and men trying in vain to extricate themselves. The horses sank to their knees in the mud, or tumbled headlong with their riders into the ditches. The spirited attack of the Ditmarskers sealed the doom of the entrapped army. The dikes were cut, and the North Sea rolled its billows over the marshy plains, while the peasants jumped around on their long poles, dealing death and destruction on every hand. The king escaped, but the army was destroyed; the Danebrog banner was lost, and enormous quantities of supplies fell into the hands of the Ditmarskers.[2]

---

[1] The statement made by old writers that the army numbered 30,000 men has long since been discarded as erroneous.

[2] Chr. Molbeck, *Historie om Ditmarskerkrigen i 1500*, Copenhagen, 1813.

King Hans' defeat made a deep impression on the whole North. In Sweden, where the people had grown restive under his rule, because he had failed to keep his promise to rule according to the charters, his discomfiture caused great excitement, and soon a well-organized revolt was set on foot. Sten Sture was again chosen regent, and the castles through the country were seized in rapid succession until only Borgholm and Kalmar remained in the hands of the king's adherents. Stockholm was ably defended by Queen Christina. The city was treacherously surrendered to Sten Sture in the fall of 1501, but not till in the spring, when all stores were exhausted, did the brave queen surrender the castle. King Hans himself arrived the day after with a fleet of thirty vessels, too late to be of any service. When Sten Sture died in 1503, Svante Sture was chosen to succeed him. An armistice was concluded, and the Councils of the three kingdoms should meet at Kalmar to negotiate a settlement of the difficulties, but Svante Sture did not appear, and in 1506 hostilities were revived.

As Denmark was again becoming a naval power, the campaigns of the next three years were largely waged on the sea. King Hans had hired ship-builders in Holland, and many vessels were added to the fleet every year. In 1502 he came to Stockholm with thirty ships; in 1505 he arrived in Kalmar with twice that number. Denmark was beginning to develop the royal navy which in future years was to be her main strength. The islands of Öland and Gothland, which were still in the hands of the Danes, afforded them a most favorable vantage ground, whence their able sea-captains, Jens Holgerssøn, Otto Rud, and Søren Norby whom the king had made chief commander of the royal fleet, harried the Swedish coasts, and swept the Baltic Sea clean of merchant vessels going to and from Sweden. Søren Norby captured Kastelholm in the Åland Islands, and Otto Rud ravaged the coasts of Finland and sacked Åbo. The plan was to destroy all commerce with Sweden, and starve the kingdom into submission. In 1509 the leaders of the Swedish uprising had to yield. They promised to pay the king 12,000 marks, and his queen, Christina, 1000 marks a year until the Councils of the three realms could assemble in joint meeting to place either King Hans or his son Christian on the throne of Sweden; but the peace did not last long. In 1510 Lübeck declared war against King Hans, and Sweden seized the opportunity to join the Hanseatic cities on the Baltic coast in a coalition against Denmark. Jens Holgerssøn, who was made commander of the Danish fleet, fought a great naval battle with the Lübeckers off Bornholm, August 9, 1511. The combat was indecisive, both sides claiming the victory. A second battle took place on the 14th of the same month near the coast of Mecklenburg with the same result. The next year Lübeck made peace on terms very favorable to Denmark; the Hanseatic cities could no longer claim naval supremacy in the North.

The creation of a navy was the one great service which King Hans rendered the kingdom of Denmark. In his efforts to subdue Sweden he was unsuccessful. Svante Sture died in 1512, but Sten Sture the Younger was chosen to succeed him as regent, and when peace was concluded in 1512, Sweden renewed the promises of 1509, but the union was not reëstablished. In 1513 King Hans died, quite suddenly, fifty-eight years of age.

14. LITERATURE AND INTELLECTUAL LIFE IN THE FOURTEENTH AND FIFTEENTH CENTURIES

In Norway, as elsewhere in the Middle Ages, the church was the custodian of the higher intellectual culture, as well as of the religious training of the people. As the kingdom had no university, the only seats of learning were the cathedral or Latin schools connected with the cathedral chapters. According to universal practice, each cathedral maintained a higher school (cathedral school) under the leadership of a scholasticus, or schoolmaster, where the students were instructed in the branches necessary for those who were to take holy orders. Most of the parish priests had received their training in the cathedral schools, aside from the private tuition by which they were prepared to enter the schools, and their own diligent study in the libraries connected with the cathedrals. Those who wished to get a university training had to go abroad. In the thirteenth and fourteenth centuries Paris, Orleans, Prague, and Bologna were much frequented by Norwegian students; and later Oxford, Cambridge, Louvain, Leyden, Cologne, Leipzig, and others were also sought.

In 1418 the University of Rostock was founded, and because of the lively commercial intercourse which the Hanseatic merchants maintained with the North, the Norwegian students found it most convenient to go to Rostock, which in a sense became the University of Norway.[1] The cathedral chapters maintained here a separate residence for the Norwegian students, the *Domus Sancti Olavi*, and the university records show that they attended in considerable numbers. Even after the University of Copenhagen was founded in 1479, the Norwegian students continued to go to Rostock,[2] until after the Reformation, when the University of Wittenberg became especially attractive to Lutherans. Not till in the seventeenth century, when the kings by royal decrees made it difficult for Norwegians and Danes to visit foreign universities, did the stream of Norwegian students turn to Copenhagen.

The union with Denmark only served to retard the development of learning and higher culture in Norway, as Copenhagen became the center of intellectual life of both kingdoms. Norway did not receive a university like Denmark and Sweden, and while the art of printing was introduced very early in Denmark, it was not brought to Norway for some time, since the books used continued to be printed in Copenhagen or other Danish or foreign cities. The historian Suhm says: "In the time of King Hans the art of printing was brought hither. In 1486 the first Latin book was printed in the city of Schleswig, in 1493 in Copenhagen, and in 1495 the first Danish book was printed in the same city, both by Godfrid of Ghenen. In Latin,

[1] Ludvig Daae, *Matrikler over nordiske Studerende ved fremmede Universiteter*, Christiania, 1885. Chr. Lange, *Matrikel over norske Studerende ved Rostocks Universitet*, Norske Samlinger, vol. I., p. 72 ff. A. Chr. Bang, *Udsigt over den norske Kirkes Historie under Katholicismen*, p. 180 ff.

Poor students could generally receive financial aid. In Catholic times the tithes were divided into four parts, so that the king, the church, the priest, and the poor should receive an equal portion; but the *bønder* reserved the right to control the portion falling to the poor, hence it was called *bondelodden, i.e.* the *bønder's* portion. By the statute of December 20, 1436, it was ordained that half of this portion should be used for the support of poor students. T. H. Aschehoug, *De norske Communers Retsforfatning før 1837*, p. 83.

[2] Peder Friedrich Suhm, *Samlede Skrifter*, VIII., p. 23. Many students from the North also attended the University of Greifswald, founded in 1456. The University of Upsala, Sweden, was founded in 1477.

Danish, and Low-German we have some chronicles from those times written in Denmark and Holstein. Christian Pedersen, Canon in Lund, was a remarkable man. He was the first to print Saxo Grammaticus in Paris. Of the New Testament we received a few Danish translations, and Wormordius translated the Psalter into Danish. Christian II. was a lover of medicine and alchemy, and he forbade any of his subjects to visit foreign universities until they had become *baccalaurei* in Copenhagen." [1] In Norway no such progress was made. A few books were, indeed, written, but they were either printed abroad — especially in Copenhagen, Paris, and Rostock — or they were left unpublished.[2] The first Norwegian printing establishment was set up in Christiania by Tyge Nielsen in 1643, in which year he printed three small books, "Encke suck," "En merkelig vise," and "En ny almanach." [3]

After the Old Norse literary period came to a close about 1350, the Norwegian language underwent a rapid change, which, in the Middle Norse period, 1350–1525, transformed it in all essential respects into modern Norwegian. This change seems to have been due in part to the almost total interruption of the old literary activity, which had hitherto maintained a literary language more or less divergent from the spoken tongue. But in general the change parallels the development of other European languages, and must be viewed as part of a great linguistic movement. The new Norwegian was not destined, however, like other modern tongues, to become a literary language. This was prevented by the union with Denmark, which grew to be intellectual as well as political. The two kingdoms had, indeed, been united on equal terms, but the king and court resided in Denmark, and after 1450 Danish was exclusively used as the official language even in purely Norwegian

---

[1] Peder Friedrich Suhm, *Samlede Skrifter*, VIII., p. 357 ff.

[2] Suhm mentions two important books which yet remained unpublished in his day; one a record of the estates of the churches of Oslo, called the "Red Book," by Canon Hans Olson, 1521; and the other a work written about Norway, *Norges Beskrivelse*, by Absalon Pedersøn Beyer about 1550, and these were not the only ones. Suhm, *Samlede Skrifter*, VII., p. 25 ff.

[3] Suhm, *Samlede Skrifter*, VII., p. 25. *Norsk Konversations-Leksikon*, vol. I., "Bogtrykkerkunsten."

affairs.[1] A Dane, Erick Valkendorf, became Archbishop of Trondhjem, 1510, Danes were appointed to other high offices both in church and state, and Danish gradually became the written language of the upper classes. The University of Copenhagen, the Danish publishing houses, and, finally, the Reformation, in the interest of which Danish religious books were introduced in Norway, contributed to make Danish the church and school language, as it had already become the official language of the kingdom. In the cities, and among the clergy and upper classes, the Danish tongue in a greatly modified form became in time also the spoken language, while Norwegian became the despised vernacular of the common people. It continued to be spoken by the great majority, especially in the country districts, but the officials, the learned classes, and the burghers allied themselves with the Danish. To speak this language even imperfectly was henceforth regarded as a sign of culture and refinement, while the Norwegian tongue became a symbol of Arcadian rusticity.

But this Danish-Norwegian city language experienced a slow growth. Professor Halvdan Koht shows that it did not become a living tongue in Norway till towards the close of the eighteenth century.[2] Through the unfortunate circumstance that higher culture in Norway began to look to Denmark as its source, and thereby became associated with a foreign language, a cleavage occurred in the intellectual life of the nation which has not yet been fully healed. Culturally the people were divided into two groups: the cities, who prided themselves in their Danish-Norwegian language and higher city culture, which was Danish in character, and grew to be clannish in spirit; and the country people, who spoke their own vernacular, lived their own intellectual life, and had no share in the higher city culture. In course of time the Danish culture, as well as the Danish language, became nationalized through the constant influence of

---

[1] The difference between Norwegian and Danish can be seen by comparing the charter granted by Karl Knutsson in Trondhjem, 1449, written in Norwegian (*Diplomatarium Norwegicum*, vol. VI., no. 531), and the charter granted by Christian I. at Bergen, 1450, written in Danish (*Diplomatarium Norwegicum*, vol. VIII., no. 345). Karl Knutsson's charter was the last constitutional charter written in Norwegian.

[2] *Syn og Segn*, September, 1907, Halvdan Koht, *Bokmaal og Bymaal.*

environment, and assumed a Norwegian character, but this transformation was slowly consummated.

The more prominent traits of intellectual life are reflected especially clearly in the literature of the period. The creative productiveness of the higher circles may be said to have ceased, but the educated classes possessed a certain diligent erudition, of which we find evidence in the numerous charters, letters, and public documents which have been published in a large series of volumes under the title "Diplomatarium Norwegicum." Another large collection of laws and other legal documents has lately been published under the title "Norges gamle Love, anden række."[1] In Iceland, where the interest in the *sagas* continued to live, some important *saga* compilations were made as the "Hrokkinskinna" and the "Flateyjarbók." A collection of Icelandic public documents has also been published under the title "Diplomatarium Islandicum." This literature, produced by the classes representing the higher culture, shows an interest in jurisprudence, in political and commercial affairs, and learned activity, but none whatever in history, poetry, and story-telling, in a word, in literature properly so called. Love for the spiritless scholastic learning had replaced the old interest for history and literary art. But poesy was not dead. It continued to flourish, where it had always flourished even before the Old Norse literature was produced, among the common people. The poesy which blossomed forth among the unlettered and unlearned classes was a direct continuation of the best features and more popular elements of the Old Norse literature. The old spirit of the Norwegian people reasserted itself in this new poesy, unguided, but also unhampered, by the arbitrary rules of art, which had finally enveloped the Old Norse poetry like a hard crust, completely arresting its development. In the Middle Period the upper classes ceased to cultivate literature. Thereby poesy emancipated itself from learning, and returned to its own haunts to frolic about the fresh fountain-heads from which it was originally led forth. It can scarcely be regarded as a misfortune that it deserted the halls and the court circles where it had been reduced to bondage, and fled back to the bosom of the common

[1] *Norges gamle Love*, anden række, edited by Professor Absalon Taranger, Christiania, 1912.

people, where it could begin to live again, because it found its own necessary environment — freedom. The Middle Period of Norwegian literature can scarcely be called the Dead Period, as some critics have ventured to suggest. It is in many ways one of the most important formative periods in Norwegian literary history, when poetry for the first time enters fully into its own; when it acquires the true universality of the art, and begins to express with charming artlessness the native mysticism, the national dreams, the joys and sorrows of the people. Even when modern Norwegian literature began to develop, it had to turn back to this period, and tune the harp to its melodies to find again the fundamental chords of true poesy which the too learned poets had forgotten. The Middle Period has not only left us one of the richest treasures among the rich stores of poesy and prose narratives in the North, which is read and admired even now to an extent which might make the masters envious, but it has done Northern literature an even greater service by rediscovering and reopening the eternal fountains of poesy, without which the great triumphs in modern literary art might never have been won. Had the upper classes continued to control the literary production, their learning might have spoiled their poetry, and we should not have had a literature so expressive of the spirit and character of the age as the folk-tales, folk-songs, and ballads of the common people. It would have been a literature for the upper classes, lacking the truly national element, and it is doubtful if it would have possessed the high value of the folk literature even when measured by modern standards of art.

The folk literature may be divided into three main groups: the folk-songs, the traditional and legendary tales (*sagn*), and the folk- and fairy-tales (*eventyr*). In all of these we find a new literary form, as well as a new literary spirit. In the folk-songs the rhyme has replaced the old alliterative verse, and the refrain is generally, though not always, employed. The folk-song has adapted itself to two new arts — music and the dance, and it is generally held, no doubt correctly, that this new poetic form had been imported together with the latter from southern Europe. In the song-dance, which gradually became the great diversion of the common people, the trio: poesy music, and dance were again united, as they had been even among the Greeks of old. This form of the dance originated quite early in Norway, and in Iceland it is mentioned even in the eleventh century.[1] It was a home dance performed in the house in winter; but in the summer generally out of doors. All could take part; young and old, men and women formed a circle by holding each others' hands. The leader sang the song, and the others joined in the refrain, while all kept time to the melody. "And as the song proceeded, all entered more and more into the spirit of it, and lived over again the *saga* which the song narrated; the dance became dramatic." The song was the chief thing in the dance, and all who took part were supposed to know it so well that they could accompany it with motions and facial expressions. Hulda Garborg says: "The song-dance strengthened and revived the interest in history, since the songs so often dealt with stories from the *sagas*. This pastime was especially entertaining and useful during the long winters when the people stayed mostly indoors. For the young people the dance also became a school, an introduction to the old life, and a strengthening of the love of home and kindred. The young people learned also through the singing of the songs the good traits which the song especially praised: courage and manhood, honesty and courtesy, chivalry, self-sacrifice in love, and friendship unto death; but shame and disgrace befell the coward and the one who was dishonest and faithless. Often the songs stimulated the people's minds by wit and sarcasm; yes, the song-dance was used even as a judicial tribunal. If a man had done something wrong, two strong men took him between them into the dance, and let him listen to verses full of spite and mockery, sung about his conduct. But he was allowed to reply as well as he could, and when they thought that he had heard enough, the case was thereby regarded as settled." In the folk-songs the epic and lyric elements are most intimately combined. The song is usually epic, as it narrates a story based on the *sagas* or other traditions, or even on mythology. The background of the narrative is often dark and mystic, but through the softer undertones breathes a deep feeling of joy or sorrow which concentrates itself in the purely lyrical refrain. The Faroe Islands have the greatest collection of purely

[1] Hulda Garborg, *Norske Folkevisor, Norske Folkeskrifter*, no. 8, Christiania, 1903; *Songdansen i Norderlandi*, 1904.

epic folk-songs found in the North. The oldest of them, and in fact the oldest folk-songs known, are the "Sjúrðarkvæði" or songs about Sigurd Fafnesbane. In Iceland the folk-songs died out, because the dance was forbidden by the church, and only fragments are now in existence.[1] From the Shetland Islands only one song has been preserved, the "Hildinakvad," written down in the eighteenth century in a language half Norse and half English. Travelers who saw the song-dance in these islands at that time state that here, as in the Faroe Islands, the songs dealt especially with episodes from Norwegian history. In Norway many large collections of folk-songs have been published, and the work of collecting them is not yet completed. Hitherto the largest and most noted collection is the "Norske Folkeviser," by M. B. Landstad.[2]

The traditional tales may be divided into two main groups: the mythological and the legendary-historical. Those of the first group form a continuation of the myths in a disguised form, especially those of the more popular features of the old faith which had become most intimately connected with the people's everyday life. Thor, the most popular of the gods, the trolls, which are but a variation of the old jøtuns, the fairy, the mountain spirits, mermaids, elves, etc., are still met with in these tales. The old gods had ceased to be regarded as divinities, but they continued to live in the popular imagination as evil spirits who exerted a powerful influence on people's lives and destiny. The conception of the powerful Thor had been too deeply ingrafted on the minds of the Norwegian people to be suddenly eradicated even by a change of faith. Though no longer

---

[1] Olafur Davíðsson, *Íslenzkir Vikvakar og Vikivakakvæði*, 1908. V. U. Hammershaimb, *Sjúrðarkvæði*, 1851. *Færøisk Antologi*, 1889.

[2] Of other Norwegian collections may be mentioned: Sophus Bugge, *Gamle norske Folkeviser*, 1858; and *Viser fra øvre Telemarken*, 1859. Jørgen Moe, *Norske Viser og Stev i Folkesproget*, 1840. Hans Ross, *Norske Viser og Stev*. Thorvald Lammers, *Norske Folkeviser med Melodier*, 1901–1902. Bernt Støylen, *Norske Barnerim og Leikar*, 1899. Rikard Berge, *Stev fraa Telemarki*, 1908.

The old folk-melodies to which the folk-songs were sung have been collected by Ludvig M. Lindeman, Catharinus Elling, and others. Ludvig M. Lindeman, *30 norske Kjæmpevisemelodier*, Christiania, 1863. Rikard Berge, *Norsk Visefugg, med Tonar nedskrivne af Arne Eggen*, Christiania, 1904. Catharinus Elling, *Norske Folkemelodier, Christiania Videnskabs-Selskabs Skrifter*, 1909.

worshiped as a god, he continued to exercise a magic influence in their lives. Thursday evening had yet its own significance; the magic plants used in medicine had to be picked on Thursday evening to have healing qualities, and food had to be placed by the barn on Thursday evening for the elves to gain their good will. Characteristic was also the belief in the *Aasgaardsrei*,[1] a fearful caravan which was thought to ride through the air on dark, wild horses. This procession consisted of the spirits of the dead who in their natural life had not done evil enough to be condemned to hell, but who were unhappy and without peace after death. Thor, as a spirit of evil, Sigurd the slayer of Fafnir, and Gudrun, who has been substituted for Hel, are the most conspicuous figures of the procession as it rides through the air to places where fights and murders occur, to fetch the souls of the slain. People were afraid to stand outdoors after dark lest the *Aasgaardsrei* should come and snatch them away; but the sign of the cross placed on the house door was a sure protection. The legendary-historical tales are especially connected with the national hero St. Olav, and the ravages of the Black Death. In these stories the red-bearded St. Olav has been substituted for the red-bearded Thor of mythology. It is St. Olav with his battle ax who wages war against the trolls and other forces of evils, as Thor swung his hammer Mjølner against the *jøtuns* of old. Some of the tales are religious and legendary, while others are so closely connected with history that it is very difficult, if not impossible, to distinguish facts from fiction. The tales relating to the Black Death have already been mentioned. To these may be added the numerous *bygdesagn*, or local traditions of more or less historic character, found in all parts of the country.[2] Ludvig Daae says of these: "The stories

---

[1] The word *Aasgaardsrei* seems to be connected with O. N. *øskranligr*, meaning fearful, and *rei* a procession on horseback, hence the fearful procession. But the meaning of the first part of the word is not clear, and it has been variously interpreted. The story of the *Aasgaardsrei* is told in a folk-song from Telemarken. See *Sagnet om Aasgaardsreien* by P. A. Munch in *Annaler for nordisk Oldkyndighed og Historie*, 1846. O. A. Øverland, *Aasgaardsreien*, "Amerika," Madison, Wis., February 27, 1901. *Folkesagn fra Sogn, Huldrefolket og Juleskreia*, "Decorah-Posten," Decorah, Ia., July 10, 1903.

[2] Andreas Faye, *Norske Folkesagn*, 1833. P. Chr. Asbjørnsen, *Norske Huldreeventyr og Folkesagn*, 1845, 1848. Ludvig Daae, *Norske Bygdesagn*, I.

which we still find preserved by the inhabitants of a certain *gaard* (farm) through generations bear the closest resemblance to the sagas of all popular traditions. These old traditions have often a great value for the history of culture; even if the individual features of the stories themselves may seem insignificant, they are of so much the greater interest, because they have been preserved through centuries." Many traditions of a more poetic character are also found, some of which seem to be of foreign origin, while others originated at home during the later romantic period of the saga literature. Of such may be mentioned the tales about Hagbart and Signe, Aslaug Kraaka, King Bele and Torstein Vikingsson, and others.[1] The resemblance which these tales bear to the sagas is especially conspicuous in the interest manifested for family relationship, and the love of historic narrative, which soon convinces us that they are pieces cut from the same cloth. But the old Norse art of story-telling, which had been developed in the saga period, is found also in the folk- and fairy-tales (*eventyr*). As to contents these tales are pure invention. If traced to their obscure origin, many of the traditions on which the stories are based may even be found to have been brought from foreign lands,[2] but this is of secondary importance. The scenery, the character, temperament, and language of the persons depicted in the narrative are not only Norwegian, but typically so. The very texture of the story is characteristic Norwegian art. In southern lands the adventure was the chief feature of the story. In the Norwegian tales the interest centers about the character of the persons depicted. Character-painting, psychological analysis, is as much the art secret in the folk- and fairy-tales as it was in the sagas, and so it continues to be in Norwegian prose narrative even to the present. The story-teller unveils to us a character, and starts him on his career. Everything, even his boldest adventures, bear the impress of his personality and follows

and II., 1870, 1872. Halvard Bergh, *Segnir fraa Valdris*. M. B. Landstad, *Gamle Sagn om Hjartdølerne*, 1880. Sir George Webbe Dasent, *Popular Tales from the Norse; Tales from the Fjeld;* and, *Norse Fairy Tales Selected and Adapted from the Translation by Sir George Webbe Dasent*, by Knowles, Lippincott Co., 1910.

[1] Svend Grundtvig, *Gamle danske Folkeviser*, vol. I.

[2] Jørgen Moe, *Samlede Skrifter*, vol. II., p. 16 ff.; *Fortale og Indledning til Norske Folkeeventyr*, 2d edition, 1852.

as a matter of course. Whatever he does, he must do, in a sense. He will do good, bad, great, mean, or foolish things, not because of circumstances, but because he is good, bad, great, mean, or foolish. His career is not a chain of romantic accidents, but the gradual unfolding of an inner law.

The most typical characters created by the Norwegian folk- and fairy-tales are the three brothers Peter, Paul, and Esben Askelad. Esben, the youngest of the three brothers, seems to be the idealized Viking chieftain lifted into the realm of poetry. Like the Viking he is the younger brother who finds his fortune only by leaving home. He is young and inexperienced and has never done anything but dig in the ashes of the fireplace. His older brothers ridicule him. He encounters the greatest difficulties, but he finally triumphs because of superior talents, patience, and perseverance, just as many a Viking chieftain had done, and wins the princess and half the kingdom. We can scarcely doubt that the Norwegian people were reviving the memories of the Viking period in these stories about Esben Askelad. After they had quit seeking adventures with the sword, they began to live over again in literature the experiences of the nation. In the sagas these experiences had been narrated as history, in these tales they reappear as poetry. Esben becomes as typical a representative of the Middle Period as the Viking chieftains and warrior kings were of the Viking Age. He is no blood-stained warrior who goes forth to kill and plunder. He is not only brave, but also kind and sympathetic, and his very kindness is a secret source of power which helps him in the greatest trials. In this respect he forms a contrast to his older brothers, who have caught nothing of the new spirit. Esben's victories were moral and intellectual victories, giving promise of a new era when moral and intellectual forces should begin to establish their superiority over brute strength. This new spirit touched the heart-strings, and gave expression to the finer feelings which the scaldic poetry had refused to recognize. The rusty portals thereby swung open to new possibilities. For the first time the poet could sing about what he had never seen, about what might and ought to be. Poesy was no longer chained by rules of art to past events, for imagination and feeling had been set free. Poverty and labor, sorrow and hardships might continue to build their prison walls; the human spirit could rise on the wings of poesy to an ideal world where no limitations existed, to that beautiful castle of its own creation, "The Castle East of the Sun and West of the Moon." [1] This enthroning of creative imagination is the beginning of poetry in a modern sense, when it becomes a vehicle for bringing the ideal world into the realm of human experience as a new force of life.

15. LOCAL AND GENERAL ADMINISTRATION

When the *lendermænd* office was abolished in 1308, the administration of internal affairs was left wholly with the *sysselmænd*, who were royal officials. In the fourteenth century, as already stated, the *sysselmænd* were called the king's *fogeds* (*vogt*, from *advocatus*, *i.e.* royal agent) and it became customary to farm out to them the royal revenues of the *syssel*, or district, in lieu of which they were to pay a certain sum to the royal purse.[2] The *syssel* might also be granted them "kvit og frit," *i.e.* without returns. As the *sysselmænd* were regarded as royal agents to whom the districts were in a way granted for administrative purposes, the *syssels* came to be called *lens*, and the *sysselmænd lensmænd*, or *lensherrer*, while the older term *foged* was applied to a class of inferior officials. The *lens* were divided into smaller administrative districts called *fogderier*, in each of which the *lensherre* appointed *fogeds* as the local administrative officers. But the *fogeds* had to swear obedience to the king, and were not the personal representatives of the *lensherre*. Under the *fogeds* stood the *bønder-lensmænd*, two in each *fylke*, who served as tax collectors and police officials. It had been ordained by the law of 1293 [3] that the *sysselmænd* should appoint these *lensmænd* from among the most intelligent and upright *bønder* of the district, hence they were called *bønder-lensmænd*, to distinguish them from the *lensmænd* proper, or *lensherrer*. The *lens* were of two kinds, principal and inferior. The principal *lens* were ten in number: Bohus,

---

[1] "Slottet østenfor Sol og vestenfor Maane," P. Chr. Asbjørnsen, *Norske Folke- og Huldreeventyr*. See also P. Chr. Asbjørnsen and Jørgen Moe, *Norske Folkeeventyr*, 1842.

[2] T. H. Aschehoug, *De norske Communers Retsforfatning før 1837*, p. 13. Ebbe Hertzberg, *Len og Veitzla*, p. 308 f.

[3] T. H. Aschehoug, *De norske Communers Retsforfatning før 1837*, p. 10.

Akershus, Brunla, Bratsberg, Agdesiden, Stavanger, Bergenhus, Trondhjem, Nordland, and Vardøhus. The *lensherre* exercised both civil and military authority in his *len*, but his office was appointive, not hereditary. He was appointed for life, for a fixed number of years, or for an indefinite period, but he might be removed by the king at any time. The royal *lensmænd* could only collect the fixed and customary dues. According to the laws of 1297, 1455,[1] 1539 they were forbidden to levy new taxes, or to change the tax rates except with the consent of the people. But this very important provision was often violated, especially by the greedy *fogeds*, who forced the people to pay more than their just dues, and if anyone resisted forcibly, he was in danger of being treated as a rebel. But when the people assembled at the *thing*, they might refuse to pay a tax even if the king had levied it. When Stig Bagge at the *fylkesthing*, in Sogndal, in 1532, read a letter from the king announcing that a new tax had been imposed, the people took the matter under advisement, whereupon they declared with uplifted swords that, as they had paid heavy taxes the last year, they would pay nothing this year until midsummer, and this resolve they maintained in spite of the threats of the royal *lensmænd*.[2] A similar action had been taken at the *fylkesthing* at Halsaa in 1484.[3] As both personal and property rights were often infringed upon by the *fogeds*, the royal *lensmænd*, and even by the king himself,[4] the people demanded that these rights should be safeguarded by the royal charters. By a royal decree of June 25, 1455, the king's *lensmænd* and other officials were forbidden to oppress the people, to impose unlawful taxes, or to seize or imprison any one without due process of law. Similar provisions are found in the Swedish charter of King Christian I., and in the charters issued by King Hans and his successors.[5]

[1] T. H. Aschehoug, *Statsforfatningen i Norge og Danmark indtil 1814*, p. 227; *De norske Communers Retsforfatning før 1837*, p. 84.

[2] T. H. Aschehoug, *De norske Communers Retsforfatning før 1837*, p. 81. *Diplomatarium Norwegicum*, II., no. 1108.

[3] *Diplomatarium Norwegicum*, IV., no. 997.

[4] At times the king did impose taxes without the advice or consent of the Council, but this does not seem to have happened very often. See T. H. Aschehoug, *Statsforfatningen i Norge og Danmark indtil 1814*, p. 253.

[5] T. H. Aschehoug, *Statsforfatningen i Norge og Danmark indtil 1814*, p. 226 ff.; *De norske Communers Retsforfatning før 1837*.

The thing-system still existed, but the power of lawmaking had been gradually assumed by the king, who in such matters was suffered to act in conformity with the advice of the Council. The people's consent expressed through the *thing* was generally, though not always, asked for, but it had ceased to be anything but a mere matter of form. Perhaps the chief reason why the *things* ceased to take an active part in legislation was that the laws were considered permanent, and the king's lawmaking power was very limited. He could issue ordinances in regard to special matters, but he had to take an oath to obey and uphold the "Code of Magnus Lagabøter," which was considered to be the essential and permanent laws of the land.

The Council of the realm shared the sovereign power with the king, and in some respects it was even placed above him. It acted, not only as an advisory body, but the king had to obtain its consent in all important matters. The charter granted by Christian I. states that "no important errand shall be undertaken or fulfilled unless a majority of the Council consents thereto." When the king died, the Council assumed full sovereign authority, and acted as a regency, or it chose a regent to act in the interim until a new king was placed on the throne. But although the king's sovereign authority was thus divided and limited, the Council was no ministry representing the will of the people, as in modern constitutional monarchies, and when we except the chancellor, who was the king's private secretary, the councilors did not assist the king as cabinet members in the routine work of his administrative duties. The members of the Council did not stay in the same place, but lived scattered through the kingdom, and because of the expenses and difficulties connected with travel in those days, they could meet only on special occasions when they were summoned by the king. How often these meetings were held cannot be determined with certainty. According to King Hans' charter, the Council should be assembled once every two years in Oslo and Bergen alternately. Because of the slow and difficult process of assembling the Council, it was stated in Karl Knutsson's charter that the king should obtain its advice except in cases of emergency, when he might act without consulting it. This was a dangerous concession, as it became possible for the king to wholly ignore the Council on the plea of emergency, and we have already observed a growing tendency on the part of the union kings to wholly disregard the Norwegian Council.

16. CHRISTIAN II. THE DAWN OF A NEW ERA

Christian, the son of King Hans, was born July 1, 1481, and was at the time of his father's death thirty-two years of age. As a child he was so wild and untractable that his father placed him in the family of a well-to-do merchant, Hans Meissenheim, but after a month had passed, the merchant's wife, a very good and conscientious woman, refused to have the responsibility of keeping him. He was then placed in the home of his tutor, but after a short time he was brought back to the palace, where he received a new tutor, the humanist Konrad of Brandenburg. Under his guidance the young prince was made acquainted with the new ideas of the Renaissance, which seem to have greatly interested the wide-awake pupil. Christian was a gifted boy; and when he grew to manhood he was especially well developed both intellectually and physically. He had lofty plans and a resolute will to accomplish great things. He was energetic and courageous, but suspicion and a tendency to faithlessness and melancholy were serious defects in his character which early manifested themselves. At the age of twenty-one he was placed in command of the army sent to Norway to quell the uprising led by Knut Alvsson, and a few years later he again returned as the ruler of the kingdom, clothed with full sovereign power. That he would become his father's successor was no longer doubtful. In 1487, while he was only six years old, the Danish Estates had hailed him as his father's successor on the throne of Denmark, two years later the Norwegian Council decided that he should succeed his father on the throne of Norway, and in Sweden he had been hailed as heir to the throne in 1499. But Sten Sture's revolt had created new difficulties. Upon the death of King Hans in 1513 the Councils of the three kingdoms were summoned to meet in Copenhagen, but only nine Swedish councilors met, and they had received such limited power that they could not settle the one great question, the attitude of Sweden to the union. The Danish and Norwegian councilors then undertook to formulate their demands in charters which the king would be asked to sign. The Norwegian councilors prefaced their demands with a complaint that the king had called himself the rightful heir to the Norwegian kingdom, although Norway was now an elective monarchy, and, furthermore, that King Hans, contrary to the oath which he had taken, had not redeemed the Orkney and Shetland Islands, or the annuities to be paid for the Hebrides and Man according to the treaty of Perth. Then follows a series of demands by which the councilors sought to safeguard the autonomy of Norway, and to maintain its equality with Denmark in the union. Towards the Danish Council the king was very condescending, but the demands of the Norwegian councilors he treated with haughty disfavor. Some he refused to grant, some he passed over in silence, and others he referred to the Danish Council. To the very reasonable request that the castles and *lens* of Norway should be granted to native lords he returned the answer through his chancellor that, since the nobility of Norway was almost extinct, he would grant the *lens* and castles of the kingdom to Danes and native-born lords. The ecclesiastical offices over which the crown exercised the right of patronage would be given to native-born Danes and Norwegians, and none but Danes and Norwegians should be appointed members of the Norwegian Council. This was tantamount to saying that Norway should be ruled by Danes, not by native-born officials. No special charter was granted Norway, but the Danish charter was to be considered as applying to both realms, a step which destroyed the equality of the two kingdoms in the union. This rather brutal disregard for the acknowledged rights of Norway he could show, because he knew that the kingdom lacked an efficient military organization, and that the Norwegian Council had no means of enforcing its demands. " But it is a question," says Sars, "if it was politically correct for Christian II. to take the greatest possible advantage of this weakness in the way he did, or if it must not rather be said that by his conduct in this instance he showed the same violent greed for power, the political short-sightedness, and lack of true statesmanship which always characterized his conduct." [1] The charter was finally

[1] J. E. Sars, *Udsigt over den norske Historie*, III., p. 178. R. Keyser, *Den norske Kirkes Historie under Katholicismen*, II., p. 616 f. *Samlinger*

accepted, and the Councils adjourned to meet again in June, 1515, for the purpose of settling the difficult question regarding Sweden. On June 11, 1514, King Christian was crowned at Copenhagen, and a little later he was also crowned at Oslo as king of Norway.

On the day of his coronation as king of Denmark, Christian II. was married to Isabella, or Elizabeth, the sister of Emperor Charles V. of Spain and Germany. At the marriage ceremony he was represented by Mogens Gjø, who acted as his proxy, as the young bride, who was only thirteen years old, did not arrive in Denmark till the following year, when the wedding was celebrated at Copenhagen. The young queen soon found that her husband was cold and indifferent. His heart still clung to Dyveke, whom he refused to give up. To the appeals which foreign ambassadors and others made to him on this point he answered with characteristic haughtiness that this was a matter with which they should not meddle. Queen Elizabeth bore her lot patiently, and proved herself a lady of such excellent qualities that she won the sympathy even of Dyveke's mother, Sigbrit, who, upon her daughter's death, transferred her motherly affections to the young queen; but many years passed before the king learned to properly esteem his legally wedded wife. In June, 1517, Dyveke died very suddenly, and the story was told that she had been poisoned by some cherries which the nobleman Torbern Oxe had sent her. For a time the king was overwhelmed with grief and mental gloom. Suspicion pointed to Torbern, who indiscreetly said things which further aroused the king's anger, and his hatred once kindled was always deadly. He did not rest until Torbern was sentenced to death, and in spite of intercessions in behalf of the condemned man he caused the death sentence to be carried out. From this time forth Dyveke's mother, Sigbrit, enjoyed the king's confidence to the fullest extent, and exercised unlimited power and influence at court. She seems to have belonged to the plain townspeople of her native city of Amsterdam, but she possessed a degree

til det norske Folks Sprog og Historie, I., Iver Hesselberg, *Christian den anden i Norge.* Karl F. Allen, *De tre nordiske Rigers Historie under Kongerne Hans, Kristian II. og Gustav Vasa. Samlinger til det norske Folks Sprog og Historie,* IV., p. 363 ff., *Kong Christiern den andens norske og danske Haandfæstning af 1513.*

of learning quite unusual among those classes at that time. She was especially well versed both in alchemy and medicine, but the real secret of her power lay in the ability to control all who came under the spell of her influence. If the courtiers and nobles had hoped to destroy her power by removing Dyveke, they were now compelled instead to wait in corridors and ante-chambers until it pleased Madam Sigbrit to admit them into the royal presence, and she did not hesitate to treat them as truant school-boys, or, upon occasion, even to chide the king himself. But she used her power with discretion. She was instrumental in bringing about the best relations between the king and his young queen whom she had learned to love as her own daughter. In the affairs of government her influence was everywhere visible, and gives evidence of the practical ability and shrewd intrigue which enabled her to play her part so successfully. Archbishop Valkendorf of Trondhjem, who had sought to remove Dyveke, had to leave his archdiocese. He repaired to Rome to lay his case before the Pope, but died there in 1522,[1] and the following year Olav Engelbrektsson, dean of the cathedral chapter in Trondhjem, was chosen his successor. Sigbrit gained full control of the customs and duties of the realm, and gradually assumed direction of all financial affairs, and she also acted in other matters as the king's chief councilor and assistant. The king did not fail to devote some attention to the Norwegian colonial possessions, but his efforts seem to have been the result of sudden and easily abandoned impulses rather than of a systematically pursued plan. For over a hundred years the colonies in Greenland had remained wholly cut off from all communication with Norway, and they were at this time well-nigh forgotten. Archbishop Valkendorf made the first attempt to reëstablish communications with Greenland. He gathered what information he could find, and wrote very detailed directions for the captains who were to make the voyage to the colonies. The king aided him enthusiastically, inspired, no doubt, by the accounts of the great voyages which were being made to the new

---

[1] Ludvig Daae, *En Krønike om Erkebiskopperne i Nidaros, Festskrift, udgivet i Anledning af Trondhjems 900 Aars Jubilæum, 1897.* H. G. Heggtveit, *Trondhjem i Fortid og Nutid,* p. 128 ff. *Diplomatarium Norwegicum,* vol. IV., no. 1080.

world, but Sigbrit's opposition to the archbishop, and his flight from his diocese, put a sudden stop to the undertaking.

The trade with Iceland continued to create complications requiring diplomatic negotiations. Commerce had not yet been reduced to the system of peaceful and well regulated intercourse between nations as in modern times, for although treaties were made for the regulation of trade, the merchants still retained too much of the spirit of belligerent navigators, or roving adventurers, to be bound by conventions either written or oral. The sixteenth century was, throughout, a period of hazardous enterprise, of sharp competition, and the use of the club-law in the harbors and upon the high seas. If Englishmen came in too close a touch with Germans, Spaniards, or other rivals, the treaty provisions were none too closely scrutinized, and many a violent encounter followed. Such brawls between Norwegian and English traders had not been unknown in the past, and they were reënacted in Iceland, where competition for the trade led to frequent outrages and serious troubles even after commerce was made free in 1490. From 1507 the complaints of the Danish and Norwegian merchants of their English competitors were constantly growing louder, until armed conflict broke out, and in 1510 or 1511 the English who had established themselves in Iceland were driven away. The following year they returned with increased forces, captured one of the royal ships, and killed one of the king's secretaries and several of the crew. When Christian II. ascended the throne, he complained of these outrages to King Henry VIII. of England, who was at that time engaged in a war with Scotland. So long as the war lasted, Henry was very polite and regretted deeply the acts of lawlessness committed by his subjects, but when peace was concluded, he suddenly changed. With a haughty air he told the ambassadors that the Icelanders had been treated as they deserved. He refused to pay any damages, and affected to be granting a special favor when he consented, in 1515, to a renewal of the treaty of 1490 by which further depredations were to be prevented.

The fifteenth century had been a time of intellectual awakening in Europe. Humanism and the Renaissance had gradually moved northward across the Alps like the coming summer, and the effect produced by the ferment of the new learning began to make itself felt, not only in art and literature, but also in the growth of new social ideas. In Germany the reform movement inaugurated by John Huss, and the subsequent wars of the Hussites, had created a religious revival tinged with a patriotic spirit. With this movement humanism allied itself on its northward march. In Germany the new learning was partly turned into religious channels, and as many of the humanists sprang from the common classes the new movement became both intellectually and socially antagonistic to the Roman hierarchy with its old scholastic learning and its aristocratic feudalistic ideas. This intellectual awakening prepared the way for the Reformation, which followed in the wake of the new learning. The reformers appealed to the common people in their own mother tongue, and proclaimed their right to govern themselves in religious affairs. The Protestant churches became national and democratic in conformity with the intellectual tendencies of the age. This important change, accompanied by greater freedom of the individual in matters of religious doctrine, finally broke the spell of the Roman incubus, and ushered in a new era of intellectual and social development. The new ideas of the Renaissance came also to the North. In Denmark, especially, very appreciable traces of humanistic activity are to be found; but as the movement was late in appearing, it received no distinct development, but was soon fused with the Lutheran Reformation which followed in its wake. In the time of Christian II. Luther began his great church reformation in Germany. On October 31, 1517, he nailed his "Ninety-five Theses" on the church door in Wittenberg, in which he attacked especially the sale of indulgences, and urged the necessity of true repentance. The attention attracted by these theses astonished even Luther himself. "In fourteen days they ran through all Germany," he says, "for all the world complained of the sale of indulgences." In 1520 Luther was excommunicated, a step which completed the rupture between him and the Roman Pontiff. Accompanied by the students of the university, he marched to the Elstergate of the city, where he publicly burned the papal bull, as a sign that he renounced all allegiance to the Pope. Luther's teachings soon became known in Denmark, and Christian II. was favorably impressed with his doctrines.[1] He had been influenced from childhood by the liberal

---

[1] R. Keyser, *Den norske Kirkes Historie under Katholicismen*, II., p. 647.

ideas of the Renaissance, and he hated the arrogant clergy, as well as the powerful nobility. He held quite advanced views with regard to the education of the common classes and the limitation of the power of the bishops and the monastic orders, but in his inclination towards the doctrines of Luther it is impossible to discover any motive but love of power and desire for gain. The new teachings would give him the longed-for opportunity to extend his power at the expense of the clergy. This would be scarcely less welcome than the opportunity to increase his revenues by suppressing the monasteries, even as his contemporary Henry VIII. did in England. His attitude to the papal agents who were selling indulgences in the North also points to this desire as the prime motive for his interest in church reform. In 1518 John Angellus Archemboldus came to the North as papal legate, ostensibly for the purpose of settling a quarrel between the Swedish bishop, Gustav Trolle, and Sten Sture the Younger, but it soon became evident that his real aim was to sell indulgences.[1] Christian II. granted him permission to carry on this trade throughout his realms in consideration of the payment of the small sum of 1120 Rhenish gulden, the legate promising to use his influence in the king's behalf in Sweden. Agents were dispatched to Bergen and even to Iceland. His chief assistant, Didrik Slagheck of Westphalia, was sent to Sweden, whither Archemboldus himself soon followed. But Sten Sture, who knew the legate's mercenary motives, soon won him to his side by bribes, and the prelate's perfidious conduct so angered King Christian that he ordered him and his assistants to be arrested. By timely flight they saved themselves, but the money and goods which they had collected and stored in various places were seized by the king's officers. Even a sum of 3000–4000 marks which had been deposited with the Bishop of Bergen was swept into the royal coffers. This episode very naturally strengthened the king's sympathy for Luther and his teachings. He was persuaded to send for a Lutheran minister to introduce Lutheranism in Denmark, and Elector Frederick of Saxony sent Martin Reinhard to Copenhagen in 1520. But Reinhard could not speak Danish, and had to employ as interpreter Paulus Eliæ (Paul

---

[1] *Diplomatarium Norwegicum*, vol. VI., no. 660, 662, 663, 664, also no. 672–677.

Ellisen), a monk from Elsinore (Helsingør), who soon became discouraged, and again accepted the Catholic faith. Reinhard could accomplish nothing, and had to return to Germany. Christian seems to have continued to be well disposed towards the Reformation, but grave political disturbances, and especially the war with Sweden, prevented him from introducing it in his realm. Norway had hitherto remained wholly untouched by the great reform movement, but the tyrannical king, who thought more of property than of faith, nevertheless secularized the two Norwegian monasteries of Dragsmark and Gimsø.

In Sweden the old feud between the rival families of Sture and Trolle was continued by Archbishop Trolle and Sten Sture the Younger. Hostilities broke out between the two factions, but Trolle defended himself successfully in his strong castle of Stäke in Mälaren. Meanwhile a greater danger threatened Sture from without. At a council in Arboga in January, 1517, he had declared that he would never recognize Christian II. as king of Sweden, and the people supported him with enthusiasm, but under the circumstances a war with Denmark was unavoidable. Christian II., who lacked funds, found difficulty in equipping an army for the campaign in Sweden. When at length he sent 4000 men and twenty ships to relieve Stäke castle, where Gustav Trolle was closely besieged, the army was defeated, the castle was destroyed, and Archbishop Trolle was deposed and imprisoned as a traitor to his country. But Christian II. would not give up the idea of conquering Sweden. On January 29, 1518, he landed an army at Stockholm, and laid siege to the city,[1] but when Sture arrived with a large force, he had to resort to peace negotiations, as he lacked provisions and ammunition, and his German mercenaries were deserting in large numbers. A year's truce was arranged, but the king planned to capture Sten Sture by treachery. He invited him to a conference and promised to give hostages, but Sture refused, and in turn invited King Christian on the same conditions. Christian accepted, but as soon as he had the hostages in his power he annulled the truce and set sail for Denmark. One of the hostages thus abducted was the young nobleman Gustav Eriksson Vasa, the later liberator of Sweden.

[1] *Diplomatarium Norwegicum*, vol. XIV., no. 271.

The increase of taxes due to Christian's warlike expeditions weighed heavily on the people, and caused much suffering and discontent. But such matters did not for a moment cause the tyrannous king to pause in the pursuit of his selfish aims.   The toll paid by the German merchants in passing the Sound was increased in flagrant violation of stipulated agreements with the German cities; soldiers were hired in Germany, France, and Scotland, and the Norwegian magnates had to furnish a certain number of armed men; the king would not halt until Sweden was subdued.   The Pope was persuaded to sanction the excommunication which Archbishop Birger had already fulminated against Sten Sture; Sweden was placed under interdict, and Christian was commissioned to inflict the requisite punishment upon the kingdom.   This gave Christian's war of conquest even a religious tinge, as he could now earn the blessing and gratitude of the Pope by winning the throne of Sweden.   In 1520 he entered Småland with a large army.   In Vestergötland the invaders encountered the Swedes under Sten Sture, who had stationed himself in the neighborhood of Bogesund.   In the battle which ensued, Sture was wounded, his army was thrown into confusion and fled from the field.   At Tiveden a second engagement was fought, and the Danes were again victorious.   The wounded Sten Sture was brought in a sleigh across Lake Mälaren towards Stockholm, but died from his wounds before reaching the city, only twenty-seven or twenty-eight years of age.   Though young in years, he was as able as he was heroic, and he is justly regarded as one of the noblest characters in Swedish history.

Under these circumstances many of the leaders lost courage and would have given up the struggle, but Sten Sture's widow, Christina Gyllenstjerna, who conducted the defense of Stockholm, refused to surrender the city.   The struggle continued, and the invaders suffered heavy losses, but when Christian II. arrived with a fleet, and blockaded Stockholm, Christina was finally forced to surrender, September 7, 1520.

17. CHRISTIAN II. THE TYRANT.   THE STOCKHOLM MASSACRE

From the moment that Sweden submitted, Christian II. treated the kingdom with the arrogance of a conqueror.   The councilors were summoned to meet in the Gray Friars monastery, where Bishop Jens Beldenak explained to them that the king was the rightful heir to the Swedish throne according to the law of St. Erik. A trace of relationship between Christian II. and St. Erik might indeed be figured out, but the claim that for this reason he was heir to the throne of an elective monarchy was a self-evident prevarication, which only illustrates how the king would respect the laws and institutions of the realm which he was henceforth to govern. On November 1, 1520, he was proclaimed king according to the principle of hereditary kingship which he had proclaimed. The coronation occurred November 4; elaborate festivities were arranged for the succeeding days, and most of the Swedish nobility had assembled in the capital for the occasion. Now that the king had reached the goal of his ambition, and the crowns of the three realms had been united on his brow, nothing could seem more natural than to seek to win the support of all for the new order of things by a conciliatory policy. The more hideous is the thought that in the midst of the coronation festivities he was conceiving the plot for one of the darkest crimes which history has recorded. The despicable creature, Didrik Slagheck, and the revengeful Gustav Trolle, the archbishop, were constantly about the king, and filled his dark mind with most pernicious counsel. On the 7th of November a large number of nobles, men and women, and a number of leading citizens were summoned to the royal palace. The doors were locked behind them, and Gustav Trolle stepped forward to accuse them of various crimes. They had driven him from his archdiocese, they had razed his castle, and had used violence against the servants of the church, he claimed. He demanded an indemnity of 500,000 marks for the losses sustained by himself and other bishops, a sum so enormous that it would have ruined all against whom he directed his charges. He further demanded that the assembled lords and ladies should be imprisoned until they could be sentenced by the king, who would receive God's reward and the praise of all Christendom for meting out punishment to these heretics. The assembled nobles were struck with consternation, as they realized but too well that a plot had been laid for their destruction. The only one who for the moment retained full composure was Sten Sture's young widow Christina Gyllenstjerna. She showed that the proceedings against Gustav Trolle had been decided by a general diet, and that if punishment should be meted out, the whole nation would have to be punished, and not only a few individual lords. But this gave the king a new opportunity. The action of the diet was interpreted as rebellion against the Pope, *i.e.* it was heresy, for which the king could punish them in the name of the church. All were hurried off to prison, and the next day, after a mock trial had been conducted, the king sentenced them to death as heretics. Now began the carnival of blood known as the Stockholm massacre, the direction of which was left to Didrik Slagheck. On the 8th of November eighty-two persons were beheaded on the public square of the city; among others, the bishops of Strängnäs and Skara, many aldermen of the city, and a large number of the leading men of Sweden. Sten Sture's body, as well as that of his dead child, was exhumed and burned with the bodies of the executed. The massacre spread also to the provinces, and it seems to have been the king's mad purpose to destroy the whole nobility of Sweden with one fell stroke. Sten Sture and his adherents had been excommunicated, and it was, therefore, possible for the king and his evil counselors to carry on their fiendish work of destruction without incurring the execration of all Christendom. When the king left Stockholm to return to Denmark, he left a trail of blood. In Jönköping several persons were executed; at Nydala monastery the abbot and several monks were drowned, and Christina Gyllenstjerna, together with many other ladies, was carried into captivity in Denmark. Christian II. had well earned the title of Christian the Tyrant. Even among the Danes themselves the king's vile deed caused general consternation. The great sea-captain Søren Norby did not conceal his ill-will even in the king's presence, and Otto Krumpen resigned as general of the army. The shock of abhorrence, which at first stunned all, was soon followed in all the realms by a storm of indignation so violent that it hurled Christian the Tyrant from the throne which he had so wantonly disgraced.

The young Gustav Eriksson Vasa, one of the Swedish nobles whom Christian II. had kidnapped and brought to Denmark, escaped from his captivity and fled to Lübeck, whence he returned to Sweden. His father was one of the victims of the Stockholm massacre, and the king engaged spies to seize the young nobleman, who henceforward bent his great energy and remarkable talents to the one great task of freeing his country from the tyrant's grasp. The accounts of his wanderings and hairbreadth escapes from his pursuers read like a romance. In vain he tried to rouse his countrymen. At Kalmar and in Småland he attempted it and failed, and even in Dalarne the peasants would give him no support, though they listened with reverence to his eloquent appeals. Hunted from place to place, wandering in disguise through remote settlements, despairing of success, he finally resolved to seek refuge in Norway. But when the Dalkarleans received proof of King Christian's cruelties, they repented and sent messengers to bring Gustav Vasa back to Sweden. On his return they chose him "Lord and chief of Dalarne and of the kingdom of Sweden " in January, 1521. At the head of a few poorly equipped peasants Gustav Vasa resolutely raised the standard of revolt against the hated tyrant, and thanks to the incompetency of Didrik Slagheck, whom King Christian II. had intrusted with the administration of Sweden, he was rapidly increasing his forces. Not till April did Slagheck and Gustav Trolle take the field against him, and they were defeated at Brunsbäk, on the Dal River. Gustav Vasa's forces soon numbered 15,000 men, and at Vesterås the government forces under Slagheck suffered a second defeat. At this critical juncture King Christian was in the Netherlands visiting his brother-in-law, Emperor Charles V., and his henchmen in Sweden were unable to cope with the rapidly spreading uprising. Gustav Vasa was unable to take Stockholm, but in the country districts the revolution had great success. Didrik Slagheck was recalled to Copenhagen,[1] and Gustav Trolle succeeded him in the management of affairs in Sweden, but he was as unable to accomplish anything as his predecessor. Before the end of the year (1521) Stockholm, Kalmar, and Åbo in Finland were

---

[1] Through Christian II.'s influence Didrik Slagheck was elected Archbishop of Lund, but when the king finally learned how he had been deceived by him, he caused him to be arrested. The hated royal favorite was tried, condemned to death and executed. C. T. Allen, *De tre nordiske Rigers Historie under Kongerne Hans, Christian II., og Gustav Vasa*, vol. III., part III., p. 225 f. Anders Fryxell, *Gustav Vasa's Historie, oversat fra det Svenske af M. Birkeland*, Christiania, 1856.

the only larger cities which had not been surrendered to Gustav. As Stockholm could not be taken without the assistance of a fleet, since the redoubtable Søren Norby, who commanded the Danish fleet, carried supplies to the city, Gustav turned to Lübeck for aid, and the merchants of that city responded by sending a fleet of ten ships to blockade the city. The king, who was hard pressed by the Hanseatic fleets, as well as by a revolt at home, could pay but slight attention to Sweden. Gustav Vasa was proclaimed king at a diet in Strängnäs June 6, 1523, and shortly afterward the surrender of Stockholm ended the struggle which terminated for all times the unfortunate union with Denmark. The sufferings caused by Christian's tyranny and the subsequent war of liberation had awakened a strong national spirit, which launched the Swedish people upon a new period of development — the era of national greatness, when Sweden under the guidance of a dynasty of great national kings rose to become one of the great powers of Europe.

King Christian's tyranny and shortsightedness had not only cost him the throne of Sweden, but he had alienated the hearts of his own people, and had created an opposition which must have made him feel uncomfortable even on the throne of Denmark. The Hollanders had been offended by the arbitrary increase of the Sound-toll, and the Lübeckers, who had supported Gustav Vasa, fought resolutely for their naval supremacy in the Baltic Sea, and in defense of their trade, which Christian sought to check by creating a strong Scandinavian trade company which could compete successfully with the Hanseatic merchants. Against his foreign enemies he could get little support at home, since he had always been an enemy both of the clergy and the nobility. He summoned the Council to meet at Copenhagen in November, but instead of obeying this summons, the councilors from Jutland met at Viborg, and formed a conspiracy to drive Christian II. from the throne. On January 20, 1523, the councilors renounced their allegiance to him, stating as their reason for this act that the king had violated the charter to which he had sworn at his coronation; that he had disregarded the Council and the nobility, and had given preferment to ignoble knaves, and especially to the wicked woman Sigbrit; that pursuant to the counsel of these he had beheaded many Swedish nobles, also, Knut Knutsson

Baat in Norway, and had driven away the Archbishop of Trondhjem, and had ill-treated many other bishops.[1] The disaffected councilors raised an army of 20,000 or 30,000 men, while Frederick, Duke of Holstein, an uncle of Christian II., who was their candidate for the throne, took the field with a force of 6000 men. Yet the situation was far from hopeless. Christian could count on the support of the common people, and he might also have raised forces in Norway, but he was as irresolute now that danger threatened him as he had been overbearing and tyrannical while his subjects remained submissive. Duke Frederick was proclaimed king of Denmark at Viborg, March 26, 1523; Jutland and Fyen joined him, Halland, Blekinge, and the Norwegian province of Viken were in the hands of Gustav Vasa, and the fleet, which the king had neglected, was unable to cope with the Lübeckers. Meanwhile Christian sat inactive in Copenhagen, nursing his own gloomy thoughts. On April 13th he sailed from the city with a fleet of twenty ships, accompanied by his family, Madam Sigbrit, and a few friends, to seek assistance in foreign lands. The occasion was a solemn one, and the people watched with tearful eyes the departure of their king. The reign of Christian II. was ended. His remaining years proved but a doleful sequel to a misspent life. Some features of his rule are, however, worthy of commendation.[2] As he was especially interested in education, he made the provision that better qualified teachers should be employed, that they should receive better salaries, and that cruel flogging of the children in the schools should be restricted. In the country districts where no schools were established, the people might send their children to be instructed by the parish priest, or some man of learning in the town. As lawmaker he sought to protect the common people against oppression. He prohibited the imposition of excessive fines, a punishment so often inflicted by the clergy for the smallest violation of the rules of the church, and the landlords were forbidden to oppress their tenants by increasing the rents. He encouraged trade, and attempted to limit the power of the Hanseatic merchants.

---

[1] *Diplomatarium Norwegicum*, vol. XIV., no. 287. Arild Huitfeldt, *Danmarks Riges Krønike*, II., p. 1196 f.

[2] C. F. Allen, *De tre nordiske Rigers Historie*. J. E. Sars, *Udsigt over den norske Historie*, III., p. 178 ff.

A uniform system of weights and measures was introduced, and the king also tried to create a postal system by hiring mail carriers, who should receive three *skillings* for carrying a letter a distance of seven miles. With his Renaissance and Reformation ideas and his solicitude for the welfare of the common people his reign might have become a new era of progress if his gloomy and bloodthirsty mind had not vitiated every nobler effort.

The Norwegians took no part in the uprising against Christian II., as the king was generally well liked in Norway. But though it has been suggested that they might have retained Christian as their king, and dissolved the union with Denmark, such a step would, undoubtedly, have been prevented by Sweden and Denmark, where he was feared as well as hated. The Norwegians were, moreover, unable to act independently at this moment. The principal cities were held by Danish commandants, Archbishop Valkendorf, the president of the Council, was dead, his successor, Olav Engelbrektsson, was in Rome to receive the consecration of the Pope, and there was, virtually, no government in the country. When the news of Christian's overthrow reached Norway, Nils Henriksson Gyldenløve of Østraat and Olav Galle of Thom met with a few others to confer regarding the affairs of the kingdom. It was decided that Nils Henriksson should take possession of Bergen and assume control of the northern part of the kingdom, while Olav Galle should act as governor of the southern part.[1] But Nils Henriksson was unable to take Bergen, which was defended by the Danish commandant Hans Knutsson, and Olav Galle was no more successful in southern Norway. Frederick I. soon gained the allegiance of the whole kingdom of Denmark, and as the three chief strategic points, the castles Akershus, Bergenhus, and Bohus, were held by the Danish commandants, who would transfer their support to the new king if the proper inducements were offered, it was quite certain that the union of the two kingdoms would be continued. King Frederick I. sent Henrik Krumedike to Norway to take charge of affairs in the southern part of the kingdom. The commandant of Bohus had already submitted to the new king, and Krumedike succeeded in winning the magnates and the cities separately by making promises which he

---

[1] *Diplomatarium Norwegicum*, I., no. 1067.

never intended to keep. The commander of Akershus submitted to King Frederick I., and before the end of 1523 nearly all of southern Norway had pledged its allegiance to him. Another prominent Danish noble, Vincence Lunge, was sent to the northern districts. He came to Bergen, where he met Nils Henriksson Gyldenløve, his noted wife, Lady Inger Ottesdatter of Østraat, and their daughters. Nils Henriksson, who was at this time an aged man, was anxious to shift the burdens to younger shoulders, as he had failed to take the castle of the city. A peaceful agreement could the more easily be arranged, since Vincence Lunge married Gyldenløve's oldest daughter, Margaret, who had been lady-in-waiting to Christian II.'s queen, Elizabeth, and had become acquainted with Lunge in Denmark. Nils Henriksson was the wealthiest and most powerful magnate in the kingdom at this time. In 1515 he became *drotsete*, and he was also appointed one of the special envoys sent to the Netherlands to bring Christian II.'s bride to Denmark.[1] His wife, Lady Inger of Østraat, was a talented, but ambitious and covetous lady. Through the marriage of her daughters to immigrated Danish nobles who had high positions in the kingdom, she exercised a unique influence, and became a leading figure in one of the most tragic chapters in Norwegian history.[2]

King Frederick's representatives came to Bergen in 1523, and Nils Henriksson died the same year. Vincence Lunge planned to take the castle still held by Christian II.'s adherents, and the king encouraged the Hanseatic merchants of the city to aid him in this undertaking. At a given signal in the still of the night the merchants sallied forth, not against the castle, but to attack their rivals, the Scotch and Norwegian merchants of the city. These were ill-treated and driven with their families into the streets; their homes were looted, and their charters destroyed. The attack was especially directed against the Scotch merchants, who suffered losses to the amount of 40,000 marks. Never since the time of the Victual Brothers, or the massacre of Olav Nilsson, had the citizens of Bergen been

---

[1] *Østeraat Herresæde fra det 11te Aarhundrede til vore Tider*, published by Axel Johannessen, Trondhjem, 1904.

[2] Her second daughter, Eline, was married to Nils Lykke in 1528, and a younger daughter, Anna, had married Erik Ugerup in 1524.

PLATE II

RUINS OF THE HAMAR CATHEDRAL.

BERGENHUS.

subjected to such indignities. But Vincence Lunge did nothing, and, probably, could do nothing to restrain his lawless allies.[1] The castle, which was held by the incompetent Hans Knutsson, surrendered, and the Norwegian Council granted Lunge the castle and royal *len* of Bergen. The new commander was a learned and able man. He had studied at several universities; he was a doctor of jurisprudence, and had been professor at the university of Copenhagen. As a member of the Norwegian Council, he naturally exercised great influence. After his marriage to Margaret Gyldenløve he accounted himself a Norwegian, and became for a period the most influential man in the kingdom, and the originator of an ultra Norwegian political policy which saved Norway from being wholly incorporated in Denmark. "But his ability," says Allen, "consisted chiefly in craft and cunning, in discovering the weakness of others, and when they had been indiscreet, he used the opportunity either to crush his opponents, or to use them for his own ends. He was flattering and ingratiating, and no one knew better than he how to act towards those whom he wanted to win, or to make it appear that he served those whom he wished to use as tools for his own purposes. As an enemy he was feared for his falsity and artifice." "To this must still be added," says Øverland, "that he was about the most covetous and greedy man of his age, and that he was proud and boastful when fortune favored him." [2]

In the month of August, 1524, the Council renounced their allegiance to Christian II., and chose Frederick I. king of Norway. A charter, to which the king would be required to subscribe,[3] specified that the king should protect the Catholic Church, its teachings, rights, and privileges; that he should maintain the laws of the kingdom, renounce the title of "Heir to the throne of Norway," acknowledge that he received the Norwegian *lens* from the Council, and agree not to grant them to any but native-born lords, or to lords married

[1] Yngvar Nielsen, *Bergen fra de ældste Tider indtil Nutiden*, 270 ff. C. F. Allen, *De tre Rigers Historie 1497–1536*, vol. IV., 2, 222. N. Nicolaysen, *Norske Magasin*, I., 548. *Norske Samlinger*, vol. II., 481 ff. *Diplomatarium Norwegicum*, vol. V., no. 1039; vol. IX., no. 515, 517; vol. VI., no. 691.

[2] *Diplomatarium Norwegicum*, vol. VIII., no. 526; IX., no. 532, 534. O. A. Øverland, *Norges Historie*, vol. V., p. 298.

[3] *Samlinger til det norske folks Sprog og Historie*, vol. I., p. 1 ff.

to native-born ladies. The Orkney and Shetland Islands were to be redeemed, and the rights and privileges granted by former charters were reaffirmed. A letter was also addressed to the king complaining of Henrik Krumedike, and giving notice that he had been deposed from his *len* and banished from the kingdom.[1] With these documents Vincence Lunge went to Denmark to King Frederick I. The king signed the charter, but Krumedike was declared innocent on the oath of twenty-four knights, and in 1529 he received again his possessions in Norway.

18. THE STRUGGLE FOR NORWAY. CHRISTIAN II.

Frederick I. had been placed on the throne of Norway, but the kingdom was controlled by the Council, in which Vincence Lunge exercised the greatest authority. Olav Galle, governor of southern Norway, and Archbishop Olav Engelbrektsson, who was president of the Council, were also influential members. The relations with Sweden were not cordial. Gustav Vasa had not evacuated Viken, though he had been requested to do so, and Swedish refugees, the opponents of King Gustav, had been well received in Norway. The hostile feeling grew still more intense when Vincence Lunge and Lady Inger of Østraat harbored and supported a Swedish pretender who claimed to be the son of Sten Sture, and sought to stir up a rebellion against King Gustav. The pretender, generally known as the "Dalejunker," was a worthless criminal by the name of Jöns Hansson, who after having operated for a time in Dalarne fled to Norway to escape capture. He came to Østraat, and succeeded in winning the confidence of Lady Inger and Vincence Lunge. The story was circulated that Gustav Vasa was dead; the pretender became engaged to one of Inger's daughters, probably Eline,[2] and the ambitious mother was dreaming lofty dreams of finally seeing her daughter as queen on the throne of Sweden. Lunge's reasons for supporting the pretender

---

[1] *Diplomatarium Norwegicum*, vol. IX., no. 537, 538, 539.

[2] R. Keyser thinks that the youngest daughter, Lucie, was betrothed to the "Dalejunker." *Den norske Kirkes Historie*, II., 679. A document later discovered states that it was Eline, but Ludvig Daae considers this to be an error, as Eline was at that time betrothed to the Danish knight, Nils Lykke, whom she married in 1528. Ludvig Daae, *Fru Inger Ottesdatter og hendes Døtre, Historisk Tidsskrift*, vol. III., p. 224 ff.

even after the fraud had been exposed must have been of the most sordid nature. Ludvig Daae thinks that he wished the young lady to marry abroad, in order that the estates which she would otherwise inherit might come into the possession of the remaining heirs. In the fall of 1527 the pretender proceeded to Dalarne to rally the people to his cause. But they had been warned by Gustav Vasa. He could accomplish nothing, and had to return with Lunge to Norway. Gustav Vasa demanded his surrender, but Lunge still claimed that he was Sten Sture's son, though Sture's widow, Christina Gyllenstjerna, had declared that he was an impostor.[1] Lunge was finally obliged to send him away from Norway, but he did it in such a way that he escaped. It was the pretender's plan to join Christian II. in the Netherlands, but in Rostock he was arrested and put to death. Vincence Lunge's conduct had offended, not only the king of Sweden, but also his own sovereign, Frederick I., who in 1528 entered into an alliance with Gustav against Christian II. King Gustav demanded that Lunge should be punished, and Frederick complied by removing him as commandant of Bergen. He did not venture, however, to risk an open rupture with the powerful noble, but granted him other possessions as a compensation, among others the Nonneseter monastery, where Lunge erected a residence called "Lungegaarden." Lunge's power was still unbroken, but a Dane, Eske Bilde, who was married to Krumedike's daughter, Sophia, became his successor in Bergen; Claus Bilde was made commandant of Bohus, and Olav Galle was deprived of Akershus, which was given to Mogens Gyldenstjerne. Contrary to the charter, the three principal castles of the kingdom were granted to Danish nobles. As the king did not seem to take the charter seriously, he was no more conscientious as to its other provisions. He had agreed that he should not ask of the Council, or of the inhabitants of Norway, that any one, either his son or any one else, should be elected as his successor in his lifetime, but in 1529 he, nevertheless, sent his son, Duke Christian, to Norway to be hailed as heir to the throne. It was clearly the king's purpose to incorporate Norway in the kingdom of Denmark, or to treat it as a

---

[1] *Diplomatarium Norwegicum*, XIV., no. 585, 587, 588, 589, 602. *Bidrag til Oplysning om Peter Kantsler og Mester Knut samt den saakaldte Dalejunker, Samlinger til det norske Folks Sprog og Historie*, I., p. 478 ff.

dependency. But this plan was frustrated by the Norwegian political policy of Vincence Lunge and Archbishop Olav Engelbrektsson, who had revived to some extent the power of the Norwegian Council. Though their motives were often sordid, and their methods reprehensible, they were fighting for Norwegian autonomy, and the outcome depended on their willingness to coöperate. But a disinterested plan of united effort could not long be pursued by the two leaders, as other circumstances would have made this impossible, even if they had been men of more lofty and unselfish purposes. Archbishop Olav was undoubtedly a patriot, who sought to defend his country's freedom and honor, but he was unable to give the struggle even a tinge of the patriot's tragic idealism, and history has unjustly veiled his name in obloquy. J. E. Sars says of him: "The name of Archbishop Olav Engelbrektsson grates unpleasantly on our ears. It is connected with the memory of Norway's deepest national humiliation in such a way that about the deepest shadow of this wholly dark picture falls upon him personally. Henrik Krumedike described him to King Frederick I. as a 'false man,' according to the statement of Vincence Lunge,[1] and in later history he has received a similar testimonial. His political policy has been described as unwise and dishonest. It has been described as showing that he had slack moral principles, a weak character, and that he lacked the proper reverence for his calling, and the conviction of the truth and justice of his cause.[2] It has even been said that such a motive as patriotism and a feeling for Norway's liberty and honor must have been wholly foreign to him, that he sought purely personal ends, or that, at best, he was only guided by a Catholic prelate's hierarchical zeal. This is evidently erroneous. Vincence Lunge would scarcely have appealed so strongly in his letters to the archbishop's patriotism if he knew that such an appeal would find no response; and the archbishop's own writings prove that his country's honor lay close to his heart, and that he deplored the state of dependency to which Norway had been brought. He did not possess the qualities of a hero or a martyr, but he was evidently not an insignificant personality.

[1] *Diplomatarium Norwegicum*, VII., no. 600.
[2] R. Keyser, *Den norske Kirkes Historie under Katholicismen*, vol. II., p. 692.

We see that he did not fail to understand what was necessary in order to defend the Norwegian kingdom and the Catholic Church against the dangers and enemies which threatened both, and that, in a way, he was always active, though he received little support from his own people. In contemplating his ambiguous, equivocal conduct we must not forget the difficult situation in which he was placed. A man of his learning and ability — and he was, according to the circumstances of the times, a learned man and loved learning — ought to have accomplished something good and lasting, but the circumstances in which he was placed were such that even an extraordinary personality would have failed. It became his duty to represent the Norwegian Catholic Church and Norway's political independence at a time when both were tottering to their fall. His position presented problems which individually, perhaps, would have transcended the greatest power given a single individual, and which in many instances clashed with one another."

Vincence Lunge inclined strongly to the Reformation movement, not only as a humanist, but also because he found an opportunity to gratify his covetousness through the secularization of monasteries and the confiscation of church property. King Frederick I., who favored the Reformation, prepared the secularization of the monasteries by appointing non-ecclesiastic managers, who should pay the king a yearly sum for this privilege, and at the same time provide the monks and nuns with the necessaries of life from the income of the estates of the monastery. Vincence Lunge had received from the king the monastery of Nonneseter, and he stretched forth his greedy hands for more. He conspired with the prior of the monastery of the Dominican Friars in Bergen, and the two plundered that institution of all its valuables, and burned the buildings to hide the crime.[1] Vincence Lunge and Archbishop Olav now became the bitterest enemies. The angry archbishop threatened to take Lunge's life, and seized all the estates belonging to Lunge and Lady Inger of Østraat in northern Norway. The king's coronation was to have taken place at Oslo, but Archbishop Olav struggled hard to prevent it. No less determined was his opposition to Prince Christian when

[1] Christian C. A. Lange, *De norske Klostres Historie i Middelalderen*, p. 337. Yngvar Nielsen, *Bergen*, p. 274.

he came to Norway to be hailed as successor to the throne, as the prince was even more outspoken in his adherence to the Lutheran Reformation than his father. In this matter the archbishop seems to have received the support of Lunge, who was also striving to maintain the political autonomy of Norway. The struggle became at once political and religious, but the quarrel between Vincence Lunge and the archbishop seems to have overshadowed all national issues. Lunge continued his seizure of church property, and was well assisted in this traffic by his greedy mother-in-law, Lady Inger. He failed in an attempt to take the monastery of Ulstein, but Lady Inger secured the cloister of Rein, and her son-in-law, Nils Lykke, gained possession of the monastery of Tautra. In Bergen the church was also suffering heavy losses. The new commandant, Eske Bilde, destroyed some of the finest edifices of the city: the Apostle church, the Christ church, the bishop's residence, and the chapter house, all built in the Gothic style of architecture. This wanton destruction was done for military purposes, to give freer range to the artillery of the fortress, but the archbishop took no step, and probably could take none, to punish this grave offense.

The Lutheran doctrine was spreading. The first Lutheran preacher, the monk Antonius, who came to Norway in 1526, seems to have received permission from King Frederick I. to preach in Bergen. Three years later two other Lutheran ministers arrived,[1] and Vincence Lunge, Lady Inger, and their influential relatives gave the reformers active support. Bergen became the center of the Reformation in Norway, but the Lutheran preachers were active also in other districts. Bishop Hoskold of Stavanger wrote to Eske Bilde that he should not tolerate or protect the damnable Lutheran heresy which had led so many astray, but he should try with all might to stamp out the false doctrine. One of the archbishop's men complained that Lutheranism was spreading also in Finmarken. Even the Council of Lübeck became alarmed, and wrote to the archbishop and the Council of Norway to act with energy against the dangerous doctrines, destructive of all social order.[2] The Reformation could make progress because the Catholic Church in Norway as elsewhere had lost its spiritual vigor. The monasteries had become hotbeds

---

[1] *Diplomatarium Norwegicum*, VIII., no. 603.　　[2] *Ibid.*, XI., no. 522, 523.

of vice and corruption,[1] and the Latin church service, which consisted chiefly of empty ceremonies, could no longer appeal to those who had caught the spirit of the new age. The fine scholar Geble Pederssøn became a convert to the Lutheran doctrine, probably in 1536.[2] He founded the Latin school at Bergen, and became the first Protestant bishop of that diocese.

In the midst of this process of disorganization Archbishop Olav's sole remaining hope was that Christian II. might return and seize the throne of Norway. The dethroned king had longed for an opportunity to return, and he had done everything possible to gain the sympathy and support of the Emperor and other princes. At Wittenberg he had heard Luther preach, and had become converted to his doctrine, but for political reasons he renounced his Lutheran faith and returned to the bosom of the Catholic Church, which he probably did without much compunction, as he seems to have been incapable of a deeper religious conviction. But his whole conduct was not very reassuring, and Emperor Charles V. would do nothing to help him. As Christian could accomplish nothing by diplomacy, he boldly entered the Netherlands, collected ships, war supplies, and a sum of 50,000 gulden, and hired an army of 7000 mercenaries for an expedition to Norway. The archbishop would not immediately declare himself for King Christian, though he had been secretly negotiating with him, but waited until he should land with his forces in the kingdom. In November, 1531, King Christian arrived on the southern coast of Norway after a stormy voyage, on which he had suffered great losses. Mogens Gyldenstjerne was asked to surrender Akershus, which he agreed to do if King Frederick I. did not send him reënforcements before the month of March, and Christian, who failed to see that the commandant was trying to gain time, agreed to a fatal armistice.[3] On November 29th he was proclaimed king of Norway at Oslo, and on the same date Archbishop Olav declared his allegiance to him. King Christian marched from Oslo with a part of his forces to Bohus, while Jørgen Hansson led another part

---

[1] A. Chr. Bang, *Udsigt over den norske Kirkes Historie under Katholicismen.*
[2] A. Chr. Bang, *Kirkehistoriske Smaastykker, Bidrag til Geble Pederssøns Levnetsløb,* 204 ff. *Norske Samlinger,* I., p. 8, 11.
[3] *Diplomatarium Norwegicum,* IX., no. 685, 688.

of the army against Bergen; but both were unsuccessful, and Christian hastened back to Oslo when he learned that Gyldenstjerne had received reënforcements. A small Danish fleet, which had been sent to Oslo, could not reach the inner harbor, which was ice-bound, but a small force was landed, and succeeded in reaching the castle of Akershus. The following day Gyldenstjerne attacked King Christian's forces, set fire to his camp, and burned the Cistercian monastery at Hovedø. Soon an army of 6000 men, Danes and Lübeckers, arrived from Denmark, Christian's fleet was destroyed, and he was obliged to resort to negotiations. It was agreed that he should go to Denmark to treat with Frederick I. in person, and if no agreement could be reached, he should be allowed to return to Norway, or to Holland. King Christian was brought to Denmark, but only to be imprisoned in Sønderborg castle as a rebel. He was finally released from his close confinement in a lonely dungeon and brought to the castle of Kalundborg, where he was better treated. Vincence Lunge and Nils Lykke, who were instructed to quell the uprising in northern Norway, came to Trondhjem, and requested Archbishop Olav to submit. As he had no alternative, he renewed his oath of allegiance to King Frederick I., and became in a way reconciled to his enemies and opponents. He was allowed to retain his office, but had to pay a heavy fine. At a meeting in the city the members of the Council, who were present, renounced their allegiance to King Christian II., and affirmed again the union with Denmark on the condition that Norway should retain its rights and liberties as before.[1] In theory the principle of equality of the two kingdoms was still maintained, but it could be nothing but empty phrases, as Norway was in reality a conquered country. The people had not even made an effort to defend their independence, and the leaders, who were animated by the destructive hatred engendered by party strife, had struggled more zealously to ruin one another than to save their country.

In Denmark King Frederick I. had been placed on the throne by the nobles, and he had been obliged to sign a charter which made him wholly dependent on the magnates, who had stipulated, among other things, that the king should not interfere in the relations between the

---

[1] *Diplomatarium Norwegicum*, XIV., no. 714.

noble landowners and their renters. Thereby the nobility secured
full jurisdiction over the peasants, who were gradually reduced to
serfdom. The Reformation was rapidly gaining ground in the
kingdom, and Frederick I. had secretly encouraged it, as he was himself a convert to Luther's teachings. Hans Tausen, a learned
man and eloquent speaker, who had studied at Rostock and Wittenberg, became the leader of the movement in Denmark, and set on
foot a great religious revival, which spread irresistibly through the
kingdom. In Copenhagen he preached with such power and persuasion that the people flocked in large numbers to hear him, and
when the clergy refused to permit them to assemble in the churches,
they gained admittance by forcing the doors. Against such a movement the Catholic clergy soon felt themselves powerless, and their
attempts at forcible resistance only aggravated the situation. Bishop
Jørgen Friis sent an armed force to arrest Tausen, but the people
drove them away. Monks were expelled, and priests who would not
accept the Lutheran faith were discharged. King Frederick, who
openly sympathized with the reformers, made Tausen his chaplain and
placed him under his royal protection, but the movement was especially encouraged by his son, Duke Christian, who was an enthusiastic supporter of the Lutheran church reform. Many nobles also
joined the movement, as they hoped to profit by the secularization
of the monasteries, and the confiscation of church property. In
the country districts they had already begun to take possession of
estates belonging to the church, as the religious enthusiasm grew
ever more fervid. In 1530 the citizens of Copenhagen submitted
their Lutheran confession to a diet assembled in the city ; the Lady's
church was broken open, and its altars and paintings were destroyed.
Even before King Frederick I. passed away in 1533, the Catholic
Church in Denmark was crumbling into ruins before the victorious
assault of this new intellectual and spiritual force.

19. THE COUNT'S WAR. CHRISTIAN III.

Frederick I. had been placed on the throne by the nobles, whose
support he had won by liberal concessions, but religious strife and
social discontent had piled high the easily ignited fuel of discord,

which at any moment might blaze forth into a general conflagration.

Under these circumstances the election of a new king was a matter causing great concern. The majority of the nobility supported Duke Christian, the oldest son of Frederick I., but as he was a Lutheran, he was opposed by a strong Catholic party led by the clergy, who favored King Frederick's younger son Hans, while the merchants and the peasants, who were sorely oppressed by the nobility, wished to place the imprisoned Christian II. on the throne. Ambrosius Bogbinder, Mayor of Copenhagen, and Jürgen Kock, Mayor of Malmö, the leaders of this party, allied themselves with Lübeck, where the leader of the common people, Jürgen Wullenwever, had been elected mayor. When the Council assembled in Copenhagen, 1533, to elect a king, little hope could be entertained of an agreement, and many important questions awaited settlement. Whether Lutheranism or Calvinism should be the future religion in Denmark, whether the union with Norway should be maintained, whether Denmark should take the side of Lübeck or of Holland in the struggle for supremacy in the Baltic, were among questions to be considered. As none of the candidates for the throne could be chosen, the election of king was postponed until the following year, but the disputes were violent, especially regarding the question of religion. Hans Tausen was summoned before the Council and sentenced to death, but the sentence could not be executed, because the angry populace threatened to mob the Catholic prelates, and the persecution of the Lutherans, which was set on foot, stranded on the people's determined resistance. As to the question of supporting Lübeck or Holland, the Council decided in favor of Holland. Wullenwever, who hoped to save Lübeck's commercial prestige by gaining power and influence in Denmark, was keeping his fleet ready, awaiting the decision, and he immediately sent an army of mercenaries into Holstein in command of Count Christopher of Oldenburg. Owing to this circumstance, this war for naval and commercial supremacy, of succession, and religious party strife is generally known as the "Count's War." Count Christopher quickly seized Seeland, Skåne, and the Danish islands. The people of Jutland rose against their lords, burned their residences, and proclaimed Christian II. king. Under these circumstances the

Council again assembled and chose Duke Christian king, but it might now be a question if they had a throne to offer him. If he wished to rule, he had to win his kingdom from his opponents. Christian III. resolutely took up the fight. As Duke of Gottorp he could rely on the support of the nobles of Holstein, who wished to become masters of Denmark. His general, John Rantzau, defeated the peasants in Jutland, and crushed the forces of the Lübeckers in Fyen, while Peder Skram, the Danish naval commander, destroyed the Lübeck fleet.[1]

King Gustav Vasa of Sweden, who was a brother-in-law and ally of Christian III., aided him in bringing Skåne to submission. Copenhagen was invested from all sides, and after a long siege, the city was forced to surrender in the summer of 1536.[2] The Lübeckers had lost their control of the Baltic, the Lutheran party had triumphed, and the nobles had crushed the uprising of the peasants, who were now wholly subjected to the tender mercies of their angry lords.

The situation in Denmark might have been an opportunity for Norway to establish her independence, but the people lacked organization and leaders. Archbishop Olav summoned a general council of the nobles and common people at Bud in Romsdal, 1533,[3] but his political prestige was gone, the religious situation made it impossible for him to unite the people politically, and the castles of the kingdom were in the hands of Duke Christian's adherents. Vincence Lunge and Archbishop Olav, who were divided both by religious and political views, could not agree to cast their country's lot with either party, or to disregard both and set up a national government. The arch-

---

[1] An account of the naval war written by Marx von Schleytz, found in *Die ersten deutschen Zeitungen*, p. 116 (Munchen library), has been published by Professor Ludvig Daae in *Historisk Tidsskrift*, første række, vol. III., p. 447 ff. C. Paludan-Müller, *Grevens Feide*, I., 430 ff.; II., 184 ff. G. Waitz, *Lübeck unter Jürgen Wullenwever*. Joh. Grundtvig, *Nye Bidrag til Sømagtens Historie i Grevens Feide*, Danske Magasin, fjerde række, III., *Bidrag til Oplysning om Grevefeidens Tid*.

[2] The siege of Copenhagen lasted over a year, and is one of the most noted sieges in history. See Ludvig Daae, *Om Kjøbenhavns Overgivelse*, *Historisk Tidsskrift*, første række, vol. III., p. 463 ff.

[3] Yngvar Nielsen, *Det norske Rigsraad*, p. 380 ff. *Diplomatarium Norwegicum*, IV., 101. C. Paludan-Müller, *Grevens Feide*, II., p. 47 f. T. H. Aschehoug, *Statsforfatningen i Norge og Danmark indtil 1814*, p. 319, 349.

bishop passively watched developments. He was in favor of Count Frederick of the Palatinate, who had married Dorothea, a daughter of Christian II., but he did not venture to espouse his cause openly. Vincence Lunge would recognize Duke Christian in the hope that a charter might be secured which would guarantee Norwegian autonomy. He assembled a few councilors from southern Norway in Oslo, and these formally elected Duke Christian king of Norway. To the document declaring his election they attached the condition that "his royal majesty shall preserve to us and to the kingdom all Christian blessings, liberties, privileges, laws, and lawful customs, according to the charter granted by Frederick I." This charter should remain in force until King Christian III. should come to Norway to negotiate with the Council and grant a new charter, whereupon he should be crowned king of Norway.[1] This proceeding was irregular and unlawful, but it was, no doubt, the wisest policy, as subsequent events proved. But the unfortunate quarrel between Lunge and the archbishop had flared up with new violence which made all coöperation impossible. Nils Lykke, Vincence Lunge's brother-in-law, was married to Lady Inger's daughter Eline. She died in 1532, and her youngest sister, Lucie, undertook to manage the household for her brother-in-law. He became enamored of the young lady, and wanted to marry her, but the Catholic Church regarded such a marriage incestuous, and Vincence Lunge, Lady Inger, and other relatives opposed the match. Archbishop Olav was for a time disposed to view it favorably, but when Lucie in 1535 gave birth to a son, he could no longer shield the unfortunate lovers. He caused Nils Lykke to be imprisoned in the castle of Steinviksholm, where the ill-fated noble was smoked to death. Lucie was later married to the Swedish nobleman Jens Tillufson Bjelke, who became owner of Østraat, and the forbear of a large and distinguished family.[2]

At Christmas time, 1535, the election of king was again to be con-

[1] *Diplomatarium Norwegicum*, XV., no. 506 ff. Archbishop Olav sanctioned the election in a letter to Bishop Hans Reff and Vincence Lunge. *Diplomatarium Norwegicum*, XII., no. 555. C. Paludan-Müller, *Aktstykker til Grevens Feide*, II., no. 30, 32, 37, 40–42, 49. *Norske Rigsregistranter*, I., p. 43 f.

[2] Axel Johannessen, *Østeraat Herresæde. Fru Inger til Austraat og hendes Døtre*, ved Henrik Mathiesen. Yngvar Nielsen, *Norges Historie*, vol. IV. I., p. 6 s. T. H. Aschehoug, *Statsforfatningen i Norge og Danmark*, p. 349 f.

PLATE III

ØSTRAAT.

RUINS OF STEINVIKSHOLM CASTLE.

sidered at a council in Trondhjem, where some of the councilors from southern Norway were present. Christian III. had also asked for a tax which was to be voted, and the people of the neighboring districts had been assembled, for the purpose, undoubtedly, of giving their consent to whatever the Council might do. But they became angry and refused to agree. Wild tumults followed. Vincence Lunge was killed, and the bishops of Oslo and Hamar were imprisoned in Tautra monastery.[1] Thereby the Norwegian Council was practically destroyed. Archbishop Olav had now no choice but to act. Since Vincence Lunge's policy had been shattered, no alternative remained but the abrogation of the act of the union with Denmark, a resolute attempt to gain possession of the fortresses of the country, and the election of Count Frederick as king of Norway. This plan was not a makeshift, but an ideal, for which the greatest sacrifices might well be made. But Archbishop Olav was wholly unfit to be a leader in a struggle of that nature, and he failed to take into account his absolute lack of preparation, organization, or resources. He dispatched Einar Tjeld with a small force to take Akershus, and Christopher Trondssøn was to seize Bergen, but both attempts failed, and the national uprising collapsed utterly. Archbishop Olav lost courage, liberated those who had been imprisoned, offered to recognize Christian III. as king of Norway, and to assemble a general council to elect him, if pardon would be granted for the uprising.

After the fall of Copenhagen King Christian was undisputed lord of Denmark. By a *coup d'état* the old constitution of the kingdom was destroyed, many councilors were turned out of the Council, and all political power was taken away from the bishops.[2] A diet was assembled at Copenhagen, where a new constitution was formulated, according to which the kingdom was to be governed by the king, the Council, and the nobility, and the Lutheran faith was formally accepted as the religion of the realm. These measures could have no force in Norway, which was still an independent kingdom, united with Denmark on stipulated terms, but a paragraph was, none the less, inserted in the charter which the king granted the Danish nobility,

---

[1] Yngvar Nielsen, *Det norske Rigsraad*, 382 ff. T. H. Aschehoug, *Statsforfatningen i Norge og Danmark indtil 1814*, p. 379.

[2] Arild Huitfeldt, *Danmarks Riges Krønike*, II., p. 1486 ff.

in which he boldly asserts his intention of making Norway a province of the Danish kingdom. Norway was to be treated as a conquered country, and no attention would be paid to the documents guaranteeing its autonomy. He says: "Since the kingdom of Norway is now so far reduced in might and power that the inhabitants are not able to support a king and lord alone, and this same kingdom is united with Denmark forever, and the greater part of the Norwegian Council, and especially Archbishop Olav Engelbrektsson, now the leading man in that kingdom, has within a short time, with the greater part of the Norwegian Council, risen against the kingdom of Denmark, contrary to their own pledges, therefore we have promised the Danish kingdom, Council, and nobility, that if God Almighty has so ordained that we gain the power over Norway, or any of its provinces, castles, or *syssels*, which belong to it, that it shall henceforth be and remain under the crown of Denmark, the same as any of the other provinces, Jutland, Fyen, Seeland, or Skåne, and it shall henceforth not be called a kingdom, but a province of the kingdom of Denmark, and subject to the Danish crown forever." [1] This was language which could not be misunderstood. Norway would have to accept the conditions dictated by Denmark. In a letter of March 5, 1536, the king threatens that if the Norwegians venture any uprising, they may be sure that he will send large numbers of warriors, both mounted and foot soldiers, and cause them to be punished as disobedient subjects, who resist their rightful king and lord, and that they must consider what injury and ruin will befall all the inhabitants if a number

---

[1] T. H. Aschehoug, *Statsforfatningen i Norge og Danmark*, p. 351 f.

R. Nyerup says of this article of the charter: "By this article in the charter, the signal was given from above for that system of oppression which *lensmænd*, *fogeds*, clergymen, and other subaltern despots continued to practice in this and the succeeding reign, and which became so well rooted that it helped little or nothing that the people continually complained of extortion and wrongs, and that the kings from time to time by charters, laws, and regulations sought to limit the numerous abuses and vexations." *Historisk-statistisk Skildring af Tilstanden i Danmark og Norge i ældre og nyere Tider*, vol. I., p. 319.

How the union with Denmark was regarded by some people in Norway in later years can be seen from a letter to P. F. Suhm, where the writer says: "About the Kalmar union no Norwegian cares to read anything. It is the source of all later misfortunes." P. F. Suhm, *Samlede Skrifter*, part XV., p. 358. Arild Huitfeldt, *Danmarks Riges Krønike*, II., p. 1316 f.

of soldiers enter the kingdom to rob, murder, and use all sorts of tyranny, and how good it is to live in peace and quiet. That Christian III. illegally usurped the power in Norway must have been manifest to all. He was not lawfully elected king, for as Norway was an elective sovereign kingdom, neither he nor the Danes had a right to determine who should be placed on the Norwegian throne. Archbishop Olav watched developments closely, but as he could see no ray of hope, nothing remained for him but to seek safety in flight. He gathered what money he could find, seized the treasures of the churches, and brought them on board his ships, and on April 1, 1537, the little fleet, carrying the archbishop and his goods and archives, left Nidaros for the Netherlands, where Olav spent his remaining years.[1] The garrisons of Steinviksholm castle and Nidarholm monastery surrendered without much resistance to Truid Ulfstand whom King Christian had dispatched to Trondhjem. After the archbishop's flight, Ulfstand marched to Hamar, where he seized Bishop Mogens, and carried him as prisoner to Denmark, where he died in 1542.[2]

Christian III. was never elected king of Norway in a regular way. No charter was issued defining the relation of the two kingdoms, and he never came to Norway to receive the homage of the Norwegian people. He regarded the two kingdoms as so intimately and permanently united that the election to the throne of Denmark made him legitimate ruler of both realms. Norway had lost her autonomy, but the Norwegian people knew nothing of the paragraph inserted in the Danish charter, and scarcely realized that any change had taken place, save that a new king had ascended the throne.[3] The

---

[1] The archives and valuables which Archbishop Olav carried with him from Norway occasioned protracted disputes. In 1548 these articles came into the possession of Count Frederick of the Palatinate. The archives were transferred to Heidelberg, and have at length been returned to the Norwegian government. *Diplomatarium Norwegicum*, V., no. 1090 ff. Ludvig Daae, *Norsk Maanedsskrift*, I., p. 270. Henr. Mathiesen, *Steinviksholm Slot og dets Bygherre.*

[2] *Hamars Beskrivelse af 1553 eller 1653.* See articles about this chronicle by Ludvig Daae and Gustav Storm, *Historisk Tidsskrift*, tredie række, vol. I.

[3] T. H. Aschehoug, *Statsforfatningen i Norge og Danmark*, p. 343. Arild Huitfeldt, *Danmarks Riges Krønike*, p. 1491. L. M. B. Aubert, *Norges folkeretslige Stilling.*

Norwegian Council disappeared, though it was not formally abolished, and the Danish Council assumed the power of acting for both realms. But since Norway had submitted to Christian III. almost without resistance, he did not carry out the threat contained in the mentioned article inserted in the charter. Norway continued to be styled a kingdom equal with Denmark. It retained its old laws and its chancellor, and its administration, which was kept separate from that of Denmark, was carried on in the old way with as little direct interference from the Danish authorities as possible. Christian III. might easily have established the hereditary principle in Norway, and thereby have strengthened his throne, but he lacked the statesmanlike foresight to do so.[1]

20. THE REFORMATION IN NORWAY

The overthrow of the Catholic Church in Denmark was, quite naturally, followed by a like change in Norway, where its power was, if possible, even more hopelessly shattered. Some of the bishoprics were vacant, and others had been vacated through the flight or imprisonment of the bishops. The Lutheran Church was established in Norway as a state church, at the head of which stood the Lutheran king. The Danish church ordinance of 1537, which was written with the assistance of Luther's friend and fellow-reformer, John Bugenhagen, became the temporary constitution of the Lutheran Church in Norway, though the king had promised to give the Norwegian church a separate ordinance, in which due consideration would be paid to local conditions. The priests should be allowed to remain in their charges, but the Catholic bishops were removed, and superintendents, or Lutheran bishops, were appointed to supervise the reformation of the doctrines of the church. Geble Pederssøn, a native

---

[1] R. Keyser, *Den norske Kirkes Historie under Katholicismen*, p. 830.

The Danish flag "Danebrog," a white cross in a red field, became the official flag of both kingdoms. The Norwegian flag, a banner with a golden lion in a red field, seems to have been used on the castles and fortresses of Norway in the sixteenth century, possibly also on Norwegian ships, but the Danish flag was used on the fleet, and became the flag of Norway during the period of union with Denmark. Yngvar Nielsen, *Norges Historie*, vol. V., p. 21.

of Helgeland (Haalogaland) in northern Norway, was appointed superintendent of the diocese of Bergen, as already stated, and the Danish church ordinance was accepted at the Oslo *lagthing* for the dioceses of Oslo and Hamar in 1539, [1] but some time passed before superintendents were appointed for all the Norwegian dioceses.[2] The estates which had hitherto belonged to the Catholic bishops were confiscated, one-half of the income from the tithes was paid to the crown, and the secularization of the monasteries, which had been begun by Christian II., was continued by Christian III. In 1555 it is mentioned as completed. The property of the monasteries had been seized by the crown, and after 1562 the last traces of Norwegian monks disappear.[3] The valuables belonging to the Norwegian churches and monasteries were seized and carried to Denmark. The king instructed Eske Bilde to see to it that nothing was removed "of chalices, plates, monstrances, jewels, silver, gilt tablets, and other such things which are and remain in churches and monasteries, that it may all be preserved, and thereby have due care for our interest and welfare." [4] In a second letter he instructs Eske to collect "articles of gilt copper belonging to churches and monasteries, whether they be basreliefs, candlesticks, or the like, and forward them to Denmark." [5] This kind of "preservation" was carried out so thoroughly that there was scarcely left sufficient of the sacred articles for the communion service. Peder Claussøn Friis (born 1545) writes: "But it is to be regretted, and it is not praiseworthy, that at the time of the introduction of the Evangelical faith they did not only take away from the churches and monasteries the articles of gold and silver, and other treasures which were used in the Catholic service, together with vestments and other such things, but they wantonly destroyed things from which they could derive no benefit;

---

[1] *Diplomatarium Norwegicum*, I., no. 1091.

[2] The first Lutheran bishop of Trondhjem, Thorbjørn Olavsson Bratt, was appointed in 1546. Of the first four Lutheran superintendents three were Norwegians; *i.e.* Thorbjørn Olavsson Bratt, of Trondhjem, Geble Pederssøn, of Bergen, and Jón Guttormsson, of Stavanger; while Hans Reff, of Oslo-Hamar, was a Dane.

[3] R. Keyser, *Den norske Kirkes Historie under Katholicismen*, p. 834 ff. Chr. C. A. Lange, *De norske Klostres Historie i Middelalderen*, p. 174 ff.

[4] *Diplomatarium Norwegicum*, III., no. 1147.   [5] *Ibid.*, I., no. 1087.

they tore down buildings, and needlessly burned valuable books and letters, and destroyed the ornaments and decorations of the churches, making God's houses cheerless and barren, which they might well have left undone, nor did they derive any benefit therefrom." [1] As a further illustration of this kind of vandalism may be especially mentioned the spoliation of the great national sanctuary of St. Olav at Trondhjem.[2] The remains of the saint were incased in a triple coffin, the inner of gilt silver, the others of wood richly studded with jewels, the outer being the ornamented cover over the real coffin. When Archbishop Olav left Trondhjem, he placed the remains of the saint in the middle coffin, and carried the other two with him to Steinviksholm castle, where he left them when he fled from the kingdom. The Danish general Ulfstand, who captured the castle, did not return them to Trondhjem, but sent them to Denmark for the profit of the royal treasury.

While the king and his assistants chiefly devoted their attention to the pecuniary benefit which they might derive from the overthrow of the Catholic Church in Norway, the reform movement itself was making slow progress. The few Lutheran bishops, who had been appointed to superintend the introduction of the new doctrine, could not reach the masses of the people, who were as yet scarcely aware that a change had been made. The Reformation, which in other lands came as a great spiritual awakening, was suddenly forced upon the Norwegian people by royal edict, hence it caused no new intellectual awakening, no spiritual regeneration. It was an affair of state to which the people finally yielded a more or less willing consent. A few Lutheran priests and a number of Danish Bibles were sent to Norway, but nothing was done to provide instruction for the people, or even to maintain the schools which already existed. Previous to the Reformation each cathedral had its school where students were prepared to pursue their studies at foreign universities, and the chapters supported a number of students who studied abroad. But shortly after the introduction of the Reformation, one of these schools, the Hamar cathedral school, was discontinued, and the prebends of the

[1] Peder Claussøn Friis, *Samlede Skrifter*, p. 350.

[2] *Ibid.*, p. 351 ff. Ludvig Daae, *Et nordtysk Sagn om Olav den helliges Ligkiste, Historisk Tidsskrift*, første række, vol. I., p. 141 ff.

cathedral from which they derived their income were seized by the king, who used the revenues derived from them to pay Danish courtiers and ecclesiastics.[1] As a result the chapters were no longer able to keep students at the universities, and after the old priests died or became unable to serve, there was a deplorable want even of ministers of the gospel. Lutheran ministers had to be sent from Denmark, but the people clung to the old faith, and the new ministers were generally ill-treated, and not a few were killed.[2] Peder Claussøn Friis, clergyman in Undal, in Stavanger *stift* (1566–1614), writes: "But at the time when the old bishops in these kingdoms were dismissed, and the religion was altered and changed, and the pure word of God, which had long been obscured by falsehood and human invention, was again restored, the inhabitants of the country were so displeased that they were filled with spite and hatred towards the Protestant clergymen and the whole ministry.[3] The tithes were not fully or regularly paid, and in some districts the people offered the government large sums of money if they would be left without ministers for some years."[4] The first effect of the introduction of the new teaching was a general deterioration of public morals, while papistical superstitions continued to live for centuries. Crucifixes and pictures of saints were believed to possess healing qualities, and receive adoration which was akin to worship. Pilgrimages were made to them from far away. Even as late as 1835 pilgrimages were made to a crucifix in Røldal.[5]

The dioceses of Oslo and Hamar were united under the superintendency of the Oslo bishop, Hans Reff, who had accepted the Lutheran faith. The ablest and in every way the worthiest of the early Lutheran superintendents in Norway was Geble Pederssøn in Bergen. He was a devoted Lutheran, and exercised a true reformatory activity

[1] J. E. Sars, *Udsigt over den norske Historie*, III., p. 302 ff. *Norske Rigsregistranter*, I., p. 242 ff.

[2] Peder Claussøn Friis, *Samlede Skrifter*, p. 235. Ludvig Daae, *Norske Bygdesagn*, I., p. 65. Vilh. Poulsen, *Fortællinger af Norges Historie*, III., p. 162. *Norske Samlinger*, I., p. 10.

[3] Peder Claussøn Friis, *Samlede Skrifter*, p. 224. Gustav Storm, *Om Peder Claussøn Friis og hans Skrifter*, introduction to *Samlede Skrifter af Peder Claussøn Friis*.   [4] Peder Claussøn Friis, *Samlede Skrifter*, p. 235.

[5] Vilh. Poulsen, *Fortællinger af Norges Historie*, III., p. 162. L. Daae, *Norske Bygdesagn, Røldals Kirke*.

in his diocese. He sought to secure Lutheran clergymen for the various parishes, and founded the Latin school at Bergen, which developed under his supervision to become an efficient institution of learning according to the new humanistic ideas. Efficient teachers were secured, and new buildings were erected through Geble's efforts. He sent students to Copenhagen, Rostock, and Wittenberg, among others Absalon Pederssøn, whom he kept at the University of Copenhagen, and later at Wittenberg, at his own expense. On his return Absalon Pederssøn became clergyman and teacher at the Latin school in Bergen, where he labored with great distinction till his death in 1574.[1]

The new principles which had been introduced by the Reformation even in church administration, though not immediately beneficial, proved an important factor in the future development. According to the church ordinance issued by Christian III., the bishops, or superintendents, should be elected by the parish priests of the cities of the diocese. When a vacancy occurred, the priests of the cities within the diocese should assemble and elect four of their number to choose a new bishop. The bishop elect should be examined by the nearest bishop, and the election should be sanctioned by the king. The parish priests should be chosen by the members of the parish. The parishioners should choose seven of their number, who should elect "a pious and learned man to be a parish priest." He should be examined by the bishop, and the election should be sanctioned by the *lensherre*. In each parish there should also be a deacon, who should give the children instruction in the Christian doctrine, help the minister to sing, ring the church bells, keep the church clean, and render other services; but no provision was made for paying the deacon for his services, and the plan suggested was not carried into effect. In 1552 the king made the provision that of the lands belonging to the church a farm (*gaard*) should be set aside for the deacon, and in the church ordinance of Christian IV. more specific provisions were made with regard to the service and pay of these officers. A special tax (*klokkertolden*) was to be paid to the deacon for his support, and he should instruct the young people in the catechism and the

---

[1] *Norske Samlinger*, I., p. 3 ff. Yngvar Nielsen, *Af Norges Historie, De norske Humanister*, I., p. 115 ff.

Christian religion once a week at such a time and place as the parish priest should designate. The deacon was appointed by the parish priest with the advice of the provost, and with the consent of six of the leading men in the parish. This was the first germ of the Norwegian public school system. The Reformation had given the people privileges and opportunities of such a kind that they could only gradually learn to understand their value and importance.[1]

If the Reformation was introduced in Norway without an accompanying change in the people's religious views, it was forced upon Iceland in a manner which recalls the scenes enacted when Christianity was first introduced in the island. The old spirit and customs still lived among the people, and the two bishops, Jón Aresson of Hólar and Agmund Paalsson of Skálholt, were not only autocratic prelates, but proud and ambitious chieftains, who brooked no resistance or interference. Vilh. Poulsen says of them: "Agmund, strong and ambitious, proud, authoritative, willful, unable to tolerate resistance, munificent to extravagance, resembles in character and conduct the old chieftains rather than a priest or bishop. Jón Aresson was a chieftain to a still higher degree; dignified in appearance, charming in manners, cheerful and spirited in good company, but a firebrand against his opponents. He knew no Latin, but 'this mattered not,' he said, 'as it was not the vernacular of the country.' But he could compose a song whenever he pleased, for he was a *scald*, at this time, perchance, the best in the land."[2] The two bishops had long been rivals and enemies. When they first met at the Althing, Bishop Agmund appeared with a force of 1300 men, and Bishop Jón of Skálholt with 900. Their quarrel was on the point of precipitating civil strife, but they finally agreed to settle their difficulty by a duel between two of their adherents. The enmity between the two prelates subsided somewhat on the appearance of the Reformation. Lutheran books had been imported by the German merchants, who had carried on trade with Iceland since 1490. Jón Einarsson, a priest of Skálholt, had become a convert to the new doctrine by reading some of Luther's books, and

[1] T. H. Aschehoug, *De norske Communers Retsforfatning før 1837*, p. 89 ff.
[2] Vilh. Poulsen, *Fortællinger af Norges Historie*, III., p. 163 f. R. Keyser, *Den norske Kirkes Historie under Katholicismen*, II., p. 844 ff.

Gissur Einarsson, whom Bishop Agmund had sent to school in Hamburg, had also become a Lutheran by hearing the great reformers in Wittenberg. In 1539 he was appointed Lutheran superintendent at Skálholt, but he was successfully opposed by the blind old Bishop Agmund, who still had the undivided support of the people. Gissur saw that he could accomplish nothing for the Reformation while Bishop Agmund lived and ruled in the diocese. He reported the situation to King Christian III., as we may believe, with all the onesidedness engendered by intense partisan spirit, and the king resolved to take measures for the introduction of the Reformation in Iceland, which proved to be far more drastic than Christian spirited. He sent Christopher Huitfeldt, the commandant of Steinviksholm, to Iceland with a military force. On his arrival Huitfeldt conferred with Gissur Einarsson, and the two seem to have agreed upon the plan to be pursued. The people were ordered to bring horses, ostensibly for the purpose of transporting goods to Skálholt, but thirteen mounted men were immediately dispatched to Hjalle, where Bishop Agmund was visiting his sister, and the aged bishop was seized and brought to Huitfeldt as a captive. Deprived of their leader, the clergy could make no resistance. The Lutheran church ordinance was accepted in the diocese of Skálholt, and after Gissur had paid a large sum of silver from the diocesan treasury in lieu of a tax demanded by the king, Huitfeldt sailed to Denmark, bringing with him Bishop Agmund, who died shortly after his arrival. As Lutheran bishop of Skálholt Gissur labored diligently to introduce the Lutheran doctrine and the new church service in southern Iceland. In the diocese of Hólar in the northern part, Bishop Jón Aresson still held sway. The enmity between the two bishops became very intense, but an open clash was averted by the death of Gissur, 1548. The Lutherans and Catholics each chose their own candidates to succeed Gissur, but the ambitious Jón Aresson, encouraged by the victories gained by Emperor Charles V. over the Protestants in Germany, thought that he could seize the bishopric and make himself the lord of all Iceland. He marched against Skálholt with a hundred armed men, but timely warning had been received, a force of three hundred men had been gathered, fortifications had been constructed, guns were mounted, and when Bishop Jón arrived, he was unable to take the bishop's residence by force, as intended. But Jón Aresson was too much of a chieftain of the old school to yield because his plan had been foiled. In 1549 he took the Lutheran bishop, Martin of Skálholt, prisoner, forced the bishop's residence to surrender, drove out the Danes from the monastery of Vedey, which had been secularized, and reinstated the abbot. The Catholic church service was reintroduced in the district of Borgarfjord, and the monastery of Helgafell, which had been made a royal estate, was reorganized. After having gained this notable success, the relentless Bishop Jón directed his attack against his personal opponents, many of whom were compelled to flee from Iceland. R. Keyser says of him : "Jón Aresson had been unscrupulous in his younger days when he sought to win the episcopal office, unscrupulous he showed himself now in his old age when the question was to hold fast with trembling hands the power once gained. He heeded neither threats nor counsel, but proceeded arrogantly in the once chosen course until the abyss of destruction yawned at his feet, and all revenues of retreat were closed." [1] He had still one powerful opponent, the chieftain Dade Gudmundsson, who was married to a sister of the imprisoned Lutheran bishop, Martin. The bishop collected an armed band of 120 men, and marched to attack Dade, but the wary chieftain met him at Saudafell with a force of trusty followers. After a determined fight, Bishop Jón and his two sons, Are and Bjørn, were made prisoners in the church where they sought refuge. As the royal commandant had returned to Denmark, Dade turned his prisoners over to his assistant, Christian Skriver, but he feared the bishop's adherents, and did not know where the prisoners could be safely kept. One morning at the breakfast table the minister, Jón Bjarnason, said to him that although he was not very wise, he knew a good way of keeping the prisoners. When asked what plan he had in mind, he answered that the ax and the grave would keep them best. This suggestion was acted upon, and the old bishop and his sons were led to execution and beheaded. The people of Bishop Jón's diocese, Hólar, bitterly resented this vile deed. They watched their opportunity, attacked Christian Skriver, and killed him and his armed escort. Later fourteen more Danes were killed, and a spirit of bitter hostility against the Danes had been kindled in all Iceland.

[1] R. Keyser, *Den norske Kirkes Historie under Katholicismen*, II., p. 868.

Sigurd Jónsson, a son of Bishop Jón Aresson, sent thirty men to Skálholt to bring the bodies home for interment. Bells were fastened to the coffins, and as they journeyed along, the church bells were ringing, and the people flocked about them to touch the coffins of the dead bishop and his sons, who were revered almost like saints. They were buried with great honors in the cathedral at Hólar.

Christian III. had dispatched a military force to Iceland even before he had received notice of Bishop Jón's death. Two hundred men were sent to the southern districts, and five hundred to the diocese of Hólar. After the bishop's death the people, who had been deprived of their leader, submitted without resistance, and took the oath of allegiance to the king at the Althing, July 1, 1551, and Olav Hjaltesson was appointed Lutheran superintendent at Hólar. The Lutheran Reformation was thereby officially accepted, but Jón Aresson was still regarded as the national hero, and generations had to pass before Lutheran Christianity could become a regenerating force in the people's intellectual and spiritual life.

Very little is known about the introduction of the Reformation in the Faroe Islands. The last Catholic bishop was Amund Olavsson, who was appointed by Frederick I. in 1533. Jens Riber was the first Lutheran bishop in the islands. In 1557 he became Bishop of Stavanger as Jón Guttormsson's successor. The diocese of the Faroe Islands was discontinued, and the islands were incorporated in the diocese of Bergen, and later in that of Seeland in Denmark.[1]

21. THE REIGN OF CHRISTIAN III.

The disappearance of the Norwegian Council, the gradual decay of the aristocracy, and, finally, the destruction of the Catholic Church and clergy left the Norwegian people without leaders, unable to assert their independence, or even to maintain their legal rights in the affairs of internal administration. The principal *lens* of the kingdom were given to Danes, with but few exceptions, bishops and ministers were sent from Denmark, the government was wholly

---

[1] R. Keyser, *Den norske Kirkes Historie under Katholicismen*, II., p. 838 f. Peder Claussøn Friis, *Samlede Skrifter*, 328. L. Debes, *Færøernes Beskrivelse*. Andreas Faye, *Christiansands Stifts Bispe- og Stiftshistorie*, Christiania, 1867, p. 120 ff.

in the hands of the king and his Danish Council, and even the courts of justice were often presided over by Danish judges appointed by the king. The Norwegian codes of law were translated into Danish, and the church laws were annulled through the introduction of the Reformation. It became customary also to appeal from the decisions of the *lagthings* to the king, who, together with his council, acted as a court of higher jurisdiction. He also sent members of his Council to Norway to hold court together with the royal *lensherrer* and *lagmænd* in order to examine complaints against *lensherrer, fogeds,* and others. This tended to undermine the authority of the old courts, and exerted a deteriorating influence on Norwegian jurisprudence.[1] The lawmaking activity was limited to the issuing of charters and the granting of trade privileges to the Hanseatic merchants, and the legal practice degenerated into a dull and formal routine, as the Danish judges were ignorant of the principles of Norwegian law as well as the detail of court procedure. During the union period Norwegian jurisprudence lost the high position which it had formerly held. Foreign rule prevented its further development, and the people themselves became indifferent, and ceased to cultivate the knowledge of the old laws.

Christian III., who was a judicious and practical king, avoided as far as possible all steps which would irritate the Norwegian people.[2] The clause which he had inserted in the charter, possibly in order to humor the Danish nobles, he suffered to remain a dead letter. The charter remained deposited in the archives unknown to most people in Denmark and, probably, to all in Norway. Two kings were laid in the grave before it became known.[3] The king's chief aim was to maintain peace, to improve the economic conditions in his kingdoms,

---

[1] J. E. Sars, *Udsigt over den norske Historie*, III., 294 ff. Gustav Storm, *Haandskrifter og Oversættelser af Magnus Lagabøters Love; Christiania Videnskabs-Selskabs Forhandlinger*, 1879, p. 22 ff. T. H. Aschehoug, *Statsforfatningen i Norge og Danmark*, p. 382 ff., 462 ff.

[2] Christian III. has been pictured by Norwegian historians as a weak and worthless king, but Professor Oscar Alb. Johnsen has shown that this view is erroneous, that he was an able, clear-minded, humane, and conscientious ruler. Oscar Alb. Johnsen, *Nogle Bemerkninger om Kristian den tredie som norsk Konge; Historiske Skrifter tilegnede og overleverede Professor Dr. Ludvig Daae*, Christiania, 1904.

[3] Yngvar Nielsen, *Norges Historie*, vol. IV., p. 40.

and to increase the revenues for the purpose of paying the big debts which had been contracted in the late war. As he felt the crown resting securely on his brow, he was in a position to carry out his administrative policy with firmness. The nobility exercised far less influence than they had expected to do, and the Norwegians remained peaceful and loyal subjects.

FIG. 3. — King Christian III.

In the Count's War King Christian had seen the importance of the fleet, and he aimed to make the dual kingdom of Denmark-Norway a naval power strong enough to control the Baltic. This would also tend to draw the two peoples closer together through a strengthened feeling of the necessity of coöperation in furthering common interests. Able sea-captains were not wanting. Men like Kristoffer von Truntheim (Christopher Trondssøn), Otto Stigssøn, Stig Bagge, and others had learned seamanship as bold corsairs and lawless rovers of the seas, but King Christian, who needed their services, was willing to condone past offenses, if they would enter the royal service in good faith, and this they were anxious enough to do. Stig Bagge of Kvinesdal in Norway was a very able captain, and the king granted him Lister *len*, but on an expedition, against the Netherlands, 1541, he was captured and put to death. He was succeeded by the no less valiant and able Christopher Trondssøn (Kristoffer von Truntheim). These two are the forerunners of a number of distinguished Norwegian naval heroes who later served in the fleet of the two kingdoms.

The king devoted special attention to the development of mining in Norway. He seems to have thought, as did Absalon Pederssøn

Beyer, that the mountains of Norway were full of silver, gold, and other precious things. Alchemy had stimulated the search for precious metals, and the growing need for money and iron, caused by the wars and the enlargement of the navy, gave a new impetus to this industry. Hitherto iron had been gathered in bogs, where small quantities of native ore could be found. King Christian II. had sought to introduce the more modern system of extracting metals from the rich mineral-bearing rock of Norway, but the attempt had led to no practical results. King Christian III. renewed this attempt, and imported miners from Germany, where the mining industry at this time was most highly developed. He made special regulations for the industry, based on German laws, and in 1537 several mines were opened in Telemarken.[1] The undertaking was very important as a first chapter in the development of a new industry, but no proper control was exercised over the rude foreign miners, whose lawless behavior so exasperated the people that a serious uprising occurred in the mining districts. The general ill-will against the Danish *fogeds* added fuel to the flame. Several of these officials were slain, and the uprising spread rapidly. Christian III., who never visited Norway after he became king, remained a stranger to all local conditions, and without inquiring further into the real cause of the disturbance, which he regarded as a rebellion, he ordered the commandants of Akershus and Bohus to suppress the uprising. They marched into Telemarken, where they met the armed *bønder*, who were persuaded to lay down their weapons. After they had thus been disarmed, the *bønder* were surrounded and taken prisoners, and a number were sentenced to death and executed. The mines were operated with profit for some years, but a decline set in during the decade from 1542 till 1552, and a few years later the work was discontinued.

The introduction of mining, though attended at first by little success, was nevertheless a harbinger of a new era of national development. Another manifestation of the awakening of the spirit of progress was the destruction of the Hanseatic trade monopoly in Bergen, and the coming into existence of a body of enterprising native

[1] M. Braun Tvethe, *Norges Statistik*, p. 74 ff. Yngvar Nielsen, *Norges Historie*, vol. IV., p. 44 ff.

merchants, who dared to enter into competition with the Germans. Though the Hanseatic League had lost its former power in the Count's War, the German merchants in Bergen continued to act with their customary arrogance, and sought to intimidate all whom they feared might become competitors.[1] Lawlessness and corrupt practices had hitherto been the means by which they had maintained their power in Norway, but Christian III. would tolerate no violence or overt disobedience. In 1556 he appointed as commandant of Bergen the resolute, calm, and fearless nobleman Christopher Valkendorf, who could neither be scared by threats, nor disheartened by open resistance. The Hanseatic merchants had mounted cannons on the tower of the St. Mary's church, and sought to frighten the new commandant, but he paid no attention to their meddling schemes. With unbending firmness he undertook to carry out the necessary reforms. Hitherto the German merchants had been a foreign nation maintaining an organized state of their own in Bergen. In order to prevent their clerks and apprentices from marrying and becoming domiciled in Norway, they encouraged immorality to the utter corruption of the social and moral life of the city. Valkendorf began his work of reform by bringing the corrupt social practices under strict control, and the merchants had to submit to the laws, and promise to live "honestly, Christian-like, and well in all respects."[2] He summoned the German artisans, and demanded of them that they should take the oath of allegiance to the king, or leave the kingdom. Hitherto they had been a colony of foreigners subject only to their own laws; henceforth they would have to become citizens amenable to the laws of Norway if they wished to stay in Bergen. The demand, though a very just one, was not heeded. The powerful merchant guild encouraged them to resist, and, emboldened by this support, they threatened that if the commandant attempted to enforce such a demand, there would soon be orphans and widows enough in Bergen. In answer to these threats Valkendorf ordered the windows of their shops to be

---

[1] Yngvar Nielsen, *Bergen fra de ældste Tider indtil Nutiden*, p. 29 f. Krag og Stephanius, *Kristian III.'s Historie*, I., 277 ff., 286 ff. Vilh. Poulsen, *Fortællinger af Norges Historie*, III., 175 f. Yngvar Nielsen, *Norges Historie*, vol. IV., p. 108 ff. C. E. Secher, *Christoffer Valkendorf*.

[2] *Bergens Fundats*, published by N. Nicolaysen in *Norske Magasin*, I., p. 555–563, 587–603. Yngvar Nielsen, *Bergen*, p. 291 ff.

closed, trained the cannons of the fortress upon them, and held his forces ready for action. The commandant's resolute action struck terror into the hearts of the artisans, and they begged for an opportunity to negotiate. A meeting was arranged in the St. Mary's church, where Valkendorf appeared accompanied by two boys, and told the artisans of the order given the garrison of the fortress to fire upon their shops if he were harmed. No one ventured to resist, and an agreement was made by which the artisans pledged themselves either to take the oath of fealty to the government, or to leave the city before the next Michaelmas, unless the king should permit them to remain on the old conditions.[1] But the king supported Valkendorf, and when the choice finally had to be made, they decided to leave Bergen (1559). The German merchants still remained, but their power was broken. Successful resistance could no longer be made to the laws and authorities of the city, and the time would soon come when they would have to submit to the government, and remain satisfied with sharing the legitimate privileges accorded all other merchants of Bergen.

Christian III. and his queen, Dorothea of Lauenburg, were both devoted Lutherans. The king was a diligent student of the Bible, and was well versed in theology, medicine, history, and natural science; but he used the German language exclusively, and never learned to speak Danish. Though not gifted above the ordinary, he conducted the administration of the kingdom of Denmark with great ability and good judgment, but the affairs of Norway were much neglected, as the king never visited that kingdom throughout his whole reign. The great changes which made his reign the harbinger of a new era are, nevertheless, ascribable, in a degree, to his active coöperation, if not to his initiative. The Reformation, the rebuilding of the navy, the destruction of the Hanseatic trade monopoly, the introduction of mining in Norway were measures which not only showed an increased

[1] *Bergens Fundats, Norske Magasin*, I., 519–563. *Diplomatarium Norwegicum*, V., no. 1133. *Norske Rigsregistranter*, I., p. 244. Yngvar Nielsen, *Bergen*, p. 295. Ludvig Holberg, *Bergens Beskrivelse*, p. 99 ff. R. Nyerup, *Skildring af Tilstanden i Danmark og Norge*, I., p. 357 ff. Paus, *Samlinger af gamle norske Love og Forordninger*, vol. III., p. 323 ff. B. E. Bendixen, *Tyske Haandverkere paa norsk Grund i Middelalderen, Skrifter udgivet af Videnskabs-Selskabet i Christiania*, 1911.

national vigor, but which gave promise of a new development born of the ideas of the Reformation and the Renaissance. King Christian's greatest merit was that he became an advocate of the new ideas, and helped to make them a factor in the national development. He died on New Year's day, 1559. His old rival, King Christian II., who had been liberated from prison in 1549, died the same month at Kalundborg in Denmark.

22. FREDERICK II. THE SEVEN YEARS' WAR WITH SWEDEN

When Christian III. died, his son, Prince Frederick, who was twenty-four years of age, ascended the throne. He had been hailed as his father's successor in Denmark in 1542, and in Norway 1548, a step which shows a growing tendency to restrict the choice of king to the members of the royal family.[1] The new king had inherited his mother's restless energy and imperious temperament, but his education had been neglected, as he cared little for books in his boyhood. The religious tone prevalent at his father's court did not appeal to him. He quarreled frequently with his parents, loved pomp and display, and exhibited great fondness for military pursuits. In the administration of the affairs of the kingdom the careful and constructive course pursued by King Christian III. was abandoned. The public policy shaped by Frederick II. became a series of hasty impulses and of ill-considered adventures, terminating in failure and general distress.

The king won his first military glory in a war with Ditmarsken. It had been constantly urged that the Danes should avenge the defeat suffered by King Hans in 1500, but Christian III. would not begin war. His two brothers, the dukes Adolph and Hans, who had always been in favor of renewing the attempt to take Ditmarsken, found no

---

[1] In the charter of 1536, which was to be regarded as a constitution for both kingdoms, the provision was made that if Prince Frederick should die before his father, and if King Christian should receive another son, the Council should elect that son as his successor, and, as heir to the throne, he should have the official title of "Prince of Denmark." It is not clear for what purpose this provision was made, as the Council still maintained the principle that Denmark should be an elective kingdom as before, but the king's oldest son was always chosen his successor till 1660. See T. H. Aschehoug, *Statsforfatningen i Norge og Danmark indtil 1814*, p. 359 ff.

difficulty in persuading their nephew, King Frederick II., to join them in the undertaking. An army of 20,000 foot soldiers and 3000 cavalry was raised, and the Ditmarskers, who could only muster a force of 7000 men, were finally overpowered in 1560 after a most heroic resistance.

King Gustav Vasa of Sweden died Sept. 29, 1560, and was succeeded by his son Erik XIV. The new king was of a warlike disposition, and, as many old grudges still existed between Sweden and Denmark, a contest for the supremacy in the Baltic was almost sure to come. King Frederick II. asserted the old claim of Denmark to Esthonia and Ösel, and sought to ward off Russian encroachments in Livonia, but Sweden took possession of Reval, and entered into open rivalry with Denmark for the control of the Baltic. The immediate cause of the Seven Years' War which soon broke out was the use of three crowns in the coat of arms both of Sweden and Denmark.[1] The three crowns was the old coat of arms in Sweden, but in Denmark they had been adopted as a sign of union of the three Northern kingdoms. As Sweden had left the union, the continued use of the three crowns in the Danish coat of arms was an indication that the kings of Denmark had not yet relinquished their claim to the throne of Sweden. Frederick I. had, indeed, dropped the three crowns from the Danish coat of arms, but they had been reintroduced by Christian III. and Frederick II. This led to protracted negotiations, but neither Erik XIV. nor Frederick II. would yield. In fact, both desired war. King Erik hoped to take Norway, and Frederick II. felt certain that the war would give him the longed-for opportunity to gain the throne of Sweden. In vain the older and more experienced men counseled him not to risk a war. He found support among the young nobles, who exercised great influence in court circles, and the torch of war was soon lighted. In the first naval engagement off Bornholm, the Swedes under Admiral Bagge, a Norwegian by birth, took the Danish admiral prisoner, and captured three of his ships. On August 9, 1563, Frederick II., who was the aggressor, issued a declaration of war. Lübeck, Poland, and Russia became his allies, and Sweden was politically isolated. The war became, to a large extent, a naval contest, as Frederick depended on the Danish-Norwegian

[1] Otto Vaupell, *Den nordiske Syvaarskrig, 1563–1570*, Copenhagen, 1891.

fleet, which his father had created. The operations on land consisted chiefly in destructive border raids, in which lives and property were destroyed, seemingly without any other plan than to swell the general sum of misery. Norway was the trophy for which King Erik XIV. was willing to do battle. In the days of Karl Knutsson and Christian I. there had been sharp rivalry between Sweden and Denmark for the possession of Norway, and although Denmark had succeeded in maintaining the union with the sister kingdom, the old jealousy was not wholly allayed. When the war broke out, the Swedes still hoped, as in the time of Engelbrecht Engelbrechtsson, that Norway would revolt and attempt to shake off the Danish yoke. This hope is expressed in the Latin poem "Querelae Swedicae" ("Swedish complaints"), written at the court of King Erik XIV.[1] The poem describes Norway's sad fate, criticizes the Danish kings and officials, and enumerates the misfortunes which Danish misrule had brought upon the country. "Oh, Sister, to be pitied art thou. After Denmark with her sweet union bitterly hast brought thee under her feet, thou complainest too late; too late dost thou take the shield after the wounds have been inflicted. Too late thou grievest, because thou hast been brought under the tight reigns of oppression. Now, unfortunate one, thou finally seest that there has been black gall beneath so sweet honey." There seemed, indeed, to be an opportunity for Norway to shake off Danish overlordship, and dissolve the union, but as nothing had been done for the creation of an efficient army, the country lacked the necessary means for the successful pursuance of such a course. The sailors and marines in the Danish-Norwegian navy had been, to a large extent, recruited in Norway, the fortresses of the country had Danish commandants, and no central organization existed which could lead a national uprising. There seems, indeed, to have been at this time in Norway a sentiment in favor of Sweden, but such a sentiment could not be strengthened by the course pursued by the Swedish king, who, in spite of expressed sympathy, sent armies across the border to raid and plunder in Norwegian territory. In the fall of 1563 a Swedish army occupied Jæmtland, but the province was recaptured by Evert Bild, the com-

---

[1] Professor Ludvig Daae thinks that King Erik XIV. is the author of the poem. *Historisk Tidsskrift*, første række, vol. III., p. 492 f.

mandant of Steinviksholm in Trøndelagen. The following year a
Swedish army of 3500 men again entered Norway. The Norwegian
commander was pursued and slain, and the *lagmand* was captured and
placed in fetters. "How cruelly they treated the people God knows,"
says an old writer. Both in Jæmtland and Herjedalen, which were
held by the Swedish troops throughout the whole war, the people
were so oppressed by the rude soldiers that they fled from their homes
to Norway in large numbers.[1] The commander of the Swedish army
was a Frenchman, Claude Collart, who after subduing Jæmtland
marched across the mountains to Trøndelagen, and laid siege to the
strong fortress of Steinviksholm, which was surrendered by the commandant, Evert Bild, almost without resistance. The people
welcomed the Swedes as friends; the Danes were driven away, and
Trøndelagen, Møre, and Romsdal accepted the Swedish king as
their sovereign. This easy victory made Claude Collart (Claudius
Gallus) very arrogant. He sent most of his forces back to Sweden,
and began to rule in a most arbitrary and oppressive way. Heavy
taxes were imposed, and gallows were erected throughout the province,
as if it were his object to wreak martial vengeance on a conquered
race. The Trondhjem cathedral was desecrated by his soldiers,
who even carried away the body of St. Olav, evidently with the intention of bringing it to Sweden, but it was finally reinterred at
Floan church in Trøndelagen.[2] The pro-Swedish sentiment which

---

[1] Edward Bull, *Bidrag til Jæmtlands Historie fra Christian III. til Christian IV.*, *Historiske Afhandlinger tilegnet Professor Dr. J. E. Sars*, Christiania,
1905.

[2] Absalon Pederssøn Beyer, *Om Norgis Rige*, published by Gustav Storm
in *Historisk-topografiske Skrifter om Norge og norske Landsdele*, p. 38.

About the later history of St. Olav's remains, Professor P. A. Munch
writes: "The middle shrine with the body remained, in the meanwhile, in
the cathedral, and was even for some decennaries suffered to stand in its
place on the altar till the above-mentioned war between Sweden and Denmark from 1563 till 1570. The Swedes then occupied the city of Nidaros
about 1564, and did great damage in the cathedral; they took the shrine,
stripped it of everything valuable, 'even to the smallest silver nail,' and
buried it at last with the body in a small country church, no longer used for
divine service since the Reformation. When they were driven back the
following year, the people asked for and got permission of the Danish governor to bring back the body to the cathedral. This was accordingly done
on the 8th of July, with great pomp; the shrine was carried to the church

the people had shown was ill rewarded by this rude soldier of fortune, and his undisciplined warriors. No course could have been more effective in turning friendship into hatred, and the people would, naturally, welcome with joy any aid which would rid them of such oppression. Aid soon came from Bergen, where the able and energetic Erik Rosenkrans had been made commandant. He dispatched troops under Erik Munk to Trøndelagen to assist the local forces. Collart was obliged to evacuate Trondhjem, and retreat to the fortress of Steinviksholm. As the Swedes did not number above 400 men, he was soon forced to surrender, and the angry *bønder* of Nordland, Trøndelagen, Nordmør, Romsdal, and Søndmør were summoned to Trondhjem, where they renewed their oath of allegiance to King Frederick II.

The campaign on the southern theater of action resulted in the capture of Elfsborg by the Danes, and in 1564 the Danish admiral, Herluf Trolle, defeated the Swedish fleet commanded by Jacob Bagge in a noted naval battle off Öland. Hitherto the advantage in the

in a procession of the clergy, the noblemen, the military officers, and the citizens, and deposited in a bricklaid grave or vault. In the spring of 1568, however, a Danish nobleman, who was in Trondhjem on a special errand from the king, caused earth to be thrown into the grave over the body, probably in order to prevent people from worshiping it, which they still were inclined to do in spite of the newly introduced Protestantism. Even then the body was tolerably well preserved. Mag. Absalon Pederssøn, who saw it himself, says in his 'Description of Norway' that 'it was not altered except the cartilage of the nose, and some parts of the eyes, which were gone, else the rest of the members were as they had been for many hundred years.' A judge in the south of Norway, who in his youth had attended school in Trondhjem, told the Rev. Peder Claussøn Friis, the first translator of Snorre Sturlason, that 'the body of St. Olav, which he had seen himself, was rather long, well preserved, with a red beard, but the nose was somewhat sunken; the wounds inflicted upon the king in his last battle were still visible, for the rest it was dry and hard as wood.' This description, as will be seen, is at some variance with the more prolix one given above. The exact place where the aforesaid bricklaid grave is to be looked for is not known, but very probably it will be found when the repairs now contemplated are begun, that is to say, if there are any signs by which it may be identified. But whether the body be found or not, it is yet a satisfaction to know that it still rests in the same church which owes its origin to the saint, and from which, during five centuries, he spread luster over the whole kingdom." P. A. Munch og H. E. Schirmer, *Trondhjems Domkirke*, p. 38 f.

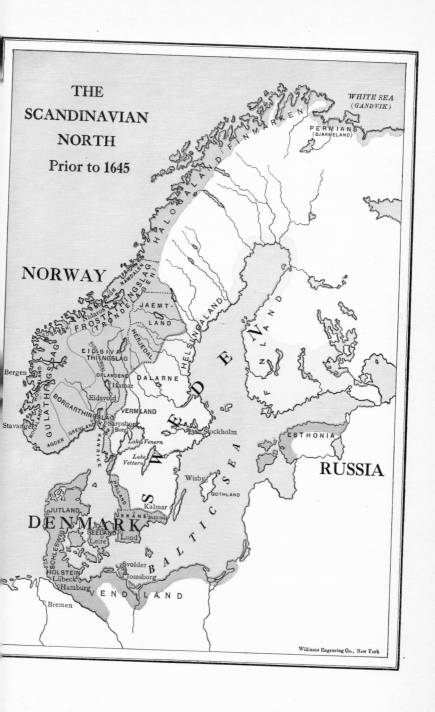

THE
SCANDINAVIAN
NORTH
Prior to 1645

WHITE SEA
(GANDVIK)

PERMIANS
(BJARMELAND)

NORWAY

SWEDEN

FINLAND

DENMARK

RUSSIA

ESTHONIA

BALTIC SEA

Williams Engraving Co., New York

struggle had inclined to the side of the Danes, but the tide turned in 1565. In the naval battle of Femern, Herluf Trolle received his death-wound, and his successor, Otto Rud, was captured in a second engagement at Bornholm. The situation became so critical that Denmark was persuaded to open peace negotiations, but King Erik XIV., who considered himself the unqualified victor, made demands which could not be accepted, and the struggle continued. The very able Danish general Daniel Rantzau defeated the Swedes at Axtorna, and the heroic Jens Holgerssøn had successfully defended Bohus against repeated attacks. In 1566 great efforts were made to increase the strength of the Danish army and navy. Soldiers were pressed into service, and the increased war contributions weighed heavily on the people both in Norway and Denmark. But of little avail were these sacrifices. A large part of the Danish-Norwegian fleet was destroyed on the coast of Gothland in a terrific storm, July 28–29. Between six and seven thousand men perished in a single night,[1] but as the Swedish fleet was also damaged in the same hurricane, the relative strength of the two powers was not materially changed. In spite of repeated misfortunes King Frederick II. "did not allow his royal courage to be shaken." Again he undertook to build a fleet, which he hoped might retrieve the losses, and bring him the coveted victory.

In 1567 King Erik XIV. directed his attack against Norway. This vain and ambitious king, who was inordinately licentious and void of any solicitude for the welfare of his people, was becoming mentally unbalanced. He still thought that the Norwegians would rise against the Danes, and he was encouraged in this belief by an adventurer, Eno Brandrøk, a son of the Norwegian naval hero Christopher Trondssøn. Eno advised Erik to attack Akershus. The Norwegians, he said, would rise in revolt as soon as the Swedes appeared, and the march from Akershus to Bergenhus would be a triumphal procession. Stories like these would, naturally, excite the diseased imagination of the almost insane king. An army under John Siggessøn was dispatched across the border into Østerdalen, and a wicked raid, accompanied by the plundering of the churches and the devastation of defenseless settlements, was begun. Østerdalen and Hedemarken were ravaged, Hamar was taken, and Hamarhus

[1] Otto Vaupell, *Den nordiske Syvaarskrig*, p. 113 ff.

castle was plundered. But when the enemy reached Oslo, the people burned their city rather than see it fall into the hands of the invaders. The districts of southeastern Norway submitted, and the people were forced to swear allegiance to King Erik XIV., but the ravages did not cease. Swedish detachments roamed over Ringerike, Romerike, Hedemarken, Gausdal, and the districts east and west of the Christiania fjord; Sarpsborg was burned, because the people refused to pay war tribute; the same fate befell Konghelle. New forces arrived constantly, and it seemed as if the plundering and burning would never stop. Akershus was invested, and Erik Rosenkrans of Bergen sought to aid the besieged fortress, but he experienced the greatest difficulty in raising forces and supplies. The war had exhausted the resources both of Norway and Denmark, and loud complaints were heard on every hand. Erik Munk was, finally, sent to Akershus with reënforcements, and the Swedes had to retire. They marched northward from Oslo, "crossed seven large rivers which were in their way, and everywhere they broke down the bridges behind them, burned everything which they found, and killed both men and women, sparing no one." On their retreat they also destroyed Hamarhus castle, and burned the Hamar cathedral. The great church was not destroyed, but suffered serious damages, which were never repaired, and the cathedral gradually fell to ruin.[1]

After the termination of the Norwegian campaign, the struggle was waged principally on Swedish soil, and Norway was not seriously molested. The war, which had exhausted all three kingdoms, was gradually drawing to a close. King Erik XIV., who had become permanently deranged, was finally deposed, and his brother, Duke John, was placed on the throne as King John III. in January, 1569. About the same time a treaty of peace had been negotiated with Denmark, but as the king and the Estates of Sweden would not ratify it, hostilities began anew. Frederick II., however, had soon spent the last strength of his two kingdoms, and peace negotiations were renewed at Stettin, July 15, 1570, and the final treaty of peace

---

[1] The cathedral, which was a structure in Romanesque style, was built in the second half of the twelfth century. Einar Orting, *Hamar Domkirke* *Symra*, vol. VII., p. 95 f. N. Nicolaysen, *Stor-Hamars Ruiner*. L. Dietrichson, *Vore Fædres Verk*, Christiania, 1906. C. Ramseth, *Hamar Bys Historie* Hamar, 1899. C. C. A. Lange, *De norske Klostres Historie i Middelalderen*

was signed December 13 of the same year. According to the terms of the treaty, Denmark should surrender all claims to Sweden. The question of the three crowns in the Danish coat of arms should be settled by a court of arbitration; but as this court was never assembled, Denmark continued to use the three crowns as before. Elfsborg should be given back to Sweden on the payment of an indemnity of 150,000 riksdaler. The Norwegian provinces of Jæmtland and Herjedalen, which had hitherto belonged to the diocese of Upsala, were joined to the diocese of Trondhjem. All ships and cannons which had been taken in the war should be returned to their respective owners, all conquered territory should be surrendered, and Lübeck should have the right to trade with Sweden. In the long struggle nothing had been gained by either power. Their relative strength, both on land and sea, remained what it had been since 1537.

23. NORWEGIAN INTERNAL ADMINISTRATION IN THE REIGN OF FREDERICK II.

From 1536 till 1572 Norway had no central government which could represent the whole people, and serve as a connecting link between the king and the royal officials, as the Council had ceased to exist, but the need of a central administrative authority within the kingdom had been keenly felt in the war with Sweden. As each *lensherre* was the highest authority within his own district, an efficient use of the country's resources in time of danger was well-nigh impossible. No army was maintained, and the Norwegians had been unable to defend themselves even against a small invading force. In 1572 the king created the office of *statholder* (viceroy) of Norway, to which position he appointed Paul Huitfeldt, commandant of Akershus. The *statholder* should have supervision of the church and clergy, the courts, and the royal demesne lands. He should exercise authority over the *lensherrer*, so that they should not oppress the people, and by a regulation of July 5, 1588, he was also placed in supreme command of the Norwegian military forces.[1] The central-

Om Hammer och Hammer Kiøbstadtz Bygning, old manuscript published by Gustav Storm in *Historisk-topografiske Skrifter om Norge og norske Landsdele*.

[1] T. H. Aschehoug, *Statsforfatningen i Danmark og Norge indtil 1814*, p. 389 ff.

ization of administrative authority was especially necessary in order
to bring better order into the finances of the kingdom, which had been
reduced to a wretched state during the war. The lands belonging
to the bishops had been confiscated by the state at the introduction
of the Reformation, and all church lands should also be administered
by the government, as the Lutheran Church was a state church.
But before the revenues could be made to flow in the proper channels,
the administrative system had to be readjusted to the altered conditions. Three subordinate officers, *stiftsskrivere*, were appointed
to supervise the buildings, property, rents, and incomes belonging to
the churches, and rules were made regarding saw-mills and the
lumber trade, the preservation of the forests, the keeping of all public
property, and the building of war galleys. Paul Huitfeldt was personally very active. He traveled about in the united dioceses of Oslo
and Hamar, and compiled a census of the property of churches and
clergymen. A copy of this document, usually called "Paul Huitfeldt's Stiftsbog," is still in existence.[1] The *lensherrer* usually received the whole income of a small *len*, but only a relatively small
share of the income from the principal *len*. The *statholder*, Paul
Huitfeldt, received for his services the income of the *len* of Tromsø,
but only 10 per cent of the income of Akershus *len*. But besides this,
he was granted, also, the necessaries for his large household, for which
he might use three hundred chickens, ten barrels of tallow for candles,
three barrels of salmon, and five hundred flounders. The cost of
maintaining these great lords, besides the taxes which had to be paid
to church and state, often made the public burdens alarmingly heavy.
In 1571 every *odelsbonde* had to pay taxes to the amount of one-half
of his whole income. This was, however, a war rate; in 1576 it was
reduced to half that amount, or 25 per cent of the income. The
revenues of the crown were derived from the following sources:[2]
The *landskyld*, or income from rented crown lands; income from lands
operated for the benefit of the crown, consisting chiefly of lumber

---

[1] Yngvar Nielsen, *Norges Historie*, vol. IV., p. 181 f.

[2] The system of taxation at this time is found clearly illustrated in an
old manuscript in the Norwegian royal archives, which contains an itemized
account of incomes and expenditures of Akershus *len* for the years 1557–1558,
and 1560–1561. Extracts from these accounts have been published by
T. H. Aschehoug in *Norske Samlinger*, vol. I., p. 161 ff.

sawed in the royal forests, the regular taxes, consisting of the *leding* tax for the coast districts and the *visøre* tax for the inland districts; *foring*, or the feeding of horses used by the government, which seems to have been a new tax, as it is mentioned for the first time in a statute of 1578; fines imposed by the court in punishment of crime; *tithes; duties*, consisting of duty on goods exported, and a certain tax or toll on ships according to their size; *sise* (excise), or import duty on ale and prydsing; and *aid* paid the crown by certain districts, probably a free donation. The taxes were collected by the provosts and *fogeds*, who usually employed the *lensmænd* (*bønder-lensmænd*) for this purpose. As money was very scarce, the taxes were, usually, paid in sheep, cattle, and produce of various kinds, which had to be transported to Akershus, or some other central point, at the expense of the crown. A part was used for the household of the *statholder* or *lensherre*, and for the payment of servants and officials; the remainder was sent to Denmark.[1]

After the war the army was neglected both in Norway and Denmark; but considerable attention was devoted to the fleet, as Frederick II. wished to maintain Danish supremacy in the Baltic. The sea was also made insecure by numerous pirates, and it was necessary to keep a strong fleet in active service to keep them at bay. Interesting incidents sometimes occurred in these pirate hunts. In 1567 Captain Aalborg sailed from Bergen to look for pirates. At Karmsund he discovered two suspicious looking vessels, which he brought to Bergen for inspection. One of the vessels was found to carry James Hepburn, Earl of Bothwell, the husband of Mary Stuart. Although a fugitive, he was courteously received by Erik Rosenkrans, commandant at Bergen, who entertained him at a banquet. In Bergen the earl met a lady to whom he had been untrue. This was Anna, the daughter of Christopher Trondssøn, who confronted him with evidence that he was her husband. In Norway she was known as "skottefruen" (the Scotch lady). She would have nothing more to do with the faithless Bothwell, and the earl was taken to Denmark, where he was imprisoned at Malmöhus, and later at Dragsholm, until his death in 1578.

[1] T. H. Aschehoug, *De norske Communers Retsforfatning før 1837*, p. 84 f. Yngvar Nielsen, *Norges Historie*, vol. IV.

One of the most noteworthy characters whose names are connected with the pirate hunts of those times is Mogens Heinessøn, who was born of Norwegian parents in the Faroe Islands, where his name still lives in stories and traditions. He had sailed as merchant between Bergen and the Faroe Islands; his ship had been robbed by pirates, and he had gone to Holland, where he enlisted in the navy. Later he returned and began again to trade with his native islands, though this trade had been made a royal monopoly. Sometimes he hunted the pirates, and at other times he was a Viking corsair, leading a life of romantic adventure, until his old enemy, Christopher Valkendorf, succeeded in throwing him into prison. Through Valkendorf's influence Heinessøn was sentenced to death and executed without proper trial. This unjust proceeding was later annulled, and Christopher Valkendorf had to pay Heinessøn's widow, and his old business partner, Hans Lindenow, a large indemnity.[1]

The problem of creating a just and efficient government in Norway, where the details of law and administration could not come under the direct control of the king and his Council, presented difficulties which were not solved even by the creation of the office of *statholder*. The old complaints of extortion and oppression by the *fogeds* and royal officials continued. Unlawful taxes were often collected, and the people felt aggrieved by many unjust and arbitrary acts on the part of the foreign royal officers, who neither understood the local conditions, nor enjoyed the good-will of the people.

However well-meaning the paternal rule of a foreign monarch may be, it is always bad. His numerous subordinates may practice a most exasperating tyranny, which he cannot mitigate without destroying the very system of which he has become the representative. In order that the king through his Council might exercise a more direct influence upon the administration and the enforcement of the laws by the courts, councils of magnates, which had hitherto been assembled on special occasions, were held more frequently. From 1568 such councils (*herredage*) may almost be regarded as a perma-

---

[1] Troels Lund, *Mogens Heinessøn*, Copenhagen, 1877. Ludvig Daae, *Om Mogens Heinessøn*, Christiania, 1869. Lucas Debes, *Feroe et Feroa reserata*, Copenhagen, 1673. J. H. Schrøter, *Færøiske Folkesagn*, *Antiquarisk Tidsskrift*, 1849–1851.

nently established institution. They were to act as a higher court, but administrative questions were also considered and settled. Some members of the Danish Council — not above five — were sent to Norway to hold such assizes. The measures adopted, and the decisions made were to be regarded as if they had been made by the Council itself, but an appeal could, nevertheless, be made to the king and the Council.[1] The king thought that all irregularities and offenses could be investigated and adjusted by the *statholder* and the Councils, so that no complaints would have to be carried directly to the throne. But the Norwegians were accustomed from very early times to bring their grievances to the attention of the king directly. He, they thought, would not shield the offender, even if he were a high official; he would give them justice, and instead of appealing to the *statholder*, they appointed committees to go to Copenhagen to lay their complaints before the king himself. The king was anxious to see justice done, but the officials and nobles against whom complaints were made, sought to revenge themselves upon those who ventured to seek justice in that way. In 1573 a committee, led by Rolv Halvardssøn, was sent to Copenhagen, and when they had presented their case, the king wrote a letter to Ludvig Munk, *lensherre* in Trondhjem, requesting him to aid the *bønder*, and to see to it that the matter was settled right. But when the committee returned, they got into trouble with Ludvig Munk and his *foged*, and Rolv Halvardssøn and his companions were unjustly condemned to death and executed.[2] The constant struggle between tyrannical officials and an angry people, whose necks could not be bent, fills the centuries of the union period with tragic episodes, and constitutes one of its most characteristic and noteworthy features. The struggle was not a war for national liberty, conducted by great leaders; it was not a general organized movement, but a dogged and persistent fight by the people for their legal rights and their freedom as individuals, without which a Norseman could not live, and out of which national liberty sprang full-grown when the union with Denmark ended.

[1] Yngvar Nielsen, *Norges Historie*, vol. IV., p. 171 and 198. T. H. Aschehoug, *Statsforfatningen i Norge og Danmark indtil 1814*, p. 382 ff.

[2] *To Herredagsdomme af 1578 og 1579 angaaende nogle Bønder i Guldalen som var henrettede for Landraadesag, Norske Samlinger*, II., p. 31 ff. Halvdan Koht, *Fyrebuing til norsk Politik, Historiske Afhandlinger tilegnet J. E. Sars*, p. 132 ff.

24. Intellectual and Social Conditions in Norway in the Sixteenth Century

The literary life in Norway in the sixteenth century, though it shows a lack of creative ability, is not wholly wanting in intellectual energy, and many valuable works were written in this period by the Norwegian humanists. Humanism, which had spread over Europe from Italy, had been temporarily interrupted by the Reformation, but after Protestantism had been established in the North, it blossomed forth again with increased vigor. In Norway, as elsewhere, the clergy, who had studied, not only in the schools at home, but at the universities abroad, and had acquired the spirit and culture of the age, became devoted adherents of the new learning. Some noblemen of literary tastes and scholarly inclinations were also enthusiastic humanists. At the bishops' seats, and also at the parsonages, small libraries were collected, though books were rare and expensive. The prevalent cosmopolitan spirit, the Latin language everywhere used by scholars, and common intellectual interests bound the humanists in all countries together with fraternal ties. They felt themselves to be a sacred brotherhood, constituting the universal kingdom of learning, and theirs was the special privilege of exploring and bringing to light the great intellectual treasures and culture of classic antiquity. They turned their attention also to the past history of their own people, and dug from obscurity and neglect the *sagas* of the kings of Norway, translated them into the modern Norse tongue, and sought to open the eyes of the people to their own past greatness. In Bergen, where the talented humanist Geble Pederssøn became the first Lutheran bishop, a circle of learned literary men sprang into existence. In Nidaros, Stavanger, Hamar, Oslo, and other places humanists were poring over old books and dusty manuscripts in their eager search for knowledge. One of the leading Norwegian humanists was Mag. Absalon Pederssøn Beyer of the Bergen Latin school, a pupil and protégé of Geble Pederssøn. Mag. Absalon wrote the "Liber Capituli Bergensis," [1] a diary which gives a picture of Bergen at

---

[1] The work is published by N. Nicolaysen, Christiania, 1860, under the title *Liber Capituli Bergensis, Absalon Pederssøns Dagbog over Begivenheder især i Bergen, 1552–1572.*

that time with great distinctness of detail. He also wrote "Norges Beskrivelse,"[1] a description of Norway which is especially remarkable because of the intense patriotic feeling expressed in it. The author bemoans in most pathetic words the loss of Norwegian independence, but he speaks with eloquent hopefulness when he refers to the country's future. The following quotation will show the general tenor of the book: "Therefore begins here Norway's old age, since she has become so old, cold, and unfruitful that she cannot give birth to royal children of her own, who could be her rulers. Her nobility, good heroes, and warriors died from her, part by the sword, and part by the pestilence during the Black Death . . . so that from that time forth the Norwegian nobility has constantly decreased in number, year by year, and day by day, since their fathers either gave their property to monasteries or churches, or forfeited it, or they wasted it themselves through marriage, or a number of bastard sons inherited it. Furthermore, the Norwegian nobility receive no grants of land belonging to the crown or the dioceses, and their own suffice little or nothing to maintain the style and extravagance which are now so common, therefore they are becoming extinct." He compares Norway to an old widow who must lean upon a staff in walking, but she is only apparently, not really, weak.

"Still Norway might awaken from her sleep if she could get a ruler, for she is not so degenerated or weakened that she could not regain her former power and glory; for these hard mountains are full of good butter, silver, gold, and other precious things. The people still possess some of the old virtue, manhood, and power, which should enable them to fight for their lord and native land, if they could daily see him and experience his favor."[2] The author's optimism regarding Norway's future development and the ability of the Norwegian people to retain their lost national greatness, rested on a correct anticipation, based on a thorough knowledge of local

[1] Published by Gustav Storm in *Historisk-topografiske Skrifter om Norge og norske Landsdele i det 16de Aarhundrede*, Christiania, 1895. Yngvar Nielsen, *Af Norges Historie, De norske Humanister*, p. 115 ff.

[2] Gustav Storm, *Historisk-topografiske Skrifter, Om Norgis Rige*, af Mag. Absalon Pederssøn Beyer, p. 21 ff. Rasmus Nyerup, *Historisk-statistisk Skildring af Tilstanden i Danmark og Norge i ældre og nyere Tider*, vol. I., p. 320 ff.

VOL. II — M

conditions. Unfortunate circumstances had, indeed, led to Norway's union with Denmark, in which perfect equality between the two sister kingdoms could not be maintained; but the Norwegian people had never been conquered, their spirit had not been subdued or broken, sometime the irksome ties would be dissolved, Norway would wake from her slumbers, the spirit of the people would reassert itself, and a new era of national progress would begin. Modern Norwegian history proves the correctness of Mag. Absalon Pederssøn's views. We shall have the opportunity to observe how this new national awakening began long before the union with Denmark was dissolved.

Peder Claussøn Friis, clergyman in Undal in Agder, was a patriot like his contemporary, Absalon Pederssøn Beyer. He wrote a work about Norway, "Norigis Beskriffuelse," a Norwegian natural history, and a description of the Norwegian island colonies.[1] He also published a translation of the "Sagas of the Kings of Norway," a most important work, through which the people learned to know their past history, as they were no longer able to read their books in the Old Norse language. Through this work Norwegian national feeling received a powerful stimulus. Mattis Størssøn,[2] who died in 1569 as *lagmand* in Bergen, translated the "Sagas of the Kings of Norway" from the "Heimskringla" and the "Codex Frisianus," and for the *lensherre* in Bergen he wrote, about 1555, "En kort Beretning om Kjøbmændene ved Bryggen" (*i.e.* a short account of the Hanseatic merchants in Bergen).[3] He complained of their encroachments, and proposed plans for improving the country's economic condition. Gustav Storm says: "He thought that Greenland in olden times had been a gold-mine for Norway, similar to what India was for the Spanish monarchy, and we probably do not err in believing that he has translated the old 'Grønlands Beskrivelse,' and has worked it into

[1] Peder Claussøn Friis, *Samlede Skrifter*, edited by Gustav Storm, Christiania, 1881.

[2] Mattis Størssøn's work is the first translation of the *sagas* into modern Danish. It was published in Copenhagen, 1594, by Jens Mortensen, and was erroneously called "Jens Mortensens Sagaoversættelse." See Gustav Storm, *Et gjenfundet Haandskrift af Mattis Størssøns Sagaoversættelse, Historisk Tidsskrift*, anden række, vol. V., p. 271 ff.

[3] Printed in *Norske Magasin*, I., p. 43–46.

Erik Valkendorf's accounts of Greenland, to be used on the expeditions of discovery which were sent out from Bergen shortly afterward." Laurents Hanssøn Bonde, who lived in the neighborhood of Bergen, translated *sagas* and wrote commentaries to the codes of church laws.[1] Erik Hansson Schønnebøl wrote "Lofotens og Vesteraalens Beskrivelse." [2] "Bergens Fundats," written by some unknown author,[3] 1559 or 1560, contains a history of Bergen till the time of Christopher Valkendorf and the subjugation of the Hanseatic merchants. "Bergens Rimkrønike," by an unknown author, narrates the history of the city till the time of the Victual Brothers, and is of importance as an historical source.[4] "Gandske Nommedals Lens Beskriffuelse Aar 1597," "Om Hammars Kjøbstads Bygning," 1553,[5] and "Norsk So" ("Die nordtsche Sau"), a bitter complaint of moral conditions in Bergen, written about 1584, are also of unknown authors.[6]

In Oslo Bishop Jens Nilssøn became the center of a large circle of

[1] *Grønlands historiske Mindesmerker*, III., p. 250–260, 490–494. *Laurits Hanssøns Sagaoversættelse*, edited by Gustav Storm, *Christiania Videnskabs-Selkabs Skrifter*, 1899.

[2] Published by Gustav Storm in *Historisk-topografiske Skrifter om Norge og norske Landsdele*. Storm has shown that Schønnebøl is the author, though the work was originally published anonymously. See *Historisk Tidsskrift*, tredie række, vol. IV., p. 173 ff.

[3] Herluf Lauritssøn has been regarded as the author of *Bergens Fundats* by Holberg, Nyerup, N. Nicolaysen, Yngvar Nielsen, and others; but Gustav Storm has shown that Lauritssøn cannot be the author. G. Storm, *Om Skriftet "Bergens Fundats" og dets forfatter*, *Historisk Tidsskrift*, tredie række, vol. IV., p. 418 ff.

[4] N. Nicolaysen, and likewise Yngvar Nielsen ("Bergen," p. 328) have held that the author of *Bergens Fundats* has used *Bergens Rimkrønike* as a source, but Gustav Storm has shown that *Bergens Rimkrønike* is based on *Bergens Fundats*. See *Historisk Tidsskrift*, tredie række, vol. IV., p. 418 ff.

[5] Published by Gustav Storm in *Historisk-topografiske Skrifter om Norge og norske Landsdele*.

[6] *Norske So*, printed in N. Nicolaysen's *Norske Magasin*, vol. II. The title was suggested by a deformed pig born at Oslo, July 7, 1581. This caused great alarm, as the superstitious people, and the no less superstitious humanistic scholars, regarded it as an evil omen signifying that the vengeance of God would fall upon the people, because of their wickedness. The poem is of importance as an historical source, as it gives us an insight into the moral depravity in Bergen at that time, though the author is guilty of extravagant exaggerations.

learned and able humanists.[1] Besides his knowledge of Greek and
Latin he was well versed in Norwegian history and Old Norse.   He
copied the manuscript of the "Jofraskinna," and wrote Latin songs,
in which he describes the scenery of Norway, and the life and customs
of the people, especially in the district of Telemarken, where the life
of the Middle Ages was still well preserved. His most important
work is his "Visitatsbøger," a record of his work as bishop of Oslo-
Hamar diocese during a period of twenty-five years, in which he describes the country, the roads, the lower nobility, clergy, peasants,
and townspeople.[2]   Fredrik Grøn says of Absalon Pederssøn Beyer,
Peder Claussøn Friis, and Jens Nilssøn: "In a larger sense the humanistic ideas were brought to Norway by these men. It was, at
all events, principally these three who brought humanistic thought
to the hitherto intellectually isolated educated circles in Norway, to
whom these thoughts were hitherto unfamiliar." [3]

Regarding the population in the North in this period only meager
data exist, as no census was taken till in the middle of the eighteenth
century. The calculations based on tax lists and the old military
system leave so much to conjecture that the results deduced by different authorities diverge very radically. Professor P. A. Munch
held that the population of Norway prior to the Black Death must
have been about 560,000. Professor J. E. Sars states as a result of
his investigations that prior to the great plague Norway had about
300,000 inhabitants, and that during the plague the number was
reduced to 200,000; at the beginning of the sixteenth century it had
again risen to 300,000, and at the end of the same century the population of Norway numbered about 400,000.[4] Troels Lund has figured
out that in the year 1600 Denmark had a population of about 1,400,000,
and that the population of Norway numbered about 600,000.   But

---

[1] Among those belonging to this circle were : Halvard Gunnarssøn, author
of Latin poems and historical works, Rector Jacob Wolf, Doctor of Medicine
Peder Flemløse, Peder Alfssøn, Claus Berg, Provost Rasmus Hjort in Tunsberg, Povel Nilssøn of Sande, and others.

[2] *Biskop Jens Nilssøns Visitatsbøger og Reiseoptegnelser*, published by
Yngvar Nielsen, Christiania, 1885. See Yngvar Nielsen, *Af Norges Historie, De norske Humanister*, p. 115 ff.

[3] Fredrik Grøn, *Nogen medicinske Forholde i Norge i det 16de Aarhundrede, Historisk Tidsskrift*, fjerde række, vol. IV., p. 399 ff.

[4] P. A. Munch, *Det norske Folks Historie*, vol. IV., p. 439 ff.

as Sars claims that this estimate is without foundation, we may take the lowest figures as the more reliable, *i.e.* the total population of Norway and Denmark in 1600 might be estimated to be about 1,500,000.[1] But relatively considered, this was a large population at that time, as Scotland did not have over 800,000 inhabitants, and the population of England did not number above 5,000,000.

City life was but little developed, as the people lived for the most part in the country. Bergen was still the largest city in the North, and the most important commercial center. The population of the leading cities in the Scandanavian kingdoms about 1600 is estimated by Troels Lund as follows: Bergen 15,000, Copenhagen 13,000, Stockholm 7000, Malmö 6000, and Trondhjem about 5000. But this estimate, which is based on military service and tax lists, seems to be largely a result of conjecture.[2] Yngvar Nielsen estimates the population of Bergen to have been six or seven thousand at the time of the introduction of the Reformation (1536)[3] while J. E. Sars thinks that at this time the population of Bergen could not have been much above 3000, Trondhjem about 1000, Oslo about 1500, and the other cities probably had, on the average, about 500 inhabitants.[4] Because of the Hanseatic trade monopoly, many of the smaller towns, such as Vaagen, Véey, Borgund, Kaupanger, and Lillehammer, had either disappeared, or had become mere market places.

From time to time foreign elements have been added to the native population in Norway, as in all other countries. This influx of new blood may, indeed, have been lighter in so distant a land than in the countries more centrally located, but in the Middle Ages the immigration became of great importance to Norway in several ways. After the union was established, a great number of Danes settled in the kingdom as officials, ministers, teachers, merchants, and even as laborers and artisans. During the Hanseatic supremacy the German merchants became an influential element in many cities, especially in Bergen, where their colony at one time is thought to have

[1] J. E. Sars, *Folkemængdens Bevægelse i Norge 13–17de Aarh.*, *Historisk Tidsskrift*, anden række, vol. III., p. 282 ff. Troels Lund, *Dagligt Liv i Norden i det 16de Aarhundrede*, vol. I., p. 52 ff.

[2] Troels Lund, *Dagligt Liv i Norden i det 16de Aarhundrede*, vol. I., p. 52 ff.

[3] Yngvar Nielsen, *Bergen*, p. 285.

[4] J. E. Sars, *Udsigt over den norske Historie*, III., p. 259 ff.

numbered about 3000 persons. In the sixteenth century many Hollanders and Englishmen settled in Norway as merchants, and many Scotchmen, who had been brought over as mercenaries, remained permanently in the country.[1] The most remarkable foreign element which came to the North in that century was the Gypsies. The origin of this people is veiled in impenetrable mystery. In course of time they have spread over the greater part of Asia and Europe, and they are also found in Africa and America. In southern Europe they appeared for the first time in 1417, and claimed to be Egyptian pilgrims who made a vow to wander about homeless for seven years to atone for the sins of their ancestors, who had refused to give Jesus, when a child, a drink of water from the Nile. By the Greeks they were called *Gyphtoi*, which has been changed in English to *Gypsies*. The story which they told of their origin created sympathy for them, and the Emperor and the Pope placed them under their special protection. But when it was learned that the Gypsies did not return to their own land, that they practiced witchcraft, and that they were not to be relied upon in word or deed, they soon became the object of hatred and persecution. In some countries they were called Tartars (N. Tater), as they were thought to be heathens from Asia. Led by their king or duke the Gypsies generally advanced in bands of three hundred persons or less. A few of the leaders were mounted, the rest of the band — men, women, and children — went on foot. They were seen for the first time in the North in 1505. A band led by Count Antonius Gagino, which had spent some months in Scotland, came to Denmark, bringing a letter of recommendation from James IV., stating that they had been peaceful. In 1511 another band led by "Junker Jørgen of Egypt" entered Schleswig.[2] In the following year the Gypsies appeared in Sweden, and they must have entered Norway

[1] The influx of foreigners into the Norwegian cities can be observed in the *Bergens Borgerbog, 1550–1751*, edited by N. Nicolaysen, Christiania, 1878. During two hundred years, from 1550 till 1750, 9279 persons had acquired the privileges of citizenship in the cities of Norway. The birthplace of 6526 is recorded. Of these 3352 were born in Norway or in the Norwegian colonies, and 2974 were foreigners: 1607 Germans, 758 Danes, 353 Englishmen and Scots, 147 Swedes, 103 Hollanders, five Frenchmen, and one Spaniard.

[2] Troels Lund, *Dagligt Liv i Norden*, p. 52 ff.

about the same time. They were at first treated with kindness, but as they were given to theft and swindle, they soon became generally hated. In 1536 they were outlawed and ordered to leave Norway within three months; any one might kill them and take their property; people were forbidden to shelter them or give them any aid; and the *lensmand* who did not arrest all the Gypsies within his district was made personally responsible for any damage which they might do.[2] "The poor Gypsies were now in dire straits," says Troels Lund. "The foxes and wolves were better situated; but they could not be expelled even by these measures. Adhering like burrs, homeless as migrating birds, shy and unsusceptible to kind as to harsh treatment, hungry as wolves, noiseless and keen-eyed like cats in the dark, they lived only for the moment. They could rejoice like children when they found a brief rest, but they could also endure hardships on their endless wanderings to a degree that no mercenary soldier had dreamt of. They did not depart; they retreated everywhere, but remained in the country. And whither should they go? If they went to France, they would be sentenced to the galleys; in Germany and the Netherlands they were outlawed. The only thing accomplished by this order issued by King Christian III. was to split them up into smaller bands, which were chased without plan from one end of the country to the other, persecuted wherever they appeared, but gone at the moment when they were to be seized; doleful, leaving no footprints, like children of the darkness." As the Gypsies had no religion, as they practiced magic arts, and were accused, though unjustly, of sacrificing human beings, the church joined the state authorities in persecuting them. In Sweden an order was

---

[1] The Code of Christian V., a lawbook prepared for the kingdom of Norway, 1687, contains the following article regarding the Gypsies: Gypsies who run about and swindle people with their cheating, lies, theft, and sorcery should be seized by the local authorities wherever they can be found, and those who are captured by the people in the country should be delivered to the nearest *bønder-lensmand*, who, with the aid of the people, shall bring them to the *foged;* and all their belongings shall be seized, and their leaders shall be punished by death; the others shall leave the kingdom by the shortest route, and if they are afterwards seen or met with in this kingdom, they shall suffer death like their leaders, and whoever houses or shelters them shall pay to his lord for every night and every person like one who shelters an outlaw. Book III., chapter 22, article 3.

issued to the parish priests in 1560 that "a priest must have nothing to do with the Taters (Gypsies). He must neither bury their dead nor baptize their children."[1] A similar order was issued by the Bishop of Fyen in Denmark, 1578. "If Gypsies come to the land, as sometimes happens, then shall no priest marry them, or give them the sacrament, but he shall let them die as if they were Turks, and they shall be buried outside of the churchyard as heathens. If they wish to have their children baptized, they must baptize them themselves."[2] But the united efforts of the church and state could not crush them.[3] Under the worst persecutions they seem to have made no attempt to leave; they were not reduced in number, nor did they adopt a different mode of life. At last the more humane spirit of modern times freed even the despised Gypsies from persecution, and suffered them to walk their own paths unmolested. But the modern humane spirit accomplished what medieval persecution did not achieve. The Gypsies no longer felt the necessity of wholly isolating themselves from the rest of mankind. They accepted into their flocks tramps and idlers of various kinds, and thereby they gradually lost their language and their identity as a people. In Denmark they have already ceased to exist as a distinct nationality, and in Sweden and Norway they are fast disappearing. The Night-men in Jutland and the *Fanter* in Norway are the last mixed remnants of the Gypsies, who through the process of amalgamation will soon be totally absorbed by the native population.[4] As to their influence on the native population Troels Lund says : "The Gypsies constituted a distinct ingredient in the life of the North in the sixteenth century, not only as viewed by themselves, but especially through their connection with the rest. Their sneaking, noiseless existence constitutes a mysterious ingredient in the motley mixture, and belongs to the shady side of its existence. They help us to understand the people's great aversion to being out after dark, the shudder which went through all when an unusual noise was heard at night, or a light was seen in

---

[1] F. Dyrlund, *Tatere og Natmandsfolk*, p. 13.

[2] Bloch, *Den fyenske Geistligheds Historie*, p. 43, quoted by Troels Lund, *Dagligt Liv i Norden*, vol. I., p. 77.

[3] Eilert Sundt, *Fante- eller Landstrygerfolket i Norge*, Christiania, 1850–1865.　　　　　　　　　　　　　　[4] *Ibid.*

the forest. One might think that the fact that they seldom appeared would have restricted this fear, but they gave name and example to a host of light-fearing tramps, crooks, loafers, and nighthawks, who even before had been a true scourge. The same was the case with the sorcery and demonolatry of the Gypsies. As they were too few to attract much attention themselves, they became the visible and tangible expression for the superstition and fear of the devil which characterized the age."

Inland travel was still attended with great difficulty. The journeys through the mountain districts had to be made on horseback, as no wagon roads existed. The narrow mountain trails which wound across the mountains and through the dense forests were often as hard to find as they were difficult to travel. This was especially the case in winter, when snow and ice made travel both difficult and dangerous. Man's best friend on these lonesome and hazardous journeys was the strong Norwegian mountain pony, who might be trusted both to find the trail and to walk it with heavy burdens, and it is not strange that the Norseman from time immemorial has felt a most tender attachment for his favorite animal. The dangers and hardships of inland travel are referred to even in the Edda poems. The "Hávamál" says:

> "Fire needs he
> who enters the house
> and is cold about the knees;
> food and clothes
> the man is in need of
> who has journeyed over the mountains."

And Skirnir, who is sent to Jøtunheim by the god Frey to woo for him the fair Gerd, says to his horse:

> "Dark it is outside,
> methinks it is time to journey
> over the damp mountains
> to the Jøtun hosts;
> but both of us shall return,
> or both shall fall into the hands of the
> powerful Jøtun."
>
>   ("Skirnismál")

A couple of logs did the service of bridge across the roaring mountain torrents. The work of keeping the roads in repair consisted in removing rocks and timber which obstructed the passage. The road overseer, appointed by the *bønder*, rode on horseback along the middle of the road with a spear sixteen feet long with loops on each end. If he could pass with this spear so that the loops did not become attached to any obstruction, the road was considered to be in order.[1] Two main routes led from eastern to western Norway over the mountains; one from Oslo to Bergen through Valdres, across Filefjeld to Sognefjord, and the other to Trondhjem through Gudbrandsdal across the Dovre mountains. Until mountain stations were erected where wayfarers might find food and shelter, these routes could be traveled only with the greatest difficulty. But the stream of pilgrims which yearly visited the shrine of St. Olav in Trondhjem prior to the Reformation made the erection of such stations a necessity. In speaking of the route across the Dovre mountains the old writer Peder Claussøn Friis says: "But in the winter people of high estate, as well as members of the court, travel mostly that way, because however deep the snow may fall, it blows together on the high mountains, and becomes so hard that men and horses can walk on it, and the *bønder* run over it on ski and snow-shoes. And there are these three stations: Drivstuen, Herdekinn, and Fogstuen, built on the same mountain, in order that travelers may find lodging there. And kings and archbishops have given cows and land to those who dwell below the mountains, in order that they shall keep the stations in proper order. And at Herdekinn dwells a man who has some cows which are given for his support, in order that he may keep the station properly, and show the travelers the way across the mountains in the winter; and it is his duty always to keep a supply of fodder and dry wood ready, for there are kettles and pots in the house, and other such utensils. And at the other stations there are implements and dry wood for making fire, so that the travelers may build themselves fire, and not suffer from cold, when they have to remain over night, and cannot find the way across the mountains." [2] On the southern route were

[1] *Historisk Tidsskrift*, IV., p. 224 ff. Troels Lund, *Dagligt Liv i Norden*, vol. I., p. 93 f.

[2] Peder Claussøn Friis, *Samlede Skrifter*, published by Gustav Storm, p. 361 f.

found Maristuen and Nystuen, and at these stations chapels were also erected for the pilgrims and travelers.[1] Because of the great inconvenience connected with inland travel, it is natural that travel by water was preferred wherever it was possible. On account of the lack of proper means of communication the inland mountain districts were thinly settled, and made slow progress. But in the sixteenth century, as in days of old, the most generous hospitality was shown every wayfarer. In the monasteries the traveler always found welcome and free lodging for charity's sake, until these institutions were closed on the advent of the Reformation. But the unwritten law of hospitality was as carefully observed by the people at large. Mag. Absalon Pederssøn Beyer writes: "Truly a pious, godfearing, and virtuous person can journey from Bohus to Vardøhus, which journey is more than three hundred miles,[2] and he shall not spend above a riksdaler, yes, they are glad, and they consider it an honor when anyone wishes to eat and drink with them. They sometimes even give people presents if they will make merry with them. A Norwegian sailed from here to Danzig, and stopped at an inn. And when he was going to leave, the hostess asked him to pay for food and ale. He asked if he should pay for ale and food, and the hostess answered yes. He said that it was not customary in his country to receive pay for ale and food, but the woman said that it was custom in her country. Then said he: 'O Norway, thou holy land! As soon as I touch thee again, I shall fall on my knees and kiss thee,' which he also did. And it is a strange thing that in other lands Norway is regarded as a barren kingdom, which it is in some respects, and still so much ale and food are given for nothing that many are astonished."[3] After the monasteries were abolished, the country parsonages became the hostelries for weary travelers, where free food and lodging were cheerfully given by the hospitable parson, who was usually an excellent host. In the cities numerous inns offered lodging, food, and ale for a small price, but they were

[1] Yngvar Nielsen, *Reisehaandbog over Norge*, *"Nystuen."* *Historisk Tidsskrift*, IV., 231–232. *Norsk Turistforenings Aarbog*, 1874, p. 78.

[2] Three hundred Norwegian miles = 2100 English miles.

[3] Absalon Pederssøn Beyer, *Om Norgis Rige*, published by Gustav Storm in *Historisk-topografiske Skrifter om Norge og norske Landsdele*, p. 40 ff.

usually low dives, where thieves and drunkards had their haunts, and where no wayfarer could feel safe. These cheap inns were especially numerous in Bergen, where they numbered four hundred in 1625. In Stavanger they multiplied so rapidly that in 1604 Christian IV. made a regulation restricting their number, as "they aroused God's anger by drunkenness, murders, and otherwise."

The chief means of inland transportation, especially of heavy goods, was the sleigh, and such transportation was carried on in the winter months when the fine sleighing facilitated traffic. The wagon was, indeed, used in the more level districts, and had been used from the very earliest times, which can be seen, among other things, from the Oseberg find from about 800 A.D., where a four-wheeled wagon has been preserved complete. But the use of the wagon as a vehicle of transportation must have been very restricted until the time when more modern roads were constructed.

The houses of the common people were much the same in the sixteenth century as they had been ever since the Viking period. On each *gaard* (farm) there were a number of houses erected for different purposes, the main one being the *stue* (*O. N. stofa*), or dwelling house, which corresponded to the *skaale*. Instead of glass, which was very scarce and expensive, windows were usually made of translucent paper or membrane. The houses were built of logs, and the walls were low. The spacious roof, which was made of birch-bark, covered with sod,[1] bore a rich crop of grass and wild flowers, and might at times serve as pasture for some nimble and enterprising goat. From the outside these houses presented no imposing appearance, but upon entering one might find the *stue* large and cozy, though the conveniences known to modern times were wanting. The abundance of fine pine timber enabled the Norwegians to build large houses, and to erect separate buildings for all sorts of purposes, so that a large *gaard* would look almost like a small village. One notable change had taken place in the *stue* or *skaale* since earlier times. The open fireplace in the center of the room (*arinn*), and the opening in the roof above it (*ljóri*), had disappeared, and an oven with chimney, built in one corner of the room, had come to serve the purpose of both. The room was lighted by burning sticks of pitch pine, or a

---

[1] Gustav Storm, Peder Claussøn Friis, *Samlede Skrifter*, p. 136 f.

PLATE IV

OLD PARSONAGE FROM VAAGE IN GUDBRANDSDAL, NOW AT LILLEHAMMER. LATER TYPE.

BONDESTUE, OLDER TYPE.

OLD CHURCH AT BORGUND.

lamp filled with train oil. The large table at the upper end of the room was built of substantial pine planks, the benches were made of the same material, the dishes, vessels, and utensils were home-made, and so were the clothes, the shoes, and even the ornaments of gold and silver. The houses of the common man were plain even to simplicity, dark and poorly ventilated, but they had their charm when the floor was strewn with twigs of evergreen for holidays or festive occasions, and not less when the family gathered about the fireplace in the evening, each with his own work, knitting, sewing, mending, wood carving, or making vessels and utensils for the house-hold. Then songs and stories unlocked the stores of adventure of ages past, and young and old lived once more with Esben Askelad, and the heroes of ballads and the *sagas*. This simple rustic life left few but strong impressions, and though its comforts were few, it fostered a vigorous and manly race.

The cities of continental Europe originated for the most part as fortified strongholds, serving as a defense against the enemy; but even in early times the Norsemen built commercial towns, and the cities of Norway are, as a rule, of commercial origin. Walls and fortifica-tions were of later construction, and with the exception of the castle, the city was never felt to be a fortress. But the general features of the European cities in the sixteenth century were, nevertheless, met with also in Norway, and a description of London or Copenhagen would, no doubt, apply in a general way also to Bergen, Oslo, and Trondhjem. The limited space inside the city walls necessitated a crowding together of the houses. Not only were the streets narrow, but the second and third stories were often extended beyond the first, shutting out both air and light.[1] The streets were poorly paved, dark, crooked, and filthy, as manure, ashes, garbage, and refuse of all sorts were thrown out of doors without much regard for comfort and well-being. Pigs were running loose, wallowing in pools of mud, and living off the garbage heaps, and when the late pedestrian sought to find the way home, he had to carry a lantern to avoid falling into the cellarways, projecting into the dark and narrow passage called the street. Numerous laws were passed to secure cleanliness and better

---

[1] Valdemar Vedel, *By og Borger i Middelalderen.* Troels Lund, *Dagligt Liv i Norden.*

order in the cities, but these were not heeded. People regarded them as an infringement on their liberty, and continued in the old ways. New lessons could only be taught by great calamities, and nature applied the lash to dull humanity in the form of conflagrations and pestilence, until the instinct of self-preservation finally produced the needed improvements. Time and again the cities, consisting as they did of wooden structures, packed closely side by side, were almost totally destroyed by fire. Patiently the suffering and impoverished inhabitants rebuilt them in the same way, until fear, at length, gave birth to the idea of constructing wide streets and public squares, and of rearing the buildings of less combustible material. The filth in the narrow passages and ill-kept streets proved an even worse enemy than fire. The summer heat turned these filthy passages into breeding places of disease, exhaling their deadly contagion upon a people who failed to obey nature's great law of cleanliness. Violent epidemics harried the North in the sixteenth century with a frequency which filled all minds with dread, and caused untold sorrow and suffering. From 1550 till 1554 a malignant pest harried the larger cities of Norway and Sweden,[1] and especially Denmark, where the university and the schools were closed, the court fled from the capital, and so many people died that it was feared that the country would be depopulated. In 1563–1566 the same plague renewed its visit in Denmark, Norway, and Sweden. Bergen, Trondhjem, and Stockholm suffered severely; the dead were thrown into big pits by day and by night; even birds and animals were poisoned by the contagion. In 1568 the pest again visited Copenhagen, in 1572 Stockholm, in 1575–1578 it harried both Denmark and Sweden, and in 1580–1581 it renewed its ravages in the whole North. Copenhagen was again visited by the dread disease in 1583, and during the next two years it spread throughout all Denmark. In Stockholm it broke out anew in 1588, in 1592 it was brought from Livonia to Copenhagen, in 1596–1598 it harried Sweden fearfully, and in 1599 it was again raging in Denmark. What sorrow and helpless misery these fearful epidemics left in their trail! But at this great cost some lessons

---

[1] Absalon Pederssøn Beyer, *Liber Capituli Bergensis, 1552–1572*, published by N. Nicolaysen, Christiania, 1860, p. 109. *Norske Magasin*, II., 645. Troels Lund, *Dagligt Liv i Norden*, II., p. 67 f.

were learned, and the instinct of self-preservation quickened human intelligence. The study of diseases, and the science of medicine and sanitation, which were to transform all human life, originated in these dark periods of human helplessness and woe.

But if the suffering due to man's ignorance cast a dark shadow over human existence, the self-inflicted horrors arising from man's credulity and superstition have often turned human society into a veritable inferno from which reason itself, and all nobler instincts, for a season seem to have fled. The sixteenth century was a period when superstition sat enthroned in the minds of all classes, high as well as low. But of all delusions which haunted man's brain, the belief in witchcraft with the attending torture and burning of witches was undoubtedly the most abominable.[1] It is not here the place to dwell upon the revolting horrors of the witchcraft craze, except so far as it has left its stain of stupid fear and brutality also in Norwegian history. As early as 1325 a witchcraft trial was conducted in Bergen against Ragnhild Tregagaas. After she had been kept in prison and chains for a long time, she was finally released on the condition that she should fast certain periods every year, amounting in all to over half the days in the year, and that she should make a pilgrimage to some sanctuary outside of Norway once every seven years. How many such cases occurred prior to the Reformation is not known,[2] but witchcraft trials and executions were numerous, especially in the latter part of the sixteenth century and the beginning of the seventeenth. The most noted case was the trial of the widow of Absalon Pederssøn Beyer, who was condemned to death, and burned as a witch in Bergen, 1590.[3] Any woman who knew more than the Lord's Prayer, *i.e.* who possessed literary culture above the average, was in danger of being persecuted for sorcery and secret association with the devil;

---

[1] One of the chief works on the history of the witchcraft craze is Soldan, *Geschichte der Hexenprocesse*, 2 vols., Stuttgart, 1880. Walter Scott, *Letters on Demonology and Witchcraft*, London, 1872 and 1884. Bætzmann, *Hexevæsen og Troldskab i Norge*, 1865. O. A. Øverland, *Norges Historie*, VI., p. 125 ff.

[2] P. A. Munch, *To Breve af Biskop Audfin betreffende en Hexeproces i Bergen Aar 1325, Samlinger til det norske Folks Sprog og Historie*, vol. V., p. 479 ff.

[3] The documents of the trial are printed in *Norske Samlinger*, vol. I., p. 529 ff.

and after the craze was once started, any prank of imagination was sufficient cause for dragging the victims of suspicion before the courts, and subjecting them to the most cruel tortures to press from them an admission of guilt. From the years 1592 to 1594 the "Bergens Raadhus-Protokol"[1] gives accounts of several witchcraft trials. Oluf Gausdal was condemned to death as a sorcerer. He claimed that he had learned his magic art of two women, Marine Haldorsgaard and Mumpe Guron, and these were burned as witches some years later. He even implicated the bishop's wife, who was saved with difficulty from sharing the fate of the others. Delis Røneke was tried for witchcraft and banished from Bergen; Johanne Jensdotter was burned at the stake, and, likewise, Anna Knutsdotter. In 1613 two women were burned, because "by their sorcery they had caused a mill in Sandvik to be destroyed," and several more women were burned at the stake, because they were thought to have caused shipwreck upon the high seas by their magic arts. Anna, the widow of Herluf Lauritssøn, the supposed author of "Bergens Fundats," was also accused of witchcraft. She was thrown into prison and on the night of the 19th of July "her neck was twisted and broken by the devil," says the account. Who the devil was that committed this outrage is not recorded. One woman was tortured with red-hot irons until she died, and another died in prison after being tortured. From Finmarken to Oslo and Christiania witchcraft trials were carried on with torture and executions.[2] As late as 1737 Ole Hoime in Slidre parish was tried as a sorcerer, but he escaped with a relatively mild punishment.[3] This seems to have closed the chapter of witchcraft trials, the ghastliest spectacle in Norwegian history, though comparatively few were executed as compared with the thousands who suffered death in all parts of Europe. No worse outrage was ever added to the woeful list of wrongs against humanity even in those days of medieval darkness, and its effect upon the finer moral and intellectual sensibilities of society was the more pernicious, because it

[1] *Uddrag av Bergens Raadhus-Protokol for Tidsrummet Juli 1592 – Mai 1594*, published by N. Nicolaysen in *Norske Samlinger*, vol. I., p. 321 ff. Daniel Thrap, *Bergenske Kirkeforholde i det 17de Aarhundrede*, Christiania, 1879.

[2] *Norske Samlinger*, I., p. 525 ff.

[3] O. A. Øverland, *Norges Historie*, vol. VI., p. 125 ff.

had been committed in the name of religion and justice. This reign of terror and superstition breeded general callousness and mental obtuseness, destroyed the regard for the sacredness of human life and the rights of man, and fostered a judicial brutality which reveals itself in all criminal jurisprudence of that period. The crude conception of the rights of the individual and his value to society is sadly conspicuous. In early days the freeman's person and honor were regarded as sacred, and this sacredness of person (*mannhelgi*) was guarded by the old laws. The greatest crimes were punished, not by straightway taking the life of the criminal, but by imposing a fine, or by declaring him an outlaw, thereby turning him over to the vengeance of those whom he had wronged, but also to the mercy of the community. In the sixteenth century the idea of sacredness of the individual seems to have disappeared. Human life had become cheap, and neither the body nor the honor of the individual citizen was any longer a sacred thing which the court was compelled to treat with respect. The trials were often accompanied by brutal torture, and capital punishment was inflicted with a frequency which made the hangman one of the leading city officials, and the public executions the amusement, not only of the jesting rabble, but of the sedate city fathers. On passing Nordnes at Bergen one might have seen, almost at any time, several bodies dangling from the gallows, exposed even after death to the jeers of idlers, probably for no greater crime than for jumping over the city wall, or stealing a few pounds of butter. The records left by Mag. Absalon Pederssøn Beyer in his diary, "Liber Capituli Bergensis," gives us an insight into the way in which crimes were punished in Bergen in the sixteenth century. A boy was beheaded for jumping over the city wall. A man who was suspected of having killed his wife was tortured till one joint of his thumb fell off. At times he admitted, but again he denied his guilt, but he was, nevertheless, executed. A baker was hanged because he had stolen butter. A *bonde* (farmer) was hanged because he had stolen some train-oil on the wharf. Two young men of old noble families, relatives of Christopher Trondssøn, were hanged because they had picked locks and stolen. A young boy who served at the castle was also hanged for theft. Examples of this kind of legal justice need not be multiplied, nor need we mention the numerous executions for what we would consider more sufficient reasons, for these alone, it seems, might have satisfied the desire of judges to inflict the favorite death penalty. Fights and drunken brawls were numerous even at weddings and other social gatherings; murders and other crimes were of frequent occurrence. When we read the descriptions of social conditions in the sixteenth century left by old writers, we feel that there was guilt enough,[1] but no shadow in the picture is deeper than that of justice forgetting to be just, and allying itself with superstition and bigoted cruelty. It is the one great evil which especially darkens the physiognomy of the sixteenth century.

But the century has also its brighter side looking forward to a new era, the first dawn of which had already broken through the medieval darkness. New elements of progress had entered the intellectual and spiritual life of the people with the Renaissance and the Reformation, while new inventions, a revival of commerce, and the growth of a native merchant class in the cities gave promise of a new development in the economic life of the nation. The destruction of the Hanseatic trade monopoly, and the development of Norwegian lumber export were the important factors in this commercial and economic development. Boards and timber had been exported, especially to Iceland and England, in very early times. King Henry III. wrote to his bailiffs in Southampton, Nov. 13, 1253, instructing them to buy two hundred Norwegian pine boards, and deliver them to the sheriff of that city, to be used for wainscoting the room of his dear son Edward in the Winchester castle.[2] At the same time mention is made of a purchase of 1000 Norwegian boards for the panelling of some rooms in the Windsor castle. "Norway planks," says Turner, "were largely imported into this country from the early period of the century (thirteenth), and perhaps, although it is not quite clear, at a still earlier term." The lumber export to England

---

[1] Peder Claussøn Friis, *Samlede Skrifter*, p. 381. Absalon Pederssøn Beyer, *Liber Capituli Bergensis. Norske So.*

[2] *Liberate Roll 37 Henry III.*, quoted in *Some Account of Domestic Agriculture in England from the Conquest to the End of the Thirteenth Century*, by T. Hudson Turner, Oxford, 1851. See L. J. Vogt, *Om Norges Udførsel af Trælast i ældre Tider, Historisk Tidsskrift*, anden række, vol. V., p. 86 ff. Alexander Bugge, *Handelen mellem England og Norge indtil Begyndelsen af det 15de Aarhundrede, Historisk Tidsskrift*, tredie række, IV., p. 138 ff.

did not become of great importance, however, till in the sixteenth century, when the English forests no longer produced the needed supply. A more important market for Norwegian lumber developed in Holland and the lower districts of northwestern Germany. In a letter issued by King Eirik Magnusson to the citizens of Hamburg, July 31, 1296, in which he grants them various trade privileges, he states that they shall have the right to carry from Norway in their own ships lumber and all other kinds of goods, upon paying a fixed export duty.[1] On August 24, 1443, the city of Amsterdam received the privilege to trade in Bergen and elsewhere in Norway, except in the Norwegian colonies,[2] and in the reign of Christian I. five similar letters were issued in six years (1452–1458), granting trade privileges to various cities in Holland,[3] an indication of the rapid growth of trade with the Netherlands. This lumber trade with Holland led to an ever widening commerce with that country, as the Hollanders did not enforce a monopoly on trade like the Hanseatic merchants, but maintained an open market, and welcomed goods brought in Norwegian ships as well as in their own. L. J. Vogt observes that on December 4, 1490, the Norwegian Council issued an order forbidding the common and ruinous practice found in many districts in southern Norway, that *bønder* have and use their own ships with which they sail to foreign lands with rafters, boards, poles, salt, and other goods, and neglect agriculture.[4] This shows that the lumber trade at this time must have been very lucrative. The boards were yet made by splitting the logs into slabs and hewing them with the ax, and they were, therefore, called *huggenbord* (hewn boards). New possibilities for this trade were developed through the invention of the saw driven by water power, which was introduced from Sweden in the early years of the sixteenth century. Vogt shows that, while the plane had been used in the North from earliest antiquity, the saw was late in making its appearance, not only because of the difficulty experienced in giving the teeth the proper shape and position, but especially in making a good saw-blade. Sawmills were soon introduced in every district, and by 1530 they seem to have been in

---

[1] *Diplomatarium Norwegicum*, vol. V., no. 33.   [2] *Ibid.*, vol. V., no. 720.
[3] L. J. Vogt, *Historisk Tidsskrift*, anden række, vol. V., p. 99.
[4] *Diplomatarium Norwegicum*, VI., no. 963.

common use. But the old method of making *huggenbord* with the ax was not discontinued.

The increasing traffic with Holland stimulated also other countries to enter into competition for the valuable Norwegian trade, as Scotland, England, Denmark, and Germany were all in need of lumber. "At the beginning of the sixteenth century," says Vogt, "it seems to have been an established custom that the export of Norwegian lumber, without the intervention of any merchant, was free from every place on the coast of Norway where a ship could be anchored and loaded."[1] The kings had sought to prohibit trade everywhere but in the cities in order to facilitate their growth.[2] A statute given by Haakon VI. about 1380 states that all goods must be brought to the cities, and foreign merchants are forbidden to buy or sell in the smaller harbors along the coast. But no native merchant class existed which possessed sufficient capital to control trade. It has already been shown that the Norwegian traders in early times belonged to the old nobility, that with the introduction of the ideas of chivalry it came to be regarded as inconsistent with the dignity of a knight or of a man of high station to carry on trade. Commerce was, accordingly, left to the poorer classes, and especially in the fifteenth century the merchant class of the cities lost both its economic strength and its social influence; the native aristocratic families disappeared, and the cities were turned over, so to speak, to the control of foreign merchants. But a new merchant class in a modern sense began to develop at the beginning of the sixteenth century, and Norwegian cities, commerce, and navigation developed with it. Professor Alexander Bugge has shown that Norway had her own merchant class about 1300,[3] but this class was almost totally destroyed by the Hanseatic merchants. At the time of the Reformation the

---

[1] L. J. Vogt, *Om Norges Udførsel af Trælast i ældre Tider II.*, *Historisk Tidsskrift*, anden række, vol. V., p. 273.

[2] *Ventilationer angaænde den nordlandske Handel*, etc., *Samlinger til det norske Folks Sprog og Historie*, vol. V., p. 590 ff.

[3] Alexander Bugge, *Handelen mellem England og Norge indtil Begyndelsen af det 15de Aarhundrede, Historisk Tidsskrift*, tredie række, IV.; *Gotlændingernes Handel paa England og Norge omkring 1300, Historisk Tidsskrift*, tredie række, vol. V. Oscar Alb. Johnsen, *De norske Stænder*, p. 42 ff. (*Christiania Videnskabs-Selskabs Skrifter*, 1906).

whole city population of Norway, according to Sars, numbered about 9000, consisting chiefly of shopkeepers, fishermen, seamen, laborers, and a few foreign traders and artisans.   Under these circumstances the cities could exercise no corporate strength at home, nor any commercial power abroad.   A new foundation had to be laid for urban life in a more modern sense.   The development was slow, but the disappearance of the old aristocracy facilitated progress, as the government of the cities was thereby naturally transferred from a circle of aristocratic families with inherited class privileges to the townsmen, who could claim no other superiority than that given them by their own energy and business insight.   The growing demand for Norwegian lumber created business activity and helped to centralize trade in the cities.   The freedom from the restraining influence of a privileged aristocracy, the democratic conditions existing in the Norwegian towns, and the growing commerce, especially in the latter half of the sixteenth century, furnished the conditions necessary for the development of the Norwegian cities along new lines.

Trade in the North was also stimulated by the attempt of the English to find a northeast passage to India.   This plan was advanced by the Spaniard Sebastian Cabot, who had entered the English service.   He had read Heberstein's account of Russia, and had studied his map, as well as Olaus Magnus' map of the North and of the *Mare Scythicum*.   A company of Merchant Adventurers was formed under the patronage of the government, and three ships were dispatched under Hugh Willoughby to discover the new route.   The expedition sailed from England May 22, 1553.   On the northwest coast of Norway the "Edward Bonaventura," under Captain Chancellor, was separated from the fleet in a severe storm.   Willoughby with the remaining two ships was driven far to the northeast, but finally he found a harbor, and landed on a barren and uninhabited coast, where he and his followers perished from hunger.   Their dead bodies and Willoughby's testament were found later.   Chancellor was more fortunate.   He rounded the northern extremity of Norway which he called North Cape, and succeeded in reaching Vardøhus, where he was well received by the commandant.   After spending a week as his guest, he sailed again to the northeast, and landed at the mouth of the Dvina, where he was received by the Russian *voivod* of the village of St. Nicolai. Chancellor received permission from the *voivod* to go to Moscow to visit the Czar, from whom he received a letter granting the English the right to trade at the mouth of the Dvina. The following year he returned to England with a cargo of Russian goods. The English lauded him as a great discoverer who had found a new route to northern Russia, though the expedition had failed to discover a new route to India. But this route to northern Russia was the old way traveled by the Norwegians ever since Ôh-thêre first discovered it in the time of Alfred the Great. Both Denmark-Norway and Holland entered into competition for this trade, and the search for a northeast passage continued for half a century.[1]

The treaty of Speier, 1544, settled the political difficulties between Denmark-Norway and Germany, resulting from Christian III.'s active coöperation with the Schmalkaldic League, and a commercial treaty was entered into by the two powers, which gave Norwegian commerce a new foundation. By this treaty unobstructed trade between Norway and Holland was assured, and Amsterdam became the chief market for Norwegian lumber, as the cities of Holland were fast becoming the center of the world's commerce, which had developed after the discovery of America and of the new routes to India. The rapid development of commerce resulting from these discoveries, the increase in ship-building, and the growth of cities greatly enhanced the demand for lumber and ship-building material. In a few years after 1584 the English merchant marine was trebled in size, and a heavy export of Norwegian timber to England developed. According to Vogt, the customs rolls show a demand for Norwegian products, and an increase in Norwegian trade to which there is no earlier parallel. In 1567 Bergen exported 206 dozen boards, in 1597 2188 dozen. From the *fogderi* of Nedenes twelve ships were cleared in 1528, 150 ships in 1560, and 277 ships in 1613. The lumber export is estimated to have risen from 102 cargoes to 1650 cargoes in 1560.[2] In the harbors where the shipping of lumber was carried on, new sea-

---

[1] Gustav Storm, *Om Opdagelsen af "Nordkap" og Veien til "det hvide Hav,"* Det norske geografiske Selskabs Aarbog, vol. V., 1873–1894, p. 911 ff.

[2] T. H. Aschehoug, *Festskrift for Oscar II.*, vol. I., p. 29 ff. A. Schweigaard, *Norges Statistik*, p. 125 ff. B. E. Bendixen, *Et Omrids af Norges Handels Historie*, Bergen, 1900. G. L. Baden, *Et Udkast til en Historie af Danmarks og Norges Handel og Næringskilder fra Oldtiden til Nutiden*, Copenhagen, 1806.

port towns (N. *ladesteder*) sprang into existence. Frederikshald, Larvik, Brevik, Kragerø, Risør, Arendal, etc., owe their origin to the flourishing lumber trade. The nationalizing of trade, which had thus begun, was an important chapter, not only in the economic development of the Norwegian people, but also in their political and intellectual progress. A Norwegian bourgeoisie was thereby created which was to play an important part in the future struggles for political independence and intellectual emancipation from the Danish tutelage, which was forced upon the Norwegian people through the union with Denmark.

25. CHRISTIAN IV. AND HIS AGE

When Frederick II. died in 1588, his son Christian was only eleven years old. The Council assumed control of the government and appointed four of their own number to act as a regency during the minority of the prince. In 1580 he had been elected heir to succeed his father as king of Denmark, and two years later a council of Norwegian nobles at Oslo acknowledged him successor also on the throne of Norway. Aksel Gyldenstjerne, member of the Council, and a prominent and able nobleman, was appointed *statholder* of Norway. As the personal representative of the king and regency he had royal power both in secular and ecclesiastical matters. He was instructed to exercise supervision over bishops and priests, so "that full concord might be maintained, and a good example might be set the parishioners." The military strength of the kingdom was to be carefully examined, and in case of war he should summon the *lensherrer* into service with the full quota of men, and assume supreme command. This attention to the military service was a laudable forethought at this time when the storm-clouds of the approaching European wars already obscured the political horizon. England's growing naval power had already encouraged her bold sea-captains to rob Spanish treasure ships, and to plunder isolated Spanish-American settlements. In 1587 Sir Francis Drake had even entered the harbors of Cadiz and Coruna, where he burned the ships and galleys which Philip II. had fitted out for an attack upon England. The Invincible Armada was ready to sail in July, 1588, three months after the death of Frederick II. England, Spain's political, commercial, and religious enemy, was to be conquered. Even Danish and Norwegian ships and crews had been hired to join the great fleet when it arrived in English waters, but owing to a remonstrance from the English ambassador in Denmark these ships were not allowed to leave the harbors. If Philip should succeed in crushing England, Denmark-Norway as a Protestant power could no longer feel safe, but the stormy sea and the bravery of the English sailors destroyed the great Armada. Many ships were driven so far north that they were wrecked on the northwest coast of Norway; five ships are said to have stranded in the neighborhood of Trondhjem; England and the Protestant North was no longer endangered by Spanish aggression.

Prince Christian, who was born April 12, 1577, was declared to be of age when he became nineteen years old in 1596. On August 29 of that year he was crowned in Copenhagen as King Christian IV., and the following year he entered upon his duties as ruling sovereign. The superstition of the age had been brought into play in connection with the birth of the prince. A peasant had visited the king to inform him that a mermaid had foretold the birth of a son to the royal pair, who should "become an excellent king and lord in these Northern lands," a prophecy which gained general credence. The mother had the chief care of the boy's education and early training. She had been reared according to the strict rules of her German home, in Mecklenburg; she loved order and economy, and took great interest in household affairs and the management of the royal estates, a love for the practical which was inherited by the son. He was well educated in the learning of the age, and could speak and write several languages, but as a student he was only moderately successful, as his interest centered chiefly on architecture, shipbuilding, seamanship, and other practical pursuits, in which he exhibited energy and talent, and a desire to see and do things in his own way. In regard to his kingly duties he entertained views resembling those of the Stuart kings in England, or of the Tudor Henry VIII. He would not only be the highest power in the state, but he would give personal attention to all details of government, so that nothing, however unimportant, might happen which did not reflect his royal will. As he possessed great courage, energy, and practical insight, and was always ready to take an active part in all administrative affairs, he instituted, at least in a practical way, a personal rule which bears the marks of his own temperament and character. He was a bold seaman, and visited Norway a greater number of times than all his predecessors together since the union was established. Professor Yngvar Nielsen has shown that he visited that kingdom not less than twenty-six times during his reign.[1] In 1599 he made a voyage to the North Cape to study conditions in northern Norway, in order that he might be able to regulate the growing commerce in those parts, and also to protect Finmarken, which both Russia and Sweden would snatch from Norway at the first opportunity. He made the voyage with a whole squadron of war vessels, and captured several Dutch merchant ships which sought to sail to Russia by way of Vardøhus.

His firm hand was soon felt also in the internal administration in Norway, where the discontent was general because of the extortions practiced by the Danish *lensherrer* and their *fogeds*, who paid little attention to the laws, and increased arbitrarily their own income and the burdens of the people. The Norwegian *bønder* did not patiently submit to injustice of that kind, but sent delegations to the king to ask for justice. The complaint was again directed against Ludvig Munk, *lensherre* in Trøndelagen, who had imprisoned and executed those who on a former occasion had served as messengers to the king. This time the old offender was made to feel the heavy hand of royal justice. He was dismissed from his office, banished to his estates in Jutland, and forced to pay a heavy fine.

During the union period Denmark had gradually established an overlordship over Norway, which for military purposes, as well as in the eyes of the world at large, made the two kingdoms one united realm, and greatly increased Denmark's prestige and power. Not only was the central government Danish, but nearly all the local officials of any importance in Norway were Danes. The Norwegian laws had been translated into Danish, which became the official language of Norway, though it was never spoken by the common

---

[1] *Historisk Tidsskrift*, første række, vol. III., p. 502 ff.; fjerde række, vol. III., p. 369.

Aage Skavlan, *Historiske Billeder fra den nyere Tid i Norge, Danmark og tildels i Sverige.*

people. The threat made by Christian III. that the kingdom of Norway should be regarded as a Danish province had, indeed, not been carried out, but intellectually as well as politically Norway now stood under the egis of Danish supremacy. But the overlordship was formal and exterior, and did not deeply affect the people's everyday life. Now as before they led their own national existence, and were governed according to their own laws and customs, and as to social conditions the people of Norway and Denmark were more widely separated in the sixteenth century than in any earlier period. If the Danish *lensherrer* and *fogeds* attempted to practice in Norway what had been regarded as common usage in Denmark, they encountered the firm resistance and vigorous protest of the people, who, though they could not place a son of their own on the throne of Norway, would defend to the utmost their individual rights.[1]

Denmark had not been able to get fully into the current of European development, which tended to bring the lower classes into active participation in political life. In Sweden Gustav Vasa had sought the support of the common people, and had made them a new political factor; in France and England the commonalty had risen into prominence, and had added new vigor to the national development; but in Denmark the aristocracy alone grew in importance, while the common classes were constantly depressed in the social scale. The aristocracy isolated themselves from the rest of society, and instead of remaining a warrior class, they became an aristocracy of birth, wealth, and titles, who would not allow their sons and daughters to marry outside of their caste, a restriction which brought about their rapid degeneration as a class. Full jurisdiction over the enslaved peasants had been established.[2] The will of the noble-born lord was the law to which they were held amenable. They had to render free service to their lords whenever they were called upon,

[1] Halvdan Koht, *Bondestrid, smaa Segner og Upskrifter fraa Nordmør*, Christiania, 1906.

[2] Arild Huitfeldt writes in his *Danmarks Riges Krønike*, p. 1252: "Frederick I. granted the nobles jurisdiction over the peasant's *boeslod*, and all cases of forty marks, as free as the nobles of the principality of Schleswig enjoyed it, which is a very great privilege, the like of which no king of Denmark has before granted. In Norway the nobles have no such power, nor in Sweden either, except those who for a short period are made counts."

and had to yield the most abject obedience, not only to the lord himself, but also to his representatives of whatever sort, even to his servants and stable-boys. In the rules made by Chancellor Nils Kaas and Treasurer Christopher Valkendorf, June 5, 1578, for the service to be rendered the "honest and noble-born" Jørgen Marsvin by the peasants, it is stated that they shall not be forced to work more than one or two days a week, except in the fall, when they shall work three days a week.[1] But this was the service rendered on a royal estate, which was much more moderate than that exacted by many an arbitrary and tyrannical lord, who could demand service of his peasants without any restriction as to time or amount. In many provinces the peasants lost even their personal liberty. They had to remain permanently on the farm where they were born, and they would have to rent such a piece of ground as the lord would grant them, and on the conditions which he prescribed.[2] The cruel hunting-laws show even more clearly to what extent the poor Danish peasants were oppressed and done to scorn by the arrogant nobles. In the statute of Christian III. of 1537, any one who catches a poacher is instructed to put out his eyes, or hang him on the nearest tree. The king's officials are instructed to watch, so that no man from the cities kill animals, either large or small, or any hares; and that no *foged*, or steward of a manor, or peasants shall keep greyhounds or retrievers, or shoot animals, large or small, on penalty of death, or the loss of their property.[3] In the statute of Frederick II., 1556, the people in the cities, preachers and peasants, are instructed that they must keep no dogs unless these are always tied, or that one of their front legs is cut off. In 1573 King Frederick II. wrote to the people of Kolding *len* that since he had learned that several of them kept many dogs, which ran about in the forests and fields, and chased away and harmed the wild animals, he wished them to take notice that no one should keep more than one dog, and that dog should have one

---

[1] Rasmus Nyerup, *Skildringer af Tilstanden i Danmark og Norge i ældre og nyere Tider*, vol. I., p. 368 ff. *Nyt dansk Magasin*, vol. II., p. 167.

[2] *Suhmske nye Samlinger til den danske Historie*, vol. I., p. 197 ff., quoted by Nyerup.

[3] Rasmus Nyerup, *Skildringer af Tilstanden i Danmark og Norge*, vol. I., p. 381 ff. Arnt Berntsen Bergen, *Danmark oc Norgis frugtbar Herlighed, 1656*, p. 147 ff.

front leg cut off above the knee. In 1577 the wild animals did so much damage that the peasants in Lem *sogn* were unable to pay their taxes. It is not strange that the Danish nobles, who were accustomed to look upon the peasants as a class possessing no rights which they were obliged to respect, should attempt also in Norway to override the laws, and oppress the people. But in Norway they did not possess the same privileges as in Denmark. Even Frederick I. had promised in his Norwegian charter to rule the Norwegian people "according to St. Olav's and the kingdom of Norway's laws and good old usages unchanged in all respects." [1] As already stated elsewhere, the freedom of the Norwegians was safeguarded in the first place by the law of *odel*, which maintained a relatively large class of free *bønder* who owned their farms.[2]

In the second place, the renters, who were more numerous, were protected by the laws as to their personal liberty and independence of their landlords. The amount of rent to be paid was fixed by law, and beyond this the renter owed no obedience or responsibility to the landlord. Since the old nobility had practically disappeared,[3] Norway had virtually become a democracy, while Denmark was the most typical exponent of aristocratic rule. This may have been the reason, also, why the principle of elective kingship was maintained in Denmark, while Norway always inclined to the hereditary principle, which had also been introduced in Sweden by Gustav Vasa. The aristocratic social organization, and the elective principle, proved a weakness which sapped Denmark's strength, and retarded her progress, though at the time she exercised dominion over Norway. On the other hand, the democratic conditions in Norway, though they had pushed the Norwegians for a season into the background, fostered powers and possibilities for a new national development.

The Danish *lensherrer* and *fogeds*, who looked upon the Norwegian

---

[1] *Kong Fredrik den førstes norske Haandfæstning af 1524, Samlinger til det norske Folks Sprog og Historie*, vol. I., p. 1 ff.

[2] Professor J. E. Sars has shown that of the ca. 30,000 farms in Norway at the time of the Reformation about 10,000 were owned by *odelsbønder*, and 20,000 were operated by renters. J. E. Sars, *Norge under Foreningen med Danmark. Om ¦Folkemængdens Bevægelse*, by the same author, in *Historisk Tidsskrift*, anden række, vol. III.

[3] Yngvar Nielsen, *Af Norges Historie*, p. 77.

laws as a restriction upon their privileges, sought to introduce the Danish system also in Norway. The crown-lands had been increased through the secularization of monasteries, and the confiscation of church-lands until the crown owned over one-fourth of all the taxable lands in the kingdom. The Danish lords began to demand service of the tenants living upon these crown-lands, and gradually also of the renters dwelling on their own estates. Many of the minor *lens* had been granted them in return for a fixed sum of money paid by them to the crown, or for service, *i.e.* for furnishing a certain number of men for the army. Some *lens* had been granted them "kvit og frit," *i.e.* so that each lord should have the whole income from his *len*. In this way the power of the *lensherre* had been greatly increased, and the king, who was far away, could have no intimate knowledge of the methods used by the *lensherrer* and *fogeds* to swell their income.

Another and, if possible, greater power was given the *lensherrer* and *fogeds* in connection with the execution of the decrees of the courts of justice. Not seldom did they influence the *fogeds* to inflict the heaviest penalties, as death or banishment, upon the offenders. The *lensherre* would then, out of kindness of heart, commute the sentence by substituting a fine which was usually so large that the offender had to deed his property to the *lensherre* in order to escape a worse fate. In this way the *lensherrer* and *fogeds* could gradually increase their personal holdings. Statholder Aksel Gyldenstjerne wrote to the government in Copenhagen, October 9, 1590: "In like manner, if any poor man commits an offense so that he has to pay the *foged* or the *lensherre* for his neck, he is not executed for such a crime, but the *lensherre* or *foged* imposes so high a fine for the offense that he cannot pay it, and a poor fellow promises willingly, in order to save his life, more than he or his family at any time can pay. Then he has to give the *lensherre* or *foged* a deed on his farm and possessions, as if the same had been bought. This has certainly happened, and it seems, therefore, advisable that a royal letter should be issued to all *lensherrer, fogeds,* and clergymen in all Norway that they should in no wise buy or confiscate any property, unless it is forfeited to the crown." [1] But with all their power and systematized

---

[1] Quoted by J. E. Sars in *Udsigt over den norske Historie*, vol. III., p. 333.

injustice the Danish lords were unable to force their system upon Norway. Their most crafty schemes and their ruthless greed proved of little avail in a contest with the martial spirit of the Norwegian *bønder* and their uncompromising love of freedom. In their mountain homes the *bønder* still retained their old character and customs. They came to the *thing* as well as to the church, armed as of old with sword, spear, battleax, shield, bow, and arrows. If they felt wronged, if their temper was aroused, the sword was their most convenient argument, and many a bloody tumult occurred at the *things* when they felt that justice had not been done. At times they assembled *things* and passed resolutions without paying any attention to the government officials. Stiff-necked and turbulent they often were, impatient of all restraint, and utterly unwilling to submit to the arbitrary rule of the Danish lords.[1] Peder Claussøn Friis, who as clergyman sympathized with the Danish officials, says of them in speaking of the origin of the Norwegian people: "However this may all be, the inhabitants of this country have their origin and descent from a hard people, because they have always been a hard, stubborn, disobedient, obstinate, restless, rebellious, and bloodthirsty people, which I cannot deny they still are, especially in places where they keep their old customs, that is, among the mountains far away from the sea; there dwells still a wild and wicked people." In another place he calls the *bønder* of Telemarken "a wicked, impious, hard, wild, and rebellious people — some shameless, devilish fellows, guilty of adultery, murder, manslaughter, heresy, licentiousness, fights, and other vices beyond any that live in this country. It was their greatest joy in olden times to kill bishops, priests, *fogeds*, and commandants, which is also shown by the fact that in one parish in that district seven clergymen have been killed, in other parishes one or two, and in some a greater number." Professor J. E. Sars remarks: "The many irksome schemes and impositions invented by the *lensherrer* and *fogeds* seem to have caused among the *bønder* a restlessness and agitation in which their strength degenerated into

---

[1] Peder Claussøn Friis, *Samlede Skrifter*, p. 225, 257 ff., 300. Fifty *fogeds* and clergymen are said to have been killed, and many others to have been driven away in Nedenes *len*. L. Daae, *Historisk Tisskrift*, første række, vol. IV., p. 305. C. F. Allen, *De nordiske Rigers Historie*, vol. I., p. 251 ff., 648.

brutality, and their combative and head-strong character assumed traits of insubordination and resistance to all forms of restraint. The efforts of the *lensherrer* and *fogeds* to reduce them to a subordination akin to that of the Danish peasants, instead of frightening or sub- duing them, only increased their defiance. They employed force against force, and throughout the whole land they seem to have risen in arms against all officials who in any way sought to exercise authority over them. . . . These irregular outbursts of a spirit of liberty, which lacks guidance and a fixed aim, do not make a pleasant impression, but it must not be forgotten that they have played a part in the country's history which is by no means unimportant. We may view as a whole the endless variety of complaints of *fogeds* and other functionaries, of riots and assaults and the violent taking of justice into their own hands on the part of the people, of which the documents of our history from that period bring evidence; where the issue seems to be trifling matters without any connection — real or imaginary injustice against some individual — and we can see in all these clashes between the *bønder* on the one side, and the *lensherrer*, *fogeds*, and clergy on the other, a single long-continued struggle in defense of what must be called the chief product of the people's earlier political development, and the most important condition for their national future — popular freedom and the right to own property. And in this struggle the Norwegian *bønder* became the unqualified victors."[1] The spirited resistance of the *bønder* compelled the *lensherrer* and *fogeds* to respect their rights, and to avoid, at least to some extent, more serious conflicts with them. The Norwegian people's bravery and love of liberty became proverbial in Denmark, and the government feared that a general uprising might take place, if the officials were allowed to unduly oppress the people. For this reason the king listened to the complaints made by the Nor- wegians, and many an offender, even of high rank, was severely punished. But many a just complaint was also left unheeded, and in too many instances the vindictive officials found opportunity to wreak vengeance on those who had sought to bring them to justice. King Christian IV. was especially anxious to win the good-will of the Norwegians. When Jørgen Friis succeeded Gyldenstjerne as *stat-*

[1] J. E. Sars, *Udsigt over den norske Historie*, vol. III., p. 336 ff.

holder, the king himself was present, and the new official had to pledge himself under oath that he would "listen and pay diligent heed to the complaints of the poor people and help them to secure justice." Towards the Estates: nobility, clergy, citizens, and common people of the kingdom, he should so act that the king should not on his account hear any complaints from the people. In 1604 the king himself held court in Bergen to decide a quarrel between the people and the lensherre, Peder Grubbe. Peder Claussøn Friis was also involved in the trial, but both Friis and the people were held to be innocent, while Grubbe was found guilty, and was removed from his len.

Even in the courts of law, justice often miscarried because the old codes were no longer understood by the lagmænd and officials. Since the union was established, the Norwegian jurisprudence had received no attention. Magnus Lagabøter's code, which was still in use, had not been revised, and many new statutes, passed from time to time, had not been incorporated in it. A revision of the code was sorely needed, and in 1602 Christian IV. ordered the Norwegian lagmænd to prepare a new code, which should be printed and put in use throughout the kingdom. The new lawbook, known as the "Code of Christian IV.," was submitted to the king in 1604,[1] and after he had caused it to be read before an assembly of nobles and lagmænd in Bergen, it was formally authorized and printed. The new code was only a translation of Magnus Lagabøter's laws, and the work was wretchedly done, as many old legal terms had been misunderstood; but it was, nevertheless, an improvement, as the laws were reduced to a code which could be read and understood, and which was everywhere accessible in printed form. The new code was also introduced in the Faroe Islands, but Iceland had its own laws, and did not adopt it, nor was it introduced in the Shetland or Orkney Islands, where the old Norse laws were still in force. The church laws were not embodied in the code, but the king caused a new church ordinance to be prepared, which was formally proclaimed at a council in Stavanger, 1607.

The religious outlook was beginning to cause no small anxiety at

[1] Kong Christian den fjerdes norske Lovbog af 1604, edited by Fr. Hallager og Fr. Brandt, Christiania, 1855.

this time. The Catholic reaction against the Reformation, organized by the Council of Trent, had gained great strength, owing to the enthusiastic propaganda of the Jesuits and the vigor of the inquisition. The Catholic Church had risen to do battle for its spiritual supremacy, to regain what it had lost. Also in the North the Jesuits began a stealthy agitation, which did not escape the attention of King Christian. A Norwegian Jesuit, Lauritz Nilssøn, with the latinized name of Laurentius Nicolai, also called *Klosterlasse* (Closterlassius) had found welcome in Sweden, where King John III. inclined toward Catholicism. A higher school was organized, where Closterlassius should teach. At first his church affiliations were to remain a secret, and he was to appear only as the learned scholar, a form of agitation adopted for the purpose of gaining influence in the schools, and of encouraging the students to attend the Catholic universities. If the students, who would become ministers in the church, could be won for Catholicism, that faith could in time be reintroduced among the common people, and great efforts were, therefore, made to create the belief that the Catholic universities were better than the Protestant, and that they enjoyed a higher reputation for learning. But Closterlassius did not accomplish much in Sweden.[1] He became arrogant, forfeited the good-will both of the king and the people, and had to leave Stockholm. The Jesuits directed their attention also to Norway, where the Reformation had still wrought but an imperfect conversion of the people to the Lutheran faith. Disguised as merchants they traveled about in the country, and sought to persuade young men to go to Catholic schools in foreign lands. After these young men had completed their studies, they often returned to Norway to be ordained as Lutheran ministers in order to be able to carry on a secret propaganda among their parishioners. Closterlassius wrote several works against Protestantism, among others, "A Letter from Satan to the Lutheran Ministers," and though he never returned to Norway, he actively supported the Jesuits there.

---

[1] Andreas Brandrud, *Klosterlasse, et Bidrag til den jesuitiske Propagandas Historie i Norden*, Christiania, 1895. M. Kubberud, *Jesuiterne i Norge*, Elverum, 1897. *Biskop Nils Glostrups Visitatser i Oslo og Hamar Stifter 1617–1637*, edited by Ludvig Daae og H. J. Huitfeldt-Kaas, p. 21. L. Daae, *Bidrag til den katholske Reaktions Historie i Norge i Christian IV.'s Tid*, *Historisk Tidsskrift*, tredie række, vol. III., p. 306 ff.

At a council in Bergen, 1604, the Norwegian bishops called the king's attention to the Jesuit agitation. He seems to have been alarmed by the reports, and issued a royal letter forbidding any one who had been educated by the Jesuits to serve in the church or schools of the kingdom. In 1606 Closterlassius was banished from Denmark, where he had arrived on a visit, and in 1613 the Jesuit priests in Norway were summoned before a council in Skien, where they were sentenced to have forfeited their office and inheritance, and they were immediately banished from the kingdom. After this time but few traces of Catholicism were found in Norway.[1]

This episode had also opened the king's eyes to the necessity of improving the schools of the two kingdoms, so that Norwegian and Danish students would not need to go to foreign institutions. In 1604 a new plan of instruction for secondary schools was prepared, and better textbooks were introduced. Gymnasiums were established at the Latin schools of Roskilde, Odense, Ribe, Aarhus, Lund, and Christiania, in order that the students could be better prepared for their university studies. Three or four professors were appointed for each gymnasium, who would give more advanced instruction in the classical languages, besides giving lectures on theology, logic, natural science, mathematics, botany, and anatomy. But this very laudable attempt to place secondary education on a higher level was unfortunately rendered abortive by later events. Only the gymnasium of Roskilde existed towards the end of the sixteenth century, and that of Odense till towards the end of the eighteenth. The academy of Sorø was founded in 1623, and the University of Copenhagen was much improved. Seven new chairs were created, and the king donated to the university a large part of his own library, in all 1100 volumes.

King Christian was a great builder and erected more castles and fortresses, and founded more cities, than any other king in the union period. In Norway he founded the city of Christiansand,[2] and when Oslo was almost totally destroyed by fire, August 17, 1624, he founded

---

[1] N. Slange, *Christian IV.'s Historie*, p. 205 f.

[2] *Af Nicolai Wergelands utrykte Christiansands Beskrivelse*, edited and published by Ludvig Daae, *Historisk Tidsskrift*, anden række, vol. III., p. 44 ff.

the new city of Christiania so near to the ruins that Oslo has long since been incorporated in the capital city of Norway. The castles of Akershus and Bohus were enlarged and surrounded by strong walls, and at Akershus he erected a palace which still lifts its towers above the city.[1]

The ever active and energetic king showed a great interest also for the Norwegian mining industry, which in the reign of Frederick II. had been wholly neglected. So great an impetus was given to this industry in this reign that it may almost be said to have been founded by Christian IV. A large number of new mines were opened, but for want of the necessary skill and science they yielded no profit.[2] The most important were the Røros copper mines, opened 1644, and the great Kongsberg silver mines, discovered in 1623, which led to the founding of the two cities, Røros and Kongsberg. As many as 4000 men were employed at Kongsberg, but the mines were often operated at a loss, till in 1830, when they began to yield profitable returns.

Christian IV., who was intensely interested in navigation, entertained a fond hope of being able to reëstablish communications with the Norse colonies in Greenland. Some attempts had been made also in the previous reign to reach the distant island. Frederick II. sent an expedition in 1579 under the English captain John Alday, and another in 1581 under Mogens Heinessøn, the great Faroe seacaptain, but both failed to reach their destination because of fog and icebergs. In 1585 the English navigator John Davis reached the west coast of Greenland, but he found no traces of white people, and thought that he was the real discoverer of the land. In 1605 King Christian sent three ships under the Danish nobleman Gødeke Lindenow and John Cunningham, a Scotchman, with the Englishman James Hall as pilot. Cunningham succeeded in landing on the west coast, and took possession of the country for the king, while Lindenow made an unsuccessful attempt to land on the east coast.[3]

---

[1] Gustav Storm, *Akershus Slot fra Midten af 17de Aarhundrede*, Christiania, 1901. *Norske Samlinger*, I., p. 633 ff.

[2] Ludvig Daae, *Det gamle Christiania*, Christiania, 1891. Joh. Dyring, *Kongeriget Norge*, p. 151 ff. I. Chr. Berg, *Aktstykker til Bergverkernes Historie, Samlinger til det norske Folks Sprog og Historie*, vol. III., p. 1 ff. Arnt Berntsen Bergen, *Danmark oc Norgis frugtbar Herlighed*, p. 274 ff.

[3] *M. M. Rosches Optegnelser fra Nordlandene 1581–1639, Norske Samlinger*, vol. II., p. 496.

Two more expeditions were sent out, one in 1606, and another in 1607, but as no traces of the colonists were found, the project was abandoned. The king turned his attention instead to the search for the northwest passage, and sent an expedition to the Hudson Bay under Jens Munk in 1619.[1] In 1636 he organized the Greenland Company to trade with Greenland, and to carry on whaling at Spitzbergen, but the trade with Greenland fell mostly into the hands of the Hollanders and the English. In harmony with the practice of the age, Christian IV. created many similar companies with exclusive trade privileges in certain parts of the world. In 1616 he chartered the "East India Company" to trade with the East India Islands, China, and Japan. This company raised a capital stock of 190,000 riksdaler, and secured Tranquebar on the Coromandel coast, which became the chief seat of its commercial operations in the far East.[2] In 1619 a company was formed to trade with Iceland, and in 1625 a Danish "West India Company" was organized.

It was King Christian's manifest ambition to increase his power at sea, and this desire was strengthened also by the necessity of being well armed both on sea and land because of the great wars waged by Philip II. in the Netherlands, and the strained relations between the Emperor and the Protestant princes in Germany. Much attention was therefore devoted especially to the navy. At his accession to the throne, Denmark-Norway had a fleet of twenty-two vessels, large and small, and some of these were very antiquated. The king hired Scotch ship-builders to assist the ablest men within his own kingdom in constructing a number of new warships of the best type, and in a few years the Danish-Norwegian fleet was by far the most powerful in the Baltic Sea. In time of war the sailors and marines serving on the new fleet seem to have numbered about six thousand.

---

[1] Daniel Bruun, *Det høie Nord, Færøernes, Islands og Grønlands Udforskning*, p. 182 ff. Two books about Greenland and the Norse colonies were written at this time: *Relation om Grønland*, by Jens Bjelke, an almost worthless product, and Lyscander's *Grønlandske Chronica*, a work of some merit.

[2] A *riksdaler* was at this time equal to a *speciedaler* (four *kroner*), or a little more than an American dollar.

26. Foreign Relations.   The Kalmar War

In internal administration Christian IV. had shown great energy and talent.   An earnest desire to increase his own personal influence and the power and prestige of his realm are features characteristic of his reign.   He showed such quickness and originality of thought and such executive ability that the people regarded him as a truly great king, to be compared with the most illustrious monarchs in history.   But this view represents nothing but the fondness with which people are wont to cherish a talented ruler who possesses charming traits, and knows how to win their admiration by a jolly straightforwardness and bold artlessness of speech and conduct.   It is true that Christian IV. instituted many useful reforms, but he was not a true reformer.   There is not to be found in his many praise-worthy undertakings and happy innovations any constructive prin-ciple aiming at the gradual uplifting of the people through a steady improvement of their social and economic condition.   He did noth-ing to rescue the Danish peasants from the wretched condition to which they had been reduced by the nobility.   He confirmed all the old statutes aiming at the preservation of the privileges of the aris-tocracy, and only increased the burdens of the poor by unnecessary wars and extravagant building projects, though in minor things he was so saving that, as he informed the Council, he could not afford to get properly married.   Morally he was weak, and intellectually not much above the ordinary.   Though a man of great courage, he was neither an able general nor a far-sighted statesman.   His ambition often led him into undertakings which were beyond both his means and his ability, and which brought upon his kingdom suffering and disaster.   He lacked the statesman's intuitive foresight.   He spent much of his time in a multitude of details in which he was unable to distinguish the important from the unimportant, and his foreign policy was often dictated by personal pique and ambition rather than by a wise forecast of political events.

In 1597 the king married Anna Catharine of Brandenburg, who bore him six children, three of whom died in childhood.   The queen died in 1612, but even before her death he had formed illicit attachments. In 1615 he acknowledged Christine Munk, a daughter of Ludvig

Munk, to be his legally wedded wife, though nothing is known of the marriage ceremony, and he never gave her the title of queen. She bore him twelve children, but the marriage was finally terminated by a divorce accompanied by a scandal.[1] He had many illegitimate children with different mothers. His illegitimate sons, Christian Ulrik, Hans Ulrik, and Ulrik Christian, received the surname of Gyldenløve. Even in that age of no very delicate tastes, the king's moral laxity must have been a constant source of scandal and offense.

In Sweden serious clashes between the Protestants and the party representing the Catholic reaction had led to important changes. King John's son, Sigismund, an ardent Catholic, who had become king of Poland, succeeded his father on the throne of Sweden, but in 1599 he was deposed because of his attempt to overthrow the Lutheran faith. The Duke of Södermanland, a younger son of Gustav Vasa, and brother of King John III., was placed on the throne as Charles IX. The new king possessed some of the ability of the great Vasa dynasty, which was to place Sweden in the front rank of European powers, but he assumed from the outset a very aggressive and uncompromising attitude towards Denmark-Norway, due in part, perhaps, to the fact that Christian IV. had shown himself a friend of Sigismund, if not an open supporter of his party. In 1610 Charles founded the city of Gottenborg, which would give the Hollanders a new harbor, where they could unload their cargoes, and avoid paying the toll for passing through the Sound. The Swedish aggressions in Finmarken, which had caused trouble in the previous reign, became more pronounced than ever. Charles IX. called himself "King of the Lapps in Nordland," collected taxes as far as Malangen and Titisfjord, a distance south of Tromsø, and gave the merchants of Gottenborg right to trade from Titisfjord to Varanger.[2] Christian IV., who wished to maintain a naval supremacy both in the Baltic and the North Sea, resisted these encroachments vigorously, but neither protests nor negotiations could influence the independent

[1] Aage Skavlan, *Historiske Billeder fra den nyere Tid.*

[2] Oscar Alb. Johnsen, *De norske Stænder*, p. 131. N. Slange, *Christian IV.'s Historie*, p. 256 ff. Amtmand G. Hammer, *Historisk Underretning om Finmarkens Handel, Samlinger til det norske Folks Sprog og Historie*, vol. III., p. 261 ff.

and haughty King Charles IX. The Northern Protestant powers were thus drifting towards open hostilities at a moment when their German brethren stood confronted by the Empire and the papacy, who were marshaling their forces for the last great assault on Protestantism, the Thirty Years' War. In 1608 the "Protestant Union" was formed with Elector Frederick of the Palatinate as Director, and the following year the "Catholic League" was organized with Elector Maximilian of Bavaria as commander-in-chief. The "Union" sought the support of Henry IV. of France, and of Christian IV. of Denmark-Norway, but King Christian chose to wage war with Sweden rather than aid his Protestant brethren in Germany. In 1611 he finally forced the Council to declare war against Sweden. It appears that he did not only intend to protect his realm against encroachments, but that he entertained a hope of being able to conquer Sweden, and to establish once more the union between the three Northern kingdoms. He invaded Sweden with an army of about 6000 men, and while he laid siege to the city of Kalmar with the greater part of his force, he dispatched Sten Sehested with a portion of it against Elfsborg. The army was supported by the fleet, which was superior to that of Sweden. The Norwegian forces were stationed in the border districts, and were instructed not to enter Swedish territory unless special orders were given.[1] On May 27 Kalmar, with the exception of the castle, was taken, an event which gave to the struggle the name of the Kalmar War, and on July 17 an undecisive battle was fought with the Swedish army under King Charles IX., who had arrived in the neighborhood of the city. The day after the battle Kalmar castle was treacherously surrendered by its commandant, and in a similar way Öland fell into the hands of the Danes, though Gustavus Adolphus, the brave son of King Charles IX., recaptured the island before the campaign was closed in the fall. On October 30 King Charles IX. died at Nyköping castle, and Gustavus Adolphus ascended the throne of Sweden. He wished to conclude peace with Denmark, but Christian IV., who dreamed of large conquests, would accept no reasonable terms, and the war was continued. In March, 1612, King Christian had greatly strengthened his army in southern Sweden, but he made the tactical mistake of

[1] *Samlinger til det norske Folks Sprog og Historie,* vol. III., p. 221.

dividing his forces, which proved of great advantage to Gustavus Adolphus, who had only a weak army of peasants, as the Swedish nobles took no part in the conflict. With his main force King Christian turned towards the city of Gottenborg, which he destroyed after having taken the fortresses of Elfsborg and Gullborg. But the fleet, though superior to the Swedish, accomplished nothing, and he had won no decisive victories. After unsuccessful operations against Jönköping, the king returned in August to Copenhagen, whence he again advanced with his fleet against Stockholm. But Gustavus Adolphus hastened to the succor of his capital, and Christian sailed away without venturing an attack on the city. This was the last important event of the war. Through the efforts of England peace was concluded at Knærød, January 20, 1613. Sweden relinquished all claims to Finmarken, and agreed to pay a war indemnity of one million riksdaler. All conquered territory was relinquished, both countries should have the right to use the three crowns in their coats of arms, and they should both enjoy the same trade privileges and freedom from tolls. The war had produced no marked result except that of destroying lives and property, of creating bitter enmity between the closely related Protestant nations of the North, and of increasing taxes and public burdens.

Some of the Norwegian forces seem to have taken part in the operations against Elfsborg, but the Norwegians were not much interested in the war. Some of the officers in charge of their forces were incompetent, and the soldiers were often disobedient and unwilling to fight. But two minor episodes occurred, one of which especially became of great importance to the Norwegian people.

In the Kalmar War both Christian IV. and Gustavus Adolphus enlisted foreign mercenaries. A Flemish officer and colonel in the Swedish army, Jan von Monkhoven, was sent by Gustavus Adolphus to the Netherlands and Scotland, where he raised a force of 1200 or 1400 men with which he hoped to capture Trondhjem. He lost one ship, but arrived at Trondhjem with the rest of the force, some 800 men; but the people defended their city well, and he sailed to Stjørdalen, where he landed his troops. A force of 250 soldiers and 1000 *bønder* which had been assembled was scattered without difficulty, as the *lensherre*, Sten Bilde, was a cowardly and incompetent man,

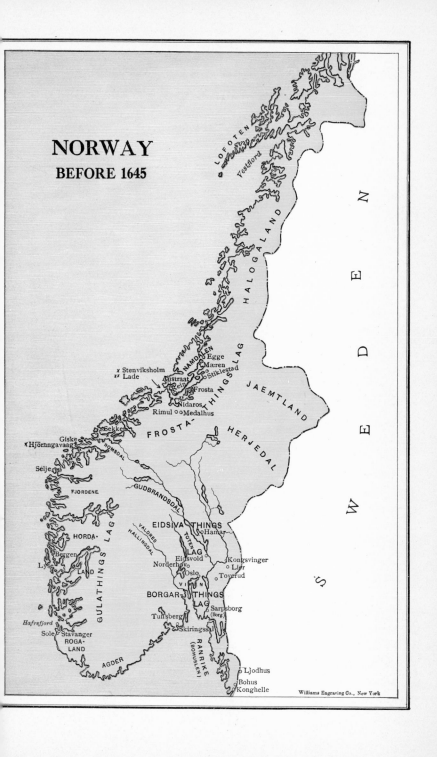

NORWAY
BEFORE 1645

Williams Engraving Co., New York

who did little or nothing for the defense of the country. Monk-hoven crossed the mountains into Herjedalen and Jæmtland, where he harried and plundered unmolested. He fought at Kalmar, and fell in the siege of Gdof in Ingermanland, 1614.[1] The second corps of mercenaries, raised in Scotland for the Swedish service, met a different fate. The enlistment was intrusted to James Spence of Wormiston, who died later as a Swedish baron. He employed Colonel Andrew Ramsey to conduct the recruiting, and James I., king of England and Scotland, who was married to King Christian's sister, Anna,[2] and probably would not have offended his brother-in-law, learned nothing of the recruiting until it was too late to prevent the enlisted soldiers from leaving. A small force, possibly 350 men, succeeded in departing, led by Lieutenant-colonel Alexander Ramsey, under whom served the captains Bruce, James Moneypenny, James Scott, George Hay, and George Sinclair. On the 19th and 20th of August, 1612, they came to anchor in the Romsdalsfjord, and landed their troops at Klungnes, near a cliff which still bears the name of *Skothammaren.* They forced two *bønder* to act as guides, and began their march through Romsdal. The people fled at their approach, and as they were a small force, they did not venture to harass the settlements through which they marched,[3] but hastened on their

[1] Chr. Lange, *Nye Bidrag til Kalmar Krigens Historie, Norske Samlinger*, vol. I., p. 262 ff.; vol. II., p. 41 ff. Yngvar Nielsen, *Nogle Notitser om Johan von Mønnichhofen, Historisk Tidsskrift*, første række, vol. IV., p. 109 ff. N. Slange, *Christian IV.'s Historie*, 312 ff. I. Chr. Berg, *Bidrag til Historien af Christian den fjerdes Krig med Sverige i Aarene 1611 og 1612, Samlinger til det norske Folks Sprog og Historie*, vol. III., p. 219 ff. Yngvar Nielsen, *Jens Bjelke til Østraat*, p. 40 ff.

[2] *Norske Samlinger*, vol. I., p. 454 ff., *Beretninger af Prindsesse Annas Giftermaal med Kong Jakob den 6te af Skotland.*

[3] The Norwegian *statholder*, Enevold Kruse, wrote to Christian Friis and Breide Rantzau, October 3, 1612: "We have also since learned that those Scots who were defeated and captured on their march through this country have absolutely neither burned, murdered, nor destroyed anything either in Romsdal or Gudbrandsdal, except only a Dane, Søfren Setnes by name, who dwells in Romsdal. From him they took a chest full of silver articles, etc." *Norske Samlinger*, vol. II., p. 288 ff.

The *Zinklar Vise*, a popular ballad written about this battle by Edward Storm (1742–1794), is based on popular traditions, and abounds in exaggerations, as ballads usually do. See H. P. S. Krag, *Sagn om Slaget ved Kringelen.* The following stanza may serve as an example:

way, and crossed the mountains into Gudbrandsdal. But news of their approach had been received, and the brave *lensmand* Lars Hage had assembled the men of Lesje, Dovre, Vaage, Fron, Lom, and Ringebu, who under the command of the *foged* Lars Gram took their position on a mountain side overlooking Kringen, where a road passes at the foot of the mountain along the Laagan River. Their exact number is not known, but in a song written shortly after the battle they are said to have numbered 500, which seems to be approximately correct. The officers who were taken prisoners stated that the Scots numbered 350 men.[1] The *bønder* gathered piles of stone and timber on the mountain side, and everything was ready when the Scots arrived on August 26, 1612. The advance guard was allowed to pass, but when the main body arrived, the signal was given,[2] and an avalanche of stone and timber swept down upon them. Many were killed outright, and many were swept into the river and drowned. The rest, attacked in front and rear, were forced to surrender. The advance guard was also captured, but most of them were put to death after they were taken prisoners. Only eighteen were escorted to Akershus, among whom were the officers Ramsey, Bruce, Moneypenny, and Scott, who were sent as prisoners to Copenhagen. Hay and Sinclair had fallen. Some of the Scots remained in Norway, and some enlisted in the Danish army. Insignificant as this episode was from a military point of view, it was, none the less, the spark which kindled the national patriotism, and roused the martial spirit of the Norwegians. Hitherto they had been too indifferent even to defend themselves; henceforth their valor became proverbial. A stone slab was erected on the battlefield of Kringen fifty years later bearing the inscription: "Here Colonel Sinclair was shot on the twenty-sixth of August, 1612." This slab was replaced

> And with him fourteen hundred men:
> On mischief all that band were bent;
> They spared nor young nor aged then,
> But slew and burnt as they went.

The song has been translated by Thomas Michell, *History of the Scottish Expedition to Norway in 1612*, part II.

[1] Olav Kringen, *Fra Snelandets Hytter*, *Decorah-Posten*, October 1, 1907.

[2] The tradition says that a girl, Pillar Guri, was stationed on a mountain top, opposite Kringen, and that she gave the signal by blowing a trumpet.

in 1733 by a wooden cross bearing a bombastic rhymed inscription which King Christian VI. read on his visit in Gudbrandsdal.[1] A new stone slab with the inscription: "In memory of the bravery of the bønder 1612" was erected in 1826.   This was again replaced by a new stone monument August 26, 1912.

King Christian had learned two things in the Kalmar War.   In the first place, that his army organization was antiquated and wholly inefficient, and secondly, that Denmark could no longer seek territorial aggrandizement in Sweden.   As soon as the war was over, he began to improve the army both in Norway and Denmark.   In 1614 he issued an order for the creation of a small national militia, which should always be ready for military service.   In Norway this force was to consist of 2100 men, but the order does not seem to have been systematically carried out, and the plan was soon abandoned.   In 1617 the firearms which had been provided for this army were finally sold to the people.   Not till after Denmark's sad

[1] This inscription reads:

> Courage, loyalty, bravery, and all that gives honor,
> The whole world 'midst Norwegian rocks can learn.
> An example is there seen of such bravery,
> Among the rocks in the North, on this very spot:
> A fully armed corps of some hundred Scots
> Was here crushed like earthen pots;
> They found that bravery, with loyalty and courage,
> Lived in full glow in the hearts of the men of Gudbrandsdal.
> Jørgen von Zinclair as the leader of the Scots,
> Thought within himself, "No one will here meddle with me."
> But, lo! a small number of bønder confronted him,
> Who bore to him Death's message of powder and ball.
> One Northern monarch, King Christian the Sixth,
> To honor on his way we have erected this;
> For him we are ready to risk our blood and life
> Until our breath goes out and our bodies lie stiff."

This not very happy translation is found in Thomas Michell's *History of the Scottish Expedition to Norway in 1612.*   The original is found in Bing's *Norges Beskrivelse*, p. 348.   H. F. Hjorthoy's *Beskrivelse over Gudbrandsdalen*, ch. II., p. 27.   H. P. S. Krag, *Sagn om Slagel ved Kringelen*, Christiania, 1838.   A. Fabricius, *Minder fra Nordens Historie*.   O. O. Olafsen, *Skottetoget efter Folkesagnet og Historien*, Molde, 1877.   *Norske Samlinger*, II., p. 288 ff.

experience in the Thirty Years' War was the plan of a better military organization carried out.[1]

In 1618 the Thirty Years' War broke out, and nearly all nations of western Europe were drawn into its bloody vortex. Bohemia became the first theater of war. In 1620 the troops of the Emperor and the Catholic League defeated the Protestants in the battle of the White Mountain, near Prague, and Frederick V. of the Palatinate, who had been chosen king of Bohemia, had to flee, and was later outlawed by the Emperor. Tilly, the general of the armies of the League, wasted the Palatinate with fire and sword; Bohemia was fearfully ravaged, and the Catholic religion was reëstablished. This encouraged the fanatic Emperor Ferdinand II. to make a general assault on the Protestants in Germany. In order to make himself independent of the League, he placed in the field a new imperial army under Wallenstein. The Protestant princes were in dire straits. Spain had also joined the Catholic alliance, and, by dangling before the eyes of King James I. of England a possible marriage between his son Charles and a Spanish princess, succeeded in keeping him inactive. France, though hostile to the House of Habsburg, was a Catholic power, and Holland lay bleeding and exhausted after the wars with Philip II. In their distress the Protestants again turned to Christian IV. Elizabeth, the daughter of his sister Anna and King James I. of England, was married to the exiled King Frederick of Bohemia. He sympathized with the Protestants, and, what possibly weighed still more, he had for some time been trying to extend his influence in lower Germany in the hope that he might be able to obtain some of the secularized bishoprics for his sons, and also to gain control of Hamburg and Bremen. He did not fear the consequences of a war with the powerful Catholic coalition, but the Council would not embark on so hazardous and expensive an undertaking. The king, however, turned a deaf ear to their remonstrance. A promise of aid from England, and the fear that Gustavus Adolphus might become the leader of a Protestant alliance, led him to decide

[1] A. C. C. Drolsum, *Det norske Folk og dets Forsvarsvæsen*, p. 25 ff. I. Chr. Berg, *Aktstykker til den staaende Hærs Historie, Samlinger til det norske Folks Sprog og Historie*, vol. III., p. 404 ff.; vol. IV., p. 1 ff. Didrik Schnitler, *Det første Aarhundrede af den norske Hærs Historie*, Christiania, 1874.

PLATE V

CHRISTIAN IV.

HANNIBAL SEHESTED.

PEDER GRIFFENFELD.

for war. In May, 1625, he entered Germany with an army of about 20,000 men, and the reënforcements sent him by the Protestant princes increased his available forces to about 30,000 men, the greater part of which consisted of German mercenaries. But Christian's operations were slow. He wasted much time in minor skirmishes which could lead to no decisive result, and nothing was accomplished in the first campaign. In 1626 Wallenstein defeated the Protestant forces under Mansfeld at Dessau, while Christian was facing Tilly with an army which was rapidly being reduced in numbers through sickness and desertions. Money was scarce, and the aid given by England was of little real value. At length Christian risked a decisive battle, August 17, at the village of Lutter am Barnberg, near Wolfenbüttel, but suffered a crushing defeat. The retreat turned into a rout; panic seized the fleeing army, and the king barely escaped falling into the hands of the enemy. When he reached Wolfenbüttel, he was accompanied by eighty horsemen, who had gathered about him in the flight. After this defeat Christian showed remarkable energy. He raised another army for the campaign of 1627, but the resistance which he could make proved useless. In July Tilly crossed the Elbe, and united his army with that of Wallenstein, and the two generals began the invasion of Denmark. The whole peninsula was soon overrun and subjected to the wildest ravages, not only by the lawless warriors of Tilly and Wallenstein, but by the mercenaries in King Christian's own army, who turned brigands and marauders. Denmark was on the verge of utter ruin, and Emperor Ferdinand II. and Wallenstein were already laying plans for extending the borders of the Empire, and of establishing its control over the Baltic and the North Sea. This grave danger brought Gustavus Adolphus into the arena. The imperial forces laid siege to the city of Stralsund, but it received help from Sweden and Denmark, whose fleets controlled the Baltic, and Wallenstein failed to take the city, though he is said to have sacrificed 12,000 men in the attempt. Gustavus Adolphus wished to form an alliance with Christian IV. for the defense of the North and the Lutheran faith, and nothing could have seemed more advantageous for Denmark at this moment, as Wallenstein offered Gustavus to partition the kingdom of Denmark and Norway in such a way that

Sweden should receive Norway, while Denmark should be the portion of the Emperor. But Christian's suspicion and jealousy prevented an alliance of the Protestant kingdoms of the North at this critical moment. It may be urged in his defense, however, that by avoiding an alliance with Sweden he could obtain more favorable terms of peace. On May 12, 1629, he signed the treaty of peace with the Emperor at Lübeck. He had to relinquish all claims to German possessions for his sons; he had to resign as commander of the Protestant forces in Germany, and had to promise not to meddle with German affairs in the future; but he lost no territory, nor was he forced to pay any war indemnity. These easy terms were not granted by the Emperor and Wallenstein from any kindness of heart, but because they wished to have their hands free for the coming struggle with Gustavus Adolphus. But though Christian had succeeded in making peace on better terms than could have been expected, Denmark had paid dearly for his participation in the war. The ravages and suffering brought upon the kingdom seem to have destroyed its vigor, and the battlefield of Luther am Barnberg marks the beginning of Denmark's national decline.

In 1628, while the realm was in its deepest distress, the king began in earnest the reorganization of the army. According to an order issued on January 18 of that year to the Norwegian *statholder* Jens Juel, four farms (*gaards*), or eight half farms, or sixteen quarter farms should form a *lægd*, which should furnish and maintain one soldier. According to this plan, an army was raised, consisting of five regiments: Trondhjem, Bergenhus, Tønsberg, Akershus, and Bohus, and three *fænniker*: Stavanger, Agdesiden, and Jæmtland. After peace was concluded at Lübeck, this organization was again abandoned, because of the resistance of the people to military burdens, but it was reëstablished by the ordinance of September 19, 1641, which united the Stavanger and Agdesiden *fænniker* into a sixth regiment. Each regiment numbered about 1000 men, and was divided into three companies, except the regiment of Bergenhus of 1300 men, which was divided into four companies. Cavalry was organized through *rostjeneste; i.e.* mounted service demanded of nobility, clergy, and *odelsbønder*. According to the military ordinance of 1641, the cavalry numbered 520 arquebusiers and 500 dragoons, but the latter, which was selected from the infantry, might be regarded as mounted infantry. Through the ordinance of 1628 fourteen city companies, each numbering about 100 men, were also organized; two in Trondhjem, four in Bergen, two in Christiania, and one in each of the cities of Fredrikstad, Tønsberg, Skien, Konghelle, Marstrand, and Udevalla. These companies totalling 1400 men were recruited among the citizens of these cities, and were to serve as a sort of garrison for their protection. The fortresses in Norway at this time were: Vardøhus, Trondhjem with Munkholmen, Bergenhus, Akershus, Bohus, Fredrikstad, Marstrand, and the redoubts of Vinger, Flekkerø, and Frøsøen in Jæmtland. These fortresses had permanent garrisons, which were greatly strengthened by Christian IV. The term of military service was fixed at three years, and no one could rent land or own or operate a farm who had not rendered the required military service.[1] Norway had thus received a national army, which in time became an invaluable aid in the struggle for national liberty, and which was of far greater value to the country in time of need than the lawless foreign mercenaries employed at that time in the wars in all countries.

27. New National Growth. Hannibal Sehested. A New War with Sweden

Immediately after the introduction of the Reformation, which destroyed what was still left of the old spirit of independence, Norway reached its lowest ebb of national weakness. But signs of a new social and economic growth soon began to manifest themselves, and before a century passed, considerable progress had been made towards a new and more vigorous national life, which was characterized, however, by a more distinct stratification of social classes. A Lutheran clergy had arisen, generally well educated, and imbued with the love of learning and the more advanced ideas of the Renaissance. A new merchant class sprang up in the cities, and a new nobility, springing partly from the old Norse nobility, and partly from im-

---

[1] Didrik Schnitler, *Det første Aarhundrede af den norske Hærs Historie.* Barstad, *Norges Landforsvar 1604–1634.* Oscar Alb. Johnsen, *Hannibal Sehesteds Statholderskab,* p. 30 ff.

migrated noblemen, also came into existence.[1] The growth of these new classes resulted, however, in increased burdens for the *bønder*, who, prior to the Reformation, had enjoyed a very high degree of social and economic independence. Christian IV., who needed money for his expensive wars and buildings, increased the taxes, and augmented the military burdens through the new army organization, while the three upper classes, whose interests were not identical with those of the *bønder*, sought to increase their own privileges and powers.[2] The *bønder*, who up to this time had virtually constituted the whole nation, were gradually reduced to the fourth and lowest estate. But their freedom was not destroyed; their spirit was not broken, nor was their economic well-being and independence seriously impaired, though they lost much of their former power and social prominence. Four distinct "estates" were gradually developed: nobility, clergy, merchants, and *bønder*, and Assemblies of Estates replaced the old *lagthings*. From 1548 such Assemblies of the four Estates were summoned to do homage to a new king, but in the latter part of the reign of Christian IV. they also took part in the levying of taxes and in the making of laws. The new social classes, though often grasping and selfish, represented in many ways a more enlightened patriotism than the *bønder*, who loved intensely their rights and freedom, but who failed to understand the demands which new ages bring, and lacked the scope of vision necessary to develop the country along national lines. The development of the four estates was a distinct organization of new forces which were to lift the nation to a higher plane both politically and intellectually. The new national army, the fortification of the cities, the creation of coast defenses, and other timely improvements were made possible through their support.

Closely associated with the development of the estates was also

[1] Oscar Alb. Johnsen, *De norske Stænder*, p. 27 ff. *Christiania Videnskabs-Selskabs Skrifter*, 1906.

[2] Lorens Berg says: "Christian IV. deserves to be branded as an oppressor of the *bønder* in spite of his many boastful phrases about 'guarding the interests of the common people.' For example: In 1640 he was on the point of stopping all the sawmills in the land by his letters of taxation. In great numbers the people sought 'gracious permission' at the *things* to shut down their sawmills." *Historisk Tidsskrift*, fjerde række, vol. V., p. 50.

the consolidation of the government officials into a distinct and influential class — a bureaucracy. In 1547 Norway received again its own chancellor, who was the keeper of the seal, and exercised supervision over the courts of law, and in 1572 the *lensherre* of Akershus was made *statholder* of Norway. Christiania, as his residence city, became the center of Norwegian administration, the place where the Assembly of Estates met, where kings were hailed,[1] where the leading men of the kingdom assembled, a center from which social and political influence began to emanate; the new city, though small, was becoming the capital of the kingdom.

In 1642 Hannibal Sehested, a Danish nobleman, was made *lensherre* of Akershus and *statholder* of Norway, and the same year he married King Christian's daughter Christiane. The new *statholder* was a gifted man of fine appearance and noble bearing. In company with one of the princes he had visited Rome, Naples, Paris, and London; he had been sent on important missions, and had become acquainted with the leading statesmen, and especially as the king's son-in-law he could appear with royal dignity in his high office, though he was yet only thirty-four years of age. On his arrival in Norway Sehested entered upon the important duties of his office with great energy and earnestness. He studied conditions closely, and aimed to make all possible improvements with the aid and advice of the Estates, which he summoned to meet in Christiania. He sought to perfect the yet incomplete military organization, to secure firearms for the army, and to aid the mining industry, which was in great need of encouragement and able assistance. In these efforts he was aided chiefly by the nobility, the clergy, and the cities, while the *bønder* held aloof or showed opposition, partly because their burdens were already heavy in proportion to their income, but partly, also, because they still lacked understanding of the value of national improvements. With his good judgment and administrative ability, Sehested might have done great things for Norway, if his work had not been suddenly interrupted by a new war with Sweden.

The crushing defeat of the Danish army in Germany, and the phenomenal victories of Gustavus Adolphus, which shed the brightest

---

[1] Assemblies of Estates were held in Christiania, 1626, 1628, 1631, 1639, 1643, 1648, 1657, and 1661. Ludvig Daae, *Det Gamle Christiania*, p. 98.

luster on Swedish arms, and filled all Europe with acclaim, suddenly changed the political aspect in the North and awakened the keenest jealousy of the ambitious King Christian. Not only was Sweden assuming political leadership in the North, but the hitherto insignificant kingdom was becoming one of the great powers of Europe, while Denmark, which but recently had treated Sweden as a dependency, was sinking into obscurity. Gustavus Adolphus' brilliant career was closed on the battlefield of Lützen, 1632, but the great Swedish generals still wielded the sword valiantly. The foreign policy of Sweden was wisely guided by the sagacious statesman Axel Oxenstjerna, and an alliance with France made her position quite secure. By pursuing a friendly policy King Christian might have profited by the new situation, but would he, could he admit that Denmark-Norway had lost the coveted leadership in the North? No bitterer chalice could be brought to the lips of so proud a king. He would still oppose Sweden; not openly, but he began to systematically annoy the Swedish government by posing as a peacemaker, and by trying to prevent Sweden from securing possessions in Germany. In the fall of 1637 he even offered the Emperor to resist with armed force any attempt of Sweden to secure German territory. In vain Peder Vibe, the Danish minister in Stockholm, warned him. The king thought that the course which he was pursuing was not dangerous. But Sweden was not in a humor at this moment to bear patiently with a jealous and meddlesome neighbor. The Kalmar War and the indemnity which Sweden had been forced to pay by the peace of Knærød were not forgotten, and Axel Oxenstjerna was much irritated by King Christian's duplicity. In 1643 orders were given the Swedish field marshal, Lennart Torstensson, to march against Denmark. The order reached him in Moravia in September, and he immediately put his army in motion. On December 12 he entered Holstein, and by New Year he stood in Jutland. Both King Christian and the Council were taken by surprise. Before the end of January the whole Danish peninsula was in Torstensson's hands, and General Gustav Horn occupied Skåne with an army of eleven thousand men. Louis de Geer was sent by Axel Oxenstjerna to the Netherlands to attempt to secure an alliance against Denmark, as the Hollanders were opposed to the Sound-toll, which hindered their commerce in the Baltic. But they did not like to see Denmark annihilated, and Sweden too powerful, and de Geer only succeeded in collecting a fleet of thirty vessels, which was sent under command of Thijssen to coöperate with the Swedish forces. In Denmark all was consternation, and no one knew what to do; the king alone retained his presence of mind. He placed his confidence in the fleet, and Norway might be able to give some assistance, since it now possessed an army. Statholder Sehested was in favor of an aggressive policy on the part of Norway, a plan also favored by King Christian, but the Norwegians strenuously opposed an attack on Sweden. The quarrel was not theirs. They would never, they said, attack Sweden, for their Swedish neighbors wished them no harm, and they well knew that if they touched Sweden, it would be to their own misfortune.[1] Their opposition to the *statholder* in this matter grew very bitter, and it must be admitted that their view was justified by the situation, as it was proven to be correct by the issue of the war. But the Danish lords cared but little for the public sentiment in Norway. Jakob Ulfeld in Jæmtland had already opened hostilities by sending forces to raid the neighboring Swedish districts, but they had to withdraw before the Swedes, who occupied Jæmtland.[2] Daniel Buschovius, a chaplain from Elfdalen, also advanced from Dalarne with 200 men into the districts of Indre and Særna in Øster-dalen, and persuaded the people to swear allegiance to Queen Christina, the daughter of Gustavus.[3] The Norwegians again advanced, captured Mørsel redoubt, and recovered Jæmtland, which remained in their possession during the rest of the war. In the meantime Sehested had made preparations to invade Vermland with a force

[1] In a letter to Admiral Gedde, January 30, 1845, Sehested wrote: "It is to be heartily deplored that the people of this kingdom are so refractory that they publicly swear and protest that they will not advance one foot across the border, neither have they been willing to be stationed here between Halland and the border of Sweden." *Samlinger til det norske Folks Sprog og Historie*, III., p. 70. *Statholder Hannibal Sehesteds Copiebog for Aaret 1645.* This was an exaggeration at the time, as the Norwegians had already made several expeditions into Sweden, but in order to make political capital, he bases this statement on the well-known fact that the Norwegians were opposed to the war.

[2] Oscar Alb. Johnsen, *Hannibal Sehesteds Statholderskab*, p. 55 ff.

[3] Yngvar Nielsen, *Om Indre og Særna, Historisk Tidsskrift*, III., p. 195 ff.

of 2000 men, assisted by a similar force under Henrik Bjelke. But he was ordered to coöperate with the king, who had already spent some time before Gottenborg. On the arrival of Sehested King Christian departed to take charge of the naval operations. On May 16, 1644, he met Thijssen's fleet, and defeated it in the battle of List Dyb, off the west coast of Schleswig, and after a second engagement a few days later, Thijssen had to return to Holland. On July 1 King Christian and Admiral Vind fought the great naval battle of Kolberger Heide, off Kiel, with the Swedish fleet under Klaes Fleming. The old king showed the greatest bravery. Even after he was so severely wounded that he lost the sight of one eye, he stood on the deck of his flagship, "Trefoldigheden," and encouraged his men. As a result of the battle the Swedish fleet was bottled up in the harbor of Kiel, but through the negligence of the Danish admiral Galt it managed to escape. Galt was sentenced to death and executed, and Eirik Ottessøn Orning, a Norwegian captain, became chief admiral. When Thijssen had repaired his ships, he again put to sea, sailed through the Sound under the thundering cannons of the Kronborg, and joined the Swedish fleet. A Danish squadron of seventeen ships under the Norwegian admiral, Pros Mund, was attacked and destroyed; only three frigates escaped into the harbor of Copenhagen.

Sehested did not engage in active operations till in June, when he attacked and destroyed the newly founded city of Vernersborg, and sent George von Reichwein across the border from Vinger and Eidskog. Morast redoubt was taken, but the Swedes dispatched Gabriel Oxenstjerna to recapture it. Sehested now joined the Norwegian forces, which numbered 2825 men with eighteen field-pieces. A serious battle was fought, in which the Norwegians were victorious; Henrik Bjelke entered Dalsland, and took the city of Åmål, but the Norwegian forces found it necessary to withdraw again to the border, and in May, Morast redoubt was the only point in Swedish territory in their possession. The newly organized Norwegian army had proven that it could render efficient service, but the active part which Norway had been forced to play in the war could not avert the disastrous outcome. After the destruction of Pros Mund's squadron, Denmark's strength was so nearly exhausted that King

Christian was compelled to negotiate for peace. The representatives of the two powers met at Brømsebro, on the border between Blekinge and Småland, where peace was finally concluded August 13, 1645. Christian had to cede permanently to Sweden the islands of Gothland and Ösel, and Halland for a period of twenty-five years. He also had to cede the Norwegian provinces of Jæmtland and Herjedalen. The districts of Indre and Særna, where the people had sworn allegiance to the queen of Sweden, were not mentioned in the treaty, but they were retained by Sweden, as they were regarded by the Swedes as a part of Herjedalen.[1]

The Norwegians, who had been dragged into the war against their will, and had defended their territory successfully, suffered the greatest loss, and might well regard themselves as the victims of Danish politics. But the peace was, none the less, welcomed with joy, because of the oppressive burdens caused by the war. In Bergen the news of peace was hailed with the firing of guns, the flying of banners, and thanksgiving services in the churches.[2]

King Christian's unfortunate wars not only destroyed Denmark's preponderance in the North, and transferred the leadership to Sweden, but they affected distinctly also the relation between Norway and Denmark. It became evident to a far-sighted statesman like Hannibal Sehested that Norway, which was making rapid commercial and economic progress, and was so near a neighbor to Denmark's powerful rival, could no longer be treated as a mere dependency, administered in the interest of Denmark, and defended by a few companies of soldiers, placed as garrisons in the leading fortresses of the kingdom. The altered situation had created new demands. Neither King Christian nor the Danish statesmen regarded the peace of Brømsebro as permanent; they would await the opportunity to regain what had been lost; but in a new conflict Norway might prove a source of weakness rather than of strength from a military point of view, if the old system was continued. Sehested would

---

[1] Yngvar Nielsen, *Om Indre og Særna, Historisk Tidsskrift*, vol. III., p. 195 ff. L. Holberg, *Danmarks Riges Historie*, III., p. 48 ff., p. 229. *Samlinger til det norske Folks Sprog og Historie*, vol. V., p. 478; vol. VI., p. 470. Yngvar Nielsen, *De nordenfjeldske Begivenheder 1657–1660*, p. 47 ff.

[2] *Norske Magasin*, II., 211. *Historisk Tidsskrift*, vol. I., p. 28. Oscar Alb. Johnsen, *Hannibal Sehesteds Statholderskab*, p. 74 ff.

institute a new policy. Norway was to be made a power with sufficient military and administrative autonomy to act of her own accord; the kingdom was not to be a weak dependency which had to be defended, but an active partner in the union. He had discovered Norway's strength in the war with Sweden, and saw that by a wise policy of administration the strength might be rapidly increased. He won the old king for his plan, and received such a plenitude of powers that he became virtually acting king of Norway. During the war the king had given him the supervision and highest authority over the Norwegian army, a power which was not curtailed even after the peace was concluded, and he soon succeeded in obtaining control also of the finances of the kingdom. He could use the money in the Norwegian treasury at his own discretion; he was authorized to levy taxes in order to improve the defenses of the kingdom, and to borrow money in the name of the king and the realm. The revenues, which, to a great extent, had been sent to Denmark, were now largely used in the kingdom, and Sehested finally convinced the king of the wisdom of using all the Norwegian revenues at home. On July 2, 1647, King Christian issued an order that all the taxes should be used in Norway for the support of the militia and for the payment of the debt. Sehested sought the active coöperation of the Norwegian Estates, as he needed their aid to carry through his reforms as well as the information which they could give him as to conditions in various parts of the country, and he summoned them often to give advice in nearly all matters touching the administration of the kingdom.[1] "At this point," says Professor Johnsen, "he appears as a third power in the government beside the king and the Council. He is more than *statholder*, more than viceroy, he is the representative of a definite political policy, the representative of the interests of a whole kingdom in direct opposition to the one power, the Council, and in alliance with the other, the king; but, in fact, the one in the alliance who takes the initiative, who is both the propelling and the guiding force."[2] In October, 1645, Sehested submitted a plan for a permanent military organization to the assembled Estates, and

[1] Oscar Alb. Johnsen, *Et Aktstykke fra Stænderforhandlingen i Christiania 1645. Historisk Tidsskrift*, fjerde række, vol. IV., p. 81 ff.
[2] Oscar Alb. Johnsen, *Hannibal Sehesteds Statholderskab*, p. 91.

the result of the deliberation was that the German cavalry which had served in the war should be kept. This cavalry was, however, dismissed by royal order in 1647. The regiments should be kept up and strengthened, and able officers should be employed. According to Sehested's proposition, sanctioned by the king, the regiments of Bohus, Akershus, and Trondhjem were to be maintained, and these were increased respectively to 2000, 3000, and 3000 men. The fortresses were to be repaired, and the garrisons strengthened, and as they were far apart, forts were also to be erected at other places. Sehested sought also to create a separate Norwegian fleet of thirty vessels, but failed to carry out the plan, as it received no general support.

The Danish nobility, and the Council led by Korfits Ulfeld, another son-in-law of King Christian, were bitterly opposed to the policy pursued by Sehested and the king in regard to Norway. They scouted the idea that Norway should have a separate army and navy, that the finances of the kingdom should be administered for Norway's own benefit, and that no contributions were to be sent to the Danish treasury. This policy, they believed, would lead to Norway's complete independence. The king was now old and weak, and when he lost his oldest son, Prince Christian, who had been elected successor to the throne by the assembled Danish Estates, the Council gained full control. The reform policy in Norway was abandoned, the expenditures for the Norwegian army were reduced, the Danish chancellor was given control of the Norwegian finances, and the *lensherrer* were instructed to send their contributions directly to Denmark. On the charge of malfeasance in office, to which he pleaded guilty, Sehested was dismissed, and lost all his possessions. But, though he was overthrown, his reform plans in Norway were destined to be revived. He had given the kingdom an army; he had organized a centralized administration separate from that of Denmark, and had placed autonomy as the goal towards which Norway should be striving. Such a lesson in self-government could not be wholly forgotten, and the Norwegian army remained as a result of what had been done, as a new repository of national strength to be used in future struggles.

28. FREDERICK III

King Christian IV. died at Rosenborg palace in Copenhagen, February 28, 1648, and as the elected successor to the throne, Prince Christian, had passed away in 1647, a new king had to be chosen. Prince Frederick, the king's next oldest son, born in 1609, seemed to be the logical candidate. He was *statholder* of the duchies of Schleswig-Holstein, to which he was the sole heir. During his brother's lingering illness both he and his ambitious wife, Sophia Amalie of Braunschweig-Lüneburg, had made it their aim to obtain the throne, if a vacancy should occur, and the prince styled himself in all public documents "Heir to the throne of Norway." But the nobles opposed him, because of his pronounced autocratic ideas. There could be no doubt that if placed on the throne, he would attempt to strengthen the royal power to the greatest extent possible, but as he was the king's only legitimate son, his election could not be prevented. On the 18th of April, 1648, he was chosen king of the united realms, and on August 24 he received the homage of the Norwegian people in Christiania.[1]

According to usage, the king had to sign a charter by which the nobility safeguarded their privileges and powers.[2] The attempt was made to introduce a stipulation with regard to Norway which would have revived the long-forgotten clause in the charter of Christian III., and would have once for all reduced that kingdom to a Danish province. The nobles proposed that Norway "shall forever remain an inseparable province under the crown of Denmark," and that the king "shall have no rights thereto either by inheritance or otherwise," but to this the king would not subscribe. The charter, as finally signed, created restrictions on the royal power which had never yet been imposed on a Danish king, but as a final compromise Norway was not mentioned. The charter became a purely Danish document. But while the Danish nobles would regard Norway as

---

[1] Andreas Højer, *Jus Publicum eller Statsforfatning og Rettigheder for Danmark, Norge og Fyrstendømmerne*, Christiania, 1783, p. 32 f. J. E. Sars, *Udsigt over den norske Historie*, vol. IV., p. 41.

[2] *Samlinger til det norske Folks Sprog og Historie*, vol. I., p. 13 ff. Yngvar Nielsen, *Frederik IIIs Hylding i Christiania 1648*, *Historisk Tidsskrift*, vol. I., p. 23 ff.

a province of Denmark, the national spirit was again awakened among the Norwegians. Through the development of the Estates they had again received a national representation, after the Norwegian Council had disappeared.[1] It is true that the Estates numbered many Danish nobles and officials, but it was, nevertheless, a representation which could speak in behalf of Norwegian interests. This they had done quite effectively when the question arose of using Norwegian revenues in the kingdom instead of paying them into the general treasury, and it is evident that the Danish government did not dare to disregard Norway's rights as a separate kingdom. When Frederick III. was to be hailed in Christiania, the Danish chancellor in a speech to the Norwegian Estates asked them to swear allegiance to the new king, but he did not mention with a word the clause which had been inserted in the "Code of Christian IV." that "whatsoever lord or prince the Danish Council, nobility, and Estates shall choose to be king of Denmark shall also be king of Norway." He offered an apology for the failure to summon the Norwegian Estates to take part in the election, but said that it was owing to the haste with which the election had to be made. The native-born Norwegian chancellor, Jens Bjelke, replied that the Norwegian Estates would take the oath of allegiance to King Frederick III. as heir to the throne of Norway, as no one had a better right to the throne than he.[2] King Frederick's position in Norway was not made clear, but the Norwegians had fearlessly maintained that

[1] Yngvar Nielsen, *Norges Historie*, vol. IV., 2, p. 269. J. E. Sars, *Udsigt over den norske Historie*, vol. IV., p. 41 ff. F. Hammerich, *Fire kjøbenhavnske Rigsdage, Nyt historisk Tidsskrift*, vol. V., p. 396 f.

[2] Yngvar Nielsen, *Frederik IIIs Hylding i Christiania 1648*, p. 40 f., *Historisk Tidsskrift*, første række, vol. I., p. 23 ff. T. H. Aschehoug, *Statsforfatningen i Norge og Danmark indtil 1814*, p. 361 f. Yngvar Nielsen, *Jens Bjelke til Østraat*, p. 365. Professor Alb. Johnsen shows that the use by various Danish kings of the title "Heir to the throne of Norway" gave them no hereditary right to the throne. He says concerning hereditary kingship in Norway: "The people clung to the hereditary kingship so long as it served their interests and the country's welfare, but they abandoned it and opposed the hereditary kingship and the hereditary principle when in the union period these were becoming a danger to the country and the nation; finally they again recognized the king's hereditary rights when, under altered conditions, the hereditary principle could promote the honor of the country and the people's happiness. When in 1814 the Norwegians refused to recog-

their kingdom was an hereditary monarchy, a position in which they were supported by the king and the *statholder*, Hannibal Sehested. The Danish nobility were clearly put on the defensive to maintain the old elective system with which their power was so closely identified. The rent thus made in the antiquated Danish policy was still to increase until the system itself was overthrown.

King Frederick III. was very unlike his father. He was quiet and given to reflection. He spoke little and wrote still less. He was much interested in literature, art, and science, and especially in alchemy, to which he devoted special attention.[1] He loved power, and felt confident that his future success was preordained by destiny. He possessed a high degree of self-control; he was a keen observer, and kept impressions well in mind; but his anger was often of the vindictive kind which might prove dangerous to those against whom it chanced to be directed. When he ascended the throne, King Christian's sons-in-law had formed a political party, and had gained full control of the government. The leader of the party was Korfits Ulfeld, who was married to Christian's daughter Leonora Christina. Much more gifted and scarcely less influential was Hannibal Sehested, *statholder* of Norway. Korfits Ulfeld rose to the highest position in the realm through royal favor, but he possessed also the royal favorite's pride and arrogance, and became generally hated by the nobility. Sehested's overthrow has already

nize Christian Frederick's hereditary right, and when in 1905 they refused to retain an hereditary king who had become unable to perform his duties as ruling sovereign, they acted in reality in perfect harmony with the policy of their forefathers." *Historisk Tidsskrift*, femte række, vol. II., p. 190 ff. *Om det norske Folks Opfatning av Tronfølgen før 1660*. G. L. Baden, *Oprindelsen til de Schleswig-Holstenske Hertugers Titel: Arving til Norge, Afhandlinger*, vol. II., p. 61.

[1] King Frederick III. wasted large sums of money on the Italian alchemist Burrhi, who instructed him in alchemy. He gave this teacher a laboratory in the palace gardens at Rosenborg. To what degree Burrhi enjoyed the king's favor can be seen from an order which he issued to General Ahlefeldt: "It is our most gracious will and command that you hereafter daily let 300 men with their officers accompany Burrhi to work in our gardens at Rosenborg and elsewhere where he may need it for our service, and that to this end you gradually change the people as you deem it necessary." P. Brock, *Den Oldenborgske Kongeslegt, især under Enevælden, belyst ved den chronologiske Samling paa Rosenborg Slot*, p. 55.

been mentioned, but he humbled himself before the king, admitted his faults, received pardon, and was destined to rise again to the highest influence and power. Ulfeld, who was stiff-necked, pursued another course, and fell to rise no more.

The relations between Korfits Ulfeld and Frederick III. were strained from the outset. The king well knew that Ulfeld was responsible for the restrictions placed upon the royal power by the charter, and the proud magnate could not gracefully submit to the authority exercised by the new king. The ambitious Queen Sophia Amalie also looked with jealous disfavor on the gifted and beautiful Leonora Christina, whom she regarded as a rival. Ulfeld secretly left Denmark, and went to Sweden, where he was well received by Queen Christina. King Frederick instituted an investigation into the way in which he had conducted his high office as steward of the kingdom, and Ulfeld, who refused to return to answer to the charges before the Danish Council, became more and more an open enemy of his king and his country. His foul treason and the long imprisonment of his innocent wife cast a dark shadow upon the reign of Frederick III.[1] The overthrow of such powerful magnates as Ulfeld and Sehested could not but weaken the Danish nobility, and render them less able to resist the king, who aimed to curtail their power, if not to destroy it. In 1650 his eldest son, Prince Christian, was elected successor to the throne, but the election was made only in behalf of Denmark, and when the royal successor was to be hailed in Christiania, 1656, the question again arose whether he was to be regarded as heir to the throne, or as elected crown prince. On this occasion a treatise entitled "Norges Rige Arve-Rige," written to prove that Norway had always been a hereditary monarchy, was submitted to the king. The author is thought to have been a Dane, Jens Dolmer,[2] who had been the tutor of King Christian's illegitimate son Ulrik Christian Gyldenløve, and who at the time of the

[1] Lenore Christine Ulfeldt, *Jammers-minde*, published by S. Birket Smith. Copenhagen. *Lenore Christine Grevinde Ulfeldt's Levned*, Copenhagen, 1870.

[2] Gustav Storm, *Om Forfatteren til det statsretslige Skrift fra 1656 "Norges Rige Arve-Rige."* *Historisk Tidsskrift*, anden række, vol. IV., p. 114 ff. Dolmer also translated the *Hirskrá, Hird-Skraa udi det gamle Norske Sprog retteligen oversat paa Danske*, Copenhagen, 1666.

festivities was granted a yearly pension from the royal purse. Professor Gustav Storm says: "When the document was submitted to the king at a Norwegian council by a man who was personally so well acquainted with him, and who a few days later received a pension from the royal treasury, it is evident that the author has written it at the instigation of the king, and expresses the views of the king and his surroundings. The treatise is, therefore, a link in the chain of utterances by the king regarding the hereditary kingship in Norway, and reveals the plans which were maturing at the court." That King Frederick should welcome such a plan to increase his power is quite natural, but he was less favorably disposed to a petition submitted by the Norwegian merchant class, or third estate, aiming at securing new improvements and privileges for Norway. The petitioners prayed that Norwegian officers might be employed in the army instead of foreigners; that Norway might get a chamber of commerce, a superior court, and a university.[1] These were all timely and useful improvements, but no attention was paid to the petition, though it was renewed the following year. Even though hereditary kingship and absolute power were established, Norway might derive but slight benefit from the change.

After the death of Gustavus Adolphus his gifted but eccentric daughter Christina succeeded to the throne of Sweden, after a regency had conducted the government during her minority. She became of age in 1644, and ruled till 1654, when she abdicated, and her cousin, Charles Gustavus, became king of Sweden as Charles X. King Frederick III. had been longing for an opportunity to regain the provinces lost in the late war with Sweden, and when Charles X., shortly after his accession to the throne, became involved in a war with Poland, he thought the time had come for the inevitable contest with the rival power. Without much preparation, and without weighing carefully the possible outcome, the king signed the declaration of war, July 1, 1657. "Seldom has a war been declared more from pure motive of revenge, and the feelings associated with it," says Professor Yngvar Nielsen.[2] In his work, "Adelsvældens sidste Dage,"

[1] Becker, *Samlinger til Danmarks Historie under Fredrik III.*, vol. I., p. 118. Quoted by Sars, *Udsigt over den norske Historie*, vol. IV., p. 43.

[2] Yngvar Nielsen, *Norges Historie*, vol. IV., 2, p. 284.

J. A. Fridericia says: "Weak and poor was the kingdom (Denmark) when the war began, dismembered and ruined when it ended. No single man can be made responsible for its weakness and poverty, the reasons for which lie deep in the people's history, in exterior misfortunes, in unfortunate errors made by kings and statesmen, in the absence of a powerful merchant class; but especially in the arrogance, demoralization, and worthlessness of the nobility. Perhaps this weakness and poverty would sooner or later have led to the same dismemberment and devastation which the kingdom now suffered, but for the misfortunes as they happened in these years, that prince whose will was the war of 1657 cannot be wholly free from blame."[1] The Norwegian army was able to render able service during the war. Attacks were made against Sweden both from Trøndelagen and from Bohuslen. Peder Vibe was commandant of Trondhjem, but the expedition against Sweden in this quarter was to be led by Jørgen Bjelke, probably the ablest officer in the Norwegian army at that moment. His forces numbered 2000 men, who had been recruited chiefly in Trøndelagen. With this force he invaded Jæmtland and Herjedalen, drove out the Swedish garrisons, and placed the two provinces once more under Norwegian administration. In the northern districts, Preben von Ahnen, commandant of Bodøgaard, raised a small force, and attacked and destroyed the Swedish silver mines at Nasafjäll and Silbojocki. The expedition from Bohuslen was led by Iver Krabbe, commandant of Bohus. He was successful in a battle at Hjertrum, but failed to effect a junction with the Danish army, which had crossed the border further south.

While Sweden was attacked by the Norwegians in Jæmtland and Bohuslen, and by a Danish force operating from Skåne, the principal Danish army was assembled in Holstein to march against Sweden's German possessions. But King Charles X. Gustavus was, above all, a warrior. He was a great tactician and a resolute and energetic general, who was always ready for new military exploits.

---

[1] J. A. Fridericia, *Adelsvældens sidste Dage*, p. 260. Yngvar Nielsen, *Kampen om Trondhjem, Festskrift, Trondhjems 900-aars Jubilæum*, 1897. Yngvar Nielsen, *De nordenfjeldske Begivenheder 1657–1660*, Christiania, 1868.

When the declaration of war reached him in Thorn in Prussia, he put his army in motion, and advanced by forced marches to the borders of Holstein. The Danish commander, Anders Bille, had kept his forces scattered, and the unexpected encounter with the Swedish main army under King Charles's own command created such consternation and disorder that no effective resistance could be made. Charles Gustavus did not stop to take the scattered fortresses throughout Holstein, but hastened forward, crossed the border of Schleswig, August 23, and pitched his headquarters at Kolding, as it was found necessary to lay siege to the important fortress of Fredriksodde.[1]

The Danish army operating in Skåne under Aksel Urup met with no success. Urup was defeated in the battle of Genevad Bro, and although he succeeded in defeating the Swedes under Gustav Stenbock at Kattorp, the advantage gained was of little value, as he failed to make a junction with the Norwegian forces in Bohuslen. At sea Denmark was more successful, though no signal victories were won. After the undecisive naval battles, September 12–14, the Swedish fleet withdrew to the harbor of Wismar, where the Danish admiral, Henrik Bjelke, succeeded in keeping it shut up for the rest of the war.

Denmark had already been placed in a most difficult situation, but new hope was created by an alliance with Poland. Austria also attacked the Swedish forces stationed in that kingdom, and Brandenburg joined the enemies of Sweden. King Charles succeeded in forming an alliance with the Duke of Gottorp, but the situation was, nevertheless, so complicated that he consented to attempt peace negotiations. Councilor Sten Bjelke, and the traitor Korfits Ulfeld, who was now in the service of Sweden, were empowered to treat with Denmark, but it could scarcely be expected that the Danish government would treat with the traitorous Ulfeld, and the attempt was abandoned. Denmark received no aid worth mentioning from her allies. On October 24 the fortress of Fredriksodde was taken by storm; 1000 Danish officers and soldiers fell, and over 4000 were made prisoners, a defeat so crushing that it filled the people with

[1] Fredrik Ferdinand Carlson, *Sveriges Historia under Konungarne af pfalziska Huset*, part I., p. 270 ff.

despair, and aroused their anger against the nobles, who were accused of incompetence and treason to the country. After the fall of Fredriksodde King Charles crossed the Little Belt on the ice to Fyen, defeated and captured the Danish army of 4000–5000 men at Tybring Vig, and seized the island. He did not tarry, but rode across the Great Belt with 2000 horsemen to Langeland, which surrendered without resistance. On the 8th of February he entered Falster, and on the 11th he stood in Seeland, where Gustav Wrangel joined him with the rest of the Swedish army. There was now nothing left for Denmark to do but to conclude peace, no matter how humiliating the terms. Peace negotiations were begun, and after a preliminary protocol had been agreed upon, the treaty was finally signed at Roskilde, February 26, 1658. Denmark had to cede Skåne, Halland, Blekinge, and Bornholm; Jæmtland and Herjedalen had to be evacuated, and Bohuslen and Trondhjems *len* in Norway were given to Sweden. King Frederick III. was, furthermore, to give King Charles 2000 horsemen; he had to agree to abrogate all hostile alliances against Sweden, and to seek to prevent any foreign fleet, hostile to either of the two realms, from passing through the Sound.[1] For the second time Norway had become the victim of a Danish foreign policy aiming solely at the maintenance of the power and glory of Denmark. Norway's interest had never been considered, and the peace of Roskilde not only alienated great portions of Norwegian territory, but almost destroyed the kingdom by dividing what remained into two dissevered halves. But in those days war was still a royal sport, and Frederick III. did not appear to be very downcast by the overwhelming misfortunes which he had brought upon his realm. He invited King Charles to visit him at Fredriksborg palace, where a great festival was arranged in his honor. For several days the two monarchs feasted, drank, chatted, and made merry; and when Charles departed from Denmark, the batteries of the Kronborg gave royal salute in honor of the victor.

[1] Fredrik Ferdinand Carlson, *Sveriges Historia under Konungarne og pfalziska Huset*, part 2, p. 324 ff. J. A. Fridericia, *Adelsvældens sidste Dage*, p. 311 ff. Yngvar Nielsen, *Kampen om Trondhjem 1657–1660; Freden i Roskilde.* C. F. Allen, *Haandbog i Fædrelandets Historie*, p. 408 f. *Danmarks Riges Historie*, vol. IV., p. 394 ff. *Sveriges Historie*, vol. III. *Norges Historie*, vol. IV., 2, p. 283 ff.

Both kings were, however, dissatisfied with the terms of the treaty of Roskilde. King Frederick III., because he had lost so much territory, and Charles Gustavus, because he did not take more when he had the opportunity. With regard to Trondhjems *len* the treaty was very vague, and King Charles claimed that the district of Romsdal as well as Nordland and Finmarken were included in the cession. Romsdal was recognized to be a part of Trondhjems *len*, but King Charles still planned to renew the war. In July, 1658, he decided in a meeting with his Council at Gottorp to attack Denmark, and Gustav Wrangel was instructed to begin operations against Copenhagen.[1] The city was invested, and a siege begun. Kronborg was surrendered to General Wrangel without much resistance, but animated by the desperate situation, the Danes concentrated their forces within their capital, which they were resolved to defend to the last extremity. The unprovoked attack, and the fear that Sweden would gain absolute control in the North, soon moved other powers to intervene in behalf of Denmark. Holland sent a fleet of forty vessels and twenty-eight transports with a force of 2200 men under Jakob van Wassenaer Opdam to Danish waters. This fleet passed through the Sound in spite of the fire from the fortresses of Kronborg and Helsingborg, defeated the Swedish fleet, joined the Danish squadron, and sent the transports with provisions and reënforcements to Copenhagen. Brandenburg and Poland also commenced war against Sweden, and sent an army into Holstein, which forced the Duke of Gottorp, King Charles's ally, to remain neutral.

King Charles Gustavus had planned this time to take possession of all Norway, but the Norwegians were determined, not only to defend their country, but to recover the lost possessions. The people of Trøndelagen regretted bitterly that they had been forced under Sweden. The Swedish commissioner, Lorentz Creutz, who acted as governor of the province, was ordered by King Charles to raise a force of 3000 men for the Swedish army, but this was so violently opposed by the people that the order could be carried out only with the greatest difficulty. Finally 2000 men were impressed to fight

<hr>

[1] J. A. Fridericia, *Adelsvældens sidste Dage*, p. 349 ff. Fredrik Ferdinand Carlson, *Sveriges Historia under Konungarne af pfalziska Huset*, part 1, p. 354 ff.

in Sweden's foreign wars. They were ordered to be sent to Livonia, and the king wrote to John Oxenstjerna to watch carefully so that the Norwegians did not desert. Many escaped, but about 1400 were transported to Livonia, few of whom ever saw their native land again. The Swedish king did nothing to win the favor of the Norwegians. His only thought had been to raise men and money in the conquered provinces. The taxes were increased, and the Trønders, who had hitherto been well disposed towards the Swedes, were now eager to aid in any undertaking which promised freedom from the foreign yoke.[1] King Charles issued a manifesto to the Norwegian people, asking them to separate from Denmark and join Sweden, but such a thought did not exist in Norway at that moment. A new national feeling had been awakened; the people would now fight for freedom from Swedish oppression, and Jørgen Bjelke, who had been placed at the head of the Norwegian army, undertook to recover Trøndelagen. As soon as the war broke out, King Frederick III. sent word to Norway to statholder Nils Trolle and to Jørgen Bjelke that they should resist to the utmost. Communications with Denmark were soon destroyed, however, and Bjelke became the leader of the military operations. His father, the old chancellor, Jens Bjelke, encouraged the people of Trøndelagen through private letters to break away from Sweden, "in which they also succeeded," says an old writer.[2] A formal manifesto signed by the statholder, the chancellor, and Jørgen Bjelke, addressed to the Estates of the lost provinces, asking them to renew their allegiance to the old government, was also published. Bjelke would lead the campaign in southern Norway, and dispatched George von Reichwein to Trøndelagen. Reichwein's forces increased as he advanced, until they numbered about 2000 men, and another force from Bergen under Reinhold von Hoven was dispatched to Trondhjem by sea to coöperate with Reichwein. Nordland also sent a detachment. The new Swedish governor, Claes Stjernsköld, felt alarmed. Everywhere the people arose against

---

[1] Yngvar Nielsen, Kampen om Trondhjem 1657–1660; Trondhjems Stad og Len under svensk Styrelse.

[2] Yngvar Nielsen, Jens Bjelke til Østraat, p. 375 ff.; Kampen om Trondhjem 1657–1660. Om Trondhjems Tilbagetagelse af de Norske, Samlinger til det norske Folks Sprog og Historie, vol. VI., p. 195 ff. H. G. Heggtveit, Trondhjem i Fortid og Nutid, p. 187 ff.

the Swedes, and the detachments which he sent out to reconnoiter met the advancing Norwegian troops, and were forced to fall back on Trondhjem. King Charles, who had not failed to understand the gravity of the situation in Trøndelagen, speedily sent a force of 500 men to reënforce Stjernsköld. If this force had reached the city, the Swedish governor might have been able to successfully defend it, as he would then have had a garrison of about 1200 men. But Eilerik Visborg, who had been sent to Værdalen with a part of the forces from Bergen, met and defeated the Swedish reënforcements,[1] and the Norwegian forces, numbering about 4000 men, laid siege to Trondhjem. The garrison of the city numbered about 750 men, but as many of these were Norwegians, desertions occurred almost daily. The supply of provisions and war material in the city was small, and after a siege lasting from October 3rd till December 11th Stjernsköld capitulated, and Trondhjems *len* again became Norwegian territory.

Jørgen Bjelke was personally leading the defense of the southern districts, where he had raised an army of about 4000 men. September 13, 1658, the Swedish general, Harald Stake, crossed the Swedish border with a force of about 1500 men, and marched upon Halden (Fredrikshald), which was defended by 900 men, of whom the greater part were volunteers. This force, led by Peder Nordmand and Mathias Bjørn, took up a position in the hills east of the town, where they resolutely attacked the Swedes when they arrived. After a battle lasting from eight o'clock in the morning till three o'clock in the afternoon, the Swedish general was forced to retreat, and he led his army back to Sweden. A second attack was commenced in February; this time by an army of 4000 men, also commanded by Stake. The town was defended by a force of 1800 men under Jørgen Bjelke and Tønne Huitfeldt, who defeated the Swedish general, and forced him to retreat to Bohuslen. After the attack had been repulsed, Huitfeldt began to construct more efficient fortifications around Halden, and Bjelke advanced into Bohuslen in the fall of 1659, and attempted to wrest that province from the Swedes. But a Swedish army of 4500 men under Marshal Kagg was advancing

---

[1] Yngvar Nielsen, *Eilerik Visborgs Kamp med de Svenske 1658*, *Historisk Tidsskrift*, første række, vol. IV., p. 286 ff.

to renew the attack on the small Norwegian fortress, and Bjelke had to return. He increased the garrison of the place to 2100 men, and placed Huitfeldt in command.[1] In January, 1660, the Swedes attempted to take the fortress by storm, but the attack was successfully repulsed. In the meantime Bjelke had raised an army of 3800 men, with which he had hoped to reënforce the garrison of Halden. The army was attacked by Kagg at Hundebunden, and a stubborn battle was fought, in which the Norwegians were victorious. A second assault on the fortress on February 13th was likewise repulsed, and a third attack on the 20th was also unsuccessful. On February 22d the siege was raised, and Kagg led his forces back to Sweden, where he received the news that the warrior king, Charles X. Gustavus, had died in Gottenborg, February 13, 1660.

The defense of Halden and the capture of Trondhjem were events of the utmost importance to Norway, Even from a military point of view they were great achievements which awakened the people's self-confidence and national pride. Hitherto the Danes had looked upon Norway as wholly incompetent in military affairs, but the late events had awakened such admiration of the bravery of the Norwegians that when Frederick IV. visited Norway about forty years later, he caused a coin to be struck, bearing the superscription: "Courage, loyalty, bravery, and all that gives honor, the whole world among the rocks of Norway can learn." This was, undoubtedly, done by the king to flatter the Norwegians, but they had shown in these wars with Sweden that they could defend their country, and that they could bring victory home from the fields of battle, even in struggles with experienced generals and the best troops of Europe. The disasters which had befallen Norway in the wars between Sweden and Denmark, and the struggles through which the people had to pass to throw off the Swedish yoke, and to defend their country, were instrumental in finally rousing them from their national lethargy. They had now regained the most important part of the lost territory, and had become animated with a new self-consciousness. The Norwegian borders had been permanently fixed, and a national aspiration, born of the people's firm resolve to lead their own free

---

[1] H. J. Huitfeldt-Kaas, *Tønne Huitfeldt til Throndstad, Historisk Tidsskrift*, tredie række, vol. II., p. 156 ff.

existence, had become deeply rooted in all hearts. An efficient army had been developed, and able and patriotic leaders had appeared. These distinct gains were doubly important since they would constitute the basis for a new national development.

The war was still continued, but the end was, nevertheless, in sight. Copenhagen resisted bravely, and when the Swedes attempted to take the city by storm they were repulsed with heavy losses. As England and France as well as Holland were interested in preserving Denmark's independence, Sweden's plan of subduing the whole kingdom was becoming ever more hopeless. Holland's great admiral, Michael de Ruyter, was dispatched to Danish waters with a large fleet, and when the Swedish army in Fyen was defeated and captured, the three western powers, Holland, France, and England, finally came to an understanding as to the terms of peace to be offered the belligerents. Norway should retain Trondhjems *len* with Romsdal; Sweden should keep Skåne, Halland, and Blekinge, together with Bohuslen; and Bornholm, where the Swedes had been driven out, should be returned to Denmark. These terms were at length agreed to, and the treaty of peace was signed at Copenhagen, May 26, 1660.

29. Hereditary Kingship. The Introduction of Absolutism

The peace of Copenhagen was hailed with joy, but the people both in Denmark and Norway had been brought to the brink of ruin, and suffering was intense in both kingdoms. An Assembly of Estates met in Copenhagen, September 10, 1660, to consider the difficult problems confronting the Danish people. The aristocracy still insisted on retaining the privilege of freedom from taxation, though the feeling against them had become very bitter; but the clergy and the third estate united and demanded equal privileges. When the nobles were finally forced to yield, the opposition had become strong enough to control the situation.[1] Under the leadership of Mayor Hans Nansen of Copenhagen and Hans Svane, Bishop of Seeland, they resolved to overthrow the rule of the aristocracy by means of a *coup d'état*. The city gates were closed, the harbor was blockaded, and the garrison was held in readiness; if the nobles should refuse

---

[1] T. H. Aschehoug, *Statsforfatningen i Norge og Danmark indtil 1814*, p. 464 ff.

to submit, force would be used. Their resistance was soon broken, and on October 13th they signed a declaration that they would join the other estates in acknowledging the hereditary principle. The charter was returned to the king as a token that the restrictions on his royal power therein expressed were annulled,[1] and on October 18, 1660, Frederick III. was formally hailed as hereditary king of Denmark. The right to the throne was vested in his family, both in the male and female line. Under the date of January 10, 1661, a document was drawn up entitled "Instrument eller pragmatisk Sanktion om Kongens Arveret til Danmarks og Norges Rige," which made the king not only heir to the throne, but granted him all royal prerogatives and sovereign privileges as absolute hereditary king. This document was circulated in the kingdom to be signed by nobles, bishops, chapters, priests, and cities, in order that formal sanction might be given to the introduction of absolutism in Denmark.

In accordance with the power which had been granted him by the assembled Estates, the king undertook to prepare the new constitution, the "Kongelov" (lex regia), which should outline in detail the various powers which he was to exercise. This document bears the date of November 14, 1665. The author of the law was Peder Schumacher (Griffenfeld).[2] The document, which was long kept secret, was finally published, and remained the constitution of Denmark and Norway till 1814. According to this document, the king had the right to change, make, and annul laws, to appoint all higher officials, to disregard all established customs, to declare war and make peace, to levy taxes and coin money. He is declared to be subject to God alone, and to be above all laws, except the fundamental laws of the realm. The second article states: "The king has the highest and most unlimited power, for he is the supreme head here on earth,

[1] The charters subscribed to by the Danish kings had long since ceased to be a guarantee for the people's liberty. Like the pacta conventa of the kings of Poland, they had become documents by which the nobles gradually destroyed the royal power, and perfected and increased their own privileges. Molesworth, An Account of Denmark as It Was in the Year 1692, p. 44 ff.

[2] A. D. Jørgensen, Peder Schumacher Griffenfeld, vol. I., p. 195 ff. Chr. Bruun, Enevældens Indførelse i Danmark, og Kongelovens Tilblivelse, p. 114. J. A. Fridericia, Kongeloven og dens Forhistorie, Dansk historisk Tidsskrift, femte række, vol. VI. O. A. Øverland, Norges Historie, vol. VII., p. 107 ff., contains thirty of the forty articles of the Kongetov.

elevated above all human laws, and he recognizes no other judge, either in secular or spiritual matters, than God Almighty." The seventeenth article states further that "he can take no oath, or make any declaration of any kind whatsoever, either orally or written, as he, being a free and unrestrained absolute monarch, cannot be bound by his subjects through any oath or obligation." [1] The Emperor of ancient China could possess no more unlimited autocratic power.

In introducing absolutism and the principle of hereditary kingship in Denmark, nothing had been said about Norway, but the king claimed that he was already heir to the throne of that kingdom. The Norwegian Estates were summoned to meet in Christiania in order to hail him as hereditary king, May 27, 1661, but as he could not be present, he sent the crown prince, Christian, together with Hannibal Sehested [2] and five commissioners to act as his representatives. A draft of a new fundamental law for the kingdom of Norway introducing absolutism was submitted, and the Estates signed the same, August 7, 1661. This was a counterpart to the Danish act, and granted the king the same absolute power as he had received in Denmark. The Norwegians had reason to be satisfied with the change. Hereditary kingship had been established, and Norway was freed from the rule of the Danish nobility, which had treated the kingdom as a province to be administered by the Danish Council for their benefit. Norway now had the same constitution as Denmark, and was, henceforth, regarded as equal in rank with the sister kingdom, as the basis for Danish supremacy, the usurped power of the Danish Council to choose a king for both realms, had been removed. [3] The two realms were usually called the "Twin Kingdoms," and the citi-

[1] Andreas Højer, *Jus Publicum eller Statsforfatning og Rettigheder for Danmark, Norge og Fyrstendømmerne forklaret ved private Forelæsninger*, Christiania, 1783. O. A. Øverland says of the *Kongelov* that it had no prototype in any European constitution. It was based chiefly on the ideas of Thomas Hobbes, expressed in his works *De Cive* and *Leviathan*.

[2] T. H. Aschehoug, *Statsforfatningen i Danmark og Norge indtil 1814*, p. 464 ff. Hannibal Sehested had again won the favor of the king, who had appointed him royal treasurer. J. A. Fridericia, *Adelsvældens sidste Dage*, p. 164, 478 ff.

[3] E. Holm, *Danmark-Norges indre Historie under Enevælden fra 1660 til 1720*, vol. I., p. 71 ff. T. H. Aschehoug, *Statsforfatningen i Norge og Danmark indtil 1814*, p. 579. L. M. B. Aubert, *Norges folkeretslige Stilling*.

zens of one realm might hold any office in the other. Under the rule of an absolute monarch the Norwegians could hope that their affairs would be more fairly and impartially dealt with than under the old régime. This they found was also done to some extent, and it would possibly have been done to a much higher degree if the absolute kings of the House of Oldenburg had been gifted men and able rulers. But their incompetence and lack of ability often rendered them unable to exercise a power in any manner answering to the fullness of their authority. Professor Sars says of them: "The most gifted of them did not rise above mediocrity; those among them who devoted themselves most diligently to administrative duties became absorbed in official routine and trifles, and never developed to become what may be termed independent and capable rulers, howsoever low a standard we may establish. A couple of them were wholly unfit to govern, and their rule was purely a nominal one. Among those who formed the immediate surroundings of these kings — their favorites, councilors, and ministers in a more special sense — only two attempted to assume in the name of the king the power which according to the constitution belonged to him, namely Griffenfeld and Struensee, and both were overthrown after a short rule." "The place which through the constitution was given the king remained in many ways vacant throughout the period here mentioned. Contrary to what might have been expected, judging from the principles expressed in the new constitution (*Kongeloven*), the government became of a very staid and impersonal character. According to the letter of the constitution, the government should have been distinctly monarchical, but in reality it became distinctly bureaucratic. Its center was not formed by the kings personally, nor by their Council (Geheimeraad, Privy Council), or their ministers in a more limited sense, but by the Colleges, placed at the head of the administrative departments. The Danish-Norwegian government in the period 1660–1814 was, with the exception of a few interruptions, essentially a government by the Colleges with all the faults and advantages which usually characterize such a rule." [1]

[1] J. E. Sars, *Udsigt over den norske Historie*, vol. IV., p. 49 f. J. A. Fridericia, *Adelsvældens sidste Dage*, p. 489 ff. Oscar Alb. Johnsen, *Norges Historie*, vol. V., 1, p. 3 ff.

Shortly after the hereditary kingship had been established, King Frederick III. created five Administrative Colleges (or committees) by the ordinance of November 4, 1660, among which the various administrative duties were divided.[1] The *Geheimeconseil* (Privy Council) was also created, consisting of the five presidents of the Administrative Colleges. The Council convened daily in the presence of the king, and exercised, quite naturally, a great influence upon his decisions. In his "cabinet" the king kept protocols and private secretaries for receiving petitions and communications. These matters would either be passed upon by the king personally, or he would turn them over to the Administrative Colleges.[2]

A new judicial tribunal, the *Høiesteret*, was also created. This was a court of final jurisdiction for Norway, the Faroe Islands, and Iceland, as well as for Denmark. It represents a very marked improvement over the old method, according to which the councils of magnates acted as a higher court. But it was an essential drawback that the new court was a purely Danish institution, which always convened in Denmark, where Norwegian cases could not be properly investigated. But the king, who exercised as absolute power in judicial matters as in other affairs, was superior even to this court, and could act as supreme judge.

The office of Statholder of Norway was retained with about the same powers and duties as before. The *statholder* was to exercise supervision over all subordinate officials, and he should so encourage the economic development of the country that the royal revenues might increase. He had to watch the relations with Sweden, keep army, fortresses, and magazines supplied with the necessary stores and equipments, and guard against the violation of treaties with foreign nations touching Norway's commerce; but he retained no power over the revenues of the kingdom, as in the days of Hannibal Sehested.

As a result of the introduction of absolutism, the nobles lost their exclusive right to the *lens*, and these might now be granted to any

---

[1] The five departments were: admiralty, war, treasury, commerce, and state, or foreign affairs.

[2] T. H. Aschehoug, *Statsforfatningen i Norge og Danmark indtil 1814*, p. 582 ff.

one whom the king might see fit to appoint. In 1662 Frederick III.
abolished the name *len*, which still reminded him of the time when
the king's power was limited, and substituted the German name
amt. As the name indicates, the *amts* became mere administrative
districts, and over these he placed officers called *amtmænd*, who were
not always of noble family. They received a fixed salary, and had
to render strict account of income and expenditures. Under Frederick's son and successor, Christian V., Norway was divided into
four *stiftsamter*: Akershus, Christiansand, Bergenhus, and Trondhjem, each of which consisted of one principal *amt* and two of subordinate rank, except in the case of Bergenhus, which had three subordinate *amts*. The power of the *amtmænd* was much more limited
than that of the *lensherrer*, who had exercised both civil and military authority within their *len*. The *amtmænd* were only civil
officials, and their power was much curtailed, as they could not appoint subordinate officials, such as *fogeds*, mayors, and councilmen,
who were all appointed by the king. Their office was, nevertheless,
one of great dignity and power, as they were the king's deputies
and personal representatives in the local administration. The
enforcement of the laws, the management of public property, and
the supervision of the work of subordinate officials were some of
the more important executive duties delegated to them. But they
should also act as the guardians of the common people in protecting
them from oppression and injustice. They were to be watchful
in preventing *fogeds* from collecting excessive taxes, and merchants
from cheating the *bønder*, and they were given special instruction
to see to it that the renters were not unjustly treated by their landlords.[1] The *stiftsamtmænd* were superior to the others in rank, and
acted as superintendents over the *amtmænd*, *fogeds*, and *skrivere*
(judges) within their *stiftsamt*. The office of Stiftsamtmand of
Akershus was connected with that of Statholder of Norway, that of
Stiftsamtmand of Christiansand with the office of Vice-statholder,
created in 1669, and in Trondhjem and Bergenhus the *stiftsamtmænd* were respectively chancellor and vice-chancellor of the kingdom. The management of the finances was left to new fiscal officials

---

[1] Edvard Holm, *Danmark-Norges indre Historie under Enevælden fra 1660
til 1720*, vol. I., p. 84 ff. Oscar Alb. Johnsen, *Norges Historie*, vol. V., 1.

called *kammererer*, later *stiftsskrivere*, who acted as local treasurers, and had to render account to the royal treasury in Copenhagen. But the collection of the taxes was left to the *fogeds*, as before.[1]

In conformity with the principles of absolutism, all officials of whatever rank, even the mayors and councilmen in the cities, now became royal officials, deriving their authority as well as their office from the king himself, who was the source and fountain of all official power. The local communities lost their autonomy. The parishes could no longer call their own ministers, and the University of Copenhagen could not appoint its professors; every change, in fact every public act, would henceforth depend on the royal will.[2] Gradually the central government left more freedom and power to the local authorities, especially in the cities, where this became quite necessary, but the fundamental idea that the king was the source of all power and authority, that the will of the people no longer existed as a factor in administration and government, could not be altered.

The transfer of political power from the aristocracy to the king and his officials resulted also in a new alignment of social classes, as the officials, especially in Norway, appeared as a new upper class, a bureaucracy.[3] This class was partly recruited from the aristocratic families, who possessed learning and culture, and still wielded a great social influence; but as rank and birth were no longer necessary qualifications, many wealthy and influential men, especially from the cities, were appointed to various higher offices.[4] As the power and

---

[1] Oscar Alb. Johnsen, *Norges Historie*, vol. IV., 1, p. 15 ff. T. H. Aschehoug, *De norske Communers Retsforfatning før 1837*, p. 182 ff.

[2] Ludvig Daae, *Trondhjems Stifts geistlige Historie*, p. 113.

[3] T. H. Aschehoug, *Statsforfatningen i Norge og Danmark indtil 1814*, p. 601 ff.

[4] "Certain it is that all sorts of places, civil and military, are filled more by foreigners than by gentlemen of the country: and in their disposal of offices it is remarkable that such as are of ordinary birth and fortunes are much sooner preferred than tho se of contrary qualities: so that there may be found several in the most profitable and honorable employments who have formerly been serving-men, and such like; and these prove the best executors of the will and pleasure of arbitrary power, and therefore are caressed accordingly. There is one further advantage in the promotion of these kind of men; that after they are grown rich by extortion, and have sucked the blood of the poor, when clamors grow loud against them, the court can with ease squeeze these leeches, laying all the blame of its own oppression at their doors; and this without the danger of causing the dis-

influence of this new class depended on their office, and not upon their rank, the development of a new aristocracy was arrested, and the aristocratic families existing in Norway at that time were too few to exercise any real power. The royal officials were haughty and arbitrary enough in their dealings with the common people, but their origin as well as their interests bound them to the common classes, and in the future political struggles for national independence and political freedom they became the leaders of the people, and showed a devotion to their cause which could not have been expected of an aristocracy.

A very important administrative reform in Norway introduced by Frederick III. was the taking of a census, and the registration and valuation of all taxable property, which should constitute a new basis for the levying of taxes. Hitherto the various taxes — *land-tax, leding, foring, tithes*, etc. — were levied upon each *gaard* (farm) without reference to its value, and a very unjust distribution of public burdens resulted. Some property was taxed too low, and some too high, so high that it had to be abandoned. The king appointed a commission of fifty members, who were instructed to list every farm, its value, its occupants, and all notable advantages, and on the basis of this census new tax tables were to be prepared. In 1669 the work was finally completed, and it was decided that the taxes should be based on the valuation of the property found in the new tax-lists. The work had been very imperfectly done, however, owing largely to the unwillingness of the people to give the necessary information, as they feared that their taxes would be increased.[1] But taxation had, finally, been based on a correct principle, and a great advance had been made towards an equitable distribution. The total income from all sources of revenue in the kingdom of Norway at this time has been estimated to be about 650,000 riksdaler ($650,000). Of this amount about 200,000 riksdaler were used in Norway for the maintenance of the Norwegian army, and the payment of officials. The balance, 450,000 riksdaler, was sent to Copenhagen to be used for the support of the joint court and navy.

content of any of the nobles upon the score of kindred or alliance." *An Account of Denmark as It Was in the Year 1692*, p. 75 f.

[1] *Historisk Tidsskrift*, vol. IV., p. 507.

Hannibal Sehested's successors in Norway, Nils Trolle and Iver Krabbe, were men of mediocre talents, who showed no trace of originality or special administrative ability. In 1664 King Frederick's illegitimate son, Ulrik Frederick Gyldenløve, was appointed *statholder*. He was a young man, accustomed to the splendor and exciting social life of the higher circles of the Danish capital, and people feared that he would be wholly unfit to shoulder the irksome burdens of this high office. But Gyldenløve, who possessed talents, as well as will and energy, became a worthy successor of Hannibal Sehested. He studied conditions in Norway very closely, and became the ardent advocate of many important reforms. Some of these had, indeed, already been suggested by Sehested, but through Gyldenløve's efforts the government was finally persuaded to take action. He advocated the simplification of the system of taxation, and the valuation and registration of taxable property. He urged the creation of a Norwegian fleet of smaller war vessels for coast defense, the improvement of Norwegian fortresses, the creation of a Norwegian superior court, from which an appeal could be made to the king alone, and, finally, the revision of the "Code of Christian IV." After encountering much indifference and opposition, he finally succeeded in persuading Frederick III. to decide in favor of some of these reforms. By royal edicts it was decreed that Norway should have a separate superior court, *Overhofretten*, from which, however, an appeal could be made to the *Høiesteret* in Copenhagen. It was also decided to revise the "Code of Christian IV.," a work which was done under Frederick's successor Christian V. Gyldenløve became very popu-

Fig. 4. — Ulrik Frederick Gyldenløve.

lar, as he knew how to win the people's favor by straightforward manners and cheerful good-will. Karl Deichman has described his popularity as follows: "The Norwegians regarded Gyldenløve as their patron saint, and they had a peculiar veneration for this lord, because of his excellent conduct, democratic spirit, brave leadership, and gay life. He extended his protection to all, especially to the common people, whom he defended against seizures and unjust impositions. He could persuade the nation to do whatever he pleased. He listened to the people's complaints, and seldom did he leave them unconsoled. The *bønder* in the mountain districts always addressed him "thou Gyldenløve." Many stories are told that he often traveled about in disguise in order to learn if the people's love for him was to be relied upon." [1] Molesworth says of him: "He is about fifty-six years of age, has been one of the handsomest, and continues one of the finest gentlemen that Denmark has produced." [2]

The Faroe Islands retained their old judicial system of six *sysselthings*, and the Lagthing as a superior court. But appeal could be made from the Lagthing to the Høiesteret in Copenhagen. Frederick III. granted these islands as a fief to his favorite Gabel and his son Frederick. These lords and their *fogeds* oppressed the people sorely, and though the king would seek to redress the wrongs when the complaints grew loud, no marked improvement was made in the people's conditions till after the death of Frederick Gabel.

Also in Iceland the old system of *sysselthings* and *lagthings* was suffered to remain; but here as in Norway and the Faroe Islands the Høiesteret in Copenhagen became the highest court of appeal, while the administrative colleges and governmental departments in Denmark gradually assumed the functions of government for the island. In 1683 a *landfoged* was appointed to receive the taxes and revenues, after these had been collected by the *sysselmænd*. The following year a *stiftsamtmand* was appointed, and two years later an *amtmand* was added to the list of crown officials, an indication that the administration was being directed from Copenhagen.[3] But as the *stiftsamt-*

---

[1] Quoted by Ludvig Daae in *Det gamle Christiania*, p. 113.

[2] Robert Molesworth, *An Account of Denmark as It Was in the Year 1692*, p. 145. Roar Tank, *Ulrik Frederik Gyldenløve og Nordmændene, Sproglige og historiske Afhandlinger viede Sophus Bugges Minde*, Christiania, 1908.

[3] Edvard Holm, *Danmark-Norges indre Historie under Enevælden*, vol. I., p. 88 ff. Jón Sigurdsson, *Om Islands statsretslige Forhold*, Copenhagen, 1855.

mand never visited the island, the royal government must have been limited principally to the collection of taxes and revenues, while the domestic affairs must have been largely left to the local authorities.

30. FOREIGN RELATIONS

Of the powers which had aided Denmark-Norway in the war with Sweden, only Holland maintained the alliance until peace was concluded. But the relations had grown less friendly as the war proceeded, and Denmark began to look around for other allies. In 1663 a treaty was formed with France, and Denmark joined the Rhenish alliance which had been formed between France, Sweden, and some of the German states for the defense of the peace of Westphalia. This step was taken by Frederick III. in the hope of being able to force France and Sweden apart. In this he failed, but France promised to pay Denmark a subsidy in case it was again attacked by Sweden. In 1665 the great naval war for commercial supremacy, which Holland and England had waged with such fury in 1652–1654, was formally renewed, after hostilities had already lasted about a year. England was jealous of Holland's commercial superiority and extensive carrying trade, which she had sought to harm by navigation acts.[1] Sweden concluded a defensive alliance with England, and the English king, Charles II., sought to form an alliance with Denmark-Norway against Holland, but Frederick III. hesitated; different opinions prevailed among his councilors, and no definite step was taken, though he secretly favored England through-

[1] Molesworth says: "The exactest computation that I have known made of the English, Dutch, and French trades to these parts in times of peace, ran thus: Of English there passed the Sound yearly, from two hundred vessels to three hundred; of Dutch from one thousand to eleven hundred; of French from ten to twelve, and the like proportion to Norway." *An Account of Denmark as It Was in the Year 1692*, p. 110. In 1656 the English trade was only one-fifth as large as Holland's, and still in 1696 Holland's merchant marine measured 900,000 tons, England's 500,000 tons, the rest of Europe 200,000 tons. O. A. Øverland, *Norges Historie*, vol. VII., p. 203. This agrees quite well with the figures given by H. von Treitschke, *Die Republik der vereinigten Niederlande*, in *Historisch und politische Aufsätze*, neue Folge II., Leipzig, 1870, p. 608; quoted by Ludvig Daae in *Nordmænds Udvandringer til Holland og England i nyere Tid*, p. 21 f.

out the war. This favor he even displayed in a manner which throws
a dark stain upon his character. As a result of their naval victories,
the English became masters of the North Sea, and in the summer of
1665 a large fleet of Holland merchantmen sought refuge in the
neutral harbor of Bergen. Sir Gilbert Talbot, the English ambassador in Denmark, suggested to Frederick III. that he should coöperate
with an English squadron in capturing this merchant fleet, and the
booty should be divided between the two kings. Frederick should
publicly protest his innocence, and Charles II. should reprimand
his admirals for violating the neutrality of Denmark-Norway.
King Frederick consented to this plot, and ordered his general Ahlefeld at Bergen to seemingly protest, but to do nothing to hinder
the English from attacking the Hollanders. But Ahlefeld received
the orders too late. He aided the Hollanders, and trained the cannons of the forts upon the English squadron, which was defeated
after a sanguinary battle. The plan had miscarried, and Denmark's
peace was greatly endangered. But Frederick's vacillating foreign
policy again changed. In 1666 he formed an alliance with Holland,
but the hostilities which broke out with England in consequence of
it were terminated by the peace of Breda, 1667.

31. Norwegian Emigration to Holland, England, Russia and America in the Seventeenth Century and Later

The great development of commerce and naval activity in Holland
and England had created a great demand for seamen. As recruiting was not yet prohibited, sailors were enlisted in large numbers
in Norway, especially for the fleets of Holland.[1] So great was the
number of young men who left their homes in the seacoast districts
that it amounted to a veritable emigration. And though some returned, by far the greater number settled permanently in Holland,
or lost their lives fighting her great naval wars.[2] Robert Moles-

[1] J. C. de Jonge, *Geschiedenis van het Nederlandsche Zeewesen*, vol. II. This
traffic was prohibited by article 7, chapter 4, book 6 of the *Code of Christian
V.*, for Norway, 1687, which imposed the penalty of death on any one who
undertook to enlist seamen in Denmark and Norway without the king's
permission.

[2] When Jens Munk made his voyage to Greenland, he went to Holland
to hire seamen for the expedition; and Christian IV. sought to persuade

worth says: "The best seamen belonging to the king of Denmark are the Norwegians; but most of them are in the service of the Dutch; and have their families established in Holland; from whence it is scarce likely they will ever return home, unless the Dutch use them worse, or the Danes better than hitherto they have done; for the Danish sea-provision is generally very bad." In 1670 Markus Gjøe, the Danish-Norwegian minister to The Hague, wrote to his government that a great number of the king's subjects lived in Holland, and that most of them were Norwegians. He added that they were sailors and officers of lower rank, as the Hollanders were too jealous to make them lieutenants or captains; but Admiral Nils Juel, who had been in the Dutch service for many years, stated a few years later that the officers who were good for anything were mostly Norwegians and Englishmen who had come to Holland to enlist.[1] Even church history shows that many Norwegians and Danes settled in Holland. In 1634 King Christian IV. gave three hundred riksdaler to a Lutheran church in Amsterdam, and in 1663 a Danish-Norwegian congregation was organized there, whose first clergyman, Christian Pedersøn Abel, published a hymnbook for his congregation.[2] Many Norwegians fled to Holland, either to escape punishment for crimes and misdemeanors, or because of religious intolerance at home; in time of war also to avoid military service.[3] But the greater number had emigrated with their families because of the higher pay and better opportunities offered in the service of the Dutch. With the growth of Norwegian lumber export to Holland, the communications with that country became very active, and young men of the seacoast districts found new oppor-

the Norwegian and Danish seamen to return home. For this purpose he issued a general pardon for those who had committed any wrong, except those who were guilty of murder and incest. In 1700 Jens Juel went to Holland and hired 500 to 600 seamen, evidently Danes and Norwegians; and Peter Tordenskjold hired 150 sailors in Holland in 1713. Ludvig Daae, *Nordmænds Udvandringer til Holland og England i nyere Tid*, p. 22 ff.

[1] Ludvig Daae, *Nordmænds Udvandringer til Holland og England i nyere Tid*, p. 14. Chr. Bruun, *Curt Sivertsen Adelaer*, p. 215 f.

[2] Andreas Faye, *Christiansands Stifts Bispe- og Stiftshistorie*, p. 255. Holger Fr. Rørdam, *Anders Christensen Arrebos Levnet og Skrifter*, vol. II., p. 161.

[3] Andreas Faye, *Christiansands Stifts Bispe- og Stiftshistorie*, p. 255 ff.

tunities for adventure and profitable employment as Dutch seamen.[1] Even in the early part of the seventeenth century many Norwegian sailors had gone to Holland, and in the war with England in the time of Cromwell (1652–1654) the Dutch had enlisted such a number of Norwegian seamen that England's jealousy was aroused. In the war of 1658–1660 the Hollanders aided Denmark-Norway against Sweden, and sought to persuade Frederick III. to cede to them Trondhjem's *len;* but the English protested, because they saw the advantage which Holland would thus be gaining. In an official English document, the following comment is made upon this attempt:

"If ye English should suffer ye Hollanders to become masters of Dronthiem there would thereby accrue to ye Hollanders an incredible strength at sea, seeing that province alone by ye occasion of ye great fishing, that is upon that coast, is able to set forth in short time some thousands of seamen, whereof ye English have the proof in ye war between ye Hollanders and them, at which time they had only ye King of Denmark's leave to leavy seamen there, and then wee may easily guesse, what is to be expected, if ye Hollanders should come to bee wholly masters there."[2]

Also in the Dutch merchant marine a large number of Norwegian sailors had found employment, and took part in the voyages to the Cape Colony, East India, Greenland, and other distant countries.

The same relations between Norway and Holland continued to exist also in the eighteenth century. The emigration to Holland continued, but the Dutch, nevertheless, deplored that a smaller number of Norwegian and German sailors flocked to their country than formerly, and recruiting officers were sent to Norway in spite of the drastic measures taken by the Danish government to stop the traffic. The emigration to Holland was greatly deplored by Norwegian and Danish writers, as well as by the government authorities. Gerhard Schøning (1758) considered this emigration one of the chief hindrances to the development of Norwegian agri-

---

[1] P. Coucheron in *Theologisk Tidsskrift*, published by Caspari, vol. I. Ludvig Daae, *Nordmœnds Udvandringer til Holland og England i nyere Tid*, p. 18 f.

[2] The passage is quoted by Ludvig Daae in *Nordmœnds Udvandringer til Holland og England i nyere Tid*, p. 13, from *Saga, et Fjerdingsaarsskrift*, published by J. S. Munch, Christiania, 1806, vol. I.

culture, and regarded it as a calamity even worse than the Black Death. As to the number of emigrants who yearly left Norway but few and incomplete statistical data exist, but we get a general idea from the statements of contemporary writers. Erik Pontoppidan (1698–1764) states that when the merchant fleets returned from the East Indies, the West Indies, Greenland, and other countries, the Norwegian, Danish, and Holstein sailors assembled in Amsterdam numbered 8000 or 9000 "by a conservative estimate." [1] "Some of these visit their homes about every three years, and finally, in their old age remain at home to live on their earnings, but a great number remain abroad all their lives, not to speak of those who lose their lives in the service." [2] L. F. Rømer, who was born in Holland, says: "We have aided the Dutch in that many thousand Norwegian, Danish, and Holstein seamen and officers yearly have left their homes to earn something abroad, since we have nothing for them to do." Such yearly losses of the ablest youth of the country would naturally be felt as a calamity, especially in the districts along the seacoast, which were most directly affected by the emigration. The government bewailed the decrease in the quota of army recruits, a truly alarming thing for the Danish kings, who "esteemed soldiers their only true riches," as Molesworth puts it. But the losses, real or apparent, caused by the emigration were probably more than compensated for in other ways. What the Norwegians needed at this time was stimulus strong enough to stir them to mental and physical action; experiences of a kind which could invigorate the phlegmatic and bloodless national organism. Such a stimulus was given by the life of adventure and enterprise in the Dutch maritime service. Many private accounts show that it was a hard service. Often the Norwegian sailors in the cities of Holland were kidnapped and brought by force aboard the ships, which were to sail around Africa to India, across the Atlantic to the West Indies or distant Greenland. The life on board was hard, and the punishments inflicted for offenses were barbarous. Often they were in danger of attack

[1] Erik Pontoppidan, *Menoza en asiatisk Prinds;* and *Det første Forsøj paa Norges naturlige Historie,* vol. II., p. 380.

[2] Ludvig Daae, *Nordmænds Udvandringer til Holland og England i nyere Tid,* p. 42 ff. L. F. Rømer, *Tilforladelig Efterretning om Kysten af Guinea,* p. 249 f., quoted by Ludvig Daae.

by pirates, or of falling into the hands of Moorish corsairs, who would carry them into slavery. But this hard school again showed the Norwegians the path to greatness — the sea. Once again, as of old, they became skillful and daring navigators, inured to the hardships of the sea, and fascinated with its freedom and adventures. New ideas, capable seamen, a spirit of enterprise, knowledge of the world and its commerce, and a desire to go abroad were the returns which Norway received for her losses. The old spirit was rekindled, and the Norwegian merchant marine was created, largely through this new impulse. Ludvig Daae says: "Historical research regarding the great, yea even remarkable development of our merchant marine will undoubtedly prove that it is due directly to the relations with Holland, which I have here tried to elucidate."[1] Holland's sea power was declining, and in the war with England, 1780, and, finally, in the French Revolution and the Napoleonic period it was crushed. But Denmark-Norway rose to new significance as a maritime and naval power. As neutrals at the time of the American Revolutionary War, they developed a great carrying trade,[2] and in course of the next century, Norway developed a merchant marine of which Joh. Dyring says that it is "of greater relative importance to the Norwegian people, even when we consider its size, than that of any other country on the globe."[3] In view of modern development we are able to see the question of the emigration to Holland in a new light, and to put the proper construction on the pessimistic views of old writers.

The emigration from Norway was not wholly limited to Holland. Many also went to England, especially because of the flourishing lumber trade with that country. Ludvig Daae cites the following interesting passage from a book of travel written by Judge Christian Gram of Christiania, who visited England and France in 1757. While he was staying at Dover, says the judge, "a strange incident occurred. A Dutch ship was brought to that city by a British privateer. The Dutch republic was indeed neutral in that war, but

---

[1] Ludvig Daae, *Nordmænds Udvandringer til Holland og England i nyere Tid*, p. 63.

[2] Jacob Aal, *Erindringer*, p. 40 ff.   B. E. Bendixen, *Et Omrids av Norges Handelshistorie*, p. 33 ff.   [3] Joh. Dyring, *Kongeriget Norge*, p. 165.

the Dutch refused to be searched by the Englishmen, and a combat followed in which hard blows were dealt on both sides, until the English privateer was finally victorious." "The remarkable thing in connection with this occurrence," he continues, "was that the captain of the English privateer, as well as of the Dutch ship, were both native-born Norwegians, who under foreign flags had given each other a thorough drubbing. The captain of the Dutch ship was a somewhat old man from the west coast of Norway, who had established himself in Amsterdam thirty years before. . . . The captain of the English privateer was a young man from Christiania."[1] This incident illustrates the situation in a striking way. The Norwegians who had begun to seek remunerative employment abroad were also found in the English service in considerable numbers, and in these wars with Holland they often fought against their own countrymen. The lumber trade also brought many Norwegian merchants to England, and the sons of rich burghers came to London to study commerce, and to form friendships, which might be of value in the carrying on of trade. A Norwegian-Danish congregation was organized, and in 1694–1696 a Norwegian Lutheran church was built in the English capital, which was described as beautiful by a traveler at the time of the Seven Years' War. Early in the eighteenth century a Norwegian-Danish club was organized in London, and towards the close of the century *Det nordiske Selskab*, a truly Scandinavian society with members from all three Northern countries, was founded.

The war between England and France during the reign of Napoleon put a sudden stop to the Norwegian emigration to Holland and England. In 1806 Holland was made a feudatory kingdom by the French Emperor, with Louis Bonaparte as king, and Holland's military forces had to join the French armies. Through Napoleon's "Continental System" Holland's commerce was destroyed, and when Louis Bonaparte abdicated in 1810, the kingdom of Holland was incorporated in the French Empire, and the Norwegian sailors in Holland were forced into the French service. The Danish diplomat

---

[1] Christian Gram, *En kort Journal eller Reise-Beskrivelse forfattet udi et Brev til en god Ven*, Christiania, ca. 1759; quoted by Ludvig Daae, *Nordmænds Udvandringer til Holland og England i nyere Tid*, p. 95 f.

J. G. Rist writes that the transportation of seamen from Holland took its beginning in the winter 1809–1810, and that at Hamburg he turned about 2000 seamen over to the French authorities. "It pained me," he writes, "to see these healthy men, of whom the greater part were Norwegians, carried as prisoners to the unhealthy Vliesingen. A mutiny broke out among the men, because of the bad treatment accorded them, and several officers who were implicated were sent home as prisoners, among others Hans Holsten. In the beginning of 1811 the crews for two warships were again sent, and these seamen remained in the French fleet till 1815." [1] England's attack on Denmark-Norway led to a war which terminated all intercourse with Great Britain. When peace was established after the downfall of Napoleon, the old relations were not reëstablished either with England or Holland with regard to emigration. New conditions had been created, and the remarkable development of the United States of America soon offered far better opportunities to the Norwegian emigrants.

Of the Norwegians staying in Holland not a few went to the Dutch colonies in America during the seventeenth century. Mr. Torstein Jahr of Washington, D.C., who has made special investigations of the Norwegian emigration to the Dutch New Netherland, shows that the great patroon Van Rensselaer, received a large tract of land near the present city of Albany, in the state of New York, on the condition that he should bring over fifty colonists within four years. In 1630, he sent nine colonists, of whom three were Norwegians. In 1631 he again made a contract with nine men to go to New Netherland. Four of these were Norwegians, but only two finally went to America. In 1636 Van Rensselaer made a contract with Albert Andriessen of Fredrikshald, Norway, who sailed from Amsterdam September 25 with the ship "Rensselaerwyck" and thirty-eight colonists, of whom many were Norwegians. Among these colonists were six women, one of whom was Captain Andriessen's wife, Annetje, who on the voyage gave birth to a child, which was baptized in England, and received the very suggestive name of Sturm van der Zee. The colonists arrived safely at Manhattan, March 4, 1637, and many

---

[1] J. G. Rist, *Lebenserinnerungen herausgegeben von G. Poel*, Gotha, 1880, quoted by Ludvig Daae, in *Nordmænds Udvandringer*, p. 123.

of Albert Andriessen's descendants still live in and about the city of Albany. Among the pioneers in Schenectady, New York, were also many Norwegians. Jahr says: "In all the Dutch settlements in New Netherland one can find more or less distinct traces of the Norwegians. Those about whom we have any knowledge were capable and honest people, who have done their share and deserve their part of the honor for the colonization of the new land, and they fostered strong and energetic descendants to continue the work of increasing the homesteads of their fathers." [1]

Among the more prominent Norwegian settlers in New Netherland the same author mentions especially Anneke Jans (Jansen) and her husband, Roelof Jansen, who came over in the ship "Eendracht" in 1630. Roelof became overseer of Van Rensselaer's farm de Laetsburg in 1632, and in 1636 he received deed to a sixty-two-acre tract of land now included between Warren and Canal streets, Broadway and the Hudson River, in the city of New York. He built a house, and began to clear and cultivate his farm, but he soon died, and his widow, Anneke, married Rev. Eberhardus Bogardus, the first regular clergyman in the colony.[2] Her mother, Trina Jonas, came to the colony in 1633 as practicing midwife in the employ of the Dutch East India Company. She received deed to a parcel of land near the foot of the present Pearl Street, where she built a house. Trina Jonas had also another daughter, Maritje, who also came to New Netherland with her husband, Tymen Jansen. These people became wealthy and influential, and Jahr observes that the New York families De Lancey, De Peyster, Gouverneur, Jay, Knickerbocker, Morris, Schuyler, Stuyvesant, Van Cortland, and Van Rensselaer became related to them through marriage, and that nearly all the old families in New York state, who pride themselves on being the genuine Knickerbockers, can trace their lineage to the Norwe-

---

[1] Torstein Jahr, *Nordmænd i Nieuw-Nederland, Symra* (Decorah, Ia.), vol. V., p. 65 ff.

[2] Torstein Jahr, *Nordmænd i Ny-Nederland, Anneke Jans fra Marstrand, hennes Farm og hennes Slekt, Symra*, vol. IX., p. 9 ff. *Nordmænd i Ny-Nederland*, in *Dagsposten* (Norway), November 19, 1905, by the same author. Torstein Jahr, *Nordmænd i Nieuw-Nederland, Ervingen* (Decorah, Ia.), vol. II., p. 1 f. I. B. Frich, *Bidrag til de Forenede Staters Kirkehistorie, Evangelisk Luthersk Kirketidende* (Decorah, Ia.), 1907, p. 211 ff., 237 ff., 265 ff., 321 ff., 348 ff., 403 ff., 430 ff., 459 ff., 487 ff.

gian midwife Trina Jonas, and her daughter Anneke Jans Bogardus. It is noteworthy in this connection that on April 7, 1909, Mrs. Mary A. Fonda began a lawsuit against the Trinity corporation of the city of New York for the possession of a part of the Trinity church property, of which she claimed she was the rightful owner, because she descended directly from Anneke Jans Bogardus.[1]

The new development of Russia in the time of Peter the Great and Catharine II. induced many Norwegians to enter the Russian service. The most noted of these is the Norwegian naval officer, Cornelius Creutz, formerly employed in Holland, who was engaged by the Czar to organize and equip the Russian navy. He received the rank of vice-admiral, and played a similar rôle in the Russian fleet as Kort Adelaer did in the navy of Denmark-Norway. He employed so many foreign naval officers that a reliable writer states in 1715: "Most of the Czar's naval officers are Hollanders, Norwegians, and Danes." Creutz was a leader of the Russian fleet in the wars with Sweden, 1705–1713, and served with great distinction. In the Russian army as well as in the navy a great number of Norwegians were employed.[2]

32. THE CLOSE OF THE REIGN OF FREDERICK III. CHRISTIAN V. THE GYLDENLØVE WAR

On February 9, 1670, King Frederick III. died. His reign had been more eventful than successful. He had accomplished much in the direction of increasing his own power, which seems to have been his chief aim, as it was the passionate ambition of his proud and pleasure-loving queen, Sophia Amalie. But in war and diplomacy he had been unsuccessful, and he did not attempt to use his great power to improve the condition of his poverty-stricken subjects. If any reforms were instituted, they were wholly due to the energy and forethought of others. He basked with self-satisfaction in the glory of his own autocratic power, which only hardened his heart against the much-abused common people, whose misery, especially in Denmark, only served to fill him with unsympathetic pride and

---

[1] *New York American*, April 8, 1909, cited by Torstein Jahr, *Nordmænd i Ny-Nederland, Symra*, vol. IX., p. 34.

[2] Ludvig Daae, *Nordmænd og Danske i Rusland i det attende Aarhundrede*.

arrogant disdain.   During the latter part of his reign he devoted himself to alchemy and fantastic speculation rather than to the care and development of his kingdom.   He used unnecessary harsh methods in collecting taxes from his impoverished subjects.   A sordid love of gain had led him into the vile bargain with Talbot, and it was probably avarice and superstition rather than true scientific interest which made him an enthusiastic alchemist.   Autocratic power had isolated him from his fellow men, and he developed symptoms of the mental eccentricity and the suspicion and fear of others peculiar to autocrats.   His people ceased to love him, and though they continued to show him the most humble courtesy, his heart must have felt that it was hollow mockery, empty ceremony. He would probably have retired more and more from the world, but the queen did not allow it.   She needed him to grace her luxurious carnivals, which were arranged with gaudy splendor.   Enormous sums were spent in royal entertainments and other like wasteful and unprofitable ways.[1]   Some nobleman or favorite might receive a present of 200,000 riksdaler, while taxes were wrung from the peasants by selling their bedclothes, their wooden chairs, and the very coats on their backs at public auction.   Molesworth says: "Yet upon the occasion of the late poll tax I heard that the collectors were forced to take from this and other towns (in lieu of money) old feather beds, bedsteads, brass, pewter, wooden chairs, etc., which they took violently from the poor people, who were unable to pay, leaving them destitute of all manner of necessaries for the use of living."[2]   But conditions were no better a decade or two earlier.   King Frederick III. and his proud queen seem to have entertained ideas of their duties as sovereigns akin to those of their younger contemporary, Louis XIV. of France, that the state existed for the monarch, not the monarch for the state.   The common people had ceased to be thought of except as soldiers, taxpayers, and common drudges.

King Christian V. was born in 1646, and was twenty-four years of age at his accession to the throne.   In character and tempera-

___

[1] "Hannibal Sehested had a present of 200,000 crowns, Svan (Svane), the superintendent or bishop, was made archbishop, and had 30,000 crowns. The president or speaker Nansen, 20,000 crowns."   Molesworth, *An Account of Denmark*, p. 68.   An English crown was a little more than a riksdaler.

[2] Molesworth, *An Account of Denmark as It Was in the Year 1692*, p. 78.

ment he resembled his grandfather, Christian IV., but he was less gifted, and lacked his interest for intellectual pursuits. He was a great hunter, a fine horseman, lively and energetic, and though he was not good-looking, he made a good impression by his fine bearing. He was friendly and good-natured, well liked, but weak in character, and easily influenced by his surroundings. In 1667 he had been persuaded to marry Charlotte Amalie of Hesse-Cassel. She was very devoted to him, learned to speak Danish, and sought to win the good-will of all. She was one of the kindliest and most popular queens which Denmark-Norway ever had, but her wedded life became an unhappy one, for even before his marriage the king seems to have become attached to a young lady, Sophia Amalie Moth, daughter of his former teacher, on whom he bestowed all his affection. Her numerous relatives, who all sought promotion through royal favor, soon came to exercise great influence at the court. His mother, the proud and imperious Sophia Amalie, also continued to wield a great influence, especially during the early part of his reign.

As a prince Christian V. had visited France, England, Holland, and Germany, where he had become acquainted with absolutism in all its splendor, and it became his aim to imitate as far as possible the great model of all autocrats, Louis XIV. of France. His coronation was celebrated with great splendor, and with all the devotional veneration and supplicant obeisance shown monarchs in that age of autocracy. Edward Holm says: "A new crown had been made, of another form than the old one, as a sign that the royal power had been changed, and it was so rich and elegant that it was at first estimated to cost 700,000 to 800,000 riksdaler. New were also the scepter, the orb, and the sword, and their value answered to that of the crown. As the royal power was the gift of God, and not of men, the king could not receive the crown and the symbols of royal authority and other regalia from human hands. He therefore placed the crown on his own head, and took the regalia before he went to church to be anointed, a ceremony which he said he regarded as an act of devotion by which he with the All-ruling God did more firmly and closely connect and unite himself. When a king was crowned in days past, the charter was read, and the king had to confirm it with an oath, but now the 'Kongelov' with its recital of the greatness of royal power was read. The one of the bishops present who took it from its cover made a deep obeisance before it. The language used by Bishop Vandel of Seeland in his speech in connection with the anointing was keyed in a lofty tone which corresponded to that used in his great work about absolutism written a few years earlier. 'It is,' he said, 'the king's right and dominion, and the people's proper subjection, that the king shall rule over the persons of his subjects — likewise that he shall rule over their goods and possessions, their fields and vineyards, their best oliveyards, their grain, cattle, and asses.' " [1] With such phrases of cringing flattery, and disavowal of every right, the people welcomed the new custodian of their destiny and welfare.

King Christian did not retain his predecessor's advisers, but chose new ones, the chief of whom were Ulrik Frederick Gyldenløve, Frederick Ahlefeld, and Peder Schumacher, the author of the " Konge-lov," a young man of rare ability, who soon became the real leader of the government. He was later raised to the nobility under the name of Griffenfeld, by which name he is generally known.[2] Through his influence, the king was persuaded to organize the Order of the Danebrog and to create two new classes of nobles; the counts (grever) and the knights (friherrer), the purpose being to gradually destroy the old nobility, which was hostile to the monarch, and to create a new one wholly subservient to him. The new nobility was, therefore, regarded as higher in rank than the old. A number of new titles were also introduced, and the royal officials were placed above the old nobility in rank. All honor and distinction was to radiate immediately from the court, as in France. In Norway the new court nobility never became very numerous, but Ulrik Frederick Gyldenløve became Count of Larvik, and Peder Count of Griffen-feld received Lem, near Tunsberg, later also the barony of Rosendal in Kvindherred.

The talented and popular Gyldenløve returned to Denmark when Christian V. mounted the throne, but his eagerness to suggest vari-ous reforms again manifested itself. In 1670 he was commissioned,

---

[1] Edvard Holm, Danmark-Norges indre Historie under Enevælden fra 1660 til 1720, vol. I., p. 12 f. R. Meiborg, Billeder fra Livet ved Christian den femtes Hof, p. 11.

[2] A. D. Jørgensen, Peder Schumacher Griffenfeld, Copenhagen, 1893.

together with Jørgen Bjelke, to propose plans for the betterment of Norway, and the two submitted a document advocating reforms in Norway's internal administration, in its defenses, in taxes and revenues, trade and commerce. The kingdom should henceforth consist of four *stifts*, four principal *amts*, nine subordinate *amts*, fifty-six *fogderier*, and nine chartered cities. They showed that by abolishing many unnecessary civil offices, and reducing the salaries of others, 30,000 riksdaler a year could be saved. They complained of the excessive burdens which had been placed upon the people, and advocated a reduction of taxes. The importance of commerce was strongly emphasized, and the building of minor warships for defense, which could also be used as merchant vessels, was urged. It was pointed out how important it was to get foreign seamen into the kingdom, and especially to prevail on the thousands of Norwegian seamen in foreign service, chiefly in that of Holland, to return to their own country. The number of civil officials was reduced, and the taxes were lowered from 236,000 riksdaler to 156,000 a year, but many of the more important suggestions were passed by. In 1673 Gyldenløve again returned to Norway as *statholder*.[1]

Griffenfeld's ambition led him to snatch for ever higher power. The system of administrative departments or colleges he found too cumbersome, especially since they checked his will and limited his influence. He persuaded the good-natured king that it would be more convenient to rule with the assistance of one "minister of quality" than with the Colleges, and in 1673 he was made count, and chancellor of the kingdom. In this high office he exercised the supreme influence in administrative and diplomatic affairs, and no important matters could be decided except with his counsel. His political views, wrought into a permanent system, and carried out in diplomacy and administration, became the chief feature of the reign of Christian V. As author of the "Kongelov," Griffenfeld had already formulated the theory on which the new absolutism was based; it was left for him as chancellor and virtual head both of internal and foreign affairs to elaborate it into a fixed policy, which

---

[1] A. D. Jørgensen, *Peder Schumacher Griffenfeld*, vol. I., p. 288 ff. Roar Tank, *Ulrik Frederik Gyldenløve og Nordmændene, Sproglige og historiske Afhandlinger viede Sophus Bugges Minde. Historisk Tidsskrift*, vol. II., p. 337.

permanently effected Denmark's future political development. According to his views the people had no rights either as individuals or as a nation, except what the king would graciously grant them. To the king belonged all the power; the kingdom and all its possessions were his. But how these possessions were originally acquired, by what rights they were held, the historical reasons for existing conditions, and the people's right as a nation to safeguard their own development and future destiny were ideas for which there was no place in the system of political science formulated by this astute politician, this keen but shortsighted statesman. He worked for the interest of the king; the welfare of the nation and the realm he never clearly understood. For the future development of the Danish people it would have been of the greatest importance to join the duchies of Schleswig-Holstein more closely to the Danish kingdom; but he did not attempt it, not because it was impossible, but because the king had some sort of title to them, and as everything was regarded as the king's personal possessions, it made no difference by what title he held them. Neither do we find that Griffenfeld with his great talents and still greater power attempted to institute any reforms which could serve to develop the nation socially and economically. He devoted his attention chiefly to diplomacy and foreign affairs, in which he had gained a great reputation and exercised great influence, but so far as Norway especially was concerned, the reforms instituted were chiefly due to the initiative of Statholder Gyldenløve.

War clouds again obscured the political horizon of Europe. Louis XIV. was preparing to seize the Spanish Netherlands, and no one could doubt that an attack would also be directed against Holland. The danger of French preponderance had for some time alarmed the statesmen, and a triple alliance of England, Holland, and Sweden had been formed in 1668 to resist the ambitions of the French king. But Louis XIV. used his excellent diplomatic service and his treasury to destroy the alliance, an effort in which he was quite successful, as Charles II. of England was induced by large subsidies to join France, and Sweden soon followed a similar course. In the meanwhile William of Orange, Stadtholder of Holland, the most sagacious statesman of his time, sought to form a new coalition against France. Frederick

William of Brandenburg and Emperor Leopold of Germany were persuaded to form an alliance with Holland, and Christian V. of Denmark-Norway was also strongly urged to join. An alliance with Holland under these circumstances would probably mean war with Sweden, the ally of France, but Christian V. nevertheless favored this course, while some of his advisers, notably Griffenfeld, advocated neutrality. The war party gained the upper hand, and on June 30, 1674, Denmark formed an alliance with Holland, and promised to place 16,000 men in the field, if France received aid from any other power. As Brandenburg and Spain soon began war against Louis XIV., and Sweden rushed troops into Brandenburg to aid France, the die was cast, and the rival Northern powers were launched upon a new struggle. It seems that this war ought to have been averted, especially since Denmark had not recovered from the ravages of the wars waged in the previous reign, but the hope of recovering Skåne and other possessions tempted Christian V. to hazard a new armed conflict.

As soon as circumstance pointed to the possibility of a new war, Gyldenløve was sent as *statholder* to Norway, 1673, to organize the military forces, and strengthen the defenses of the kingdom. He made a tour of inspection through the country, and found that neither the army nor the fortresses were in so good a condition as they ought to be, but the recommendations for improvements which he submitted were opposed, especially by Griffenfeld, until the war was on the point of breaking out, when some concessions had to be made. Griffenfeld seems to have feared that Gyldenløve was becoming too powerful in Norway, and he sent a trusted friend, Jens Juel, to assist him, and to watch his movements. But to Gyldenløve, who needed help in his many duties, Juel was not unwelcome. Together with the generals Russenstein and Løvenhjelm the two formed a council of war, which henceforth directed all military preparations in Norway. In the summer of 1675, 1800 men were kept at work on the fortresses of Akershus, Fredrikstad, and Fredrikshald, and the king authorized the creation of a war fund of 100,000 riksdaler to be used in case of emergency.[1] Instructions were also

---

[1] I. Gulowsen, *Gyldenløvefeiden 1675–1679, Christiania Videnskabs-Selskabs Skrifter,* 1906.

given in a royal proclamation regarding Bohuslen, that the people of that province should be induced "by fair promises" to leave Sweden, and renew their allegiance to the government of Denmark-Norway.

However faulty the military organization might be in minor details, Norway was much better prepared for the war at this time than in any of the previous conflicts with Sweden. The army numbered about 12,000 men, consisting of five regiments of infantry, six companies (800) of cavalry, and an artillery division of seventy-six field pieces. A sixth regiment of infantry, numbering 1000 men, had been sent to Denmark. The war between the Scandinavian countries was fought partly in Germany and partly in Skåne and along the Norwegian border. In Danish history it is called the War in Skåne, in Norway it is generally known as the Gyldenløve War, because the *statholder* was commander in chief of the Norwegian forces.[1]

Denmark had, especially, been making progress as a naval power under the able management of the great admiral Kort Sivertson Adelaer, who was placed in supreme command of the Danish-Norwegian navy by Frederick III. in 1663. Adelaer was a Norwegian by birth, but like many of his countrymen he had gone to Holland, where he enlisted in the navy, and became an able seaman. In time he became the owner of a ship with which he entered the service of the Venetian Senate, and upon his return to Holland he became very prominent. Frederick III. invited him to Denmark, made him chief admiral of the Danish navy, granted him a large salary, and finally raised him to the nobility. Adelaer possessed great administrative ability, and brought the fleet to a point of efficiency which soon made Denmark-Norway a great naval power. He died shortly after the war broke out, and was succeeded by Admiral Nils Juel, the great Danish naval hero.[2] Christian V. had

---

[1] Didrik Schnitler, *Det første Aarhundrede af den norske Hærs Historie*, p. 52 ff. Oscar Alb. Johnsen, *Norges Historie*, vol. V., 1. I. Gulowsen, *Gyldenløvefeiden*, *Christiania Videnskabs-Selskabs Skrifter*, 1906. C. O. Munthe, *Fredrikshalds og Fredriksstens Historie indtil 1720*, p. 321 ff.

[2] Kort Adelaer's achievements have been variously estimated. He has had his enthusiastic admirers and his bitter opponents among the historians. See A. F. Fabricius, *Minder fra Nordens Historie*, "Kort Adeler."

planned to direct his first attack against Sweden's German provinces,[1] and war began in August, 1675, when a Danish army of 16,000 men marched into Mecklenburg. The main part of this force advanced into Pomerania, while some minor detachments besieged Wismar, which was taken before the campaign closed for the year. In Bremen a smaller Danish force had coöperated with the allies, and a greater part of the bishopric was taken. The operations along the Norwegian border had commenced with minor skirmishes in which the combatants tested each other's strength. The Swedish general Ascheberg had taken a position at Svarteborg with 2000 men, and a similar army of reserves was quartered in Vermland, while the Norwegians concentrated 4000 men at Fredrikshald under General Russenstein, and kept the mountain passes well guarded. No important battle was fought in this campaign. Gyldenløve sent a force of 1000 men on galleys along the coast of Bohuslen with orders to land at Saltkällan, and cut off Ascheberg's retreat, but the Swedish general had been informed of the plan, and both Swedes and Norwegians went into winter quarters in the border districts. The success gained by the Danes in Germany was undoubtedly due in a large measure to the superiority of the Danish-Norwegian fleet, which under Kort Adelaer had gained full control of the Baltic Sea. At this time the Swedish fleet was in such a wretched condition that it could not even seriously attempt to maintain communications with Germany, which had become the theater of war, and where its armies were in need of reënforcements; a situation which shows that Sweden was ill prepared to expose her scattered dominions to the dangers of a new war. A young and untried king, Charles XI., had just ascended the throne, and the armies in the field had been hampered in their operations through jealous rivalry among the generals.

The success gained in the first campaign strengthened the influence of the Danish war party. Duke John Adolph of Pløen was chosen commander-in-chief of the army, and a vigorous campaign

Chr. Bruun, *Curt Sivertsen Adelaer.* Axel Larsen, *Dansk-Norske Heltehistorier,* "Curt Sivertsen Adelaer," and "Nils Juel."

[1] By the treaty of Westphalia, 1648, Sweden received the city of Wismar and the greater part of Pomerania, together with Rügen, and the bishoprics of Bremen and Verden, but not the city of Bremen.

for the conquest of Skåne, supported by an attack on the Swedish border provinces by the Norwegian army, was planned for the following year. Griffenfeld, being an advocate of peace, not only opposed the war, but he sought still through diplomatic negotiations to maintain friendly relations with France, the ally of Sweden. Great power, flattery, and royal favor had made him very arrogant, so that he even offended the king himself, and aroused the hatred of the nobles. He continued to take bribes in spite of continued warnings, and as his diplomacy and statesmanship began to take a course ever more opposed to the policy of the king and his generals, who were determined to push the war with vigor, it became easy for his enemies to undermine his influence, and bring about his overthrow. His most powerful opponents were General Frederick Arenstorf and the king's mistress, Sophia Amalie Moth, who was created Countess of Samsø, and became the head of a court camarilla, which virtually controlled the king. But Griffenfeld also had numerous personal enemies, especially in the court circles, and no man in so exalted a position possibly ever had fewer real friends. On the morning of March 11, 1676, when the chancellor arrived at the palace to lay the latest letters before the king, he was accosted by General Arenstorf, who informed him that he had been ordered by the king to arrest him. His house was placed under guard, his papers were seized, and the distinguished prisoner was locked up in the citadel. After being tried on several grave charges, among others, perjury, simony, treason, extortion, and the taking of bribes, he was sentenced to be executed, and to have forfeited all his honors, titles, and possessions. He had already placed his head on the block, when he was pardoned by the king, and his sentence was changed to life imprisonment. Griffenfeld was undoubtedly innocent of many of the gravest offenses with which he was charged, and the sentence was manifest'y unjust, but he had himself created the conditions which brought about his fall, and by his conduct in his high office he had made himself justly liable to severe punishment. For twenty-two years he remained imprisoned. In 1680 he was transferred from Frederikshavn to the castle of Munkholmen, near Trondhjem, where he stayed till 1698, when he was liberated from prison, and allowed to stay in the city, because of his failing health. He died in Trondhjem, March 12, 1699, and his body was brought to Denmark, where it rests in the cemetery of Vaer church in Jutland.[1]

The Swedish king, Charles XI., exerted himself to the utmost to bring Sweden's military forces, both on sea and land, to the highest state of efficiency for the next campaign. He would send a fleet to Germany with sufficient reënforcements to protect his German provinces, while an army should attack Seeland, and carry the war to the very heart of the Danish kingdom. But Nils Juel, who had succeeded Kort Adelaer as admiral of the Danish-Norwegian fleet, seized Gothland and concentrated his whole fleet of twenty-six ships near Bornholm. The Swedish fleet of fifty vessels carrying 1100 guns advanced to attack him, but as Juel had strict orders not to engage in battle with a greatly superior force, he retreated towards the coast of Skåne, and anchored behind Falsterbo Reef, followed closely by the Swedes. Here he received reënforcements of five Danish and four Dutch ships, but had to turn over the chief command to the Hollander Cornelius Tromp. After some maneuvering the two fleets finally joined in battle off Öland, June 1, 1676, where the Swedes suffered a serious defeat. Both flagships were destroyed, the two admirals, Creutz and Ugga, lost their lives, and many ships were captured. This defeat so crippled the Swedish fleet that the contemplated invasion of Skåne could be undertaken without fear of serious opposition. Gyldenløve fortified the pass of Kvistrum, and seized Uddevalla without encountering much opposition. Venersborg was also taken after a sharp engagement. An attempt to seize Gottenborg was unsuccessful, but Gyldenløve turned towards Bohus, where he was joined by reënforcements under Tønne Huitfeldt, which increased his forces to 5000 men. In their operations in Skåne the Danes were very successful, as their countrymen in that province welcomed them as liberators. Helsingborg opened its portals to the invaders, Landskrona was taken without great resistance, and Kristianstad was forced to surrender after a severe engagement. As the people of Skåne also rose in arms, and organized bands of guerillas (Snaphanerne), who everywhere attacked the Swedes,

<hr/>

[1] A. D. Jørgensen, *Peder Schumacher Griffenfeld.* Paludan-Müller, *Griffenfelds Stigen og Falden,* Copenhagen, 1879. O. Vaupel, *Rigskantsler Grev Griffenfeld,* 1880. O. A. Øverland, *Norges Historie,* vol. VII., p. 226 ff., 348 ff.

Charles XI. was obliged to withdraw from the province. Sweden had been placed in a most critical position. Its German provinces, with the exception of the strongest fortresses, were held by the armies of the allies, its fleet was unable to render efficient service, Gothland and Skåne had been seized by the Danes, and Bohuslen was occupied by the Norwegians under Gyldenløve. The time seemed to have come when Denmark would get revenge for past defeats and losses, but Christian V., who appears to have had a jealous and irritable temper, threw away the final victory at the moment when it seemed to be within reach. Having taken offense at Duke Pløen's haughty bearing, he lent such willing ear to his opponents that the duke resigned as commander-in-chief of the Danish armies. The king himself assumed command, but proved to be wholly incompetent, and misfortunes befell the Danish arms in rapid succession. A force which had been sent into Halland under the Scotch general Duncan was destroyed by Charles XI. at Fyllebro. Duncan fell, and only a few hundred men escaped from the field. This victory, which gave the Swedes new hope, and increased their confidence in their king, was of no slight military importance, as it prevented any further coöperation between Gyldenløve and the Danish army in Skåne. When he heard that a large Swedish army was approaching to attack him, Gyldenløve raised the siege of Bohus, and withdrew from Bohuslen. More disastrous still was the battle of Lund, December 4, 1676. When Charles XI. learned that the Norwegians had left Bohuslen, he advanced into Skåne, and sought to surprise the Danes in their winter quarters. His movements were discovered in time, but a bloody battle ensued, in which the Danes were defeated with a loss of several thousand men, together with artillery and baggage.[1] This victory reëstablished the self-confidence and reputation of the Swedes, and gave the Danes a stunning blow from which it was difficult to recover. The people of Skåne submitted to King Charles XI., and Helsingborg received a Swedish garrison. But some

---

[1] O. Vaupel, *Den danske og norske Hærs Historie*, vol. I., p. 136 ff. Abraham Cronholm, *Skånes politiske Historia*, vol. II., p. 181 ff. Fredrik Ferdinand Carlson, *Sveriges Historia under Konungarne af pfalziska Huset*, part II. I. Gulowsen, *Gyldenløvefeiden*. G. Bjørlin, *Kriget mot Danmark 1675–1679*, p. 111 ff.

sinews of strength still remained to Christian V., his superior fleet and the undefeated Norwegian army.

King Charles' plan for the campaign of 1677 was to strengthen his fleet to such an extent that he could reëstablish communications with his army in Pomerania under Königsmark, and by an attack on Seeland force the Danes to withdraw from Skåne. But Christian V., who aimed to regain what had been lost by the defeat at Lund, hurried reënforcements across the Sound as soon as the campaign opened in the spring. During the winter the Norwegian army had been increased to 17,000 men. In July Gyldenløve with a small Norwegian force captured the fortress of Marstrand, and advanced to join General Løvenhjelm, who was marching into Bohuslen with the main Norwegian army. At Uddevalla they encountered a Swedish army of 8000 men under General de la Gardie. In the battle which ensued the Swedish general was outmaneuvered, and ordered a retreat which soon turned into a disastrous flight. A great part of his force were made prisoners of war; his artillery and nineteen standards fell into the hands of the Norwegians, who gained control over the whole of Bohuslen with the exception of Bohus castle. This defeat also affected the campaign in Skåne, where the Swedes had continued to make progress. The siege of Kristianstad was raised, and Charles XI. hastened into Halland to forestall an invasion by the Norwegian forces in Bohuslen. In August of the same year a force of 2000 men from Trøndelagen under Reinhold von Hoven and Christian Schultz marched into Jæmtland, and drove out the Swedish detachments under Count Sparre. But though they were well received by their countrymen, no effort was made to take permanent possession of this old Norwegian province, as General von Hoven soon withdrew his forces in obedience to an order from the king.

At sea the united forces of the two kingdoms were very successful, and won some of the greatest victories in Danish-Norwegian naval history. In the battle of Rostock, or Møen, Admiral Nils Juel almost annihilated a Swedish squadron under Admiral Sjöblad, and on July 1 he fought the memorable naval battle of Kjøge Bay with the Swedish main fleet under Admiral Horn. The Swedes suffered an overwhelming defeat. Their admiral lost twenty ships with 700 cannons, and

3000 men were killed or captured. After the great battle many of the foreign captains who served under the great admiral were court-martialed for incompetence or negligence. Jan Peppe was dismissed, Jan Vogel escaped a worse fate by timely flight, and three others were sentenced to pay fines. But the Norwegians had served with great distinction, notably Mickel Tennissen, Morten Pedersen, Hans Schønnebøl, Thomas Seerup, and Hans Garstensen Garde.[1] These, and many other brave Norwegian officers, had learned their seamanship in Dutch and English service, and their bravery and competence to a large extent made these victories possible. The great naval wars between Holland and England had been a severe military school, in which the Norwegian sailors and sea-captains had been such apt pupils that they often surpassed their teachers in bold adventure and clever seamanship.[2]

The success gained by the Norwegian army and the fleet was, however, neutralized by new defeats inflicted on the Danish land forces in Skåne. In a fruitless attack on Malmö Christian V. sacrificed 4000 men, and after a crushing defeat at Landskrona, the plan of capturing Skåne had to be abandoned. In the next campaign confidence would chiefly be placed in the Norwegian army, which was reënforced with Danish troops, and efforts would be made to occupy new Swedish territory in Germany. Already in September, 1677, Christian V. seized the island of Rügen with an army of 6000

---

[1] Ludvig Daae, *Nordmænds Udvandringer til Holland og England i nyere Tid*, p. 25 ff.

[2] Attempts were repeatedly made to induce the Norwegian and Danish seamen in Holland to return home. Daae says: "The same attempt was repeated during the war in Skåne, and from among those who returned, the officers for the fleet were chosen."

In 1690 the higher officers in the Danish-Norwegian fleet, with the exception of admirals, schoutbynachts, and cadets, numbered sixty-seven persons. In Nils Juel's *Conduiteliste over Marinens Officerers Personale, Anno 1690* four commander-captains, three second-class captains, two third-class captains, one captain-lieutenant, and seven lieutenants, in all seventeen, are especially mentioned as Norwegians. There was possibly a similar number of Danes; the rest were foreigners. Ludvig Daae, *Nordmænds Udvandringer til Holland og England i nyere Tid*, p. 28. J. E. Sars says: "The Norwegian marines constituted throughout one-half of the total complement of men in the fleet, and even more, and it is certain that they were not the least able and respected part." *Udsigt over den norske Historie*, vol. IV., p. 113.

men, but General Königsmark defeated the Danes, and recaptured the island. Gyldenløve entered Bohuslen, and laid siege to Bohus castle. All the outer works were carried, the stronghold would have been taken, but he was so embarrassed in his operations by orders from the Danish Council of War, and by the disloyal conduct of the generals Giese and Degenfeld, who commanded the Danish auxiliary forces, that the opportunity was wasted, and when a large Swedish army under Otto Stenbock approached, he raised the siege, and retreated to Uddevalla. Hostilities continued also during the next year, but no important military event occurred. The two powers still held the same territory as before the war, but the border districts of Skåne and Bohuslen had been severely harried by the plundering soldiers, both friend and foe. The hope which Christian V. had entertained of humbling Sweden, and recovering the lost provinces, gradually but surely vanished with the breaking up of the coalition against France. The peace of Nimwegen between Holland and Louis XIV. was signed July 1, 1678, after protracted negotiations, and in January of the next year the German Emperor concluded peace with France and Sweden. Only Elector Frederick William of Brandenburg now supported Denmark-Norway against France and Sweden, and it was certain that Louis XIV. would subscribe to no terms of peace derogatory to the interests of his ally. When Brandenburg also concluded peace with France, and a French army threatened the duchies of Schleswig-Holstein, the situation became critical. But the war spirit had finally ebbed away, and peace between Denmark and France was signed at Fontainebleau, August 23, 1679, stipulating that all territory taken from Sweden should be returned, and that the terms of the peace of Roskilde should remain in force. In September, 1679, a peace between Denmark-Norway and Sweden was signed in Lund, reaffirming the conditions already established in the treaty of Fontainebleau, and providing also for a defensive alliance between the Northern kingdoms, which should remain in force for a period of ten years. The unfortunate war had ceased, but only after the three Scandinavian peoples had wasted the strength which they should have employed in peaceful development, or which they might have preserved for resisting more dangerous foreign foes.

33. Internal and Foreign Affairs in the Reign of Christian V.

In civil as in military affairs Christian V. sought to retain all power and influence in his own hands in conformity with the principles of absolutism, but he lacked the ability to develop an efficient personal rule. He hated the old nobility, as he suspected that they would use any favorable opportunity to reëstablish their former power, and after the overthrow of Griffenfeld, he was also careful lest any of his councilors should become too powerful. Among his advisers were many from the commons whom he had elevated to high positions besides the prominent men of noble birth like Ahlefeld and Gyldenløve, but no one enjoyed his full confidence. As he hated any restrictions upon his own personal influence, the Administrative Colleges were not allowed to exercise any independent activity, but in all matters the decision was to be left to the king. In military affairs he demanded an account even of the minutest details of the service, not even the purchase of necessaries for the fleet exceeding 500 riksdaler would be valid without royal sanction. In diplomacy and foreign affairs he was equally careful to centralize all influence in his own hands. After the fall of Griffenfeld his instructions to his new chancellor, Frederick Ahlefeld, were, that all communications with representatives of foreign courts, "how insignificant soever the matter may be," should bear his own signature, and that all dispatches from abroad should be placed before him without delay.[1] The creation of commissions which gradually absorbed the greater part of the duties of the Administrative Colleges was a part of the general plan to strengthen his own influence, as these commissions, which could be dissolved at any moment, would be in the highest possible degree subservient to the royal will.

King Christian had a jealous dislike for those who could win popular favor and exercise great influence. He would not only wield all power, but he could not bear any one who towered above him intellectually, a weakness not uncommon in small minds. Of Griffenfeld, the special object of his hatred, he could have said as Macbeth did of Banquo :

[1] E. Holm, *Danmark-Norges indre Historie under Enevælden*, p. 51.

> "He hath a wisdom that doth guide his valour
> To act in safety.   There is none but he
> Whose being I do fear: and under him
> My Genius is rebuk'd, as it is said
> Mark Antony's was by Cæsar."

And Griffenfeld, the only statesman who possessed sagacity enough to guide the state through this stormy period, was overthrown at a moment when his experience and insight was most indispensable.

Duke Pløen, the general who successfully conducted the campaign in Skåne, was dismissed, because the king did not like him.   Christian himself would be chief general, a position for which he was as little qualified as for that of diplomat.   Armies were destroyed, and opportunities wasted through lack of competent leadership, until Louis XIV. could dictate the terms of peace.   In matters of internal administration, his efforts to play autocrat and emulate the great French king only brings to light a lack of ability which forms a glaring contrast to his unlimited power.   During a long reign of twenty-nine years he was unable to develop a well-systematized form of administration, and we look in vain for new ideas, or an effort to create better economic and social conditions.   By the wars with Sweden, and the extravagance of the court, public burdens had been increased to an almost unbearable degree, and as the peasants were unable to pay the taxes, the government resorted to the scheme of making the larger landowners responsible for the revenues, in return for which they were exempted from taxation.   The German-born nobles, who had emigrated to Denmark in large numbers, owned a great portion of the largest estates, but they resided in Copenhagen, and their estates were managed by overseers (ridefogeds), whose business it became to extort the taxes from the peasants.   The wooden horse and other instruments of torture were invented by them, and the condition of the peasants grew even worse under the rule of the nobles.   Agriculture fell into decay, and no progress was made by the cities.   Rather than to seek to ease the people's burdens, and to further economic and social development, he would maintain old social conditions, and play guardian of his people in minor domestic affairs, where his meddlesome interference could do nought but harm. The king showed no interest for scientific research, but his solicitude for the religious and moral life of his people was of the most anxious kind. He ordered that the daily hours of devotion in the city churches should be better attended, and that in the country districts the people with their children and servants should spend some time in prayer both morning and evening. If people did not go to church, it was to be regarded as sacrilege, and by the ritual of 1685 the deacons were instructed to be present and observe who went to communion, and to write their names in a book kept for the purpose. Against luxury of all kinds the king instituted a vigorous campaign,[1] and sought to regulate in detail the people's daily life. Regulations were issued regarding funerals, describing in what sort of coffins people of the various classes should be buried, and the ceremonies to be used for each class. To give food and drink to those who carried the coffin to the grave was forbidden, likewise also the burning of candles, or excessive decorations of the house of mourning. Funeral orations could be delivered only if the deceased were persons of quality, and if the funeral took place in the evening, the oration should not last over fifteen minutes.

Still more annoying were the royal orders issued by Christian V. in 1683 regarding attire, weddings, parties, etc. In a solemn introduction the king declares that he "perceives how the extravagance in attire as well as food and drink at weddings, confinements, and parties is carried to such extremes that God thereby must be highly offended, and as one will not be inferior to the other in such matters, they waste their means until they are utterly ruined." He then proceeds to lay down rules, says Holm, as to "who are to be allowed to wear gold and silver embroidery, precious stones, lace, gold, and silver brocade, flowered velvet, rings above a certain price, etc. Only those belonging to the highest classes were numbered among these especially favored ones. There was one kind of attire; for example,

---

[1] Efforts to limit luxury had been made also in the previous century both by the kings and the clergy. The sixteenth century was especially the period of luxury-laws. France took the lead, and other nations followed her example. In thirty years, from 1545 till 1575, not less than eight statutes were issued against luxury in France. In Denmark Frederick I. began to legislate against luxury in 1528, and laws on this subject appeared at brief intervals, but usually to no purpose. See Troels Lund, *Dagligt Liv i Norden*, vol. IV., p. 130 ff.

black or plain colored velvet, which all persons of rank, as well as the nobles, might wear. Regulations were also made how *promoti doctores in theologia* and *promoti doctores* in other faculties should be attired. Those who had studied abroad, the principal royal officers who were not of 'rank,' the thirty-two members of the city council of Copenhagen, etc., were regarded as equal to these. Those who belonged to this class might wear mantels of black velvet or other suitable attire of silk, grofgrøn, tersonel, ferandin, taffeta, and other plain silks manufactured in this country, and likewise, also, all kinds of India silks which are brought hither with the Company's ships, and rings to the value of a hundred riksdaler; lynx, martin, and squirrel, and other lining of reasonable price. All others were forbidden to wear silk, nor could they wear any rings save plain gold rings. Regulations were made as to the length of the train of ladies' dresses according to rank, what ornaments they should wear, what kind of braid people should use on the uniforms of their lacqueys, what kind of carriages they should drive in, etc. A series of regulations for weddings, banquets, and childbirth parties were made to correspond. It was stipulated how everything was to be done at engagement feasts and weddings, according to people's rank, and a fixed gradation was established regarding the decorations of the bridal bed, from gold and silver fringes for privy councilors, counts, and knights, down to craftsmen and servants, who were permitted to use 'woolen cloth which can be made in this country, but without fringes, tassels, or braids.' People were in general allowed to invite twelve couples to a wedding, besides their nearest relatives, but a limit was placed on the number of meals to be served, and it was expressly forbidden to offer the guests more than eight different dishes, and no pyramids of confectionery were allowed to be placed among the victuals. Craftsmen and servants should not invite more than six couples, and they should serve a frugal meal of only four dishes. Not more than eight couples should be invited to a country wedding, and not above six ordinary dishes should be served. A general provision, which was made binding upon all, specially forbade the giving or receiving of wedding presents by any one whatsoever; but parents might give their children presents according to their means, and wedding presents might also be given to servants." [1]

---

[1] E. Holm, *Danmark-Norges indre Historie under Enevælden*, vol. I., p. 300.

But while the king sought to limit so strictly what he termed the luxury of the common people, he would not in any way curtail his own pleasures, or the excessive extravagance of the nobility. The old hunting laws were kept in force, as it was the king's chief care to preserve the game and maintain the pleasures of the chase. Whether the wild animals destroyed the people's grain fields, or the fox killed their geese and chickens was a matter about which the royal conscience felt no compunction. But such barbaric punishments were inflicted on all poachers, i.e. any one outside the privileged classes who ventured to kill a bird or animal, that it seemed a less offense to kill a human being than a deer or a partridge. Ordinary poaching was punished by flogging, branding, or life imprisonment. If a landowner who possessed the right to hunt, killed a deer on the royal hunting grounds, the fine was 1000 riksdaler, for a bird 200 riksdaler, but if the offender was a servant he would be punished by death even for shooting a snipe.

In order to carry numerous provisions of this kind into effect it was necessary also to increase and extend the police service of the kingdom. In 1682 Christian V. appointed the first chief of police in Copenhagen, and delegated to him such a multitude of duties that it would have required a whole army of police officers to attend to all. He was not only to maintain general order in the city, but all servants were placed under his special supervision, and it was his duty to punish disobedience, dishonesty, and carelessness on their part. The cleaning and lighting of the streets, the waterworks, and the fire department were also placed under his command. It was his duty to prevent strangers from staying in the city on an unlawful errand, and he should give good heed that no cheating was done with coin, weight, or measure; that the lawful prices were maintained, and that the rules for crafts and guilds were enforced. He should also watch over the Lutheran Church, so that no writings against religion, or other forbidden books were offered for sale, and that no lampoons were published; and he was especially delegated to insure the proper observance of the royal decrees regarding weddings, parties, funerals, rank, and wearing apparel. But his activity should not only extend to the city, but to the whole kingdom of Denmark. He should watch lest any unlawful trade was carried on in any city in the kingdom, that travelers were carried from place to place at the stipulated rates, that inns and taverns along the main routes were properly equipped, etc. In this way a police régime was created which possessed some good features, but which in many respects would have been intolerable if it had been in any degree efficient. The kind of administration created by Christian V. shows the king's own mental caliber, and illustrates in general the character of the seventeenth century absolutism. The government was chiefly occupied with a multitude of trifles which ought to have been intrusted to the care of local authorities, if they could not be left, as they ought to have been, to the good judgment of the private citizen. Not only was all political liberty destroyed, but the most private domestic affairs were to be controlled by royal decrees to an extent which made the state resemble a well-regulated home for orphans. Society was stratified into ever more sharply demarcated classes, based on rank, titles, and special privileges, and as no encouragement was given to individual enterprise, as small room was found within this system for originality and real ability, the government suffered in nearly all departments from a dull incompetence which made it unable to meet a crisis with resolute energy. Royal favor was looked upon as the source of promotion rather than talent and energetic individual effort. Titles, pensions, or even a smile or nod from the absolute sovereign was esteemed of more value than solid achievements in art or industry, a most serious impediment to true social progress. Some improvements might occasionally be made, but they were happy accidents rather than part of a systematically pursued plan of national development.

Among such improvements must especially be mentioned the "Code of Christian V.," a new lawbook prepared for the kingdom of Norway. The "Code of Christian IV." of 1604 which, as already stated, was but a wretched translation of the "Code of Magnus Lagabøter" (Landsloven) of 1276, had become so antiquated that it had become almost useless, and the plan of preparing a new code had been considered even by Hannibal Sehested and Jens Bjelke. Many changes had also resulted from the introduction of absolutism, and the need was more imperative than ever of bringing the laws into harmony with the new conditions. In Denmark the preparation of a new code, which had been begun in 1661, was finally completed in 1683. After some abortive attempts four Norwegians, among whom was the able and learned jurist Christian Stockfleth, were appointed to prepare a new lawbook for Norway.[1] This was indeed an important concession, as the judicial affairs of the two kingdoms would thereby remain separated, and special attention would be paid to local social environment in Norway. The work submitted by this commission was naturally based on the laws of Norway, but the king, who favored strongly a uniform system of laws for both kingdoms, subjected it to revisions which brought it into close harmony with Danish jurisprudence. But the law of *odel* and other laws governing the tenure of land in Norway were, nevertheless, retained, and in regard to hunting the Norwegian code contains few and very liberal provisions. The code was completed 1687. The following year it was put into use in Norway and the Faroe Islands and in part, also, in Iceland. In conformity with the spirit of the times it prescribed the most cruel punishments for crime. A long list of offenses was punishable by death, while maiming, banishment, and life imprisonment were frequently inflicted for no very grave crimes.[2] But the code contains some good features. It attempts especially to maintain the principle of equality before the law, and to insure a degree of personal liberty quite uncommon in those times. The code was received in Norway with general good-will, as it met a long-felt want, but much confusion was caused by the introduction of Danish laws which were not adapted to Norwegian local conditions. It must also be regarded as a distinct national loss that the old system of Norwegian jurisprudence, the codes of St. Olav and Magnus Lagabøter, had been discarded, and the Norwegian code had been based on principles largely foreign to the people.

[1] N. Prebensen og Hj. Smith, *Forarbeiderne til Kong Christian den femtes norske Lov.*

[2] "Whosoever is engaged to one and afterward marries another shall leave the king's realms and domains." *Kong Christian den femtes norske Lov* (Code of Christian V.), Christiania, 1883, book vi., ch. 13, article 23.

"Whosoever is convicted of blasphemy against God or his holy name, word, or sacrament, his tongue shall be cut from his mouth while he lives, his head shall be cut off, and together with his tongue shall be placed on a stake." *Ibid.*, book VI., ch. I., article vii.

During King Christian's reign the Norwegian army and defenses were greatly strengthened. At the outbreak of the war in Skåne, 1675, the Norwegian army numbered 12,000 men, by 1683 it had been increased to 16,300, and in 1700 it had reached a total of 21,000 men.[1]

The joint Danish-Norwegian fleet experienced an even greater development under the efficient leadership of Kort Adelaer and Nils Juel. Through purchase, as well as by the building of new ships, a relatively strong fleet was created before the outbreak of the war with Sweden, and by encouraging the Norwegian merchants to construct ships which could be converted into war vessels, a valuable auxiliary squadron of "defense ships" had been created, which was to be used for the protection of the Norwegian coast. In 1674 the fleet, together with the "defense ships," numbered sixty-three vessels, of which seventeen carried fifty guns, and forty-six were "defense ships." By 1679 the fleet had been increased to 107 vessels, of which only seventeen were "defense ships." In 1700, after some reduction had been made in the number of vessels, it still numbered thirty-three ships of the line, carrying 2778 guns. Denmark-Norway had become one of the leading naval powers.[2]

The fortresses of the kingdom were much improved, and new forts were built under the direction of Gustav Wilhelm Wedel, a German by birth, who was made commander-in-chief in Norway, 1681, during the absence of Statholder Gyldenløve. Fredriksten was strengthened by the building of new forts, and the Glommen River was made a strong line of defense through the construction of several fortresses and redoubts, a work which proved to be of great value in the next war with Sweden. Vinger was completed in 1682, Kristiansfjeld, Blakjær, and Basmo were founded the following year, and the Kongsvinger and Sponviken fortifications were also erected at this time.

In 1685 Christian V. visited Norway, and the people welcomed him on all occasions with enthusiastic loyalty. From Christiania he journeyed across the Dovre Mountains to Trondhjem, and after

---

[1] J. Chr. Berg, *Aktstykker til den staaende Hœrs Historie, Samlinger til det norske Folks Sprog og Historie*, vol. IV. Didrik Schnitler, *Det første Aarhundrede af den norske Hœrs Historie.*

[2] Edvard Holm, *Danmark-Norges indre Historie under Enevœlden*, vol. I., p. 455 ff. Robert Molesworth, *An Account of Denmark*, p. 131 ff. Oscar Alb. Johnsen, *Norges Historie*, V, 1, p. 127 ff.

visiting Bergen, Stavanger, and the towns of southern Norway, he returned home.

King Christian was neither broad-minded nor very gifted, but he was conscientious, and devoted himself with great diligence to the numerous routine duties which devolved upon him as absolute ruler. He was a lover of moderation, always kind and good-natured, and by his gentle manners he won the hearts of the people to quite an unusual degree. Molesworth speaks of him as a prince of singular ability and good nature, but adds that "he is often overruled by those about him, to whom he leaves the whole management of affairs, because he neither loves nor has a genius for business." [1] He died August 25, 1699, at the age of fifty-three.

Touching his policy of internal administration in Norway Professor Oscar Alb. Johnsen says: "He regarded Norway and his other possessions with a feeling akin to that with which a landed proprietor looks upon his estates and his subordinates. Everything existed for the benefit of himself and his family, and was to be administered in such a way that it yielded him and his family the greatest and most lasting profit. He sought to promote the interests of the bønder, because they were good taxpayers. He was interested in shipping, for without it there would be no able seamen to serve in the wars. From his diary it is clear that it was principally the more elementary features of administration which interested him, — the defenses, taxation, and economic conditions." [2]

With regard to Norway, he pursued a policy of political amalgamation with a definite aim to obliterate as far as possible the national existence of the Norwegians, and to reduce the two kingdoms to one country. This policy comes to view especially in the Norwegian code of laws, which is based almost exclusively on the laws of Denmark. He wished to introduce a uniform code for both kingdoms, and the same laws were henceforth made to apply as far as possible to both kingdoms, even when they were not adapted to Norwegian local conditions. In the administration the two countries were also treated as one estate, and the specific Norwegian interests were often ignored or neglected. Norway received no university or central administration, though an earnest desire for these very necessary im-

---

[1] *An Account of Denmark*, p. 139.   [2] *Norges Historie*, vol. V., 1, p. 130 f.

provements had long been expressed, neither did the kingdom have a bank or a capital city,[1] all features which would have tended to unite its scattered cities and separate communities into a more firmly consolidated state, and would have given a new impetus to the development of national patriotism. But the kings of the period of absolutism, like the kings during the union period from the time of Queen Margaret, wanted a strong Denmark, not a strong Norway. The kingdom united with Denmark should lose its own individuality, in the hope that it would gradually become an integral part of that realm. This short-sighted statesmanship, which was of no benefit to either kingdom, often resulted in a wanton neglect of Norway's most vital interests, and retarded, though it could not wholly arrest, the national development of the Norwegian people. The absolute kings, like their earlier predecessors in the union period, did not attempt to further the true development of either nation. Their interests were personal, dynastic, and wholly self-centered, which made their rule a monotonous routine, or a greedy desire for lands and revenues, usually barren of all good results.

In Sweden the late wars had caused great losses. The fleet had been destroyed, cities burned, and the German provinces, as well as the border districts of the kingdom, had been devastated by repeated raids. A great public debt had been created, and the burdens upon the common people were excessively heavy, while the nobles were still exempted from paying taxes. A change had also taken place in the government. Though the old forms were to all appearances maintained, the Council had been pushed into the background, and the king had begun to act with more independence than before, partly because the stress of circumstances had made it necessary, but partly also because his growing popularity enabled him to assume more direct control of the affairs of government. In order to meet as well as possible the exigencies of the situation, the Estates were assembled at Stockholm in 1680. The commons demanded that the crown-lands which had been given or sold to the nobles should be confiscated and that the royal power should be strengthened. The Council and the nobles had to yield, and the king became virtually absolute also in Sweden.

[1] J. E. Sars, *Historisk Indledning til Grundloven*, p. 78 f.

34. ECONOMIC AND SOCIAL CONDITIONS IN NORWAY IN THE SEVENTEENTH CENTURY

After the overthrow of the Hanseatic merchants, the Norwegian cities found new opportunities to develop, and they gradually assumed a character very different from the surrounding rural communities, from which they had at first been but slightly differentiated as to economic interests and mode of life.[1] The development once begun struck a rapid pace, and soon wrought an important change in the social as well as the economic life of the nation. At the assembly of the Estates in Oslo, 1591, the burghers and the *bønder* appeared for the first time as two distinct estates,[2] and this division of the commons into two separate classes with diverging social tendencies and economic interests grew even more distinct, until it developed into a social struggle of far-reaching importance.[3]

The cities had been regarded from the outset as a part of the district in which they were situated, and the rural communities had been the local units of government and religious life.[4] In course of time the new urban development inverted the order, and the cities through their growing influence and power became commercial, social, and cultural centers to which the rural districts were attached as tributary territories. The burghers were rapidly rising, and the *bønder* were correspondingly depressed in the social scale. The growth of the cities was favored, not only by an increasing commerce, but especially through privileges granted by the kings, who became their special patrons, and sought to force their development. Limited privileges had been granted the cities by various statutes from quite early times, and from 1299 the right of the rural districts to carry on trade was restricted in favor of the cities.[5] But more radical measures were taken by Christian IV., who, among other things,

[1] T. H. Aschehoug, *De norske Communers Retsforfatning før 1837*, p. 19 f.

[2] Oscar Alb. Johnsen, *De norske Stænder*, p. 112, 115 f.

[3] Halvdan Koht, *Bonde mot Borgar i nynorsk Historie, Historisk Tidsskrift*, femte række, vol. I., p. 29 ff.

[4] Absalon Taranger, *Oslos ældste Byprivilegium, Historiske Afhandlinger tilegnet J. E. Sars.* Alexander Bugge, *Studier over de norske Byers Selvstyre og Handel.* L. J. Vogt, *Historisk Tidsskrift*, anden række, vol. V., p. 80 ff., 273 ff.

[5] T. H. Aschehoug, *De norske Communers Retsforfatning før 1837*, p. 19.

issued a royal decree commanding the people of the neighboring towns to move into the new cities of Christiania and Christiansand, which he had founded.[1] Each city was to have its own fixed district, inside of which it had a trade monopoly, and all harbors within a distance of twenty-one miles should be abandoned. Christiansand was especially favored, as the kings were determined to make it a metropolis in southern Norway. The bishop's seat, the Latin school, and the *stiftsamtmand* were moved from Stavanger to Christiansand by royal decree; all the smaller towns in its neighborhood except Mandal, Arendal, Østerrisør, and Flekkefjord were abandoned, and Stavanger's city charter was revoked. In 1685 Christian V. even decreed that all inhabitants in Mandal, Arendal, Østerrisør, and Flekkefjord who did not move to Christiansand before New Year should pay a double amount of taxes. "It was manifestly the plan of the government," says Holm, "that the four *stift* cities (*i.e.* Christiania, Christiansand, Bergen, and Trondhjem) should be the trade centers of the kingdom. Bergen occupied the same privileged position in Bergens *stift* as Christiansand did in its *stift*, and farther to the north the four so-called "sjø-len" (naval districts) (*i.e.* Romsdal, Nordmør, Fosen, and Namdalen) as well as the coast along the Trondhjemsfjord belonged to the trade district of Trondhjem.[2] In the privileges granted this city March 7, 1682, it was stipulated that the inhabitants of the thriving towns of Molde and Fosen (Christiansund), who lived as burghers, should either move to Trondhjem, or build within that city in a year a home as good as the one in which they were living. The villagers and those who dwelt by the harbors in the neighborhood were also ordered to move to the city." But although towns were not allowed except at a certain distance from the chief cities, the burghers were instructed to erect trading posts at convenient places within their district, in order to facilitate trade and to enable the people to reach a market.

The government also issued regulations regarding the importation of goods and the carrying on of trade. The wares should be

[1] Edvard Holm, *Danmark-Norges indre Historie under Enevælden*, vol. I., p. 245 ff.

[2] *Ibid.*, vol. I., p. 253. I. Chr. Berg, *Ventilationer angaaende den nordlandske Handel, Samlinger til det norske Folks Sprog og Historie*, vol. V., p. 655. A. Schweigaard, *Norges Statistik*, p. 126 ff.

bought directly from the producers, or where it was most natural and convenient to obtain them. Wine should be imported from Spain and Portugal, French wines and salt from France, Rhenish wine from Holland, iron and steel from Sweden and Prussia, etc. Any one could engage in wholesale trade who could handle the required amount of goods, but the retail trade was governed in detail by a multitude of regulations aiming at the prevention of encroachment by one kind of merchants upon the other. In most cities the merchants were divided into classes having exclusive right to deal in certain specified commodities. The merchants of Trondhjem agreed to organize into fourteen classes. In Christiania a similar arrangement was made, but not in Bergen. This classification and close supervision was in harmony with the activity of the absolute government in all other lines, and coincided in general with the spirit of the cities where guilds and crafts still flourished; but it did not prevent the development of a powerful class of merchant princes, who sought to gain full control of all lucrative trade. In Christiania the complaint was made as early as 1643 that "there was not thirty solvent merchants who without debt could carry on their small trade," and in 1653 the cry was raised that "some of the rich burghers had usurped all the trade with feathers, elk skins, goatskin, butter, tallow, and caraway, by purchasing these articles in the country," and the city magistrate proposed that such purchasing in the country districts should be stopped.[1] It is natural that the more opulent merchant class, whose influence was increasing with their wealth, would not rest satisfied until they had gained control of the more important branches of trade. In 1656 and 1661 they formulated special demands for the whole burgher class of the kingdom, and as a result, a series of privileges were granted in 1662 to all Norwegian cities, which marks a new epoch in Norwegian commercial jurisprudence.[2] The two chief articles of export on which Norwegian commerce largely depended were: the fish trade in the northern and western districts, and the lumber trade in the southern and eastern districts. The lumber trade with England was rapidly increasing

---

[1] Ludvig Daae, *Det gamle Christiania*, p. 51.

[2] Halvdan Koht, *Bonde mot Borgar i nynorsk Historie, Historisk Tidsskrift*, femte række, vol. I., p. 31. Ludvig Daae, *Det gamle Christiania*, p. 55.

at this time, as Norwegian pine lumber was in great demand for ship-building. Even Milton alludes to it in his "Paradise Lost" (1658–1665), where he says:

> His spear to equal which the largest pine
> Hewn on the Norwegian hills, to be the mast
> Of some great ammiral, were but a wand.[1]

A new stimulus was given this trade by the great fire in London, September 3, 1666, which destroyed eighty-nine churches and 13,000 houses. Three hundred streets, about two-thirds of the city, were laid in ashes. Lumber for the rebuilding of the city was eagerly sought, and the greater part of it was imported from Norway. Bishop Jens Bircherod writes in his diary March 7, 1667: "I heard a captain, who had come from Norway, tell of the great profit which the inhabitants of Norway had of the great fire which occurred in London last fall, and that their timber, which was needed for the rebuilding of the city, was constantly exported in unusual large quantities, so that the people could ask as high a price as they wished to demand. For although there should at present be war between us and England, our king, nevertheless, permitted such export of timber from Norway, because of the good money which was brought to the country. And it had already become a proverb among the Norwegians that the Norsemen have warmed themselves well at the London fire." "This communication with England," says Daae, "did not cease with the rebuilding of London, but continued uninterrupted through ages, and became an important factor in the development of Norway."

By the privileges of 1662 the merchants of the cities received exclusive right to carry on lumber trade, and clergymen, *fogeds*, and judges (*sorenskriver*) were forbidden to carry on trade. This tended to concentrate the lumber trade in the cities, and to give the merchant class greater solidity and strength.[2]

In order to gain still greater advantage, the merchants demanded that the *bønder* should bring the timber to the city, where they again

---

[1] *Paradise Lost*, book I., v. 292 ff.

[2] Ludvig Daae, *Nordmænds Udvandringer til Holland og England i nyere Tid*, p. 100 ff. P. E. Bendixen, *Et Omrids av Norges Handelshistorie*, p. 23 ff.

used the opportunity to pay a very low price. In order to protect the *bønder* from this crying injustice, the king gave them permission to sell their timber to foreign buyers, if the merchants would not pay the full value, and receive it at the customary places of delivery. Later fixed prices were established, but with the proviso that the right to the lumber trade should remain with the cities and their inhabitants, and the attempts to regulate the trade were generally lame and unsuccessful.

In the northern districts the situation was still more unfavorable to the *bønder*. We have already seen how the Hanseatic merchants of Bergen had gradually reduced the small native traders, the *Nordfarer*, who brought fish from Nordland to Bergen, to a sort of commercial serfdom by keeping them continually in debt, and these conditions were not improved when the native merchants gained control. They had learned from the German merchants how to take advantage of the fishermen from Nordland, who every year brought their catch to the great central market of Bergen, where they also bought their supplies for the coming year. In Peter Dass' descriptive poem of Nordland, the "Nordlands Trompet," from about 1700, the swindle and extortion practiced by the Bergen merchants in their dealings with the fishermen of Nordland are described with great vividness, sometimes with humor, but always with characteristic sympathy for the oppressed.[1] Occasionally the king sought to put a stop to their cheating and extortion. He even reduced the amount of indebtedness of the *bønder*,[2] and sometimes even cancelled their old debts, but these attempts at regulation did not alter the general relation between the burgher class and the *bønder*.

In the early part of the seventeenth century until the loss of Bohuslen, Norway had ten chartered cities (*kjøbstæder*), ranking as follows, according to a tax levied in 1599 to pay the bridal outfit

---

[1] Halvdan Koth, *Bonde mot Borgar i nynorsk Historie*. A. E. Erichsen, *Peter Dass' Samlede Skrifter*, vol. I., p. 11 ff. Alexander Bugge, *Nordlands skiftende Skjæbne, Historisk Tidsskrift*, fjerde række, vol. V., p. 423 ff. Amund Helland, *Nordlands Amt*, p. 210 ff., *Norges Land og Folk*. Erik Hansen Schønnebøl, *Lofotens og Vesteraalens Beskrivelse, Historisk-topografiske Skrifter om Norge og norske Landsdele*, edited by Gustav Storm.

[2] I. Chr. Berg, *Ventilationer angaaende den nordlandske Handel, Samlinger til det norske Folks Sprog og Historie*, vol. V., p. 659 ff. Edvard Holm, *Danmark-Norges indre Historie under Enevælden*, vol. I., p. 168 f.

for one of the princesses: *Bergen* (250 riksdaler), *Christiania* (125), *Trondhjem* (100), *Marstrand* (100), *Fredrikstad* ($37\frac{1}{2}$), *Tunsberg* (25), *Stavanger* (25), *Kongelv* (25), *Skien* ($12\frac{1}{2}$), *Oddevald* or *Uddevalla* ($12\frac{1}{2}$). With the loss of Bohuslen in 1660 the number was reduced to seven, as Marstrand, Kongelv, and Uddevalla were located in that province; but before the close of the century the number had been increased to eleven, the new cities being: *Fredrikshald, Kragerø, Drammen,* and *Larvik.* Of the more important towns *Moss, Holmestrand, Østerrisør, Arendal, Molde, Lille-Fosen (Christiansund),* and *Trømsø* became cities in the eighteenth century.[1] The population of the cities at this time cannot be determined with any degree of accuracy. J. E. Sars has estimated that in the latter part of the seventeenth century Christiania had between 3000 and 3500 inhabitants,[2] but Ludvig Daae considers this estimate too low.[3] Roar Tank holds that the population of Christiania in 1683 was about 4000,[4] which agrees in the main with the estimate of A. Collett, who thinks that the population of the city in 1654 was about 4000.[5] The population of Fredrikstad is estimated by Tank to have been 900 in 1683.[6] According to the tax levied in 1599, Bergen would have 8000 to Christiania's 4000, and Trondhjem and Stavanger would have 3500 and 800, respectively. Oscar Alb. Johnsen estimates that before 1660 Marstrand had 1400 inhabitants, Kongelv 500, and Uddevalla less, probably about 400.[7] Skien probably had a similar number. It is clear, however, that the

[1] I. Chr. Berg, *Ventilationer angaaende den nordlandske Handel, Samlinger til det norske Folks Sprog og Historie,* vol. V., p. 613 ff. Ludvig Daae, *Bidrag til Christiansands Historie indtil 1814, Historisk Tidsskrift,* tredie række, vol. II., p. 293 ff. Molde and Lille-Fosen were chartered as cities in 1742, and Lille-Fosen was called Christiansund. In 1701 Lille-Fosen is estimated to have had 600 inhabitants. O. C. Bull, *Adskilligt om Kjøbstaden Molde, Topografisk-statistiske Samlinger udgivet av Selskabet for Norges Vel,* vol. I., p. 73 ff.

[2] *Norge under Foreningen med Danmark,* p. 99.

[3] *Det gamle Christiania,* 2d edition, p. 51.

[4] *Studier i Christiania Bys Folkemængde i det syttende Aarhundrede, Historisk Tidsskrift,* fjerde række, vol. V., p. 478 ff.

[5] *Gamle Christiania Billeder,* p. 98.

[6] *Fredrikstad 1660-1699, Historisk Tidsskrift,* fjerde række, vol. V., p. 284 ff.

[7] Oscar Alb. Johnsen, *Befolkningsforholdene i Bohuslen før Afstaaelsen, Historisk Tidsskrift,* fjerde række, vol. III., p. 247.

burgher class was rapidly growing in number, not only through the increase of the population of the old cities, but also through the rise of new ones.[1]

A danger to the independence of the *bønder*, greater than any other, was the practice of the wealthy burghers to buy land in the country districts. After they had gained control of the lucrative lumber trade, their next attempt was to get possession of the forests, and when crown-lands were sold, they were the heaviest buyers. In the latter part of the seventeenth century a number of large private estates (*proprietærgods*) were created, and the areas of land owned by the burgher class was rapidly increasing. Lorens Berg has shown that in Brunla *len* they owned fourteen per cent of the land in 1661, and eighteen per cent in 1703, while the holdings of the *bønder* did not increase.[2] At this time not above one-third of the *bønder* were freeholders, the rest were renters. A large part of the soil was owned by the crown, which had gradually acquired possession of the estates of the Catholic Church and of the old noble families who became extinct.[3] The crown finally owned about one-third of all the land in the kingdom, while the rest belonged to the noblemen, officials, burghers, and rich landowners among the *bønder*.[4] During the wars with Sweden these opulent classes had loaned money to the crown, and the kings, who were generally short of funds, hit upon the idea of paying their creditors with lands. What remained after these debts were liquidated, they sold in order to replenish their treasury. From 1660 till 1670 crown-lands were thus disposed of for the amount of 1,300,000 riksdaler, mostly to rich burghers, officials, and noblemen.[5]

---

[1] Many towns which have later become cities arose at this time along the southern coast. Fredrikshald, Moss, Soon, Drøbak, Bragernes, Holmestrand, Larvik, Brevik, Kragerø, Risør, and Arendal owe their existence to the flourishing lumber trade. A. Schweigaard, *Norges Statistik*, p. 126.

[2] Lorens Berg, *Historisk Tidsskrift*, fjerde række, vol. V., p. 202 f. *Ibid. Andabu*, p. 56, 276, 327 ff., 336 ff.

[3] Oscar Alb. Johnsen, *Fraa Leilending til Sjølveigar, Syn og Segn*, 1910, p. 349 ff. L. J. Vogt, *Om Norges Udførsel og Trælast i ældre Tider, Historisk Tidsskrift*, anden række, vol. V., p. 306 ff.

[4] Henrik Heliesen, *Udsigt over Beløbet af offentlig Jordegods i Begyndelsen af det 17de Aarhundrede, Norske Samlinger*, vol. I., p. 513 ff.

[5] Oscar Alb. Johnsen, *Fraa Leilending til Sjølveigar, Syn og Segn*, 1910, p. 281 ff.

A class of rich landowners thus sprang into existence, and the *bønder*, who were forced to rent lands from them, soon found that they were worse off under these greedy masters than they had been as tenants under the crown. In order to make their investments as profitable as possible, these landlords increased the rents, and introduced methods of oppression resembling those in vogue in Denmark, and the bitterest resentment was awakened among the Norwegian *bønder*, who understood that they were threatened with complete subjugation. Their spirit of resistance was aroused, and according to old custom they brought their complaints directly to the king. Deputations were sent to Copenhagen to ask for redress of grievances, but as the request involved the redemption of the alienated lands, the king neither would nor could grant the relief sought. Finally Statholder Gyldenløve, who foresaw that serious troubles might arise, espoused the cause of the *bønder*, and urged the king to grant them relief by curbing the greed of the landowners. "In Norway," he said on a later occasion, "the government differs so much from that of other lands that there it consists of the *bønder*, and is maintained by them." — "The prosperity of the *bønder* is the main thing, the root and basis for the preservation of the whole kingdom," [1] a statement pregnant with a fundamental truth, which had been clearly perceived by the *statholder*. So long as Griffenfeld remained in power, Gyldenløve's advice remained unheeded, as he was opposed by the powerful chancellor, but after the king assumed more direct control of affairs, he took steps to insure the Norwegian *bønder* against oppression by the landlords. In 1684–1685 regulations were published fixing the rate of rent to be charged, and limiting the amount of free service to be rendered by the peasants.[2] The farm had to be leased with all its conveniences to the leaseholder for his whole lifetime, the rent had to be stipulated by mutual contract, and fixed prices were established for the products by which the farmer paid his rent. The jurisdiction exercised by Danish landlords over their

---

[1] *Norske Samlinger*, vol. I., p. 549, *Forslag og Betænkning angaaende Lettelser for den norske Almue, Statholder Gyldenløves Forslag af 2den Januar 1693.*

[2] These laws remained in force only a short time, as they were replaced by the laws for tenants in the *Code of Christian V.*, of 1687, book III., ch. 14.

peasants was not allowed in Norway. Heavy fines were imposed on any landlord who charged excessive rents, or in any way wronged or abused the leaseholders, and the main provisions of these laws could not be abrogated even by contract. Some features of these laws were so favorable to the leaseholders that they could not be enforced at once, but they served to insure the renters fair treatment. Under these conditions the landowners found it little profitable to own extensive areas, and they sold the greater part of their holdings in smaller portions to their renters, thereby increasing the number of freeholders.

"The struggle with the landlords had in general a wholesome effect upon the renters," says Professor Johnsen. "It roused them from their slumber. Now for the first time they understood the importance of owning their own farms, and they saved money so that they could buy land. After 1680 the king again began to sell land, but what he now sold was mostly separate farms, small places, and parts of farms, and the *bønder* bought the greater share."

The laws of 1684-1685 were also intended to protect the *bønder* against extortion and injustice practiced by the royal officials. After the *lensherrer* had been replaced by *amtmænd*, who could exercise but slight control over their subordinates, who also ranked as royal officials, abuses of that sort had been increasing.[1] In order to right these wrongs the laws established fixed rates of charges for clergymen and other officials, and imposed other necessary restrictions. But as the laws were to be enforced by the selfsame officials whom they were supposed to govern, it is natural that in too many instances they were allowed to remain inoperative. The *bønder* were hard pressed both by the officials and by the burgher class. They were not only reduced to a worse situation socially and economically than in any earlier period, as the burghers and officials gradually intrenched themselves in a position of power such as no class outside of the old nobility had hitherto enjoyed, but they were also forced into the background politically, after absolutism had eliminated all partici-

---

[1] T. H. Aschehoug, *Aktstykker om Finmarken i Aaret 1667, Norske Samlinger*, vol. I., p. 120 ff. L. Daae, *Fem Dokumenter til Oplysning om Avgifternes Beløb i det syttende Aarhundrede, Samlinger til det norske Folks Sprog og Historie*, vol. V., p. 485 ff. These documents consist of supplications and complaints of the people of various districts in the kingdom.

pation of the people in affairs of administration and government. But the *bønder* had awakened to the realization of the situation, and a determined struggle began, which constantly increased in bitterness.[1] Scattered uprisings grew more frequent, able popular leaders appeared in various districts, and the growing social conflict stirred the people's love of their rights and liberties, not to a momentary enthusiasm, but into a permanent attitude of mind, which was destined to shape all future national development in Norway. This school of adversity made the Norwegian *bønder* vigilant patriots, and their national independence was cradled in these bitter local struggles against oppression and injustice which were waged with ever increasing intensity, especially throughout the eighteenth century.

The struggle between the *bønder* and the new upper classes was aggravated, also, by the fact that the burghers, as well as the officials, consisted largely of foreigners, who came to Norway to seek new opportunities. They felt in no direct touch with the common people, and treated them with an offensive haughtiness, and not infrequently with an insolent arrogance which engendered the most innate class hatred. J. E. Sars says: "The Norwegian burgher class, which arose under the union with Denmark, was to a large extent of foreign origin. Danes, and still more frequently Germans and merchants from Schleswig-Holstein, moved to the Norwegian cities, and because of their good connections they were often able to play a leading rôle. Danish had become the spoken language in the cities after the Reformation, and thereby the burgher class, whether they were foreigners or native-born, became separated from the rest of society by a deep chasm, so that they stood over against the rest of the people as half foreigners.

"The same was true, even in a higher degree, of the official class. In the period immediately following the Reformation the lack of higher schools in Norway, and the generally neglected and benumbed intellectual conditions, resulted in the frequent appointments of Danes to office in the kingdom. Afterwards when Norway was better able to shift for herself in this respect, it continued to be a general practice to give the Norwegian offices to Danes, while Nor-

[1] *Nedenes Lens Opsætsighed mod Øvrigheden 1658–1659, Norske Samlinger,* vol. II., p. 81.

wegians were frequently appointed to office in Denmark. The government had a fixed purpose, which was constantly becoming more clearly defined, of commingling as far as possible the two peoples so that they might learn to feel as one. At every period of the union with Denmark the Norwegian official class was, therefore, strongly mixed with Danish elements, especially in the higher and leading circles. Of the Norwegian members of this class, as well as the Danish, it was true that they had studied at the University of Copenhagen; that they had spent their happiest and most important years in the Danish capital, and had often formed friendships there which lasted through their whole lifetime. The higher they rose intellectually, the stronger they must have felt attracted by the memories of their youth spent among friends, both Danes and Norwegians, in study and in the intellectual pastime of the clubs, while they must have felt almost as strangers, as exiles, when they became established at home as officials in the lonely country districts, or in a small Norwegian town, where the people's minds were occupied with freight rates and lumber prices." [1]

The new classes were, nevertheless, of great importance to the future development of the Norwegian people. They gradually came to represent the economic strength of the nation, and as they established close relations with the outside world, not only commercially but also intellectually, they were in position to transplant to Norwegian soil new ideas from abroad, elements of higher culture, intellectual interests, and taste for art and elegance which had an elevating and stimulating influence on the otherwise so democratic Norwegian society. After a generation or two those who were of foreign descent learned to feel as native-born citizens, and were ready to bear their full share in defending the kingdom, and in building its institutions; but the social conditions which have been outlined made them unable to deal justly with the bønder, nor were they able to realize what secret strength lay hidden in the ardent love of freedom and the unsubdued will of the common people.

The commercial activity was chiefly controlled by three principal cities: Bergen, Trondhjem, and Christiania. Bergen especially had developed a considerable commerce and a strong class of merchants,

[1] J. E. Sars, *Historisk Indledning til Grundloven*, p. 88 f.

who maintained trade with all western countries of Europe. They even ventured into the Mediterranean Sea in spite of the Barbary pirates, and attempts were made to carry on trade with the West Indies, Greenland, America, and the west coast of Africa. Trondhjem retained the right to trade in the four "sjølen," Namdalen, Fosen, Nordmør, and Romsdal, but the trade with Nordland was open to the merchants of both cities. Bergen received the trade monopoly and the control of the local administration in Finmarken, but this great power was so abused by the Bergen merchants that after six years of systematic extortion an *amtmand* was again appointed for the province.[1]

In the southern towns and cities the lumber trade was growing rapidly. In the last decade of the seventeenth century, when England and Holland were carrying on war with France, the commerce of these powers decreased, and Norwegian trade received an impetus which marks a new epoch in the development of Norway's merchant marine. The trade with France increased steadily, as the Norwegian articles of export, tar, lumber, masts, iron, and fish,[2] were in great demand. England and Holland sought to stop this trade, but in 1691 the Northern kingdoms formed an alliance in defense of neutral trade, and both powers had to abandon their attempts at interference with the trade of neutral nations. Home industry was encouraged through protective tariff or the exclusion of foreign wares, and the high duties placed on goods imported in foreign vessels also favored Norwegian trade. Christiania had a fleet of twenty-three merchant vessels in 1696. Bergen's merchant fleet rose from forty-six ships in 1680 to 146 in 1690, and similar progress was made by other cities and towns. In 1707 the Norwegian merchant marine numbered 568 ships,[3] a remarkable increase from fifty merchant vessels in 1648. Also in the fisheries considerable progress is noticeable in this

[1] Amtmand Frederik Schort of Finmarken wrote in 1667 that besides the profit made in selling the fish, the Bergen merchants made $33\frac{1}{3}$ per cent in buying it from the *bønder;* that they also cheated them on the weight, and that for these reasons the *bønder* could not pay their taxes. *Aktsykker om Finmarken, Norske Samlinger*, vol. I., p. 120.

[2] Robert Molesworth, *An Account of Denmark as It Was in 1692*, p. 63. B. E. Bendixen, *Et Omrids af Norges Handelshistorie*, p. 23 ff.

[3] Oscar Alb. Johnsen, *Norges Historie*, vol. V., 1, p. 106. A. Schweigaard *Norges Statistik*, p. 127 f.

period. The catching of ling and halibut on the Storeggen banks, about a hundred and ten miles from the coast, was begun at this time, the gill net and other implements for the cod-fisheries were invented, and the export of lobster, especially to Holland, was begun. The whale-fisheries near the coast of Greenland and Iceland were encouraged, and stations for the manufacture of train-oil were built. The commerce with the East Indies, which had long been interrupted, was again revived through the organization of a new East India Company, and a West India Company was also organized.

Industry was making slow progress for want of the necessary capital and experience, but some attempts were made which show a growing spirit of enterprise, and the influx of new ideas. Jørgen thor Møhlen of Bergen was especially active in originating new industrial enterprises in his home city. In 1684 he was also instrumental in founding the Bergen chamber of commerce. He erected rope, salt, soap, and train-oil factories in Bergen and neighborhood, canvas and woolen mills, tanneries and cooper shops, powder mills, and nail factories. He managed the trade with Finmarken and Greenland, and carried on commerce with Guinea and the West Indies. These attempts were in complete harmony with the mercantile economic ideas of the times, and he was generously encouraged by the government in the hope that factories might soon be erected in different cities to supply the demand for manufactured articles. But Møhlen engaged in too hazardous ventures. Before the end of the century he was financially ruined, and the enterprises which he established soon proved unsuccessful. Some lasting progress was, nevertheless, made. About 1700 the first oil mill was built in Norway, and about the same time the first paper mill was also erected. This marks the beginning of the paper industry, which was destined in time to become one of the best paying branches of Norwegian manufacture. In full accord with the mercantile spirit was also the encouragement of mining, as well as the restrictions placed upon the number of sawmills in the interest of the preservation of the forests. These restrictions would, naturally, tend to eliminate the small producers. Lumbering became a monopoly controlled by rich dealers and mill owners, who grew to be a class of capitalists.[1]

[1] A. Schweigaard, *Norges Statistik*, p. 118 ff. Oscar Alb. Johnsen, *Norges Historie*, vol. V., 1, p. 117 ff.

35. NORWEGIAN LITERATURE IN THE SEVENTEENTH CENTURY

The seventeenth century or, more correctly, the period from 1620 till 1720 was a century of lifeless formalism and unproductive learned pedantry in Norwegian literature as well as in that of many other countries of Europe. In Germany the literary and intellectual life which had begun to flourish at the beginning of the century was crushed by the ravages of the Thirty Years' War, and poetry became the servantmaid of Latin learning and Protestant theology. German had, indeed, replaced Latin as the literary language, but Latin learning and classical mythology still constituted the chief contents of most of the poetry written. The pedantic metric laws formulated by Martin Opitz had gained an absolute authority,[1] which checked all development of verse and meter, and the poets imitated, as well as they could, the empty bombast of the Italian poet Marino, and the hollow pathos of the Frenchman Ronsard, and the French tragedy, fostered in the atmosphere of the court of Louis XIV. A fine literature of hymns and religious songs was produced by poets like Spee, Scheffler, Gerhardt, Tersteegen, Rist, Dach, and others. Religious prose writers like Arnd, Spener, and Scriver wrote works which have exercised a lasting influence upon religious life and thought also in the North, but the secular poetry consisted largely of songs for birthday parties, weddings, funerals, or in congratulation of princes and persons of wealth and quality, whose favor was sought through the most servile flattery. At the same time the poet considered it essential to make a boastful display of his own learning through frequent classic allusions, the use of mythological elements, and phrases and expressions borrowed from classic authors. The drama was represented by traveling companies of entertainers who adopted to their own use selections from Italian, French, Spanish, Dutch, English, and Latin writers.

In the North the German literature exercised a great influence, and in Sweden, especially, Martin Opitz was accepted as the great pattern and authority. In Norway local conditions did not favor a systematic adherence to foreign patterns, but German influence made itself felt both directly and indirectly, and the literary taste

[1] Martin Opitz, *Buch von der deutschen Poeterey*, 1624.

and spirit of the age gained full control. In 1664 sixteen German comedians came to Bergen and acted almost daily near the custom-house, "and the students of the cathedral school played 'heathen histories' in the New Church." [1] During Lent mysteries and miracle plays were also presented in the churches. But the German literary influence was principally exerted indirectly through Denmark, where the Norwegian students received their higher school training at the University of Copenhagen, and where German intellectual culture had made a profound impression, especially after the introduction of the Reformation. We find, accordingly, also in Norwegian litera-ture of this period the customary varieties of poetic productions — didactic poems, lamentations, religious poems, songs for various occasions, and rhymed descriptions of different parts of the king-dom, much of it almost wholly devoid of poetic merit. By contem-poraries this kind of poetry must have been received with favor, possibly even with generous praise, but the interest which it awakened was transient, and a literary historian has aptly characterized it as "the forgotten literature," [2] as most of it has long since been rele-gated to oblivion. Few really gifted poets graced literature at this time. Most of those who devoted themselves to poetic production were mere rhymers, who might weave their couplets deftly enough into light verses for a festive occasion, or who, with infinite patience, tortured their muse in the vain effort to produce a great epic on a subject which could better be dealt with in a prose treatise; but in most of these efforts we discover the author's erroneous idea that poetry is the art of making rhyme according to an acknowledged system of metric rules.

But the "forgotten literature" of the seventeenth century repre-sents the first faltering steps in modern poesy, aside from the popular ballads and folk-tales, and it is not without its interest and value to the modern student who would understand the intellectual culture and social life of this period.

The first poet of this period, and, in a sense, the originator of this class of poetry in Norway, was, characteristically enough, a Dane,

---

[1] L. Dietrichson, *Omrids af den norske Poesis Historie*, p. 58.

[2] *Ibid.*, p. 51 ff. Peter Friedrich Suhm, *Samlede Skrifter*, part VII., *Om de Norskes Fortjenester i Henseende til Videnskaberne.*

Anders Christensen Arrebo (1587–1637), a gifted and dashing young scholar, a favorite of King Christian IV., who had been made Bishop of Trondhjem, and according to J. H. Schlegel "deserves to be compared with his contemporary Opitz." [1] Arrebo could not at the outset have been influenced by Opitz, as his "Kong Davids Psalter," a paraphrase of the Psalms of David, was completed in 1623, a year before the "Buch von der deutschen Poeterey" was published, but Rørdam says that "it is clear enough that Opitz' useful effort to purify his countrymen's taste and their poetic style has exerted a beneficial influence upon him towards the close of his career." [2] The socially inclined bishop with the poetic temperament mixed with unrestrained mirth in the frolicsome merry-makings which in those days were the chief features of weddings and social gatherings. He was guilty of no moral wrongdoing, but his powerful enemies Tage Thott, royal *lensmand* of Trondhjem, and Peder Lauritsen, the city *foged*, found an opportunity to accuse him of conduct unbecoming a bishop, and he was dismissed from his high office, 1622. After a few years he became clergyman in Vordingborg in Denmark, where he died in 1637, fifty years of age. The disgrace and sorrow which had thus darkened Arrebo's life brought his poetic gifts to full maturity. He completed his paraphrase of the Psalms of David in 1623, and after 1629 he was persuaded to undertake a translation of Guillaume Barat's epic poem "La première Sepmaine." Arrebo did not translate the poem, but gave a free elaboration of its theme and thoughts in his "Hexaëmeron," a poem about the creation, in Alexandrine verse, which became very popular, and continued to be held in high esteem even in the following century. The poem was not published till twenty-four years after the author's death, but it gained for him a great reputation, especially among younger contemporaries.

Through Arrebo's works, especially his paraphrase of the Psalms, which was first published, a great stimulus was given to poetry. He found many imitators in Denmark, and in Norway numerous versifiers appeared. Michel Mogenssøn (1590–1654), clergyman at Nærø

---

[1] J. H. Schlegel's *Werke*, vol. V., p. 267.

[2] Holger Fr. Rørdam, *Anders Christensen Arrebos Levnet og Skrifter*, part I., p. 244.

in Namdalen, wrote a lamentation over a storm which caused great loss of lives and property along the seacoast,[1] and poems of that type continued to grow in number. Hans Mortensen Maschius, engraver and clergyman at Jølster, has left an engraving of the Trondhjem cathedral, to which he has added a poem lamenting the ruin of the great church.[2] Claus Hansen Gantzius, or Gaas, clergyman at Ulvsteen in Søndmør, wrote a lamentation about a great avalanche,[3] and Dorothea Engelbrechtsdatter of Bergen wrote poems about the great fire in that city.

Samuel Bugge (1605–1663), and Roland Knudson, city *foged* in Kragerø, wrote didactic poems, and religious songs were written, especially by Samuel Olsen Bruun [4] and Dorothea Engelbrechtsdatter [5] (1635–1716). By contemporaries Dorothea was lauded in the most extravagant terms. She was called the tenth muse, the wonder of the North, etc., but her productions are mostly dull and trivial rhymes expressing a fervent religious feeling, but lacking the qualities of great art. Only a few songs, or, rather, fragments of songs, in which she has succeeded in striking deep and true chords of religious sentiment, still continue to be numbered among the cherished Lutheran hymns. Dorothea Engelbrechtsdatter was the daughter of a Bergen clergyman. At the age of seventeen she married her father's successor, Ambrosius Hardenbech, with whom she became the mother of nine children. But she experienced many sorrows, as she survived her husband and all her children. She died at Bergen in 1716, eighty-one years of age.

The barren monotony of the seventeenth century as to literary

---

[1] *Threnologia Numdalensis eller Numdal, Tenck derpaa. Det er et sørgeligt Klagemaal om den store Haffsnød oc Søskade i Numdals Len udi Throndhjems Stift,* Copenhagen, 1627.

[2] *Norwegia religiosa eller Norrig gudelig tildreven beseer og beklager sin Herrens Huus,* Christiania, 1661.

[3] *En Klage Dicht offuer det Tilfald i Bergenshuus Lehn paa Sundmøer d. 6 Februar, 1679,* Copenhagen, 1681.

[4] Samuel Olsen Bruun, *Siungende Tidsfordriv eller Korsets Frugt,* 1695. The work appeared in many new editions in Copenhagen.

[5] Dorothea Engelbrechtsdatter, *Sjælens Sangoffer,* 1678; *Taareoffer for bodfærdige Syndere,* 1685, together with a new edition of *Sjælens Sangoffer; Et christeligt Valet fra Verden og Længsel efter Himmelen,* 1698, united with the two first works in a new edition, 1699. See Nordahl Rolfsen, *Norske Digtere,* and Henrik Jæger, *Norsk Literaturhistorie,* vol. I., p. 204 ff.

life is, nevertheless, relieved by one distinguished name, Petter Dass, the first truly great poet in modern Norwegian literature. His father, Peter Dundas, fled from Scotland to Norway during the religious persecutions in the time of Charles I., and settled in Bergen, where he became a merchant. After his marriage to Maren Falch, a daughter of the *foged* Peter Falch in Helgeland, he moved to his father-in-law in Nord-Herø, where his son Petter Dass was born in 1647. Petter attended the Latin school at Bergen, and in 1665 he entered the University of Copenhagen. His father died, and as his mother was left with five children in straitened circumstances, he could continue his studies only two years, whereupon he received holy orders, and after serving for sixteen years as curate, he was appointed rector of the church of Alstahaug in Nordland in 1689.[1] His whole life work both as rector and poet is inseparably connected with this part of the country. He was a born leader, a man of unique talents, who through his powerful personality and amiable traits of character became, not only the favorite poet, but the personified ideal of the people of Nordland. He was a dignified and earnest rector, strong in faith, firm in convictions, unbending in authority, and exercised a powerful influence as spiritual adviser and moral teacher. He was also an eminently capable man in all practical affairs, to whom the people could always turn for advice. The impression became general among his parishioners that he could control even the powers of evil, and numerous tales were told of his struggles with the devil, in which he was always victorious. The custom still prevalent among the Nordland fishermen of fastening pieces of black cloth to their sails as a token that they mourn the loss of Petter Dass shows to what extent he had become the hero of the common people.[2] As rector of the largest parish in Norway, an extensive region which at present embraces eight parishes with over 30,000 inhabitants, he had many assistants and was in fact a real

---

[1] His biography has been written by his grandson, Albert Dass, in the introduction to his edition of the *Nordlands Trompet*, Copenhagen, 1763.

[2] Petter Dass, *Samlede Skrifter*, edited by A. E. Erichsen, introduction, p. i-lxxv. J. S. Welhaven, *Digteren fra Alstahaug, Petter Dass; Samlede Skrifter*, vol. VI., p. 109 ff. Dr. A. Chr. Bang, *Kirkehistoriske Smaastykker*, p. 232 ff. L. Dietrichson, *Den norske Poesis Historie*, p. 76 ff. Henrik Jæger, *Norsk Literaturhistorie*, vol. I., p. 240 ff.

chieftain. But in this large district, where all travel had to be done by boat among the shoals and breakers of a storm-swept seacoast, he had to lead a life full of hardships and hazards which taxed his strength and courage to the utmost, and he refers to it ironically by saying that "the clergymen of Nordland do not dance on violets and roses." He was always of good cheer, social and full of sparkling humor, but the constant struggles with the angry sea he describes in many places with touching pathos and powerful realism. He shows how the fishermen sail through the roaring breakers until their boats are upset, the usually unsuccessful attempts to ride the upturned boat to safety, how the people gather on the shore where the empty boats have stranded, and count the knives which their dying fathers, husbands, and brothers have plunged into the upturned boat to learn how many have found a grave on the stormy deep. So clearly and truthfully are the social conditions, the environment, life, and character of the people of Nordland reflected in the poetry of Petter Dass, that it becomes true of him in a very special sense that he who wishes to understand the poet must know the land which fostered him. But the converse is no less true, that he who wishes to become acquainted with Nordland and its people as they were in the seventeenth century must study Petter Dass.[1]

His pastoral duties and the religious instruction of his parishioners were always his chief care, and he wrote several collections of religious songs in order to give the Christian doctrines a pleasing and striking form.[2] The most popular of these works are his "Katekismus Sange," i.e. Luther's Catechism turned into songs, which have remained the cherished reading of the common people. But his principal work, and the one on which his reputation as a poet chiefly rests, is the "Nordlands Trompet," which retains its place

---

[1] Bjørnstjerne Bjørnson wrote after a visit in Nordland: "Every traveler in Nordland must own the 'Nordlands Trompet,' but it should not be read until one is on the return voyage, and knows how incomparably true it is." Petter Dass, Samlede Skrifter, edited by A. E. Erichsen, introduction, p. LV.

[2] His principal works of this kind are: Aandelig Tidsfordriv eller bibelsk Vise-Bog; Dr. Morten Luthers lille Katekismus forfattet i bekvemme Sange under føielige Melodier; Epistler og Evangelier sangvis forfattet udi bekvemme Melodier; Trende bibelske Bøger, nemlig Ruth, Ester, og Judith, udi dansk Rim forfattet.

among the classic productions in Norwegian literature. Although it is a description of Nordland and its people which pictures with the minuteness of a geography the nature and the climate, the economic and social conditions of the people, it is written with a taste and skill which makes it a true work of art. "It is a book more popular than any other secular work in our literature," writes A. E. Erichsen; and Just Bing says that "the people's life and work has fascinated Petter Dass, and his description of nature turns into a picturing of the life of the people. It would be futile to attempt to distinguish between nature and the people in his works, as he has viewed them together, not apart. Yes, it is when nature bears a direct relation to human life that it becomes interesting, according to his opinion, and their point of contact is, so to speak, the basis of operation in his nature-description. At the point where nature begins to influence the lives and deeds of man, Petter Dass dwells upon natural phenomena, and the reader gets the full impression of the great might of nature, its activity and power. At this point, also, the reader's imagination forms a clear picture. It is not the description of nature itself which makes us shudder, however strong expressions the author might use, — but when we hear how the storm has caused death and sorrow in many families; when we see that all human power, as compared with the storm, is a mere nullity which is swept away; when we see men's vain efforts to save their lives, how they strive convulsively to gain the bottom of the upturned boat, to cling fast to it, and that the waves, nevertheless, carry them away; when we see corpses and wreckage drifting in the sea, the picture becomes powerful. We feel the great might of the elements, we see them overwhelm men irresistibly, destroying the happiness of one generation after the other. In other words, the description of nature becomes impressive when we see the power of nature pictured in its effect upon the inhabitants of the country." [1] Some of Petter Dass' minor poems have become favorite folk-songs; as, "Norsk Dalevise" and "Jephtæ Løfte." [2]

Of other poets who flourished towards the end of the period may be mentioned especially Povel Juul, an eccentric person of real

[1] Just Bing, *Norske Digte og Digtere*, p. 154 ff.
[2] J. S. Welhaven, *Samlede Skrifter*, vol. VI., p. 147 ff.

poetic talent, who wrote "Et lyksaligt Liv" and "En god Bonde og hans Gjerning"; and Ole Camstrup, who became known as the writer of humorous verses for various festive occasions. His most typical poem is a song written in the Norwegian dialect about a wedding. This song was later imitated very successfully by Nils Heyberg in the very popular ditty, "Bonden i Bryllaupsgarden," written in 1734.[1]

Norse history, literature, and runic inscriptions were diligently studied by the Danish scholar Ole Wormius, who in 1643 published his "Monumenta Danica," a large work on the runic inscriptions. In his study of old Norse literature he was ably assisted by Bishop Brynjulf Sveinsson of Skálholt, and the learned Icelander Arngrim Jónsson, "the Restorer of Icelandic Literature." In Sweden Olof Verelius (1618–1682), and Olof Rudbeck, the author of "Atlantica s. Manheim Japheti Sedes et Patria," were emphasizing with one-sided enthusiasm the importance of the Scandinavian countries in history. This revival of interest in Northern studies led to the creation of a new historical school in the North, whose most prominent members were the Icelanders Arni Magnusson, the originator of the great collection of Icelandic manuscripts which bears his name, and Thormod Torfæus, the most distinguished name in the prose literature of this period. In 1662 Torfæus was sent by Frederick III. to Iceland to collect manuscripts, a work in which he was very successful. In 1682 he was made royal historiographer, and in 1711 he published his large and in many respects important work "Historia Rerum Norwegicarum," a history of Norway from the earliest times till 1387. The Dane Arnoldus de Fine also undertook to write a history of Norway in Latin, but left the work unfinished. Of great value to modern scholars are the historical typographical writings and shorter annals of this period, works which were left unpublished at the time, but which of late years have been edited and published in the interest of historical research. Edvard Edvardssøn, conrector of the Bergen Latin school, wrote an elaborate history and description of the city of Bergen.[2] Melchior Augustinussøn wrote annals of Trondhjem and Trøndelagen, 1670–1705, and Hans Lillienskjold (1703) wrote a

[1] L. Dietrichson, *Den norske Poesis Historie*, p. 95 f.
[2] *Norske Samlinger*, vol. I., *Uddrag af Edvardssøns Bergens Beskrivelse*.

large and still unpublished work "Speculum Boreale" an historical-geographical description of Finmarken. Gert Henriksen Miltzow is the author of several local personal-historical works dealing with Bergens *stift*, but most of his writings have been lost; and Diderich Brinch in Nordland published in 1683 "Discriptio Lacefodæ Norwegia." Hans Noble's "Indberetning til Kongen om Forholdene i 1716," "Aktstykker om Finmarken 1667," by Frederik Schort, and Johan Vilhelm Klüver's "Beretning om den Norske Hærs Indfald i Sverige 1719" may be classified as public documents.[1] An extensive religious prose literature was also produced, consisting chiefly of sermons and devotional books. Among the common people the folk-poesy continued to flourish, and throughout this dull period it maintained an untutored literary life, and fostered the true instinct for poetic art, which formed a healthful contrast to the pedantic rules and lifeless learning of the age.

As true poesy in this period is chiefly to be sought in the folk-literature of the common people, so art was still found mainly as handicrafts among the *bønder*, who from very early ages had been skilled wood carvers, goldsmiths, etc. Fine embroidery, and especially the weaving of fine tapestry, which had been the pride and pastime of ladies of rank in early ages, was at this time, and still continues to be, a highly developed art in Norway. The carving of wood and ivory was brought to a state of perfection which has never been excelled in the North. Even country lads, using no other tools than their knife, were able to produce real pieces of art, which are still preserved as treasures in the art museums. The most noted name in this field is that of Magnus Berg of Gudbrandsdal (1666–1739), of whose wonderful carvings in ivory thirty-eight pieces are still preserved in Rosenborg palace in Copenhagen. Nearly every district had its own adepts in the various arts and handicrafts, who wrought with rare genius such works of beauty and imagination that many a trained artist would find difficulty in imitating them.[2]

---

[1] *Norske Samlinger*, vol. I., p. 121 ff., 136 ff., 176 ff., and 153 ff.

[2] See Kristofer Visted, *Vor gamle Bondekultur*, Christiania. O. A. Øverland, *Norges Historie*, vol. VIII., p. 113 ff. Erik Pontoppidan, *Det første Forsøg paa Norges naturlige Historie*, vol. II., p. 392 ff. L. Dietrichson, *Den norske Elfenbensskjærer Magnus Berg*, Christiania, 1912.

36. EDUCATION AND THE CHURCH

Norway had no university, but secondary or Latin schools were found in nearly all the principal cities in the kingdom. The main stress was laid on the study of Latin, which the pupils should learn to read, write, and speak; but Greek was also read, and in the highest class Hebrew, logic, metaphysics, and rhetoric were studied. Much time was devoted to devotional exercises and singing, but mathematics and history were almost wholly neglected, and until 1668 no schoolbook existed in the mother tongue,[1] and no attention was paid to it. The discipline was very severe. Corporal punishment was often inflicted, and fines were imposed on the scholars for various offenses. This bred a rude and insolent spirit in the pupils, and the school became the scene of constant jarrings between scholar and schoolmaster, who regarded each other as hostile forces. Ludvig Holberg says with the characteristic exaggeration of the humorist: "Every schoolmaster was at that time a sovereign, and the pupils lived in profound awe. Their lacerated backs, their swollen foreheads, their bruised cheeks proclaimed that every school was like a Lacedemonian gymnasium." At the head of the school stood the rector, who was assisted by the conrector. According to royal decree of March 17, 1675, no one could become rector or instructor unless he had received the degree of *baccalaureus artium*.[2] It has already been stated that one-fourth of the tithes, the *bondelut*, was used for the support of poor students, but at a meeting in Skien,

[1] Erik Eriksson Pontoppidan, Bishop of Trondhjem, 1673–1678, wrote *Grammatica Danica* in Danish, 1668. Nyerup og Kraft, *Literatur-Leksikon*. Andreas Faye, *Christiansands Stifts Bispe- og Stiftshistorie*, p. 266. R. Nyerup, *Tilstanden i Danmark og Norge i ældre og nyere Tider*, vol. III. The church ordinances of 1537 made the provision that there should be one Latin school in each city, and that all other primary schools should be closed. Only Latin should be taught, "as the Latin schools are easily spoiled by the Danish and German schools, since those who have founded these schools have looked more to their own profit than to the welfare of the children." See W. Rein, *Encyklopädisches Handbuch der Pädagogik*, Langensalza, 1903, vol. I., p. 933 ff., *Deutsches Schulwesen*. A. V. Heffermehl, *Folkeundervisningen i Norge indtil omkring 1700*, Christiania, 1913.

[2] Ludvig Holberg, *Bergens Beskrivelse*, p. 194 ff. E. Holm, *Danmark-Norges indre Historie under Enevælden*, vol. I., p. 384 ff. A. Faye, *Christiansands Stifts Bispe- og Stiftshistorie*, p. 265.

PLATE VI

WOODCARVING ON AN OLD
CHURCH DOOR IN SOGN.

WOODCARVING ON AN OLD CHURCH
PORTAL AT HURUM.

1575, of the nobles, bishops, *lagmænd*, and leading *bønder* it was decided that a *spand* [1] of grain should be paid for each *mandsverk* [2] for the maintenance of the school, while the *bondelut* should be kept by the *bønder* for the support of the poor. This was ratified by royal decree of 1578, but the *bønder* were often unwilling to pay the school tax, and it could not always be collected.

The Reformation brought no marked improvement in primary education, as the reformers both in Norway and Denmark were chiefly concerned with the education of ministers for the Lutheran Church. No public schools were organized, and the education of the common people was so far neglected that not above one-tenth could read and write.[3] Some provision was, nevertheless, made for the religious instruction of the people. Bishop Palladius of Seeland says in his "Visitatsbog": "The congregation has two servants, one especially for the older, and the other for the younger church. As the clergyman teaches and instructs the old, so the sexton should teach the young. When he has rung the church bell for the first time on Sunday, then he shall strike the bell fifteen or sixteen times as a signal to the children. The young people shall come to church and seat themselves on the first benches, and the sexton shall stand in the midst of them, and instruct them with pleasure and kindness according to a sexton's book published in Copenhagen, and he shall also teach them religious songs. But to those who do not dwell in a church village, the sexton shall come at least once a month, when the sun shines brightly, and the children can be out of doors. He shall encourage the parents to send their children to the sexton, but if they will not come, they shall then be forced with the whip to do so." This system of religious teaching, which was the same both in Norway and Denmark, must be regarded as the first attempt at systematic public instruction, the germ of the common schools. As an aid to ministers and sextons in instructing the children, Bishop

---

[1] *Spand* = en sjællandsk skjeppe (Faye, *ibid.*, p. 174) = 17.372 liter, or about half a bushel. J. Brynildsen, *Norsk- engelsk Ordbog*.

[2] *Mandsverk*, a certain area of land. *Norges gamle Love*, anden række, vol. I., *Ord og Sagregister* by Oscar Alb. Johnsen. Daniel Thrap, *Bergenske Kirkeforholde i det 17de Aarhundrede*, p. 101 ff.

[3] W. Rein, *Encyklopädisches Handbuch der Pädagogik*, vol. VI., p. 287 ff. A. V. Heffermehl, *Folkeundervisningen i Norge indtil omkring 1700*, 1913.

Palladius published a translation of Luther's Catechism, 1538, to which he added, in 1542, "Brevis Expositio Catechismi pro Parochis Norwegiæ," a work which was translated into Danish in 1546. But as the majority of the people could not read, and as they had difficulty in understanding the Danish language, they could not derive much direct benefit even from books of this kind.[1] The great disadvantage of the prevailing illiteracy was keenly felt, especially by the clergy, and in the preliminary drafts of the church ordinance issued by Christian IV. the desire was expressed that the people in the larger towns should keep a school teacher, that they should build a schoolhouse, and that the more well-to-do citizens should make donations for this purpose. It is clear that there was a growing demand for popular education, and that some attempts were made to provide for the instruction of the common people, but because of frequent wars and oppressive taxes, slight progress was made in the seventeenth century.

Through the introduction of absolutism changes had also to be made in the laws and ritual of the church. In 1685 a new ritual was published, which was introduced in Norway in 1688, and about the same time the Danish-Norwegian Church also received a new hymnbook, published by the great psalmist Thomas Kingo, Bishop of Fyen. In Catholic times, and even after the introduction of the Reformation, the old Latin hymns were sung in the churches, but Hans Thomissøn's "Danske Salmebog" of 1569 had gradually come into general use, and so many additions had been made to it that it was deemed necessary to get a new hymnbook. Thomas Kingo was commissioned by the king to edit one. The first part of Kingo's hymnbook appeared in 1689, but the book was not authorized for general use till in 1699.

The bishops and many other ecclesiastics were men of learning and high character, who wrote collections of eloquent sermons, devotional books,[2] hymns and religious songs, and who labored earnestly

---

[1] A. Faye, *Christiansands Stifts Bispe- og Stiftshistorie*, p. 138.

[2] Bishop Jørgen Erichsson of Stavanger published in 1592 a collection of sermons, "Jonae Prophetes skjønne Historia udi 24 Prædigener begreben," about which A. Faye says: "This collection of sermons is not only the most remarkable religious work written in Norway in the century of the Reformation, but it is one of the best collections of sermons which even till the present

to improve the religious and intellectual life of the people, but the church as a whole was, none the less, in a rather deplorable state. "Everything was for sale," says Andreas Faye. "In Denmark not only the churches were sold to the highest bidder, but even the right to appoint clergymen for the parishes in which they were located. In Norway the king had at his free disposal the revenues of the church, which were often used for military purposes. The income of the church was farmed out, or granted, in part, as donations. Christian V. granted, among other things, the rich estates of the provosty of Tunsberg to Peder Griffenfeld, and after his downfall, to U. F. Gyldenløve, together with the right to make all ecclesiastical appointments in the counties of Jarlsberg and Larvik. At times one was granted the tithes of a church, another its fees or its estates. . . .

The public church service was looked down upon, and this, together with the ridiculous passion for rank, led to private communion, to marriages and baptisms at home among the finer classes, who imitated French language, manners, and customs, while the attention of the common people was especially directed to the exorcising of the devil, to witchcraft, and other superstition."

time has been written in this country." Christen Bang, clergyman at Romedal in Hedemarken, 1621–1657, published an explanation of Luther's Catechism in ten volumes, and many devotional books. Michael Leigh, rector of the Stavanger Latin School, and later clergyman at Thvet, wrote "Guds Børns Herlighed her i Naaden og hisset i Æren" (1680), and "Gileads Slave" (1682), books which were published in many editions. Of psalmists may be mentioned Niels Arctander, of Overnes, who became Bishop of Viborg, author of "Psalmer og aandelige Viser" (1607); Peder Mathieson Ofrid, of Indherred, who wrote a collection of hymns called "Aandens Glæde"; Peder Olufsson Svenning, clergyman at Stordøen 1648–1671, left a collection of hymns "Aurora eller den nye Morgenrøde"; John Brunsmand of Trøndelagen, author of "Aandelige Sjunglyst" (1676) and "Sjungende Himmellys" (1687); Erik Eriksson Pontoppidan, Bishop of Trondhjem, author of "Sjelens Opløftelse til Herren"; Knud Sevaldsen Bang prepared a hymnbook for his congregation in Toten (1662). See Andreas Faye, *Christiansands Stifts Bispe- og Stiftshistorie*, p. 272 f. Erik Pontoppidan, *Norges naturlige Historie*, vol. II., p. 397 ff.

Translations of the Bible both into Danish and Icelandic had long existed. In 1550 the whole Bible, translated from Luther's German Bible by Christiern Pedersøn, was printed in Danish. A new revised folio edition of this translation was published in 1589. In 1607 a literal translation of the Bible from the original languages was published, and in 1633 a large folio edition of Frederick II.'s Bible of 1550, the Bible of Christian IV., appeared.

The period was one of general moral laxity and lack of religious spirit, and among the common people drunkenness and coarse manners were prevalent. Bishop Jørgen Erichsson of Stavanger says in his first sermon of "Jonae Prophetes skjønne Historia": "What vices and offenses against God Almighty are to be found among the lower classes, the common people know well enough how to complain of; for there are very few married folks who live together in peace and good understanding. Parents and older people give the children poor training, and rather set them a bad example in everything which is contrary to God's holy commandments. Children and servants will not be governed by any one, but resent all chastisement and rebuke. Among the people cursing and swearing, immorality, theft, cheating, falsehood, and slander, and other such evils prevail; for they are so wicked and perverse that we see among all classes sin and vice prevail in the highest degree and most damnable form, so that we must complain with the holy Polycarpus: O Lord, why didst thou suffer us to live in such pitiful and miserable times?" Though this is a piece of pulpit oratory, other evidence shows that it can be taken more literally than is usually the case with religious complaints about the wickedness of mankind. Even the clergymen were often rude and violent, and not seldom intemperate and immoral. In the year 1594 four rectors in Christiansands *stift* alone were dismissed for grave offenses of that kind. The seventeenth century was the age of orthodoxy. The Lutheran Church laid great emphasis on the purity of doctrine, and its teachings were adhered to by all classes with the firmest faith and conviction. But the spiritual life of the people was not deeply affected by the cold formalism and lifeless reiteration of dogmas into which the church service had degenerated. Bishop A. Chr. Bang says: "As people believed without scepticism, they also observed diligently all religious ceremonies. They had time and patience to listen to a sermon which lasted for five hours, but the faith and the religious exercises, which in a manner were sincerely enough meant, were able to exert but slight influence. The people of those times were all dualists to a greater or less degree. They were divided into two personalities, the pious and the licentious, and they seemed to live happily in this dualism without being aware of its inconsistency. They were equally orthodox, equally pious, even if they were at times caviling and quarreling, and given to fighting and drunkenness, to barbaric rudeness and a moral licentiousness which, to say the least, was half pagan."[1] But the church itself was largely responsible for these conditions. Bishop Bang continues: "As a people is, so are their priests, says the prophet. In the age of orthodoxy the clergy were in every way imbued with the spirit of the times, the character of the age. The sermons which they delivered can, as a rule, not be rated very high. They were often earnest in chastising the people for their sins and vices, but these legal philippics frequently degenerated into pure invective, not to mention the instances when the preacher would thunder the anathemas of his wrath upon his audience, and wish that the devil himself might take them all. . . . On the whole, the sermon in the age of orthodoxy was unpractical, uncultured, pedantic, and long drawn out. The Christian truth which it undoubtedly contained was drowned in the circumlocutions, introductions, and subdivisions, the examples and learned quotations which belonged to the style of preaching in that age. . . . The views of religion, society, and government were largely that of the Old Testament, and the Bible was, therefore, regarded as one of the chief codes of law. People were sentenced to death, not only according to the civil laws, but also according to the Deuteronomy, and they also sought and found in the Deuteronomy the rules for waging war in a manner pleasing to God." That this type of preaching and Christian instruction should fail to produce a true spiritual regeneration is not strange, especially as the ministers themselves were often addicted to drunkenness and immorality. On March 27, 1629, an ordinance "Regarding the Office of the Church and its Authority over the Impenitent, together with some Conditions of the Clergy" was published. The complaint is made that the preaching of the gospel, the royal ordinances, and the sharpened threats and punishments had been of small avail, and that wickedness has so daily increased "that the people in the clear evangelical light kindled in these countries lead a more reckless, offensive, and godless life, a great number with the idea that the true service of

---

[1] A. Chr. Bang, *Udsigt over den norske Kirkes Historie efter Reformationen*, p. 52 f. See also Edvard Holm, *Danmark-Norges Historie fra den store nordiske Krigs Slutning til Rigernes Adskillelse*, vol. I., p. 556 ff.

God consists in the exterior church service, the use of the sacraments, singing, praying, etc." Various remedies are prescribed by the ordinance. The rectors were to choose some of the best members of the congregation as assistants (*medhjelpere*), and in the country districts the *lensmand* and *provost* should appoint two of the best men as *kirkeverger* to assist the rector in his duties. Those who swore and cursed should be put in the pillory, and the ministers should preach according to the church ordinance, so that their sermons did not become too long and tiresome. Baptisms and marriages should be solemnized in the churches, and not in the private homes. This was a well-meant effort to remedy the evils in church and society, but there is no evidence that the conditions were improving in the seventeenth century. Government regulations or other coercive measures have not the power to impart new life or to create new ideals. The forces which are to regenerate society and lift it to a higher intellectual and moral level must have a higher source, and the Norwegian people were destined to wait another century before the great spiritual awakening came which made faith a matter of the heart, and turned Christianity into a new spiritual and social force.

37. Frederick IV. The Great Northern War

When Christian V. died, August 25, 1699, his son, Frederick, who was twenty-eight years of age, ascended the throne as Frederick IV. The prince had taken little or no part in public affairs, and his education had been much neglected. A. Højer says that King Christian V. was persuaded by his ministers, Gabel, Knuth, and others, who had not much opportunity to study in their youth, that a prince did not need to be educated, that it only tended to obscure his natural ability if his brain was filled with too much learning, but these arguments only served to conceal the thought that they and their families would be more indispensable to the future sovereign if he remained ignorant and without understanding of his royal duties.[1] Frederick's greatest fault, however, was not his scant educa-

[1] A. Højer, *Friederich des 4ten glorwurdigstes Leben.* G. L. Baden, *De danske Kongers og det oldenborgske Hus Karakteristiker.* Edvard Holm, *Danmark-Norges indre Historie under Enevælden*, vol. II., p. 15 f. Niels Ditlev Riegels, *Forsøg til fjerde Friederichs Historie*, vol. I., p. 48.

tion or lack of literary interests, but his frivolity and disgracefully immoral life. In 1695 he married Louise of Mecklenburg, but his open cohabitation with various mistresses proved that he was devoid of moral feeling, a lascivious wanton, who wholly ignored the laws, which if broken by his subjects would bring upon the offender the severest punishment. The most noteworthy of his mistresses was Anna Sophia Reventlow, daughter of Count Reventlow, the king's chancellor. The king had met the young countess at a masquerade, and though her mother tried to prevent it, he enticed her from her home, and she became formally "wedded" to the king's left hand while his queen still lived, the marriage service being read by a conrector, who was liberally rewarded for his pliable conscience. In a similar way he had been "wedded" to Helen Viereck, who died not long after the marriage. This form of illegal polygamy could give the union neither legality nor sanctity, but this gave the king no concern, as he considered himself elevated above all laws. His queen, Louise, died in 1721, and he was formally wedded to Anna Reventlow on the day after the funeral.[1] The reports of these events, following so closely upon each other, caused a great scandal. One day the funeral of the good Queen Louise, and the king's "profound grief" were described in eloquent terms; the next day the king's marriage and his "great joy" was heralded in glowing colors. His brother Charles and his sister Hedevig were so offended that they left the court, and a permanent estrangement resulted between the king and his son and successor, Christian. King Frederick IV. was of a weak and sickly appearance; he was not very gifted, and he possessed no graces which could serve to distinguish him, but his goodness and great kindness of heart won for him the love of the common people. In his duties as king he was energetic, diligent, and conscientious, though somewhat stubborn and narrow-minded. "Frederick IV. belonged to those kings who, while void of any higher intellectual range, can view many relations soundly and ably, and he also had a marked interest for administrative matters, especially if they pertained to financial and military affairs."[2] He wished to become

[1] Edvard Holm, *Danmark-Norges Historie fra den store nordiske Krigs Slutning til Rigernes Adskillelse*, vol. I., p. 34 ff.

[2] Edvard Holm, *Danmark-Norges indre Historie*, vol. II., p. 25.

personally acquainted with conditions in his realms, and he was actively engaged in introducing needed reforms. The not very great honor seems to be due him of being regarded as one of the best kings of the house of Oldenborg.

In Norway Frederick's accession to the throne led to the retirement of Statholder Gyldenløve, who, because of advancing age, was no longer as energetic or mindful of official duties as formerly. He resigned from his office, and retired to Hamburg, where he spent the closing years of his life. No new *statholder* was appointed, but Frederick Gabel, who was made *vice-statholder*, was placed in temporary charge, and G. V. Wedel was made commander-in-chief of the Norwegian army.

FIG. 5. — Frederick IV.

The first half of the eighteenth century was a period of almost constant warfare, in which nearly all nations of Europe took part. The great struggle of England, Holland, and Germany against France was being waged for the Spanish succession and the maintenance of the principle of balance of power, and in eastern Europe Sweden fought the Great Northern War against Russia, Poland, and Denmark-Norway for the preservation of her prestige as a great power. It is not strange that in so critical a period the chief features of the reign of Frederick IV. should be those of war and diplomacy rather than of administration.

Ever since the wars with Sweden in the sixteenth century, when the princes of the part of Schleswig called Gottorp gained full autonomy, a hostile feeling existed between these princes and the kings of Denmark-Norway. This hostility was intensified by the support which Sweden always gave the dukes of Gottorp. From Sweden's

German provinces armies might easily be sent against Denmark, and past experience had shown that Gottorp would serve as an open door through which they could enter. Christian V. had tried to establish Danish overlordship over Gottorp in 1675, but he was forced to acknowledge the full autonomy of the dukedom in the treaty of Lund, 1679, after the war with Sweden.[1] The desire of Denmark to gain control of Gottorp seems a rather excusable ambition, especially when we view it in the light of European politics of that age. It was not only in perfect accord with the general policy of land-grabbing, so universally practiced in the eighteenth century, but it would increase the king's revenues, and greatly lessen the chances of an attack on the southern border of the kingdom. If a favorable opportunity should present itself, the temptation to renew the attempt against the duchy would be very strong, and such an opportunity seemed to have come when the seventeen-year-old Charles XII., who was considered to be a gay and incompetent youth, ascended the throne of Sweden in 1697. The relations between Gottorp and Denmark-Norway again became strained, and Sweden showed as active a sympathy with the duke as ever. In 1698 Christian V. formed an alliance with August II. of Poland, and Saxony, and in 1699 with Czar Peter of Russia against Sweden. No special cause of war existed, and no valid reason for an attack on Sweden at this moment could be given, but such considerations did not weigh much with eighteenth century monarchs. They found the moment opportune, and the negotiations were carried on with the greatest secrecy, in order that Sweden might be surprised and overwhelmed by an unexpected attack. If the plot proved successful, Poland should receive Livonia and other provinces which Sweden had seized, Russia hoped to get some Baltic seaports, and Frederick IV. would subjugate Gottorp, and probably recover some of the provinces lost in the late wars.

At the beginning of the year 1700 a Danish army of 18,000 men was concentrated at Rendsburg in Holstein. The Norwegian army was also mobilized, and four regiments were sent to Denmark, partly to reënforce the Danish army, and partly to render service on the fleet. When spring came, a Saxon army invaded Livonia, and the

---

[1] Robert Molesworth, *An Account of Denmark*, p. 184 ff.

Great Northern War, destined to continue for over twenty years, had begun. The Danes took the forts of Husum and Stapelholm, but failed to take the fortress of Tønningen, and when an army of Swedes and Lüneburgers arrived, they had to raise the siege and withdraw. But the war now took a rather unexpected turn. As both England and Holland were greatly concerned about maintaining peace in the North, they viewed with alarm and resentment this unwarranted attack on Gottorp, and sent a large fleet of thirty-nine ships under the English admiral Rookes to the Baltic. This fleet joined the Swedish fleet numbering thirty-eight ships, and a naval force thus suddenly appeared with which the Danish-Norwegian fleet was unable to cope. Seeland and Copenhagen were almost wholly unprotected, and Charles XII. seized the opportunity to land a force of 10,000 men in the neighborhood of Copenhagen. But before he could begin the bombardment of the city, Frederick IV., who had already begun peace negotiations, succeeded in concluding the peace of Traventhal in Schleswig, August 18, 1700. He agreed to pay the Duke of Gottorp an indemnity of 260,000 riksdaler, and to acknowledge his independence. To these terms Charles XII. had to accede, and the war between Sweden and Denmark-Norway was terminated without much loss or gain to either side. The administration in Norway had been severely criticized by Commissioner of War Hans Rosencreutz in a report to the king, and later by Vice-statholder Gabel, who pointed out that the administration of Norwegian affairs was wholly dictated by the regard for the interests of Denmark and a few royal officials, whereas it ought to be conducted in such a way that it could subserve the best interests both of the king and the realm. King Frederick realized that some change ought to be made in the Norwegian administrative system, and in 1704 a commission was created in Christiania called "Slotsloven paa Akershus," consisting of one military and four civil members, who should assist the *vice-statholder*, and in general perform the duties which the *statholder* had hitherto had. The military member was a German officer, Tritzschler, and three of the civil members were Norwegians, who might be supposed to have more direct knowledge of Norwegian affairs. But Slotsloven showed little competence or interest. They were satisfied with adhering to the old system, and no improvement could be noticed either in the military or civil service.

The same year King Frederick also visited Norway, where he was received with great honors. On the souvenir coins struck in honor of his visit he caused the following motto to be inscribed: *Mod, troskab, tapperhed og hvad der giver ære, al verden kan blandt norske klipper lære.* This was, perhaps, done in acknowledgment of the efficient service which the Norwegians had rendered in past wars, but possibly also to stimulate their warlike spirit, so that military service should be more willingly rendered when the gates of war should again swing open, or when the king should deem it profitable to sell more mercenaries to fight in the bloody wars raging on the Continent.

In 1701, when England, Holland, and the German Empire began the great struggle against France, known as the War of the Spanish Succession, both sides sought the support of Denmark-Norway. Frederick IV. avoided any active participation in the war, but he favored the opponents of France. In return for a yearly subsidy and the promise of aid in case of need, he hired 20,000 mercenaries to the English king, about 6000 of whom were Norwegians. This system of sacrificing the young men of the kingdoms on foreign battlefields for no worthier purpose than to secure a few million crowns for the royal treasury was quite universally practiced at that time, and had been resorted to also by Christian V. Molesworth says that the Danes sent 7000 soldiers to England "which are yet in His Majesty's pay." [1] These were losses far exceeding those caused by the emigration to Holland and England, but none raised a voice to bemoan it as a calamity "worse than the Black Death," or to proclaim it the "cause of the decline of Norwegian agriculture." We cannot but feel the truth of Molesworth's rather bitter words: "At present soldiers are grown to be as salable ware as sheep and oxen, and are as little concerned when sold; for provided the officers be rendered content by the purchaser, in having liberty to plunder the laborious and honest country people in their marches, and a fat winter quarter, with a permission to defraud their own men of their pay; the common soldier goes with no more sense than a beast to

---

[1] *An Account of Denmark*, p. 200.

the slaughter; having no such sentiment as love of honor, country, religion, liberty, or anything more than fear of being hanged for a deserter." [1] Even during the intervals of peace the nation's best blood was being shed on distant battlefields, and these poor mercenaries could not even feel that they were giving their lives for their country.

After the peace of Traventhal Charles XII., "the Swedish lion," turned against Russia and Poland, and fought a series of brilliant campaigns which dazzled Europe. After he had crushed the Russians at Narva, he marched into Poland, drove out August II., and placed Stanislaus Leszczynski on the throne. He then entered Saxony, and forced August II. to conclude a humiliating peace at Alt-Ranstädt. In 1707 he again turned against Russia with an army of 40,000 men, probably the best drilled and officered army in Europe at that time. The situation became critical, and both Czar Peter and August II. implored Frederick IV. to come to their aid. Frederick was still hostile to Sweden, and he continued to quarrel with Gottorp, but he would not risk a new war with Charles XII. until the situation should be more favorable. He made instead a pleasure trip to Italy, which was prolonged till 1709, when he returned by way of Saxony. He met King August II., and an alliance was now concluded between the two kings. August II. should again receive the throne of Poland, and Frederick IV. should seek to recover the provinces which Sweden had taken from Denmark-Norway.

While hard pressed by the Swedish armies, Czar Peter of Russia had offered Frederick IV. the sum of 300,000 riksdaler and a yearly subsidy of 100,000, if he would come to his aid, but Frederick, who hoped to get still more, did not accept the offer. Now the situation was wholly changed. On July 8, 1709, Charles XII. was defeated at Pultava, and his army was destroyed. Russia replaced Sweden as the leading power in the North, and the Czar withdrew his offer. Frederick, who realized that he had lost his opportunity, nevertheless entered into an alliance with him, on the best terms obtainable, and began war with Sweden in November of the same year by sending an army of 15,000 men under Count Reventlow into Skåne. The Norwegian army was also mobilized, and received orders to support

---

[1] *An Account of Denmark*, p. 118.

the Danes by invading the Swedish border districts. Seven thousand men were concentrated at Fredrikstad, but after Gyldenløve's retirement, the Norwegian army had been so woefully neglected that it was in no condition to render active service. Not only were soldiery, cavalry, and commissariat in a deplorable state, but all efficient leadership had disappeared through the mischievous practice of appointing to the higher military offices in Norway old men who were incapable of active military service, and considered their appointment only as a sinecure. In the Swedish wars at the time of Sehested and Gyldenløve the Norwegians had distinguished themselves, but this time they had to take the field without proper arms, equipments, or leaders. The *vice-statholder*, Vibe, was a sickly man, over seventy years of age. H. E. Tritzschler, who was appointed commander-in-chief, was utterly incompetent, and General Schultz, who commanded the forces in northern Norway, was an aged man, over seventy-seven years old. The campaign became a ludicrous example of hesitation and procrastination. All opportunities were wasted, and nothing was accomplished. So wholly incompetent were the commanders that the Norwegian troops spent all their time in camp, and could not even hold in check any of the Swedish forces who under the able general Magnus Stenbock advanced against the Danes in Skåne. In the battle of Helsingborg, February 28, 1710, the Danes suffered a crushing defeat, losing 5000 men dead and wounded, and 2600 who were made prisoners of war. Skåne was speedily evacuated by the remnant of the Danish army, which retreated across the Sound to Seeland. Even after this defeat Frederick IV. would have sent a new army into Sweden, but he was prevented by the Swedish fleet.

Not many important naval engagements occurred in this war, but on October 4, 1710, an undecisive naval battle was fought in Kjøge Bay, which was made memorable by the death of the Norwegian naval hero Ivar Huitfeldt, who anchored his burning ship, "Danebrog," so as not to endanger the rest of the fleet, and continued to fight until the vessel was destroyed by the explosion of its powder-magazines. The attempt of seizing Skåne was not renewed, and Frederick was prevented by various circumstances from taking further active part in the war till 1712.

The utter incompetence of the Norwegian administration, which had been one of the contributory causes of the disastrous defeat at Helsingborg, had been brought to the king's attention in various ways. H. C. Platen, whom he sent to Norway to examine conditions, wrote: "There is not the proper energy and vivacity in the administration, nor the subordination which there ought to be, for though there is much talking and arguing, very little is done." The king, therefore, appointed a new *statholder*, U. F. V. Løvendal, an able and experienced general, son of the former *statholder* Ulrik Frederick Gyldenløve. Løvendal soon brought new order and energy into the Norwegian administration, and persuaded the king to send more warships to Norway for the protection of the Norwegian coast and commerce.[1] In 1711 he was instructed to make an attack on Sweden for the purpose of holding in check the Swedish forces, and of preventing reënforcements from being sent to Pomerania, where the allies intended to make their next attack on Charles XII. These instructions he carried out successfully by leading an army of 7000 men into Bohuslen, which was occupied by a strong Swedish force under Burenskjöld. No battles of importance were fought, but the object of the expedition was, none the less, attained. In popularity as well as ability Løvendal resembled his noted father, but he did not remain long in Norway. Already in 1712 he was recalled to Denmark, and he soon returned to Poland, where he became King August II.'s minister and lord high steward.

After the battle of Pultava Charles XII. sought to fight his adversaries with the assistance of the Turks, and Magnus Stenbock attempted to come to his aid with an army of 17,000 men. But the transportation of such an army across the sea and through territory occupied by the enemy was connected with insurmountable obstacles. At Gadebusch in Mecklenburg he defeated the Danes, but large armies of Saxons and Russians blocked his way. Turning west, he burned Altona, and entered Holstein, but mild weather made the roads impassable, and he retired to the fortress of Tønningen, which was opened to him by the Duke of Gottorp. On May 16, 1713, he was forced to surrender with his whole army, and after four

---

[1] I. Gulowsen, *Fra Valdemar Løvendals Tid, Historisk Tidsskrift*, fjerde række, vol. VI., p. 90 ff.

years of close confinement the great general died in a Danish prison, 1717.[1]

Stenbock's defeat and capture exhausted Sweden's last strength, and made further resistance impossible. Charles XII. was a prisoner in Turkey, and after the situation became so critical that the Estates threatened to conclude peace if the king did not return, Charles left Turkey, and reached Stralsund in November, 1714. He hoped to defend Pomerania against his enemies, but Frederick IV. formed an alliance with George I. of England-Hanover, and Frederick William of Prussia, and while the Danish-Norwegian fleet made it impossible to send reënforcements across the Baltic, a Danish-Prussian army besieged the city, which was forced to capitulate, December 23, 1715.

38. KING CHARLES XII. IN NORWAY

Two days before Stralsund capitulated, King Charles XII. boarded a Swedish man-of-war and set sail for Sweden. He succeeded in eluding the Danish-Norwegian fleet, and landed at Trelleborg at daybreak on Christmas eve, 1715. The homecoming was not a joyful one. The condition of the kingdom was deplorable in the extreme, and the people desired peace at any cost, but King Charles had not yet abandoned hope of success, and refused to listen to any proposals of that kind. Through proscriptions, forced loans, and other coercive methods he succeeded also this time in raising the required forces. The attack was to be directed against Frederick IV., against whom he felt a special resentment. Had the winter been cold enough, he would have crossed the Sound on the ice, and invaded Seeland, but this plan had to be abandoned because of mild weather, and he decided to seize Norway, which he hoped to take by a swift and energetic attack.

After the departure of Løvendal, the Norwegian administration, directed by Slotsloven and the new *vice-statholder*, Frederick Krag, had relapsed into its old inactivity and incompetence. General Hausman, the commander-in-chief of the army, and the military

---

[1] *Felttoget i Skaane 1709–1710, ved den danske Generalstab*, Copenhagen, 1903. Paludan-Müller, *Omrids af Kong Fredrik IV's Kamp med Grev Magnus Stenbock og Baron Görtz, Dansk historisk Tidsskrift*, fjerde række, vol. VI. Still, *Kriget i Skåne*, Stockholm, 1903.

member of Slotsloven, who had proven himself both able and conscientious, and had brought the army into a fairly high state of efficiency, was dismissed shortly before the war broke out, because the government feared lest his warlike spirit should lead him to act with too much haste. The country was ill prepared for war, though the military burdens, as well as the size of the army, were continually augmented until they passed all reasonable limits.[1] The treasury was empty, and the army, which numbered 24,000 men, of whom 4000 had been sent to Germany, lacked clothes, medicine, tents, and provisions. The officers were, to a large extent, foreigners, often without military experience, and devoid of interest for the country's welfare. The new commander-in-chief, Lutzow, was a German by birth, but he had married a Norwegian lady, and had settled permanently in the kingdom. He was upright and competent, but extremely cautious, and not very energetic. When the report was received that Charles XII. might attack Norway, some efforts were made to mobilize the Norwegian army, but there was a conspicuous lack of promptness and energy. Lutzow and his assistants, as well as Slotsloven, felt convinced that Charles would not begin a new campaign in the winter, and nothing of importance was done to safeguard the country against invasion. But Charles XII. was used to take advantage of situations of that kind. His army of invasion, consisting of 12,000 men, was ready to march at any moment, and in the beginning of March he started from Vermland with a corps of 3000 men, infantry and cavalry. It was his aim to march straightway upon Christiania. General Carl Gustav Mørner, governor of Bohus, was ordered to advance to his support with a force of 4000 men, and General Aschenberg was instructed to operate against Fredrikshald and Fredriksten with a third division. On the night before the 9th of March, 1716, the burning *varder* on the mountain-

---

[1] At the beginning of Frederick's reign the Norwegian army numbered 10,000 men. In 1727 it was increased to 18,000, and through new enlistments, and especially by adding a force of reserves of 9300, it was raised to 30,000 by 1742. The length of the required term of military service was increased from three to ten years, so that many remained in the army from sixteen to twenty years. J. E. Sars says that scarcely a government in Europe drew so heavily on the people's strength for military purposes. Sars, *Udsigt over den norske Historie*, vol. IV., p. 68 ff. J. C. Berg, *Om Landværnet*, p. 32 ff. A. C. Drolsum, *Det norske Folk og dets Forsvarsvæsen*, p. 40 ff.

tops suddenly announced that the enemy had entered the country. Charles XII. had crossed the border with a force of 1000 men, and as he found all strategic points unguarded, and the road open, he hastened forward with a cavalry troop of 600 men to Høland parsonage. The Norwegian troops stationed there under Lieutenant-Colonel Brüggemann and Colonel Kruse were quartered on different farms in the neighborhood.

Brüggemann was surprised and captured with eighty-two men without being able to make resistance, but Kruse, who had collected 200 men, attacked the Swedes, and a bloody battle ensued, in which King Charles' favorite, General Poniatovski, and his brother-in-law, Prince Frederick of Hessen, were severely wounded, and Charles himself barely escaped being captured. But the tide of battle soon turned. Kruse was wounded and captured, and his small band was scattered. He was treated with

Fig. 6. — Charles XII.

the greatest courtesy by the chivalric Swedish king. His bravery was admired by all, but he had acted in too precipitous a haste. Had he waited a few hours, and collected all his forces, which numbered 700 to 800 men, he might have won an important victory, and King Charles might have been made prisoner. Kruse was tried by a court-martial, and sentenced to pay a fine, but Frederick IV. accorded him full pardon.[1]

[1] A. Faye, Carl XII. i Norge. O. A. Øverland, Borgerne paa Fredrikshald. Oscar Alb. Johnsen, Norges Historie, vol. V., 1, p. 164 ff. Fredrik Ferdinand Carlson, Sveriges Historia under Konungerna af pfalziska Huset, part II. Voltaire, Histoire de Charles XII. Robert Nisbet Bain, Charles XII. and the Collapse of the Swedish Empire. King Oscar II., Charles XII. Anders Fryxell, Carl den tolftes Historia.

King Charles' unexpected approach caused the greatest consternation in Norway, where the members of Slotsloven had neglected to take proper steps even for protecting Christiania. King Charles was now only thirty-five miles away, but cold and stormy weather prevented him from pursuing his march for some days. This delay enabled the government to collect an army of about 7000 men in the city, but when King Charles had effected a junction with Mørner, who was advancing from Bohus, General Lutzow and other members of Slotsloven considered it prudent not to risk a battle. A garrison of 3000 men was placed in the fortress of Akershus, Lutzow evacuated Christiania, and retired to Gjellebek, in the neighborhood of Drammen, and the Swedes occupied the city without resistance, March 21, 1716.

So far Charles had been successful. Christiania had been taken, and he had found ample stores of provisions, and good quarters for his soldiers during the inclement season of early spring. But serious obstacles were soon thrown in his way. For want of artillery he could not besiege Akershus castle, which trained its guns upon the city, and killed many of his men by firing along the streets. The people were everywhere hostile, a circumstance which soon made all his operations difficult. Foraging parties had to fight with the *bønder*, and the smaller isolated detachments were often attacked and destroyed. A force of over 400 men which he had left at Moss in charge of the commissariat was annihilated by Henrik Jørgen Huitfeldt, and large quantities of ammunition were taken, though the greater part of the stores had already been removed. In the latter part of March a cavalry force of 600 men under Axel Løven was dispatched by King Charles into Hakedal, Hadeland, and Ringerike to burn stores, and also to destroy the rich silver mines at Kongsberg.[1] They were everywhere opposed by the *bønder*, who felled trees across the roads, and offered what resistance they could without fighting any pitched battle, and they were so delayed that they did not reach Norderhov parsonage till ten o'clock in the evening, March 28.

---

[1] A. Faye, *Bidrag til den norske Krigs-Historie under Kong Fredrik IV, Samlinger til det norske Folks Sprog og Historie*, vol. III., p. 182 ff. Haakon H. Breien, *Svensketoget til Norderhov i 1716, Historisk Tidsskrift*, fjerde række, vol. V., p. 454 ff.

Here they were surprised by the Norwegians under Oetken. Colonel Løven and a large number of his men were taken prisoners, and the rest of the force was scattered. A fairly well founded tradition relates how the parson's wife, the brave Anna Colbjørnsdatter, entertained the Swedish officers while word was sent to the Norwegians to hasten to Norderhov.[1] Through these and similar mishaps King Charles' position soon became critical. General Aschenberg had retreated across the border, his line of communication had been broken, and the Norwegians destroyed roads and bridges. The Norwegian forces were constantly increased, and when the regiments which had been sent to Germany returned, and Danish reënforcements had been received, the commanders resolved to block King Charles' line of retreat, and to isolate him in the district between Christiania and the Glommen River. An attempt which Charles made to turn the flank of the Norwegian army failed, and Moss was taken by Vincence Budde and Henrik Jørgen Huitfeldt. Falkenberg, the Swedish commander, was mortally wounded, and the garrison of 800 men were killed, captured, or scattered. Charles now found the situation so critical that he suddenly left Christiania in the night of April 29, and marched across the Glommen River to Fredrikshald. The townspeople of that city made a determined resistance under the leadership of the brothers Peter and Hans Colbjørnsen, half-brothers of Anna Colbjørnsdatter, but King Charles seized the city, and hoped to capture the citadel, the fortress of Fredriksten.[2] On the night of July 3 he sought to take it by storm, but the citizens fired the town, so that the enemy could find no shelter, and the attack was repulsed, King Charles losing 500 men and many of his best officers.[3] He now decided to lay siege to the fortress, as soon as his fleet of transports should arrive with the

---

[1] Bernt Moe, *Aktstykker til den norske Krigshistorie under Kong Fredrik den fjerde*, vol. II., p. 3 ff. A. Faye, *Carl XII. i Norge*, p. 48 ff. Oscar Alb. Johnsen, *Norges Historie*, V., 1, p. 171. Haakon H. Breien, *Svensketoget til Norderhov, Historisk Tidsskrift*, fjerde række, vol. V., p. 455 ff.

[2] C. O. Munthe, *Fredrikshalds og Fredrikstens Historie indtil 1720. Officielle Raporter og Meldinger, Norske Samlinger*, vol. I., p. 403 ff. Bernt Moe, *Aktstykker til den norske Krigshistorie under Kong Fredrik den fjerde*, vol. II., p. 37 ff.

[3] The whole city was burned. In all, 330 houses were destroyed. Only a few houses in the southern part of the city remained.

necessary siege guns and war material, but this hope was shattered by the Norwegian naval hero Peter Tordenskjold.

This remarkable man, the son of John Wessel, a sea-captain and later innkeeper and alderman in Trondhjem, was born in 1690, and was at this time about twenty-six years of age. In his boyhood he was placed in school, but he loved adventure and the sea more than books, and several episodes from his school-days reveal the temper of the future sea-fighter. One day a larger boy had given him a beating, but Peter Wessel vowed that he would have his revenge. The next day he returned to the combat with his hair cut close and his head greased, and this time he worsted his opponent. When Frederick IV. visited Norway in 1704, the restless youth found an opportunity to follow his retinue to Denmark, where he hoped to become a cadet. Failing in this, he hired out as a sailor, and later as mate on a ship going to the East Indies. On his return to Denmark, the war with Sweden had begun, and he became officer on the fleet, with the rank of lieutenant. A little later he was sent to Norway with dispatches to Baron Løvendal, who liked the young officer so well that he made him captain of a small privateer, an opportunity which enabled Wessel to develop his talents unhampered by superiors. He rendered such valuable service that Løvendal soon placed him in command of a new ship of some size, "Løvendals Gallei," of eighteen guns, and on his first cruise he captured a Swedish ship of nine guns, which was also placed under his command under the new name of "Norske Vaaben." He was soon ordered to rejoin the Danish fleet under Admiral Gyldenløve, and he distinguished himself to such a degree that he won the admiral's lifelong friendship and the special favor of the king. Again he was allowed to return to the coast of Norway to fight the enemy. His remarkable exploits, his distinguished service in the regular fleet, the number of prizes which he captured cannot be dwelt upon in detail, but the king so admired his rare talents that in spite of powerful opponents and jealous rivals who sought to harm the young officer, he raised him to the nobility with the name of Tordenskjold, February 24, 1716, before he had reached the age of twenty-six years.[1] In the month of

---

[1] W. Carstensen og O. Lütken, *Tordenskjold*. Constantinus Flood, *Tordenskjold*. Jacob Børresen, *Kontreadmiral Tordenskjold*, Christiania, 1901. W. Coucheron-Aamot, *Tordenskjold*.

June of that year Tordenskjold submitted to the king and the admiralty a plan for the defense of Fredrikshald, and for an attack on the Swedish coast squadron, which was bringing supplies to Charles XII. The plan was accepted, and the king ordered a small squadron to be placed under Tordenskjold's command for its execution. On July 2 he weighed anchor, and sailed for the Swedish coast with seven small vessels, including his flagship the "Hvide Ørn," which he had captured from the Swedes, and a small frigate, "Vindhunden," commanded by his chief companion in arms, Lieutenant-Captain Grip. When he approached the coast of Bohuslen, he learned from some fishermen that the whole Swedish squadron of over forty sail under Rear Admiral Strömstjerna lay anchored in the harbor of Dynekilen, about twenty miles from Fredrikshald. This was the fleet transporting siege guns and supplies to Charles XII., on which the outcome of the Swedish king's attack on Fredrikshald and Fredriksten at this moment depended. But could Tordenskjold with seven small vessels attack so formidable a fleet, anchored in a harbor where the narrow entrance was well defended both by infantry and shore batteries? It was a daring adventure of the kind which always tempted Tordenskjold. At daybreak, July 8, he set sail for Dynekilen, and had almost passed the narrow entrance, which is about three miles long, before the signal of his approach reached the Swedish fleet. But before he could enter the inner harbor he was met with a brisk fire from the fleet, and also from the battery of six twelve-pound guns planted on an island in such a way that its fire could rake the entire mouth of the harbor. Tordenskjold did not return the fire till he could place his vessels as close as possible to those of the enemy. The real combat then began, and the ships were soon enveloped in a thick smoke of gunpowder which made all maneuvers difficult. After the incessant roar of cannons had continued for about three hours, the fire from the Swedish fleet began to weaken, and when Captain Tønder at about one o'clock captured the battery on the island, Tordenskjold closed in on the enemy, and at three o'clock in the afternoon, after a battle lasting seven hours, he was master of the harbor. The Swedes ran their ships aground and fled, leaving only a few men on each vessel to set it on fire, or to blow up its powder-magazines. But the situation was still critical, as Swedish troops and artillery had been stationed along the narrow entrance channel, which is only 160 to 180 paces wide. Also the capture of the ships, even after they had been abandoned, could be accomplished only with the greatest difficulty, as most of them had been mined or set on fire. But the work was undertaken by Tordenskjold's men with the most resolute daring. Nine war vessels and five transports with ammunition and supplies were towed out of the harbor; the others had been sunk, beached, or crippled.[1] The proud squadron had been destroyed, and with it disappeared King Charles' hope of taking Fredrikshald. Upon receiving the discouraging news he withdrew from Norway. His campaign had failed, not because of any great ability shown by General Lutzow and Slotsloven, who had distinguished themselves chiefly by their inactivity, but because a nation had risen against him to fight for their country and their homes.

39. KING CHARLES XII.'s SECOND INVASION OF NORWAY

The unsuccessful Norwegian campaign and the losses it entailed would in themselves have been sufficient at this moment to create a critical situation in Sweden, but new dangers now threatened to overwhelm the kingdom with general ruin. Before King Charles retreated from Norway, he had received the news that Wismar, his last German possession, had fallen into the hands of his enemies, Finland and the Swedish Baltic provinces were in the hands of Czar Peter the Great, and both Russia and Denmark were ready to invade Sweden with large armies. Charles' available forces did not exceed 20,000 men, of whom many had endured the greatest privations, and his country seemed to have exhausted its last strength in a hopeless and uneven struggle. But neither dangers nor misfortunes could make the king yield to peace proposals. His mind was of that strange kind which under the pressure of ill fortune becomes more rigidly fixed in its resolves even to a point of eccentricity. Victory,

---

[1] Oscar Alb. Johnsen, *Norges Historie*, vol. V., 1, p. 175, and O. A. Øverland, *Norges Historie*, vol. VIII., p. 251, state that nine war vessels and five transports were taken. The statement made by W. Coucheron-Aamot, *Tordenskjold*, p. 15 ff., and A. Faye, *Carl XII. i Norge*, p. 7, that eleven war vessels were captured, seems to be incorrect. See also W. Carstensen og O. Lütken, *Tordenskjold*, 1902.

which in his early career had accompanied him on many a battle-field, continued in his hours of adversity to buoy him up as a hope, but it had long since changed into a mad delusion which goaded him onward to his tragic end. With incredible energy, which was only equaled by the harshness of his methods, he succeeded in a short time in raising an army of 60,000 men, of which 48,000 should be used in an attack on Norway. In order to secure well-protected depots for supplies, he fortified Strömstad, which together with Marstrand and Gottenborg would constitute a line of communications easily defended. Neither the Danish government nor the higher military authorities in Norway understood the significance of this step, but the alert Peter Tordenskjold saw it, and tried to frustrate the plan. On May 14, 1717, he made an attack on Gottenborg, and July 19 on Strömstad, but at both places he was repulsed, though the attacks had been well planned.

The situation now seemed more hopeful for Charles XII. As Czar Peter had ceased to coöperate with Frederick IV., there was no immediate danger of an attack from Russia; he could turn his whole army against Denmark-Norway, and a second invasion of Norway was begun in the fall of 1718. An army under General Armfelt was sent into Trøndelagen with instructions to seize Trondhjem, and the main army of invasion under the king's own command advanced a little later towards Fredrikshald.[1] The city was invested, fort Gyldenløve fell December 6th after a bloody struggle, and trenches were dug towards the main fortress. But on December 11th, while watching the progress of this work, the king was hit by a bullet from the fortress and instantly killed.[2]

[1] The size of these armies has been variously estimated. O. A. Øverland in a treatise, *Armfeldts Tog nordenfjelds 1718, Historisk Tidsskrift*, anden række, vol. II., p. 193 ff., shows that Armfelt's forces, according to the general's own statement, numbered 14,540 men. See also *Danmarks Riges Historie*, vol. V., p. 77, and H. G. Heggtveit, *Trondhjem i Fortid og Nutid*, p. 233. *Sveriges Historia*, edited by Hildebrand, vol. III.-2, p. 365, and Oscar Alb. Johnsen, *Norges Historie*, V., 1, p. 177, state that Armfelt's army numbered 7500 men. *Danmarks Riges Historie* says that Armfelt should march into northern Norway with about 14,000 men, and Charles would soon advance with 30,000 men into southern Norway. See also A. Faye, *Carl XII. i Norge*, p. 129, footnote.

[2] The story, which was given some credence by older historians, that Charles

The grief which filled the hearts of his brave soldiers and companions when the news of his tragic death passed from mouth to mouth was accompanied by a sigh of relief and a feeling of satisfaction that the fearful drama of war, perchance, was over, and that thoughts of home and peace might again be entertained. The words attributed to the Frenchman Megret, who was with the king when he fell, seem expressive of a general sentiment: " *La pièce est finié, allons souper!*" The body was brought back to Stockholm, and buried in the Riddarholm church. In 1860 a fine monument was erected by the Swedish army at the place where he fell.

In northern Norway General Armfelt had advanced against Trondhjem, which was held by Vincence Budde, who commanded an army of 6900 men. His march had been slow, as he had been opposed at every turn by the people, as well as by the Norwegian military forces. Provisions could be secured only with great difficulty, the Swedish soldiers were dissatisfied to a point of mutiny, and the long northern winter was at hand. He reached Trondhjem and laid siege to the city, but sickness decimated his ranks, and reduced the efficiency of his forces to such a degree that instead of risking an attack on the fortifications he felt compelled to withdraw into Værdalen, where he could await reënforcements and supplies. King Charles gave the brave general a sharp reprimand, and ordered him to take the city immediately, but when he again advanced, the garrison had been reënforced, and four warships had anchored in the harbor.[1] Armfelt isolated Trondhjem by cutting off all com-

XII. was slain by an assassin, is now considered to be wholly unfounded. Henrik Wergeland, *Notitser om Carl den tolvtes Felttog i Norge 1716–1718 fra E. M. Fant, Samlinger til det norske Folks Sprog og Historie*, vol. III., p. 193 ff. Bernt Moe, *Aktstykker til den norske Krigshistorie under Fredrik den fjerde*, p. 248 ff. C. O. Munthe, *Fredrikshalds og Fredrikstens Historie indtil 1720*, p. 696 ff. P. A. Munch, *Den sidste Undersøgelse af Kong Carl XII.'s Lig tilligemed Bemerkninger om hans Dødsmaade, For Hjemmet*, vol. II., p. 385. *Illustreret Nyhedsblad*, vol. VIII., p. 161. *Langes Tidsskrift*, vol. IV., p. 317. Paludan-Müller, *Nyt historisk Tidsskrift*, I. S. A. Sørensen, *Karl XII.'s Fald ved Fredriksten, Historisk Tidsskrift*, fjerde række, vol. II., p. 158 ff. *Norske Samlinger*, vol. II., p. 560 ff.

[1] O. A. Øverland, *Armfelts Tog nordenfjelds 1718, Historisk Tidsskrift*, anden række, vol. II., p. 193 ff. Yngvar Nielsen, *De gamle Kampe om Trondhjem, Trondhjem i Fortid og Nutid*, edited by H. G. Heggtveit. *Norske Samlinger*, vol. II., p. 517 ff.

munications with the inland districts, but supplies could reach the
city from the sea, and General Budde sent out light detachments
which constantly harassed the enemy. The final assault had to be
postponed from time to time, and sickness reduced Armfelt's available forces to 4000 men, who were compelled to camp in the open, in
want of clothes, food, and proper shelter. The besieged city also
suffered severely, and of the garrison alone 1500 are said to have
died. When Armfelt received the news of the death of Charles XII.
during the last days of December, he immediately began his retreat
across the mountains to Sweden; but severe storms and cold weather
made his passage across the pathless mountains in the middle of the
winter resemble Napoleon's retreat from Moscow. His sick and
hungry soldiers dropped from cold and exhaustion, and a large part
of his force perished on the way.[1] Emahusen, who led a detachment
of Norwegian ski-runners in pursuit of the enemy, says: "I am unable to describe the destruction of the Swedish army as I saw it.
On the whole mountain no wood was to be found, and when the last
companies arrived there, a storm began which lasted three days. It
was a sad and fearful sight! The soldiers lay dead in groups of
thirty, forty, fifty, or more, in full uniform, with their knapsacks
on their backs, some with their guns in their hands; others lay
dead by the wayside with food in their hands and even in the
mouth; the cavalry-men stood on their heads in the snowdrifts,
as they had been thrown from their horses. Some had broken the
stocks of their muskets to build a fire, — no, I cannot describe it!
The farther we came up the mountains, the more dead men and
horses we saw. Only a few either of the cavalry or the infantry

---

[1] The number of those who perished on the homeward march has been
variously estimated and often grossly exaggerated. Yngvar Nielsen says:
"The probability is that the statement is correct which gives the following
figures: 600 dead, 200 injured by cold, 300 sick, besides the drivers of the
baggage wagons. It has been said that 4000, and even 7000 perished on the
mountains." *De gamle Kampe om Trondhjem, Trondhjem i Fortid og Nutid*,
by Heggtveit, p. 239. Professor Oscar Alb. Johnsen thinks that probably
2500 men perished. *Norges Historie*, vol. V., 1, p. 182. *Sveriges Historia*,
edited by Hildebrand, says: "More than 2200 men, almost a third of the
whole force, froze to death. Horses, artillery, and baggage were totally
destroyed. Only remnants of the army, partly unfit for further military
service because of frozen limbs, returned to Swedish soil."

could have gotten across the mountains, and those who did must be hurt, of what rank soever they may be, for the weather and the cold were too penetrating." [1]

With the retreat of the Swedish armies from Norway, military operations ceased for a time, as neither Norway nor Denmark were prepared to follow up the discomfiture of the enemy with an aggressive movement.

In Sweden the fall of Charles XII. led to important changes. That Sweden's dream of empire had vanished had to be admitted, and the sentiment of the whole nation was united in a desire to obtain peace on any acceptable terms whatsoever. The absolute power of the sovereign was abolished, and King Charles' younger sister, Ulrika Eleonora, was placed on the throne with very limited power; not through the recognized right of inheritance, but by election, the guidance of state affairs being intrusted chiefly to the *Rigsdag*, or Estates of the realm, in which the nobility exercised marked preponderance. The allies which had hitherto fought against Sweden were no longer on friendly terms. England's jealousy of Russia's growing power had developed into open hostility, a circumstance which enabled Sweden to conclude peace with England by ceding Bremen and Verden, November 20, 1719. Peace was also made with Prussia, which received the larger part of Swedish Pomerania, Usedom, Wollin, Damm, and Gollnow, by paying Sweden two million crowns. But no such concessions were offered King Frederick IV. of Denmark-Norway, who was instead asked to make concessions to Sweden, a rather strange demand under the circumstances. The war was continued, and Frederick now planned a new invasion of Sweden to be undertaken from Norway, where he collected an army of 34,000 men. In June he came to Norway accompanied by the crown prince, and in July, 1719, he led his army into Bohuslen. When the king had established his headquarters at Strömstad, Tordenskjold succeeded, through a brilliantly executed attack, in capturing Marstrand with its citadel Carlsten. Securing entrance to the fortress disguised as a vender of fish, he found opportunity to examine the fortifications, and to determine the strength of the garrison. The attack was as skillfully carried out as it was daringly planned. On

[1] Heggtveit, *Trondhjem i Fortid og Nutid*, p. 241.

June 23 he seized the five batteries defending the harbor, captured the city, and destroyed the Swedish squadron of warships stationed under its guns. Four warships and one merchant vessel were taken, and the remaining vessels were sunk in the harbor. The citadel of Carlsten could not be taken by assault, but by a ruse Tordenskjold prevailed on the commandant to surrender the stronghold. King Frederick was so pleased that he made Tordenskjold vice-admiral.

The capture of Marstrand was the only important event of the campaign. Frederick IV. had become politically isolated through the breaking up of the coalition against Sweden, but as England exerted her influence to bring about peace, both powers finally yielded to her solicitations, and a treaty of peace was signed at Fredriksborg, July 3, 1720. Sweden was to pay 600,000 riksdaler, and Denmark-Norway was to evacuate the Swedish possessions Rügen, Pomerania, Wismar, and Marstrand. Frederick IV. retained the possessions of the Duke of Gottorp in Schleswig, and united these with the duchy, and Sweden

FIG. 7. — Peter Tordenskjold

promised never again to aid the duke against Denmark. The peace treaty with Russia was signed at Nystad, 1721. Russia received Ingermanland, Esthonia, Livonia, Ösel, and southeastern Karelen, with Viborg *len* in Finland. Sweden had lost her position as a great power; her warrior king, who made her final struggle for supremacy so dramatic, had met his death in a foreign country in the darkest hour of national misfortune. But Peter Tordenskjold, his great antagonist, was also snatched away in the noonday of life, in the height of his glory. At the age of thirty he fell in a duel in

Hamburg, four months after peace had been concluded at Fredriksborg.[1]

Throughout the war the Norwegians had distinguished themselves both on sea and land. The attack on their country had been repulsed at every point, and not a foot of territory had been lost; but economically the kingdom had suffered a noticeable decline. The great military burdens, together with heavy taxes, exhausted the energy as well as the means which should have been employed in industry and trade. The flourishing export trade which had been developed before the war, though not destroyed, was greatly reduced, and all business was crippled, as all available means were employed for military purposes. The city of Fredrikshald had been burned; Trøndelagen and the districts of southeastern Norway, the most productive sections of the country, had been harried by hostile armies until the people were reduced to beggary. Still, these hardships were borne with patience and fortitude, as the war had developed into a national struggle. The invasion of the country by large armies made a deep impression, and an intense patriotism was engendered, as the people felt the war to be their own cause. For the first time in centuries the nation had been stirred to heroic efforts, and great leaders showed the way to victory and national honor. Norway had received a new national hero, Tordenskjold, who, like another Olav Tryggvason, came from the unknown, dazzled with his brilliant achievements, and died young. Deeds of valor, and heroic sacrifices like the burning of Fredrikshald, which made those days memorable, have continued to live in song and story till the present. If Norway lost in national well-being, she gained in national regeneration. Time and again the Norwegians had been compelled to fight battles, and to suffer losses for the sole interest of their partner in the union, but the Great Northern War taught them the lesson of patriotism, which became the starting-point of a new national development.

[1] Kong Carl og han, de skulde følges sammen
i livets tvedragt og i dødens fred,
i daadens glans og rygtets evighed;
thi de var tvilling-skud af asastammen.

(C. Ploug.)

40. The Closing Years of the Reign of Frederick IV.
Social and Economic Conditions

The Great Northern War closed an epoch in the history of the Scandinavian kingdoms. Sweden had succeeded Denmark as the leading power in the North, but her preponderance, which had lasted since the Thirty Years' War, was now destroyed, and an equilibrium had been established which would be the best guarantee for the maintenance of peace. Both Sweden and Denmark had been reduced to their natural boundaries, and their old rivalry for supremacy would have to be abandoned. Russia had become a powerful and dangerous neighbor to the east, and as conditions had so changed that they could no longer hope to play a prominent part in European affairs, an opportunity would be given for the development of the pursuits of peace. When the dream of empire had vanished, and the paths to martial glory had been closed, the people's energy and talents could be devoted to the improvement of economic and social conditions, and the creation of the high intellectual culture, which was destined to shed a more benign luster upon the three sister kingdoms.

Frederick IV. was in no respect a great ruler. He was very suspicious, and entertained an almost superstitious fear of the nobility, but he lacked the ability to free himself from the influence of intriguing officials and court favorites. The Norwegian *bønder*, however, enjoyed the king's special good-will. They had won his heart by their bravery and fidelity in the war with Sweden, and he was always inclined to favor them, and to take their part against the grasping and unjust officials.

After the war with Sweden some changes were made in the Norwegian administration. "Slotsloven paa Akershus," which had proven inefficient, was abolished, and Ditlev Vibe was appointed to succeed Baron Krag as *statholder*. Vibe was a man of ability and fine character, but as he was inclined to favor the common people when he found that they suffered injustice, he was opposed by the corrupt bureaucracy, and especially by the rather unscrupulous Bishop Deichmann of Christiania. The bishop succeeded for a while in ingratiating himself with the king by arousing his suspicion against

Vibe, and a commission was appointed to examine conditions among the royal officials in Norway. Vibe was shown to be wholly innocent, but corruption was revealed on every hand. Malversation and the taking of bribes had become a common practice among the under-paid royal officials, who could urge in their defense that their salaries were too small to afford them an honest living. Among those who were guilty of these corrupt practices was Bishop Deichmann himself, who seldom refused a bribe. The king sought to remedy these defects by increasing the salaries of many officials, and by restricting the sale of public offices which had hitherto been so common.

The king had placed Deichmann at the head of a commission to prepare a new tax register for Norway, a work which involved the listing and valuation of all real estate in the kingdom. It was an important undertaking, but as it was done with little care, the work when completed suffered from many serious defects, and it was not accepted. It is, nevertheless, important as a document throwing light on the conditions of agriculture in Norway at the time.

During the last ten years of his reign King Frederick devoted special attention to the revenues of the kingdom, and the paying of the national debt, which had been increasing during the long war. The war indemnity of 600,000 riksdaler paid by Sweden, and the acquisition of the Gottorp provinces in Schleswig, had been a welcome aid, but as the king succeeded in reducing the debt by several million riksdaler, besides maintaining a large standing army, he found that the revenues were too small in spite of the very heavy taxes, and the sale of property belonging to the crown was again resorted to. In Norway the remaining crown-lands were sold in smaller parcels, and as the purchasers usually were the renters and tillers of the lands, the class of freeholding *bønder* was increased by these sales. The king's chief care, however, was to replenish his treasury; the care for the well-being of the individual citizen seemed to be purely accidental. Not only were the crown-lands sold, but also the church-lands and the churches themselves. With the introduction of the Reformation the state assumed control of all church property, the idea being that the state should administer it for the benefit of the church. But the kings soon swept the incomes from the church-lands into their own coffers. The absolute kings regarded themselves even as the owners of the churches, and when the sale of crown-lands was resumed, Frederick IV. sold the churches with their lands and revenues to the highest bidder. In all, 620 churches were sold, some to the congregations, but the greater number were bought by private individuals who wished to get possession of the lands and incomes belonging to the churches. The understanding was that the purchasers should spend a part of the revenue in keeping the churches in repair, but as the kings themselves had been remiss in the performance of this duty, it could scarcely be expected that the individual purchaser should be more conscientious, and the churches were most deplorably neglected. A great change was, nevertheless, taking place in religious life and thought. Pietism, which had been developed in Germany by pious and able men like Johan Arnd and Christian Scriver, was finally promulgated as a regenerated system of Christian faith by Philip Jacob Spener and August Hermann Francke. It demanded that Christianity should not consist only in orthodox Christian faith, but that faith should express itself as a living force in human life and conduct, a truth which, together with the strong appeals to the heart and the feelings, and the often undue emphasis laid on the sentimental side of religious life, made Pietism appear as a violent reaction against the dead formalism of orthodoxy. The time for such a reaction had come, and Pietism swept through the North as a spiritual tidal wave which culminated in the reign of King Frederick's successor, Christian VI. The first important manifestations of the change are noticeable in King Frederick's reign in a tendency among many of the ablest men to emphasize especially the ethical side of Christianity. Even the king himself inclined towards Pietism during his later years, though his lax morals conformed little to the cardinal principles of the new teaching. Pietism awakened a new religious life, which soon manifested itself in a very earnest and successful missionary activity. The two great missionaries whose work was of special importance were Hans Egede, who carried Christianity to the Eskimos in Greenland, and Thomas v. Westen, who began missionary work among the Finns in northern Norway.

Egede was born on the Lofoten Islands in northern Norway,

January 31, 1686. He became a clergyman in these islands, but very early he became enthusiastically interested in a plan to reëstablish commercial relations with Greenland, and to become a missionary in the old Norse colonies, which he thought still existed there. In 1721 he finally succeeded in obtaining from people in Bergen the necessary aid to fit out an expedition. On May 3d he set sail for Greenland, and landed two months later on the island of Imeriksok, where he founded the colony of Godthaab. The Council of Missions had appointed him a missionary, and the Greenland Company of Bergen had made him manager of the commerce with Greenland, but neither the government nor any one else understood the importance of his undertaking, and he received but little assistance. Aided by his faithful wife, Gertrude Rask, Egede labored for fifteen years among the Eskimos under the greatest privations and difficulties. His own words may be placed as a motto over the self-sacrificing life-work of this devoted couple. "God's honor alone, and the enlightenment of the ignorant people has been, is, and shall ever be my sole aim, yes, my heart's constant desire until my death." His hope of finding the old Norse colonists was not realized. He discovered the ruins of their homes and churches, but not a white man was found in the island. But his work was crowned with success both religiously and commercially, and led to the recolonization of Greenland. The Greenland Company was dissolved in 1727, but the king had become interested in the undertaking, and sent other missionaries to Greenland to assist Egede. When his wife died in 1735, Egede left his son Paul Egede in charge of the mission and returned to Denmark. He was created bishop and devoted his remaining years to the writing of several works about Greenland.[1]

Hans Egede was an adherent of orthodoxy, but his contemporary, Thomas v. Westen, born in Trondhjem in 1682, was strongly influenced by Pietism. In 1709 Westen was appointed rector of Véey church in Romsdal, and found opportunity to coöperate with

---

[1] Hans Egede, *Det gamle Grønlands nye Perlustration eller Naturhistorie*, Copenhagen, 1741. *Omstændelig Relation angaaende den grønlandske Missions Begyndelse og Fortsættelse*, Copenhagen, 1738. *Kort Beretning om den grønlandske Missions Beskaffenhed*, Copenhagen, 1737. Eilert Sundt, *Egedes Dagbog i Udtog*, Christiania, 1860. Hans Fenger, *Hans Egede og den grønlandske Missions Historie 1712–1760.* Gustav Nieritz, *Hans*

several other Pietist ministers of that district. This little fraternity, known as "Syvstjernen," constituted a sort of *collegium pietatis*. They met to discuss ways and means for improving the people's moral and religious life, they distributed hymnbooks and collections of sermons among their parishioners, and urged the government to sell Bibles and catechisms so cheap that the people could afford to buy them, an appeal which led to the reduction of the price of Bibles from ten to one riksdaler. They pictured the ignorance and moral depravity of the people in the very darkest colors, and urged that schoolmasters should be employed, at least one in each parish. Thomas v. Westen writes as follows: "The common people are for the most part so little versed in Christian knowledge that they do not even know who Christ is. Many do not believe in the immortality of the soul or the resurrection of the body, while others, who are educated, are usually given to pride, drunkenness, covetousness, hardness of heart, disregard of God's word, cursing, and breaking of the Sabbath. . . . All this is the kingdom of the devil; therefore we demand, and Christ through us, that, for the sake of the first named, catechizing and schools be everywhere instituted, and that, for the sake of the others, church discipline be revived in its old apostolic vigor; that, for the sake of both, priests be appointed who are filled with the spirit of God, and can set their flock a good example." [1] The demand raised by the Pietists for better popular education bore no immediate fruit, but their suggestion and agitation brought the matter to the attention of the government in such a way that steps were soon taken to improve conditions.

In 1716 Thomas v. Westen began his missionary work among the Finns (Lapps). From 1716 till 1722 he made three trips to Finmarken to bring the gospel to these nomads. The efforts which had hitherto been made to Christianize them had been of small importance, and they were yet almost wholly heathen. Thomas v. Westen urged

Egede, Missionary to Greenland, translated from the German by Rev. Wm. H. Gotwald, Philadelphia, 1873. Daniel Bruun, *Det høie Nord,* p. 188 ff. Edvard Holm, *Danmark-Norges Historie fra den store nordiske Krigs Slutning til Rigernes Adskillelse,* vol. I., p. 563 ff. *De norske Findlappers Beskrivelse,* Copenhagen, 1790. J. Quigstad, *Historisk Oversigt over Oplysningsarbeidet blandt Finnerne i Finmarken,* 1907.

[1] Daniel Thrap, *Thomas von Westen og Finne-missjonen,* Christiania, 1882.

strongly that missionary work among them should be done in their own language, and he succeeded in organizing a *Seminarium Lapponicum* in connection with the Trondhjem Latin school, where missionaries might be properly educated. When he died in 1727, no one was found who at once could continue his work, but he had opened a new field for missionary activity, and had laid foundations for successful work in the future.

In his old age Frederick IV. was wholly converted to Pietism, which in his gloomy mind developed into religious pessimism, and a fanatic solicitude for the spiritual welfare of his subjects. He felt that the state ought to take more drastic measures to make people pious and moral, and in 1730 he issued his notorious Sabbath ordinance, which virtually destroyed every vestige of religious freedom. Fines were imposed for not attending church, and those who failed to pay the fines should be pilloried; "for which purpose pillories shall be provided by the church-owners for all churches where none such are found," says the ordinance. This is the beginning of the reign of fanaticism, and the violent interference with people's private life in the interest of religion which characterizes the age of Pietism. King Frederick IV. died October 12, 1730, at Odense, and was succeeded by his son, Christian VI.

41. CHRISTIAN VI. THE AGE OF PIETISM

Prince Christian was thirty-one years of age when he ascended the throne of Denmark-Norway. He had been reared according to the strict precepts of Pietism, and was morally better trained and also better educated than his father. He was of a retiring disposition, pious and moral, and as his queen, the German princess Sophia Magdalena of Kulmback-Baireuth, shared his views and tastes, they led a felicitous married life. Both physically and intellectually Christian VI. was undersized, thin and small of frame, with a shrill and piping voice. He became easily excited, and blushed and stuttered in company, but towards his companions and subordinates he showed his authority even to harshness and pedantry. He was, on the whole, better qualified to enter a monastery than to ascend a throne. He had not traveled, he knew little about military affairs, and still less about finances, and as he had assumed an almost hostile attitude to his father, because of his moral laxity, and especially because of his marriage to Anna Sophia Reventlow, he reversed as far as possible the policy hitherto pursued, even to the extent of discarding its good features. A number of discontented nobles and men of rank who had gathered about the crown prince during his father's reign were now appointed to the highest offices, and became prominent as the king's chief advisers. Baron Iver Rosenkrans was made chancellor, though without special title, since the office had been abolished. Kr. Ludvig Plessen was placed at the head of the exchequer, Paul Løvenørn became secretary of war and navy, and Count Christian Rantzau was appointed *statholder* in Norway. King Frederick's widowed queen, Anna Sophia Reventlow, and all his adherents were made to feel the king's displeasure. Bishop Deichmann of Christiania was dismissed from his office, and a Norwegian, Peder Hersleb, was appointed as his successor. Anna Sophia Reventlow was given a pension, but had to retire from court to her private estate, Klausholm.

Christian V. and Frederick IV. had developed a sort of cabinet system of government, and the Colleges created by the ordinance issued by Frederick III., November 4, 1660, had been reduced to mere administrative bureaus. Christian VI. revived the old system, and raised the Colleges to their former importance. In administrative affairs he seldom deviated from their recommendations, though in his relation to his advisers he maintained an independence which seems out of proportion to his limited talents. Men of real ability he could not tolerate. Many of those whom he had himself appointed to high offices had to withdraw, and even Christian Rantzau, Statholder of Norway, a generous and highly cultured nobleman, who had become very popular because of his affability and sense of justice, was soon retired on a pension, and the office of *statholder* was abolished.

In 1733 King Christian and his queen, accompanied by a large retinue, made a journey through Norway, and the people received the royal pair with great enthusiasm. In the cities triumphal arches were erected, songs were written to their honor, and everything possible was done to express the profound veneration and loyalty accorded royal personages in those times. The journey across the mountains was made with wagons, but as the roads were still very poor, the progress was slow and difficult. To the people along the route the entertaining of such a large retinue became a heavy burden, and though the king was highly pleased with his successful and only visit to Norway, the people remembered him as the ruler who took their property without paying for it, and whose visit had only brought them labor and loss.

Christian VI. evidently meant to rule well. He began his reign by reducing the taxes, but as he knew nothing about economy, he spent with lavish hands the surplus in the treasury which his father had created, and when the money was spent, he was again forced to increase the taxes. His reign was a period of unbroken peace, but the diplomatic relations with foreign nations became a strange medley of weakness, vacillation, and ambitions unrealized, as the king was unable to formulate a clearly defined foreign policy, or to adhere with firmness to a position once taken. His advisers often disagreed; some preferring an alliance with England, others with France, and no one seemed to possess the ability or authority to act with energy at the critical moment.

In order to safeguard the Gottorp provinces in Schleswig which had lately been acquired, King Christian formed an alliance with Russia, and signed the Pragmatic Sanction, promulgated by Emperor Charles VI. of Austria in favor of his daughter Maria Theresa. Thereby he won the favor of both these powers, who had hitherto favored Gottorp, but an attempt to secure an alliance with Sweden failed. Between France and England a very hostile feeling was developing, which finally culminated in the War of the Austrian Succession, and the struggle between the two rival powers for supremacy in India and America. In 1734 an alliance with England was concluded for three years, but some of the king's advisers favored France, and labored to secure a closer friendship with that power. This made matters complicated, as both powers had guaranteed to Denmark the possession of the Gottorp provinces, and had a claim to the Danish king's friendship and gratitude. But though the relations of the two western powers were delicate, it was of less vital importance than the question which developed in connection with a new struggle between Sweden and Russia.

After Czar Peter's death, the Russian fleet had been neglected, and rival candidates for the throne were maintaining a struggle which paralyzed the arm of the government. In Sweden the patriotic war party, *hatterne* (the hats), had gained the power, and they found the moment opportune for a war with Russia, in which some of the lost provinces might be recovered. In 1741 General Levenhaupt was sent into Finland with an army, and war against Russia was declared. Elizabeth, the daughter of Peter the Great, who was plotting to wrest the throne from the child Czar, Ivan VI., solicited the aid of the Swedes, and Levenhaupt crossed the Russian border; but before he reached St. Petersburg, Elizabeth had been made Empress of Russia, and she immediately ordered him to withdraw from Russian territory. Instead of acting with energy, the Swedish general concluded an armistice, and retreated to Finland, and the opportunity for obtaining any concessions was lost. After a campaign in which they suffered many losses, the Swedes were forced to withdraw even from Finland, which was overrun by the Russians.

Under these circumstances the Swedes had turned to Denmark-Norway for aid, and suggestions were made which filled Christian VI. with high hopes. His son, Crown Prince Frederick, might be chosen king of Sweden to succeed Ulrika Eleonora, who died in 1741, and Denmark, Norway, and Sweden might again be united. After the expiration of the treaty with England, 1742, King Christian had concluded a treaty with France, and received from that kingdom 400,000 riksdaler as a yearly subsidy. He raised the Danish-Norwegian army to war-footing, and held the fleet ready for immediate service to coöperate with Sweden in case Frederick should be chosen king. The Swedish peasants were enthusiastically in favor of the Danish-Norwegian crown prince, but Russia supported Adolph Frederick of Holstein-Gottorp, and promised to return nearly all of Finland to Sweden, if he were elected. When the Riksdag assembled at Stockholm, the Dalkarlean peasants marched in force to the city to secure the election of Prince Frederick of Denmark-Norway, but they were dispersed by the military forces of the city, and Adolph Frederick of Holstein-Gottorp was chosen king of Sweden, July 3, 1743. Christian VI. now demanded that Adolph Frederick should formally relinquish all claims to the Gottorp provinces which had been given to Denmark, but even this simple plan of safeguarding his kingdom against undue encroachment of united Sweden and Gottorp he was persuaded to abandon. His diplomacy had failed at every point; his numerous alliances proved to be harmless stage thunder accompanying a political farce, and his enemies had restored the relations existing between Gottorp and Denmark prior to the Great Northern War.

But if King Christian was no statesman, financier, or warrior, he had at least the satisfaction of knowing that he excelled in piety. Frederick the Great had remarked that as Frederick IV. attempted to conquer Sweden, Christian VI. sought to conquer heaven. In his father's time Pietism had been gaining a foothold in the North, and during the early years of the reign of Christian VI. it waged a final contest with orthodoxy, which resulted in a complete triumph for Pietism, owing largely to the support of the king, who was an adherent of the new movement. Queen Sophia Magdalena was of a pious and melancholy disposition, and as the king himself became devotedly absorbed in religious matters, the gayety of the court circles soon gave way to the grave and joyless austerity of Pietism, which forced all social and religious life into stern forms and somber colors. The king considered it to be his special mission to drive all his subjects into the sackcloth and ashes of repentance, that as many as possible might escape eternal perdition, and he instituted a vigorous campaign against all forms of amusements which were considered sinful. According to the views of the Pietists, nearly all public pastimes were regarded as worldly pleasures. Dancing, smoking, comedies, and operas were categorically condemned, and even laughter was regarded as sinful. August Hermann Francke says: "All laughter is not forbidden, for it happens, indeed, that even the most pious may so heartily rejoice, not over worldly, but over heavenly things, that his lips may show evidence of his mental delight in a faint laughter. But it easily becomes sinful, and paves the way for great distraction of the mind, which soon discovers that it has become too unthoughtful when it again wishes to meekly turn to God." [1] According to these principles Christmas parties were wholly interdicted,

---

[1] Christen Brun, *Pietismens Begreb og Væsen*, p. 59, quoted from Francke's *Schriftmässige Lebensregeln*.

amusements on Sundays and holidays were prohibited, and the playing of comedies on Saturdays, Sundays, and holidays was forbidden. It is true, as Edvard Holm points out,[1] that the king did not forbid comedies, dances, and masquerades except on the days mentioned, but it is very doubtful if we can infer from this that the people could dance as much as they pleased on the remaining five days of the week. The king created a church college (*kirkeinspections kollegiet*), which possessed most extensive powers in matters of church discipline, and the bishops and clergy labored hard to suppress all such amusements. Finally, in 1738, the king issued an order that "no comedians, funambulists, jugglers, or operators of games of hazard must henceforth appear in Denmark or Norway to show their plays or exercises."[2] The king's attitude to the players of comedies may also be seen from his letter to J. S. Schulin, dated August 30, 1735, in which he says: "In Glückstadt there are said to be some comedians who pull money out of people's pockets. It would be well if the magistrate were instructed to get rid of them, for nothing good comes of it." In 1735 the king published a new Sabbath ordinance very similar to the one issued by Frederick IV. in 1730. Persons who without valid reason remained absent from public worship were fined, and if they were *bønder*, they should be put in the pillory. That this attempt to teach people Christian piety and good morals by means of the pillory and the police force would breed deceit and hypocrisy is quite natural. Conversation and conduct assumed of a sudden a religious tone which in too many instances only seemed to hide moral corruption and intellectual dishonesty.

Pietism had come as a violent reaction against the moral laxity of the age of orthodoxy, and such a movement usually passes the bounds of fairness and good policy. It is like a fever which reacts against the disease, and saves life, but destroys tissue and reduces the vitality. Orthodoxy had failed to lay proper stress on the moral side of Christian life, and moral corruption and rude manners had flourished to an almost intolerable degree. To cure this evil, Pietism raised moral life into a prominence which made a deep impression on the age, and greatly elevated its moral tone, but it arrested the

---

[1] *Danmark-Norges Historie*, vol. II., p. 644 ff.
[2] Georg Brandes, *Ludvig Holberg, et Festskrift*, p. 278.

growth of dramatic art, destroyed many of the finer features of intellectual and social life, and robbed society of the spirit of optimism and the sense of beauty. It cannot be denied, however, that viewed against the background of what preceded it, Pietism represents progress along many lines. It was the first religious revival which the Norwegian people had ever experienced, and through the emphasis which it laid on piety and moral conduct it chastened the people's moral feelings, and taught them gentleness, temperance, and a higher regard for things spiritual. It gave also a new impetus to intellectual development through a keen interest for popular education. If the people were to become truly pious, they would have to read the Scriptures, and learn the chief Christian doctrines. The religious instruction which the people had hitherto received had been so meager that few understood even the cardinal Christian teachings, and among the common people it was regarded as a wonder if a person could read. In 1736 *confirmation* was introduced by law both in Denmark and Norway. In Akershus *stift* it had been introduced in 1734 by Bishop Peder Hersleb. The young communicants were now required to formally renew their baptismal vow before their first communion, after being catechised in church in presence of the congregation to prove that they possessed the required Christian knowledge. About the same time the important religious textbook, Bishop Erik Pontoppidan's "Sandhed til Gudfrygtighed," an explanation to Luther's Catechism arranged in questions and answers, was introduced. As the children were expected to commit these answers to memory, they would have to learn to read, and steps were taken to provide the necessary instruction. By the ordinance of January 23, 1739, "About the country schools in Norway" the government attempted to establish a system of public schools, and to enforce compulsory attendance of all school children between seven and twelve years of age. Instruction should be given from six to seven hours daily, at least during three months of each year; the schoolbooks should be Luther's Catechism, Pontoppidan's Explanation, the Bible, and the hymnbook. The bishops and *stiftsamtmænd* were instructed to appoint teachers, and the people were encouraged to build schoolhouses. If no schoolhouse could be provided, the school was to be kept in private houses by itinerant teachers. If this law had been enforced, it would have marked a great advance in popular education, but the people did not understand the value of the reform, and offered such resistance that the government had to substitute a new ordinance in 1741 which made it optional for the congregation to provide instruction for the children. Opposition and indifference had retarded progress, but the bishops and priests could bring great pressure to bear on the people, as they could refuse to confirm the children who did not possess the required knowledge. The resistance was gradually broken, and several public schools were organized before the close of the reign of Christian VI.

42. MERCANTILISM AND COMMERCIAL STAGNATION

With regard to the economic conditions in Denmark-Norway in the time of Frederick IV. and Christian VI. we may observe the futile attempts to increase the wealth and revenues of the realms by enforcing the arbitrary principles of mercantilism by means of despotic royal power. The government assumed the initiative and direction of industrial enterprises, sought to encourage their growth by various artificial stimuli, and exhibited an activity and paternal solicitude which resembled wisdom and generosity, but which was so selfish and narrow that it produced stagnation where it sought to foster new life and activity. Companies organized to trade with the West Indies, Guinea, Morocco, and other distant lands were granted monopolies and other special privileges, but at the same time a system of protective tariff, export duties, and the exclusion of various foreign goods subverted the most fundamental laws of trade. Importation of grain to Norway from any other country than Denmark was forbidden, though the supply was often inadequate, the quality poor, and the prices exorbitant. This restriction was especially damaging to Norway's commerce with England, as Norwegian lumber and fish had been exported to England in exchange for grain. The carrying trade was obstructed by the English navigation laws and the mercantile system of political economy everywhere adhered to. Prices on lumber and fish fell, and Norwegian commerce suffered a serious decline. The commercial companies proved to be of comparatively little importance, as the few individuals constituting them used their monopoly chiefly to plunder the colonies with whom they were trading. The Iceland Company paid 8000 riksdaler, and later 16,000 riksdaler, for their privileges, and they used their opportunity to fleece the Icelanders. The Asiatic Company carried on trade in India and China; the West-India-Guinea Company with Africa and the West Indies. The trade with Greenland was granted to a single man, Jacob Severin, who founded the colonies of Kristianshaab, Jakobshavn, and Fredrikshaab. The small and precarious trade carried on by these Danish companies at the ends of the earth could in no way compensate for the general decline in Norwegian commerce. In 1736 the merchant fleet of Bergen was scarcely one-third of what it had been in 1700, and even the carrying of Norwegian articles of export to foreign markets was largely in the hands of the Dutch and English.

The efforts of the government, in harmony with the mercantilistic ideas of the times, to encourage manufacture by protective tariff, monopolies, and the subsidizing of various industries failed to produce the results desired. Several minor factories were started, but the depressed economic conditions, and the lack of capital and enterprise, rendered the attempt to produce a new industrial development an almost fruitless experiment.

In Denmark the peasants were more severely oppressed, especially in the reign of Christian VI., than in any previous period. Frederick IV. had abolished serfdom in 1702, but this very praiseworthy reform was rendered nugatory by the revival of the old system of compulsory military service which made it possible for the landed proprietors to virtually enslave the peasants under the pretext of furnishing the required number of men for the army. Christian VI. reëstablished villeinage in all Denmark, and increased the burdens of military service to such an extent that Riegels calls the 900 Danish manorial estates "plantations with white negro slaves." No peasant between fourteen and forty years of age was allowed to leave the estate to which he belonged, and the proprietor could even inflict the most severe corporal punishment upon him at will. "The lash was in constant activity," says Sars. "The system of beating the peasants was so well established that it was practiced even on the estates of humane and kindly disposed proprietors as something necessary which could not be otherwise.   It was regarded as a matter of course that the proprietors had the right to inflict corporal punishment on the peasants; cudgeling was even the least; he could cause them to be thrown into the dungeon; he could put them into the pillory; he could place them in the 'Spanish cloak,' or compel them to ride the wooden horse; in short, the greater number of Danish peasants were reduced to the condition of slaves." With good reason the same author calls the reign of Christian VI. "one of the worst which Denmark ever had." [1]

The freeholding Norwegian *bønder* could not be subjected to such oppression.   It has already been shown that the number of freeholders had been greatly increased in Norway through the sale of crown-lands, and the kings had even shown them special favor, though the old feuds continued to be waged between the *bønder* and the royal officials.   The economic well-being of the *bønder* would, probably, not have been impaired, but in 1740 and 1742 crop failures produced a famine, which was also accompanied by serious epidemic diseases, so that in the latter year the number of deaths exceeded the births by 16,000.   These calamities, together with a serious decline of commerce, made the period one of general depression.

43. DEVELOPMENT OF MODERN DANISH-NORWEGIAN LITERATURE
THE AGE OF LUDVIG HOLBERG

The Reformation had been accompanied by no spiritual awakening in Norway, and the Renaissance had reached the North only as a faint swell caused by the great revival which it had produced in southern Europe.   No new intellectual life had been kindled in the Scandinavian countries, and literature still slumbered in its old dusty folds.   In the universities and the secondary schools the learning was chiefly limited to Latin grammar and disputations, a lifeless pedantry from which no new impulses could come, and the same unprogressive stolidity and vain love of display which characterized learning might be observed in all higher social classes.   Every imagined preëminence was displayed with arrogant self-conceit; jealous rivalries, love of empty titles, narrow-mindedness, snobbish-

---

[1] J. E. Sars, *Udsigt over den norske Historie*, vol. IV., p. 77 ff.

ness, and a crude imitation of everything foreign and *bon ton* had become distinct features of the intellectual life of the age, especially in Denmark, where society had become most thoroughly stratified into distinct classes. The native Danish culture was held in slight esteem, and the mother tongue was so far neglected that persons of quality seldom used it except when talking to their servants. Robert Molesworth, who speaks from personal observation, says: "The king, great men, gentry, and many burghers make use of the High Dutch in their ordinary discourse, and French to strangers. I have heard several in high employment boast that they could not speak Danish."[1] It was the time of Louis XIV. and Louis XV., the era of affectation and long wigs. In literature Petter Dass had, indeed, relieved the general dullness, but with this exception scarcely a note of true poesy found its way into the lifeless pages of the verse-makers. "Few or no books are written," says Molesworth, in speaking of Denmark. "Not so much as a song or a tune was made during three years that I stayed there." In this age of dullness and affectation Holberg appeared to found in Denmark-Norway, not only a new literature, but a new intellectual life. Parallel with the religious awakening which found its expression in the Reformation and the revival of literature, learning, and art in the Renaissance, a new astronomy and natural science had been developed, which demanded freedom of thought and respect for human reason as the ultimate authority in scientific investigation. These new movements were parts of the same general progress of the human mind, but as they advanced along diverging paths, scientific thought not only sought to free itself from religious control, but it soon became hostile to revealed religion, and challenged its genuineness and authority. This school of thought, generally known as deism, because it postulated the existence of God, originated in England, and is traceable in its inception to the philosophical writings of Francis Bacon (1561–1626), though its most prominent representatives were John Locke (1632–1704) and David Hume (1711–1776). From England deism was brought to France, where Voltaire and Rousseau became its chief representatives. It had directed its attack especially against the dominion of the church in the field of scientific investigation,

[1] *An Account of Denmark*, p. 91.

but a similar revolt against religious authority also took place in other fields. Throughout the Middle Ages philosophy had been regarded as the handmaid of theology, and jurisprudence had been dominated by the principles of the Old Testament and the canon law. The emancipation of these branches of learning marks an important step in the victorious progress of scientific thought. In Holland and Germany Hugo Grotius (1583–1645), Pufendorf (1632–1694), and Thomasius (1655–1728) developed a new system of jurisprudence, the *Naturrecht*, based on reason and man's innate sense of justice, and Christian Wolff (1679–1754) elaborated the critical thought of the age into a rationalistic view of life in his philosophic system, based on the work of Leibnitz. The ground had thus been well prepared, and the influence of English deism, both directly from England and indirectly through France, soon made itself strongly felt. This system of critical scientific thought, and rationalism in religion and ethics, which dominated intellectual life in the latter half of the eighteenth century, is probably best known by the German name of *Aufklärung*. Its influence extended to every field of intellectual activity, and expressed itself as clearly in literature and statescraft as in science and philosophy. Frederick the Great applied its principles in his *aufgeklärte despotismus*, according to which he ruled as a benevolent despot.[1] Lessing, the founder of modern German literature and intellectual life, became one of its chief representatives, but passed beyond it in spirituality and broadness of view.[2] In America Benjamin Franklin became its most noted representative, and no one has expressed the common-sense utilitarian view of the *Aufklärung* in a more popular way than America's statesman-philosopher.

In the North Ludvig Holberg (1684–1754) became the pioneer in this field of thought. He was a native of Bergen, and received his early school training in his home town. In 1702 he was sent to the University of Copenhagen, where he completed the required course, and after spending two years at the University of Oxford, and travel-

[1] Other benevolent despots were: Catharine II. of Russia, Gustavus III. of Sweden, Charles III. of Spain, Archduke Leopold of Tuscany, and Emperor Joseph II. of Austria.

[2] Christen Brun, *Oplysningens Tidsalder*, Christiania, 1886. W. E. H. Lecky, *History of the Rise and Influence of Rationalism in Europe*.

ing for some time on the Continent, he returned to Copenhagen, where he spent five years in writing a number of historical works, through which he introduced into history-writing the rationalistic thought of Grotius, Pufendorf, and Thomasius, whom he declares to be his "constant pattern." The most important of these works are: "Introduction til de europæiske Rigers Historier," and "Introduction til Naturens og Folkerettens Kundskab, uddragen af de fornemste Juristers, besynderlig Grotii, Pufendorf og Thomasii Skrifter." In 1714 he was appointed titular professor without salary. Again he spent almost two years abroad studying, especially in Paris, and, finally, in 1717 he was made regular professor of metaphysics, a branch which he especially hated, because of the pedantry of Latin disputations and learning. But it was the only vacancy, and he accepted the position. "There he stands," says Georg Brandes, "the poor professor of metaphysics, against his will, and teaches, to make a living, things in which he does not believe, and with which he can associate no thought, and the black-gowned students in front of him write down the wisdom, and commit it to memory, while round about in the lecture rooms the learned corps with profound gravity defends, demonstrates, concludes, and proves the arrant nothing. Is not the situation ironical, Mephistophelian, or tragicomic?" Holberg was a keen observer, a deep and critical thinker, and a dramatic talent of the first rank. On his mind the burlesque of the situation was not lost. He, the representative of the most advanced scientific thought, who had returned from the greatest centers of learning with rich stores of the best knowledge of the age, was not allowed to teach his students anything worth knowing, because the learned circles loved the shadow rather than the substance of knowledge. And was not all society blinded by pedantry and conceit? Did he not meet it on every street corner? Did not snobbishness and pretense make themselves broad in every thoroughfare? He knew but too well the intellectual pride, the mental dullness, the bigotry, the snobbishness and conceit which masqueraded as civic virtue on every hand. "Is it a wonder," continues Georg Brandes, "if irony becomes the predominant mood of this soul; if a smile, a suppressed smile, curls these lips? or is it not quite natural that the new professor gets a peculiar impression

PLATE VII

PETTER DASS.

LUDVIG HOLBERG.

PEDER CLAUSSØN FRIIS.

of this temple of learning, and the land of which it is the intellectual center; yea, of the whole world? It is comical, this world which he now sees."[1] The great master of comedy has seen the foibles and inconsistencies of the age; it stirs his poetic talents, and launches him upon his career as a poet. From this time forth he enters upon his life work with as high a purpose as any other reformer, though he undertakes his task with no fervent enthusiasm, but rather with a fixed purpose founded on reflection. The pedantry, the conceit, the social foibles must perish; mental sobriety, love of truth, and true esteem of the real value rather than the outward appearance of things must be substituted. This is a lesson which the whole people must learn before the professor can mount his cathedra and teach his students anything worth while. With superb humor he began to show the people the comedy of their own lives. If ever a poet held the mirror up to nature it was Holberg, and human foibles have never been delineated by a more clever pen. He wrote the burlesque epic "Peder Paars," showing the humorous inconsistence of the pretended greatness and the real ability and achievements of his countrymen. It aroused a storm of indignation, but the king was amused by the poem, and refused to imprison the author to appease the wrath of the angry citizens. But though the poem created a veritable sensation, Holberg knew that it would be read by few, and he chose the comedy as the more popular and suitable vehicle for his thoughts.

Before Holberg's time no dramatic literature and no real theater existed in Denmark. The old school comedy had gone out of use, and at court only light operas and French tragedies were performed. In 1721 King Frederick IV. dismissed a company of players, two of whom, Montagu and Capion, received permission to build theaters. Montagu hit upon the idea of building a Danish theater, hoping that this would be more popular and bring a larger income, and in 1722 the first Danish theater was opened, an event which proved to be of more than ordinary importance, as it marks the beginning of dramatic literature and art in Denmark-Norway. During the first year Hol-

[1] Georg Brandes, *Ludvig Holberg, et Festskrift*, p. 99. J. S. Welhaven, *Samlede Skrifter*, vol. VI., p. 155 ff. H. Lassen, *Oplysninger til Literaturhistorien*.

berg gave the new theater his five first comedies which were all performed; and before the end of the following year he wrote ten more. In six years (1722–1728) he wrote no less than twenty-eight plays, the masterpieces which have made his name immortal. But the theater yielded small returns, the owners labored under great financial difficulties, and when Christian VI. ascended the throne, and Pietism gained full control, it had to close its doors. It was reopened in 1747, and Holberg wrote his last five comedies. What he might have written in the interval under favorable circumstances may be inferred from his productivity during the years when the theater was operated. But even during that period he was not inactive. He wrote "Nils Klim," a satire on European society in the strain of "Gulliver's Travels," a church history till the time of the Reformation, and a history of Denmark in two volumes. His work in this field marks the beginning of a new epoch in history-writing in the North, but Holberg was not a great historian. He describes events and social conditions without prejudice, in a clear and lively narrative, but he did not devote himself to historic research. He fails to judge each age by its own standards, and establishes the standards of his own time and his own good judgment as the criterion according to which he estimates the value of past institutions and events. He was a dramatist and reformer of the first rank. He gave the intellectual life of the North the first great impulse which it had received since the Viking Age, destroyed the old idols of pedantry and conceit, founded modern Scandinavian literature and dramatic art, and launched his people upon a new era of intellectual progress. "He began by being a lonely stranger who was against all and all against him, who was unlike all his surroundings, and who differed from them in all respects, but he ended as the master whom all followed, and to whom all submitted. What he consigned to forgetfulness was forgotten, and the new which he introduced became the foundation on which Danish-Norwegian intellectual life has since been building." [1]

The events of the late war with Sweden, in which the Norwegians had successfully resisted the attacks of Charles XII., and the fact that Norway could produce men like Ludvig Holberg and Peter

[1] J. E. Sars, *Udsigt over den norske Historie*, vol. IV., p. 124.

Tordenskjold proved a great stimulus to the national self-consciousness, and helped to kindle a new patriotism. Throughout the union period Danish influence had dominated all higher culture in Norway; now the tide had turned, and Norway was giving to Denmark new vigor and intellectual life. After centuries of dormant inactivity, the Norwegian people were regaining their national and intellectual strength. It was the beginning of a new awakening.

44. FREDERICK V.

When Christian VI. died, August 6, 1746, his son, who was twenty-four years of age, ascended the throne as Frederick V. The prince had been educated by foreign teachers who had not only neglected to interest him in the language of his own people, but had even sought to prevent him from learning it, an effort in which they had not succeeded. Frederick had learned to speak Danish, and he even regarded that language as his native tongue, to the chagrin of his German mother, who considered it too common. Also in other respects the labors of his teachers had borne little fruit. The Pietistic gloom and rigor which surrounded the prince from childhood made him averse to all restraint, and when he could escape the watchful eyes of his parents and teachers, he abandoned himself to licentious pleasures in company with profligate courtiers, who visited low dives, and taught him even from youth to lead a life of debauchery. In 1743 he was married to Louise, the daughter of George II. of England, a very charming princess, but even then he was unable to abandon his vicious habits, though the marriage does not seem to have been an unhappy one. Both King Frederick and Queen Louise were very popular, as they surrounded themselves with a Danish court and mingled freely with the people. The restrictions which had been placed on public amusements were removed. The theaters were reopened, the people were allowed to return to their old merry ways, and the court circles were again made bright by balls and soirées, a welcome change from the joyless gloom of the preceding reign.

The relations to Gottorp, which had again become a political question of importance in his father's reign, caused the young king some anxiety, especially since the successors to the thrones of Russia and Sweden were both princes of the House of Gottorp. It became his first care to bring about a final settlement of this question, and to trade Oldenburg and Delmenhorst for the Gottorp part of Holstein, so that the southern boundary of the kingdom could become properly rounded out. After prolonged negotiations this was accomplished by the treaty of 1750, in which the heir to the throne of Sweden, Adolph Frederick of Gottorp, renounced for himself and his heirs all claims to the island of Femern and the part of Schleswig which had belonged to his family. The Gottorp part of Holstein should be ceded to Denmark in return for Oldenburg and Delmenhorst, and 200,000 riksdaler, if Karl Peter Ulrik, successor to the Russian throne, should die without heirs. This treaty practically eliminated the troublesome Gottorp question from politics, and made it possible to maintain friendly relations with Sweden. The boundary dispute between Norway and Sweden was also settled. Norway retained Kautokeino and Karasjok in Finmarken, and a commission was established to survey and mark the boundary line throughout its entire length.

The people had hoped that their liberal-minded and popular king would institute many needed reforms, but his suavity of manners was associated with moral weakness and mental ineptitude rather than with originality of thought. His irregular life sapped his physical strength, and enveloped his mind in the intoxication of sensual pleasures. He gradually became unfit for systematic work, and the direction of state affairs devolved upon his ministers. In 1751 Johan Hartvig Ernst Bernstorff became minister of foreign affairs, a position for which he was eminently qualified. He was a man of great ability and high character, and though only thirty-nine years of age he was an experienced diplomat. In the administration of domestic affairs he sought to realize the liberal and benevolent ideas of the *Aufklärung* to a moderate degree, and in his foreign policy he was an avowed friend of peace. "War," he said, "if begun without valid reason, yea without necessity, is one of the most deplorable steps which a human being can take." During the naval war between France and England in 1755, caused by the rivalries of these powers in India and America, and during the Seven Years'

War, 1756–1763, in which Prussia and England were pitted against Austria, Russia, France, and Sweden, Bernstorff maintained the neutrality of Denmark-Norway, though with great difficulty. Thirteen thousand five hundred twenty men of the Norwegian army were stationed in Holland for the defense of the duchies of Schleswig-Holstein, and an alliance of neutrality was concluded with Sweden, according to which the two powers agreed to keep a joint fleet in the North Sea to protect their commerce, while the Baltic Sea was to be closed to the war vessels both of England and France. This alliance, however, proved of little value, as Sweden, in 1757, joined Austria, Russia, and France in their war against Frederick the Great. The protection of commerce against English privateers proved a most difficult task, as England regarded nearly all products exported from the neutral kingdoms as contraband of war, and the government was loath to resort to drastic measures for fear of becoming involved in the war. But with remarkable tact and prudence Bernstorff succeeded in saving Denmark-Norway from being drawn into the vortex of the great struggle.[1]

The new ideas of the *Aufklärung* began to exert their influence on the more progressive minds, and the charm of discovering that there was something besides war and diplomacy which was worth while turned the attention of many to the pursuits of peace. Bernstorff devoted special attention to the development of trade, manufactures, arts, sciences, and agriculture. Treaties were concluded with Turkey and the Barbary States, which enabled Denmark-Norway to develop an extensive carrying trade in the Mediterranean Sea, and the trade with the West Indies began to flourish when the monopoly of the West India Company was annulled. In 1753 only seven vessels were engaged in the commerce with these islands, but in 1766 the number had been increased to thirty-eight. The neutrality maintained during the Seven Years' War contributed greatly to the growth of Danish-Norwegian commerce, and the East India Company developed a flourishing trade during the war.

In order to develop manufacture, foreign artisans and skilled

---

[1] Regarding Bernstorff's policy see *Dansk historisk Tidsskrift*, R. IV., p. 672 ff. *Danske Samlinger*, vol. IV., p. 292 ff. *Danmarks Riges Historie*, V., p. 203 ff.

laborers were employed, monopolies and special privileges were granted, and the importation of manufactured articles was greatly restricted. In these measures the ideas of mercantilism are still clearly noticeable; but more attention was also paid to agriculture than hitherto, as the ideas of the French Physiocrats were gaining ground.[1] This new economic doctrine, which was tinged with the ideas of Rousseau and other French political philosophers, who maintained that government exists for the good of the governed, that freedom and equality are man's birthright, and that a return to nature was necessary if man wished to find true happiness, gave the agricultural classes a hitherto unknown importance. New sociological ideas were being developed which were destined to produce great changes. Hitherto these ideas had been scouted as dangerous theories, if they had not been regarded as idle dreams, but already in the reign of Frederick V. they were beginning to exert a distinct influence. In 1757 King Frederick appointed a commission to examine the conditions of husbandry, and to submit recommendations for the encouragement and improvement of agriculture. The king's mother, Queen Sophia Magdalena, abolished villeinage on her estate of Hirschholm, Bernstorff followed her example, and before the close of the reign the liberation of the peasants in Denmark had been adopted as the future program of the government.

In Norway the national awakening created new activity, and shaped new demands in many fields. In 1760 the first scientific society in Norway, *Det Trondhjemske Videnskabs-Selskab*, was founded in Trondhjem by the three distinguished scholars: Peter Friedrich

[1] The Physiocratic School of political economy was originated in France by François Quesnay (1694–1774). According to their views the government should only administer justice and defend the rights of the citizens. The liberty of the individual should not be restricted, nor should the government exercise any control over commerce and industry. Their economic doctrine was based on the cardinal principle that nature is the source of all good. Since all wealth comes from the soil and the atmosphere, agriculture is the great productive employment. Manufacture, being only a change in the form of the material, does not change its value. Commerce, being only an exchange, does not add to the value of things. As an economic system it was one-sided and wholly unscientific, but it rendered good service through the importance it ascribed to agriculture, which had hitherto been generally neglected.

Suhm, a Dane by birth, who had settled in Trondhjem, and the two native-born Norwegians, Gerhard Schøning and Johan Ernst Gunnerus. The historical writings of Suhm, especially his "Historie af Danmark," from the earliest times till 1400, reveals a new scholarly spirit in history-writing, a love for scientific inquiry which comes to view even more plainly in Schøning's "Norges Riges Historie," in three volumes, from the earliest times till 955. Schøning has written his work from a Norwegian point of view, and has advanced a theory of the earliest migrations into Norway, which was elaborated seventy years later by R. Keyser and P. A. Munch, the founders of the Norwegian historical school,—a theory which has served as the general basis for the views of Norwegian scholars as to the origin and early antiquity of the Norwegian people. Gunnerus was a theologian, and became Bishop of Trondhjem, but he distinguished himself also in philosophy and mathematics. It is noteworthy that this society of scholars devoted much attention to the discussion of agriculture, and that several treatises on this subject appeared in the society's journal. The stimulus imparted by this new organization to the interest for higher intellectual culture was accompanied, also, by an active agitation for the founding of a Norwegian university. Suhm wrote, 1761, in "Trondhjemske Samlinger," a periodical published by him in Trondhjem: "In no land in Europe are the conditions for the development and spread of the sciences more unfavorable than here, since we have not even a university." [1] And in 1768 Bishop Gunnerus said in an address before the society: "There is no want in Norway of patriotic thoughts, or of the desire, courage, and high spirit to do useful and praiseworthy things, even at the cost of personal loss, but there is lack of effectual encouragement and necessary guidance and direction in many ways. We have four cathedral schools, but there is in the whole kingdom no public library and no university. The journey to Copenhagen is long and expensive. The greater number of students are, moreover, poor, and howsoever many rich foundations there be at the said university for the benefit of such students, all cannot be supported there. This is the reason why so many Norwegians of this class, who, on account of the

---

[1] *Trondhjemske Samlinger, udgivet af Philaletho*, vol. I., p. 41, quoted by J. E. Sars, *Udsigt over den norske Historie*, vol. IV., p. 183.

public examinations, have been at the university two or three times, have scarcely remained longer than a few months. This can, indeed, be called to visit, but not to study at the university, and every one will understand what great harm this is to the cultivation and development of higher learning in Norway." In 1771 Suhm published an anonymous pamphlet, in which he indulges in bitter invective against the Danish government for failing to make provision for higher education in Norway. "It seems to me," he says, "that the Danes from mean-spirited jealousy and unfounded fear seek to perpetuate ignorance in this country. There is no academy, no university, no public library. The Norwegians who wish to study must go to Denmark." Several pamphlets appeared, urging the founding of a Norwegian university, and Ove Gjerløv Meyer subjected the question to a more systematic examination in two treatises published in 1771. He argued that though the two kingdoms were so firmly united that they could never be separated, yet the question of a university was a matter of national concern to the Norwegian people. The agitation for a university was becoming somewhat of a national cause, but the Danish government failed to grant the demand. During the following reign the liberal Struensee favored the plan, but when he was overthrown, the government again became reactionary, and the matter was dropped.[1] The strict censorship of the press, which was still maintained in spite of the king's otherwise liberal views, also stood in the way of carrying through important measures of reforms. Two newspapers had been founded in Norway: "Norske Intelligenssedler," which began to appear in May, 1763, and "Efterretninger fra Adresse Contoret i Bergen," first published in 1765, but neither paper ventured to speak a word in behalf of national issues or to criticize the course pursued by the government. The press had not yet become a factor in political life. If the people wished to express their opinion on public measures,

---

[1] *Det kongelige Fredriks Universitet 1811–1911*, vol. I., p. xii ff. Arne Bergsgaard, *Striden for Universitetet, Syn og Segn*, September, 1911. Halvdan Koht, *Universitete og det norske Folk, Syn og Segn*, September, 1911. *Essay sur l'etat present des sciences, des belles lettres et des beaux arts dans le Dannemark et dans la Norwège.* Suhm, *Samlede Skrifter*, vol. VI., p. 422 ff. O. A. Øverland, *Norges Historie*, vol. IX., p. 319 ff. J. E. Sars, *Udsigt over den norske Historie*, vol. IV., p. 43 f., 183 ff.

they still had to avail themselves of more drastic means, such as the riots caused by the new tax levy of 1762. The armed neutrality which had been maintained during the Seven Years' War had cost large sums, which, together with the support given to manufacture in the form of loans and subsidies, as well as the great extravagance of the court, had placed the government in great financial difficulty. In order to pay the interest and term payments on large loans, a new tax of eight skilling was imposed on every person twelve years of age. In Norway this caused the greatest ill-will, and serious disturbances occurred. In Bergen a force of *bønder*, which was estimated at two thousand, attacked the residence of the *stiftsamtmand*, insulted and ill-treated him, and forced him to refund them the tax which had been collected.[1] In Stavanger and Christiansund, in Romsdal, and many other places serious riots occurred, as the *bønder*, who suffered because of high prices and hard times caused by the war, refused to pay the extra tax.

No very noteworthy changes had been effected during this reign, but Bernstorff's policy in administration and diplomacy had been liberal-minded as well as prudent, and he had given the awakening national feeling an opportunity to grow without exploiting it in the interest of a radical liberalism.

King Frederick V. paid a brief visit to Norway shortly after his accession to the throne, but instead of studying the needs and customs of the kingdom, he spent the time in gambling and making merry with his courtiers. Any higher conception of his duties to his realm and his subjects he never seemed to have entertained. He died in 1766, forty-three years of age.

45. CHRISTIAN VII. AND QUEEN CAROLINA MATHILDA
THE STRUENSEE PERIOD

When King Frederick's son and successor, Christian VII., ascended the throne amid the plaudits of the populace, the truckling seekers of royal favors pronounced the most extravagant panegyrics upon the virtues of the prince, whom they declared to be wiser than Augustus and better than Trajan. But thoughtful men, who knew the young

---

[1] Yngvar Nielsen, *Bergen*, p. 449 ff.

king, shook their heads and mused upon what the future might bring. They knew that he was a moral degenerate; that his mild appearance and frail physique hid the most unbridled passions; that his weak mind might even be wrecked by excess, and leave him a mental imbecile if not a helpless maniac. Christian had not had the good fortune to enjoy proper care in his childhood. His mother, Queen Louise, died December 19, 1751, before he was three years of age, and Juliane Marie, who became King Frederick's second queen half a year later, does not seem to have had much affection for the motherless child. The king was as unfit to watch over his son's early training as he was to govern his kingdoms, and the education of the prince was intrusted to Count Reventlow, an honest and upright, but rude and brutal man. The little prince was forced to go to church twice every Sunday, and to recite at home the contents of the sermons which he had heard. If he failed to satisfy the stern count, he received a thorough flogging. The philosophy of Wolff and the deism of Matthews Tindal were the subjects which his teachers tried to force into his child-mind by diligent application of the rod. In free hours he was left without proper care to associate with corrupt courtiers, who led him into a life of moral degradation which he learned to hide with falsehoods and deceit.[1] The sudden change from a helpless pupil under the dominion of tyrannous masters to an absolute monarch, to whom all showed the most obsequious homage, did not inspire the seventeen-year-old prince with any feeling of responsibility, but only made him feel that the hour of freedom had come at last, when he could throw restraints to the winds, and plunge into wild pleasures without being obliged to hide his waywardness by clever lies. To his physician Wallert he declared shortly after his accession to the throne that he would "rage for two years," and rage he did like no other king that ever wore the royal purple in Denmark. In 1766 he married Princess Carolina Mathilda of England, daughter of Frederick, Prince of Wales, the eldest son of George II.; but this political marriage of the seventeen-year-old king to a princess who was only fifteen years old, and whom he had never before seen, did not in any way improve his wayward private

---

[1] Chr. Blangstrup, *Christian VII. og Caroline Mathilde*, Copenhagen, 1894. Karl Wittich, *Struensee, edited by Blangstrup.*

life. "The society which was found assembled inside the palace walls of Christiansborg," says his biographer, Blangstrup, "endeavored to the best of their ability to become a copy of the world whose fame spread from Versailles over all Europe. One meets here the same kind of characters and thoughtless persons, the same forms of culture, the same frivolous social tone, the same moral laxity. And this circle of richly attired lords and ladies of the court, who move about with the graceful steps of the dance, accost one another with flattery and compliments, and an affected French *esprit*, despising thoroughly the language and culture of their own country, seek to live, also, according to the rules of convenience, and to imitate their model in feelings and ideas, as well as in costumes and demeanor. It was especially necessary to make marriage the object of ridicule and wanton remarks. One cannot read memoirs or accounts of court life of those times without meeting cynical expressions which show how little marriage was esteemed in all higher society. Love and fidelity in married life was regarded as narrow-mindedness and foolish prejudice." [1] Christian VII. had acquired this view of life in the court circles where he had been reared, and he openly confessed that he regarded marriage as a burden.[2] In company with the mischief-loving and dissolute nobles, who became his friends, he roamed about in disguise at night, visiting low dives, breaking windows, throwing furniture into the streets, fighting with the police, and reveling in disorder like the rudest vagabond. The capital was horrified, but Christian smiled in complacent glee over every new escapade like a wayward child. His education, though apparently thorough and profound, was of the most superficial and useless sort. He had learned nothing about statesmanship, military affairs, or finances, nor of the conditions of the kingdoms which he was to govern. His ministers, instead of aiding him to become acquainted with the work of the administration, preferred to keep matters in their own hands, and Bernstorff continued to conduct the affairs of government until he was overthrown by the intriguing Struensee in 1770. As absolute monarch King Christian was the personification

---

[1] *Christian VII. og Caroline Mathilde*, p. 87.

[2] Friedrich von Raumer, *Europa vom Ende des siebenjährigen bis zum Ende des amerikanischen Krieges*, vol. I., p. 138.

of sovereignty, in whose name every act of government was performed, but he exercised no direct influence either on diplomacy or domestic administration. In life and thought as well as in manners and appearance he was more like a French coxcomb than a real king.

The young queen, who had been brought to this corrupt court at so tender an age, and had been married to a young voluptuary for whom she could entertain no other feeling than aversion and disgust, felt lonesome and unhappy. After the birth of Crown Prince Frederick, January 29, 1768, the king treated her with studied disrespect, and even dismissed her duenna and first lady-in-waiting, Lady Plessen, who attempted to guide the young queen, and sought to shield her from the corrupting influences of the court. The unhappy relation between the royal pair developed into an open hatred, and the *ennui* and feeling of unhappiness were undermining the queen's health. In the spring of 1769, when she became really ill, the king finally advised her to consult his physician, Struensee. At first she refused to see the doctor, as she feared that he was like the rest of the king's companions and favorites, but she finally consented to an interview. Struensee, a German by birth, was thirty-two years of age, a man of fine learning and appearance, who knew the art of being agreeable.[1] His culture, intelligence, and sympathy made a most favorable impression on the queen. His visits were repeated, and she soon found in his company and conversation the understanding which she had so ardently longed for. He brought about a reconciliation between her and the king, a help for which she was very grateful. She learned to regard him as her true friend, and the friendship soon ripened into passionate love. The king was rapidly sinking into mental imbecility, and Struensee, who had gained full control over him, was in position to seize the reins which were dropping from his enervated hands. On September 15, 1770, Bernstorff was dismissed from office at the instigation of Struensee, who now assumed full control of the government, together with his two friends, Rantzau-Ascheberg and Enevold Brandt. The king's special favorite and companion, Count Conrad Holck, was banished from the court,

---

[1] Reverdil, *Struensée et la cour de Copenhague*, p. 151, calls him "un homme aimable et insinuant," "un très bel homme, renomé par ses succès aupres des femmes, chasseur et voyageur infatigable."

a number of the highest officials were dismissed, friends of the usurper were appointed to the most important positions, and Brandt was placed in Holck's former position as the king's companion, with the duty of arranging all festivities and amusements at court. The Geheimekonceil was abolished, the Colleges lost their importance, and a government by cabinet orders, *i.e.* orders issued by Struensee and signed by the king, was substituted. In 1771 Struensee persuaded the king to appoint him cabinet minister, a position which virtually made him regent with unlimited power. He now superseded King Christian as ruler, as he had already superseded him in the affections of Queen Mathilda. That he was her paramour was no longer a secret, but the imbecile king, who was as incapable of jealousy as he was of love, seems to have been well satisfied.

Personal ambition was, undoubtedly, the chief motive in Struensee's daring usurpation of royal power, but it is quite clear that he hoped to justify his course in the eyes of the world by doing great things for the realms over which he exercised dominion. He was an adherent of the *Aufklärung*, and as soon as he assumed control of the government, he introduced a series of reforms embodying liberal and progressive ideas. The press was granted complete liberty, patriotic and able men were appointed to public office, the number of empty titles was restricted, and many useless offices and pensions were abolished. Greater economy was practiced at court, so that the public expenditures should not exceed the income, a stricter control was exercised over public officials, and Struensee was an avowed friend of religious toleration.[1] To us these and similar reforms seem very praiseworthy and necessary, but as they were introduced into a society which was as yet unable to understand their value, they proved to be in many cases worse than useless, productive of nothing but grief and harm to their author. Reverdil seems to state it correctly when he says of Struensee's activity as a reformer that his aims were high and noble, but his methods were often ill chosen, and his worst fault was that he believed that people can be reformed by ordinances.[2] It is evident that Struensee had launched his reforms without duly considering his chances of success. The

[1] Jens Krag Høst, *Struensee og hans Ministerium.*
[2] *Struensee, Memoirs de Reverdil*, p. 160 f., 227.

VOL. II — 2 A

old bureaucracy was offended by the stricter control of officials, the cutting down of pensions, and the abolishing of old and useless offices ; the idlers at court, by the introduction of a system of stricter economy and fewer titles, the clergy, by Struensee's religious toleration, while the common classes, steeped in superstition and illiteracy, were none the wiser, and, probably, none the happier because of the attempted reforms. The dissatisfied were those who could speak, those who shaped public opinion, and they took advantage of the freedom of the press to publish lampoons against Struensee, and to stir up public sentiment against him by giving publication to insipid gossip and malignant falsehoods, until he found it necessary to restrict again the freedom of the press.

The Norwegians had remained rather indifferent to Struensee's attempts at reforms, especially since he had wounded their feelings by dismissing the popular *statholder*, Jakob Benzon. But they had formulated certain specific demands which seem to have been favorably regarded by the cabinet minister, and after he had remained in power long enough, there is reason to believe that they would have been granted. To the agitation for a university they added a demand for a separate Commercial College for Norway, and the privilege to found a Norwegian bank with a capital of 500,000 riksdaler, an institution which must have been sorely needed, when we consider the volume of Norwegian commerce. They also demanded the abolition of the extra tax which had been levied in 1762 without the people's consent, and the revocation of the laws prohibiting the importation of grain to Norway from any country but Denmark. Struensee favored the plan of establishing a Norwegian bank, but as the directors of the Danish-Norwegian bank in Copenhagen opposed it, he dropped the matter. The laws restricting grain import were not revoked, but by special order free importation of grain was allowed for a limited period. None of the requested reforms was carried through at this time, but they had been formulated as a distinct demand, and we cannot fail to see in them an effort to separate Norwegian internal affairs from direct Danish control.

Struensee's measures of reform reveal clearly the weakness and short-sightedness characteristic of the *Aufklärung*. As social progress was not to originate in the intelligence and patriotism of the people at large, but was to be brought about artificially by ordinances issued by an enlightened and benevolent despot, no regard was had for the conditions of the society which these reforms were intended to benefit, and the sympathy and national spirit of the people were not enlisted in their support. Struensee was wholly unnational. He despised Danish, and used German exclusively. Like many other despotic reformers of that age, he failed to realize that a people's social and intellectual progress must spring from their own national life, that the incorporating of new ideas as a living force in the old social organism can be accomplished only by the slow progress of moral and intellectual growth. Largely because of his misconception of the true nature of reform he failed to carry through even the most moderate and useful measures. But his work was not wholly in vain. He had brought the liberal views of the *Aufklärung* from the realm of speculation into the more practical one of statescraft and social reform, and had thereby given valuable aid to the progress of liberal political ideas.

That Struensee would be able to exercise permanently his usurped power could not be expected, even if he had been a man of far greater prestige and more influential connections; but as a mere foreign adventurer he could receive no support from the upper classes, who, aside from the king, exercised all power in the realm. He lacked, moreover, many of the qualities which make men truly great, and his lack of prudence and real courage hastened his downfall.[1] He had won to his side one important person, the young queen, who, prompted by love, hazarded all for his sake; but others who might have been won were repelled by his arrogance, or offended by his recklessness. The moral tone of the court was not improved by Struensee, and he took no care to conceal his relation to the queen. Emboldened by her affections for the usurper, and the spirit of the circles in which she moved, she abandoned her former modest ways, and indulged in imprudent frolic, which gave great offense, and became the topic of damaging gossip. She appeared in public in male attire, she rode her horse *à califourchon*, and played other gay pranks which were little in keeping with the dignity of a queen. Struensee, who was now guiding both her destiny and his own,

[1] Karl Wittich, *Struensee*, p. 94 ff.

ought to have been her mentor, as the preservation of her good name should have been a matter of great concern to him, if for no higher motive than the promotion of his own selfish aims. But instead of wisely restraining her, who would gladly have yielded to any suggestion from him, we are forced to believe that he was responsible for her conduct, that it conformed to his peculiar ideas of liberty, and his utter disregard for all institutions, ideas, and conventionalities which did not represent his own views. In the treatment of the king he showed the same lack of foresight and true nobleness. Though all his great powers were still delegated to him by the king, he even encouraged Brandt to illtreat the imbecile and helpless monarch. These things were soon noised abroad, and became effective weapons in the hands of his enemies. The rumors that the king was being illtreated, and that the royal family was being disgraced by Struensee, created a storm of ill-will which emboldened his opponents. A plot was formed to overthrow him, the leader of which was his own faithless friend Rantzau, who was aided by Ove Høeg-Guldberg and Queen Juliane Marie. In the early morning of January 17, 1772, after a ball at the court, the conspirators gained entrance to the palace, and placed Struensee, Brandt, and the queen under arrest. The success of the plot was hailed with general delight, and the only thought of the leaders was to punish the offenders as severely as possible. Struensee and Brandt were condemned to death and executed after a trial which was declared by many to be a travesty on justice.[1] It is true that the charge of *crimen laesae majestatis* could be but lamely maintained against Struensee, since the king himself had placed him in power, and the cabinet minister had performed every official act by order of the king. It is also true that Guldberg, one of the conspirators, should not have been made one of the judges at the trial. The king might, indeed, have good

[1] H. Walpole says in his *Journal of the Reign of King George III.*, vol. I., p. 115: "The sentences . . . instead of satisfying the public have excited a general compassion for them, and an abhorrence of their barbarous execution; and, in short, they are now looked upon as victims of the state, sacrificed to the ambition and hatred of their enemies."

In a letter of July 6, 1772, the Danish diplomat, Count Rochus Fr. Lynar, condemns the execution of the count in the strongest terms, and says that "in all Europe they ridicule this decision, which, to Denmark's disgrace, has been translated into nearly every language."

reason to feel offended at the prisoners, but he had made no complaint, though he was finally prevailed upon to sign their death warrants. The vindictive character of the prosecution, and the barbaric punishment inflicted, shows that the conspirators were bent on destroying their opponents rather than securing even-handed justice. Queen Carolina Mathilda was placed in Kronborg castle, where she was allowed to communicate only with persons selected for her company. Her marriage to Christian VII. was annulled by the court, a decree which was not only harsh, but impolitic and unwise. If she had erred, she was still infinitely better than her worthless husband, who was long since unfit to marry again. She had come to the Danish court while very young; she was given in marriage to a worthless rake; she was surrounded from the outset by the evil influences of an immoral court, and had fallen into the snares of an artful seducer, who in the hours of trouble had won her confidence as a friend and adviser. Her misfortunes should have palliated many of her mistakes, but the obdurate judges, who could spell wisdom only from the dull letters of the law, rendered a decision which could not garnish the corrupt Danish court with a virtue which it did not possess, but only served to offend her brother, King George III., and to awaken among the English people a hostility to Denmark-Norway which may have been responsible for many later unhappy events. Her divorce and imprisonment were regarded in England as a violation of English national honor, and a storm of indignation was aroused. A letter in the "Public Advertiser" demanded that a fleet should be immediately dispatched to Copenhagen to frighten Queen Mathilda's enemies, and Junius, the anonymous author of the famous "Letters of Junius," plied his eloquent pen in violent criticism of the "Northern Vandals" and the "shameful remissness" of Lord North, who, according to the writer, failed to take energetic measures for her protection.[1] It had been the plan of the conspirators to keep the queen in a mild imprisonment at Aalborg, but when the English government protested, they decided to turn her over to the English authorities. Her dowry of £80,000 should be refunded her, she should retain the title of queen, but she had to part with her children, who were regarded as members of the

---

[1] Karl Wittich, *Struensee*, p. 146.

Danish royal family. Two English frigates were sent to Copenhagen to carry her from Denmark. On May 30, 1773, Queen Carolina Mathilda sailed away from the land which had witnessed her misfortunes, but which still harbored the treasures of her heart. She was carried to Celle in her brother, King George's, Hanoverian possessions, where she was to reside. In that city she died May 10, 1775, twenty-four years of age. "Thus ended this drama of which she had been the heroine," says Professor Wittich. "History could have numbered this high-minded and lovable woman among the worthiest of princesses, if destiny had not linked her to so miserable a prince without consulting her heart. But even in her delinquencies she rose to a self-denial and a nobility of soul which make her tower high above her surroundings, and especially above the man who betrayed her."

46. PRINCE FREDERICK AND OVE HØEG-GULDBERG
A PERIOD OF REACTION

After the overthrow of Struensee, Prince Frederick, a half-brother of Christian VII., the son of Queen Juliane Marie, became regent, but the leading spirit in the government was Ove Høeg-Guldberg, one of the conspirators. He was a man of small ability, a pedant and reactionary, who was carried into power on the crest of the wave of loyalty to the king, and opposition to reform which culminated in the palace revolution of January 17, 1772. Like every pedant he had a system, and it happened to be very acceptable to those who had now gained control, and sought to undo every reform which had been introduced by his fallen predecessor. He considered the progressive and liberal ideas of the age as idle vagaries, and regarded education of the common classes as harmful and dangerous. "Humanity," he said, "can bear only a certain amount of knowledge, and each class must, therefore, have its proper share. More than that intoxicates. The peasant children," he continues, "acquire knowledge of Christianity and their duties; they become acquainted with the Bible; they learn to write, and, if they must do so, to figure a little. Other knowledge they do not need, neither is it profitable for them. I shudder for everything else which these flatulent times have taught, and with which they would spoil everything." [1] He did not openly proclaim the maxim that the subjects exist for the sake of the king, but this is the standpoint from which he generally reasoned, says Sars. On the whole, his theory of statesmanship was of the most antiquated sort, and it is true, as his son observes, that he was a product of the spirit of 1660.[2] The first concern of the new government was to bring everything back into the old conditions. The Geheimekonceil was reëstablished, and the step taken by Struensee to abolish serfdom, and to limit the amount of free service to be rendered by the peasants, was annulled, and the aristocracy were again allowed to lord it over the peasants, "according to old usage." A strict censorship of the press was reëstablished, and at court the old abuses and extravagance were reintroduced with the granting of titles, pensions, offices, gifts, and gratuities to truckling seekers of royal favors. The old mercantile protective system, which Struensee had sought to abolish, was again adopted. Monopolies and special favors were freely employed to encourage various private undertakings, and large sums were expended to aid useless commercial and industrial enterprises in the old mercantile spirit. The reaction was thorough in its work, enthusiastic in its efforts to stop every wheel of progress, and to turn the clock of the ages back to the "good old days," when liberal ideas had not yet disturbed those who possessed all privileges and power.

But even this reactionary government granted one important reform. As Struensee was a German, and the German language was always used at court, the overthrow of the foreigner was regarded as a sort of national victory, and the use of Danish, which had been so forcibly brought to the people's attention through the comedies of Holberg, was now urged as a patriotic demand. Suhm wrote to the king: "Let us again hear our own dear language in your commands. You are a Dane, and I know that you can speak Danish. Let the foreign language be a sign of the vile traitor who was too indolent to learn our language, too scoffing to show us so great a

[1] *Dansk historisk Tidsskrift*, IV. R., vol. I., p. 184, quoted by J. E. Sars, *Udsigt over den norske Historie*, vol. IV., p. 194.

[2] Edvard Holm, *Nogle Hovedtræk af Trykkefrihedens Historie 1770–1773*, p. 129, quoted by Sars.

condescension." [1] On February 3, 1772, the German words of command in the army were abolished by royal order,[2] and by an order of February 13th of the same year it was ordained that Danish should be the official language of the realm. Another important measure sustaining the awakening national spirit was the ordinance of January 15, 1776, *Indfødsretten*, by which it was decreed that only native-born citizens, and those who could be counted equal to them, should be appointed to office, or to positions of honor in the kingdom.

But while the government aided and encouraged the national spirit in Denmark, it pursued the very opposite policy in Norway, where the national awakening was manifesting itself in many ways. When P. F. Suhm wrote a brief history of Denmark, Norway, and Holstein, Guldberg himself examined the manuscript, and canceled or changed every passage in which the author referred to the equality of Norway and Denmark, returning the mutilated work with the remarks that "no Norwegian exists. We are all citizens of the kingdom of Denmark. Do not write for the despicable Christiania raisoneurs." Such insolent disregard for a people's sentiments and honor can only awaken resentment, and strengthen their national feeling. In Norway Guldberg became generally hated. His name is enrolled in the index to "Samlinger til det norske Folks Sprog og Historie" with the remark that he "was a learned and narrow-minded statesman." The former epithet is probably accorded him from courtesy, that the truth of the latter may appear with better grace.

While Guldberg was the leading spirit in the government, A. P. Bernstorff, a nephew of the older Bernstorff, was placed in charge of foreign affairs. Besides the ill-will which had been created in England by the imprisonment of Queen Mathilda, the attitude of Sweden was also causing alarm. King Gustavus III., who succeeded his father, Frederick Adolph, on the throne of that kingdom, February 12, 1771, made the royal power almost absolute by a successful *coup d'état*, August 19, 1772, and although he hastened to assure the neighboring powers that he desired to maintain peace and friendly relations, it soon became

---

[1] Quoted by O. A. Øverland, *Norges Historie*, vol. IV., p. 449.

[2] *Dansk historisk Tidsskrift*, IV. R., vol. II., p. 738. See Karl Wittich, *Struensee*, p. 216.

evident that he planned to gain possession of Norway. The Norwegian army and defenses had been neglected since 1763, and the Danish government was well aware that dissatisfaction was widespread in the sister kingdom. General Huth was, accordingly, dispatched to Norway to take charge of the military preparations, and Prince Carl of Hessen, who was married to King Christian's sister Louise, was made commander-in-chief of the Norwegian army, with the understanding that he should reside in Christiania, where he should maintain a court in order to stimulate the loyalty of the Norwegian people.[1] The hated extra tax of 1762 was also abolished to gain their good-will. Active war preparations were now carried on both in Norway and Sweden. In 1773 Denmark-Norway formed an alliance with Russia for joint operations against Sweden, but Empress Catherine II. was at that time at war with Turkey, and no aggressive step could be taken until this war was ended. The peace was not interrupted, and friendly relations were again established when the Northern kingdoms had to defend their rights as neutrals in the great naval war precipitated by the American Revolution (1775–1783).

As soon as the war with America began, English privateers seized neutral merchant vessels, and brought them to English ports on the charge that they were carrying contraband of war. As no rules had yet been established as to what should be considered contraband of war, this threatened to destroy neutral commerce, especially after France became the ally of the American colonies, and the English privateers extended their operations to all parts of the world. Sweden and Holland, as well as Denmark-Norway, protested against this infringement on the rights of neutrals, and the principle that a "free ship makes a free cargo" was advanced with so much greater force, because the English themselves had maintained it against the Barbary States. It was also urged that a port should be considered blockaded only when all traffic with it was cut off by warships actually present, and that all neutrals should be treated alike. Fearing that an alliance between England, Russia, and Denmark-Norway might be brought about by the negotiations carried on relative to these

---

[1] Prins Carl af Hessen, *Optegnelser, translated from the French by C. J. Anker,* Christiania, 1893, p. 77 ff.

points, Sweden proposed a defensive alliance between the three Northern kingdoms in defense of their trade, but Bernstorff, who feared that this might lead to war with England, did not favor this plan. In 1780 Catherine II., acting upon the advice of her minister Panin, issued a declaration that she would organize a league of all the neutral states for the support of the following points: Ships of neutrals should have the right to enter ports and harbors of the nations at war, a free ship should make free cargo, excepting articles which should be regarded as contraband of war, and these should be defined according to the existing treaties. No port should be regarded as blockaded unless the blockade was made effective by warships actually present, and the decision as to whether a neutral ship had been rightfully seized should be based on these principles. These were the same points which Bernstorff had already urged, and Sweden, Holland, Denmark-Norway, Prussia, Portugal, the two Sicilies, and even the German Emperor joined Russia in the proposed league. But Bernstorff nevertheless signed the treaty with reluctance, as he knew that the coalition was directed against England. Five days before Denmark-Norway entered the league, he concluded with England a special treaty, in which more favorable rules were made relative to contraband of war; but this step offended Catherine II., and he was forced to retire from office. England did not venture to resist this powerful league of neutrals, and the principles which they had laid down were respected throughout the war, but they were not accepted as a recognized part of international law.

The great naval war had, none the less, produced for the neutral nations quite extraordinary commercial advantages, in spite of the losses and impediments due to the operations of privateers. The Norwegian merchant marine nearly doubled its tonnage during the war, and while the total export in 1773 was estimated at 1,370,492 riksdaler, it amounted in 1782 to 2,084,913 riksdaler. But the flourishing times due to this sudden increase of traffic could not last, as the return of peace and normal conditions was sure to produce a serious reaction.

47. Crown Prince Frederick and A. P. Bernstorff. Increasing Unrest in Norway. Chr. J. Lofthus. War with Sweden, 1788

When Bernstorff resigned, the reactionary government conducted by Prince Frederick, Ove Guldberg, and Queen Juliane Marie became more pedantic than ever, and forfeited the respect of all thinking people. The support of those who enjoyed the benefits of such a régime created a feeling of security among those in power, but a desire for a change was rapidly growing, even though the strict press censorship prevented any expression of the spreading feeling of discontent. In order to retain their power they delayed the confirmation of Crown Prince Frederick, and planned to keep him under the control of the Council, which consisted of their own partisans. But the day came, April 14, 1784, when the crown prince, being sixteen years old, should take his seat in the Council. As soon as the king was seated, the prince read a paper in which he asked him to abolish the Council, and to appoint as his advisers A. P. Bernstorff, Rosencrants, Huth, and Stampe. Amid the violent protests of Prince Frederick, the regent, the king was persuaded to sign the document. The old régime was overthrown by this well-planned *coup de théâtre*, and the greatest excitement prevailed in the palace. But the English government, as well as a majority of the people of Denmark, probably felt a secret satisfaction that Queen Caroline Mathilda's son had driven from power those who had imprisoned and banished his mother.

Crown Prince Frederick, who now became regent, was inexperienced, not very gifted, and but indifferently educated, but he loved fairness and justice, and his choice of ministers shows that he favored progressive and liberal ideas. The leadership in the new government naturally devolved on the experienced statesman A. P. Bernstorff. Assisted by his able associates, E. Schimmelmann, C. D. Reventlow, and Christian Colbjørnsen, he inaugurated an era of reform which may be characterized as a period of social reconstruction, though the changes were made with due caution and moderation. Even as to the theory of government, Bernstorff entertained very liberal views, maintaining that the will of the people should be the king's law, a principle which, if carried out, would make the king the servant of the people instead of the virtual owner of the state.   But this could be done only by creating a national legislature where the will of the people could be expressed by their chosen representatives, and such a reform he probably never thought of, or even desired. In his work as reformer he was still the benevolent despot, whose phrases about the will of the people only indicate his wish to improve their social condition.

With regard to industry and commerce, Bernstorff abandoned the old mercantile system, and abolished monopolies and special privileges. The freedom of the press was reëstablished, and censorship of literature was done away with.   In his most important reforms, which aimed at the emancipation of the Danish peasants, he was ably assisted by the very competent and liberal-minded Christian Colbjørnsen.   This gifted statesman was a Norwegian by birth, a relative of the Colbjørnsen brothers of Fredrikshald, who won fame in the Great Northern War.   He had come to Denmark in his early youth, and became intensely devoted to the doctrines of the rights of man and the liberal ideas of the age.   "Liberty," he said, "is nature's first and most glorious gift to the noblest of her creatures."   "No feeling is more deeply imprinted in human nature than the love of liberty."   It is natural that these ideas should make him a friend of the oppressed Danish peasants, and when he was made secretary of a commission of sixteen members, appointed in 1786 to examine the whole relation between landlords and peasants, he became their ablest spokesman.   As a result of the recommendation of this commission serfdom was abolished in Denmark, and the amount of free service to be rendered by the peasants was limited and defined by ordinances issued June 20, 1788, and June 24, 1791.   These reforms, which freed the almost enslaved peasants, had a tendency to alter social conditions fundamentally.   They represent the first important step in a new social and economic development in Denmark.[1]

In Norway no serfdom had existed, and as the *bønder* enjoyed great social and economic independence, there was no need of the kind of reforms instituted in Denmark.   But the struggle which had

---

[1] E. Holm, *Kampen om Landreformerne i Danmark.* J. A. Fridericia, *Den danske Bondestands Frigjørelse.*

always been waged between the people and the greedy Danish officials grew more intense as the national spirit developed, and liberal ideas were disseminated. The Norwegians had at all times been very loyal to the king, whom they fondly regarded as *their* king, but they had also been very intolerant of oppression at the hands of royal officials, who were often guilty of extortionate and unlawful practices. Excessive taxes imposed against the will of the people, and harmful trade monopolies which increased the prices on the necessities of life, added fuel to the smoldering discontent, and when the *bønder* gathered about their hearthstones they had many grievances to complain of, and many a violent clash with the officials to narrate. But these clashes never assumed the dimensions of a revolt. They were isolated occurrences produced by local conditions, violent resistance to oppression, but no national uprising aiming at independence; for even the leaders lacked the scope of vision to conceive such a plan. Among the many tragic episodes in this more intense than dramatic struggle was a movement in Nedenes *amt* in southern Norway in 1786 and 1787, led by Chr. J. Lofthus.

The people in that mountain district felt grievously oppressed by the heavy taxes, and the rapacity of the officials, as well as by the laws governing the importation of grain, which had increased the prices on that commodity. A commission appointed to examine into the causes of the almost incessant complaints gave a very gloomy picture of the situation. A report in which the popular *foged*, Weidemann, also concurred, states: "We unite our prayer with that of the *foged*, and recommend the people to your Majesty's favor. As long as they could, they willingly paid, but inability is no crime." The commission also found that the royal officials had oppressed and wronged the people by extortionate charges, and two judges, *sorenskrivere*, were removed from office, a sufficient proof that the complaints were well founded. With the return of peace after the American Revolution, Norwegian commerce decreased, hard times followed, and the large numbers of unemployed in the coast districts helped to swell the general discontent. The oppressed people soon found a leader and spokesman in Chr. J. Lofthus, a *bonde* in Moland. Among his neighbors he was highly respected, and well known for his energy and intelligence, but also for the tenacity with which he defended his legal rights.[1] Lofthus would go to Denmark and complain to Crown Prince Frederick of the government officials in his district. But although Bernstorff had said that the people's will should be the king's law, the ordinance of 1685, forbidding the Norwegian *bønder* to petition the king, on the penalty of loss of liberty and property, and the royal edict of 1744, which threatened any Norwegian who came to Denmark with a complaint or petition not signed by the *amtmand* with imprisonment in the citadel, still threatened with destruction any one who ventured to bring the people's will to the attention of the government in Copenhagen. But the Norwegians had confidence in the king's good-will; for it had often happened that he had heard their complaints, and had granted them relief without paying attention to the unjust laws. In 1785 the people of Telemarken and other districts sent three representatives to Copenhagen to petition the king for redress of grievances, and the following year Hans Kolstad was sent on a similar mission. The government did not punish them. The tall men in uniform who served as the king's bodyguard were their countrymen; the Norwegian people's courage and love of liberty had inspired respect in Denmark. They were allowed to return home, and the government instructed the *fogeds* in Norway that they should be guided in their charges by the tax-lists and the rules regulating fees. In 1786 Lofthus went to Denmark with a written complaint bearing 329 signatures. The crown prince received him in audience, and after having heard the complaint, told him that more conclusive proof would be required. Lofthus returned home, had a meeting with those who had signed the complaint, and received from them a certificate of the genuineness of the signatures, and of his own appointment as a special delegate to the king. With these documents he returned to Copenhagen, but he met the same objection as before. The crown prince, however, gave him his word of honor that if he could furnish adequate proof the matter would be investigated. Lofthus returned home, and, acting as a self-constituted tribune of the people, he assembled meetings of the *bønder* in his own home, and traveled about from place to place to collect evidence, and to

[1] Henrik Wergeland, *Samlede Skrifter*, vol. VIII., p. 150, *Almuestalsmanden Christian Jensen Lofthus*.

secure new signatures. This activity was considered by the authorities of the districts to be rebellious, and steps were taken to arrest him. But as he was aided by the *bønder*, he was able to elude the officers, and to continue to hold secret meetings with the people. At the meeting with the *amtmand* the *bønder* demanded that Lofthus should not be arrested, and that he should receive a passport to go as their representative to Copenhagen, a request which was finally granted. In October Lofthus started for Copenhagen with the signed document in company with thirty men, who should act as witnesses. But the *amtmand* notified the government about what had happened, and said that Lofthus had organized a very dangerous uprising. The government immediately issued orders to the *amtmand* to arrest Lofthus, and place him in the fortress of Christiansand, and the chief of police of Copenhagen was instructed to seize him and his band, if he had already arrived in that city. In the meantime Lofthus and his thirty companions marched along the Swedish coast towards Helsingborg, where they would cross the Sound to Denmark. When they arrived in that city, they learned of the orders issued for their arrest. Lofthus sent a number of his men to Denmark to secure a safe-conduct, but before their return he decided to start homeward with a few followers. As soon as he arrived in Nedenes, the *amtmand* made strenuous efforts to arrest him, but through the people's aid Lofthus always evaded his pursuers. The *bønder* gathered in large numbers to defend him, but no acts of violence were committed, and there is no evidence that they had any rebellious intentions. In the meantime Lofthus' companions who had been sent to Copenhagen had secured a safe-conduct for their leader, and a royal commission was appointed to investigate the troubles in Nedenes. This commission assembled in Christiansand, and Lofthus, together with a large number of *bønder*, met and submitted their complaints, supported by most damaging evidence against the accused. The commission found the charges to be true. They found the people to be peaceful and loyal, and they did not get the impression that Lofthus was a dangerous character. But Judge Smith and Captain Hammer, together with a lawyer, Salvesen, formed a secret plot to arrest Lofthus, who wandered about in the neighborhood, and sometimes returned to his own home for a short visit. Watching their opportunity, they fell upon him with a band of armed men, bound him, and threw him into a boat. In a raging storm they escaped from the angry *bønder* who pursued them, and succeeded in carrying their prisoner to Christiania, where he was imprisoned in the fortress of Akershus. Five years he spent in this dungeon before the court finally decreed that he should remain in prison for life; probably as unjust a decision as a judicial tribunal ever rendered. An appeal was made to the superior court, and that tribunal, after deliberating seven years upon the final verdict, sustained the decree of the lower court, two years after the defendant had breathed his last in his prison cell at Akershus. The unjust officials, who were the cause of the deplorable affair, escaped with light punishment. Two of the worst offenders, the judges Smith and Brønsdorph, had to pay a fine together with the expenses of the trial; the diocesan prefect, Adeler, was removed from office and pensioned; the rest escaped all punishment. Those who had arrested Lofthus were liberally rewarded. Such a miscarriage of justice is explainable when we bear in mind that the government officials of whatever title constituted a bureaucracy, consolidated by intermarriage, friendship, and common interests into a distinct social class. The extortion and corruption of which some might be accused were, perchance, practiced in a greater or less degree by all, and when an offender was made to answer in a court consisting of his own friends and colleagues, the procedure was usually a hollow mockery. When the *bønder* were goaded to open resistance, the officials used their power with vindictive harshness to terrorize them, and keep them at bay; hence the deep-rooted hatred and the intense struggle between the two classes, which never ceased until the Norwegian bureaucracy had disappeared.

The disturbance in which Lofthus had become the central figure made a deep impression in Norway. It was a local affair, like many a similar episode, but it occurred at a time when the national spirit was awakening, when the atmosphere of despotic Europe was surcharged with ideas which struck at the very root of the old régime, and when destiny had brought the hour of national freedom closer to the Norwegian people than they supposed. It took place even within the dawn of the great national daybreak, some light of which was later reflected upon it. The episode ended in a groan of pain, but it stirred the people's spirit, and taught them to understand the value of independence. The political situation might have given it an even greater significance, if the moment had been opportune. We have observed that the desire for national autonomy in educational and business affairs had grown strong in Norway, that liberal ideas were spreading among the upper classes,[1] and that the *bønder* were growing more restive than ever under the irksome burdens placed upon them by the bureaucracy. Gustavus III. of Sweden had long entertained the hope that he might be able to profit by these circumstances, and some day gain possession of Norway. He had for many years carried on a secret agitation in the eastern districts of the kingdom, but at the time of the mentioned episode he was inactive. "Had the Lofthusian movement happened fourteen years earlier, or four years later," says Øverland, "there might have been danger for the Danish-Norwegian state."[2]

Gustavus III. watched events in Norway very closely, and even appointed a consul-general in Christiania to act as a secret diplomatic agent for the purpose of strengthening the pro-Swedish sentiment. But a visit of Crown Prince Frederick in 1788, and the removal of the restrictions on the importation of grain by the ordinance of January 6th of that year, tended to satisfy the always loyal Norwegians, though their demand for a bank and a university had not been granted. King Gustavus III. was now planning to attack Russia, in the hope of regaining southern Finland, as Catherine II. was engaged in a war with the Turks. Denmark-Norway had formed an alliance with Russia in 1773, but without being able to secure the neutrality of his near neighbor, Gustavus invaded Finland, and laid siege to Nyslot and Frederickshamn. The Russian troops had been withdrawn from the northern provinces, and even St. Petersburg had been left without a garrison, but no attack could be made on the capital after the Swedish fleet had failed to gain a decisive victory

---

[1] Ludvig Daae, *Det gamle Christiania*, p. 185 ff. Yngvar Nielsen, *Gustav III's norske Politik, Historisk Tidsskrift*, anden række, vol. I., p. 5 ff.

[2] *Norges Historie*, vol. X., p. 32. Yngvar Nielsen, *Gustav III's Politik, Historisk Tidsskrift*, anden række, vol. I., p. 1 ff. J. Hellstenius, *Konung Gustaf den tredjes danska politik, Nordisk Universitets Tidsskrift för 1861–62*.

over the Russians at Hogland, July 17th. This undecisive battle and the tiresome siege of Frederickshamn caused great dissatisfaction in the Swedish army. The higher officers organized a mutiny, and Gustavus was forced to give up the campaign. He returned to Sweden, punished the offenders, and by a new *coup d'état* he gained even more absolute power than before.

By the treaty of alliance Denmark-Norway had engaged to assist Russia in case of war, but it was now recognized that any increase in the power of that steadily growing Empire would be prejudicial to the safety of the whole North. Bernstorff was aware of this, and granted grudgingly the least assistance possible under the terms of the treaty. A Norwegian army of 12,000 men under Prince Carl of Hessen was sent into Bohuslen to make a diversion on the Swedish border. Crown Prince Frederick, who had become enthusiastic over the opportunity of participating in a war, accompanied the army. After a minor engagement at Kvistrum Bro, where a Swedish detachment was captured, Prince Carl intended to seize Gottenborg, but as England and Prussia threatened to intervene, the Norwegian army was withdrawn from Swedish territory, and peace was restored in November, 1788.[1]

The struggle between Sweden and Russia was renewed in 1789, but although Gustavus won a great naval victory in Svensksund, July 9 and 10, 1790, where he captured thirty ships and 6000 men, he was unable to pursue his advantage, and the outcome of the war was doubtful. The events of the French Revolution had also made a deep impression on the imaginative king. He hastened to conclude the peace of Verela on the basis of *statu quo*, and proposed an alliance with Russia against the Revolution.

Gustavus III. was bitterly offended at the Danish government because of the aid which it had given to Russia, and when peace was restored, he renewed his agitation in Norway. Through his favorite, Armfelt, and his secret agent, Manderfelt, who was stationed in Copenhagen, he entered into negotiations with a few Norwegians who desired independence of Denmark. Carsten Tank and three others met the Swedish agents, March 11, 1790, but their meeting,

---

[1] Chr. Blangstrup, *Begivenhederne i Norden i Efteraaret 1788.* E. Holm *Danmarks Politik under den svensk-russiske Krig fra 1788-1790.*

which was repeated later at Karlstad, produced no definite result.[1] Armfelt said of Tank that he was a man whose head was full of political sophisms and enthusiastic ideas of liberty, and King Gustavus suspected, undoubtedly with a good reason, that what the Norwegians desired was not union with Sweden, but independence and a republican government. The ideas of the French Revolution had found adherents also among the Norwegians, who desired separation from Denmark, not for the purpose of joining another foreign kingdom equally despotic, but in order to establish republican freedom according to their own ideas. Why, then, should he support them when he had made it his special aim to combat the French Revolution. In 1792 King Gustavus was shot down by an assassin, and all Swedish agitation in Norway ceased.

48. DANISH-NORWEGIAN LITERATURE IN THE SECOND HALF OF THE EIGHTEENTH CENTURY

The separatistic tendencies and growing national spirit in Norway, of which distinct manifestations have been observed especially in connection with the agitation for a university, comes even more clearly to view in the literature of the later half of the eighteenth century. Ludvig Holberg, who by his reformatory activity and great genius became the founder of modern Danish-Norwegian literature, had introduced the new thought and liberal ideas of the *Aufklärung*, and had brought intellectual life in the North under the influence of French and English thought. In his day the new movement was still in its beginning, but in the field of history, philosophy, and politics a school of young writers, such as J. S. Sneedorff and P. F. Suhm, followed the paths which he had discovered, and became the disciples of the great French writers, especially of Montesquieu. So sudden was the change that Holberg in his old age grew somewhat alarmed over the movement which he had started, and began to

---

[1] "The family Anker were regarded as Swedish sympathizers," says Prince Carl of Hessen in his *Optegnelser* (Memoires de mon temps), 1744–1784, p. 84. Carsten Anker was prominently connected with the events of 1814. When the prince states that there were some leaders who wished to make Norway an independent kingdom and choose him king, he is probably guilty of a misunderstanding.

revise some of his earlier expressions regarding the placidity and moderation of his countrymen. Sars points out that in one of his epistles Holberg refers to an earlier description of the Danes as a people who do not easily go to extremes, but generally walk in the middle of the road, a description which was considered true at the time, as the Danish people actually possessed such a trait. But if the work should again be published, says the author, we would have to add a foot-note stating that in the last twenty or thirty years they have changed character so completely that they are no longer recognizable.[1] That the leaven had begun to work became manifest in the growing unrest and increased intellectual activity; and as it produced a new era of development, it also brought to light a difference in temper and character in the peoples of the two kingdoms which would soon bring about a dissolution of the literary partnership which had hitherto existed. Holberg, who was a Norwegian by birth, but had done his great life work in Denmark, had pointed out this difference with characteristic keenness of observation. The Danes, he thinks, have a "strange modesty" and are inclined to follow the middle path, while the Norwegians are haughty, and, like the English, inclined to go to extremes. That the free unfolding of the native traits and tendencies of each people should produce an ever-increasing divergence between them is quite natural. Holberg's cosmopolitan interests and broad scope of vision made him look upon Danish-Norwegian literature as a possession common to both peoples, in which a slight difference in national spirit could be left out of account. But these irreconcilable traits of national character soon entered into the new development as a most important factor. The trend of literary progress was soon to be determined by two distinct kinds of foreign influence which divided the writers into two camps, as they associated themselves with one or the other of the two prevailing tendencies. In 1751 the German poet Klopstock was invited to Copenhagen, where he stayed for twenty years, and became the center of a large circle of German and Danish admirers. Many sought to imitate his bombastic odes and his declamatory pathos. Such homage was paid him by his enthusiastic adherents that he exercised the influence of a literary monarch.

[1] J. E. Sars, *Udsigt over den norske Historie*, vol. IV., p. 162.

His most important disciple was the gifted poet Johannes Ewald, who became the chief exponent of German influence in Denmark. Ewald and his followers organized *Det danske Literatur-Se skab*, and this circle of young poets sought to give the views of their leader full currency in Danish literature.   But while the German influence gained preponderance among the Danish poets, the Norwegians continued to look to England and France for their models.   The first English novelists, and especially the fervid and imaginative description of nature in the "Seasons" of James Thomson, had kindled an enthusiastic love of nature which in Germany, Norway, and elsewhere created a new literary taste.[1]   Even Rousseau had gathered ideas from this source, and his slogan, "return to nature," was in perfect accord with the views of the English poets.   In Norway Christian Braunmann Tullin wrote a long descriptive poem, "Maidagen," in the strain of Thomson's "Seasons."   Measured by modern standards it is a production of no exceptional merit, but in the midst of the insipidity and dullness of the literature of that day it was hailed with enthusiasm as a literary event of the first magnitude.   Tullin, who represented the English-French influence as truly as Ewald represented the German, had hoisted the standard about which the Norwegian poets were to rally in opposition to Ewald and his party.[2] In Copenhagen the Norwegians organized in 1772 *Det norske Selskab*, a literary club which numbered among its members Johan Nordahl Brun, Nils Krog Bredal, Claus Fasting, Johan Herman Wessel, Claus Frimann, and his brother Peder Frimann, Jens Zetlitz, Jonas Rein, and others.   Even the names of the two societies which had suddenly appeared as rivals show that national spirit, no less than literary taste, tended to bring about a gradual separation of Danes and Norwegians in the field of literature, and the poetry written in the two clubs was soon to dispel all doubt on this point.   Ewald chose for many of his productions national themes, as in the drama "Rolf Krage," and pointed the way to Danish heroic tradition and early history.   The Norwegians lauded in patriotic songs the freedom and

[1] Knut Gjerset, *Der Einfluss von James Thompson's "Jahreszeiten" auf die deutsche Literatur des achtzenten Jahrhunderts*, Heidelberg, 1898.
[2] J. S. Welhaven, *Samlede Skrifter*, vol. VIII., *Om Betydningen af det norske Selskabs Opposition mod den Ewaldske Poesi.*

grandeur of their country. Johan Nordahl Brun, the most ardent patriot, said in a song to "Norway the motherland of heroes" that the Norwegians would some day awaken and break all chains and fetters. These fetters could only be the union with Denmark, but it is possible that extravagant expressions of this sort were little more than rhetorical flourishes. The Norwegians prided themselves no less on their loyalty to the king than on their love for their fatherland, whose ancient glory they had just begun to discover. But an era of storm and stress had come, when great feelings were expressed in vehement language, while the ideas had not yet clarified themselves into definite principles. A higher intellectual life had been kindled, a new patriotism had been awakened among the higher classes, who possessed learning and ability enough to speak for the whole nation, who could view the life of their people in its historic aspect. They knew that Norway had been great in the past, and felt sure that its vigor would return, that it would rise again from dependency to new national greatness. The thought was inspiring, intoxicating. Their patriotic songs grew as vehement as their enthusiasm was intense. They had no specific aim, no definite plan, but they felt their own worth, and knew that their countrymen, if given a fair opportunity, would attain a position no less honorable than that which they had occupied of old. This conviction found support, not only in memories of the past, but in conditions of their own age. Were not the Norwegians a free people throughout the whole union period, as compared with the Danes, and were they not lauded for their courage and their irrepressible love of liberty? Had they not shown that they possessed both vigor and talent?[1] The members of *Det norske Selskab* had not forgotten that Tordenskjold, Adelaer, and Huitfeldt were Norwegians, that Ludvig Holberg, the greatest genius of his age in the North, was their countryman, that in the Danish capital their own club embraced, with the single excep-

[1] In conformity with the Rousseauan ideas current in the latter half of the eighteenth century, thinkers and poets had pointed to the Norwegian *bønder* as a model people owning their own farms and leading a healthful rustic life in freedom and contentment. There was some truth in this, though the picture was generally overdrawn. Tyge Rothe, Denmark's leading thinker at that time, says: "Praiseworthily proud are the sons of Norway, and who wonders that the *bønder* are so, when he knows that among

tion of Ewald, the best poetic talent in the realm. There was the incomparable satirist Wessel, the rare epigrammatist Fasting, the fine lyric poet Claus Frimann, the noted Johan Nordahl Brun, and many others who added luster to the literature of this period. As they were fully conscious of these things, there was from the start a ring of victory, yea often of boastfulness, in their lines. They might write dramas according to French models, as did Bredal and Brun, or they might, like Fasting, use their keen wit in epigrams, or in biting satire, like Wessel, who destroyed the French dramatic influence in Danish-Norwegian literature by his incomparable parody " Kjær- lighed uden Strømper." [1] These things were of importance in litera- ture, but their songs to liberty and Norway, their poems about the Norwegian people, about mountain scenery and country life in their own native land touched the hearts of their countrymen in a different way. They gave the people the opportunity for the first time to sing out in bold triumphant tones their love of liberty and fatherland. The verses lived in their lives, and traced deep sentiments on their hearts. It was the first lesson in true patriotism. Though often offensively bombastic, and faulty enough when measured by the highest literary standards, these songs were of greater importance than the more sumptuous literary efforts of the age.

Besides the patriotic songs, a new kind of popular poems began to appear, written in the strain of the folk-songs. Many of Brun's best productions, and several collections of songs by Claus Frimann, belong to this kind of popular lyrical poesy. Especially noteworthy is also the collection of poems, " Gudbrandsdalske Viser," by Edward Storm. These poems are written in the Norwegian vernacular, and describe home, love, and nature with fervent sentiment and great accuracy of local coloring. The author also wrote many popular ballads, of which the best known is "Zinclars Vise." Many songs

their number are those who descend from kings, and that they through suc- ceeding generations have dwelt on their farms, which they own by right of *odel;* that they have been true warriors and defenders of their country. Is it a wonder that also the Norwegians of other classes understand what national honor is. He who lives in the pure mountain atmosphere; he with his traditions of the past; he with the thought that his country has been a land of freedom, not of aristocracy or serfdom." Quoted by J. E. Sars, *His- torisk Indledning til Grundloven*, p. 108.

[1] Introduction to J. H. Wessel's *Samlede Digte*, edited by J. Levin.

written by these poets are so truly national both in spirit and contents that they have continued to live among the people as real folksongs. Of such may be mentioned: Brun's "Bor jeg paa det høie Fjeld," "For Norge Kjæmpers Fødeland"; Claus Frimann's "Ondt ofte lider den Fiskermand," "Saa knytter jeg Traad"; Edward Storm's "Os ha gjort, kva gjerast skulde," "Markje grønnast, Snjogen braana," and many others. Though linked to Denmark with every tie of loyalty, the new school of poets had become ardent Norwegian patriots. They had rediscovered the true fountains of song, and had expressed with beauty and truthfulness the inmost thoughts and feelings of their people relative to home, nature, and fatherland. In Denmark they had exercised so predominant an influence upon literary life, and had developed in their poetry so distinct a national spirit, that, as L. Dietrichson says, "it must have been evident to all at the end of the period that a nation, not a province, spoke through the Norwegian poets."

The growing national sentiment received support, also, in the Norwegian press, which began to develop in this period. The first Norwegian paper of any importance was the "Christiania Intelligentssedler," founded in 1763. The paper was a weekly, but prior to 1814 it took no definite stand in political matters. In 1805 it began to appear twice weekly, and in 1830 it became a daily.[1] "Trondhjemske Samlinger af Philaletes," a literary and scientific periodical, published in Trondhjem by P. F. Suhm, was founded in 1767, and in 1775 Hans Storm in Søndmør began to publish "Tilskueren paa Landet," a periodical which was printed in Copenhagen. In Bergen a number of periodicals were founded, but they were generally short-lived and of little real importance.[2] A publication of high merit was Claus Fasting's "Provincial-blade," published in Bergen from 1778 to 1781. In 1808 the poet Jonas Rein became clergyman in Bergen, and together with Christian Magnus Falsen and Herman Foss he began the publication of "Den norske Tilskuer."

---

[1] *Dagbladet*, Christiania, May 25, 1913.

[2] *Decorah-Posten*, Decorah, Ia., June 13, 1913. L. Dietrichson, *Omrids af den norske Poesis Historie*, p. 146 ff.

49. REVOLUTION AND DESPOTISM. DENMARK-NORWAY'S FOREIGN POLICY, 1792–1814

The liberal ideas which had broken through the crust of eighteenth century despotism had created a feeling of unrest which was rapidly spreading over all Europe. Serious attention had been paid to the conditions of the common classes, who were yet drudging under feudalistic oppression, and a desire had been awakened for greater freedom and better social conditions. The neglected and enslaved masses had begun to feel that the hour of liberation was approaching, and poets and thinkers were dreaming of the millennium which would be ushered in when liberty and justice should regenerate the world. The charm of the new ideas regarding liberty and equality, of social regeneration and the rights of man; the self-evident truths regarding the injustice and iniquity of oppression and corrupt social institutions, so eloquently and fearlessly proclaimed, had for a moment touched all hearts, as if a new revelation had suddenly burst upon the age. Even the despots themselves had become benefactors of the people. The French Revolution brought this feeling to a climax. Gray-haired scholars became enthusiastic, and those who possessed learning and foresight enough to interpret the meaning and possible results of political events hailed it as the coming of that new era of which poets had dreamed and sages prophesied. But the crowned heads, and the privileged classes, who were intrenched in power, suddenly grew alarmed when they realized that the first sacrifice demanded for the attainment of this new social felicity would be their own privileges and despotic power. To them the Revolution was a rude shock which awakened them from their dreams. The cherub of liberty had suddenly changed into the demon of rebellion. They forgot their quarrels, and hastened to unite to arrest the spread of so dangerous a movement. Revolution became the terror of the age, and every liberal idea, yea every useful reform was soon classified as revolt against established authority.

No one felt more alarmed than Gustavus III. of Sweden. He hastened to terminate his war with Russia, and on October 19, 1791, he concluded a treaty with the Russian Empress, Catherine II., for joint operation against the French Revolution. His untimely death prevented him from carrying out his plans, and Catherine II. was rather indifferent, as she was still occupied with the war with Turkey. But Austria and Prussia had also formed an alliance to oppose the Revolution, and on April 20, 1792, King Louis XVI. was persuaded to begin war against these powers. The two allies tried to prevail on the lesser powers to join them in a general coalition against France, and Denmark-Norway was also invited. But Bernstorff declined, as he held that every nation ought to have a right to determine for itself its form of government, and that foreign powers had no right to interfere with the internal affairs of France. An invitation extended by Catherine II. of Russia was also declined. The fate of Poland convinced Bernstorff that the great powers would not hesitate to swallow up the smaller states at the first opportunity, and he saw that their only safety lay in neutrality in the great struggle which had begun. But to remain neutral became difficult enough, especially after England and Holland joined the enemies of France after the execution of Louis XVI. Commerce was exposed to the greatest dangers, and slight regard was paid by the belligerent powers even to the limited rights which neutrals were supposed to have. Catherine II. of Russia, who had maintained that the flag protected the ship and its cargo, that the blockade of a port, in order to be respected, must be made effective; who in 1780 had organized the great coalition for the protection of the rights of neutrals, now boldly announced that she had discarded these principles, that the neutrals would be given the choice of discontinuing all trade with France, or of joining the coalition against that country. France was to be starved into submission. It was a piece of perfidy characteristic of that age of dishonest diplomacy and disregard of pledges and treaties. In order to enforce her demand, Catherine sent a fleet of thirty war vessels to Denmark, and announced both in Stockholm and Copenhagen that this fleet would cruise in the North Sea, and seize all ships sailing under the French flag; that the ships of neutrals, sailing to French ports, would be searched and turned back. England took a similar stand, but Bernstorff could not be intimidated. He told both England and Russia that their demands would not be complied with, and Danish-Norwegian ships continued to sail. The Russians did not molest them, in spite of the threats which had been made, but the English continued their old practice of sending out privateers to prey upon neutral commerce.

After the death of Gustavus III. the relations between Sweden and Denmark became more friendly. Duke Carl of Södermanland, King Gustavus' brother, who became regent during the minority of the crown prince, was less gifted but more careful than his brother, and as he was anxious to maintain the neutrality of Sweden, a treaty of alliance was concluded between Sweden and Denmark-Norway in 1794. They agreed to make the Baltic Sea neutral waters, and to place a joint fleet in the North Sea for the protection of their commerce, but the treaty should not include the German provinces of the two powers, as these could not be kept neutral. The relations with England grew very strained, as the English continued to annoy the allied Northern kingdoms with all sorts of unreasonable demands; among others, that proof should be given that the cargoes carried by their ships were their own property, that French privateers should be excluded from Norwegian harbors, etc. The English ambassador to Denmark-Norway, Hailes, was also a very impudent and disagreeable gentleman. But the presence of the joint fleet of the neutrals had a tranquilizing effect, and as the English became gradually more reasonable, a hostile collision was averted.

The results obtained through Bernstorff's wise policy of neutrality and alliance with Sweden, and the evident danger to weaker states, as illustrated by the fate of Poland, changed the hatred and mistrust between the Northern kingdoms into a feeling of friendship. The idea that the three sister nations should draw closer together had long been growing, and eloquent political leaders advocated a distinct Scandinavian policy, which should secure the permanent coöperation of the three kingdoms for their own protection. In an address before the Scandinavian club, "Nordiske Forening," in London January 28, 1792, the Danish historian F. Sneedorff said in speaking of the political situation in the North: "You will notice that Russia has gained control of the commerce of the Black Sea, and it is no imagined danger if you fear the same in the Baltic." "When Germany and Russia," he continued, "join hands across the Baltic Sea, it will be too late for us in the North to unite. There will then be nothing left for us but to die, or to hide among the mountains, even as our fathers hid behind their shields, and to disappear as states. But what power can be dangerous to a united Scandinavia? Our mountains, our islands, our united fleets, our severe climate, our love of liberty, of our fatherland, and our kings will make it impossible for any power on earth to deprive us of our independence." [1] Similar thoughts were expressed by many others, notably by the Danish statesman Ove Høeg-Guldberg, the Norwegian poet Zetlitz,[2] and the Swedish poet Franzén. In 1796 *Det skandinaviske Literatur-Selskab* was organized to foster a closer literary fellowship in the North, but it numbered only forty members; and although it continued to exist till 1840, it was never popular, and did not exercise any important influence. This Pan-Scandinavian movement had emanated chiefly from Denmark. The Swedes remained rather indifferent, and among the military officers and the higher classes the old jealousy and ill-feeling had not wholly disappeared. Even the relations between the two governments were not as cordial as might have been expected, since the Swedish regent seemed unable to avoid political indiscretions by which he irritated both Catherine II. and England. The most serious of these was the recognition of the French Republic in 1795, a step which greatly increased the

[1] O. A. Øverland, *Norges Historie*, vol. X., p. 90 ff. Julius Clausen, *Skandinavismen historisk fremstillet*, p. 7 ff.

[2] In a song to the united fleet Zetlitz says:

> Vi Danmarks mænd, vi Sverges mænd,
> Vi Norges mænd,
> Vi havets mænd, vi krigens mænd,
> Vi hædersmænd,
> Vi hørte vore fyrsters bud
> Om ledingstog,
> Vi løд, omfavned far og brud
> Og fro bortdrog;
> Thi se, vore fyrster er fædre!
>
> Paa høien mast det danske flag
> Urørt skal staa!
> Paa høien mast det svenske flag
> Urørt skal staa!
> Thi gother elske vaabenbrag,
> Kjækt cimbrer slaa,
> Og nordmænd ingen, ingen dag
> Forsagte saa;
> Thi er vore fyrster ei fædre?

gravity of the situation for the neutrals. The first coalition against France was broken up that same year, and Prussia and Spain withdrew. But England, Austria, and Sardinia still continued the struggle, and Catherine II. of Russia declared her willingness to join them. Under these circumstances it was as necessary as ever for the Northern nations to coöperate in the defense of their neutrality. Catherine II. sought to force them apart. She attempted to persuade Denmark-Norway to join the coalition, and made very tempting offers, but Bernstorff declined, though the situation was growing more difficult than ever. In 1796 he recognized the French Republic, but this proved to be of no advantage, as the French also began to send out privateers to prey upon neutral commerce. The right of search claimed by the English, and the slight regard for the precarious rights of neutrals, made the situation almost unbearable, but Bernstorff, who regarded war as the greatest calamity which could befall a nation, clung tenaciously to his policy of peace. The foreign policy of Sweden, which was now conducted by the minister of state, Reuterholm, continued to be vacillating. He abandoned the policy of Gustavus III., and sought an alliance with France. When this failed, he attempted to win the friendship of Russia by the marriage of the crown prince to Alexandra, a granddaughter of Catherine II., but the match failed because of a disagreement regard-

Vi krigens mænd, vi havets mænd,
Vi hædersmænd,
Vi Sverges mænd, vi Danmarks mænd,
Vi Norges mænd,
Vi all stolte Nordens mænd
Er et igjen;
Vi se det: Gud i himmelen
Er Nordens ven.
O, er vore fyrster ei fædre?

Som dug for sol alt indbildt had
Er svundet hen;
Se cimbren favner gothen glad
Som gammel ven.
Trohjertig nordmand begge ta'r
Med lyst i haand:
"Gud signe den, som tvundet har
Det skjønne baand,
De tvillingrigernes fædre."

ing the right of the future queen to worship according to the Greek faith. In November, 1796, the Swedish crown prince became of age, and ascended the throne as Gustavus IV. Catherine II. died the same month, and no further attempt was made to establish closer relations between the two nations.

In 1797 the great statesman Bernstorff died, an irreparable loss for Denmark-Norway in those critical times. The crown prince appointed as his successor his son Christian Bernstorff, an able and humane man, who lacked his father's experience as a statesman.

By his remarkable Italian campaign Napoleon Bonaparte forced Austria to conclude peace at Campo Formio, 1797, but England continued the struggle, and a second coalition was formed the following year. The war was renewed, and the commerce of the neutral Northern nations was so harassed by the English, French, and Spanish privateers that every merchant vessel had to be convoyed. The eccentric Emperor Paul of Russia, who had succeeded his mother Catherine II. on the throne, also assumed a most threatening attitude towards Denmark-Norway, and the government finally yielded to his demands, and joined the coalition against France. Actual hostilities were, however, avoided. Bonaparte, who at this time returned from Egypt, and made himself first consul, maintained friendly relations with the Northern kingdoms, and also with Emperor Paul of Russia, who had already changed his mind, and had suddenly become very hostile to England. The situation, though not much improved, was no worse than before, and prudent statesmanship would have adhered to the course so successfully pursued by A. P. Bernstorff. But the government arranged instead a new alliance of neutrality between Denmark-Norway, Sweden, Russia, and Prussia, and reaffirmed the principles of the rights of neutrals which had been formulated by A. P. Bernstorff and Catherine II. The step proved to be a mistake, as it aroused the resentment of the English government, which regarded the new alliance as a coalition hostile to England. In March, 1801, an English fleet of fifty-three warships under Admiral Hyde Parker, with Lord Nelson second in command, was sent to the Baltic. That war was imminent was now apparent, but Sweden had neglected to make preparations, and Denmark-Norway had to meet the attack of the great English fleet

alone. On March 30th the fleet passed the Sound, and took up a position before the Copenhagen roadstead, where the Danish-Norwegian fleet was anchored, wholly unprepared for active service. On
April 2, 1801, was fought the battle of Copenhagen, one of the most
memorable struggles in the history of Denmark-Norway.[1] Admiral
Nelson with the main fleet of thirty-five ships, 1192 guns, and 8885
men, was ordered to attack the Danish-Norwegian fleet, which was
much smaller both in size and armament. The part of the fleet
retained by Parker under his own immediate command should act
as reserve. The battle grew furious, as the combatants fought at
close quarters, and no attempt was made to withdraw a vessel from
the battle line until it was almost demolished. The Danes and Norwegians suffered terrible losses, but they entertained no thought
of yielding. Seven English vessels ran aground, and many were
severely damaged; the outcome of the struggle seemed very prob-
lematic, and as the whole English fleet was in the gravest danger,
Admiral Parker signaled to Nelson to stop the battle and retreat.
But this humiliation Nelson would not suffer. He put the field glass
to his blind eye, said he could see no signal, and let the battle continue. In order to bring the combat to a speedy close, he resorted
to a clever stratagem. He dispatched an officer with the following
letter to the crown prince, who was watching the battle from the
shore: "Lord Nelson has instructions to spare Denmark when no
longer resisting, but if the firing is continued on the part of Denmark, Lord Nelson will be obliged to set on fire all the floating batteries he has taken, without having the power of saving the brave
Danes who have defended them."[2] A second letter was dispatched
immediately after the first, in which he stated that he made this
appeal from humanitarian motives, that he would regard it as the
greatest victory he ever won, if his flag of truce might be the signal
for a permanent and happy union between his sovereign and the
king of Denmark. The threat in the first letter was, of course, only
a ruse, but he succeeded in disheartening the crown prince, who
immediately ordered a flag of truce to be hoisted. The last great

[1] Jacob Aal, *Erindringer*, p. 20 ff.

[2] The letter, which is dated on board the ship "Elephant," April 2, 1801,
is found in the Danish archives, *Danmarks Riges Historie*, vol. V., p. 502.

battle in which the Danes and Norwegians were destined to fight side by side was over, and a preliminary peace was concluded April 9th. The alliance with Russia had only brought war and disaster, and Denmark-Norway had good reasons to feel that they had been left to shift for themselves at a critical juncture. On March 23 Emperor Paul was assassinated, and his successor, Emperor Alexander I., concluded a treaty of alliance with England without consulting the other allies, waiving nearly every right claimed by the neutrals. But even under these circumstances Denmark-Norway felt compelled to join the new alliance in order to recover their lost American and Asiatic colonies, which had been seized by England.

In 1802 peace was concluded between France and England at Amiens, but both powers felt that it could be nothing but a truce, and a year had scarcely passed when hostilities were renewed. The danger to Denmark now became more imminent, as Bonaparte seized the Electorate of Hanover, which belonged to the king of England. The theater of war had thus been moved closer to the Danish border, and the crown prince advanced into Holstein with an army of 16,000 men to protect the kingdom. The mounting ambition of Napoleon, manifested by his proclamation as Emperor of France in 1804, made all Europe regard him as a common enemy, and a new coalition was soon formed against him, consisting of England, Russia, and Austria. Napoleon crushed the Austrians at Ulm, and the united forces of Russia and Austria at Austerlitz, but England dealt his naval power a deadly blow at Trafalgar. In 1806 the Confederation of the Rhine was organized under the protectorate of the Emperor, and the old German Empire ceased to exist. Prussia declared war, only to be crushed at Jena and Auerstadt, and Napoleon occupied Berlin. In rapid succession the continental powers had been vanquished, but England was still defiant, and as her proud navy controlled the sea, he would have to strike at her only vulnerable spot — her commerce. In 1806 he issued his noted Berlin Decree, declaring the British Isles to be in a state of blockade, and interdicting all trade with England, not only in France, but in all ports of Europe over which he exercised authority, including the Netherlands, western Germany, Prussia, and Italy. After the treaty of Tilsit, 1807, he also subjected Russia to his "Continental System." In December, 1807, he issued a second decree from Milan, in which he threatened to seize any ship which touched at a British port. The English retaliated by Orders in Council, declaring the ports of France and her allies to be in a state of blockade, but allowing neutral vessels to carry on trade between these ports and Great Britain. The crown prince, who had been stationed in Holstein, where he had gathered an army of 20,000 men, finally withdrew the greater part of his force across the Eider. It seemed to have been his purpose to maintain neutrality as long as possible, and to cast his lot with England if he were finally forced into the struggle. The situation was constantly growing more critical, as any move which the government might make was interpreted as unfriendly either by Napoleon or England. In direct contravention of the concessions which had been made to neutral powers in 1801, the English government issued new Orders in Council, forbidding neutral ships to trade between the ports of France or her allies. This new restriction would damage Danish-Norwegian commerce very seriously; but although sharp diplomatic encounters followed, no redress of wrongs could be obtained. The ultimate rupture with one or the other of the belligerents could evidently not long be averted even by the most watchful prudence. After the battle of Friedland and the peace of Tilsit, Napoleon succeeded in winning to his side the imaginative Emperor Alexander I. of Russia. Alexander promised to attempt to negotiate peace between France and England, but if the English government should refuse to accept the terms on which the two emperors had agreed, Russia should join France. Denmark-Norway, Sweden, and Portugal would be requested to close their ports to English commerce, and if they refused, they should be treated as enemies. This cunning stroke of Napoleon shattered the policy of neutrality, and forced the smaller nations to choose sides in the conflict.

The news of the alliance between France and Russia and their plans regarding the neutral nations caused the greatest alarm, not only in Copenhagen, Stockholm, and Lisbon, but also in England. The English government imagined that Denmark-Norway was a secret partner to the compact, and without even taking the time to ascertain the real state of affairs, a large fleet was immediately dispatched to Denmark. On August 6th the English diplomat Sir

Francis Jackson arrived in Kiel, where the crown prince and Christian Bernstorff were staying, and presented an English ultimatum. As a guarantee that Denmark-Norway would be the ally of England they should turn their fleet over to the English, who would use it during the war, and return it to the owners after the peace had been concluded. Forty thousand English troops should coöperate with the Danes against France, and in return for the aid which Denmark-Norway should give England, they might receive a few English colonies. The crown prince and Bernstorff were so taken by surprise that they lost their presence of mind, and the negotiations became a scene of almost pitiable confusion. So much they, nevertheless, succeeded in making clear to the English ambassador that the ports of the realm would not be closed to English commerce, and that Denmark-Norway would enter into an alliance with England. But the English demanded the fleet, as if they were negotiating with criminals, whose words and pledges could not be relied upon. Even an alliance would not be accepted as sufficient guarantee. No more humiliating terms could have been offered an independent people, but it was folly for the crown prince to make open resistance. The English forces concentrated on Seeland under Lord Cathcart numbered 31,000 men, commanded by the most experienced English generals, among others General Wellesley, the later Duke of Wellington. The fleet commanded by Admiral Gambier consisted of twenty-five ships of the line, forty frigates, and a large number of smaller vessels and transports. To subject the capital with its antiquated defenses to the bombardment and attack of such a force, when it was defended only by some 14,000 men, of whom not above 6000 belonged to the regular army, appears like a Don Quixotic adventure, even under such circumstances. From the second to the fifth of September Copenhagen was bombarded until it looked like a sea of flames. Large portions of the city were laid in ruins, and between two and three thousand people were killed. The commandant, General Peymann, was forced to capitulate, and the Danish fleet, of seventy vessels, which was lying in the harbor wholly unprepared for active service, was taken.[1]

---

[1] Jacob Aal, *Erindringer*, p. 29 ff. Constantinus Flood, *Under Krigen 1807–1814*, p. 127 ff.

But England had gained nothing and lost much by her precipitate haste. The unprovoked attack on Denmark was not only an outrage on a friendly nation, but it was a political mistake of the worst sort. The assumption advanced by English historians that Napoleon planned to seize the fleet of Denmark-Norway to use it against England, and that his plan was frustrated only by the prompt action of the English government, must be dismissed as pure hypothesis. Napoleon was taking steps to coerce Denmark-Norway to submit to the demands of France and Russia. If the English fleet had not arrived when it did, a rupture with France would have followed, and Denmark-Norway would have become the ally of England; their fleet would have coöperated with that of England, and their army, which was already stationed on the southern border to protect the kingdom against French attack, would have been ready to coöperate with whatever forces the English government could have placed in the field against Napoleon. But by this ill-starred event the Danish-Norwegian fleet had been destroyed as a fighting force, and in her despair Denmark formed an alliance with France. The English government was much disappointed at the outcome of the expedition to Copenhagen. Even after the capture of the fleet, attempts were made to persuade the Danish government to enter into an alliance with England. This might have been the wisest policy for Denmark-Norway even at that moment, but it must be granted that such a step would require a degree of self-abnegation which is not usually given to human nature. The English attack had not only brought about the destructive bombardment of Copenhagen and the loss of the fleet, but by forcing Denmark-Norway into an alliance with Napoleon it resulted in still greater disasters to the twin kingdoms.

By a treaty of alliance concluded at Fontainebleau, October 31, 1807, Denmark-Norway agreed to coöperate with France and Russia and to close all ports against English commerce. On November 4th England declared war against the two kingdoms. It was a dark moment for Denmark-Norway. The English had not only taken the fleet, but all the military stores in Copenhagen, and because of the suddenness of the attack, they were also able to seize about a thousand Danish and Norwegian merchant vessels in their own harbors and elsewhere. They had also occupied the island of

Helgoland, a step which Denmark-Norway could not prevent, as they had been deprived of all means of defending themselves at sea. The interruption of commerce, and the destruction of lives and property incident to the war, brought upon the North a period of intense suffering. This was especially the case in Norway, where the necessary quantity of grain cannot be produced, and where the cessation of import trade finally added famine to the many trials of those dark years. But the otherwise gloomy picture is brightened by the intense patriotism and high courage with which the peoples of both kingdoms waged the long struggle with their powerful enemy. The English had estimated that the fleet and supplies seized at Copenhagen represented a value of £2,000,000. During the war they captured about 1500 Danish-Norwegian merchant vessels and smaller craft, but in balancing accounts at the end of the war, they still found that the struggle had netted them a considerable loss.

After the loss of the fleet Denmark-Norway still had two ships of the line which were not at Copenhagen at the time of the bombardment, and with resolute energy they set to work to create a fleet of small vessels, each carrying a couple of guns. With this flotilla of gunboats manned with experienced seamen they began a guerilla warfare at sea which proved destructive to English commerce in the Baltic. The lighthouses remained dark, and the buoys were moved to misguide the stranger, while the gunboats and privateers [1] lay in ambush behind the rocks and skerries of the dark coast, ready to swoop down upon the enemy at any given opportunity. The dangers became so great that the English merchant vessels had to unite into fleets under convoy of men-of-war. But these naval caravans moved slowly, as the whole fleet had to stop whenever a vessel was to make port, and even such convoys were in danger of

[1] On September 14, 1807, before the English had left Copenhagen, a permit was issued to the *stiftsamtmœnd* and the chief military officers in each stift to license privateers to any extent which they might deem advantageous, and these should be permitted to seize English property on land or sea wherever they might find it. Swarms of privateers were sent out, and the traffic became so profitable that stock companies were organized to promote it. Constantinus Flood, *I Krigsaarene*, p. 95. Ludvig Daae, *Det gamle Christiania*, p. 306 ff.

being attacked by the gunboats. In 1808 the gunboat flotilla attacked an English convoy at Malmö, and captured or destroyed eleven merchant vessels. Many valuable prizes were taken from time to time. According to documents in the Danish archives the value of prizes brought into Danish-Norwegian harbors amounted to 28,081,013 riksdaler, and the value of those which were actually confiscated amounted to 14,933,119 riksdaler.[1] In all, 2000 English merchant vessels were seized by the Danes and Norwegians during the war. At times successful battles were also fought with English men-of-war. On March 14, 1808, the Norwegian brig "Laugen" defeated the English brig "Childers," and on June 19th the same year, the "Laugen" captured the English brig "Seagull," which was incorporated in the Norwegian fleet. But such moments when victory brightened the melancholy aspect of the unequal struggle must have been few and far between. The English men-of-war swept along the coast and picked up every little craft which sought to steal across to Denmark to fetch food for those who were starving at home, and the daring voyagers who would risk all to relieve the growing distress were carried off as prisoners of war, and huddled together with like unfortunates in the dreadful English prison-ships. The Norwegian privateers did valiant service in the guerilla warfare, but officers and crew would often pay for their daring by languishing for years in the unsanitary military prison-pens, which sometimes harbored whole armies of those unfortunate victims of war. The English themselves disliked this war with Denmark-Norway, which was waged for no definite purpose, which proved so expensive, and so destructive to their commerce, and which cut off their supply of Norwegian lumber and ship-building material.

The old insane king Christian VII. died March 13, 1808, and the crown prince, who had long acted as regent, ascended the throne at Frederick VI. The political situation was so extremely difficult that he might have needed the assistance and advice of the ablest men, but he preferred to exercise unlimited autocratic power, even

---

[1] Constantinus Flood, *Under Krigen 1807-1814*, p. 131. Constantinus Flood, *I Krigsaarene*, p. 93 ff. S. C. Hammer, *Da det gjaldt*, Christiania, 1909. Constantinus Flood, *For otti Aar siden*. H. P. Holmboe, *Briternes Krigsforetagender langs Norges Kyster fra 1808 til 1814*, *Samlinger til det norske Folks Sprog og Historie*, vol. II., p. 246 ff.

to an extent hitherto unknown. Not till in 1813, when utter ruin threatened the realm, did he summon his ministers for consultation. He sought with great earnestness and uprightness of purpose to promote the welfare of the people, but he entertained very extravagant notions as to his own ability as a ruler, and looked with jealous disfavor upon any minister who exhibited any independence of mind, and ventured to offer suggestions or advice. His overweening self-esteem, which made him unnecessarily despotic in affairs of government, was fully equaled by his confidence in his military ability and his love for martial adventure and display. These traits of character, which rendered his statesmanship venturesome and ill-advised, were particularly unfortunate at a critical juncture, when the state policy should have been dictated by the greatest wisdom and prudence.

Fig. 8. — Frederick VI

To the Norwegians the war with England was ruinous. Their coasts were blockaded, and their lucrative commerce destroyed; yet the struggle, which was as useless as it was hopeless, was, nevertheless, waged for a cause. But when King Frederick also declared war against Sweden, 1808, as it appears, for no cause whatever, except that Sweden opposed France and Russia, it must be regarded as sheer madness. It was clear that the Norwegians would also be compelled to bear the brunt of this war, though they lacked, not only military stores, but the necessities of life. While their unprotected coasts were ravaged by the English, they would also have to guard their extensive borders against the Swedes; and it must have been evident to the king that any hope of aid from Denmark was precluded from the outset, as the Danes had no navy, and the Norwegian coast was patrolled by English warships.[1] It had, further-more, been evident for a long time that the Swedish kings sought to gain possession of Norway, and no better opportunity could be offered than a war under such circumstances. The immediate dan-ger was, however, less than might have been expected, as Gustavus IV. of Sweden, who was tottering on the brink of insanity, brought upon his country such disasters that its very existence was threat-ened. He could not be persuaded to submit to the Continental System. He regarded Napoleon as the beast of the Apocalypse, against whom relentless war ought to be waged, and as he believed himself to be a reincarnation of Charles XII., he did not hesitate to join England against France and Russia. By a war against these powers Sweden would gain nothing, and with a blindness which finds an explanation only in his insanity he thereby exposed Finland to the attack of Russia, which was becoming an ever greater danger to the Scandinavian kingdoms. On February 21, 1808, Alexander I. sent an army of 16,000 men to occupy Finland, without the formality of a warning or a declaration of war. On February 29th King Frederick VI., persuaded by his French and Russian allies, declared war on Sweden. Regarding the feeling which this step created in Norway the contemporary Norwegian statesman Jacob Aal says in his memoirs: "It was regarded even by those who were most de-voted to the Danish government as a great mistake in Danish politics, and a presentiment was felt of the possible results which in the full-ness of time might reveal themselves. This war prepared the way for the separation of Denmark and Norway, and some Norwegians began, though vaguely, to think of the advisability of a union with Sweden, the very possibility of which had hitherto wounded their innermost feelings."[2]

On account of the interruption of communications with Denmark, the king was now obliged to create a special government for Nor-way, a Government Commission (Regjerings-Kommissionen for Norge), at the head of which stood Prince Christian August of August-enborg, commanding general in southern Norway.[3] Count Wedel-

---

[1] Ludvig Daae, Det gamle Christiania, p. 306 f.
[2] Jacob Aal, Erindringer, p. 136.
[3] Yngvar Nielsen, Lensgreve Johan Caspar Wedel-Jarlsberg, vol. I., p. 115.

Jarlsberg was placed at the head of a subsidiary commission which should seek to provide the country with the necessary supplies, a most difficult task under the circumstances. A superior court was also created in 1807, *Overkriminalretten*, which should meet in Christiania, and should be the highest court of appeal in all criminal cases. This gave Norway an autonomy in judicial and administrative affairs which it had not enjoyed for centuries.

While Russia attacked Finland, Napoleon ordered Marshal Bernadotte to march through Denmark and attack Sweden. In 1808 an army of about 23,000 men was sent to Jutland. A Danish force of about 14,000 men was to join it in Seeland, but what might easily have been foreseen happened. The army could not be transported across the Sound, which was patrolled by English warships, and the plan had to be abandoned. Denmark was cut off from both her adversaries, and Norway was left to fight her battles alone.

The Swedish forces in active service at this time numbered about 100,000 men. But owing to the war with Russia in Finland, and a possible attack on southern Sweden, only the western army of 13,400 men under General G. M. Armfelt, and a smaller detachment in Jæmtland of 2000 men under Colonel Bergenstråle, could operate against Norway. The Norwegians could mobilize only about one-half of their southern army of 17,000 men, and so poor were the equipments that the soldiers had to wear old uniforms which had been in use in the war of 1788.[1] Ragged and half naked these defenders of their country were sent against the superior invading force. But the people resolved to hold the enemy at bay, and from their scant supplies they provided the soldiers with food and clothing, as far as this could be done under the circumstances Well-to-do citizens organized volunteer companies, and equipped them at their own expense, and many *bønder* reënlisted as volunteers when the term of required military service had expired. Enevold de Falsen, Count Herman Wedel-Jarlsberg, and other leading men labored with untiring zeal to provide means for carrying on the defense of the country,

Jacob Aal, *Erindringer*, p. 105 ff. Gustav Peter Blom, *Norges Statsforandring i Aaret 1814*, ch. I. ff. Erik Vullum, *Hvorledes Norge blev frit*, p. 16 ff.

[1] J. E. Sars, *Udsigt over den norske Historie*, vol. IV., p. 302. Jacob Aal, *Erindringer*, p. 135 ff. Didrik Schnitler, *Episoder fra Krigen 1808–1809*. Constantinus Flood, *I Krigsaarene*. O. A. Øverland, *Norges Historie*, vol. XI.

and Prince Christian August, commander of the military forces, gained the love and confidence of the soldiers by his democratic ways and true soldierly spirit. The patriotism and love for their leader which inspired the Norwegians made them formidable in a border war of the kind which had just begun, and as the Swedish general, G. M. Armfelt, divided his forces into different columns instead of concentrating them for a main attack, it became possible for Christian August to meet and defeat each detachment in turn. On April 15th General Armfelt attacked the Norwegians at Lier, not far from the Glommen River, south of Kongsvinger, and drove them back across the river.[1] But this was to be his only success. At Toverud one of his flying columns under Count Axel Mörner was defeated and captured, April 20th, by a Norwegian force under Major Weibye, and at Trangen another detachment under Major Gahn was captured by Major Staffeldt. These victories aroused great enthusiasm, and the people contributed liberally to the support of the army. Jacob Aal writes: "Every one hastened to place his offering on his country's altar. Provisions, money, and clothing poured in for the army on the border, and the merchant John Collett in Christiania distinguished himself especially by collecting or sending provisions, and by personally contributing to the maintenance of the army. Nearly every number of 'Budstikken'[2] published lists of contributions of this kind. In that first war with Sweden private charity made good the deficiency in the provisions made by the public authorities, due to the lack of means and the depleted and impoverished condition of the country. After the war had lasted two weeks, Collett could announce that fifty-five, mostly two-teamed, wagons had been sent to the army."[3]

The unsuccessful engagements already fought made it clear to King Gustavus IV. that further operations against Norway with the forces then available would prove unsuccessful, and he ordered General Armfelt to retreat to the border. The Swedish general concentrated his forces at Enningdalen, but he suffered new losses in an engagement at Prestebakke, June 10th, where over 400 men and twenty-seven offi-

[1] Jacob Aal, *Erindringer, Bilag 24.*
[2] A newspaper published in Christiania by Enevold Falsen.
[3] Jacob Aal, *Erindringer*, p. 14.

cers were taken prisoners. This was the last engagement of any importance between the Swedes and Norwegians in this war. Sweden had to employ all her strength against the advancing Russians in Finland, and the Norwegians did not wish to carry on an offensive war against Sweden. The friendship which had been developing between the two peoples had manifested itself quite clearly at the time when they sought as allies to defend their neutrality, but in the present war it was shown in a still more emphatic way. The Norwegians would defend their country with every possible means, but they made it quite clear that, although they had been forced into war, they entertained none but the kindliest feelings for their Swedish neighbors.

The war with Finland had brought Sweden into great peril. Her armies, indeed, won brilliant victories at Lappo, Juutas, and other places, and several of her generals, as Adlercreutz, Döbeln, and Sandels, had greatly distinguished themselves; but the lack of proper support from home, and the treasonable surrender of the strong fortress of Sveaborg with military stores, a hundred vessels of the coast fleet, and a garrison of 7000 men made the situation critical. On September 14, 1809, General Adlercreutz suffered a crushing defeat at Oravais, and before the end of the year the Swedes were expelled from Finland, which was turned into a Russian province.

In 1809 the Russians prepared to follow up their advantage by an invasion of Sweden. National peril and disaster intensified the growing ill-will against the incompetent and mentally unbalanced King Gustavus IV., who had involved the kingdom in this disastrous war. It had long been evident that he was mentally unfit to direct the affairs of government, and a conspiracy was formed to depose him. One of the leaders of this movement was George Adlersparre, commander of the right wing of the Swedish army operating against Norway.[1] He determined to lead his forces against Stockholm, but the situation was so critical that this could not be done without the greatest hazard, unless he could persuade the Norwe-

---

[1] Armfelt was removed after his many failures, and Cederström was made chief commander of the army. Carl Henrik Posse, commander of the left wing of the army, did not coöperate actively with Adlersparre, but promised not to oppose him.

gians to suspend operations. Christian August was expected to attack Sweden at the same time that the Russians were preparing to advance from the east. The Russian general Schuvaloff had already entered northern Sweden by crossing Torneå River, Barclay de Tolly occupied Umeå, and Russian cossacks from the Åland Islands had appeared in Stockholms *len*.[1] Prince Christian August hesitated. He saw Sweden's plight, and reflected upon the consequences to the North if the kingdom should be overwhelmed by Russia. Would not the Scandinavian peninsula share the fate of Finland? When Adlersparre turned to him with the request to refrain from aggressive operations against Sweden, he promised that he would not cross the border unless he received peremptory orders from Frederick VI. to do so, and even then he would not enter Swedish territory without giving a ten days' notice. This was more than a courtesy;

FIG. 9. — Prince Charles August

it was rendering an enemy a service so important that it might have been construed as treason if it were not for the exigencies of the situation and the friendship which really existed between the two peoples. In Sweden it was officially stated that Prince Christian August had shown the country a greater service than had ever been rendered it by a foreigner.[2] The prince had risked this step

---

[1] Yngvar Nielsen, *Wedel-Jarlsberg*, vol. I., p. 191. Gustaf Montgomery, *Kriget emellan Sverige och Ryssland 1808 och 1809*, vol. II., p. 208 ff. Gustav Peter Blom, *Norges Statsforandring i Aaret 1814.*

[2] *Handlingar rörande Sveriges Historia*, vol. IV., p. 59 ff.; quoted by Yngvar Nielsen, *Wedel-Jarlsberg*, vol. I., p. 189.

for Sweden's sake, and no one has ever questioned his patriotism and loyalty.

Frederick VI. failed to comprehend the situation. Time and again he ordered the Norwegian army to invade Sweden and join the advancing Russians on Swedish soil, but Christian August, who saw that such a step would be suicidal, always found new pretexts for postponement, and the army never crossed the border. As soon as Adlersparre had received assurances from Christian August, he hastened to Karlstad, where he raised the standard of revolt, and new troops constantly joined him on his march. But even before he reached Stockholm the king was arrested by General Adlercreutz, who had just returned from Finland.[1] The Estates were summoned, Duke Charles of Södermanland was placed on the throne as King Charles XIII., and a constitution was adopted which made Sweden a limited constitutional monarchy.

The victorious advance of the Russians, which, as Frederick Sneedorff had predicted in 1792, had become more than an imaginary peril to the North, revived again the Pan-Scandinavian sentiment. Swedish politicians began to consider the advisability of choosing Frederick VI. of Denmark-Norway Swedish crown prince, as the newly elected King Charles XIII. had no heirs. The plan, which would lead to the union of the three kingdoms, was supported by Prince Christian August and many leading men in Norway, especially by Count Herman Wedel-Jarlsberg; but King Frederick himself soon defeated it by his prejudice and narrow-minded absolutism, as he would not accept the crown if Sweden had a constitution limiting the power of the king.[2] In the meantime Adlersparre, who at this moment was the most influential man in Sweden, was endeavoring to secure the election of Christian August as heir to the Swedish throne. The prince was very popular in Norway, and it was hoped that the Norwegians could easily be persuaded to make him their

---

[1] King Gustavus IV. and his heirs were declared to have forfeited the throne. The king and his family were sent to Germany, and were not allowed to return to Sweden. He received a pension of 10,000 riksdaler, and was allowed to keep his private property. He assumed the name of Gustafson and spent the rest of his life in Germany and Switzerland.

[2] Carl Th. Sørensen, *Fredrik den sjettes fortrolige Brevveksling med Norge i Aaret 1809*, p. 64.

king, and a union between Norway and Sweden would thus be established.[1] For this plan he received the enthusiastic support of Prince Christian August's chief adviser, Count Wedel-Jarlsberg, who soon abandoned his Pan-Scandinavian ideas, and developed a political policy which aimed at a united Scandinavia. That the position taken by the count strained to the breaking-point the ties of loyalty to King Frederick VI. seems quite apparent, but Norway had paid dearly enough for the political blunders of the Oldenborg kings. The time had come when the Norwegians would safeguard the interests of their own country in any way which they might deem expedient. To protect Norway against possible Russian aggression, to secure peace with England and Sweden, and to save the country from impending famine seemed more important to Count Wedel-Jarlsberg and his associates than to earn the compliments and good-will of the king. The count proposed to Christian August that the Norwegians should declare themselves independent of Denmark, and elect him king of Norway; but the Prince would agree to no plan which seemed treasonable. He promised the Swedish messengers, however, that he would accept the election as Swedish crown prince if King Frederick VI. would grant him leave to do so. In July, 1809, he was elected crown prince of Sweden as Charles August, and King Frederick granted him permission to accept the proffered honor. On September 17th of that year a treaty of peace between Sweden and Russia was signed at Fredrikshamn, by which Finland was ceded to Russia, and Sweden had to submit to the Continental System. On December 10th peace was also concluded between Sweden and Denmark-Norway at Jönköping. The war with England continued, but in order to appease the Norwegians, King Frederick agreed to a proposal made by the Council of Regency to raise the embargo on commerce between Norway and England by a mutual agreement with the English government, according to which Norwegian merchant ships could sail to English harbors, if they purchased in London a license which would insure them against attack by English privateers and men-of-war. This "license trade," or "neutral commerce," helped greatly to relieve the distress in Norway,

---

[1] B. von Schinkel, *Minnen ur Sveriges nyare Historia*, published by C. W. Bergman, vol. V., p. 118 ff.

as grain and other commodities could be imported, and the export of timber and other articles could be resumed.[1]

In 1810 Prince Charles August left Norway for his future kingdom. His departure was celebrated with great festivities, and the people showed him the most devoted affection. Count Wedel-Jarlsberg, who accompanied him across the border, had been unable to persuade the prince to head a Norwegian uprising, but he had not relinquished the hope of bringing about a union between Norway and Sweden.[2]

At the time of his election as crown prince, Charles August was less than forty-one years of age, but he was not destined to ascend the throne of Sweden. On May 28, 1810, while attending military maneuvers in Skåne, he died suddenly of an apoplectic stroke. This opened anew the difficult question of the election of a Swedish crown prince, destined to produce such important political changes in the North.

50. The Gradual Dissolution of the Danish-Norwegian Partnership

The demand for national autonomy created by the suffering which Norway had to undergo during the war with England and Sweden did not culminate in an attempt to sever the bonds of union with Denmark by a revolutionary uprising, but the growing love of independence nevertheless effected a thorough change in the relations between the two kingdoms. The old idea that Norway sustained a quasi provincial relation to Denmark both politically and intellectually had vanished in the powder smoke of the great wars. Forced to rely on themselves in a most critical period, the Norwegians had become conscious of their own ability to defend themselves, and of the necessity of relying on their own strength in days of trial. A wave of patriotism swept over the country, due in part to the experiences in the war, but partly also to the nationalism which had been kindled throughout Europe in the struggle against Napoleon. The French Revolution had endued nationality with a new meaning,

[1] Yngvar Nielsen, *Wedel-Jarlsberg*, vol. I., p. 305 ff.
[2] Jacob Aal, *Erindringer*, p. 190. Yngvar Nielsen, *Wedel-Jarlsberg*, vol. I., p. 332.

as it had fundamentally changed the conception of the rights of man. With the rights of the individual, so vehemently proclaimed, was associated as a necessary corollary the right of every people to lead their own independent national existence, and this principle was being employed as a new weapon against Napoleon in Spain, Germany, and Italy. "And the idea, once proclaimed, spread with astonishing rapidity," says Alison Phillips; "till in all Europe there was not a race with a grievance, real or fancied, against the established order but based its resistance on the national right of a nation to be mistress of its own destinies."[1] The Norwegian leaders were enthusiastic adherents of these ideas, and the national struggle which had hitherto been a dogged resistance of the *bønder* against the oppression of Danish officials, an effort of the common people to preserve their personal freedom, now entered upon a new stage. New leaders from the upper classes had appeared, men of learning and high culture, who united the ideals of liberty and national independence with the old spirit of personal freedom, and aimed to rear the Norwegian state once more on its own foundation. They would henceforth control the destinies of the nation, and were determined to secure for it sufficient autonomy to insure its unhampered development.

When Prince Charles August left Norway, they seized the opportunity to organize, after the pattern of the German *Tugendbund*,[2] a national society of which a Swedish contemporary writer has given the following account: "As soon as Count Wedel, after several unsuccessful attempts, realized the impossibility of persuading Prince Augustenborg to agree to the plan of separating Norway from Denmark, and uniting it with Sweden, he determined to act independently. For this purpose he originated the plan for *Selskabet for Norges Vel*, a sort of masonic order which extended its ramifications to all parts of the country and to nearly all classes. The apparent aim of the society was to promote agriculture and different branches of

---

[1] *Modern Europe*, p. 6.

[2] The *Tugendbund* was organized in Königsberg, Prussia, in 1808. Its aim was to work for the reorganization of the Prussian army, and for the proper physical and moral training of the young men of the country; to encourage patriotism, and to prepare the way for the throwing off of the French yoke.

Norwegian industry, but Wedel had in reality no less a plan than to make it the nucleus of a representative body, to prepare the minds of the people for the new order of things which he would establish in his country. . . . None but the principal leaders of the society knew the secret purpose of its organization." [1]

Not till after the society had been organized did Count Wedel and his father-in-law, Peter Anker, ask King Frederick to grant it his royal protection. This the king did, though he disliked the spirit of independence shown by the Norwegian leaders. Before a year had passed, the society had 2000 members. It still exists, and continues to be of great service in aiding and encouraging undertakings of national importance.

In 1809 a new agitation for a Norwegian university had been set on foot, as the need of a higher institution of learning had become more pressing than ever, since the war had destroyed the communications with Denmark. The demand for such an institution had been so long and urgently pressed that it had become a national issue, and as soon as *Selskabet for Norges Vel* was organized, it gave this cause its earnest support. "This time such large means were made available, the nation's demand was expressed in such vigorous terms, and the desire was backed with such large subscriptions that the Danish king, who loved Norway, found it hazardous to postpone the granting of so reasonable a request. . . . Furthermore, there had been formed in the kingdom a body of men who took it upon themselves to speak about important matters, who stood united with regard to plans which they considered beneficial to the country, and who, on approaching the government authorities, had to a certain degree dispensed with the formalities of an absolute monarchy," writes Jacob Aal.[2]

Selskabet for Norges Vel offered a prize of 1000 riksdaler for the best treatise to be written on the question of a Norwegian university. Nine were submitted to the judges, who awarded the first prize of 800 riksdaler to the author of "Mnemosyne," who proved to be Nicolai Wergeland, the father of the later poet and patriotic leader

¹ B. von Schinkel, *Minnen ur Sveriges nyare Historia*, vol. V., p. 88. Yngvar Nielsen, *Wedel-Jarlsberg*, vol. I., p. 344 f. Erik Vullum, *Hvorledes Norge blev frit*, p. 88 ff.   ² *Erindringer*, p. 228.

Henrik Wergeland.[1] "Mnemosyne" was much praised by some. The king gave the author 300 riksdaler as a token of his esteem; the people of Drammen presented him with 1200 riksdaler, and in Tunsberg the people gave him a church offering of 900 riksdaler. But his treatise has been severely criticized, among others by the Norwegian historian Ludvig Daae. In Denmark the learned jurist A. S. Ørsted assailed it because of the bitter criticism of Denmark indulged in by the author. This only served to intensify Nicolai Wergeland's anti-Danish feelings, and on a later occasion he found an opportunity to express it in an even more acrimonious way. The Danish government found that they could no longer wholly disregard the demand of the Norwegians, but they would compromise, and offered to grant them permission to establish a sort of seminary. This offer was not accepted, and the solution seemed as distant as ever when matters suddenly took a new turn.

It had been rumored at court that Count Wedel was a traitor who planned to separate Norway from Denmark, and the king, who gave credence to these reports, summoned Wedel to Denmark. The count hastened to present himself before the king, and demanded to know why he had been called. The king, who possessed no evidence of his disloyalty, was disconcerted by his sudden appearance, and as a plausible excuse he said that he wished to confer with him regarding a Norwegian university. By a rescript of March 1, 1811, the directors of the University of Copenhagen were instructed to confer with the count, who submitted a declaration regarding the sentiment in Norway, which moved the directors to advise the granting of the Norwegian demand. In June of the same year *Selskabet for Norges Vel* started a subscription among the wealthier classes to raise means for the founding of the new institution of learning. The subscription, which was continued for two years, brought the sum of 782,000 riksdaler, and a yearly contribution of 13,382 riksdaler. In 1813 the university, which was located at Christiania, was able to begin its work. The Norwegian poets in Denmark had already returned to their own country from patriotic motives. In 1812 the *Norske Selskab* in Copenhagen was dissolved, and when the university in Christiania opened its doors, the academic and literary

---

[1] Arne Bergsgaard, *Nicolai Wergeland*, Christiania, 1908.

partnership with Denmark must be regarded as terminated. A new national literature had begun to develop in Denmark in 1802, but in Norway a new literary epoch did not begin till 1830. Of the poets who flourished in the decades prior to 1814 the former members of the *Norske Selskab* in Copenhagen, Jonas Rein, Jens Zetlitz, and Claus Frimann, continued to write in the spirit of the eighteenth century, and their younger associates, Lyder Sagen, Johan Storm Munch, Conrad Schwach, and Simon O. Wolff, shared their views. They wrote bombastic patriotic songs and sentimental lyrics, but as they were strangers to the life and sentiments of their own people, they were so dominated by foreign models that their verse lacked the true national qualities. A new spiritual movement had, indeed, stirred the Norwegian people, but it was of a purely religious character, and had in no way influenced the literary tastes of the higher classes.

While the conquests of Napoleon absorbed all attention in the field of politics, and while a flourishing commerce prior to the war with England and Sweden created great traffic and prosperity, especially in the cities, the people throughout many of the rural districts were roused by a great revival which permanently influenced religious life in Norway. Rationalism, which had followed in the wake of Pietism, had almost destroyed all true piety in the Lutheran state church. The cultured upper classes had in general accepted the views of the *Aufklärung*, and the greater part of the clergy did not believe the gospel which they were to preach. Some clergymen even substituted for the sermons discourses on purely secular matters, and sang popular ditties in their churches for the edification of their parishioners. Among the common people, who believed the Bible teachings in a literal way, Christian faith lived despite the lack of proper religious instruction, but their deeper religious sentiments had never been stirred by an appeal to their faith as a dominant force in their moral and social life. Religion had become associated with a lifeless formalism which exercised no power over the hearts of the people, and the rationalistic state church lacked all regenerating power. It was left for the great revival set on foot by Hans Nielsen Hauge to make their Lutheran faith a living force strong enough to shape new ethical and social views.

PLATE VIII

THE UNIVERSITY OF CHRISTIANIA.

Hauge was an untutored country lad, born in the neighborhood of Sarpsborg in 1771. His parents were pious God-fearing people, who gave their children a thorough Christian training, and Hans Nielsen, who was a very gifted boy, quiet, introspective, and given to reflection, exhibited even in boyhood a fervent religious spirit. An accident in his thirteenth year in which he nearly lost his life by drowning increased his fervor. He devoted himself sedulously to the study of the Bible, and became convinced that God had appointed him to preach the gospel to his countrymen. Finally, after much hesitation, he began, in 1796, the great task of reviving and purifying the people's religious faith. He entered upon his work with the most self-sacrificing earnestness, but also with a modesty which always employed the most quiet methods, and avoided all disturbance and excitement. In six years he traveled over 10,000 miles, mostly on foot, preached from two to four times a day, and wrote hundreds of pamphlets and devotional books. His love for the common people was of the most genuine sort, and as he possessed great practical ability as well as rare talents, he was often able to render them valuable assistance even in purely secular matters. He taught them to found mills and factories, he even established himself as merchant in Bergen, and developed a lucrative trade with Trondhjem and Nordland to aid his adherents by his business insight. Hauge preached no new doctrine. He did not even attempt to organize his followers into a new religious body, but contented himself with preaching the gospel according to the confession of the Lutheran state church. But this was regarded as a crime, since no one but ordained ministers were authorized to preach.[1] Under the Conventicle Act of 1741, Hauge was prosecuted by the state officials and the clergy of the state church. He was repeatedly arrested, and had to spend a large part of his life in prison. In 1804 he was transported in chains to Christiania, where he remained incarcerated till 1814. In 1808, when the Council of Regency found great difficulty in securing provisions and supplies because of the blockade, and great anxiety was felt because of the shortage of salt, Hauge offered

[1] A. Chr. Bang, *Hans Nielsen Hauge og hans Samtid*, Christiania, 1874. *Hans Nielsen Hauges Reisen, Schicksale und denkwürdige Ereignisse von ihm selbst beschrieben*, übersetzt, Christiania, 1819.

to erect salt-works which could produce salt from the sea water, if they would liberate him. They accepted the offer, and Hauge built several salt-works which supplied the country with that necessary commodity, but as soon as he had accomplished this, he was remanded to prison to await his final trial. Not till after he had spent ten years in the prison cell did the court see fit to render its decision by which he was adjudged guilty of the following offenses: (a) That contrary to the ordinance of 1741 he had traveled about

Fig. 10. — Hans Nielsen Hauge

the country and preached the word of God; (b) that he had encouraged others to do the same; (c) that he had used invectives against the clergy, which were not considered to emanate from ill-will, and which, when taken in their proper connection, did not seem as offensive as when they were torn out of their connection. The judges paid no attention to the fact that Hauge had already spent a decade in prison without being convicted of any wrongdoing. They decided that he ought to pay a fine of 1000 riksdaler and the cost of the trial; but this considerable sum exhausted his scant means. He left the prison penniless and broken in health, physically unable to resume his great religious work which he had so unselfishly performed. His adherents, the *Haugianer*, who were now numbered by the thousands all over the country, bought him a small farm in the neighborhood of Christiania, where he resided until his death in 1824. Hauge lived, however, to see the fruits of his labor. The revival which he had set on foot caused a great awakening, which for the first time made the Christian faith a dominant force in the people's spiritual life. He roused them even socially to greater diligence and earnestness, and imbued them with an ardent desire to manage their own local affairs, as they had learned to govern themselves in religious matters. The nation's conscience had been awakened, and before Hauge was liberated from prison some of the more fair-minded among the clergy began to call attention to the beneficial results of his work. In 1812 Claus Pavels wrote in his diary: "I believe that Hans Hauge has done much more good than harm in Norway. His apostolic itineracy, his foolish writings, his followers' and partly also his own fanatic conduct is no longer seen; but that he has founded a sect which still exists, the members of which distinguish themselves by piety, virtue, good order, diligence, and peacefulness, in short, nearly everything which constitutes civic virtue, and tends to strengthen society, none but the most biased can deny." [1]

"After Hauge had moved to Bredtvedt," says his biographer, Bishop Bang, "this place may truly be said to have been the center of religious life in Norway. From Bredtvedt he issued a number of letters of religious contents and sent them to all parts of the country, and the influence of Hauge's religious letters of that time can scarcely be truly estimated at present. To Bredtvedt flocked also year by year large numbers of Hauge's adherents from all parts of the country." Even the clergy of the state church began to recognize the true importance of the great evangelist. In 1815 two theological professors, two bishops, and fifteen clergymen visited him in his home. Hauge was already regarded by many as a sage and a martyr. " When I saw Hauge, bent and suffering from all sorts of ailments, I had to say to him in my heart: this you have suffered for Christ's sake," said Bishop Bugge, who himself had been one of his opponents.[2] By the law of July 27, 1842, the ordinance of 1741 was repealed, and full freedom in religious matters was established. "This was mainly due," says Bang, "to the clearer understanding among the common classes of the great cause of religious liberty, due to the labor and suffering of Hauge and his friends."

[1] *Dagbøger for Aarene 1812–1813*, p. 225.
[2] A. Chr. Bang, *Hans Nielsen Hauge og hans Samtid*, p. 486. V. Ullmann, *Hans Nielsen Hauge, Nordmænd i det 19de Aarhundrede.*

51. Events Leading to the Separation of Norway and Denmark

After the death of Prince Charles August, the Swedish government had to choose a new successor to the throne. The party which had been in favor of the prince and the ultimate union of Norway and Sweden proposed to elect his brother, the Duke of Augustenborg; the party representing the Pan-Scandinavian idea of uniting the three Scandinavian countries favored King Frederick VI. of Denmark-Norway;[1] some preferred the Prince of Oldenburg, but the choice finally fell upon one of Napoleon's marshals, Bernadotte, Prince of Pontecorvo, who became Swedish crown prince under the name of Charles John. It was thought that by this choice Sweden would gain the friendship of Napoleon, and Bernadotte was, furthermore, a man of many excellent qualities; a great general, an experienced and talented statesman, who would act with energy, and whose word would have weight in the councils of the nations.[2]

The problems which Charles John had to deal with were not easy. Sweden had suffered much in the late war. Its commerce and industry were disorganized, and its finances were in confusion. He could not speak Swedish, and he was a stranger both to the people and the country. At first he had to remain a silent spectator, but in a relatively short time he became the real leader in the government, and brought dispatch and energy both into diplomacy and administration.

Sweden had not observed the rules of the Continental System very strictly, and as Napoleon in 1810 made special efforts to compel obedience to his demands on this point, he issued an ultimatum requiring the Swedish government to declare war against England, their old ally, within five days. Refusal to comply would have gravely imperiled the kingdom, and war was, accordingly, declared; but through a secret understanding with the British authorities it was agreed that it should only be a sham war, and that amicable

[1] Many prominent Danes wrote pamphlets to show the advantage of a united Scandinavian North. Among these were: Grundtvig, Schimmelman, Moltke, Høst, and others. Schinkel, *Minnen*, vol. V., p. 268 ff.

[2] *Minne af Statsministeren Greve Gustaf af Wetterstedt, Svenska Akademiens Handlingar,* 1888, p. 140. Jacob Aal, *Erindringer*, p. 247 f.

relations should continue. Charles John was resolved from the outset to uphold the rights and dignity of his kingdom, and was in no way inclined to submit to the humiliating dictates of Napoleon. He saw, probably more clearly than any one else, that the great Emperor's power rested on a very weak foundation, and that a new coalition would soon be organized against him. The growing estrangement between France and Russia in 1811 also convinced him that he would soon have to choose sides in a war between these two leading Continental powers. Almost from the time of his election in 1810 he had seen the necessity of gaining the friendship of Russia as a support against the aggression of Napoleon, and Emperor Alexander was making friendly advances to secure his coöperation in case of a war with France. Charles John would take no definite stand, but circumstances soon compelled him to incline more strongly towards the powerful eastern neighbor. In conformity with this policy he soon abandoned the plan of recovering Finland, a hope entertained by many leading men in Sweden at the time, and revived instead the plan of uniting Norway and Sweden, which in his mind was equivalent to extending the Swedish borders to the North Sea.

When Napoleon found that Charles John would not submit to every demand, the relations between France and Sweden soon grew strained. In 1811 the French ambassador was recalled from Stockholm, and French and Danish privateers attacked Swedish merchant vessels in the Baltic.[1] Under these circumstances Sweden might be expected to join the enemies of France for her own protection in case new encroachments should aggravate the situation. In 1811, prior to his invasion of Russia, Napoleon seized Swedish Pomerania, an overt act of hostility which led to an alliance between Sweden and Russia, concluded April 5, 1812. In this compact Emperor Alexander promised definitely to aid Charles John in securing Norway as a compensation for Finland. In a spirited letter to Napoleon, Charles John had demanded to know why Pomerania had been occupied by the French, contrary to all treaties. "Without seeking the honor and power which surrounds your Majesty," he wrote, "I only ask not to be considered your vassal. Your

<hr/>

[1] Yngvar Nielsen, *Indberetninger fra østerrigske Gesandter i Kjøbenhavn 1807–1812, Forhandlinger i Videnskabs-Selskabet i Christiania*, 1882, p. 64.

Majesty rules over a large part of Europe, but your dominion does not extend over the country to which I have been called. To defend this land is the extent of my ambition, and I consider this the task which Providence has given me." [1] Napoleon's only answer was further encroachments, and Charles John found it necessary to cement still closer his friendship with Russia. Peace was concluded between Sweden and England, and also between Russia and England at Örebro. By a convention at Åbo, August 30, 1812, Alexander promised that not only Norway but also Seeland should be given to Sweden, and Charles John was to receive an army of 35,000 Russians, of which 25,000 should be concentrated in Skåne for an attack on Denmark,[2] as he wished to secure possession of Norway before taking part in a general war against France.[3] He encouraged Alexander to pursue the Fabian tactics of avoiding pitched battles with Napoleon, but by retreating and laying the country waste, to lure him ever further from his base of operations. The expedition against Denmark could not be undertaken that year, however, as the summer was already far advanced, and before the next campaign opened, the situation was wholly changed through the destruction of Napoleon's Grand Army on the snow-covered plains of Russia.

At this juncture Denmark was still the ally of Napoleon. In December, 1812, both Russia and England had made overtures to King Frederick VI. to join them in the war against France. Norway would have to be surrendered to Sweden, but compensation would be given in northern Germany, possibly even in Holland. This plan did not appeal to King Frederick, and he refused.[4] But the retreat of Napoleon and the destruction of his army made the situation critical for Denmark-Norway, as a general uprising throughout northern Germany brought the war to the very border of the kingdom, and France could give Denmark no protection against the large armies which advanced in pursuit of Napoleon's shattered forces. In Norway an army could scarcely be brought into the field, as the

[1] Yngvar Nielsen, *Aktmæssige Bidrag til Sveriges politiske Historie 1812*, *Forhandlinger i Videnskabs-Selskabet i Christiania*, 1876. B. von Schinkel, *Minnen*, vol. VI., p. 113.

[2] *Recueil de lettres de Charles Jean*, Stockholm, 1825, p. 55.

[3] B. von Schinkel, *Minnen*, vol. VII., p. 12.

[4] Carl Th. Sørensen, *Kampen om Norge i Aarene 1813 og 1814*, p. 44 ff.

country was suffering from a serious famine, due to the almost total crop failure in 1812. But Charles John attempted even now without success to persuade King Frederick VI. to cede Norway; neither could he be prevailed upon to change his political policy to the extent of seeking a reconciliation with England, though he was urged to do so by his most influential minister, Rosencrantz, and even by Prince Christian Frederick, heir to the throne of Denmark. He decided instead to remain neutral, though this did not meet with the approval of the allied powers.

Charles John had not been able to take active measures towards securing Norway, and he knew that a long delay might wreck his plans. Denmark's *chargé d'affaires* in Stockholm had suggested that the bishopric of Trondhjem should be ceded to Sweden; from Russian sources it had been hinted that a change in the plans was necessary, and England remained indifferent and would not support his designs on Norway unless he used his forces on the Continent in co-operation with the allies. Circumstances forced him to yield. He promised to raise a force of 30,000 men, which together with 35,000 Russians should coöperate with the allies against Napoleon under his own command, and in return England agreed to support his demand for the cession of Norway. But his plan might still be shattered. Austria supported Denmark, as the great statesman Metternich wished to attach to himself the smaller European states in the hope that as soon as Napoleon was vanquished he might secure for Austria the leadership in European politics. In that event the legitimate princes would be restored to their thrones and possessions, and he was not disposed to destroy an old legitimate monarchy for the benefit of Charles John, the parvenu who emerged from obscurity to enter the charmed circle of the crowned heads of Europe. Both in St. Petersburg and London Metternich had protested against an attack on Denmark at a moment when all the European powers had begun to talk of peace. Even Russia began to show signs of Danish sympathy. Prince Dolgorouki was sent to Copenhagen with a letter from Emperor Alexander, stating that at the time when he sanctioned Sweden's plan of securing Norway, he did not know Denmark's real position; that he had thought that Denmark would gladly part with Norway in return for more valuable possessions in northern Germany; but since this did not please the king, he would now postpone the matter. King Frederick was urged to join the allies, and take active part in the operation against Napoleon, and Dolgorouki added enough orally to make it quite clear that the question of ceding Norway would be dropped altogether if Denmark would coöperate with the allies. But King Frederick would not join the coalition in active war operations unless the possession of Norway was definitely guaranteed to him.[1] At this moment Charles John seems to have abandoned the hope of securing the whole of Norway. On April 10, 1813, he dispatched an ultimatum to King Frederick, stating that unless he ceded the bishopric of Trondhjem to Sweden, and joined the coalition in active operations against Napoleon, he would attack Denmark-Norway.[2] While awaiting a reply, he received the news of Dolgorouki's secret mission. He also learned that the 35,000 Russian troops which had been promised had been ordered to march in another direction. This palpable breach of faith on the part of Russia drove Charles John into violent fury. He wrote to Emperor Alexander demanding the troops which had been promised. He also asked that Dolgorouki should be recalled from Copenhagen, and that diplomatic relations between Russia and Denmark should cease. The Swedish ambassador at Copenhagen was immediately recalled, as Denmark refused to cede any part of Norway. Thus matters stood when operations against Napoleon began in the spring of 1813.

On April 15th Napoleon left Paris and took personal command of the large army which he had organized, and the decisive campaign of 1813 was begun. A Swedish army of 30,000 men had landed in Pomerania, with which Charles John was to coöperate with the allied forces, but he refused to take part in active operations until Russia should place under his command the 35,000 men which had been promised. He was willing, however, to make one concession with regard to Norway. Instead of demanding the whole kingdom he

---

[1] Yngvar Nielsen, *Aktmæssige Bidrag, Forhandlinger i Videnskabs-Selskabet i Christiania*, 1876, no. 7, p. 31 ff. Carl Th. Sørensen, *Kampen om Norge*, p. 100 ff.

[2] B. von Schinkel, *Minnen*, vol. VII., p. 61 ff. *Correspondence, Dispatches, and Other Papers of Viscount Castlereagh*, vol. VIII. *Minne af Statsministeren Greve Gustaf af Wetterstedt*, p. 206 ff.

would be satisfied with the bishopric of Trondhjem, which should be permanently incorporated in Sweden. But Russia demanded that he should immediately join the allies without further conditions. On May 21st Napoleon defeated the armies of the coalition at Bauzen, and the allies were highly displeased because Charles John remained inactive. On June 4th both Russia and Prussia concluded an armistice with Napoleon at Poischwitz without consulting either England or Sweden. But in a personal interview with Emperor Alexander and King Frederick William III. of Prussia at Trachenberg, near Breslau, Charles John again won the favor of the two monarchs. Again they renewed their assurances to Sweden, and they also adopted his plan for the next campaign in case peace with Napoleon could not be arranged. According to this plan, the forces of the allies should be divided into three armies. The Northern army of Swedes, Russians, and Prussians under the command of Charles John should form the right wing, the Silesian army of Prussians and Russians under General Blücher should form the center, and the Bohemian army of Austrians, Russians, and Prussians under the Austrian field marshal, Prince Schwartzenberg, should form the left wing. These armies, forming a half-circle, should converge on the point where Napoleon was stationed. When the armistice expired, August 16th, Austria joined the allies, whose armies in the field now numbered 479,000. Against these forces Napoleon could place an army of about 440,000, mostly raw recruits. In his attempt to break this half circle of iron which threatened to crush him, he was not successful. He inflicted a crushing defeat on Schwartzenberg, August 26th and 27th, but his marshals were unable to carry out successfully the parts assigned to them. Macdonald was defeated by Blücher at Katzbach, and Marshal Vandamme was defeated and captured at Kulm. Oudinot failed to take Berlin, and Ney, who was sent to take charge of the operations, was defeated at Dennewitz. The armies of the allies pressed forward into Saxony, where the decisive battle of Leipzig was fought, October 16th to 19th, in which Napoleon was defeated.

The Swedish troops had taken little part in the actual fighting, as Charles John evidently sought to save his forces for an attack on Denmark. But after his retreat Napoleon himself said to the

Swedish general Sköldebrand, who had been made prisoner of war: "No one has done me so much harm as your crown prince. Do you believe that if it were not for him I should have been here at this moment? I should still have been in northern Germany. I myself tell you so, and you may believe my word."[1]

King Frederick VI. continued to the last to exercise a paternal care for his kingdom of Norway to the greatest extent possible under the circumstances. Prince Frederick of Hessen, who had succeeded Charles August, was an inactive man, who did not win the favor of the people, and in the spring of 1813 Prince Christian Frederick was dispatched to Norway, in the hope that this young and talented heir to the throne might arouse the people's love for the union.[2] In his instruction to the prince the king said: "Since Norway is far distant, it makes it difficult for the sovereign himself to be present in the kingdom. They need therefore, especially in time of war, to have a person who can rule the realm, otherwise it cannot be expected that any system can be established in the administration. This, then, is the thing especially required of you, and you are requested to continually travel about and seek to prevail on the people to show the love which they owe me. Whenever they complain, you must answer them that your presence as *statholder* and commander of the military forces is a new evidence of my regard and love for the Norwegian people. This important tie, without which no nation can long endure, the love of the people for their sovereign, and *vice versa*, you must attempt to strengthen." In his effort to counteract Swedish influence in Norway Prince Christian Frederick was quite successful. The twenty-six-year-old prince[3] was gifted, well educated, jovial, and pleasing. He had fine features, loved merry company,[4] and maintained a greater dignity and stricter etiquette

[1] A. F. Sköldebrand, *Memoiren.*

[2] A. Faye, *Norge i 1814*, p. 2 ff. Henrik Wergeland, *Norges Konstitutions Historie, Samlede Skrifter*, vol. IX. Yngvar Nielsen, *Bidrag til Norges Historie i 1814.* Carl Th. Sørensen, *Kampen om Norge*, vol. I., p. 135.

[3] Prince Christian Frederick was a son of Prince Frederick, a younger half-brother of Christian VII., and heir presumptive to the throne of Denmark-Norway. He was the nearest heir to the throne, as Frederick VI. had no male heir.

[4] Claus Pavels, *Dagbogs-Optegnelser for Aarene 1812–1813*, p. 102. Ludvig Daae, *Det gamle Christiania*, p. 341 f.

than his predecessors. He soon gained the love and admiration of the people, but he was not able to win to his side the most influential man in the kingdom, Count Wedel-Jarlsberg. The two met in Tunsberg, and Wedel told Prince Christian Frederick that if he would become king of Norway as an independent kingdom, he would support him to the last, that he must either drive the Swedish crown prince from the North, or allow himself to be driven out. But so decisive a step the prince would not take, and Count Wedel remained an inactive spectator, who placed no confidence in the ability of Prince Christian Frederick to solve the difficult problems confronting him. In a conversation with Jacob Aal, Count Wedel said: "We shall now see who will rule the North, Charles John or Christian Frederick," and there is no doubt that his sympathy was with the former.[1]

The arrival of Christian Frederick in Norway had a wholesome effect, and tended to strengthen the people's loyalty to the union. But the king's attempt to protect the Norwegian coast against the English was not only a failure, but a mistake. The English did not plan any attack on Norway. English privateers hovered around the coast, and seized Norwegian vessels, but the regular commerce with England, which was as advantageous to the English as to the Norwegians, was not seriously interfered with at this time. King Frederick, nevertheless, dispatched to the coast of Norway a new battleship, the "Najad," which had been recently built. Several smaller vessels were added, and this flotilla was placed in the command of an able captain, H. P. Holm. The Norwegians frowned at this, as they realized that it would only challenge the English to more active hostilities, and the venture ended, as might be expected, in speedy disaster. An English man-of-war, the "Dictator," with sixty-four guns, in command of the young captain Steward, accompanied by several smaller vessels, discovered the "Najad," and pursued it into a narrow gap near Lyngør, where a fierce duel was fought

---

At the age of twenty, Prince Christian Frederick was married to Charlotte Frederikke of Mecklenburg-Schwerin, who bore him two sons, one of whom died in childhood. The other became King Frederick VII. of Denmark. The prince and his wife were divorced before he came to Norway.

[1] Yngvar Nielsen, *Wedel-Jarlsberg*, vol. II., p. 17. Jacob Aal, *Erindringer*, p. 308. J. H. Vogt, *Optegnelser*, p. 35 ff.

in which the Danish ship was destroyed. The Norwegian gunboat flotilla was notified, but arrived too late to prevent the "Dictator" from escaping through the same narrow passage where it entered.[1]

After the battle of Leipzig, Charles John was to advance with the northern army against Marshal Davout, who was stationed on the lower Elbe with an army of 25,000 men. To this plan he willingly agreed, as it gave him an opportunity to follow out his own designs against Denmark. He felt that the moment had now come when he must secure possession of Norway, or leave the question to a general peace conference, where he would have small chance of being supported by the legitimate princes. He dispatched some Prussian and Russian forces against the French, and with his own army he turned northward to attack Holstein. An invasion of Denmark could now be undertaken without incurring any blame, since Frederick VI. had declared war against Russia and Prussia before he received the news of Napoleon's defeat at Leipzig. Holstein was quickly overrun, and in order to prevent an invasion of Schleswig and Jutland the Danish commander, Prince Frederick of Hessen, concluded an armistice. Charles John now renewed his original demand for the cession of the whole of Norway, and the situation made him anxious to reach a speedy agreement. Austria, which still supported Denmark, had sent a special envoy, Count Bombelles, to Copenhagen to advise King Frederick to cede the bishopric of Trondhjem, but the king still hoped that the intervention of Austria might change the situation. He sent a special envoy, Edmund Bourke, to Kiel, accompanied by Bombelles, to negotiate with Charles John for a prolongation of the armistice. The crown prince would not grant a long respite, but he agreed to extend the time till January 5th, in order that Bourke might confer with his government. He also submitted his ultimatum in which he demanded either the cession of the bishopric of Trondhjem at once, and the rest of Norway when a general peace conference assembled, or the whole of Norway at once, in which case Denmark would receive Swedish Pomerania and one million riksdaler as a compensation.[2] Bourke and Bombelles returned

[1] Jacob Aal, *Erindringer*, p. 281 ff.
[2] Schinkel, *Minnen*, vol. VII., p. 313 ff. *Minne af Statsministeren Greve Gustaf af Wetterstedt*, p. 287 ff. Yngvar Nielsen, *Norge i 1814.*

to Copenhagen, and Charles John also dispatched a letter to King Frederick, urging him to accept the terms offered. All hope of an intervention of Austria finally vanished. Russia and England remained firm in demanding the cession of Norway, and Austria was at last obliged to support this demand to avoid a rupture with her allies. On January 4th Bourke again arrived in Kiel to open peace negotiations, and Charles John declared in a speech to the assembled diplomats that if the treaty of peace was not signed within forty-eight hours he would renew hostilities, and the Danish monarchy would be destroyed. It was necessary for him to push matters to a hasty conclusion, for the English minister, Castlereagh, had sent an imperative order that he should immediately cross the Elbe and join in the operations against Napoleon. This order was received January 13th, and the peace was not yet signed. Disobedience might cost him the friendship of England and shatter his whole plan.[1] He prevailed on the English ambassador, Thornton, not to make the order known for twenty-four hours, and during the night the work on the treaty was carried on with the greatest possible speed. On January 14, 1814, the treaty of Kiel[2] between Sweden and Denmark was signed. Peace was also concluded between Denmark and England.

By the treaty of Kiel Frederick VI. ceded Norway to the king of Sweden, and according to article IV. of the treaty Norway should remain a kingdom united with Sweden. Because of the haste with which the treaty was drawn up, the Norwegian possessions, Iceland, Greenland, and the Faroe Islands, were not included in the cession. Through this oversight these possessions were separated from Norway, and continue to remain united with Denmark. The king of Sweden ceded to Denmark Swedish Pomerania and the island of Rügen. He promised as king of Norway to pay to Denmark that part of the Danish-Norwegian state debt which would justly fall on Norway, and to use his influence in the general peace congress to secure further compensation for Denmark.[3]

[1] *Kong Christian VIII's Dagbog fra Regenttiden i Norge*, p. 7 f. Wetterstedt, *Minne*, p. 302.

[2] Gustav Peter Blom, *Norges Statsforandring i Aaret 1814*, Bilag III., p. 254. L. M. B. Aubert, *Norges folkeretslige Stilling*, p. 69 ff. C. A. Broberg, *For ikke 100 Aar siden.*

[3] L. M. B. Aubert, *Norges folkeretslige Stilling*, p. 69 ff.

On the 15th of January Charles John wrote to his son, Prince Oscar: "My dear child: Peace has been concluded. Norway is united with Sweden, and forms a separate and independent kingdom." This was an unreserved recognition of the full meaning of the treaty, but he also seems to have entertained other ideas regarding the relation of the two kingdoms, which did not presage well for the future. The same day he wrote to Count Essen in Stockholm that the Norwegian fortresses of Fredrikshald, Kongsvinger, Fredrikstad, and Akershus should at once be occupied by a force of 6000 men. "I believe," he concludes, "that a larger force will not be needed, as Norway is to be taken possession of, not as a province, but only to be united with Sweden in such a way as to form with it a single kingdom."

THE MODERN PERIOD

52. NORWAY GAINS HER NATIONAL INDEPENDENCE IN 1814

IN an open letter of January 18, 1814, King Frederick VI. announced to the Norwegian people that their country had been ceded to the king of Sweden. He released them from their oath of loyalty, and bid them farewell in terms which reveal the deepest emotion.[1] In Norway the news did not immediately become known. The communications between the two kingdoms had been interrupted by the war, and as the Norwegian newspapers contained little or nothing but local news items, the people had to gather what they knew of foreign affairs largely from rumors, which were often exaggerated and contradictory. They knew that the outcome of the war waged in southern Denmark would be of importance to Norway, but no reliable reports had revealed the true state of affairs, when the paper "Tiden" on January 25th suddenly brought the glad tidings that peace had again been established in the North. The conditions were not mentioned, though the editor had been informed of the treaty through a private letter; but when the truth became known, the first outburst of joy gave way to anger and resentment, as the people felt that they had been bartered away in a manner disgraceful to a free people. They had not been consulted by either of the contracting parties, hence the treaty of Kiel could not be binding on them. To countenance it would be national dishonor.

The strong national spirit and love for constitutional liberty which had been awakened in Norway, as well as in other parts of Europe, in the closing decades of the eighteenth century and the opening of the nineteenth had long since been tinged with a desire for national autonomy, if not for independence. At the time when the peace of

[1] Gustav Peter Blom, *Norges Statsforandring i Aaret 1814, Bilag*, p. 257. A. Faye, *Norge i 1814*, p. 9 ff.

Kiel was concluded, there was no general desire for a union with Sweden on any terms, and when the union with Denmark was terminated, the Norwegians felt that they were free to work out their own national destiny. Denmark might dissolve the old union, but it could not create for Norway a new union with Sweden without the consent of the Norwegian people.[1] The presence of Prince Christian Frederick also buoyed up their courage. He could give the country a stable government, and around him as a legitimate successor to the throne they could rally in defense of their independence.

On the evening of January 24th, the day before the news was broached by "Tiden," King Frederick's first courier, C. L. V. Rømer, reached Christiania, and submitted to Prince Christian Frederick the terms of the treaty of Kiel, together with an order that he should surrender Norway to the Swedish authorities, and return to Copenhagen. This order the prince refused to obey. In his diary he wrote: "That the king can believe that the Norwegians will surrender voluntarily — that he thinks that I would be mean enough to desert them now — I do not understand it. They would, indeed, be justified in throwing stones at me, if I could desert a people who love me, and place their whole confidence in me. And I should leave even without attempting to defend them — Never! not while I live!" He left Christiania, visited one of his most influential advisers, Peter Anker, at Eidsvold, and journeyed through Gudbrandsdal to Trondhjem. Everywhere the people welcomed him with great enthusiasm as their deliverer, as it had now become generally known that Norway had been ceded to Sweden, though it had not yet been officially announced. In Trondhjem they even requested him to call an Assembly of Estates to frame a constitution for the kingdom. He returned to Christiania resolved to ascend the throne, and to rule according to the old "Kongelov" until he could find opportunity to grant a new constitution.[2]

But the friends of popular sovereignty and government by the people did not remain inactive. Inspired by the example of the North American colonies and the French Revolution, they resolved not only to declare their independence, but to frame a constitution

---

[1] L. M. B. Aubert, *Norges folkeretslige Stilling*, p. 95 ff.
[2] Yngvar Nielsen, *Norge i 1814.*

which should embody the principles of democracy which had been proclaimed by the fathers of the American Republic and the French political philosophers. Christian Magnus Falsen, son of the patriot and poet Enevold Falsen, invited Peter Anker, Professor George Sverdrup, L. S. Platau, and Joh. G. Adler to a meeting at his country residence, Vollebæk, near Christiania, where he read to them the draft of a constitution which he had framed with the assistance of Adler, and not long afterwards Professor Sverdrup and Peter Anker were invited to attend an Assembly of Notables which had been summoned by Christian Frederick to meet at Eidsvold, February 16, 1814.[1]

A number of the leading men in Norway assembled at Eidsvold. Prince Christian Frederick proposed that he should be placed on the throne by right of succession, but this was opposed by a strong party, whose chief spokesman was Professor Sverdrup. In a private conversation with the prince he implored him not to seize the crown in a manner contrary to the wishes of all the enlightened men of the nation. "The rights which Frederick VI. has renounced reverts to the people," he added. "From the hands of the people you will receive the crown, which will be the more lustrous since the people have given it to you." In the assembly the members declared that as free men they would not submit to the provisions of the treaty of Kiel. Regarding the question of succession to the throne many supported Sverdrup, and Christian Frederick yielded to the general desire on this point.[2] He was chosen regent *ad interim*, and agreed to summon a general constituent assembly to meet at Eidsvold. When a constitution had been framed, a king would be placed on the throne by election to exercise executive powers accord-

---

[1] A. Faye, *Norge i 1814*, p. 22. Jacob Aal, *Erindringer*, p. 340 ff. Henrik Wergeland, *Norges Konstitutions Historie, Samlede Skrifter*, vol. IX., p. 95. T. H. Aschehoug, *Norges nuværende Statsforfatning*, vol. I., p. 5 ff.

The official paper, "Tiden," published, immediately after the cession of Norway to Sweden had been announced, an offer of a premium for a treatise on the best form of government for Norway. A request was also made for the loan of the constitutions of all free countries, and commentaries on the same, together with Adam's *Defense of the Republican Government*, and *Journal for Rigsforfatning og Lovgivning*. Henrik Wergeland, *Norges Konstitutions Historie, Samlede Skrifter*, vol. IX., p. 14.

[2] T. H. Aschehoug, *Norges nuværende Statsforfatning*, vol. I., p. 6 ff.

ing to its provisions. Circumstances had made it necessary for the scion of the autocratic Oldenburg dynasty to bow to the sovereign will of the people.

In an open letter, dated February 19th,[1] Prince Christian Frederick announced in the customary autocratic phraseology that since the assembly at Eidsvold had declared that they would not submit to Sweden, he had placed himself at the head of the nation, had assumed the title of regent, and would do everything in his power to prevent disorder, and to maintain peace with every foreign power which should not attempt to trample on the rights of the Norwegian people. In the same letter he also published the rules according to which the members of the Constituent Assembly should be chosen. After religious services had been held in the principal churches in each parish, the people should take an oath to maintain the independence of Norway, and to sacrifice, if need be, their lives for the fatherland; whereupon two electors should be chosen in each parish, one of which should be a *bonde* (farmer). These electors should meet in each *amt* and choose three delegates to the Constituent Assembly, one of whom should be a *bonde*. Also the army and navy should send delegates, a truly unique step,[2] probably taken by the prince to identify these important organizations more closely with the national cause.[3]

After concluding the treaty of Kiel, Charles John led the northern army westward to coöperate with the allies against France. He had

---

[1] Gustav Peter Blom, *Norge i 1814*, p. 99.

[2] Yngvar Nielsen, *Norge i 1814*, p. 46 ff. Gustav Peter Blom, *Norge i 1814*, p. 140. A. Faye, *Norge i 1814*, p. 23 ff. T. H. Aschehoug, *Norges nuværende Statsforfatning*, vol. I., p. 6 ff.

[3] The stand taken by Norway was applauded even by the English press. *The Morning Post* and *The Courier* contained articles commenting on events in Norway, and expressing sympathy with the attempt of the Norwegian people to establish their independence. *The Morning Post* said: "We did not deem it just to guarantee Norway to Sweden, as we could easily see that the hatred between the two nations would make the union a source of civil strife and internal war. . . . The resolute will of the Norwegian nation has now been so clearly expressed that we hope it will not be disregarded. Sweden would only have gained rebellious subjects, whereas it can now gain a brave ally." See Gustav Peter Blom, *Norge i 1814*, p. 264. *The Courier* stated that England "only reluctantly gave her consent to the eager desire of Sweden to annex Norway." Henrik Wergeland, *Samlede Skrifter*, vol. IX., p. 124.

secured Norway by treaty, but the task of taking possession of it was left to the Swedish government, at the head of which stood the old King Charles XIII. and his minister of state, Lars von Engeström, both of whom failed to understand the real nature of the situation. They seemed to think that the acquisition of Norway was now an accomplished fact, and that the work of bringing the country under Swedish administration could be done at leisure. The idea that the Norwegians might re-sist did not occur to them, neither did they know the sentiment and real char-acter of the Norwegian people. Yngvar Nielsen says: "At this important moment few men in Sweden had any knowl-edge of the Norwegian people; and only few un-derstood what steps they might be inclined to take. . . . Only a small minor-ity remembered what had led to the election of Charles August, and little gratitude was expressed to the people which in 1809 had helped to save Sweden.

Fig. 11. — Charles XIII

On this point the majority was blind, a fact which produced its result, and in its blindness the government sur-passed the rest." Count von Essen was appointed governor-general of Norway. George Adlersparre, one of the leaders of the revolution in 1809, was offered the position of governor-general in the two north-ern provinces, but he declined, as he did not favor the plan of attempt-ing to rule Norway by Swedish governors. Against this unwise policy he repeatedly warned the government, but his advice was not heeded. Count von Rosen, who had been appointed governor of Trøndelagen, was forthwith dispatched to Christiania by Governor General von Essen to negotiate with Prince Christian Frederick regarding the transfer of Norway to the Swedish authorities, but he was told by the prince that his mission was useless, as the Norwegians had declared their independence, and were resolved to maintain it.

On Sunday, February 25th, a special service was conducted in the church of Our Savior in Christiania, and the congregation took an oath to maintain the independence of the country.[1] Similar services were conducted in all parishes throughout the kingdom according to the open letter which the prince had addressed to the Norwegian people. The taking of the oath, and the solemn invocation of God's blessing, brought the question of national independence close to the people's hearts, and inspired them with a most earnest devotion to the national cause.

Hitherto Prince Christian Frederick had sought the advice of influential private citizens, but before entering upon his duties as regent he created a royal council or cabinet,[2] the members of which should act as his official advisers, and assist him in his administrative duties. General Gottschalk Haxthausen was made minister of finance, Jonas Collett minister of the interior, M. O. L. Sommerhjelm minister of justice, Niels Aal minister of commerce, and Carsten Anker minister of manufacturing and mining. A department of foreign affairs was to be created later, and education was to be placed in charge of a committee consisting of Professor Sverdrup, Professor Treschow, and Bishop Bech. Carsten Anker did not take charge of the department to which he had been appointed. He was sent instead as special envoy to England,[3] as Prince Christian Frederick hoped that England might be moved to look with favor upon the Norwegian people's struggle for independence, and that the English government might possibly undertake to mediate between Norway and Sweden. Anker was well acquainted in England, where he had many connections both with business houses and statesmen, but his mission proved unsuccessful. The English prime minister, Lord Liverpool, told him that if the Norwegians persisted in keeping the Danish prince, and continued their struggle for independence, England would be obliged to help Sweden. Though Anker was disheartened, he

---

[1] Kong Christian VIII., *Dagbog fra Regenttiden i Norge*, p. 49.

[2] F. Bætzmann, *Det norske Statsraad 1814–1884.*

[3] Yngvar Nielsen, *Aktstykker vedkommende Stormagternes Mission, Skrifter udgivne af Videnskabs-Selskabet i Christiania*, 1897, p. 15 ff.

did not leave England immediately, and he was soon prevented from departing, as he was placed under arrest for an old debt which the Danish Asiatic Company owed some English merchants. He was soon released, but had to remain in London for a time. This gave him time to renew his diplomatic activity, but nothing could be accomplished, as the English government remained obdurate, and refused to negotiate with him.

53. THE MEETING OF THE CONSTITUENT ASSEMBLY AT EIDSVOLD. THE FRAMING OF THE NORWEGIAN CONSTITUTION

The delegates to the Constituent Assembly were summoned to meet at Eidsvold, Carsten Anker's beautiful country seat, April 10, 1814. The roads in Norway at that time were still in poor condition, and a spring thaw had made them almost impassable, still the delegates succeeded in reaching their destination in time. Prince Christian Frederick also arrived from Christiania to be present at the opening of the assembly. "He came accompanied by his cabinet," says Jacob Aal,[1] " and a few light infantry, mounted and on foot, paraded before him. His whole conduct during his stay in Norway prior to his election as king was exceedingly plain. He kept but few horses and no expensive equipages. At his table there was no luxury, and he was not extravagant in regard to expenditure. He conducted himself as a private citizen, and acquainted himself with the simple Norwegian customs. Though he did not shun pleasure, he did not seek it in the expensive forms prevalent at the courts, and he displayed no princely pomp. One cannot compare the prince-regent, or even the king of Norway, with those kings who seem to seek protection for their royal privileges in the splendor of their throne. His democratic manners were in keeping with the customs of the country, whose throne he hoped to ascend."

After attending religious services in the old Eidsvold church, the delegates assembled in Carsten Anker's spacious mansion. The

---

[1] Jacob Aal, *Erindringer*, p. 386. V. C. W. Sibbern, *Dagbog paa Eidsvold 1814*, *Historisk Tidsskrift*, første række, vol. I., p. 208 ff. W. F. K. Christie, *Dagbog under Rigsforsamlingen paa Eidsvold fra 10de April til 11te Mai 1814; Norske Samlinger*, vol. II., p. 563 ff. H. J. Næss, *Den norske Grundlovs Historie fortalt for Folket.*

first day was devoted to the examination of the credentials of the delegates, and in the evening they all assembled for a festive supper. "Here could be seen representatives from all parts of the country, of all classes and dialects," writes Nicolai Wergeland, one of the delegates, "courtiers, bønder, amtmænd, lensmænd, ministers, deacons, colonels, corporals, learned and unlearned, of high and low estate, officials, merchants, and landed proprietors. All had assembled for the sacred purpose of laying the foundation for the regeneration of their country. Though they were not equal in knowledge, they were all equally upright in purpose, and equally worthy of respect." "It was a picture of Norway," says Yngvar Nielsen, "as it was and as it was to be." [1]

The "men of Eidsvold," as the members of the Constituent Assembly have been called, numbered one hundred and twelve, though no delegates arrived from the two northern districts, Nordland and Finmarken. Among them were found the most able leaders in the kingdom, men like Christian Magnus Falsen, W. F. K. Christie, Wedel-Jarlsberg, George Sverdrup, Nicolai Wergeland, Jacob Aal, Peter Motzfeldt, Severin Løvenskiold, Peter Anker, and others. A serious divergence of opinion on very fundamental questions soon manifested itself. The question whether the prince had been elevated to the regency because of an inherited right to the throne, by virtue of which he possessed sovereign power, or whether sovereignty was now exercised by the Assembly as the representatives of the people, threatened to cause a serious clash. The question had been raised by Nicolai Wergeland in connection with a vote of thanks to be addressed to the prince.[2] He desired to have a motion passed by which it would be made evident that the Assembly exercised sovereign power, but even those who agreed with him in principle would not make this question an issue at that moment, and Wergeland's motion was lost.

After the Assembly had disposed of this matter, a committee of fifteen was elected to draft a constitution which should form the basis

[1] *Norge i 1814*, p. 114.

[2] Nicolai Wergeland, *En politisk Tale til det norske Folk, med Bilag af dem Forfatteren fremsagde i Rigsforsamlingen paa Eidsvold*, Christiania, 1814, p. 56 ff. Henrik Wergeland, *Norges Konstitutions Historie, Samlede Skrifter*, vol. IX., p. 155.

PLATE IX

EIDSVOLD IN 1814.

THE EIDSVOLD CONSTITUENT ASSEMBLY.

for the deliberations of the Assembly.[1] Among the members of this committee were: Falsen, Sverdrup, Aal, Wedel-Jarlsberg, Wergeland, and Diriks. Eleven fundamental principles were soon agreed upon and submitted to the Assembly, ten of which were adopted in the following form:

1. Norway is to be a limited hereditary monarchy: it shall be a free, independent, and indivisible kingdom, and the regent shall have the title of king.

2. The people shall exercise the lawmaking power through their representatives.

3. The people shall have the right to tax themselves through their representatives.

4. The right to declare war and conclude peace shall be vested in the regent.

5. The regent shall possess the power of pardon.

6. The judicial department shall be separate from the legislative and executive departments.

7. Freedom of the press shall be established.

8. The Evangelical-Lutheran Church shall be the state church of Norway, but all religious sects shall have the right to worship according to their own faith. Jews shall be excluded from the kingdom.

9. The freedom of industry shall not be limited by further restrictions.

10. No personal, mixed, or hereditary privileges shall hereafter be granted.

The eleventh point, proposing uniform compulsory military service, was not adopted.[2]

After the main features of the constitution had thus been outlined, the labor of drafting the instrument itself was carried forward with great vigor. The committee based its work on the constitution which had been framed by Falsen and Adler prior to the meeting of the notables at Eidsvold. But this document, which was

---

[1] Gustav Peter Blom, *Dagbog under Rigsforsamlingen paa Eidsvold, Historisk Tidsskrift*, tredie række, vol. I., p. 83 ff. N. J. Gregersen, *Norges Historie i 1814*, p. 69 ff.

[2] J. H. Darre, *Dagbog under Rigsforsamlingen i 1814, Historisk Tidsskrift*, første række, vol. IV., p. 399 ff.

patterned on the French constitution framed at the time of the Revolution, was a work of no great merit,[1] and its whole tenor was changed. The committee sought to eliminate all revolutionary spirit and to avoid the pitfalls of obscure language and doctrinaire liberal ideas of revolutionary theorists, which might create endless discussion and insuperable difficulties. The Eidsvold constitution is clear and concise, features which are nowhere more desirable than in a document of that kind. It is, also, more conservative than the original draft submitted by Falsen and Adler, even to such an extent that some features which seem essential to true democracy, as for example that of trial by jury, and unrestricted suffrage of adults, were not included in it. But minor defects of this kind, which usually adhere to all such documents in their original form, were easily remedied by amendments and later legislation. On the whole, the constitution framed by the "men of Eidsvold" is one of the most remarkable instruments of the kind ever written, whether we consider the sound democratic principles which it embodies, or the clearness and calm dignity with which they are expressed. The authors were members of the official upper classes, who possessed both the learn-

[1] J. E. Sars, *Norges politiske Historie 1815–1885*, p. 87. Ludvig Kr. Daa, *K. Magnus Falsen, Et Bidrag til Norges Konstitutions Historie*, p. 23. Yngvar Nielsen, *Christian Magnus Falsen, Nordmænd i det 19de Aarhundrede*. Henrik Wergeland, *Norges Konstitutions Historie, Samlede Skrifter*, vol. IX., p. 203.

A part of this constitution is found in Jacob Aal's *Erindringer, Bilag 73*, p. 757. The principles of popular sovereignty are stated very clearly:

7. The sovereignty is lodged in the people. No part of the people can exercise the power of the whole people.

8. All power has its origin in the people.

14. The people cannot be bound by laws except those which they themselves create through their chosen representatives.

15. The laws are a free and solemn exercise of the will of the people.

As a statement of general principles these paragraphs are very lucid, but they are too abstract to become part of a constitution. Several other delegates prepared outlines of constitutions, among others Nicolai Wergeland. See *Historiske Samlinger udgivne af den historiske Kildeskriftkommission*, vol. III., *Nicolai Wergelands Grundlovsudkast udgivet af G. Tank*. This draft was long considered lost. See Yngvar Nielsen, *Bidrag til Norges Historie i 1814*, vol. I., p. 241. Erik Vullum, *Kristian Magnus Falsen, Grundlovens Fader*, p. 11. J. E. Sars, *Historisk Indledning til Grundloven*. T. H. Aschehoug, *Norges nuværende Statsforfatning*, vol. I., p. 13 ff. Erik Vullum, *Hvorledes Norge blev frit*, p. 253 ff.

PLATE X

HERMAN WEDEL-JARLSBERG.

W. F. K. CHRISTIE.

GEORG SVERDRUP.

CHRISTIAN MAGNUS FALSEN.

ing and the influence necessary to insert whatever provisions they might desire. They were in the majority in the Assembly, and enjoyed the full confidence of the people. They possessed the power, and had the opportunity to perpetuate that power by constitutional provisions, which would have aroused no resentment. But they understood that liberty was the Norwegian people's ancient heritage, a fruit of their own unremitting struggle through the ages, and they knew, even as Statholder Gyldenløve had perceived over a century earlier, that a free kingdom of Norway could only be maintained by the *bønder*, who represented the strength of the nation, and who had preserved the freedom of the people through the centuries of the union with Denmark. True to these principles, which had been reënforced by the republican ideals of a government by the people and for the people, they chose with unselfish patriotism to make a constitution for the kingdom so truly democratic in spirit that it lodged all power in the hands of the common people, and deprived both king and upper classes of the power of exercising political leadership. So clear are its provisions on this point, that although it has had to undergo the severest test of analytical controversial interpretation for well-nigh a hundred years, the closest scrutiny has only revealed how thoroughly it has insured to the people full liberty, sovereign power, and democratic popular government.

With regard to the question of establishing a constitutional government, and of insuring the autonomy of the kingdom, full unanimity of opinion prevailed among the delegates. But on the vital question of absolute independence they were divided into two parties. A large group, to which belonged such influential leaders as Wedel-Jarlsberg, Nicolai Wergeland, Peter Anker, Jacob Aal, Severin Løvenskiold, and Gustav Peter Blom, preferred union with Sweden, as they feared that Norway, with its limited resources, would not be able to support a government, or to maintain an army and navy. The course pursued by those who desired complete independence would, in their opinion, ruin the already disorganized finances of the country, and would throw away the military and commercial advantages which could be gained through a union with Sweden. Their opposition to the will of the great powers might even jeopardize the opportunity of securing a constitution, and if they succeeded in placing Christian Frederick on the throne, they would only bring about a new union with Denmark, as the prince was heir to the Danish throne. But the independence party stood firm and self-confident, as it was supported by public sentiment, and embraced the majority of the delegates. Its leader was the ardent liberalist Christian Magnus Falsen,[1] a disciple of Noailles and Mirabeau, chairman of the constitutional committee, and the most influential man in the Assembly. He has even been styled "the father of the constitution," an epithet arising from the fact that he had submitted the Falsen-Adler draft. He was Prince Christian Frederick's special friend and supporter, and had bent his energy on securing full independence for Norway in the hope that the prince would be placed on the throne, an effort in which he was ably assisted by other leaders within his party.[2]

As no difference of opinion existed regarding the question of constitutional government and national autonomy, no difficulty was experienced in adopting the constitution. On May 16th it was read in its final form and accepted by the Assembly, after all its provisions had been carefully considered in detail.

The British politician and writer Samuel Laing says of the Norwegian constitution: "There is not probably in the history of mankind another instance of a free constitution, not erected amidst ruins and revolutions, not cemented with blood, but taken from the closet of the philosopher, and quietly reared and set to work, and found to be suitable without alteration to all ends of good government. The reason of this apparent singularity is, that all the essential parts of liberty were already in the country. The property was in the hands of the whole people. The ancient laws and institutions affecting property were in full operation, and were conceived and administered in the very spirit of liberty. As far as regards property, these laws and institutions left nothing for the most liberally consti-

---

[1] Ludvig Kr. Daa, *Bemerkninger om Begivenhederne i Norge i Aaret 1814, Forhandlinger i Videnskabs-Selskabet i Christiania 1858*, p. 190 ff. Yngvar Nielsen, *Christian Magnus Falsen, Nordmænd i det 19de Aarhundrede.* Erik Vullum, *Kristian Magnus Falsen, Grundlovens Fader.*

[2] Gustav Peter Blom, *Norges Statsforandring i 1814*, p. 121 ff. A. Faye, *Norge i 1814*, p. 59 ff. J. E. Sars, *Historisk Indledning til Grundloven*, p. 159 ff. Jacob Aal, *Erindringer*, p. 354 ff.

tuted assembly to legislate upon. As far as regards personal rights, the mild and enlightened administration of Denmark, although under an arbitrary form, had left few general grievances to be redressed. There was nothing in the condition of the people, the state of property, the civil or religious establishments which did not fit in with a free constitution, in which legislative power was vested in the people. These had all emanated from the people in ancient times; and, there being no hereditary privileges, and power, or property vested in any class of the community, had been handed down unbroken through ages. The new constitution was but a superstructure of a building of which the foundations had been laid and the lower walls constructed, eight centuries before, by the ancestors of the present generation." [1]

The main features of the government established by the Eidsvold constitution and later amendments are, briefly, as follows: The Storthing (the National Legislative Assembly) consists of 123 representatives elected by the people for the period of three years. The kingdom is divided into elective districts, but if more than one representative is chosen from a district, it is divided into as many sub-districts as there are representatives. All citizens, men and women, who are twenty-five years of age have the right to vote.[2] A representative to the Storthing must be thirty years of age. He must have resided in the kingdom ten years, and must have the right to vote in the district where he is elected. One who has been member of a ministry may also be elected to represent a district in which he has no right to vote. The Storthing assembles on the first week-day after the 10th of January each year, and remains in session so long as it finds it necessary. Under extraordinary circumstances it may be summoned into extra session by the king at any time. Though all members are chosen in the same way and at the same time, they organize themselves into two branches according to article seventy-

[1] Samuel Laing, *Journal of a Residence in Norway during the Years 1834, 1835, and 1836* (London, 1854), p. 304.

[2] In 1901 all women who paid taxes to the amount of 400 kroner in the cities and 300 kroner in the country received the right to vote in local elections. In 1907 they received the right to vote also in general elections, but with considerable restrictions. In 1913 these restrictions were removed, and women received the right of suffrage on the same conditions as men.

three of the constitution. "The Storthing selects from its members one-fourth to form the Lagthing; the remaining three-fourths constitute the Odelsthing." This organization remains for the three years' term for which the members are elected. Each branch chooses its own president and secretary. Two-thirds of the members of each constitute a quorum. All bills must be introduced in the Odelsthing, either by a representative or by the ministry. If it receives a majority vote it is sent to the Lagthing, and if it is passed also in this branch of the Storthing, it is sent to the ministry to be signed or vetoed by the king. If the Lagthing does not pass the bill, it is returned to the Odelsthing, which may again return it to the Lagthing with or without amendments. If the two houses fail to agree, they meet in joint session to discuss the measure, which may then be passed if it receives two-thirds of the votes. A measure vetoed by the king becomes a law if it is passed in the same form by three separately elected Storthings.

The king chooses his own ministers, who are responsible to the Storthing, and whose advice he must hear in all important questions. The ministry consists of the minister of state, and not less than seven other ministers, all of whom are heads of administrative departments. The ministers may take part in the deliberations of both branches of the Storthing, but they have not the right to vote. The parliamentary form of government prevails, according to which the ministry must have the confidence and support of a majority in the Storthing. Throughout the period of union with Sweden, 1814–1905, the ministry consisted of two parts. The minister of state and two other ministers should always stay in Stockholm, the rest of the ministry should remain in Christiania. The king might appoint his eldest son viceroy of Norway, or he might appoint a *statholder*, who might be either a Swede or a Norwegian.

The Judiciary. — Commissions of arbitration (*forligelseskommissioner*) are found in all *herreds* and cities, and in all villages of more than twenty families. Before a suit is brought into court, an attempt must be made by the parties to the quarrel to arrive at a settlement by appearing before this commission. The object of this very useful institution is to avoid expensive and useless litigation.

A lower court, corresponding in a general way to our justice court, is the *meddomsret*. The judge of this court selects by lot two men to assist him in rendering the decision. Most cases may be appealed from this court to the *lagmandsret*, or jury court. Further appeal may be made to the superior courts and the High Court of Justice, *høiesteret*.

After the constitution had been adopted, the Eidsvold Assembly might have secured peace with England and the allied powers, by pursuing the more conservative policy advocated by the union party. They could have offered the Norwegian crown to Charles John on the condition that he should accept the Eidsvold constitution, a demand which would have been supported by the English government. England's treaty obligations would thereby have been fulfilled, and as the popular sentiment in Great Britain was strongly in favor of the Norwegians, a union with Sweden could have been formed on terms most favorable to Norway. But the independence party, led by the ardent Falsen, who was strongly attached to Prince Christian Frederick, would countenance no compromise, or remain satisfied with anything short of absolute independence. This was, indeed, a high and worthy aim, in perfect accord with the liberal and national tendencies of the age, but it is doubtful if it was the wisest policy to hazard everything, even the constitution itself, for the sake of obtaining a form of independence which cool judgment could scarcely regard as within the realm of possibility. Such a course would inevitably lead to war with Sweden, and the English government had already declared to Carsten Anker that under those circumstances England would support Charles John.[1]

But however wisely prudence may reason, it is not always on the side of absolute justice. The undaunted spirit of freedom which looks to the ideal, and refuses to be fettered by compromises, may justly claim our sympathy, and the world will forever pay homage to those who in the darkest hours of a nation's existence ask only the one question, what is right, and sacrifice all to maintain it. Of such a spirit of courage and devotion liberty and progress are ultimately born, and no statesman can analyze its subtle and far-reaching influence. The Norwegian people felt once more their old strength; they had experienced the first raptures of independence, and a new

---

[1] N. J. Gregersen, *Norges Historie i 1814*, p. 121 ff.

age had whispered hopes of new national greatness. Hesitation could no longer halt their steps, or reconcile them to a national independence only half accomplished. All would be sacrificed that all might be gained; a solemn resolve which sheds its own enduring luster on the memories of Eidsvold. The constitution was dated May 17, 1814, and on the same date the Assembly elected Christian Frederick king of Norway. The work was finished, and the president, George Sverdrup, announced in solemn voice: "Reared within the confines of Norway is the old Norwegian throne on which Haakon Adelstein and Sverre were seated, and from which they ruled the kingdom with wisdom and power. . . . God save Norway!" And the Assembly repeated the refrain.

With the choice of independence followed also the problem of defending it, and this became the more difficult because the supply of money as well as of provisions and war material was very limited. Prince Christian Frederick had already issued unsecured paper money to the amount of three million riksbankdaler, but this could only serve as a temporary makeshift. Early in the session the Assembly had appointed a committee to examine the financial conditions of the kingdom, and this committee submitted a report which after much spirited discussion led to the adoption of the "Eidsvold guarantee," a measure which provided that the Assembly should guarantee the existing public debt, provided that the new lawmaking assembly, the Storthing, should give its sanction. A like guarantee was also given for the issue of paper money to the amount of fourteen million riksdaler, the estimated budget for the coming year.[1] This proved the willingness of the people to shoulder all burdens necessary to maintain their newborn independence.

54. THE WAR OF 1814. THE CONVENTION OF MOSS AND UNION WITH SWEDEN

Up to the time when he was elected king of Norway, Prince Christian Frederick had played successfully his part as leader of the independence movement. He was in sympathy with the liberal ideas embodied in the constitution, and so long as the problem had been

[1] Yngvar Nielsen, *Wedel-Jarlsberg*, vol. II., p. 207 ff.

to rouse the patriotic sentiment of the Norwegian people his best qualities, his eloquence, his youthful enthusiasm, and lofty sentiments had shone with charming luster. But he was wholly unfit to lead the kingdom through the period of storm and struggle which now confronted it, and which he himself had been instrumental in creating. He was, above all, a man of peace, who clung with visionary optimism to the evanescent hope that some fortunate circumstance might save Norway. From the start he placed all his hope in diplomatic negotiations, and several envoys were sent to England and other countries in the attempt to gain the favor of the great powers. All these efforts were unsuccessful, but he was so devoid of love and talent for military affairs that he did not even use the time and opportunity to put the army in condition for efficient service, though he must have foreseen that if he allowed matters to come to the final issue a clash with Sweden would be unavoidable.[1] On May 18th, before he had formally accepted the Norwegian throne, he received letters that envoys from Russia and Prussia were on their way to Norway to declare on behalf of those powers that they would never recognize Norway as an independent kingdom, and that they would help Sweden to subdue Norway. Similar declarations had been received from England. "For two hours I walked up and down in my room," says the prince in his diary. "'Is this a warning, or is it a trial sent by heaven?' I asked myself. 'Can I hesitate? It is, after all, only words, threats. It is quite natural that the great powers desire peace. . . . If they see that I and the Norwegian people stand firm, they will, perchance, hesitate to destroy a peaceful people and again light the torch of war in the North.'"[2] After having consoled himself with this kind of reasoning he decided "to make a great resolve," i.e., to accept the crown; for, he adds, "what will not one do for a people's welfare through faith in God?" And what had he done for the people's welfare? He had, indeed, brought matters to a crisis, but in that crisis he soon lost courage. He was unable to make the high resolve of obtaining a peaceful settlement of the difficulty on terms advantageous to Norway, and then to

---

[1] Carl Th. Sørensen, *Kampen om Norge*, vol. II., p. 215. J. E. Sars, *Udsigt over Norges Historie*, vol. IV., p. 342 f.

[2] *Kong Christian VIII's Dagbog fra Regenttiden i Norge*, p. 113 ff.

depart from the kingdom; neither was he able to act with energy in attempting to carry out his own plans. He accepted the throne rather with the hope that some fortuitous circumstance might enable him to keep it.[1] The thought of fighting to the last trench in defending it does not seem to have been a part of his resolve. The available military forces in Norway at that moment numbered not less than 20,000 men, while Sweden could muster only about 16,000, so long as Charles John was still on the Continent. A resolute leader would scarcely have suffered such an opportunity to pass without attempting an aggressive movement, when it was clear that war could not be averted. But this thought found no favor with the timid king. According to the plan for military operations outlined by the king and his staff, the war was to be wholly defensive. The Norwegian army should be stationed on the Glommen River to oppose the Swedes, if they should attempt an invasion, an event which was rapidly approaching.

After Napoleon had been deposed, April 1, 1814, the Russian Emperor promised Charles John an army of 30,000 men for the purpose of subjugating Norway. England promised ample subsidies, and agreed to blockade the Norwegian coast with six men-of-war, and Austria and Prussia would send envoys to inform Christian Frederick that the decision of the powers with regard to the union of Norway and Sweden was irrevocable. Having received such assurances of support, Charles John returned to Sweden accompanied by some troops collected in Germany. "The reënforcements which I bring you number almost 30,000 men," he wrote to Count Hessen, "among others the regiment of *Royal Suedois* which is organized in Germany, and which to-morrow lands at Carlshamn. . . . I will have from 15,000 to 20,000 Russians, and about 10,000 or 12,000 Prussians; but I fear that the want of provisions will compel me to reduce the number in active service. I have also asked Emperor Alexander to send a corps of 5000 or 6000 men from Archangel to

---

[1] The hope which Charles John seems to have entertained of being placed on the throne of France after the fall of Napoleon was shared by Christian Frederick, who in that event might have been chosen crown prince of Sweden. The three Northern kingdoms might then again have become united under the same king. See *Kong Christian VIII's Dagbog*, p. 112. Jacob Aal, *Erindringer*, p. 369.

Trondhjem. When Norway is attacked at once at three or four places, it is reasonable to suppose that the fight will soon be over." He immediately mobilized the available Swedish forces, which were dispatched to the Norwegian border, reënforced by the auxiliary troops which he had brought.

King Christian Frederick continued to the very last to hope that England might intervene in behalf of Norway. When he received no further dispatches from Carsten Anker, he sent Peter Anker, his brother, to London; later also Christie and P. V. Rosenkilde. But all these efforts were of no avail. The Norwegian commissioners were ordered to leave England, and I. P. Morier was sent to Norway to communicate the only terms which the English government would offer.[1] If Norway would consent to a union with Sweden, England would use her influence to secure for the Norwegian people a guarantee of their constitutional liberty. This offer was not accepted, and the English blockade of the coast of Norway was begun on May 31st.

In England public sentiment was strongly opposed to the course pursued by the government. The noted Sir Philip Francis wrote to Lord Grey on May 9th with regard to Norway, asking if any one could mention a situation when the king of England would have the right to give Ireland to France, whether such a transfer would give France the right of ownership, and if it would be treason for the Irish to defend their independence.[2] Lord Grenville called it a cruel injustice to attempt to coerce the honest and innocent Norwegian people. The aim of the blockade, he said, could only be to produce a famine in Norway. But if this was the first use which England would make of her good fortune, she ought to adopt the new doctrine that profit is to be preferred to moral right and the established laws of all nations. In the House of Lords, Grey championed the cause of Norway with great eloquence, but when the question was voted upon, the ministry was sustained with a hundred and fifteen votes to thirty-four.[3] In the House of Commons, Sir Ch. Wynne, James

---

[1] Claus Pavels *Biografi og Dagbøger*, edited by Claus Pavels Riis, p. 197. Yngvar Nielsen, *Bidrag til Norges Historie i 1814*, vol. II., p. 133 ff.

[2] Henrik Wergeland, *Norges Konstitutions Historie, Samlede Skrifter*, vol. IX., p. 362 ff.

[3] Among the lords who voted in favor of Norwegian independence were: Grey, Essex, Sussex, Grenville, Roslyn, Clifton, Glocester, Fitzwilliam, Stanhope, Lauderdale, and Norfolk. A. Faye, *Norge i 1814*, p. 122 ff.

Mackintosh, and others spoke with great effect in support of the Norwegians. Lambton declared that he viewed with abhorrence the sacrifice of a brave people on the altar of political agreements. Both in prose and poetry the people of England expressed their sympathy with the Norwegian people in their struggle for independence, but the government stood firm, supported by a majority in both houses.[1]

The Danes, too, sympathized with their Norwegian brethren, and many a sailor who was able to elude the blockading squadron brought his cargo of grain from the Danish coast. "When winter passed, and the sea became navigable with small vessels," says Henrik

[1] Charlotte Wardle wrote a poem in praise of Norwegian freedom, and on May 17, 1814, the following poem appeared in *The Star:*

Norwegia to Britain

Lovest thou thy freedom — by her holy shrine,
If yet a drop of British blood be thine,
O Britain! I conjure thee — spare the brave!
Nor join the crew, that would my realms enslave!
Blast not the laurel, which thy fathers wore,
By foul invasion of my Norway's shore,
Whose hardy sons, like those of Runnymede,
For freedom pant, and dare, like them, to bleed!

O! let not history stain her honest page,
Bright with the triumphs of the present age,
With the sad tale, that Britain drew her sword
To bend Norwegians to a foreign lord.
That she, who fought, all Europe's realms to free,
Uplifts her arm — to murder liberty;
And aims her steel to stab her in the cell,
Where still she deigns amid wild woods to dwell,
Beneath the snow-clad pines and mountain's shade,
For nature's free-born sons by nature made.

Blush, Britain, at the deed! With conscious pride,
Call back to memory how thy Sidney died!
And, emulous of all the noble fires,
That warm'd with holy zeal thy patriot sires,
Stand forth the champion of my sons' great cause,
While Heaven and Earth unite in loud applause!
To save — not vanquish — speed across the waves,
And chaunt with them: "We never will be slaves."

Henrik Wergeland, *Samlede Skrifter*, vol. IX., p. 378.

Wergeland, "a secret path stretched from northern Jutland, where open boats might cross the stormy sea, swarming with privateers. And in the rear of these boats, half buried in grain, many a young man with his jacket collar turned up and his pipe in his mouth would survey the broad expanse of the sea, and with anxious heart he would try to penetrate the ocean mists, not for fear of death — for trim sail! trim sail! was the word — but in order to catch the first glimpse of the Norwegian coast."

On June 30th the envoys of the great powers arrived in Christiania: Count von Steigentesch from Austria, General Orloff from Russia, August Forster from England, and Count Martens from Prussia, to demand of Christian Frederick that he should abide by the treaty of Kiel, as the great powers would never recognize him as king of Norway. They offered an armistice of three months' duration, and a partial suspension of the blockade on condition that the three Norwegian fortresses Fredriksten, Fredrikstad, and Kongsvinger should be surrendered to the Swedes, that the Norwegian forces should evacuate the district between these fortresses and the Glommen River, and that Christian Frederick should surrender to the Constituent Assembly all the powers which had been conferred upon him. The king summoned his cabinet and a few other leaders to a meeting at his summer residence. He told them of the terms offered by the envoys, and as he regarded them as favorable, he declared his willingness to abdicate, if thereby a great calamity might be averted, but he was willing to die for the cause, if the representatives of the nation should choose war with all Europe rather than union with Sweden, based on a guarantee of the rights and liberties of the Norwegian people. The cabinet members as well as the other leading men present were all agreed that the Norwegian fortresses could not be surrendered to Sweden, as this would be a violation of the constitution, and might cause internal disturbances.

In answer to the ultimatum of the powers the king sent a courteous note to the envoys, in which he indicated his willingness to yield on certain conditions. He outlined some modifications of their demands which would be acceptable, and also the main features of the union with Sweden, and the changes which would be required in the Norwegian constitution, in case an agreement should be reached.[1] The foreign envoys then left Norway, accompanied by the two Norwegian commissioners, Colonel Peterson and Captain Holstein, who were empowered to negotiate an armistice. They found Charles John in Uddevalla. The crown prince refused to accept the terms offered, and he was impatient with Orloff, who spoke in favor of the Norwegians,[2] but he prevailed on the envoys to return to Norway and attempt once more to arrange a peaceful settlement. In a second interview with Christian Frederick at Moss, they told him that Charles John demanded the surrender of the three fortresses before an armistice could be arranged. This he could not grant, and no further negotiations were attempted. In proclamations to the Norwegian people and the Norwegian army King Christian Frederick announced that Charles John had demanded his abdication and the cession of the fortresses, that the negotiations for a peaceful settlement had failed, that Swedish troops had already entered Norwegian territory, and that valiant fight for freedom and fatherland was now their sole remaining hope.

At the same time King Charles XIII. issued a proclamation to the Norwegian people, exhorting them to pause and reflect, lest the innocent and guilty should alike be overwhelmed by the unavoidable disasters of war. Their effort to maintain their independence, he said, was contrary to their own interests as well as to the true and unchangeable principles of political science. He declared the Constituent Assembly which had been assembled at Eidsvold by Christian Frederick to be unlawful, a violation of the undisputable rights of Sweden, of all lawful governments, and of the rights of the Norwegian people themselves.[3]

The Swedish fleet left Strömstad July 26th, and landed a force at Hvaløerne to take possession of these islands, from which the small Norwegian garrison had already been withdrawn. The fleet then proceeded to Kragerøen, in the neighborhood of the fortress of Fredrikstad, where an army of 6000 men was landed without opposi-

---

[1] Jacob Aal, *Erindringer*, p. 473 ff.   A. Faye, *Norge i 1814*, p. 128.   B. von Schinkel, *Minnen*, vol. VIII., p. 350, contains Charles John's answer to a letter sent by Christian Frederick on the same occasion.

[2] Schinkel, *Minnen*, vol. VIII., p. 190 ff.

[3] Jacob Aal, *Erindringer*, p. 482 ff.   Niels Aal, *Erindringer fra 1814*. Gustaf Björlin, *Kriget i Norge i 1814*.

tion. Lieutenant-Colonel Hjerman, who held this important place with a garrison of 1200 men, retreated in precipitate haste without offering resistance. The Swedes placed batteries in position on the island, and began the bombardment of Fredrikstad. The fortress was old, and could, probably, not have withstood a long siege, but its disgraceful surrender even before a single man of the garrison had been hurt gave the Swedes a great advantage at the very beginning of the campaign, and served to dispirit the Norwegian army. "The remarkable thing about this capitulation," says B. von Schinkel, "is that Christian Frederick himself advised the commandant to surrender the fortress by a dispatch written the same date (August 3d) by his adjutant, Colonel Brock; that Brock himself brought the dispatch, though the fortress had capitulated even before his arrival." It was a piece of military cowardice only equaled by later acts of the faint-hearted king.

A Swedish detachment of 2500 men under General Gahn was sent against the Norwegian border at Solør with instructions to march to Kongsvinger, and attack the Norwegian army in the rear. On his march he encountered a Norwegian force of about the same size under Lieutenant-Colonel Krebs, who retreated slowly to a fortified position at Lier. Gahn attacked the Norwegians on August 2d, but was repulsed with considerable loss. He then retreated to Matrand, where he pitched his camp, but Krebs resolved to surprise him. In the night a force of 800 men approached Matrand from the front, while a force of 1000 men were making a detour through the mountains to fall upon the rear of the Swedish army. The battle which began in the early morning of August 5th was bloody and stubborn. The detachment making the detour had to march farther than expected, and arrived an hour too late, but they seized the baggage trains, and Gahn was able only with great difficulty to extricate his forces. Fourteen officers and 312 men were taken prisoners. The entire baggage, including eighteen wagon loads of ammunition, together with one field piece and sixty horses, fell into the hands of the Norwegians.[1]

Gahn's defeat at Lier and Matrand proved that under able officers the Norwegian forces were able to contend successfully even with the veteran armies of Sweden, but the chief leadership was hopelessly incompetent. The king, who acted as commander-in-chief, was not only the very personification of timidity, but he selected for the highest positions those who pleased him, rather than those who were most competent and best qualified for the place. Seiersted, who became his chief of staff, and Haxthausen, in whom he placed special confidence, were agreeable, but not very able men. Those who had served with distinction in former wars, but were of a sterner type, like Staffeldt, Stabell, and Krebs, were kept in subordinate positions.

But even the ablest leaders would scarcely have been able to carry to a successful issue the war with Sweden supported by the allied powers both on land and sea. The forces under Charles John already numbered 40,000 men, while the Norwegian army did not exceed 27,000. At sea the situation was still more unfavorable. Sweden had four ships of the line, five frigates, one brig, and eighty-five smaller war vessels, while Norway had only eight brigs, one schooner, and one hundred and eight smaller craft. An English squadron blockaded the coast, and Russia and Prussia were ready to send additional troops to help Sweden. B. von Schinkel very aptly observes that Krebs' victory at Lier and Matrand "shows clearly what the enthusiasm and warlike spirit of the Norwegians might have accomplished under other circumstances; now it was only an *ignis fatuus* glimmering in a hopeless night."

The Swedes advanced steadily, and no serious effort was made to stop them. When Field Marshal Essen approached with the second corps of the Swedish army through Enningdalen, the small Norwegian force under Sprøck had to retreat, and General Vegesack laid siege to Fredriksten with an army of 6000 men. Butenschøn, who was stationed at Svinesund with another small force, was compelled to withdraw to avoid being cut off by Essen's advancing army. King Christian Frederick hastened forward to Rakkestad, where a large part of the Norwegian army had been concentrated, but instead of fighting a battle, he ordered a general retreat, and the Norwegians had to withdraw across the Glommen River. In the meanwhile several engagements were fought, but none of them was of any great

PLATE XI

CHARLES JOHN (BERNADOTTE).

CHRISTIAN FREDERICK.

significance. After the withdrawal of the Norwegian army across the Glommen River, Charles John again resorted to negotiations in the hope of bringing the war to a speedy close. Hitherto he had been successful, but experience in the Napoleonic wars had shown him that a united people who were determined to defend their liberty and independence to the last extremity were capable of a resistance which might prove dangerous. The sympathy expressed for the Norwegians both in England and elsewhere must also have convinced him that the aid of the allies, who were developing their reactionary system of political readjustment of Europe in the interest of the legitimate princes and the maintenance of peace, might be an uncertain factor to depend upon if the struggle should be too long drawn out. On August 7th Carsten Tank, one of King Christian Frederick's former ministers, and Provost Hount, a member of the Eidsvold Constituent Assembly, arrived at the king's headquarters with peace propositions from Charles John. He offered to conclude an armistice, and to accept the Eidsvold constitution only with such modifications as would be necessitated by a union of Sweden and Norway, if Christian Frederick would call a special session of the Storthing, deliver his crown into the hands of the ministers, and leave Norway. These were essentially the same conditions which he had rejected before the war. The king called a meeting of his cabinet and some of the leading officers of the army to consider the peace proposal. General Seiersted, his chief of staff, stated that the army would be unable to defend Christiania, and General Haxthausen, head of the commissariat, informed them that the available army supplies would not last above a week. Under these circumstances the cabinet counseled him to yield, and he dispatched a letter to Charles John, stating that he would surrender his crown to the Storthing, if he could insure thereby the liberty and happiness of the Norwegian people.[1] He now transferred his headquarters to Moss, where the negotiations were continued. To the members of his cabinet and other leading men, including Falsen, Christie, Sverdrup, and Diriks, he described the truly alarming situation. He showed that in case

---

[1] B. von Schinkel, *Minnen*, vol. VIII., p. 203 ff. Jacob Aal, *Erindringer*, p. 503 ff. A. Faye, *Norge i 1814*, p. 153 ff. Yngvar Nielsen, *Bidrag til Norges Historie i 1814.*

of an attack Christiania would have to be abandoned, and that the reserves commanded by Armfeldt had provisions only for two days. He considered further resistance hopeless, and ordered two of his ministers, Jonas Collett and Niels Aal, to negotiate with the Swedish envoy, General Björnstjerna, who had arrived in Moss. Before evening the same day, August 13th, they were ready to submit to the king and his cabinet the terms under which an armistice could be arranged. King Christian Frederick was to abdicate immediately, and to transfer the executive authority to his cabinet, who should exercise it until the Storthing could find opportunity to make provisions for a temporary administration. Hostilities should cease, and the blockade should be raised. Sweden should guarantee to Norway the Eidsvold constitution without any other changes than those which a union of the two kingdoms would necessitate, and which the Storthing should deem acceptable. The fortress of Fredriksten, which was still defending itself bravely against the Swedes, was to be surrendered.[1] These conditions were accepted by Christian Frederick and his cabinet, and the armistice was signed at Moss, August 14, 1814. The same day he dispatched his adjutant, Major Brock, to Charles John, who ratified the agreement concluded by his representatives. On August 30th King Charles XIII. of Sweden issued a proclamation ratifying the promises made by the crown prince,[2] according to which "the kingdom of Norway, without being regarded as a conquered country, in the future shall be an independent state united with Sweden; and its present constitution shall be properly protected, after the changes necessitated by the union of the two countries shall have been made."

During the negotiations at Moss King Christian Frederick was in a very distressed state of mind. "He suffered such mental agony," writes Blom, "that it was feared that he would lose his reason." His

---

[1] Yngvar Nielsen, *Norge i 1814*, p. 337 ff. Jacob Aal, *Erindringer*, p. 503. A. Faye, *Norge i 1814*, p. 156. Yngvar Nielsen, *Om Konventionen i Moss, Historisk Tidsskrift*, tredie række, vol. V. *Historiske Samlinger udgivne af den norske historiske Kildeskriftkommission, Diplomatiske Aktstykker fra 1814*, vol. III., p. 215 ff.

[2] *Kong Christian VIII's Dagbog fra Regenttiden i Norge*, p. 183 ff. Yngvar Nielsen, *Om Konventionen i Moss, Historisk Tidsskrift*, tredie række, vol. V. Oscar Joseph Alin, *Den svensk-norska Unionen*, vol. I., p. 46 ff.

last official act as king was to issue a rescript through which he assembled the Storthing for an extra session. He did not preside at its opening, but retired almost heart-broken to the royal residence at Ladegaardsøen, and on October 11th the president of the Storthing read a communication from the king in which he announced his abdication, and released the Norwegian people from their oath of allegiance. Shortly after he boarded a ship and returned to Denmark. "He was followed across the island (Ladegaardsøen) by persons of his nearest surroundings," says Blom, "and as it was late in the evening, he was escorted by torch-bearers. When he had bidden farewell to those who followed him, he boarded the yacht, and the torches were extinguished in the sea. It resembled a procession of mourning, and both he and those who followed him were, undoubtedly, deeply moved." [1]

Prince Christian Frederick had proven himself a weak leader. Count Wedel-Jarlsberg, who had always been opposed to him, called him "the petticoat king," [2] and A. Faye observes that the expression of a prominent man before the bar of the supreme court that "he was a declaimer without energy, a boaster without courage, and a charmer without actuality" expressed quite accurately the people's opinion of him shortly after the great drama was ended.[3] But, however weak his leadership, and however faulty his management of affairs during his short reign of less than five months, he had rendered Norway an important service in her struggle for independence, which entitles him to grateful remembrance. The repudiation of the treaty of Kiel, the organization of the popular sentiment into a definite movement with a fixed purpose, and the calling of the Constituent Assembly at Eidsvold were important steps which were made possible because the people could rally about him as the scion of the old royal family. By lending his royal name and influence to the national cause, and by supporting it with liberal-minded enthusiasm, he gave it, in the eyes of the people, a consecration which it never could have received without the presence of a leader of royal blood.

After King Christian Frederick's abdication the four remaining

[1] Gustav Peter Blom, *Norges Statsforandring*, p. 228.
[2] Yngvar Nielsen, *Wedel-Jarlsberg*, vol. II., p. 264.
[3] A. Faye, *Norge i 1814*, p. 165.

members of his cabinet, Rosencrantz, Sommerhjelm, Collett, and Niels Aal, were to act as a regency *ad interim*. Their first care was to prevent any violation of the armistice, and to protect the Storthing in its deliberations; but they also sought to secure supplies, and to make necessary preparations in case hostilities should be resumed.[1]

On October 13th the Swedish commissioners met with the Storthing to negotiate concerning the union of the two kingdoms.[2] Many of the representatives, among others Count Wedel-Jarlsberg, spoke in favor of union, but all were agreed that it could not be based on the provisions of the treaty of Kiel, but that the Storthing would decide the question of its own free accord. The armistice would terminate on October 21st, but the deliberations were continued until the 20th, when the question was finally submitted to a vote, with the result that only the four representatives from Bergen voted in the negative in obedience to instructions from their constituents. Of these the able and well-poised Christie, president of the Storthing, was one, but he was personally in favor of union, and declared that he would abide loyally by the decision made. He was made a member of the committee which together with the Swedish commissioners should undertake the revision of the constitution, necessitated by the union with Sweden.[3] For this task he possessed the best qualifications. His great talents and extensive knowledge, his dignified presence, and courteous and pleasing manners had made him a great favorite even among the Swedish commissioners, and he soon became the leading spirit in the committee. The work advanced without very serious difficulty, and on November 4th the Storthing ratified the revision, as completed by the committee. On the same day Charles XIII. of Sweden was elected king of Norway. On November 9th Charles John arrived in Christiania to submit the king's oath, and in the presence of the Storthing the crown prince himself took the same oath to uphold the Norwegian constitution.[4] November 4, 1814,

[1] Yngvar Nielsen, *Wedel-Jarlsberg*, vol. II., p. 265. *Historisk Tidsskrift*, tredie række, vol. IV., p. 150 ff.

[2] *Storthings-Efterretninger 1814–1833*, vol. I., p. 121 ff.

[3] Erik Vullum, *Unionen og dens Fremtid*, p. 70. Yngvar Nielsen, *Det første overordentlige Storthing, Optegnelser og Aktstykker*.

[4] L. M. B. Aubert, *Kieler-Traktatens Opgivelse*, p. 7 ff.; ibid., *Norges folk-eretslige Stilling*, p. 91 ff.

marks the completion of the union between Norway and Sweden, though the "Act of Union" (Rigsakten),[1] in which the conditions of union are fully outlined, was not adopted until the following year. This document was prepared by the constitutional committee of the Swedish Rigsdag, and contained the provisions which had been inserted in the Norwegian constitution regarding the union of the two kingdoms. It was submitted to the Norwegian Storthing, which ratified it July 31st. The Swedish Rigsdag approved it August 6, 1815. The Act of Union, like the constitution of Norway, recognized the union as resting, not on the treaty of Kiel, but on the free consent of the Norwegian people, and the complete equality of the two realms. In a government bill presented to the Swedish Rigsdag April 12, 1815, the king says: "When two peoples of their own free will submit to the same government, everything tending to produce a difference between them in their relations to the common ruler should be carefully cleared away. Otherwise the union will sooner or later be disrupted, and one people will oppress the other, or their violent separation will sow the seeds of discord, which will produce serious dissensions for centuries. If grave consequences have resulted from the lack of attention to this principle, which experience has shown to be true, how much the more necessary is it not to pay due heed to it at present when it is our aim, not only to create a Scandinavian power of two free nations which have long been enemies, but also to create mutual confidence and true friendship between them. For the attainment of this object perfect equality between them should be established by determining their mutual rights without regard to the number of inhabitants or the products of each country." The perfect equality was, nevertheless, not established

"The treaty of Kiel," says Samuel Laing, "if it had even been founded on any just or admitted principle of the law of nations, was renounced by this acceptance as a ground of right to the sovereignty of the Norwegian nation. At the present day, when the excitement and occasion which gave rise to the nefarious treaty are past, and its object has been accomplished upon just principle, no Swedish cabinet could, in the face of civilized and moral nations, have the effrontery to claim rights over the Norwegian people as emanating from a treaty so repugnant to all principle." *Journal of a Residence in Norway during the Years 1834, 1835, and 1836.*

[1] A. C. Drolsum, *Das Königreich Norwegen als souveräner Staat*, Berlin, 1905.

in practice, as diplomacy and foreign affairs, as well as the representation of both kingdoms at foreign courts, remained in the hands of the Swedish government. But this was a practice based on no express right, as no such privilege was granted Sweden by the Act of Union.[1]

55. Sentiments and Conditions after 1814

The union with Sweden had been forced upon Norway by the European powers, who had not yet learned to pay attention to the principle of nationality as an important factor in international politics. In the North and elsewhere they were carving out states by geographical metes and bounds on their military charts without regard for the character and sentiment of the people, that great force which was to carry Europe through the extraordinary development of the nineteenth century. The Norwegians entered the union with dignified loyalty, but the new relation had no root in their deeper sentiments. They accepted it as an unavoidable destiny, but with sadness, not with joy, as they felt that their ideals had been bedimmed, and their right to work out their own destiny had been infringed upon. In the storms and struggles of 1814 they had succeeded in winning constitutional liberty and political independence, while the nations of Europe were yet groaning under the oppression of a medieval political and social system. No country in Europe had been so fortunate, and no people had better reason to rejoice. But the disappointment arising from the military fiasco of the war, due to Christian Frederick's incompetence, and the necessity of entering into a union with Sweden under compulsion eclipsed for a period every advantage which had been gained, and filled the minds of the people with sadness and bitter thoughts. Many did not even stop to consider that full liberty and independence had been guaranteed the Norwegian people under the Eidsvold constitution and the Act of Union. They thought that since the king of Sweden was also to be king of Norway, they had been subjected to Sweden in the same way in which they had before stood under Danish overlordship, an erroneous idea which for a time caused Norwegian patriots many

[1] J. E. Sars, *Norges Historie*, vol. VI., 1, p. 145. J. Utheim, *Grundloven om Norges Utenrigsstyre.*

heartaches. The great financial distress and the unfavorable economic conditions also began to be felt more keenly after the excitement of the struggle was over, and the routine of peaceful vocations was resumed in the customary way. The private fortunes even of the wealthiest families had been wrecked during the long period of war and blockade, and crop failures had produced great suffering. From 1815 to 1818 the crops were also very poor, and the fisheries failed, so that the export of codfish was reduced to almost one-half of what it had been before the war. The lumber trade with England was declining, as the English government had begun to encourage importation of lumber from Canada. The importation of grain from Denmark was also rendered difficult, because Norway was placed among the least favored nations in regard to trade with that country. The finances of the kingdom were wholly disorganized, and it had no public credit. About twenty-five million riksdaler of unsecured paper money was in circulation, and this currency was steadily falling in value, though the Eidsvold guarantee had established a ratio of 3.75 paper riksdaler to every silver riksdaler. This guarantee had proven useless, and a hundred specie riksdaler was already worth 1500 riksbank paper daler. Claus Pavels, chaplain at Akershus, writes in his diary, January 10, 1815, that besides his fuel bill he had used for his household that year 37,137 riksdaler, that besides this sum he had spent 5000 or 6000 riksdaler of his own money, and yet he had not lived extravagantly.[1] The people were unable to pay their taxes, the treasury was empty, and clergymen and government officials did not receive their salaries. Under these circumstances the warm sympathies for Denmark and its royal house soon gave way to a feeling of hostility and bitterness, as it was thought that the Danish government was responsible for much of the economic distress from which the country was suffering.[2]

The first problem confronting the government was how to reorganize the finances and to bring about a revival of commerce in order that the most acute distress might be relieved. The Swedish

[1] Claus Pavels, *Dagbogs-Optegnelser 1815–1818*, p. 6.
[2] The most violent expression of anti-Danish feeling was a treatise published by Nicolai Wergeland in 1816 entitled, *En sandfærdig Beretning om Danmarks politiske Forbrydelse mod Norge Aar 995 til 1814.*

Field Marshal Henrik von Essen had been appointed *statholder* in Norway to exercise the highest administrative authority in the name of the king. Peter Anker was placed at the head of the ministry as minister of state, his associates being Professor Treschow, minister of church and education; Sommerhjelm, minister of justice; Diriks, minister of the department of police; Collett, minister of the interior; Wedel-Jarlsberg, minister of commerce and finance; Hegermann, minister of war; and P. Motzfeldt and Christian Krohg, members of the Swedish branch of the Norwegian ministry.[1] Count Wedel-Jarlsberg had received the most difficult portfolio, but no one was so well qualified to wrestle with the difficult financial situation, and he became the virtual head of the ministry.[2] But the ministers exercised in the beginning very limited power beyond what pertained to the routine work of their own departments. The king was accustomed to exercise the administrative power, and the *statholder*, acting in his name, became the real head of the administration, as the ministers were not yet accustomed to assert their rights arising from their duties and responsibilities under the constitution. The Storthing alone could be relied upon to carry through the needed reforms.

The first regular Storthing which assembled in July, 1815, passed several bills for the reorganization of the finances. The unsecured paper money should be withdrawn from circulation, but the question whether the bills should be redeemed at their par value of 3.75 riks-

---

[1] The Eidsvold constitution provided a minimum number of five departments, but by the revision of November 4, 1815, the number was changed to eight, with the further provision that the minister of state and two other ministers should always stay in Stockholm. The king also had the right to make his eldest son viceroy of Norway, or he might appoint a statholder, who might be either a Swede or a Norwegian. In 1815 a department for the marine was created, but in 1818 the number of ministers was reduced to five, as the departments of justice and police were consolidated, and likewise also the departments of the interior and of justice and finance. In 1822 an auditing department was added, and these six departments remained unchanged during the reign of Charles John. F. Bætzmann, *Det norske Statsraad*. T. H. Aschehoug, *Norges nuværende Statsforfatning*, vol. I. Erik Vullum, *Unionen og dens Fremtid*, p. 93 ff.

[2] J. E. Sars, *Norges Historie*, vol. VI., 1, p. 144 ff. Yngvar Nielsen, *Grev Herman Wedel-Jarlsberg, Nordmænd i det 19de Aarhundrede*. J. E. Sars, *Norges politiske Historie 1815–1885*, p. 270 ff.

daler in paper to 1.00 riksdaler in specie was long debated, and it was finally decided that since the Eidsvold guarantee had proven a failure, it should be left out of consideration, and a special tax should be levied for their redemption at current value. This was equivalent to declaring a state bankruptcy, but it was, undoubtedly, necessary in order to forestall utter chaos, as the public burdens already exceeded the people's ability to pay taxes. The budget for the year represented the large sum of 3,600,000 specie daler, and as the treasury was empty, and the credit exceedingly poor, this sum would have to be raised by taxes. It was also decided to create a new specie currency with the specie daler as the monetary unit,[1] and a Bank of Norway was to be organized with a capital stock of not less than two million, and not more than three million specie daler, to be divided into shares of 200 specie daler each. These were to be sold to private individuals, but only 3791 shares could be disposed of, and the levying of an extra tax had to be resorted to in order to secure the minimum capital stock.[2]

Christie, who had served as president of the Storthing till 1818, retired at the close of that session, highly honored by his countrymen as a great patriot. All realized that he had guided the deliberations of that body with great tact and ability, as he had been one of the ablest leaders in the days of 1814.

No parties had yet developed, but a divergence of opinion and interests between the official classes and the *bønder* had manifested itself as a distinct reaction against the liberalism of the men of Eidsvold. The great reactionary movement which after the downfall of Napoleon spread over all Europe, the political creed of Metternich, accepted by the Holy Alliance as the infallible guide for all true statesmen, could not but exert an influence also upon Norway. The democratic principles embodied in the constitution represent the ideals of the most liberal-minded and far-sighted patriot leaders. In the critical days of Eidsvold they had dared to pursue the thought of consti-

---

[1] The specie daler was equal to four kroner, or about $1.08. It was divided into five *ort* and 120 *skilling*.

[2] *Storthings-Efterretninger 1814–1833*, vol. I., p. 462 ff. Yngvar Nielsen, *Wedel-Jarlsberg*, vol. III. J. E. Sars, *Norges Historie*, vol. VI., 1, p. 157 ff. Yngvar Nielsen, *Herman Wedel-Jarlsberg, Nordmænd i det 19de Aarhundrede.* B. E. Bendixen, *Et Omrids av Norges Handelshistorie*, p. 45 ff.

tutional freedom to its logical conclusion, a free nation, a government by the people and for the people. But the era of high ideals and great feelings was now past, and social conditions were not as democratic as the provisions in the constitution. The old class spirit reasserted itself, and the official class, failing to grasp the full meaning of what had been done at Eidsvold, settled down to their accustomed ways in the belief that they would continue to enjoy their old powers and privileges. The *bønder* were not yet able to assert the rights and powers granted them by the constitution, and it was possible for the upper classes during the first session of the Storthing to legislate in their own interest as if no democratic government existed. The constitutional provision regarding general and uniform military service was wholly disregarded, and in the Storthing of 1816 Judge Weidemann proposed that the soldiers should be recruited among the *bønder*, but that the officers should be chosen from the bureaucracy. A motion to maintain the provision of the constitution was voted down, and a bill was passed providing that only the young men of the country districts should be compelled to serve in the army. Other equally reactionary measures were proposed. Only officials were appointed to the Lagthing, as it appears, in an effort to create an aristocratic upper house, and this body also passed a bill providing that allowances and mileage for the representatives should be figured according to their social standing, "so that all might live according to their rank." A constitutional amendment was also proposed, according to which the representatives of the rural districts should not constitute above one-third of the total number of representatives, and the other two-thirds should be distributed among the remaining "four estates": civil officials, clergy, military officers, and the merchant class. These very distinct traces of reactionary autocratic ideas show that the Norwegian democracy was yet in its infancy, but it developed rapidly because of the powers and privileges granted the common people by the constitution.

56. THE REIGN OF CHARLES JOHN. THE RELATION TO SWEDEN

King Charles XIII. died February 5, 1818, at the age of seventy, and was succeeded by Charles John, who since his return from the

Napoleonic wars had exercised the leading influence, especially in diplomacy and foreign affairs. In Sweden he enjoyed great popularity. He had earned a well-merited reputation as a military leader, the Norwegian campaign had been swiftly terminated, and he had secured Norway, as many believed, as a compensation for Finland.[1] The Swedish people greeted his accession to the throne with enthusiasm, feeling that henceforth there would be only one kingdom and one people on the Scandinavian peninsula. But those who were better informed, and had watched events more closely, were not so well pleased. They realized that Norway had become an independent state, that it was in no sense a part of Sweden, and that Charles John had but imperfectly fulfilled the long-cherished hope of Sweden of getting compensation for Finland. They could reconcile themselves to what had happened only on the supposition that the work of consolidating the two kingdoms would be continued until Norway should be fully incorporated in Sweden. Axel Gabriel Silverstolpe expressed quite a general Swedish sentiment when he said that the two kingdoms might, indeed, be regarded as one country, but it was left to make the Swedes and Norwegians one people.[2] Charles

[1] A great divergence of views regarding the nature of the union between Norway and Sweden soon manifested itself. The Swedes regarded the treaty of Kiel as the basis of the union. According to this theory, Sweden had been granted possession of Norway with full title of ownership. H. L. Rydin held that by the treaty of Kiel Sweden only secured permission or right to secure Norway, that the union rested on the treaty of Moss, not on that of Kiel. See Herman Ludvig Rydin, *Föreningen mellan Sverige och Norge*. But Oscar Joseph Alin and the younger school of Swedish historians held that the basis of the union was the treaty of Kiel. See Oscar Joseph Alin, *Den svensk-norska Unionen;* C. A. Reuterskiöld, *Til Belysning af den svensk-norska Unions Författningen och des tidligare Utvecklingshistoria;* Otto Varenius, *Unionsförfatningen ur svensk och norsk Synspunkt;* Nils Edén, *Die schwedisch-norwegische Union und der Kieler Friede.* The Norwegians, who refused to accept the provisions of the treaty entered into by Sweden and Denmark, claimed, properly enough, that the union was based on the treaty of Moss, by which Sweden agreed to accept the Eidsvold constitution, and to recognize Norway as a sovereign kingdom united with Sweden under a common king. See J. E. Sars, *Den norsk-svenske Unions historiske Retsgrund; Den norsk-svenske Unionsstrid*, and other essays on this subject, *Samlede Verker*, vol. III., p. 610 ff.

[2] *Sveriges Historia*, edited by Emil Hildebrand, vol. V., part IX., p. 286 ff.

John was well aware of the brewing discontent, but he felt sure that he would be able to carry through amendments to the Norwegian constitution which would destroy the sovereignty of the people, and subject them to the supremacy of Sweden. He thought that the Norwegians possessed neither the power nor the ability to resist him on this point, and his constant onslaught on the Norwegian constitution is one of the important features of this reign.

But the hindrances in the way of an amalgamation of the two peoples or a consolidation of the two kingdoms were far greater than Charles John had anticipated. The statement made by a contemporary observer that Norway and Sweden were "like two twins grown together in the back, and therefore continually turning away from one another, the one looking eastward and the other westward,"[1] expresses a truth which has been of the greatest significance in the development of the two nations. Sweden, facing eastward, has stood under the influence of central Europe; Norway, facing westward, has been strongly influenced by the more liberal French and English ideas. Sweden had been a great military power, and was ruled by a proud and powerful nobility; the Norwegians were a nation of freeholding *bønder* accustomed to a high degree of personal freedom, and they were rapidly developing under their newly won political independence to become one of the most democratic peoples in the world. And as for their ability to defend their constitutional liberties, the king found that they possessed a skill in statescraft, and a resolute determination to defend their rights, which he had not expected. Finally there was the most conspicuous obstacle, the constitution itself, which the king had sworn to uphold, a charter of liberty as firmly established and as solemnly approved as any document of the kind that ever existed. In the face of such obstacles an attempt at amalgamation must seem impolitic if not imprudent. Samuel Laing says: "If there be any meaning in the word amalgamation, it must be to render Norway an integral part of the kingdom of Sweden, governed by the same laws, with the same constitution, and subject to the same taxes. It was forgotten by the Swedish ministry, that the very structure of society and property in the two countries is founded on totally different principles: in the one on the feudal,

[1] *Sveriges Historia*, vol. V., part II., p. 286 ff.

in the other on the udal (odel) principle; so that even if both desired it, they could not assimilate their institutions without such a total subversion of all social arrangements and rights of property in one or other, as would exceed the most violent revolution in modern times. The Swedish legislative body consists of nobility, clergy, burgesses of towns, and peasantry, forming distinct chambers, and voting by chambers, at a general diet. To give to a legislative body or diet, so constituted, the power to impose taxes and frame laws affecting the property of a nation having no representatives in such a diet, and no similar classes of the community in its social structure, could not be attempted by the most arbitrary government, in an age when property, especially in a commercial country connected with others as Norway is, must be respected." [1]

Even before ascending the throne, Charles John seems to have given encouragement to the discontent of Norwegian *bønder*, due to the heavy taxes and the hard times, no doubt in the hope that if the Norwegian government became unpopular, a change in the constitution could be more easily effected. In 1816 a man by the name of Röslein, who represented himself as his secret agent, came from Sweden, and traveled about in the eastern districts of the kingdom, telling the people that the Storthing, which was a very expensive institution, was the cause of the high taxes and the hard times, that if the king received more power, everything would be different. In several districts the people held public meetings and indulged in loud complaints and seditious talk. Halvor Hoel in Hedemarken even collected a band of about two hundred followers, and marched against Christiania, but they were met by a military force, and were persuaded to return home. Hoel himself was later tried and sentenced to prison for the term of three years, but he was soon pardoned by the king. The disturbance was not of a serious character, but Charles John was suspected of having aided it, and this caused an anti-Swedish feeling which proved very unfavorable to an amalgamation policy. The same is true of another unfortunate incident.

[1] Samuel Laing, *Journal of a Residence in Norway*, p. 85 f. J. E. Sars, *Norges politiske Historie 1815–1885*, p. 39 ff. Yngvar Nielsen, *Carl Johan som han virkelig var og som han skildres af J. E. Sars.*
The Swedish system of a legislature of four Estates mentioned by Laing existed till 1863, when the bicameral system was introduced.

John Everth, member of an English firm, and their agent, C. J. Gerss, who had established a trading station at Nyholmen in the harbor of Bodø, where they were allowed to occupy some government buildings, had turned smugglers, and carried on their traffic on a large scale. The government officials attempted to arrest the two men, and after some resistance they were finally lodged in jail, and their goods were confiscated. After a short time the smugglers were released, and some time later John Everth succeeded in decoying a part of the guards at Nyholmen on board his ships, where they were detained while he landed with twenty men, drove away the remaining guards, brought the goods on board his two vessels, and sailed away. Somewhere in the North Sea he placed the imprisoned guards in a frail boat in which they succeeded in reaching shore. This flagrant violation of all laws was to be settled by diplomatic negotiations between the English and Swedish governments. Everth not only claimed that he was innocent, but he demanded a large indemnity, which the Swedish government awarded him without making any very serious attempt to defend the rights and dignity of Norway. The people felt that the Swedish ministers, to whom the foreign affairs of both kingdoms were intrusted, had been very negligent, and that their country had been treated, not as a sovereign kingdom, but like a province.[1]

Because of the amalgamation policy pursued by Charles John the Storthing was not only in danger of being forced to agree to a revision of the constitution, but the Norwegians were not accorded their full rights as a sovereign nation in all respects equal with Sweden. They had no flag which was generally recognized, and south of Cape Finisterre, Norwegian merchant vessels had to use the union flag, which was the Swedish flag with a white cross in a red field as a union sign in the upper left-hand corner.[2] On the seals and in public documents even in Norway the name of Sweden always preceded that of Norway, and the diplomatic and consular service was wholly Swedish.[3]

---

[1] J. E. Sars, *Norges politiske Historie 1815–1885*, p. 43 f. *Samlinger udgivne af den norske historiske Kildeskriftkommissionen 1900, Aktstykker om Bodøsagen.* B. von Schinkel, *Minnen*, vol. XI., p. 247 ff. Yngvar Nielsen, *Bodøsagen. Storthings Efterretninger*, vol. II., p. 622 ff., vol. III., 375 ff.

[2] J. C. Anker, *Tegninger af Norges Flag*, Christiania, 1888.

[3] Munch Ræder, *Unionen og egen Udenrigsminister.* Sam Clason, *Redo-*

Even the attempts of the Storthing to carry out the express provisions of the constitution met with determined resistance. In 1815 a bill was passed abolishing the Norwegian hereditary nobility, as the few representatives of this class were of recent and foreign origin, and as the existence of such a class, however insignificant, could not very well be reconciled with the democratic spirit of the Norwegian institutions. The king refused to sanction the bill, but it was passed again in 1818. If it should be passed a third time in 1821, it would become law without the sanction of the king, according to article seventy-nine of the Norwegian constitution,[1] and the principle that the king's veto power was only suspensive would be established also in practice. The king brought all possible pressure to bear on the Storthing to postpone the passage of the bill. He declared that the European powers would not tolerate such a step, that war would be sure to follow, and that if the Storthing insisted on passing the bill, they would also have to provide means for making the army and navy ready for war. He might punish the members of the Storthing as traitors, he said, if they ventured to pass a law which he had not sanctioned. But he preferred not to take so drastic a step. He would sign the bill if they would consent to postpone the matter till some other time. Threats and intimidations did not avail, however, as the Storthing felt that the constitution itself was on trial. The bill was passed a third time, and became law without royal sanction.

Another and more serious question to be settled was whether Norway should pay her share of the joint state debt of Denmark-Norway.[2] By the treaty of Kiel it had been promised the king of

gjörele for Unionsfrågans tidligere Skeden, p. 11 f. J. Utheim, Grundloven om Norges Udenrigsstyre.

[1] "If a bill has been passed in the same form by three regular Storthings, constituted after three successive elections, and separated from each other by at least two intervening sessions of the Storthing, no contrary resolutions in the meantime having been passed by any session of the Storthing from the time of the introduction of the bill till its final passage, and it is then placed before the king with the request that His Majesty will not refuse to sanction the measure which the Storthing after so mature deliberation considers useful, it shall become a law even if the sanction is not granted before the Storthing adjourns." Article 79.

[2] B. von Schinkel, Minnen, vol. X., p. 210 ff. Eidsvold Constitution,

Denmark that Norway should pay her share in proportion to the population and resources of the two kingdoms. But the Norwegians did not recognize that treaty, and did not feel obligated by a promise which the Swedish king had made without their knowledge or consent. Denmark, however, turned to the Quadruple Alliance, which had assumed control of the political and international affairs of all Europe, and welcomed such an opportunity to show its zeal and authority. At the congress of Aix la Chapelle, where neither Denmark nor Sweden was represented, the great powers issued strict orders to Charles John to bring this dispute to a speedy close, an undue interference with the private affairs of a sovereign state which he very promptly resented.[1] But on September 1, 1819, an agreement was made with Denmark, according to which Norway should pay the sum of three million riksdaler. Many still thought that Norway ought to refuse to pay, as the principle of recognizing the treaty of Kiel was involved, but the majority considered it unwise under the circumstances to repudiate the debt, and the Storthing passed a bill May 29, 1821, providing that Norway should pay the amount stipulated in the agreement of 1819. Thereby all danger of foreign intervention disappeared, and the matter ought to have been regarded as settled, but Charles John seemed determined to strike a telling blow in favor of his long-cherished hope of changing the Norwegian constitution. Six thousand Swedish and Norwegian troops were assembled for maneuvers on the plain of Etterstad in the neighborhood of Christiania. It was also discovered that the Swedish soldiers had been supplied with ball cartridges, as if they were in an enemy's country. As soon as the army had assembled, a Swedish squadron, carrying 300 guns and a crew of 2000 men, entered the harbor of Christiania, and on July 17th the king himself started for Norway, accompanied by a number of admirals, generals, and foreign diplomats. The assembling of such forces around the capital at a moment when the financial distress of the kingdom did not warrant large expenditures for military display could have been undertaken only for the most sinister purposes. It seems

Article 93. Yngvar Nielsen, *Stormagternes Forhold til Norge og Sverige 1815–1819*, p. 4 ff.; *Diplomatiske Aktstykker vedkommende Opgjør med Danmark.*

[1] Yngvar Nielsen, *Stormagternes Forhold til Norge og Sverige 1815–1819*, p. 81 ff.

almost certain that the king contemplated a *coup d'état*, by which he would overthrow the Norwegian government and consolidate Norway and Sweden. On June 1, 1821, he had issued a circular note to the powers, in which he violently assailed the Norwegians for disloyalty and ingratitude, as if to justify the step he had decided to take. The whole document is evidently written for the purpose of arousing the prejudice of the great powers against Norway. "The course lately pursued by the Norwegian Storthing," he says, "could not fail to attract the king's most serious attention. The insurrectionary spirit of southern Europe seems to have infected the minds also in the North." [1] After he had been granted full power over Norway by the treaty of Kiel, he says, he granted the Norwegians a free constitution, but his kindness had been rewarded with ingratitude, and he had not been able to persuade the Storthing not to pass the bill abolishing the Norwegian nobility, which was contrary both to the laws and constitution. He would, no doubt, be acting within the scope of his right, he continues, if he said to the Norwegian people: "You violate on your side the agreement to which I have given my consent; thereby I am reinstated in the full possession of the rights granted me by the treaty of Kiel, and I deprive you of the liberty which I once granted you, but which you have so sadly misused. Or I might say: You wish to place upon Sweden the burden of your public debt, although Sweden has claims against you arising from the common expenditures of the united realms. In this wise you raise the question of the consolidation of the two kingdoms, and I only follow the example you have set when I carry out this consolidation. But faithful to that system of forbearance from which the king will not depart, His Majesty will not employ either the one or the other of these ways, but if egotism and blindness continue to disregard his counsel, he shall be obliged to reconstruct the Norwegian constitution on foundations which give greater assurance of general safety." [2]

---

[1] In the spring of 1821 the Austrians had suppressed the liberalist uprising in Naples, and the attempt of the army in Piedmont to organize a revolt in favor of constitutional government was also crushed. It was the high tide of reaction, and the Quadruple Alliance was eagerly watching to suppress liberal movements everywhere.

[2] B. von Schinkel, *Minnen*, vol. X., p. 201 ff. J. E. Sars, *Norges politiske Historie*, p. 62 ff.

A catastrophe seemed imminent, but the king did not strike the threatened blow. He had reflected upon the possible consequences, and the thought made him pause, the more so because the reply of the powers to his circular note had not been quite as favorable as he had expected. Charles John was of an impulsive nature, easily stirred to wrath, but his anger was of the passionate kind which quickly subsided. He was kind-hearted and generous, never truly happy unless he felt that he enjoyed the love and admiration of his subjects, and the loyalty shown him on all occasions had helped to calm his temper. The great maneuvers ended with parades, balls, and dinners, and the king returned to Stockholm without having accomplished much more than recovering his good humor. As to the changes to be made in the Norwegian constitution, he contented himself with proposing certain constitutional amendments to the consideration of the Storthing. The chief features of these were: that the king should be granted absolute veto, and the right to dissolve the Storthing and order new elections when the session had lasted over three months, the right to appoint the presidents of the Storthing, the right to remove from office all officials, with the exception of judges, and the right to create a new hereditary nobility. Christian Magnus Falsen, "the father of the constitution," also proposed some amendments, which aimed to destroy the political power of the common people, democratic features of the constitution which he had once labored so hard to establish, and which had made his name illustrious. This strange fickleness put a stain upon his character which tarnished his reputation and committed his name to obscurity.[1]

[1] J. E. Sars, *Norges politiske Historie 1815–1885*, p. 72 ff., 87 ff: Yngvar Nielsen, *Christian Magnus Falsen, Nordmænd i det 19de Aarhundrede*. Erik Vullum, *Kristian Magnus Falsen, Grundlovens Fader*, p. 81 ff. King Charles John proposed:

1. A change of article XV. of the constitution, so that the two Norwegian ministers, who should always be in Stockholm, should not be changed yearly, as the constitution provides, but according to the king's pleasure.

2. A change in article LVIII., whereby the Storthing should be made to assemble in the summer, and the king should be allowed to convene it in any Norwegian city.

3. A change in article LXXI., by which the king should receive the right to dissolve the Storthing and order new elections.

The proposed amendments became the issue in the political campaign of 1824. They were vigorously assailed by the best writers, and new papers, like "Patrouillen," edited by the able liberalist Ludvig Mariboe, were founded to wage the fight for the constitution. Only Falsen supported the amendments, to the further detriment of his already tarnished reputation. The elections returned to the Storthing a number of the most experienced leaders who had been prominent in the Eidsvold Constituent Assembly, and care was taken to appoint as members of the constitutional committee men of broad experience and recognized talents. The learned jurist Christian Krohg was made chairman of the committee, the other members being George Sverdrup, Wedel-Jarlsberg, C. G. Hornemann, and the great orator and parliamentary leader Ingebret Knudssøn. King Charles John used all his influence to carry his amendments. He used threats and intimidations. In a letter to Statholder Sandels he wrote: "It is to the interest of the Storthing that I reserve to myself the power to dissolve it so soon as circumstances demand it, and I will be obliged to do so unless I am granted absolute

4. A change in article XXII., by which the king should be allowed to dismiss from office all government officials, except judges, without investigation or trial.

5. A change in article LXXIV., allowing the king to appoint the presidents and vice-presidents of the two branches of the Storthing from among its members, and that the Storthing should choose as secretaries persons not elected as representatives.

6. A change in article LXXV., necessitated by the change in article LVIII.

7. The canceling of article LXXIX., which provides that a law can be passed over the king's veto.

8. A change in article LXXXI., necessitated by the canceling of article LXXIX.

9. The canceling of paragraphs e. and i. in article LXXXII.

10. A change in article XCII., necessitated by the change in article LXXXII.

11. Introduction of a new article providing that an extra session of the Storthing should consider only such matters as the king should lay before it.

12. An addition to article XXIII., by which the king should receive the power to create a new hereditary nobility.

13. A change in articles LXXXVI., and LXXXVII., providing for a different organization of the *Rigsret*, or Court of Impeachment.

Kampen mellem Norges Storthing og Regjering, from *Dagbladet*, Christiania, 1882. P. Flor, *Bemerkninger over de paa det tredie ordentlige Storthing fremsatte Konstitutionsforslag*, Drammen, 1823.

veto power, for the eyes of the absolute monarchies are resting upon us." This and other like epistles were brought to the attention of the Storthing, but nothing availed. Pursuant to the recommendations of the constitutional committee the amendments were voted down. Some of the more essential points, as that of absolute veto, were again brought forward in 1827, but when the king found that they could not be carried, he withdrew his proposals with the understanding that they should again be considered in 1830. He had been compelled to yield, and although these amendments were continually placed before the Storthing throughout his whole reign, his threats had lost their terror, and the amendments were never passed. King Charles John's crusade against the constitution had failed. He had only taught the Norwegian people to treasure more highly this great document, and to preserve it unimpaired as the charter and bulwark of their liberty.

The struggle waged by the king against the celebration of the Norwegian national holiday, the Seventeenth of May, was no more successful. In 1827 the Storthing impeached Jonas Collett, member of the Norwegian ministry, because he was responsible for the promulgation of unconstitutional ordinances and the expenditure of money in excess of what had been granted by the Storthing. This aroused the king's temper to an unusually high pitch, and he thundered like the angry Jove against what he regarded as an undue usurpation of power by the national legislature. But his anger was soon appeased, and he departed from Christiania in the best of humor. The trial of Collett was allowed to proceed, and the minister was finally acquitted. But the king's displeasure was again kindled when he learned of attempts to celebrate the Seventeenth of May.

Prior to 1824 no celebration had taken place,[1] but in that year the university students had arranged a festival, and during the succeeding years it became customary to hoist flags on the ships in the harbor, and to arrange private parties in honor of the day. In March, 1827, before the king departed from Christiania, Statholder Sandels had asked that the people be allowed to celebrate the Seventeenth of May, and the king had given an answer which

---

[1] B. von Schinkel, *Minnen*, vol. XI., p. 265 ff. J. E. Sars, *Norges politiske Historie 1815–1885*.

the *statholder* understood to be favorable. As the royal ban was now supposed to be raised, the festivities were more general than they had been on any previous occasion, and even the Storthing arranged a public dinner in their assembly rooms, where toasts were drunk to the health of the king and various members of the royal family. But, to the surprise of all, the king flew into a rage when he heard of the celebration, and when a miserable Swedish drama, which was played at the Christiania theater the following fall, was hooted off the stage by a few young men who felt that it would reflect on their intelligence to see such an exhibition without protest, he felt sure that a revolution was on the point of breaking out. Statholder Sandels was dismissed from office, and in his place was appointed B. B. von Platen, who was thoroughly in favor of the policy of amalgamation and the consolidation of the two kingdoms. But instead of seeking to further his plan of amalgamation by attempting to win the favor and good-will of the Norwegian people, he was determined to suppress all manifestations of a distinct national spirit, and especially to wage war on the celebration of the Seventeenth of May. In a circular letter to the higher officials of the kingdom he attempted to show that because of the rights which Sweden had secured by the treaty of Kiel, and because of the magnanimity of Charles John towards the Norwegian people, either August 14th, when the treaty of Moss was concluded, or October 14th, when the Storthing declared in favor of union with Sweden, or November 4th, when the union was established, ought to be made a joint holiday for both countries, but May 17th ought to be forgotten. His efforts were, however, in vain, as he could issue no instructions to the officials which they were obliged to heed.

On January 29, 1828, the king called an extra session of the Storthing, ostensibly for the purpose of considering some very urgent matters. But as none of the proposals submitted could be regarded as very urgent measures, it was clear that the real purpose of the extra session had not yet come to light. Sars thinks that he would prevail on the Storthing to annul the decree of the court in the impeachment case against Collett, and to give sanction to the prerogatives which he believed belonged to him; but when he found that the constitution did not permit such a course, he dropped the matter, and his lofty plans, which brought him to summon the Storthing into extra session, and to journey to Christiania, dwindled down to an attack on the Seventeenth of May. He summoned the presidents and vice-presidents of the Storthing, and delivered a speech to them, in which he declared the celebration of the Seventeenth of May to be an insult to the union and the constitution of November 4, 1814. In his long career he could recall many bitter moments, he said, but the bitterest of all were these three: first, when he was forced to draw his sword against France, his native land, where he had won his military reputation; second, when he had to enter Norway, sword in hand, though he loved the Norwegian people; third, when he learned that the Storthing had celebrated the Seventeenth of May by arranging a public dinner.[1] In order to please the king on this rather trivial point, the Storthing resolved not to celebrate the Seventeenth of May. The people throughout the country, even the students, heeded the resolution passed by the Storthing, so that even Statholder von Platen complimented them on their loyalty. Had the *statholder* acted with tact and good judgment, it is possible that the people might have been persuaded to abandon the idea of making that day a national holiday. But the following year an event occurred which made the matter a national issue, and rendered all restraint useless.

In 1829 the Students' Union (*Studentersamfundet*) decided to make the Seventeenth of May one of their regular holidays, and a private festival was arranged for in the apartments of the club. This affair was conducted in the most quiet way, and nothing happened which could attract any attention. The day was warm and beautiful. Many people were assembled at the wharf to see the steamer "Constitutionen," which just arrived in port, and as a steamer was rather an uncommon sight in those days, the vessel was greeted with hurrahs and the singing of national songs. Later in the afternoon many people, especially women and children, numbering in all about 500, assembled in the public square to enjoy the fresh air and the fine weather. The authorities grew nervous and ordered them to go home, but this warning was not heeded, as the people failed to see why such an order should be issued. In the evening, about nine

---

[1] B. von Schinkel, *Minnen*, vol. XI., p. 274 ff.

o'clock, the chief of police caused the riot act to be read, and a force of cavalry and infantry was sent from the fortress of Akershus to clear the streets. Several persons were ridden down, but, fortunately, no one was seriously hurt. The people returned to their homes, and the "battle of the market-place" was over, but great indignation prevailed, as they felt that an outrage had been committed against a peaceful and law-abiding public. At the inquiry which was instituted it was proven that the people had not disturbed the peace or done anything unlawful. The wrath of the offended people was especially turned against Statholder von Platen, who, as commander-in-chief of the Norwegian army, was responsible for the conduct of the military. He left Christiania shortly after the affair, but when he returned in the fall he was met with such ill-will that the situation became intolerable. In a short time he took sick and died, and it is thought that this was due in part to chagrin and disappointment. The commission of inquiry had decided that twelve of the leaders who had arranged the celebration, among others the poet Henrik Wergeland, who was a leader among the students, should be prosecuted, and the commandant of Akershus should be censured for indiscretion. But the people of Christiania vowed that they would have their rights. They sent a memorial to the Storthing protesting against the outrage. This was referred to the constitutional committee, with the result that the Storthing issued an address to the king, defending the celebration of the Seventeenth of May as a right belonging to the people. During the following years the day was publicly celebrated, and the Storthing joined in the festivities without further interference from the king. The Seventeenth of May had become a recognized national holiday.

The king's attempt to prevent the Norwegians from celebrating the Seventeenth of May was a part of a systematic effort to reduce Norway to a Swedish province, inaugurated by the attack on the Norwegian constitution. What he sought to do, says J. E. Sars, was "to carry out the Swedish views of the relation between the two kingdoms in the union. In both instances he appeared as Swedish king, as representative of the will of the Swedish people, Swedish political and national interests and views, not as king of Norway. . . . He appeared as Norwegian king only when he was to receive appanages, and when he was to be greeted with hurrahs and triumphal arches. The kingdom and Sweden, the union and the kingdom, Sweden and the union, appeared to him as one and the same thing, or as the necessary and combined powers in opposition to the Norwegian democracy."[1]

This policy of amalgamation, the attempt to strengthen the union at the expense of Norway, became an issue which forced the two peoples ever farther apart, and created a prolonged political struggle which culminated in the separation of the two countries.

57. YOUNG NORWAY. HENRIK WERGELAND AND JOHAN SEBASTIAN WELHAVEN. LITERARY AND INTELLECTUAL REVIVAL

One of the names which had been most frequently mentioned during the excitement connected with the celebration of the Seventeenth of May, 1829, was that of Henrik Wergeland, a son of Nicolai Wergeland, at that time only twenty-one years of age. He had cried hurrah for the steamer "Constitutionen," and in the evening a cavalryman had struck him across the back with his saber. This stain of oppression he regarded as such a disgrace to his student's uniform that he sent it in a basket to the commandant of Akershus.[2] In this strange episode the young patriot makes his first début in the history of his people, in which he was destined to play so singular a part, and to win a name with which no other can be fully compared. "Who is Henrik Wergeland, under whose silent supremacy we live?" writes Erik Vullum. "He has become for us what the household deity was to the ancients. They might hate or love the god, it mattered not, for all had to worship him, and bring their offerings, and all were aided by him in their work. We may be supporters or opponents of the ideas which Wergeland advocated, but we must have him with us. It is as though we felt that there is no hope of success for an undertaking in our country unless it has the consecration of the name and spirit of Wergeland, and all like to make him their own. He is disrobed or attired according to the needs of the hour and the party. Are there ten of us who have the same conception of

---

[1] J. E. Sars, *Norges politiske Historie 1815-1885*, p. 125 ff.
[2] Henrik Wergeland, *Samlede Skrifter*, vol. VII., p. 550.

the great indispensable one, who unites under his sway the young republicans and the staid and dignified department officials?

" It is not through his poetry he has won this power over us. A poet may be loved by all, but he is not equally indispensable to all. Wergeland has exerted a deeper influence on our lives than rhyme and rhythm can produce if they be as perfect and melodious as the music of the spheres. Not through his stormy life, or his beautiful death, nor even through his genius has he won the immortal glory which he now enjoys, of sitting enthroned in sympathetic and believing human hearts as the prince of patriots. His undying fame he has earned by patient drudgery devoted to the national needs of the hour." [1]

The cleavage in Norwegian society caused by the Reformation when the Danish language was introduced as the church and literary language still existed. The city population and the official class, including the clergy, which were strongly mixed with foreign elements, had thoroughly assimilated the Danish language and culture, while the rural population still spoke their own tongue, and adhered to their old customs. Under the shelter of absolutism in the period of the union with Denmark, which fostered a distinct aristocratic spirit among the cultured classes, this condition had assumed a rigid permanence, and the bønder had become sharply differentiated from the city population and official class, not only in customs and language, but also in views and sympathies. The men of Eidsvold had created liberal political institutions suited to the most democratic society, but during the great European reaction, 1814–1830, it became evident that the old spirit of class prejudice, desire for special privileges, and antipathy to the common people still prevailed in higher social circles. The officials showed strong bureaucratic tendencies, and continued to rule in the old spirit, even under the new constitution. Their views and tastes remained to a large extent unchanged, and they were glad to settle down to the old ways, not thinking that the great political change would necessitate a radical social readjustment. What the result would be when the bønder should assume political leadership was a thought which had not yet dawned upon their mind, as they do not seem to have

[1] Erik Vullum, *Henrik Wergeland i Digt og Liv.*

VOL. II — 2 H

considered such a state of affairs to be within the realm of possibility. In literature no progress had been made since *Det norske Selskab* flourished in Copenhagen, and poets like Schwach, Johan Storm Munch, S. O. Wolff, and H. A. Bjerregaard were not even as well known as Johan Nordahl Brun, Johan Herman Wessel, Claus Frimann, and other members of *Det norske Selskab*. An intellectual and social revival would have to rouse the people to new life and national self-consciousness, before they would be able to enter into full possession of their liberty, or to begin the new development which their independence and free institutions made possible. This revival came in 1830 with Henrik Wergeland, who in patriotism and aspirations was the personification of young Norway.

Romanticism, which had caused a new intellectual awakening in Germany and Denmark, had not reached Norway, though the higher classes still thought that their country continued to be dependent upon Denmark for higher intellectual culture and refined literary and artistic taste. If they had been able to realize their theory in practice, the same impulses which stirred the Danish people to new activity could also have been transmitted to Norway, and some progress might have been made, but they were content with the old ideas which had flourished in Denmark several decades earlier. These ideas, which represented the good old intellectual stock in trade which had been inherited from the union period, had become associated with everything æsthetic and *bon ton*. They could produce no new growth, but satisfied the wants of a limited number of aristocratic families who desired to live in intellectual repose on their well-garnished cultural provision chest. The few new ideas which were imported from Denmark were of the romantic kind, which dreamed of the faded glories of a remote past, and hence harmonized perfectly with the tranquillity and refined taste which already existed in the higher circles, and which were regarded as the acme of cultural perfection. In the midst of this sedate and self-satisfied autocratic elegance Henrik Wergeland appeared as a huge storm center, causing an intellectual upheaval such as the nation had not yet experienced. Long cherished literary views were challenged, and old social ideas were given a rude shock. It was a storm which electrified and cleansed the atmosphere, and stirred the germs of life into new growth.

Wergeland was a representative of that spirit of the age which manifested itself in the struggle for nationality and liberty in nearly all parts of Europe, and which in England found its best expression in the poetry of Shelley and Byron. The effort of the human spirit to free itself from political and social oppression, and to break through the narrow systems of conventional views and arbitrary rules of art, engendered a feeling of *weltschmertz*, but created also the charming hope that liberty once established would regenerate the world and usher in the millennium. The struggle of the Greeks for freedom had become the cause of all Europe, which Byron had glorified in his poetry and consecrated with his death. On no one had these events made a more profound impression than on the perfervid genius of Wergeland. He, too, would have hastened to the aid of the Greeks, if he had been a wealthy and powerful lord instead of a young student, the son of the poor clergyman of Eidsvold. In 1827 he wrote: "When I think of the future everything grows dark — I tremble. I said to my father that I must go to Greece, that my life may not be wholly in vain." And after the death of Canning he wrote a poem in praise of England, which "like a sharp-beaked sea-eagle rises from her foggy nest to aid the Greeks." [1] His ardent devotion to the cause of liberty was further strengthened through extensive reading of French literature, and finally by the July Revolution in Paris in 1830, which revived the drooping spirit of all liberalists in Europe. In 1831 he visited France, where he came into personal contact with the most advanced liberal ideas. Hitherto the liberalists had sought to win political liberty, but the English naturalists, and still more the French romanticists, emancipated themselves from established rules also in regard to literature, art, and social conditions. St. Simon laid the foundations of Socialism, and Victor Hugo and his followers declared the right of the individual to disregard all recognized rules of art, and to express his thoughts and feelings in his own way, unhampered by any established authority. Under the influence of English and French literature and liberal ideas Henrik Wergeland had developed his political and literary theories and his whole view of life. " As Norwegian liberty in 1814 sprang from the great French Revolution," says Halvdan

[1] Erik Vullum, *Henrik Wergeland i Digt og Liv*, p. 36.

Koht, "so germs of the new French revolutionary ideas had blown to Norway, where they found opportunity to grow in the mind of the man who produced the great awakening of his people." [1]

Wergeland laid no new foundations, but he was the chief architect who reared the cultural structure of Norway on the foundations laid by the Eidsvold men, and continued to work in their spirit. They had adopted the liberal and progressive ideas which had their origin in English political institutions and scientific thought, and which found their full development in the revolutionary struggles of America and France; he made these ideas the living force in the new national development. They had made the people supreme in theory; he would make them supreme in practice. They had acted for the people; he taught the people to act for themselves. The resolute resolve to lead a free national existence which enabled the Eidsvold men to achieve such great things in the darkest hours of the people's history should inspire every citizen, and Norway would rise triumphant from her humiliation to new national greatness. It became his task to create new national life and self-confidence, to unite the people in the effort to make themselves truly independent, and to create a literature and higher culture of their own. For this work he was qualified, not only by a rare literary genius, but also through his ability for hard work, his love for everything national, and his profound sympathy for all who were poor and needy, traits which made him the national leader and invincible idol of the common people. His father, Nicolai Wergeland, describes him as follows:

"Henrik Wergeland has been from his earliest youth an ardent liberalist, philanthropist, and patriot, and he has not yet (1843) proven untrue to this character. He has been inspired by love for the freedom and happiness of his fatherland and for the enlightenment and well-being of the people. No one has loved the people so well, and no one has sought to a like degree in all possible ways to serve them. No one has so unselfishly espoused their cause without regard for the annoyance and misfortunes which he reaped from it. He always considered how he might serve the people, and when he found an opportunity, he acted with energy without fear or regard for any hindrance, and without any thoughts of loss or profit to

---

[1] *Henrik Wergeland*, p. 67.

PLATE XII

HENRIK WERGELAND.

himself. In 1825 his father deposited for him in the savings bank a hundred specie daler, and he earnestly begged that of this sum he might give his poor uncle fifty specie daler. 'If we saw,' he said, 'a good mill standing idle for want of water, would we not open the mill race? Let me have the joy to start this mill.' He divided his bread with the poor; he took his coat off and gave it to the one who had none. 'I gave what I had,' he wrote once, 'two specie daler and a new shirt. I ran out and secured six or seven customers for the man. The food grows bitter in my mouth when I think of all the misery. It seems to me that I have no right to satisfy my hunger.'" "When the people learned," continues his father, "that Henrik Wergeland was their honest, fearless, and unselfish friend, all who were in need or considered themselves wronged or oppressed came to him to seek help, counsel, and protection. This increased more and more after the year 1830. Not only from Eidsvold, but from other parts people sought him, and still (1843) they come from far away on such errands." [1] The people had at last found a leader whose name became their battle cry, the sign by which they were destined to conquer.

The signal for the great national struggle which was now precipitated was the publication of Wergeland's greatest literary work, "Skabelsen, Mennesket og Messias." Shortly after the appearance of this work, on August 15, 1830, "Morgenbladet" printed an anonymous poem, "Til Henrik Wergeland," which assailed the poet in the bitterest terms, and concluded by declaring that he belonged to the Parnassian madhouse candidates. The author of the poem was the young poet Johan Sebastian Welhaven, born in 1807, and by one year Wergeland's senior.[2] Welhaven also wished to bring about

[1] Halvdan Koht, Henrik Wergeland, p. 25, 75. Hans Tønsager, Barndoms- og Ungdomsminder om Henrik Wergeland. Gerhard Gran, Henrik Wergeland, Nordmænd i det 19de Aarhundrede. J. E. Sars, Samlede Verker, vol. IV., p. 102 ff., 154 ff. Gerhard Gran, Norges Dæmring, p. 221 ff. Hartvig Lassen, Henrik Wergeland og hans Samtid. Henrik Jæger, Illustreret norsk Literaturhistorie, vol. II., p. 87 ff. J. E. Sars, Norges politiske Historie 1815-1885, p. 131 ff. Just Bing, Norsk Literaturhistorie, p. 77 ff. Olav Skavlan, Henrik Wergeland, Afhandlinger og Brudstykker. Kristian Prestgard, Norske Kvad, Decorah, Ia., p. 9 ff.

[2] Arne Løchen, J. S. Welhaven, Liv og Skrifter. Gerhard Gran, J. S. Welhaven, Nordmænd i det 19de Aarhundrede. J. S. Welhaven, Samlede Skrifter,

a revival in Norwegian intellectual life, and in regard to the theory of poetry he represented new ideas, as he was influenced by the Danish romanticists. But he agreed with the conservative upper classes that higher culture had to be introduced from Denmark, and as to poetic form and diction he clung with scholastic fidelity to the old rules. The attack on Wergeland did not remain unanswered, and soon the literary battle between these two leaders waxed furious, and attracted widespread attention. In 1832 Welhaven published a critique of Wergeland's poetry, entitled "Henrik Wergelands Digtekunst og Polemik ved Aktstykker oplyste," in which he lays down the rules for lyric poetry, and tries to show that, as Wergeland's poems do not conform to these rules, he is not a poet. But his rules are so narrow that they could not be followed without serious detriment to the poetic art, and his critique shows that personal animosity has obscured his vision, and has rendered him unable to recognize the great genius of his rival. Welhaven regarded poesy as beautiful images and tender sentiment wrought into harmonious and elegant verse. He wrote as with a painter's pencil, tracing his own inner life and feelings with so refined a taste that his lines are capable of creating like feelings in others, and his poetry excels in descriptive beauty and lyric tenderness. Wergeland's rugged force and frequent disregard for form offended him. He regarded his scope and depth as obscurity, his freedom in diction and versification as formlessness and chaos.

To Wergeland poetry was not lyric sentiment or lovely fancy-bred images perched in serene tranquillity above the clouds. It was an expression of the storms and struggles, the joys and sorrows, of life itself. To him poesy was the sword in the fight, the implement in his daily labor, the expression of his whole personality in vigorous activity. His poems are wrought from the thoughts and experiences of the hour. There are living heartbeats in his rhymes and rhythms, tears and triumph, battle shouts and joyous laughter in his lines. It is doubtful if ever another poet to a like degree has succeeded in making life poetry and poetry life — the real secret of his greatness and his unique influence.

vol. I., p. 15 ff. J. E. Sars, *J. S. Welhaven, Samlede Verker*, vol. IV., p. 130 ff.

In taste and character the two poets were as different as in their theories. Welhaven, who was the son of a Bergen clergyman, belonged in every way to the upper classes, while Wergeland belonged both by training and sympathies to the common people, with whom he became ever more closely identified. The two represented the incompatibility which has always existed between the *bønder* and the officials, and their friends and supporters soon formed two distinct parties, the first in modern Norwegian history, and in a direct line the forerunners of the two great political parties which appeared later. Welhaven's friends, among whom were found nearly all the officials, were called the Intelligence party, as they posed as the representatives of refined taste and higher intellectual culture, while Wergeland's party, which, besides a few literary friends, embraced the common classes, were called Patriots, because of their strictly national program. The clashes between the two groups soon led to a split in the Students' Union (Studentersamfundet). Fifty-six members, including many of the most talented leaders, like A. Schweigaard, F. Stang, P. A. Munch, J. S. Welhaven, Bernhard Dunker, and U. A. Motzfeldt, seceded in 1832 and formed a new students' union (Studenterforbundet). They also began to publish a periodical, "Vidar," but it received no support from the public and had to be discontinued two years later. In the meantime, Welhaven was preparing for a new onslaught on the Patriots. In 1834 he published his long critical poem "Norges Dæmring" ("The Dawn of Norway"), in which he attacked the semi-culture, narrow-mindedness, and blind and boisterous patriotism which he attributes to his opponents. It was a violent assault, full of invective and bitterness, and the Patriots considered it an attack on their country's honor, though it is certain that the author had no such intention.[1] The storm of controversy rose to a veritable tempest, and as both parties had begun to publish their own papers, the effects of the struggle were felt in wider circles than hitherto. In 1836 the Intelligence party began the publication of a daily paper, "Den Constitutionelle." The Patriot party organ, "Folkebladet," founded in 1831 by P. P. Flor, had ceased to appear, but the more radical opposi-

[1] Gerhard Gran, *Norges Dæmring*. Arne Løchen, *J. S. Welhaven, Liv og Skrifter*, p. 179 ff.

tional paper "Statsborgeren" ("The Citizen") was still in full activity. This was, however, a scurrilous sheet, whose editor, P. P. Soelvold, was convicted of libel and dismissed. In order to help the unfortunate man, Henrik Wergeland undertook to edit the paper, though he thereby exposed himself to the bitterest attacks of his opponents, who would make him responsible for everything which had ever appeared in its columns.

The conflict between the two parties, at first only literary, gradually assumed also a social and political character. It was Wergeland's aim to place the power in the hands of the common people, according to the provisions of the constitution, while the leaders of the Intelligence party wished to maintain the predominance of the upper classes in political as well as in intellectual and social life. Both parties were patriotic, both wished to advance, but along different routes. It was a question whether the new national life should be aristocratic or democratic, whether the new cultural development should be based on foreign elements, the heritage of a refined upper class, or if it should issue from the life and individuality of the people themselves. As the leaders were young and talented men, the struggle was waged with intense bitterness, and it reached a dramatic climax in the memorable "Campbeller battle" in 1837. A prize had been offered for the best drama to be written for the dedication of a new theater in Christiania. Of the twelve pieces submitted, A. Munch's "Kong Sverres Ungdom" was regarded as the best, but it was also decided that the second best, Wergeland's "Campbellerne," should be played. On the evening when the piece was to be played for the first time, the friends of Welhaven appeared at the theater in force to hoot it off the stage, but Wergeland's friends had also assembled to applaud the play. As soon as the curtain rose, the din of rough-music began, which drowned every word, and when order could not be restored, a fierce hand-to-hand struggle was precipitated, in which Welhaven's followers were thoroughly beaten and ejected from the theater. It is difficult to understand why the Intelligence party, who vaunted their refinement, should resort to such arguments in which they were no match for their more brawny opponents. It is no doubt safe to ascribe their conduct to overconfidence and youthful arrogance. But the episode taught them that whatever they might think of æsthetic theories, there existed a robust young Norway which was determined to solve its cultural problems without foreign interference either directly or indirectly. As ludicrous as the episode may appear to a distant observer, it was, like the "battle of the market-place," a victory for the national program of the Patriots, which stimulated the common people to a most resolute attitude.

"Campbellerne" was played for the third and last time February 12, 1838, for the benefit of the author, who received about 400 specie daler, a sum which enabled him to buy a cottage and a piece of ground, "Grønlien," in the outskirts of the city. The following year he married the lady of his choice, Amalie Sophie Bekkevold, but his income was so small that he learned from experience to know the bitterness of poverty. He had studied theology, and hoped to get a curacy, but his career as a liberalist stood in the way, and all his attempts had been unsuccessful. Wergeland had always been an admirer of King Charles John, "the son of the Revolution." The king had also learned to love the gifted and impulsive poet, but the only thing which he could do for him at this time was to offer him a gratuity of 200 specie daler from his private purse for two years, a gift which Wergeland accepted on the condition that he might repay it by promoting the education of the poor.[1] All unbiased people would agree that it was perfectly honorable for him to receive this present from his king, though he was himself a republican, but his enemies used the opportunity to accuse him of accepting a bribe, of selling himself to King Charles John. Even his own adherents were offended, and when he was appointed Keeper of the Rolls, a rather modest position in the government archives, they felt convinced that he had forsaken his republican principles. Ludvig Kr. Daa, his best friend, turned his back upon him as a traitor, and Wergeland soon found himself deserted and alone. Even his sister, Camilla Collett, a gifted author, and the originator of the woman's movement in Norway, seems to have agreed with his antagonist Welhaven in literary views and tastes, if she did not sympathize with the Intelligence party in their whole campaign. At home Wergeland was happy with his young wife, his flowers, and his animal pets,

---

[1] Henrik Wergeland, *Samlede Skrifter*, vol. VIII., p. 625 ff.

all alike the object of his most tender affection, and as he had built a new home, "Grotten," in the city, a romantic spot with a natural grotto which he especially loved, he might have enjoyed the full measure of contentment. But the feeling that he was forsaken by his friends, and unjustly regarded as a traitor, filled his hours with a bitterness against which he sought solace in a most intense work. At this time he wrote his large history of the Norwegian constitution, a work of high merit in which he shows the continuity of the historic development of the Norwegian people, and the intimate connection between their new national life and their past history, a thought of fundamental importance to the correct understanding of Norwegian history. Wergeland showed that the same circumstances which led to the downfall of the old nobility, resulting in Norway's weakness in the union period, enabled the *bønder* to preserve their liberty, and created conditions favorable to a new national development. The thought was, however, too new and original to be much heeded by historians at the time. He also waged a determined fight to secure the passage of an amendment to the constitution which should grant the Jews the right to reside in Norway with all the privileges enjoyed by other citizens.[1] This amendment was finally adopted in 1851, six years after his death.

His sorrows and hardships only tamed his too ardent spirit, and gave his character greater repose. His poetic spirit was chastened, and he wrote during these years some of the finest productions which adorn Norwegian poetic literature, like "Et Blomsterstykke" and "Den engelske Lods." But this, the most productive period of his life, was destined to be very brief. He was tall, strong, and athletic, but in the spring of 1844 he contracted a severe cold which confined him to his bed. On the Seventeenth of May he could not be persuaded to remain quiet. He hastened forth into the damp and cold spring weather to take part in the celebration, an imprudence which threw him again upon the sick-bed. The illness turned into consumption, and it was soon evident that the shadows of death were gathering about the great poet. The news created the profoundest grief throughout the whole kingdom, and his friends, who had long

---

[1] Henrik Wergeland, *Jødesagen i det norske Storthing*, *Samlede Skrifter*, vol. VIII., p. 435 ff.

PLATE XIII

J. S. WELHAVEN.

HENRIK WERGELAND'S MONUMENT IN CHRISTIANIA.

CAMILLA COLLETT.

remained indifferent, hastened to his bedside to implore his forgiveness and to renew their pledges of friendship. The reconciliation with his friends gave him even in these dark hours a joyous presentiment of victory which robbed death of its bitterness, and made him look forward to the end with a smile of contentment. He continued to the last to ply his pen with the greatest diligence, and his most pathetic lyrics are those written on his death-bed.[1] About one o'clock in the night, July 12, 1845, he awoke from a short slumber and said: "Now I dreamed so sweetly; I dreamed that I rested in my mother's arms." These were his last words. A few minutes later he breathed his last at the early age of thirty-seven. The next morning the street was filled with throngs of men, women, and children who came to cast a last look upon their friend and benefactor. Some came from far away to see him, and so many thousands followed his bier that the capital had never witnessed such a funeral procession. The bitterness of party strife had passed away, and the nation stood sorrowing at the grave of the leader whose life and influence proved to be "the dawn of Norway."

[1] The following poem, translated by Ole O. Lien, is the dying poet's farewell to the wallflower blossoming in his window:

To My Wallflower (*Til Min Gyldenlak*)

My flower bright, before thy colors fade,
Then I am that of which the world was made;
Before thou part with thy crown of gold, —
Then I am — mold.

When last I look to the window up,
My parting glance greets thy golden top;
My soul doth kiss thee when, free and bright,
He takes his flight.

I seal our parting with kisses two;
One is for thee — for our love is true —
The other token of friendship close
Is for the rose.

Full-blown, the rose I no more shall see;
But bring a greeting to her from me; —
And say — I wish that upon my grave
Her blossoms wave.

And I desire that upon my breast
A rose be placed when in death I rest. —
And, flower bright, be in death and night
The bridal light.

58. Political Progress. New Men and Measures

In the period 1814 till 1830 no marked change had taken place in the political situation. The members returned to the Storthing in 1830 were of the same class as in all previous sessions, but two new leaders, Ludvig Mariboe [1] and Jonas Anton Hjelm,[2] now made their appearance for the first time, and the influence of the great Wergeland-Welhaven controversy as well as of the liberal movement awakened throughout Europe by the July Revolution in France aroused the political leaders to new activity. Both Mariboe and Hjelm were liberalists. Hjelm was a keen and profound constitutional lawyer and a powerful parliamentary debater, well qualified to open the battle for Norway's constitutional rights. The Storthing, which had hitherto pursued a purely defensive policy, had sought to prevent the king from changing the constitution and reducing the kingdom to a Swedish dependency; but the time had come when the people would begin to exercise their political rights, and when an attempt would be made to establish in practice Norway's sovereignty and recognized equality with Sweden. In the discussion of the constitutional amendments proposed by Charles John, Hjelm stated very clearly his views regarding the relation between the two realms. He showed that Norway as a sovereign kingdom could not be compelled to leave its diplomatic and consular service in the hands of the Swedish government, and that although such an arrangement actually existed, it was temporary, and in no wise consonant with the true interests of the realm. He showed that the Swedish government authorities could assume charge of no Norwegian affairs whatsoever, except in cases where such a power was granted by specific provisions in the constitution or the Act of Union, and that all doubtful cases had to be interpreted on the fundamental principle expressed in the first paragraph of both these instruments, that Norway was a sovereign kingdom. The aim of the Norwegian people should be, not to obtain full equality with Sweden in the union, so that Norway might enjoy the same right as Sweden in the management both of foreign and other affairs, but to carry out in practice

---

[1] Henrik Wergeland, *Samlede Skrifter*, vol. VIII., p. 126 ff.
[2] Ibid., vol. VIII., p. 446. J. E. Sars, *Samlede Verker*, vol. IV., p. 73 ff.

the sovereignty or political independence of the kingdom, so that the Norwegian people could manage their own affairs without any interference from Swedish authorities, a right which Norway unquestionably possessed. This was a clear statement of the nature of the union and the rights which Norway expected to maintain and enjoy in the new relation. Hjelm was welcomed as a leader, but the Storthing did not dare to accept his logical and clearly outlined national program. Regarding the all-important question of the relation of the two kingdoms in the union there still existed much uncertainty among the representatives, and they sought to dodge the question which had been raised by resorting to temporary makeshifts. Sweden had requested Norway to pay to the Swedish treasury her full share of the expenses connected with the diplomatic service. This request was not fully complied with, but the Storthing voted to increase the contribution, a half measure which for the moment evaded the issue.

At the time when Wergeland began his great struggle against the Intelligence party and the privileges of the upper classes, the bønder were also roused to greater activity in political life by one of their own class, John Neergaard, from Nordmør in western Norway. Neergaard, who had been a representative in the Storthing in 1827, traveled through the country, and assembled the bønder to political meetings, where he spoke to them on the political issues. He also sold his book, "Olaboka," in which he described the hard times, showing that these were due to the upper classes, who had hitherto had the power in the Storthing, and had used it to increase the taxes. His campaign was so successful that of ninety-six representatives elected to the Storthing in 1833 forty-five were bønder,[1] and as they could count on support from several representatives from the rural districts who did not belong to their own class, and also from some of the representatives from the cities, they had a majority in the national legislature for the first time. Besides John Neergaard himself and other leaders among the bønder, like Teis Lundegaard, who had been a member of the Eidsvold Constituent Assembly, Ole Haagenstad,[2] who had been a representative in the

---

[1] Halvdan Koht, Bondestrid, p. 70 ff.
[2] Henrik Wergeland, Samlede Skrifter, vol. VIII., p. 1 ff.

Storthing of 1815, and Fauchald from Toten, who was now elected for the first time, Johan Gabriel Ueland, who became the great leader of the *bønder* in the Storthing, was also elected. Ueland was a self-made man, a born leader, a clever tactician, skillful in debate, with a penetrating, logical mind; always careful, pursuing a diplomacy tinged with cunning. He did not possess the statesmanlike views of Hjelm, and he cared little for the questions arising from Norway's relation to Sweden. He directed his attention mainly to the internal affairs, and to the organization of the *bønder* into political opposition to the official class. In this field of work he showed exceptional ability. It was his aim from the outset to limit the power of the officials, and to carry into effect the system of democratic government also in local affairs.

The "Code of Christian V." had destroyed all self-government in the rural communities. The people no longer assembled at the *thing*, unless they were summoned by royal order for some specific purpose.[1] The *lagrette* was no longer selected from the best *bønder* for life, but for a year at the time, and they had ceased to be the people's spokesmen and leaders. All local government was conducted by the *amtmænd* and *fogeds;* for although the people were often consulted on minor matters, especially in church affairs, they exercised but small influence on the administration of public affairs. The Eidsvold constitution of 1814 wrought no change in the system of local administration, but since a democratic national government had been established, it was a manifest anomaly that the old bureaucratic system should still prevail in local government. Until the people could govern themselves in local as well as in national matters, the principle of popular sovereignty could not be said to be realized.

Attempts made in 1821 and 1830 to secure local self-government had failed, but in 1833 the matter became the campaign issue, and as the *bønder* secured a majority of the representatives, the passage of the measure in some form was assured. The king, who attempted by his proposed amendments to the constitution to destroy the people's sovereignty in the national government, was naturally opposed to popular government in local affairs, but in order to forestall a more radical measure, he proposed a plan of local administration

---

[1] T. H. Aschehoug, *De norske Communers Retsforfatning før 1837*, p. 182.

which would still leave the people almost powerless.   The ministry also submitted a plan which would grant the local authorities more power, but the measure passed by the Storthing gave the people more complete control of local affairs, and it was accordingly vetoed by the king.   The aim of the supporters of the measure would now be to secure its passage according to article seventy-nine of the constitution, which would make it a law without the king's sanction.   In 1836 the *bønder* again secured a majority in the Storthing, and their leaders Hjelm, Ueland, Fauchald, and Neergaard were all returned. Before the new Storthing assembled, a commission had been appointed to investigate the matter of popular local self-government.   This commission proposed a very liberal plan, and as the king was persuaded to yield, this was submitted to the consideration of the Storthing, apparently with good chances of being passed.

Another equally important issue brought before the Storthing in 1836 was the principle so clearly set forth by Jonas Anton Hjelm regarding Norway's equality with Sweden in the union, and the right of the Norwegian people to manage their own national affairs without interference from Swedish state authorities.   This very fundamental issue, together with a proper system of local self-government and the exercise by the people of their political rights according to the spirit of the constitution, was the national political program of Wergeland and Hjelm.   It is clear that this was a very sound and conservative position, that they only sought to make operative the principles and institutions which had been most solemnly established, and that they deserved the support of all loyal men.   But the *bønder* did not understand Hjelm's broad-minded statesmanship. They regarded themselves as belonging to his party while he was aiding them in securing the passage of the bill for local self-government, but they had failed to support him in 1830 and likewise, also, in 1833.   The Norwegian ministry had even surrendered the very principles for which he contended by resorting to a compromise with the king, by which they imagined that they would make a substantial gain, when, in fact, they only acknowledged Norway's inferiority to Sweden, and gave up the strong position taken by Hjelm.   In 1834 they addressed a memorial to the king, in which they made certain demands, which were, in part, granted.   By a royal resolution of

April 13, 1835, it was stipulated that the Norwegian minister of state in Stockholm should be present when Norwegian diplomatic affairs, or diplomatic matters of interest to both kingdoms, were considered by the Cabinet Council for Foreign Affairs, which was otherwise a purely Swedish institution. By resolutions of 1836 it was also provided that Norwegian consuls should be appointed with the advice of the Swedish-Norwegian ministry, and that they should take their oath of office as Norwegian officials. But this arrangement only accentuated the inferiority of Norway.[1] The Swedish minister of state should preside even when purely Norwegian matters were considered, and even then the Swedish ministers were in the majority. When Swedish affairs were considered, the Norwegian minister should not be present. It must be regarded as weak and reprehensible statesmanship, that the Norwegian government asked as a concession from the king what they already possessed as a full right according to the constitution, and that they were willing to surrender so important a principle, in order to obtain a concession which practically amounted to nothing whatsoever.

It had been decided in 1833 that Hjelm's plan should be submitted to the following Storthing, and the matter was, accordingly, brought up in 1836, but not in the original form and spirit. Other liberal leaders, like Sørenssen, Holst, and Rye, who were more inclined to compromise, assumed management of affairs, and Hjelm, who undoubtedly saw that the time had not come when such a policy would gain general support, made no effort to secure the passage of his measure. The other leaders, who also wished to maintain the principle of equality between the two kingdoms, centered their efforts on obtaining the passage of a law which should insure the use of the Norwegian flag of the same design as at present in all parts of the world. Because no treaty had been concluded between Norway and the Barbary States, it had hitherto been necessary to substitute the Swedish flag with the union sign for the Norwegian south of Cape Finisterre, in order to avoid attack from the pirates. A memorial was also to be addressed to the king in regard to a Norwegian man-of-war flag. Hitherto a Swedish flag with a union sign,

---

[1] B. Dunker, *Om Revision af Foreningsakten mellem Sverige og Norge*, p. 7 ff. T. H. Aschehoug, *Norges nuværende Statsforfatning*, vol. I., p. 60.

consisting of a white cross in a red field, had been used on Norwegian fortresses and war vessels, a manifest symbol of Swedish overlordship.[1] But before the pending measures could be acted upon, the king suddenly prorogued the Storthing, an unexpected and extraordinary step, which he claimed was made necessary by the hostile attitude of Russia. No evidence, however, can be adduced to show that Russia paid any attention whatever to the measures introduced in the Norwegian Storthing. The statement must be regarded as a subterfuge, by which he sought to conceal the real reason — his own determined opposition to all measures aiming at asserting Norway's sovereign rights and equality with Sweden. Even though surprised, the Storthing acted with calmness and dignity. During the last moments of the session which came to so abrupt a close, the Odelsthing passed a bill impeaching the minister of state Løvenskiold, who had not opposed the step taken by the king. The reactionary minister suffered the humiliation of being found guilty of a misdemeanor, and of being sentenced to pay a fine of 1000 specie daler, together with part of the cost. The king was very angry, because the Storthing had again ventured to use its power of impeachment against one of his advisers, but as he had abandoned the idea of forcibly overthrowing the government, the episode closed without further complications.

After the death of B. B. von Platen the office of *statholder* had remained vacant, but in 1836 the king appointed as a new incumbent Count Wedel-Jarlsberg, a choice in every way agreeable to the Norwegian people. They rejoiced to see one of their leading men in this important office, but they hated the office itself, since it put the stamp of dependence and inferiority upon their country, and its abolition soon became a national issue. In the fall of the year the Storthing was assembled in extra session, and the measures pending at the time of adjournment were again introduced. The bill establishing popular local self-government was passed, and it received the king's signature, January 14, 1837. This great measure, constituting a bulwark of democratic liberty second in importance only to the constitution itself, had finally become a law.[2] It made the old *thinglag*,

---

[1] C. J. Anker, *Tegninger af Norges Flag.*
[2] *Storthings Efterretninger*, vol. II., p. 535 ff., 814 ff. ; vol. III., p. 561 ff.

or local administrative districts, in most instances identical with the parishes, and called them *formandskabs-distrikter*, a name which was changed to *herred* in 1863. The people of each *herred* should elect a *herredsstyre*, or body of select men, of not less than twelve or more than forty-eight members. This body chooses one-fourth of their members as a committee, *formandskab*, which together with the magistrate determines what improvements are to be undertaken by the *herred* each year, and what taxes are to be levied. All matters of common interest to the *herreds* are decided by the *amtsthing*, which consists of the chairmen of the *herredsstyre* in all *herreds* in the *amt*, with the *amtmand* acting as chairman.

Hjelm's policy aiming at establishing a diplomatic and consular service in harmony with Norway's dignity as a sovereign power did not receive general support, but a memorial was addressed to the king, showing how the equality of the two kingdoms established by the constitution and Act of Union had hitherto been ignored in practice. Norway had no man-of-war flag, Sweden's name always preceded that of Norway on all seals and documents, and the foreign and diplomatic affairs of both kingdoms were exclusively in the hands of Sweden. Pursuant to the views expressed in this memorial, a government bill was introduced in the Storthing, February 14, 1837, providing for the creation of two committees with an equal number of Swedish and Norwegian members, the one to consider the question of a separate Norwegian man-of-war flag, the other what modifications of the constitution and the Act of Union would be necessary in order that foreign affairs could be conducted in a manner agreeing with Norway's right as a sovereign state. The bill regarding the exclusive use of the Norwegian merchant flag in the Norwegian merchant marine on all seas was also pending. By a royal decree issued April 11, 1838, it was finally ordained that the Norwegian merchant flag should be used in all waters. This was the only direct result of Hjelm's efforts to maintain Norway's sovereign rights in the union. It was not a great triumph, but it was hailed as a very welcome victory,[1] especially by the political leaders, who could point to it as a result of their efforts to promote the welfare of their constituents.

[1] H. J. Næss, *Flagsagens Historie.* Henrik Wergeland's poems: *Hurra for Jonas Anton Hjelm. Nu hvil dig, Borger! det er fortjent.*

Hitherto Charles John had exercised a strong personal rule. The ministers had, indeed, acted as his advisers, but they had been so dominated by his strong will that they had been able to exert but small influence. The two last Swedish incumbents in the office of *statholder*, Sandels and Platen, also acted as his personal adherents,[1] and sought to make the royal power supreme in the government. These conditions had proven very unfavorable to the development of democratic institutions and popular government, but the selection of Count Wedel-Jarlsberg as *statholder* wrought a marked change, though it is quite certain that the king did not intend to alter his policy. Even as minister of finance, Count Wedel had exercised such influence in the ministry that he was regarded as its real head, but as *statholder* he also became minister of state, and as a leading Norwegian statesman he could lend great support to the pending issues. No one had played a more conspicuous part in political affairs than Wedel, but in the Eidsvold Constituent Assembly he advocated the consolidation of Norway and Sweden under a common government with a joint system of taxation and finance, and as the independence party prevailed, he became unpopular. For a few years he was pushed into the background, but his great ability as minister of finance brought him again into prominence. That he was a loyal patriot could not be doubted. After the union with Sweden he earnestly supported the constitution, he opposed the amendments proposed by Charles John, and as *statholder* he was ready to uphold to the full extent the rights of the Norwegian people. In the performance of the duties of his high office he showed great tact and ability, good judgment, and regard for the opinions of his colleagues. "Wedel gave the administration dignity, life, and system," writes a contemporary. "No one was better qualified to be a leader." [2] His second ministry developed sufficient independence

[1] Yngvar Nielsen, *Wedel-Jarlsberg*, vol. III., p. 180. J. E. Sars, *Norges politiske Historie 1815–1885*, p. 274 ff. F. Bætzmann, *Det norske Statsraad.*

[2] *Vogts Optegnelser*, quoted by J. E. Sars, *Norges politiske Historie*, p. 275. F. Bætzmann, *Det norske Statsraad*, p. 49 ff.

"At the time when Wedel was minister, and I was secretary of state, I had learned to esteem his great ability, quick perception, and more than ordinary knowledge in different fields; and after he became head of the ministry, I was forced to admire the self-control and rare conduct which he exhibited on so many occasions," writes Paul Christian Holst. "He conto exert a definite influence on the government as a connecting link between the king and the people. The time had come when the ministry was becoming the organ of the sovereign will of the nation, whose wish the king would not dare to ignore. Time and circumstances had also wrought a change in the attitude of Charles John to his Norwegian subjects. In Sweden he had been attacked by a vituperative pamphleteer, M. J. Crusenstolpe, and the press had wounded the feelings of the sensitive king by its rather hostile tone, while the Norwegians had always spoken of him in the most endearing terms. In 1838 he made a prolonged visit in Norway, and he was greatly pleased with the enthusiastic loyalty shown him. He had always coveted popularity, and never had the words of flattery been more pleasing than now when old age had turned his vision backward upon the events of a most remarkable career. He found that the Norwegians were very loyal and agreeable, that they knew how to appreciate his ability and great achievements, and he was more inclined to listen to their demands than hitherto. The reins were slipping from his hands, and the ministry gradually began to exert a leading influence in shaping the policy of government. It might seem that the time had come when an attempt would be made to establish the necessary safeguards for Norway's rights as a sovereign power, but the progress was halted by the reactionary spirit of the age.

The national movement led by Wergeland and Hjelm had grown out of a strong liberal idealism, and it had created issues which the conservative upper classes opposed, and which the *bønder* had failed to understand. The people had, indeed, been roused to participation in political life, important measures like local self-government and a Norwegian national flag had been carried through, but the liberal tidal wave had already spent its force, and many of the most important features of the national program stranded on the shoals of reactionary public sentiment. In France the agitation carried on by

ducted the deliberations of the ministry with great wisdom; he sought to harmonize conflicting views and to create concord. In order to accomplish this he sometimes sacrificed even his own opinion, as he undoubtedly knew that frequent minority reports would weaken the recommendations of the ministry; and I am fully convinced that in his reports to the king he never sought to oppose the opinion once agreed upon." *Efterladte Optegnelser*, p. 276 f.

the radicals for the economic emancipation of the lower classes, and their defiance of all established rules and authorities, caused society to react for its own protection. Liberalism was branded as lawlessness, and peace and social order became the slogan. In Norway this new reaction received a ready welcome, not only among the official class, but even among the *bønder*, who still clung with characteristic conservatism to the old order of things. Faithful obedience to the established rules was once more regarded as the highest civic virtue. In literature the regular rhythm and polished verse of Welhaven were preferred to the more original and irregular style of Wergeland. "Statsborgeren," the only oppositional paper, had to be discontinued in 1837 for want of subscribers, and in the election of 1839 fifty-two officials and only thirty-five *bønder* were returned to the Storthing. The autocratic upper class had won a decided victory. The leaders of the *bønder*, Ueland, Fauchald, Neergaard, and Haagenstad, had been reëlected, but the liberalist leader, Hjelm, refused to accept reëlection, as he felt convinced that he could accomplish nothing against the reactionary majority. More conservative men like Sørenssen, Foss, and Riddervold became leaders in the Storthing. Sørenssen had become a conservative, Foss, "the idol of the nation," pursued a middle-of-the-road policy, and tried to bring about a reconciliation between the adherents of Wergeland and Welhaven, while the somber and dignified Riddervold was opposed to liberalist agitation both from principle and temperament. The issues which had been raised by Hjelm were allowed to rest. The Storthing of 1839 devoted its attention to economic questions and routine affairs about which no serious controversy could arise, and no stormy party debates disturbed the peace and quiet of the assembly. The king's constitutional amendments were, nevertheless, voted down as usual, and a new attempt was also made to repeal the Conventicle Act of 1741, which restricted religious liberty by forbidding laymen to preach the gospel. Under this act Hans Nielsen Hauge had been prosecuted and imprisoned, and it was justly regarded as a remnant of absolutism wholly foreign in spirit to the free institutions of Norway. A bill for the repeal of this law, passed in 1836, had been vetoed by the king, and when it was passed a second time in 1838 in the same form, the king again vetoed the measure.

In 1840 Count Wedel-Jarlsberg died, and King Charles John appointed as his successor another Norwegian nobleman, Løvenskiold, at that time Norwegian minister of state in Stockholm. The choice was undoubtedly made with the best intention, but it was less welcome than that of his popular predecessor. Løvenskiold was a man of limited talents and haughty bearing, who took a delight in being unpopular, and in thwarting the will of the people. He had advised the king to prorogue the Storthing; he had opposed the local self-government bill, and though he had held a number of high offices, it was generally thought that his arrogance far exceeded the services which he had rendered the state His chief associate in the ministry was J. H. Vogt, a capable official, who usually succeeded in carrying through the measures which he happened to favor. He could give the ministry the character of trustworthy administrative ability, but in his official duties as well as in character he was a spiritless pedant and typical reactionary, who never strayed from the old bureaucratic routine.[1] Both were ultra-conservative in their views, and sought to revive as far as possible the political policies and administrative practices of a bygone age. But as no organized party of opposition existed, the Vogt-Løvenskiold ministry remained in power during a long period.

The Storthing of 1842 was of the same general complexion as the one of 1839. The official class again received a safe majority, the elections returning fifty of their class and only forty-two bønder. The great issues were again carefully avoided, and attention was directed exclusively to such practical affairs as would arouse no serious conflict. The bill for the repeal of the Conventicle Act was passed a third time, and became a law without the king's signature. The adoption of a new criminal code was also a much needed reform, but the most important legislative work accomplished by this Storthing was the passage of laws establishing freedom of trade and industry. These laws were originated by A. M. Schweigaard, prominent as leader of the Intelligence party in the Wergeland-Welhaven controversy, who now appeared in the Storthing for the first time together with another new leader, Ludvig Kr. Daa, one of Wergeland's leading supporters. Both were very gifted men and editors

---

[1] Thv. Boeck, *Statsraad Jørgen Herman Vogt.*

of the leading party organs, Daa of "Granskeren," and Schweigaard of "Den Constitutionelle." And as they had been opponents in their student days because of different political and literary views, they found a new battleground on the floor of the Storthing. Hjelm had also been elected, but he was too feeble to take any active part in the work, and the leadership of the liberal faction naturally devolved on Daa, whose paper, "Granskeren," had become the organ of the opposition. Daa and his followers were accused of radicalism, but he had adopted the program of the Whig party of England, and, judged by modern standards, his liberalist ideas must be regarded as very moderate. He advocated a parliamentary form of government, the participation of the ministers in the deliberations of the Storthing, unrestricted religious liberty, the introduction of the jury system, and the maintenance of Norway's political independence in the union, measures which became the future political program of Norway, and which, in time, were carried through in conformity with the growth of democratic ideas. He opposed the bureaucratic spirit of the government, but he was distinctly conservative when he opposed complete industrial freedom and the parceling out of the lands of the *bønder*, which, in course of time, would have destroyed their power as a privileged class of landed proprietors.

Schweigaard was a man of extraordinary ability, but he was a learned jurist and political economist rather than a statesman. As professor of jurisprudence he had won a great and well-merited reputation. "The students of jurisprudence," says Sars, "were the leaders in academic and fashionable circles in the capital, and to them Schweigaard was the teacher and master above all others. He possessed to an eminent degree the qualities of the distinguished practical jurist — lucidity of thought, precision, sober realistic judgment, the ability to criticise and to analyze every question of jurisprudence so that the characteristic features could come clearly to view in every instance. He represented in such a perfect and almost ideal way the jurist's view of life and society that by his younger colleagues he was regarded as a sort of oracle, by whose words they could swear without further investigation." [1] In poli-

---

[1] J. E. Sars, *Norges politiske Historie 1815–1885*, p. 299. Ebbe Hertzberg, *Nordmænd i det 19de Aarhundrede, A. M. Schweigaard.*

tics he was a Conservative, representing views akin to those of Løvenskiold and Vogt, and it was certain that he would be opposed to the issues raised by the liberalists relative to Norway's rights in the union. But as political scientist he held very advanced views, and in this field he rendered his country services which proved to be of epoch-making importance. As member of the royal commissions appointed in 1838 and 1839 to revise the laws of commerce, and to readjust the tariff schedules, he elaborated a system of free trade which he succeeded in incorporating in the new tariff law of 1842. The principle of free competition in trade and industry was now substituted for the mercantile system of protective tariff, trade monopolies, and special privileges hitherto adhered to. In the field of economics Schweigaard was so opposed to all artificial restraint that even Daa, who was in favor of free industry in a general way, regarded him as a radical whose views were revolutionary. But the principle of free competition once established brought about a rapid increase in the volume of trade, and laid the foundation for a new era of prosperity, so sorely needed in Norway at that time. A measure like the new tariff law was passed without much opposition, as it harmonized with the views and business spirit of the age. A betterment of conditions after so serious a financial and industrial depression must have appeared like a godsend, and Schweigaard became the hero who was able to lead the nation out of the slough of economic despond. Daa was less fortunate. The political policy of which he became the advocate could reckon but few supporters. It embraced the same views which Wergeland and Hjelm had sought in vain to make the platform of a strong liberal party organization; but the *bønder* had failed to grasp the significance of these issues, and as their group in the Storthing formed an organized opposition of which Daa became one of the leaders, he was no better situated than Hjelm had been before him, nor did he become any more successful. All important measures which he advocated, the *bønder* refused to support. Even a proposed amendment to the constitution for the repeal of the article excluding the Jews from the kingdom was vigorously resisted. Their narrow-minded policy of promoting the interests only of their own class made the organization of a liberal party impossible, and forced Daa like Hjelm into tragic political isolation.

The *bønder* were yet too wrapped up in their old class hatreds, too clannish, and too jealous of their own special rights to understand Daa's statesmanlike policy, or to attempt to consolidate all available forces into a strong liberal party.

59. Oscar I. Romanticism and Pan-Scandinavianism

The struggle between the king and the Storthing, which once occupied the attention of all political leaders in Norway, had now subsided, partly because of the more conciliatory attitude of the aged king, but partly also because of the reactionary character of the ministry and the Storthing, and when Charles John died, March 8, 1844, at the age of eighty, he was deeply mourned by all parties and classes. His successor, Oscar I., who was forty-five years of age, was in every way a contrast to his robust, majestic, impulsive, and energetic father. He was very quiet, thin, pale, and of a sickly appearance. He had visited Norway several times. For a period he had even been viceroy. He was well known, but because of his quiet ways no one knew his views, and it was generally feared that he was in sympathy with the Swedish aristocracy, who were believed to entertain no friendly feelings for the liberal political institutions of Norway. P. C. Holst, member of the Norwegian ministry in Stockholm, says that during Charles John's last illness their conversation often centered on the very improbable supposition that the crown prince might wish to play the same rôle in Norway as did King Ernest in Hanover; that he might refuse to take an oath on the constitution, unless some modifications were made in it, as, for example, that the king should receive absolute veto. "That we could suppose anything of the kind," he says, "or even entertain a thought of the possibility, was due to our knowledge of the hostile attitude of the Swedish aristocracy, and, perhaps, in part also to the reticence which the crown prince, no doubt from good policy, always maintained towards all Norwegians. We also agreed upon what we should do if so unexpected a situation should develop." [1] Oscar I. proved, however, to be a fair-minded and well-intentioned king. He did not venture upon great undertakings, but even his first acts as ruler served to dispel all lingering mistrust. So soon

[1] P. C. Holst, *Efterladte Optegnelser*, p. 314 f.

as he had taken his oath as king, he issued an order that in all Norwegian documents the name of Norway should precede that of Sweden, and not long afterward it was decreed that on the union coat of arms the Norwegian coat of arms should occupy one-half instead of one-third of the field as hitherto. Norway also received her own man-of-war flag. These concessions, which the king called his dowry to the Norwegian people, were of importance as showing his good intentions, but their real value was materially reduced, since they were to be looked upon as a present from the king rather than as a right justly claimed by Norway as a sovereign kingdom. The not very welcome provision was also attached that a union sign should be inserted in all flags both in Norway and Sweden.

It has already been observed that after the political reaction had ended the storm and stress caused by the clashes of parties and the animated discussions of great issues in the Storthing, an era of peace and good feeling, such as Welhaven had been longing for, finally came. The Patriot agitation had died away, the ultra-national program had, for the time being, lost its charm, and the Intelligence party could cultivate "good taste" practically unopposed. Their society "Kringla" dominated social life in the capital, and no sound of robust laughter or noise of national merrymaking was allowed to penetrate to their exclusive and refined morning and evening parties. Only the most conservative refinement and the taste for foreign elegance could be tolerated in these élite circles, where the life of Paris and Copenhagen was reproduced even in manners and conversation. The social tone harmonized with the general revival of aristocratic spirit. In literature a similar love of polished conformity to rule prevailed, as the younger poets had accepted the poetic-æsthetic views of Welhaven, who acted as the *arbiter elegantiarum* of the upper classes.

But the intellectual forces, which had been stimulated to activity by the events of 1814 and the great patriotic revival of Henrik Wergeland, were producing a new creative epoch in Norwegian art and literature. The dreamy mysticism of the romanticists had also reached Norway. Their love of heroic traditions of the past, of the sentimental, the supernatural, became associated with an intense interest in nature, and the admiration for the national customs and

PLATE XIV

OLE GABRIEL UELAND.

A. M. SCHWEIGAARD.

OSCAR I.

JOHN NEERGAARD.

LUDVIG KRISTENSEN DAA.

rural virtues of the common people so diligently fostered by Henrik Wergeland. The young artists and writers turned with rapture to their own picturesque mountain scenery, and the charming freedom and simplicity of the rural life among the pineclad mountains, where folk-songs and fairy-tales lived on the people's lips like a fountain of poesy which had welled in primeval purity from remote ages. Welhaven himself had prophesied that there the sources of true poesy were to be found, and he led the way into the new region of art in his ballads, in which he expressed with rare truth and beauty the dramatic episodes and deep feeling of the popular traditions. Gradually the rich stores of folk-literature were discovered, like some prehistoric mound made to yield its unique treasures. In 1833 A. Faye published his "Norske Folkesagn," traditions from early times, which still lived among the people. These echoes from the past were given a warm welcome by the romanticists, and Welhaven chose from this work the themes for many of his ballads and romances. In 1840 Jørgen Moe published a small collection of folk-songs, "Norske Viser og Stev," but far more important is M. B. Landstad's great collection, "Norske Folkeviser," which appeared in 1853, and Sophus Bugge's smaller collection, "Gamle norske Folkeviser," of 1858. Landstad, who was clergyman at Kviteseid, and later at Seljord and Fredrikshald, was a gifted poet, and he is especially noted as a psalmist. His hymnbook is still in universal use in Norway, and is regarded as a work of rare excellence.

For some years the two friends Jørgen Moe and P. Chr. Asbjørnsen had been engaged in collecting fairy-tales, and in 1842 they began the publication of their first collection, "Norske Folkeeventyr samlede og fortalte af Asbjørnsen og Moe." At first the literary circles were skeptical, as they considered these stories a literature only fit for the nursery, but the skepticism vanished when they discovered in these tales the humor, poesy, and fascinating life of the common people, and learned to know Norway as the land of charming scenery, such as they had never before seen. Every year during the summer months the two friends traveled through the more remote districts in search of new stories, but in 1853 Moe abandoned the work to accept a curacy in Sigdal. In 1863 he became clergyman in Drammen, and later bishop of the diocese of Christiansand. He was a gifted poet, and though his poetical works are not voluminous, they contain many highly cherished productions. Asbjørnsen, who was a natural scientist, and loved to roam about in the mountains and forests, continued the work begun by the two. He advanced beyond the views and tastes of the romanticists, as he acquired a more thorough knowledge both of nature and of the life of the people, and in his "Norske Huldreeventyr og Folkesagn" [1] he contributed a series of sketches and short stories in which he depicts nature and the life of the people with charming realism. The work is of such rare excellence that it surpasses anything written in that field by his contemporaries. Through the work especially of Asbjørnsen and Moe the doors were opened to the charming mountain scenery and tranquil peasant life of Norway. The vast perpetual snowfields on the inland mountain plateau, the *Jøtunheim*, were discovered, and tourist life took its beginning. The city people, who hitherto had scarcely been known to cross their own city limits, now spent the summer among the mountains, where new raptures met the eye at every turn. Poets and prose writers like B. Herre, Andreas Munch, P. A. Jensen, Theodor Kjerulf, C. P. Riis, Nicolai Østgaard, Hans Schultze, and other members of the romantic school, had become charmed with the thought of nature and the quaint fairy (*Hulder*) who herded her cattle in the woods, and paid her mystic visits to the herdsmen and the dairymaid when night threw her mantle over the mountains, or when the sun smiled among the trees in the forest. When the evening shadows fell, the *Fossegrim* could be heard playing his fiddle in the waterfall, and the love-sick *Nøk* would sob beside the brook. These ideas of the common people, now for the first time revealed to the imagination of the cultured classes in the midst of so unique a natural scenery, proved to be a most powerful stimulus to poetic sentiment. The better they learned to know the hitherto unknown common people, the more of old art and culture they found to study and to preserve. The folk-melodies, no less charming than the folk-tales, were collected by L. M. Lindeman, and soon their quaint strains were reëchoed in the musical compositions of Nordraak, Halvdan Kjerulf, and Ole Bull.[2] The arts of woodcarving,

---

[1] Henrik Jæger, *Norske Forfattere.*
[2] *Nordmænd i det 19de Aarhundrede, Ole Bull, Halvdan Kjerulf.*

PLATE XV

JØRGEN MOE.

P. CHR. ASBJØRNSEN.

IVAR AASEN.

A. O. VINJE.

tapestry weaving, rose painting, and the like, which flourished among the *bønder*, were made subjects of special study, and became the source of new inspiration in national painting and decorative art. In architecture a new departure was created through the study of the distinctively Norwegian style of wood architecture especially developed in the old wooden churches, of which many are still found in the mountain valleys of Norway.[1] In 1844 a society, *Foreningen til norske Fortidsmindesmerkers Bevaring*, was organized to preserve these venerable structures from destruction or decay. The new intellectual awakening caused by the national regeneration had produced a creative era in every field. The art of painting also received its masters. J. C. Dahl, Hans Gude, and Adolph Tidemand painted the scenery of fjords and mountains, national costumes, life, and character of the people with unexcelled beauty of composition and delicacy of coloring. The national spirit had asserted its own sovereignty, and whatever might be the opinion regarding literature and art as such, the view of Henrik Wergeland that all true national development must spring from the people's own thought and sentiment could no longer be a subject of controversy.

Where the poets and artists led the way, the more analytic spirit of scientific research followed, as the new material which had suddenly been brought to light offered rare opportunities for scholarly activity in many fields, especially in archæology, philology, folklore, and mythology. Especially noteworthy are two distinctively new movements which developed under the influence of romanticism, but which soon found their own paths, and continued to grow, wholly independent of it. Being devoted to critical research, these penetrated deeper, and were able to show the continuity of the historical development of the Norwegian people, and their former literary and intellectual achievements, at that time greatly obscured and generally misunderstood because of Norway's unfortunate position during the long union with Denmark. These movements were the Norwegian historical school, developed by R. Keyser and P. A. Munch, and the national linguistic movement, originated by the philologist Ivar Aasen. Keyser and Munch had become coworkers in the

[1] L. Dietrichson, *De norske Stavkirker; Vore Fædres Verk, Norges Kunst i Middelalderen.*

field of Norwegian history.[1] Keyser, who was appointed lecturer in history, and later professor in the University of Christiania, introduced the study of Old Norse language and literature, and exerted great influence, as well through his carefully prepared lectures as through his historical works. He was the originator of the new theory regarding the prehistoric migrations to the Scandinavian peninsula, which, though no longer regarded as the correct view, proved to be a valuable working hypothesis. It attempted to show that the Norwegians from the most remote times had been a distinct people, even because of their origin, since they were supposed to have come from the regions east of the Baltic, and not from the south, as hitherto believed. It did great service by destroying the older and wholly unscientific views of the Danish historian Suhm, and by placing historical research on a strictly scientific basis. His pupil and younger associate, P. A. Munch, seems for a time to have shared his opinions on all essential points, but he soon passed beyond his older associate to more advanced views. Munch possessed most remarkable talents and versatility. Not only is he the most voluminous writer in Norwegian literature, though he died in his fifty-third year, but his capacity for work, his memory, his intuitive insight and ability to trace the hidden meaning in every old relic and manuscript were all alike extraordinary. When we consider, not only his historical writings, but also his work as critical scholar in various fields, the tribute paid him on a later occasion by his erstwhile opponent the Danish scholar C. A. E. Jessen that he was "the greatest historian in the North" seems well merited. In the fields of archæology, geography, mythology, philology, and runology he carried on extensive original research, and contributed works of great value. But more important still are his treatises on various historical problems, in four large volumes, his critical editions of numerous historical sources, a work in which he and Keyser coöperated with C. R. Unger, and his discovery and collection of new sources, especially in the archives of the Vatican. His chief work, "Det norske Folks His-

---

[1] P. A. Munch, *Om den saakaldte historiske Skole i Norge.* J. E. Sars, *Samlede Verker*, vol. IV., p. 192 ff. Chr. Brinchmann, *P. A. Munch. Nordmænd i det 19de Aarhundrede, P. A. Munch.* Laura Larsen-Naur, *P. A. Munch, Levnet og Breve.*

PLATE XVI

P. A. MUNCH.

NIELS HENRIK ABEL.

OLE BULL.

EDVARD GRIEG.

torie," in eight large octavo volumes, is a repository of scholarly knowledge which will always continue to be one of the chief sources of Norwegian history.[1]

It became Munch's great task to show Norway's true position in the historical and cultural development of the North, to lift the veil of obscurity which had fallen upon the nation because of unfortunate political circumstances in the union period. It had hitherto been customary to regard the mythology, the Eddas, and sagas as products of an ancient culture, produced by the Germanic spirit in a past so remote that the Scandinavian race was still a unit. These treasures were, therefore, regarded as a heritage common to all the Northern peoples, in which, however, Norway was supposed to have little or no share. Old scholars had developed a theory no longer doubted at the time, that the Edda songs, the myths, and the sagas, had originated as oral traditions in southern Sweden and the Danish islands, the home and center of ancient Scandinavian culture, it was thought, and that the already finished product had been accidentally committed to writing in Norway and Iceland. This theory Munch proved to be wholly untenable. He showed that the original Northern tongue had been divided into three distinct dialects: the old Norse (including the Old Icelandic), the Old Danish, and Old Swedish; that mythological and heroic traditions had been divided in the same way, before the Edda mythology originated; that it is wholly Norwegian, and not a common Northern heritage. He showed further that the myths, as they now exist, are of no very great antiquity, but that many show distinct traces of Christian influence. The Eddas and the sagas he proved to be purely Norwegian-Icelandic literature, and showed that the theory of a joint Northern heritage has to be wholly discarded. His views at first caused most determined opposition, as they were regarded as revolutionary, as an attempt to rob the sister nations of their proudest possessions; but his theory was soon confirmed by other distinguished

---

[1] As a motto to this work he has chosen the following words from Niebuhr: "Ich werde suchen die Kritik der Geschichte nicht nach dunkelen Gefühlen, sondern forschend, auszuführen, nicht ihre Resultate, welche nur blinde Meinungen stiften, sondern die Untersuchungen selbst in ihren ganzen Umfange fortragen."

scholars, like Konrad Maurer, Sophus Bugge, C. A. E. Jessen, Finnur Jónsson, and others. The Norwegian people thus entered into their own possessions, and instead of being the poorest in ancient intellectual culture, they had suddenly appeared as the richest. By the verdict of the scholars they had been given full title to their own past achievements, a fact which strengthened the national spirit, and created new confidence in the worth of their own native culture. This confidence was further strengthened through the national linguistic movement originated by Ivar Aasen.

This untutored peasant boy, born in most humble circumstances, too poor to attend school, rose by his own efforts and native genius to be one of the most learned scholars and influential leaders of his age. Professor Halvdan Koht says of him : "Ivar Aasen — scholar and leader of the people — leader of the people because he was a scholar — is so strange a phenomenon in history that it may well cause wonder. A poor peasant boy, who never took a single examination, advances to leadership in philology, and brings a whole new language into the realm of scientific study. This quiet, retiring investigator originates a movement which divides a whole nation, creates a new literature, stirs up a growing struggle in state and community, in church and school. One cannot understand the history of Norway during the last sixty years without knowing Ivar Aasen, the father of Norwegian philological study, of the *Landsmaal* and the *maalstræv*." [1]

Aasen was born in 1813 in Søndmør.[2] At the age of twelve he became an orphan, and for the next five years he had to work on the little homestead where he was reared. With passionate love for study he read all the books to which he had any access, and in 1831 he was appointed teacher in his home parish. This gave him better opportunity for study, and with the assistance of Provost Thoresen, he devoted himself to the study of German, French, English, and Latin. His favorite study was grammar, he writes in his autobiography, and when in 1835 he became private tutor

---

[1] *Symra*, Decorah, Ia., vol. IX., p. 145 ff.

[2] Ivar Aasen, *Skrifter i Samling*, vol. I., p. 1 ff., *Selvbiografi*. Arne Garborg, Anders Hovden, Halvdan Koht, *Ivar Aasen, Ei Minneskrift um Livsverke hans.*

in the home of Chaplain Daa, he conceived the idea of attempting
to write the grammar of some language. "The language selected,"
he says, "was the one which I could call my own, and which I did
not find treated in any grammar. Why, I thought, are not the
Norwegian dialects treated like other languages? Why do we
not find grammatical works and dictionaries where the forms of the
words, their genders and conjugations, are given? Is not our dialect
or the pure old Norwegian tongue worthy of more thorough investigation? Such a work, I thought, can only be done by one who is
born in a peasant's cottage, and I will attempt it." In order to
better qualify himself for this task he also studied Old Norse and
Swedish, and in 1839 he wrote a grammar of his own dialect. He
also devoted himself to the study of botany, and gathered and classified a large collection of plants from his own neighborhood. A
desire to see the world, or rather, perhaps, a deep yearning to find
some suitable opportunity to employ his talents, drove him to visit
Bergen,[1] where he was introduced to Bishop Neumann, who examined his grammar and herbarium. The bishop marveled at the
learning of the unschooled peasant lad, and wrote an article about
him in the "Bergen Stiftstidende." This attracted the attention of
the able philologist F. M. Bugge, rector of the cathedral school
in Trondhjem, who soon discovered in Ivar Aasen an extraordinary
linguistic talent, the kind of man he had been looking for, who could
devote himself to the study of the Norwegian dialects. He secured
for him a small yearly stipend from the *Kongelige norske Videnskabs-
Selskab*, of which he was the president, and during the next four years
Aasen traveled through nearly all parts of the country, studying the
dialects, and gathering material for his great works. In 1848 he
published "Det norske Folkesprogs Grammatik," and in 1850 appeared his dictionary of the dialects, "Ordbog over det norske
Folkesprog," works which opened new domains for linguistic research,
and gave new vigor to the growing national spirit. Of the grammar
P. A. Munch said: "This work is not only an ornament to our literature, but it is a work of national importance, of which the whole
nation may well be proud. It reveals the Northern nationality of

¹ Ivar Aasen, *Dagbog paa en Reise til Bergen, Skrifter i Samling*, vol. II.,
p. 75 ff.

the Norwegian people more clearly than any work which has hitherto appeared; it shows that the more than thousand-year-old Norse tongue still lives among the people with a purity of accent which we do not find even in Iceland. This we learn in such a way that we not only have a vague feeling of it, as hitherto, but it is clearly, thoroughly, and systematically shown and proven, so that no shadow of doubt can exist. . . . For us it is a source of pride and consolation to know that in spite of unfortunate circumstances we have been able to preserve our language in so original a form."

About Aasen's dictionary he wrote: "The dictionary furnishes proof of the existence of the Old Norse language among us in an almost unchanged form. It shows clearly that it is only the grammatical forms which have disappeared from the now spoken language, while nearly the whole vocabulary has been preserved unchanged. . . . The dictionary in connection with the grammar is a national monument, to whose author every patriotic Norwegian owes the deepest gratitude." In 1853 followed a third work: "Prøver af Landsmaalet i Norge." "These three works," says Koht, "constitute the foundation for his work. They contain both his great scholarly achievement and his new linguistic program. They made him renowned; they carried his name even to foreign lands, and laid the foundation for a new national work." [1]

Ivar Aasen was not only a scholar, but a patriot. He had begun his career with a desire to see his own tongue accorded the same respect as other languages, and his study of the dialects had shown him that in them the old Norwegian language was still preserved. Norse had once been the greatest literary language of the North; why should it now be despised? In the introduction to "Det norske Folkesprogs Grammatik" he says: "This language might have been cultivated as a literary language, and might have had a large literature; but it may also for the present be regarded as the vernacular of the common people without any literature. In all events this is the true Norwegian language. We see no reason why it should be regarded as inferior to Swedish or Danish; we find no justification for calling it undeveloped and unfit for higher purposes. We can

---

[1] Ivar Aasen, *Atterførsla, Skrifter i Samling*, vol. II., p. 194 ff. *Ivar Aasen og Verket hans, Syn og Segn*, August, 1913.

not understand that it should contribute to the honor of the common people to despise this language, and to seek to change it for another." Aasen studied the dialects, not only from scientific interest, but with a fixed purpose to restore to the Norwegians their own language, that also in this field they might enter into full possession of their own. As early as 1836 he wrote in an article entitled "Om det norske Sprog," that since the three Northern peoples can not have the same language, each ought to have their own. "As we have lately been freed from an overlordship of another kingdom," he says, "and have the right to establish our own household, the time might now be opportune to think of this." [1] In order to realize this plan he not only collected the dialect words and idioms, but by selecting the forms most commonly used, and the ones which corresponded most closely to the Old Norse, he was able to systematize the dialects into a uniform language — the *Landsmaal*. This language, which contains as nearly as possible the essential features of all the dialects, could readily be adopted by all, he thought. The people in the rural districts would recognize it as their own tongue, and it would gradually replace the official Danish language, which continued to be Danish even though its vocabulary had been enriched by many Norwegian words.

It was clear that the efforts to introduce the *Landsmaal* as the official and literary language would precipitate a struggle of the most determined sort between the officials and the *bønder*, or, rather, between the city people, who favored the Danish-Norwegian official language, and the country people, who spoke their own Norwegian vernacular. The *bønder* demanded, not only their political rights under the constitution, but they would also claim the right to use their own language, and to have their own native culture duly respected. This new issue, the *maalstræv*, precipitated the conflict between the *bønder* and the officials on both flanks, so to speak, and Aasen and Ueland, both of humble parentage, became the leaders of the rural population in this cultural and political struggle.

If any one had doubted that a literature could be produced in the *Landsmaal*, he was soon to be disillusioned. Aasen himself, who was a gifted poet as well as a scholar, has left poetic works of rare value

[1] Ivar Aasen, *Skrifter i Samling*, vol. III., p. 65.

written in this language. His somewhat younger contemporary, A. O. Vinje, a peasant boy like himself, and one of the greatest lyric poets in Northern literature, wrote exclusively in the *Landsmaal*. Many authors both in prose and poetry soon appeared who gave strength to the new movement. Hitherto unknown and unused forces, which had been lying dormant in the people's national life and character, had been stirred to creative activity by Aasen's work. The revived national vigor had created new demands, but it also added great treasures to the nation's store of intellectual culture. The *Landsmaal* seems to have small chance of being adopted as the language of Norway, but it has inaugurated a new development of the Danish-Norwegian language which is constantly reducing the chasm between the two forms of speech, and ultimately, it is hoped, the two will merge in one literary language.[1]

Another movement quite closely associated with romanticism was the Pan-Scandinavianism, which developed especially during this period. The dream of a united North was to a large extent of a sentimental nature. It flourished almost exclusively among the students, and found nourishment in the same interest for the traditions of the past which formed the basis of the whole romantic movement. In some respects, however, it was a revival in a new form of a feeling which had grown strong on several earlier occasions, that the Scandinavian North ought to stand united for its own protection. It has already been observed how the Danish historian F. Sneedorff in 1792 had advocated a political Pan-Scandinavian program, lest Russia and Germany should "join hands across the Baltic Sea." Prominent men in all three countries supported the idea, and the words *Scandinavia, Scandinavian,* and *Scandia* came into common use at that time.[2] In 1809–1810 great enthusiasm was developed for the union of the three kingdoms under one king, and an attempt was made to elect King Frederick VI. of Denmark-Norway successor to the Swedish throne. Again the fascinating thought was eagerly supported by many of the ablest writers, especially by N. F. S. Grundtvig, distinguished scholar and ecclesiastic, the man of

---

[1] Moltke Moe, *Nationalitet og Kultur, Samtiden,* January, 1909.

[2] Julius Clausen, *Skandinavismen historisk fremstillet.* J. Løvland, *Den politiske Skandinavisme, Samtiden,* 1904.

great visions, who looked upon the North as one country with one language, the Northern mother tongue. In general, however, the Danish people were not much in favor of the union of the three Scandinavian countries under a common king. It was not a movement based on a general desire of the people, but a political plan supported by poets and theorists, a hothouse-engendered idea which could not be transplanted into practical life. Frederick VI. was not elected Swedish crown prince, and the plan of a dynastic union of the Scandinavian countries quickly collapsed.

After Denmark had been forced to cede Norway by the treaty of Kiel, 1813, the relation between Sweden and Denmark remained hostile for a time, but romanticism, which had created a new interest in the traditions of the past, awakened again the Pan-Scandinavian sentiment, especially among the students of the Northern universities. After 1837 the students and professors at the universities of Lund and Copenhagen began to pay each other friendly visits. These were repeated on ever larger scale, and soon grew into a movement of great proportions. The climax seems to have been reached in 1843, when the students of Copenhagen and Lund visited Upsala, and in 1845, when another great festival was held in Copenhagen, where the students from Upsala, Lund, and Christiania were the guests of their Danish friends. On the latter occasion the father of Danish romanticism, the poet Adam Oehlenschlæger, was greeted as the greatest champion of the Scandinavian idea. It was stated that by reviving the interest for the traditions of the past he had aroused the young men of the North to new enthusiasm and love for achievements, that he had renewed the ties of friendship between the sister nations. In Sweden the historian Geijer and the poet Tegnér had exerted a like influence as Oehlenschlæger and Grundtvig in Denmark. A romantic literature had been created in both countries, largely based on the sagas and Northern heroic traditions. Tegnér's "Fridtjofs Saga," and Oehlenschlæger's dramas, "Axel og Valborg," "Haakon Jarl," "Helge," "Tordenskjold," and others, reveal a literary Pan-Scandinavianism, which comes even more clearly to view in the lyric poesy of the age. Typical are songs like : "Længe var Nordens herlige Stamme " and "Unge Gjenbyrds Liv i Norden," by the Danish poet C. Ploug, and "Mulmet sank det svale," by C.

Hostrup. In Norway, J. S. Welhaven and Andreas Munch wrote songs of like contents, and the Scandinavian idea even fired the enthusiasm of Bjørnstjerne Bjørnson.[1]

In so far as the Scandinavian movement tended to create a friendly feeling, to sweep away old misunderstanding, and foster a livelier intercourse between the Northern peoples, it exerted a beneficial influence. It rested, it is true, on no firmer foundation than a wave of evanescent sentiment, and even as a theory it suffered from the

[1] In a song written as a dedication to a collection of poems published in 1870 the following stanzas are especially noteworthy in this connection:

Jeg sender disse sange hen
paa venners bøn til kvinner, mænn
i Nordens trende lande.
At Finlands folk blandt dem er med
paa sangen under Nørreled,
maa jeg med tak jo sanne.

    *   *   *   *   *

Selv gaar jeg paa min sanger vei
med ærefrygt først ind til dig,
du største aand i Norden,*
som vred profetisk varsled gry
bak Nordens tunge morgensky,
der skalv i lyn og torden.

Men siden blid bag hav og hæld
av sagas og av troens væld
paa bondens sæd har spillet; —
nu snefjæll-hvit paa nitti aar
av tidens strøm tilbake faar
dit eget høie billed!

Til dig saa, i hvis sanger-vaar
"de tusen sjöars" Finland staar
og vemodsmægtig toner!†
Vor stammes aand i evig sus
gaar grænsevakt i sangens brus
mot Østens millioner.

Men staar jeg i vor egen gaard,
et stjernebilled øiet slaar
med alt sit rike under.
Det lyser HENRIK WERGELAND
utover Norges bleke land
i mindets klare stunder.

  * N. F. S. Grundtvig.   † John Ludvig Runeberg.

very serious defect of allowing no room for the distinct national individuality of the three peoples. But it had sounded a chord of sympathy and friendship which might have continued to reverberate with still deeper meaning, if the whole idea had not been wrecked by the attempt to press it into a service for which it was not adequately adapted. In Denmark, the real home of the movement, the hope seems to have been entertained from the outset that the Scandinavian sentiment would culminate in a political union, which might be used by the Danes in repelling German aggression in Schleswig-Holstein. To them this sentiment assumed the character of a distinct political program, to which the more sanguine leaders could pin their hope of successfully maintaining a dynastic policy, which was represented to be identical with the safety and welfare of the whole North. In a speech at the students' festival in 1843, C. Ploug outlined this program as follows: "It is especially this fear for the existence of the Northern nationalities, very strong among the Danes, which moves us to join you to-day rather than to-morrow. The fight has already begun. It rages on the border in the beautiful land between the Eider and the Kongeaa. Through negligence as well on the part of the government as of the people, the Germans have been able in the course of the last fifty years to occupy one-half of old Schleswig, and they threaten arrogantly to plant their victorious banner on the farthest point of Skagen. The battle is not ours alone. It is also yours. Our common nationality is at stake, and if we should need your help against a powerful and active party led by a Most Serene Highness with a bodyguard of aristocrats and lawyers, you must be ready." This appeal was repeated with renewed fervor in 1845 by the fiery Danish orator Orla Lehmann. He stirred the excitable students to the wildest enthusiasm, and in the midst of this ecstasy he exacted from them a solemn vow to support the common cause even unto death. The safety of Denmark was, indeed, a matter of the greatest concern to all Scandinavians, and the desire to aid the sister state in the hour of danger was the outgrowth, not only of a praiseworthy national sentiment, but of a correct political instinct. But the enthusiastic pledges of an assemblage of students proved to be but a weak support for a political policy which sooner or later would embroil the whole North in a war with the great continental powers. Outside of the academic circles the Swedes were not much in sympathy with the political program of the Danes, and in Norway the Scandinavian sentiment did not gain much strength until after 1848. The romantic idealism, which gave the movement its real charm, had then grown so strong that the Scandinavian idea received general and earnest support. But it turned people's attention away from the vital issues at home to chimerical plans abroad, and served mainly to strengthen the growing reactionary spirit. The most vital interests of Norway were not identical with those of Denmark.[1] Past experiences had shown it, and coolheaded statesmen would hesitate to involve the country in new wars, from which no benefit could be derived. When the hour of trial came, Scandinavianism vanished like a fair delusion, and left Denmark alone with her troubles and disappointments.

60. POLITICAL REACTION. THE LABOR MOVEMENT

Neither J. A. Hjelm nor Ludvig Kr. Daa had succeeded in rallying the opposition in the Storthing to the support of the Norwegian political policy which they advocated. Their ideas had been too lofty, their views too statesmanlike to be fully understood and appreciated. In 1845 Ueland, the leader of the *bønder*, found an able assistant in Søren Jaabæk, who now took his seat in the Storthing for the first time, and Daa was succeeded by A. B. Stabell, editor of "Morgenbladet," a shrewd and cunning tactician, who cared little for general principles of statesmanship, but watched his opportunity to gain such victories as circumstances would allow. The *bønder* representation in the Storthing had increased in strength, and through the aid of some representatives from other classes they controlled a majority of the votes. But instead of directing their attention to the question of the relation to Sweden, they raised the issue of greater economy in the administration, and attacked the privileges still enjoyed by the officials. But the attempt of the *bønder* to exercise the right granted them by the constitution was vigorously resisted by the bureaucracy, who were still intrenched in power. They feared nothing so much as a government by the people. They

[1] J. Løvland, *Den politiske Skandinavisme, Samtiden*, 1904.

saw their power and privileges threatened, and looked upon the effort of the *bønder* to gain political power as a grave danger to the good old social order. They began to look upon the constitution, not as a bulwark of constitutional liberty, but as a people's charter which deprived them of their rights and privileges. In a book "Om den norske Konstitution," published in 1845, the great jurist Bernhard Dunker apparently sought to defend the constitution, when in reality the work is a vigorous attack upon it. He would not blame the constitution alone for the deplorable political situation, he said. He thought that, if interpreted in the right way, it might prove a very satisfactory fundamental law, *i.e.* if so interpreted that the bureaucrats would retain their power. But it would be especially necessary, he thought, to repeal article seventy-nine, which gave the Storthing the power to pass laws without the king's sanction. The king should be given absolute veto, so that "the enlightened part of the nation might have full confidence in the work of the national legislature and regard it as their representative." [1] The bureaucracy no longer feared that the king might infringe on the rights of the Norwegian people. They began to regard him as the chief representative of the old social order, with whom they must unite in order to successfully oppose the growing democratic spirit and the power of the people. This reactionary tendency was clearly shown in connection with the impeachment of J. H. Vogt, one of the leading members of the ministry, for advising the king to veto a bill passed by the Storthing. The impeachment was based on two charges, but Vogt was acquitted, though only on the supposition that he had misunderstood the provisions of the constitution. The trial showed that the Storthing was determined to defend its honor and dignity; that a minister who should attempt to disregard its authority would be promptly called to account. But the bureaucrats hailed Vogt as a martyr whose just rights had been infringed upon, who had been victimized by unscrupulous demagogues. The tension between the conservative officials and the *bønder* had developed into an antagonism, which grew even more determined during the next session in 1848. The *bønder* could again control a majority of the votes,

---

[1] J. E. Sars, *Norges politiske Historie 1815–1885*, p. 386. Erik Vullum, *Kristian Magnus Falsen*, p. 57 ff.

and they felt that the time had come for more aggressive tactics against the reactionary Vogt-Løvenskiold ministry and its supporters. It was clear that the ministry no longer represented the views of the majority, that its administrative policy no longer conformed to the will of the people as expressed through the national legislature. In 1845 some members of the opposition, including Ueland and Fauchald, had attempted to prepare a memorial to the king, expressing lack of confidence in the ministry, but their courage finally failed them, and the matter was dropped. In 1848 the attempt was renewed. Fauchald, Ueland, Krogness, and Stabell prepared a memorial to the king, in which they stated very forcibly the principle of parliamentary government, and showed that the Storthing could no longer have confidence in a ministry which had become the representative of a bureaucratic coterie. But before the memorial was considered by the Storthing, it was printed in "Morgenbladet," and aroused a storm of indignation among the Conservatives. The leaders of the opposition again lost courage, and were satisfied to let the matter be buried by the committee to which it had been referred. The *bønder* and their leaders had again shown that they lacked the necessary experience and self-confidence to carry through in practice the principles of popular government in opposition to the able reactionary bureaucracy. But their greatest weakness was, perhaps, that they were in reality not a liberal party, but a faction opposed to many of the essential features of true democracy. They had prevented the passage of a constitutional amendment granting the Jews the right to reside in the kingdom with the same privileges as other citizens, and they would not grant the ministry the right to participate in the deliberations of the Storthing, an essential feature of parliamentary government.[1]

By some writers the Norwegian *bønder* have been called peasants, but this is quite misleading. They are the freeholders, the landowners of the nation, who until quite recently exercised in their districts all power and influence not specifically delegated to the

---

[1] The feature in the Norwegian constitution that the members of the cabinet should not be present in the Storthing was borrowed from the American constitution, says Bjørnstjerne Bjørnson, *Den norske Forfatningskamp*, p. 17.

government, and who, after 1814, waged the battle with the clergy and the officials of the crown for political supremacy. Many bønder are landed proprietors of considerable wealth, and in some districts they constitute a sort of untitled rustic aristocracy. But as a class they are not wealthy. Their farms are usually small, and they are obliged to work hard to support their families. In no country has property been more evenly distributed than in Norway, but at this time the distribution of land was not so thorough as it needed to be in a country where the tillable area is small. A large and dependent peasant class, the husmænd, still existed who owned no land, but leased small parcels from the bønder, for which they were to render a certain amount of service at a stipulated price. As the right to vote was restricted by the provision that all voters in the rural districts should be owners of land, neither the husmænd nor the laboring class in general had the right of suffrage. For them no room had yet been provided in the Norwegian political and social democracy, but the time would come when they would not be satisfied to remain deprived of all political rights.

The February Revolution in France in 1848 ushered in a new period of social unrest in Europe, and the despotic rulers found difficulty in subduing the growing liberal spirit. Since 1830 new and hitherto unknown revolutionary forces had been at work creating a hostile opposition to all existing order and ideas. General discontent accompanied by disregard for the hitherto acknowledged rules and authorities was increasing among the lower classes. They discovered that modern industrialism, the organization of capital, and the use of steam power and modern inventions in manufacture placed them face to face with economic and social conditions which threatened to reduce them to a serfdom no less galling than that from which political liberty was supposed to free them. Socialism, originated by St. Simon, and the communistic ideas of Fourier were spreading. The struggle had begun between the established feudalistic ideas and modern social tendencies. Capital and labor had clashed in their first great encounter, and the demand for social and economic equality raised by the French theorists was rapidly adopted by the struggling laboring classes as a doctrine foreshadowing a more felicitous future.

This social ferment, destined to produce so many changes, was first brought to Norway by a young student, Markus Thrane, born in Christiania in 1817. Thrane belonged to a good family, but his parents, though once wealthy, were early plunged into misfortune and poverty. As a young man Thrane had traveled in France and Switzerland, where he became acquainted with socialism, but because of poverty he was sent back to his native land as a vagabond. In 1840 he became a student at the University of Christiania, but he soon married, discontinued his studies, and founded a school at Lillehammer, where he lived for some years in most straitened circumstances. When the news of the French February Revolution reached Norway in 1848, an article signed "A Voice from the Country" appeared in "Morgenbladet," which attracted general attention. This "Voice" was Markus Thrane, who now made his début as a socialistic agitator. In 1848 he was made editor of "Drammens Adresse," which he soon made the most radical paper in the country, as he advocated French socialistic ideas, and raised his voice in behalf of the *husmænd* and laborers. He held that constitutional government, as it had been practiced, served to intrench the upper classes in power. In Norway the bureaucracy had been forced to divide their power with the *bønder*, but both classes had used their political power for their own advantage, and the so-called liberal opposition was nothing but an aristocracy struggling for their own freedom and power. He demanded universal suffrage, as "a so-called democratic constitution which deprives the poorer classes of all influence is a most deplorable and demoralizing form of government." Such ideas fearlessly expressed fairly startled the publishers and readers of "Drammens Adresse," and Thrane was discharged. But this only turned his energies into more practical channels. He was not a dreamer, as many supposed, but a talented agitator and an able organizer. He undertook to unite the laborers and the *husmænd*, and to organize them into clubs and societies so that they might learn to coöperate. But social conditions in Norway were not yet ripe for labor agitation. The city population was small, only 160,000 in all, and as the industries were undeveloped, the laboring classes in the cities numbered only 17,700 persons, 6700 industrial laborers, and 11,000 engaged in various other pursuits. In the country districts there were 47,000 laborers and 145,000 servants. In fact, the laboring class was still only a servant class, to whom modern labor conditions were unknown. But the *husmænd* numbered 58,049 as against 77,780 freeholders and 25,047 renters, and they were increasing in number, though the circumstances under which they were living were miserable enough. Their pay was only a few pennies a day and board. In the eastern districts they demanded, in 1850, that they should not be compelled to work more than five days a week for their landlord, and that the working day should be shortened to eleven hours. That reforms were much needed was evident, but before they could hope for much improvement, they would have to learn to organize and coöperate in support of their demands. Thrane aimed to organize them, but they were so timid, so little used to act independently that it was only with great difficulty that he was able to organize the first labor society in Drammen in December, 1848. The following year he founded "Arbeiderforeningernes Blad," an organ published in the interest of the labor movement. He traveled from district to district working for the cause, and before another year had passed, he had organized one hundred societies, and he had also addressed to the king a petition bearing 12,833 signatures, asking that the right of suffrage should be extended to the laboring classes. On July 31, 1850, a convention of labor delegates was assembled in Christiania, and a general program, or platform, was agreed upon.[1] The demands were: free trade, the abolition of trade privileges, restriction of the liquor trade, a better regulation of the relations between *bønder* and *husmænd*, better public schools, universal suffrage, and universal military service. With this program Thrane hoped to be able to influence the election of members to the Storthing, but this influence was noticeable only in Larvik, where Johan Sverdrup was elected.

The government authorities watched for an opportunity to arrest Thrane, whom they regarded as a dangerous person; but as they could find no just complaint, they finally accused him of blasphemy, a charge which the superior court set aside. If his adherents had been prudent, he might have been able to continue his work without molestation, but many of the peasants failed to understand the real

---

[1] Halvdan Koht, *Den fyrste norske Arbeiderrørsla, Den 17de Mai*, 1911.

nature of Thrane's views. They began to divide the land among themselves, to cut timber in the forests, to put into practice the ideas of socialism in a way which they thought conformed with his ideas. Thrane sought to prevail on them to abstain from all radical measures, but he was unable to fully control the movement which he had started. When he found that he could not prevent disorder, he turned his paper over to his assistant, F. S. Abildgaard, and retired as leader. At a new labor convention, *Lillethinget*, which assembled in Christiania in June, 1851, he took little part in the deliberations, but was mainly active in counseling moderation. But the government had determined to destroy the whole movement without further delay. The leaders were arrested, and a special commission was appointed to investigate the plans and doings of the whole organization. One hundred and forty-nine persons were indicted for various offenses. Of these only eleven were acquitted, the rest were fined or imprisoned, some even for terms of fifteen years. An appeal resulted in the acquittal of six others, and the modification of some of the severest punishments, but, as a whole, the decree of the lower court was sustained. Thrane and Abildgaard were sentenced to prison for a period of four years, and their paper, which had been repeatedly suppressed, had to be discontinued in 1856. In 1863 Thrane emigrated to America, where he spent the greater part of his remaining years in Chicago as publisher of various radical papers : "Den norske Amerikaner," "Dagbladet," and "Den nye Tid." The closing days of his life he spent with his son, Dr. Thrane, in Eau Claire, Wisconsin.[1]

The labor movement collapsed with the disappearance of its leaders, but the demands for political and social reforms proved to be more than a passing caprice. The peasants had been stirred to thought and political activity. Their economic emancipation and social development had begun, and they would henceforth appear as a class whose rights and interests would demand attention. The specter of socialism had stalked through the land ; the labor question had been raised ; the effects of the French Revolution of 1848

---

[1] J. E. Sars, *Norges politiske Historie 1815–1885*, p. 398 ff. O. A. Øverland, *Thraniterbevægelsen*. Zakarias Hermansen, *Arbeiderbevægelsen i Norge*, *Norsk Folkebibliothek*, vol. XVII., p. 28 ff.

had been distinctly felt, and the political leaders, who had been able to decipher the handwriting on the wall, grew alarmed. The Conservatives became reactionary, and sought to save state and society from what they considered to be impending ruin by opposing every liberal idea. A. M. Schweigaard in the Storthing of 1851 went to almost ridiculous lengths in attempting to forestall the spread of radical ideas, and even A. B. Stabell, and "Morgenbladet," of which he was the editor, now joined the Conservative ranks. But the Liberals, headed by new leaders, formulated demands which even many of the old party of opposition refused to support, and the cleavage between Conservatives and Liberals — the Right and the Left — was widening. Johan Sverdrup, the future liberal leader, who had been elected with the aid of the labor element as representative from Larvik, now made his first appearance in the Storthing, and he soon attracted attention as the originator of many important reform measures. In encounters with the Conservatives he showed great ability and presence of mind. "Even his appearance," says Sars, "his small but athletic and wiry frame, his black hair, his dark complexion, his quick movements, lively gesticulation, and somewhat theatrical pose gave him so completely the air of a foreigner, a stranger, that one would necessarily notice him." [1] This striking appearance and southern temperament he had inherited from his French mother. It soon appeared that this strange-looking man, who spoke with rhetorical elegance, and carried himself with the punctilious dignity of a grand seignior, possessed a will-power, a fiery zeal, an energy, and talent for organization which made him a peerless leader. Ever since his student days he had been an opponent of the bureaucratic tendencies and conservative ideas of the official classes. He was a stanch advocate of democratic principles and the rights of the people, and through reading in many languages he had acquired a broad culture and thorough familiarity with liberal political ideas. "The name of no other Norwegian politician has been identified with so many important reform measures and great political questions, and no one has equaled him as a powerful parliamentary debater," says J. Løvland. "He regarded

[1] *Storthinget i 1851 og Partiernes Stilling i vort Land.* J. E. Sars, *Norges politiske Historie 1815–1885*, p. 420 ff.

the Storthing as the chief organ for the nation's political life, and no one has done so much to maintain dignity and discipline in that body, to elevate the deliberations, and to uphold its power and authority."[1] Another liberal leader who appeared in this Storthing was F. G. Lerche, representative from Trondhjem, a robust and jovial man of the earlier Patriot type.

It is true that the labor movement started by Thrane was vigorously opposed by nearly all the members of the Storthing. A petition presented by the central committee of the labor organization before it was destroyed by the arrest of its leaders was turned down with the remark that some of the demands made were unreasonable, and some had already been granted in some other form. But the need of reform was, nevertheless, recognized, and some useful measures were passed. The still remaining tariff on grain was reduced by one-half, and a law was made giving the *husmænd* better protection against undue oppression by the *bønder*. Many important liberal issues were raised. It was proposed to extend the right of suffrage, to introduce trial by jury, and to grant the ministry the right to participate in the deliberations of the Storthing. But the reactionary spirit was strong, and the liberal leaders did not yet possess sufficient influence to secure the passage of these important measures. A successful attempt was, however, made in 1854 to secure an equal distribution of military burdens, which had hitherto rested only on the rural districts. A law was passed establishing the principle of universal military service in conformity with the provisions of the constitution, but the law was to such an extent a compromise measure that it was of little practical value, since a clause allowing the hiring of substitutes still made it possible for all but the poorer classes to escape military service. A law abolishing the very important office of *statholder*, which made Norway appear like a Swedish province, was also passed, but failed to get royal sanction. A bill providing for the introduction of trial by jury, passed in 1857, suffered the same fate. The liberal opposition was yet in its teens, so weak that for some years it almost seemed to

---

[1] *Nordmænd i det 19de Aarhundrede, Johan Sverdrup.* J. E. Sars, *Samlede Verker,* vol. IV., p. 176 ff. *Norsk Folkebibliothek,* vol. XVII., *Fra Johan Sverdrups Storthingsliv.*

PLATE XVII

JOHAN SVERDRUP.

FREDRIK STANG.

have disappeared, but in 1859 it began to show signs of new activity. Shortly after the opening of the session, *Reformforeningen*, a club consisting of representatives in the Storthing, was organized with over thirty members. This was an attempt to organize a distinct liberal party whose platform should be: yearly sessions of the Storthing, the maintaining of Norway's separate rights as a sovereign kingdom, opposition to the centralization of power, local self-government, trial by jury, and an independent development of the school system. The appearance of such an organization created the greatest excitement among the politicians. It was claimed to be a most wanton violation of good old usage, a revolutionary movement by which the liberal leaders Ueland, Sverdrup, and Joh. Steen, the "triumvirate," would fetter even the mind and conscience of the representatives. So bitter was the opposition that the leaders lost courage and disbanded the club.

The French February Revolution and the subsequent uprisings throughout Europe was followed by a period of reaction and nervous dread of social and political radicalism. In Norway this fear of revolutionary ideas was so increased by the alarm caused by Thrane's labor agitation that even Ludvig Kr. Daa forsook his liberal and national patriotic views, and became a political conservative and an ardent adherent of Pan-Scandinavianism. Reaction triumphed, the national and liberal issues were lost sight of, and the union with Sweden was lauded as the one great blessing. The Scandinavian sentiment, which was growing strong in Norway at this time, also strengthened the love for the union, and in 1854 the Union Day, November 4th, was celebrated in Christiania as a national holiday. To strengthen the bonds which, it was thought, would ultimately unite the three kingdoms, to protect the country against the spirit of revolution, which, like a dreaded specter, made the conservative pillars of European society quake with fear, and to dream undisturbed the Pan-Scandinavian dream became the chief desire of those who considered themselves the guardians of the nation's welfare. For the realization of this program they began to organize a distinct conservative party, whose political policy gave expression to this reactionary tendency. In opposition to the national issues which had been raised by the Liberals they desired to strengthen the power of the king, and to so modify the Act of Union as to create a centralization of power which might serve as a protection against the growing influence of the common people.

In 1839 the king had appointed a committee to examine the relations between the two kingdoms regarding the flag and other matters which were not satisfactory to the Norwegians. This committee requested that the scope of its work should be so enlarged that they might undertake a revision of the whole Act of Union. To this the Norwegian ministry consented, and the committee drafted in 1844 a new act of union, containing no less than one hundred and fifty articles.[1] According to the Act of 1815, the union between Norway and Sweden was a compact between two wholly independent kingdoms, according to which the only common affairs were a joint sovereign, and the joint action of both kingdoms in declaring war and making peace. According to the plan proposed in the draft of 1844 nearly all important interests, save distinctly local affairs, should be common. The principle in the document of 1815 was decentralization of power in the union, perfect equality and equal sovereignty of the two kingdoms. The new plan proposed political amalgamation and the creation of a common government superior to the individual governments of the two realms.[2] There should be a joint minister of foreign affairs, responsible to a committee consisting of an equal number of Norwegian and Swedish members to be chosen by the national legislature of each country; three joint cabinets should be created, one for foreign affairs, one for military affairs, and one for joint matters; and a joint congress should be established, consisting of twelve members of the Norwegian Storthing and twelve members of the Swedish Rigsdag, which should meet from time to time to deal with matters of common interest. The principle of full equality between the two realms should be maintained in all matters. This draft was submitted to the ministry, which examined the document and recommended the canceling of several articles.[3] Finally in

---

[1] *Underdanigst Forslag til Forenings-Act imellem Kongerigerne Norge og Sverige, udarbeidet af den ved kongelig Resolution af 30te Januar, 1839, naadigst anordnede Committee*, Christiania, 1856. *Aktstykker angaaende Revision af Foreningen*, Christiania, 1862.

[2] B. Dunker, *Om Revision af Foreningsakten mellem Sverige og Norge*, vol. II., p. 14 ff.

[3] *Angaaende en Foreningsakt mellem Kongerigerne Norge og Sverige. Den*

1848 a joint session of the Swedish and Norwegian ministers recommended that the matter should be dropped for the time being. The Norwegians probably feared the consequences of so far-reaching a change, and the Swedes looked with disfavor upon the principle of full equality between the two kingdoms. This drastic measure had failed, but more moderate steps were taken in the direction of political amalgamation. Efforts were made to create a joint Swedish-Norwegian army. The Norwegian cadets were stationed at Stockholm, and Norwegian and Swedish troops were even mingled in large military maneuvers. Commissions were appointed to propose new laws for the regulation of trade and tariff between the two countries, and for carrying into execution in one kingdom decrees rendered in the courts of the other. These propositions were rejected by the Storthing, but the Conservatives viewed this policy of strengthening the union and centralizing the power of government as "the organic beginning of an articulation of civilized human society which we regard as the task of the new age," as Professor Monrad expressed it.

During this period of slight political activity the attention was mainly turned to economic questions. The removal of monopolies and special privileges had facilitated development, and the interest in all phases of material progress was stimulated by modern inventions, and also by the great expositions in London and Paris, in 1851 and 1855. In 1845 Frederick Stang, a learned jurist, who at the age of twenty-five had become lecturer of jurisprudence at the University of Christiania, was placed at the head of the new department of the interior, a position in which he showed such initiative and energy that his term of office (1845–1856) became a new era in Norway's economic development. This was not due wholly to Stang's own ability, as the circumstances were favorable, and the time had come for a new advance in this field, but the services which he rendered his country as minister of the department were, nevertheless, of the greatest importance.[1] An extensive system of excellent roads penetrating to all parts of the kingdom was now planned, and the work was carried on with vigor. Stang was also active in promoting

norske Regjerings underdanigste Indstilling af 27de Februar, 1847, til Hs Majestæt Kongen, etc.

[1] Nordmænd i det 19de Aarhundrede, Fredrik Stang.

the construction of the first Norwegian railway from Christiania to Eidsvold, for which provision had been made by the Storthing in 1851. In 1854 the road was opened for traffic. The first telegraph line was constructed from Fredrikshald to Mandal, and a law establishing uniform postage completed a series of reforms in the postal system. Much attention was especially devoted to the improvement of farming. Agricultural schools were founded, and a loan office was created,[1] where the farmers might secure loans at a low rate of interest. The fisheries received encouragement, new lighthouses were built, and state subsidies were paid to private steamship lines. The repeal of the English navigation laws in 1849 opened new fields of commerce, and foreign merchant vessels could carry on an unrestricted traffic with England and her colonies. Holland also removed all restrictions on commerce, and during the Crimean War (1854–1856) Norwegian carrying trade was growing rapidly. In six years, from 1849 to 1856, the Norwegian merchant marine was increased by 900 vessels. The lumber trade was very profitable, the fisheries yielded good returns; manufacturing was increasing, and the growing trade yielded large revenues to the government treasury.

The rapid economic development was accompanied by a corresponding growth of population. According to the census of 1825 the population of Norway numbered 1,195,000. In 1845 it had increased to 1,328,000, in 1855 to 1,490,000, and in 1865 to 1,702,000. The specter of radical liberalism had vanished. Prosperity and the growing sympathy for the union fostered by the reactionary tendencies of the times created a feeling of contentment among the upper conservative classes. Only the foreign relations still caused some anxiety.

King Charles John had maintained throughout his reign very friendly relations with Russia, but the relations with that power grew very unfriendly in the reign of Oscar I. The ambitious Czar Nicholas I. sought to revive the policy of conquest of his predecessors, and aimed to seize parts of northern Norway. From early times the Norwegian Finns had driven their herds of reindeer into

---

[1] J. Smitt, *Det norske Landbrugs Historie.* B. E. Bendixen, *Et Omrids af Norges Handelshistorie.*

Russia in the winter, and in the summer the Russian Finns had crossed northern Norway with their flocks in order to reach the districts by the Arctic Ocean, where the gnats were less troublesome. These privileges were safeguarded by a special treaty, but the Russian government now made the demand that the Russian Finns should have the right to fish on the coast of Norway, and that a district by the Varangerfjord should be ceded to them. When King Oscar I. refused to grant this concession, the Czar forbade the Norwegian Finns to enter Russia, and Sweden-Norway retaliated by prohibiting the Russian Finns from entering Norway. At the time of the Crimean War King Oscar I. formed an alliance with France and England, promising not to cede a foot of territory to Russia, and the two western powers agreed to aid Norway and Sweden in case of need. King Oscar, who was devoted to the Scandinavian idea, desired a defensive alliance between the Northern kingdoms, and always remained a warm friend of Denmark. At the time of Denmark's first war with Prussia, 1848–1850, he stationed Swedish and Norwegian troops in northern Schleswig, after an armistice had been arranged in 1849, and he did not withdraw them until the peace was signed at Berlin in 1850. In 1857 he even offered to form an alliance with Denmark in order to defend the Eider River as the southern Scandinavian boundary. As he had always been in delicate health, he was obliged, in 1857, to hand the reins of government to his son, Crown Prince Charles, viceroy of Norway, who was made regent with full royal authority. He lingered in a state of growing physical and mental weakness till 1859, when he passed away, July 8th, at the age of sixty years.

61. KING CHARLES XV. BEGINNING OF A NEW LITERARY DEVELOPMENT

At the age of thirty-three Crown Prince Charles ascended the throne as King Charles XV. of Sweden and Charles IV. of Norway. He was a man of fine physique, robust, jovial, talented, and very popular, resembling in many respects his grandfather, King Charles John.[1] He shared his father's Pan-Scandinavian ideas, and took great

---

[1] *Kong Karl og Dronning Louise, Træk af det kongelige Pars Livshistorie.* Christiania, 1873. *Sveriges Historia,* edited by Hildebrand, part X., p. 68 ff.

interest in military affairs. Even as regent he had used his influence to further the organization of a joint system of defense for the Scandinavian peninsula, and in uniting Norwegian and Swedish troops in great military maneuvers. The policy of political amalgamation and the strengthening of the union which had found support in the Scandinavian sentiment and the reactionary spirit of the age would, naturally, be continued by the new king, as such a policy, aided by the active sympathy of the conservative majority in the Storthing, and supported by an energetic and popular ruler, might be expected to meet with unqualified success. But a new era of political and intellectual progress had already signaled its approach. A transition was coming which in another decade or two was to effect a thorough change in the political situation, and produce a new and more patriotic public spirit. It soon became clear that the parties which had waged their first great fight under the leadership of Wergeland and Welhaven would again clash in a new struggle to be waged on a more extensive scale. The political activity of the *bønder*, and the late movement among the *husmænd* and laborers, had roused these classes to interest and active participation in public affairs. Politically the *bønder* would ally themselves with the Liberals, and as they were intensely national in spirit, accustomed from time immemorial to defend their own rights, and to adhere with tenacity to their freedom and native customs, they would naturally oppose a policy which aimed to strengthen the power of the king, to maintain the privileges of the upper classes, to weaken their own political influence, and to obliterate the features of Norwegian nationality by a system of amalgamation aiming at the ultimate consolidation of the two kingdoms. The national spirit of the people was further stirred to intense activity by the new literary movement, which also this time played an essential part in the whole national development. In 1857 Bjørnstjerne Bjørnson published his "Synnøve Solbakken," a beautiful idyl, picturing the life and character of the *bønder*. It is as charmingly free from all spirit of controversy as the dawn of a summer morn, but it was the beginning of a new development in Norwegian literature, and it is undoubtedly true, as Chr. Collin puts it, that it exerted an even greater influence on the political than on the literary life of the age. Hitherto the description of the country people had served only as literary ornament, as it had been the diversion of the romanticists, who loved to linger in the mystic twilight of the strange and the unknown. But in "Synnøve Solbakken" Bjørnson made the Norwegian *bønder* the center of literary interest.[1] Throughout the centuries they had preserved their liberty, the traits and traditions of the nation; they were still its most typical representatives, and a literature which could depict their life, and express properly their sentiments, would be a Norwegian national literature in quite a new sense. Bjørnson saw that a literature can reflect nothing more important than the life and character of the people for which it is produced, and he realized that hitherto Norwegian literature had dealt but sporadically and imperfectly with this central interest. His discovery proved to be a literary revolution, for he of all poets possessed the genius to express the people's thoughts and feelings in song and story. With dramatic realism he has pictured the customs and character of the country people among whom he was reared, and this classic portraiture of real life he has woven into a delicate framework of romantic nature painting which gives even the most scarred and drawn features an almost youthful charm. The people could see themselves as in a mirror, and by discovering their own worth they gained new confidence in themselves and their native culture. No more powerful stimulus could be imparted to the awakening national sentiment. Other stories of the same kind appeared, as "Arne," "En glad Gut," "Fiskerjenten," etc.; and other masters followed Bjørnson, until a new literature had been produced, not only for the Norwegian people, but about them. Henrik Ibsen had already approached the same subject from another side. In 1850, when only twenty-two years of age, he had published his first drama, "Catalina," in which the dissatisfied and philosophizing youth represents the Roman conspirator as a liberalist and patriot. When he reached his full maturity he hurled his thunderbolts at the sluggish indifference and romantic indolence of the Norwegian people in his great masterpieces "Brand" and "Peer Gynt," in which nature painting and character study has reached a never excelled degree of artistic perfection.

[1] Chr. Collin, *Bjørnstjerne Bjørnson.*

Even before Ibsen and Bjørnson had gained a reputation as poets they had become prominent as leaders of a movement to create a national theater. Hitherto Norway had been dependent on Denmark both for her actors and her dramatic literature. Through the efforts of Ole Bull a theater was built in Bergen in 1850, and the following year Ibsen was employed as stage manager. In Christiania a national theater was erected in 1851 to compete with the Christiania theater, which had a Danish director, and which employed only Danish actors. But the rivalry with the older competitor became difficult for the new playhouse, and when the director of the Christiania theater continued to employ Danes, the students lost patience. When a new Danish actor was to appear, they assembled under the leadership of Bjørnstjerne Bjørnson to the number of 600 and started such a tumult that nothing like it had been heard since the "Campbeller battle" in the days of Wergeland. Two days later Bjørnson wrote an article in "Morgenbladet" outlining the program and demands of the young patriots. "A theater in the capital," he says, "is an outpost of nationalism against foreign supremacy. The capital witnesses the most severe clashes between that which is foreign and that which is our own. It has to wage an important fight; it has great responsibility, and needs forces and vigilant sentinels. . . . We have made rapid progress, but in regard to theater we have until lately been a dependency. Our immortal Henrik Wergeland, who in this matter, as in many others, was far ahead of his time, spoke for the first time with great force and earnestness in behalf of a Norwegian theater. We are grateful to the Danish artists, and we are not yet prepared to lose them. They do not oppose our nationality much, as they are acclimated. But new foreigners, always new ones, result not only in the destruction of what we are doing and have done, but it is an insult, not against us alone, but against the power which is above us all, our country. . . . Our beloved Henrik Wergeland should have seen an evening like that of last Tuesday. He would have rejoiced to have heard the storm of rough-music which shook the old prejudices. In his time he was in the minority, the smallest possible, for he alone was the minority. Now he would have been in the majority, a large and powerful majority. We have progressed

PLATE XVIII

BJØRNSTJERNE BJØRNSON.

possibly faster than he expected." [1] Bjørnson carried to a successful issue the fight for a Norwegian theater in Christiania, though he was at the time only twenty-three years of age. He showed even at this time the great qualities which soon placed him at the head of the liberal movement as its peerless leader, the greatest since the time of Henrik Wergeland. Professor Gerhard Gran describes him as follows: "I have already mentioned that his literary works were weapons, implements in his battles and his work. But his great poetic genius endowed him also with other more direct auxiliaries for his work as ruler. His sovereign command of language enabled him to coin in the heat of the conflict sudden surprising pictures, in which his thoughts shone before the eyes of his subjects, both sympathizers and opponents. Striking words flowed from his lips, entered irresistibly into the minds of the listeners, and chased around the country in search for new proselytes. The dramatic element in his nature turned the political campaigns under his leadership into exciting episodes, made the situation strained, and urged all lines of thought and action forward to a solution, a catastrophe. To this must still be added his great talent as an actor — the plastic art of speech, and the no less beautiful and commanding figure, the orchestra of a voice which had a chord for every sentiment, and which was trained to an art of elocution which never suffered a modulation to escape. So endowed was this chieftain. Seldom have so many qualities of the leader been united in the same person. With a patriotism tendér as love, a faith which could move mountains, a power of personality which overcame all obstacles, an intuition which penetrated into the future, a practical judgment and an ability to act which was always ready to solve the nearest questions, a sense of justice which balanced all values, and, shed over all, a poetic genius which poured its radiance on all his works and spread its luster to many lands." [2]

Among the great leaders who made this age illustrious and created a new era of intellectual and social progress must also be mentioned Camilla Collett, Henrik Wergeland's gifted sister. She did not equal Ibsen or Bjørnson in literary influence, but she was a gifted

[1] Henrik Jæger, *Illustreret norsk Literaturhistorie*, vol. II., p. 596 ff.
[2] Gerhard Gran, *Bjørnstjerne Bjørnson, Høvdingen*, p. 46 ff.

writer and an original thinker, and rose to special prominence as the founder of the woman's rights movement in Norway. In her excellent novel "Amtmandens Døtre" she attacked the conventional view of marriage which paid slight heed to woman's feelings and her rights as a personality, and regarded the marriage institution chiefly as a means of securing her daily bread. In her later works, "Sidste Blade," "Fra de Stummes Leir," and "Mod Strømmen," she discussed woman's rights in all relations of life. Her works were battle signals which roused the women of Norway, freed them from the old prejudices, and called them into a field of widened activity as a distinct force in the new intellectual and social progress.

These movements in various fields emanated from a vigorous national spirit which attempted to realize its ideals, and sought to rear a social structure conforming to its needs. The great liberal national movement in Norway in the nineteenth century was not a political struggle alone, but a distinct attempt of the nation's genius to reassert itself after centuries of partial inactivity and foreign tutelage. The Norwegian historical school, the collection and study of folk-tales, art, and traditions of the past, the *Landsmaal* movement, the realistic literary school, and, finally, the organization of a Liberal political party which overcame all reactionary opposition, and maintained Norway's rights to lead her own free and sovereign existence, are phases of a development in which all vital forces of the nation were concentrated. The great political struggle grew out of the attempt of the Bernadotte kings to rule Norway as a dependency, but the vigor and determination with which the struggle was waged was wholly due to the spirit of liberty and progress created by the new national development.

62. New Political Struggles. Proposed Revision of the Act of Union

Through the revision of the Eidsvold constitution by the extra session of the Storthing in 1814, the king was given the right to appoint a *statholder* for Norway, but this institution was very unpopular, and efforts were soon made to abolish it. In 1818 a bill was introduced in the Storthing for this purpose, but it received no support. The attempt was renewed in 1848 and 1854. In 1854 the measure was passed, but it was promptly vetoed by the king. When Charles XV. ascended the throne in 1859, he resolved to sanction the bill, which had again been introduced in the Storthing. He gave the representatives to understand that if the measure was adopted, it would receive his sanction, and the bill was passed by an almost unanimous vote. This "dowry" to the Norwegian people the king had, undoubtedly, intended as a token of his good-will, which should serve to strengthen still further the sympathy of the Norwegian Conservatives for a closer union between the two kingdoms. After Løvenskiold had resigned in 1855, the office remained vacant and lost all real importance. Birch-Reichenwald, who in 1858 succeeded Vogt as the leading man in the ministry, favored the amalgamation

Fig. 12. — Charles XV

policy, and everything seemed to augur well for the attempt to draw the two realms into closer union. But the sentiment in Sweden was not so friendly as the Scandinavian movement seemed to indicate. It had become evident to all that the union with Norway did not constitute a compensation for Finland in a manner compatible with Swedish interests, and the attempts hitherto made to modify the terms of the union had proved unavailing. On November 2, 1859, Anckarsvärd introduced a measure in the Swedish Rigsdag, in which he launched forth into a philippic against the existing form of union, and proposed that it should be so modified as to be more satisfactory to both peoples. His motion was applauded and supported by the

Swedish press, and when it was learned that the Storthing had passed a bill to abolish the office of *statholder*, the feeling grew intensely hostile. It was clear that Norway would yield to no demand for Swedish overlordship based on the treaty of Kiel, and the move of the Storthing was regarded by some as rebellion. In the Rigsdag Dalman introduced a motion declaring the article in the Norwegian constitution regarding the office of *statholder* to be a part of the union compact, which could not be altered without the consent of

FIG. 13. — Queen Louise

Sweden. This view was, undoubtedly, erroneous, as the terms of union had been embodied in another document, and as a sovereign and independent nation unquestionably possesses the right to amend its constitution without asking the consent of another power.[1] But both Anckarsvärd's and Dalman's motions were adopted by the Rigsdag. It was also decided to undertake a revision of the Act of Union, evidently for the purpose of creating a Swedish supremacy over Norway, and the question of Norwegian *statholder* was to be regarded as a union affair. To the latter proposition no Norwegian ministry could agree, as it would establish Swedish authority over the Norwegian constitution, but the king was intimidated by the hostile attitude of the Swedish leaders, and as the Swedish ministry threatened to resign unless he accepted their view, he finally refused to sanction the measure passed by the Storthing. That Sweden had won a victory in a purely Norwegian affair was evident, and the episode did not tend to increase the Norwegian people's love for the

[1] B. Dunker, *Flyveblad No. 4 og No. 5. Om Statholderposten.*

union. The Norwegian press maintained on the whole a very calm tone in discussing the matter, but that deep resentment had been aroused by this unexpected manifestation of anti-Norwegian feeling in Sweden was clearly apparent. In the Storthing a committee of fifteen, which was appointed to consider the situation, drafted an address to the king, stating clearly and forcibly the right of the Norwegian people to exercise full control over their constitution. The first part of the document, written by Schweigaard, closes with these words: "Against the claims advanced by the Swedish Estates that the measure abolishing the office of *statholder* should be treated as a matter with which Sweden is concerned, the Storthing hereby submits to Your Majesty their respectful protest." The second part of the address, written by Aal, states that a revision of the Act of Union cannot be undertaken by the Norwegians on any other basis than that of full equality between the two kingdoms, and the right of each nation to manage its own affairs in all matters not specifically designated as common interests. The third part, written by Johan Sverdrup, is an eloquent appeal to the king, closing with the statement that it would be the duty of His Majesty and the new session of the Storthing to bring the question of the office of *statholder* to a successful issue. After being carefully considered, the address was passed by the Storthing in the night of April 23, 1860, as a solemn protest against the attempt of the sister kingdom to impair the sovereign right of Norway. In conformity with this address the Norwegian ministry refused to agree to the proposed revision. But the following year the Swedish minister of justice, De Geer, submitted to the combined Swedish-Norwegian ministry a proposal that the revision of the Act of Union should be undertaken according to the motions of Anckarsvärd and Dalman passed by the Rigsdag. The principle of equality between the two kingdoms should be maintained, he said, but this should not be an absolute, but a relative, equality. The share of each kingdom in the common government should be made proportionate to the amount contributed by each toward the defraying of joint public expenses, and the joint legislative assembly should consist of representatives from each kingdom in proportion to the population. Sweden would demand "to be regarded as *primus inter pares* in all matters in which the principle of equality could not be maintained." [1] The resolution passed by the Storthing, that "no Norwegian who loved his country and his honor could agree to a revision of the Act of Union on any basis save that of Norway's absolute equality with Sweden," was disregarded, and the Norwegian government was invited to join in the work of revision as if nothing had been said. The Norwegian ministry unanimously refused to accede to the request, but disagreement arose over certain expressions in their report, and Birch-Reichenwald and two of his colleagues resigned. The ministry was then reorganized with Frederick Stang as its real head, and the new ministry assumed a different attitude to the question of revision.

After Birch-Reichenwald's resignation, and before Stang had taken his seat in the new ministry, the report was finally purged of the disputed expressions and submitted to the king, February 18, 1862. Point by point it controverted the reasons for revision assigned by the Swedish ministers. It reiterated the opinion of the Storthing, expressed in the address of 1860, and declared that the Norwegians could not agree to the proposed revision. De Geer sought to refute the points in the report by reasserting the principle which had already been declared, but he would not urge the revision at that moment on account of the prevailing sentiment in Norway. He declared, however, that he favored revision, and he expressed the hope that the matter was only postponed, and that the time would soon come when the revision could be carried out. A formal declaration was added, stating that the king desired the revision to be undertaken at a more opportune time, and that it should be carried out without any obstruction from previously announced principles. It was long thought that De Geer was the author of this declaration,[2] but he has stated in his memoirs that the author was Stang himself. From this circumstance it is clear that the Norwegian ministry had already consented to a revision, but this could not be undertaken while the resolution which had been passed in the Storthing was still in force. An attempt was, therefore, made to secure the repeal of this resolution, but the constitutional committee to which the

---

[1] Aug. Chr. Manthey, *Dagbøger for Aarene 1856–1874*, p. 191 ff. O. A. Øverland, *Norges Historie 1814–1902*, p. 94 ff.

[2] *Om Revision af Foreningsakten mellem Sverige og Norge*, vol. I., p. 175 ff.

matter was referred did not agree. A compromise measure was adopted which, though very vague, was interpreted to mean that a revision might be undertaken whenever the king should find the moment opportune, but the principle of full equality between the two kingdoms should be adhered to. The new constitutional committee to which the work of revision was to be intrusted was appointed February 6, 1865, and consisted of seven Norwegian and seven Swedish members.

During these strange political maneuvers, by which Sweden had succeeded in forcing through a measure wholly repugnant to the Norwegian people, the Liberal leaders had made no protest. J. E. Sars says that this strange silence was due to a desire to secure the passage of some measures which they regarded as especially important. These measures were, the introduction of the jury system, and especially the question of yearly sessions of the Storthing, about which Sverdrup said: "Let us all unite in working for yearly sessions of the Storthing; this is the greatest service we can show our country; all other things are only palliatives." Both the king and the ministry seemed favorably inclined to these reforms, but neither one was passed at this time.

The Norwegian members of the constitutional committee were: O. V. Lange, G. P. Harbitz, N. Vogt, E. Saxlund, N. K. Irgens, T. H. Aschehoug, and O. G. Ueland. The first two soon withdrew, and K. Platau and H. Th. Meinich were appointed in their place. The committee was instructed to agree to no changes in the Act of Union except such as might improve that document in minor details. But the amalgamation policy of the Stang ministry, and the influence of "Morgenbladet," whose gifted editor, Chr. Friele, was Stang's personal friend and supporter, made them yield to a general revision. Such a step was favored by the conservative spirit and desire for centralization of power represented by Stang and his colleagues, and also by the Scandinavian sentiment, which at this time was very strong.

The Pan-Scandinavian ideas had been stated in very vague terms, and even the leaders of the movement could probably not have defined their real aim. The enthusiastic talk about a united North proved to be little more than a sentiment, which could not be reduced to anything so prosaic as a distinct purpose. The feeling that the three nations are in reality one people had been appealed to, and it was thought that it constituted a bond of union so strong that it would insure coöperation in case either should be attacked by a foreign foe. Beyond this purely theoretical stage Scandinavianism never advanced. The thought was beautiful, but it proved to be too purely poetic to be of much practical value in time of great emergencies.

When the Schleswig-Holstein question threatened to embroil Denmark in war with Austria and Prussia, the sympathy for the sister state grew very intense both in Norway and Sweden. King Charles XV. conferred with Frederick VII. of Denmark, and negotiations were carried on between the three realms with the aim of creating a defensive alliance for defending the Eider as the southern border of Denmark.[1] The plan was opposed by leading cabinet members both in Sweden and Norway. The Swedish minister of finance, John August Gripenstedt, showed the king how dangerous it would be to engage in war with Germany merely for the sake of a vague sentiment, and pointed to Charles XII. and Gustavus IV. as examples. Sibbern, Norwegian minister of state in Stockholm, and Stang, head of the Norwegian ministry, were also opposed to an alliance with Denmark unless the coöperation of the great powers was assured. An earnest appeal was addressed to England, France, and Russia to aid Denmark, but as no encouraging answer was returned, Charles XV. was forced to abandon the plan of an alliance with Denmark. King Frederick VII. died shortly afterwards, and his successor, Christian IX., signed the new constitution for Denmark-Schleswig, a step which immediately led to war with the two German powers Austria and Prussia, who refused to allow the duchy of Schleswig to be incorporated in the Danish kingdom. A German army entered Holstein, and in February, Prussian and Austrian troops crossed the Eider. This brought matters to such

[1] Halvdan Koht, *Die Stellung Norwegens und Schwedens im deutsch-dänischen Konflikt*, Christiania *Videnskabs-Selskabs Skrifter*, 1907, p. 119 ff. Aug. Chr. Manthey, *Dagbøger*, vol. I., p. 330. John August Gripenstedt, *Minnen*, vol. I., p. 250 f. *Det Stangske System, Aftryk af Dagbladet.* Halvdan Koht, *Unionen og Freden. En historisk Udredning av svensk Krigspolitik siden 1814*, p. 69.

a crisis that it appeared as if Norway and Sweden would be involved in the war. The Swedish Rigsdag placed three million rigsdaler at the disposal of the government to place the army on war footing, and the Storthing passed a bill submitted by the government, empowering the king to use the army and navy of Norway in defense of Denmark. Attached to this measure, however, were the conditions that in case of an alliance with Denmark the forces used for its defense would have to approximate those of the enemy in strength, and Norway's extensive commerce would have to be protected. These conditions were so exacting that they almost voided the measure itself. Some preparations were made, and a Norwegian-Swedish squadron cruised in the Baltic, but no alliance was concluded, and Denmark was left to her fate. Neither the Norwegian nor the Swedish ministry would assume the responsibility for a war, and the Storthing passed a declaration that "the majority of the Norwegian people did not desire closer political relations with Denmark." This gave the political Pan-Scandinavianism its death blow. Denmark was soon compelled to yield, and Lauenburg, Holstein, and Schleswig were ceded to the German allies. The Scandinavian sentiment still continued to live, and Scandinavian societies were organized in all three kingdoms, but when the Norwegian Storthing in 1871 refused to agree to the proposed revision of the Act of Union, political Scandinavianism vanished. Before the close of King Charles's reign the societies had disappeared, and Pan-Scandinavianism as a distinct movement was dead.

The fate of Denmark in 1864 was a new illustration of the dangers to which the smaller states are always exposed, and though the Pan-Scandinavian idea had been rudely shattered, it is evident that the need of closer coöperation was keenly felt both in Norway and Sweden at the time. The revision committee, which labored under the influence of this sentiment, was finally able to submit a draft of a new Act of Union in 1867.[1] Instead of the confederation of two independent kingdoms established in 1815, the new document

---

[1] *Underdanigst Betænkning angaaende Revision af Foreningsakten mellem Norge og Sverige afgiven af den ved kongelig Resolution af 6te Februar, 1865, naadigst nedsatte Committee. Forslag til Foreningsakt mellem Norge og Sverige.*

proposed a federal union, in which Sweden should have predominance. The king should reside permanently in Stockholm, and the Swedish minister of foreign affairs should have charge of the foreign affairs of both countries. The number of matters to be regarded as union affairs was also to be greatly increased in both countries. This would have turned the development into paths leading to ultimate consolidation of the two realms, and leading men in Sweden hoped that a union parliament could soon be established if this act was adopted. In 1869 the measure was proposed to the Storthing as a government bill to be taken up for consideration at the next session. The measure seemed to have the best chance of being passed. Ueland, the great leader of the *bønder*, was a member of the committee which had framed it, and the other leader of the *bønder*, Jaabæk, who since 1865 had been actively engaged in organizing societies among his followers, the *bondevenforeninger*, and who was chiefly interested in the question of an economic administration, advised his friends to have nothing to do with this measure, as it was "higher politics," with which they were not concerned. There seemed to be a real danger that Norway's independence might be destroyed. But the proposed bill became an issue which called into active opposition the ablest leaders, and served to hasten the organization of the great Liberal party, the "Left" (*Venstre*). Bernhard Dunker assailed the proposed act in his work "Om Revision af Foreningsakten mellem Sverige og Norge," second part (1868), and "Norsk Folkeblad" and "Dagbladet" joined in the attack. T. H. Aschehoug, who had been a member of the committee, sought to defend the measure,[1] but the opposition was rapidly growing. In the debates in the Storthing Ketil Motzfeldt and Johan Sverdrup led the attack, and the measure was defeated by a vote of ninety-two to seventeen, 1871. Repeated failures had shown that the character of the union could not be changed, and the attempt to revise the Act of Union was not renewed.

[1] T. H. Aschehoug, *Om Unionskomiteens Udkast til en ny Rigsakt.* This work first appeared as a series of articles in *Morgenbladet*.

63. IMPORTANT REFORM MEASURES PASSED IN THE REIGN OF CHARLES XV. THE RISE OF THE LIBERAL OR VENSTRE PARTY

Though the questions regarding the office of *statholder* and the revision of the Act of Union had raised issues which for many years attracted the chief attention of the lawgivers, many important measures were passed which contributed to general progress. In 1860 a new school law was passed, based on recommendations submitted by Hartvig Nissen, by which a public school system was created for the kingdom.[1] All *herreds* and parishes should be divided into school districts, and compulsory school attendance was established for all children between eight and fourteen years of age. In all districts where the homesteads were so situated that thirty pupils could attend daily, permanent schools should be erected, and in districts where this was not the case, instruction should be given in their homes by itinerant teachers.

A new regulation was also made regarding the relative number of representatives from rural and urban districts. The constitution provides that the country districts should elect two-thirds, and the cities only one-third, of the total number of representatives to the Storthing, but because of prevailing rules of election, this ratio had not been maintained. In 1857 the cities secured forty-four and the rural communities only sixty-seven seats. In 1860 a bill, introduced by Schweigaard, was passed, establishing in practice the provisions of the constitution. The country districts were given seventy-four representatives, and the cities only thirty-seven. This tended to strengthen the opposition party, and gave the *bønder* increased political influence. A royal commission was appointed to examine the jury system, but the bill finally submitted providing for its introduction was defeated in the Lagthing, and the matter was allowed to rest. Attempts were also made by the Stang ministry to improve the military organization, and many bills were introduced for this purpose. A new military code was adopted in 1866, and the same year a new law for the regulation of the military service was passed, but the majority in the Storthing was opposed to a new army organization. The management of army and navy was so

---

[1] W. Rein, *Encyklopädisches Handbuch der Pädagogik*, vol. VI., p. 319 ff.

severely criticized that the heads of those departments, General Storm Wergeland and W. W. Hafner, resigned. The opposition was rapidly growing. Jaabæk continued with great success to organize societies among the *bønder*, the *bondevenforeninger*, and his paper, "Folketidende," became the most widely circulated newspaper in the country. His clamor for public economy found general support in the rural districts, and as he resisted every measure which he feared might tend to increase the burdens of the rural population, he was able to prevent additional military appropriations. The ministry were also opposed by the Liberals, who desired reforms of various kinds, and who were dissatisfied with its bureaucratic tendencies and the position which it had taken on the revision question. The different groups had their own organs. The "Folketidende" of Jaabæk and his adherents had found a still more influential successor in "Verdens Gang," edited by O. Thommesen. The organ of the Liberals was "Dagbladet," edited by H. E. Berner, and the leading Conservative papers were "Morgenbladet," edited by Chr. Friele, and "Aftenposten," edited by A. Schibstead.

It had become the aim of the Liberal leader, Johan Sverdrup, to introduce the parliamentary system and to lodge the supreme power in the Storthing. His slogan was: "All power is to be united in this assembly." "It is especially necessary," he said, "to make the framework of our government as perfect for the future as possible. This work cannot stop, if our political life is to be a blessing for our country." So long as the opposition forces were divided into distinct factions more or less unwilling to coöperate, the Storthing could not be strong, and Sverdrup's first aim was to unite the opposition groups into a large Liberal party. He won Jaabæk to his side, and the consummation of the work was hastened by the revival of the issue of yearly sessions of the Storthing which had first been raised in 1857. Bills for establishing this reform had been repeatedly introduced, but they had not been passed, as it was feared that it would lead to the introduction of the parliamentary system. When the measure was again brought before the Storthing in 1869, A. M. Schweigaard, who in 1866 had voted for the bill, arose and declared that he would now vote against it. He was one of the most honored and influential leaders, and his opinion had great weight, but Sverdrup waged the fight for the measure with great skill. "It will be regarded as one of the greatest triumphs which has ever been won on the path of progress in this country," he declared. The bill was passed with eighty-one against thirty votes. "Sverdrup was the hero of the hour," says Løvland. "When he stepped into the street he was greeted with cheers by the populace. A liberal majority had been created, the party of the Left (Venstre), and Sverdrup had become its leader." [1]

When Ueland and Schweigaard died in 1870, Frederick Stang alone remained of the older leaders, and as head of the Conservative forces he was to wage a long and losing fight against his doughty antagonist. Yearly sessions of the Storthing and the existence of the Liberal party made it possible to approach other issues with greater chance of settling them according to the will of the people. The question regarding the participation of the cabinet in the deliberations of the Storthing had been an issue ever since Christian Magnus Falsen in 1821 submitted a bill for amending the constitution on that point. In 1824 his bill had been laid on the table even without discussion, and repeated attempts to pass the measure had proven unsuccessful. A bill embodying this reform, introduced by P. K. Gaarder, was passed in 1851 by a large majority, but it was vetoed by the king, and later efforts in behalf of the measure had failed. In 1869 this reform was again proposed in a bill introduced by C. Motzfeldt. It was moved for consideration in 1872, and an intense struggle between Conservatives and Liberals was precipitated. In his famous speech on the measure Sverdrup urged with great force the necessity of introducing the parliamentary system. This measure has become "a necessary corollary to the constitutional provision establishing yearly sessions of the Storthing, through which a new political system is necessarily established in our country," he declared. "It is necessary for both branches of the government; for the Storthing no less than for the ministry." "The responsibility of the ministers will follow as a natural consequence when the ministers are obliged to answer for their own acts and those of their colleagues whenever it is demanded." The leader of the Conservatives in the Storthing, Professor T. H. Aschehoug, maintained that the

[1] *Nordmænd i det 19de Aarhundrede*, p. 111.

measure involved the introduction of the parliamentary system like that of England, and that this might lead to a tyrannous rule by the majority, against which other countries had found it necessary to provide safeguards in the form of an upper house which could protect the minority. A hostile attitude between the ministry, led by Frederick Stang, and the liberal majority of the Storthing, led by Sverdrup, soon developed. It became evident that a struggle had begun which would decide whether the Storthing or the crown should exercise the highest authority. The provision of the constitution on this vital point would be put to the severest test. The bill was passed, March 9th, with a majority of eighty against twenty-nine votes, but Stang and a majority of his colleagues in the ministry advised the king to veto it. Two of the ministers who favored the measure, O. J. Brock and N. K. Irgens, resigned. The veto caused great excitement, and increased the growing tension between the Storthing and the ministry. An address to the king was adopted, in which the Storthing expressed its lack of confidence in the Stang ministry, and gave utterance to the surprise and disappointment caused by the veto. As a result, the ministers expressed their willingness to resign, but when the king stated that he saw no reason why he should change advisers, they remained in office, showing that they regarded themselves as responsible to the king and not to the Storthing. Only Riddervold, minister of ecclesiastical affairs, retired.

64. Oscar II. The Office of Statholder Abolished. The Veto Question

King Charles XV. was a strong man, but his health had been impaired, and on returning from the baths of Aix la Chapelle, where he had sought relief, he died at Malmö, September 18, 1872, at the age of forty-six. As he left no male heir,[1] his brother, Oscar Frederick, Duke of Östergötland, succeeded him on the throne as Oscar II. It was the aim of the new king to secure a settlement of the union question, and to bring about a better understanding between

---

[1] Queen Louise died in March, 1871, and Prince Charles, born in 1852, passed away in 1854. Only a daughter survived the king, Princess Louise, who married Crown Prince Frederick of Denmark in 1869.

the Norwegian ministry and the Storthing. The question regarding the office of *statholder* had been repeatedly brought up. In 1873 a bill was again passed, abolishing the office, and creating instead that of minister of state for Norway, who should be the recognized head of the Norwegian ministry, a real prime minister. The king sanctioned the measure, and Frederick Stang, who was already the leader of the Norwegian ministry, was appointed to the new office.[1]

The issue regarding the participation of the ministers in the deliberations of the Storthing was still pending, and as King Oscar retained the Stang ministry, there was no prospect of more friendly relations between the two parties in Norway. The election of 1874 became a real trial of strength between Conservatives and Liberals. The Liberal party secured a majority in the Storthing, and a bill providing for the seating of the ministers was passed by a vote of seventy-four to thirty-five. The measure was again vetoed, but it had now been passed twice, though not in a strictly unaltered form, as the word *statsministeren* was changed to *statsministrene*, because of the creation of the new office of minister of state for Norway. In the elections of 1877 the Liberals were again victorious, and the bill was passed a second time in an unchanged form with increased majority, but it was promptly vetoed as before. The political campaigns grew more intensely bitter, and the leaders of both parties did their utmost to rally their adherents. The leading Conservative organ, "Morgenbladet," was predicting a change in the situation. The *bønder*, it was claimed, were awakening to see that Sverdrup was guiding them along paths leading to a republic and socialism; they would soon turn and support the Conservative party. But the election of 1880 resulted in a new victory for the Liberals, and the bill for seating the ministers was passed a third time, with ninety-three votes against twenty. Since the Moderates, and even some of the Conservatives, joined the Liberals in voting

---

[1] Up till 1905, when Norway was separated from Sweden, the Norwegian ministry consisted of two branches: The division in Stockholm, consisting of a minister of state and two other ministers, and the Norwegian cabinet in Christiania, at first headed by the *statholder*. When that office was abolished, the office of minister of state for Norway was created. This new official received the same rank as the minister of state in Stockholm, and was the head of the ministry.

for the measure, it was evident that the reform was supported by a general public sentiment. But the Stang ministry, which paid no heed to the will of the people, again caused the bill to be vetoed. The same day that the veto was announced to the Storthing, the president, Johan Sverdrup, submitted a resolution that since the measure had been passed in an unchanged form by three separate Storthings, it should be declared law without the king's sanction, and that it should be sent to the ministry to be proclaimed as law in the manner prescribed for constitutional amendments. The resolution was passed June 9th by a large majority. But this only precipitated a new issue regarding the extent of the king's veto power. The constitution provides that a bill passed in an unchanged form by three successively elected Storthings becomes a law without the king's signature; but this measure was a constitutional amendment, and the constitution did not explicitly state that such a measure could become law without royal sanction. To the resolution passed by the Storthing on June 9th the ministry returned the answer that since the bill had not been sanctioned, and had, therefore, not become a part of the constitution, it could not be proclaimed as such.

The question regarding the king's veto power in cases of constitutional amendments had been answered in different ways by the best authorities.[1] The constitutional committee of 1824 with the

---

[1] Among those who thought that the king had absolute veto in cases of amendments to the constitution were: T. H. Aschehoug, *Norges nuværende Statsforfatning*, vol. II., p. 231, first edition. Statsminister Stang, *Om den kongelige Sanctionsret efter Norges Grundlov*. Professor Ludvig Daae, who characterized the resolution of June 9th as revolutionary, in a speech delivered at Ramnæs, September 29, 1883. Johannes Berg, who defended Selmer and his colleagues in the impeachment trial, *Den nye Statsskik, Tillid til Johan Sverdrup*. L. Raknerud, *Sanktionsretten i Grundlovssager og den politiske Situation*. H. L. Rydin, *Unionen och Konungens Sanktionsrätt i norska Grundlagsfrågor*.

Among those who opposed absolute veto may be mentioned: H. N. Stenbuch, professor of jurisprudence, *Bemerkninger over Norges Grundlov*, Trondhjem, 1815. P. P. Flor, President of the Lagthing, *Bemerkninger over de paa 3die ordentlige Storthing 1821 fremsatte Konstitutionsforslag*, Drammen, 1823. Professor Fredrik Stang, *Systematisk Fremstilling af Kongeriget Norges konstitutionelle grundlovsbestemte Ret*, Christiania, 1833. H. H. Foss, member of the Storthing, member of the cabinet, etc., *Angaaende de til Afgjørelse paa 7de ordentlige Storthing fremsatte Konstitutionsforslag og hvad der om samme offentlig er ytret*, Christiania, 1833. Ole Munch Ræder, *Den*

learned jurist Chr. Krohg as chairman had expressed the opinion that the king must be regarded as possessing absolute veto in cases of constitutional amendments. And in an address to the king of the same year the Storthing itself had expressed the same view, saying: "The National Legislature admits that your Royal Majesty possesses an absolute veto in cases of amendments to the constitution." But Jonas Anton Hjelm held that the king had no such power. Ueland and Sverdrup were of the same opinion, and Stang in his work on the constitution, "Systematisk Fremstilling af Kongeriget Norges constitutionelle eller grundlovsbestemte Ret," 1833, held that in constitutional amendments, as in case of other bills, the king had only a suspensive veto.[1] The king requested the faculty of the department of law of the University of Christiania to submit an opinion on the veto question, and with only one member dissenting they stated that according to their understanding of the constitution it could not be amended without the king's sanction.[2] But

norske Statsforfatnings Historie og Væsen, Copenhagen, 1841. A. S. Ørsted, leading Danish jurist, and judge of the supreme court of Denmark, P. K. Gaarder, jurist, *Fortolkning over Grundloven og de øvrige Love som danne Norges Riges offentlige Ret*, Christiania, 1845. S. Jaabæk, *Den høieste Magt i Staten*, Mandal, 1883.

[1] J. E. Sars, *Norges politiske Historie 1815–1885*, p. 634.

[2] *Sth. Prp. No. 20 (1881) angaaende Kongens Sanktionsret ved Grundlovsforandringer. Om Kongens Sanktionsret, Uddrag af det juridiske Fakultets Betænkning af 23de Marts, 1881.*

N. L. Brækstad, *The Constitutional Crisis in Norway*, London, 1883. Ole Ring, *Imødegaaelse af Vetobetænkningen*, Christiania, 1881. C. Winter-Hjelm, professor of jurisprudence, *Om Grundlovens Principer og den Aand hvori de under gjensidig Begrænsning er gjennemførte i dens enkelte Bestemmelser*, Christiania, 1863. Bjørnstjerne Bjørnson, *Tale, Om Folkesuveræniteten. Tale, Om den norske Forfatningskamp.* J. Belsheim, *Lidt om det kongelige Magtomraade i hvert af de forenede Riger; Mod det absolute Veto, Udtalelser af navnkundige Jurister og Storthingsmænd i ældre Tid; Om Magtfordelingen i Grundloven og mod absolut Veto.*

The member of the faculty of jurisprudence of the University of Christiania who did not agree with his colleagues in the opinion submitted was Professor F. Brandt. He declared that under the circumstances he would agree to decide in favor of absolute veto, but he added that he found the question so doubtful, and the reasons for holding that the king's veto in cases of constitutional amendments was merely suspensive to be so strong that the doubt as to the real character of the veto ought to be removed by an amendment to the constitution. *Kampen mellem Norges Storthing og Regjering, Aftryk af Dagbladet*, Christiania.

after all had been said, the fact remained that the framers of the constitution had failed to state what the power of the king should be in the given instance. The best jurists stood divided, some claiming that he had no veto power, as none had been specifically granted him, others inferring that he had absolute veto. Under these circumstances the view taken by Stang that he had a suspensive veto as in the case of all other bills might have been accepted, as J. E. Sars suggests, as a fair compromise. When the ministry refused to accept this view of the situation, and assumed an uncompromising attitude in favor of absolute veto, a deadlock was created which could only be broken by the defeat either of the Storthing or the ministry, and the ultimate triumph of the one or the other of the more extreme views.

The resolution of June 9th had scarcely been expected by Stang. He realized that a determined struggle would be waged by the Storthing, and as he was getting old, and feared the consequences of the impending conflict, he resigned. He was a highly gifted man, and in his long public career he had rendered his country eminent service as professor of jurisprudence, as lawyer, and especially as head of the department of the interior. But he was not a great statesman. He was in spirit a bureaucrat, who loved to be shown implicit obedience. His legal learning made him look at all questions from a jurist's point of view, and under the influence of his conservative friends he had developed as minister of state a decidedly reactionary policy. He retired from office with all outward show of honor, says Sars. "The king expressed his appreciation of the valuable services which he had rendered his country and his sovereign. But these and other honors shown him could not conceal from his own contemporaries, or from posterity, the fact that he retired from office as a defeated man, whose political policy had miscarried, because it rested on erroneous premises."

After Stang's retirement a new ministry was formed by C. A. Selmer, who had been representative in the Storthing and member of the Stang ministry. Hitherto he had not been conspicuous as a political leader, his only special qualification being his stanch adherence to the policy of Stang and "Morgenbladet," who considered it to be the chief object of the cabinet to defend the royal prerogatives.

PLATE XIX

CHR. AUG. SELMER.

EMIL STANG.

OSCAR II.

JOHANNES STEEN.

SØREN JAABÆK.

The position taken by the Storthing was enthusiastically supported by a great majority of the people. A few days after the resolution of June 9th had been passed, many thousands marched to Sverdrup's residence and thanked him for his great service. Throughout the country the representatives who had voted for the resolution received a joyous welcome, and were lauded by the press and at public political meetings. The ninth of June became for a time a national holiday.[1]

Instead of attempting to allay the controversy between ministry and Storthing, Selmer pursued a narrow bureaucratic policy which only aggravated the situation. In 1878 a bill was passed transferring the power of appointing *lensmænd* from the *amtmand* to the *herredstyre*, a very timely and useful reform, but the measure was vetoed. Other controversies also arose which served to increase the hostility between ministry and Storthing. In 1880 the Storthing instructed the committee on military affairs to prepare a plan for a new army organization to be submitted to the next session, but the ministry claimed that committees of the Storthing could not continue their work between sessions, and refused to pay the allowances granted the members. In 1868–1869 a commission had been appointed to propose plans for the extension of the suffrage, but when a bill was finally passed, in 1881, proposing to restrict male suffrage only by a slight property qualification, the measure was vetoed. The following year an appropriation bill was passed, granting financial aid to the *folkevæbningssamlag*, or *skytterlag*, a national organization of rifle clubs, aiming at training the people in the use of firearms. But also this measure was vetoed, as it was feared that the rifle clubs, organized for the purpose of strengthening the national defense, were the beginning of a parliamentary army created for the sake of supporting the Storthing in case of emergency. A bill providing for a central railway commission, six members of which should be appointed by the Storthing, was sanctioned in part, but the last clause, describing in what manner the members should be chosen, was vetoed. It was evident that the dictatorial attitude of the ministry, if allowed to pass unchallenged, would destroy the prestige and impair the power of the Storthing. Not only had the ministers

---

[1] Erik Vullum, *Følgerne af den 9de Juni.*

undertaken to settle by their own fiat the mooted question of the king's veto power in cases of constitutional amendments, but the veto had been extended even to bills of appropriation, and had been used in a way which would make the crown the supreme power in all affairs of government. Instead of being the servants of the people, carrying out the behests of the national legislature, the ministry had become the representatives of the king, who regarded the will of the people as a hostile force, which had to be checked and curbed in order that the royal prerogatives might be preserved. If a system should be allowed to develop, under which the executive department should arrogate to itself the power of successfully resisting the will of the people, expressed by its chosen representatives, the principle of democratic government would be destroyed. The royal preroga- tives, which might constantly be enlarged by inference and cabinet interpretation, would be elevated to the dignity of a constitution, which in doubtful cases would be given the preference over the written fundamental law. Progress was hindered, and the efficiency of the administrat on greatly reduced by the continual rivalry be- tween the executive and legislative departments. True develop- ment would demand that the king and the ministry should cease to stand in opposition to the people; that the executive and adminis- trative department should become the organ, not of the will of the ruler, but of the sovereign will of the people, in harmony with the constitution. By vesting in the Storthing the power of impeachment, which might be used against any minister who pursued a course deemed to be inimical to the interests of the country, the men of Eidsvold had placed in the hands of the people a weapon which had already been used on several occasions against recalcitrant members of the cabinet. This sword might again have to be used to sever the Gordian knot, but before resorting to so drastic a measure the leaders of the Liberal party would place the issue before the country at the next election, 1882. The king arrived in Christiania, and in a speech from the throne he openly censured the Storthing for its attitude on the veto question. The excitement throughout the country grew very intense, and the campaign became one of the stormiest ever witnessed in Norway. The Liberal leaders — Johan Sverdrup, Johannes Steen, Bjørnstjerne Bjørnson, and other able speakers — urged the people to rally to the defense of their political rights, and to support the resolution of June 9th. As the suffrage was restricted to landowners, many who on this account were disfranchised secured the rights to vote by acquiring title to marshy and otherwise useless land. By the Conservatives they were called in derision fagot-voters (*myrmænd*).[1] The Liberals won a decisive victory, returning eighty-three members to the Storthing while the Conservatives secured only thirty-one seats. But even after this overwhelming defeat, the ministry showed no inclination to resign. Impeachment was, therefore, the sole remaining constitutional remedy to which the Storthing could resort. The precaution was taken to choose only Liberals to the Lagthing, and on March 30, 1883, a measure was introduced in the Odelsthing instituting impeachment proceedings against the members of the cabinet for having advised the king to veto a bill passed by three Storthings, and for refusing to promulgate the bill as law upon the request of the Storthing. As the constitution provides that the king is blameless, and that all responsibility falls upon his ministers, they alone could be called to account.[2] An attempt to negotiate a compromise between the ministry and the leaders of the majority in the Storthing failed. The Conservatives were unwilling to agree to the retirement of the ministry, and demanded that the Liberals should concede nearly every point in the controversy, among other things that they should accept the theory of the king's absolute veto. Such a demand left no room for compromise, and the bill of impeachment was passed with fifty-three votes against thirty-two, April 23, 1883.

The impeachment proceedings began May 18th before the *Rigsret*, a tribunal consisting of thirty-eight members, *i.e.* nine judges of the High Court of Justice, and the members of the Lagthing numbering twenty-nine.[3] The accused used their right to challenge

---

[1] K. Lous, *Det radikale Parti og Myrmandsvæsenet.* Bjørnstjerne Bjørnson, *Om Folkesuveræniteten eller det norske Folks Husbondsret,* 1882.

[2] Jakob Sverdrup, *Ministeransvarligheden og Rigsretten, Særavtryk af Vestlandsposten,* 1883.

[3] *Rigsretten, dens Sammensætning og forfatningsmæssige Myndighed,* Christiania, 1880. Hartvig Lassen, *Det radikale Parti og Rigsretten.* G. Blom, *Mere om det radikale Parti og Rigsretten.* Haakon Løken, *Minder fra Rigsretstiden.* Yngvar Nielsen, *Under Oscar II's Regjering,* p. 222 ff.

and dismiss one-third of the members. The remaining twenty-six conducted the trial, which lasted till February 18, 1884. All the ministers were found guilty. The minister of state, J. A. Selmer, was dismissed from office, and had to pay the cost of the trial. His associates, Vogt, Holmboe, Helliesen, Jensen, Munthe, and Bachke, were dismissed from office. Johansen, who in 1880 had opposed the veto of the measure in question, and Chr. Schweigaard and Hertzberg, who had become members of the ministry after the measure was vetoed, escaped with a fine.

For some time after the decree had been rendered, the greatest excitement prevailed, as it was rumored that the king would disregard the decision of the court. In the London "Pall Mall Gazette" a correspondent writes, October 10, 1883:

"Rumors have reached England that the decision of the tribunal now engaged in trying the Norwegian ministry — in case the verdict should be the dismissal of the ministers from their office — will be set aside or disregarded, and that the king will express his confidence in the ministers, and retain them in his Council, or that he may even appoint a new Conservative ministry. But surely this, in a constitutional country, is the first step towards revolution, and I cannot believe the Executive entertains such treasonable designs. This court is, unquestionably, a national tribunal, and the judgment there expressed is the will of the people, which history teaches us it is not well to tamper with. A *coup d'état* on the part of the king has also been spoken of, and more than once recommended by the Conservative papers in the country. It is surely too late in the day for any constitutional king to think of forcing an absolute veto, which is now really the bone of contention, upon his people at the point of the bayonet, and if the Norwegians do not belie their traditions, there seems but little chance of success for the king, if he were to attempt to thwart the national will by force of arms. The Norwegian people, who in 1814 took the bold and resolute step of standing up for their liberty, and declaring themselves a free and independent nation, may in the present year of grace, or whenever occasion demands it, prove themselves as valiant as their forefathers to defend their liberty. All the reports circulated about a rupture with Sweden, the object of the majority in the Storthing to establish the republic, and about civil war, may be entirely overlooked.

"The anxiety displayed by the Conservative press of the country at the prospect of a change of the ministry is almost amusing to Englishmen, who have become pretty accustomed to such political vicissitudes; these reactionary organs predict the ruin of the country if the Liberals were to win the day, and the country be blessed with a ministry who would work in harmony and good earnest with the people's representatives. If the Norwegian people will have a Liberal ministry, let the king by all means appoint such a one. Surely the well-known honorable and sedate character of the Norwegians is more than sufficient guarantee that the welfare and the liberty of the country will be as zealously guarded in such an event as by any Conservative ministry."

Many strange acts on the part of the government increased the excitement, and gave further support to the belief that the decision of the court of impeachment would not be respected. It became known that Selmer had presided as minister of state after the decision of the court had been rendered. It was rumored that loaded cannons were mounted on the fortress of Akershus, and that the army rifles belonging to the national troops in many places had been rendered useless, for fear, as it was said, of a rebellious uprising. But this nervous alarm was finally allayed when on March 11th the king dismissed Selmer in obedience to the decision rendered by the court. The Storthing had won the battle. Its supreme authority could no longer be questioned, nor could it be doubted that the parliamentary system, according to which the cabinet must coöperate with the majority in the legislative assembly, or retire, would henceforth be carried out in practice. The king, it is true, did not recognize this principle, and appointed a new Conservative ministry headed by Emil Stang, leader of the Conservative party. But the Storthing continued to follow up its victory. The bill regarding the appointment of *lensmænd*, which had been vetoed in 1878 and 1881, was passed a third time. The minister of the war department, Dahl, and his successor, Munthe, were summoned before the Storthing to explain the strange occurrences in their department at the time of the trial of Selmer and his colleagues. The Liberal majority demanded of the new ministry that they should promulgate as law the bill regarding the seating of the ministers, according to the resolution of June 9th, and that the decision of the court of impeachment should be accepted in all its parts. If this was not done, impeachment proceedings would immediately be instituted against them. The Stang ministry, finding that they could not resist the majority in the Storthing, resigned. The king now requested O. J. Broch to form a coalition ministry, but this attempt failed, and he advised the king to intrust the task of forming a new ministry to the Liberal leader, Johan Sverdrup. A compromise was agreed upon, and Sverdrup formed a Liberal ministry which quickly settled the pending issues. The appropriations to the rifle clubs were sanctioned; so also the bill providing for a change in the method of appointing *lensmænd*. The bill providing for a central railway commission was also signed without any modification. But with regard to the bill providing for the seating of the ministers, which involved the question of the king's veto power, a compromise was arranged. The measure should again be introduced in the Storthing with the additional clause providing that members of the cabinet should be made eligible to the Storthing from districts in which they do not reside. The bill was introduced by Levius Smitt, and was promptly passed and sanctioned. On July 2, 1884, the Sverdrup ministry took their seats in the Storthing, and were bidden welcome by President Johannes Steen. The parliamentary principle had been formally recognized.

65. Further Development of the Norwegian Literary and Cultural Renaissance

The great political struggles stirred the Norwegian people to intense thoughts and feelings, and roused them to a new national life. During the exciting conflicts waged for the defense of their liberty and independence they had become active participants in events which involved their most vital social and national interests. The newborn independence had brought increased privileges and opportunities, but it had also made new demands on the vigilant intelligence of the individual. Every boy had begun to consider himself a politician; in every household the conversation centered on the great issues, the popular political leaders, the technical points in the all-absorbing controversy. Business interests and economic questions were pushed into the background. From year to year the mind followed the deepening conflict with anxious fascination, or joyous controversial interest. The poets who lived through this exciting period as young men and political leaders imbibed the strongly realistic spirit and love for the solution of great problems, the distinguishing features of the intellectual as well as of the political life of the age. At first they had been influenced by romanticism. They had stood in romanticism to the waist, as Brandes says of Ibsen.[1] But the age of vague symbolism and sentimental ballads had passed, and they developed under the influence of the national conflict a modern novel and drama dealing with social and psychological problems. Ibsen and Bjørnson, who were the founders of the new realistic school, were soon joined by their great contemporaries Jonas Lie, Alexander Kielland, and Arne Garborg. In "Peer Gynt" Ibsen makes the visionary romanticist the mark of his superb satire. Peer, the gifted dreamer, never accomplishes anything, never even attempts it. He goes through life waiting for good luck to perform the miracle of making him great. A more worthless caricature of a man has never stirred an audience to laughter, but even the mirth is tinged with sadness. The trifling with life's most solemn duties, the dreamy hallucinations of greatness in the midst of poverty and indolence, the wasting of gifts and opportunities, the ludicrous self-centered egotism which destroys his soul and his happiness, because he refuses to contribute to the happiness of others, become a profound tragedy when viewed against the background of the struggling and suffering which surround him. So useless are the romanticists in this practical world of ours, Ibsen would say. This philosophy that the poet, the artist, the great man is a divinely inspired individual who does not need to exert himself, who triumphs by virtue of his genius, which is thrown like a witch's dowry into his cradle, is destroyed with one fell stroke. In "The Pretenders" and "Brand" Ibsen had already set up another philosophy, in which he makes the will and the character the central forces in life, the true source of greatness. Success, or even great-

---

[1] Georg Brandes, *Henrik Ibsen.* Henrik Jæger, *Henrik Ibsen og hans Verker.* Anathon Aal, *Henrik Ibsen als Dichter und Denker.* Just Bing, *Norske Digte og Digtere.* Henrik Jæger, *Norske Forfattere.*

ness itself, is not a gift which luck drops into the lap of the indolent; it is a trophy won by the one who has the resolute will, the courage to conquer. Life is a perpetual conflict between things as they are and as they ought to be. Into this conflict we must all enter, and as a strong, undaunted, truth-loving character is the only true qualification for a useful life, so an indolent and compromising spirit is the source of our undoing. Brand raises the demand of "all or nothing." You must not compromise with sin and injustice. You must do what is right to the full extent of the demand of the divine law. The will is the main thing. "Willingly and joyfully you must suffer every anguish," says Brand to Agnes, and when she feels her inability to fulfill such a demand, and leans her head upon his shoulder, he consoles her by saying: "That you can't will be forgiven, but never that you lack the will." In "The Pretenders" he shows the conflict between the doubting, hesitating, plotting Skule Jarl and the upright and self-confident King Haakon. Both desire to accomplish great things. Achievements are their fascination. The ability to do great deeds they regard as the true worth of life, the measure of success. "Who is the greatest man?" asks Bishop Nikolas. "The one who is the most courageous," replies Skule. "So says the chieftain," answers the bishop. "A priest would say the most pious, a sage would say the most learned, but it is neither of them, Jarl. The happiest man is the greatest. The happiest is he who does the greatest deeds, he to whom the demands of the age come like a passion, and create in him thoughts which he cannot understand, points out to him the way which he does not know whither it leads. But he must continue on the way until he hears the people shout for joy; and he looks about with staring eyes, wonders, and realizes that he has done a great deed." This is a characterization of Ibsen himself and of his age. In his epigrammatic sentences, into which he has compressed fundamental truths regarding life, character, personality, truth, right, the mission of the individual, we find expressed the spirit of the age which waged war against oppression, desired a life of freedom, solved great problems, and assailed with youthful vigor the crumbling bulwarks of antiquated political and social ideas.

The old social forms in Norway did not conform to the new polit-

PLATE XX

HENRIK IBSEN.

ical ideas, neither did they meet the wants of the kind of personality which Ibsen and his contemporaries demanded. Sedate respectability and decorous, time-honored forms from which long since all spirit had fled served as a cloak of hypocrisy and dishonesty. Old prejudice stood in the way of the recognition of talent and ability; closer scrutiny revealed falsehood and hidden corruption in all relations of life. Against this spiritual weakness and moral depravity in high places as in low the great writers declared relentless war in their social dramas and novels. Society was to be purged of its falsehood and corruption; the life of the community as of the individual should be based on truth and purity; the relations in love, marriage, home, and state should be rendered sacred, not by conventional forms, but by true affection, chastity, and honesty. In social as in political life there was need of men and women who could do great deeds. Only through a regeneration of society could the development of free, moral, intelligent personalities become possible. Every phase of life was scrutinized by Ibsen's searching eye in "Love's Comedy," "The Pillars of Society," "A Doll House," "Ghosts," "An Enemy of the People," and the whole list of his modern social dramas. Bjørnson ceased writing idyllic descriptions of country life, and turned his attention to social problems. In his novel "Magnhild," in which he treats of woman's position in married life and the mission of the individual, both scenery and people have assumed somber traits which remind us of Ibsen's "Brand" rather than of "Synnøve Solbakken." It has all the characteristic features of the new philosophizing, reforming realism, and in his succeeding works, as "The New System," "Leonarda," "A Mitten," "A Bankruptcy," etc., he deals with various features of social and moral life with great dramatic force.

Among the great masters of this period no one excelled Alexander Kielland in elegance of style and mastery in narrative and character painting. At thirty he wrote his first novel, and at forty his literary career was closed, but during this short period of ten years he enriched Norwegian literature with a series of masterpieces in which he sharply attacked the prevailing social wrongs. About his first novel, "Garmann and Worse," Henrik Jæger writes:[1] "This son of

---

[1] *Illustreret norsk Literaturhistorie*, vol. III., p. 841 ff.

a Stavanger patrician, who for a number of years had been manager of some tile works, had early discovered the fatal contrast in modern society between capitalist and laborer; the contrast between the fortunate ones who sleep in their soft beds, and those who never sleep on anything but chaff and straw; the contrast between those who have a taste for oysters and champagne, and can satisfy their taste, and those who during their whole life never learn to know what oysters and champagne are, who are condemned to live on the shady side of life; the contrast between that which is fine, but can be simple, and that which is simple and still may be fine; the contrast between opulence and want, between wealth and poverty; the contrast between those who dance on the floor, and those who cause the same floor to tremble with the hatred of millions; the contrast between those who are buried with the singing of hymns and the tolling of bells, and those who are buried as paupers about in the same way that a dead cat is put into the ground, only with the difference that in the former instance the minister speaks a few words at the grave. About these contrasts Kielland speaks in his first novel. His attacks on vice and corruption are often very severe, but he never stoops to anything coarse or indelicate." Professor J. E. Sars says: "The works of Alexander Kielland are, as all know, singularly free from everything coarse and impure. In his descriptions he never attempts to unduly stimulate the senses, nor does he ever overstep the boundaries which the strictest modesty may draw. His satire is unusually sharp and poignant, but it is never directed against anything but falsehood and humbug, the vicious and ridiculous, which without controversy ought to be removed from the positions of honor into which it has been able to climb. His works show no anti-Christian tendency; on the contrary, they must be said to reveal a deep sympathy with the genuine spirit of piety, and an appreciation of all true Christianity." [1] Kielland was a novelist, less versatile than Bjørnson, but no less a master in his chosen field. In popularity as an author he is only excelled by Jonas Lie, who has won the hearts of the Norwegian people to an unusual extent. Lie's first novel, "The Clairvoyant" ("Den Fremsynte"), was a literary triumph which suddenly made him known as a great

---

[1] *Norges Historie*, vol. VI., 2, p. 12 ff.

PLATE XXI

ARNE GARBORG.

JONAS LIE.

ALEXANDER L. KIELLAND.

author.   From the depths of his mystic mind he had brought forth
one of the finest pieces of art in narrative literature.   He began
late, as he was slow in discovering his own talents.   But he soon
captivated the whole North, and won world-wide fame through his
matchless sea-tales, "The Pilot and his Wife," "Rutland," and
other novels, in which he has contributed the best that the world
literature owns in that field.   The scope and true greatness of his
genius reveals itself in his novels dealing with family life, especially
"The Family of Gilje," in many ways his greatest work.   The
various phases of social life he has treated in a series of novels, as
"A Life Convict," "Maisa Jons," "Niobe," and other works.[1]

Arne Garborg, the youngest of the five leading authors of this
period, was born in 1851.   He is a deep and original thinker, a
doubting, searching, critical, introspective soul of the type of Leo
Tolstoi.   "That which constitutes myself," he says, "is a contempla-
tor in ceaseless hope and struggle, with a faith which every day vanquishes doubt, and a doubt which, nevertheless, pulls the foundation from under my faith, so that I must move further and further
upland whenever the river swallows up the sod which I believed to
be a sure foothold."[2]   No one in Norway has wielded a better
pen, and no one has been his superior as a polemicist.   His lyrical
productions have a rare charm, and his prose writings excel in brilliant idiomatic style and rare descriptive power.   Very early in
his career he chose the *Landsmaal* as his literary language, but his
paper "Fedraheimen," which began to appear in 1877 in this language,
lived only seven years.   Later he founded "Den 17de Mai," which
has become one of the leading papers.   He has been an active liberal
politician and journalist, intensely interested in every public issue.
His contributions to the various questions of the day would fill
volumes, and constitute an important part of his literary work.
In some of his best books, like "Kolbotnbrev" and "Knudaheibrev,"
he narrates the story of his own quiet family life in his humble log
cabin among the lonely mountains of Østerdalen and on the heath-
ery heaths of his native district of Jæderen.   In these charming
narratives he has achieved the highest in description of country life

---

[1] Arne Garborg, *Jonas Lie*.   Erik Lie, *Jonas Lie, Oplevelser*.   *Jonas Lie,
et Festskrift*.   [2] Ivar Mortensen, *Arne Garborg*, p. 116.

and scenery. But his musing spirit has especially dwelt on the often ghastly problems of social life, which have yielded themes for works like "Bondestudentar," "Trætte Mænd," "Fred," "Hjaa ho Mor," etc. "Garborg is at the same time romanticist and rationalist, ascetic and a lover of beauty, ironist and believer. As author and journalist, politician and agitator for the *Landsmaal*, atheist and Christian advocate, he has shown tireless flexibility and alertness. He has been at the same time the most impressible and most inflexible spirit in our literature," writes Reider Øksnevad. He manifested early the strong will, the undaunted courage, and self-confidence of the leader, who never shrinks from the conflict. For many years he was the recognized head of the *Landsmaal* movement, and through his intensely national spirit he became an inspiration to the young people, who flocked in great numbers to his standard.[1]

These great authors and their contemporaries, like Jon Klæbo, Elias Blix, Kristofer Jansen, John Lie, Theodor Caspari, Peer Sivle, and others, created a literature which gave Norway rank among the great nations in the field of higher intellectual culture. The power and originality of this literature was soon recognized, and it has exerted a great influence on the nineteenth century literary art throughout the whole world. The creative Norse mind, freed from political and social obstructions, has again given the nations a heritage equaling that of the Eddas and sagas of old.

In all fields of intellectual activity the creative spirit showered its wealth upon this age. A new national school of music was originated by Norway's greatest composers, Edward Grieg,[2] Johan Svendsen, and other contemporaries, and in painting, a new realistic school was founded by J. F. Thaulow, Christian Krohg, G. Munthe, and E. Werenskiold. In sculpture, Stephan Sinding, Vigeland, and Utsond have won great fame. In the various branches of higher learning the same productivity and originality may be observed as in literature and art. In mathematics Norway has twice produced a genius whose name is forever linked to the highest achievements in this field. The first was Niels Henrik Abel, who died in 1829, less than twenty-seven years old, but who at that youthful age had won

---

[1] *Arne Garborg*, T. Mauland, Hulda Garborg, and others, in *Syn og Segn*, January, 1911.   [2] Henry T. Finck, *Edward Grieg*.

world-wide fame as one of the greatest lights in the field of mathematics.[1] The other was Sophus Lie, who after having been tossed about for some time with uncertainty as to his calling, suddenly rose to greatness as a mathematician. "Yet in 1867 Lie was groping around in uncertainty as to himself and his destiny," writes his biographer, Holst. "Two years later he was the leader among the mathematicians of his age. Every new work was like a stroke of the sword, which won new territory for his science, and new renown for himself and his country. His mathematical productions are very extensive. In his chief work, "Theori der Transformationsgruppen," in three large volumes, he has opened a new field in mathematical science. In 1886 he was called as regular professor of mathematics to the University of Leipzig, but in 1894 the Norwegian Storthing offered him a salary of 10,000 kr. per year if he would return. He accepted the offer, but died in 1899 in Christiania.

In the field of philology Sophus Bugge has won world-wide reputation. Of the many able men which Norway has produced in this field no one has quite equaled him in renown. His researches cover nearly all phases of Indo-Germanic philology, but especially important are his interpretations of the runic inscriptions, his theory regarding the origin of the runic alphabet, and his work on the origin of the Northern myths, "Studier over de nordiske Gude- og Heltesagns Oprindelse," which has created a new epoch in the study of Northern mythology. Bugge opened new fields of research in Northern history and tradition. Through his new viewpoints and profound scholarship he fostered an intense scholarly interest and strictly scientific methods, and contributed much to the awakening of a national spirit.

A most typical exponent of the spirit of this age is the great historian J. E. Sars, one of the most influential leaders of the national liberal movement. The founders of the Norwegian historical school, R. Keyser and P. A. Munch, had developed a scientific historical research, and had formulated the fundamental theories of Norwegian nationality, on which later historians have continued to build. They had written great works on the earlier periods of Norwegian

---

[1] *Nordmænd i det 19de Aarhundrede, Niels Henrik Abel.* Abel's works, edited by Sylow and Sophus Lie, were published in the French language in Christiania, 1881, at the expense of the government.

history, but a systematic exposition of the national development of the Norwegian people was still lacking. All the older historians had regarded the history of Norway as consisting of two parts, to which they might with profit devote their attention; the earlier period up to the time of the Kalmar union, and the modern period after 1814. The period of union with Denmark was regarded as an era of dependence and national stagnation, about which they preferred to keep silent. In 1834 Henrik Wergeland had characterized the situation as follows: "Modern Norway and ancient Norway appear like two halves of a broken ring which fit exactly together; the middle period is but the bogus soldering which we must break away to restore the genuine parts." This view was correct in so far as it recognized the intimate relation between ancient and modern Norwegian culture, but it was wholly erroneous as an explanation of the historic development of the Norwegian people. The unbroken continuity and general character of this development, the national warp and woof in the whole social and historic fabric was first fully shown by Sars in his leading work, "Udsigt over den norske Historie." Henrik Wergeland first indicated it in his "Norges Konstitutions Historie," but Sars made it the basis of a new interpretation of Norwegian history. He showed that the Norwegian people in early times did not consist only of *bønder* under a patriarchal rule, but that an aristocracy had been developed, more powerful than that of Sweden and Denmark. When Harald Haarfagre united all Norway under his rule, the *herser*, or chieftains, lost their former power, but the struggle between the kings and the aristocracy continued until the chieftain class was destroyed. When the old royal line died out, Norway entered the union with Denmark without a warlike aristocracy strong enough to be the leaders of the people. Norwegian society had become democratic at a time when Sweden and Denmark were ruled by a strong warlike aristocracy. This explains the inferior position of Norway during the period of union. But the destruction of the aristocracy was in many ways a benefit to Norway. There was no longer any powerful upper class which could oppress and enslave the people, as in Sweden and Denmark. The *bønder* retained their land and their personal freedom. Social conditions were created which were most favorable

PLATE XXII

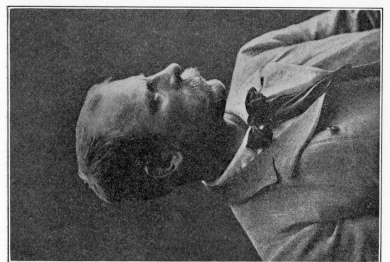

FRIDTJOF NANSEN.

J. E. SARS.

to a national development along new lines, and when the modern era dawned, Norway quickly outstripped Denmark and Sweden in the development of democratic social conditions and free political institutions. When seen in the proper light, the period of union with Denmark was an era of slow inner growth which shaped conditions favorable to a new national development. The apparently sudden change brought about in 1814 was the culmination of a long social evolution, and the rapid progress made by the Norwegian people during the last century finds its explanation in conditions which had shaped themselves in the union period. The political development of the Norwegians under their own representative government after 1814 is treated by Sars in his second great work, "Norges politiske Historie 1815–1885." These two works became household books in Norway, and as their spirit was not only historical, but national, they strengthened the patriotic sentiment, dispelled the Pan-Scandinavian dream, and inspired the people with pride in their own history, and confidence in their ability to restore to their kingdom its ancient glory. What the Norwegian historical school had begun, Sars had continued, until Norway could now be said to have recovered the once lost legacy of her own past history.

The national development had also awakened new interest in popular and higher education, and the improved schools in turn became the intellectual arsenals which equipped the people with new ideas and mental force for the solution of their cultural problems. Great stimulus was given popular education by the folk-high-schools, which began to flourish in the seventies. These schools were built in the country districts for the use of the rural population, and were organized according to the plan originated in Denmark by N. F. S. Grundtvig. They represented a strong patriotic movement, and are in reality not high-schools in any sense of the word. Their aim is not to impart instruction in such a way as to make the pupil learned, but to awaken intellectual life, to kindle interest by lectures on history and literature and the study of the mother tongue. Classical and foreign languages are banished. There are no fixed courses of study and no examinations. The pupils attend at intervals, especially during the winter months, when they have time, usually one or two winters. It was found that long courses of study often monopolize the attention and interest of the young people; hence short periods of attendance are preferred, as the school is to fit them for a successful life in their own home environment. Great stress is laid especially on the development of character and personality. Christopher Bruun, one of the leaders of this movement in Norway, writes: "As Norway has received her great poets, so we hope that she may receive her great statesmen, great thinkers, great warriors, — if they should be needed, — great spirits in all fields. But what we especially desire is men who know how to work for a cause, not only for wife and children, who understand how to sacrifice for it, to fight for it, and carry it to victory. Even if we do not lack such strong men nowadays, it cannot be denied that they are few enough, and that we need many more. The education which our young people receive in our higher schools cannot produce such a spirit. They learn a number of things which are worth little, but of that which is most important they learn little and learn it poorly." [1]

The folk-high-schools have exerted a very beneficial influence, but as they are private schools, their number has always been limited. In 1877 the government took steps to organize a system of secondary schools for the young people of the rural districts. These were of two kinds, the evening schools and the *amt* schools, supported partly by the government and partly by the local districts.

In 1865 a new school commission was created with Hartvig Nissen as chairman, and as a result of the labors of this body, the school law of 1869 was passed, creating a new system of secondary schools. The *middelskole*, or higher public school, with a course covering a period of six years, was opened for children between the ages of nine and fifteen years who had finished the grades of the primary public schools. By the law of 1896 this course was shortened to four years. The *middelskole* prepares for the *gymnasium*, where the regular course covers a period of three years. A reorganization of the public school system was effected by the law of 1889, which still forms the basis of public school organization in Norway, though it has been modified by later legislation.[2]

---

[1] Christopher Bruun, *Folkelige Grundtanker*, p. 137.

[2] W. Rein, *Encyklopädisches Handbuch der Pädagogik*, vol. VI., p. 287 ff. David Allen Anderson, *The School System of Norway*, Richard Badger Publishing Company, Boston.

66. The Sverdrup Ministry. Norway under Parliamentary Government

Johan Sverdrup formed a ministry including a number of the most influential Liberal leaders. Ole Richter became Norwegian minister of state in Stockholm, Ludvig Daae minister of war, Aimar Sørenssen minister of justice, Sofus Arctander minister of the interior, Baard Haugland minister of finance, Elias Blix, noted scholar and poet, minister of education and church affairs, and Birger Kildal minister of the auditing department. All these were men of ability, who enjoyed the full confidence of the people. But Sverdrup's two nephews, J. Stang and Jakob Sverdrup, who became members of the Swedish branch of the ministry, were not very prominent, and enjoyed no special confidence. Their appointment was looked upon with disfavor, and proved to be a mistake, as the Liberals favored the able and popular Johannes Steen, who was second only to Sverdrup himself in influence. It soon became evident that the hitherto prevailing harmony might be disrupted for no very serious reason. So long as the Liberal party had to fight a strong and determined Conservative opposition, it had presented a united front, but after this opposition had been almost destroyed, the various groups which had united under the leadership of Sverdrup might cease to coöperate. Jaabæk still led a large faction of the bønder, whose favorite issue was economy in the administration; and the church reform group, who were opposed to atheism and modern European ideas, was growing very strong in the southwestern districts. The first serious discord between these factions occurred in connection with a proposal submitted to the Storthing by Bjørnson and Jonas Lie, that Alexander Kielland should receive a similar poet's salary which had already been granted Bjørnson, Ibsen, and Lie. There could be no doubt that Kielland's reputation as an author entitled him to this recognition, but the committee to which the petition was referred considered it inadvisable "to give official sanction to a literature which was opposed to the prevailing views on religion and morality." When the measure was brought up in the Storthing by the dissenting chairman of the committee, it was defeated by a small majority. Bjørnson brought the matter also before the next Storthing in 1886, but it was again defeated, as a faction of the Liberal party voted with the Conservatives. Lars Oftedal, a very influential clergyman from Stavanger, was especially active in opposition to this measure, though he had on former occasions praised Kielland's works. He was leader of the church reform group, and editor of "Vestlandsposten," a paper which had gained considerable circulation. Jakob Sverdrup, member of the ministry, who belonged to the same group, proposed a reform by which the congregations were to receive greater influence in the administration of church affairs. Each congregation should elect a council, which might propose a candidate for clergyman in case of vacancy, and might grant permission to others than the clergyman to speak in the church. This was a purely administrative reform, but Oftedal and his group sought to bring it forward as a general issue, on which a new Christian Liberal party could be organized to oppose those who favored atheism and anti-Christian views. Christianity and morality was to be associated with the proposed reform as a campaign issue, but in this he did not succeed, as all other factions of the Liberal party opposed it.

The Sverdrup ministry entered the campaign of 1885 on the issue of parliamentary government, and reforms in the judicial system, the army, the administration, and the public school system. "Full confidence in Johan Sverdrup" became the campaign cry which carried the Liberal party to victory. When the Storthing assembled, Sverdrup controlled a safe majority, and he secured the adoption of the proposed plan for a new army organization as well as the passage of a bill providing for the introduction of the jury system, July 1, 1887. Other important measures might have been carried through but for the attempt to establish the church reform proposed by Jakob Sverdrup. This had aroused bitter opposition, and the larger part of the Liberal party were in favor of postponing the matter for a time. Johan Sverdrup himself, however, insisted on presenting the bill to the Storthing. It was already too late to consider it at that session, but when it was brought up in 1887, it was rejected almost unanimously.[1] As the bill had been originated by a member of the cabinet, its overwhelming defeat raised the question if the

---

[1] A. M. St. Arctander, *De Sverdrupske Ministerkriser.*

ministry should resign. Three ministers, Astrup,[1] Arctander, and Kildal, demanded that Jakob Sverdrup, who had originated the bill, should retire, but the other members did not consider this necessary. The ministry might remain unchanged, they thought, as the bill was not a leading measure, on which they had all united. Jakob Sverdrup did not retire, and the three tendered their resignation. They were persuaded, however, to remain in office until the matter could be brought before the next session of the Storthing, when the question of parliamentary principles would be discussed. The Liberal majority in the Storthing prepared to question the ministry in regard to its attitude to these principles, but a majority of the ministers had agreed that no definite answer should be given. To this course Astrup, Arctander, and Kildal would not agree, and they retired from the ministry. Blix also resigned a few days later. To the questions of the Liberal majority as to his position regarding parliamentary principles, Johan Sverdrup returned only evasive answers, but he promised to reconstruct the ministry in harmony with the Liberal majority, such as he considered that majority to be constituted. A split had already taken place in the Liberal party. Against the supporters of Sverdrup, who called themselves National Liberals, or Moderate Liberals, stood the Pure Liberals, led by Johannes Steen. The confidence in Sverdrup was shaken, and when he reconstructed his ministry by appointing as members many who had not been prominent in political affairs, the prestige of the old chieftain rapidly waned. The Pure Liberals demanded that the principles of the parliamentary system should be carried out, and Sverdrup's great reputation could no longer shield him from attack, when it became evident that he had forsaken these principles, which had been the issue in the whole political conflict. The tragic death of Ole Richter, Norwegian minister of state in Stockholm, increased the ill-will against the ministry. He had opposed Sverdrup's tactics in the church reform question and the manner in which the ministry had been reconstructed. He held that the position of the ministry

---

[1] When Ludvig Daae retired from the ministry in April, 1885, the departments of war and navy were united into one department of defense, and H. R. Astrup was placed at the head of the new department of labor which was now created.

was untenable, that by remaining in office they violated the parliamentary principles, which they had made their main issue. Circumstances had forced him into opposition to his chief, but he was unable to break off all relations with him, and resign. The attempt to coöperate with a ministry with which he could no longer agree involved him in contradictory courses of action which rendered the situation unbearable. He finally resigned, June 6, 1888, bid farewell to his colleagues, and was going to return home. But before leaving Stockholm he committed suic de in his hotel. This news caused a great sensation, and the Pure Liberals attempted to overthrow the Sverdrup ministry by a vote of lack of confidence, but the motion brought was not considered, because of the approaching elections. In 1888 the Conservatives, led by Emil Stang, secured fifty-one seats, the Pure Liberals thirty-eight, and the Moderate or National Liberals, who supported the ministry, only twenty-two. It was evident that Sverdrup no longer enjoyed the confidence of the people, and in the face of so overwhelming a defeat he ought to have retired. But he preferred to remain in power, and was able to do so for a time, as the Conservatives gave him their support, not because they agreed with their old adversary, but because they might derive some advantage from prolonging the life of the ministry. Finally, on June 26, 1889, the Conservative leader, Emil Stang, proposed a vote of lack of confidence in the Sverdrup ministry, and Sverdrup and his colleagues resigned before the resolution was put to a vote. A Conservative ministry was now formed under the leadership of Emil Stang. The split in the Liberal party had become permanent, and the two Liberal groups waged a bitter fight against one another. The Pure Liberals were especially acrimonious in their attacks on Johan Sverdrup, whom they regarded as a renegade· The intense party feeling led them, as Sars says, "not only to greatly misjudge Sverdrup, who despite his weakness and errors must be regarded as one of Norway's greatest men, but they slandered their own party, and threw a dark shadow upon its past history." Johan Sverdrup's public career was now closed. In 1891 he was elected representative to the Storthing from Stavanger *amt*, but he died before the session opened, February 17, 1892.

The parliamentary principle had gained undisputed recognition.

By the proposed vote of lack of confidence in the Sverdrup ministry the Conservative leader himself had accepted the view that no ministry can remain in power without the support of the majority in the Storthing. Many of the great issues, like the establishing of parliamentary government, the introduction of the jury system, the extension of the suffrage, the reform of the school system, etc., had also been carried through before the Liberal party had been swept from power. But one difficult question yet remained unsettled, that of Norway's equal rights with Sweden in dealing with diplomatic and foreign affairs. According to existing provisions, the Cabinet Council for Foreign Affairs, which should deal with diplomatic matters affecting both countries, should consist of the Swedish minister of state and one other member of the Swedish cabinet, together with the Norwegian minister of state in Stockholm, or, in case of his inability to be present, another member of the Norwegian ministry in Stockholm. In 1885 the Swedish Rigsdag changed the Swedish constitution in such a way as to disturb this relation, without conferring with the Norwegian government. According to this change, Sweden should have three members in the Council to Norway's one, and the diplomatic affairs, which had hitherto been reported by the king, should be reported by the Swedish minister of foreign affairs. This was such an undisguised attempt to treat Norway as a dependency that the Swedish government saw the necessity of taking steps to prevent a new union controversy. The Swedish minister of justice proposed in a joint session of the Swedish-Norwegian ministry in Stockholm that Norway should be represented in the Council by two ministers. But this attempt at compromise stranded on the protests from the Norwegian members, who opposed the consideration of a purely Norwegian affair in joint session.

After the king had sanctioned the measure passed by the Rigsdag, he proposed that the relative number of Swedish and Norwegian members in the Cabinet Council for Foreign Affairs should be fixed by a new clause to be added to the Act of Union. The Norwegian ministers in Stockholm, Ole Richter and Jakob Sverdrup, proposed that the Council should consist of six members, three from each kingdom. To this plan the Swedish ministry consented, with the understanding that the Swedish minister of foreign affairs should report all joint diplomatic matters, a condition which the Norwegian ministers accepted. When the plan was proposed to the Storthing, it caused prolonged and animated debate. It was clear that the relative number of members in the Council was not the main feature of the measure, for Swedish supremacy would be virtually conceded by making the Swedish minister joint minister of foreign affairs. This feature of the measure was vigorously opposed. Johan Sverdrup said at the time: ' The amendment which is to be inserted in our constitution must not be made to depend on the action of Sweden as to whether the proposed measure will become a part of the Act of Union. It has its own value, and it will produce consequences which are unavoidable." When the matter was brought up in the joint ministry in 1886, the Swedish members demanded that the Swedish minister should be made joint foreign minister, but to this the Norwegian members refused to agree. On June 21st the Storthing passed the following resolution:

"In accordance with repeated and concordant declarations, by which former Storthings have upheld Norway's equal rights with Sweden in the union, the present session of the Storthing expresses the conviction that the Norwegian people, in loyalty to the king and country, will defend the rights and honor of the kingdom, and support the government and the Storthing in their efforts to secure for Norway the share in the administration of foreign affairs which rightfully belong to her by virtue of her position as an independent kingdom placed on equal footing with Sweden in the union."

In 1891 the Stang ministry reached an understanding with the Swedish government, and a new proposal was submitted. The question as to whether the minister of foreign affairs should be a Swede or a Norwegian should this time be omitted, and should be settled by later negotiations, a provision which led the Swedish Rigsdag to reject the plan, as they thought that too great concessions had been made to the Norwegians. When it was brought up in the Storthing, the Liberal leader, Carl Berner, proposed the following resolution: "In accordance with declarations of earlier Storthings, the present session of the Storthing maintains Norway's equality with Sweden in the union, and the right of the kingdom to manage its own foreign affairs in a manner warranted by the constitution; and expresses the confident belief that the Norwegian people will never agree to an arrangement which may prove a hindrance to the exercise of Norway's full rights on this point." The resolution was passed by fifty-nine votes against fifty-five, both groups of the Liberal party supporting it, and the Stang ministry immediately resigned.

67. The Demand for a Separate Norwegian Foreign Office and Consular Service

When Emil Stang and his colleagues resigned, a new ministry was formed by Johannes Steen, leader of the Pure Liberals, 1891. It was clear that the chief problem awaiting solution was the question regarding the administration of Norway's foreign affairs. Recent events had shown that no attempt to strengthen Sweden's position in the union could succeed, as Norway resolutely demanded complete independence in all matters not designated as union affairs.[1] That the Norwegians desired to get their own minister of foreign affairs was well understood by the Liberal leaders, but they were uncertain as to what extent this desire should be made the issue in the coming campaign. The platform drafted by the Pure Liberals in Christiania contained clauses advocating universal suffrage, the abolition of the office of viceroy of Norway to which the king's oldest son could be appointed, the organization of the administration of Norwegian foreign affairs in such a way as to bring it under control of the Norwegian government, etc. But in spite of the hesitation of the leaders the question of a separate Norwegian foreign department became the leading issue, and the Pure Liberals, who had been a minority when the new ministry was organized, secured a safe majority in the next session. A bill passed by the Storthing abolishing the office of viceroy was sanctioned by the king, June 30, 1891, but this was a measure of secondary importance. The question as

---

[1] Otto Varenius, *Den gemensamme Utenrigsministern och Likställigheten.* Rudolf Kjellén, *Unionen sådan den skapades och sådan den blifit. I Utenrigsministerfrågan. Udenrigsstyret historisk fremstillet.* H. L. Brækstad, *The Norwegian Swedish Contest, a Reply to Constance Sutcliff's article* "*Scandinavia and her King,*" in *The Fortnightly Review* of October, 1897. I. Floodström, *Unionen och Unionsdocumenten; Sverige och Norges Utriksstyrelse.*

to what the ministry should do in regard to a separate Norwegian foreign department was the topic of all-absorbing interest.[1]

The Liberal leaders saw that although the people desired a foreign minister, it would be useless to attempt to carry such a measure at that time, as it would be opposed by the Conservative party as well as by Sweden. Instead of raising so difficult an issue, the Steen ministry resolved to make the more modest demand for a separate Norwegian consular service, about which it could not be successfully urged that it was a union affair.[2] This was a matter of vital importance, as it affected Norway's economic interests in a most direct way. Norway contributed $41\frac{2}{3}$ per cent of the joint expenses for consular and diplomatic service, but her trade interests were often poorly cared for. The two kingdoms were to a large extent commercial rivals, and as all consuls were appointed by the Swedish government, many salaried consuls were kept in places where Norway had no use for them, and in many places where Norway had a large trade, no consuls were found. Bernhard Dunker, a strict Conservative, wrote in 1866, that the past twenty years had proven the advisability for each kingdom in certain instances to use the right to appoint its own consuls. "But Sweden," he adds, "has been so jealous regarding the diplomatic representation in foreign countries that there could never be a question of appointing Norwegian consuls in places where Norway alone has commercial interests. But since Norway's commerce is now twice as large as that of Sweden,

[1] Munch Ræder, *Unionen og egen Udenrigsminister*. Arne Garborg, *Norges Selvstændighetskamp*, p. 55 ff. *Det norske Venstre fra 1884 til 1909*, *Utenrigsminister-Spørgsmaalet, Konsulatsaken*. L. M. B. Aubert, *Norges folkeretslige Stilling*, p. 214 ff. J. Belsheim, *Selvstændighet og Union*, p. 51 ff. J. Utheim, *Grundloven om Norges Udenrigsstyre*. Marcellus, *Bidrag til den Skandinaviska Unionens Historia*. N. Höier, *Statsforbundet mellan Sverige och Norge*. H. C. Berner, *Norsk eller fælles Udenrigsminister*.

[2] "While the *Act of Union* does not mention the consular service, the revised Norwegian constitution of November 4th has two paragraphs (22 and 92) which show that the consuls were to be regarded as purely Norwegian officials." Sigurd Ibsen, *Unionen*, p. 149. J. Utheim, *Grundloven og eget Udenrigsstyre*. Fridtjof Nansen, *Norway and the Union with Sweden*, p. 48 ff. The views of the Conservatives are stated by Professor Bredo Morgenstjerne, in *Norges nuværende Statsforfatning*, vol. I., p. 152 ff. K. Nordlund, *Den Svensk-Norska Krisen*, p. 7 ff. Oscar Alin, *Unionskomiténs Resultat*. Sigfried Wieselgren, *Sammenslutning eller Skilsmässa*.

Norwegian merchants, shipowners, and seamen have always desired consuls in some places where Sweden has not considered it necessary to have any." [1] At the request of the Storthing the ministry appointed a committee to investigate the consular service and report on the necessity of separate Norwegian consuls. The committee found that the interests of Norway demanded separate consuls. But the Swedish ministry declared the consular service to be a union affair, which could be settled only by mutual agreement.[2] This view was rejected by the Storthing, which passed on March 1, 1892, a resolution introduced by Moursund, declaring the organization of a separate consular service to be a purely Norwegian affair to be settled by the Norwegian authorities, though the conditions growing out of the existing arrangement had to be adjusted according to mutual agreement. The department of the interior concurred in the findings of the committee, and submitted a plan for separate Norwegian consuls which was passed by the Storthing. The ministry advised the king to sanction the measure, but he submitted instead a written document which he claimed contained his opinion in the matter. The ministers pointed out that he could submit no such opinion except by the advice of his cabinet, and further action was postponed until the king should arrive in Christiania, when he would discuss the measure with his ministers. After his arrival they learned in a private interview that he would not sanction the bill, and at the formal meeting of the ministry they tendered their resignation. They consented, however, to remain in office temporarily until a new ministry could be organized. Several attempts to form a new ministry failed, and the Storthing advised Steen and his colleagues to accede to the king's request and remain in office, with the understanding that the question of separate consular service should remain in abeyance for a time. To this the ministry consented, on condition that the consular question should be regarded as a purely Norwegian affair, and that the ministry might bring it up at any time. Both the Norwegian Storthing and the Swedish Rigsdag remained firm on the pending issue, the one

---

[1] B. Dunker, *Om Revision af Foreningsakten mellem Sverige og Norge*, p. 151 f.

[2] H. L. Rydin, *Antekningar om den norska Vensterns Unionspolitik.*

holding that Norway had the right to organize a separate consular service whenever it should be deemed necessary, the other asserting that the consular service was intimately connected with the diplomatic service, that it was a union affair, which could only be settled by mutual agreement. As there was no prospect of any immediate change in the situation, and as the king still refused to sanction the bill providing for Norwegian consuls when it was again proposed by the ministry, Steen and his colleagues retired from office, April 22, 1893.[1]

It would, undoubtedly, have been the wiser policy for the Steen ministry to have remained in office for a time according to the advice of the Storthing, without attempting to revive the question of separate consuls before the elections of 1894. But Steen, who was otherwise a very able leader, showed an anxiety to act in harmony with the majority which approached timidity, and made him the servant instead of the leader of his party. His resignation at this time made it impossible to form a ministry supported by the Liberal majority, and Emil Stang formed a Conservative ministry, "in order to avert the danger," as he explained it, "of leaving the king without advisers, and the country without a government." Lack of support naturally confined the work of the new ministry to routine affairs, and its existence was threatened from the outset. The Liberal press attacked it with bitterness and scathing sarcasm, claiming that it was organized in opposition to parliamentary principles for the purpose of helping the king to defeat the measure for a separate Norwegian consular service. In the Storthing the Liberal majority met them with undisguised hostility. Ullmann, one of the leading Liberals, said that the Stang ministry was conceived in sin and born in iniquity, that the wages of sin is death, and that the ministry would die a very violent death. A motion of lack of confidence in the new ministry was immediately passed, and a resolution was adopted, stating that the measure passed by the Storthing regarding the consular service would have to be acted upon by the king before the close of the fiscal year. A bill was also passed July 3, 1893, providing for the removal of the union sign from the Norwegian

---

[1] C. H. Schweigaard, *Konsulatsagen som politisk Middel.* Alfred Mohn, *Une Page d'Histoire de la Civilisation la Suède et la Revolution Norwegienne.*

flag, but the measure was vetoed by the king. A few days later the appanages of the king and the crown prince were reduced from 336,000 kroner and 80,000 kroner respectively to 256,000 and 30,000 kroner, and the allowance for table expenses for the two ministers of state, 15,000 kroner in Stockholm and 10,000 kroner in Christiania, was canceled. The refusal of the king to sanction the bill providing for a separate Norwegian consular service, and the selection of a body of advisers opposed by the Liberal majority in the Storthing, created an intensely hostile feeling. A bill was passed, providing that the joint consular service should terminate January 1, 1895, and the budget for this service for the year 1893–1894 was allowed only on the condition that the ministry should announce to the Swedish government the dissolution of the joint consular system, and should submit to the Storthing a plan for the organization of a separate Norwegian consular service. But the bill was not sanctioned. The money for the consular budget, which was not allowed, because the conditions were not complied with, was taken from the fund for incidental expenses, and when the Storthing passed a new bill withdrawing the contribution to the legation in Vienna, the king decided, contrary to the advice of the ministry, to continue that legation, and Norway's share of the expenses was to be advanced by Sweden.

In the elections of 1894 the Pure Liberals secured fifty-nine seats, and the Conservatives and Moderate Liberals fifty-five. The victory was not so decisive as might have been expected, but the Stang ministry immediately retired from office. They had accepted their portfolios, as Stang explained, only to avert the danger of being without a government, and it had been their aim to attend to the routine duties only until the election could be held. Their inability to settle the pending consular issue must have been evident to all, and the accusation that they attempted to prevent such a settlement, and that they disregarded the parliamentary principles, was as unjust as it was unfounded. Stang had already shown that he was in full sympathy with parliamentary practice, and he again demonstrated this when he resigned immediately after the elections. The vituperative attacks on him and his colleagues by the Liberal press and the majority in the Storthing only harmed the Liberal cause, as it was evident that the blame for the unfortunate situation could not attach to those who had undertaken the burdens of government only until the people could get the opportunity to express their opinion through the election. Stang's statement that he wished to avert the danger of being without a government had been ridiculed, but after his resignation it soon became apparent that there was real danger of such a situation. The king invited the Liberal leader Steen to form a new ministry, but attached such conditions that Steen refused. Several other leaders, both Conservative and Moderate, were approached, but no one found that he was equal to the task, and Stang was compelled to remain in office for a time against his wish.[1]

The Swedish Rigsdag assumed a more hostile and uncompromising attitude. Bitter expressions were indulged in both by the Rigsdag and by the Swedish press, and it was urged that a new act of union would have to be adopted, "which should reconstruct the Norwegian constitution on a safer foundation," as Charles John had expressed it. The war budget was doubled, war supplies were stored in large quantities near the Norwegian border, and troops were stationed in the border provinces. The Swedish minister of foreign affairs, Lewenhaupt, who had shown a disposition to extend a brotherly hand to the Norwegians, resigned, as it appears, according to the wish of minister of state Bostrøm, head of the Swedish ministry, and in his place was appointed the uncompromising Count Douglas. Everything indicated that there was grave danger of an open rupture between the kingdoms. Leading Swedish politicians who sympathized with Norway wrote to their Norwegian friends, and warned them to be on their guard against the warlike spirit of the Swedish ministry. One prominent Swedish leader, probably Adolf Hedin, wrote: "It is believed that the government, which has a new act of union in its pocket, will call an extra session of the Rigsdag. The new act of union is to be adopted by the Rigsdag, and will then be submitted to the Storthing. If Norway remains without a government, and no agreement can be reached with the majority in the Storthing, the Swedish army is to march against Norway. These are said to be the main features of the plan."[2] The Swedish

---

[1] *Forholdet mellem Norge og Sverige, vor Selvstændighedskamp i de sidste tyve Aar*, Bergen, 1905. [2] J. E. Sars, *Norges Historie*, vol. VI., 2, p. 153 ff.

plan was not to declare war, but to seize Christiania and Trondhjem. This would have crippled the Norwegian defense, and would have enabled Sweden to dictate terms. The plan might have succeeded, as Norway's defenses and military affairs had been sadly neglected.[1] The feeling of grave danger cooled to some extent the ardor of party strife, and a petition was sent to the Storthing from Christiania, signed by twenty-five Conservatives, twenty-two Pure Liberals, five Moderate Liberals, and four Independents, asking the representatives not to refuse to negotiate with Sweden regarding a settlement of the controversy, as such a course would be political imprudence, and would forfeit the sympathy of the European powers. A similar petition was sent from Bergen, signed by men like Sofus Arctander and Christian Michelsen. "These petitions," says Sars, "may be regarded as the beginning of a coalition of the parties with regard to foreign politics which was to carry the cause of independence to ultimate victory." Even the parties in the Storthing began to show a more conciliatory spirit. On June 7, 1895, a joint motion submitted by members of all the parties declaring in favor of negotiations with Sweden was passed with ninety votes against twenty-four, and appropriations were also made covering Norway's share of the expenses connected with the diplomatic and consular service. After several unsuccessful attempts the king finally succeeded in the fall of that year to form a new ministry of prominent men from all parties, headed by the conservative leader, Fr. Hagerup.

The policy of the Liberal party regarding the consular question had failed, and they had suffered a defeat which was regarded by all as a national humiliation.[2] Sweden had won a signal victory, and leading Swedish statesmen felt sure that the Norwegians would soon learn to see the futility of the struggle in which they had engaged; they would offer to negotiate, and a new act of union could

[1] Threats of war found expression both in the Conservative and Liberal Swedish press. The *Göteborgs Handels- och Sjöfarts-Tidning*, one of the leading Liberal organs, wrote in November, 1894: "If we should finally deem it necessary to appeal to the God of Hosts in order to maintain the union, we should place as a motto on our flags: 'Not the union as it is, but union with a joint foreign minister, Norwegian or Swede, etc.'" *Den svenske Krigsplan mod Norge*, Christiania, 1895.

[2] J. E. Sars, *Svenske Seire, norske Nederlag i Unionspolitiken, Samtiden,* 1905.

be carried through which would answer to the demands of Sweden. They felt sure that the defeat of the Liberals would split their party, and would greatly strengthen the Conservatives, who favored a strong union. They were soon to learn, however, that their calculations had been based on false premises; that instead of weakening the Liberals, their defeat had only strengthened them, and that even the Conservatives began to waver in the strong union policy which they had hitherto advocated. In course of time the reasons which had led the Conservatives to favor a closer union with Sweden had disappeared one by one. The attempt of the old official bureaucracy to perpetuate their political power and social influence by seeking the support of the king against the growing democratic spirit had failed utterly, as the common people had gained complete control. The Pan-Scandinavian sentiment had vanished, and even the economic benefit of the union, to which they had pointed with pride and confidence, proved to be an illusion. The lack of a separate consular service was a serious obstacle to the growth of Norwegian commerce, and as Sweden developed a system of protective tariff, while Norway introduced free trade, no very intimate relations between the two kingdoms could be maintained. In 1874 the *Mellemrigslov* was passed, which admitted to Sweden a number of Norwegian articles free of duty. It was renewed in 1890, but in 1895 it was repealed, and Norway's commercial relations with Sweden were no more intimate than with any other foreign power. The growing national spirit, the desire of removing all obstacles which stood in the way of Norway's free development tended to strengthen the Liberals, to lessen party differences, and to change the demand for a separate consular service from a party issue to a national cause.

The new ministry appointed in 1895 a committee of seven to negotiate with a similar Swedish committee regarding the pending consular issue.[1] During the negotiations between these committees quiet prevailed both in the press and in the Storthing. A bill for the removal of the union sign from the Norwegian flag, passed by the

---

[1] The members were: Getz, Schweigaard, Blehr, Thorne, Olai Olsen, Sivert Nielsen, and W. Konow. Olsen and Nielsen resigned, and Fritz Hansen and J. Løvland were appointed in their place. The Swedish members were: Ehrenheim, Sparre, Restadius, Olof Jonson, von Steyern, and the professors Alin and Trygger.

Storthing for the second time, was vetoed, but no other important measure was introduced. In the elections of 1897 the Liberal party won a decisive victory, securing seventy-nine seats, while the Conservatives retained only twenty-five, and the Moderate Liberals ten. The Hagerup ministry resigned, and Steen was invited to form a new Liberal ministry.

On March 26, 1898, the union committee submitted to the Storthing the result of their negotiations. Both the Norwegian and the Swedish members had split into two groups, and four different plans for the solution of the difficulty were submitted, neither of which had the slightest chance of being adopted.[1] The Swedish and Norwegian cabinets agreed after a short conference that nothing further could be done in the matter.[2]

The bill providing for the removal of the union sign from the flag was passed a third time in 1898. It was vetoed by the king, but according to article seventy-nine of the constitution it was promulgated as law. An intense agitation against this step was carried on in the Swedish press and by Swedish historians, who declared that it was "the beginning of the end," that in this measure the dissolution of the union was to be found "like the embryo in the seed."[3] The Swedish foreign minister, Douglas, refused to announce the change to foreign powers, but he was asked by his chief, Bostrøm, to resign, and Lagerheim, who succeeded him, gave due notice to consuls and foreign powers of the change in the Norwegian flag.[4]

Though supported by a large majority, the new ministry did not reopen the consular question. The experience of past years had proven that the most careful preparation was necessary, and they undertook instead to increase the nation's sinews of strength for the conflict which could not long be avoided. It was their aim to introduce universal suffrage in order that the people might participate

---

[1] *Underdanig Betænkning afgiven af den til Udarbeidelse af Forslag til forandrede Bestemmelser om Norges og Sveriges Forening ved kongelig Resolution af 13de November 1895 nedsatte Komite, tilligemed de af Komiteens enkelte Medlemmer udarbeidede Forslag,* Christiania, 1898.

[2] Oscar Alin, *Unionskomiténs Resultat.*

[3] *Flagfrågan.* R. Kjellén, *Ret och Sanning i Flagfrågan.*

[4] Rudolf Peersen, *Rent Flag.*

more directly in political and public affairs. By the law of 1898 full right of suffrage was extended to all men twenty-five years of age who had resided in the country five years, still resided there, and were not receiving aid as paupers, nor had received such aid for one year prior to the election. In 1901 women received the right to vote in local elections, if they had an income of 400 kroner in the cities or 300 kroner in the country, or, in case of married women, if their husbands had that income. By these laws the numerous working classes in the cities were enfranchised. In 1898 the time for the meeting of the Storthing was changed from February to the first week-day after the 10th of October. This made it possible to hold longer sessions, as the representatives from the country districts could more easily stay away from home during the winter months.

Since the crisis of 1895, special attention was also devoted to the army and navy, which had hitherto been neglected. Large military budgets were voted for both branches of the service, aggregating about twenty million kroner, and the work of improving the defenses of the kingdom was carried forward with great energy by successive ministers of the department of defense: Olssøn, Holst, and Georg Stang. A fleet of four armored warships and many torpedo boats and smaller vessels was provided, and modern fortifications were constructed for the defense of the seacoast cities. The efficiency of the army was greatly increased, large stores of ammunition and war material were collected, and in 1901 an appropriation of 3,380,000 kroner was made for fortresses to be erected on the Swedish border from Fredrikshald to Kongsvinger. This plan was carried out by the energetic Lieutenant-Colonel Georg Stang. Many modern forts were built which might have made a Swedish invasion difficult.[1]

In the election of 1900 the Liberals were again victorious, and the Steen ministry could remain in office supported by a large majority. In 1902 Steen retired, and Otto Blehr formed a new ministry. In that year the question of the consular service was again brought up, this time by the Swedish minister of foreign affairs,

---

[1] These border forts were divided into four groups: 1. Kongsvinger, 2. Urskog, 3. Ørje, 4. Fredriksten. See *Karta öfer neutrala Zonen och norska Gränsfästningarne jämte Delegerades Förslag til Öferenskommelser,* Stockholm, 1905.

Lagerheim. He proposed that a joint Swedish-Norwegian committee should be appointed to investigate how a separate consular service for the two kingdoms might be organized. A joint committee of two Norwegians and two Swedes was appointed in January, 1902, and on July 26th they submitted their report stating that no serious obstacles to the organization of separate consular service for the two kingdoms could be found, that separate Swedish and Norwegian consuls could be appointed, responsible to their respective governments, and that the supervision hitherto exercised by the Swedish foreign minister over Norwegian consuls could be dispensed with. On the basis of this report the two governments resumed their negotiations, and in 1903 they reached a preliminary agreement, dated March 24th, containing the following points : (1) Separate consular service is to be created for Sweden and Norway. The consuls of each kingdom are to be responsible to the authorities in their own country which its government may designate. (2) The relation of the consuls to the minister of foreign affairs is to be regulated in both kingdoms by identical laws, which cannot be altered or repealed except with the consent of the governments of both. The question regarding the minister of foreign affairs they agreed not to discuss.[1] The difficult question seemed to be fairly on the way to a satisfactory solution, but some points in the agreement made the Norwegians hesitate. The Norwegian consular service should not be wholly emancipated from Swedish control. To some extent the Norwegian consuls would still be subject to the Swedish minister of foreign affairs, who was to act as foreign minister for both kingdoms; and this relation should be regulated by laws which could not be changed or repealed. That such an arrangement might serve to rivet upon Norway a sign of dependence and inferiority was justly feared. But it was hoped that by continued negotiations all difficulties might be overcome, and an effort was made to unite all parties in support of this program. Bjørnstjerne Bjørnson himself became an earnest advocate of negotiations,[2] and "Verdens Gang"

---

[1] A. C. Drolsum, *Das Königreich Norwegen als souveräner Staat,* p. 26 ff. S. C. Hammer, *Det merkelige Aar 1905. Underdanig Betænkning afgiven af den under 18de Januar, 1902, nedsatte Konsulatkomite.*

[2] Bjørnstjerne Bjørnson, *Forhandling, bare Forhandling eller det som kan føre til Krig,* Samtiden, 1904. J. Castberg, *Om Begivenhederne i 1905.*

and other Liberal organs supported this policy. In the elections of 1903 Liberals and Conservatives united and formed the Coalition party (*Samlingspartiet*), which favored negotiations with Sweden, a program which gained such support that the party received a majority in the new Storthing. The Blehr ministry resigned, and a new Coalition ministry was formed with Hagerup as minister of state. Norway had met Sweden's advances with all possible manifestations of friendly spirit, and it was hoped that the negotiations officially instituted between the two governments would result in a speedy settlement of the difficulty. In a meeting of the joint ministry in Stockholm, December 11, 1903, Lagerheim reported the agreement of March 24th of that year. This was accepted both by the Swedish and the Norwegian ministers present, and it was ratified by the Norwegian Storthing, and approved by the king. This made it an officially established compact between the two governments. The protocols and documents from the meetings of the cabinets were sent to the Storthing, which referred them to the constitutional committee. The committee reported that official documents showed that full unanimity existed between the two governments and the king regarding the agreement reached March 24th, *i.e.* that separate consuls should be appointed for the two kingdoms, and that the relation of these officials to the diplomatic service should be regulated by identical laws. Nothing seemed now to stand in the way of a speedy settlement of the question. The Storthing took steps to organize a Norwegian consular service, and drafted a bill embodying the identical laws which were to govern the relations between the consuls and the minister of foreign affairs. The bill was forwarded to the Swedish minister of state, Boström, May 28, 1904, but he waited till September before he undertook to examine it. This long delay aroused suspicion, and it was feared that the plan might miscarry. This fear became almost a certainty when Lagerheim, the Swedish foreign minister, resigned, because Boström disagreed with him regarding the proposed settlement of the consular question.[1] On November 23d Boström arrived in Christiania, and submitted to the two Norwegian ministers of state, Hagerup and Ibsen, his "Reasons," a document in which he laid

---

[1] Yngvar Nielsen, *Norge i 1905*, p. 159 f.

down the fundamental principles for the identical laws. These principles were widely different on many essential points from the agreement already reached. He demanded, among other things, that the Swedish minister of foreign affairs should be made joint foreign minister, while the agreement left this question in abeyance. He also demanded that the Cabinet Council for Foreign Affairs should have the power to dismiss Norwegian consuls, a provision which would violate the constitution, and reduce Norway to a dependency. The two ministers refused to accept the principles proposed by Boström, and there seemed to be little hope of arriving at a new agreement. But Hagerup still made an attempt. In December, 1904, he went to Stockholm, where the Swedish ministry submitted to him the laws which had been drafted regarding the consular service. These laws had been based on the principles of Boström, and contained among other provisions the six "dependency clauses" (5, 6, 8, 11, 16, and 19). 5. provided that the authorities governing the consular service should, in case of vacancy, give the minister of foreign affairs all desired information regarding the candidates for the position. 6. provided that in consular reports the name of Sweden should always precede that of Norway. 8. The authorities governing the consular service should issue no instructions to the consuls which should come in conflict with the decisions of the minister of foreign affairs. 11. If the minister of foreign affairs should learn that a consul disturbed the good relations of the two united kingdoms and a foreign power, he should report this to the Cabinet Council for Foreign Affairs or the joint ministry, whereupon the king should examine the matter in the presence of the ministry of the kingdom in question. 16. Under certain circumstances a consul should be dismissed by the minister to the country where he was stationed, and a consul so dismissed could not be reappointed without royal order upon report of the minister of foreign affairs.[1] 19. In some countries the joint consular service should continue. The Norwegian ministers would not accept these paragraphs, and asked Boström to omit them. This he would not do, and the negotiations terminated. Why Boström should consider it worth while to submit these conditions, which would have reduced Norway to a

[1] N. Gjelsvik, *Hvem har begaat Traktatbrud? Aftenposten*, July 25, 1905.

Swedish dependency, and which he must have known would never be accepted, it is difficult to explain, except by assuming that he chose this way of breaking off negotiations, as he did not wish to consent to a separate consular service for Norway.[1]

The failure of the negotiations so auspiciously begun created great disappointment in Norway, and precipitated a crisis which united all parties. The minister of state, Hagerup, said in reporting the result to the Storthing: "Our people are anxious to maintain the peace and good understanding which are equally important to both nations. But the present condition is unbearable, and it cannot last long without endangering the good understanding which has hitherto existed between them. The aim must, therefore, be to establish to the fullest degree such conditions as will give Norway the position which rightfully belongs to her as a sovereign kingdom, a cause in the defense of which all Norwegians have stood, and henceforth will stand united."[2] "If this cannot be done in the existing union, it will be necessary to consider the creation of such new and freer forms for the coöperation of both nations and the promotion of their mutual interests as all shall wish to preserve, and to a higher degree than institutions constitute the lasting and valuable foundation for a union between free peoples." These words from a leading Conservative show that recent events had caused the best friends and supporters of the union to ally themselves with the Liberals. The Conservative papers, like "Aftenposten" and "Morgenbladet," were no less indignant than the Liberal press, and urged that, since all negotiations had failed, the Storthing should take matters into its own hands, and that Norway's honor and independence should be defended at any cost. From all parts of the country petitions were sent to the Storthing advocating decisive measures, and giving assurance that the people would make any sacrifice necessary to defend their liberty and independence.[3]

---

[1] Forh. Statsraad Chr. Knudsen, *Spredte Minder fra 1905.*

[2] J. E. Sars, *Norges Historie*, vol. VI., 2, p. 220. *Det norske Venstre fra 1884 til 1909, En politisk-historisk Oversigt utgit av Norges Venstreforening*, Christiania, 1909, p. 22 f.

[3] Numerous resolutions of that kind are found in *Unions Opløsningen* by F. V. Heiberg, 1905, p. 125 ff. This work is a collection of official documents connected with the events of that year.

The Storthing had appointed a special committee of nineteen to examine the protocols and documents dealing with the negotiations, and to submit plans for further action. Several had been suggested. Some favored renewed negotiations, but all parties finally agreed that the Storthing should pass a law establishing a separate consular service. Such a law might be made by passing it in three separately elected Storthings, but this would take many years, and such a delay might be dangerous. But a bill might also be passed containing a clause stating that at a certain future date it would be proclaimed as law. This, the quickest and most direct way, was recommended by the special committee.[1]

As to the manner of meeting the crisis the ministry stood divided. Hagerup himself, professor of jurisprudence, a scholar, and a man of great ability, lacked resoluteness and decision. As a last resort he would abrogate the Act of Union, and make a joint king the only bond of union. But he hesitated to take so decisive a step, and favored negotiations. Christian Michelsen and J. Schøning, who preferred immediate and energetic action, resigned, and the ministry was forced to retire.[2] A new ministry representing all parties was formed by Michelsen, who selected as his associates J. Løvland, minister of state in Stockholm, Sofus Arctander, minister of commerce, General W. Olssøn, minister of defense, Gunnar Knudsen, minister of finance, Christopher Knudsen, minister of ecclesiastical affairs and education, A. H. Vinje, minister of agriculture, E. Hagerup Bull and H. Bothner, members of the branch of the Norwegian ministry in Stockholm. All party differences had been dropped, and all stood united in support of the new ministry which was to guide the nation through so perilous a crisis.

Because of ill health King Oscar II. had temporarily turned the government over to his son, Crown Prince Gustaf, who was to act as regent. When it became evident that the consular question threatened to disrupt the union, the regent took steps to open new negotiations. While on a visit in Christiania, he sent a letter to the special committee, in which he urged them to take no step which might imperil the union. On his return to Stockholm, the

[1] F. V. Heiberg, *Unionens Opløsning 1905*, p. 117 ff. *Unionens Opløsning, en Dagbog, Særavtryk av Aftenposten*, 1905. [2] *Ibid.*, p. 29 f.

Swedish Rigsdag appointed a special committee to confer with the ministry, and on April 5, 1905, the regent invited the cabinets of both kingdoms to resume negotiations with a view to create a joint foreign minister, who might be either a Swede or a Norwegian, and to establish separate consular service for both kingdoms in such a way that in all matters touching foreign relations the consuls should be responsible to the minister of foreign affairs. Boström resigned, and Ranstedt, who had been member of the ministry, and was supposed to be more favorably disposed towards the Norwegian demands, was placed at the head of the Swedish cabinet. But these apparent concessions did not change the situation. Ranstedt had voted in favor of the "dependency clauses" in Boström's document, and there was no evidence of any change in the Swedish point of view. The Norwegian government refused to renew the negotiations until a separate Norwegian consular service should be established. This condition was not accepted, and nothing further could be done in regard to the matter. By these offers of continued negotiations Sweden succeeded, however, in gaining some sympathy among foreign powers, while Norway's refusal to negotiate was interpreted as wrong-headedness and obstinacy.[1] But several able Norwegian writers, as Fridtjof Nansen, A. C. Drolsum, and H. L. Brækstad, pleaded Norway's cause in foreign countries with such success that the tide of sentiment turned, and sympathy for Norway became pronounced in France and Germany, and, finally, also in England.[2] A foreign loan of forty million kroner was also floated on very favorable terms, and it was resolved by the Storthing that this sum should

[1] In England The Daily Graphic declared that jealousy and vanity had led the Norwegians to dissolve the union, and other leading papers like The Daily Express, The Daily Mail, and The Standard spoke in a similar strain. Only the Liberal Westminster Gazette sided with Norway. The leading French papers like Le Temps and Journal des Débats sympathized with Norway, as did also many of the leading Russian papers. S. C. Hammer, Det merkelige Aar 1905, p. 64.

[2] Fridtjof Nansen, Norwegen und die Union mit Schweden; Norway and the Union with Sweden. H. L. Brækstad, The Constitutional Crisis in Norway; The Norwegian-Swedish Conflict; The Constitution of Norway. A. C. Drolsum, Sovereign Norway and her State Rights; Das Königreich Norwegen als souveräner Staat; together with a German translation of the Norwegian Constitution; Skal Norge bære Skylden for Ufreden i Norden?